	SYMBOL	ATOMIC NUMBER	ATOMIC WEIGHT
NEODYMIUM	Nd	60	144.24
NEON	Ne	10	20.179
NEPTUNIUM	Np	93	237.0482[a]
NICKEL	Ni	28	58.71
NIOBIUM	Nb	41	92.9064
NITROGEN	N	7	14.0067
NOBELIUM	No	102	(254)[b]
OSMIUM	Os	76	190.2
OXYGEN	O	8	15.9994
PALLADIUM	Pd	46	106.4
PHOSPHORUS	P	15	30.9738
PLATINUM	Pt	78	195.09
PLUTONIUM	Pu	94	(242)[b]
POLONIUM	Po	84	(210)[b]
POTASSIUM	K	19	39.102
PRASEODYMIUM	Pr	59	140.9077
PROMETHIUM	Pm	61	(147)[b]
PROTACTINIUM	Pa	91	231.0359[a]
RADIUM	Ra	88	226.0254[a]
RADON	Rn	86	(222)[b]
RHENIUM	Re	75	186.2
RHODIUM	Rh	45	102.9055
RUBIDIUM	Rb	37	85.4678
RUTHENIUM	Ru	44	101.07
SAMARIUM	Sm	62	150.4
SCANDIUM	Sc	21	44.9559
SELENIUM	Se	34	78.96
SILICON	Si	14	28.086
SILVER	Ag	47	107.868
SODIUM	Na	11	22.9898
STRONTIUM	Sr	38	87.62
SULFUR	S	16	32.06
TANTALUM	Ta	73	180.9479
TECHNETIUM	Tc	43	98.9062[a]
TELLURIUM	Te	52	127.60
TERBIUM	Tb	65	158.9254
THALLIUM	Tl	81	204.37
THORIUM	Th	90	232.0381[a]
THULIUM	Tm	69	168.9342
TIN	Sn	50	118.69
TITANIUM	Ti	22	47.90
TUNGSTEN	W	74	183.85
URANIUM	U	92	238.029
VANADIUM	V	23	50.9414
XENON	Xe	54	131.30
YTTERBIUM	Yb	70	173.04
YTTRIUM	Y	39	88.9059
ZINC	Zn	30	65.37
ZIRCONIUM	Zr	40	91.22
		104	(260)[b]
		105	(260)[b]

[a]Mass of most commonly available, long-lived isotope.
[b]Mass number of most stable or best known isotope.

CHEMISTRY
A Conceptual Approach

SECOND EDITION

Cover photograph:

Photomicrograph of stilbene. Photographed with the use of a "Polychromator," which is a special compensator designed by Kage.

CHEMISTRY
A Conceptual Approach

SECOND EDITION

CHARLES E. MORTIMER

Muhlenberg College
Allentown, Pennsylvania

D. VAN NOSTRAND COMPANY
New York   Cincinnati   Toronto   London   Melbourne

D. Van Nostrand Company Regional Offices:
New York   Cincinnati   Millbrae

D. Van Nostrand Company International Offices:
London   Toronto   Melbourne

ISBN: 0-442-25561-6

Published by D. Van Nostrand Company
450 West 33rd Street, New York, N.Y. 10001

Published simultaneously in Canada by
Van Nostrand Reinhold Ltd.

10   9   8   7   6   5   4

To
J. S. M. and C. E. M.[II]

Preface

In this text, I have attempted to present a balanced treatment of modern theoretical and descriptive chemistry. The preparation of freshman chemistry students varies widely, and the book was written to meet the needs of the majority. A primary objective was to make the material understandable to the student without distortion or over-simplification. The use of calculus has been avoided since most freshmen lack an adequate background in this subject. A comparatively large amount of theory basic to analytical chemistry has been included to support laboratory instruction.

No fundamental changes in objectives, organization, level, or manner of presentation have been made in this edition. However, material has been added to keep the book up to date, and many sections have been rewritten in the interest of greater clarity. In general, the changes are designed to increase the pedagogical utility of the text, and many of them are in response to comments received from teachers who have used the text. The number of problems has been approximately doubled, and very few of the old problems have been retained. The longer chapters (Chemical Bonding, The Nonmetals, and Ionic Equilibria) have been divided for greater convenience.

The chapter on thermodynamics has been largely rewritten so that the treatment focuses on chemical reactions rather than on physical changes. Both matter *and* energy are the proper concern of chemistry, and thermodynamics is of pervasive importance to the science. Therefore, I have continued the practice of introducing thermodynamic concepts (e.g., heats of reaction, Born-Haber cycles) throughout the text where they pertain. The modest increase in the length of these discussions is designed to make them more lucid, not to increase the degree of difficulty.

It has been gratifying to learn that the first edition has been successfully used in a number of courses in which the sequence of topics is different from that of the book. A text should aid, not restrain, a creative teacher. Minor changes in organization can be made, such as the presentation of all the sections concerned with thermodynamic concepts (including Chapter 13) as a unit or the incorporation of material from Chapter 21 (Nuclear Chemistry) into the discussion of Chapter 2 (Atomic Structure). A major change in organization involves starting the course with stoichiometry (Chapter 5), then discussing the states of matter (Chapters 6 and 7), oxidation-reduction (parts of Chapter 8), solutions (Chapter 9), and electrochemistry (Chapter 10), thus leading to an earlier discussion of thermodynamics (Chapter 13). In a course of this type, consideration of atomic structure and chemical bonding is postponed until after the properties of macroscopic matter have been discussed.

No matter how a course is organized, it is unlikely that any course would incorporate all of the material contained in this book. However, the scope of a course can be expanded by the assignment of some sections for independent study. Many of the descriptive topics (e.g., metallurgy) readily lend themselves to such treatment.

I sincerely thank the following for their comments and suggestions: Professors Craig M. Baker, Jon M. Bellama, Robert C. Brasted, Duane F. Burow, William B. Guenther, David W. Herlocker, Frederic J. Kakis, Benjamin F. Naylor, Harry H. Sisler, Calvin A. VanderWerf, and Kenneth W. Whitten. I am also grateful to many others who have generously sent me comments based on their experience with the first edition. That it is impossible to mention everyone to whom I am indebted is a matter of much regret.

Charles E. Mortimer

Contents

INTRODUCTION

Chemistry may be defined as the science that is concerned with the characterization, composition, and transformations of matter. This definition, however, is far from adequate. The interplay between the branches of modern science has caused the boundaries between them to be so vague as to make it almost impossible to stake out a field and say "this is chemistry." Not only do the interests of scientific fields overlap, but concepts and methods find universal application. Moreover, this definition fails to convey the spirit of chemistry, for it, like all science, is a vital, growing enterprise, not an accumulation of knowledge. It is self-generating; the very nature of each new chemical concept stimulates fresh observation and experimentation leading to progressive refinement as well as the development of other concepts. In the light of scientific growth, it is not surprising that a given scientific pursuit frequently leads across artificial, human-imposed boundaries.

Nevertheless, there is a common, if somewhat vague, understanding of the province of chemistry, and we must return to our preliminary definition; a fuller understanding should emerge as this book unfolds. Chemistry is concerned with the structure of substances—of what they are composed and how their components are put together. The physical properties of substances are studied since they provide clues for structural determinations, serve as a basis for identification and classification, and indicate possible uses for specific materials. The focus of chemistry, however, is probably the chemical reaction. The interest of chemistry extends to every conceivable aspect of these transformations and includes such considerations as: detailed descriptions of how and at what rates reactions proceed, the conditions required to bring about desired changes and to prevent undesired changes, the energy effects accompanying chemical changes, the syntheses of substances that occur in nature and those that have no natural counterparts, and the quantitative mass relations between the materials involved in chemical changes.

1.1 Measurement

The **metric system** of measurement is used in all scientific studies. It is a decimal system that employs several basic units, defined by international agreement; the names of other, related units are derived from those of the basic units by the addition of prefixes (Table 1.1). Thus 1 decimeter (1 dm)

Table 1.1

Prefixes Used to Modify Unit Terms in the Metric System

Prefix	Abbreviation		
tera-	T-	1 000 000 000 000 ×	(10^{12})
giga-	G-	1 000 000 000 ×	(10^{9})
mega-	M-	1 000 000 ×	(10^{6})
kilo-	k-	1 000 ×	(10^{3})
deci-	d-	0.1 ×	(10^{-1})
centi-	c-	0.01 ×	(10^{-2})
milli-	m-	0.001 ×	(10^{-3})
micro-	μ-	0.000 001 ×	(10^{-6})
nano-	n-	0.000 000 001 ×	(10^{-9})
pico-	p-	0.000 000 000 001 ×	(10^{-12})

is 0.1 meter; 1 centimeter (1 cm) is 0.01 meter; and 1 millimeter (1 mm) is 0.001 meter. Conversion of a measurement from one unit into another in the **English system** (e.g., 1 yard $= 3$ feet $= 36$ inches) is unwieldy and time consuming; a decimal system is much to be preferred. Conversion factors between

several units of the English system and the metric system are given in Table 1.2.

Table 1.2

Some Conversion Factors

	English System		Metric System
1	pound (advp)	453.59	gram[a]
1	inch	2.5400	centimeter
1	quart	0.94633	liter
2.2046	pound (avdp)	1000	gram[a]
0.39370	inch	1	centimeter
1.0567	quart	1	liter

[a] The pound is a unit of weight, and the gram is a unit of mass. See Section 1.3.

Almost all units of measurement can be derived from units of length, mass, and time. The metric standard of length is the **meter**, which was originally meant to be one ten-millionth of the distance along a meridian from the north pole to the equator and was defined as the distance between two etched lines, at 0°C, on a platinum-iridium bar kept at the International Bureau of Weights and Measures at Sèvres, France. The meter is now defined as 1,650,763.73 wavelengths of the orange-red spectroscopic line of $^{86}_{36}Kr$. For the measurement of very small objects, the Ångstrom unit (A, 10^{-8} cm or 10^{-10} m) is frequently employed.

The primary standard of mass is the **kilogram**, which is defined as the mass of a cylinder of a platinum-iridium alloy deposited at the International Bureau of Weights and Measures. The **second** is defined by means of astronomical observations. Two methods are used to derive additional units (Section 1.4) from those of length, mass, and time: the meter-kilogram-second (**mks**) system, which is used by most physicists; and the centimeter-gram-second (**cgs**) system, which is preferred by most chemists. The two methods, however, may be used interchangeably.

Volume may be measured in terms of the volume of a cube 1 cm on a side (1 cubic centimeter, 1 cm^3). However, the unit of capacity employed most frequently in chemistry is the **liter**. The liter is now defined as 1 cubic decimeter (1 dm^3). Hence, 1 liter equals exactly 1000 cm^3, and 1 milliliter (1 ml) equals 1 cm^3. The liter was originally defined as the volume of exactly 1000 g of pure water under normal atmospheric pressure and at 3.98°C (the temperature of maximum density of water). Based on the old definition, 1 liter equaled 1000.028 cm^3. For most purposes, the difference is unimportant.

The selection of a primary standard for a system of measures is arbitrary, and throughout the history of science many different standards have been used. The criteria for the selection of a primary standard are that it be reproducible, unchanging, and capable of being used for precise measurement. A table of the values of important constants in terms of metric units appears in the Appendix.

1.2 Significant Figures

In scientific studies, the number of figures recorded for a measured quantity must reflect the precision with which the measurement has been made and thus the degree of certainty that can be attributed to the reported value. In short, all the figures must be **significant**; the value must provide as much usable information as is possible but must also avoid giving misinformation.

For example, let us suppose that the mass of an object is determined to be 12.3456 g. The analytical balance commonly employed in chemistry is capable of measuring the mass of an object to a sensitivity of 0.0001 g, and therefore all the figures reported are significant; the value has six significant figures. There is some uncertainty in the last figure (6), but it is of value, and therefore significant, because it tells us that the true mass lies closer to 12.3456 g than 12.3455 g or 12.3457 g. This is the most precise value we can secure; it is impossible to derive a value containing seven significant figures for the mass of this particular object using a balance with a sensitivity of 0.0001 g.

If we add a zero to the measurement, we indicate a value of *seven* significant figures (12.34560), which is incorrect and misleading. The conclusion to be drawn from the value 12.34560 g is that the true mass lies between 12.34559 g and 12.34561 g, a much closer tolerence than that indicated by the properly reported value, whereas, in fact, we have no idea of the magnitude of the integer of fifth decimal place. A zero does not indicate the fact that the fifth decimal place is unknown or undetermined; rather, the zero is interpreted to be as significant as any other figure in the number. A properly determined and recorded mass, such as 42.5630 g, may legitimately include a zero as a significant figure.

Zeros used to locate the decimal place, however, are not significant. The number 0.0005030 has four significant figures; two of the zeros are significant, whereas those preceding the numeral 5 are not. Expressing the diameter of a particle as 0.00000001 cm, rather than 1 Å, does not render the measurement any more precise.

Occasionally, difficulty arises in interpreting the number of significant figures in a term such as 6000. Are the zeros significant, or do they merely serve to locate the decimal point? One solution to the problem is to indicate the position of the decimal point as a power of 10 and include only those zeros that are significant in the other portion of the number. Thus, if the value 6000 has, indeed, been determined to four significant figures, it is indicated as 6.000×10^3; otherwise fewer zeros are placed after the decimal point.

Certain values, such as those arising from the definition of terms, are exact. Thus there are *exactly* 1000 ml in 1 liter, and the number 1000 may be considered to possess an infinite number of significant zeros following the decimal point. Other values are not so precise as might normally be expected. For example, if a balance with a sensitivity of 0.0002 g is used to determine 12.3456 g as the mass of an object, the measurement should be recorded as 12.3456 ± 0.0002 g. The uncertainty range (± 0.0002 g) gives the reliability of the determination. The last figure of a value recorded without an uncertainty range is understood to be precise plus or minus one digit.

Frequently, the values used in a calculation have different numbers of significant figures. The method used to determine the proper number of significant figures in the answer depends upon the mathematical operation performed. The result of an **addition** or **subtraction** should be given to the same number of decimal places as that of the term with the least number of decimal places. The answer for the addition

$$\begin{array}{r} 161.032 \\ 5.6 \\ \underline{32.4524} \\ 199.0844 \end{array}$$

should be recorded as 199.1 since the number 5.6 has but one digit following the decimal point.

The answer to a calculation involving **multiplication** or **division** is rounded off to the same number of significant figures as is possessed by the least precise term used in the calculation. Thus the result of the multiplication

$$152.06 \times 0.24 = 36.4944$$

should be reported as 36, which conforms to the limitations imposed by the term 0.24. As a matter of fact, this answer is slightly more precise than the least precise term. The value 0.24 indicates a precision of 1 part in 24, whereas the answer indicates the slightly greater precision of 1 part in 36.

The values to be used in a calculation involving several steps should be rounded off before the mathematical operations are performed. Each value that has an excess number of significant figures is rounded off to *one more* significant figure than the number of significant figures required to express the answer. For example, the answer to the computation

$$1.267 \left(\frac{4.353178}{56} \right)$$

should contain only two significant figures since this is the level of precision of the value 56. Therefore, the values to be used in the calculation should be rounded off to *three* significant figures, and the answer should be rounded off to *two* significant figures. Thus,

$$1.27 \left(\frac{4.35}{56} \right) = 0.099$$

1.3 Matter

Science interprets nature in terms of energy (which is discussed in Section 1.4) and matter. **Matter**, the material of which the universe is composed, may be defined as anything that occupies space and has mass. Mass is a measure of quantity of matter. A body that is not being acted upon by some external force has a tendency to remain at rest or, when it is in motion, to continue in uniform motion in the same direction. This property is known as **inertia**, and the mass of a body is proportional to the inertia of that body.

The mass of a body is invariable; the weight of a body is not. **Weight** is the gravitational force of attraction exerted by the earth on a body, and the weight of a given body varies with the distance of that body from the center of the earth. The weight of a body is, of course, directly proportional to its mass as well as the earth's gravitational attraction. Therefore, at any given place, two objects of equal mass have equal weights.

The mass of an object may be determined by means of an analytical balance; standard masses are placed on one pan of the instrument to balance the object of unknown mass placed on the other pan. When the instrument is "in balance," the gravitational force on one pan equals that on the other, the weights on the two pans are equal, and hence, the masses on the two pans are equal.

The terms mass and weight have long been used interchangeably in chemistry. Such usage is strictly incorrect but is somewhat firmly established through such terms as atomic weight, molecular weight, and weight-percent. Mass determinations are made through weight comparisons and, in writing and speaking, the verb "weigh" is usually less awkward than the phrase "determine the mass." Actually, the pound is a weight unit in the English system, whereas the gram is a mass unit in the metric system. In general, no significant errors arise through this loose usage, and the precise meaning is almost invariably evident from the context in which the terms are used.

Matter exists in three physical states: gaseous, liquid, and solid. A **gas** maintains neither volume nor shape; it completely fills any container into which it is introduced and may be expanded or compressed between relatively wide limits. A **liquid** also has no fixed shape. However, a liquid assumes the shape of the container only within the limit of the volume that the sample occupies, and volumes of liquids do not vary greatly with changes in temperature and pressure. A **solid**, under ordinary conditions, maintains both volume and shape. Observed variations in the volumes of solids with changes in temperature and pressure are of a very low order.

Changes in state (such as the melting of a solid and the vaporization of a liquid), as well as changes in shape or state of subdivision, are examples of **physical changes**, which may be defined as changes that do not involve the production of new chemical species. Physical means (such as filtration and distillation) may be used to separate the components of a mixture, but a substance that was not present in the original mixture is never produced by such means. **Chemical changes**, on the other hand, are transformations in which substances are converted into other substances.

A material may be characterized by its **intrinsic properties**—attributes that distinguish it from all other types of matter. Properties such as density, color, physical state, melting point, and electrical conductivity are known as physical properties because they can be observed without causing any change in the chemical composition of the specimen. The **chemical properties** of a substance are those that describe the chemical changes, or reactions, that the substance undergoes. Properties, such as mass, length, and temperature, that are not characteristic of any particular type of matter, are known as **extrinsic properties**.

A distinct portion of matter that is uniform throughout in terms of composition and intrinsic properties is called a **phase**. If a material consists of only one phase, it is said to be **homogeneous**; if it consists of more than one phase, it is classified as **heterogeneous**. Thus iron, salt, and a solution of salt in water are homogeneous; wood, granite, and a mixture of ice and water are heterogeneous.

The phases of heterogeneous matter have distinct boundaries and are usually easily discernible. In granite, for example, it is possible to identify pink feldspar crystals, colorless quartz crystals, and shiny black mica crystals. When the number of phases in a sample is being determined, all the portions of the same kind are counted as a single phase. Thus, granite is said to consist of three phases.

Heterogeneous materials do not have fixed compositions and are, therefore, **mixtures**. The relative proportions of the three phases of granite vary from specimen to specimen. An infinite number of heterogeneous mixtures are possible, since there are no restrictions on the proportions in which the various components may be present.

Homogeneous mixtures are called **solutions**, and the single phase in which a solution occurs may be gaseous, liquid, or solid. Air, salt dissolved in water, and a silver-gold alloy are examples of gaseous, liquid, and solid solutions. All gases mix with one another in all proportions, but for solid and liquid solutions, there are usually limits on the solubility of one substance in another. Nevertheless, the compositions of solutions are variable; more than

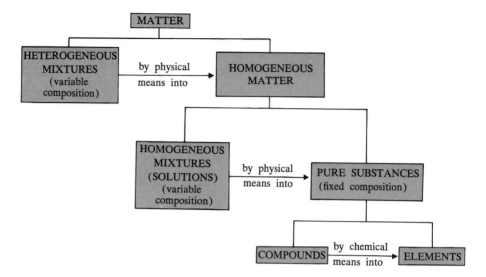

Figure 1.1   Classification of matter.

one solution is possible for each group of components from which a solution may be prepared; and solutions are, therefore, mixtures.

Each phase of a heterogeneous mixture has its own properties. A homogeneous mixture has but a single set of intrinsic properties, but each of these properties depends upon the composition of the mixture. The density, taste, boiling point, and electrical conductivity, for example, of aqueous salt solutions vary with the proportion of salt and water present.

Pure substances are homogeneous materials that have fixed compositions and invariable intrinsic properties. There are two types. An **element** is a pure substance that cannot be decomposed into any simpler pure substance. A **compound** is a pure substance that is composed of two or more elements in fixed and definite proportion. Thus, hydrogen and oxygen are elements; water is a compound composed of 11.19% hydrogen and 88.81% oxygen. Preparation of a compound from the constituent elements is known as **synthesis**, and decomposition of a compound into the component element is called **analysis**.

The classification of matter is summarized in Figure 1.1.

1.4   Energy

Energy is usually defined as the capacity to do work. Work is done when a body is displaced by a force, and the amount of work is equal to the product of the displacement, d, and the magnitude of the force in the direction of the displacement, f.

$$w = fd$$

A given force is directly proportional to the acceleration, a, it causes in a body (increase in velocity per unit time); the mass of the body, m, is the proportionality constant.

$$f = ma$$

In the cgs metric system, the unit of force is the dyne when mass is expressed in grams and acceleration in cm/sec^2.

$$1 \text{ dyne} = 1 \text{ g cm/sec}^2$$

One erg is the work done when a force of 1 dyne acts through 1 cm.

$$1 \text{ erg} = 1 \text{ g cm}^2/\text{sec}^2$$

In the mks system, the unit of force is the newton, N, which is defined as the force that gives to a mass of 1 kg an acceleration of 1 m/sec^2.

$$1 \text{ N} = 1 \text{ kg m/sec}^2$$

The unit of work is the newton-meter, or joule.

$$1 \text{ joule} = 1 \text{ N m} = 1 \text{ kg m}^2/\text{sec}^2$$

Since 1 kg equals 10^3 g and 1 m is 10^2 cm,

$$1 \text{ joule} = 10^3 \text{ g } (10^2 \text{ cm})^2/\text{sec}^2 = 10^7 \text{ g cm}^2/\text{sec}^2$$

and therefore

$$1 \text{ joule} = 10^7 \text{ erg}$$

There are many forms of energy (Section 13.1) such as heat energy, electrical energy, kinetic energy (energy of motion), and potential energy (intrinsic energy of an object due to the position of the object). Under appropriate circumstances, one form of energy can be converted into another form; in these transformations, energy is conserved (Section 13.1).

The chemist frequently expresses quantities of energy in terms of their heat equivalents (calories) rather than their mechanical equivalents (ergs). The direction of heat transfer is determined by temperature; heat flows from a body at a higher temperature to one at a lower temperature. The **Celsius** (or **centigrade**) temperature scale, named for Anders Celsius, a Swedish astronomer, is employed in scientific studies. This scale is based on the assignment of 0° to the normal freezing point of water and 100° to the normal boiling point of water. On the **Fahrenheit** temperature scale (named for G. Daniel Fahrenheit, a German instrument maker), the normal freezing point of water is 32° and the normal boiling point of water is 212°. Since there are 100 Celsius degrees and 180 Fahrenheit degrees between the freezing and

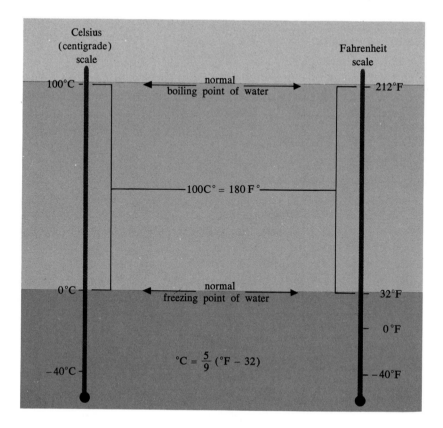

Figure 1.2 Comparison of the Celsius (centigrade) and Fahrenheit temperature scales.

boiling point of water, 5 Celsius degrees equal 9 Fahrenheit degrees. In Figure 1.2, these two temperature scales are compared and the formula for converting a reading on one scale to the other is given. The international temperature scale, or Kelvin scale, is described in Section 6.4.

The specific heat of a substance is the amount of heat required to raise the temperature of 1 g of the substance 1 Celsius degree. The specific heat of water is the original standard for the **calorie**, which may be defined as the quantity of heat required to raise the temperature of 1 g of water from 14.5°C to 15.5°C. Since specific heat changes slightly with temperature, it is necessary to specify the temperature interval. For many purposes, however, the specific heat of water may be assumed to be constant over the entire temperature range of liquid water. The calorie is now defined by its joule equivalent.[1]

$$1 \text{ cal} = 4.1840 \text{ joules (exactly)}$$

Very precise determinations of energy, in terms of joules or ergs, may be

---

[1] The "15 degree calorie" is actually equal to approximately 4.1855 joules.

made by electrical measurements, and hence the joule is a better primary standard than the specific heat of water (Section 13.1).

The unit of heat energy in the English system is the **British thermal unit (Btu)**. It is defined as the amount of heat required to raise the temperature of 1 pound of water from 62°F to 63°F; 1 Btu equals approximately 252 calories.

SOME SUGGESTED READINGS

Asimov, I., *A Short History of Chemistry*, Garden City, N.Y., Anchor, 1965 (paper).

Farber, E., *The Evolution of Chemistry—A History of Its Ideas, Methods, and Materials*, 2nd ed., New York, Ronald, 1969.

Ihde, A. J., and Kieffer, W. F., *Selected Readings in the History of Chemistry*, Easton, Penna., Chemical Education Publishing Co. (paper).

Partington, J. R., *A Short History of Chemistry*, New York, Harper, 1960 (paper).

Platt, J. R., *The Excitement of Science*, Boston, Houghton Mifflin, 1962 (paper).

Toulmin, S., and Goodfield, J., *Architecture of Matter*, New York, Harper, 1966 (paper).

One of the theories that has, in large measure, provided the impetus for the rapid advance of chemistry is the modern atomic theory. Chemical phenomena can effectively be interpreted and correlated on the basis of atoms. In this chapter, concepts of atomic structure and the development of these concepts are discussed.

ATOMIC STRUCTURE

2.1 The Atom

Through the ages men have been intrigued with the problem of the ultimate constitution of matter. Credit for the first "atomic" theory is usually given to the ancient Greeks; however, this concept may have had its origins in even earlier civilizations. Aristotle (fourth century B.C.) held that matter was continuous and hence, hypothetically, could be divided and subdivided endlessly into smaller and smaller particles. The atomistic school, principally of Leucippus, Democritus, and Epicurus (sixth to fourth centuries B.C.), believed that the subdivision of matter ultimately would yield atoms (from the

Greek *atomos*, meaning uncut or indivisible), which could not be further reduced. In the first century B.C., the atomic concept was eloquently presented by the Roman poet-philosopher Lucretius in his *De Rerum Natura* (*The Nature of Things*).

The ancient's theories were based on abstract thinking alone and not on planned experimentation. Hence, for nearly 2000 years the atomic theory was mere speculation. It formed a part of the thinking of Robert Boyle in his book *Sceptical Chymist* (1661) and of Isaac Newton in his works *Principia* (1687) and *Opticks* (1704). However, it remained for John Dalton to propose an atomic theory (1803–1807) that was a landmark in the progress of chemistry. Dalton's theory, based on experimentation and chemical laws known at that time, assigned weights and combining capacities to the postulated atoms. Because of its quantitative nature, his theory convincingly interpreted many observed facts and stimulated new work and thought. Dalton's theory in its broad outline is still valid; however, some of the particulars must be modified in the light of modern discovery.

Today, we know that the division of matter, of any type from any source, into the smallest particles capable of independent prolonged existence would result in the separation of only about 300 different kinds of atoms (naturally occurring **nuclides**). Some of these nuclides are very similar chemically, and if the 300 nuclides are grouped according to chemical characteristics, about 100 sets result. The atoms of a given set are isotopes of the same element (Section 2.8).

2.2 Subatomic Particles

Although Dalton, like the Greeks, regarded the atom as indivisible, it is now known that the atom consists of even smaller particles into which it may be divided. In fact, certain radioactive atoms spontaneously disintegrate into smaller fragments.

At the present time, approximately 35 different **subatomic particles** have been identified from the subdivision of atoms. Many of these particles are unstable, existing for only a split second, and their status relative to the atom is not completely understood. To add to the confusion, Albert Einstein has shown (Section 2.9) that matter and energy are equivalent; some of the particles identified are probably not particles in any sense of the word, but merely bundles of energy.

Three types of particles—the **electron, proton,** and **neutron** (see Table 2.1)—are regarded as "fundamental." Whether this term is wisely chosen is questionable since the particles may arise from some lesser species and one of them, the neutron, breaks down spontaneously when isolated. However, for

Table 2.1

Fundamental Subatomic Particles

| Particle | Mass | | Charge[b] |
	Grams	Unified Atomic Mass Units[a]	
electron	9.1091×10^{-28}	0.000548597	1−
proton	1.67252×10^{-24}	1.00727663	1+
neutron	1.67482×10^{-24}	1.0086654	0

[a] The unified atomic mass unit (u) is 1/12 the mass of a ^{12}C atom (Section 2.9).
[b] The unit charge is 1.60210×10^{-19} coulomb or 4.80298×10^{-10} esu.

purposes of the study of chemistry, atomic structure is quite adequately explained on the basis of these three fundamental particles.

2.3 The Electron

The **electron** is the lightest of the fundamental particles, and it has a negative charge (the unit electrical charge). The magnitude of the unit electrical charge may be expressed as 1.602×10^{-19} coulomb or 4.803×10^{-10} esu. A **coulomb** is the quantity of charge that passes a given point in an electrical circuit in 1 sec when the current is 1 amp, and 1 coulomb is 2.998×10^9 esu.

The definition of the **electrostatic unit** (esu) is derived from **Coulomb's law.** The force of attraction, or repulsion, F, between two charges q_1 and q_2 separated by a distance d is

$$F = \frac{q_1 q_2}{D d^2}$$

where the constant D, is the dielectric constant. The value of D depends upon the medium between the charges; for a vacuum, $D = 1$. The electrostatic unit is defined as that charge that will repel another identical charge by a force of exactly 1 dyne when the charges are separated by exactly 1 cm in a vacuum.

All substances contain electrons; many chemical transformations are the result of electron exchange or electron sharing by atoms. Many of the properties of metals (e.g., electrical conductivity) can be explained on the basis of the mobile electrons characteristic of metals.

In 1832–1833, Michael Faraday's studies on chemical electrolysis convincingly demonstrated the electrical nature of matter and the equivalence between chemical transformations and the flow of electricity (Chapter 10). The term electron (from the Greek meaning *amber*—so called because of the effect of friction on this substance) was first applied by Johnston Stoney in 1874 to the unit of electrical charge that he thought was associated with atoms.

Much of the information about electrons comes from the study of **cathode rays**, which were discovered by Julius Plücker in 1859 (Figure 2.1). When a high voltage is impressed across two electrodes sealed in a glass tube from which the air is almost completely withdrawn, rays emanate from the negative electrode (cathode). These rays cause the walls opposite the cathode to glow.

In the forty years after their discovery, the nature of these cathode rays was extensively investigated, especially by Johann Hittorf (1869), William Crookes (1879), and Joseph J. Thomson (1897). Experiments showed cathode rays to be streams of fast-moving, highly energetic, electrons. These electrons, which originate from the metal comprising the negative pole, are the same no matter what material is employed for the electrode. An object placed in the path of these cathode rays casts a shadow. Also, the rays, when focused on thin metal foils, heat the foils to incandescence.

Since unlike charges attract, these streams of electrons are attracted to the positive plate when two charged plates are placed on either side of them, and hence the rays are deflected from their usual straight-line path. The higher the charge on any such particle the greater is the attraction and the greater is the deflection. The magnitude of the deflection also depends *inversely* upon the mass of the particles, since a light particle is deflected much more than a heavy one in a given electrical field. Hence, the degree of deflection of these particles under the influence of an electrical field is determined by the ratio of

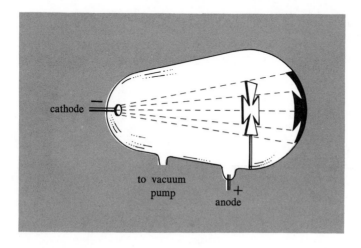

Figure 2.1   Cathode-ray tube.

charge to mass, e/m. Cathode rays are deflected in magnetic fields also; in this case, however, deflection is at right angles to the applied field.

In 1897, J. J. Thomson determined the ratio of the charge of the electron to its mass, e/m, by studying the deflection of cathode rays in magnetic and electric fields. Since they are electrically charged, electrons in motion constitute a current of electricity, and magnetic fields interact with electric currents. When an electron of charge e and mass m, moving with a velocity v, enters a magnetic field, it is deflected from its usual straight-line path into a circular path of radius r (Figure 2.2). The deflection occurs at a right angle to the field, and the electron continues in a straight line when it leaves the field.

The value of r is given by:

$$r = \frac{mv}{He} \tag{1}$$

where H is the magnetic field strength. The larger the field strength or the larger the charge on the electron, the greater the deflection from a straight-line path. A large deflection, however, means that the value of r is small. Therefore, H and e are *inversely* proportional to r. On the other hand, comparatively large values of r, indicating little deviation from a straight line, would be given by a particle with a large mass or one that is moving rapidly. Hence, m and v are *directly* proportional to r.

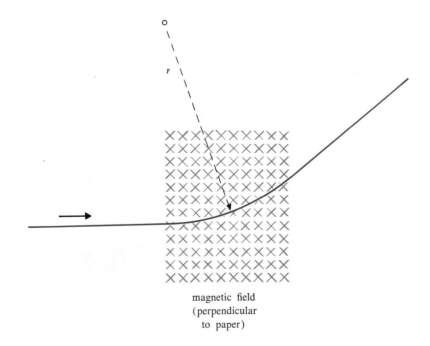

magnetic field
(perpendicular
to paper)

Figure 2.2 Path of an electron in a magnetic field.

Thomson measured the values of *r* for the deflections of cathode rays in magnetic fields of known strengths and was thereby able to get *e/mv*. From (1),

$$\frac{e}{mv} = \frac{1}{Hr} \qquad (2)$$

In order to get *e/m*, however, the velocity of the electron, *v*, had to be determined. One of the methods Thomson used to find *v* involved the study of cathode rays in a tube around which magnetic and electric fields, perpendicular to each other, could be simultaneously applied (Figure 2.3).

Electrons describe a parabolic path in an electric field; deflection occurs toward the positive plate. Under the influence of the electric field alone, the electron would strike the tube at point (c). The force causing this deflection is proportional to the charge of the electron but not to its velocity;

$$F = Ee \qquad (3)$$

where the proportionality constant, *E*, is the electric field strength. Under the influence of the magnetic field alone, the cathode ray in Figure 2.3 would strike the tube at point (a); the force causing the magnetic deflection, however, is proportional to both the charge and the velocity of the electron:

$$F = Hev \qquad (4)$$

Figure 2.3 Thomson's determination of *e/m* for the electron.

Thomson balanced the intensities of the electric and magnetic fields, when they were applied simultaneously, so that there was no net deflection and the impact of the ray was at point (b). Then

$$Hev = Ee \qquad (5)$$

$$v = \frac{E}{H} \qquad (6)$$

Multiplication of e/mv by v gives the value of e/m.
The value is

$$e/m = -5.273 \times 10^{17} \text{ esu/g}$$

Robert A. Millikan in 1909 determined the absolute value of the charge on the electron, e. When X rays irradiate the atoms of which air is composed, they knock electrons off these atoms. In Millikan's experiment (Figure 2.4), such electrons are picked up by a spray of very fine oil drops. These drops are allowed to settle between two horizontal plates. By the use of a telescope, the rate at which a single drop falls under the influence of gravity can be measured and the size of the drop calculated.

When the plates are charged, the rate of fall of the drop is altered by the attraction of the negatively charged drop for the positive plate. Measurement of the rate of fall of the drop in these circumstances enables calculation of the

oil drops

Figure 2.4 Millikan's determination of the charge on the electron.

charge on the drop. Since a given drop of oil can pick up one or more electrons, the charges thus calculated are not identical. They are, however, all simple multiples of the same value, 4.803×10^{-10} esu, which is assumed to be the charge on a single electron.

Combining this value for e with the value for e/m, one may calculate the mass of the electron. Thus:

$$\frac{e}{m} = -5.273 \times 10^{17} \text{ esu/g}$$

$$\frac{-4.803 \times 10^{-10} \text{ esu}}{m} = -5.273 \times 10^{17} \text{ esu/g}$$

$$m = 9.109 \times 10^{-28} \text{ g}$$

2.4 The Proton

If a single electron is removed from an atom, the residue has a charge equal to that of the electron removed but opposite in sign. When the lightest of all atoms, hydrogen, loses its lone electron, a particle which is called a **proton** (Greek, *first*) remains. It has a mass 1836 times that of the electron, and it bears a unit positive charge, $+4.803 \times 10^{-10}$ esu.

Like electrons and cathode rays, protons and positive rays arise in electric discharge tubes. The action of cathode rays rips electrons from atoms of the gas present in the tube, forming **ions** (Greek, *to go*). These ions, being positively charged, move in a direction contrary to that of the cathode rays (which are negatively charged), away from the positive pole toward the cathode. Many of them simply pick up electrons and again become neutral atoms. Some of them, however, reach the cathode and, if a hole has been bored in this electrode, go through it and beyond. These positive rays, or canal rays, were first discovered in 1886 by Eugen Goldstein (Figure 2.5).

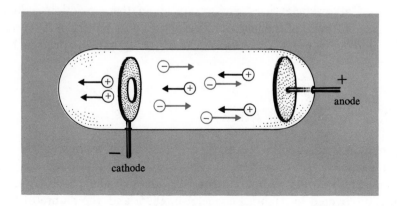

Figure 2.5 Positive rays.

In 1898 positive rays were studied by Wilhelm Wien, who determined approximate value of e/m for the positive particles comprising these rays by observing their deflection in magnetic and electrostatic fields. By using essentially the same method that he devised for the study of cathode rays, J. J. Thomson in 1906 refined Wien's estimates for e/m for these positive particles.

The positive particles comprising positive rays differ depending upon the gas present in the discharge tube, unlike the electrons of the cathode rays which are identical no matter from what material they arise. When particles have the same size charge, the value of e/m increases with a decrease in the mass of the particle. Hence, for the electron, the value of e/m is large. All positive ions have much smaller e/m values than the electron, and the value of e/m obtained depends upon the gas present in the discharge tube.

When hydrogen is used in the tube, the largest of all e/m values for positive ions is observed; it is assumed that positive ions from this source are the fundamental particles—protons. The mass of the proton is 1.673×10^{-24} g. The positive charge on the proton is of exactly the same magnitude as the negative charge on the electron ($1+$ and $1-$ in terms of the unit electrical charge).

2.5   The Neutron

Since atoms are electrically neutral, a given atom must contain as many electrons as protons. To account for the total masses of atoms, the existence of an uncharged particle was predicted by Ernest Rutherford around 1920. Since this particle is uncharged, it was difficult to detect and characterize. However, in 1932 James Chadwick published the results of his work which established the existence of the **neutron** (from Latin, *neutral*). He was able to calculate the mass of the neutron from data on certain nuclear reactions (see Chapter 21) in which neutrons are produced. By taking into account the masses and energies of all particles used and produced in these reactions, Chadwick determined the mass of the neutron. It is very slightly larger in mass than the proton; the neutron has a mass of 1.675×10^{-24} g and the proton, 1.673×10^{-24} g.

2.6   The Nuclear Atom

Certain atoms apparently represent unstable combinations of the fundamental particles. These atoms spontaneously emit rays and are thereby **transmuted** into atoms of different chemical identity. This process, **radioactivity**, was discovered by Henri Becquerel in 1896, and the nature of the rays produced was subsequently elucidated by Rutherford. The three types of rays emitted by naturally occurring radioactive materials (others have now been identified from man-made atoms) were named alpha (α), beta (β), and gamma (γ).

Alpha rays consist of particles made up of two protons and two neutrons. They are ejected from the radioactive atom at speeds around 10,000 miles/sec, carry a 2+ charge (from their two protons), and have a mass approximately four times that of the proton. Beta rays are streams of electrons (1— charge) that travel at approximately 80,000 miles/sec. Gamma radiation is essentially a highly energetic form of light; these rays are uncharged and are similar to X rays.

By the use of α particles, Rutherford, in 1911, presented convincing evidence for a nuclear construction of the atom. A radioactive source of α rays was placed behind a lead shield. A thin beam of α rays emerged through a hole bored in the thick lead shield. This beam was directed against very thin (ca. 0.0004 cm) foils of gold, platinum, silver, or copper. About 99.9% of the α particles went right through the foil in use; however, some were deflected from their straight-line path, and a few were sent back toward their source.

Rutherford explained the results of these scattering experiments by postulating the existence of a nucleus in the center of the atom. Most of the mass and all of the positive charge of the atom (the protons and neutrons) are concentrated in this nucleus. The electrons, which occupy most of the total

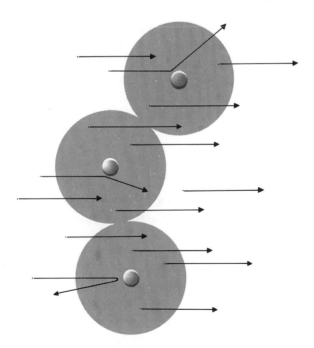

Figure 2.6 Deflections and recoil of α particles by nuclei of metal foil in Rutherford's experiment (not to scale).

volume of the atom, are outside of this nucleus and in rapid motion around it.

It is important that one grasp the scale of this model. If an atom had a diameter of 1 mile, its nucleus would have a diameter on the order of only $\frac{2}{3}$ in. Thus it is easily seen that most of the α particles in a scattering experiment would pass undeflected through an atom—most of the volume of an atom is empty space. This is true even though the target foils are about 1000 atoms thick.

If an α particle scores a direct hit on a nucleus, it recoils in the direction of its source; such recoils, though few in number, were observed. A near miss with a close approach of a positively charged α particle to a positively charged nucleus would result in repulsion of the α particle and thus deflection from its straight-line path (Figure 2.6). The comparatively light electrons do not cause the deflection of the heavier, fast-moving α particles.

The composition and stability of the nucleus is discussed in Chapter 21.

2.7 Atomic Symbols

An atom may be identified by two numbers: the atomic number, Z, and the mass number, A. The atomic number (Section 2.12) represents the number of unit positive charges on the nucleus and hence is equal to the number of protons in the nucleus, since each proton carries a $1+$ charge. An atom, being electrically neutral, must have as many electrons (at $1-$ each) as it has protons (at $1+$ each). Hence, the atomic number also gives the number of electrons in the neutral atom under consideration.

The mass number of an atom is the total number of neutrons and protons (**nucleons**) in the nucleus of the atom. Thus to obtain the number of neutrons in a given nucleus, one must subtract the atomic number (the number of protons) from the mass number (the number of neutrons and protons).

$$\text{number of neutrons} = A - Z$$

It must be emphasized that these are *numbers* of particles and not weights. Hence, the mass *number* represents the total *number* of nucleons in a nucleus and not the mass of the nucleus. However, since the mass of both the proton and the neutron are approximately equal to 1 u (Section 2.9), the mass number is generally a whole number approximation of the atomic masses expressed in atomic mass units. An atom of sodium with an atomic number of 11 and a mass number of 23 would have 11 protons and 12 neutrons in a nucleus in the center of the atom and 11 electrons in motion about that nucleus.

Chemical reactions involve only the extranuclear electrons, and the chemical characteristics of a neutral atom depend largely upon the number of electrons that it has. All neutral atoms with 11 electrons behave the same chemically, and all such atoms are given the same chemical name—sodium. We shall see later that it is possible to have, within limits, atoms with 11 protons and 11 electrons but a varying number of neutrons. Nevertheless, all atoms with 11 protons in the nucleus and 11 electrons around the nucleus are sodium atoms and comprise what is spoken of as the element sodium.

Each element is given a symbol, a practice introduced by the Swedish chemist Jöns Berzelius in the early 1800's. The names of the elements have been decided upon by international agreement, and the symbols are usually the initial letters of the names. Where more than one element begins with the same letter, a second letter (not necessarily the second letter of the name) is added to distinguish them. Most of the symbols for the elements correspond closely to their English names. However, the symbols of some of the elements, known and characterized long ago, have been assigned on the basis of their Latin names (see Table 2.2). The symbol for tungsten, W, is derived from the German name for the element, wolfram.

Table 2.2

Symbols of Elements Derived from Latin Names

English Name	Latin Name	Symbol
antimony	stibium	Sb
copper	cuprum	Cu
gold	aurum	Au
iron	ferrum	Fe
lead	plumbum	Pb
mercury	hydrargyrum	Hg
potassium	kalium	K
silver	argentum	Ag
sodium	natrium	Na
tin	stannum	Sn

A specific type of atom (nuclide) is designated by using the chemical symbol for the element with the atomic number placed at the lower left corner of the symbol and the mass number placed at the upper left corner. (The other two corners are reserved for other designations: the upper right for the charge if the atom has lost or gained one or more electrons and become an ion; the lower right corner for the number of atoms present in a formula unit of a compound.) Thus the sodium atom previously described would be designated $^{23}_{11}Na$. An atom with the symbol $^{35}_{17}Cl$ has 17 protons and 18 neutrons in the nucleus and 17 extranuclear electrons. An atom of uranium with the designation $^{238}_{92}U$ has 92 protons and 146 neutrons in its nucleus and 92 electrons in motion about this nucleus.

2.8 Isotopes and Isobars

One of the postulates of Dalton's atomic theory is that every atom of a given element is identical in all respects (including mass) to every other atom of that element. By the early twentieth century, however, it was clear that an element may consist of several varieties of atoms that differ from one another in atomic mass. Frederick Soddy proposed the name **isotopes** (Greek, *same place*) for atoms of the same element that differ in this respect.

The most fruitful method of studying isotopes is by use of a **mass spectrograph**. Instruments of this type were first constructed by Francis W. Aston (1919) and A. J. Dempster (1918) who followed principles developed by J. J. Thomson in 1913. The mass spectrograph (Figure 2.7) separates ions according to their charge-to-mass ratios; these ions are caused to impinge at different positions on a photographic plate. If an element consists of several types of atoms varying in mass, then ions from that element will have various charge-to-mass ratios.

When the instrument is operated, atoms of the vaporized material to be studied are converted into positive ions as a result of bombardment by streams of electrons (Section 2.4). These ions are next accelerated by passage through an electric field of several thousand volts. Provided the voltage is held constant, all ions of the same e/m value emerge into a magnetic field with about the same velocity. This velocity, as well as the e/m value and the strength of

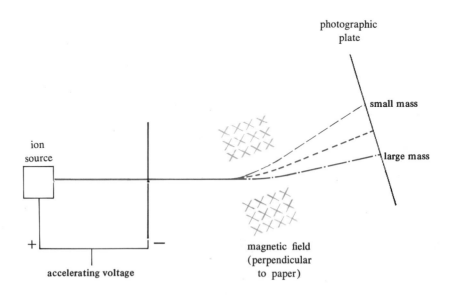

Figure 2.7 Essential features of a mass spectrograph.

the magnetic field, determines the radius of the path of the ion in the magnetic field.

Hence, if the strength of the magnetic field and the accelerating voltage are held constant, particles of the same e/m will be focused at definite positions on the photographic plate. These positions may be altered by changing the potential used to accelerate the ions. When an electrical device that measures the intensities of the ion beams is substituted for the photographic plate, the instrument is known as a **mass spectrometer**.

Isotopes are atoms with the same atomic number but different mass numbers. They have very similar chemical properties, in most cases, indistinguishable. Thus, in nature, there are two types of atoms of chlorine: $^{35}_{17}Cl$ and $^{37}_{17}Cl$. Both these atoms have 17 protons and 17 electrons. The first, however, has 18 neutrons, and the chlorine-37 atom has 20 neutrons. Thus isotopes differ in the number of neutrons in the nucleus. In nature, some elements exist in only one isotopic form (e.g., sodium, beryllium, and fluorine); however, most elements have more than one isotope—tin has ten. The term **nuclide** is used for atomic species in general.

Isobars are nuclides that have the same mass number but different atomic numbers. Thus $^{36}_{16}S$ and $^{36}_{18}Ar$ are isobars. The total numbers of nucleons in each of these isobars is the same, but the numbers of protons and neutrons are different. Thus the sulfur isotope has 16 protons and 20 neutrons making a total of 36 nucleons, whereas the argon isotope has 18 protons and 18 neutrons making the same total. Isobars are not alike chemically since chemical characteristics depend principally upon the number of electrons, which is determined by the atomic number.

2.9 Atomic Weights

The usual standards of mass are not convenient for the measurement of the very small nucleons and nuclides, since they give rise to very small numbers. Therefore a standard of mass has been adopted for the measurement of these particles that is on a scale commensurate with them.

The **atomic mass unit** (u) is defined as one-twelfth the mass of the nuclide $^{12}_{6}C$. Note that this gives approximate values of unity to the proton and the neutron. The assignment of the value of 12 u to this isotope of carbon is quite arbitrary; other nuclides could have been used, and, indeed, others have been used at other times (Dalton used hydrogen as his standard). At the present, the masses of all nuclides are expressed as a ratio of their masses to the mass of $^{12}_{6}C$ taken as exactly 12 u.

On this scale the mass of the proton is 1.007277 u; the neutron is 1.008665 u; the electron is 0.0005486 u. Given these values one might expect that the mass of any nuclide could be calculated from its atomic number and mass number; such, however, is not the case. For example, the mass of $^{35}_{17}$Cl would be expected to equal the sum of the masses of 17 protons, 18 neutrons, and 17 electrons. Thus:

$$17(1.007277) \text{ u} + 18(1.008665) \text{ u} + 17(0.0005486) \text{ u} = 35.289005 \text{ u}$$

The mass of $^{35}_{17}$Cl has been accurately determined, however, to be 34.96885 u. The difference between the two values is:

$$35.28901 \text{ u} - 34.96885 \text{ u} = 0.32016 \text{ u}$$

This difference in its energy equivalent is spoken of as the **binding energy** of the nuclide in question.

Einstein has shown that energy and mass are equivalent:

$$E = mc^2$$

where E is energy, in ergs; m is mass, in grams; and c is the speed of light, 3.00×10^{10} cm/sec. Thus the energy equivalent of 1 g of matter is

$$E = (1.00 \text{ g})(3.00 \times 10^{10} \text{ cm/sec})^2$$
$$= 9.00 \times 10^{20} \text{ g cm}^2/\text{sec}^2 = 9.00 \times 10^{20} \text{ ergs}$$

Since 1 cal $= 4.184 \times 10^7$ ergs,

$$E = 2.15 \times 10^{13} \text{ cal} = 2.15 \times 10^{10} \text{ kcal}$$

Therefore 1 g of matter is equal to over 20 billion kcal of energy.

Binding energy is generally interpreted in terms of the particles of the nucleus. If it were possible to pull the nucleus apart, this would be the energy required to do the job. The reverse process, the condensation of nucleons into a nucleus, would release the binding energy with the attendant decrease in mass.

The removal of electrons from an atom, or the addition of electrons to an atom, also involves energy changes which, of course, have mass equivalents. However, these mass equivalents are extremely small; in most cases, it is perfectly valid to assume that the mass of the electron does not change when the electron assumes a position in an atom. The energy effects attributable to the particles of the nucleus are very much larger than those caused by the addition or removal of electrons.

For every atom except $^1_1$H (the nucleus of which consists of a single proton), the sum of the masses of the constituent particles exceeds the actual mass of the nuclide. Thus every nucleus consisting of two or more nucleons has a binding energy. Binding energy is discussed more fully in Section 21.6.

Most naturally occurring elements consist of a mixture of isotopes, and chemical calculations would be hopelessly complicated except for the fact that, with very few exceptions, these mixtures are of constant composition. The element chlorine consists of a mixture of 75.53% $^{35}_{17}$Cl and 24.47% $^{37}_{17}$Cl.

Any sample of chlorine from any source will consist of these two isotopes in this proportion.

It is convenient to use a weighted average for the atomic weight of chlorine. This average may be obtained from the isotopic masses by multiplying each by its fractional abundance and adding the values obtained. Thus

$$0.7553 \,(34.97 \text{ u}) + 0.2447 \,(36.95 \text{ u}) = 35.45 \text{ u}$$

The accepted value for chlorine is 35.453 ± 0.001.

There is no atom of chlorine that weighs 35.453 u, but it is convenient to think in terms of one. In even a very small sample of matter there is a huge number of atoms. (There are more atoms in a drop of water than there are people on the face of the earth—a sobering comparison for the behavioral sciences.) Even though a very small sample may be used in an experiment, a very large number of atoms is included, and no mistake is made in assuming in most calculations that the sample consists of only one type of atom with the average mass. The term **atomic weight** is applied to this average.

Prior to 1961, two different standards were employed for atomic and nuclear masses. Chemists based their scale on the assignment of exactly 16 to the average mass of oxygen atoms as they occur in nature. The physical scale was based on $^{16}_{8}O$, this isotope being assigned a mass of exactly 16. Since naturally occurring oxygen consists of three isotopes (of mass numbers 16, 17, and 18), the average value for oxygen is 16.0044 on the physical scale. The $^{12}_{6}C$ scale, called the **unified scale**, was developed to eliminate this duality.

Readers must be careful to note, therefore, what standard an author employs. To aid in the distinction, the National Bureau of Standards suggests the use of the symbol u for the unit of the new unified scale; the symbol amu (atomic mass unit) was previously employed (somewhat ambiguously) for both the physical and chemical scales.

2.10 Electromagnetic Radiation

Much has been learned about atomic structure through studies of the absorption and emission of radiant energy by atoms. An appreciation of these investigations requires that the nature of radiant energy be understood.

Radiant energy may be considered to consist of fluctuating electric and magnetic fields propagated through space in a wave motion (Figure 2.8). The distance from crest to crest (or trough to trough) is called a **wavelength**, λ; the height of the wave, or its **amplitude**, a, is related to the **intensity** of the radiation.

Matter is not needed for the propagation of these waves. In a vacuum, all waves, regardless of wavelength, move with a velocity of 2.9979×10^{10} cm/sec. This velocity, called the speed of light, is usually given the symbol c.

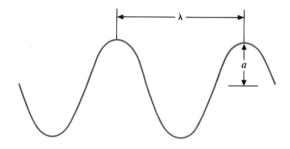

Figure 2.8 Wavelength, λ, and amplitude, a, of a wave.

If the speed of light (in cm/sec) is divided by the wavelength of a given wave (in cm/cycle), the result gives the number of waves of that type that pass a given spot in a second (in cycles/sec). This value is the frequency, ν, of the radiation. Thus,

$$\nu = \frac{c}{\lambda}$$

or

$$c = \lambda\nu$$

The electromagnetic spectrum is shown in Figure 2.9. Seemingly diverse types of radiation are in reality electromagnetic radiations of different wavelength. Thus, radio waves have very long wavelengths, radiant heat (infrared rays) have moderate wavelengths, and γ rays (from radioactive decay) have

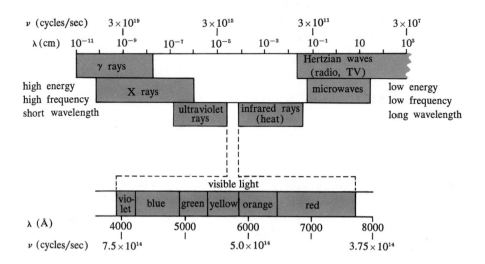

Figure 2.9 Electromagnetic radiation. Note that the approximate ranges of electromagnetic radiations are plotted on a logarithmic scale in the upper part of the diagram; the spectrum of visible light is not plotted in this way.

extremely short wavelengths. White light consists of radiations with wavelengths in the range of from 4×10^{-5} cm to 7.5×10^{-5} cm.

The wave theory successfully interprets some properties of electromagnetic radiation (particularly diffraction and mode of propagation); however, other properties require that such radiation be considered as consisting of particles. One such property involves the radiation emitted by hot bodies. The temperature of the body determines the range of wavelengths of the light emitted, and, at each temperature, a maximum intensity is observed at a characteristic wavelength. As the temperature of the incandescent body increases, the maximum shifts to shorter wavelengths. Thus the body glows red at first, then orange, yellow, white, and blue. According to the wave theory, a maximum should not be observed at any temperature.

In 1900, Max Planck proposed the **quantum theory** of radiant energy to explain these observations. Planck suggested that radiant energy could be absorbed or emitted only in discrete quantities, or quanta. The energy of each quantum is directly proportional to the frequency of the radiation.

$$E = h\nu$$

where the proportionality constant, h, is Planck's constant, 6.6256×10^{-27} erg sec. Thus, when the temperature is low, the energy of an emitted quantum is low, the frequency is low, and the wavelength is relatively long (red). At higher temperatures, the frequency is higher, and the wavelength shorter (blue).

In 1905, Einstein used and extended Planck's quantum theory to explain the photoelectric effect, which consists of the emission of electrons from the surface of a metal when the metal is irradiated by light. According to the wave theory, the energies of the ejected electrons should be proportional to the intensity of the light beam. Instead, the energies of the photoelectrons are proportional to the frequency of the radiation, with each metal requiring a characteristic frequency before electrons are ejected at all. Increasing the intensity of the light dislodges more electrons but does not affect their energies.

Einstein proposed that Planck's quanta represented discontinuous bits of energy, later called **photons**, and that the interaction of a photon with an electron of the metal caused the photoelectric effect. In a collision, the photon vanishes and all the energy is given to the electron. In order to dislodge the electron, the photon has to have a certain minimum energy (given by its frequency), and any excess energy over that needed to disengage the electron is imparted to the electron as kinetic energy. Increasing the intensity of light of a given frequency increases the number of photons but does not increase the energies of the photons. Hence, when the intensity of the light is increased, more electrons are ejected, but the energies of these electrons are not altered.

Radiant energy, therefore, may be described in two ways: as waves of energy or as streams of photons. Each concept has the support of experimental observation, and which model is used for a given purpose depends upon which is more convenient. In Section 2.14, the dual character of matter is discussed.

2.11 Atomic Spectra

Since the extranuclear electrons of an atom determine its chemical characteristics, the arrangement of these electrons is of primary importance. Rutherford, as well as others, postulated that the electrons are in rapid motion in spherical orbits around the nucleus similar to the way the planets travel around the sun (but with the important distinction that the units of the solar system are not charged). The postulated rapid motion was supposed to overcome, by centrifugal force, the attraction on the negative electron by the positive nucleus.

This simple picture did not stand the close scrutiny of classical physics. According to electromagnetic theory, a charged particle moving under the influence of an attractive force should continuously emit energy, and therefore the electron should follow a spiral path until it finally falls into the nucleus. The atom should, with the emission of energy, ultimately collapse. The study of atomic spectra led to an answer to this problem.

When a ray of electromagnetic radiation is passed through a prism, the ray is bent. The degree of refraction depends upon the wavelength of the ray; short wavelengths are refracted more than long wavelengths. Thus a prism can be used to resolve radiation, consisting of different wavelengths, into its component wavelengths. Since ordinary white light consists of all the wavelengths in the visible range, it is spread out into a wide band of colors called a **continuous spectrum** (Figure 2.10). This spectrum is a rainbow of colors with no discontinuities—violet merges into blue, which merges into green, etc.

When gases or vapors of chemical substances are heated by an electric arc or spark or a Bunsen flame, light is emitted. The resolution of a ray of such light by a prism produces a **line spectrum** (Figure 2.10). This spectrum is not continuous; it consists of a number of lines of various colors, each line representing a definite wavelength or energy. Each element has its own characteristic line spectrum; there are similarities, but each is unique. The frequencies of the lines emitted by hydrogen in the visible region of the spectrum (the Balmer series) can be expressed by the formula

$$\nu = 3.29 \times 10^{15} \text{ cycles/sec} \left(\frac{1}{2^2} - \frac{1}{n^2} \right)$$

where n is an integer equal to, or greater than, 3.

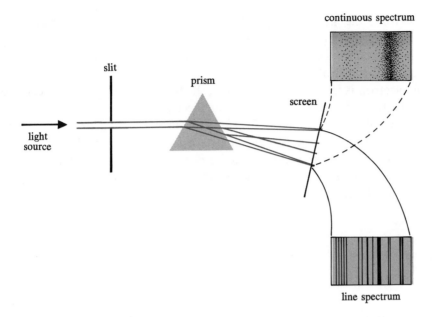

Figure 2.10 The spectroscope.

In 1913, Niels Bohr proposed a theory, which was based on the spectrum of hydrogen and which used the quantum concept of Planck, to explain the configuration of electrons in atoms. The radiation emitted in a spectral study is thought to arise from electronic transitions within atoms. Since the line spectrum of hydrogen shows that radiation is emitted only in discrete quanta, it is logical to assume that the energy of the electron of hydrogen is quantized and that a transition from a high energy state to a lower energy state results in the emission of the energy difference in the form of a quantum of light.

According to Bohr, the electron of hydrogen can exist only in certain spherical orbits (or energy levels, or shells), which are arranged concentrically around the nucleus. These orbits are subject to a quantum restriction: the angular momentum of an electron in an orbit (mvr, where m is the mass of the electron, v is its velocity, and r is the radius of the orbit) must be an integral multiple of the quantity $h/2\pi$.

$$mvr = n\frac{h}{2\pi} \qquad n = 1, 2, 3, \ldots$$

Thus an electron moving in any orbit has a definite energy characteristic of that orbit. As long as an electron remains in a given orbit, it neither absorbs nor radiates energy.

Thus the K level ($n = 1$) is the shell closest to the nucleus and is of the smallest radius and lowest energy. The next shell (L; $n = 2$) has a larger radius, and electrons moving in it have higher energies. With increasing distance from the nucleus $(K, L, M, N, O; n = 1, 2, 3, 4, 5)$, the radius of the shell increases, and the energy of electrons in that shell increases. No electron in an atom can have an energy that would place it somewhere between the permissible orbits.

If an electron is in an orbit of radius r, the force of attraction between the nucleus (with a charge of $+Ze$) and the electron (with a charge of $-e$) is given by Coulomb's law as $-Ze^2/r^2$. This force of attraction causes the electron to deflect from a straight-line path to a circular path around the nucleus, and therefore the coulomb force is a centripetal force. The formula for centripetal force is $-mv^2/r$, where the minus sign indicates attraction inward. Therefore,

$$\frac{mv^2}{r} = \frac{Ze^2}{r^2} \qquad (7)$$

Thus,

$$v^2 = \frac{Ze^2}{mr} \qquad (8)$$

If we solve Bohr's quantum condition for v, we get

$$mvr = \frac{nh}{2\pi} \qquad n = 1, 2, 3, \ldots \qquad (9)$$

$$v = \frac{nh}{2\pi mr} \qquad (10)$$

Squaring equation (10) and combining the result with equation (8) gives

$$\frac{Ze^2}{mr} = \frac{n^2h^2}{4\pi^2m^2r^2} \qquad (11)$$

$$r = \frac{n^2h^2}{4\pi^2mZe^2} \qquad n = 1, 2, 3, \ldots \qquad (12)$$

If we solve this expression for the smallest orbit $(n = 1)$ of hydrogen $(Z = 1)$, we get

$$r = 0.529 \times 10^{-8} \text{ cm} = 0.529 \text{ Å}$$

This quantity is called the **Bohr radius** and is sometimes given the symbol a_0.

The total energy of an electron is equal to the sum of its kinetic energy $(mv^2/2)$, which is attributable to its motion, and its potential energy $(-Ze^2/r)$, which results from its position in the field of the nucleus.

$$E = \frac{mv^2}{2} - \frac{Ze^2}{r} \qquad (13)$$

From equation (8),

$$mv^2 = \frac{Ze^2}{r} \qquad (14)$$

and therefore

$$E = \frac{Ze^2}{2r} - \frac{Ze^2}{r} = -\frac{Ze^2}{2r} . \qquad (15)$$

Substitution of the value of r from equation (12) into equation (15) gives

$$E = -\frac{2\pi^2 m Z^2 e^4}{n^2 h^2} \qquad n = 1, 2, 3, \ldots \qquad (16)$$

By means of equation (16) it is possible to calculate the energy of an electron in each of the Bohr orbits.

When the electrons of an atom are arranged as close to the nucleus as possible (in the case of hydrogen, one electron in the K level), they are in the condition of lowest possible energy; such is called the **ground state** or **ground level**. In a spectroscope, the electrons of the material being investigated absorb energy from the electric arc or spark and hence jump to outer, more energetic levels. Such a condition is called an **excited state**.

When an electron falls back to a lower orbit, it emits a definite amount of energy—the difference between the energy required by the outer level, E_o, and the energy required by the inner level, E_i. This energy is emitted as radiation, and since it is a definite amount, it has a characteristic frequency (and wavelength) and produces a characteristic spectral line.

The energy of the photon radiated by the atom is

$$h\nu = E_o - E_i \qquad E_o \rightarrow E_i$$

Substitution of the values of E from equation (16) into this expression gives

$$h\nu = \left(-\frac{2\pi^2 m Z^2 e^4}{h^2} \right)\left(\frac{1}{n_o^2} \right) - \left(-\frac{2\pi^2 m Z^2 e^4}{h^2} \right)\left(\frac{1}{n_i^2} \right) \qquad (17)$$

$$= \frac{2\pi^2 m Z^2 e^4}{h^2} \left(\frac{1}{n_i^2} - \frac{1}{n_o^2} \right) \qquad (18)$$

and

$$\nu = \frac{2\pi^2 m Z^2 e^4}{h^3} \left(\frac{1}{n_i^2} - \frac{1}{n_o^2} \right) \qquad (19)$$

If the constants of this equation are evaluated for hydrogen ($Z = 1$), the frequencies of photons emitted by transitions to the $n = 2$ level from higher levels is given by

$$\nu = 3.29 \times 10^{15} \text{ cycles/sec}\left(\frac{1}{2^2} - \frac{1}{n^2} \right)$$

which agrees with the empirically derived equation describing the spectral lines of the Balmer series.

The relation between some of the electronic transitions of the hydrogen atom and the spectral lines is illustrated in Figure 2.11. Since electron transitions to the $n = 1$ level (Lyman series) release more energy than those to the

Figure 2.11 The relation between some electronic transitions of the hydrogen atom and spectral lines of the visible region.

$n = 2$ level, the wavelengths of the lines of this series are shorter than those of the Balmer series, and the lines of the Lyman series occur in the ultraviolet region. On the other hand, the lines of the Paschen series, which represent transitions to the $n = 3$ level, occur at wavelengths longer than the Balmer series, and the Paschen lines appear in the infrared region. Certain wavelengths of light are not emitted because there are no corresponding energy drops for an electron in the atom. The removal of an electron to an infinite shell amounts to **ionization**, and the **ionization energy** is the minimum amount of energy required for this process (Section 3.2).

Since atoms differ in size, charge on the nucleus, number of electrons, etc., the spectrum of each element is different. The Bohr theory successfully interprets the spectra of atoms containing only one electron, such as H, He$^+$, and Li^{2+}.

2.12 Atomic Numbers and the Periodic Law

Early in the nineteenth century, chemists became interested in the relationships among the elements. In 1817 and 1829, Johann W. Döbereiner published articles in which he examined certain sets of elements that he called triads (Ca, Sr, Ba; Li, Na, K; Cl, Br, I; and S, Se, Te). The elements of each set have similar properties, and the atomic weight of the middle element is approximately the arithmetic mean of the other two.

Period	I a	I b	II a	II b	III a	III b	IV a	IV b	V a	V b	VI a	VI b	VII a	VII b	VIII a	VIII b(0)
1	H 1.0															He 4.0
2	Li 6.9		Be 9.0			B 10.8		C 12.0		N 14.0		O 16.0		F 19.0		Ne 20.2
3	Na 23.0		Mg 24.3			Al 27.0		Si 28.1		P 31.0		S 32.1		Cl 35.5		Ar 39.9
4	K 39.1		Ca 40.1		Sc 45.0		Ti 47.9		V 50.9		Cr 52.0		Mn 54.9		Fe 55.8 · Co 58.9 · Ni 58.7	
		Cu 63.5		Zn 65.4		Ga 69.7		Ge 72.6		As 74.9		Se 79.0		Br 79.9		Kr 83.8
5	Rb 85.5		Sr 87.6		Y 88.9		Zr 91.2		Nb 92.9		Mo 95.9		Tc		Ru 101.1 · Rh 102.9 · Pd 106.4	
		Ag 107.9		Cd 112.4		In 114.8		Sn 118.7		Sb 121.8		Te 127.6		I 126.9		Xe 131.3
6	Cs 132.9		Ba 137.3		La * 138.9		Hf 178.5		Ta 180.9		W 183.9		Re 186.2		Os 190.2 · Ir 192.2 · Pt 195.1	
		Au 197.0		Hg 200.6		Tl 204.4		Pb 207.2		Bi 209.0		Po		At		Rn
7	Fr		Ra		Ac **											

*	Ce 140.1	Pr 140.9	Nd 144.2	Pm	Sm 150.4	Eu 152.0	Gd 157.3	Tb 158.9	Dy 162.5	Ho 164.9	Er 167.3	Tm 168.9	Yb 173.0	Lu 175.0
**	Th 232.0	Pa	U 238.0	Np	Pu	Am	Cm	Bk	Cf	Es	Fm	Md	No	Lr

Figure 2.12 Periodic table based on the Mendeleev chart of 1871. Elements that were not known in 1871 appear in the darker squares.

In the years following, many chemists made attempts to discern regularities in the properties of elements, and several charts and arrangements of the elements were proposed. The work of John A. R. Newlands is significant. In the years 1863–1866, Newlands proposed and developed his law of octaves, in which he compared the elements to the notes of octaves in music. He stated that if the elements are arranged in order of increasing atomic weight, any given element is similar to the eighth element following it. Newlands assigned a serial number, based on increasing atomic weight, to each element with hydrogen assigned the number 1. These numbers may be regarded as early atomic numbers, although no physical significance could be attached to them at that time. Furthermore, Newlands' values do not correspond to modern values, since some of the elements had not yet been discovered and since some of the atomic weights he used were incorrect.

The periodic classification of the elements was first proposed in polished form in 1869 by both Julius Lothar Meyer and Dmitri Mendeleev working independently. The modern **periodic law** states that the chemical and physical properties of the elements are periodic functions of atomic number; that is, when the elements are arranged in order of increasing atomic number and the properties of each element are studied in turn, similarities recur periodically (Section 2.13). The original statement of the periodic law was based on atomic weights, not atomic numbers. However, even in this form, it was a promising and useful generalization, since atomic numbers and atomic weights increase in a parallel manner with only three exceptions (K, Ni, and I). Mendeleev prepared a periodic table in which similar elements were listed under one another and in which blanks were left for missing elements (see Figure 2.12). On the basis of his system, Mendeleev was able to predict the existence, as well as the properties, of some of the elements that had not been discovered at that time (e.g., Sc, Ga, and Ge).

Figure 2.13 X-ray tube.

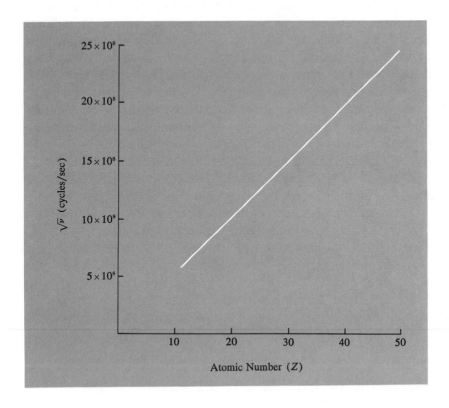

Figure 2.14 Relationship between frequency of characteristic X-ray lines and atomic number.

Subsequent study of Mendeleev's periodic classification convinced many that some fundamental atomic property other than atomic weight is the cause of the periodicity observed. It was proposed that this fundamental property is in some way related to atomic number, which at that time was only a serial number derived from the periodic classification. The work of Henry G. J. Moseley in the years 1913 and 1914 solved this problem. To explain his results, Moseley drew upon Bohr's theory, which had just been published.

When high-energy cathode rays are focused on a target, X rays are produced (Figure 2.13). This X radiation can be resolved into its component wavelengths, and the line spectra thus obtained can be recorded photographically. Different X-ray spectra result when different elements are used as targets; each spectrum consists of only a few lines.

Moseley studied the X-ray spectra of 38 elements with atomic numbers between number 13 (aluminum) and number 79 (gold). Using a corresponding spectral line for each element, he found that there is a linear relationship between the square root of the frequency of the line and the atomic number of the element (Figure 2.14). In other words, the square root of the spectral line increases by a constant amount from element to element when the elements are arranged by increasing atomic number.

Moseley was able, therefore, to assign the correct atomic number to any element on the basis of its X-ray spectrum. In this way, he settled the problem involving the classification of elements that have atomic weights out of line with those of their neighbors (K, Ni, and I). He also stated that there should be 14 elements in the series from $_{58}$Ce to $_{71}$Lu (found at the bottom of the chart in Figure 2.12), and he established that these elements should follow lanthanum in the periodic table. Moseley's diagrams indicated that 4 elements before $_{79}$Au remained to be discovered (numbers 43, 61, 72, and 75).

In the production of X rays, the cathode rays rip electrons from the inner shells of the target atoms. When outer electrons fall into the vacancies thus produced, photons of high energy are emitted, which have the high frequencies and short wavelengths characteristic of X rays. Since the Bohr equation, number (19) of Section 2.11, shows that the frequency of a spectral line is directly proportional to the square of the number of unit charges on the nucleus, Z^2, Moseley proposed that the atomic number of an element is the number of units of positive charge on the atomic nucleus.

2.13 The Periodic Law and Electronic Structures

The most popular form of the periodic table is the long form that is found inside the back cover of this book. The **periods** consist of those elements that are arranged in horizontal rows in the table. The organization is such that elements of similar chemical and physical properties (called **groups** or **families**) appear in vertical columns. In this table, the set of elements appearing at the bottom and called the lanthanides should actually appear in the body of the chart in proper order by atomic number so that the sixth period has its requisite 32 elements. For convenience in reproduction this is not done; but, properly, the chart should be vertically cut, the sections separated, and the lanthanides inserted in their proper positions. For the actinides, which appear below the lanthanides at the bottom of the periodic table, the same considerations pertain; they should be inserted in the seventh period (as yet incomplete).

The first period consists of only two elements, hydrogen and helium. Subsequent periods have 8, 8, 18, 18, and 32 elements. With the exception of the first period, each complete period begins with an **alkali metal** (group I A)—a highly reactive, light, silvery metal—and ends with a **noble gas** (group 0)—an unreactive, colorless gas. The element before the noble gas of each complete period (again, excepting the first period) is a **halogen** (group VII A)—a very reactive nonmetal.

There is a general pattern for each of the periods after the first. Starting with an alkali metal, the properties change from element to element—the metallic properties fading and being gradually replaced by nonmetallic characteristics. After a highly reactive nonmetal, a halogen, is reached, each complete period ends with a noble gas.

Since the periodic table classifies atoms by chemical behavior, and since chemical behavior is determined by electronic configuration, the periodic table may also be said to classify atoms by electronic configuration. The maximum number of electrons that each energy level may hold is given by $2n^2$, where n is the principal quantum number of the shell in question. Hence for the $n = 1$ shell, the maximum number is $2(1)^2$ or 2; for the $n = 2$ level, this number is $2(2)^2$ or 8; these maximum electron populations for the first five shells are given in Table 2.3.

Table 2.3

Maximum Number of Electrons for Each Shell

Shell	n	$2n^2$
K	1	2
L	2	8
M	3	18
N	4	32
O	5	50

In this discussion all elements are considered in their ground states. The first element, hydrogen, has one electron in the K level; the second, helium, has two electrons in this shell. This completes the $n = 1$ shell and the first period. The third element, lithium, has a complete K shell and one electron in the L level. Each succeeding element in the period adds one electron to this level. The second period ends with the noble gas neon ($Z = 10$) which has two electrons in the $n = 1$ level and a complete $n = 2$ level of eight electrons.

A striking fact is encountered in the third period. The initial element of this period, sodium, has completed K and L shells of two and eight electrons, respectively, and an additional electron in the next level, the M level ($n = 3$). One notes that in the first group of elements, lithium and sodium both have one electron in the outer shell. Likewise the second elements of these periods both have two electrons in their outer shells; beryllium has a configuration (by shells) of 2, 2, and magnesium has a configuration of 2, 8, 2.

By comparing the third period elements with the second period elements, we see that the number of electrons in the outer shells (called the **valence**

shells) is the same for elements of the same group and that this number is the same as the group number. This similarity in number of valence electrons accounts for the similarities in properties. These facts may be derived from Table 2.4.

Table 2.4

Electronic Configurations by Shells for the First Three Periods

Electronic Levels	Group Number							
	I A	II A	III A	IV A	V A	VI A	VII A	0
	H							He
K	1							2
	Li	Be	B	C	N	O	F	Ne
K	2	2	2	2	2	2	2	2
L	1	2	3	4	5	6	7	8
	Na	Mg	Al	Si	P	S	Cl	Ar
K	2	2	2	2	2	2	2	2
L	8	8	8	8	8	8	8	8
M	1	2	3	4	5	6	7	8

The electronic **configurations** of the element of the fourth and subsequent periods are **not easily understood** in terms of the electronic shells alone; a number of questions arise that may be answered only in **terms** of concepts that will be discussed later. The fourth period begins with potassium, number 19, which is a member of group I and has one valence electron in the *N* ($n = 4$) level, thus giving potassium a configuration of 2, 8, 8, 1. This poses a question. Since the *M* level can hold a maximum of 18 electrons, why should the final electron of potassium be placed in the *N* level before the *M* level has been filled?

Calcium, number 20, has the configuration 2, 8, 8, 2. The next element, scandium ($Z = 21$), has the electronic configuration 2, 8, 9, 2; it differs from the preceding element, calcium, by the addition of an electron not in the outer (or *N*) level but rather in the second from the outer level—the *M* level. This element, scandium, is not a member of group III A because it does not have three valence electrons, and it is not placed below aluminum in group III A. Scandium is called a **transition element**, and because the "last" electron was added to the second from the outer shell, it is said to undergo **inner building**. These transition elements (numbers 21 through 30 in the fourth period) are placed in the center of the periodic table, and their groups are given B designations. Inner building cannot be explained on the basis of electronic shells alone.

The electronic configurations of the noble gases also pose a question. The first noble gas, helium, has a completed first shell; the second noble gas, neon ($Z = 10$), has a configuration of 2, 8 representing two completed shells (K and L); the third noble gas, argon ($Z = 18$), has the configuration 2, 8, 8. One might suppose that these elements of extremely low chemical reactivity would have all of their electronic shells complete; this must not be a requisite for electronic stability, however, since the third level in argon is not complete but has only an octet of electrons. We shall see later that all of the noble gases have eight electrons in their outer shells with the exception of helium which has the maximum number of electrons that the K level can hold—two.

2.14 Dual Nature of the Electron

In the same way that electromagnetic radiation has both a wave and a corpuscular character, matter has a dual nature. We have seen that the energy of a photon, E, is related to its frequency, v, and its wavelength, λ.

$$E = hv = h\frac{c}{\lambda} \tag{20}$$

Using Einstein's equation, $E = mc^2$, we derive

$$mc^2 = \frac{hc}{\lambda} \tag{21}$$

or

$$\lambda = \frac{h}{mc} \tag{22}$$

The term mc is equal to the momentum of the photon (mass times velocity).

In 1925, Louis de Broglie postulated that a wavelength can be assigned to an electron:

$$\lambda = \frac{h}{mv} \tag{23}$$

where m is the mass of an electron, and v is its velocity. This postulate has been confirmed by a variety of experimental data.

The application of the postulate to the Bohr theory produces an interesting result. The Bohr restriction

$$mvr = n\frac{h}{2\pi}$$

may be rearranged to

$$2\pi r = n\frac{h}{mv}$$

and therefore

$$2\pi r = n\lambda$$

Thus a standing wave can be accommodated in the Bohr orbit since the circumference of the orbit, $2\pi r$, is an integral multiple of the wavelength of the electron, $n\lambda$.

Consideration of the electron as a wave is very important because the Heisenberg **uncertainty principle** (1927) demonstrates the ultimate futility of any attempt to make the Bohr model more exact and comprehensive. The precise prediction of the path of a moving body requires that both the position and the velocity (the latter denoting direction as well as speed) of that body be known at a given time. Werner Heisenberg showed that it is impossible to measure simultaneously the exact position and exact velocity of a body as small as an electron.

The determination of the position of an object depends upon our ability to observe it, either by noting the interference in the light rays that illuminate the object or, more indirectly, by noting the variation in some other test signal. Since there is an uncertainty in the position of an object, Δx, approximately equal to the wavelength of the light used to illuminate it,

$$\Delta x \approx \lambda$$

radiation of extremely short wavelength would be needed to detect the position of an object as small as an electron with any degree of precision. Such radiation is very energetic (the shorter the wavelength, the more energetic), and hence, when it impinges on an electron, the impact causes the direction and speed of the tiny electron to change.

Solving equation (23) for the momentum of a photon, we get

$$mc = \frac{h}{\lambda}$$

In the collision of a photon with an electron, a part, or all, of the momentum of the photon is imparted to the electron. Therefore, the uncertainty in the momentum of an electron, Δmv, after collision is

$$\Delta mv \approx \frac{h}{\lambda}$$

Photons of longer wavelength (less energetic) have less effect on the momentum of the electron but, because of their longer wavelength, are less precise in indicating the position of the electron. Therefore, the two uncertainties are related. An approximate mathematical statement of the Heisenberg uncertainty principle is

$$\Delta x \, \Delta mv \approx \lambda \frac{h}{\lambda} = h$$

The mass of the electron is approximately 9×10^{-28} g, and according to the Bohr model, the velocity of the electron in the $n = 1$ shell of hydrogen is approximately 2×10^8 cm/sec. The momentum of the electron obtained by multiplying these values is

$$(9 \times 10^{-28} \text{ g})(2 \times 10^8 \text{ cm/sec}) = 2 \times 10^{-19} \text{ g cm/sec}$$

If the measured momentum is permitted to be in error by 100%,

$$\Delta x \, \Delta mv \approx h$$

$$\Delta x(2 \times 10^{-19} \text{ g cm/sec}) \approx 6.6 \times 10^{-27} \text{ g cm}^2/\text{sec}$$

$$\Delta x \approx \frac{6.6 \times 10^{-27} \text{ g cm}^2/\text{sec}}{2 \times 10^{-19} \text{ g cm/sec}} = 3 \times 10^{-8} \text{ cm} = 3 \text{ Å}$$

This value is approximately three times the Bohr diameter of the $n = 1$ shell of the hydrogen atom. (If the value $h/2\pi mr$, from the Bohr theory, is used for the velocity of an electron in the $n = 1$ shell and m is used for the mass of the electron, the result is $\Delta x \approx 2\pi r$, or the circumference of the Bohr orbit.)

It appears, then, that a precise description of the path of an electron in a Bohr orbit is impossible. The wave postulate of de Broglie was used by Erwin Schrödinger to develop a differential equation describing the electron in terms of its wave character.

The **Schrödinger equation** (1926) is the keystone of **wave mechanics**. It reconciles the idea of the quantum restriction on the energy of the electron, originally imposed by Bohr, with the idea of the electron as a standing wave which may be described mathematically in much the same way as the waves of a vibrating guitar string. By means of the Schrödinger equation, a function may be derived that describes an electron as a wave of energy or a cloud of negative charge, denser in some parts than in others.

Max Born proposed an interpretation of the wave equations based on probabilities. If one imagines a corpuscular electron in motion about a nucleus, the wave equations may be interpreted in terms of the probability (or relative chance) of finding that electron at any given distance from the nucleus. The chance of finding an electron is high in a region where the cloud is dense. This interpretation does not fix electron position nor does it describe electronic paths; it merely predicts where an electron is most likely to be found. Insofar as a corpuscular interpretation of the electron is concerned, it is the best that wave mechanics has to offer.

For an electron in the $n = 1$ state of the hydrogen atom, the charge cloud has its greatest density near the nucleus and becomes thinner as the distance from the nucleus increases (Figure 2.15). More information about this electronic distribution can be obtained from an examination of the probability curves of Figure 2.16.

In curve (a), the probability of finding an electron in a small segment of volume in space is plotted against distance from the nucleus. This probability is greatest near the nucleus, but there is a finite probability at all points in

Figure 2.15   Cross section of charge cloud of an electron in the $n = 1$ state of the hydrogen atom.

space that are finite distances from the nucleus. Curve (b) is a radial probability distribution. Imagine a group of spherical shells of very small thickness arranged concentrically around the nucleus; the total probability of finding the electron in such a shell is plotted against the distance of the shell from the nucleus in curve (b) of Figure 2.16. The probability per unit volume is greatest close to the nucleus, but the volume of a shell that is close to the nucleus is less than the volume of a shell that is farther out. Hence, the plot shows a maximum at 0.529 Å, or the Bohr radius, a_0. The total probability of finding an electron at all points of distance r from the nucleus is greatest when r is equal to a_0. In terms of the charge cloud concept, a greater amount of the total charge of the electron is found in the spherical shell radius a_0 than is found in any other shell.

Since there is a probability of finding an electron at all finite distances from the nucleus, the three-dimensional representation of an $n = 1$ electron

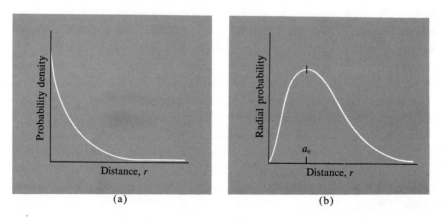

Figure 2.16   Probability curves for an electron in the $n = 1$ state of the hydrogen atom. (a) Probability of finding the electron per unit volume versus distance from the nucleus. (b) Probability of finding the electron at a given distance versus distance from the nucleus.

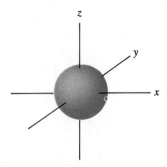

Figure 2.17 Boundary surface representation of an electron in the $n = 1$ state of the hydrogen atom. Volume encloses 90% of the electron density. Nucleus is at the origin.

of the hydrogen atom poses a problem. Such representations, however, are important aids for interpreting chemical phenomena. It is not possible to depict a geometric shape that will encompass a region of 100% probability. However, a surface can be drawn that connects points of equal probability and encloses a volume in which there is a high probability (e.g., 90%) of finding the electron (Figure 2.17). Alternatively, the figure can be interpreted as representing a contour that encloses a high percentage (90%) of the electronic charge.

2.15 Quantum Numbers

Bohr explained spectral lines on the basis of electronic energy shells or levels, assigning each shell a **principal quantum number**, n. Wave mechanics uses this quantum number as well as three additional numbers to describe electrons. We can consider that Bohr's shell represents a region where the probability of finding an electron is high. The value of n gives an indication of the position of the shell relative to the nucleus; the larger the value of n, the farther that shell is from the nucleus. These shells must be regarded as discrete in terms of energy, and the only permissible electron transitions are between shells, which, according to Bohr, accounts for the spectral lines.

The use of better spectroscopes, however, showed that the spectral lines first observed actually consist of groups of fine lines (fine structure). To account for all of these lines, more permissible electron states were necessary; Arnold Sommerfeld in 1916 proposed that Bohr shells consisted of subshells of slightly different energies—that the level of Bohr was actually a group of sublevels. Sommerfeld proposed this in terms of the Bohr quantum theory; however, his idea is incorporated into the modern wave mechanical treatment.

Each principal shell has as many subshells as its value of n; there is only one sublevel for the $n = 1$ level, but there are two sublevels for the $n = 2$ level, three for the $n = 3$ level, etc. A **subsidiary quantum number**, l, is introduced, and each subshell is assigned an l value. For each quantum level, n, there are values of l corresponding to every term in the series

$$l = 0, 1, 2, 3, \ldots (n - 1)$$

Thus when $n = 1$, the only value of l is 0, and there is only one subshell; when $n = 2$, there are two sublevels having l values of 0 and 1, respectively; and when $n = 3$, the three sublevels have l values of 0, 1, and 2. Notice that the values of l are referred back to the n value of the level in question.

By convention, other letters are used at times to denote sublevels. Thus the $l = 0$ sublevel is designated as an s sublevel; $l = 1$, p; $l = 2$, d; and $l = 3$, f. These spectroscopic notations are the initial letters of adjectives formerly used to describe spectral lines: sharp, principal, diffuse, and fundamental. For l values larger than 3, the letters used proceed alphabetically—g, h, i, etc.; however, for the ground states of the known elements, no value of l higher than 3 (f) need be used. Combining the principal quantum number with these spectroscopic symbols gives a convenient way to denote the subshells as is indicated in Table 2.5 for the first four shells.

Table 2.5

Subshell Notations

n	l	Spectroscopic Notations
1	0	$1s$
2	0	$2s$
2	1	$2p$
3	0	$3s$
3	1	$3p$
3	2	$3d$
4	0	$4s$
4	1	$4p$
4	2	$4d$
4	3	$4f$

The maximum number of electrons in each level is given by the formula $2n^2$. How these electrons of each level are distributed among that level's sublevels is made clear by examining the remaining two quantum numbers.

The **spin quantum number**, s, characterizes the spin of an electron on its own axis and may have a value of either $+\frac{1}{2}$ or $-\frac{1}{2}$, since only two directions of spin are possible. A spinning charge generates a magnetic field, and an electron has a magnetic moment associated with it that may be attributed to electron spin. The magnetic moments of two electrons with different spins ($+\frac{1}{2}$ and $-\frac{1}{2}$) oppose and cancel each other.

The wave function associated with an electron is termed an **orbital** to distinguish it from the path or orbit of the Bohr theory. Each orbital may hold two electrons, and electrons thus paired in a single orbital have opposed spins. The $n = 1$ level has a maximum electron population of two and but one sublevel ($1s$) to hold them. The $1s$ sublevel must, therefore, consist of a single orbital.

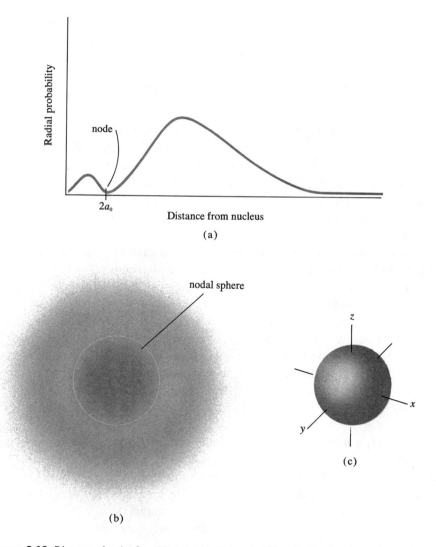

Figure 2.18 Diagrams for the $2s$ orbital. (a) Radial probability distribution. (b) Cross section of electron charge cloud. (c) Boundary surface diagram.

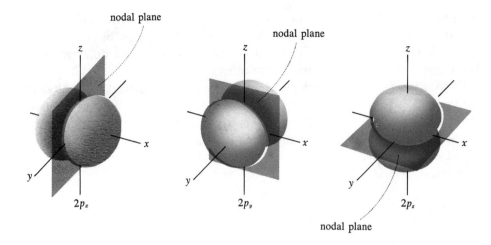

Figure 2.19 Boundary surface diagrams for the 2p orbitals.

The radial probability distribution for the $2s$ orbital is shown in Figure 2.18a. Notice that at the point where r is equal to $2a_0$, the radial probability drops to zero (a node). In the cross section of the electron density of this orbital (Figure 2.18b), this point shows up as a nodal sphere where electron density is zero. However, the conventional boundary surface of the $2s$ orbital, shown in Figure 2.18c, appears the same as that of the $1s$ orbital (Figure 2.17) only larger.

There are three $2p$ orbitals (Figure 2.19), and each has a nodal plane passing through the nucleus at the origin. Each p orbital consists of two lobes that may be considered to be oriented along the x, y, or z axis; hence they are sometimes given the designations $2p_x$, $2p_y$, and $2p_z$.

The number of orbitals in a sublevel may be inferred from the fourth quantum number—the **magnetic quantum number**, m. A magnetic field has no effect on an s electron since an s orbital is spherically symmetrical. If such an orbital were turned in a magnetic field, no effect would be observed because a sphere presents the same aspect toward the lines of force no matter what its orientation. This observation is true for all of the s orbitals—$1s$, $2s$, $3s$, etc.

However, a p orbital is not spherically symmetrical. Each p sublevel consists of three differently oriented p orbitals. These p orbitals are identical in terms of energy, and no distinction may be noted between electrons occupying different p orbitals in the absence of a magnetic field. However, if spectral studies are run with the source of emission in a magnetic field, certain spectral lines are split into several lines (Zeeman effect)—an effect that disappears when the magnetic field is removed.

For any sublevel, values of the magnetic quantum number, m, are given by the terms in the series

$$m = +l, +(l-1), \ldots, 0, \ldots, -(l-1), -l$$

Since m values indicate possible orientations in space for nonspherically symmetrical orbitals, the number of such values for a given sublevel reflects the number of orbitals in that sublevel. Each orbital is capable of holding two electrons of opposed spin. Thus, for $l = 0$, $m = 0$. For $l = 1$, the m values are $+1, 0$ and -1—indicating three orbitals. When $l = 2 (d$ subshell), m may have values of $+2$, $+1$, 0, -1, and -2—describing five orbitals each oriented differently in space. Notice that the values of m depend upon the value of l for the subshell under consideration.

The conventional boundary surfaces of the five $3d$ orbitals are shown in Figure 2.20. The shape of the d_{z^2} orbital is different from the others, but all these orbitals are energetically equivalent.

Each electron, therefore, may be described by a set of four quantum numbers—n giving the relative distance of the electron from the nucleus, l giving the subshell and the shape of the orbital for the electron (each orbital of a given subshell is equivalent in energy), m designating the orientation of

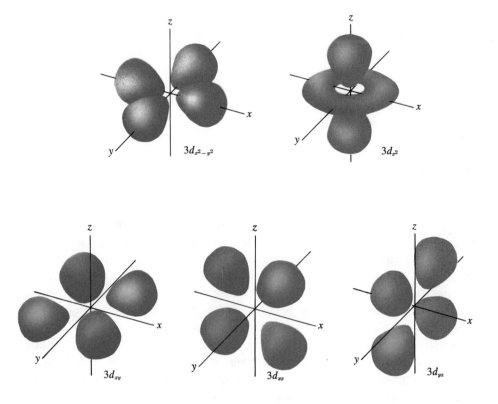

Figure 2.20 Boundary surface diagrams for the $3d$ orbitals.

the orbital in space, and s stating the spin of the electron. The **exclusion principle** of Wolfgang Pauli states that no two electrons in the same atom may have identical sets of all four quantum numbers; electrons so described would be indistinguishable. Even if two electrons have the same values for n, l, and m, they will differ in their s values. The quantum numbers are summarized in Table 2.6 by use of the 32 electrons of the $n = 4$ level as an example.

Table 2.6

Quantum Numbers for the Electrons of the $n = 4$ Level

n	l	m	s	Number of Electrons by Subshells
4	0 (s)	0	$\pm\frac{1}{2}$	2
	1 (p)	+1	$\pm\frac{1}{2}$	
		0	$\pm\frac{1}{2}$	6
		−1	$\pm\frac{1}{2}$	
	2 (d)	+2	$\pm\frac{1}{2}$	
		+1	$\pm\frac{1}{2}$	
		0	$\pm\frac{1}{2}$	10
		−1	$\pm\frac{1}{2}$	
		−2	$\pm\frac{1}{2}$	
	3 (f)	+3	$\pm\frac{1}{2}$	
		+2	$\pm\frac{1}{2}$	
		+1	$\pm\frac{1}{2}$	
		0	$\pm\frac{1}{2}$	14
		−1	$\pm\frac{1}{2}$	
		−2	$\pm\frac{1}{2}$	
		−3	$\pm\frac{1}{2}$	

2.16 Magnetic Moment

There are a number of types of magnetic behavior; **diamagnetism, paramagnetism,** and **ferromagnetism** are the most important. Diamagnetic substances are weakly repelled by a magnetic field, while paramagnetic materials are drawn into a magnetic field. Ferromagnetism, exhibited by iron, is a comparatively rare phenomenon and is an extreme form of paramagnetism.

A single spinning electron behaves like a small magnet (Section 2.15). Two electrons that are paired in an orbital have opposed spins, and their magnetic moments oppose each other and cancel. However, the magnetic properties of **unpaired electrons** (electrons occupying orbitals singly) cause atoms containing such electrons to be paramagnetic, and the larger the number of unpaired electrons, the greater the magnetic moment.

There are actually two effects that contribute to the paramagnetism of an atom: the spin of the unpaired electrons and the orbital motion of the electrons. The magnetic moment associated with the orbital motion of electrons is related to the orientation of the orbitals in regard to the magnetic field and hence is related to the magnetic quantum number, m. In the same way that a pair of electrons has no net spin magnetic moment (and the sum of the s values equals zero), a filled or half-filled subshell has no resultant *orbital* magnetic moment, and the sum of the values of m for all of the electrons of the subshell is zero. A half-filled subshell, however, has a magnetic moment attributable to the spins of the unpaired electrons it contains.

The magnetic properties of some atoms are the result of both effects; this is true for the lanthanides, in which the unpaired f electrons lie deep within the atom and are well shielded from the surface. For many atoms, however, the effect of the orbital motion is quenched by the environment of the atom, and this contribution is negligible. In such cases, the total magnetic moment is equal to the spin magnetic moment. The number of unpaired electrons (n in the following equation) and the spin magnetic moment (in Bohr magnetons) are approximately related by the expression:

$$\text{spin magnetic moment} = \sqrt{n(n+2)}$$

A material is diamagnetic if all of its electrons are paired. Diamagnetism is a universal property of matter, but it is obscured by the stronger paramagnetic effect when unpaired electrons are present. Diamagnetism arises from the interaction of the magnetic field with filled orbitals and is a function of the electronic charge density.

Magnetic measurements have helped to determine the electronic configurations of many elements and thereby to establish the hypothetical order in which the orbitals may be assumed to fill. The electronic configurations, by orbitals, of the first five elements are given in Table 2.7. A question arises

Table 2.7

Electronic Configurations of the First Five Elements

		$1s$	$2s$	$2p$
$_1$H		1		
$_2$He		2		
$_3$Li		2	1	
$_4$Be		2	2	
$_5$B	/	2	2	1

concerning the electronic distribution of the sixth element, carbon. Since there are three $2p$ orbitals, does the next electron belong in the $2p$ orbital already holding one electron, or does it belong in another $2p$ orbital?

Hund's rule of maximum multiplicity, which has been confirmed by magnetic measurements, provides an answer for this and similar questions. Hund's rule states that electrons are distributed among the orbitals of a subshell in such a way as to give the maximum number of unpaired electrons. Hence, each of the two $2p$ electrons of carbon must assume its own orbital instead of pairing with the other in a single orbital. The six electrons of carbon may be considered to have the sets of quantum numbers indicated in Table 2.8.

Table 2.8

Quantum Numbers for the Electrons of Carbon

n	l	m	s
1	0	0	$+\frac{1}{2}$
1	0	0	$-\frac{1}{2}$
2	0	0	$+\frac{1}{2}$
2	0	0	$-\frac{1}{2}$
2	1	+1	$+\frac{1}{2}$
2	1	0	$+\frac{1}{2}$

The next electron added, for nitrogen, would have the quantum numbers $2, 1, -1, +\frac{1}{2}$.

In Figure 2.21, the orbitals are represented by circles, and the order of filling for the first ten electrons is shown by the numbers entered in these circles. Electrons are negatively charged and repel each other. Hence, they spread out and occupy the $2p$ orbitals singly before they begin to pair. After each of the $2p$ orbitals holds one electron, pairing occurs because less energy is required to overcome the interelectronic repulsion and add an electron to an orbital

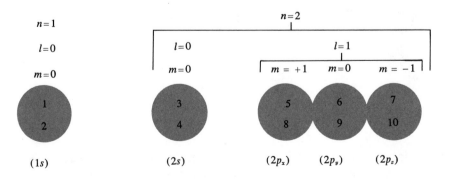

Figure 2.21 Order in which the orbitals of the $n = 1$ and $n = 2$ shells are filled.

already holding an electron than is required to place an electron in the next-higher empty orbital—a $3s$ orbital. This general order of orbital filling is observed for all subshells.

The spectroscopic notations for electronic configurations convey this information in a different form. The spectroscopic terms for the subshells are used with superscripts indicating the number of electrons in each subshell. Thus the electronic configuration of carbon may be indicated as $1s^2\,2s^2\,2p^2$. This notation clearly presents the first two quantum numbers—the number stands for n and the letter may be related to l—but the second two quantum numbers must be inferred indirectly.

Someone unfamiliar with this system must guard against interpreting all even-numbered superscripts as indicating a situation where all electrons are paired. This is not the case. In carbon, for example, we know that there are two unpaired electrons despite the fact that all of the superscripts are even numbers.

A way of circumventing this difficulty is to repeat the designation for each orbital of an incompete subshell. Thus the electronic configuration of carbon would be indicated as $1s^2\,2s^2\,2p_x{}^1\,2p_y{}^1$; that of the following element, nitrogen, would be $1s^2\,2s^2\,2p_x{}^1\,2p_y{}^1\,2p_z{}^1$; and that of the next element, oxygen, would be $1s^2\,2s^2\,2p_x{}^2\,2p_y{}^1\,2p_z{}^1$. After some experience with this spectroscopic system of notation, such a device is unnecessary.

2.17 Electronic Structures of the Elements

We are now in a position to show how the periodic table relates to electronic structure and thus to answer the questions raised in Section 2.13. To do this we shall use the **aufbau (building) principle** of Pauli. In this *hypothetical process*, the electronic structure of an element is correctly deduced by successive addition of electrons into orbitals arranged in order of increasing energy until the proper number of electrons for that element has been accommodated.

It is assumed that each electron enters the lowest energy level available to it, and, since all of the orbitals of a given sublevel have equivalent energies, this amounts to an arrangement by sublevels. It is possible for a simple orbital of one level (e.g., a 4s) to have a *lower* energy than a more complicated orbital of an *inner* level (e.g., a 3d), and hence the 4s sublevel fills before the 3d. The order of filling, then, is not by increasing value of n, but may be derived from the energy level diagram for atomic orbitals given in Figure 2.22. In the use of this diagram, one may consider the orbitals as being filled starting at the bottom of the chart and proceeding upward. Remember that there are three orbitals in a p sublevel, five orbitals in a d sublevel, and seven orbitals in an f sublevel.

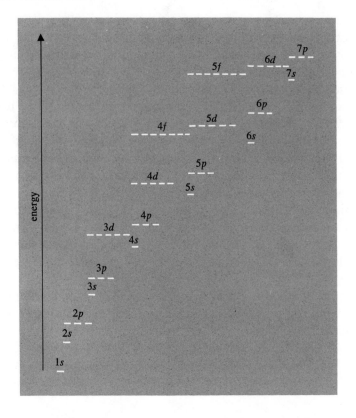

Figure 2.22 Energy-level diagram for atomic orbitals.

In the following discussion, the electronic configurations of the elements will be surveyed using the aufbau order. In a few cases the resulting configurations are in error but never by more than one or two electrons. The correct configurations are given in Table 2.9. Use a periodic table to follow the discussion.

The spectroscopic notations for the electronic structures of the elements of the first three periods are easily written since the symbols occur in order of principal quantum number. A few typical notations for elements of these periods are:

$$
\begin{array}{lll}
\text{He } (Z = 2) & \quad 1s^2 \\
\text{Li } (Z = 3) & \quad 1s^2\, 2s^1 \\
\text{N } (Z = 7) & \quad 1s^2\, 2s^2\, 2p^3 \\
\text{Ne } (Z = 10) & \quad 1s^2\, 2s^2\, 2p^6 \\
\text{Na } (Z = 11) & \quad 1s^2\, 2s^2\, 2p^6\, 3s^1 \\
\text{P } (Z = 15) & \quad 1s^2\, 2s^2\, 2p^6\, 3s^2\, 3p^3 \\
\text{Ar } (Z = 18) & \quad 1s^2\, 2s^2\, 2p^6\, 3s^2\, 3p^6
\end{array}
$$

In discussing the configurations of the remaining elements, we shall indicate only the outer orbitals. The first overlap of orbital energies is observed with potassium ($Z = 19$), the first element of the fourth period, and the configuration is ... $3s^2\ 3p^6\ 4s^1$ despite the fact that $3d$ orbitals are vacant. Likewise, calcium ($Z = 20$) has the configuration: ... $3s^2\ 3p^6\ 4s^2$. With scandium ($Z = 21$) the $3d$ sublevel comes into use: ... $3s^2\ 3p^6\ 3d^1\ 4s^2$, and with the series from scandium to zinc this sublevel is gradually filled. The configuration of zinc ($Z = 30$) is ... $3s^2\ 3p^6\ 3d^{10}\ 4s^2$. The elements 21 to 30 are the first transition series (B families) and are spoken of as exhibiting inner building, since in each case the last electron was added to the second from the outer shell. With element 31, gallium, the $4p$ sublevel begins: ... $3s^2\ 3p^6\ 3d^{10}\ 4s^2\ 4p^1$, and the fourth period ends with krypton: ... $3s^2\ 3p^6\ 3d^{10}\ 4s^2\ 4p^6$.

The fifth period starts with rubidium ($Z = 37$), the additional electron over krypton being added to the $5s$ subshell. A second transition series follows, starting with yttrium ($Z = 39$) and adding electrons to the $4d$ sublevel: ... $4s^2\ 4p^6\ 4d^1\ 5s^2$. This period ends with the series from indium to xenon with electrons being added to the $5p$ level. Xenon has the configuration: ... $4s^2\ 4p^6\ 4d^{10}\ 5s^2\ 5p^6$.

The sixth period is much more complicated as far as orbital overlap is concerned. The first element, cesium ($Z = 55$), adds one electron in the $6s$ sublevel to the xenon core: ... $4d^{10}\ 5s^2\ 5p^6\ 6s^1$, and the second element, barium ($Z = 56$), has an additional electron that completes the $6s$ sublevel. We here come upon one complication of the aufbau procedure. The $4f$ and $5d$ sublevels are so close in energy that the next electron (for lanthanum, $Z = 57$) is added to the $5d$ level (thus lanthanum is a transition element), but the next succeeding electron (for cerium, $Z = 58$) adds to the $4f$ sublevel and the electron added for lanthanum falls back into the $4f$ sublevel. Thus for La we have: ... $4d^{10}\ 5s^2\ 5p^6\ 5d^1\ 6s^2$, and for Ce: ... $4d^{10}\ 4f^2\ 5s^2\ 5p^6\ 6s^2$. For the elements 58 to 70 (cerium to ytterbium), the electrons are added to the $4f$ sublevel.

These elements are called **inner-transition** elements; for such elements, electron addition occurs in the third from the outer shell. After the $4f$ sublevel has been filled, the next electron adds to the $5d$ sublevel. Thus for lutetium ($Z = 71$), we have ... $4d^{10}\ 4f^{14}\ 5s^2\ 5p^6\ 5d^1\ 6s^2$. This third transition series is completed and the $5d$ shell filled with element 80, mercury: ... $4d^{10}\ 4f^{14}\ 5s^2\ 5p^6\ 5d^{10}\ 6s^2$. The period ends with electrons being added to the $6p$ sublevel in elements 81 to 86.

The seventh period is incomplete and includes many artificial man-made elements. This period follows the pattern established by the sixth period with 87 and 88 adding electrons to the $7s$ sublevel, 89 adding an electron to the $6d$ sublevel, elements 90 to 103 constituting a second inner-transition series and exhibiting an electron buildup of the $5f$ sublevel, and the transition elements 104 and 105 (as yet unnamed) adding electrons to the $6d$ sublevel.

Table 2.9

Electronic Configurations of the Elements

Element	Z	1s	2s	2p	3s	3p	3d	4s	4p	4d	4f	5s	5p	5d	5f	6s	6p	6d	7s
H	1	1																	
He	2	2																	
Li	3	2	1																
Be	4	2	2																
B	5	2	2	1															
C	6	2	2	2															
N	7	2	2	3															
O	8	2	2	4															
F	9	2	2	5															
Ne	10	2	2	6															
Na	11	2	2	6	1														
Mg	12	2	2	6	2														
Al	13	2	2	6	2	1													
Si	14	2	2	6	2	2													
P	15	2	2	6	2	3													
S	16	2	2	6	2	4													
Cl	17	2	2	6	2	5													
Ar	18	2	2	6	2	6													
K	19	2	2	6	2	6		1											
Ca	20	2	2	6	2	6		2											
Sc	21	2	2	6	2	6	1	2											
Ti	22	2	2	6	2	6	2	2											
V	23	2	2	6	2	6	3	2											
Cr	24	2	2	6	2	6	5	1											
Mn	25	2	2	6	2	6	5	2											
Fe	26	2	2	6	2	6	6	2											
Co	27	2	2	6	2	6	7	2											
Ni	28	2	2	6	2	6	8	2											
Cu	29	2	2	6	2	6	10	1											
Zn	30	2	2	6	2	6	10	2											
Ga	31	2	2	6	2	6	10	2	1										
Ge	32	2	2	6	2	6	10	2	2										
As	33	2	2	6	2	6	10	2	3										
Se	34	2	2	6	2	6	10	2	4										
Br	35	2	2	6	2	6	10	2	5										
Kr	36	2	2	6	2	6	10	2	6										
Rb	37	2	2	6	2	6	10	2	6			1							
Sr	38	2	2	6	2	6	10	2	6			2							
Y	39	2	2	6	2	6	10	2	6	1		2							
Zr	40	2	2	6	2	6	10	2	6	2		2							
Nb	41	2	2	6	2	6	10	2	6	4		1							
Mo	42	2	2	6	2	6	10	2	6	5		1							
Tc	43	2	2	6	2	6	10	2	6	6		1							
Ru	44	2	2	6	2	6	10	2	6	7		1							
Rh	45	2	2	6	2	6	10	2	6	8		1							
Pd	46	2	2	6	2	6	10	2	6	10									
Ag	47	2	2	6	2	6	10	2	6	10		1							
Cd	48	2	2	6	2	6	10	2	6	10		2							
In	49	2	2	6	2	6	10	2	6	10		2	1						
Sn	50	2	2	6	2	6	10	2	6	10		2	2						
Sb	51	2	2	6	2	6	10	2	6	10		2	3						

Table 2.9 Continued

Electronic Configurations of the Elements

Element	Z	1s	2s	2p	3s	3p	3d	4s	4p	4d	4f	5s	5p	5d	5f	6s	6p	6d	7s
Te	52	2	2	6	2	6	10	2	6	10		2	4						
I	53	2	2	6	2	6	10	2	6	10		2	5						
Xe	54	2	2	6	2	6	10	2	6	10		2	6						
Cs	55	2	2	6	2	6	10	2	6	10		2	6			1			
Ba	56	2	2	6	2	6	10	2	6	10		2	6			2			
La	57	2	2	6	2	6	10	2	6	10		2	6	1		2			
Ce	58	2	2	6	2	6	10	2	6	10	2	2	6			2			
Pr	59	2	2	6	2	6	10	2	6	10	3	2	6			2			
Nd	60	2	2	6	2	6	10	2	6	10	4	2	6			2			
Pm	61	2	2	6	2	6	10	2	6	10	5	2	6			2			
Sm	62	2	2	6	2	6	10	2	6	10	6	2	6			2			
Eu	63	2	2	6	2	6	10	2	6	10	7	2	6			2			
Gd	64	2	2	6	2	6	10	2	6	10	7	2	6	1		2			
Tb	65	2	2	6	2	6	10	2	6	10	9	2	6			2			
Dy	66	2	2	6	2	6	10	2	6	10	10	2	6			2			
Ho	67	2	2	6	2	6	10	2	6	10	11	2	6			2			
Er	68	2	2	6	2	6	10	2	6	10	12	2	6			2			
Tm	69	2	2	6	2	6	10	2	6	10	13	2	6			2			
Yb	70	2	2	6	2	6	10	2	6	10	14	2	6			2			
Lu	71	2	2	6	2	6	10	2	6	10	14	2	6	1		2			
Hf	72	2	2	6	2	6	10	2	6	10	14	2	6	2		2			
Ta	73	2	2	6	2	6	10	2	6	10	14	2	6	3		2			
W	74	2	2	6	2	6	10	2	6	10	14	2	6	4		2			
Re	75	2	2	6	2	6	10	2	6	10	14	2	6	5		2			
Os	76	2	2	6	2	6	10	2	6	10	14	2	6	6		2			
Ir	77	2	2	6	2	6	10	2	6	10	14	2	6	7		2			
Pt	78	2	2	6	2	6	10	2	6	10	14	2	6	9		1			
Au	79	2	2	6	2	6	10	2	6	10	14	2	6	10		1			
Hg	80	2	2	6	2	6	10	2	6	10	14	2	6	10		2			
Tl	81	2	2	6	2	6	10	2	6	10	14	2	6	10		2	1		
Pb	82	2	2	6	2	6	10	2	6	10	14	2	6	10		2	2		
Bi	83	2	2	6	2	6	10	2	6	10	14	2	6	10		2	3		
Po	84	2	2	6	2	6	10	2	6	10	14	2	6	10		2	4		
At	85	2	2	6	2	6	10	2	6	10	14	2	6	10		2	5		
Rn	86	2	2	6	2	6	10	2	6	10	14	2	6	10		2	6		
Fr	87	2	2	6	2	6	10	2	6	10	14	2	6	10		2	6		1
Ra	88	2	2	6	2	6	10	2	6	10	14	2	6	10		2	6		2
Ac	89	2	2	6	2	6	10	2	6	10	14	2	6	10		2	6	1	2
Th	90	2	2	6	2	6	10	2	6	10	14	2	6	10		2	6	2	2
Pa	91	2	2	6	2	6	10	2	6	10	14	2	6	10	2	2	6	1	2
U	92	2	2	6	2	6	10	2	6	10	14	2	6	10	3	2	6	1	2
Np	93	2	2	6	2	6	10	2	6	10	14	2	6	10	4	2	6	1	2
Pu	94	2	2	6	2	6	10	2	6	10	14	2	6	10	6	2	6		2
Am	95	2	2	6	2	6	10	2	6	10	14	2	6	10	7	2	6		2
Cm	96	2	2	6	2	6	10	2	6	10	14	2	6	10	7	2	6	1	2
Bk	97	2	2	6	2	6	10	2	6	10	14	2	6	10	8	2	6	1	2
Cf	98	2	2	6	2	6	10	2	6	10	14	2	6	10	10	2	6		2
Es	99	2	2	6	2	6	10	2	6	10	14	2	6	10	11	2	6		2
Fm	100	2	2	6	2	6	10	2	6	10	14	2	6	10	12	2	6		2
Md	101	2	2	6	2	6	10	2	6	10	14	2	6	10	13	2	6		2
No	102	2	2	6	2	6	10	2	6	10	14	2	6	10	14	2	6		2
Lr	103	2	2	6	2	6	10	2	6	10	14	2	6	10	14	2	6	1	2

Figure 2.23 Aufbau order for filling sublevels.

Many mnemonic devices have been proposed to help remember the order of filling of subshells. One such system is illustrated in Figure 2.23. The spectroscopic notations for the subshells are written in indented fashion; when these symbols are joined by downward vertical lines, the proper sequence emerges.

Probably the best memory aid is the periodic table itself. In the schematic periodic table of Figure 2.24 certain areas of the chart are marked with subshell notations. The electron added to make an element different from its preceding neighbor (the so-called differentiating electron) in any region of the chart is of the type indicated for that region. The principal quantum number of this final electron is given by the period number for the A family elements, the period number minus one for the transition elements, and the period number minus two for the inner-transition elements.

To determine the electronic configuration of any element, one starts with hydrogen and on the basis of the periodic table accounts for every electron added until the desired element is reached. Thus for tungsten ($Z = 74$): the first period gives $1s^2$; the second period, $2s^2\,2p^6$; the third, $3s^2\,3p^6$; the fourth, $4s^2\,3d^{10}\,4p^6$; and the fifth, $5s^2\,4d^{10}\,5p^6$. The sixth period—in which tungsten is found—starts with $6s^2$ for cesium and barium, adds $4f^{14}$ for the inner-transition series, and the final term is $5d^4$, since tungsten is the fourth element in the $5d$ transition series. Rearranging these terms in sequence gives: $1s^2\,2s^2\,2p^6\,3s^2\,3p^6\,3d^{10}\,4s^2\,4p^6\,4d^{10}\,4f^{14}\,5s^2\,5p^6\,5d^4\,6s^2$.

The aufbau method is convenient and gives fairly accurate results (Section 2.18); however, it has an inherent danger As one thinks in terms of the

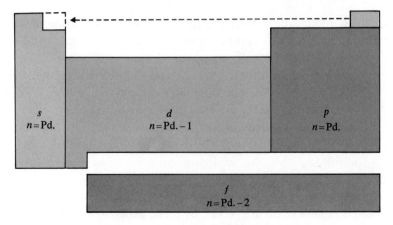

Figure 2.24 Type of differentiating electron related to position of the element in the periodic chart.

addition of electrons to build up atoms, it is all too easy to ignore the attendant addition of protons and neutrons to the nucleus and the fact that an electron added in any step of the procedure is not isolated but is entering a field dominated by an increasingly larger and larger number of electrons. Thus the order of sublevels, based on energy, changes from element to element in the periodic table. There is no one standard order of sublevels that accurately describes the conditions existing in all atoms. The aufbau order reflects the order of filling and the relative energy positions of the orbitals as one encounters them in this hypothetical filling procedure.

In processes involving the loss of an electron (ionization), frequently the electron lost is not the last one added. Thus the configuration of iron ($Z = 26$) is $1s^2\, 2s^2\, 2p^6\, 3s^2\, 3p^6\, 3d^6\, 4s^2$, and, upon ionization, the first electron removed is a $4s$ electron even though the last electron added by the aufbau procedure is a $3d$ electron. One must conclude that for iron the $3d$ subshell has a lower energy than the $4s$ subshell—a conclusion contrary to the aufbau order. Hence the aufbau order should be regarded as what it is—an artificial device to permit us to correlate electronic configurations.

In general this need not bother us. The aufbau principle may be used to arrive at a satisfactory electronic configuration for an element. In ionization procedures, electrons are not necessarily lost in the reverse of the aufbau order and therefore spectroscopic notations should be written by increasing value of n and not by any hypothetical order of filling.

2.18   Half-filled and Filled Subshells

The electronic configurations predicted by the aufbau procedure are confirmed by spectral and magnetic studies for most elements. There are a few, however, that exhibit slight variations from the standard pattern. In certain instances, it is possible to explain these variations on the basis of the enhanced stability of a filled or half-filled subshell.

The predicted configuration for the $3d$ and $4s$ subshells in the chromium atom is $3d^4 4s^2$, whereas the experimentally derived configuration is $3d^5 4s^1$. Presumably the stability gained by having one unpaired electron in each of the five $3d$ orbitals (half-filled subshell) accounts for the fact that the $3d^5 4s^1$ configuration is the one observed. The existence of a half-filled subshell also accounts for the fact that the configuration for the $4d$ and $5s$ subshells of molybdenum is $4d^5 5s^1$ rather than the predicted $4d^4 5s^2$.

For copper the predicted configuration for the last two subshells is $3d^9 4s^2$, whereas the accepted structure is $3d^{10} 4s^1$. The explanation for this deviation lies in the superior stability of the $3d^{10} 4s^1$ configuration resulting from the completed $3d$ subshell. Silver and gold also have configurations with completely filled d subshells instead of the $(n-1)d^9 ns^2$ configurations predicted. In the case of palladium, two electrons are involved—the only case with a difference of more than one electron. The predicted configuration for the last two subshells of palladium is $4d^8 5s^2$; the observed configuration is $4d^{10} 5s^0$.

That half-filled and filled subshells contribute to the stability of atoms is also borne out in cases where the aufbau order is followed. Thus nitrogen, phosphorus, and arsenic show unusual properties (e.g., unexpectedly high ionization potentials) because of the fact that they all have half-filled p subshells. Zinc, cadmium, and mercury have properties that can be traced to the fact that all of their subshells are filled. The noble gases have unusually stable configurations with all of their subshells complete.

Some deviations from predicted configurations are observed other than those that can be accounted for on the basis of filled or half-filled subshells, particularly among elements of higher Z. For our purposes such exceptions are not important. The chemistry of the elements is, in the main, satisfactorily explained on the basis of the predicted configurations.

2.19 Types of Elements

We may classify the elements according to their electronic configurations into four types.

1. *The noble gases.* In the periodic table, the noble gases are found at the end of each period in group 0. They are colorless gases, chemically unreactive and diamagnetic. An examination of Figure 2.22 shows that the arrangement $ns^2 np^6$ is exceptionally stable. Discontinuities in the energy-level diagram occur after these configurations are attained. The next electron added is added with a much higher energy to a quantum level of the next higher n. With the

exception of helium ($Z = 2$), all the noble gases have outer configurations of $ns^2\, np^6$. No atom has a complete outer shell with the exception of helium and neon.

2. *The representative elements.* These elements comprise the A families of the periodic table used in this book and include metals and nonmetals. They exhibit a wide range of chemical behavior and physical characteristics. Some of the elements are diamagnetic and some are paramagnetic; the compounds of these elements, however, are generally diamagnetic and colorless. They are characterized as having all of their electronic shells either complete or stable (e.g., $ns^2\, np^6$) except their outer shells to which the last electron may be considered as having been added. This outer shell is termed the valence shell; electrons in it are valence electrons. The number of valence electrons for each atom is the same as the group number. The chemistry of these elements depends upon these valence electrons.

3. *The transition elements.* These elements are found in the B families of the periodic table. They are characterized by inner building—the "last" electron being an inner d electron. Electrons from the two outermost shells are used in chemical reactions. All these elements are metals; most of them are paramagnetic and form highly colored paramagnetic compounds.

4. *The inner-transition elements.* These elements are found at the bottom of the periodic table and properly should follow group III B. The sixth-period series that follows lanthanum (14 elements) is called the lanthanide series; the seventh-period series is known as the actinide series. The last electron added to each element is an f electron added to the third from the outer shell. Hence, the outer three shells may be involved in the chemistry of these elements. All of the inner-transition elements are metals. The elements are, in general, paramagnetic, and the compounds derived from them are paramagnetic and highly colored.

SOME SUGGESTED READINGS

Day, M. C., Jr., and Selbin, J., *Theoretical Inorganic Chemistry*, 2nd ed., New York, Van Nostrand Reinhold, 1969.

Gamow, G., *The Atom and Its Nucleus*, Englewood Cliffs, N.J., Prentice-Hall, 1961 (paper).

Gamow, G., *Thirty Years that Shook Physics*, Garden City, N.Y., Doubleday, 1966.

Harvey, K., and Porter, G., *Introduction to Physical Inorganic Chemistry*, Reading, Mass., Addison-Wesley, 1963.

Hochstrasser, R. M., *Behavior of Electrons in Atoms*, New York, Benjamin, 1964 (paper).

Lagowski, J. J., *The Structure of Atoms*, Boston, Houghton Mifflin, 1964 (paper).

Sisler, H. H., *Electronic Structure, Properties, and the Periodic Law*, New York, Van Nostrand Reinhold, 1963 (paper).

Thomson, G., *The Atom*, New York, Oxford University Press, 1962 (paper).

PROBLEMS

The more difficult problems are starred.

2.1   How does the radius of deflection of a charged particle in a magnetic field (Figure 2.2) vary with an increase in each of the following? (a) The magnetic field strength, H; (b) the mass of the particle, m; (c) the charge of the particle, e; (d) the velocity of the particle, v.

2.2   Complete the following table:

Symbol	Atomic Number	Mass Number	Protons	Neutrons	Electrons
Sr	38	88			
As		75			
	65	159			
Rn				136	86
Mo		98		56	
Au$^+$				118	
	16			16	18

2.3   The isotopes of neon were the first to be identified by Aston. What is the mass number and charge corresponding to each of the following e/m values obtained for neon ions: 1.314×10^{13} esu/g, 1.377×10^{13} esu/g, 1.446×10^{13} esu/g, 2.629×10^{13} esu/g, 2.892×10^{13} esu/g. The charge on the electron, e, is 4.80×10^{-10} esu and 1 u is 1.66×10^{-24} g.

2.4   There are two naturally occurring isotopes of copper: ^{63}Cu, which has a mass of 62.930 u, and ^{65}Cu, which has a mass of 64.928 u. The atomic weight of copper is 63.546. What is the percent abundance of each of the isotopes?

2.5   If element X consists of 60.4% of atoms with a mass of 68.9 u each and 39.6% of atoms with a mass of 70.9 u each, what is the atomic weight of X?

2.6   Naturally occurring carbon consists of two isotopes: ^{12}C, which is assigned a mass of exactly 12 u, and ^{13}C, which has a mass of 13.003 u. The atomic weight of carbon is 12.011. What is the percent abundance of each of the isotopes?

2.7   The binding energy of one $^7_3$Li atom is 6.258×10^{-5} erg. The masses of the fundamental particles are: electron, 0.0005 u; proton, 1.0073 u; neutron, 1.0086 u. Since 1 u equals 1.49×10^{-3} erg, what is the actual mass (in u) of a $^7_3$Li atom?

2.8   The isotope $^{16}_8$O constitutes 99.759% of naturally occurring oxygen and has a mass of 15.995 u. What is the binding energy, in calories, of a $^{16}_8$O atom? Use the data given in Problem 2.7 plus the fact that 1 cal equals 4.18×10^7 erg.

2.9 Use the information in Section 2.9 and the fact that the atomic weight of oxygen on the unified scale is 15.9994 to determine the ratios that should be used to convert readings on the old chemical scale and the old physical scale to unified scale values. Which of the three mass units is the largest?

2.10 What is the frequency and energy per quantum of red light with a wavelength of 7000 Å and of violet light with a wavelength of 4000 Å?

2.11 What are the masses of photons that have wavelengths of 7000 Å and 4000 Å?

2.12 (a) According to the Bohr theory, what is the radius of the H atom in the ground state? (b) The radii of many nuclei may be calculated by means of the formula $r = (1.3 \times 10^{-13} \text{ cm})A^{1/3}$, where A is the mass number. What is the radius of a H nucleus? (c) Use your answers from parts (a) and (b) to determine the percentage of the total volume of the H atom of Bohr that is occupied by the nucleus.

2.13 What is the interpretation of the meaning of the Bohr radius, a_0, in terms of the Bohr theory and in terms of wave mechanics?

*2.14 (a) The equation for the radius, r, of a Bohr orbit (Section 2.11) may be simplified to $r = n^2 a_0/Z$, where n is the principal quantum number, a_0 is 0.529 Å, and Z is the atomic number. Calculate the radii of the $n = 1$, $n = 2$, and $n = 3$ orbits of the hydrogen atom. (b) E, the energy of an electron in a given orbit, is given by $E = -Ze^2/2r$, where e, the charge on an electron, is 4.80×10^{-10} esu; 1 esu $= 1 \text{ g}^{1/2}\text{cm}^{3/2}/\text{sec}$. Calculate the energy of an electron in each of the $n = 1$, $n = 2$, $n = 3$ orbits. (c) Use your answers from part (b) to calculate the frequencies and wavelengths corresponding to electron transitions from the $n = 3$ level to the $n = 1$ level, from the $n = 3$ to the $n = 2$ level, and from the $n = 2$ level to the $n = 1$ level.

*2.15 Make the calculations described in Problem 2.14 for the helium ion, He^+.

*2.16 Moseley found that the frequency, v, of a characteristic line of the X-ray spectrum of an element is related to the atomic number, Z, of the element by the formula: $\sqrt{v} = a(Z - b)$, where a and b are constants. A characteristic X-ray wavelength for $_{25}$Mn is 2.11 Å and for $_{50}$Sn is 0.495 Å. (a) Convert these wavelengths into frequencies and determine the values of a and b in the formula. (b) What is the atomic number of an element that has a corresponding X-ray line at a wavelength of 0.675 Å? (c) What is the wavelength of the analogous X-ray line for $_{30}$Zn?

2.17 (a) According to the Bohr theory, the velocity of an electron in the $n = 1$ level of a hydrogen atom is 2.19×10^8 cm/sec. What is the de Broglie wavelength for this electron? The mass of an electron is 9.11×10^{-28} g; Planck's constant is 6.63×10^{-27} g cm^2/sec. (b) What is the de Broglie wavelength of a proton moving at the same velocity? The mass of a proton is 1.67×10^{-24} g.

2.18 (a) Use the approximate expression for Heisenberg's uncertainty principle, $\Delta x \, \Delta mv \approx h$, to determine the uncertainty in the velocity of a particle with a mass of 1.0 g when the uncertainty in the particle's position is 1.0 Å. Planck's constant is 6.6×10^{-27} g cm^2/sec. (b) Perform the same calculation for the electron (mass, 9.1×10^{-28} g).

2.19 Give the values for all four quantum numbers for each electron in nitrogen ($Z = 7$).

2.20 What is the maximum number of electrons in a single atom that can have a set of quantum numbers containing the following: (a) $n = 3, l = 2$; (b) $n = 3, l = 0, m = -1$; (c) $n = 4$; (d) $n = 4, \ l = 4$; (e) $n = 5, l = 1$; (f) $n = 5, l = 3$; (g) $n = 5, l = 3, m = 0$.

2.21 In the ground state of $_{36}$Kr, how many electrons have $m = +1$ as one of their quantum numbers? How many electrons have $l = 1$ as one of their quantum numbers?

2.22 Draw boundary surface diagrams for the $1s$, $2p$, and $3d$ orbitals.

2.23 Write spectroscopic notations for the ground-state electronic configurations of: (a) $_6$C, (b) $_{17}$Cl, (c), $_{20}$Ca, (d) $_{24}$Cr, (e) $_{27}$Co, (f) $_{29}$Cu, (g) $_{48}$Cd, (h) $_{55}$Cs, (i) $_{58}$Ce, (j) $_{96}$Cm, (k) $_{98}$Cf.

2.24 Which of the atoms in Problem 2.23 has unpaired electrons in the ground state?

2.25 Write ground-state spectroscopic notations for the electronic configuration of (a) $_{13}$Al, (b) $_{18}$Ar, (c) $_{33}$As, (d) $_{51}$Sb, (e) $_{85}$At, (f) $_{89}$Ac, (g) $_{95}$Am.

2.26 Write spectroscopic notations for the following ions: (a) $_{19}$K$^+$, (b) $_{21}$Sc^{3+}, (c) $_{26}$Fe^{2+}, (d) $_{26}$Fe^{3+}, (e) $_{28}$Ni^{2+}, (f) $_{35}$Br$^-$.

2.27 (a) State the number of unpaired electrons in each of the ions listed in Problem 2.26. (b) Which of these ions would you predict to be diamagnetic and which paramagnetic?

2.28 Describe how the ground-state electronic configurations of the elements of a period compare to one another and how the ground-state electronic configurations of the elements of a group are related.

2.29 Identify the atoms that have the following ground-state electronic configurations in their outer shell or shells: (a) $5s^2 5p^2$, (b) $3s^2 3p^6 3d^5 4s^2$, (c) $4s^2 4p^6 4d^{10} 5s^2$, (d) $4s^2 4p^6 5s^2$, (e) $5s^2 5p^5$.

2.30 Describe how each of the following contributed to the theory of atomic structure: Chadwick, Rutherford, Dalton, de Broglie, Schrödinger, and Moseley.

2.31 Define the following: orbital, excited state, electrostatic unit of charge, diamagnetism, photoelectric effect, periodic law, photon.

2.32 Define, describe the characteristics of, and give examples of: (a) representative elements, (b) transition elements, (c) inner-transition elements, (d) noble gases.

CHEMICAL BONDING

It is the electrons of atoms that are responsible for chemical bonding. **Ionic**, or **electrovalent**, **bonding** is characterized by electron transfer; one of the reacting atoms loses one or more electrons, and the other atom gains one or more electrons. In **covalent bonding**, electrons are not transferred but are shared; a bond so formed consists of a pair of electrons shared by two atoms. Pure ionic bonding and pure covalent bonding are seldom encountered. Most bonds are of intermediate character, somewhere between these two extremes, although many bonds are predominantly ionic or covalent.

An understanding of electronic configuration, a principal topic of the last chapter, is therefore fundamental to an understanding of chemical bonding. Other properties of the elements, such as atomic size, are also important to a discussion of chemical bonding and will be considered in the opening sections of this chapter. These properties are effectively correlated by the periodic table in the same way that the periodic table systematizes electronic configuration.

3.1 Atomic Sizes

The determination of atomic sizes poses a problem. If the atom is viewed as a sphere, the radius of the atom should be the distance from the center of the nucleus to the outer reaches of the last electron. But the electron cloud of an atom has a varying intensity, and the probability of finding an electron extends to infinity. It is impossible to isolate and measure a single atom.

The most useful approach to the problem of atomic size is that which determines so-called **atomic** (or **covalent**) **radii**. It is possible to measure the distance between the nuclei of two covalently bonded atoms by diffraction or spectroscopic methods. This bond distance is then apportioned between the bonded atoms to arrive at values for atomic radii. For example, a radius of 0.99 Å is derived for the chlorine atom by dividing the distance from chlorine nucleus to chlorine nucleus in the Cl—Cl bond (1.98 Å) by two. In like manner, dividing the Br—Br bond distance (2.28 Å) by two gives a value of 1.14 Å for the atomic radius of bromine.

Atomic radii thus calculated may be added to give bond distances that agree fairly well with those that have been directly determined. Thus the atomic radius of chlorine, 0.99 Å, may be added to the atomic radius of bromine, 1.14 Å, to arrive at a value of 2.13 Å for the Cl—Br bond distance. This procedure may also be reversed; the atomic radius of chlorine, 0.99 Å, may be subtracted from the C—Cl bond distance, 1.76 Å, to derive the atomic radius of carbon, 0.77 Å.

Changing the environment of an atom may cause its effective size to vary; hence, discrepancies sometimes arise when this method of assigning atomic radii is used. Nevertheless, such data are useful in establishing trends and making generalizations.

Atomic radius is plotted against atomic number in Figure 3.1. Within a group of the periodic table, an increase in atomic radius is generally observed from top to bottom. The alkali metals (group I A) and the halogens (group VII A) are labeled in Figure 3.1, and the increase in size within each group is clearly evident. Such a trend is expected since the larger atoms of a group employ more electron levels than the smaller atoms.

Figure 3.1 also shows a general decrease in atomic radius from left to right across any period. The outermost electrons of the elements of a given period all have the same principal quantum number. As the atomic number increases from element to element across a period, the additional electron is added to the same level or to an inner level, and it is important to remember that the number of protons in the nucleus is also increased. This increase of positive charge on the nucleus tends to draw in the electron shells, and the result is that atoms decrease in size.

The transition elements and inner-transition elements show some minor variations. For the transition elements, the differentiating electrons fill inner *d*

Figure 3.1 Atomic radii of the elements.

orbitals. The effect of nuclear charge on outer, size-determining electrons is reduced by the **screening effect** of inner electrons. Therefore for a transition series, the gradual buildup of electrons in inner *d* orbitals at first retards the rate of decrease in atomic radius and then, toward the end of the series when the inner *d* subshell is nearing completion, causes the radius to increase. In addition, at the conclusion of a transition series, the next electron must enter the *p* orbital of the next higher principal quantum level.

In general, the lanthanides (elements 58 to 71) exhibit a slow but significant decrease in atomic radius called the **lanthanide contraction**. The differentiating

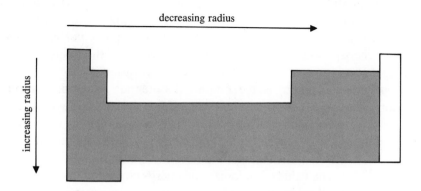

Figure 3.2 General trends in atomic radius in relation to the periodic classification.

electrons of these elements are added to the third level from the outside (the 4f sublevel). These electrons screen the increasing nuclear charge from the outer 6s electrons but are not completely efficient, and therefore the steady reduction in size is observed. The transition elements following the lanthanides exhibit a typical transition-element pattern; however, the effect of the lanthanide contraction is such that these elements are approximately the same size as the corresponding elements of the preceding period. Thus hafnium ($Z = 72$) has an atomic radius of 1.44 Å, and that of zirconium ($Z = 40$) is 1.45 Å.

The general trends in atomic radius are summarized in Figure 3.2.

3.2 Ionization Potentials

The amount of energy required to remove the most loosely held electron from an isolated gaseous atom in its ground state is the **ionization energy** of the element.

$$A(g) \longrightarrow A^+(g) + e^-$$

The symbol (g) indicates a gaseous species.

Conventions regarding the assignment of signs to energy terms must be noted. When a system absorbs energy, the term is given a positive sign. If the system evolves energy, the value is given a negative sign. Since energy is absorbed in the ionization process described, ionization energies have positive signs.

Ionization energies are usually determined by spectroscopic methods (Section 2.11). Figure 2.11 shows that the electronic energy levels converge to a limit. The ionization energy is the energy required to raise an electron to this limit, or it is the energy emitted when an electron falls from this limit back to the ground state. The limit is readily identified from the spectrum since beyond this point, in the direction of shorter wavelengths, the spectrum no longer consists of lines but is continuous. An electron is not restricted to quantized energy states after it has been removed from the atom and hence produces a continuous spectrum under these circumstances.

The **ionization potential** is the minimum potential required to produce ionization. The ionization potential of an atom is measured in volts (Section 10.1); however, it is numerically equal to an ionization energy expressed in electron volts, which are energy units. One electron volt is the energy acquired by an electron when it falls through a potential difference of 1 v; 1 ev equals 3.83×10^{-20} cal. The value of an ionization energy expressed in electron volts is customarily called an ionization potential; even though this terminology is not strictly correct, it is widely employed and is used in this book.

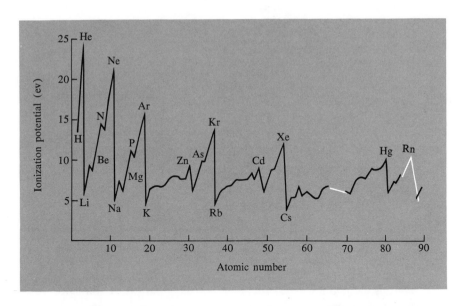

Figure 3.3 First ionization potentials of the elements versus atomic number.

Certain atoms produce negative ions by the addition of one or more electrons. The terms ionization energy and ionization potential pertain *only* to the production of positive ions by the *removal* of an electron. Some of the positive ions thus described (such as ions derived from the noble gases or from elements that commonly form only negative ions) are never produced in ordinary chemical reactions.

In Figure 3.3 the ionization potentials of the elements are plotted against atomic number. Particularly striking are the maxima of the curve that occur at the atomic numbers of the noble gases and the minima that represent the ionization potentials of the group I A elements. Also evident are the general upward trends for each period.

The magnitude of the ionization potential of an element depends upon several factors. The larger the atomic radius, the easier it is to remove an electron and the smaller the ionization potential. In larger atoms, the electron to be removed is on the average at a greater distance from the positively charged nucleus. Therefore, increasing ionization potential roughly parallels decreasing atomic radius; the smallest potential of a period is on the left, and the smallest potential of a group is on the bottom (Figure 3.4).

The magnitude of the positive charge on the nucelus is another factor of importance. An enhanced nuclear charge would be expected to make it more difficult to remove an electron. Such an effect is observed across a period where increasing nuclear charge parallels decreasing size, and hence ionization potential increases from left to right in any period. However, the nuclear charge is partially screened by inner electrons. The ionization potentials of

Figure 3.4 General trends in ionization potential in relation to the periodic classification.

the transition elements do not increase across a period at the same rate as those of the representative elements; the ionization potentials of the inner-transition elements remain almost constant. The screening effect of the inner electrons accounts for these observations.

The screening effect is operative in all multiple electron atoms. The ionization potential of lithium is much lower than that of helium (Figure 3.3) despite the fact that the nuclear charge of Li (which is $3+$) is higher than that of He $(2+)$. In He, one electron is not effectively screened by the other since they both occupy the same subshell. Not only is the Li atom larger than the He atom, but also in Li, the two $1s$ electrons strongly shield the nuclear charge from the electron that is removed (a $2s$ electron).

In going from lithium to neon, the nuclear charge increases from $3+$ to $10+$. Since electrons are being added to the same level (the outer level), they do not significantly increase the screening effect, and the ionization potential increases. The ionization potential of Ne, however, is lower than that of He. In general, ionization potential decreases in going from the lighter to the heavier members of a group (notice the values for the noble gases and the I A metals in Figure 3.3). The effect of increasing nuclear charge is greatly reduced by the increasing number of inner electrons, and ionization potential decreases as atomic radius increases.

Electronic configuration is the last factor to be considered. We noted in Section 2.18 that certain configurations are unusually stable. Thus the noble gases have high ionization potentials owing, in part, to their very stable electronic arrangements. We shall return to this important fact in Section 3.4. Other elements have relatively stable electronic arrangements. Elements with filled subshells (e.g., Be, Mg, Zn, Cd, and Hg) have high ionization potentials which are out of line with those of the other elements of their period. Nitrogen, phosphorus, and arsenic have unexpectedly high ionization potentials because in each case it is necessary to break up a half-filled p subshell to remove an electron.

It must be remembered that ionization potential is related to the energy *required* to remove an electron. Thus the elements most active in losing electrons (metallic behavior) are those with the *lowest* ionization potentials and are found in the lower left of the periodic table. This reactivity in terms of electron loss decreases as one moves upward or to the right from this corner of the chart.

What we have described here are **first** ionization potentials. The **second** ionization potential of an element relates to the energy required to remove *one* electron from a $1+$ ion of that element.

$$A^+(g) \longrightarrow A^{2+}(g) + e^-$$

The *third* ionization potential pertains to a process in which *one* electron is removed from a $2+$ ion.

$$A^{2+}(g) \longrightarrow A^{3+}(g) + e^-$$

Even higher ionization potentials may be determined. When the term ionization potential is not further qualified, it is understood that the first ionization potential is meant.

Predictably, for any given element, the third ionization potential is higher than the second, and the second is higher than the first. It is more difficult to remove an electron ($1-$ charge) from a $2+$ ion than from a $1+$ ion; likewise, it is more difficult to remove an electron from a $1+$ ion than from a neutral atom. The high values observed for third and fourth ionization potentials indicate that few highly charged positive ions exist under ordinary conditions.

3.3 Electron Affinities

The energy effect accompanying the process in which an electron is added to an isolated atom in its ground state is called an **electron affinity**. In these processes, energy is usually evolved, and therefore most of these values have negative signs. Electron affinity is frequently defined as energy released, and in sources that employ such a definition, electron affinity values relating to the liberation of energy are given positive signs. This sign convention is the reverse of the one that we employ; we shall consistently use negative signs for energy released and positive signs for energy absorbed.

It should also be noted that electron affinity pertains to a process in which a *negative ion* is formed from a *neutral atom*.

$$e^- + Cl(g) \longrightarrow Cl^-(g)$$

The process described is not the reverse of the process that determines ionization potential.

$$Cl(g) \longrightarrow Cl^+(g) + e^-$$

The numerical value of the electron affinity of chlorine, however, is the same as the ionization potential of the negative chloride ion.

The electron affinity of an element is usually determined indirectly by calculation from thermodynamic data (Section 5.10); uncertainties in the values employed in the calculation lead to electron affinities of questionable accuracy. Values are available for only a few elements.

On the basis of electron affinity data that are available, predictions based on reasoning analogous to that used in discussing ionization potentials appear generally to be borne out. A small atom should have a greater tendency to add an electron than a large atom since the added electron is, on the average, closer to the positively charged nucleus in a small atom. This trend is roughly followed from left to right in any period (Table 3.1).

Table 3.1

Electron Affinities (ev)

H −0.7							He 0
Li −0.5	Be ~0	B −0.3	C −1.1	N ~0	O −1.5 (+7.3)[a]	F −3.6	Ne 0
Na −0.7	Mg ~0	Al −0.4	Si −1.9	P −0.8	S −2.1 (+3.4)[a]	Cl −3.8	Ar 0
						Br −3.5	Kr 0
						I −3.2	Xe 0

[a] Values in parentheses are total energy effects for the addition of two electrons.

In the second period, however, exceptions may be noted for beryllium (filled $2s$ subshell), nitrogen (half-filled $2p$ subshell), and neon (all subshells filled). Similar exceptions may be noted for analogous elements of the third period. Elements with relatively stable electronic configurations do not accept additional electrons readily. Since the electronic configuration of each of the group VII A elements is one electron short of a noble gas configuration, each element of group VII A has the greatest tendency toward electron gain of any element of its period.

Group trends are best illustrated by reference to the halogens. Electron attracting ability, except for that of fluorine, tends to increase from bottom to top within the group in conformity with decreasing atomic size. However, the effect of small size may be partially negated by the repulsion of electrons already present in the atom. The exception noted for fluorine, as well as for other second period elements, may be, in part, explained by such repulsions. The concentration of negative charge in a very small shell is greater than the concentration obtained when the same number of electrons is placed in a larger shell.

Some second electron affinities have been determined. These values refer to processes in which an electron is added to a negative ion; for example,

$$e^- + O^-(g) \longrightarrow O^{2-}(g)$$

Since there is an electrostatic repulsion between a negative ion and an electron, energy is required, not released, and second electron affinities have positive signs.

3.4 The Ionic Bond

When an element that has a comparatively low ionization potential and an element that has a relatively high electron affinity combine, electrons are transferred, and an **ionic** (or **electrovalent**) **compound** is produced. For example, in the reaction of a sodium atom with a chlorine atom, an electron is transferred from sodium to chlorine, and charged particles, or ions, result. The sodium ion has a charge of $1+$ since it has a nuclear charge of $11+$ and only 10 electrons; the chloride ion has a $1-$ charge since its nucleus contains 17 protons and it has 18 electrons. Positive ions are called **cations**, and negative ions are called **anions**. These names are derived from the terminology of electrochemistry (Chapter 10).

The reactions and compounds of the A family elements are at times conveniently indicated by using the symbols of the elements under consideration together with dots for their valence electrons. For A family elements, the valence electrons are the only ones involved in chemical reactions. The positions of the dots around the symbol have no significance; electrons are distributed in three dimensions and in the manner previously discussed. Using such a notation, the equation for the reaction of sodium and chlorine is

$$\text{Na} \cdot + \cdot \overset{\cdot\cdot}{\text{Cl}} \colon \longrightarrow \text{Na}^+ + \colon\overset{\cdot\cdot}{\underset{\cdot\cdot}{\text{Cl}}} \colon^-$$

Care must be exercised in interpreting such equations since not all the electrons present in the atom or ion are shown. The electronic configuration of sodium is $1s^2\, 2s^2\, 2p^6\, 3s^1$, and that of chlorine is $1s^2\, 2s^2\, 2p^6\, 3s^2\, 3p^5$. After the reaction, the sodium ion attains a configuration identical with that of neon ($1s^2\, 2s^2\, 2p^6$), and the configuration of the chloride ion is the same as that of argon ($1s^2\, 2s^2\, 2p^6\, 3s^2\, 3p^6$). The sodium and chloride ions may be said to be **isoelectronic** (of the same electronic configuration) with neon and argon, respectively.

In ionic reactions, most of the representative elements attain an electronic configuration isoelectronic with a noble gas (the post-transition metals such as gallium and indium cannot attain them). Much has been made of this fact. Undoubtedly, the $ns^2\, np^6$ (octet) arrangement of electrons in the outer shell of a noble gas is very stable; this, in part, accounts for the values of the ionization potentials and electron affinities observed for the A family elements and the stabilities of their ionic compounds. Important as this generalization is, however, we shall see later that the attainment of a noble-gas configuration is not the most fundamental driving force for the ionic reaction. Nevertheless, an A family element generally reacts through the loss or gain of electrons in such a way as to secure an octet of electrons in its outer shell; for those ions where the $n = 1$ shell is the only one present, two electrons form a stable structure (compare the first noble gas, helium).

In the reaction of sodium and chlorine, the total number of electrons lost by sodium must equal the total number of electrons gained by chlorine. Thus, the number of sodium ions produced is the same as the number of chloride ions produced. These ions attract each other to form a **crystal** (Figure 3.5).

The **lattice energy** is the energy effect associated with the condensation of positive and negative ions into a crystal (Section 7.13). Since energy is evolved in these processes, lattice energies have negative signs. For a particular

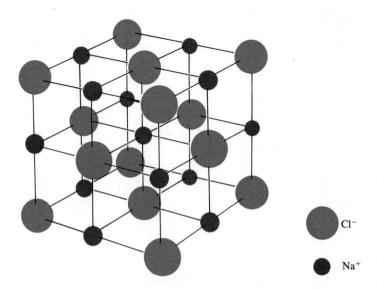

Cl$^-$

Na$^+$

Figure 3.5 Sodium chloride crystal lattice.

crystal, the lattice energy, with the sign changed, is the amount of energy required to separate the positive and negative ions of the crystal.

Even though there are the same number of sodium ions as chloride ions in a sodium chloride crystal, no pair of ions may be considered as belonging to each other. Rather, each sodium ion is surrounded by six chloride ions and each chloride ion is surrounded by six sodium ions; the geometry of the crystal is such that the repulsion of like-charged ions is more than compensated for by the attraction of oppositely charged ions. This mutual attraction of positive and negative ions is what holds the crystal together; indeed, the ionic bond may be considered to be just this.

The formula for this ionic compound, sodium chloride, is NaCl. From our examination of the sodium chloride crystal, we can see that this formula does not describe a unit of one sodium ion and one chloride ion, for such does not exist under ordinary conditions. Rather, the formula of an ionic compound gives the simplest ratio of ions present in a crystal; the actual number of ions present in any crystal (which would be very large) depends upon the size of the crystal under study.

When oxygen undergoes an ionic reaction, each oxygen atom (electron configuration $1s^2\,2s^2\,2p^4$) accepts two electrons and attains the neon configuration ($1s^2\,2s^2\,2p^6$); the oxide ion has a charge of $2-$. In the reaction of sodium with oxygen, two atoms of sodium are required for every one atom of oxygen since it is necessary that there be a balance between electrons lost and electrons gained. Thus the equation for this reaction is

$$2\text{Na}\cdot + \ddot{\underset{\cdot\cdot}{\text{O}}}\colon \longrightarrow 2\text{Na}^+ + \colon\ddot{\underset{\cdot\cdot}{\text{O}}}\colon{}^{2-}$$

The formula of the product, sodium oxide, is Na_2O. In the formula the subscript 2 for sodium and the subscript 1 (understood) for oxygen indicate the simplest ratio of ions present in any crystal of this substance. The geometry of the sodium oxide crystal is different from that of the sodium chloride crystal and is such that these ions are accommodated in the ratio of two sodium ions to one oxide ion.

The **electrovalence number** of an element is the charge (including sign) of the ion derived from that element after an electrovalent reaction. If we follow the octet principle, the electrovalence number of any of the group I A elements should be $1+$; group VII A, $1-$; group II A, $2+$; group VI A, $2-$. These charges are derived from the number of valence electrons characteristic of any element of a given group and the number of electrons that need to be lost (positive electrovalence) or gained (negative electrovalence) in order for the element to attain a noble-gas configuration.

From these ionic charges, formulas may be derived on the basis of the fact that the *total* positive ionic charge of any compound must equal the *total* negative ionic charge of that compound. Calcium is a group II A metal has two valence electrons and has an electrovalence number of 2+. We have already determined that the electrovalence number of chlorine is 1− and that the electrovalence of oxygen is 2−. Thus the formula of calcium chloride is $CaCl_2$ and that of calcium oxide is CaO. In a similar manner one can derive the formulas of aluminum oxide (Al_2O_3), sodium sulfide (Na_2S), and potassium nitride (K_3N) from the predicted electrovalence numbers of aluminum (3+), oxygen (2−), sodium (1+), sulfur (2−), potassium (1+), and nitrogen (3−). We shall see later that not all the compounds predicted by this method exist, and not all those that do exist are truly ionic in character.

Metals are elements that tend to lose electrons in an ionic reaction, whereas nonmetals, if they enter into an ionic reaction at all, gain electrons. Whether two atoms will react to form an ionic compound depends upon several energy considerations. The three most important to the present discussion are the ionization energy of the metal, the electron affinity of the nonmetal, and the lattice energy of the resulting crystal.

The ionization of a sodium atom absorbs energy (ionization energy).

$$1.96 \times 10^{-19} \text{ cal/atom} + Na(g) \longrightarrow Na^+(g) + e^-(g)$$

Energy is evolved when a chlorine atom gains an electron (electron affinity).

$$e^-(g) + Cl(g) \longrightarrow Cl^-(g) + 1.46 \times 10^{-19} \text{ cal/atom}$$

But the amount is insufficient to supply that required for the ionization of a sodium atom. The deficit is supplied by the condensation of the two ions into a crystal lattice (lattice energy).

$$Na^+(g) + Cl^-(g) \longrightarrow NaCl(\text{crystal}) + 3.04 \times 10^{-19} \text{ cal}$$

Thus energy is evolved by the overall process.

$$Na(g) + Cl(g) \longrightarrow NaCl(\text{crystal}) + 2.54 \times 10^{-19} \text{ cal}$$

This is a simplification. Other factors are involved (Section 5.10) such as the energy required to separate the sodium atoms from the form in which they customarily occur.

Two additional considerations should be borne in mind. First, the ionization potentials plotted in Figure 3.3 are **first** ionization potentials. For a bivalent ion such as Ca^{2+}, the second ionization potential must also be considered; second- and higher-order ionization potentials are always larger than first ionization potentials. Second, when more than one electron is added to an atom in the preparation of a negative ion, energy is *required*, not released. Thus for the formation of the oxide ion, the addition of the first electron releases energy, but the addition of the second electron requires energy

(Section 3.3); for the overall process, energy is required, not evolved. In the reaction of sodium with oxygen, therefore, the lattice energy of sodium oxide would have to supply the energy required for the formation of the oxide ion as well as that needed for the ionization of sodium.

Certain metals fulfill the requirements for reaction but still cannot possibly produce ions that are isoelectronic with noble gases. The electronic configuration of the last two shells of zinc is $\cdots 3s^2\, 3p^6\, 3d^{10}\, 4s^2$. In order for zinc to attain the configuration of argon ($\cdots 3s^2\, 3p^6$), it would have to lose 12 electrons. An electron loss of this magnitude is never observed; the energy required is unobtainable in any known process. Nevertheless, zinc does react with nonmetals, but an ion with a $2+$ charge is produced in these reactions.

The electronic configuration of the Zn^{2+} ion is one of some stability (although not so stable as a noble-gas configuration); all the subshells present are filled ($1s^2\, 2s^2\, 2p^6\, 3s^2\, 3p^6\, 3d^{10}$). Ions that have $ns^2\, np^6\, nd^{10}$ configurations in their outer shells are called **pseudo-noble-gas ions**. Examples are: Cu^+, Ag^+, Au^+, Zn^{2+}, Cd^{2+}, Hg^{2+}, Ga^{3+}, In^{3+}, and Tl^{3+}.

Another type of ion with a regular electronic configuration is the **inert-pair ion** in which a pseudo-noble-gas arrangement is overlayed by a pair of s electrons in the next higher quantum level. Examples of inert-pair ions include: In^+, Tl^+, Sn^{2+}, Pb^{2+}, Sb^{3+}, and Bi^{3+}.

It is impossible for most of the transition elements to produce ions with any of these types of electronic configuration. Sc^{3+}, Y^{3+}, and La^{3+} have noble-gas configurations, and some of the ions of elements of the copper family (group I B) and the zinc family (group II B) have pseudo-noble-gas structures. For the remainder, however, the attainment of a noble-gas, pseudo-noble-gas, or inert-pair structure is impossible since the existence of any ion with a charge higher than $3+$ is doubtful under ordinary conditions.

Most of these metals (although not all of them) exhibit more than one electrovalence number. Thus, depending upon reaction conditions, iron forms either the Fe^{2+} ion or the Fe^{3+} ion. The configuration of Fe^{2+} is $1s^2\, 2s^2\, 2p^6\, 3s^2\, 3p^6\, 3d^6$ and that of Fe^{3+} is $1s^2\, 2s^2\, 2p^6\, 3s^2\, 3p^6\, 3d^5$; Fe^{3+} is more stable than Fe^{2+} since Fe^{3+} has a half-filled $3d$ subshell. Notice that for the transition elements, more than the outer shell of electrons may be used for chemical bonding. Some other common transition element ions are Cr^{2+}, Cr^{3+}, Mn^{2+}, Co^{2+}, Co^{3+}, and Ni^{2+}. Copper forms the Cu^{2+} ion in addition to the pseudo-noble-gas ion Cu^+. The most common electrovalence number of the inner-transition elements is $3+$.

Some of the compounds we have discussed are not purely ionic in character; this will be a topic for Section 3.8. Nevertheless, the ionic concept here applied is a convenient and important generalization. Ion types are summarized in Table 3.2.

Table 3.2

Types of Ions

Ion Type	Electronic Configuration of Outer Shell(s)	Examples
noble-gas	$ns^2\,np^6$	Na^+, Ca^{2+}, Al^{3+} Cl^-, O^{2-}, N^{3-}
pseudo-noble-gas	$ns^2\,np^6\,nd^{10}$	Ag^+, Zn^{2+}, Ga^{3+}
inert-pair	$(n-1)s^2\,(n-1)p^6\,(n-1)d^{10}\,ns^2$	Tl^+, Sn^{2+}, Bi^{3+}

3.5 Ionic Radius

The radii of ions have been determined by X-ray diffraction of ionic crystals. Such studies give the distances between the centers of adjacent ions, and it is a problem to apportion these distances. When bond distances of covalent molecules are apportioned to secure covalent radii (Section 3.1), one starts with a bond between two like atoms which can be divided equally. In ionic crystals the positive and negative ions are, of necessity, different sizes.

One solution to this problem is to study a crystal of a compound with a very small cation and a very large anion, such as lithium iodide (Figure 3.6a). The assumption is then made that the iodide ions touch each other, and the iodide–iodide distance (d in the illustration) is divided in half to give the radius of the iodide ion. Such an apportionment of the anion–anion distance (d) is impossible for a crystal of the more common type illustrated in Figure 3.6b since there is no anion–anion contact. Once the radius of the iodide ion has been fixed as a standard, other ionic radii can be calculated by subtracting the radius of the standard ion from the cation–anion distance (d' in Figure 3.6b) of another crystal. For example, the radius of the potassium ion could be

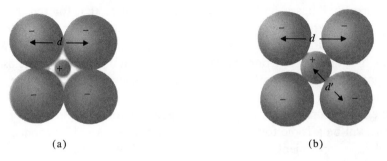

(a)   (b)

Figure 3.6 Determination of ionic radii. (See text for further discussion.)

Table 3.3

Ionic Radii (*in angstrom units*, Å)

	I A	II A	III A	VI A	VII A
	Li^+ 0.60	Be^{2+} 0.31		O^{2-} 1.40	F^- 1.36
	Na^+ 0.95	Mg^{2+} 0.65	Al^{3+} 0.50	S^{2-} 1.84	Cl^- 1.81
	K^+ 1.33	Ca^{2+} 0.99	Ga^{3+} 0.62	Se^{2-} 1.98	Br^- 1.95
	Rb^+ 1.48	Sr^{2+} 1.13	In^{3+} 0.81	Te^{2-} 2.21	I^- 2.16
	Cs^+ 1.69	Ba^{2+} 1.35	Tl^{3+} 0.95		

calculated by subtracting the radius of the iodide ion from the K^+ to I^- distance in the potassium iodide crystal. Table 3.3 lists some ionic radii.

A positive ion is always smaller than the neutral atom from which it is derived (Figure 3.7). Thus the radius of Na is 1.57 Å; the radius of Na^+

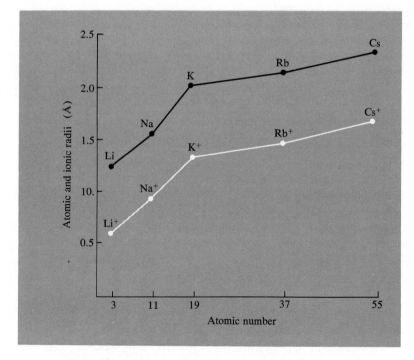

Figure 3.7 Atomic and ionic radii of the group I A elements.

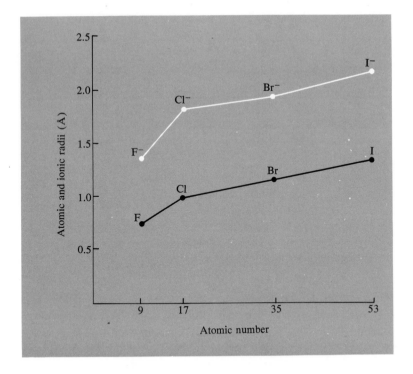

Figure 3.8 Atomic and ionic radii of the group VII A elements.

is 0.95 Å. In the formation of the sodium ion, the loss of an electron represents the loss of the entire $n = 3$ shell of the sodium atom. Furthermore, the loss of an electron creates an imbalance in the proton–electron ratio; since the protons outnumber the electrons in the positive ion, the electrons of the ion are drawn in closer to the nucleus.

For similar reasons, a 2+ ion is larger than a 3+ ion. Thus

$$\text{Fe} = 1.17 \text{ Å} \qquad \text{Fe}^{2+} = 0.75 \text{ Å} \qquad \text{Fe}^{3+} = 0.60 \text{ Å}$$

A negative ion is always larger than its parent atom. Thus the radius of the fluorine atom is 0.72 Å, and that of the fluoride ion is 1.36 Å (Figure 3.8). In the formation of the fluoride ion, the addition of an electron to the $2p$ subshell causes an enhanced repulsion between electrons, and the $n = 2$ shell expands. The fluoride ion has nine protons and ten electrons.

Within a period, isoelectronic positive ions show a decrease in ionic radius from left to right. This is because of the increasing nuclear charge. The same trend is observed for the isoelectronic negative ions of a period; ionic radius decreases from left to right.

Within a group of the periodic table, similarly charged ions increase in size from top to bottom of the group. The ions of the heavier members of the group employ more electron shells than those of the lighter members.

3.6 The Covalent Bond

When two nonmetals react, a covalent compound is produced. The characteristic of this bond is that electrons are shared by the bonded atoms; electron transfer does not occur. Since nonmetals have high ionization potentials, they do not lose electrons in chemical reactions. Rather, in a successful reaction between two nonmetals, each of the reacting elements has an attraction for additional electrons (Section 3.3). Thus two atoms of helium (which does not exhibit this attraction) do not bond to each other; rather, helium exists as a monatomic gas.

On the other hand, two atoms of hydrogen combine to form a **molecule**, H_2, for which the symbol H **:** H is frequently used. Each of the bonded atoms supplies one electron to the covalent bond. One covalent bond consists of a pair of electrons, with spins paired, that is shared by both of the bonded atoms. Although the electrons must be considered as belonging to the molecule as a whole, each hydrogen atom can now be thought of as having the noble-gas configuration of helium. This consideration is based on the premise that both shared electrons contribute to the stable configuration of each hydrogen atom. Remember that for both hydrogen and helium, only the $n = 1$ shell is involved; this shell is complete when occupied by two electrons. Another designation used to show the bonding in the hydrogen molecule is H—H, where the dash depicts one covalent bond (two electrons).

In a hydrogen atom, the electron is symmetrically distributed around the nucleus; in a hydrogen molecule this distribution is altered so that electronic charge is concentrated between the two nuclei (Figure 3.9). The strength of this

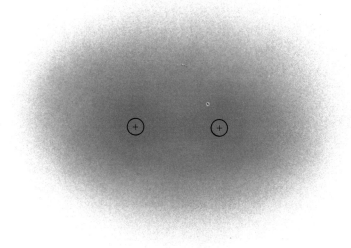

Figure 3.9 Representation of the electron distribution in a hydrogen molecule.

bond comes from the attraction of the positively charged nuclei for the negative electron cloud of the bond; electron–electron and nucleus–nucleus repulsions are more than compensated for by this attraction.

The formula, H_2, describes a discrete unit—a molecule—and hydrogen gas consists of a collection of such molecules. There are no molecules in strictly ionic materials. The formula Na_2Cl_2 is incorrect because sodium chloride is an ionic compound, and the simplest ratio of ions in a crystal of sodium chloride is 1 to 1; a molecule of formula Na_2Cl_2 does not exist. However, for covalent materials a formula such as H_2O_2 can be correct; here, the formula describes a molecule containing two hydrogen atoms and two oxygen atoms.

The hydrogen molecule can be described as being **diatomic** (containing two atoms). Certain other elements also exist as diatomic molecules. An atom of any group VII A element has seven valence electrons. By the formation of a covalent bond between two such atoms, each atom attains an octet configuration characteristic of the noble gases. Thus fluorine gas consists of F_2 molecules.

$$:\ddot{\text{F}}\cdot + \cdot\ddot{\text{F}}: \longrightarrow \ :\ddot{\text{F}}:\ddot{\text{F}}:$$

Only the electrons between the two atoms are shared and form a part of the covalent bond (although the molecular orbital theory considers that all of the electrons affect the bonding—Section 4.4).

More than one covalent bond may form between two atoms. A nitrogen atom (group V A) has five valence electrons.

$$:\dot{\text{N}}\cdot + \cdot\dot{\text{N}}: \longrightarrow \ :\text{N}:::\text{N}:$$

In the molecule, N_2, six electrons are shared in three covalent bonds (usually called a triple bond). Notice that, as a result of this formulation, each of the nitrogen atoms can be considered as having an octet of electrons.

The nonmetallic elements that exist as diatomic molecules are H_2, F_2, Cl_2, Br_2, I_2, N_2, and O_2. (Oxygen is a special case and will be discussed in Section 4.4.) These elements are always indicated in this way in chemical equations.

The electron-dot formulas we have been using are called **valence-bond structures** or **Lewis structures**, named after Gilbert N. Lewis who proposed this theory of covalent bonding in 1916. The Lewis theory emphasized the attainment of noble-gas configurations on the part of atoms in covalent molecules. On this basis, and since the number of valence electrons is the same as the group number for the nonmetals, one would predict that VII A elements, such as Cl, would form one covalent bond to attain a stable octet; VI A elements, such as O and S, two covalent bonds; V A elements, such as N and P, three covalent bonds; and IV A elements, such as C, four covalent bonds. These predictions are borne out in many compounds containing only simple covalent bonds.

$$H\cdot + \cdot \ddot{\underset{\cdot\cdot}{Cl}}: \longrightarrow H:\ddot{\underset{\cdot\cdot}{Cl}}:$$

hydrogen chloride

$$2H\cdot + \cdot \ddot{\underset{\cdot}{O}}: \longrightarrow H:\ddot{\underset{H}{O}}:$$

water

$$3H\cdot + \cdot \ddot{\underset{\cdot\cdot}{N}}\cdot \longrightarrow \overset{H}{\underset{\cdot\cdot}{H:N:H}}$$

ammonia

$$4H\cdot + \cdot \dot{\underset{\cdot}{C}}\cdot \longrightarrow \overset{H}{\underset{H}{H:C:H}}$$

methane

Notice that for these molecules, the hydrogen atoms can be considered as having a stable $n = 1$ shell; the other atoms have characteristic noble-gas octets.

'The covalent bonding of compounds is also conveniently indicated by dashes. Remember that each dash represents a pair of electrons. The electrons not engaged in bonding may, or may not, be shown. In each of the following, the number of covalent bonds on each atom agrees with our predictions.

$$:\ddot{\underset{\cdot\cdot}{Cl}}-\ddot{\underset{|}{P}}-\ddot{\underset{\cdot\cdot}{Cl}}: \qquad :\ddot{\underset{\cdot\cdot}{Cl}}-\ddot{\underset{\cdot\cdot}{O}}-\ddot{\underset{\cdot\cdot}{Cl}}: \qquad \overset{H\quad H}{\underset{H\quad H}{H-C-C-H}}$$
$$:\underset{\cdot\cdot}{Cl}:$$

phosphorous trichloride dichlorine oxide ethane

The following are examples of molecules that contain double and triple bonds.

$$:\ddot{\underset{\cdot\cdot}{O}}: + :C: + :\ddot{\underset{\cdot\cdot}{O}}: \longrightarrow :\ddot{\underset{\cdot\cdot}{O}}::C::\ddot{\underset{\cdot\cdot}{O}}:$$

carbon dioxide

$$2H\cdot + \cdot\dot{\underset{\cdot}{C}}: + :\dot{\underset{\cdot}{C}}\cdot + 2H\cdot \longrightarrow \overset{H\quad H}{H:C::C:H}$$

ethylene

$$H\cdot + \cdot C: + :C\cdot + \cdot H \longrightarrow H:C:::C:H$$

acetylene

The structures of these compounds may also be represented by dash formulas.

$$:\ddot{O}=C=\ddot{O}: \qquad \begin{matrix} H & H \\ | & | \\ H-C=C-H \end{matrix} \qquad H-C\equiv C-H$$

Notice that in each compound the number of covalent bonds on each atom agrees with that predicted.

3.7 Formal Charge

In the formation of certain covalent bonds, *both* of the shared electrons are furnished by *one* of the bonded atoms. For example, in the reaction of ammonia with a proton (a hydrogen atom stripped of its electron), the un-shared electron pair of the nitrogen atom of NH_3 is used to form a new covalent bond.

$$H:\overset{\cdot\cdot}{\underset{H}{N}}:H + H^+ \longrightarrow \left[H:\overset{H}{\underset{H}{N}}:H \right]^+$$

A bond formed in this way is frequently called a "coordinate covalent" bond, but it is probably unwise to do so. The coordination *process* of covalent-bond formation is a useful distinction—particularly in the study of coordination complexes (Chapter 19) and in interpreting certain acid-base reactions (Section 15.7). However, labeling a specific *bond* as a "coordinate covalent" bond, different from other covalent bonds, has little justification.

All electrons are alike no matter what their source. All the bonds in NH_4^+ are identical, and it is impossible to distinguish between them. Furthermore, the mode of formation of a covalent bond does not affect its nature. We can *imagine* any covalent bond as having been formed by electron pairing

$$2H\cdot + \cdot\overset{\cdot\cdot}{\underset{\cdot}{O}}: \longrightarrow H_2O$$

or electron-pair donation

$$2H^+ + \left[:\overset{\cdot\cdot}{\underset{\cdot\cdot}{O}}: \right]^{2-} \longrightarrow H_2O$$

Notice, however, that the number of covalent bonds on the N atom of NH_4^+ does not agree with the number predicted in the preceding section. Since a nitrogen atom has five valence electrons (group V A), it would be expected to satisfy the octet principle through the formation of three covalent bonds. This prediction is correct for NH_3; it is not correct for NH_4^+.

An answer to this question may be obtained by calculating the formal charges of the atoms in NH_4^+. A **formal charge** is calculated by apportioning the bonding electrons equally between the bonded atoms, one electron to each atom for each covalent bond, and then comparing the number of electrons that a given atom has in the structure with the number of valence electrons that this atom would have when electrically neutral.

In NH_4^+, the N atom may be considered to have four electrons—one each from the division of each of the covalent bonds. Since a neutral N atom has five valence electrons, the N atom in NH_4^+ is assigned a formal charge of $1+$. Each H atom of the NH_4^+ ion has the same number of electrons in the structure that it has as a neutral atom and hence carries no formal charge. We can indicate the formal charge on the N atom of NH_4^+ as follows.

$$
\begin{array}{c}
\text{H} \\
| \\
\text{H} - \overset{\oplus}{\text{N}} - \text{H} \\
| \\
\text{H}
\end{array}
$$

Thus the discrepancy between the predicted and actual number of bonds on the N atom in NH_4^+ may be explained on the basis of formal charge since the hypothetical N^+ would have four unpaired electrons and be able to form four covalent bonds.

In the assignment of formal charges, the assumption is made that the electron pair of any covalent bond is shared equally by the bonded atoms. Such an assumption is usually not true (Section 3.8), and formal charges must be interpreted carefully. The electron density on the N atom in NH_4^+ is less than that on the N atom in NH_3, but the actual charge is much less than a full positive charge because the bonding electrons are not equally shared. In addition, molecular polarity occurs in some molecules in which the formal charges of all atoms are zero (Section 3.10).

Lewis structures may be assigned without reference to the source of the bonding electrons. For example, one could proceed in the following way to diagram the structure of the sulfur dioxide molecule, SO_2. This theory of covalent bonding offers no way to predict the arrangement of atoms in a molecule; such an arrangement must be derived from experimental evidence. In the SO_2 molecule, the O atoms are joined to a central S atom, and the molecule is angular.

$$
\begin{array}{c}
\text{S} \\
\text{O} \quad \text{O}
\end{array}
$$

There is a total of eighteen valence electrons to be distributed between the atoms (twelve from the two O atoms plus six from the S atom). If we place single bonds between the atoms, the addition of these two bonds would use up four of our electrons, leaving fourteen. These fourteen must be distributed in such a way as to give an octet to each of the atoms.

In an attempt to accomplish this division, we derive the structure

$$:\ddot{O}. \overset{\overset{..}{S}}{\diagdown} .\ddot{O}:$$

Both the O atoms in this structure have the proper number of electrons associated with them, but the S atom has only six. We can remedy this situation by switching an electron pair from one of the O atoms in such a way as to make a double bond between it and the S atom.

$$:\ddot{O}. \overset{\overset{..}{S}}{\diagup} = \ddot{O}:$$

For the calculation of formal charge, the S atom may be considered to have five electrons—two that are not engaged in bonding and three from the division of the three covalent bonds on that atom. Since a neutral S atom has six valence electrons (group VI A), the S atom is assigned a formal charge of $1+$. The right-hand O atom has the same number of electrons in the structure that it has as a neutral atom, and hence it carries no formal charge. The O atom on the left has seven valence electrons in the structure (six unshared electrons plus one from the covalent bond), and since the neutral O atom has six valence electrons, this O atom is assigned a formal charge of $1-$.

A structure for SO_2 may be diagramed as follows.

$$^\ominus:\ddot{O}. \overset{\overset{..}{S}^\oplus}{\diagup} = \ddot{O}:$$

However, the bonding in SO_2 is not adequately represented by a single structure of this type, and, as we shall see in Section 4.1, a further refinement is necessary.

3.8 Transition Between Ionic and Covalent Bonding

Chemical reactions and physical measurements support the belief that most chemical compounds are intermediate in character between the purely ionic and the purely covalent. The best examples of ionic bonds are found in compounds between the metals of low ionization potential of the lower left of the periodic table and the nonmetals of high electron affinity found in the upper right of the periodic table. In such compounds, electron transfer is definite and complete; these compounds exist as a collection of ions in ionic crystals (Section 3.10).

ionic bond distorted ions polarized covalent bond covalent bond

Figure 3.10 Transition between ionic and covalent bonding.

A pure covalent bond is found only in molecules formed from two *identical* atoms, such as Cl_2. The electron-attracting ability of one chlorine atom is exactly the same as the electron-attracting ability of any other, and the electron cloud of the bond is distributed equally between the two chlorine atoms. Or, one could say that the bonding electrons are shared equally by the chlorine atoms.

Most compounds fit somewhere between these two extremes. If two spherical ions of opposite charge are brought together, the positively charged ion attracts and deforms the electron cloud of the anion. The electron cloud of the anion is drawn toward the cation, and, in extreme cases, such ion deformation can lead to the formation of molecules and predominantly covalent compounds (Figure 3.10). The degree of covalent character that a compound exhibits may be considered to correspond to the extent of ion distortion in the compound.

The ability of a cation to distort the electron cloud of a neighboring anion depends upon the charge concentration of the cation; a small cation with a high positive charge is very effective in this respect. On the other hand, large multicharged anions are the most readily distorted since the outer electrons are relatively far from the nucleus in ions of this type. Cations are usually smaller and more compact than anions, and therefore the distortion of a cation by an anion is usually negligible.

Boron (group III A—three valence electrons) has a small atomic radius, is a nonmetal, and forms covalent compounds. If a B^{3+} ion were to form, its small size and high positive charge would cause such distortion in an anion that a predominantly covalent compound would result. Likewise, aluminum chloride is a predominantly covalent material (consisting of Al_2Cl_6 molecules in the vapor state). Truly ionic compounds containing cations with a charge of 3+ or higher are rare, and such exist only when the cation is a very large one. Certain highly charged cations exist, in hydrated form, in water solution, however (Sections 9.2 and 9.3).

Tin and lead are group IV A elements and are metallic in character. These elements are frequently said to form 2+ and 4+ ions in such compounds as $SnCl_2$, $SnCl_4$, $PbCl_2$, and $PbCl_4$. The compounds with "4+ cations" are undoubtedly not ionic at all but covalent; this is not unexpected, since Sn.

and Pb both have four valence electrons, and the formation of four covalent bonds gives them noble-gas structures. The compounds of Sn^{2+} and Pb^{2+} (inert-pair ions) have more ionic character because of the lower charges on the cations.

Likewise, the metals antimony and bismuth, of group V A, are reported to form $3+$ and $5+$ "ions." Such compounds are probably even more covalent than those of tin and lead, particularly those in which antimony and bismuth have $5+$ charges. Ion-distortion and enhanced covalence is also observed in transition metal compounds.

Another approach to the problem of bonds of intermediate character is that which considers the polarization of covalent bonds (Figure 3.10); in this view, the ionic bond is an extreme case of the polarization of a covalent bond by the dislocation of electron charge density.

Two *like* atoms form a pure covalent bond in which the bonding electrons are shared exactly equally. However, when two *different* atoms are joined by a covalent bond, the electrons of the bond are not shared equally. No matter how similar such atoms may be, there will be some difference in their electron-attracting abilities. As predicted by electron affinities (Section 3.3), chlorine has a larger attraction for electrons than does bromine. Thus in the molecule BrCl the electrons of the covalent bond are more strongly attracted by the chlorine atom than the bromine atom, and the electron cloud of the bond is distorted toward the chlorine atom. Therefore the chlorine end of the molecule is negative with respect to the bromine end of the molecule. The molecule as a whole is electrically neutral, since it contains as many protons as electrons; however, polarity arises from an unequal distribution of the bonding electrons in the molecule. The Br—Cl bond is spoken of as a polar covalent bond. Since the charges of this polar bond are not as large as the $1+$ or $1-$ charges found on ions, they are usually indicated by the symbols δ^+ and δ^-.

Obviously, the greater the difference in electron-attracting ability between two atoms joined by a covalent bond, the more polar the bond will be. Reading Figure 3.10 from right to left shows that if this unequal sharing is carried to an extreme, a situation arises where one of the bonded atoms has all of the bonding electrons, and separate ions result.

Many of the physical properties of certain covalent compounds reflect the polar nature of their molecules—for example, melting point, surface tension, heat of vaporization, bond energy, and dipole moment. These properties will be studied in later chapters. A molecule with positive and negative charge centers is spoken of as a dipole, and the dipole moment of the molecule may be defined as the product of the charge times the distance between the positive and negative centers. The dipole moment of a compound may be calculated from the measurement of the compound's dielectric constant. In an electric field, polar molecules orient themselves with their positive ends toward the negative plate and their negative ends toward the positive plate (Figure 3.11).

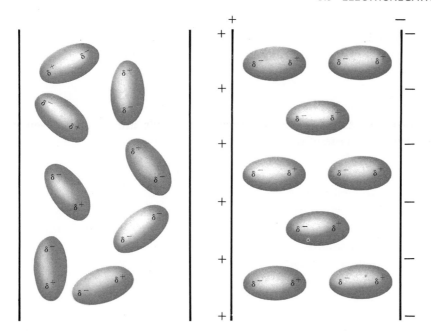

Figure 3.11 Effect of an electrostatic field on the orientation of polar molecules.

This orientation influences the amount of charge that a pair of electrically charged plates can hold. The dielectric constant of a compound can be determined by comparing the charge on a pair of plates with the compound between them to the charge on the plates when they are separated by a vacuum, voltage constant.

The dipole moments of nonpolar molecules, such as H_2, Cl_2, and Br_2, are zero. The more polar the bond of a diatomic molecule, the larger is the dipole moment of the molecule. Linus Pauling has used the dipole moment of a compound to calculate the **partial ionic character** of its covalent bond. Dipole moment, μ, is defined as the product of the distance separating equal charges of opposite sign and the magnitude of the charge. If hydrogen chloride were completely ionic, the H^+ and Cl^- ions would each bear a unit charge (1.60×10^{-19} coulomb). Since the bond distance between the H and Cl atoms of hydrogen chloride is 1.27 Å, the dipole moment of the hypothetical, completely ionic, HCl would be:

$$\mu = (1.60 \times 10^{-19} \text{ coulomb})(1.27 \times 10^{-8} \text{ cm})$$
$$= 2.03 \times 10^{-27} \text{ coulomb cm} = 6.10 \text{ D}$$

Dipole moments are customarily expressed in debye units; $1 \text{ D} = 3.33 \times 10^{-28}$ coulomb cm. The experimentally derived dipole moment of HCl is 1.03 D. Thus the observed dipole moment is 0.17 times the value calculated for the hypothetical, ionic, compound.

$$\frac{1.03 \text{ D}}{6.10 \text{ D}} = 0.17$$

Based upon dipole moment measurements, the HCl bond appears to be 17% ionic. Bonds with a partial ionic character of over 50% should be classed as ionic.

3.9 Electronegativity

The ability of an atom in a molecule to attract electrons to itself is called the relative **electronegativity** of the atom. Thus the polarity of the HCl molecule may be said to arise from the difference between the electronegativity of hydrogen and that of chlorine; since chlorine is more electronegative than hydrogen, the chlorine end of the molecule is the negative end of the dipole. In general, electronegativities of the elements are related to the same atomic parameters as are ionization potentials, and trends in electronegativities approximately parallel those in ionization potentials.

Unlike ionization potentials, however, electronegativities cannot be determined by a definite, direct, measurement. There is no agreement as to how they should be calculated, and many systems of measurement have been proposed. Several electronegativity scales have been derived from atomic radii and electronic configurations. Electronegativity determinations have been based on measurements of dipole moments; this scheme employs the same type of data as that used for the determination of the partial ionic character of the HCl bond.

A system has been devised using the average of the ionization potential and the electron affinity of each element as the electronegativity of that element. It is logical that a measure of the electron-attracting ability of an atom of a covalent bond can be based on these measurements. Thus, a large electronegativity value is observed when the atom has a high ionization potential (small tendency to lose an electron completely) and a high electron affinity (great tendency to gain an electron completely). Unfortunately, electron affinities have been calculated for only a few elements, and some of these values are of questionable accuracy.

The electronegativity scale devised by Pauling is the one most used (Table 3.4) and is based on experimentally derived values of **bond energies**. The bond energy of the Cl—Cl bond, for example, is the energy required to separate the Cl_2 molecule into two atoms of chlorine (*not* ions).

$$9.63 \times 10^{-20} \text{ cal/bond} + \overset{\cdot\cdot}{\underset{\cdot\cdot}{Cl}} \overset{\cdot\cdot}{:} \overset{\cdot\cdot}{\underset{\cdot\cdot}{Cl}} : \longrightarrow 2 : \overset{\cdot\cdot}{\underset{\cdot\cdot}{Cl}} \cdot$$

This bond energy relates to a pure covalent bond in which the electrons are shared equally, and there is no polarity. In like manner, the bond energy of the H—H bond, another nonpolar bond, can be experimentally determined.

$$1.73 \times 10^{-19} \text{ cal/bond} + H : H \longrightarrow 2H \cdot$$

An expected value of the bond energy of the H—Cl bond can be calculated by taking the arithmetic mean of the bond energies of the H—H and Cl—Cl bonds.

$$\frac{0.96 \times 10^{-19} \text{ cal/bond} + 1.73 \times 10^{-19} \text{ cal/bond}}{2} = 1.35 \times 10^{-19} \text{ cal/bond}$$

The experimentally determined value of the bond energy of the H—Cl bond, however, is larger than this calculated value.

$$1.71 \times 10^{-19} \text{ cal/bond} + H\!:\!\ddot{C}l\!: \longrightarrow H\!\cdot + \!:\!\ddot{C}l\!\cdot$$

The difference between the two values is given the symbol Δ.

$$\Delta = 1.71 \times 10^{-19} \text{ cal/bond} - 1.35 \times 10^{-19} \text{ cal/bond}$$
$$= 3.6 \times 10^{-20} \text{ cal/bond}$$

The calculated value is based on equal electron sharing; the actual bond is polar. The energy that must be expended to separate the electrons of a covalent bond when they are closely associated with one of the bonded atoms is larger than that required when the bonding electrons are equally shared. One can think in terms of the need to overcome the attraction of the δ^+ and δ^- produced in the case of unequal sharing.

Thus, for a polar bond, the experimental bond energy is always larger than the calculated bond energy, and the magnitude of the difference, Δ, depends upon the degree of polarity of the bond. For highly polar bonds, which result when atoms of widely different electron attracting abilities are joined, Δ is large. Hence, calculated values of Δ have been empirically related to electronegativities of Table 3.4. The electronegativity difference between two bonded atoms is not directly proportional to the Δ for the bond; rather, Pauling has shown that the difference in electronegativities is directly related to the square roots of the Δ values.

Table 3.4 Electronegativities of the Elements[a]

1 H 2.1																	2 He —
3 Li 1.0	4 Be 1.5											5 B 2.0	6 C 2.5	7 N 3.0	8 O 3.5	9 F 4.0	10 Ne —
11 Na 0.9	12 Mg 1.2											13 Al 1.5	14 Si 1.8	15 P 2.1	16 S 2.5	17 Cl 3.0	18 Ar —
19 K 0.8	20 Ca 1.0	21 Sc 1.3	22 T 1.5	23 V 1.6	24 Cr 1.6	25 Mn 1.5	26 Fe 1.8	27 Co 1.8	28 Ni 1.8	29 Cu 1.9	30 Zn 1.6	31 Ga 1.6	32 Ge 1.8	33 As 2.0	34 Se 2.4	35 Br 2.8	36 Kr —
37 Rb 0.8	38 Sr 1.0	39 Y 1.2	40 Zr 1.4	41 Nb 1.6	42 Mo 1.8	43 Tc 1.9	44 Ru 2.2	45 Rh 2.2	46 Pd 2.2	47 Ag 1.9	48 Cd 1.7	49 In 1.7	50 Sn 1.8	51 Sb 1.9	52 Te 2.1	53 I 2.5	54 Xe —
55 Cs 0.7	56 Ba 0.9	57–71 La–Lu 1.1–1.2	72 Hf 1.3	73 Ta 1.5	74 W 1.7	75 Re 1.9	76 Os 2.2	77 Ir 2.2	78 Pt 2.2	79 Au 2.4	80 Hg 1.9	81 Tl 1.8	82 Pb 1.8	83 Bi 1.9	84 Po 2.0	85 At 2.2	86 Rn —
87 Fr 0.7	88 Ra 0.9	89– Ac– 1.1–1.7															

[a] Based on Linus Pauling, *The Nature of the Chemical Bond, Third Edition,* © 1960 by Cornell University Press. Used with the permission of Cornell University Press.

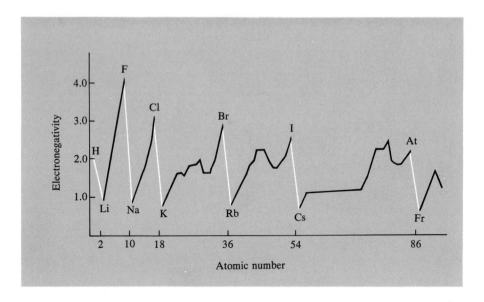

Figure 3.12 Electronegativity versus atomic number.

The electronegativity values obtained by any of the methods described are quite similar, indicating that the concept of electronegativity is a valid, if inexact, one. In general, electronegativity increases from left to right across any period (with increasing number of valence electrons) and from bottom to top in any group (with decreasing size). Thus the most highly electronegative elements are found in the upper right corner of the periodic table (ignoring the noble gases) and the least electronegative elements are found in the lower left corner of the chart. These trends parallel those noted for ionization potentials and electron affinities. The electronegativities of the elements are plotted against atomic number in Figure 3.12.

Metals are elements that have small attractions for valence electrons (low electronegativities); except for the noble gases, nonmetals have large attractions (high electronegativities). Thus electronegativities (as well as ionization potentials and electron affinities) can be used to rate metallic reactivities and nonmetallic reactivities, and the positions of the elements in the periodic table are helpful in making predictions concerning chemical reactivity (Figure 3.13).

Electronegativities can be used to predict the type of bonding to be found in a compound. When two elements of widely different electronegativity combine, an ionic compound is produced; thus, the electronegativity difference between sodium and chlorine is 2.1, and NaCl is an ionic compound.

Covalent bonding occurs between nonmetals where the electronegativity differences are not so large. In such cases, the electronegativity differences give

Figure 3.13 The relation between position in the periodic classification and metallic or nonmetallic reactivity.

an indication of the degree of polarity of the covalent bonds. If the electronegativity difference is zero or very small, an essentially nonpolar bond with equal, or almost equal, sharing of electrons can be assumed. The larger the electronegativity difference, the more polar is the covalent bond, the bond being polarized in the direction of the atom with the larger electronegativity. Thus, from electronegativities, we can predict that HF is the most polar, and has the largest bond energy, of any of the hydrogen halides (see Table 3.5).

Table 3.5

Some Properties of the Hydrogen Halides

Hydrogen Halide	Dipole Moment (D)	Bond Energy (cal/bond)	Electronegativity of Halogen	Electronegativity Difference Between Hydrogen and Halogen
HF	1.91	2.24×10^{-19}	F = 4.0	1.9
HCl	1.03	1.71×10^{-19}	Cl = 3.0	0.9
HBr	0.78	1.45×10^{-19}	Br = 2.8	0.7
HI	0.38	1.18×10^{-19}	I = 2.5	0.4

The type of bonding that occurs between two metals (the metallic bond), where electronegativity differences are also relatively small, will be considered in Section 4.6.

3.10 Properties of Ionic and Covalent Compounds

The properties of ionic compounds are best understood on the basis of the structure of the ionic crystal (Section 3.4, Figure 3.5). The electrostatic forces between the ions in such a crystal are moderately strong forces. Thus ionic crystals are hard. In the process of melting, thermal energy must be supplied to overcome these forces sufficiently for the crystal to liquefy, and therefore ionic substances have relatively high melting points. The boiling points of ionic materials are high since the vaporization of ionic liquids is opposed by the strong electrostatic attractions between ions.

The ions in a crystal are held in a definite geometric pattern. The structure is such that the electrostatic attractions between positive and negative ions more than compensate for the repulsions that exist between ions of like charge. Thus **ionic crystals** are brittle because the stability of the crystals depend upon the preservation of their geometric patterns (Figure 3.14). Ionic compounds are good conductors of electricity when molten or in solution (but not in the crystalline state where the ions are not free to move); also, ionic materials are very soluble in polar solvents (Chapter 9).

Molecules occupy the lattice points in a crystal of a covalent compound. Polar molecules are held in the crystal lattice by the orientation of their dipoles—the negative end of one molecule attracting the positive end of another (Figure 3.15). Such forces of attraction are not nearly so strong as those encountered in ionic crystals. Nonpolar molecules are held in a crystal

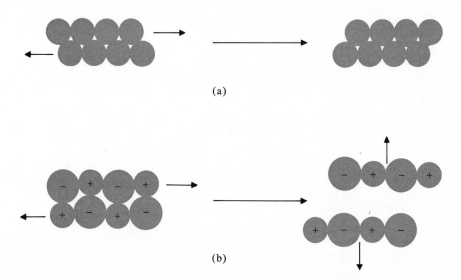

(a)

(b)

Figure 3.14 Effect of deformation on (a) a metallic crystal, and (b) an ionic crystal.

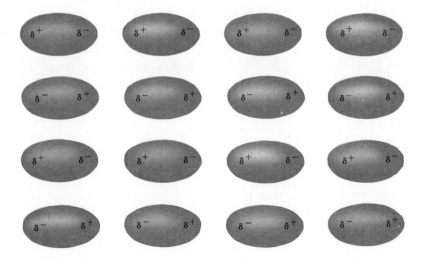

Figure 3.15 Orientation of polar molecules in a crystal.

lattice by van der Waals forces. These forces are extremely weak (and are common to all matter); they are thought to be caused by the motion of electrons and are sometimes called fluctuating dipoles. Hence, at a given instant one portion of an otherwise neutral molecule may have a very small negative charge associated with it because it has a slightly higher than average concentration of electrons. At the next instant, however, that same portion may be relatively positive because of a slight deficiency of electronic charge.

Because of the very weak nature of the forces holding **nonpolar molecular crystals** together, such crystals are soft and have low melting points. Liquids of nonpolar materials are quite volatile and have low boiling points; compounds of this type are usually gases under normal conditions. Nonpolar compounds do not conduct electricity in the liquid state or in solution because of the absence of charged particles to respond to the electric field. Nonpolar liquids are poor solvents for ionic compounds.

Polar covalent compounds have properties intermediate between those of ionic compounds, and nonpolar covalent compounds. Because of the dipole attractions, polar compounds have higher melting points and boiling points and are less volatile than nonpolar materials. **Polar molecular crystals** are harder than nonpolar molecular crystals. These properties are not so extreme as those of ionic substances. Polar covalent compounds are not conductors of electricity, however, because the negative and positive charges of the dipole are contained in the same particle, and this particle is consequently attracted toward both poles of an electric field equally. The best solvents for ionic materials are in this classification of substances.

It is relatively simple to predict the degree of polarity of a given diatomic molecule by means of electronegativities. For molecules containing more than two atoms, it is essential that the geometry of the molecule also be known before a prediction as to the overall polarity of the compound can be made. Thus, for a molecule of the type A_2B, two geometric arrangements are possible: angular (I) or linear (II).

$$A-B$$
$$\mid$$
$$A \qquad A-B-A$$

structure I structure II

Let us assume that atom A is more electronegative than atom B. Hence, in either structure, the A—B bonds are polar, but there are two such bonds to consider in each structure. In structure I, the center of gravity of positive charge coincides with the center of the B atom, while the center of gravity of negative charge lies at some point equidistant between the two A atoms. Since the molecule exhibits charge separation, it is polar. In structure II, however, the center of gravity of negative charge lies at the same point as that of the positive charge—the center of the B atom. Hence, the dipoles of the two bonds effectively neutralize one another, and the molecule is nonpolar. CO_2 is a nonpolar molecule corresponding to structure II; H_2O and SO_2 are polar molecules corresponding to an angular arrangement of atoms such as that of structure I.

More complicated molecules lend themselves to similar analysis. Thus BF_3 is a nonpolar molecule even though the individual B—F bonds are strongly polar. The reason for this is that BF_3 is a planar molecule:

All of the bond angles are equivalent, and all of the bond distances are equal; the dipoles of the three bonds cancel one another. The centers of positive and negative charge coincide in the center of the B atom. The compound NF_3, on the other hand, is polar. The difference in electronegativity between boron and fluorine is much larger than that between nitrogen and fluorine, but in NF_3 the dipoles of the bonds do not cancel one another because the molecule is arranged in a three-dimensional trigonal pyramid:

Even though the total polarity of the molecule is reduced by the effect of the unshared electron pair on the N atom (Section 4.3), the NF_3 molecule has a resultant dipole with the negative end in the direction of the base of the pyramid.

Network, or **atomic, crystals** are crystals in which the lattice points are occupied by atoms that are joined by a network of covalent bonds. It is impossible to distinguish molecules or ions; in fact, the entire crystal may be visualized as one giant molecule. An example of such a crystal is the diamond in which carbon atoms are joined by covalent bonds in a three-dimensional structure (Figure 3.16). Such materials have high melting points, high boiling points, low volatilities, and are extremely hard because of the large number of covalent bonds that would have to be ruptured to destroy the crystal structure. They are also nonconductors of electricity.

The **metallic crystal** is discussed in Section 4.6. However, as a first approximation, we can imagine such a crystal as being made up of a lattice of positive ions together with mobile electrons in such a proportion as to make the whole electrically neutral. Only the outermost electrons of the metal atoms are involved in the bonding, and these electrons move freely throughout the lattice of positive ions, binding it together. This attraction is strong, as evidenced by the close-packed arrangement of the positive ions and the high densities and high melting points of most metals (but not all metals—there are

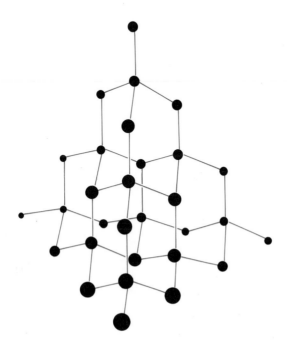

Figure 3.16 Arrangement of atoms in a diamond crystal.

other factors to be considered, such as atomic radius and number of vacant electron orbitals).

Like the ionic bond, the metallic bond is essentially nondirectional; the covalent bond is always a directional bond in molecules and in atomic crystals. Unlike ionic crystals, however, the positions of the positive ions can be altered without destroying the crystal because of the uniform charge distribution provided by the mobile electrons (Figure 3.14). Thus metallic crystals are usually deformed easily, and most metals are malleable (capable of being pounded into shapes) and ductile (capable of being drawn into wire). The properties of the types of crystalline solids are summarized in Table 3.6.

Table 3.6

Types of Crystalline Solids

Crystal	Particles	Attractive Forces	Properties	Examples
ionic	positive and negative ions	electrostatic attractions	high m.p. hard, brittle good electrical conductor in fused state	NaCl, BaO, KNO_3
polar. molecular	polar molecules	dipole–dipole	low m.p. soft poor electrical conductor	H_2O, BrCl, SO_2
nonpolar molecular	nonpolar molecules	van der Waals forces	very low m.p. soft, extremely poor electrical conductor	H_2, Cl_2, CO_2, CCl_4
network	atoms	covalent bonds	very high m.p. very hard nonconductor of electricity	C (diamond) SiC, AlN, SiO_2
metallic	positive ions mobile electrons	metallic bonds	fairly high m.p. hard or soft malleable and ductile good electrical conductor	Ag, Cu, Na, Fe, K

3.11 Nomenclature of Binary Compounds

Common, or **trivial**, **names** of compounds are those that have been assigned by popular usage; they usually give no clue as to the exact chemical composition of the compound. If all chemical compounds were named in such a way, it would be an almost impossible task to learn the names of the materials with which the chemist works. Instead, **systematic** nomenclature is used; systematic names follow rules designed to relate the name of a compound to its composition. Certain common names such as water, H_2O, and ammonia, NH_3, are so firmly entrenched that they continue to be employed.

Ionic binary compounds are named with the metal first and the nonmetal second; covalent binaries are usually named with the less electronegative element first. For all binary compounds, the ending *-ide* is substituted for the usual ending of the element appearing last in the name. All compounds ending in *-ide*, however, are not binaries; there are a few exceptions, such as the cyanides (e.g., NaCN) and the hydroxides (e.g., NaOH). Thus the name of Na_2O is sodium oxide, $CaCl_2$ is calcium chloride, AgBr is silver bromide, ZnS is zinc sulfide, and HF is hydrogen fluoride.

However, some metals (particularly the transition metals) have more than one valence. Thus there are two chlorides of iron: $FeCl_2$ and $FeCl_3$. One way of dealing with this problem is to change the suffix of the name of the metal (Latin names are employed when the symbol derives from the Latin); the ending *-ous* is used to indicate the lower valence of the metal, and *-ic* is used for the higher valence state. Thus $FeCl_2$ is ferrous chloride, and $FeCl_3$ is ferric chloride. Difficulties arise in the use of this method since some element pairs form more than two compounds. Furthermore, the system requires that all the possible valences of a metal be known in order to assign the proper suffix. The $2+$ state of iron is its lower (ferrous); the $2+$ state of copper is its higher (cupric).

In a system of nomenclature proposed by Albert Stock, the valence of the metal, in Roman numerals, is indicated after the English name of the metal; suffixes for the metals are not employed. Thus: $FeCl_2$ is iron(II) chloride; $FeCl_3$ is iron(III) chloride; Cu_2O is copper(I) oxide; and HgS is mercury(II) sulfide. The number applies to the valence of the metal (or more properly the oxidation number—see Chapter 8) and not to any numbers appearing as subscripts in the formulas.

A system of nomenclature that is particularly useful for series of compounds formed between two nonmetals employs Greek prefixes. One of the prefixes: *mono-* (1), *di-* (2), *tri-* (3), *tetra-* (4), *penta-* (5), *hexa-* (6), *hepta-* (7), *octa-* (8), etc., is added to the name of each element to indicate the number of atoms of that element in the molecule being named. The prefix *mono-* is frequently omitted. Hence, the names of the oxides of nitrogen are:

N_2O	dinitrogen oxide
NO	nitrogen oxide
N_2O_3	dinitrogen trioxide
NO_2	nitrogen dioxide
N_2O_4	dinitrogen tetroxide
N_2O_5	dinitogen pentoxide

Stock nomenclature can also be used to name the binary compounds of the nonmetals. The method used to derive the oxidation numbers of the nonmetals is described in Section 8.5.

3.12   Ternary Compounds

Many compounds are known in which both electrovalent and covalent bonding occur. Usually these are ternary compounds (containing three elements) with oxygen as one of the constituent elements. Sodium sulfate, Na_2SO_4, is such a compound.

A crystal of sodium sulfate consists of sodium ions, Na^+, and sulfate ions, SO_4^{2-}, arranged in a crystal lattice in the proper stoichiometric ratio of 2 to 1. When sodium sulfate is dissolved in water, these ions separate from the crystal and move about independently of one another in solution. The sulfate ion is held together, as an entity, by covalent bonding; it does not break apart in water solution.

Such polyatomic, covalently bonded anions are common, and some are listed in Table 3.7. On the other hand, only a few polyatomic cations are of

Table 3.7

Common Polyatomic Anions

Formula	Name	Formula	Name
$C_2H_3O_2^-$	acetate	ClO^-	hypochlorite
AsO_4^{3-}	arsenate	OH^-	hydroxide
AsO_3^{3-}	arsenite	NO_3^-	nitrate
BO_3^{3-}	borate	NO_2^-	nitrite
CO_3^{2-}	carbonate	ClO_4^-	perchlorate
ClO_3^-	chlorate	MnO_4^-	permanganate
ClO_2^-	chlorite	PO_4^{3-}	phosphate
CrO_4^{2-}	chromate	SO_4^{2-}	sulfate
CN^-	cyanide	SO_3^{2-}	sulfite
$Cr_2O_7^{2-}$	dichromate		

importance, for example, the ammonium ion, NH_4^+ and the bismuthyl ion, BiO^+. (This excludes complex ions, which are discussed in Chapter 19.)

In aqueous solution, each ion is closely associated with a few water molecules; in fact, the formation of these hydrated ions is primarily responsible for the process of solution of ionic compounds in water. These aqueous, or hydrated, ions are usually indicated by the symbol (aq), placed after the formula; the number of water molecules closely associated with a given ion is not indicated thereby and in many cases is not known. In addition to a primary sheath of water molecules, other water molecules are loosely associated. The solution process is described in Section 9.2, and the nature of hydrated ions is the topic of Section 9.3.

Certain compounds of hydrogen, which are covalent when pure, dissolve in water to produce solutions containing ions. In these cases, a reaction occurs which may be indicated:

$$HNO_3 + H_2O \longrightarrow H_3O^+ + NO_3^-$$

or

$$HNO_3 \longrightarrow H^+(aq) + NO_3^-(aq)$$

Compounds that dissociate in water solution to produce H_3O^+, or H^+ (aq), ions are called **acids**.

Because of its large charge to radius ratio, the unassociated proton (H^+) does not exist in ordinary chemical systems; in pure acids, the hydrogen atom is covalently bonded to the rest of the molecule, and in aqueous solutions the proton is hydrated. There is evidence that the proton bonds to a water molecule by means of a pair of electrons of the oxygen atom to form an ion, H_3O^+, called the **hydronium ion**. The three hydrogen atoms of the H_3O^+ ion are equivalent, and the ion is in the form of a trigonal pyramid with the oxygen atom at the apex. The hydronium ion is known to occur in a few crystalline hydrates of acids such as H_3O^+, ClO_4^-; H_3O^+, Cl^-; and H_3O^+, NO_3^-.

Thermal and electrical conductivity experiments indicate that the H_3O^+ ion is associated with three additional water molecules (by means of hydrogen bonds, Section 8.11) in water solution, and a pyramidal $H_9O_4^+$ ion has been postulated (Figure 3.17). Other types of experimental evidence tend to

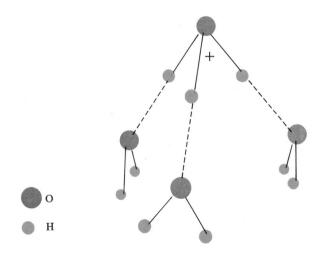

O

H

Figure 3.17 Proposed structure of $H_9O_4^+$ ion.

support the idea that several types of hydrated species exist simultaneously in solution. We shall represent the hydrated proton as H^+(aq) unless it is especially convenient to employ the formula H_3O^+, as it is in the discussion of the Brønsted theory (Section 15.3).

Alkalies are compounds containing a metal cation and the hydroxide ion, OH^-. An alkali and an acid react in water by a **neutralization** reaction.

$$H^+(aq) + OH^-(aq) \longrightarrow H_2O$$

A salt composed of the cation of the alkali and the anion of the acid may be obtained by evaporating a solution derived from a neutralization reaction.

The usual ternary acids derived from oxygenated anions are named according to the name of the central element (the element other than oxygen) to which the ending -ic is added. Thus H_3BO_3 is boric acid. Often there are two ternary acids containing the same elements. In such instances, the endings -ic and -ous are used to distinguish between them, the -ous ending denoting the one with the lower number of oxygen atoms. Thus HNO_3 is nitric acid, and HNO_2 is nitrous acid.

There are a few series of acids for which two names are not enough. The prefix per- can be used to denote one additional oxygen; the prefix hypo- can be used to denote one less oxygen. Thus perchloric acid, $HClO_4$, has one more oxygen than chloric acid, $HClO_3$; hypochlorous acid, HOCl, has one less oxygen than chlorous acid, $HClO_2$. A system of nomenclature for more complicated polyatomic ions is discussed in Section 19.3.

The names of the polyatomic anions (Table 3.7) themselves are derived from the acid names by changing the -ic ending to -ate and the -ous ending to -ite. Hence, NO_3^-, the nitrate ion, is derived from HNO_3, nitric acid; ClO^-, the hypochlorite ion, is derived from HOCl, hypochlorous acid. Salts are named by combining the cation name with the anion name; $NaNO_2$ is sodium nitrite.

Some binary compounds function as acids in water solution. The combination of the prefix hydro- and the suffix -ic is used to indicate a water solution of a binary acid. For example, a water solution of hydrogen chloride, HCl, is called hydrochloric acid. The names of salts of binary acids have the customary -ide ending.

SOME SUGGESTED READINGS

Barrow, G. M., *The Structures of Molecules*, New York, Benjamin, 1963 (paper).
Companion, A., *Chemical Bonding*, New York, McGraw-Hill, 1964 (paper).
Day, M. C., Jr., and Selbin, J., *Theoretical Inorganic Chemistry*, 2nd ed., New York, Van Nostrand Reinhold, 1969.

Drago, R. S., *Physical Methods in Inorganic Chemistry*, New York, Van Nostrand Reinhold, 1965.

Gray, H. B., *Electrons and Chemical Bonding*, New York, Benjamin, 1964 (paper).

Harvey, K., and Porter, G., *Introduction to Physical Inorganic Chemistry*, Reading, Mass., Addison-Wesley, 1963.

Lagowski, J. J., *The Chemical Bond*, Boston, Houghton Mifflin, 1966 (paper).

Luder, W. F., *The Electron-Repulsion Theory of the Chemical Bond*, New York, Van Nostrand Reinhold, 1967 (paper).

Lynch, P. F., *Orbitals and Chemical Bonding*, Boston, Houghton Mifflin, 1966 (paper).

Pauling, L., *The Nature of the Chemical Bond*, 3rd ed., Ithaca, N. Y., Cornell University Press, 1960.

Ryschkewitsch, G. E., *Chemical Bonding and the Geometry of Molecules*, New York, Van Nostrand Reinhold, 1963 (paper).

Sebera, D. K., *Electronic Structure and Chemical Bonding*, Waltham, Mass., Blaisdell, 1964 (paper).

Sisler, H. H., *Electronic Structure, Properties, and the Periodic Law*, New York, Van Nostrand Reinhold, 1963 (paper).

PROBLEMS

The more difficult problems are starred.

3.1 Which member of each of the following pairs would you predict to be larger? (a) As or Br, (b) Sn or As, (c) Ru or Cd, (d) La or Hf, (e) Na or Be, (f) Mg or Mg^{2+}, (g) S or S^{2-}, (h) Tl^+ or Tl^{3+}.

3.2 Explain why a minimum is observed in each curve obtained by plotting atomic radius against atomic number for the members of each transition series.

3.3 Which member of each of the following pairs would you predict to have the higher first ionization potential? (a) Ne or Xe, (b) S or Cl, (c) Mg or Sr, (d) Na or Mg, (e) F or I, (f) Br or Kr, (g) P or O.

3.4 Discuss the atomic parameters that influence ionization potential.

3.5 Of the elements of the fourth period (K through Kr): (a) which has the largest atomic radius? (b) which has the highest first ionization potential? (c) which has the highest first electron affinity? (d) which is the most reactive metal? (e) which is the most reactive nonmetal? (f) which is the most unreactive chemically?

3.6 Why is it incorrect to say that the chemistry of an element depends entirely upon the number and arrangement of the extranuclear electrons in the atoms of that element?

3.7 Explain the meaning of the values recorded in Table 3.1 for oxygen. Why are the signs different? What is the value of the second electron affinity of oxygen?

3.8 Define the following terms: (a) lanthanide contraction, (b) network crystal,

(c) isoelectronic ions, (d) lattice energy, (e) screening effect, (f) electrovalence number, (g) dipole moment, (h) anion–anion contact, (i) hydronium ion.

3.9 Identify the noble-gas ions, the pseudo-noble-gas ions, and the inert-pair ions that are included in the following list: Al^{3+}, Ga^{3+}, Pb^{2+}, K^+, Ba^{2+}, Cu^+, Sc^{3+}, Cd^{2+}, Tl^+, Bi^{3+}.

3.10 Draw Lewis structures for the following: (a) H_2NNH_2, (b) O_2NONO_2, (c) PH_3, (d) O_2NCl, (e) O_2SF_2, (f) H_3COH.

3.11 Draw Lewis structures for the following: (a) PO_4^{3-}, (b) ClO_4^-, (c) NO_3^-, (d) ClO_3^-, (e) OCN^-, (f) HCO_2^-, (g) O_2^{2-}.

3.12 Draw Lewis structures for the following: (a) $HONO_2$, (b) S_2Cl_2, (c) CO, (d) S_8 (a ring structure), (e) $PbCl_4$, (f) $H_2NC(O)NH_2$.

3.13 On the basis of anion deformation, predict which compound of each of the following pairs is the more covalent. (a) $SbCl_3$ or $BiCl_3$, (b) BeO or BeS, (c) Tl_2O or Tl_2O_3, (d) SnS or PbS, (e) HgF_2 or HgI_2, (f) $CrCl_2$ or $CrCl_3$.

3.14 Discuss the relationship between bond energy and bond polarity.

3.15 The bond distance between the H and I atoms of hydrogen iodide is 1.62 Å, and the dipole moment of HI is 0.38 D. Calculate the partial ionic character of HI.

3.16 Which bond is more polar: a S—H or a Se—H bond? a S—F bond or a Se—F bond? Use the data of Table 3.4 and indicate the direction of polarization of each bond by using δ^+ and δ^- signs.

3.17 On the basis of electronegativity (Table 3.4) state whether you think the bonds formed between the following pairs of elements would be ionic or covalent, and if covalent, estimate the degree of polarity of the bond. (a) C, I, (b) Hg, I, (c) Al, Cl, (d) S, Cl, (e) K, Cl, (f) C, S, (g) Cs, S, (h) N, Cl, (i) Ca, O, (j) Be, Br.

*3.18 Given the following bond energies:

F—F, 37 kcal/mole	O—F, 44 kcal/mole
O—O, 33 kcal/mole	C—O, 84 kcal/mole
C—C, 83 kcal/mole	C—H, 99 kcal/mole
H—H 104 kcal/mole	

A mole consists of 6.02×10^{23} of the items being considered. (a) Use the bond energies of the F—F and the O—O bonds to calculate an average bond energy for the O—F bond (in kcal/mole). In the same way, calculate average bond energies for the C—O and C—H bonds. (b) Calculate the difference, Δ, between each value obtained in the preceding part and the actual bond energy or the corresponding bond. (c) The difference in electronegativity between two bonded atoms is approximately $0.18\sqrt{\Delta}$. Calculate the difference in electronegativity between O and F, C and O, and C and H. (d) Use the values obtained in the preceding part to determine the electronegativities of O, C, and H based upon the assignment of 4.0 to F. Compare your results with the values given in Table 3.4.

3.19 Carbon and silicon are both members of group IV A, but Si, unlike C, does not form multiple bonds with atoms of nonmetallic elements. Carbon dioxide sublimes at $-78.5°C$, and silicon dioxide melts at $1713°C$. Describe and compare the structures and expected properties of CO_2 and SiO_2.

3.20 Use the data of Table 3.4 and the melting points listed beside the following formulas to determine what type of crystal each substance forms. (a) $BaCl_2$, $962°C$, (b) $PbCl_4$, $-15°C$, (c) Pd, $1552°C$, (d) Si, $1410°C$, (e) ICl, $97°C$.

3.21 Briefly describe how the determination of the dipole moment of a molecule that conforms to the general formula A_2B can help to determine the arrangement of atoms in the molecule.

3.22 Discuss the origin and effect of van der Waals forces. Why are these forces common to all substances? Why are the van der Waals forces between I_2 molecules stronger than those between Cl_2 molecules?

3.23 Define, and discuss the difference in meaning between the terms *electron affinity* and *electronegativity*.

3.24 Give formulas for the oxides, chlorides, phosphates, sulfates, and dichromates of: sodium, magnesium, and aluminum.

3.25 Give formulas for: (a) iron(II) oxide, (b) potassium oxide, (c) magnesium nitride, (d) magnesium nitrite, (e) pentasulfur dinitride, (f) thallium(I) sulfide, (g) calcium permanganate, (h) ferric sulfite, (i) lead(II) chromate, (j) silver(I) dichromate.

3.26 Name the following: (a) $CuCrO_4$, (b) $Fe(ClO_4)_3$, (c) BaO, (d) Au_2O_3, (e) P_4S_3, (f) Cl_2O_7, (g) ZnS, (h) HOCl, (i) $Ca_3(AsO_3)_2$, (j) $CrCl_2$.

*3.27 Use the Bohr equation: $v = 3.29 \times 10^{15}$ cycles/sec $\left(\dfrac{1}{n_i^2} - \dfrac{1}{n_0^2}\right)$ to evaluate

the ionization potential of hydrogen (in electron volts). One electron volt is equal to 1.60×10^{-12} erg.

It is impossible to derive Lewis structures for some molecules. Furthermore, in many instances, the observed properties of a molecule (such as bond distance and molecular polarity) are not satisfactorily represented by the Lewis structure assigned to the molecule. Since a characteristic of the covalent bond is that it is directed in space, the lack of correlation between a Lewis structure and the geometry of the molecule that it represents is a serious shortcoming. The newer theories of the covalent bond supply answers to these problems and are more informative; they represent, therefore, better descriptions of covalent bonding.

MOLECULAR GEOMETRY AND THE COVALENT BOND

4.1 Resonance

The Lewis structure for SO_2 (Section 3.7) does not represent the true character of the molecule.

$$\overset{\ominus}{:}\overset{..}{O}: \overset{\overset{..}{S}^{\oplus}}{=} \overset{..}{O}:$$

The structure depicts the S atom to be bonded

to one O atom by a double bond and to the other O atom by a single bond. Double bonds are characteristically shorter than single bonds, yet experimental evidence shows both S to O linkages to be the same length. The structure also shows one of the O atoms to be more negative than the other, but it is known that both of the O atoms are equivalent in this respect.

In a case of this type, two or more valence-bond structures can be used, in combination, to depict the molecule. The molecule is said to be a **resonance hybrid** of the electronic structures, which are called **resonance forms**. For SO_2,

$$\ominus :\ddot{O} - \overset{\overset{\displaystyle ..}{\oplus}}{S} = \ddot{O}: \quad \longleftrightarrow \quad :\ddot{O} = \overset{\overset{\displaystyle ..}{\oplus}}{S} - \ddot{O}: \ominus$$

There is only one type of SO_2 molecule; the above notation does not mean that this substance is a mixture of two types of molecules. Nor does the symbolism denote a situation where electrons oscillate in such a way as to make the molecule appear in one form at one moment and in the other at the next. The symbol ($\leftrightarrow$) does not denote motion. Neither resonance form alone adequately represents the molecule, but the one *single* structure of the SO_2 molecule can be imagined by superimposing both resonance forms.

Thus resonance shows the O atoms of the molecule to be equally negative and the S to O linkages of SO_2 to be identical—intermediate between a single and a double bond. The problem is one of representation within the framework of the classical valence-bond approach, and the problem arises because the approach is limited—not because of any freakishness on the part of resonating molecules.

All resonance forms of a given species must have the *same configuration of nuclei* and be *energetically similar*. The resonance forms of the linear molecule nitrous oxide, N_2O, are

$$\overset{\ominus}{:}\overset{..}{N} = \overset{\oplus}{N} = \overset{..}{O}: \quad \longleftrightarrow \quad :N \equiv \overset{\oplus}{N} - \overset{..}{\underset{..}{O}}: \overset{\ominus}{}$$

These forms correlate well with the observed bond distances and dipole moment of the molecule. Measurement shows the N to N bond distance (1.13 Å) to be intermediate between that of a double bond (1.19 Å) and a triple bond (1.06 Å). In addition, the N to O bond distance (1.19 Å) falls between that of an N to O single bond (1.36 Å) and that of an N to O double bond (1.15 Å). The dipole moment of the compound is observed to be close to zero; in the resonance hybrid, the polarities of the individual forms cancel, since the positive and negative centers of charge coincide.

Another possible resonance form of N_2O is rejected.

$$\overset{2-}{} :\overset{..}{\underset{..}{N}} - \overset{\oplus}{N} \equiv O: \overset{\oplus}{}$$

A form in which a comparatively high negative charge is placed on the end N atom and at the same time a positive charge is forced on the more highly electronegative O atom is a form of comparatively high energy. In addition, the O atom and the adjacent N atom are shown with formal charges of the same sign, a condition that would tend to disrupt the bond between these two atoms. Therefore this form does not contribute appreciably to the resonance hybrid. Resonance tends to delocalize charge, not build up centers of high charge.

The delocalization of charge in an ion is illustrated by the resonance of the carbonate ion, CO_3^{2-}. The ion is planar, all bonds are equivalent (between single and double bonds), and all oxygen atoms are equally negative. The formal charges add up to the charge on the ion.

As depicted by resonance, the charge is delocalized; it is impossible to locate the exact position of the "extra" two electrons that give the ion its negative charge.

It is also possible, although usually not necessary, to use the concept of resonance to indicate the charge distribution of a polar molecule. The structure of hydrogen chloride can be illustrated in the following way:

Calculations from dipole moment measurements show HCl to have a 17% partial ionic character (Section 3.8). We conclude that structures I and II contribute to the resonance hybrid in a ratio of 83 to 17.

Resonance hybrids are always more stable than a single valence-bond representation of a molecule would indicate. Thus the energy required to break the H—Cl bond is more than that calculated for a structure in which the bonding electrons are equally shared (Section 3.9). This difference is called the **resonance energy**.

4.2 Hybrid Orbitals

Resonance can, properly applied, serve to adjust the valence-bond theory into closer accord with reality, but certain other extensions need to be applied to the valence-bond view. We have seen that certain ions exist that do not have noble-gas configurations and that some of these ions are relatively stable. Some molecules exist in which atoms have configurations other than those the octet principle would lead us to expect.

There are a few molecules that have an odd number of valence electrons to be distributed among the constituent atoms (Section 4.4). It is manifestly impossible to divide an odd number of electrons in such a way as to give each atom of the molecule a configuration of eight electrons (an even number). There is a resonance treatment for this type of molecule in which the embarrassing odd electron is delocalized, but the molecular orbital description of these species is more satisfactory (Section 4.4). There are not many stable odd electron molecules; usually odd electron species are very reactive and, consequently, short-lived.

More common are the molecules that have an even number of valence electrons but contain atoms with valence shells of less than, or more than, eight electrons. Examples of this are BF_3, where the central boron atom has six valence electrons

$$:\ddot{F}:$$
$$|$$
$$B$$
$$:\ddot{F}\cdot \quad \cdot\ddot{F}:$$

and PCl_5 and SF_6 where the phosphorus and sulfur atoms have ten and twelve valence electrons, respectively.

For the elements of the second period, only four bonding orbitals are available ($2s$ and $2p$), and thus the maximum covalence of these elements is limited to four. But the elements of the third and subsequent periods have many more orbitals available in their outer electron shells; compounds are known in which these elements form four, five, six, or (infrequently) an even higher number of covalent bonds. In valence-bond structures representing compounds containing elements of the third and subsequent periods, therefore, the octet principle is frequently violated. It appears that the criteria for covalent bond formation should be centered on the electron pair rather than the attainment of an octet.

When a covalent bond forms, the atomic orbitals used in the bonding interpenetrate, or overlap (Figure 4.1). The electron clouds reinforce each other in the bonding region between the two nuclei, and electronic charge is concentrated in this region. The strength of the bond comes partly from the

Figure 4.1 Overlap of the 1s orbitals of two hydrogen atoms.

spin neutralization of the electron pair but more from the attraction of the positively charged nuclei for the electron cloud of the bond.

Therefore, the strongest bonding occurs when the orbital overlap is at a maximum within the limits imposed by the internuclear forces of repulsion. Hence, the atoms must not only approach each other as closely as possible but also the orbitals in certain cases must be aligned properly. All $1s$ orbitals are spherically symmetrical so that in the formation of H_2, the alignment of the $1s$ orbitals of the atoms is not crucial. The p orbitals of an atom, however, can be considered to be directed in space along the Cartesian coordinates x, y, and z (Figure 2.19). The electronic configuration of fluorine is $1s^2\ 2s^2\ 2p^2\ 2p^2\ 2p^1$; and in the formation of a covalent bond between two fluorine atoms, the axes of the p orbitals used in the bonding must be aligned. The atoms are directed along this axis in the resulting F_2 molecule.

In the vapor state, beryllium chloride consists of linear $Cl-Be-Cl$ molecules. Both covalent bonds of the molecule are equivalent in terms of strength and bond length. A p orbital of each Cl atom is used in forming a bond with the central Be atom, but what type of Be orbitals are employed? The electronic configuration of Be is $1s^2\ 2s^2$, and it appears that in the ground state beryllium should not form covalent bonds at all. The excited state $1s^2\ 2s^1\ 2p^1$ provides two unpaired electrons for bonding, but it too is inadequate in explaining the bonding of the molecule.

If the $2p$ orbital of the excited state of Be is used to form a covalent bond with a $3p$ orbital of a Cl atom, these two atoms would be aligned along the bonding axis of the p orbitals. For the $2s$ orbital of the Be atom, all directions are equivalent, and therefore the $Be-Cl$ bond formed by utilizing this orbital would be essentially undirected. Even if this second bond were assumed to take a position 180° away from the other bond, thus producing a linear arrangement, the two bonds would not be similar. The bond lengths would be dissimilar, since the bonds would have been produced by a p orbital of a Cl atom overlapping a $2s$ Be orbital in one instance and a $2p$ Be orbital in the other. In addition, the two bonds would not be energetically equivalent, since the $2s$ and $2p$ orbitals of Be are not energetically equivalent.

It is assumed that the $2s$ and $2p$ orbitals of the Be atom are blended, or **hybridized**, into two new **hybrid orbitals**. These hybrid orbitals, called *sp* **orbitals**, have one-half s character and one-half p character, are equivalent, and are directed at 180° from one another (Figure 4.2). Use of the *sp* hybrid orbitals of Be results in the formation of two perfectly equivalent covalent bonds (Figure 4.3). The *sp* orbitals extend farther along the x axis than either the s or the p orbital (Figure 4.2), and greater orbital overlap results when an *sp* hybrid orbital is used instead of a pure s or a pure p orbital. Calculations show that stronger bonds result from the use of hybrid orbitals.

The formation of $BeCl_2$ may be summarized as follows:

$2p$ _ _ _ $2p$ ⥮ _ _ $2p$ _ _

                                                    sp ⥮ ⥮

$2s$ ⥮⥯ $2s$ ⥮

$1s$ ⥮⥯ $1s$ ⥮⥯ $1s$ ⥮⥯

Be (ground state)   Be (excited state)   Be (hybrid state)

The energy required to produce the excited state as well as that required for the hybridization is more than supplied by the energy released when two comparatively strong covalent bonds are formed.

Why doesn't Be form a molecule $BeCl_4$ in which all four of the Be electrons occupy orbitals singly and in which these four orbitals are hybridized? Hybridization of orbitals that have greatly different energies is not possible. The $2s$ and $2p$ orbitals are comparatively close together in terms of energy, whereas there is a large energy difference between these two and the $1s$ orbital. The orbitals most commonly used in the bonding of molecules are the s, p, and d orbitals of the outer shell and, in some cases, the d orbitals of the next to the outer shell. With the exception of these inner d orbitals, electrons of inner orbitals are usually bound too tightly to be involved in covalent bond formation.

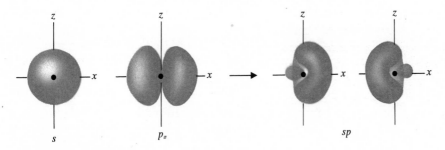

Figure 4.2 Hybridization of s and p orbitals to produce sp hybrid orbitals. Nuclei at origins; s and p orbitals should be superimposed, and sp orbitals should be superimposed.

Figure 4.3 Formation of $BeCl_2$. Shapes of orbitals simplified for clarity.

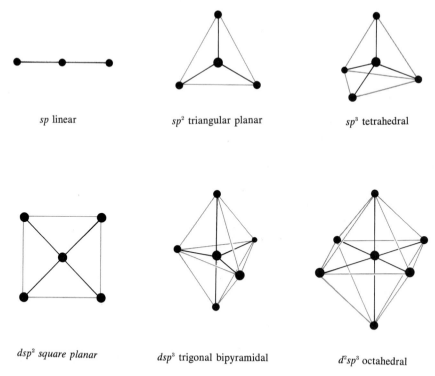

sp linear   *sp²* triangular planar   *sp³* tetrahedral

dsp² square planar   *dsp³* trigonal bipyramidal   *d²sp³* octahedral

Figure 4.4 Directional characteristics of hybrid orbitals.

Other types of hybrid orbitals are known (Figure 4.4). In the description of molecules of the type AB_n, where n is two or more, attention is directed to the bonding orbitals of the central atom, A, since it is these orbitals that determine the overall geometry of the molecule.

The atoms of boron trifluoride lie in the same plane, the angle formed by any two bonds is 120°, and the three bonds are equivalent.

$$\begin{array}{c} F \\ | \\ B \\ F \quad F \end{array}$$

It is assumed that *sp²* **hybrid orbitals** of B are used in the formation of the molecule and that each orbital has $\frac{1}{3}s$ character and $\frac{2}{3}p$ character (Figure 4.5).

2p 1 _ _	2p 1 1 _	2p _
		sp² 1 1 1
2s ⥮	2s 1	
1s ⥮	1s ⥮	1s ⥮
B (ground state)	B (excited state)	B (hybrid state)

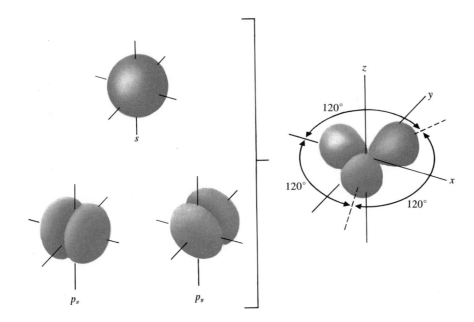

Figure 4.5 Formation of hybrid sp^2 orbitals. The hybrid orbitals are coplanar. Shapes of the hybrid orbitals have been simplified for clarity.

All molecules in which the central atom uses sp^2 hybrid orbitals for bonding are triangular (trigonal) planar, and all sp^2 hybrid orbitals have the orientation shown in Figure 4.5.

An important, and relatively common, type of hybridization is found in methane, CH_4. In this molecule, an s and three p orbitals are mixed to produce four equivalent sp^3 **hybrid orbitals**, each one with $\frac{1}{4} s$ character and $\frac{3}{4} p$ character.

$$2p\ \underline{\uparrow}\ \underline{\uparrow}\ \underline{\ \ } \qquad 2p\ \underline{\uparrow}\ \underline{\uparrow}\ \underline{\uparrow}$$

$$sp^3\ \underline{\uparrow}\ \underline{\uparrow}\ \underline{\uparrow}\ \underline{\uparrow}$$

$$2s\ \underline{\uparrow\downarrow} \qquad 2s\ \underline{\uparrow}$$

$$1s\ \underline{\uparrow\downarrow} \qquad 1s\ \underline{\uparrow\downarrow} \qquad 1s\ \underline{\uparrow\downarrow}$$

C (ground state)   C (excited state)   C (hybrid state)

The sp^3 hybrid orbitals are directed to the corners of a regular tetrahedron (Figure 4.6), and the CH_4 molecule has this geometry. In CH_4, all the H—C—H bond angles are 109° 28′, the so-called tetrahedral angle, and chemical and physical evidence show that all of the C—H bonds are equivalent.

It might seem logical that carbon would form a CH_2 molecule with hydrogen in which two pure p orbitals of the ground state of C would be used to

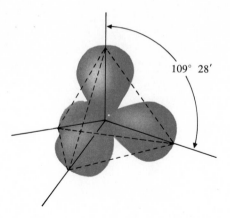

109° 28′

Figure 4.6 Orientation of the sp^3 hybrid orbitals.

bond two H atoms and in which the H—C—H bond angle would be 90° in conformity with the orientation of the p orbitals of C used in the bonding. The formation of such a CH_2 molecule would not require that energy be used to promote electrons and hybridize orbitals.

The bonds formed by using the hybrid orbitals of C are stronger than any formed by using simple atomic orbitals—a greater overlap of bonding orbitals is possible. Furthermore, *four* of the comparatively stronger bonds are formed in the preparation of CH_4 and only *two* of the weaker bonds are formed when CH_2 is prepared. Therefore, on balance, it is energetically more favorable to supply the energy required for the promotion and hybridization in order to get the larger energy return when CH_4 forms.

The nitrogen atom of NH_3 is assumed to use sp^3 hybrid orbitals for bonding with one of the orbitals occupied by an unshared pair of electrons. The atoms of NH_3 form a trigonal pyramid, but the four N orbitals are arranged approximately in the form of a tetrahedron (see Figure 4.8 given subsequently).

$2p$ ↑ ↑ ↑

sp^3 ↑↓ ↑ ↑ ↑

$2s$ ↑↓

$1s$ ↑↓

$1s$ ↑↓

N (ground state) N (hybrid state)

The H—N—H bond angle of NH_3 (107.3°) is close to the tetrahedral angle (109.5°). The N atom could conceivably use its three $2p$ orbitals for bonding. In this instance, however, the bond angle would be 90°, since p orbitals are directed along Cartesian coordinates. The observed bond angle is closer to the tetrahedral angle than it is to 90°. The use of sp^3 hybrid orbitals results in stronger bonding than would be obtained if pure p orbitals were employed.

In like manner, the oxygen atom of the H_2O molecule is assumed to use sp^3 hybrid orbitals in the bonding of the molecule with two of the hybrid orbitals occupied by unshared electron pairs.

$$2p\ \underline{\uparrow\downarrow}\ \ \underline{\uparrow}\ \ \underline{\uparrow}$$

$$sp^3\ \underline{\uparrow\downarrow}\ \ \underline{\uparrow\downarrow}\ \ \underline{\uparrow}\ \ \underline{\uparrow}$$

$$2s\ \underline{\uparrow\downarrow}$$

$$1s\ \underline{\uparrow\downarrow} \qquad\qquad 1s\ \underline{\uparrow\downarrow}$$

$$\text{O (ground state)} \qquad \text{O (hybrid state)}$$

The atoms of the H_2O molecule are arranged in angular form with a bond angle of 104.5°, which is closer to the tetrahedral angle of 109.5° than it is to the 90° angle expected if pure p orbitals were used.

There are several types of hybridization that involve d orbitals. The most important of these are the d^2sp^3, or octahedral, the dsp^3, or trigonal pyramidal, and the dsp^2, or square planar, types (Figure 4.4). The sulfur atom of sulfur hexafluoride, SF_6, employs d^2sp^3 **hybrid orbitals** in the bonding of the molecule (Figure 4.7).

$$3d\ \underline{\ }\ \underline{\ }\ \underline{\ }\ \underline{\ }\ \underline{\ } \qquad 3d\ \underline{\uparrow}\ \underline{\uparrow}\ \underline{\ }\ \underline{\ }\ \underline{\ } \qquad 3d\ \underline{\ }\ \underline{\ }\ \underline{\ }$$

$$d^2sp^3\ \underline{\uparrow}\ \underline{\uparrow}\ \underline{\uparrow}\ \underline{\uparrow}\ \underline{\uparrow}\ \underline{\uparrow}$$

$$3p\ \underline{\uparrow\downarrow}\ \underline{\uparrow}\ \underline{\uparrow} \qquad 3p\ \underline{\uparrow}\ \underline{\uparrow}\ \underline{\uparrow}$$

$$3s\ \underline{\uparrow\downarrow} \qquad\qquad 3s\ \underline{\uparrow}$$

$$\text{S (ground state)} \qquad \text{S (excited state)} \qquad \text{S (hybrid state)}$$

The d^2sp^3 hybrid orbitals are directed to the corners of a regular octahedron (Figure 4.4).

Phosphorus pentafluoride, PF_5, is a trigonal bipyramidal molecule (Figure 4.4), and dsp^3 **hybrid orbitals** are used in the formation of it.

$$3d\ \underline{\ }\ \underline{\ }\ \underline{\ }\ \underline{\ }\ \underline{\ } \qquad 3d\ \underline{\uparrow}\ \underline{\ }\ \underline{\ }\ \underline{\ }\ \underline{\ } \qquad 3d\ \underline{\ }\ \underline{\ }\ \underline{\ }\ \underline{\ }$$

$$3p\ \underline{\uparrow}\ \underline{\uparrow}\ \underline{\uparrow} \qquad 3p\ \underline{\uparrow}\ \underline{\uparrow}\ \underline{\uparrow} \qquad dsp^3\ \underline{\uparrow}\ \underline{\uparrow}\ \underline{\uparrow}\ \underline{\uparrow}\ \underline{\uparrow}$$

$$3s\ \underline{\uparrow\downarrow} \qquad\qquad 3s\ \underline{\uparrow}$$

$$\text{P (ground state)} \qquad \text{P (excited state)} \qquad \text{P (hybrid state)}$$

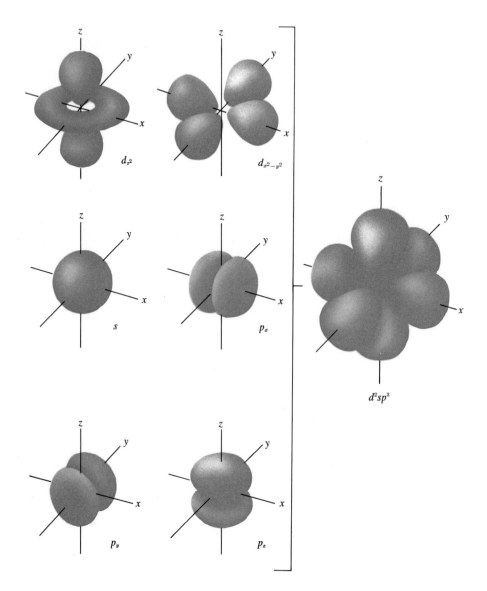

Figure 4.7 Formation of d^2sp^3 hybrid orbitals. Shapes of the hybrid orbitals have been simplified for clarity.

The $d_{x^2-y^2}$ atomic orbital is not used in the formation of dsp^3 hybrid orbitals, but the other atomic orbitals shown in Figure 4.7 are blended in the formation of this type of hybrid.

The $Ni(CN)_4^{2-}$ complex ion is square planar (Figure 4.4), and is prepared by the reaction of the Ni^{2+} ion with excess cyanide ion.

$$Ni^{2+} + 4CN^- \longrightarrow Ni(CN)_4^{2-}$$

The bonding in the complex may be considered to arise from *empty dsp^2* **hybrid orbitals** of Ni^{2+} being occupied by unshared electron pairs of the C atoms of the four cyanide ions, $:C\equiv N:^-$. The $3d$ orbitals are not far removed, in terms of energy, from the $4s$ and $4p$ orbitals, and a $3d$ orbital is used for the formation of the hybrid.

$$4p \; \_ \; \_ \; \_ \qquad\qquad 4p \; \_$$

$$dsp^2 \; \_ \; \_ \; \_ \; \_$$

$$4s \; \_$$

$$3d \; \uparrow\downarrow \; \uparrow\downarrow \; \uparrow\downarrow \; \uparrow \; \uparrow \qquad 3d \; \uparrow\downarrow \; \uparrow\downarrow \; \uparrow\downarrow \; \uparrow\downarrow$$

$$Ni^{2+} \text{ (ground state)} \qquad Ni^{2+} \text{ (hybrid state)}$$

The $d_{x^2-y^2}$, s, p_x, and p_y orbitals are used in the formation of dsp^2 hybrid orbitals (compare Figure 4.7).

4.3 Electron Pair Repulsions and Molecular Geometry

The orientation that a set of atoms assumes in the formation of a given molecule may be explained qualitatively on the basis of electrostatic repulsions between electron pairs. In the application of this concept, attention is directed to the valence level of the central atom of the molecule, and the diagrams for the examples that follow show only the electrons of this level of the central atom.

Mercury has two electrons in its valence level ($6s^2$); these are used to form two covalent bonds with two chlorine atoms in the mercuric chloride molecule, $HgCl_2$. The molecule is linear:

$$Cl : Hg : Cl$$

The $HgCl_2$ molecule assumes a configuration such that the two electron-pair bonds are as widely separated as possible, thus minimizing the electrostatic repulsion between them. Molecules of the type $B : A : B$ are invariably linear; beryllium, zinc, cadmium, and mercury form such molecules.

The boron trifluoride molecule is triangular and planar.

$$\begin{matrix} F \\ \cdot\cdot \\ \cdot B \cdot \\ F \; \cdot\cdot \; F \end{matrix}$$

Each of the bond angles of the molecule is 120°, and this arrangement provides the greatest possible separation between the three electron pairs.

In the methane molecule, CH_4, the central carbon atom has four pairs of electrons in bonds. The Lewis structure, which does not depict the molecular geometry, is

$$\begin{array}{c} \text{H} \\ \cdot\cdot \\ \text{H}:\text{C}:\text{H} \\ \cdot\cdot \\ \text{H} \end{array}$$

The electrostatic repulsions between the bond pairs are at a minimum when the bonds are directed toward the corners of a regular tetrahedron (Figure 4.8); in this configuration, all of the bonds are equidistant from one another.

The structure of ammonia

$$\begin{array}{c} \cdot\cdot \\ \text{H}:\text{N}:\text{H} \\ \cdot\cdot \\ \text{H} \end{array}$$

can also be related to the tetrahedron (Figure 4.8). The nitrogen has three electron pairs engaged in bonding and a fourth pair, which is called a **lone pair of electrons**. The representation used to show a lone pair of electrons in the figures should not be interpreted in the same manner as the boundary surface diagrams of the atomic orbitals; the lone pairs bear a closer relationship to the electrons in hybridized orbitals (Section 4.2). The four pairs of NH_3 assume a slightly distorted tetrahedral configuration which causes the atoms of the molecule to have a trigonal pyramidal arrangement. The bond pairs, which are under the influence of two positive charge centers, are more localized and take up less volume than the lone pair, which is under the influence of but one positive charge center. In addition, the charge concentration of the lone pair is closer to the central atom than that of a bond pair. Hence, the lone pair exerts a greater repulsion on a bond pair than a given bond pair exerts on another bond pair. As a result, the three bonds of the NH_3 molecule are forced slightly closer together than is normal for the tetrahedral arrangement. Thus each of the $H-N-H$ bond angles is $107.3°$ rather than the tetrahedral angle of $109.5°$.

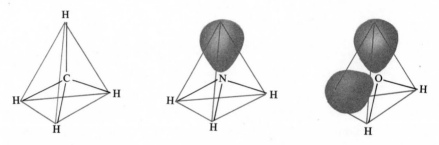

Figure 4.8 Geometries of methane (CH_4), ammonia (NH_3), and water (H_2O) molecules.

The NF_3 molecule has a structure similar to that of NH_3.

$$\overset{\displaystyle \overset{..}{N}}{\underset{\displaystyle F}{F \diagdown | \diagup F}}$$

In this molecule, the very electronegative fluorine atoms attract the bonding electrons strongly, and the regions of high charge concentration of the bonds are farther from the nitrogen atom in NF_3 than they are in NH_3. As a result, a N—F bond is contracted compared to a N—H bond, and, because of the repulsion due to the lone pair, the N—F bonds are closer together than the N—H bonds. The F—N—F bond angles in NF_3, therefore, are only 102.1° rather than 107.3° as are the H—N—H bond angles in NH_3.

The lone pair also influences the polarity of the NF_3 molecule (Section 3.10). Nitrogen trifluoride has a dipole moment of only 0.24 D, a surprisingly low value in view of the highly polar nature of the N—F bonds. Each of the N—F bonds is polarized so as to give the molecule a dipole with the negative end in the direction of the base of the NF_3 pyramid. The contribution of the lone pair to the dipole moment, however, works in the opposite direction and reduces the total polarity of the molecule.

The water molecule has two bond pairs and two lone pairs.

$$\overset{\displaystyle ..}{\underset{\displaystyle \overset{..}{H}}{:\overset{}{O}:H}}$$

The four electron pairs are arranged in an approximately tetrahedral manner (Figure 4.8), so that the atoms of the molecule have a V-shaped configuration. The bond angle of the water molecule (104.5°) is less than the H—N—H bond angle of NH_3. For the reasons discussed previously, the strengths of the repulsion forces decrease in the general order: lone pair–lone pair (L–L) > lone pair–bond pair (L–B) > bond pair–bond pair (B–B). Hence, the two lone pairs of the H_2O molecule force the O—H bond together more closely than the N—H bonds of the NH_3 molecule, which are influenced by only one lone pair.

The central atoms of some ions and molecules have six electron pairs (bond pairs or lone pairs), and the geometries of these species are related to the octahedron. An example is the SF_6 molecule in which the central S atom has six bond pairs.

$$\underset{\displaystyle \underset{F}{F \diagup | \diagdown F}}{\overset{\displaystyle F}{\underset{\displaystyle S}{F \diagdown | \diagup F}}}$$

A S atom has six valence electrons; in SF_6 each of these electrons forms a covalent bond with an electron from a F atom. The molecule adopts the

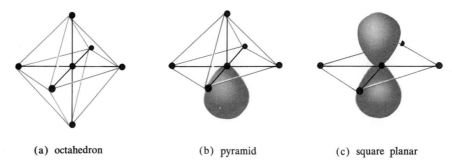

(a) octahedron   (b) pyramid   (c) square planar

Figure 4.9 Geometries of molecules and ions in which the central atom has six electron pairs.

geometry of a regular octahedron (Figure 4.9a) in which the bonds are equidistant and all positions are equivalent. In this configuration, the electrostatic repulsions are as small as possible for this type of molecule, and all bond angles are 90°.

The I atom of IF_5 has five bond pairs and one lone pair.

$$F\diagdown\underset{\textstyle F}{\overset{\textstyle ..}{\underset{|}{I}}}\diagup F$$

An I atom has seven valence electrons; in IF_5, five of these electrons are engaged in bonding five F atoms, and the other two constitute a lone pair. The electron pairs are directed to the corners of an octahedron. Since all the positions of an octahedron are equivalent, the atoms of the molecule form a square pyramid (Figure 4.9b), which may be slightly distorted.

The Br atom of the BrF_4^- ion has four bond pairs and two lone pairs.

$$F\diagdown\underset{\textstyle F}{\overset{\textstyle ..}{\underset{..}{Br}}}\diagup F^-$$

To account for the charge on the ion, we can consider that the central Br atom gains an electron becoming a Br^- ion with eight valence electrons. Four of these electrons are then used to form four covalent bonds with F atoms (four bond pairs), and the other four electrons constitute two lone pairs. Since the total number of electron pairs is six, the electron pairs of this ion also assume octahedral positions. The lone pairs assume positions that are 180° from one another (Figure 4.9c) which minimizes the L–L repulsion. The atoms of the molecule, therefore, have a square planar geometry.

The analysis of species with five electron pairs on the central atom is less straightforward. The configuration that minimizes electron-pair repulsions is the trigonal bipyramid (Figure 4.10a); this is the arrangement assumed by the PCl_5 molecule in which the five valence electrons of a P atom form five

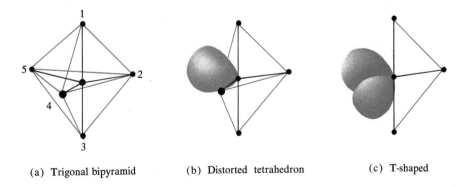

(a) Trigonal bipyramid   (b) Distorted tetrahedron   (c) T-shaped

Figure 4.10 Geometries of molecules in which the central atom has five electron pairs.

bond pairs with electrons from five Cl atoms. In this configuration, however, the polar positions (numbers 1 and 3 of the diagram) are different from the equatorial positions (numbers 2, 4, and 5). Equatorial atoms are coplanar, and any bond angle formed by two equatorial atoms and the central atom is 120°. The polar atoms are at right angles to the equatorial plane; any bond angle defined by a polar atom, the central atom, and an equatorial atom is 90°.

The Te atom of $TeCl_4$ has four bond pairs and a lone pair. Tellurium (group VI A) has six valence electrons; in $TeCl_4$, four of these form bond pairs with electrons from four Cl atoms, and the other two electrons constitute a lone pair. The structure of the molecule may be related to that of a trigonal bipyramid in which the lone pair occupies an equatorial position (Figure 4.10b). The L–B repulsions are far more significant than B–B repulsions. In an octahedral configuration, all the bond angles are 90°, whereas in a trigonal bipyramidal configuration, there are bond angles of 90° and 120°. If the lone pair were directed toward a polar position, it would form angles of approximately 90° each, with three equatorial bond pairs. In an equatorial position, the lone pair forms angles of approximately 90° each, with only two bond pairs (those directed toward the polar atoms).

The Cl atom of ClF_3 has three bond pairs and two lone pairs. Three of the seven valence electrons of the Cl atom are used to bond the three F atoms, and the remaining four electrons constitute two lone pairs. Molecules with three bond pairs and two lone pairs, such as ClF_3 and BrF_3, have both of their lone pairs in the equatorial plane, giving the atoms of the molecule a T-shape (Figure 4.10c). Why the two lone pairs are not directed toward polar positions, at a 180° angle from one another, is not immediately obvious. Only the interactions between electron pairs that are directed at an angle of 90° need to considered; interactions at 120°, or wider angles, are negligible in comparison. With the lone pairs directed toward polar positions, six 90°

L–B repulsions occur. With the lone pairs directed toward equatorial positions, however, there are only four 90° L–B repulsions and two B–B repulsions (which are much smaller than L–B repulsions). If one lone pair were to be directed toward a polar position and the second toward an equatorial position, the molecule would have one 90° L–L repulsion (the strongest type of repulsion), three 90° L–B repulsions, and two 90° B–B repulsions. Therefore, the configuration that minimizes electrostatic repulsions is that with both lone pairs in the equatorial plane.

4.4 Molecular Orbitals

Molecular structure has so far been depicted by forms that relate back to the electronic configurations of the constituent atoms. The **method of molecular orbitals** is an alternative approach. In this method, orbitals are associated with the molecule as a whole, and the configuration of the molecule is obtained by entering electrons into these molecular orbitals in an aufbau order analogous to that employed in the filling of atomic orbitals. Corresponding to the practice of indicating atomic orbitals by the letters s, p, and d, molecular orbitals are assigned the similar Greek letter designations σ (sigma), π (pi), and δ (delta).

A hydrogen atom has one electron in a $1s$ orbital. When two such atoms are separated by a relatively large distance, the electrons do not interact, and the energy of the system may be taken as zero. As the two atoms are brought together and the orbitals begin to overlap, the energy of the system decreases because of the attraction of the nuclei for the increasing electronic charge that is accumulating in the bonding region (lower curve of Figure 4.11). However, at very small internuclear distances, the repulsive force between the two positive nuclei causes the energy of the system to increase rapidly. The minimum in the curve occurs at an equilibrium internuclear distance, R_0, which is the bond distance of the molecule (0.74 Å for the H_2 molecule). The atoms of the molecule vibrate about this position. The dissociation energy, d, is approximately the bond energy of the molecule (1.73×10^{-19} cal/bond for H_2). Actually, slightly less energy than d is required to separate the bonded atoms because the atoms are not at rest; they possess kinetic energy and vibrate about the distance R_0.

In Figure 4.12, electron density is plotted against distance along a line joining the nuclei of a H_2 molecule. The curve labeled $\sigma 1s$ shows the concentration of electronic charge in the region between the two nuclei. The $1s$ atomic orbitals may be considered to have combined into a **molecular orbital**, which extends over the nuclear system of the molecule as a whole, unlike an atomic orbital which is centered around a single nucleus. The molecular orbital of H_2 is called a **sigma (σ) bonding orbital**, and a boundary surface

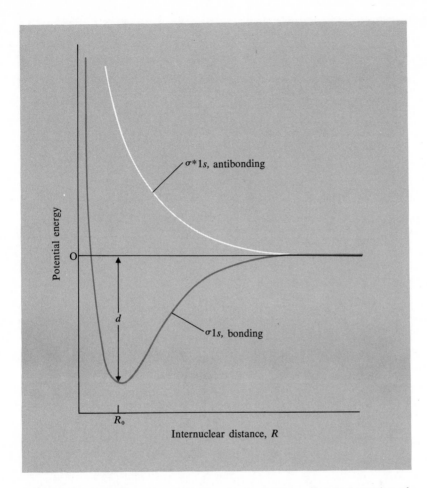

Figure 4.11 Potential energy versus internuclear distance for the formation of the molecular orbitals of H_2 from the atomic orbitals of two hydrogen atoms. In the ground state of H_2, only the bonding orbital is occupied. The dissociation energy, d, and the equilibrium internuclear distance, R_0, are indicated.

diagram is shown in Figure 4.13. Sigma orbitals are symmetrical around an axis joining the two nuclei, rotation of the molecule about this axis causes no observable change in the orbital shape.

A molecular orbital, like an atomic orbital, is filled by two electrons of opposed spin. In the hypothetical construction of the $\sigma 1s$ bonding orbital, two atomic orbitals, which together could accommodate four electrons, were used. The combination should, therefore, provide for four electrons, or two molecular orbitals, and mathematical combination of the wave equations of two $1s$ atomic orbitals does indeed give two different solutions.

The first solution pertains to the $\sigma 1s$ bonding molecular orbital already described, and the second solution pertains to what is called a **sigma (σ*)**

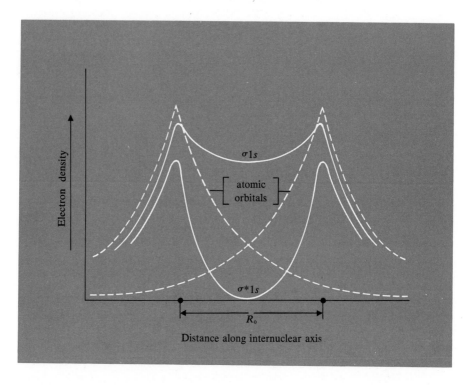

Figure 4.12 Electron density plotted against distance along an axis joining the nuclei of H_2 for the $1s$ atomic orbitals of two nonbonded hydrogen atoms and the σs and $\sigma^* s$ molecular orbitals of H_2.

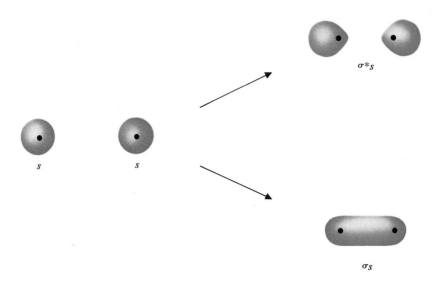

Figure 4.13 Formation of σs and $\sigma^* s$ molecular orbitals from $1s$ atomic orbitals.

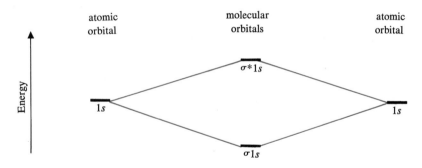

Figure 4.14 Energy-level diagram for the formation of σ and σ^* molecular orbitals from the $1s$ orbitals of two atoms.

antibonding molecular orbital (Figure 4.11). The electron density of the anti-bonding orbital is low and falls to zero in the internuclear region (Figure 4.12); most of the electron density is found at the ends of the molecule (Figure 4.13). Such an electron distribution does little to counteract nuclear repulsion, and thus the net effect is disruptive. The σ^*1s orbital, like the $\sigma1s$ orbital, is symmetrical about the internuclear axis.

A qualitative energy-level diagram for the formation of $\sigma1s$ and σ^*1s molecular orbitals from the $1s$ atomic orbitals of two atoms is shown in Figure 4.14. The energy of the σ bonding orbital is lower than that of either atomic orbital from which it may be considered to have been derived, whereas the energy of the σ^* antibonding orbital is higher. When two atomic orbitals are combined, the resulting bonding molecular orbital represents a decrease in energy, and the antibonding molecular orbital represents an increase in energy; s atomic orbitals from any quantum level give rise to σ and σ^* molecular orbitals.

The following notation may be used to represent the formation of the H_2 molecule:

$$2H(1s^1) \longrightarrow H_2[(\sigma1s)^2]$$

The superscripts denote the number of electrons in each orbital. One-half the difference between the number of bonding electrons and the number of antibonding electrons gives the number of bonds in the molecule. In the ground state of H_2, there are no antibonding electrons and, therefore, $\frac{1}{2}(2 - 0) = 1$.

If an attempt is made to combine two helium atoms, a total of four electrons must be placed in the two molecular orbitals resulting from the combination of the two $1s$ orbitals of the He atoms. The $\sigma1s$ orbital is filled with two electrons, so that the other two must be placed in the higher σ^*1s orbital.

$$2\,He(1s^2) \longrightarrow He_2[(\sigma1s)^2(\sigma^*1s)^2]$$

The number of bonds indicated by this notation is $\frac{1}{2}(2 - 2) = 0$, and the net effect is no bond. If the diagram of the $\sigma1s$ orbital is superimposed on the diagram of the $\sigma*1s$ orbital, the electron distribution is roughly the same as that of two He atoms, and He_2 does not exist.

The combination of two $2s$ orbitals produces σ and $\sigma*$ molecular orbitals similar to those formed from $1s$ orbitals, but the molecular orbitals derived from $2p$ atomic orbitals are slightly more complicated. The three $2p$ orbitals of an atom are directed along the Cartesian coordinates x, y, and z. If we consider that a diatomic molecule is formed by the atoms approaching each other along the x axis, the p_x atomic orbitals approach each other head on and overlap to produce $\sigma2p$ bonding and $\sigma*2p$ antibonding molecular orbitals (Figure 4.15). All sigma orbitals are symmetrical about the internuclear axis;

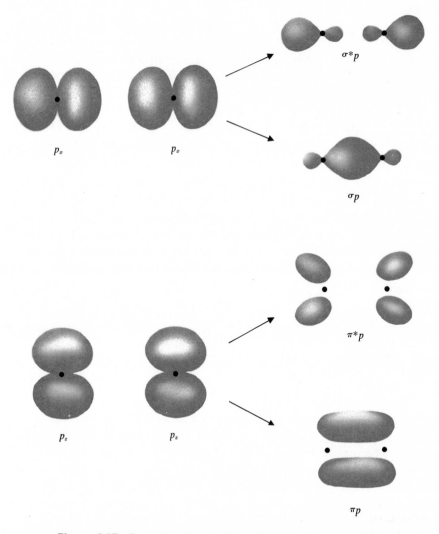

Figure 4.15 Formation of molecular orbitals from p atomic orbitals.

the $\sigma 2p$ and $\sigma*2p$ orbitals have shapes that are similar to those of the $\sigma 1s$ and $\sigma*1s$ orbitals.

In the formation of the diatomic molecule, the p_z atomic orbitals approach each other side to side and produce what are called **pi (π) bonding and antibonding molecular orbitals**. (Figure 4.15). Pi orbitals are not symmetrical about the internuclear axis. The electron density of a π bonding orbital is zero in a plane that includes both nuclei of the molecule, but charge is concentrated in two regions above and below this plane and between the two nuclei. The $\pi*$ orbital reduces electronic density in the internuclear region.

The p_y orbitals, which are not shown in Figure 4.15, also approach each other sideways. Consequently another set of π and $\pi*$ molecular orbitals, at right angles to the set resulting from the overlap of p_z orbitals, can be produced. The two $\pi 2p$ orbitals are **degenerate**, or of equal energy, and the two $\pi*2p$ orbitals are degenerate. Therefore, six molecular orbitals arise from the two sets of p orbitals—one $\sigma 2p$, one $\sigma*2p$, two $\pi 2p$, and two $\pi*2p$.

In what order are these orbitals filled in the formation of a diatomic molecule? Figure 4.16 shows the order that is followed by atoms in which there is a large energy difference between the $2s$ and $2p$ orbitals. The three $2p$ orbitals of the isolated atoms are degenerate. This degeneracy is split in the

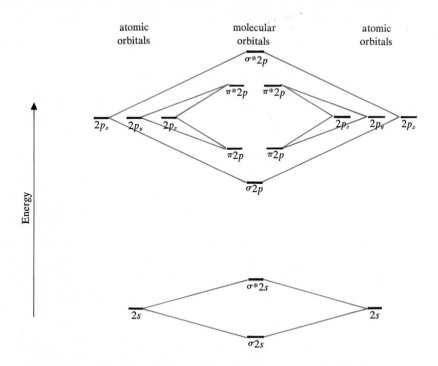

Figure 4.16 Energy-level diagram for the formation of molecular orbitals between identical atoms in which there is a large difference in energy between the $2s$ and $2p$ orbitals.

formation of molecular orbitals; the σ bonding orbital (derived from p_x atomic orbitals) has a lower energy than either of the two degenerate π bonding orbitals (derived from p_y and p_z atomic orbitals). In diatomic molecules formed from atoms with more than one electronic shell, the inner shells do not appreciably affect the bonding; such electrons are called **nonbonding electrons**.

The order shown in Figure 4.16:

$$\sigma 2s \quad \sigma^*2s \quad \sigma 2p_x \quad \genfrac{|}{|}{0pt}{}{\pi 2p_y}{\pi 2p_z} \quad \genfrac{|}{|}{0pt}{}{\pi^*2p_y}{\pi^*2p_z} \quad \sigma^*2p_x$$

is followed in the formation of F_2 and O_2 (Figure 4.17). The notation for the F_2 molecule is

$$2F(1s^2\ 2s^2\ 2p^5) \quad \longrightarrow \quad F_2[K\,K\ (\sigma 2s)^2\ (\sigma^*2s)^2\ (\sigma 2p)^2\ (\pi 2p)^4\ (\pi^*2p)^4]$$

The symbols $K\,K$ indicate nonbonding electrons, and the subscripts x, y, and z have been omitted. The number of bonds here represented is $\frac{1}{2}(8-6)$ or 1.

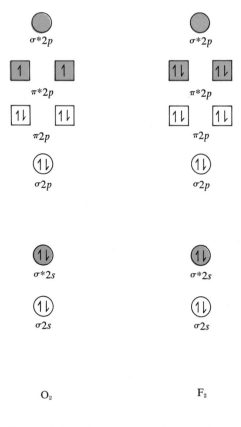

O₂   F₂

Figure 4.17 Molecular orbital energy-level diagrams for O_2 and F_2.

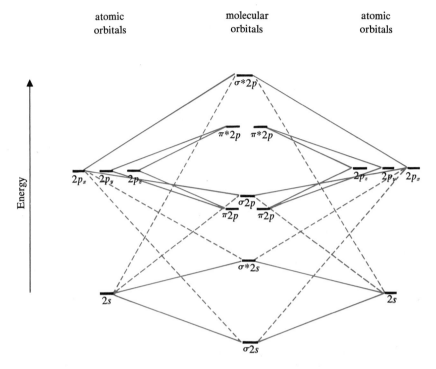

Figure 4.18 Energy-level diagram for the formation of molecular orbitals between identical atoms in which the $2s$-$2p$ energy difference is not large.

The notation for O_2 is

$$2O(1s^2\ 2s^2\ 2p^4) \longrightarrow O_2[K\ K\ (\sigma 2s)^2\ (\sigma^*2s)^2\ (\sigma 2p)^2\ (\pi 2p)^4\ (\pi^*2p)^2]$$

The number of bonds is $\frac{1}{2}(8-4)=2$. The Lewis structure for O_2, $:\ddot{O}::\ddot{O}:$, depicts the double bond but does not show that oxygen is paramagnetic (two unpaired electrons). The last term of the molecular orbital designation, $(\pi^*2p)^2$, accounts for the two unpaired electrons of the oxygen molecule. There are two antibonding π orbitals available (π^*2p_y and π^*2p_z); the two electrons do not pair but occupy these orbitals singly according to Hund's rule (Figure 4.17).

For the other diatomic molecules of the second period, formed from atoms in which the difference in energy between the $2s$ and $2p$ orbitals is smaller, the order shown in Figure 4.18 prevails.

$$\sigma 2s\ \sigma^*2s\ \begin{Bmatrix}\pi 2p_y\\ \pi 2p_z\end{Bmatrix}\ \sigma 2p_x\ \begin{Bmatrix}\pi^*2p_y\\ \pi^*2p_z\end{Bmatrix}\ \sigma^*2p_x$$

The principal difference between this and the previous order is that the $\sigma 2p_x$ orbital has been switched from below the degenerate $\pi 2p$ pair to above this pair.

In the development of the first order given, it was assumed that a $2s$ orbital interacted only with another $2s$ orbital and that the $2p_x$ orbitals interacted only with each other; this assumption is approximately valid if there is a large energy separation between the two types of atomic orbitals. When the combining $2s$ and $2p_x$ orbitals (the ones that form sigma molecular orbitals) are close in energy, however, interaction can occur between these different atomic orbitals as well as between like atomic orbitals ($2s$—$2s$ and $2p_x$—$2p_x$). The result is a type of hybridization in which the $\sigma 2s$ and $\sigma^* 2s$ become more stable (of a lower energy) and the $\sigma 2p$ and $\sigma^* 2p$ become less stable (higher energy). The most important result, as far as orbital order is concerned, is that the $\sigma 2p$ orbital is shifted.

In Figure 4.19, energy-level diagrams are given for B_2, C_2, and N_2, which utilize the order in which the two $\pi 2p$ orbitals lie below the $\sigma 2p$ orbital. One confirmation of this fact is afforded by magnetic susceptibility measurement of B_2. This molecule has two unpaired electrons (one in each of the two $\pi 2p$ orbitals), and B_2 is paramagnetic. Utilization of the aufbau order

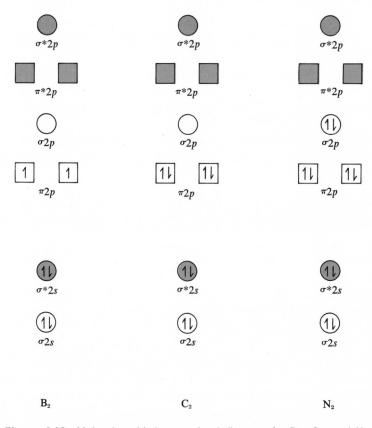

Figure 4.19 Molecular orbital energy-level diagrams for B_2, C_2, and N_2.

employed for F_2 would have given a diamagnetic B_2 molecule with the last two electrons paired in a $\sigma 2p$ orbital.

Table 4.1

Diatomic Molecules of the Elements of the Second Period

Molecule	Number of Electrons in Molecular Orbitals						Bond Order	Bond Length (Å)	Dissociation Energy (ev)	Unpaired Electrons
	$\sigma 2s$	$\sigma^* 2s$	$\pi 2p$	$\sigma 2p$	$\pi^* 2p$	$\sigma^* 2p$				
^{a}Li$_2$	2						1	2.67	1.1	0
^{b}Be$_2$	2	2					0	—	—	0
^{a}B$_2$	2	2	2				1	1.59	3.0	2
^{a}C$_2$	2	2	4				2	1.31	6.5	0
N$_2$	2	2	4	2			3	1.09	9.8	0
	$\sigma 2s$	$\sigma^* 2s$	$\sigma 2p$	$\pi 2p$	$\pi^* 2p$	$\sigma^* 2p$				
O$_2$	2	2	2	4	2		2	1.21	5.1	2
F$_2$	2	2	2	4	4		1	1.43	1.6	0
^{b}Ne$_2$	2	2	2	4	4	2	0	—	—	0

^{a} Exists only in the vapor state at elevated temperatures.
^{b} Does not exist.

A summary of the diatomic molecules of the second period elements is given in Table 4.1. As the number of bonds increases, the bond distance shortens and the bonding becomes stronger. The molecule bonded most strongly is N_2, which is held together by a triple bond (Figure 4.19). The molecules for which the method of molecular orbitals assigns a bond order of zero (Be$_2$ and Ne$_2$) do not exist.

In heteronuclear diatomic molecules, the clouds of the bonding orbitals are distorted so that more electronic charge is found around the more electronegative atom than around the other atom; antibonding orbitals have their largest electron density in the regions close to the lesser electronegative atom. For molecules such as CO and NO, the same types of molecular orbitals, slightly distorted, are formed as occur in homonuclear diatomic molecules. Either aufbau order may be used in most cases with the same qualitative results; the actual order is uncertain.

Since CO is isoelectronic with N_2 (each molecule has ten valence electrons), the molecular orbital notation for CO is similar to that for N_2 (Figure 4.19). Carbon monoxide, therefore, has a bond order of 3. The dissociation energy of the CO molecule is about the same as that of the N_2 molecule.

We have said that it is impossible to diagram a valence-bond structure utilizing the octet principle for a molecule with an odd number of valence

Figure 4.20 Molecular orbital energy-level diagram for NO.

electrons. Nitrogen oxide, NO, is such a molecule. Since five valence electrons are contributed by the N atom and six valence electrons by the O atom, the total number of valence electrons is eleven. An energy-level diagram for the molecular orbitals of NO is given in Figure 4.20. Since there are eight bonding electrons and three antibonding electrons shown in the diagram, a bond order of $\frac{1}{2}(8 - 3)$, or $2\frac{1}{2}$, is indicated. Nitrogen oxide is paramagnetic; the NO molecule has one unpaired electron in a π^*2p orbital.

4.5 Molecular Orbitals in Polyatomic Molecules

Molecular orbital concepts can be applied to polyatomic molecules, and such application is particularly advantageous for molecules containing multiple bonds. Consider the series

$$\begin{array}{c} H \quad H \\ | \quad | \\ H-C-C-H \\ | \quad | \\ H \quad H \end{array}$$

ethane

ethylene

$$H-C\equiv C-H$$

acetylene

Each C atom in ethane utilizes sp^3 hybrid orbitals in the formation of σ bonds with the other C atom and with three H atoms (Figure 4.21). Thus, all bond angles are 109.5°, the tetrahedral angle. Since σ bonding orbitals are symmetrical about the internuclear axis, free rotation about each bond i possible. Rotation about the C—C bond causes a changing atomic configuration (Figure 4.21).

There can only be one σ bond between any two bonded atoms; any additional bonds must be π bonds. The σ bonding skeleton of ethylene, therefore, is

$$\begin{array}{c} H \qquad H \\ \diagdown \qquad \diagup \\ C-C \\ \diagup \qquad \diagdown \\ H \qquad H \end{array}$$

and the C atoms utilize sp^2 hybrid orbitals in forming this skeleton. This type of hybridization leads to a planar configuration of hybrid orbitals in which the orbitals form angles of 120° with each other. The ethylene molecule is planar with H—C—H bond angles of 118° and H—C—C bond angles of 121° (Figure 4.22).

Each C atom of ethylene has one electron in a p_z orbital that is not involved in σ bond formation. The p_z orbitals overlap to produce a π bonding orbital. The electron density of the π bond is above and below the plane of the molecule, and hence free rotation about the C=C linkage is impossible without breaking the π bond.

The bonding skeleton of acetylene is

$$H-C-C-H$$

Each C atom forms two σ bonds, and sp, or linear, hybrid orbitals of C are employed in the formation of these σ bonds. The $2p$ carbon orbitals that are

Figure 4.21 Rotation about the C—C bond in ethane.

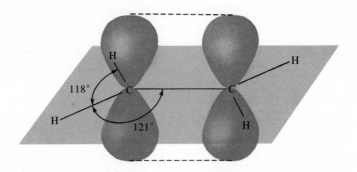

Figure 4.22 Geometric configuration of ethylene. Shapes of the *p* orbitals which overlap to form a π bond are simplified.

not involved in the hybridization and σ bond formation overlap to form two π bonding molecular orbitals (Figure 4.23). The structure is much like that of N_2.

The multiple bonds of ethylene and acetylene may be considered to be localized between two nuclei. In some molecules and ions, **multicenter** or **delocalized**, **bonding** exists in which some bonding electrons serve to bond more than two atoms together. The description of these species by the valence bond approach requires the use of resonance structures.

An example of delocalized bonding is afforded by the bonding in the carbonate ion (Figure 4.24). The ion is triangular planar, and each $O—C—O$ bond angle is 120°. The C atom may be assumed to use sp^2 hybrid orbitals in the formation of the σ bonding skeleton leaving one $2p$ orbital unhybridized. This p orbital of C overlaps similar p orbitals of the O atoms forming a π bonding *system* that encompasses all of the atoms of the ion.

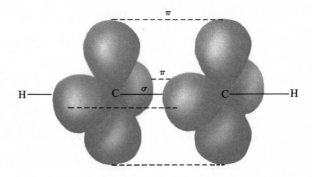

Figure 4.23 Formation of the π bonds of acetylene. Orbital shapes simplified.

Figure 4.24 Multicenter π bonding system of the carbonate ion and the relationship to resonance structures.

The CO_3^{2-} ion has a total of twenty-four valence electrons. Six are used in the formation of the three σ bonds of the ion, and placement of two pairs of unshared electrons on each O atom accounts for twelve more. The remaining six electrons are placed in the molecular orbitals of the π bonding system. It must be understood that a molecular orbital, like an atomic orbital, can hold only two electrons. Hence, a π bonding system involves two or more contiguous molecular orbitals.

The structures of sulfur trioxide, SO_3, and the nitrate ion, NO_3^-, are similar to the structure of the carbonate ion, and the resonance forms of these species are also similar. The π bonding system of sulfur dioxide, SO_2, is shown in Figure 4.25; ozone, O_3, and the nitrite ion, NO_2^- have similar structures.

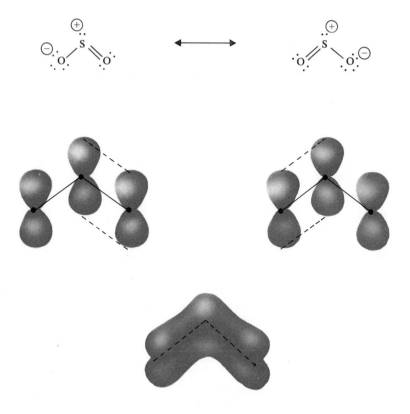

Figure 4.25 Relation of the π bonding system of sulfur dioxide to the resonance forms of the molecule. Orbital shapes simplified.

4.6 The Metallic Bond

Both resonance and the method of molecular orbitals have been used to interpret the **metallic bond**—the attraction that holds metallic crystals together. The most characteristic chemical and physical properties of metals are derived from their low ionization potentials and low electronegativities. Hence, the outer electrons of metal atoms are relatively loosely held, and, in a metallic crystal, the lattice positions are occupied by positive metal ions which are held together by mobile electrons.

Only the most loosely held electrons of the metal atoms are used in the metallic bonding. In the case of many metals this includes only the electrons of the outer shell, but for the transition and inner-transition metals, some of the electrons of the inner orbitals may be involved as well. An examination of ionization potentials shows that the electrons of inner orbitals are held tightly and therefore are associated with the individual positive metal ions and not the crystal as a whole. The first to fourth ionization potentials of some A family metals are listed in Table 4.2. Notice that after the valence

Table 4.2

Ionization Potentials of the Third-Period Metals

		Ionization Potentials (ev)			
Metal	*Group*	*First*	*Second*	*Third*	*Fourth*
Na	I A	5.1 $\mid$	47.3	71.7	98.9
Mg	II A	7.6	15.0 $\mid$	80.1	109.3
Al	III A	6.0	18.8	28.4 $\mid$	120.0

electrons have been removed, there is a decided jump in the level of the energy required to remove the next electron (this place is marked with a vertical line).

Metallic crystals are close-packed structures; each of the positive ions has a comparatively large number of close neighbors. It is impossible for an atom to form simultaneously as many covalent bonds as would be needed to bind such an arrangement of atoms together, particularly metal atoms, all of which have few valence electrons.

The bonding in metals may be regarded as an extreme type of nonlocalized bonding encorporating all of the atoms of the metallic crystal, and a resonance treatment has been postulated. In a lithium crystal, each atom has eight close neighbors and one valence electron. The crystal may be approximately represented as a resonance hybrid of such structures as the following. Whereas only four atoms are shown in these structures, the actual bonding includes all of the atoms of the crystal and is three-dimensional.

$$
\begin{array}{ccccccc}
\text{Li—Li} & & \text{Li} \quad \text{Li} & & \text{Li}^+ \quad \text{Li} & \\
& \longleftrightarrow & | \quad | & \longleftrightarrow & | & \longleftrightarrow \\
\text{Li—Li} & & \text{Li} \quad \text{Li} & & \text{Li —Li}^- & \\
\quad \text{I} & & \quad \text{II} & & \quad \text{III} &
\end{array}
$$

$$
\begin{array}{ccccccc}
\text{Li —Li}^- & & \text{Li} \quad \text{Li}^+ & & \text{Li}^-\text{—Li} & \\
| & \longleftrightarrow & | & \longleftrightarrow & | & \\
\text{Li}^+ \quad \text{Li} & & \text{Li}^-\text{—Li} & & \text{Li} \quad \text{Li}^+ & \\
\quad \text{IV} & & \quad \text{V} & & \quad \text{VI} &
\end{array}
$$

In structures III, IV, V, and VI, ionic forms are indicated, and one lithium atom (the one holding a negative charge) in each of these structures is shown as bonded to two other atoms. Hence, it appears that more than one valence orbital of each lithium atom must be involved in the metallic bonding. Lithium has the electronic configuration $1s^2 2s^1$, and it is assumed that a vacant $2p$ orbital (which is not far removed energetically from the $2s$) is used; this orbital is called the **metallic orbital**.

The quantum mechanical treatment of the metallic crystal proceeds by combining the wave functions of the atomic orbitals into sets of orbitals

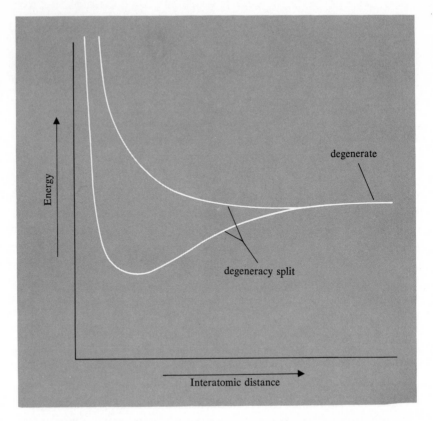

Figure 4.26 Energy of the 2s orbitals of two lithium atoms as a function of interatomic distance.

(or **bands**) for the entire crystal, much like the method of molecular orbitals. The process is more complicated, however, because the orbitals of a large number of atoms must be considered (all of the atoms in the crystal) unlike the situation in a covalent molecule where the orbitals of a comparatively few atoms need to be taken into account.

The 2s orbitals of two lithium atoms are degenerate when the atoms are very far apart. However, when the two atoms are brought together, this degeneracy is split into two levels by the interaction of the atoms (Figure 4.26), and the magnitude of the splitting increases as the distance between the atoms decreases. The Li_2 molecule exists in the vapor state; the curve of Figure 4.26 showing the higher energy level may be regarded as that for a σ^* antibonding molecular orbital, whereas the curve for the lower energy level may represent a σ bonding orbital. In Li_2, only the bonding orbital is occupied.

If seven lithium atoms are brought together, the degeneracy of the orbitals of the isolated atoms is split into seven levels (Figure 4.27). Each atom con-

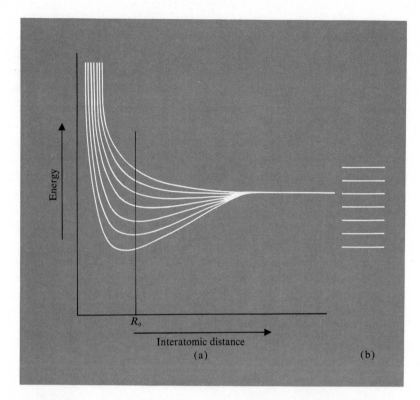

Figure 4.27 (a) Energy of 2s orbitals versus interatomic distance for a collection of seven atoms. (b) Energy-level diagram corresponding to the interatomic distance R_0.

tributes one level to the aggregate, which is called a band. In a large number (N) of isolated lithium atoms, the 2s orbitals are of equal energy, but this degeneracy is removed as the atoms are brought together, giving rise to N levels of slightly different energies. Each level of this band may accommodate two electrons of opposed spin.

As long as a fairly large number of atoms is considered, the spread between the levels is not significantly widened by an increased number of atoms. With uniform interatomic spacing, the orbital overlap is not significantly altered when the number of atoms is increased, and it is this orbital interaction that produces the effect on the energy levels. The gradual addition of atoms causes the increasing number of levels of the band to be more and more crowded together rather than affecting the spread of the band. As a result, the separation in energy between the levels of a band is very small even for samples of extremely small size. Even at very low temperatures, the electrons have enough energy to move from level to level within a band, and for all practical purposes the band represents a continuum of energy.

Each level of a band may accommodate two electrons of opposed spin. If N atoms contribute N levels to a band, the band is capable of holding $2N$ electrons. Since N lithium atoms have a total of N valence electrons, it would appear that half of the levels of the lithium valence band should be unoccupied. However, the band derived from the $2p$ orbitals of lithium must also be considered.

In an isolated lithium atom, the three $2p$ orbitals are only slightly higher in energy than the $2s$ orbital. The band derived from the $2p$ orbitals fans out and overlaps the band from the $2s$ orbitals (Figure 4.28). At the normal equilibrium interatomic distance, R_0, the two bands may be considered to form one. Since each atom contributes three $2p$ orbitals and one $2s$ orbital, the band resulting from the combination of N atoms would consist of $4N$ levels capable of holding $8N$ electrons. Hence the lithium band is only one-eighth filled.

If this band overlap did not occur, the valence band of beryllium (electronic configuration, $1s^2\,2s^2$) would be full, and beryllium would not conduct

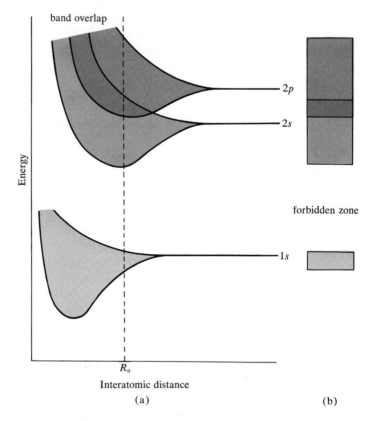

Figure 4.28 (a) Overlap of $2s$ and $2p$ bands. (b) Energy-level diagram for the interatomic distance R_0.

electricity. Beryllium is a metallic conductor because the band resulting from the overlap of the 2s and 2p orbitals is only one-quarter filled.

Metallic bonding generally arises from the interaction of the orbitals of the valence shell only. The interatomic spacing of a metallic crystal is determined by the overlap of the valence orbitals, and the orbitals of the inner shells do not interact appreciably at this distance. Consequently, the bands derived from inner orbitals, which are completely occupied, are narrow (Figure 4.28). In a crystal, no electron can have an energy that does not fall within the limits of a band; hence the region of an energy-level diagram between the bands is called a **forbidden energy zone**.

In a metallic crystal, therefore, the valence electrons are held by all of the atoms of the crystal. These electrons are highly mobile; the valence band that they occupy is overlapped by an unfilled conduction band, and the valence band itself may be only partially filled. Transference of an electron to a higher level of a band requires the addition of very little energy, since the levels are close together within a band. Thus the valence electrons of a metal can move to higher levels by absorbing light of a wide range of wavelengths. When electrons fall to lower energy levels, light is radiated. The lustrous appearance of metals, therefore, is caused by electron transitions.

The high order of electron mobility of metallic crystals also accounts for the high electrical conductivities of metals. Furthermore, metals are also excellent conductors of heat. The valence electrons take up heat energy as kinetic energy, and, since their motion is relatively unrestricted, they transfer energy rapidly to all parts of the metal. The low thermal conductivities of solids in which electrons are localized may be explained by the fact that conduction of heat by these materials takes place through the motion of ions or molecules— a much slower process.

Energy-level diagrams for **conductors, insulators,** and **intrinsic semiconductors** are shown in Figure 4.29. In the diagram for the conductor, the valence band is overlapped by an empty conduction band, and these are separated from an upper conduction band by a forbidden energy zone. The upper conduction band, which arises from higher atomic orbitals, is of slight significance. Electrical conduction takes place by means of the motion of electrons in the lower conduction band; there is no need to supply the energy required to bridge the forbidden zone in order to use the upper conduction band.

The diagram for the insulator, however, shows a completely filled valence band widely separated from a conduction band by a forbidden energy zone. Electron motion, and hence electrical conductivity, is only possible if energy is provided to promote electrons to the conduction band across the comparatively large forbidden zone. Normally such promotion does not occur, and hence the conductivities of insulators are extremely low. The diamond,

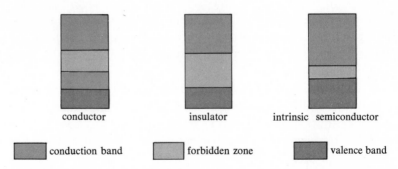

Figure 4.29 Energy-level band diagrams for three types of solids.

which is an insulator, has been described as a network crystal with localized bonding between atoms (Figure 3.16). In the construction of the band model for the diamond crystal, the symmetry of the atomic spacings imposes limitations on the orbital overlap so that a large forbidden zone is generated between a filled valence band and a conduction band. Band overlap, particularly for heavier atoms, is at times much more complicated than presented here.

An intrinsic semiconductor is a material that has a low electrical conductivity, intermediate between that of a conductor and an insulator; this conductivity increases markedly with increasing temperature. For a semiconductor, the forbidden zone is sufficiently narrow that electrons can be raised from the valence band to the conduction band by thermal excitation (see Figure 4.29). The vacancies left by the removal of electrons from the valence band permit electrons remaining in the valence band to move under the influence of an electric field, and thus conduction takes place through the motion of electrons in the valence, as well as in the conduction, band.

The electrical conduction of a metal is not dependent upon thermal excitation of electrons. Whereas the conductivity of an intrinsic semiconductor increases with increasing temperature, the electrical conductivity of a metal decreases with increasing temperature. Presumably, the increased temperature brings about increased vibration of the metal ions of the crystal lattice which, in turn, impedes the flow of conduction electrons. Other properties of semiconductors are discussed in Section 7.14.

SOME SUGGESTED READINGS

Barrow, G. M., *The Structure of Molecules*, New York Benjamin, 1963 (paper).
Companion, A., *Chemical Bonding*, New York, McGraw-Hill, 1964 (paper).
Day, M. C., Jr., and Selbin, J., *Theoretical Inorganic Chemistry*, 2nd ed., New York, Van Nostrand Reinhold, 1969.

Drago, R. S., *Physical Methods in Inorganic Chemistry*, New York, Van Nostrand Reinhold, 1965.

Gray, H. B., *Electrons and Chemical Bonding*, New York, Benjamin, 1964 (paper).

Harvey, K., and Porter, G., *Introduction to Physical Inorganic Chemistry*, Reading, Mass., Addison-Wesley, 1963.

Lagowski, J. J., *The Chemical Bond*, Boston, Houghton Mifflin, 1966 (paper).

Luder, W. F., *The Electron-Repulsion Theory of the Chemical Bond*, New York, Van Nostrand Reinhold, 1967 (paper).

Lynch, P. F., *Orbitals and Chemical Bonding*, Boston, Houghton Mifflin, 1966 (paper).

Pauling, L., *The Nature of the Chemical Bond*, 3rd ed., Ithaca, N. Y., Cornell University Press, 1960.

Ryschkewitsch, G. E., *Chemical Bonding and the Geometry of Molecules*, New York, Van Nostrand Reinhold, 1963 (paper).

Sebera, D. K., *Electronic Structure and Chemical Bonding*, Waltham, Mass., Blaisdell, 1964 (paper).

Sisler, H. H., *Electronic Structure, Properties, and the Periodic Law*, New York, Van Nostrand Reinhold, 1963 (paper).

PROBLEMS

4.1 Draw Lewis structures for the following ions and indicate the formal charge of each atom of each structure NO_2^-, NO_3^-, SO_3^{2-}, ClO_4^-, SO_4^{2-}, PO_4^{3-}.

4.2 The azide ion, N_3^-, is linear and symmetrical. Diagram the resonance forms of N_3^-.

4.3 Diagram the resonance forms of the formate ion, HCO_2^-, in which the C atom is the central atom and the two C to O bonds are of equal length.

4.4 In the oxalate ion, $C_2O_4^{2-}$, the two C atoms are bonded to each other, and each C atom has two O atoms bonded to it. The structure is symmetrical, and all C—O bond distances are equal. Diagram the resonance forms of $C_2O_4^{2-}$.

4.5 The O_2NCl molecule is triangular planar with the N atom as the central atom. The two N to O bonds are of equal length. Diagram the resonance forms of the O_2NCl molecule.

4.6 Crystalline PCl_5 consists of an ionic lattice formed from PCl_4^+ and PCl_6^- ions. In the vapor and liquid states, however, the compound exists as PCl_5 molecules. What types of hybrid orbitals does P employ in PCl_4^+, PCl_6^-, and PCl_5? What are the geometric configurations of these species?

4.7 Draw boundary surface diagrams to show how the component atomic orbitals are hybridized into a dsp^2 set.

4.8 The following species have been identified in aqueous solutions of cadmium bromide: Cd^{2+}, $CdBr^+$, $CdBr_2$, $CdBr_3^-$, $CdBr_4^{2-}$. For each of the bromine-containing species, indicate the type of hybrid orbitals employed and describe the geometric configuration.

4.9 For each of the following molecules, indicate the type of hybrid orbitals employed in the bonding and the geometric configuration. (a) $CdCl_2$, (b) Cl_2O, (c) $GaCl_3$, (d) AsH_3, (e) AsF_5, (f) CCl_4, (g) $SnCl_4$, (h) $SnCl_2$.

4.10 Interpret the configurations of the molecules given in Problem 4.9 on the basis of electron-pair repulsions. Which of the molecules would have dipoles?

4.11 Use the concept of electron-pair repulsions to predict the geometric configurations of the following. (a) $CuCl_2{}^-$, (b) $SeBr_2$, (c) $ICl_2{}^-$, (d) $ICl_4{}^-$, (e) $SeBr_4$, (f) SiF_6^{2-}.

4.12 Use the concept of electron-pair repulsions to predict the geometric configurations of the following. (a) SbF_5^{2-}, (b) TeF_6, (c) $BF_4{}^-$, (d) $SnF_3{}^-$, (e) PF_3, (f) IF_3.

4.13 Describe the geometric configuration of each of the following ions. (a) ClO^-, (b) $ClO_2{}^-$, (c) $ClO_3{}^-$, (d) $ClO_4{}^-$.

4.14 Ozone, O_3, is an angular molecule, and the two O to O linkages are the same length. Describe the bonding of O_3 in terms of resonance and also on the basis of molecular orbitals and delocalized bonding.

4.15 By means of molecular orbital energy-level diagrams, describe the bonding · of the homonuclear diatomic molecules of the first ten elements.

4.16 Draw molecular orbital energy-level diagrams for CO and NO. Use your diagrams to determine the bond order of CO, CO^+, CO^-, NO, NO^+, and NO^-. Which of these species are paramagnetic?

4.17 Draw a molecular orbital energy-level diagram and determine the bond order for each of the following. (a) H_2, (b) $H_2{}^+$, (c) HHe, (d) He_2, (e) $He_2{}^+$.

4.18 When sodium is reacted with oxygen, sodium peroxide (Na_2O_2) is obtained. The reaction of potassium and oxygen yields potassium superoxide (KO_2). (a) Give molecular orbital designations for the peroxide ion, O_2^{2-}, and the superoxide ion, $O_2{}^-$. (b) State the number of bonds in each ion, (c) Predict whether the ions would be paramagnetic or diamagnetic.

4.19 Use energy-level diagrams to explain the difference between conductors, insulators, and semiconductors.

4.20 Define the following: hybrid orbital, antibonding orbital, π orbital, conduction band, tetrahedral angle, forbidden energy zone, formal charge.

CHEMICAL EQUATIONS AND QUANTITATIVE RELATIONS

We have discussed the assignment of symbols to represent elements and formulas to represent compounds. This convenient shorthand can be extended into representations of chemical reactions, which are known as chemical equations. Symbols and their derivatives—formulas and equations—are not merely abbreviations; rather, the chemist greatly extends their utility through a method of interpretation which will be one of the principal topics of this chapter. **Stoichiometry** is that branch of chemistry that deals with the weight relations between elements and compounds as represented by formulas and equations.

5.1 The Gram Atom, Avogadro's Number

Ignoring the isotopic composition of the elements for the moment, let us consider that we have one atom of fluorine that weighs 19.0 u and one atom of hydrogen that weighs 1.0 u.[1]

[1] For most problem work, atomic weights will be rounded off to the first figure following the decimal point.

The fluorine atom is 19 times heavier than the hydrogen atom. If we take 10 atoms of each, the collection of fluorine atoms weighs 190.0 u, and the collection of hydrogen atoms weighs 10.0 u; the ratio of the sample weights is 19 to 1. If we take N atoms of fluorine and N atoms of hydrogen, the two samples will weigh $19.0 \cdot N$ u and $1.0 \cdot N$ u, respectively, and the total weights will still be in the ratio of 19 to 1. Provided that we take an equal number of atoms of each element, the ratio of the total weights of the two samples will be constant and the same as the ratio of the weights of the individual atoms.

We can turn this around to get a more valuable statement. If we have samples of fluorine and hydrogen in a weight ratio of 19.0 to 1.0 (the ratio of their atomic weights), there is an equal number of atoms in each sample. This is true regardless of what units of weight are used. Thus a sample of fluorine weighing 19.0 lb will contain the same number of atoms as a sample of hydrogen weighing 1.0 lb. A 19.0 g sample of fluorine will contain the same number of atoms as a 1.0 g sample of hydrogen.

The quantity of an element having a weight in grams numerically equal to that element's atomic weight is the **gram atomic weight** of that element; or more briefly, such a sample of an element is called a **gram atom**. A gram atom of any element contains the same number of atoms as a gram atom of any other element. The number of atoms in a gram atom is called **Avogadro's number** (N), named for Amadeo Avogadro who first interpreted the behavior of gases in terms of the number of reacting atoms (Section 6.7). The value of Avogadro's number has been determined by electrochemical and crystallographic techniques as 6.023×10^{23}.

The magnitude of Avogadro's number is difficult to imagine. If all the atoms in a gram atom were converted into 1 in.³ ice cubes, there would be enough ice cubes to cover the 50 states of the United States to a depth of about 650 miles! In the preceding discussion, we used the atomic weight of an element as the weight of a single atom of that element. The atomic weight of an element, however, usually is not the weight of any individual atom; rather, the atomic weight of an element is an average and takes into account the existence of isotopes (Section 2.9). It is easily seen that there is virtually a 100% chance of getting a collection of atoms of an element with an average weight equal to the atomic weight of that element since there is such a large number of atoms in even a very small sample. We do not work with solitary atoms; therefore, we may continue to think in terms of atoms with weights equal to atomic weights. The relations thus derived are perfectly valid for samples of a realistic size.

5.2 The Mole

The molecular weight of a compound can be obtained by adding the atomic weights of the constituent atoms. A **gram molecular weight** is that quantity of a compound that has a weight, in grams, numerically equal to the compound's molecular weight. The terms molecular weight and gram molecular weight are employed for substances formed from more than one atom whether or not they consist of molecules. Truly ionic species contain no molecules, and the terms formula weight and gram formula weight are sometimes applied to them. We shall not follow such a procedure. It is impossible to classify all substances as either ionic or molecular (Section 3.8); this questionable distinction is of less value than a uniform treatment.

A gram molecular weight of a compound contains Avogadro's number of the units described by the formula of the compound. The formula HF indicates a molecule formed from one atom of hydrogen and one atom of fluorine. Thus, a 1.0 u hydrogen atom combines with a 19.0 u fluorine atom to produce a molecule that weighs 20.0 u. If we take 6.023×10^{23} atoms of hydrogen (1.0 g—a gram atom), this sample will require 6.023×10^{23} atoms of fluorine (19.0 g—a gram atom) to produce 6.023×10^{23} molecules of hydrogen fluoride (20.0 g—a gram molecular weight).

That quantity of a substance that contains Avogadro's number of the units indicated by the formula of the substance is called a **mole**. The term can be applied to a wide variety of items—for example, atoms, molecules, ions, collections of ions, electrons, or chemical bonds. Hence, a mole of oxygen atoms contains 6.023×10^{23} oxygen atoms, weighs 16.0 g, and is a gram atom. A mole of molecular oxygen consists of 6.023×10^{23} O_2 molecules, weighs 32.0 g, and is a gram molecular weight. A mole of calcium chloride (111.1 g, a gram molecular weight) is 6.023×10^{23} $CaCl_2$ units, which all together contain 6.023×10^{23} Ca^{2+} ions (40.1 g) and $2(6.023 \times 10^{23})$ Cl^- ions (2×35.5 g). Thus a mole of calcium chloride consists of 1 mole of calcium ions and 2 moles of chloride ions.

5.3 Chemical Calculations

The units of measure must be included as an integral part of any meaningful measurement. It makes very little sense to say that an object weighs 9.0, for this could mean 9.0 lb, 9.0 g, 9.0 oz, or any of a host of other weights. Furthermore, any terms employed in a calculation should include proper labels, and these should undergo the same mathematical operations as the numbers. In any calculation, if the units appearing in both numerator and denominator are canceled, those remaining will appear as a part of the answer and will give the answer its true dimension. If the answer does not have the units sought, then a mistake has been made in the calculation setup.

The use of dimensions in solving problems is illustrated in the following examples:

▶ EXAMPLE 5.1 Given the conversion: $454 \text{ g} = 1.00 \text{ lb}$, how many pounds are there in 1.00 kg (1000 g)?

Solution   One would probably reason as follows:

$$454 \text{ g} = 1.00 \text{ lb}$$

Therefore,

$$1.00 \text{ g} = \left(\frac{1}{454}\right) \text{ lb}$$

and

$$1000 \text{ g} = 1000 \left(\frac{1}{454}\right) \text{ lb} = 2.20 \text{ lb}$$

The same line of reasoning can be followed using a properly labeled conversion factor. From

$$454 \text{ g} = 1.00 \text{ lb}$$

the factor

$$\left(\frac{1.00 \text{ lb}}{454 \text{ g}}\right)$$

can be derived. Since the numerator and denominator are equivalent, this factor is equal to unity. Our problem can be stated:

$$? \text{ lb} = 1000 \text{ g}$$

By the use of the factor, we can solve the problem:

$$? \text{ lb} = 1000 \text{ g} \left(\frac{1.00 \text{ lb}}{454 \text{ g}}\right) = 2.20 \text{ lb}$$

Notice that the gram labels have canceled leaving the answer in the desired units, pounds.[2]

We have noted that the factor is equal to unity. A second, perfectly valid factor (454 g/1.00 lb)—the reciprocal of that used in the preceding solution—can also be derived. The use of this factor leads to a rather peculiar result:

$$? \text{ lb} = 1000 \text{ g} \left(\frac{454 \text{ g}}{1.00 \text{ lb}}\right) = 454,000 \text{ g}^2/\text{lb}$$

The answer, although mathematically correct, is not particularly useful nor does it answer the question. Since this answer does not have the desired label, it is immediately obvious that a mistake has been made.

---

[2] Cancellation will not be indicated in future examples.

Several factors may be used, in series, in the setup for the solution of a problem.

▶ **EXAMPLE 5.2**   How many grams are there in 0.0150 ton?

Solution   We can state the problem:

$$? \text{ g} = 0.0150 \text{ ton}$$

To convert tons to pounds, we use 1.00 ton = 2000 lb and derive the factor (2000 lb/1.00 ton). The problem now reads:

$$? \text{ g} = 0.0150 \text{ ton} \left(\frac{2000 \text{ lb}}{1.00 \text{ ton}} \right)$$

The factor to convert pounds to grams is (454 g/1.00 lb), and thus

$$? \text{ g} = 0.0150 \text{ ton} \left(\frac{2000 \text{ lb}}{1.00 \text{ ton}} \right) \left(\frac{454 \text{ g}}{1.00 \text{ lb}} \right)$$
$$= 13,600 \text{ g}$$
$$= 1.36 \times 10^4 \text{ g}$$

5.4 The Law of Constant Composition

The law of constant composition (or the law of definite proportions) was first proposed by Joseph Proust in 1799 and states that a pure compound always consists of the same elements combined in the same proportions by weight. In the preceding sections the assumption is tacitly made that compounds are of definite composition, and, indeed, such is a logical consequence of modern atomic and molecular theory.

The composition of a given compound can be determined by chemical analysis, and the formula of the compound is usually derived from these analytical data (Section 5.5). However, the calculation of the percent composition from a formula is sometimes necessary and is readily accomplished.

▶ **EXAMPLE 5.3**   What is the percent composition by weight of Fe_2O_3 ?

Solution   One mole of Fe_2O_3 contains

$$\begin{array}{ll} 2 \text{ gram atoms of Fe} = (2 \times 55.8) \text{ g} = & 111.6 \text{ g} \\ 3 \text{ gram atoms of O} = (3 \times 16.0) \text{ g} = & \underline{48.0 \text{ g}} \\ & 159.6 \text{ g} \end{array}$$

The percent Fe is

$$\frac{111.6 \text{ g Fe}}{159.6 \text{ g Fe}_2\text{O}_3} \times 100\% = 69.9\% \text{ Fe in Fe}_2\text{O}_3$$

The percent O is

$$\frac{48.0 \text{ g O}}{159.6 \text{ g Fe}_2\text{O}_3} \times 100\% = 30.1\% \text{ O in Fe}_2\text{O}_3$$

(The same result, of course, could have been obtained by subtracting 69.9% from 100.0%.)

Other simple stoichiometric problems can be solved by use of the proportions represented by formulas.

▶ EXAMPLE 5.4   What weight of oxygen must be combined with 100 g of iron to produce Fe_2O_3 ?

Solution

$$1 \text{ gram atom Fe} = 55.8 \text{ g Fe}$$

Therefore, 100 g Fe is

$$100 \text{ g Fe} \left(\frac{1 \text{ gram atom Fe}}{55.8 \text{ g Fe}}\right) = 1.79 \text{ gram atom Fe}$$

from the formula Fe_2O_3,

$$2 \text{ gram atom Fe} = 3 \text{ gram atom O}$$

Hence,

$$1.79 \text{ gram atom Fe} \left(\frac{3 \text{ gram atom O}}{2 \text{ gram atom Fe}}\right) = 2.69 \text{ gram atom O}$$

Since 1 gram atom O = 16.0 g O,

$$2.69 \text{ gram atom O} \left(\frac{16.0 \text{ g O}}{1 \text{ gram atom O}}\right) = 43.0 \text{ g O}$$

The entire calculation can be performed in one step:

$$? \text{ g O} = 100 \text{ g Fe} \left(\frac{1 \text{ gram atom Fe}}{55.8 \text{ g Fe}}\right) \left(\frac{3 \text{ gram atom O}}{2 \text{ gram atom Fe}}\right) \left(\frac{16.0 \text{ g O}}{1 \text{ gram atom O}}\right)$$

$$= 43.0 \text{ g O}$$

A similar, but shorter, way to solve this problem is to note the ratio of weights of oxygen to iron in Fe_2O_3 as in the calculation of Example 5.3.

$$? \text{ g O} = 100 \text{ g Fe} \left(\frac{48.0 \text{ g O}}{111.6 \text{ g Fe}}\right) = 43.0 \text{ g O}$$

▶ **EXAMPLE 5.5** An iron ore contains 70.0% Fe_2O_3. What weight of iron, in pounds, can theoretically be obtained from 1.00 ton of the ore?

Solution A factor can be derived from the fact that the ore is 70.0% Fe_2O_3. Thus

$$70.0 \text{ lb } Fe_2O_3 = 100 \text{ lb ore}$$

From the formula Fe_2O_3,

$$2 \text{ lb atom Fe} = 1 \text{ lb mole } Fe_2O_3$$

or

$$111.6 \text{ lb Fe} = 159.6 \text{ lb } Fe_2O_3$$

The solution of the problem is

$$? \text{ lb Fe} = 2000 \text{ lb ore} \left(\frac{70.0 \text{ lb } Fe_2O_3}{100 \text{ lb ore}} \right) \left(\frac{111.6 \text{ lb Fe}}{159.6 \text{ lb } Fe_2O_3} \right)$$

$$= 979 \text{ lb Fe}$$

5.5 Determination of Formulas

The **simplest**, or **empirical**, formula is that derived from the simplest ratio of atoms in a compound. The **molecular formula** of a particular compound is based on the actual numbers of atoms that comprise a molecule of that compound. For some compounds, the molecular and the simplest formulas are identical, for example, H_2O, CO_2, NH_3, and SO_2. For many compounds, however, the molecular and simplest formulas are different. The molecular formulas N_2H_4, $B_3N_3H_6$, C_6H_6, and $C_6H_{12}O_6$ correspond to the simplest formulas NH_2, BNH_2, CH, and CH_2O. Notice that the atomic ratio for a simplest formula may be obtained by reducing the atomic ratio of the molecular formula to the lowest possible set of whole numbers.

Obviously, there is no molecular formula for an ionic compound since there are no molecules. Formulas of ionic compounds are, in reality, simplest formulas and state the simplest ratio of ions in an ionic crystal.

To determine the simplest formula of a compound, an experimentally determined analysis of the compound is needed.

▶ **EXAMPLE 5.6** A sample of a compound contains 6.30 g of carbon and 5.60 g of oxygen. What is the simplest formula of the compound?

Solution The analysis states a weight ratio; formulas are based on atomic ratios. Since a gram atom of any element contains 6.023×10^{23} atoms, conversion of the weight ratio to a gram atom ratio gives the atomic ratio desired.

$$? \text{ gram atom C} = 6.30 \text{ g C} \left(\frac{1 \text{ gram atom C}}{12.0 \text{ g C}} \right) = 0.525 \text{ gram atom C}$$

$$? \text{ gram atom O} = 5.60 \text{ g O} \left(\frac{1 \text{ gram atom O}}{16.0 \text{ g O}} \right) = 0.350 \text{ gram atom O}$$

Dividing both numbers by the smaller number gives the ratio (C to O) 1.5 to 1, or, in whole numbers, 3 to 2. Therefore the simplest formula is C_3O_2.

▶ **EXAMPLE 5.7** What is the simplest formula of an oxide of phosphorus containing 43.6% phosphorus and 56.4% oxygen?

Solution In 100 g of compound there would be 43.6 g P and 56.4 g O.

$$? \text{ gram atom P} = 43.6 \text{ g P} \left(\frac{1 \text{ gram atom P}}{31.0 \text{ g P}} \right) = 1.41 \text{ gram atom P}$$

$$? \text{ gram atom O} = 56.4 \text{ g O} \left(\frac{1 \text{ gram atom O}}{16.0 \text{ g O}} \right) = 3.53 \text{ gram atom O}$$

Dividing by the smaller number gives the atomic ratio 1.0 to 2.5. The simplest whole number ratio, therefore, is 2 to 5, and the formula is P_2O_5.

Additional information is necessary to assign a molecular formula to a compound. The number of atoms that constitute a molecule can be ascertained by diffraction techniques, or the molecular weight of the compound can be experimentally determined.

▶ **EXAMPLE 5.8** What is the molecular formula of the compound described in Example 5.7 if the compound has a molecular weight of 284?

Solution The weight obtained by adding the atomic weights indicated by the simplest formula, P_2O_5, is 142. Since the actual molecular weight is 284, there must be twice as many atoms present in a molecule as is indicated by the simplest formula. Therefore the molecular formula is P_4O_{10}.

5.6 Chemical Equations

Chemical equations are representations of reactions in terms of the symbols and formulas of the elements and compounds involved. The reactants are indicated on the left and the products on the right. An arrow is used instead of the customary equal sign of the algebraic equation; it may be considered as an abbreviation for the word "yields."

The **law of conservation of mass** states that there is no detectable change in mass during the course of an ordinary chemical reaction.[3] This law was first stated formally by Antoine Lavoisier in his work *Traite Elementaire de Chemie* (1789), although the quantitative methods of prior workers assumed such a principle. Insofar as chemical equations are concerned, the law of conservation of mass means that there must be as many atoms of each element, combined or uncombined, indicated on the left of an equation as there are on the right.

Chemical equations report the results of experimentation. One of the goals of chemistry is the discovery and development of principles that make it possible to predict the products of chemical reactions; careful attention will be given to any such generalizations. However, all too often the products of a particular set of reactants must be memorized, and any prediction is subject to modification if experiment dictates. What may appear reasonable on paper is not necessarily what occurs in the laboratory.

The first step, then, in writing a chemical equation is to ascertain the products of the reaction in question. Carbon disulfide, CS_2, reacts with chlorine, Cl_2, to produce carbon tetrachloride, CCl_4, and disulfur dichloride, S_2Cl_2. To represent this, we write

$$CS_2 + Cl_2 \longrightarrow CCl_4 + S_2Cl_2$$

This equation is not correct quantitatively and violates the law of conservation of mass. Although one carbon atom and two sulfur atoms are indicated on both the left side and the right side of the equation, only two chlorine atoms (one Cl_2 molecule) appear on the left to balance the six chlorine atoms shown on the right. The equation can be balanced[4] by indicating that three molecules of chlorine should be used for the reaction. Thus

$$CS_2 + 3Cl_2 \longrightarrow CCl_4 + S_2Cl_2$$

The simplest types of chemical equations are balanced by trial and error as the following examples will illustrate. When steam is passed over hot iron, hydrogen gas and an oxide of iron having the formula Fe_3O_4 are produced. Thus

$$Fe + H_2O \longrightarrow Fe_3O_4 + H_2$$

---

[3] This is demonstrably untrue for nuclear transformations. In these cases, Einstein's postulate of the equivalence of mass and energy (Section 2.9) satisfactorily accounts for the conversion of a small amount of mass into energy. Rigorously, a law of conservation of mass–energy should be stated. The energy changes observed in ordinary chemical reactions may be the result of concomitant mass changes, but such changes in mass are too small to be experimentally detected. Therefore, the law of conservation of mass, as stated, is valid for all reactions except those involving nuclear change (Chapter 21).

[4] Strictly speaking, the expression is not an "equation" until it is balanced.

It is tempting to substitute another oxide of iron, FeO, for the Fe_3O_4, since that would immediately produce a balanced equation. Such an equation, however, would be without value; experiment indicates that Fe_3O_4, not FeO, is a product of the reaction. Balancing an equation is never accomplished by altering the formulas of the products of the reaction. In the equation for the reaction of iron and steam, three atoms of Fe and four molecules of H_2O must be taken to give the iron and oxygen atoms required for the formation of Fe_3O_4.

$$3Fe + 4H_2O \longrightarrow Fe_3O_4 + H_2$$

The equation is now balanced except for hydrogen, and the hydrogen may be brought into balance as follows:

$$3Fe + 4H_2O \longrightarrow Fe_3O_4 + 4H_2$$

In much the same manner we can balance an equation for the complete combustion of ethane (C_2H_6) in oxygen. The products of this reaction are carbon dioxide and water.

$$C_2H_6 + O_2 \longrightarrow CO_2 + H_2O$$

To balance the two carbon atoms of C_2H_6, the production of two molecules of CO_2 must be indicated, and the six hydrogen atoms of C_2H_6 require that three molecules of H_2O be produced.

$$C_2H_6 + O_2 \longrightarrow 2CO_2 + 3H_2O$$

Only the oxygen remains to be balanced; there are seven atoms of oxygen on the right and only two on the left. In order to get seven atoms of oxygen on the left, we would have to take $3\frac{1}{2}$ (or $\frac{7}{2}$) molecules of O_2.

$$C_2H_6 + \tfrac{7}{2}O_2 \longrightarrow 2CO_2 + 3H_2O$$

Customarily, equations are written with whole number coefficients. By multiplying through by two, we get

$$2C_2H_6 + 7O_2 \longrightarrow 4CO_2 + 6H_2O$$

5.7 Problems Based on Chemical Equations

An equation can be interpreted in several different ways. Consider, for example,

$$2H_2 + O_2 \longrightarrow 2H_2O$$

On the simplest level, this equation shows that hydrogen reacts with oxygen to produce water. On the atomic-molecular level, it states that two molecules of hydrogen react with one molecule of oxygen to produce two molecules of water. In more practical, quantitative, terms, it can be read as a statement that 2 moles of hydrogen react with 1 mole of oxygen to produce 2 moles of water, or, in terms of actual weights, 4.0 g of hydrogen react with 32.0 g of oxygen to produce 36.0 g of water. Pound moles, ton moles, or any other type of moles can be used as long as the use of units is consistent. The weights derived from chemical equations can be interpreted as simple weight ratios; they can be used with any units of weight. Thus, the equation states that 4.0 lb of hydrogen react with 32.0 lb of oxygen to yield 36.0 lb of water.

Stoichiometric problems, then, are readily solved by reference to the equation describing the chemical change in question.

▶ **EXAMPLE 5.9** How many grams of HCl are required to produce 15.0 g of Cl_2, according to the following reaction?

$$MnO_2 + 4HCl \longrightarrow MnCl_2 + Cl_2 + 2H_2O$$

Solution The equation states that 4 moles of HCl (molecular weight, 36.5) produce 1 mole of Cl_2 (molecular weight, 71.0). Thus

$$? \, g \, HCl = 15.0 \, g \, Cl_2 \left(\frac{4(36.5) \, g \, HCl}{71.0 \, g \, Cl_2} \right) = 30.8 \, g \, HCl$$

Notice that this method of solution actually condenses three steps into one. We could proceed in the following way:

$$? \, mole \, Cl_2 = 15.0 \, g \, Cl_2 \left(\frac{1 \, mole \, Cl_2}{71.0 \, g \, Cl_2} \right) = 0.211 \, mole \, Cl_2$$

$$? \, mole \, HCl = 0.211 \, mole \, Cl_2 \left(\frac{4 \, mole \, HCl}{1 \, mole \, Cl_2} \right) = 0.844 \, mole \, HCl$$

$$? \, g \, HCl = 0.844 \, mole \, HCl \left(\frac{36.5 \, g \, HCl}{1 \, mole \, HCl} \right) = 30.8 \, g \, HCl$$

▶ **EXAMPLE 5.10** One of the reactions occurring in a blast furnace used to reduce iron ore is

$$Fe_2O_3 + 3CO \longrightarrow 2Fe + 3CO_2$$

What weight of CO, in pounds, is needed to reduce 100 lb of Fe_2O_3?

Solution From the equation, 1 mole of Fe_2O_3 (molecular weight, 159.6) reacts with 3 moles of CO (molecular weight, 28.0). Thus

$$? \, lb \, CO = 100 \, lb \, Fe_2O_3 \left(\frac{3(28.0) \, lb \, CO}{159.6 \, lb \, Fe_2O_3} \right) = 52.6 \, lb \, CO$$

Quantities of two or more reactants are given in some problems. In such cases, it would be unusual if the reactants were added in the exact stoichiometric ratio. The amount of one material usually limits the quantity of products obtainable, and the other materials are present in excess over what is required.

▶ EXAMPLE 5.11   What weight of P_2I_4 can be prepared from 5.00 g P_4O_6 and 8.00 g I_2 according to the following reaction?

$$5P_4O_6 + 8I_2 \longrightarrow 4P_2I_4 + 3P_4O_{10}$$

Solution   The first step is to determine which reactant limits the quantity of P_2I_4 produced. To do this, we first determine the number of moles of each reactant present before reaction.

$$? \text{ mole } P_4O_6 = 5.00 \text{ g } P_4O_6 \left(\frac{1 \text{ mole } P_4O_6}{220.0 \text{ g } P_4O_6}\right) = 0.0227 \text{ mole } P_4O_6$$

$$? \text{ mole } I_2 = 8.00 \text{ g } I_2 \left(\frac{1 \text{ mole } I_2}{253.8 \text{ g } I_2}\right) = 0.0315 \text{ mole } I_2$$

Hence the reactants are present in the ratio of 0.0227 mole P_4O_6 to 0.0315 mole I_2, or 1 mole P_4O_6 to 1.4 mole I_2.

The equation states that 5 moles of P_4O_6 require 8 moles of I_2—a ratio of 1 mole P_4O_6 to 1.6 mole I_2. Therefore, there is insufficient I_2 present to react with all of the P_4O_6, and the amount of P_2I_4 that may be obtained is limited by the quantity of I_2 used.

$$? \text{ g } P_2I_4 = 0.0315 \text{ mole } I_2 \left(\frac{4 \text{ mole } P_2I_4}{8 \text{ mole } I_2}\right) \left(\frac{569.6 \text{ g } P_2I_4}{1 \text{ mole } P_2I_4}\right) = 8.97 \text{ g } P_2I_4$$

▶ EXAMPLE 5.12   How many grams of P_4O_6 are left unreacted at the conclusion of the reaction described in Example 5.11?

Solution   We first find out how much P_4O_6 is required to react with the I_2 employed.

$$? \text{ g } P_4O_6 = 0.0315 \text{ mole } I_2 \left(\frac{5 \text{ mole } P_4O_6}{8 \text{ mole } I_2}\right) \left(\frac{220.0 \text{ g } P_4O_6}{1 \text{ mole } P_4O_6}\right) = 4.33 \text{ g } P_4O_6$$

Since we started with 5.00 g P_4O_6, $(5.00 - 4.33) = 0.67$ g P_4O_6 remains unreacted.

5.8   Heat of Reaction

The heat that is liberated or absorbed in the course of a chemical reaction is an important and integral part of the reaction. Reactions that evolve heat are called **exothermic** reactions; those that absorb heat are called **endothermic** reactions. Under constant pressure, a **heat of reaction** can be regarded as a manifestation of the difference in **heat content**, or **enthalpy**, H, between the products of a reaction and the reactants, and is therefore given the symbol ΔH. For an exothermic reaction, the products have a lower enthalpy than the reactants, and thus the heat of the reaction, ΔH, is negative; the system evolves heat. The products of endothermic reactions have a higher enthalpy than the reactants; ΔH is positive, and heat is absorbed.

The heat contents of chemical substances depend upon the temperature and pressure. By convention, ΔH values are generally reported at 25°C (298°K) and standard atmospheric pressure (Section 6.2). In other words, for exothermic reactions, all the heat above that necessary to maintain the temperature of the chemical substances at 25°C goes into what is called the heat of reaction. For endothermic reactions, the heat of reaction is the heat required to secure products at 25°C from reactants at the same temperature. If a ΔH value pertains to a reaction run at a temperature other than 298°K, the temperature is usually appended to the symbol as a subscript (e.g., ΔH_{300}).

Thermochemical data may be given by writing an equation for the reaction under consideration and listing beside it the ΔH value for the reaction *as it is written*. The value of ΔH used is that required when the equation is read in gram molar quantities. Contrary to usual practice, fractional coefficients may be used to balance the chemical equation; a fractional coefficient indicates a fraction of a mole of the substance in question. Thus,

$$H_2(g) + \tfrac{1}{2}O_2(g) \longrightarrow H_2O(l) \qquad \Delta H = -68.3 \text{ kcal}$$

The state of each substance used or produced by the reaction must be indicated in the equation; one of the designations: (g) for gas, (l) for liquid, (s) for solid, or (aq) for in water solution is placed after each formula. The need for this convention may be demonstrated by considering the reaction:

$$H_2(g) + \tfrac{1}{2}O_2(g) \longrightarrow H_2O(g) \qquad \Delta H = -57.8 \text{ kcal}$$

Notice that 10.5 kcal less heat is liberated by this reaction than by the first reaction because of the heat used in converting $H_2O(l)$ to $H_2O(g)$.

When an equation is reversed, the sign of ΔH is changed; a reaction that is endothermic in one direction is exothermic in the other.

$$H_2(g) + I_2(s) \longrightarrow 2HI(g) \qquad \Delta H = +12.40 \text{ kcal}$$
$$2HI(g) \longrightarrow H_2(g) + I_2(s) \qquad \Delta H = -12.40 \text{ kcal}$$

Problems involving heat effects are solved in much the same way that simple stoichiometric problems are solved.

▶ **EXAMPLE 5.13** How much heat is liberated by the preparation of 100 g of iron by the following reaction?

$$2Al(s) + Fe_2O_3(s) \longrightarrow 2Fe(s) + Al_2O_3(s) \qquad \Delta H = -202.6 \text{ kcal}$$

Solution The data show that 202.6 kcal is liberated when 2 gram atoms of Fe(s) are produced. Therefore,

$$? \text{ kcal} = 100 \text{ g Fe} \left(\frac{1 \text{ g atom Fe}}{55.8 \text{ g Fe}} \right) \left(\frac{202.6 \text{ kcal}}{2 \text{ g atom Fe}} \right) = 182 \text{ kcal}$$

A device called a **calorimeter** is used to measure heats of reaction. In the typical calorimeter, a reaction vessel is placed in the center of a larger, well-insulated vessel containing a weighed quantity of water. The reaction is run between known quantities of reactants, and the heat evolved increases the temperature of the water and the calorimeter. The rise in temperature is determined by a sensitive thermometer. The number of calories liberated by the reaction is the product of the rise in temperature and the total heat capacity of the calorimeter and its contents.

The **heat capacity** of a substance is the amount of heat required to increase the temperature of the substance by 1°C. Since the specific heat of water is known (ca. 1 cal/g°), the amount of heat absorbed by the water in the calorimeter is readily calculated. However, some heat is absorbed by the calorimeter as well, and therefore the heat capacity of the calorimeter must be determined by experiment. This value is usually expressed as a "water equivalent," which is the weight of water that the calorimeter equals in terms of heat capacity.

▶ **EXAMPLE 5.14** A bomb-type calorimeter is used to determine the heat of combustion of sulfur; 0.1000 gram atom of sulfur is put in the bomb which is then filled with oxygen under pressure. The bomb is placed in the calorimeter vessel which is filled with 900.0 g of water. The calorimeter has a water equivalent of 214.0 g. The reaction mixture is ignited electrically, and the reaction causes the temperature of the water to increase from 22.105°C to 28.474°C. From these data, calculate the heat of combustion of sulfur. Assume that the specific heat of water is 1.000 cal/g° over the temperature range of the experiment.

Solution The rise in temperature is

$$28.474°C - 22.105°C = 6.369°C$$

The number of calories evolved by the reaction is

$$? \text{ cal} = (900.0 + 214.0) \text{ g } H_2O \ (6.369°C) \left(\frac{1 \text{ cal}}{1 \text{ g } H_2O \ 1°C} \right) = 7095 \text{ cal}$$

This value is the amount of heat liberated by the combustion of 0.1 gram atom of sulfur. For 1 gram atom,

$$? \text{ kcal} = 1.000 \text{ gram atom S} \left(\frac{7095 \text{ cal}}{0.1000 \text{ gram atom S}} \right) \left(\frac{1 \text{ kcal}}{1000 \text{ cal}} \right) = 70.95 \text{ kcal}$$

$$\Delta H = -70.95 \text{ kcal/mole}$$

There is no significant increase, or decrease, in pressure accompanying this reaction. For reactions in which there is an attendant pressure change (e.g., those in which there are more moles of gaseous products than there are moles of gaseous reactants), the determination of the enthalpy of reaction requires that a correction be made to the value obtained by the method outlined above. Enthalpy is defined as the heat effect under constant pressure; the calorimeter bomb determines the heat effect under constant volume.

5.9 Law of Hess

The basis of many thermochemical calculations is the **law of constant heat summation** established experimentally by G. H. Hess in 1840. This **law of Hess** states that the change in enthalpy for any chemical reaction is constant, whether the reaction occurs in one step or in several steps. Thus, thermochemical data may be treated algebraically. As an example, consider the calculation of the ΔH of a reaction in which methane, CH_4, is prepared from the constituent elements carbon and hydrogen; it is impossible to measure this change in enthalpy directly.

The heats of combuston of $CH_4(g)$, $H_2(g)$, and C(graphite) are directly measurable. A standard **heat of combustion** of a substance is the ΔH at 25°C and 1 atm for the reaction in which the substance in its standard state is completely oxidized into products in their standard states. The **standard state** of a substance is that state in which the substance normally exists at 25°C and 1 atm, and the symbol $\Delta H°$ is used to indicate enthalpy changes of reactions involving only materials in their standard states. Heats of combustion are given in terms of kcal/mole of reactant, and the three equations are written accordingly.

$$CH_4(g) + 2O_2(g) \longrightarrow CO_2(g) + 2H_2O(l) \qquad \Delta H° = -212.8 \text{ kcal} \qquad (1)$$
$$H_2(g) + \tfrac{1}{2}O_2(g) \longrightarrow H_2O(l) \qquad \Delta H° = -68.3 \text{ kcal} \qquad (2)$$
$$C(\text{graphite}) + O_2(g) \longrightarrow CO_2(g) \qquad \Delta H° = -94.1 \text{ kcal} \qquad (3)$$

Notice that the standard state of water is $H_2O(l)$, not $H_2O(g)$.

The desired $\Delta H°$ can be obtained by reversing equation (1), multiplying equation (2) by 2, and then adding the equations. In the addition, terms common to both sides of the final equation are canceled. Whatever is done to a chemical equation must be reflected in the ΔH° of the reaction. Thus,

$2H_2O(l) + CO_2(g)$	$\longrightarrow$ $CH_4(g) + 2O_2(g)$	$\Delta H^\circ = +212.8$ kcal	(4)
$2H_2(g) + O_2(g)$	$\longrightarrow$ $2H_2O(l)$	$\Delta H^\circ = -136.6$ kcal	(5)
$C(graphite) + O_2(g)$	$\longrightarrow$ $CO_2(g)$	$\Delta H^\circ = -94.1$ kcal	(3)
$C(graphite) + 2H_2(g)$	$\longrightarrow$ $CH_4(g)$	$\Delta H^\circ = -17.9$ kcal	(6)

The standard **heat of formation** (ΔH_f°) of a compound is the change in enthalpy for the reaction in which 1 mole of a compound in its standard state is formed from its constituent *elements* in their standard states. Equation (2) of the preceding discussion is the equation for the heat of formation of $H_2O(l)$, equation (3) gives the heat of formation of $CO_2(g)$, and equation (6) represents the heat of formation of $CH_4(g)$. Notice that equation (2) may be described as giving the heat of combustion of $H_2(g)$ or the heat of formation of $H_2O(l)$. When a compound cannot be made directly from its constituent elements, the law of Hess may be used to calculate the ΔH_f° of the substance.

Heats of formation are convenient to use for thermochemical calculations. Thus the heat of hydrogenation of ethylene, $C_2H_4(g)$,

$$C_2H_4(g) + H_2(g) \longrightarrow C_2H_6(g)$$

can be calculated from the heat of formation of ethane, $C_2H_6(g)$, and the heat of formation of ethylene. The thermochemical equation for the formation of ethylene, which is endothermic, is written in reverse form and the sign of the heat effect adjusted accordingly.

$2C(graphite) + 3H_2(g)$	$\longrightarrow$ $C_2H_6(g)$	$\Delta H_f^\circ = -20.2$ kcal
$C_2H_4(g)$	$\longrightarrow$ $2C(graphite) + 2H_2(g)$	$\Delta H_f^\circ = -12.5$ kcal

Addition of these equations gives

$$C_2H_4(g) + H_2(g) \longrightarrow C_2H_6(g) \qquad \Delta H_f^\circ = -32.7 \text{ kcal}$$

Examination of the preceding problem, as well as similar problems, reveals that a heat of reaction can be calculated by subtracting the sum of the heats of formation of the reactants from the sum of the heats of formation of the products. Notice that compounds alone are assigned ΔH_f° values. To calculate the heat of reaction for

$$Fe_2O_3(s) + 3CO(g) \longrightarrow 2Fe(s) + 3CO_2(g)$$

the heats of formation of the compounds represented in the equation are treated in the following manner.

$$\Delta H^\circ = 3 \Delta H_f^\circ(CO_2) - [\Delta H_f^\circ(Fe_2O_3) + 3 \Delta H_f^\circ(CO)]$$
$$\Delta H^\circ = 3(-94.1) - [(-196.5) + 3(-26.4)]$$
$$\Delta H^\circ = -282.3 + 275.7 = -6.6 \text{ kcal}$$

5.10 Born-Haber Cycle

The law of Hess is the justification for a method of analysis of thermochemical processes developed independently by Max Born and Fritz Haber in 1919. A **Born-Haber cycle** shows how a reaction, or a physical process, may be considered to be made up of several component steps. By a relatively simple calculation, the heat effect of one of the steps, or the entire process, may be determined. In addition, Born-Haber cycles may be useful in analyzing reactions, or groups of reactions, in order to see how they are affected by variations in one of the individual steps.

The calculation of the lattice energy of the sodium chloride crystal will serve as an illustration of a Born-Haber cycle. The heat of formation of NaCl(s) is -98 kcal/mole.

$$Na(s) + \tfrac{1}{2}Cl_2(g) \longrightarrow NaCl(s) \qquad \Delta H_f^\circ = -98 \text{ kcal}$$

We can *imagine* 1 mole of NaCl(s) to be prepared by the following series of steps.

1. Crystalline sodium metal is sublimed into gaseous sodium atoms; 26 kcal of heat is *absorbed* per mole of Na.

$$Na(s) \longrightarrow Na(g) \qquad \Delta H_{subl.} = +26 \text{ kcal}$$

2. *One-half mole* of gaseous Cl_2 molecules is dissociated into 1 *mole* of gaseous Cl atoms; 58 kcal of heat is *absorbed* per *mole* of $Cl_2(g)$. This value is called the bond energy of the Cl—Cl bond, or the heat of dissociation of $Cl_2(g)$.

$$\tfrac{1}{2}Cl_2(g) \longrightarrow Cl(g) \qquad \tfrac{1}{2}\Delta H_{diss.} = \tfrac{1}{2}(+58 \text{ kcal}) = +29 \text{ kcal}$$

3. The gaseous sodium atoms are ionized into gaseous sodium ions; the amount of heat *required* is derived from the ionization potential of sodium.

$$Na(g) \longrightarrow Na^+(g) + e^- \qquad \Delta H_{i.p.} = +118 \text{ kcal}$$

4. Electrons are added to the gaseous chlorine atoms to produce gaseous chloride ions. The amount of heat *liberated* per mole of Cl(g) is the electron affinity of chlorine.

$$Cl(g) + e^- \longrightarrow Cl^-(g) \qquad \Delta H_{e.a.} = -87 \text{ kcal}$$

5. The gaseous ions condense into 1 mole of crystalline sodium chloride. This heat effect is defined as the lattice energy.

$$Na^+(g) + Cl^-(g) \longrightarrow NaCl(s) \qquad \Delta H_{l.e.} = ?$$

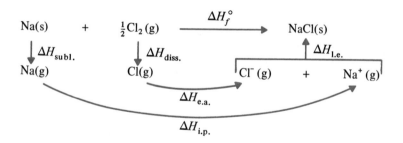

Figure 5.1 Born-Haber cycle for NaCl(s).

According to the law of Hess, the total ΔH for all of the steps of the hypothetical preparation should equal the value of ΔH_f° for NaCl(s), -98 kcal/mole. Therefore,

$$\Delta H_f^\circ = \Delta H_{subl.} + \tfrac{1}{2}\,\Delta H_{diss.} + \Delta H_{i.p.} + \Delta H_{e.a.} + \Delta H_{l.e.}$$
$$-98 \text{ kcal} = +26 \text{ kcal} + 29 \text{ kcal} + 118 \text{ kcal} - 87 \text{ kcal} + \Delta H_{l.e.}$$
$$-98 \text{ kcal} = +86 \text{ kcal} + \Delta H_{l.e.}$$
$$\Delta H_{l.e.} = -184 \text{ kcal}$$

The Born-Haber cycle for NaCl(s) is summarized in Figure 5.1.

For the NaCl Born-Haber cycle, all the thermal values except the lattice energy can be directly measured, and hence the cycle may be used, as we have used it, to calculate the lattice energy of NaCl. However, the direct determination of electron affinity is difficult; accurate values have been directly obtained for only a few elements. For a given cycle, therefore, both lattice energy and electron affinity may be unknown. In such a case, a lattice energy value calculated from crystal parameters may be employed (Section 7.13) and the cycle used to secure an electron affinity.

Other types of thermochemical cycles are of theoretical importance. By means of these cycles, energy effects of processes may be determined that cannot be evaluated by direct experimentation nor by theoretical computation.

SOME SUGGESTED READINGS

Butler, J. N., Dunell, B. A., and Harrison, L. G., *Problems for Introductory University Chemistry*, Reading, Mass., Addison-Wesley, 1967 (paper).

Kieffer, W. F., *The Mole Concept in Chemistry*, New York, Van Nostrand Reinhold, 1962 (paper).

Nash, L., *Stoichiometry*, Reading, Mass., Addison-Wesley, 1966 (paper).

PROBLEMS

The more difficult problems are starred.

5.1 What is the weight (in grams) of a single $^{12}_{6}C$ atom? How many atoms are present in a 1.00 g sample of $^{12}_{6}C$?

5.2 If one atom of element X weighs 1.42×10^{-22} g, what is the atomic weight of element X?

5.3 The element californium does not occur in nature. The first isotope of the element to be prepared, $^{245}_{98}Cf$, was identified using a total of approximately 5000 atoms. Assume that one atom of $^{245}_{98}Cf$ weighs 245 u, and calculate the number of grams that this quantity of the element would weigh.

5.4 How many moles and how many molecules are present in 10.0 g of each of the following? (a) H_2, (b) H_2O, (c) NH_3, (d) CH_4.

5.5 How many atoms are present in each of the samples described in Problem 5.4?

5.6 Arrange the following in order of increasing copper content: $CuSO_4$, $Cu_3(PO_4)_2$, Cu_2S, CuO, $CuCO_3$, $Cu(OH)_2$.

5.7 What percentage of wolframite, $FeWO_4$, is tungsten?

5.8 What percentage of the mineral ilmenite, $FeTiO_3$, is titanium? iron?

5.9 What weight of Bi is combined with 5.00 g of selenium in the compound bismuth(III) selenide, Bi_2Se_3?

5.10 How many pounds of zirconium is theoretically obtainable from 1.00 ton of zircon ore that is 73.0% $ZrSiO_4$?

5.11 How many pounds of beryllium is theoretically obtainable from 1.00 ton of beryl ore that is 65.0% $Be_3Al_2(SiO_3)_6$?

5.12 What weight of chromium(III) sulfide, Cr_2S_3, is theoretically obtainable from 10.0 g of Cr and 10.0 g of S?

5.13 (a) An oxide of arsenic consists of 75.7% As and 24.3% O. What is the empirical formula of the compound? (b) The molecular weight of the oxide is 395.6. What is the molecular formula of the compound?

5.14 What is the empirical formula of a compound that is 35.2% S, 43.9% O, and 20.9% F?

5.15 What is the empirical formula of a compound that is 30.5% Si, 60.8% N, and 8.68% H?

5.16 A sample of a compound that contains only C and H was burned in oxygen, and 16.5 g of CO_2 and 8.10 g of H_2O were obtained. (a) How many gram atoms of C and H were present in the sample? (b) What is the empirical formula of the compound? (c) What was the weight of the sample that was burned?

5.17 Upon heating 5.32 g of a hydrate of yttrium nitrate, $Y(NO_3)_3 \cdot xH_2O$, the water was driven off and 3.82 g of anhydrous $Y(NO_3)_3$ remained. (a) How many moles of $Y(NO_3)_3$ were present in the anhydrous sample? (b) How many moles of water were driven off? (c) What is the value of x in the formula $Y(NO_3)_3 \cdot xH_2O$?

5.18 Determine the molecular formulas of the compounds for which the following empirical formulas and molecular weights pertain. (a) S_3Cl, 263.6; (b) AsS, 428.0; (c) P_4S_7, 348.7; (d) CH_2O, 90.0; (e) BH_2, 76.8; (f) B_5H_4, 232.0; (g) SNF, 260.4; (h) TeF_5, 445.2.

5.19 Write balanced chemical equations for the following reactions.
(a) Hydrogen sulfide (g) and oxygen (g) yield water and sulfur dioxide (g).
(b) Sodium (s) and sulfur hexafluoride (g) yield sodium sulfide (s) and sodium fluoride (s).
(c) Titanium(IV) chloride (l) and water yield titanium(IV) oxide (s) and hydrogen chloride (g).
(d) Naphthalene, $C_{10}H_8$(s), and oxygen (g) yield carbon dioxide (g) and water.
(e) Niobium pentabromide (g) and niobium (s) yield niobium tetrabromide (g).
(f) Aluminum (s) and hydrochloric acid (aq) yield hydrogen (g) and aluminum chloride (aq).

5.20 The reaction of $Ca_3(PO_4)_2$ with H_2SO_4 can be made to yield H_3PO_4 and $CaSO_4$ or $Ca(H_2PO_4)_2$ and $CaSO_4$. (a) Write balanced chemical equations for both reactions. (b) What weight of H_2SO_4 is needed for each of the reactions using 1.00 kg of $Ca_3(PO_4)_2$ in each case?

5.21 By the addition of the proper amount of water to P_4O_{10}, any one of a number of phosphoric acids may be prepared. (a) Write the equation for the preparation of pyrophosphoric acid, $H_4P_2O_7$, from P_4O_{10} and H_2O. (b) Calculate the weight of water and the weight of P_4O_{10} needed to prepare 100 g of $H_4P_2O_7$.

5.22 Antimony(III) sulfide reacts with iron at high temperatures to give antimony and iron(II) sulfide. (a) Write the chemical equation for the reaction. (b) What weight of iron is required to react with 650 g of Sb_2S_3? What weight of Sb is produced by the reaction?

5.23 Iodine(V) oxide, I_2O_5, is used as a reagent for the determination of carbon monoxide. The reaction of CO and I_2O_5 produces I_2 and CO_2. (a) Write the chemical equation for the reaction. (b) What weight of CO would be indicated by the liberation of 12.5 g of I_2 from excess I_2O_5?

5.24 Sodium azide, NaN_3, may be produced by the reaction:

$$3NaNH_2 + NaNO_3 \longrightarrow NaN_3 + 3NaOH + NH_3$$

(a) What weight of NaN_3 should theoretically be obtained from the complete reaction of 5.00 g of $NaNH_2$? (b) If 1.81 g of NaN_3 is isolated from the reaction mixture, what percentage of the theoretical yield is obtained?

5.25 A metal oxide has the formula XO_3 and reacts with H_2 to give the free metal, X, and H_2O. (a) Write the equation for the reaction. (b) If 15.99 g of XO_3 yields 6.00 g of H_2O, what is the molecular weight of XO_3? (c) What is the atomic weight of X?

5.26 Phosphorus trifluoride may be prepared by the reaction:

$$2PCl_3 + 3PbF_2 \longrightarrow 2PF_3 + 3PbCl_2$$

What weight of PF_3 should be obtainable from a mixture of 75.0 g of PCl_3 and 100 g of PbF_2 ?

5.27 The reaction of TiO_2, carbon, and chlorine yields $TiCl_4$ and CO_2. (a) Write the balanced chemical equation for the reaction. (b) What weight of titanium(IV) chloride is theoretically obtainable from 10.00 g of TiO_2 and 9.00 g of Cl_2 if an excess of C is present?

*5.28 The reaction of P_4O_{10} and PCl_5 yields $POCl_3$ as the only product. (a) Write the chemical equation for the transformation. (b) What weight of $POCl_3$ is theoretically obtainable from a mixture of 2.00 g of P_4O_{10} and 7.00 g of ′ PCl_5 ?

*5.29 A mixture of sodium oxide, Na_2O, and barium oxide, BaO, that weighs 6.50 g is dissolved in water, and this solution is then treated with dilute sulfuric acid, H_2SO_4. Barium sulfate, $BaSO_4$, precipitates from the solution, but sodium sulfate, Na_2SO_4, is soluble and remains in solution. The $BaSO_4$ is collected by filtration and, when dried, is found to weigh 7.61 g. What percentage of the original sample of mixed oxides is BaO?

*5.30 A 4.70 g sample of a mixture of calcium carbonate, $CaCO_3$, and calcium sulfate, $CaSO_4$, is heated to decompose the carbonate.

$$CaCO_3(s) \longrightarrow CaO(s) + CO_2(g)$$

Calcium sulfate is not decomposed by heating. The final weight of the sample is 3.16 g. What percentage of the original mixture is $CaCO_3$?

*5.31 A 4.000 g sample of a mixture of $CaCO_3$ and $NaHCO_3$ is heated and the $CO_2(g)$ and $H_2O(g)$ driven off. The compounds decompose as follows:

$$CaCO_3(s) \longrightarrow CaO(s) + CO_2(g)$$
$$2NaHCO_3(s) \longrightarrow Na_2CO_3(s) + CO_2(g) + H_2O(g)$$

What percentage of the original mixture was $CaCO_3$ if the sample weighs 2.325 g after ignition?

5.32 A 2.50 g sample of sucrose, $C_{12}H_{22}O_{11}$, was burned in excess oxygen in a calorimeter which contained 1.95 kg of water. The temperature of the calorimeter and contents increased from 18.22°C to 22.73°C. The calorimeter had a water equivalent of 240 g. Determine the heat of combustion of sucrose in kcal/mole.

$$C_{12}H_{22}O_{11}(s) + 12O_2(g) \longrightarrow 12CO_2(g) + 11H_2O(l)$$

5.33 The heat of combustion of glutaric acid, $H_2C_5H_6O_4(s)$, is 514.9 kcal/mole. The heat from the combustion of 1.50 g of glutaric acid is evolved in a calorimeter with a water equivalent of 530 g and containing 1250 g of water. What is the final temperature of the calorimeter and contents if the original temperature was 20.00°C?

5.34 (a) The reaction of $MnO_2(s)$ and $Al(s)$ yields $Mn(s)$ and $Al_2O_3(s)$. Write the balanced chemical equation for this reaction. The standard heat of formation of $MnO_2(s)$ is −124.5 kcal/mole and of $Al_2O_3(s)$ is −399.1

kcal/mole. What is the value of $\Delta H°$ for the reaction? (b) What quantity of heat is liberated, or absorbed, when 1.00 kg of Mn is prepared?

5.35 (a) Calculate the value of $\Delta H°$ for the following reaction:

$$Cu_2S(s) + 2Cu_2O(s) \longrightarrow SO_2(g) + 6Cu(s)$$

The values of $\Delta H_f°$ are: $Cu_2S(s)$, -19.0 kcal/mole; $Cu_2O(s)$, -39.8 kcal/mole; $SO_2(g)$, -71.0 kcal/mole. (b) What quantity of heat is liberated, or absorbed, in a reaction in which 50.0 g of Cu is prepared?

5.36 For the reaction:

$$2NiS(s) + 3O_2(g) \longrightarrow 2NiO(s) + 2SO_2(g)$$

the value of $\Delta H°$ is -223.8 kcal. The standard heat of formation of $SO_2(g)$ is -71.0 kcal/mole and of $NiS(s)$ is -17.5 kcal/mole. What is the standard heat of formation of $NiO(s)$?

5.37 Calculate $\Delta H°$ for the reaction:

$$C(graphite) + H_2O(g) \longrightarrow CO(g) + H_2(g)$$

The heat of formation of $H_2O(g)$ is -57.8 kcal/mole. The heat of *combustion* of $CO(g)$ to $CO_2(g)$ is -67.6 kcal/mole, and the heat of formation of $CO_2(g)$ is -94.1 kcal/mole.

5.38 Determine the heat of formation of $COCl_2(g)$, in kcal/mole, and write the chemical equation corresponding to the value. Given:

$$CO(g) + Cl_2(g) \longrightarrow COCl_2(g) \qquad \Delta H = -26.88 \text{ kcal}$$

The heat of combustion of $CO(g)$ is -67.63 kcal/mole, and the heat of combustion of $C(s)$ is -94.05 kcal/mole.

5.39 Given the following heats of reaction:

$$4NH_3(g) + 5O_2(g) \longrightarrow 4NO(g) + 6H_2O(l) \qquad \Delta H = -279.4 \text{ kcal}$$
$$4NH_3(g) + 3O_2(g) \longrightarrow 2N_2(g) + 6H_2O(l) \qquad \Delta H = -365.8 \text{ kcal}$$

Calculate the heat of formation of $NO(g)$.

*5.40 (a) Calculate the heat of formation of hydrazine, $N_2H_4(l)$, from the following data:

$$2NH_3(g) + 3N_2O(g) \longrightarrow 4N_2(g) + 3H_2O(l) \qquad \Delta H = -241.4 \text{ kcal}$$
$$N_2O(g) + 3H_2(g) \longrightarrow N_2H_4(l) + H_2O(l) \qquad \Delta H = -75.7 \text{ kcal}$$
$$2NH_3(g) + \tfrac{1}{2}O_2(g) \longrightarrow N_2H_4(l) + H_2O(l) \qquad \Delta H = -34.2 \text{ kcal}$$
$$H_2(g) + \tfrac{1}{2}O_2(g) \longrightarrow H_2O(l) \qquad \Delta H = -68.3 \text{ kcal}$$

(b) Write the chemical equation for the combustion of $N_2H_4(l)$ to $N_2(g)$ and $H_2O(l)$. What is the heat of combustion of $N_2H_4(l)$?

5.41 Use the following data to calculate the lattice energy of NaI(s). The heat of formation of NaI(s) is -68.8 kcal/mole. For Na: the heat of sublimation is $+26.0$ kcal/mole and the first ionization energy is $+118.1$ kcal/mole. For I_2 : the first electron affinity is -73.8 kcal/mole of I atoms and the value of ΔH for the reaction $I_2(s) \rightarrow 2I(g)$ is $+51.0$ kcal.

5.42 Use the following data to calculate the first electron affinity of fluorine. For KF: ΔH_f° is -134.5 kcal/mole and the lattice energy is -190.4 kcal/mole. For K: $\Delta H_{subl.}$ is $+21.5$ kcal/mole and $\Delta H_{i.p.}$ is $+99.2$ kcal/mole. For F_2: $\Delta H_{diss.}$ is $+37.8$ kcal/mole.

5.43 Use the following data to calculate the lattice energy of MgO(s). The heat of formation of MgO(s) is -143.8 kcal/mole. For Mg: $\Delta H_{subl.}$ is $+35.9$ kcal/mole, the first ionization energy is $+175.5$ kcal/mole, and the second ionization energy is $+345.0$ kcal/mole. For O_2 : the heat of dissociation is $+118.3$ kcal/mole, the first electron affinity is -34.6 kcal/mole of O atoms, and the second electron affinity is $+202.9$ kcal/mole of O atoms. Magnesium oxide melts at 2800°C and NaCl melts at 801°C. Explain the difference in melting point.

5.44 For Ca, $\Delta H_{subl.}$ is $+46$ kcal/mole, and the first and second ionization energies are $+140$ kcal/mole and $+273$ kcal/mole, respectively. For Cl_2, $\Delta H_{diss.}$ is $+58$ kcal/mole and $\Delta H_{e.a.}$ is -87 kcal/mole of Cl atoms. The ΔH_f° of $CaCl_2(s)$ is -190 kcal/mole. Calculate the lattice energy of $CaCl_2(s)$. If Ca^+ and Cl^- formed a crystal lattice similar to that of NaCl, the lattice energy of the hypothetical CaCl crystal would be approximately -180 kcal/mole. Use this value to calculate an approximate ΔH_f° of CaCl. Compare the heats of formation and lattice energies of $CaCl_2$ and the hypothetical CaCl.

GASES

Under suitable conditions, most substances can be made to exist in any of the three states of matter—solid, liquid, or gaseous. However, only ten nonmetallic elements (F_2, Cl_2, O_2, N_2, and the noble gases) and certain covalent compounds (generally of low molecular weight) are gases under ordinary conditions of temperature and pressure.

6.1 The Gaseous State

A study of the properties of gases leads to the conclusion that gases consist of widely separated molecules in rapid motion. The most familiar gas, air, is actually a mixture of gases. Experiments show that any two (or more) gases can be used in any proportion to prepare a perfectly homogeneous mixture; no such generalization can be made for liquids. This fact can be explained by the assumption that the molecules of any gas are separated by comparatively large distances, making it possible for one gas to accommodate molecules of other gases. This molecular model can also be used to explain the compressibility of gases; compression is the forcing of gas molecules closer together.

A gas diffuses throughout any container into which it is introduced. Odorous gases released in a room can soon be detected in all parts of the room. The premise that gas molecules are in constant, rapid motion accounts for the diffusion of gases. Furthermore, gas molecules in their random motion strike the walls of the container, and these myriad impacts explain the fact that gases exert pressure.

6.2 Pressure

Pressure is defined as force per unit area. Thus the pressure of a gas is the force the gas exerts on the walls of the container divided by the surface area of the container. Pressure is frequently expressed in dynes per square centimeter or pounds per square inch.

The atmosphere exerts a pressure on the surface of the earth. The instrument used to measure atmospheric pressure is called a **barometer** and was first devised by Evangelista Torricelli, a pupil of Galileo. A long tube, sealed at one end, is filled with mercury and inverted in an open container of mercury (Figure 6.1). If the tube is sufficiently long, the mercury falls in the tube. However, it will not completely run out; the pressure of the atmosphere on the surface of the mercury in the dish supports the column. Practically no pressure is exerted on the upper surface of the mercury in the column. Since mercury is not very volatile at room temperature, the amount of mercury vapor in the space above the liquid mercury in the tube is small; air has been

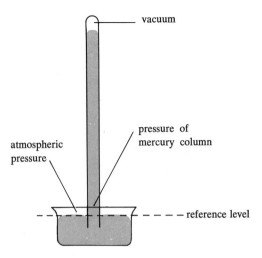

Figure 6.1 Barometer.

excluded. A vacuum obtained in this manner is called a Torricellian vacuum. The pressure inside the tube and above the reference level indicated in Figure 6.1 is due only to the weight of the mercury column; this pressure is equal to the atmospheric pressure outside the tube and above the reference level.

The height of mercury in the tube serves as a measure of the atmospheric pressure, and pressure is frequently recorded in centimeters, or millimeters, of mercury. Remember that pressure is force *per unit area*. Whether the tube has a relatively large or small cross-sectional area, a given atmospheric pressure will support the mercury in a tube to the same height.

The pressure of the atmosphere changes from day to day at a given altitude and also changes with altitude itself. A **standard atmosphere** (atm) is defined as the pressure that will support a column of mercury to a height of 76.0 cm at 0°C and sea level. It is necessary to specify the temperature and altitude, since the density of mercury varies with temperature and the force of gravity varies with altitude; both these factors affect the height of the mercury in the column. A pressure of 1 mm of mercury at 0°C and sea level is referred to as 1 **torr** (named for Torricelli).

Centimeters, or millimeters, of mercury can readily be converted into other pressure units. For example, a column of mercury 76.00 cm high and 1.000 cm^2 in cross section has a volume of 76.00 cm^3. This volume of mercury weighs 1034 g, since mercury has a density of 13.60 g/cm^3 (at 0°C). At sea level the acceleration of gravity is 980.7 cm/sec^2, and, therefore, the force ($f = ma$) at the base of the mercury column is

$$1034 \text{ g} \times 980.7 \text{ cm/sec}^2 = 1.013 \times 10^6 \text{ g cm/sec}^2$$
$$= 1.013 \times 10^6 \text{ dynes}$$

Since this force is acting on 1 cm^2, the pressure indicated is 1.013×10^6 dynes/cm^2. In the English system, 1 atm is 14.7 lb/in.^{2}

A **manometer**, a device used to measure the pressure of a sample of gas (Figure 6.2), is patterned after the barometer. In Figure 6.2, the right arm of the manometer is open to the atmosphere; thus atmospheric pressure is exerted on the mercury in this arm. The left arm is connected to a container of gas, allowing the gas sample to exert pressure on the mercury. Since the mercury level is lower in the left arm than that in the right, the illustration indicates a situation where the gas pressure is greater than atmospheric pressure. If the gas sample were under a pressure equal to atmospheric pressure, the mercury would stand at the same level in both sides of the U tube. In the experiment illustrated in Figure 6.2, the difference in height between the two mercury levels (in mm) must be added to the atmospheric pressure (in torr) to obtain the pressure of the gas. If the pressure of the gas were less than atmospheric, the mercury in the left arm would stand higher than that in the right arm, and the difference in height would have to be subtracted from atmospheric pressure.

* difference in height of mercury levels

Figure 6.2 A type of manometer.

6.3 Boyle's Law

The quantitative relationship between the volume and pressure of a sample of gas was first summarized by Robert Boyle in 1662. **Boyle's law** states: at constant temperature, the volume of a sample of gas varies inversely with the pressure under which it is measured. If the pressure is doubled, the volume is reduced to half its former value; if the pressure is cut in half, the volume is doubled. Mathematically,

$$V \propto \frac{1}{P}$$

$$V = \frac{k}{P} \quad \text{or} \quad PV = k$$

The value of the constant depends upon the size of the sample and the temperature. The pressure–volume curve for this equation (Figure 6.3) is the first quadrant branch of a hyperbola (negative values for volumes and pressures do not exist). A plot of V versus $1/P$ is a straight line through the origin with a slope equal to the constant.

▶ EXAMPLE 6.1 A sample of a gas occupies 360 ml under a pressure of 625 torr. At constant temperature, what volume will the sample occupy under a pressure of 750 torr?

Solution Gas law problems of this type can be solved through the use of correction factors. For this problem, a factor must be used to correct the volume

Figure 6.3 Pressure–volume curve for an ideal gas (Boyle's law).

for the change in pressure. Two pressure-correction factors can be derived from the data given: (625 torr/750 torr) and (750 torr/625 torr). Which one should be used?

Since the pressure *increases* from 625 torr to 750 torr, the volume must *decrease* a proportional amount, and the pressures must appear in a factor of less than unity. Therefore,

$$? \, ml = 360 \, ml \left(\frac{625 \, torr}{750 \, torr}\right) = 300 \, ml$$

▶ EXAMPLE 6.2   At 0°C and 5.00 atm pressure, a given sample of a gas occupies 100 liters. If the gas is compressed to 30.0 liters at 0°C, what will be the final pressure?

Solution   The volume decreases from 100 to 30.0 liters. Therefore the pressure increases, and the factor must be greater than unity.

$$? \, atm = 5.00 \, atm \left(\frac{100 \, liters}{30.0 \, liters}\right) = 16.7 \, atm$$

6.4   Charles' Law

Boyle's law describes the behavior of gas under conditions of constant temperature. Studies to determine the effect of temperature change on the volume and pressure of a gas sample were first undertaken by Jacques Charles (1787), and this work was considerably extended by Joseph Gay-Lussac (1802).

Experimental data show that for each Celsius degree rise in temperature, the volume of a gas expands $\frac{1}{273}$ of its value at 0°C, if the pressure is held constant. When a 273 ml sample of gas at 0°C is heated to 1°C, the volume of the sample increases by $\frac{1}{273}$ of 273 ml, or 1 ml. At 10°C, the volume of the sample would be 283 ml; at −1°C, the sample would occupy 272 ml.

Let V equal the volume of a gas sample at temperature t (in °C) and V_0 equal the volume of the sample at 0°C. Then

$$V = V_0 + \frac{1}{273} t V_0$$

or

$$V = V_0 \left(1 + \frac{t}{273}\right) = V_0 \left(\frac{273 + t}{273}\right)$$

It is convenient to use the absolute temperature scale, on which temperatures are measured in degrees Kelvin (°K). A reading on this scale is obtained by adding 273 to the Celsius value; temperatures on the absolute scale may be denoted by T. Thus:

$$T = t + 273$$

Substituting T for $(273 + t)$ in the equation for the dependence of volume on temperature, we get

$$V = V_0 \left(\frac{T}{273}\right) = \left(\frac{V_0}{273}\right) T$$

Since the volume of a given gas sample at 0°C is a constant under contant pressure, this relation can be expressed as

$$V = kT$$

The numerical value of k depends upon the size of the gas sample and the pressure.

Charles' law states, therefore, that the volume of a sample of gas varies *directly* with the *absolute* temperature. Volume is not directly proportional to the *Celsius* temperature. Thus doubling the absolute temperature doubles the volume of the gas; doubling the Celsius temperature does not.

The absolute temperature scale was first proposed by William Thomson, Lord Kelvin (1848), and the unit is named in his honor. Any absolute measurement scale must be based on a zero point that represents the complete absence of the property being measured; on such scales, negative values are impossible. Thus, 0 cm represents the complete absence of length, and one can say that 10 cm is twice 5 cm in length because these are absolute measurements. The Celsius temperature scale is not an absolute one; 0°C is the

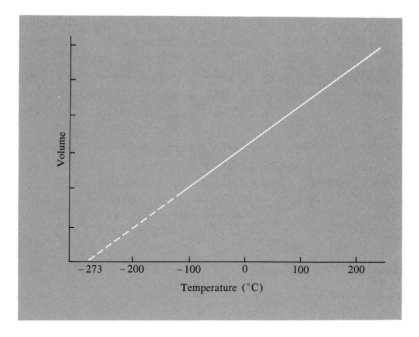

Figure 6.4 Temperature–volume curve for an ideal gas (Charles' law).

freezing point of water, not the lowest possible temperature. Because of this, negative Celsius temperatures are possible. On the other hand, the Kelvin scale is absolute; $0°K$ is the lowest possible temperature, and negative Kelvin temperatures are as impossible as negative volumes or negative lengths.

If volume versus temperature is plotted for a sample of gas, a straight line results such as illustrated in Figure 6.4. Since volume is directly proportional to absolute temperature, the volume of the gas *theoretically* should be zero at absolute zero (Section 6.13). Upon cooling, gases liquefy and then solidify before temperatures this low are reached; no substance exists as a gas at a temperature near absolute zero. However, the straight-line curves can be extrapolated to zero volume. The temperature that corresponds to zero volume is $-273.15°C$; many lines of experimental evidence have confirmed this as absolute zero. The Kelvin degree is the same size as the Celsius degree; however, for the Kelvin scale, the zero point is moved to $-273.15°C$. Conversion to the Kelvin temperature scale can be accomplished, therefore, by adding 273.15 algebraically to the Celsius reading. For most problem work, this value can be rounded off to 273 without entailing significant error. The Kelvin, Celsius, and Fahrenheit temperature scales are compared in Figure 6.5.

In like manner, the relationship between pressure and temperature can be derived; a temperature-pressure curve is similar to the temperature-volume curve illustrated in Figure 6.4. The pressure of a gas varies directly with boiling point of water   373.15°K   100°C   212°F

freezing point of water   273.15°K   0°C   32°F

absolute zero   0°K   −273.15°C   −459.67°F

Kelvin   Celsius   Fahrenheit

Figure 6.5 Comparison of temperature scales.

absolute temperature, volume constant:

$$P = kT$$

It is convenient to define standard reference conditions for work with gases. By convention, **standard temperature and pressure (STP)** are 0°C (273°K) and 760 torr (1 atm) pressure; values for properites of gases are recorded at STP unless otherwise specified.

▶ EXAMPLE 6.3   A sample of gas has a volume of 79.5 ml at 45°C. What volume will the sample occupy at 0°C, pressure constant?

Solution   Since the temperature decreases from 318° to 273°K, the volume must decrease. A factor of less than unity must be employed.

$$? \text{ ml} = 79.5 \text{ ml} \left(\frac{273°\text{K}}{318°\text{K}}\right) = 68.3 \text{ ml}$$

▶ EXAMPLE 6.4   A 10.0 liter container is filled with a gas to a pressure of 2.00 atm at 0°C. At what temperature will the pressure inside the container be 2.50 atm?

Solution   Since the pressure increases, the temperature must increase. Thus

$$? °\text{K} = 273°\text{K} \left(\frac{2.50 \text{ atm}}{2.00 \text{ atm}}\right) = 341°\text{K (or } 68°\text{C)}$$

6.5 Ideal Gas Law

By combining Boyle's law and Charles' law, it is possible to solve problems in which all three variables—volume, temperature, and pressure—change.

▶ **EXAMPLE 6.5** A gas measures 462 ml at 35°C and 800 torr. Calculate the volume of the gas at STP.

Solution A combined gas law problem is best solved by considering each of the changes in conditions independently. First, the temperature decrease from 308° to 273°K would call for the volume to decrease by a factor of 273/308. Second, the pressure decreases from 800 to 760 torr. Since volume is inversely proportional to pressure, such a change in pressure would increase the volume by a factor of 800/760.

$$? \text{ ml} = 462 \text{ ml} \left(\frac{273°\text{K}}{308°\text{K}}\right) \left(\frac{800 \text{ torr}}{760 \text{ torr}}\right) = 431 \text{ ml}$$

We can derive a mathematical statement for the combined gas law. Since $V \propto 1/P$ and $V \propto T$,

$$V \propto \frac{T}{P}$$

This proportionality can be changed to an equality by the use of a constant:

$$V = k\frac{T}{P}$$

or

$$PV = kT$$

The value of k in this equation depends upon the size of the gas sample. When 1 mole of gas is used, the constant is given the designation R and has the numerical value 0.08206 liter atm/°K mole provided the volume is expressed in liters, the pressure in atmospheres, and the temperature in degrees Kelvin. Other values for R are used when other dimensions for these variables are employed. The general form of the equation is

$$PV = nRT$$

where n is the number of moles of the gas under investigation. A gas that follows this equation exactly is called an **ideal gas**; the equation is known as the equation of state for an ideal gas.

▶ **EXAMPLE 6.6**   What volume will 10.0 g of carbon monoxide occupy at STP? Assume that CO is an ideal gas.

Solution   The molecular weight of CO is 28.0, and 10.0 g constitutes 10.0/28.0, or 0.357, mole. The problem is solved by substituting in the equation of state.

$$PV = nRT$$

$$(1 \text{ atm}) \ V = (0.357 \text{ mole})(0.0821 \text{ liter atm/}^\circ\text{K mole})(273^\circ\text{K})$$

$$V = 8.00 \text{ liters}$$

▶ **EXAMPLE 6.7**   A 500 ml sample of a gas weighs 0.326 g at 100°C and 380 torr. What is the molecular weight of the gas?

Solution   The number of moles of gas in the sample, n, is equal to the weight of the sample, g, divided by the molecular weight of the gas, M. Therefore,

$$PV = \left(\frac{g}{M}\right) RT$$

The units used for P, V, and T must correspond to those in which R is expressed. The pressure is 380 torr/760 torr, or 0.500 atm; the volume is 0.500 liter; the temperature is 373°K.

$$(0.500 \text{ atm})(0.500 \text{ liter}) = \left(\frac{0.326 \text{ g}}{M}\right)(0.0821 \text{ liter atm/}^\circ\text{K mole})(373^\circ\text{K})$$

$$M = 39.9 \text{ g/mole}$$

6.6   Kinetic Theory

So far we have examined the laws that correlate observed facts concerning the behavior of gases. The theory that offers a model to explain these laws and observations is known as the **kinetic theory** of gases. This theory was first proposed in substantially the following form by August Krönig (1856) and Rudolf Clausius (1857). However, the theory had its roots in the previous work of many others, notably Daniel Bernoulli (1738) and James Joule (1845–1851); also, later workers, in particular James Clerk-Maxwell (1860) and Ludwig Boltzmann (1871), did much to extend the concept.

The kinetic theory postulates the following for an ideal gas:

1. Gases consist of molecules widely separated in space. The total volume of the molecules is negligible in comparison with the volume of the gas as a whole. Certain gases, for example the noble gases, are monatomic. In discussions of the kinetic theory of gases, the word molecule is used to designate the smallest particle of any gas.

2. Gas molecules are in constant, rapid, straight-line motion colliding with each other and their container. These collisions are perfectly elastic; energy may be transferred from molecule to molecule, but there is no net decrease in kinetic energy.

3. Gas molecules translate heat energy into kinetic energy. At a given instant, different molecules have different kinetic energies; however, the average kinetic energy of the molecules depends upon the temperature and increases as temperature increases. The molecules of any gas have the same average kinetic energy at a given temperature.

4. No attractive forces exist between the molecules of an ideal gas.

According to the kinetic theory, the gas pressure is caused by molecular collisions with the walls of the container. Therefore, the larger the number of molecules per unit volume—the molecular concentration—the larger is the number of collisions and the higher is the pressure. Reducing the volume of a gas crowds more molecules into a given space, resulting in larger molecular concentration and a porportionally higher pressure. Hence, the kinetic theory accounts for Boyle's law.

The average kinetic energy of the molecules of a gas is proportional to the absolute temperature. At absolute zero, the molecules are at rest, and since the molecular volume of an ideal gas is negligible, the volume of an ideal gas at absolute zero is theoretically zero. As the absolute temperature is increased, the molecules move at increasing speeds. Hence, as the temperature increases, collisions of gas molecules with the walls of the container are more vigorous and more frequent, which accounts for the increased pressures observed when gases are heated. If the pressure is not permitted to change when a gas is heated, then its volume must increase so that the number of collisions will be reduced to compensate for the increased intensity of the collisions.

The equation of state for an ideal gas may be derived as follows. Consider a sample of gas containing N molecules having a mass of m each. If this sample is enclosed in a cube l cm on a side, the total volume of the gas is l^3 cm^3. Although the molecules are moving in every possible direction, the derivation is simplified if we assume that one-third of the molecules ($\frac{1}{3} N$) are moving in the direction of the x axis, one-third in the y direction, and one-third in the z direction. For a very large number of molecules, this is a valid simplification since the velocity of each molecule may be divided into an x component, a y component, and a z component.

The pressure of the gas on any wall (surface area l^2 cm^2) is due to the impacts of the molecules on that wall. The force of each impact can be calculated from the change in momentum per unit time. Consider the shaded wall in Figure 6.6 taking only those molecules moving in the direction of the x axis into account. A molecule moving in this direction will strike this wall every $2 \times l$ cm of its path, since after an impact it must go to the opposite wall (a

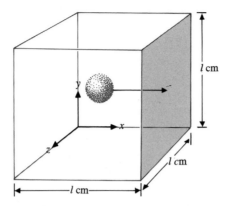

Figure 6.6 Derivation of the ideal gas laws.

distance of l cm) and return (a distance of l cm) before the next impact. If the molecule is moving with a velocity of u cm/sec, in 1 sec it will have gone u cm and have made $u/2l$ collisions with the wall under consideration.

Momentum is mass times velocity. Before an impact, the momentum of the molecule is mu; after an impact, the momentum is $-mu$ (the sign is changed because the direction is changed—velocity takes into account speed and direction). Therefore the *change* in momentum equals $2mu$.

In 1 sec, a molecule makes $u/2l$ collisions, and the change in momentum per collision is $2mu$. Therefore, in 1 sec, the total change in momentum per molecule is

$$\left(\frac{u}{2l}\right) 2mu = \frac{mu^2}{l}$$

The total change in momentum (force) for all of the molecules striking the wall in 1 sec is

$$\frac{N}{3} \times \frac{mu^2}{l}$$

In this expression, u^2 is the average of the squares of all of the molecular velocities.

Pressure is force per unit area, and the area of the wall is l^2 cm². Therefore the pressure on the wall under consideration is

$$P = \frac{Nmu^2}{3l} \times \frac{1}{l^2} = \frac{Nmu^2}{3l^3}$$

Since the volume of the cube is l^3cm³, $V = l^3$, and

$$P = \frac{Nmu^2}{3V} \quad \text{or} \quad PV = \tfrac{1}{3}Nmu^2$$

This equation can be written

$$PV = (\tfrac{2}{3}N)(\tfrac{1}{2}mu^2)$$

The kinetic energy of any body is one-half the product of its mass times the square of its speed. The average molecular kinetic energy, therefore, is $\tfrac{1}{2}mu^2$. By substitution,

$$PV = \tfrac{2}{3}N(KE)$$

The average molecular kinetic energy, KE, is directly proportional to the absolute temperature, T, and the number of molecules, N, is proportional to the number of moles, n. Substitution of these terms requires the inclusion of a constant since these are proportionalities and not equalities. The required constant can be combined with the $\tfrac{2}{3}$ (also a constant), and thus

$$PV = nRT$$

6.7 Avogadro's Principle

According to the kinetic theory, the molecules of two different gases at the same temperature have the same average kinetic energy. If we allow the subscript to relate the measured property to gas A and gas B,

$$KE_A = KE_B$$

and

$$\tfrac{1}{2}m_A u_A^2 = \tfrac{1}{2}m_B u_B^2$$

or

$$m_A u_A^2 = m_B u_B^2$$

If we take equal volumes of these two gases, and if these are collected at the same pressure as well as the same temperature,

$$P_A V_A = P_B V_B$$

From the relationship $PV = \tfrac{1}{3} Nmu^2$,

$$\tfrac{1}{3}N_A m_A u_A^2 = \tfrac{1}{3}N_B m_B u_B^2$$

or

$$N_A m_A u_A^2 = N_B m_B u_B^2$$

But, $m_A u_A^2 = m_B u_B^2$, and therefore

$$N_A = N_B$$

We conclude, therefore, that equal volumes of any two gases at the same temperature and pressure contain the same number of molecules. This is a statement of **Avogadro's principle**, which Avogadro derived in a much more empirical manner than described here.

Conversely, equal numbers of molecules of any two gases under the same conditions of temperature and pressure will occupy equal volumes. A mole of any substance contains 6.023×10^{23} molecules (Avogadro's number—Sections 5.1 and 5.2) and occupies 22.414 liters at STP; this volume is called the **STP molar volume**. For most calculations, the value is rounded off to 22.4 liters.

Avogadro's principle was almost entirely ignored after its presentation in 1811. Stanislao Cannizzaro was the first to see the full significance of this principle, and he was largely responsible for its universal acceptance (1858–1864) after the death of Avogadro. This principle enables the introduction of the weight of a gas sample as one of the variables in a calculation. Furthermore, the molecular weight of a gas can be calculated from the density of the gas.

▶ **EXAMPLE 6.8** What is the density of fluorine gas at STP?

Solution The molecular weight of F_2 is 38.0. At STP, 38.0 g of F_2 occupies 22.4 liters. Therefore the density is: 38.0 g/22.4 liters = 1.70 g/liter.

▶ **EXAMPLE 6.9** What volume will 10.0 g of carbon dioxide occupy at 27°C and 2.00 atm?

Solution The molecular weight of CO_2 is 44.0. Therefore at STP, 22.4 liters of CO_2 will weigh 44.0 g. To find the volume of 10.0 g of CO_2 at STP:

$$? \text{ liters} = 10.0 \text{ g} \left(\frac{22.4 \text{ liters}}{44.0 \text{ g}} \right) = 5.09 \text{ liters}$$

To convert this volume from STP to the conditions specified in the problem:

$$? \text{ liters} = 5.09 \text{ liters} \left(\frac{300°K}{273°K} \right) \left(\frac{1.00 \text{ atm}}{2.00 \text{ atm}} \right) = 2.80 \text{ liters}$$

This problem can also be solved by use of the equation of state, $PV = nRT$. The number of moles, n, is 10.0/44.0, or 0.227.

$$(2.00 \text{ atm}) \, V = (0.227 \text{ mole})(0.0821 \text{ liter atm}/°K \text{ mole})(300°K)$$
$$V = 2.80 \text{ liters}$$

▶ **EXAMPLE 6.10** A gas has a density of 0.991 g/liter at 91°C and 750 torr. What is the molecular weight of the gas?

Solution If we take 0.991 g of the gas, the sample will occupy 1.00 liter under the conditions specified. Converting this volume to STP, we get

$$? \text{ liter} = 1.00 \text{ liter} \left(\frac{273°K}{364°K} \right) \left(\frac{750 \text{ torr}}{760 \text{ torr}} \right) = 0.740 \text{ liter}$$

Therefore at STP, 0.740 liter of the gas weighs 0.991 g. The weight of 22.4 liters of the gas at STP is the gram molecular weight.

$$? \, g = 22.4 \text{ liters} \left(\frac{0.991 \text{ g}}{0.740 \text{ liter}} \right) = 30.0 \text{ g}$$

This problem can also be solved by means of the equation of state (Example 6.7).

Cannizzaro was the first to use data on gas densities to assign atomic weights. He based his atomic weight scale on hydrogen and assigned the hydrogen atom a weight of 1, a value which is close to that currently used for hydrogen. Thus, since carbon dioxide gas has a density 22 times greater than that of hydrogen gas, CO_2 was assigned a molecular weight of 44, comparable to $H_2 = 2$. Carbon dioxide contains 27.3% carbon; therefore one molecular weight of carbon dioxide must contain 12 units of carbon. Similar data for other gaseous compounds containing carbon are summarized in Table 6.1. Notice that the smallest weight of carbon in a molecular weight of any compound is 12, and that the other weights are multiples of 12. One concludes, therefore, that carbon has an atomic weight of 12, and that the compounds of Table 6.1 contain 1, 2, 2, 1, 1, and 3 atoms of carbon per molecule, respectively.

Table 6.1

Composition of Some Carbon Compounds

	Molecular Weight	% Carbon	Weight of Carbon per Mole (g)
carbon dioxide	44	27.3	12
cyanogen	52	46.2	24
ethane	30	80.0	24
hydrogen cyanide	27	44.4	12
methane	16	75.0	12
propane	44	81.8	36

6.8 Gay-Lussac's Law of Combining Volumes

In 1808, Gay-Lussac reported the results of his experiments with reacting gases. When measured at constant temperature and pressure, the volumes of gases used or produced in a chemical reaction can be expressed in ratios of small whole numbers. This is a statement of **Gay-Lussac's law of combining volumes**.

For the reaction

$$H_2(g) + Cl_2(g) \longrightarrow 2HCl(g)$$

Gay-Lussac found that a given volume of hydrogen reacts with an equivalent volume of chlorine to produce twice this volume of hydrogen chloride. For example, at fixed temperature and pressure, 10 liters of hydrogen will react with 10 liters of chlorine to produce 20 liters of hydrogen chloride. The law is applicable only to gases; the volumes of liquids or solids cannot be treated in a comparable fashion.

The equation shows that equal numbers of hydrogen and chlorine molecules are required for the reaction. According to Avogadro's principle, equal numbers of hydrogen and chlorine molecules are contained in equal volumes of these gases. Also, the number of hydrogen chloride molecules produced by the reaction is twice the number of hydrogen molecules used, and therefore the volume of hydrogen chloride produced is twice the volume of the hydrogen used.

The total volume of the reacting gases need not equal the volume of the gases produced. This fact is illustrated by another of Gay-Lussac's examples:

$$2CO(g) + O_2(g) \longrightarrow 2CO_2(g)$$

For this reaction, two volumes of carbon monoxide and one volume of oxygen are required to produce two volumes of carbon dioxide. The equation for the reaction shows a molecular ratio of carbon monoxide to oxygen to carbon dioxide of 2 to 1 to 2, which is the same as the observed volume ratio. These observations, as the previous ones, are consistent with Avogadro's principle. Thus if 2 liters of carbon monoxide contain $2x$ molecules, such a sample would require 1 liter of oxygen (x molecules) to produce 2 liters of carbon dioxide ($2x$ molecules).

Historically, Gay-Lussac's law of combining volumes preceded Avogadro's principle, and Avogadro derived his statement to explain Gay-Lussac's law.

Simple problems involving volumes of gases can be solved by the use of Gay-Lussac's law of combining volumes.

▶ **EXAMPLE 6.11** What volume of ammonia can be prepared, theoretically, from the reaction of 15 liters of hydrogen and 15 liters of nitrogen? All gases are measured at STP.

Solution The equation for the reaction shows that one volume of nitrogen reacts with three volumes of hydrogen to produce two volumes of ammonia.

$$N_2 + 3H_2 \longrightarrow 2NH_3$$

The complete reaction of the nitrogen supplied is impossible since 15 liters of nitrogen would require 45 liters of hydrogen, and we have only 15 liters of hydrogen. The hydrogen, therefore, is the limiting factor, and the nitrogen is present in excess.

$$? \text{ liters NH}_3 = 15 \text{ liters H}_2 \left(\frac{2 \text{ liters NH}_3}{3 \text{ liters H}_2} \right) = 10 \text{ liters NH}_3$$

The amount of nitrogen required for this reaction is

$$? \text{ liters N}_2 = 15 \text{ liters H}_2 \left(\frac{1 \text{ liter N}_2}{3 \text{ liters H}_2} \right) = 5 \text{ liters N}_2$$

which means that there are 10 liters of unreacted nitrogen left over from the original 15 liters supplied.

6.9 Weight-Volume Relationships in Reactions

Gay-Lussac's law of combining volumes does not contradict the law of conservation of mass. Listed beneath each formula of the following equation are three equivalent terms derived from the equation. Volumes given are measured at STP.

$$2CO(g) + O_2(g) \longrightarrow 2CO_2(g)$$

2 moles	1 mole	2 moles
2(22.4)liters	22.4 liters	2(22.4) liters
2(28) g = 56 g	32 g	2(44) g = 88 g

The total weight of the reactants (56 g + 32 g = 88 g) equals the weight of the product (88 g), but the total volume of the reactants (67.2 liters) does not equal the volume of the product (44.8 liters). Each of the three gases involved in the reaction has a different density. In a reaction such as this one, where the volume decreases, the average density increases.

The fact that a gram molecular weight of a gas occupies 22.4 liters at STP can be utilized in stoichiometric calculations.

▶ EXAMPLE 6.12   How many grams of iron are needed to produce 100 liters of hydrogen gas (at STP)?

Solution   The equation for the reaction is

$$3Fe(s) + 4H_2O(g) \longrightarrow Fe_3O_4(s) + 4H_2(g)$$

According to this equation, 3 gram atoms of iron (167.5 g) produce 4 moles of hydrogen (89.6 liters). Therefore

$$? \text{ g Fe} = 100 \text{ liters H}_2 \left(\frac{167.5 \text{ g Fe}}{89.6 \text{ liters H}_2} \right) = 187 \text{ g Fe}$$

English units of measure can be employed in calculations of this type. A pound molecular weight, or pound mole, contains 2.732×10^{26} molecules and occupies 359 ft^3 at STP.

▶ **EXAMPLE 6.13** How many cubic feet of carbon monoxide (measured at STP) are needed to reduce 1.00 ton of Fe_2O_3 ?

Solution   The equation

$$Fe_2O_3(s) + 3CO(g) \longrightarrow 2Fe(s) + 3CO_2(g)$$

shows that 1 pound mole of Fe_2O_3 (159.6 lb) requires 3 pound moles of CO (3 × 359 ft^3). Thus

$$? \ ft^3 \ CO = 2000 \ lb \ Fe_2O_3 \left(\frac{1077 \ ft^3 \ CO}{159.6 \ lb \ Fe_2O_3} \right) = 13{,}500 \ ft^3 \ CO$$

6.10 Dalton's Law of Partial Pressures

The behavior of a mixture of gases that do not react with one another is frequently of interest. The partial pressure of a component of such a gaseous mixture is the pressure that the component would exert if it were the only gas present in the volume under consideration. **Dalton's law of partial pressures** (1801) states that the total pressure of a mixture of gases is equal to the sum of the partial pressures of the component gases. If the total pressure is P_{total}, and the partial pressures are $p_1, p_2, p_3, \ldots$, then,

$$P_{total} = p_1 + p_2 + p_3 + \cdots$$

Suppose we have 1 liter of gas A at 0.2 atm pressure and 1 liter of gas B at 0.4 atm pressure. If these two gases are mixed in a 1 *liter container*, temperature constant, the pressure of the mixture is 0.6 atm.

According to the kinetic theory, at constant temperature, molecules of gas A have the same average kinetic energy as molecules of gas B. Furthermore, the kinetic theory states that there are no attractive forces between gas molecules that do not react chemically. Hence, the act of mixing two or more gases does not change the average kinetic energy of any of the component gases, and each gas exerts the pressure that it would exert if it were the only gas present in the container.

For a mixture of gas A and gas B, let the pressure of gas A equal p_A, the number of moles of gas A equal n_A, the number of moles of gas B equal n_B, and the total pressure equal P_{total}. Then,

$$p_A V = n_A RT$$

or

$$\left(\frac{RT}{V}\right) = \left(\frac{p_A}{n_A}\right)$$

The total number of moles is $n_A + n_B$, and therefore,

$$P_{total} V = (n_A + n_B)RT$$

$$P_{total} = (n_A + n_B)\left(\frac{RT}{V}\right)$$

Thus

$$P_{total} = (n_A + n_B)\left(\frac{p_A}{n_A}\right)$$

Solving for p_A gives

$$p_A = \left(\frac{n_A}{n_A + n_B}\right) P_{total}$$

In like manner,

$$p_B = \left(\frac{n_B}{n_A + n_B}\right) P_{total}$$

The quantity $n_A/(n_A + n_B)$ is called the **mole fraction** of A; it is the ratio of the number of moles of gas A to the total number of moles of gas present. The partial pressure of a component of a gaseous mixture is equal to the mole fraction times the total pressure.

The preparation of gas mixtures at constant pressure is a less common situation. When gases are mixed at constant pressure, the total volume of the mixture is equal to the sum of the volumes of the component gases at that pressure. Thus if 200 ml of oxygen at 1 atm pressure is mixed with 800 ml of nitrogen at 1 atm pressure, the resulting mixture occupies 1000 ml at a pressure of 1 atm. The composition of this mixture approximates that of air. In this final mixture, the oxygen exerts a partial pressure of 0.2 atm, and the nitrogen exerts a partial pressure of 0.8 atm.

In the laboratory, it is often convenient to collect a gas over water. In such experiments, water vapor is mixed with the collected gas, and the total pressure of the gas sample must be corrected by subtracting the pressure due to the water vapor. In Figure 6.7, the total pressure of the gas sample is equal to the barometric pressure, since the water stands at the same level inside the bottle as outside it. To obtain the pressure of the gas being investigated, it is necessary to subtract the vapor pressure of water at the temperature of the experiment (Table 6.2) from the barometric pressure.

Figure 6.7 Collection of a gas over water.

Table 6.2

Vapor Pressure of Water

Temperature (°C)	Pressure (torr)	Temperature (°C)	Pressure (torr)
0	4.6	25	23.8
1	4.9	26	25.2
2	5.3	27	26.7
3	5.7	28	28.3
4	6.1	29	30.0
5	6.5	30	31.8
6	7.0	31	33.7
7	7.5	32	35.7
8	8.0	33	37.7
9	8.6	34	39.9
10	9.2	35	42.2
11	9.8	40	55.3
12	10.5	45	71.9
13	11.2	50	92.5
14	12.0	55	118.0
15	12.8	60	149.4
16	13.6	65	187.5
17	14.5	70	233.7
18	15.5	75	289.1
19	16.5	80	355.1
20	17.5	85	433.6
21	18.7	90	525.8
22	19.8	95	633.9
23	21.1	100	760.0
24	22.4	105	906.1

▶ EXAMPLE 6.14   A 370 ml sample of oxygen is collected over water at 23°C and 753 torr. What volume would this sample of oxygen occupy dry and at STP?

Solution   At 23°C, the vapor pressure of water is 21.1 torr. The initial pressure of the oxygen, therefore, is 753 torr minus 21 torr, or 732 torr; the initial temperature is 296°K. A pressure change to 760 torr would decrease the volume by 732 torr/760 torr; changing the temperature to 273°K would cause the volume to decrease by a factor of 273°K/296°K. Thus

$$? \text{ ml} = 370 \text{ ml} \left(\frac{732 \text{ torr}}{760 \text{ torr}}\right) \left(\frac{273°\text{K}}{296°\text{K}}\right) = 329 \text{ ml}$$

▶ EXAMPLE 6.15   A mixture of 40.0 g of oxygen and 40.0 g of helium has a total pressure of 900 torr. What are the partial pressures of oxygen and helium in the mixture?

Solution   The molecular weight of O_2 is 32.0; 40.0 g of O_2 is 40.0/32.0, or 1.25, mole. Helium is a monatomic gas; atomic weight = 4.00. Therefore 40.0/4.0, or 10.0 moles are present in the mixture. The total number of moles of gases is 11.25. The partial pressure of O_2 is

$$? \text{ torr} = \left(\frac{1.25 \text{ moles}}{11.25 \text{ moles}}\right) 900 \text{ torr} = 100 \text{ torr}$$

The partial pressure of He is

$$? \text{ torr} = \left(\frac{10.00 \text{ moles}}{11.25 \text{ moles}}\right) 900 \text{ torr} = 800 \text{ torr}$$

6.11   Molecular Velocities

In Section 6.6, we derived the expression

$$PV = \tfrac{1}{3}Nmu^2$$

For 1 mole of a gas, the number of molecules, N, is Avogadro's number, and N times the mass of a single molecule, m, is the molecular weight, M.

$$PV = \tfrac{1}{3}Mu^2$$

Also for 1 mole, $PV = RT$, and thus

$$RT = \tfrac{1}{3}Mu^2$$

Rearranging and solving for the molecular velocity, we obtain

$$u = \sqrt{\frac{3RT}{M}}$$

The velocity, u, in this equation, as in previous equations, is the root-mean-square velocity. This is the value obtained by taking the square root of the average of the squares of all of the molecular velocities, and it represents the velocity of a molecule possessing average kinetic energy at the temperature under consideration.

In order to solve the equation for the root-mean-square velocity, R must be expressed in appropriate units. R equals 8.3143×10^7 g cm²/sec² °K mole, a fact that may be derived from the ideal gas law by substituting P in dynes/cm² (which is g/cm² sec²) and V in cm³. The root-mean-square velocity of hydrogen at 0°C is 1.84×10^5 cm/sec or 1.84 km/sec. This represents a speed of about 4100 miles per hour!

The diffusion of one gas through another gas does not occur at speeds commensurate with this. Although a given molecule travels at a high speed, its direction is continually being changed through collisions with other molecules. At 1 atm pressure and 0°C, a hydrogen molecule, on the average, undergoes about 1.4×10^{10} collisions in 1 sec. The average distance traveled between collisions is only 1.3×10^{-5} cm; this value is called the **mean free path** of hydrogen.

Not all the molecules of a gas possess the same kinetic energy, and the velocities of molecules are distributed over a wide range. The nature of this distribution is described by the **Maxwell-Boltzmann distribution law**. Figure 6.8 shows the distribution of molecular velocites of a gas at two temperatures.

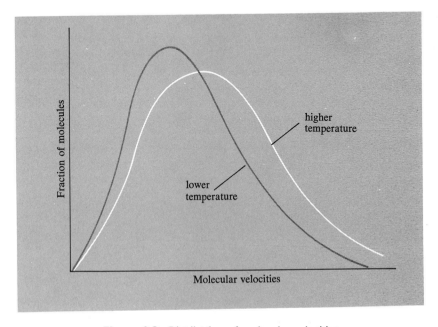

Figure 6.8 Distribution of molecular velocities.

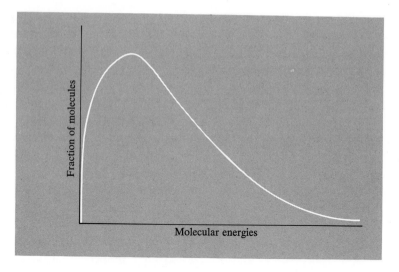

Figure 6.9 Distribution of molecular energies.

Because of the collisions of molecules and consequent exchange of energy, the velocity of a given molecule is continually changing. However, since a large number of molecules is involved, the distribution of molecular velocities of the total collection is constant. At the higher temperature, the curve is broadened and shifted to higher velocities. A typical curve for the distribution of molecular energies is shown in Figure 6.9.

6.12 Graham's Law of Effusion

Suppose that two gases, A and B, are confined in identical containers under the same conditions of temperature and pressure. Molecules of two different gases at the same temperature have the same average kinetic energy, and therefore

$$\tfrac{1}{2}m_A u_A^2 = \tfrac{1}{2}m_B u_B^2$$

or

$$m_A u_A^2 = m_B u_B^2$$

Rearranging this equation, we obtain

$$\frac{u_A^2}{u_B^2} = \frac{m_B}{m_A}$$

Extracting the square root of both sides of the equation, we get

$$\frac{u_A}{u_B} = \sqrt{\frac{m_B}{m_A}}$$

If there is an identical, and extremely small, orifice in each container, molecules will escape. The rate of escape, *r*, which is called the rate of **molecular effusion**, is equal to the rate at which molecules strike the orifice, and this in turn is roughly proportional to the average molecular velocity. In addition, the ratio of the molecular masses, m_B/m_A, is the same as the ratio of the molecular weights, M_B/M_A. Thus

$$\frac{r_A}{r_B} = \sqrt{\frac{M_B}{M_A}}$$

Since the density of a gas, *d*, is proportional to its molecular weight, this relation may also be written

$$\frac{r_A}{r_B} = \sqrt{\frac{d_B}{d_A}}$$

Thomas Graham experimentally derived this **law of effusion** in his studies of 1828–1833. For molecular effusion, the orifice must be small in comparison to the mean free path of the molecules. If high pressures and large orifices are employed, collisions of the molecules while passing through the orifice cause the gas to escape in the form of a jet that does not obey Graham's law.

It is not surprising that of two molecules with the same kinetic energy, the lighter one will move more rapidly than the heavier one. Graham's law confirms this and gives the quantitative relationship. The molecular weights of oxygen and hydrogen are 32 and 2, respectively; hence, hydrogen molecules will effuse $\sqrt{32/2}$ or 4 times faster than oxygen molecules under the same conditions.

This principle has been used for the separation of isotopes. Naturally occurring uranium consists of 0.7% ^{235}U and 99.3% ^{238}U, and therefore, the uranium hexafluoride produced by the reaction of uranium and fluorine consists of a mixture of $^{235}UF_6$ and $^{238}UF_6$. This mixture is heated above its boiling point (56°C) and passed, at low pressure, through a porous barrier. The lighter $^{235}UF_6$ effuses 1.004 times faster than $^{238}UF_6(\sqrt{352/348})$; hence, the emerging gas has a higher $^{235}UF_6$ content than the original mixture. This procedure must be repeated thousands of times to effect a significant separation.

6.13 Deviations from the Ideal Gas Laws

The gas laws describe the behavior of an ideal or perfect gas—a gas defined by the kinetic theory. Under ordinary conditions of temperature and pressure, real gases follow the behavior expressed by these laws rather closely. This is not true, however, at high pressures and low temperatures.

The kinetic theory assumes that gas molecules are points in space and that their volume is negligible; hence, at 0°K, at which temperature molecular motion ceases, the volume of an ideal gas is zero. Real gases, of course, do not have zero molecular volumes, and, although the space between the molecules can be reduced by increasing the pressure, the molecular volume cannot be compressed. At pressures up to a few atmospheres, the gas molecules are widely separated, and the free space between the molecules is large in comparison to the molecular volume. Under such conditions, neglecting the volume of the molecules does not introduce a large error. However, at high pressures, the molecules of a gas are relatively close together, and the molecular volume constitutes a significant fraction of the total volume. Under these conditions, the volume of a real gas is materially larger than that predicted for an ideal gas.

The kinetic theory also assumes that there are no attractive forces between gas molecules. This assumption is belied by the fact that all gases can be liquefied. At high temperatures, gas molecules move so rapidly that the attractive forces between molecules are effectively overcome. On the other hand, at low temperatures, the forces of attraction pull the molecules together so that the volume observed is less than that predicted by the ideal gas law.

It is interesting to note that these two effects work in opposite directions—one to increase the volume and the other to decrease the volume. Thus, under moderate conditions, the ideal gas law is followed fairly closely by real gases. However, under more extreme conditions, the net deviation depends upon which of the effects is dominant.

The equation of state for an ideal gas was modified to take into account these two sources of error by Johannes van der Waals in 1873. The **van der Waals equation** is

$$\left(P + \frac{n^2a}{V^2}\right)(V - nb) = nRT$$

The numerical values of the constants a and b are determined by experiment; these values are specific to the gas under consideration (see Table 6.3).

Table 6.3

van der Waals Constants

	a (liter^2 atm/mole^2)	b (liter/mole)
H_2	0.244	0.0266
He	0.0341	0.0237
N_2	1.39	0.0391
O_2	1.36	0.0318
Cl_2	6.49	0.0562
NH_3	4.17	0.0371
CO	1.49	0.0399
CO_2	3.59	0.0427

The constant b, multiplied by n, is subtracted from the total volume of the gas to correct for that portion of the volume that is not compressible because of the intrinsic volume of the gas molecules. If the molecules are assumed to be spherical and of radius r, the excluded volume per molecule is not merely the volume of the molecule, $\frac{4}{3}\pi r^3$. The closest approach of *two* molecules is $2r$ (Figure 6.10), and hence the excluded volume for *two* molecules is $\frac{4}{3}\pi(2r)^3$, or $8(\frac{4}{3}\pi r^3)$. For one molecule, this volume is $4(\frac{4}{3}\pi r^3)$, or four times the molecular volume. Hence, for a mole of molecules, N molecules,

$$b = 4N(\tfrac{4}{3}\pi r^3)$$

where b is given in cm^3/mole and r is given in cm.

The pressure term of the equation is corrected by a factor $n^2 a/V^2$ to take into account the intermolecular attractions, which are called van der Waals attractions (Section 3.10). These attractive forces draw the gas molecules together. Hence, this effect augments pressure in reducing the volume of the gas, and the correction term is added to P.

The term (n/V) represents a concentration (moles/liter). If x molecules are confined in a liter, there are $(x - 1)$ ways for a given molecule to collide, or interact, with another molecule since it cannot collide with itself. This factor applies to all the molecules, making a total of $\frac{1}{2}x(x - 1)$ possible interactions for the entire collection of molecules. The fraction $\frac{1}{2}$ is added so that a given interaction is not counted twice—once for each of the molecules entering into it. If a large number of molecules are present, $(x - 1)$ is approximately equal to x, and the proportionality is $\frac{1}{2}x^2$ to a good approximation. Hence the number of interactions between gas molecules is proportional to the *square* of the concentration. The van der Waals constant a may be regarded as a proportionality constant (incorporating the $\frac{1}{2}$), and the correction term is $n^2 a/V^2$.

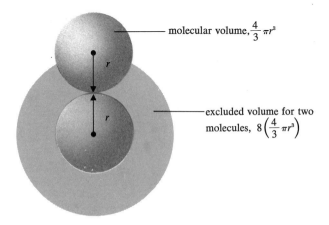

molecular volume, $\frac{4}{3}\pi r^3$

excluded volume for two molecules, $8\left(\frac{4}{3}\pi r^3\right)$

Figure 6.10 van der Waals correction, b, for excluded volume.

When the volume of a mole of gas is large (and pressure is low), the effect of subtracting nb from the volume is negligible, as is the magnitude of the correction term n^2a/V^2. Under such conditions, gases follow the ideal gas law.

6.14 Liquefaction of Gases

Liquefaction of a gas occurs under conditions that permit the intermolecular attractive forces to bind the gas molecules together in the liquid form. If the pressure is high, the molecules are close together, and the effect of the attractive forces is appreciable. The attractive forces are opposed by the motion of the gas molecules; thus liquefaction is favored by low temperatures where the average kinetic energy of the molecules is low. The behavior of a gas deviates more and more from ideality as the temperature is lowered and the pressure is raised. At extremes of these conditions, gases liquefy.

The higher the temperature of a gas, the more difficult it is to liquefy and the higher the pressure that must be employed (Table 6.4). For each gas,

Table 6.4

Pressures Needed to Liquefy Carbon Dioxide

(Vapor Pressures of Liquid CO_2)

Temperature (°C)	Pressure (atm)
−50	6.7
−30	14.1
−10	26.1
10	44.4
20	56.5
30	71.2
31	72.8

there is a temperature above which it is impossible to liquefy the gas no matter how high the applied pressure. This temperature is called the **critical temperature** of the gas under consideration. The **critical pressure** is the minimum pressure needed to liquefy a gas at its critical temperature. The critical constants of some common gases are listed in Table 6.5.

The critical temperature of a gas gives an indication of the strength of the intermolecular attractive forces of that gas. A substance with weak attractive forces would have a low critical temperature; above this temperature, the molecular motion is too violent to permit the relatively weak forces to hold the molecules in the liquid state. The substances of Table 6.5 are listed in order of increasing critical temperature; the magnitude of the intermolecu-

Table 6.5

Critical Point Data

Gas	Critical Temperature (°K)	Critical Pressure (atm)
He	5.3	2.26
H_2	33.3	12.8
N_2	126.1	33.5
CO	134.0	35.0
O_2	154.4	49.7
CH_4	190.2	45.6
CO_2	304.2	72.8
NH_3	405.6	111.5
H_2O	647.2	217.7

lar attractive forces (related to the *a* of Table 6.3) increases in this same order. Helium, which has weak attractive forces, can exist as a liquid below 5.3°K only; the strong attractive forces of water permit it to be liquefied up to a temperature of 647.2°K. The critical constants have been used to evaluate the constants of the van der Waals equation.

The data of Table 6.5 show that it is necessary to cool many gases below room temperature (ca. 295°K) before these substances can be liquefied. Commercial liquefaction procedures make use of the **Joule-Thomson effect** to cool gases. When a compressed gas is allowed to expand to a lower pressure, as for example, through an orifice, the gas cools. In the expansion, work is done against the intermolecular attractive forces. The energy used in performing this work must be taken from the kinetic energy of the gas molecules themselves; hence, the temperature of the gas decreases. This effect was studied by James Joule and William Thomson (Lord Kelvin) in the years 1852–1862. The liquefaction of air is accomplished by first allowing cooled compressed air to expand. The temperature of the air falls to a lower level. This cooled air is used to precool entering compressed air, and the expansion of this compressed air results in the attainment of even lower temperatures. The cooled expanded air is recycled through the compression chamber. Eventually, the cooling and compression produce liquid air.

SOME SUGGESTED READINGS

Hildebrand, J. H., *An Introduction to Molecular Kinetic Theory*, New York, Van Nostrand Reinhold, 1963 (paper).

Kauzmann, W., *Thermal Properties of Matter: Kinetic Theory of Gases*, New York, Benjamin, 1966 (paper).

Parsonage, N. G., *The Gaseous State*, Elmsford, N.Y., Pergamon, 1966 (paper).

PROBLEMS

The more difficult problems are starred.

6.1 The space above the liquid mercury in a column of a barometer is occupied only by mercury vapor. The vapor pressure of mercury at 25°C is 0.00156 torr. Assuming mercury vapor to be an ideal monatomic gas, calculate the number of atoms of mercury per milliliter at this temperature and pressure.

*6.2 If a barometer were constructed using water instead of mercury, to what height (in inches) would the water rise at 0°C and a pressure of 1.00 atm? The vapor pressure of water at 0°C is 4.6 torr. Assume that the density of water at 0°C is 1.00 g/cm³.

6.3 A container is filled with a gas to a pressure of 10.0 atm at 20°C. (a) What pressure will develop inside the sealed container when it is warmed to 100°C? (b) At what temperature would the pressure be 20.0 atm?

6.4 The volume of a gas sample is 100 ml at 100°C. If the pressure is held constant, at what temperature will the sample have a volume of 200 ml?

6.5 The volume of a sample of a gas is 2.50 liters at 2.50 atm. If the temperature is held constant, what will be the volume of the sample at (a) 1000 torr, (b) 2500 torr, (c) 1.00 atm?

6.6 For each of the following pairs of variables, which apply to measurements made on a sample of an ideal gas, draw a rough graph to show how one quantity varies with the other. (a) P vs. V, T constant; (b) T vs. V, P constant; (c) P vs. T, V constant; (d) PV vs. V, T constant.

6.7 The volume of a gas sample is 175 ml at 30°C and a pressure of 740 torr. Calculate the volume of the sample at STP.

6.8 If a sample of a gas occupies 4.48 liters at STP, what volume will it occupy at 25°C and 500 torr?

6.9 The volume of a gas sample is 500 ml at 50°C and a pressure of 700 torr. What is the temperature when the volume of the sample is 300 ml and the pressure is 800 torr?

6.10 A sample of a gas occupies 300 ml at 10°C and a pressure of 700 torr. What pressure must be applied in order to change the volume of the gas sample to 200 ml at 50°C?

6.11 A sample of oxygen, collected over water at 20°C, occupies 150 ml and exerts a pressure of 758 torr. What volume would the sample occupy if dry and under standard conditions? The vapor pressure of water at 20°C is 18 torr.

6.12 What volume would 4.00 g of carbon monoxide gas, CO, occupy at 100°C and a pressure of 746 torr?

6.13 A sample of an ideal gas, collected over water, at 29°C occupies a volume of 200 ml. The wet gas exerts a pressure of 634 torr. The sample of gas, when dried, occupies the same volume and exerts the same pressure, 634 torr, at 44°C. From these data, calculate the vapor pressure of water at 29°C.

6.14 What is the density of $F_2(g)$ at 50°C and a pressure of 800 torr?

6.15 What is the total pressure (in atm) of a mixture of 10.0 g of $H_2(g)$ and 10.0 g of He(g) confined to a volume of 50.0 liters at 0°C?

6.16 Calculate the molecular weight of a gas that has a density of 0.743 g/liter at 90°C and a pressure of 600 torr.

6.17 A 501 ml sample of a gas collected at 20°C and a pressure of 700 torr weighs 1.23 g. What is the molecular weight of the gas?

6.18 If the temperature is held constant at 0°C, at what pressure will the density of Ar(g) be 1.00 g/liter?

6.19 A 1.00 liter sample of oxygen gas is collected over water at 25°C and a total pressure of 765 torr. The vapor pressure of water is 23.8 torr at 25°C. (a) What weight of water is present in the sample? (b) What weight of oxygen is present in the sample?

6.20 Calculate the number of molecules in 1.00 liter of O_2 gas at 56°C and 821 torr.

6.21 Nitrosyl fluoride, ONF(g), can be prepared by the direct union of NO(g) and $F_2(g)$. (a) Write the chemical equation for the reaction. (b) What volume of ONF(g) can be prepared from 17 liters of NO(g) and 7 liters of $F_2(g)$? Assume that all gases are measured at the same temperature and pressure.

6.22 The complete combustion of ethane, $C_2H_6(g)$, in $O_2(g)$ yields $CO_2(g)$ and $H_2O(l)$. (a) Write the equation for the reaction. (b) If all gases are measured under the same conditions, what volume of $O_2(g)$ is needed to burn 15.0 liters of $C_2H_6(g)$? (c) What volume of $CO_2(g)$ is produced in the reaction described in part (b)?

6.23 What volume of NO(g) results from the reaction of 20.0 liters of $NO_2(g)$ with excess water if the volumes of both gases are measured at STP?

$$3NO_2(g) + H_2O \longrightarrow 2HNO_3(aq) + NO(g)$$

How many moles of HNO_3 are produced by the reaction?

6.24 The complete combustion of 11.2 liters of a gaseous compound that contains only carbon and hydrogen requires 50.4 liters of $O_2(g)$ and produces 33.6 liters of $CO_2(g)$ and 27.0 g of $H_2O(l)$. All gas measurements are made at STP. (a) For each substance involved in the reaction, calculate the number of moles used or produced. (b) Use your answers from part (a) to derive the whole-number coefficients of the balanced chemical equation for the reaction. (c) Determine a formula for the hydrocarbon and write the equation for the reaction.

6.25 A mixture of 100 ml of $C_2H_6S(g)$ and 900 ml of $O_2(g)$ is placed in a 1.00 liter container at a total pressure of 1.00 atm. The mixture is ignited and reacts according to the equation:

$$2C_2H_6S(g) + 9O_2(g) \longrightarrow 4CO_2(g) + 6H_2O(g) + 2SO_2(g)$$

Assume that the temperature is constant throughout the experiment and is such that all substances involved in the reaction are gaseous. What is the pressure after the reaction? What is the partial pressure of each gas present in the final mixture?

6.26 A 0.145 g sample of a compound that contains only carbon and hydrogen was burned to $CO_2(g)$ and $H_2O(l)$. The CO_2 gas from the combustion occupied a volume of 224 ml at STP, and 0.225 g of water was collected. (a) What is the empirical formula of the hydrocarbon? (b) If the original sample of the hydrocarbon occupied a volume of 56 ml at STP, what is the molecular formula of the hydrocarbon?

6.27 The complete combustion of carbon disulfide, $CS_2(l)$, in $O_2(g)$ yields $CO_2(g)$ and $SO_2(g)$. (a) Write the equation for the reaction. (b) What volume of oxygen gas (measured at STP) is needed to burn 10.0 g of CS_2? (c) What total volume of $CO_2(g)$ and $SO_2(g)$, measured at STP, is produced? (d) What are the partial pressures of $CO_2(g)$ and $SO_2(g)$ in the mixture?

6.28 What volume of phosphine (measured at STP) would be formed by the reaction of 100 g of calcium phosphide with water?

$$Ca_3P_2(s) + 6H_2O \longrightarrow 3Ca(OH)_2(s) + 2PH_3(g)$$

6.29 The reaction of coke and steam yields a mixture of $CO(g)$ and $H_2(g)$ called water gas.

$$C(s) + H_2O(g) \longrightarrow CO(g) + H_2(g)$$

What weight of coke is needed to prepare 250 liters of water gas if the volume of this gaseous mixture is measured at 1.20 atm and 50°C?

6.30 A sample of sodium azide, NaN_3, is decomposed by heating and 462 ml of N_2 gas, measured at 24°C and 745 torr, is obtained. What did the sample of NaN_3 weigh?

$$2NaN_3(s) \longrightarrow 2Na(l) + 3N_2(g)$$

6.31 Magnesium and aluminum react with aqueous acids to give hydrogen gas.

$$Mg(s) + 2H^+(aq) \longrightarrow H_2(g) + Mg^{2+}(aq)$$
$$2Al(s) + 6H^+(aq) \longrightarrow 3H_2(g) + 2Al^{3+}(aq)$$

What volume of $H_2(g)$ measured at 20°C and a pressure of 770 torr can be obtained from 4.00 g of an alloy that is 70.0% Mg and 30.0% Al?

*6.32 A 3.90 g sample of an alloy that contains only Mg and Al reacts with dilute acid to give 4.47 liters of hydrogen gas (measured at STP). The equations for the reactions are given in Problem 6.31. What percentage by weight of the alloy is aluminum?

*6.33 A mixture of $CaCO_3$ and $NaHCO_3$ is heated and the compounds decompose.

$$CaCO_3(s) \longrightarrow CaO(s) + CO_2(g)$$
$$2NaHCO_3(s) \longrightarrow Na_2CO_3(s) + CO_2(g) + H_2O(g)$$

If 784 ml of CO_2, measured at STP, and 0.396 g of H_2O were obtained from the decomposition of the sample, what weight percentage of the original sample was $CaCO_3$? What did the original sample weigh?

6.34   A mixture of 7.70 g of $CO_2(g)$ and 7.70 g of $N_2(g)$ exerts a pressure of 770 torr. What is the partial pressure of each gas?

6.35   The partial pressures of $He(g)$ and $O_2(g)$ in a mixture of the two gases are 608 torr and 152 torr, respectively. (a) What is the mole fraction of $He(g)$ in the mixture? of $O_2(g)$? (b) If the mixture occupies a volume of 44.8 liters at STP, what is the total number of moles of gas present? (c) What is the composition of the mixture by weight? (d) What is the weight percent of $He(g)$ present in the mixture?

*6.36   Dinitrogen tetroxide gas dissociates into nitrogen dioxide gas; the extent of the dissociation depends upon the temperature and pressure.

$$N_2O_4(g) \rightleftharpoons 2NO_2(g)$$

The mixture of NO_2 and N_2O_4 that results from the dissociation of 1.00 mole of N_2O_4 at 70°C and 1.00 atm pressure occupies a volume of 47.6 liters. (a) What is the total number of moles of gas in the mixture? (b) Each mole of N_2O_4 that dissociates produces 2 moles of NO_2. How many moles of each type of gas are present in the mixture? (c) What molar percentage of the original quantity of N_2O_4 is dissociated? (d) What mole fraction of the final gas mixture is NO_2? (e) What are the partial pressures of N_2O_4 and NO_2 in the final mixture of gases?

6.37   Given 1.00 mole of $He(g)$ and 1.00 mole of $H_2(g)$ measured under the same conditions. Compare quantitatively the He sample to the H_2 sample in terms of each of the following properties. (a) Number of molecules, (b) mass of a single molecule, (c) root-mean-square velocity of a molecule, (d) change in momentum for a single molecular collision with the wall of the container, (e) total number of collisions with the wall per unit time, (f) total change in momentum for all molecular collisions with the wall per unit time.

6.38   Calculate the root-mean-square velocity of a helium atom at 100°K and at 200°K.

6.39   Use Graham's law to calculate the molecular weight of a gas if a given volume of the gas effuses through an apparatus in 282 sec and the same volume of nitrogen, under the same conditions of temperature and pressure, effuses through the apparatus in 215 sec.

6.40   Under certain conditions of temperature and pressure, the density of oxygen gas is 1.30 g/liter; a volume of 21.0 ml of $O_2(g)$ effuses through an apparatus in 1.00 sec; and the rate of effusion of gas X through the same apparatus is 15.0 ml/sec. Calculate the density of gas X under the experimental conditions.

6.41   Calculate the pressure exerted by 1.00 mole of O_2 gas confined to a volume of 1.00 liter at 0°C by (a) the ideal gas law and (b) the van der Waals equation.

6.42   Calculate the pressure exerted by 1.00 mole of O_2 gas confined to a volume of 10.00 liters at O°C by (a) the ideal gas law and (b) the van der Waals equation. Compare the results to each other and to those obtained in Problem 6.41.

*6.43 Use the equation that is given in Section 6.13 and that relates the radius of a gas molecule to the value of the van der Waals constant b to calculate the radius of the helium atom. At STP, what percentage of the total volume of helium gas is molecular volume?

6.44 The radius of the argon atom is 1.47Å. (a) Calculate the value of the van der Waals constant b in liters/mole. (b) Calculate a value for the van der Waals constant a from your value for b and the fact that 1.00 mole of Ar(g) confined to a volume of 1.00 liter at 27°C exerts a pressure of 24.1 atm.

LIQUIDS AND SOLIDS

As a gas is cooled, the molecules come together, under the influence of the intermolecular attractive forces, and form a liquid. Molecular motion is more restricted in the liquid state than in the gaseous state. The molecules are closer together in liquid than in gas, and hence the attractive forces exert a stronger influence. Further cooling produces a solid. In crystalline solids, the molecules assume positions in crystal lattices, and the motion of the molecules is restricted to vibration about these fixed points.

7.1 The Liquid State

The liquid state is intermediate in character between the complete molecular randomness that characterizes gases and the orderly arrangement of molecules typical of crystalline solids. In liquids, the molecules are moving sufficiently slowly for the intermolecular forces of attraction to hold them together in a definite volume; however, the molecular motion is too rapid for the attractive forces to fix the molecules into the definite positions of a crystal lattice. Hence, a liquid retains its volume but not its shape; liquids flow to assume the shape of the container.

The space between the molecules of liquids is reduced almost to a minimum by the intermolecular attractions; a change in pressure has almost no effect on the volume of a liquid. An increase in temperature, however, increases the volume of most liquids slightly and consequently decreases the liquid density. As the temperature of a liquid is increased, the kinetic energy of the molecules increases, and this increased molecular motion works against the attractive forces. This expansion is, however, of a much lower order than that observed for gases in which the effect of the attractive forces is negligible.

Two miscible (mutually soluble) liquids will diffuse into each other when placed together. If a liquid is carefully overlaid with a second, less dense liquid, a sharp boundary line is observed between the two. This boundary gradually becomes less distinct, and, in time, disappears completely as the molecules of the two liquids mix. The diffusion of liquids, however, is a much slower process than the diffusion of gases. Since the molecules of liquids are relatively close together, the mean free path of liquid molecules is relatively short; liquid molecules suffer many more collisions per unit time than do gas molecules.

Any liquid exhibits resistance to flow, a property known as **viscosity**. One way of determining the viscosity of a liquid is to measure the time that it takes for a definite amount of the liquid to pass through a tube of small diameter under a given pressure. Resistance to flow is largely due to the attractions between molecules, and the measurement of the viscosity of a liquid gives a simple estimate of the strength of these attractions. Allowance should be made, however, for other factors, such as molecular weight and the structure of the molecules. Liquids with large, irregularly shaped molecules are generally more viscous than liquids with small, spherical molecules. In general, as the temperature of a liquid is increased, the cohesive forces are less able to cope with the increasing molecular motion, and the viscosity decreases. On the other hand, increasing the pressure generally increases the viscosity of a given liquid.

Another property of liquids related to the intermolecular forces of attraction is surface tension. A molecule in the center of a liquid is attracted equally in all directions by surrounding molecules. However, molecules on the surface of a liquid are attracted only toward the interior of the liquid (Figure 7.1). Therefore, the surface molecules are pulled inward, and the surface area of a liquid tends to be minimized. This accounts for the spherical shape of liquid drops. **Surface tension** is a measure of this inward force on the surface of a liquid, the force which must be overcome to expand the surface area. The surface tension of a liquid decreases with increasing temperature since the increased molecular agitation tends to decrease the effect of the intermolecular cohesive forces.

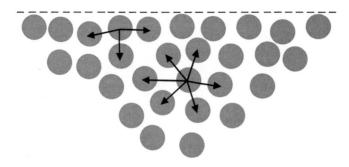

Figure 7.1 Schematic diagram indicating the unbalanced intermolecular forces on the surface molecules of a liquid.

7.2 Evaporation

The kinetic energy of the molecules of a liquid follows a Maxwell–Boltzmann distribution similar to the distribution of kinetic energy among gas molecules (Figure 7.2). The kinetic energy of a given molecule of a liquid is continually changing as the molecule collides with other molecules, but at any given instant, some of the molecules of the total collection have relatively high energies and some have relatively low energies. The molecules with kinetic energies sufficiently high to overcome the attractive forces of surrounding molecules can escape from the liquid and enter the gas phase if these high-energy molecules are close to the surface and moving in the right direction; they use part of their energy in working against the attractive forces when they escape.

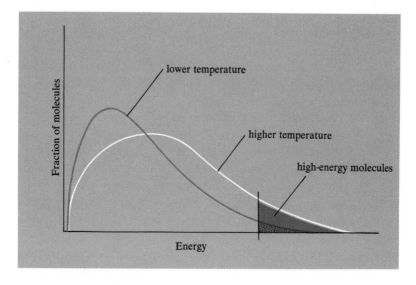

Figure 7.2 Distribution of kinetic energy among molecules of a liquid.

In time, the loss of a number of high-energy molecules causes the average kinetic energy of the molecules remaining in the liquid to fall, and the temperature of the liquid falls proportionately. When liquids evaporate from an open container at room temperature, heat flows into the liquid from the surroundings to maintain the temperature of the liquid. Thus the supply of high-energy molecules is replenished, and the process continues until all of the liquid has evaporated. The total quantity of heat required to vaporize a mole of liquid at a given temperature is called the **molar heat of vaporization** of that liquid. For example,

$$9.7 \text{ kcal} + H_2O(l) \longrightarrow H_2O(g)$$

The transfer of heat from the surroundings explains why a swimmer emerging from the water becomes chilled as the water evaporates from his skin. Likewise, the regulation of body temperature is, in part, accomplished by the evaporation of perspiration from the skin. Various cooling devices have made use of this principle; a water cooler of the Middle East consists of a jar of unglazed pottery filled with water. The water saturates the clay of the pottery and evaporates from the outer surface of the jar, thus cooling the water remaining in the jar.

The rate of evaporation increases as the temperature of a liquid is raised. When the temperature is increased, the average kinetic energy of the molecules increases, and the number of molecules with energies high enough for them to escape into the vapor phase constitutes an increased fraction of the total number of molecules (Figure 7.2).

7.3 Vapor Pressure

When an evaporating liquid is confined in a closed container, the vapor molecules cannot escape from the vicinity of the liquid, and in the course of their random motion, some of the vapor molecules return to the liquid.

$$H_2O(l) \rightleftharpoons H_2O(g)$$

The rate of return depends upon the concentration of molecules in the vapor; the more vapor molecules per unit volume, the greater the chance that some of them will strike the liquid and be recaptured. Thus a situation develops in which the vaporization of the liquid is opposed by the condensation of the vapor. Eventually, the system reaches a point where the rate of condensation equals the rate of vaporization.

Such a condition, in which the rates of two exactly opposite tendencies are equal, is called a state of **equilibrium**. At equilibrium, the concentration of molecules in the vapor state is constant because molecules are leaving the vapor through condensation at the same rate that molecules are being added to the vapor through vaporization. Similarly, the quantity of liquid is a constant.

It is important to note that equilibrium does not imply a static situation; in any system, the numbers of molecules present in both phases are constant because the two opposing changes are taking place at equal rates and not because vaporization and condensation have ceased. In a closed container, equilibrium is the only situation that can prevail for any length of time. If the rate of vaporization were greater than the rate of condensation for an extended period, all the substance would eventually become vapor. The reverse situation is equally improbable; all the material would end as liquid.

The pressure of vapor in equilibrium with a liquid at a given temperature is called the **vapor pressure**. If the temperature of a liquid–vapor system is constant, the vapor pressure will be constant. The pressure of the vapor depends upon the average kinetic energy of the vapor molecules (which is constant since the temperature is constant) and the concentration of vapor molecules. The concentration of vapor molecules, as well as their average kinetic energy, is fixed by temperature since the vapor concentration must be such that the rate of condensation is equal to the rate of vaporization, and the rate of vaporization is dictated by the temperature.

For any sample of a liquid at a given temperature, then, the equilibrium concentration of vapor is constant, regardless of the size of the sample or the dimensions of the container. The absolute quantity of vapor may not be the same from system to system, but the vapor concentration is. If the volume of vapor is changed, the consequent alteration of the vapor concentration causes the rate of condensation to increase or decrease until the concentration is reestablished at its former, equilibrium, value. Hence, vapor pressure is fixed by temperature alone; volume changes do not alter it. A list of the vapor pressures of water at various temperatures appears in Table 6.2.

As the temperature is increased, the vapor pressure of a liquid increases. We have noted that an increase in temperature causes the rate of vaporization to increase; equilibrium is possible only if the rate of condensation increases proportionately, and this will occur only when the concentration of vapor molecules becomes adjusted to a higher level. This factor and the augmented kinetic energy of the vapor molecules accompanying a rise in temperature account for the observed increase in vapor pressure.

Figure 7.3 shows the temperature–vapor pressure curves for ethyl ether, ethyl alcohol, and water. The curve for each substance could be extended to the critical temperature of that substance; at this point, the vapor pressure would equal the critical pressure. Above the critical temperature, only one phase—the gas phase—can exist.

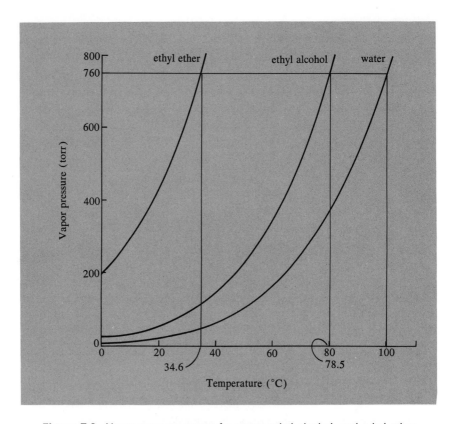

Figure 7.3 Vapor pressure curves for water, ethyl alcohol, and ethyl ether.

Liquids with weak intermolecular attractive forces have relatively high vapor pressures. Thus at 20°C, ethyl ether has a vapor pressure of 442 torr, and water has a vapor pressure of 17.5 torr; these data indicate that the forces of attraction are stronger in water than in ethyl ether.

7.4 Boiling Point

The temperature at which the vapor pressure of a liquid equals the atmospheric pressure is called the **boiling point** of the liquid. At this temperature, vapor produced in the interior of a liquid results in the bubble formation and turbulence characteristic of boiling. Bubble formation is impossible at temperatures below the boiling point; the atmospheric pressure on the surface of the liquid prevents the formation of bubbles with internal pressures that are less than atmospheric.

The temperature of a boiling liquid remains constant until all the liquid has been vaporized. In an open container, the maximum vapor pressure that can be attained by any liquid is the atmospheric pressure. We have noted in the preceding section that the vapor pressure or a liquid is determined by temperature alone; hence, if the vapor pressure is fixed, the temperature is fixed. Heat must be added to a boiling liquid to maintain the temperature, because in the boiling process the high-energy molecules are lost by the liquid. If the rate of heat addition is increased above the minimum needed to maintain the temperature of the boiling liquid, the rate of boiling increases, but the temperature of the liquid does not rise.

The boiling point of a liquid changes with changes in external pressure. For example, water will boil at 97.7°C at a pressure of 700 torr and at 101.4°C at 800 torr; only at a pressure of 760 torr will water boil at 100°C. The **normal boiling point** of a liquid is defined as the temperature at which the vapor pressure of the liquid equals 760 torr. Boiling points given in reference books are understood to be normal boiling points.

The normal boiling points of ethyl ether (34.6°C), ethyl alcohol (78.5°C), and water are indicated on the vapor pressure curves of Figure 7.3. The boiling point of a liquid can be read from its vapor pressure curve by finding the temperature at which the vapor pressure of the liquid equals the prevailing pressure.

The fluctuations in atmospheric pressure at any one geographic location cause a maximum variation of about 2°C in the boiling point of water. However, from place to place, the variations can be greater than this. The average barometric pressure at sea level is 760 torr; at higher elevations, average barometric pressures are less. Thus, at an elevation of 5000 feet above sea level, the average barometric pressure is 635 torr; at this pressure, water boils at 95.1°C. Water boils at 90.1°C at 528 torr, which is the average atmospheric pressure at 10,000 feet above sea level.

If a liquid has a high normal boiling point or decomposes when heated, it can be made to boil at low temperatures by reducing the pressure. Such a procedure is followed in vacuum distillation; water can be made to boil at 10°C, which is considerably below room temperature, by adjusting the pressure to 9.2 torr (see Table 6.2 and Figure 7.3). Many food products are concentrated by removing unwanted water under reduced pressure; in these procedures, the product is not subjected to temperatures that bring about decomposition or discoloration.

The normal boiling point gives a general indication of the strength of the intermolecular cohesive forces of a liquid (Section 3.10). The boiling point of nonpolar materials, which are held together by van der Waals forces, generally increases with increasing molecular weight. High molecular weight materials have a large number of electrons to participate in the formation of the fluctuating dipoles that characterize van der Waals forces. However, predictions of the boiling point of a substance based on molecular weight must be made with caution. On the basis of molecular weight alone, one would predict a boiling point for water (molecular weight, 18) about 200 to 300 degrees less than the observed 100°C; water is a polar material with exceptionally strong forces of attraction (Section 8.11).

7.5 Heat of Vaporization

The **molar heat of vaporization**, ΔH_v, is that quantity of energy that must be supplied to vaporize a mole of a liquid at a specified temperature. Heats of vaporization are usually recorded at the normal boiling point in kcal/mole (Table 7.1).

Table 7.1

Heats of Vaporization of Liquids at their Normal Boiling Points

Liquid	t_b Normal Boiling Point (°C)	ΔH_v Heat of Vaporization (kcal/mole)	$\Delta S_v = \Delta H_v/T_b$ Entropy of Vaporization (cal/°K mole)
water	100.0	9.72	26.0
benzene	80.1	7.35	20.8
ethyl alcohol	78.5	9.22	26.2
carbon tetrachloride	76.7	7.17	20.5
chloroform	61.3	7.02	21.0
carbon disulfide	46.3	6.40	20.0
ethyl ether	34.6	6.21	20.2

In Section 7.2, a kinetic picture of the vaporization process was presented, and the heat of vaporization was interpreted from this viewpoint. A slightly different interpretation follows, based on a consideration of the heat content (or enthalpy, H) of the vapor and of the liquid. The temperature of a vapor is the same as the temperature of the liquid with which it is in equilibrium; hence, the molecules of each phase have the same average kinetic energy. However, the phases differ in total internal energy, which includes potential energy as well as kinetic energy. The molecules of the liquid are held together by cohesive forces; the molecules of the vapor are essentially free. When the liquid is converted into a gas, energy must be supplied to separate the molecules. Thus the energy of the gas phase is higher than that of the liquid phase by the amount of this difference.

The difference in heat content of the phases (ΔH) takes into account another factor. The volume of a gas is considerably larger than the volume of the liquid from which it is derived (e.g., about 1700 ml of steam is produced by the vaporization of 1 ml of water at 100°C); energy must be supplied to do the work of pushing back the atmosphere to make room for the vapor. The heat of vaporization includes both the energy required to overcome the inter-molecular cohesive forces and the energy needed to expand the vapor.

When a mole of vapor is condensed to a liquid, the difference in heat content of the phases is released rather than absorbed. In this instance, the heat effect is called the **molar heat of condensation**; it has a negative sign but is numerically equal to the molar heat of vaporization at the same temperature.

The heat of vaporization of a given liquid decreases as the temperature increases and equals zero at the critical temperature of the substance. This parallels an increase in the fraction of high-energy molecules; at the critical temperature, all the molecules have sufficient energy to vaporize.

In general, the higher the heat of vaporization of a substance, the stronger are the intermolecular forces of attraction; this relationship is similar to that between the normal boiling point and these forces. Frederick Trouton, in 1884, discovered that for many liquids the heat of vaporization, in calories per mole, divided by the normal boiling point, in °K, is a constant: 21 cal/°K mole (**Trouton's rule**). Thus

$$\frac{\Delta H_v}{T_b} = 21 \text{ cal/°K mole}$$

The rule is only approximate, as the values listed in Table 7.1 attest.

The value ($\Delta H_v/T_b$) of Trouton's rule is called the **molar entropy of vaporization** and is given the symbol ΔS_v. The **entropy**, S, of a system is a measure of the system's randomness, or disorder (Section 13.5). A positive change in entropy, ΔS, indicates an increase in disorder; a negative value of ΔS indicates that the system has become more ordered.

The change from liquid to vapor involves an increase in molecular randomness. The extent of this increase is about the same for all nonpolar liquids, and therefore the values of ΔS_v are about the same, 21 cal/°K mole. In liquid water and ethyl alcohol, the intermolecular forces of attraction are unusually strong (Section 8.11); hence ΔS_v values for these liquids are comparatively large (Table 7.1), since they represent changes from liquids that are more highly ordered than usual.

The entropy of vaporization of a given liquid, like the heat of vaporization, decreases as the temperature is increased. With increasing temperature, the molecular randomness of the liquid phase increases and approaches that of the gas phase; at the critical temperature, they are equal, only one phase exists, $\Delta H_v = 0$, and $\Delta S_v = 0$.

7.6 The Freezing Point

As a liquid is cooled, the molecules move more and more slowly. Eventually, a temperature is reached where some of the molecules have sufficiently low kinetic energies to allow the intermolecular attractions to hold them in a crystal lattice; the substance then starts to freeze. Gradually, the low-energy molecules assume positions in the crystal lattice; the molecules remaining in the liquid have a higher temperature because of the loss of these low-energy molecules. Heat must be removed from the liquid to maintain the temperature.

The **normal freezing point** of a liquid is the temperature at which solid and liquid are in equilibrium under a total pressure of 1 atm. At the freezing point, the temperature of the solid–liquid system remains constant until all of the liquid is frozen. The quantity of heat that must be removed to freeze a mole of a substance at the freezing point is called the **molar heat of crystallization**. It represents the difference in the heat content (ΔH) between the liquid and the solid.

At times, the molecules of a liquid, as they are cooled, continue the random motion characteristic of the liquid state at temperatures below the freezing point; such liquids are referred to as **undercooled** or **supercooled**. These systems can usually be caused to revert to the freezing temperature and the stable solid–liquid equilibrium by scratching the interior walls of the container with a stirring rod or by adding a seed crystal around which crystallization can occur. The crystallization process supplies heat, and the temperature is brought back to the freezing point until normal crystallization is complete.

Some undercooled liquids can exist for long periods, or permanently, in this state. When they are cooled, molecules solidify in a random arrangement typical of the liquid state rather than in an orderly geometric pattern of a crystal. Such substances have relatively high viscosities and are generally of a complex molecular form for which crystallization would be difficult. They are frequently called amorphous solids, vitreous materials, or glasses; examples include glass, tar, and certain plastics. Some materials (e.g., glass) can be obtained in the crystalline form by careful cooling and can revert very slowly to this form from the undercooled state. Amorphous solids have no definite freezing or melting point; rather, these transitions take place over a temperature range. They exhibit conchoidal fracture rather than the cleavage along definite planes at definite angles shown by crystalline materials.

When a crystalline substance is heated, the temperature at which solid–liquid equilibrium is attained under air at 1 atm pressure is called the **melting point**; it is, of course, the same temperature as the freezing point of the substance. The quantity of heat that must be *added* to melt a mole of the material

at the melting point is called the **molar heat of fusion** and is numerically equal
to the heat of crystallization.

The molar heats of fusion and **molar entropies of fusion** of several substances
are listed in Table 7.2. The transition from solid to liquid represents an

Table 7.2

Heats of Fusion of Solids at the Melting Point

Solid	t_f Melting Point (°C)	ΔH_f Heat of Fusion (kcal/mole)	$\Delta S_f = \Delta H_f / T_f$ Entropy of Fusion (cal/°K mole)
water	0.0	1.44	5.26
benzene	5.5	2.35	8.44
ethyl alcohol	−117.2	1.10	7.10
carbon tetrachloride	−22.9	0.60	2.40
chloroform	−63.5	2.20	10.50
carbon disulfide	−112.1	1.05	6.52

increase in disorder, and, consequently in entropy, in the same way that the
transition from liquid to gas does. Entropies of fusion, however, are generally
of a lower order than entropies of vaporization because molecular disorder
is greater in the gaseous state than in the liquid or solid states. The variation
in ΔS_f values from substance to substance is not large, indicating a rough
similarity in the extent of increase of disorder when solids melt. However,
ΔS_f values are not nearly so constant as ΔS_v values.

7.7 Vapor Pressure of a Solid

Molecules in a crystal vibrate about their lattice positions. There is a distribution of kinetic energy among these molecules similar to that for liquids and
gases but on a lower level. Energy is transmitted from molecule to molecule
so that the energy of any molecule is not indefinitely constant. The high-
energy molecules on the surface of the crystal can overcome the attractive
forces of the crystal and escape into the vapor phase. If the crystal is in a
closed container, equilibrium is eventually reached in which the rate of the
molecules leaving the solid equals the rate of the vapor molecules returning
to the crystal. The vapor pressure of a solid at a given temperature is a
measure of the number of molecules in the vapor at equilibrium.

Every solid has a vapor pressure, although some pressures are of very low
order. The magnitude of the vapor pressure is inversely proportional to the
strength of the attractive forces; thus ionic crystals have very low vapor
pressures.

Since the ability of molecules to escape the intermolecular forces of attraction depends upon their kinetic energies, the vapor pressure of a solid increases as the temperature increases. The temperature–vapor pressure curve for ice is illustrated in Figure 7.4. This curve intersects the vapor pressure curve for water at the freezing point. In the absence of air, the normal freezing point of water (1 atm total pressure) is 0.0025°C. *In air*, however, and under a total pressure of 1 atm, the freezing point of water is 0.0000°C, which is the commonly reported value. The difference in freezing point is caused by the presence of dissolved air in the water (Section 9.9). The vapor pressures plotted in Figure 7.4 are the partial pressures of H_2O in air with the total pressure equal to 1 atm. Freezing points are usually determined in air; however, in any event, any change in freezing point of a given substance caused by the presence of air is generally very small.

At the freezing point, the vapor pressures of solid and liquid are equal. If this were not true, one form would gradually be converted into the other. For example, if the vapor pressure of the liquid were higher than that of the

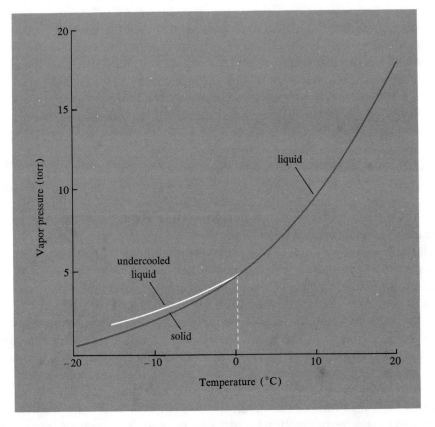

Figure 7.4 Vapor pressure curves for ice and water near the freezing point. Vapor pressures are partial pressures of H_2O under air at a total pressure of 760 torr.

solid, the vapor concentration would be higher than the equilibrium value for the solid–vapor system.

$$\text{solid} \rightleftharpoons \text{vapor}$$

In this circumstance, the rate of crystallization would increase, the amount of solid would increase, and the concentration of vapor would decrease. This decrease in the concentration of vapor would cause more of the liquid to vaporize in order to reestablish the equilibrium vapor pressure of the liquid.

$$\text{liquid} \rightleftharpoons \text{vapor}$$

The process would continue until all the liquid was converted into solid. At a given temperature, the stable form is that which has the lower vapor pressure.

7.8 Phase Diagrams

The temperature–pressure phase diagram for water conveniently illustrates the conditions under which water can exist as solid, liquid, or vapor, as well as the conditions that bring about changes in the state of water. Figure 7.5 is a schematic representation of the water system; it is not drawn to scale, and some of its features are exaggerated to give prominence to important details. Every substance has a unique phase diagram which describes only systems in equilibrium and which must be derived from experimental observations.

The diagram of Figure 7.5 relates to what is called a **one-component system**; that is, it pertains to the behavior of water in the absence of any other substance. Thus the total pressure of any system described by the diagram cannot be due in any part to the pressure of a gas other than water vapor. The vapor pressure curves plotted in Figure 7.4 (measured in air under a constant total pressure of 1 atm) therefore deviate slightly, but only very slightly, from the vapor pressure curves of Figure 7.5 (for which the vapor pressure of water is the *total* pressure). The easiest way to interpret the phase diagram for water is to visualize the total pressure acting on a system in mechanical terms, for example, as a piston acting on the material comprising the system contained in a cylinder.

In Figure 7.5, curve OC is a vapor pressure curve for liquid and terminates at the critical point, C. Any point on this line describes a set of temperature and pressure conditions under which liquid and vapor can exist in equilibrium. The extension DO is the curve for undercooled liquid; systems between liquid and vapor described by points on this line are **metastable**. (The term metastable is applied to systems that are not in the most stable state possible at the temperature in question.) Curve AO is a vapor pressure curve for solid and represents a set of points that describe the possible temperature and

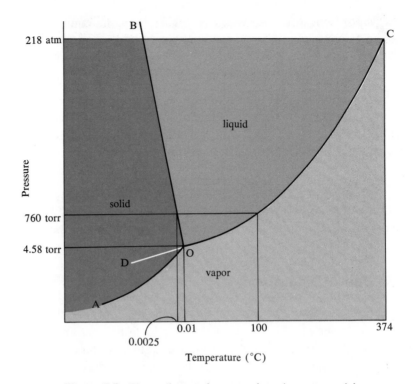

Figure 7.5 Phase diagram for water (not drawn to scale).

pressure conditions for solid–vapor equilibria. The line BO, the melting point curve, represents conditions for equilibria between solid and liquid.

These curves intersect at point O, the **triple point**. Solid, liquid, and vapor can exist together, in equilibrium, under the conditions represented by this point: 0.01°C (273.16°K) and a pressure of 4.58 torr due to the vapor. When a point described by the temperature–pressure coordinates falls in one of the regions labeled solid, liquid, or vapor, a situation is indicated where only one phase can exist under the conditions described.

The slope of the melting point (or freezing point) curve, BO, shows that the freezing point decreases as the pressure is increased. A variation of this type is observed for only a few substances such as antimony, bismuth, and water; it indicates an unusual situation where the liquid expands upon freezing. At 0°C a mole of water occupies 18.00 cm³, and a mole of ice occupies 19.63 cm³. Thus there is an expansion when 1 mole of liquid water freezes into ice. An increase in pressure on the system would oppose this expansion and the freezing process. Hence, the freezing point of water is lowered as the total pressure is increased. In Figure 7.5, the slope of the line BO is exaggerated.

Phase changes brought about by temperature changes at constant pressure may be read from a phase diagram by interpreting a horizontal line drawn at the reference pressure like the line drawn at 760 torr in Figure 7.5. The point where this line intersects curve BO indicates the normal melting, or freezing, point, and the point where the 760 torr line intersects curve CO represents the normal boiling point. Beyond this point, only vapor exists.

In like manner, phase changes brought about by pressure changes at constant temperature may be read from a vertical line drawn at the reference temperature. If the pressure is increased at, for example, 0.0025°C (Figure 7.5), the point where the vertical line crosses AO is the pressure where vapor changes to solid, and the point where the vertical line crosses BO represents the pressure where solid changes to liquid. Above this point, only liquid exists.

For materials that contract upon freezing (i.e., the solid phase is more dense than the liquid phase), the freezing-point curve inclines in the opposite direction, and the freezing point is increased as the pressure is increased. Such is the case for most substances and is seen in the phase diagram for carbon dioxide in Figure 7.6.

The process whereby a solid goes directly into a vapor without going through the liquid state is known as **sublimation**; this process is, of course, reversible. The phase diagram for carbon dioxide is typical of that for

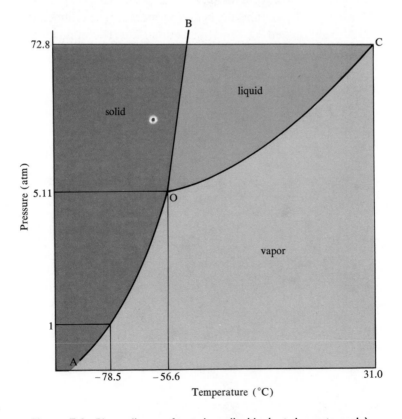

Figure 7.6 Phase diagram for carbon dioxide (not drawn to scale).

substances that sublime at ordinary pressures rather than melt and then boil. The triple point of the carbon dioxide system is $-55.6°C$ at a pressure of 5.11 atm, and, therefore, liquid carbon dioxide exists only at pressures greater than 5.11 atm. When solid carbon dioxide (dry ice) is heated at 1 atm pressure, it is converted directly into gas at $-78.5°C$; the **molar heat of sublimation** is the heat that must be added to a mole of solid to convert it into a gas.

7.9 Crystals

The orderly arrangement of atoms, ions, or molecules in a crystalline solid was discussed in Section 3.10. The constituent particles of a crystal are arranged in a repeating three-dimensional pattern called a **crystal** (or **space**) **lattice**. The smallest section of a crystal lattice that can be used to describe the lattice is the **unit cell**. A crystal can be reproduced, in theory, by stacking its unit cells in three dimensions.

Crystal lattices may be grouped, according to symmetry, into six **crystal systems** (Figure 7.7). A crystal system may be described by the dimensions of a unit cell along its three axes (a, b, c) and the sizes of the three angles between the axes (α, β, γ). The hexagonal system is sometimes divided into two, symmetrically related, systems: hexagonal and rhombohedral. Crystals have the same symmetry as their constituent unit cells.

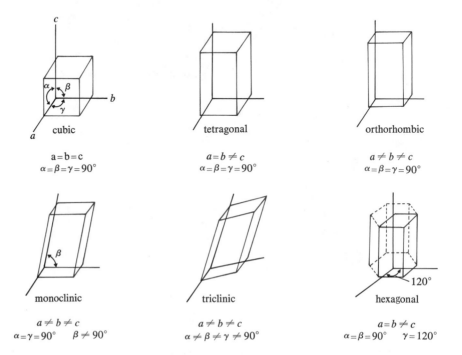

cubic
$a=b=c$
$\alpha=\beta=\gamma=90°$

tetragonal
$a=b\neq c$
$\alpha=\beta=\gamma=90°$

orthorhombic
$a\neq b\neq c$
$\alpha=\beta=\gamma=90°$

monoclinic
$a\neq b\neq c$
$\alpha=\gamma=90°\quad\beta\neq 90°$

triclinic
$a\neq b\neq c$
$\alpha\neq\beta\neq\gamma\neq 90°$

hexagonal
$a=b\neq c$
$\alpha=\beta=90°\quad\gamma=120°$

Figure 7.7 Crystal systems.

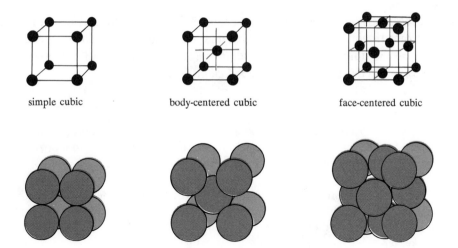

simple cubic   body-centered cubic   face-centered cubic

Figure 7.8 Cubic lattices.

In illustrations of crystal lattices, dots are customarily used to indicate the centers of the ions, atoms, or molecules. Six such point lattices can be drawn by indicating points at the corners of the unit cells shown in Figure 7.7. However, it is possible to have points at positions other than the corners. Thus three cubic lattices are known (Figure 7.8): simple cubic, body-centered cubic, and face-centered cubic. Altogether, there are 14 possible lattices in which each point is surrounded in an identical manner by other points.

In counting the number of atoms per unit cell, one must keep in mind that atoms on corners or faces are shared with adjoining cells. Eight unit cells share each corner atom, and two unit cells share each face-centered atom (Figure 7.9). Therefore, the simple cubic unit cell contains the equivalent of

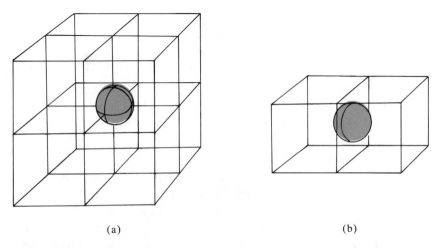

(a)   (b)

Figure 7.9 In cubic crystals, (a) a corner atom is shared by eight unit cells, and (b) a face-centered atom is shared by two unit cells.

only one atom (8 corners at 1/8 each). The body-centered unit cell contains two atoms (8 corners at 1/8 each and one unshared atom in the center). The face-centered unit cell contains the equivalent of four atoms (8 corners at 1/8 each and 6 face-centered atoms at 1/2 each).

▶ **EXAMPLE 7.1** Nickel crystallizes in a face-centered cubic crystal; the edge of the unit cell is 3.52 Å. The atomic weight of nickel is 58.7, and its density is 8.94 g/cm³. From these data, calculate Avogadro's number.

Solution There are four nickel atoms in each unit cell. If we let N = Avogadro's number, the weight of one atom is $(58.7/N)$ g. The weight of one unit cell is $4\,(58.7/N)$ g. The volume of one unit cell is $(3.52 \times 10^{-8})^3$ cm³. The density of nickel is

$$\frac{4(58.7/N)\ \text{g}}{(3.52 \times 10^{-8})^3\ \text{cm}^3} = 8.94\ \text{g/cm}^3$$

Therefore

$$N = 6.02 \times 10^{23}$$

An alternative solution follows:

$$? \text{atoms} = 58.7\ \text{g Ni} \left(\frac{1\ \text{cm}^3}{8.94\ \text{g Ni}}\right) \left(\frac{4\ \text{atoms}}{(3.52 \times 10^{-8})^3\ \text{cm}^3}\right)$$

$$= 6.02 \times 10^{23}$$

7.10 X-Ray Diffraction of Crystals

Much of what is known about the internal structure of crystals has been learned from X-ray diffraction experiments. Two X-ray waves that are in phase reinforce each other and produce a wave that is stronger than either of the original waves (Figure 7.10a). The resultant wave has a greater amplitude than either of the primary waves, but the wavelength, λ, remains the same. Two waves that are completely out of phase cancel each other; the resultant is of negligible intensity (Figure 7.10b).

Figure 7.11 illustrates the determination of crystal spacings by the use of X rays of a single wavelength. The rays impinge upon parallel planes of the crystal at an angle ϕ; the angle of reflection equals the angle of incidence. Some of the rays are reflected from the upper plane, some from the second plane, and some from lower planes. A strong reflected beam will result only if all of the rays are in phase. In the illustration, the ray *DFH* travels farther than the ray *ABC* by an amount equal to *EF* + *FG*. These rays will be in phase at

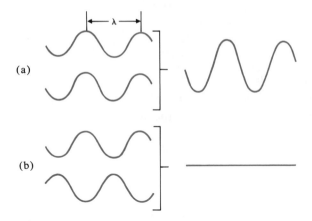

Figure 7.10 (a) Reinforcement of in-phase waves.
(b) Destructive interference of out-of-phase waves.

CH only if this difference equals a whole number of wavelengths. Thus

$$EF + FG = n\lambda$$

where n is a simple integer.

The line *BE* is drawn perpendicular to *DF*. Angle *BEF*, therefore, equals 90°. The sum of the other two angles (*EBF* and *EFB*) of the triangle *BEF* must also equal 90°, since the sum of the angles of any triangle equals 180°.

$$\angle EBF + \angle EFB = 90°$$

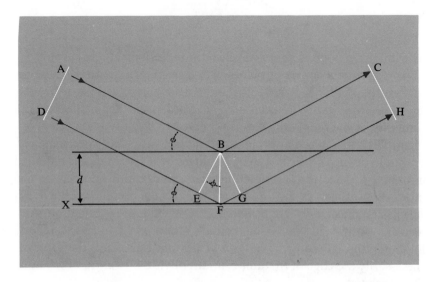

Figure 7.11 Derivation of the Bragg equation.

Angle *XFB* is a right angle, and angle *XFE* is ϕ; therefore angle *EFB* is equal to 90° minus ϕ. Consequently,

$$\angle EBF + (90° - \phi) = 90°$$

and angle *EBF* equals ϕ.

The sine of this angle, ϕ, is equal to *EF/BF*, and since *BF* is equal to *d* (the distance between the planes of the crystal),

$$\sin \phi = \frac{EF}{d}$$

or

$$EF = d \sin \phi$$

Likewise,

$$FG = d \sin \phi$$

and therefore,

$$EF + FG = 2d \sin \phi$$

or

$$n\lambda = 2d \sin \phi$$

This equation was derived by William Henry Bragg and his son William Lawrence Bragg in 1913.

The Bragg equation can be rearranged:

$$\sin \phi = \frac{n\lambda}{2d}$$

Thus with X rays of a definite wavelength, reflections at various angles will be observed for a given set of planes with a spacing equal to *d*. These reflections correspond to $n = 1, 2, 3$, etc., and are spoken of as first order, second order, third order, etc. With each successive order, the angle ϕ increases, and the intensity of the reflected beam is observed to weaken.

Figure 7.12 is a schematic representation of an X-ray spectrometer. An X-ray beam, defined by a slit system, impinges on a crystal that is mounted on a turntable. A detector (photographic plate, ionization chamber, or Geiger counter) is positioned as shown in the figure. As the crystal is rotated, strong signals flash out as angles are passed that satisfy the Bragg equation. Any set of regularly positioned planes that contain atoms can give rise to reflections and not only those that form the faces of the unit cells. Thus the value of *d* is not necessarily the edge of the unit cell, although the two are always mathematically related.

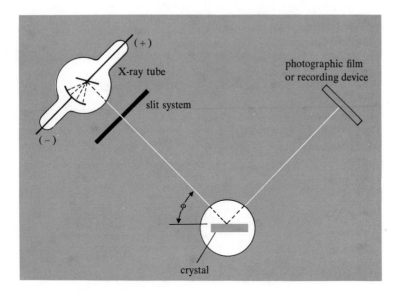

Figure 7.12 X-ray diffraction of crystals (schematic).

▶ **EXAMPLE 7.2** The diffraction of a crystal of barium with X radiation of wavelength 2.29 Å gives a first-order reflection at 27° 8′. What is the distance between the diffracted planes?

Solution Substitution into the Bragg equation gives:

$$n\lambda = 2d \sin \phi$$
$$1(2.29 \text{ Å}) = 2d(0.456)$$
$$d = 2.51 \text{ Å}$$

7.11 Crystal Structure of Metals

In the overwhelming majority of cases, metal crystals belong to one of three classifications: body-centered cubic (Figure 7.8), face-centered cubic (Figure 7.8), and hexagonal close packed (Figure 7.13). The geometric arrangement of atoms in the face-centered cubic and the hexagonal close-packed crystals is such that each atom has a coordination number of 12 (is adjoined by 12 other atoms). If the atoms are viewed as spheres, there is a minimum of empty space in these two types of crystals (about 26%), and both of the crystal lattices are spoken of as close-packed structures. The body-centered cubic arrangement is slightly more open than either of the close-packed arrangements (about 32% empty space); each atom of a body-centered cubic crystal has a coordination number of 8.

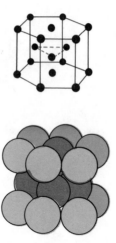

Figure 7.13 Hexagonal
close-packed structure.

The difference between the two close-packed structures may be derived from a consideration of Figure 7.14. The shaded circles of the diagram represent the first layer of spheres which are placed as close together as possible. The second layer of spheres (open circles of Figure 7.14) are placed in the hollows formed by adjacent spheres of the first layer. The first two layers of both the face-centered cubic and the hexagonal close-packed arrangements are the same; the difference arises in the third and subsequent layers.

In the hexagonal close-packed arrangement, the spheres of the third layer are placed so that they are directly over those of the first layer; the sequence of layers may be represented as *ababab*.... However, in the face-centered cubic structure, the spheres of the third layer are placed over the holes (marked *x* in Figure 7.14) formed by the arrangements of the first two

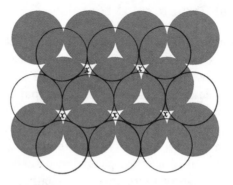

Figure 7.14 Schematic representation of the first two layers of the close-packed arrangements.

layers. The spheres of the fourth layer of the face-centered cubic structure are placed so that they are directly over those of the first layer, and the sequence of layers is *abcabc*....

The holes that the *second* layer of spheres cap are called **tetrahedral holes** because each is formed by four spheres. The *x* holes are **octahedral holes**, and each is surrounded by six spheres. In an extended three-dimensional model of either close-packed structure, there are the same number of octahedral holes as spheres and twice as many tetrahedral holes as spheres. The importance of these holes is discussed in Section 7.12.

The crystal structures of metals are summarized in Table 7.3. The division

Table 7.3

Crystal Structures of Metals

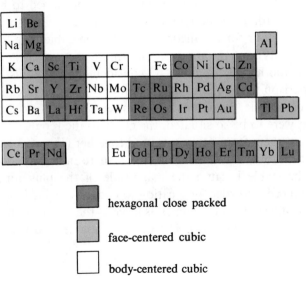

between the three structures: hexagonal close packed, face-centered cubic, and body-centered cubic, is about even. The close packing of most metallic crystals helps to explain the relatively high densities of metals. The structures of a few metals (for example, manganese and mercury) do not fall into any of the three categories, and the symbols for these metals do not appear in the table. Some metals exhibit **crystal allotropy**; that is, different crystal forms of the same metal are stable under different conditions. For example, a modification of calcium exists in each of the three structures. The form of each metal that is indicated in Table 7.3 is the one that is stable under ordinary conditions. In addition to many metals, the noble gases also crystallize in the face-centered cubic lattice.

7.12 Ionic Crystals

Ionic lattices are more complicated than metallic lattices. An arrangement must accommodate ions of opposite charge and different size in the proper stoichiometric ratio and in such a way that electrostatic attractions outweigh electrostatic repulsions.

For most ionic compounds, the anion is larger than the cation, and it is advantageous to look at an ionic crystal as being composed of a lattice of anions with cations placed in lattice holes. Three types of lattice holes are illustrated in Figure 7.15. By imagining that the lattice points of the diagrams expand into spheres that touch, one can get an idea of the actual appearance of these holes.

If cations were placed in the spots marked y in the diagrams of Figure 7.15, the number of anions around each cation (and presumed to be touching it) would vary according to the type of hole occupied: eight for cubic, six for octahedral, and four for tetrahedral. Clearly, the cubic hole is best in terms of crystal stability brought about by plus-minus attractions.

However, another factor must be considered: the radius of the cation, r^+, in comparison to the radius of the anion, r^-. If a large cation were to be placed in a cubic hole, the anions of the lattice could be forced apart, but if a small cation were to be so situated, the electrostatic repulsions of the anions would prevent them from being squeezed together (Figure 3.5). In this latter case, the cation could not touch each anion surrounding it, and the structure would not be stable because the magnitude of the plus-minus attractions would be reduced. In order for a cation to occupy a cubic hole, the radius of the cation must be at least 0.73 times as large as the radius of the anion (radius ratio, r^+/r^-, greater than 0.73). The value 0.73 is derived from a calculation based on solid geometry.

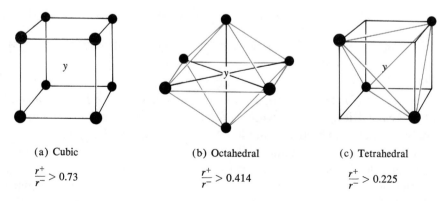

(a) Cubic	(b) Octahedral	(c) Tetrahedral
$\dfrac{r^+}{r^-} > 0.73$	$\dfrac{r^+}{r^-} > 0.414$	$\dfrac{r^+}{r^-} > 0.225$

Figure 7.15 Types of holes in crystal lattices and radius ratio criteria for cation occupancy.

If a cation is too small for a cubic hole, the next best bet is the slightly smaller octahedral hole (coordination number, 6). In order to maintain cation-anion contact, the radius of a cation filling an octahedral hole must be at least 0.414 times as large as the anion radius.

The tetrahedral hole is the smallest of the three, but its coordination number is only 4. Cations that are small in relation to the size of the anions of the lattice fill tetrahedral holes; the critical radius ratio is only 0.225.

The three most common crystal types for compounds of formula MX are shown in Figure 7.16. In each diagram, there are as many cations shown as belonging to a unit cell as there are anions (1 each in CsCl, 4 each in both NaCl and ZnS, taking into account sharing by adjacent unit cells). Therefore, a 1 : 1 stoichiometric ratio is represented in each case.

Compare the diagrams of Figure 7.15 with those of Figure 7.16. In the **cesium chloride** type crystal, the chloride ions form a simple cubic lattice with cesium ions filling cubic holes. In the **sodium chloride** crystal, the chloride ions assume a face-centered cubic lattice, and the sodium ions fill octahedral holes. The sulfide ions of the **zinc blende** structure also form a face-centered cubic lattice, but the zinc ions fill alternate tetrahedral holes. There are twice as many tetrahedral holes as spheres in a close-packed structure (Section 7.11), and therefore the zinc ions of ZnS fill only half of the total number of such holes.

Predictions based on radius ratio alone are sometimes not borne out, because the hard sphere model of ions that we have used fails to take ion distortion into account (Section 3.8). Many ionic compounds occur in the three structures we have discussed; examples are given in Table 7.4.

Analysis of the crystal forms of compounds of formula MX_2 or M_2X proceeds along similar lines. The antifluorite and rutile structures are shown in Figure 7.17. In the **antifluorite** form, cations occupy all the tetrahedral holes in a face-centered cubic anion lattice. The **fluorite** structure (named for the mineral fluorite, CaF_2) is not shown in Figure 7.17; it is similar to the

Cesium chloride
CsCl

Sodium chloride
NaCl

Zinc blende
ZnS

Figure 7.16 Crystal structures of ionic compounds of the MX type. Colored circles represent cations.

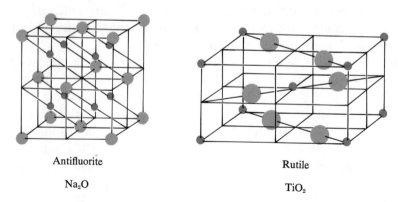

Antifluorite

Na_2O

Rutile

TiO_2

Figure 7.17 Crystal structures of ionic compounds of the MX_2 type. Colored circles represent cations.

Table 7.4

Crystal Structures of Some Ionic Compounds

Structure	Examples
cesium chloride	$CsCl$, $CsBr$, CsI, $TlCl$, $TlBr$, TlI, NH_4Cl, NH_4Br
sodium chloride	halides of Li^+, Na^+, K^+, Rb^+
	oxides and sulfides of Mg^{2+}, Ca^{2+}, Sr^{2+}, Ba^{2+}, Mn^{2+}, Ni^{2+}
	AgF, $AgCl$, $AgBr$, NH_4I
zinc blende	sulfides of Be^{2+}, Zn^{2+}, Cd^{2+}, Hg^{2+}
	$CuCl$, $CuBr$, CuI, AgI, ZnO
fluorite	fluorides of Ca^{2+}, Sr^{2+}, Ba^{2+}, Cd^{2+}, Pb^{2+}
	$BaCl_2$, $SrCl_2$, ZrO_2, ThO_2, UO_2
antifluorite	oxides and sulfides of Li^+, Na^+, K^+, Rb^+
rutile	fluorides of Mg^{2+}, Ni^{2+}, Mn^{2+}, Zn^{2+}, Fe^{2+}
	oxides of Ti^{4+}, Mn^{4+}, Sn^{4+}, Te^{4+}

antifluorite structure except that cation and anion positions are exchanged. The **rutile** unit cell is not cubic and is difficult to describe. Notice, however, that the titanium ion in the center of the unit cell fills an octahedral hole formed by oxide ions.

7.13 Lattice Energy

The lattice energy of an ionic compound may be calculated if the crystal geometry and distances between the ions in the crystals are known. An expression for the electrostatic interactions of the ions may be derived by treating the charges of the ions as though they were located entirely at points in the centers of the ions. The expression for the potential energy of interaction of point charges—that is, the energy associated with bringing charges together from an infinite distance to a separation distance, d—may be derived from Coulomb's law (Section 2.11).

$$PE = \frac{q_1 q_2}{d} \tag{1}$$

If the charges are of like sign (both positive or both negative), then the potential energy will be positive, indicating that energy is absorbed by the process. On the other hand, if the charges have unlike signs, then they will attract each other, and the potential energy will be negative; energy is evolved by the process.

In a sodium chloride crystal, the distance between neighboring Na^+ and Cl^- ions is 2.8 Å, which we shall designate as r. The Na^+ and Cl^- ions have charges of $+e$ and $-e$, respectively, where $-e$ is the charge on the electron $(-4.803 \times 10^{-10}$ esu). Calculation of the electrostatic potential of a single sodium ion proceeds by determining the contributions to the potential energy from interactions with all the surrounding ions of the crystal.

As a greatly simplified example, we shall consider the potential energy of the sodium ion (dark circle) in the center of the extremely small crystal fragment illustrated in Figure 7.18. The fragment is a cube $2r$ on a side and may be considered to be made up of eight smaller cubes each r on a side. Notice

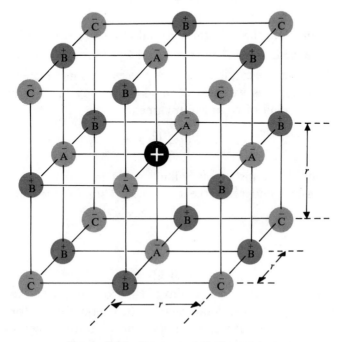

Figure 7.18 Fragment of NaCl crystal.

that the diagonal of a face of one of the smaller cubes is $r\sqrt{2}$ and that the cube diagonal of the smaller cube is $r\sqrt{3}$. These facts may be confirmed by use of the Pythagorean theorem.

The nearest neighbors of the reference ion are the six Cl^- ions that are labeled A in the diagram and which are at a distance of r from the Na^+ ion. The potential energy contributed by six of these ions is:

$$PE = 6\frac{(+e)(-e)}{r} = -\frac{e^2}{r} \text{ (6)} \qquad (2)$$

The next nearest neighbors of the central Na^+ ion are the twelve Na^+ ions that are labeled B in Figure 7.18. Each of these ions is situated at a distance $r\sqrt{2}$ from the central Na^+ ion (along face diagonals of the small cubes). Since the charge on each of these ions is the same as that of the reference ion, a positive potential energy, or repulsion, is indicated. The total contribution from this group of ions is:

$$PE = 12\frac{(+e)(+e)}{r\sqrt{2}} = -\frac{e^2}{r}\left(-\frac{12}{\sqrt{2}}\right) \qquad (3)$$

The eight Cl^- ions that are labeled C in Figure 7.18 are at a distance of $r\sqrt{3}$ from the central Na^+ ion (along cube diagonals of the small cubes). Their contribution is therefore

$$PE = 8\frac{(+e)(-e)}{r\sqrt{3}} = -\frac{e^2}{r}\left(\frac{8}{\sqrt{3}}\right) \qquad (4)$$

If we continued in this way for a crystal of a more realistic size, we would find that there were six Na^+ ions at $2r$, 24 Cl^- ions at $r\sqrt{5}$, 24 Na^+ ions at $r\sqrt{6}$, etc. However, we can illustrate the process by summing expressions (2), (3), and (4) as long as we keep in mind that many more terms would be required for any kind of complete treatment. Thus,

$$PE = -\frac{e^2}{r}\left(6 - \frac{12}{\sqrt{2}} + \frac{8}{\sqrt{3}} - \cdots\right) \qquad (5)$$

The sum of the terms of the infinite series in parentheses is called the **Madelung constant** and given the symbol A. Thus for the reference ion (a sodium ion):

$$PE = -\frac{e^2}{r}A \qquad (6)$$

The expression for the chloride ion is identical.

A mole of sodium chloride contains N Na^+ ions and N Cl^- ions, where N is Avogadro's number. The total electrostatic energy for the formation of a mole of NaCl, however, is not $2N$ times expression (6), since this procedure would count each interaction twice—once for the Na^+ ion and again for the

Cl^- ion. Hence, the electrostatic potential energy per mole is one-half of $2N$, or N, times equation (6)

$$PE = -\frac{e^2}{r} NA \tag{7}$$

Notice that energy is evolved (minus sign) in the formation of a crystal from its constituent ions.

Equation (7) is a general expression for any type of crystal in which both ions bear unit charges. Differences in crystal geometry are reflected in the terms of the series used to derive the Madelung constant, and the value of the constant, therefore, depends upon the crystal structure. For crystals of the NaCl type, A is 1.748; for zinc blende crystals, A is 1.638; for CsCl type crystals, A is 1.763.

For crystals formed between ions that do not both have unit charges, equation (7) becomes

$$PE = -\frac{(Z_c)(Z_a)e^2}{r} NA \tag{8}$$

where Z_c and Z_a are the number of unit charges on the cation and anion, respectively. These numbers do not include signs. The value of A for the fluorite structure is 5.039 and for the rutile structure is 4.816.

Equations (7) and (8) give values for lattice energies that are about 10% too high. Ions in crystals are not charges at fixed points in a lattice. The electron clouds of ions interact, and there are repulsive forces (even between ions of unlike sign) caused by this electronic interaction. A more exact calculation of lattice energy includes a correction for these repulsions—the magnitude of the correction factor being determined by measurement of the extent to which the crystal resists compression. More highly refined calculations include more corrections (for example, one that takes van der Waals forces into account). The importance of lattice energy calculations in relation to the Born–Haber cycle has been discussed in Section 5.10.

7.14 Defect Structures

Few crystals are perfect; many have some type of lattice defect. **Dislocations** are crystal imperfections where planes of atoms are misaligned. For example, one type of dislocation is caused by the insertion, perpendicular to a face, of an extra plane of atoms part way through a crystal. Atoms in the part of the crystal containing the extra plane are compressed.

Point defects are caused by missing or misplaced ions. One type of defect consists of a cation that has been moved from its proper position (thus creating a vacancy) to a place between regular lattice sites (an **interstitial**

position). Another type of point defect consists of a pair of vacancies—one cation and one anion; the ions for these lattice positions are missing from the structure completely. These defects do not alter the stoichiometry of the crystal.

Certain crystals are imperfect because their compositions are not stoichiometric. Thus, samples of iron(II) oxide, FeO, usually contain more oxygen atoms than iron atoms, whereas zinc oxide, ZnO, usually has an excess of zinc atoms over oxygen atoms. These departures from stoichiometry are usually quite small, on the order of 0.1%. There are several causes for **nonstoichiometry**, and in each the electrical neutrality of the crystal is preserved. Extra metal *atoms* or nonmetal *atoms* may be included in interstitial positions between the *ions* of the crystal (such as extra Zn atoms in ZnO). In addition, metal *atoms* or nonmetal *atoms* may assume regular lattice positions in place of *ions*; in these cases, ionic vacancies exist in the crystal lattice so that the whole is electrically neutral. For example, in FeO oxygen atoms assume positions normally occupied by oxide ions, and there are missing Fe^{2+} ions so that a 1 to 1 cation-anion ratio is maintained. It is postulated that in some crystals of this type (e.g., KCl), electrons from the "extra" metal atoms occupy the holes created by the anion vacancies. Nonstoichiometric substances are sometimes referred to as **berthollides**, named for Claude Louis Berthollet, who believed that the compositions of compounds varied continuously within limits. Joseph Proust, who upheld the law of definite proportions, engaged Berthollet in an argument of eight years' duration (1799–1807) concerning the composition of compounds.

The presence of **impurities** frequently accounts for crystal defects. For example, a Mg^{2+} ion may occur in a lattice position in a NaCl crystal in place of a Na^+ ion; electrical neutrality requires that another lattice position be vacant, since the charge of the Mg^{2+} ion is twice that of the Na^+ ion.

The addition of impurities to certain crystals produces conduction effects. Pure silicon and germanium function as intrinsic semiconductors (Section 4.6, Figure 4.29). Both these elements crystallize in the diamond-type network lattice in which each atom is bonded to four other atoms (Figure 3.16). At room temperature, the conductivity of either silicon or germanium is extremely low, since the electrons are fixed by the bonding of the crystal. However, at higher temperatures, the crystal bonding begins to break down; electrons are freed and are able to move through the structure, thereby causing the conductivity to increase.

The addition of small traces of certain impurities to either silicon or germanium enhances the conductivity of these materials and produces what are called **extrinsic**, or **impurity**, **semiconductors**. For example, if boron is added to pure silicon at the rate of one B atom per million Si atoms, the conductivity is increased by a factor of approximately one hundred thousand (from 4×10^{-6}/ohm cm to 0.8/ohm cm at room temperature). Each Si atom has four valence electrons that are used in the bonding of the network lattice. A boron atom, however, has only three valence electrons. Hence, a B atom that assumes a position of a Si atom in the crystal can form only three of the four bonds required for a perfect lattice, and an electron vacancy, or hole, is introduced. An electron from a nearby bond can move into this vacancy, thus completing the four bonds on the B atom but, at the same time, leaving a vacancy at the original site of the electron. In this way electrons move through the structure, and the holes move in a direction opposite to that of the conduction electrons.

This type of extrinsic semiconductor, in which holes enable electron motion, is called a *p*-**type** semiconductor; the *p* stands for positive. The term is somewhat misleading, however, since the crystal, formed entirely from neutral atoms, is electrically neutral. The structure is electron deficient only with regard to the covalent bonding requirements of the lattice; it never has an excess of positive charge.

In addition to boron, other III A elements (Al, Ga, or In) can be added, in small amounts, to pure silicon or germanium to produce *p*-type semiconductors. Impurities that owe their effect to their ability to accept electrons by means of the holes they produce in the crystal lattice are known as **acceptor impurities**.

The energy-level band diagram for *p*-type semiconductors is shown in Figure 7.19. Electron vacancies are responsible for the addition of *empty*

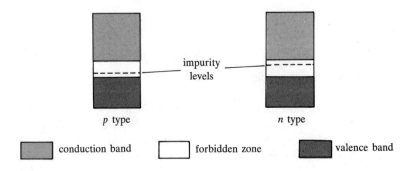

Figure 7.19 Energy-level band diagrams for extrinsic semiconductors.

impurity levels, just above the filled valence band, to a diagram that otherwise would be characteristic of an intrinsic semiconductor. Promotion of electrons from the valence band to the unoccupied impurity levels requires the addition of comparatively little energy, and conduction takes place in this manner.

Traces of group V A elements (P, As, Sb, or Bi) when added to silicon or germanium produce a second type of extrinsic semiconductor known as an *n*-**type**; the *n* stands for negative. In this instance, each impurity atom has five valence electrons—one over and above that required by the bonding of the host crystal. The extra electron can move through the structure and function as a conduction electron. Impurities of this type are known as **donor impurities**, since they provide conduction electrons. The *n*-type semiconductor is negative only in the peculiar sense that more electrons are present than are required by the bonding scheme of the crystal; the substance is electrically neutral.

The energy-level diagram for the *n*-type semiconductor is shown in Figure 7.19. *Filled* impurity levels are introduced just below the empty conduction band by the addition of donor impurities. The electrons from these levels are easily excited into the conduction band by heating, and conduction occurs by this means. Semiconductors find use in photocells and transistors.

SOME SUGGESTED READINGS

Dreisbach, D., *Liquids and Solutions*, Boston, Houghton Mifflin, 1966 (paper).
Evans, R. C., *An Introduction to Crystal Chemistry*, 2nd ed., New York, Cambridge University Press, 1964 (paper).
Findlay, A., *The Phase Rule and Its Applications*, 9th ed., New York, Dover, 1951 (paper).
Hildebrand, J. H., *An Introduction to Molecular Kinetic Theory*, New York, Van Nostrand Reinhold, 1963 (paper).

PROBLEMS

The more difficult problems are starred.

7.1   Briefly explain how and why each of the following gives an indication of the strength of the intermolecular forces of attraction: (a) critical temperature, (b) surface tension, (c) viscosity, (d) vapor pressure, (e) heat of vaporization, (f) heat of fusion, (g) normal boiling point, (h) molecular weight.

7.2   Compare and contrast: (a) enthalpy, entropy; (b) boiling point, normal boiling point; (c) freezing point of water, triple point of water; (d) crystalline solid, vitreous solid; (e) *p*-type semiconductor, *n*-type semiconductor.

7.3   By the use of Trouton's rule, estimate the heat of vaporization of a compound, C_9H_{20}, that has a normal boiling point of 141°C. Give the answer in kcal/mole and in cal/g.

7.4   The heat of vaporization of S_2Cl_2 at the normal boiling point is 63.9 cal/g. Use Trouton's rule to predict the normal boiling point of this compound (in °C).

7.5   The heat of vaporization of ethyl chloride is 92.5 cal/g at the normal boiling point of the compound, 13°C. By use of Trouton's rule estimate the molecular weight of ethyl chloride.

7.6   A compound has: a normal boiling point of 88°C, a heat of vaporization at the boiling point of 77 cal/g, and an empirical formula of CH_2. What is the molecular formula of the compound?

7.7   Calculate the amount of heat required to change 1 mole of H_2O from ice at $-10°C$ to steam at 110°C. The heat of vaporization of H_2O at 100°C is 540 cal/g and the heat of fusion of H_2O at 0°C is 79.9 cal/g. The specific heat of a substance is the amount of heat required to raise the temperature of 1 g of the substance 1°C. The specific heat of ice is 0.492 cal/g°, of liquid water is 1.00 cal/g°, and of steam is 0.484 cal/g°.

7.8   Explain why the entropy of vaporization of a substance is considerably larger than the entropy of fusion of that substance (see Tables 7.1 and 7.2).

7.9   Figure 7.5 is the phase diagram for water. Describe the phase changes that occur, and the approximate pressures at which they occur, when the pressure on a H_2O system is gradually increased (a) at a constant temperature of $-1°C$, (b) at a constant temperature of 50°C, (c) at a constant temperature of $-50°C$.

7.10 Refer to Figure 7.5 and describe the phase changes that occur, and the approximate temperatures at which they occur, when water is heated from $-10°C$ to 110°C (a) under a pressure of 1 torr, (b) under a pressure of 400 torr, (c) under a pressure of 800 torr.

7.11 Refer to Figure 7.6 and describe the phase changes that occur and the approximate pressures at which they occur when the pressure on a CO_2 system is gradually increased (a) at a constant temperature of $-60°C$, (b) at a constant temperature of 0°C.

7.12 Refer to Figure 7.6 and describe the phase changes that occur, and the approximate temperatures at which they occur when carbon dioxide is heated (a) at a constant pressure of 2.0 atm; (b) at a constant pressure of 6.0 atm.

7.13 Briefly explain how and why the slope of the melting-point curve of a phase diagram for a substance depends upon the relative densities of the solid and liquid forms of the substance.

7.14 Use the following data to draw a rough phase diagram for krypton. Normal boiling point, $-152°C$; normal melting point, $-157°C$; triple point, $-169°C$, 133 torr; critical point, $-63°C$, 54.2 atm; vapor pressure of solid at $-199°C$, 1.00 torr. Which has the higher density at a pressure of 1 atm: solid Kr or liquid Kr?

7.15 Sublimation is sometimes used to purify solids. The impure material is heated and the pure crystalline product condenses on a cold surface. Is it possible to purify ice by sublimation? What conditions would have to be employed?

7.16 The dimensions (in angstrom units) and the axial angles of the unit cells of five minerals are listed in the following table. To what crystal system does each belong?

	a	b	c	α	β	γ
marcasite	3.35	4.40	5.35	90°	90°	90°
muscovite	5.18	9.02	20.04	90°	95°30′	90°
rhodonite	7.77	12.45	6.74	85°10′	94°4′	111°29′
rutile	4.58	4.58	2.95	90°	90°	90°
quartz	4.90	4.90	5.39	90°	90°	120°

7.17 In the diffraction of a gold crystal using X rays with a wavelength equal to 1.54 Å, a first-order reflection is shown at an angle of 22°10′. What is the distance between the diffracted planes?

7.18 In the diffraction of a crystal using X rays with a wavelength equal to 1.54 Å, a first-order reflection is found at an angle of 16°. What is the wavelength of X rays that show this same reflection at an angle of 20°20′?

7.19 At what angle would a first-order reflection be observed in the X-ray diffraction of a set of crystal planes for which d is 3.03 Å if the X rays used have a wavelength of 0.710 Å? At what angle would a second-order reflection from this same set of planes be observed?

7.20 Copper crystallizes in a face-centered cubic lattice. The density of copper is 8.93 g/cm^3. What is the length of the edge of a unit cell?

7.21 Tantalum crystallizes in a cubic system and the edge of the unit cell is 3.30 Å. The density of Ta is 16.6 g/cm^3. How many atoms are contained in one unit cell of Ta? What type of cubic unit cell does Ta form?

7.22 The density of platinum is 21.5 g/cm^3 and Pt crystallizes in a face-centered cubic lattice with the edge of the unit cell equal to 3.92 Å. Calculate the atomic weight of Pt from these data.

7.23 Vanadium crystallizes in a body-centered cubic lattice, and the length of the edge of a unit cell is 3.05 Å. What is the density of V?

7.24 Lithium crystallizes in a body-centered cubic lattice; the length of the edge of the unit cell is 3.50 Å. The atomic weight of Li is 6.94 and the density of Li is 0.534 g/cm^3. From these data, calculate Avogadro's number.

7.25 Potassium crystallizes in a body-centered cubic unit cell with the length of an edge equal to 5.33 Å. Calculate the dimensions of a cube that would contain exactly one gram atomic weight of K.

7.26 Aluminum crystallizes in a face-centered cubic unit cell with the length of an edge equal to 4.05 Å. Assume that the atoms are identical hard spheres and that a face-centered atom touches each of the four corner atoms of its face. (a) Calculate the length of the diagonal of a face. (b) By means of your answer to part (a), calculate the radius of the hard-sphere atoms that comprise the crystal.

7.27 Use the data given in Problem 7.26 and the answer to Problem 7.26 to calculate: (a) the volume of a unit cell of Al, (b) the total volume of the hard-sphere atoms contained in one unit cell, (c) the percentage of the volume of a unit cell that is empty space.

7.28 Sodium crystallizes in a body-centered cubic unit cell with the length of an edge equal to 4.30 Å. Assume that the atoms are identical hard spheres and that the body-centered atom touches all eight corner atoms. (a) Calculate the length of the body diagonal of the cube. (b) By means of your answer to part (a), calculate the radius of the hard-sphere atoms that comprise the crystal.

7.29 Use the data given in Problem 7.28 and the answer to Problem 7.28 to calculate: (a) the volume of a unit cell of Na, (b) the total volume of the hard-sphere atoms contained in one unit cell, (c) the percentage of the volume of a unit cell that is empty space. Compare your answer to the answer to Problem 7.27.

*7.30 Assume that hard-sphere atoms of radius r comprise a simple cubic unit cell. Calculate: (a) the length of the edge of a unit cell, (b) the volume of a unit cell, (c) the total volume of the atoms comprising one unit cell, (d) the percentage of the volume of a unit cell that is empty space. Compare your final answer to answers for Problems 7.27 and 7.29.

*7.31 Make the calculations described in Problem 7.30 for the face-centered cubic unit cell and the body-centered cubic unit cell.

7.32 Xenon difluoride, XeF_2, *molecules* crystallize in a body-centered tetragonal lattice (see Figure 7.7). The base of the unit cell is a square 4.32 Å on a side, and the height of the unit cell is 6.99 Å. In counting the number of *molecules* per unit cell, assume that *molecules* occupy lattice positions. What is the density of XeF_2?

*7.33 Consider the cubic hole depicted in Figure 7.15. Assume that a cation (radius, r^+) is inserted in the position marked y, and that this cation touches all of the anions (radius, r^-) of the structure. Also assume contact between any two anions that are adjacent along an edge of the cube. By calculating the body diagonal of the cube, determine the value of the radius ratio, r^+/r^-, that is consistent with the criteria given.

*7.34 Consider the octahedral hole depicted in Figure 7.15. Assume that a cation (radius, r^+) is inserted in the position marked y, and that this cation touches all of the anions (radius, r^-) of the structure. Also assume contact between any two anions that are adjacent along an edge of the octahedron. By calculating the diagonal of the square formed by the four anions in the center of the structure, determine the value of the radius ratio, r^+/r^-, that is consistent with the criteria given.

*7.35 Consider the tetrahedral hole depicted in Figure 7.15. The anions (radius, r^-) along the diagonal of a face of the cube shown touch one another, and therefore the diagonal of a face of the cube is $2r^-$. (a) What is the length of an edge of the cube shown in terms of r^-? (b) What is the length of the body diagonal of the cube in terms of r^-? (c) Assume that a cation (radius, r^+) is placed in the position marked y in the figure. The body diagonal of the cube is equal to $(2r^+ + 2r^-)$. Calculate the radius ratio, r^+/r^-, for the tetrahedral hole.

7.36 (a) How many ions of each type are shown in the unit cell of the zinc blende structure depicted in Figure 7.16? (b) The density of ZnS is 4.10 g/cm³. What is the length of the edge of the unit cell shown in the figure?

*7.37 (a) How many ions of each type are shown in the unit cell of the sodium chloride structure depicted in Figure 7.16? (b) The length of the edge of the cube shown in the figure is 5.638 Å, and the density of NaCl is 2.165 g/cm³. Calculate the apparent molecular weight of NaCl to four significant figures. (c) The difference between the calculated value for the molecular weight of NaCl and the actual value (58.44) may be ascribed to a type of lattice defect in which Na atoms replace Na^+ ions in the crystal and an equal number of Cl^- ions are missing from lattice positions. On the basis of your answer to (b), calculate the percentage of anion sites that are vacant.

7.38 The distance between a Na^+ ion and a Cl^- ion, r, in a NaCl crystal is 2.82 Å, and the Madelung constant for crystals of the sodium chloride type is 1.75. (a) Calculate the electrostatic potential energy per mole for NaCl (in kcal/mole). The value of e is 4.80×10^{-10} esu (or $cm^{3/2} g^{1/2}/sec$); 1 erg = 1 g cm²/sec²; 1 joule = 10^7 erg; 1 cal = 4.18 joule. (b) In Section 5.10, a Born-Haber cycle was used to derive a value of -184 kcal/mole for the lattice energy of NaCl. Compare your answer from part (a) to this value of the lattice energy. By what percent does the electrostatic potential energy differ from the lattice energy? What are the sources of the deviation?

7.39 For cesium chloride, the length of the unit cell (shown in Figure 7.16) is 4.12 Å. (a) What is the distance, r, from the center of a Cs^+ ion to the center of an adjacent Cl^- ion? (b) The Madelung constant for crystals of the cesium chloride type is 1.76 and the value of e may be taken as 2.35×10^{-15} $kcal^{1/2}$ $cm^{1/2}$. Calculate the electrostatic potential energy for CsCl in kcal/mole. (c) The lattice energy of CsCl is -149 kcal/mole. Compare your result with this value.

7.40 In a given crystal, the distance between the centers of a cation and a neighboring anion is approximately equal to the sum of the ionic radii of the relevant ions. Some ionic radii are: Mg^{2+}, 0.65 Å; Na^+, 0.95 Å; K^+, 1.33 Å; Ba^{2+}, 1.35 Å; F^-, 1.36 Å; O^{2-}, 1.40 Å; and I^-, 2.16 Å. Arrange the following (each of which crystallizes in a sodium chloride lattice) in order of decreasing magnitude of lattice energy: NaF, MgO, KF, KI, and BaO.

7.41 List and describe the types of lattice defects found in crystals.

OXYGEN
AND HYDROGEN

Oxygen and hydrogen are probably the most important of all the elements. Oxygen is essential for the maintenance of life. Hydrogen forms more compounds than any other element (carbon is a close second). Water is the most common solvent and reaction medium. The classical acid-base scheme is based on water, and many analytical procedures depend upon the solubility of substances in water.

8.1 Occurrence and Preparation of Oxygen

Oxygen is the most abundant element (Table 8.1). Free oxygen makes up about 23.2% by weight of the atmosphere, or about 21.0% by volume. Water is approximately 89% oxgyen, and most minerals contain oxygen in the combined state. Silica, SiO_2, is a common ingredient of many minerals and the chief constituent of sand. Silicon is second to oxygen in the order of natural abundance because of the widespread occurrence of silica. Other oxygen-containing minerals are oxides, sulfates, and carbonates. Oxygen is a constituent of the compounds that make up plant and animal matter; the human body is more than 60% oxygen.

Table 8.1

Abundance of the Elements
(Earth's crust, bodies of water, and atmosphere)

Rank	Element	Percent by Weight
1	O	49.2
2	Si	25.7
3	Al	7.5
4	Fe	4.7
5	Ca	3.4
6	Na	2.6
7	K	2.4
8	Mg	1.9
9	H	0.9
10	Ti	0.6
11	Cl	0.2
12	P	0.1
13	Mn	0.1
14	C	0.09
15	S	0.05
16	Ba	0.05
	all others	0.51

Oxygen may be prepared by the thermal decomposition of certain oxygen-containing compounds. The oxides of metals of low reactivity (e.g., Hg, Ag, and Au) decompose on heating to give oxygen and the free metals.

$$2HgO(s) \longrightarrow 2Hg(l) + O_2(g)$$

Some higher oxides, upon heating, release only a part of their oxygen and go to lower oxides.

$$2PbO_2(s) \longrightarrow 2PbO(s) + O_2(g)$$
$$3MnO_2(s) \longrightarrow Mn_3O_4(s) + O_2(g)$$

Oxygen and the oxide ion are produced when the peroxide ion, O_2^{2-}, is heated.

$$2\left[:\ddot{O}:\ddot{O}:\right]^{2-} \longrightarrow 2\left[:\ddot{O}:\right]^{2-} + O_2$$

Thus

$$2Na_2O_2(s) \longrightarrow 2Na_2O(s) + O_2(g)$$
$$2BaO_2(s) \longrightarrow 2BaO(s) + O_2(g)$$

(Note that PbO_2 and MnO_2 are not peroxides.) If sodium peroxide is added to water, oxygen and a solution of sodium hydroxide result.

$$2O_2^{2-}(aq) + 2H_2O \longrightarrow 4OH^-(aq) + O_2(g)$$

Certain other compounds release all, or part, of their oxygen upon heating. Nitrates of the I A metals form nitrites.

$$2NaNO_3(l) \longrightarrow 2NaNO_2(l) + O_2(g)$$

Potassium chlorate loses all its oxygen; a catalyst (MnO_2) is generally used to lower the temperature required for this decomposition.

$$2KClO_3(s) \longrightarrow 2KCl(s) + 3O_2(g)$$

Small amounts of pure oxygen are produced commercially by the electrolysis of water.

$$2H_2O \xrightarrow{\text{electrolysis}} 2H_2(g) + O_2(g)$$

Most of the oxygen produced industrially, however, is obtained from the liquefaction of air. The principal components of air are nitrogen (78% by volume) and oxygen (21% by volume). In the fractionation of liquid air, nitrogen (boiling point, $-196°C$) is boiled away from the oxygen (boiling point, $-183°C$).

8.2 Properties of Oxygen

Oxygen is a colorless, odorless, and tasteless gas under ordinary conditions. The normal boiling point of oxygen is $-182.9°C$, and the normal melting point is $-218.4°C$; solid and liquid oxgyen are pale blue in color. The critical temperature of oxygen is $-118°C$, and the critical pressure is 49.7 atm.

At STP, the density of oxygen gas is 1.429 g/liter. Approximately 31 ml of the gas will dissolve in 1 liter of water under ordinary conditions; evidently this small amount is enough to sustain fish and aquatic plant life under water.

There are three naturally occurring isotopes of oxygen: $^{16}_{8}O$ (99.759%), $^{18}_{8}O$ (0.204%), and $^{17}_{8}O$ (0.037%). The isotopes ^{14}O, ^{15}O, ^{19}O, and ^{20}O are artificial and unstable.

The reactions of oxygen are often more sluggish than would be predicted from the fact that oxygen is a very electronegative element (3.5), second in this property only to fluorine (4.0). The reason for this slowness is that the bond energy of oxygen is high (118 kcal/mole), and therefore reactions that require the oxygen-to-oxygen bond to be broken occur only at high temperatures. Many of these reactions are relatively highly exothermic and therefore produce sufficient heat to sustain themselves after having once been initiated by external heating.

Whether self-sustaining or not, most oxygen reactions occur at temperatures considerably higher than room temperature. The most facile reactions of oxygen are those in which the oxygen-to-oxygen bond of the O_2 molecule is not completely broken. Examples of this type of reaction are afforded by the reactions of oxygen in which peroxides are prepared. Oxygen forms three different anions: the superoxide, peroxide, and oxide ions. Molecular orbital diagrams for oxygen, the superoxide ion, and the peroxide ion are given in Figure 8.1. The **superoxide ion**, O_2^-, can be considered as arising from the addition of one electron to the (π^*2p) orbital of the O_2 molecule, which reduces the number of unpaired electrons to 1 and the bond order to $1\frac{1}{2}$. The **peroxide ion**, O_2^{2-}, contains two additional electrons (in the (π^*2p) orbitals) over and above the O_2 molecule; hence, the bond order is reduced to 1, and

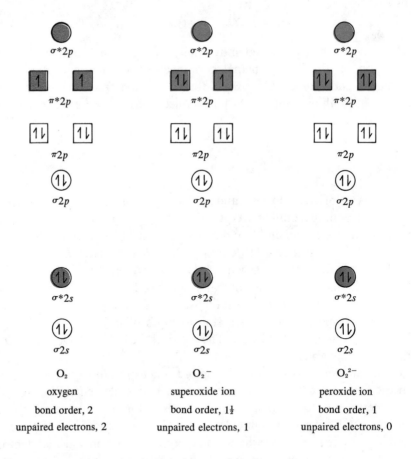

Figure 8.1 Molecular orbital energy-level diagrams for oxygen, the superoxide ion, and the peroxide ion.

the ion is diamagnetic. The **oxide ion**, O^{2-}, is isoelectronic with neon and is diamagnetic.

All metals except a few of the less-reactive metals (e.g. Ag, and Au) react with oxygen. Oxides of all metals are known but some must be made indirectly. The most reactive metals of group I A (and those with largest atomic radii): Cs, Rb, and K, react with oxygen to produce superoxides. For example,

$$Cs(s) + O_2(g) \longrightarrow CsO_2(s)$$

Sodium peroxide is produced by the reaction of sodium with oxygen.

$$2Na(s) + O_2(g) \longrightarrow Na_2O_2(s)$$

Lithium metal forms a normal oxide with O_2 rather than a peroxide or a superoxide because the small Li^+ ion cannot form a stable lattice with the larger O_2^{2-} or O_2^- ions.

$$4Li(s) + O_2(g) \longrightarrow 2Li_2O(s)$$

Generally, oxides form at much higher temperatures than either peroxides or superoxides. The normal oxides of potassium, rubidium, and cesium can be obtained by heating oxygen with an excess of the metal.

With the exception of barium (which reacts with oxygen to yield barium peroxide), the remaining metals generally produce normal oxides in their reactions with oxygen.

$$2Mg(s) + O_2(g) \longrightarrow 2MgO(s)$$
$$4Al(s) + 3O_2(g) \longrightarrow 2Al_2O_3(s)$$

Analogous reactions can be written for the preparation of CaO, CuO, ZnO, PbO, and other oxides. The reaction of mercury and oxygen is reversible.

$$2Hg(l) + O_2(g) \rightleftharpoons 2HgO(s)$$

For metals that have more than one electrovalence number, the oxide produced generally depends upon the quantity of oxygen, the quantity of the metal, and the reaction conditions. Thus the reaction of iron and oxygen can be made to yield FeO (low pressure of oxygen, temperature above 600°C), Fe_3O_4 (finely divided iron, heated in air at 500°C), or Fe_2O_3 (iron heated in air at temperatures above 500°C). Hydrated Fe_2O_3 is iron rust.

Except for the noble gases and the group VII A elements, all the nonmetals react with oxygen. Oxides of the halogens and of the heavier members of the noble gas family (Section 11.2) have been prepared by indirect means. The reaction of hydrogen produces water. The product of the reaction of carbon with oxygen depends upon the proportion of carbon to oxygen employed.

$$2C(s) + O_2(g) \longrightarrow 2CO(g)$$
$$C(s) + O_2(g) \longrightarrow CO_2(g)$$

In like manner, the product of the reaction of phosphorus and oxygen depends upon whether phosphorus is reacted in a limited oxygen supply (P_4O_6) or in excess oxygen (P_4O_{10}). Sulfur reacts to produce SO_2.

$$S(s) + O_2(g) \longrightarrow SO_2(g)$$

The reaction of nitrogen with oxygen requires extremely high temperatures. The following reaction occurs in a high-energy electric arc.

$$N_2(g) + O_2(g) \longrightarrow 2NO(g)$$

Additional important oxides of sulfur (e.g., SO_3) and nitrogen (e.g., NO_2 and N_2O_5) are prepared by means other than the direct combination of the elements. Lower oxides can be reacted with oxygen to produce higher oxides. For example,

$$2Cu_2O(s) + O_2(g) \longrightarrow 4CuO(s)$$
$$2CO(g) + O_2(g) \longrightarrow 2CO_2(g)$$

Most reactions of compounds with oxygen yield the same products that would be obtained if the individual elements comprising the compounds were reacted directly. Thus

$$2H_2S(g) + 3O_2(g) \longrightarrow 2H_2O(g) + 2SO_2(g)$$
$$CS_2(l) + 3O_2(g) \longrightarrow CO_2(g) + 2SO_2(g)$$
$$2C_2H_2(g) + 5O_2(g) \longrightarrow 4CO_2(g) + 2H_2O(g)$$
$$C_2H_6O(l) + 3O_2(g) \longrightarrow 2CO_2(g) + 3H_2O(g)$$

The reaction of zinc sulfide with oxygen illustrates a metallurgical process known as roasting; many sulfide ores are subjected to this procedure (Section 18.3).

$$2ZnS(s) + 3O_2(g) \longrightarrow 2ZnO(s) + 2SO_2(g)$$

The products of the reaction of a hydrocarbon with oxygen depend upon the amount of oxygen supplied. Thus when natural gas (methane) is burned, at least three reactions can be identified.

$$CH_4(g) + O_2(g) \longrightarrow C(s) + 2H_2O(g)$$
$$2CH_4(g) + 3O_2(g) \longrightarrow 2CO(g) + 4H_2O(g)$$
$$CH_4(g) + 2O_2(g) \longrightarrow CO_2(g) + 2H_2O(g)$$

8.3 Acidic and Alkaline Oxides

Many of the oxides of metals and nonmetals react with water to produce alkalies and acids. Thus the oxides of the group I A metals and calcium, strontium, and barium dissolve in water to produce hydroxides. All these oxides are ionic; when one of them dissolves in water, it is the oxide ion that reacts.

$$O^{2-}(aq) + H_2O \longrightarrow 2OH^-(aq)$$

Hydroxides of other metals exist, but they are prepared by other methods, since the corresponding oxides, as well as the hydroxides, are insoluble in water. When heated, most hydroxides are converted to oxides.

$$Mg(OH)_2(s) \longrightarrow MgO(s) + H_2O(g)$$

Many covalent, nonmetal oxides react with water to produce acids.

$$SO_3 + H_2O \longrightarrow H_2SO_4$$
$$P_4O_{10} + 6H_2O \longrightarrow 4H_3PO_4$$
$$Cl_2O + H_2O \longrightarrow 2HOCl$$
$$N_2O_5 + H_2O \longrightarrow 2HNO_3$$
$$SO_2 + H_2O \longrightarrow H_2SO_3$$

Most of the polyatomic anions listed in Table 3.7 are derived from acids that can be prepared in this manner. Binary acids, of course, are not derivable from oxides.

The oxides of metals, therefore, are frequently called **alkaline oxides**, and the oxides of the nonmetals are called **acidic oxides**. The oxides themselves can be made to undergo neutralization reactions. Thus barium sulfate can be prepared by the action of sulfuric acid on either barium hydroxide or barium oxide.

$$2H^+(aq) + SO_4^{2-}(aq) + Ba^{2+}(aq) + 2OH^-(aq) \longrightarrow BaSO_4(s) + 2H_2O$$
$$2H^+(aq) + SO_4^{2-}(aq) + BaO(s) \longrightarrow BaSO_4(s) + H_2O$$

The insoluble Fe_2O_3 will react with acids, even though it will not react with water to produce a hydroxide.

$$6H^+(aq) + Fe_2O_3(s) \longrightarrow 2Fe^{3+}(aq) + 3H_2O$$

Oxides of nonmetals will neutralize alkalies. In the reaction with sodium hydroxide, SO_2 produces the same product as its counterpart H_2SO_3.

$$H_2SO_3(aq) + 2OH^-(aq) \longrightarrow SO_3^{2-}(aq) + 2H_2O$$
$$SO_2(g) + 2OH^-(aq) \longrightarrow SO_3^{2-}(aq) + H_2O$$

Some oxides react with both acids and alkalies. Such oxides are called **amphoteric** and are generally derived from elements in the center of the periodic table, on the borderline between the metals and the nonmetals.

$$ZnO(s) + 2OH^-(aq) + H_2O \longrightarrow \underset{\text{zincate ion}}{Zn(OH)_4^{2-}(aq)}$$
$$ZnO(s) + 2H^+(aq) \longrightarrow Zn^{2+}(aq) + H_2O$$
$$Al_2O_3(s) + 2OH^-(aq) + 3H_2O \longrightarrow \underset{\text{aluminate ion}}{2Al(OH)_4^-(aq)}$$
$$Al_2O_3(s) + 6H^+(aq) \longrightarrow 2Al^{3+}(aq) + 3H_2O$$

8.4 Ozone

The existence of an element in more than one form in the same physical state is called **allotropy**, and the forms are called **allotropes**. A number of elements exhibit allotropy, for example, carbon, sulfur, and phosphorus. Oxygen exists in a triatomic form, ozone, in addition to the common diatomic modification.

The ozone molecule is diatomic and has an angular structure. Both oxygen-to-oxygen bonds have the same length (1.27 Å), which is intermediate between the double-bond distance (1.10 Å) and the single-bond distance (1.48 Å). The molecule may be represented as a resonance hybrid:

Ozone is a pale blue gas with a characteristic odor; predictably, its density is $1\frac{1}{2}$ times that of O_2. The normal boiling point of ozone is $-112°C$, and the normal melting point is $-250°C$. It is slightly more soluble in water than is O_2.

Ozone is produced by passing a silent electric discharge through oxygen gas. The reaction proceeds through the dissociation of an O_2 molecule into oxygen atoms and the combination of an O atom with a second O_2 molecule.

$$\frac{1}{2}O_2 \longrightarrow O \qquad \Delta H = +59 \text{ kcal}$$
$$O + O_2 \longrightarrow O_3 \qquad \Delta H = -25 \text{ kcal}$$

The energy released in the second step, in which a new bond is formed, is not sufficient to compensate for the energy required by the first step, in which a bond is broken. Hence, the overall reaction for the preparation of ozone is endothermic:

$$\frac{3}{2}O_2 \longrightarrow O_3 \qquad \Delta H = +34 \text{ kcal}$$

Ozone is highly reactive; it is explosive at temperatures above 300°C or in the presence of substances that catalyze its decomposition. Ozone will react with many substances at temperature not sufficiently high to produce reaction with O_2. The higher reactivity of O_3 in comparison to O_2 is consistent with the higher energy content of O_3.

8.5 Oxidation Numbers

The term oxidation was originally applied to reactions in which substances combined with oxygen.

$$2Zn(s) + O_2(g) \longrightarrow 2ZnO(s)$$

Reduction was defined as the removal of oxygen from a substance.

$$ZnO(s) + C(s) \longrightarrow Zn(g) + CO(g)$$

The meanings of the terms have gradually been broadened. At first, they were extended to include the gain and loss of other nonmetals in reactions that are obviously analogous to those involving oxygen.

$$Zn(s) + Cl_2(g) \longrightarrow ZnCl_2(s)$$
$$2AgCl(s) + H_2(g) \longrightarrow 2Ag(s) + HCl(g)$$

Today, even wider definitions of these terms are employed, and many more types of reactions are classified as oxidation-reduction reactions (Section 8.6). These enlarged definitions are based on the assignment of **oxidation numbers** to the atoms, combined or uncombined, that are involved in a given reaction.

The oxidation number of an atom in a binary electrovalent compound is the same as the charge on the ion derived from that atom (the electrovalence number). Thus the oxidation number of sodium in $NaCl$ is $1+$, and that of chlorine is $1-$. In K_2S, the oxidation number of potassium is $1+$ (a total of $2+$ for both potassium atoms), and the oxidation number of sulfur is $2-$. In Al_2O_3, the oxidation number of aluminum is $3+$ (total, $6+$), and that of oxygen is $2-$ (total, $6-$). Note that the sum of the oxidation numbers of the atoms of each compound equals zero; this is true of all compounds since they are electrically neutral.

By the use of some arbitrary rules, oxidation numbers can be assigned to the atoms of covalent compounds as well as those of electrovalent compounds derived from more than two elements. For example, if in the covalent compound SO_2 the oxidation of oxygen is $2-$ (a total of $4-$ for the two oxygen atoms), then sulfur is arbitrarily assigned an oxidation number of $4+$. It must not be assumed that this number represents an actual charge on the sulfur atom or that the SO_2 molecule will break apart into monatomic ions under any circumstances, for neither is true.

Oxidation numbers are convenient and useful; this is the only justification for such an arbitrary concept. Later sections will show that oxidation numbers can be used to facilitate writing formulas, recognize and organize oxidation-reduction phenomena, balance oxidation-reduction equations, construct a simplified method for solving stoichiometric problems involving oxidation-reduction changes, and systematize the chemistry of the elements.

The following rules can be used to assign oxidation numbers.

1. Any uncombined atom, or any atom in a molecule of an element, is assigned an oxidation number of zero.
2. The sum of the oxidation numbers of the atoms in a compound is zero.
3. The oxidation number of a simple, monatomic ion is the same as the

charge on the ion (electrovalence number). The sum of the oxidation numbers of the atoms comprising a polyatomic ion equals the charge on the ion.

4. The oxidation number of fluorine, the most electronegative element, is 1− in all fluorine-containing compounds.

5. In most oxygen-containing compounds, the oxidation number of oxygen is 2−. There are a few exceptions. In peroxides, each oxygen has an oxidation number of 1−. For example, the two oxygens of the peroxide ion, O_2^{2-}, are equivalent, and each must be assigned an oxidation number of 1− so that the sum equals the charge on the ion. In superoxides, O_2^{-}, each oxygen has an oxidation number of $\frac{1}{2}$−. In OF_2, the oxygen has an oxidation number of 2+.

6. The oxidation number of hydrogen is 1+ in all its compounds except the metallic hydrides (e.g., CaH_2 and NaH) in which hydrogen is in the 1− oxidation state.

The oxidation states of the constituent elements of most compounds can be determined through the use of these rules. The oxidation numbers of the atoms of H_3PO_4 must add up to zero. If each hydrogen is assigned 1+ (total, 3+) and each oxygen is assigned 2− (total, 8−), the phosphorus must have an oxidation number of 5+. The same conclusion can be reached by examining the ion derived from phosphoric acid, the phosphate ion, PO_4^{3-}. Here, the sum of the oxidation numbers must be the same as the charge on the ion, 3−. Since each oxygen has an oxidation number of 2− (total, 8−), the phosphorus must have an oxidation number of 5+.

In the dichromate ion, $Cr_2O_7^{2-}$, the seven oxygen atoms have a combined oxidation number of 14−. Since the charge on the ion is 2−, the oxidation numbers of the two chromium atoms must add up to 12+, and the oxidation number of chromium is 6+. The usual practice is to report the oxidation state of an element in a compound on the basis of the oxidation number of a single atom. It would be misleading to say that oxygen is in an oxidation state of 2− in H_2O and 4− in SO_2; in both compounds, oxygen has an oxidation number of 2−.

Fractional oxidation numbers are possible. Calculation of the oxidation number of iron in Fe_3O_4 gives a value of $2\frac{2}{3}$+. (Since the oxygens add up to 8−, the irons must add up to 8+, and 8+ divided by 3 is $2\frac{2}{3}$+.) This compound can be considered to be formed from FeO and Fe_2O_3. Hence, two iron atoms at 3+ each and one iron atom at 2+ average out to $2\frac{2}{3}$+. When an element has a fractional oxidation number in a particular compound, this often means that the compound contains two (or more) atoms of the element that are not perfectly equivalent.

Frequently, an element displays, in its compounds, a range of oxidation states. For example, in the compounds of nitrogen, this element exhibits oxidation numbers of from 3− (e.g., in NH_3) to 5+ (e.g., in HNO_3). Since the number of valence electrons of an A family element is the same as its group number, the highest positive charge (even a hypothetical one) that can logically be assigned to an A family element is the same as its group number. The highest oxidation number of an A family element is, therefore, its group number.

The lowest oxidation number of an A family element is its electrovalence number. Thus the highest oxidation number of sulfur (group VI A) is 6+ (e.g., in H_2SO_4) and the lowest oxidation number of sulfur is 2− (e.g., in H_2S). The highest oxidation number of sodium (group I A) is the same as the lowest oxidation number, 1+. There are exceptions to these generalizations, however (e.g., fluorine and oxygen).

8.6 Oxidation-Reduction Reactions

Oxidation and reduction may be defined on the basis of change in oxidation number. **Oxidation** is the process in which an atom undergoes an algebraic increase in oxidation number and **reduction** is the process in which an atom undergoes an algebraic decrease in oxidation number. On this basis, oxidation-reduction is involved in the reaction

$$\overset{0}{S} + \overset{0}{O_2} \longrightarrow \overset{4+2-}{S\,O_2}$$

whereas oxidation-reduction is not involved in the reaction

$$\overset{4+2-}{S\,O_2} + \overset{1+2-}{H_2\,O} \longrightarrow \overset{1+4+2-}{H_2\,S\,O_3}$$

The oxidation number of each type of atom is written above its symbol. In the first reaction, sulfur is oxidized, and oxygen is reduced.

It is apparent, from the manner in which oxidation numbers are assigned, that neither oxidation nor reduction can occur alone; furthermore, each process must occur to the same extent in a given reaction. According to the rules by which oxidation numbers are assigned, the sum of the oxidation numbers of any chemical species equals the charge on that species (zero if the entire compound is considered). In any reaction, the sum of the charges of the reactant species (zero for reactions involving only molecules) must equal the sum of the charges of the product species (again zero for reactions involving only molecules). Charge conservation demands, therefore, that any oxidation (increase in oxidation number) be accompanied by a commensurate reduction (decrease in oxidation number).

Since one substance cannot be reduced unless another is simultaneously oxidized, the material that is reduced is responsible for the oxidation; as such it is called the **oxidizing agent** (or **oxidant**). Because of the interdependence of the two processes, the converse is also true: the material that is itself oxidized is the **reducing agent** (or **reductant**). Therefore

$$\overset{0}{S} + \overset{0}{O_2} \longrightarrow \overset{4+2-}{SO_2}$$

oxidized   reduced
reducing agent   oxidizing agent

Equations for oxidation-reduction reactions are usually more difficult to balance than those for reactions that do not entail oxidation and reduction (such as neutralization reactions). It is advantageous to balance oxidation-reduction equations systematically, and there are two methods that are commonly used to balance them: the oxidation-number method and the ion-electron method. Both of these methods will be discussed. For clarity, the physical state of the atoms, molecules, and ions will not be indicated in the examples that follow. In addition, the symbol H^+, instead of $H^+(aq)$ or H_3O^+, will be employed; it should be kept in mind, however, that all ions are hydrated in aqueous solution.

There are three steps in the **oxidation-number method** of balancing oxidation-reduction equations. An example of oxidation-reduction is afforded by the reaction of nitric acid with hydrogen sulfide; the unbalanced expression for this change is:

$$HNO_3 + H_2S \longrightarrow NO + S + H_2O$$

1. The oxidation numbers of the atoms in the equation are determined in order to identify those undergoing oxidation or reduction. Thus

$$H\overset{5+}{N}O_3 + H_2\overset{2-}{S} \longrightarrow \overset{2+}{N}O + \overset{0}{S} + H_2O$$

2. Coefficients are placed before the appropriate formulas so that the total decrease in oxidation number equals the total increase in oxidation number. In this example, nitrogen is reduced ($5+$ to $2+$, a decrease of 3) and sulfur is oxidized ($2-$ to 0, an increase of 2). Thus it is necessary that 2 molecules of HNO_3 and 2 molecules of NO, as well as 3 molecules of H_2S and 3 atoms of S, be indicated. In this way the total increase in oxidation number will be 6 which will equal the total decrease in oxidation number of 6.

$$2HNO_3 + 3H_2S \longrightarrow 2NO + 3S + H_2O$$

3. Balancing is completed by inspection; this method takes care of only those materials that undergo oxidation-number change. In this example, there are now 8 hydrogen atoms on the left, and therefore, $4H_2O$ molecules must be indicated on the right.

$$2HNO_3 + 3H_2S \longrightarrow 2NO + 3S + 4H_2O$$

The final, balanced, equation should be checked to ensure that there are as many atoms of each element on the left as there are on the right.

Nitric acid is frequently employed as an oxidizing agent, and it functions in this capacity in this reaction (the nitrogen of HNO_3 is reduced). The sulfur of H_2S is oxidized, and therefore, H_2S is acting as a reducing agent.

The oxidation-number method may be used to balance **net**, or **ionic, equations**, in which only those ions and molecules that actually take part in the reaction are shown. For example, the K^+ ion does not take part in the reaction of potassium chlorate, $KClO_3$, with iodine and is not shown in the equation. The steps in balancing are:

1.
$$H_2O + \overset{0}{I_2} + \overset{5+}{Cl}O_3{}^- \longrightarrow \overset{5+}{I}O_3{}^- + \overset{1-}{Cl}{}^- + H^+$$

2. *Each* iodine atom undergoes an increase of 5 (0 to 5+), but there are *two* iodine atoms in I_2. The increase in oxidation number is therefore 10. Chlorine undergoes a decrease of 6 (5+ to 1−). The lowest common multiple of 6 and 10 is 30. Therefore, $3I_2$ molecules must be indicated (a total increase of 30) and $5ClO_3{}^-$ ions are needed (a total decrease of 30). The coefficients of the products, $IO_3{}^-$ and Cl^- follow from this assignment.

$$H_2O + 3I_2 + 5ClO_3{}^- \longrightarrow 6IO_3{}^- + 5Cl^- + H^+$$

3. Ignoring H_2O, there are now 15 oxygen atoms on the left and 18 oxygen atoms on the right. To make up 3 oxygen atoms on the left, $3H_2O$ molecules must be indicated. It then follows that the coefficient of H^+ must be 6 to balance the hydrogens of the H_2O molecules.

$$3H_2O + 3I_2 + 5ClO_3{}^- \longrightarrow 6IO_3{}^- + 5Cl^- + 6H^+$$

An ionic equation must indicate charge balance as well as mass balance. Since the algebraic sum of the charges on the left, 5−, equals that of the right, 5−, the equation is balanced.

Reactions in which electrons are transferred are clearly examples of oxidation-reduction reactions. In the reaction of sodium and chlorine, a sodium atom loses its valence electron to a chlorine atom.

$$2\overset{0}{Na} + \overset{0}{Cl_2} \longrightarrow 2\overset{1+}{Na}{}^+ + 2\overset{1-}{Cl}{}^-$$

For simple ions, the oxidation number is the same as the charge on the ion. It follows, then, that electron loss represents a type of oxidation, and electron gain represents a type of reduction. This equation can be divided into two **partial equations** representing **half reactions**.

$$\begin{aligned} \text{Oxidation:} \quad & 2Na \longrightarrow 2Na^+ + 2e^- \\ \text{Reduction:} \quad & 2e^- + Cl_2 \longrightarrow 2Cl^- \end{aligned}$$

The **ion-electron method** of balancing oxidation-reduction equations employs partial equations. Only those ions that are involved in the reaction are shown; un-ionized (or slightly ionized) species and insoluble substances that take part in the reaction are written in molecular form. The equation for the reaction between dichromate ion and chloride ion in acid solution will be used to illustrate the steps of the method.

1. Two skeleton partial equations for the half reactions are written, and the central element of each partial equation is balanced.

$$Cr_2O_7^{2-} \longrightarrow 2Cr^{3+}$$
$$2Cl^- \longrightarrow Cl_2$$

2. The hydrogen and oxygen atoms are then balanced. Since this reaction occurs in acid solution, H^+ and H_2O can be added where needed. For each oxygen atom that is needed, one H_2O molecule is added to the side of the partial equation that is deficient. The hydrogen is then brought into balance by the addition of $2H^+$ to the opposite side. Thus 7 oxygens must be added to the right side of the first partial equation; the second partial equation is already in material balance.

$$14H^+ + Cr_2O_7^{2-} \longrightarrow 2Cr^{3+} + 7H_2O$$
$$2Cl^- \longrightarrow Cl_2$$

3. The next step is to balance the half reactions electrically. In the first partial equation, the net charge is $12+$ on the left side of the equation ($14+$ and $2-$) and $6+$ on the right side. Six electrons must be added to the left. The second equation is balanced electrically by the addition of 2 electrons to the right.

$$6e^- + 14H^+ + Cr_2O_7^{2-} \longrightarrow 2Cr^{3+} + 7H_2O$$
$$2Cl^- \longrightarrow Cl_2 + 2e^-$$

4. The number of electrons lost must equal the number of electrons gained. Therefore the oxidation equation is multiplied through by 3.

$$6e^- + 14H^+ + Cr_2O_7^{2-} \longrightarrow 2Cr^{3+} + 7H_2O$$
$$6Cl^- \longrightarrow 3Cl_2 + 6e^-$$

5. Addition of the two partial equations gives the final equation.

$$14H^+ + Cr_2O_7^{2-} + 6Cl^- \longrightarrow 2Cr^{3+} + 3Cl_2 + 7H_2O$$

These steps are illustrated as follows, for the reaction in which As_4O_6 reacts with MnO_4^- to produce H_3AsO_4 and Mn^{2+}

1.
$$MnO_4^- \longrightarrow Mn^{2+}$$
$$As_4O_6 \longrightarrow 4H_3AsO_4$$

2. The first partial equation can be brought into material balance by the addition of $4H_2O$ to the right side and $8H^+$ to the left side. In the second partial equation, $10H_2O$ must be added to the left side to make up the needed 10 oxygens. If we stopped at this point, there would be 20 hydrogen atoms on the left and 12 on the right; therefore $8H^+$ must be added to the right.

$$8H^+ + MnO_4^- \longrightarrow Mn^{2+} + 4H_2O$$
$$10H_2O + As_4O_6 \longrightarrow 4H_3AsO_4 + 8H^+$$

3. To balance the net charges, electrons are added.

$$5e^- + 8H^+ + MnO_4^- \longrightarrow Mn^{2+} + 4H_2O$$
$$10H_2O + As_4O_6 \longrightarrow 4H_3AsO_4 + 8H^+ + 8e^-$$

4. The first partial equation must be multiplied through by 8 and the second by 5 so that the same number of electrons are lost in the oxidation partial equation as are gained in the reduction.

$$40e^- + 64H^+ + 8MnO_4^- \longrightarrow 8Mn^{2+} + 32H_2O$$
$$50H_2O + 5As_4O_6 \longrightarrow 20H_3AsO_4 + 40H^+ + 40e^-$$

5. When these two partials are added, water molecules and hydrogen ions must be canceled as well as electrons. It is poor form to leave an equation with $64H^+$ on the left and $40H^+$ on the right.

$$24H^+ + 18H_2O + 5As_4O_6 + 8MnO_4^- \longrightarrow 20H_3AsO_4 + 8Mn^{2+}$$

Equations for reactions that take place in alkaline solution are balanced in a manner slightly different from those that occur in acidic solution. All the steps are the same except the second one; H^+ cannot be used to balance equations for alkaline reactions. As an illustration, consider the following reaction that takes place in alkaline solution.

1.
$$Cr(OH)_6^{3-} \longrightarrow CrO_4^{2-}$$
$$HO_2^- \longrightarrow OH^-$$

2. For reactions occurring in alkaline solution, OH^- and H_2O are used to balance oxygen and hydrogen. For each oxygen that is needed, $2OH^-$ ions are added to the side of the partial equation that is deficient, and one H_2O molecule is added to the opposite side. For each hydrogen that is needed, one H_2O molecule is added to the side that is deficient, and one OH^- ion is added to the opposite side.

In the first partial equation, the right side is deficient by 2 oxygen atoms. We add, therefore, $4OH^-$ to the right side and $2H_2O$ to the left. *This addition takes care of oxygen balance only.*

$$2H_2O + Cr(OH)_6^{3-} \longrightarrow CrO_4^{2-} + 4OH^-$$

We need (as we originally needed) 6 more hydrogen atoms on the right and therefore add $6H_2O$ to the right and $6OH^-$ to the left.

$$6OH^- + 2H_2O + Cr(OH)_6^{3-} \longrightarrow CrO_4^{2-} + 4OH^- + 6H_2O$$

We can consolidate our additions:

$$2OH^- + Cr(OH)_6^{3-} \longrightarrow CrO_4^{2-} + 4H_2O$$

The second partial is brought into material balance by the addition of $2OH^-$ to the right and one H_2O to the left.

$$H_2O + HO_2^- \longrightarrow 3OH^-$$

3.
$$2OH^- + Cr(OH)_6^{3-} \longrightarrow CrO_4^{2-} + 4H_2O + 3e^-$$
$$2e^- + H_2O + HO_2^- \longrightarrow 3OH^-$$

4.
$$4OH^- + 2Cr(OH)_6^{3-} \longrightarrow 2CrO_4^{2-} + 8H_2O + 6e^-$$
$$6e^- + 3H_2O + 3HO_2^- \longrightarrow 9OH^-$$

5.
$$2Cr(OH)_6^{3-} + 3HO_2^- \longrightarrow 2CrO_4^{2-} + 5H_2O + 5OH^-$$

As a final example, consider the following skeleton equation for a reaction in alkaline solution.

$$Br_2 \longrightarrow BrO_3^- + Br^-$$

In this reaction, the same substance, Br_2, is both oxidized and reduced. Such reactions are called **disproportionations** or **auto-oxidation-reduction reactions**.

1.
$$Br_2 \longrightarrow 2BrO_3^-$$
$$Br_2 \longrightarrow 2Br^-$$

2.
$$12OH^- + Br_2 \longrightarrow 2BrO_3^- + 6H_2O$$
$$Br_2 \longrightarrow 2Br^-$$

3.
$$12OH^- + Br_2 \longrightarrow 2BrO_3^- + 6H_2O + 10e^-$$
$$2e^- + Br_2 \longrightarrow 2Br^-$$

4.
$$12OH^- + Br_2 \longrightarrow 2BrO_3^- + 6H_2O + 10e^-$$
$$10e^- + 5Br_2 \longrightarrow 10Br^-$$

5.
$$12OH^- + 6Br_2 \longrightarrow 2BrO_3^- + 10Br^- + 6H_2O$$

When the ion-electron method is applied to a disproportionation reaction, the coefficients of the resulting equation usually are divisible by some common number since one reactant was used in both partial equations. The coefficients of this equation are all divisible by 2 and should be reduced to the lowest possible terms.

$$6OH^- + 3Br_2 \longrightarrow BrO_3^- + 5Br^- + 3H_2O$$

Most oxidation-reduction equations may be balanced by use of the ion-electron method, which is especially convenient for electrochemical reactions and reactions of ions in water solution. However, several misconceptions that can arise must be pointed out. Half reactions cannot occur alone, and partial equations do not represent complete chemical changes. Even in electrochemical cells, where the two half reactions take place at different electrodes, the two half reactions always occur simultaneously.

Whereas the partial equations probably represent an overall, if not detailed, view of the way an oxidation-reduction reaction occurs in an electrochemical cell, the same reaction in a beaker may not take place in this way at all. The method should *not* be interpreted as necessarily giving the correct mechanism by which a reaction occurs. It is, at times, difficult to recognize whether a given reaction is a legitimate example of an electron-exchange reaction. The reaction

$$\overset{4+}{S}O_3^{2-} + \overset{5+}{Cl}O_3^- \longrightarrow \overset{6+}{S}O_4^{2-} + \overset{3+}{Cl}O_2^-$$

looks like an electron-exchange reaction, can be made to take place in an electrochemical cell, and can be balanced by the ion-electron method. However, this reaction has been shown to proceed by direct oxygen exchange (from ClO_3^- to SO_3^{2-}) and *not* by electron exchange.

8.7 Equivalent Weights

It is often convenient to use equivalent weights for stoichiometric calculations. The definition of equivalent weight depends upon the type of reaction being considered; however, the definition is always framed in such a way that one equivalent weight of a given reactant will react with exactly one equivalent weight of another. Therefore, unlike mole ratios, there is always a simple 1:1 stoichiometric ratio between numbers of equivalents entering into a reaction.

Two important types of reactions for which equivalent weights are defined are neutralization reactions and oxidation-reduction reactions. For neutralization reactions, equivalent weights are based on the fact that one proton reacts with one hydroxide ion.

$$H^+(aq) + OH^-(aq) \longrightarrow H_2O$$

Thus the weight of an acid that supplies 1 gram molecular weight of H^+ is the gram equivalent weight of that acid. A gram equivalent weight of a hydroxide is the weight that will supply 1 gram mole of OH^-. It is obvious, then, that 1 gram equivalent of an acid will completely neutralize 1 gram equivalent of an alkali. Table 8.2 lists the equivalent weights of three acids

Table 8.2

Equivalent Weights of Some Acids and Bases
(Complete Neutralization)

Compound	Molecular Weight	Equivalent Weight
HNO_3	63.01	63.01
H_2SO_4	98.07	49.04
H_3PO_4	98.00	32.67
NaOH	40.00	40.00
$Ca(OH)_2$	74.09	37.05
$Al(OH)_3$	78.00	26.00

and three hydroxides; these values can be derived by dividing the molecular weight of the compound by the number of replaceable hydrogens or hydroxides per formula unit. In some instances, polyprotic acids undergo reactions where not all the hydrogens are neutralized; for such a reaction, the equivalent weight of the acid must be calculated on the basis of the number of hydrogens that are neutralized.

▶ **EXAMPLE 8.1** Using equivalent weights, calculate the weight of NaOH required to produce Na_2HAsO_4 from 10.0 g of H_3AsO_4.

Solution The equivalent weight of NaOH is the same as the molecular weight, 40.0. The equivalent weight of H_3AsO_4 is the molecular weight, 141.9, divided by 2, or 71.0, since only 2 hydrogens are replaced in this neutralization reaction.

$$?\text{g NaOH} = 10.0 \text{ g } H_3AsO_4 \left(\frac{40.0 \text{ g NaOH}}{71.0 \text{ g } H_3AsO_4} \right) = 5.63 \text{ g NaOH}$$

In an oxidation-reduction reaction, the total increase in oxidation number of one species must equal the total decrease in the oxidation number of another species. Therefore a system of equivalent weights for oxidizing and reducing agents is based on oxidation number changes. The equivalent weight of a compound functioning as an oxidizing or reducing agent is defined as the molecular weight of the compound divided by the total decrease or increase in oxidation number of all the atoms in one formula unit of the compound under consideration. Obviously, 1 gram equivalent weight of an oxidizing agent requires 1 gram equivalent weight of a reducing agent for complete reaction.

Thus in the reaction

$$\overset{0}{I_2} + 10\,H\overset{5+}{N}O_3 \longrightarrow 2\,H\overset{5+}{I}O_3 + 10\,\overset{4+}{N}O_2 + 4H_2O$$

each iodine atom undergoes an increase in oxidation number of 5, making a total increase of 10 per molecule of I_2. The molecular weight of I_2 is 253.81, and in this reaction, therefore, the equivalent weight of iodine is 253.81/10, or 25.381. In this reaction each nitrogen atom of HNO_3 undergoes a decrease in oxidization number of 1; therefore the equivalent weight of HNO_3 is the same as its molecular weight, 63.01.

The stoichiometric weight ratio of reductant (I_2) to oxidant (HNO_3) derived from equivalent weights is the same as that derived from the balanced chemical equation. Thus the balanced chemical equation for the reaction of I_2 and HNO_3 shows 1 mole of I_2, which is 10 equivalents, reacting with 10 moles of HNO_3, which is also 10 equivalents.

It is also possible to use half equations to derive equivalent weights; the increase or decrease in oxidation number is the same as the number of electrons indicated as being lost or gained in the partial equations.

The equivalent weight of an oxidizing agent or a reducing agent is not invariant; for different reactions, a given compound may have different equivalent weights. When potassium permanganate serves as an oxidizing agent in acid solution, the partial equation for the reduction of permanganate ion is

$$5e^- + 8H^+ + \overset{7+}{Mn}O_4^- \longrightarrow Mn^{2+} + H_2O$$

The equivalent weight of $KMnO_4$ for this reaction is the molecular weight (158.04) divided by the change in the oxidation number of Mn (5), or 31.61.

The partial equation for the use of $KMnO_4$ as an oxidizing agent in alkaline solution is

$$3e^- + 2H_2O + \overset{7+}{Mn}O_4^- \longrightarrow \overset{4+}{Mn}O_2 + 4OH^-$$

Hence, the equivalent weight of $KMnO_4$ for this reaction is 158.04/3, or 52.68.

Some analytical determinations employ solutions containing a known concentration of a given oxidant or reductant. The concentrations of such solutions and the mathematical treatment of such analyses are usually based on equivalent weights. The preparation and use of these solutions are described in later chapters.

▶ **EXAMPLE 8.2** What weight of $KMnO_4$ is needed to oxidize 15.0 g of As_4O_6 in acidic solution? The products of the reaction are Mn^{2+} and H_3AsO_4.

Solution The equivalent weight of $KMnO_4$ (to Mn^{2+}) is 31.6 (see preceding discussion). When As_4O_6 is transformed into H_3AsO_4, *each* As atom undergoes an increase in oxidation number of 2 (from 3+ to 5+). The total change for 4As atoms is 8, and the equivalent weight of As_4O_6 is 395.6/8, or 49.5.

$$?g \ KMnO_4 = 15.0 \ g \ As_4O_6 \left(\frac{31.6 \ g \ KMnO_4}{49.5 \ g \ As_4O_6} \right) = 9.58 \ g \ KMnO_4$$

The equivalent weights of elements are of historical importance. The concept was usually applied to simple binary compounds, although it can be extended to more complicated types of compounds. In the formation of any binary compound from its constituent elements, the total increase in oxidation number of one element must equal the total decrease in oxidation number of the other. Since uncombined elements are assigned oxidation numbers of zero, the equivalent weight of an element in a compound is given by the atomic weight of the element divided by the absolute value of the oxidation number of the element in the compound under consideration. Equivalent weights can be experimentally determined with great accuracy and have been used to establish atomic weights. The atomic weight is, of course, the product of the equivalent weight of the element and the absolute value of the oxidation number of the element.

8.8 Hydrogen Peroxide

In addition to water, hydrogen and oxygen form a compound called hydrogen peroxide, H_2O_2. This compound is a blue liquid with physical properties much like those of water; it boils at 150.2°C and freezes at −0.43°C. The molecule is diamagnetic. The approximate geometry of the molecule is shown in Figure 8.2. The arrangement shown suggests that the O atoms employ sp^3 hybrid orbitals for bonding.

Hydrogen peroxide is the hydride of the peroxide ion (Section 8.2), and therefore may be made by treating peroxides with acids.

$$BaO_2(s) + 2H^+(aq) + SO_4^{2-}(aq) \longrightarrow BaSO_4(s) + H_2O_2(aq)$$

In this preparation, the barium sulfate, which is insoluble, can be removed by filtration.

The peroxide linkage is found in other covalent compounds and ions in addition to H_2O_2 and the peroxide ion itself. For example, the peroxydisulfate

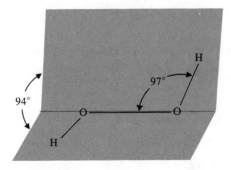

Figure 8.2 Approximate structure of hydrogen peroxide.

ion, $S_2O_8^{2-}$, which is produced as an intermediate in a commercial preparation of H_2O_2, contains such a linkage. The following half reaction occurs at the anode in the electrolysis of either sulfuric acid or ammonium hydrogen sulfate under suitable conditions.

$$2HSO_4^- \longrightarrow \begin{bmatrix} & O & & O & \\ & | & & | & \\ O-S-O\!-\!\!-\!O-S-O \\ & | & & | & \\ & O & & O & \end{bmatrix}^{2-} + 2H^+ + 2e^-$$

The peroxide linkage is shown in boldface type. The peroxydisulfate ion reacts with water to produce hydrogen peroxide.

$$S_2O_8^{2-} + 2H_2O \longrightarrow H_2O_2 + 2HSO_4^-$$

Hydrogen peroxide is also made commercially by the hydrogenation, oxidation, and subsequent reaction with water of an organic intermediate, 2-ethylanthraquinone.

The dilute solutions of hydrogen peroxide produced in the preceding processes are concentrated by distillation under reduced pressure (Section 7.4), since hydrogen peroxide readily decomposes.

$$2H_2O_2 \longrightarrow 2H_2O + O_2$$

This decomposition, which is catalyzed by traces of heavy metal ions, is an example of an auto-oxidation-reduction reaction.

Because the oxygen of H_2O_2 can be either oxidized or reduced, H_2O_2 can function as an oxidizing agent or a reducing agent. As an oxidizing agent, the oxygen of H_2O_2 is reduced to the normal 2− oxidation state.

$$2H^+(aq) + H_2O_2(aq) + 2I^-(aq) \longrightarrow I_2(s) + 2H_2O$$
$$2OH^-(aq) + H_2O_2(aq) + Mn^{2+}(aq) \longrightarrow MnO_2(s) + 2H_2O$$

Oxidations are often slow in acid solution; they generally occur more rapidly in alkaline solution.

Hydrogen peroxide only serves as a reducing agent with materials that are themselves strong oxidizing agents. In such reactions, the oxygen of the H_2O_2 is oxidized to O_2.

$$6H^+(aq) + 5H_2O_2(aq) + 2MnO_4^- \longrightarrow 2Mn^{2+}(aq) + 5O_2(g) + 8H_2O$$

Reactions in which hydrogen peroxide functions as a reducing agent in alkaline solution are rarely encountered.

Hydrogen peroxide is a weak acid in water solution. One or two hydrogens of H_2O_2 can be neutralized by sodium hydroxide to produce either $NaHO_2$ (sodium hydroperoxide) or Na_2O_2 (sodium peroxide).

8.9 Occurrence and Preparation of Hydrogen

In the crust, bodies of water, and atmosphere of the earth, hydrogen constitutes less than 1 % of the weight of the whole and ranks ninth of all elements in order of abundance (Table 8.1). The most important naturally occurring compound of hydrogen is water, which is the principal source of the element. Hydrogen forms a series of compounds with carbon known as the hydrocarbons; these occur in coal, natural gas, and petroleum. A few minerals, such as clay and certain hydrates, contain hydrogen. Compounds of hydrogen (with carbon, oxygen, and occasionally other elements) constitute the principal part of all plant and animal matter. Free hydrogen occurs in nature only in negligible amounts (e.g., as a component of volcanic gases).

The very reactive metals (Ca, Sr, Ba, and the group I A metals) react with water at room temperature to produce hydrogen and solutions of hydroxides.

$$2Na(s) + 2H_2O \longrightarrow 2Na^+(aq) + 2OH^-(aq) + H_2(g)$$
$$Ca(s) + 2H_2O \longrightarrow Ca^{2+}(aq) + 2OH^-(aq) + H_2(g)$$

At high temperatures, some additional metals, of slightly lower reactivity, will displace hydrogen from water (steam); in these cases, metal oxides (the anhydrides of hydroxides) are obtained instead of metal hydroxides.

$$Mg(s) + H_2O(g) \longrightarrow MgO(s) + H_2(g)$$

The reaction of iron and steam serves as a commercial source of hydrogen.

$$3Fe(s) + 4H_2O(g) \longrightarrow Fe_3O_4(s) + 4H_2(g)$$

A still longer list of metals (including, e.g., Mg, Al, Mn, Zn, Cr, Fe, Cd, Co, Ni, Sn, and Pb) will react with aqueous solutions of acids to produce hydrogen. This method is a convenient laboratory preparation, but it is too expensive to be of commercial importance. The very reactive metals react too violently to be useful.

$$Zn(s) + 2H^+(aq) \longrightarrow Zn^{2+}(aq) + H_2(g)$$
$$Fe(s) + 2H^+(aq) \longrightarrow Fe^{2+}(aq) + H_2(g)$$
$$2Al(s) + 6H^+(aq) \longrightarrow 2Al^{3+}(aq) + 3H_2(g)$$

The anions of certain acids (e.g., nitric acid) react with the metals as well as hydrogen itself; such acids cannot be used to prepare pure hydrogen.

The reactions of metals and acids are examples of a type of oxidation-reduction reaction known as a **displacement reaction**; the metals are said to displace hydrogen from its compounds, the acids. Displacement reactions in which metals participate are often electron-exchange reactions. For example, in the reaction

$$Mg(s) + Cu^{2+}(aq) \longrightarrow Mg^{2+}(aq) + Cu(s)$$

the more reactive metal, magnesium, loses its valence electrons to the ion of the lesser reactive metal, copper. Certain electrochemical determinations provide a measure of the tendency of a given metal toward electron loss and the tendency of a given metal ion toward electron gain; these **electrode potentials** are a topic of Chapter 10.

Coke and steam react at high temperatures (1000°C) to produce a gaseous mixture known as **water gas**.

$$C(s) + H_2O(g) \longrightarrow CO(g) + H_2(g)$$

This mixture is used as a fuel. Since it is difficult to separate hydrogen from carbon monoxide, the water gas is subjected to a second step if hydrogen alone is desired. Water gas, mixed with additional steam, is passed over a catalyst at a temperature of about 500°C; this converts the carbon monoxide into carbon dioxide.

$$CO(g) + H_2O(g) \longrightarrow CO_2(g) + H_2(g)$$

The carbon dioxide and hydrogen are separated by taking advantage of the solubility of carbon dioxide in cold water under pressure.

Hydrocarbons react with steam, in the presence of suitable catalysts, to give mixtures of carbon monoxide and hydrogen.

$$CH_4(g) + H_2(g) \longrightarrow CO(g) + 3H_2(g)$$

The production of hydrogen and water gas from these reactions is industrially important.

Hydrogen is obtained from the catalytic decomposition of hydrocarbons at high temperatures.

$$CH_4(g) \longrightarrow C(s) + 2H_2(g)$$

In gasoline refining, petroleum hydrocarbons are "cracked" into compounds of lower molecular weight; hydrogen is a by-product.

Very pure, but relatively expensive, hydrogen is commercially prepared by the electrolysis of water containing a small amount of sulfuric acid or sodium hydroxide.

$$2H_2O \xrightarrow{\text{electrolysis}} 2H_2(g) + O_2(g)$$

Hydrogen is a by-product (as is chlorine) in the industrial preparation of sodium hydroxide by the electrolysis of concentrated aqueous solutions of sodium chloride.

$$2Na^+(aq) + 2Cl^-(aq) + 2H_2O \xrightarrow{\text{electrolysis}} 2Na^+(aq) + 2OH^-(aq) + H_2(g) + Cl_2(g)$$

Certain metals and nonmetals displace hydrogen from alkaline solutions.

$$Zn(s) + 2OH^-(aq) + 2H_2O \longrightarrow H_2(g) + \underset{\text{zincate ion}}{Zn(OH)_4^{2-}(aq)}$$

$$2Al(s) + 2OH^-(aq) + 6H_2O \longrightarrow 3H_2(g) + \underset{\text{aluminate ion}}{2Al(OH)_4^{-}(aq)}$$

$$Si(s) + 2OH^-(aq) + H_2O \longrightarrow 2H_2(g) + \underset{\text{silicate ion}}{SiO_3^{2-}(aq)}$$

8.10 Properties of Hydrogen

Hydrogen is a colorless, odorless, tasteless gas. It has the lowest density of any chemical substance; at STP, 1 liter of hydrogen weighs 0.0899 g. The two atoms of hydrogen of the H_2 molecule are joined by a single covalent bond, giving each atom a stable helium electronic configuration. The molecule is nonpolar; the weak nature of the intermolecular forces of attraction is indicated by the low normal boiling point ($-252.7°C$), the normal melting point ($-259.1°C$) and the critical temperature ($-240°C$ at a critical pressure of 12.8 atm). Hydrogen is virtually insoluble in water; approximately 2 ml of hydrogen will dissolve in 1 liter of water at room temperature and atmospheric pressure.

There are three isotopes of hydrogen. The most abundant isotope, $_1^1H$, constitutes 99.985% of naturally occurring hydrogen; deuterium, $_1^2H$ (or $_1^2D$) constitutes 0.015%; and the radioactive tritium, $_1^3H$ (or $_1^3T$) occurs only in trace amounts.

The bond energy of the H—H bond is 103 kcal/mole. In the course of most reactions, this bond must be broken so that the H atoms can form new bonds with other atoms. Since this bond energy is relatively high, most of the reactions of hydrogen take place at elevated temperatures.

Hydrogen reacts with the metals of group I A and the heavier metals of group II A (Ba, Sr, and Ca) to form **saltlike halides**. The hydride ion, H⁻, of these compounds, is isoelectronic with helium and achieves this stable configuration by the addition of an electron from the metal. Since the electron affinity of hydrogen is low (-0.7 ev), hydrogen reacts in this manner only with the most reactive metals.

$$2Na(s) + H_2(g) \longrightarrow 2NaH(s)$$
$$Ca(s) + H_2(g) \longrightarrow CaH_2(s)$$

The saltlike hydrides react with water to form hydrogen.

$$H^- + H_2O \longrightarrow H_2(g) + OH^-(aq)$$

With certain other metals, such as platinum, palladium, and nickel, hydrogen forms **interstitial hydrides**. Many of these hydrides are nonstoichiometric, the apparent formulas of the hydrides depending upon the conditions under which they were prepared. Palladium can absorb up to 900 times its own volume of hydrogen. The interstitial hydrides resemble the metals from which they are derived; the crystal structures of the metals do not change (or change only slightly) as hydrogen is added. Whether these substances should be regarded as compounds is debatable; the name, interstitial hydrides, arises from the view that the hydrogen is only absorbed into the interstices of the metallic crystal.

However, magnetic studies indicate that electron pairing of some sort is involved in the formation of these hydrides. Many of the metals have unpaired electrons and, hence, are paramagnetic. A gradual loss of paramagnetism is observed as the hydrides form from the metal. Since the electrons of molecular hydrogen are paired, these studies imply that the hydrogen is incorporated into the crystal in atomic form. This would account for the catalytic activity of platinum, palladium, nickel, and other metals for many reactions of hydrogen; if the H—H bond is broken, or even only weakened, the absorbed hydrogen should be much more reactive than ordinary H_2 gas.

Complex hydrides of boron and aluminum are important and useful compounds for chemical syntheses. Important examples are sodium borohydride and lithium aluminum hydride.

$$Na^+ \left[\begin{array}{c} H \\ H\!:\!\overset{\cdot\cdot}{B}\!:\!H \\ H \end{array} \right]^- \qquad Li^+ \left[\begin{array}{c} H \\ H\!:\!\overset{\cdot\cdot}{Al}\!:\!H \\ H \end{array} \right]^-$$

Since these compounds, as well as the saltlike hydrides, react with water to liberate hydrogen, they are prepared by reactions in ether.

$$4LiH + AlCl_3 \longrightarrow Li[AlH_4] + 3LiCl$$

Hydrogen forms covalent compounds with most of the nonmetals. It reacts with the halogens to form colorless, polar covalent gases.

$$H_2(g) + Cl_2(g) \longrightarrow 2HCl(g)$$

Reactions with fluorine or chlorine will take place at room temperature or below, but the reactions with the less reactive bromine or iodine require higher temperatures (400°C to 600°C).

The reaction or hydrogen and oxygen is highly exothermic and is the basis of the high temperature (ca. 2800°C) produced by the oxyhydrogen torch. The reaction with sulfur is more difficult and requires high temperatures.

$$H_2(g) + S(g) \longrightarrow H_2S(g)$$

Hydrogen reacts with nitrogen at high pressures (300 to 1000 atm), at high temperatures (400°C to 600°C), and in the presence of a catalyst to produce ammonia (Haber process).

$$3H_2(g) + N_2(g) \longrightarrow 2NH_3(g)$$

Hydrogen does not react readily with carbon, but at high temperatures, hydrogen can be made catalytically to react with finely divided carbon (Bergius process); hydrocarbons are produced.

$$2H_2(g) + C(g) \longrightarrow CH_4(g)$$

The ionization potential of hydrogen is relatively high (13.60 ev). In none of the compounds formed between hydrogen and the nonmetals does hydrogen exist as positive ions; the bonding in all such compounds is polar covalent.

Hydrogen reacts with many metal oxides to produce water and the free metal.

$$CuO(s) + H_2(g) \longrightarrow Cu(s) + H_2O(g)$$
$$WO_3(s) + 3H_2(g) \longrightarrow W(s) + 3H_2O(g)$$
$$FeO(s) + H_2(g) \longrightarrow Fe(s) + H_2O(g)$$

Certain of these reactions are employed in the metallurgy of oxide ores; for example, in the commercial production of tungsten metal, WO_3 is reduced to the free metal by hydrogen.

Carbon monoxide and hydrogen react at high temperatures and high pressures in the presence of a catalyst to produce methyl alcohol.

$$CO(g) + 2H_2(g) \longrightarrow CH_3OH(g)$$

8.11 The Hydrogen Bond

The intermolecular attractions of certain hydrogen-containing compounds are unusually strong. Such attractions occur in compounds in which hydrogen is covalently bonded to highly electronegative elements of small atomic size. In these compounds, the electronegative element exerts such a strong attraction on the bonding electrons that the hydrogen is left with a significant δ^+ charge. In fact, the hydrogen is almost an exposed proton, since this element has no screening electrons. The hydrogen of one molecule and a pair of un-shared electrons on the electronegative atom of another molecule are mutually attracted and form what is called a **hydrogen bond**. Because of its small size, each hydrogen atom is capable of forming only one hydrogen bond. The association of HF, H_2O, and NH_3 by hydrogen bonds (indicated by dotted lines) can be roughly diagramed as follows:

$$
\begin{array}{ccc}
& & \overset{\displaystyle H}{\underset{\displaystyle H}{|}} \quad \overset{\displaystyle H}{\underset{\displaystyle H}{|}} \\
H{-}F\cdots H{-}F\cdots & H{-}\overset{..}{\underset{|}{O}}\cdots H{-}\overset{..}{\underset{|}{O}}\cdots & H{-}N\cdots H{-}N\cdots \\
& H \qquad H & H \qquad H
\end{array}
$$

Unusual properties are characteristic of compounds in which hydrogen bonding occurs. In Figure 8.3, the normal boiling points of the hydrogen compounds of the elements of groups IV A, V A, VI A, and VII A are plotted.

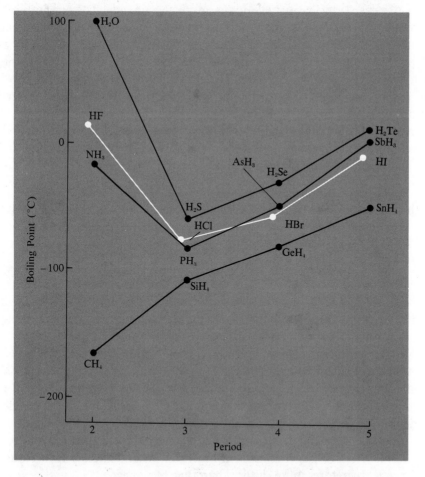

Figure 8.3 Boiling points of the hydrogen compounds of the elements of groups IV A, V A, VI A, and VII A.

The series CH_4, SiH_4, GeH_4, and SnH_4 illustrates the expected trend in boiling points; the boiling point increases as the molecular weight increases (Section 7.4). However, the first member of each of the other three series of compounds has a boiling point that is 100 to 200 degrees higher than the boiling point that would be predicted on the basis of molecular weight alone. The boiling points of hydrogen fluoride, water, and ammonia are unusually high because of hydrogen bonding, which increases the difficulty in separating molecules from the liquid state. Methane, CH_4, does not form hydrogen bonds; the carbon of CH_4 has no unshared electron pair. In addition to high boiling points, compounds that are associated by hydrogen bonding have abnormally high melting points, heats of vaporization, heats of fusion, and viscosities; the crystalline solids of such compounds are unusually hard.

Hydrogen bonds are much stronger than ordinary van der Waals intermolecular attractions and have energies around 5 kcal/mole, which is about 5 to 10% as strong as average ionic or covalent bonds. The strength of the hydrogen bond depends in part upon the electronegativity of the element to which hydrogen is covalently bonded; the strength of the hydrogen bonds, $N-H\cdots N < O-H\cdots O < F-H\cdots F$, parallels the increasing electronegativity of the elements, $N < O < F$. The electronegativity of carbon is too low for carbon compounds to form hydrogen bonds readily. However, in certain compounds, the hydrogen bonded to a carbon can participate in intermolecular hydrogen bonding if highly electronegative groups are also bonded to the carbon; such hydrogen bonds are relatively weak, however. For example, the hydrogen of the chloroform molecule, $HCCl_3$, forms hydrogen bonds

with an electron pair of the oxygen of the acetone molecule, $CH_3\overset{\displaystyle O}{\overset{\|}{C}}CH_3$,

$$
\begin{array}{ccc}
\text{Cl} & & \text{CH}_3 \\
| & & | \\
\text{Cl}-\text{C}-\text{H} & \cdots \text{O}= & \text{C} \\
| & & | \\
\text{Cl} & & \text{CH}_3
\end{array}
$$

and chloroform-acetone mixtures have higher boiling points than either pure component.

Another requirement for the formation of strong hydrogen bonds is that the element covalently bonded to the hydrogen must have a small atomic size. Really effective hydrogen bonds are formed only by fluorine, oxygen, and nitrogen compounds. Chlorine compounds form weak hydrogen bonds as evidenced by the slight displacement of the boiling point of HCl (Figure 8.3). Chlorine has approximately the same electronegativity as nitrogen; however, a chlorine atom is larger than a nitrogen atom, and the electron cloud of chlorine is, therefore, more diffuse than that of nitrogen.

An examination of Figure 8.3 will show that hydrogen bonding has a greater effect on the boiling point of water than on the boiling point of hydrogen fluoride. This effect is observed even though the $O-H\cdots O$ bond is only about two-thirds as strong as the $F-H\cdots F$ bond. There are twice as many hydrogen bonds per molecule possible in water as there are in hydrogen fluoride. The oxygen of each water molecule has two hydrogen atoms and two electron pairs, and each molecule can, therefore, form hydrogen bonds with four other water molecules. The HF molecule has three free electron pairs that can bond with hydrogen atoms from other molecules, but only one hydrogen atom with which it can form a hydrogen bond; hence, a maximum average of two hydrogen bonds per molecule is possible in any aggregate of HF molecules.

There are other properties of water that are affected to an unusual degree by hydrogen bonding. The tetrahedral arrangement of the hydrogen atoms and the unshared electron pairs of oxygen in water (Section 4.3) cause the hydrogen bonds of the ice crystal to be arranged in this manner and leads to the open structure of the ice crystal. Ice, therefore, has a comparatively low density. In water at the freezing point, the molecules are arranged more closely together, and hence water has a higher density than ice—an unusual situation. It should be noted that H_2O molecules are associated by hydrogen bonds in the liquid state but not to the same extent, nor in the rigid manner, as they are associated in ice.

Hydrogen bonding also accounts for the unexpectedly high solubilities of some compounds containing oxygen, nitrogen, and fluorine in certain hydrogen-containing solvents, notably water. Thus ammonia and methanol dissolve in water through the formation of hydrogen bonds.

$$
\begin{array}{cc}
\mathrm{H} & \mathrm{H} \\
| & | \\
\mathrm{H-N}\cdots\mathrm{H-O} \qquad & \mathrm{H-C-O}\cdots\mathrm{H-O} \\
|\qquad| & |\quad| \qquad | \\
\mathrm{H}\qquad\mathrm{H} & \mathrm{H}\ \ \mathrm{H}\qquad\mathrm{H}
\end{array}
$$

In addition, certain oxygen-containing anions (e.g., sulfate, SO_4^{2-}) dissolve in water through hydrogen-bond formation.

The water molecule is polar and forms dipole–dipole interactions with certain other polar molecules. The essential difference between these interactions and the hydrogen bond is that the latter is much stronger and exerts a more pronounced effect upon the properties of the materials in which it occurs. Both these intermolecular interactions are essentially electrostatic in character. The extra strength of the hydrogen bond comes about because of the highly concentrated positive charge on the hydrogen which attracts the electronegative element of another molecule strongly; in addition, the small size of the hydrogen atom permits the second molecule to approach closely. An extreme (and not typical) case is the HF_2^- ion, $F-H\cdots F^-$, in which the hydrogen is thought to be exactly midway between the two fluorine atoms.

The hydrogen bond of the HF_2^- ion is so strong that this ion, formed from a fluoride ion and a HF molecule, can be considered as an entity in aqueous solution or in such crystalline materials as KHF_2.

Rather than the somewhat random arrangement of some polar molecules with the usual dipole–dipole attractions, there is some evidence that the hydrogen bond is directional. It is assumed, at least in certain cases, that the hydrogen atom of one molecule approaches the second molecule in the direction of the hybrid orbitals of the unshared electron pair (Section 4.2). This directional character accounts for the tetrahedral structure observed in the ice crystal as well as the zigzag arrangement of HF molecules in solid hydrogen fluoride.

$$H \diagup \overset{F}{\cdots} \diagdown \overset{\cdot}{H} \diagup \underset{F}{\cdots} \diagdown \overset{F}{\cdots} \diagup \overset{\cdot}{H} \diagdown H \diagup \underset{F}{\cdots}$$

Hydrogen bonding plays an important role in determining the structures and properties of molecules of living systems. For example, the fibrous proteins (such as are found in silk, hair, and muscle) consist of high molecular-weight, long-chain protein molecules, which are organized in bundles held

Figure 8.4 Schematic representation of the structure of DNA. Dots indicate bonding between subunits of the chains of the double helix.

together by hydrogen bonding. In deoxyribonucleic acid (DNA), two long spiral chains form a double helix, and the hydrogen bonding which occurs between subunits of these chains holds the structure together (Figure 8.4). One theory proposed to account for the replication of DNA molecules assumes that the chains first come apart through the breaking of the hydrogen bonds. Next, each chain of the pair forms a new complementary chain from simpler molecules existing in the cell. In this respect, the parent chain acts as a template for the formation of the daughter chain; the geometry of the parent, including the very important factor of the location of active sites for hydrogen bonding, determines the molecular structure of the daughter. The process ends with two double helices where one had been before.

SOME SUGGESTED READINGS

Cotton, F. A., and Wilkinson, G., *Advanced Inorganic Chemistry*, 2nd ed., New York, Wiley, 1966.

Johnson, R. C., *Introductory Descriptive Chemistry*, New York, Benjamin, 1966 (paper).

Jolly, W. L., *The Chemistry of the Non-Metals*, Englewood Cliffs, N. J., Prentice-Hall, 1966 (paper).

Lavoisier, A., *Elements of Chemistry*, New York, Dover, 1965 (paper).

Pauling, L., *The Nature of the Chemical Bond*, 3rd ed., Ithaca, N. Y., Cornell University Press, 1960.

Weeks, M. E., and Leicester, H. M., *Discovery of the Elements*, 7th ed., Easton, Penna., Chemical Education Publishing Co., 1968.

PROBLEMS

The more difficult problems are starred.

8.1 Write chemical equations for the preparation of oxygen from (a) HgO, (b) BaO_2, (c) Na_2O_2 and H_2O, (d) $NaNO_3$, (e) $KClO_3$, (f) H_2O.

8.2 Write chemical equations for the preparation of hydrogen from (a) Na and H_2O, (b) Mg and steam, (c) Fe and steam, (d) Zn and $H^+(aq)$, (e) Zn and $OH^-(aq)$, (f) C and steam.

8.3 Write a chemical equation for the reaction of each of the following with oxygen: (a) Cs, (b) Na, (c) Li, (d) C, (e) S, (f) Cu_2O, (g) P_4.

8.4 Write chemical equations for the complete combustion, in oxygen, of (a) C_6H_6, (b) C_4H_6S, (c) $C_4H_{10}O$.

8.5 Write a chemical equation for the reaction of each of the following with hydrogen: (a) Na, (b) Cu_2O, (c) Cl_2, (d) CO, (e) WO_3, (f) N_2.

8.6 Write a chemical equation for the reaction of each of the following with water: (a) CaH_2, (b) $Li[AlH_4]$, in which the hydroxides of Li and

Al are two of the products, (c) SO_3, (d) CaO, (e) Na_2O, (f) N_2O_3.

8.7 What are the anhydrides of the following: (a) LiOH, (b) $Ba(OH)_2$, (c) $Ga(OH)_3$, (d) HOCl, (e) HNO_2, (f) $HClO_4$, (g) HNO_3, (h) H_3BO_3.

8.8 Complete and balance the following equations: (a) $CaO(s) + H^+(aq) \rightarrow$, (b) $SO_2(g) + OH^-(aq) \rightarrow$, (c) $BaO(s) + CO_2(g) \rightarrow$, (d) $H_2O_2(aq) + OH^-(aq) \rightarrow$.

8.9 Describe the structure and properties of (a) salt-like hydrides, (b) interstitial hydrides, (c) complex hydrides, (d) covalent hydrides.

8.10 Define the following: (a) disproportionation reaction, (b) allotrope, (c) hydride, (d) hydrate, (e) para hydrogen, (f) deuterium, (g) roasting.

8.11 State the oxidation number of:

(a) Sb in Sb_4O_6 (e) Fe in $BaFeO_4$
(b) Ti in $K_2Ti_2O_5$ (f) N in N_2H_4
(c) I in H_5IO_6 (g) N in O_2NF
(d) S in $S_2O_5Cl_2$ (h) Ge in Mg_2GeO_4

8.12 State the oxidation number of:

(a) Pb in $PbCl_6^{2-}$ (e) Bi in BiO^+
(b) Sn in $Sn_2F_5^-$ (f) N in $(NH_3OH)^+$
(c) Re in ReO_4^- (g) Mo in $(Mo_6Cl_8)^{4+}$
(d) Xe in $HXeO_4^-$ (h) W in $(H_2W_{12}O_{40})^{6-}$

8.13 Balance the following equations for oxidation-reduction reactions by the oxidation-number method:

(a) $H_2O + MnO_4^- + ClO_2^- \rightarrow MnO_2 + ClO_4^- + OH^-$
(b) $H^+ + Cr_2O_7^{2-} + H_2S \rightarrow Cr^{3+} + S + H_2O$
(c) $H^+ + IO_3^- + SO_3^{2-} \rightarrow I_2 + SO_4^{2-} + H_2O$
(d) $H_2O + P_4 + HOCl \rightarrow H_3PO_4 + Cl^- + H^+$
(e) $OH^- + Cl_2 \rightarrow ClO_3^- + Cl^- + H_2O$

8.14 Balance the following equations for oxidation-reduction reactions by the oxidation-number method:

(a) $Cu + H^+ + NO_3^- \rightarrow Cu^{2+} + NO + H_2O$
(b) $H_2O + NiO_2 + Fe \rightarrow Ni(OH)_2 + Fe(OH)_3$
(c) $PbS + H_2O_2 \rightarrow PbSO_4 + H_2O$
(d) $PbO_2 + HI \rightarrow PbI_2 + I_2 + H_2O$
(e) $H_2O + CrI_3 + Cl_2 \rightarrow CrO_4^{2-} + IO_3^- + H^+$

8.15 Complete and balance the following equations for oxidation-reduction reactions by the ion-electron method. All the reactions occur in acid solution.

(a) $ReO_2 + Cl_2 \rightarrow HReO_4 + Cl^-$
(b) $HgI_4^{2-} + N_2H_4 \rightarrow Hg + I^- + N_2$
(c) $Te + NO_3^- \rightarrow TeO_2 + NO$
(d) $UO^{2+} + Cr_2O_7^{2-} \rightarrow UO_2^{2+} + Cr^{3+}$
(e) $Zn + H_2MoO_4 \rightarrow Zn^{2+} + Mo^{3+}$

8.16 Complete and balance the following equations for oxidation-reduction reactions by the ion-electron method. All the reactions occur in acid solution.

(a) $AsH_3 + Ag^+ \rightarrow As_4O_6 + Ag$

(b) $Sb + NO_3^- \rightarrow Sb_4O_6 + NO$

(c) $Mn^{2+} + BiO_3^- \rightarrow MnO_4^- + Bi^{3+}$

(d) $NO + NO_3^- \rightarrow N_2O_4$

(e) $MnO_4^- + HCN + I^- \rightarrow Mn^{2+} + ICN$

8.17 Complete and balance the following equations for oxidation-reduction reactions by the ion-electron method. All the reactions occur in acid solution.

(a) $S_2O_3^{2-} + IO_3^- + Cl^- \rightarrow SO_4^{2-} + ICl_2^-$

(b) $Se + BrO_3^- \rightarrow H_2SeO_3 + Br^-$

(c) $H_3AsO_3 + MnO_4^- \rightarrow H_3AsO_4 + Mn^{2+}$

(d) $H_5IO_6 + I^- \rightarrow I_2$

(e) $Pb_3O_4 \rightarrow Pb^{2+} + PbO_2$

*8.18 Complete and balance the following equations for oxidation-reduction reactions by the ion-electron method. All the reactions occur in acid solution.

(a) $Hg_5(IO_6)_2 + I^- \rightarrow HgI_4^{2-} + I_2$

(b) $MnO_4^- + Mn^{2+} + H_2P_2O_7^{2-} \rightarrow Mn(H_2P_2O_7)_3^{3-}$

(c) $CS(NH_2)_2 + BrO_3^- \rightarrow CO(NH_2)_2 + SO_4^{2-} + Br^-$

(d) $Co(NO_2)_6^{3-} + MnO_4^- \rightarrow Co^{2+} + NO_3^- + Mn^{2+}$

(e) $HClO_2 \rightarrow ClO_2 + ClO_3^- + Cl^-$

8.19 Complete and balance the following equations for oxidation-reduction reactions by the ion-electron method. All the reactions occur in alkaline solution.

(a) $Cr(OH)_4^- + BrO^- \rightarrow CrO_4^{2-} + Br^-$

(b) $Al + NO_3^- \rightarrow Al(OH)_4^- + NH_3$

(c) $P_4 \rightarrow H_2PO_2^- + PH_3$

(d) $Bi(OH)_3 + Sn(OH)_4^{2-} \rightarrow Bi + Sn(OH)_6^{2-}$

(e) $Ni^{2+} + Br_2 \rightarrow NiO(OH) + Br^-$

8.20 Complete and balance the following equations for oxidation-reduction reactions by the ion-electron method. All the reactions occur in alkaline solution.

(a) $MnO_4^- + CN^- \rightarrow MnO_2 + CNO^-$

(b) $S \rightarrow SO_3^{2-} + S^{2-}$

(c) $Al + OH^- \rightarrow Al(OH)_4^- + H_2$

(d) $HXeO_4^- + O_3 \rightarrow XeO_6^{4-} + H_2O$

(e) $I_2 + Cl_2 \rightarrow H_3IO_6^{2-} + Cl^-$

8.21 Complete and balance the following equations for oxidation-reduction reactions by the ion-electron method. All the reactions occur in alkaline solution.

(a) $As + OH^- \rightarrow AsO_3^{3-} + H_2$

(b) $S_2O_3^{2-} + I_2 \rightarrow SO_4^{2-} + I^-$

(c) $Br_2 \rightarrow Br^- + BrO_3^-$

(d) $S + HO_2^- \rightarrow SO_4^{2-} + OH^-$

(e) $CO(NH_2)_2 + OBr^- \rightarrow CO_2 + N_2 + Br^-$

*8.22 There are apparently several ways in which the equation for the reaction of XeF_4 and H_2O can be balanced. For example,

$$4XeF_4 + 8H_2O \longrightarrow 2XeO_3 + 2Xe + O_2 + 16HF$$

$$6XeF_4 + 12H_2O \longrightarrow 2XeO_3 + 4Xe + 3O_2 + 24HF$$

$$8XeF_4 + 16H_2O \longrightarrow 2XeO_3 + 6Xe + 5O_2 + 32HF$$

(a) Under what conditions would you expect such a situation to arise?

(b) How can the correct equation be established?

8.23 What fraction of a mole is the equivalent weight of each of the following substances?

(a) H_5IO_6 in a reaction in which $IO_3{}^-$ is produced.

(b) H_5IO_6 in a reaction in which $Na_3H_2IO_6$ is produced.

(c) $K_2Cr_2O_7$ in a reaction in which Cr^{3+} is produced.

(d) $Ca(OCl)_2$ in a reaction in which Cl^- is produced.

(e) $K_3[Fe(CN)_6]$ in a reaction in which $K_4[Fe(CN)_6]$ is produced.

8.24 What fraction of a mole is the equivalent weight of each of the following substances?

(a) H_3PO_3 in a reaction in which $CaHPO_3$ is produced.

(b) KIO_3 in a reaction in which I^- is produced.

(c) $Na_2S_2O_3$ in a reaction in which $S_4O_6^{2-}$ is produced.

(d) Mo_2O_3 in a reaction in which H_2MoO_4 is produced.

(e) $Ca(C_2O_4)$ in a reaction in which CO_2 is produced.

8.25 What is the equivalent weight of a metal oxide if 5.33 g of H_2SO_4 completely neutralizes 2.50 g of the oxide?

8.26 The reaction of AsH_3 and $AgNO_3$ yields As_4O_6 and Ag. (a) What are the equivalent weights of AsH_3 and $AgNO_3$ for this reaction? (b) What weight of AsH_3 is needed to react with 5.00 g of $AgNO_3$?

8.27 The reaction of I_2O_5 and CO yields I_2 and CO_2. (a) What are the equivalent weights of I_2O_5 and CO for this reaction? (b) What weight of CO is present in a sample that requires 2.50 g of I_2O_5 for complete reaction?

8.28 (a) What is the equivalent weight of $KBrO_3$ (in a transformation producing Br^-), of Se (in a transformation producing H_2SeO_3), and of Se (in a transformation producing H_2SeO_4)? (b) In a reaction between $KBrO_3$ and Se, 1.02 g of $KBrO_3$ react with 0.725 g of Se. What is the formula of the selenium-containing product of the reaction?

*8.29 A 4.00 g sample of an ore of Bi_2S_3 was reacted with acid and a quantity of H_2S released equivalent to the amount of Bi_2S_3 present in the ore. The H_2S was reacted with I_2 yielding S and I^-; the complete reaction required 3.04 g of I_2. (a) What are the equivalent weights of H_2S and I_2 for the second reaction? (b) What weight of H_2S is equivalent to 3.04 g of I_2? (c) What percent of the ore is Bi_2S_3?

8.30 The effect of hydrogen bonding on the properties of the following hydrides falls in the order: $H_2O > HF > NH_3$. Explain this observation.

8.31 Diagram the structures of the following molecules and use the diagrams to show how the water solubility of each compound is enhanced by hydrogen bonding. (a) NH_3, (b) H_2N-NH_2, (c) CH_3CH_2OH, (d) $CH_3\overset{\displaystyle O}{\overset{\|}{C}}-OH$.

8.32 (a) Use Figure 8.3 to estimate what the normal boiling point of water would be if H_2O followed the trend established by H_2S, H_2Se, and H_2Te. (b) By means of Trouton's rule (Section 7.5), calculate the molar heat of vaporization of water that would be expected on the basis of the boiling point from part (a). (c) The actual molar heat of vaporization of water is 9.72 kcal/mole. What explanation may be offered to account for the difference between the actual value and that derived from Trouton's rule?

8.33 (a) Calculate the molar entropy of vaporization at the boiling point, in cal/°K mole, for acetic acid. The normal boiling point of acetic acid is 118°C and the heat of vaporization of acetic acid is 96.8 cal/g. How does your answer compare to the Trouton's rule value of 21.0 cal/°K mole? (b) Acetic acid vapor at temperatures near the boiling point consists of double molecules, or dimers, of two

molecules joined by hydrogen bonds. Diagram the acetic acid dimer. How does the existence of these dimers in acetic acid vapor explain the result obtained in part (a)?

Solutions are homogeneous mixtures (Section 1.3). They may be classified according to their physical state; gaseous, solid, and liquid solutions may be prepared. Gaseous solutions, of which air is an example, are mixtures of molecules of two or more gases. Dalton's law of partial pressures describes the behavior of gaseous solutions. Certain alloys are solid solutions; coinage silver is copper dissolved in silver, and brass is a solid solution of zinc in copper. Not all alloys, however, are solid solutions; some are heterogeneous mixtures, and some are intermetallic compounds. Liquid solutions are the most common and probably the most important to the chemist.

SOLUTIONS

9.1   Nature of Solutions

The component of a solution that is present in greatest quantity is usually called the **solvent,** and the other components are called **solutes**. Such terminology is loose and arbitrary. It is sometimes convenient to designate a component as the solvent even though it is present in only small amount; at other times, the assignment of the terms solute and solvent has little significance (e.g., in characterizing gaseous solutions).

Certain pairs of substances are miscible in all proportions. Complete miscibility is characteristic of the components of all gaseous solutions and some pairs of components of liquid and solid solutions. However, for most materials, there is a limit on the amount of the substance that will dissolve in a given solvent. The **solubility** of a substance in a particular solvent at a specified temperature is the maximum amount of the solute that will dissolve in a definite amount of the solvent and produce a stable system.

For a given solution, the amount of solute dissolved in a unit volume of solution (or a unit amount of solvent) is the **concentration** of the solute. Solutions containing a relatively low concentration of solute are spoken of as **dilute** solutions; those of relatively high concentrations are called **concentrated** solutions.

If an excess of solute (more than will normally dissolve) is added to a quantity of a liquid solvent, an equilibrium is established between the pure solute and the dissolved solute.

$$\text{solute}_{pure} \rightleftharpoons \text{solute}_{dissolved}$$

The pure solute may be a solid, liquid, or gas. At equilibrium in such a system, the rate at which the pure solute dissolves equals the rate at which the dissolved solute comes out of solution. The concentration of the dissolved solute, therefore, is a constant. Such a solution is called a **saturated** solution, and the concentration of the solution is the solubility of the solute in question.

That such dynamic equilibria exist has been shown experimentally. If small crystals of a solid solute are placed in contact with a saturated solution of the solute, the crystals are observed to change in size and shape. Throughout this experiment, however, the concentration of the saturated solution does not change, nor does the quantity of excess solute decrease or increase.

An **unsaturated** solution has a lower concentration of solute than a saturated solution. Unsaturated solutions cannot exist in contact with excess solute. Instead, when pure solute is added to an unsaturated solution, some solute dissolves, and the concentration of the solution increases until equilibrium is attained and the solution is saturated.

It is sometimes possible to prepare a **supersaturated** solution, a metastable state. The concentration of solute in a supersaturated solution is higher than that of a saturated solution of the same solute. The additional solute, over that needed to saturate the solution, comes out of solution when pure solute is placed in contact with the supersaturated solution. The system quickly establishes a condition of equilibrium between solute and saturated solution.

Solutes exist in solution as molecules, atoms, or ions, which is one reason for running chemical reactions in aqueous solution. Such reactions are usually rapid since: the reactants are in a small state of subdivision, the attractions between the particles (molecules, atoms, or ions) of the pure solute have been at least partially overcome, and these particles are free to move about through the solution. In addition, it is convenient to measure quantities of reactants volumetrically, which is possible when these reactants are in solution (Section 9.6). Because of their importance, liquid solutions containing gases, liquids, or solids as solutes will be the principal topic of this chapter.

9.2   The Solution Process

The molecules of a nonpolar covalent material, such as carbon tetrachloride, are held together by the weak fluctuating dipoles called van der Waals forces. On the other hand, polar covalent substances have relatively strong inter-molecular attractions derived from the permanent dipoles of the molecules; the intermolecular attractions of water are unusually strong (Section 8.11). Nonpolar substances and polar substances are generally immiscible; for example, carbon tetrachloride is insoluble in water. The attraction of one water molecule for another water molecule is much greater than any attraction between a carbon tetrachloride molecule and a water molecule. Hence, carbon tetrachloride molecules are "squeezed out," and these two substances form a two-liquid-layer system.

Iodine is a nonpolar material and is soluble in carbon tetrachloride. The attractions between I_2 molecules in solid iodine are approximately of the same type and magnitude as those beetween CCl_4 molecules in pure carbon tetra-chloride. Hence, significant I_2–CCl_4 attractions are possible, and iodine molecules can mix with carbon tetrachloride molecules. The resulting solution is a random molecular mixture.

Methyl alcohol, CH_3OH, like water, consists of polar molecules that are highly associated. In both pure liquids, the molecules are attracted to one another through hydrogen bonding.

$$
\begin{array}{ccc}
\text{H}-\text{O} \cdots & \text{H}-\text{O} \cdots & \text{H}-\text{O} \\
| & | & | \\
\text{H}-\text{C}-\text{H} & \text{H}-\text{C}-\text{H} & \text{H}-\text{C}-\text{H} \\
| & | & | \\
\text{H} & \text{H} & \text{H}
\end{array}
\qquad
\begin{array}{ccc}
\text{H}-\text{O} \cdots & \text{H}-\text{O} \cdots & \text{H}-\text{O} \\
| & | & | \\
\text{H} & \text{H} & \text{H}
\end{array}
$$

Methyl alcohol and water are miscible in all proportions. In solutions of methyl alcohol in water, CH_3OH and H_2O molecules are associated through hydrogen bonding.

$$
\begin{array}{ccc}
\text{H}-\text{O} \cdots & \text{H}-\text{O} \cdots & \text{H}-\text{O} \\
| & | & | \\
\text{H} & \text{H}-\text{C}-\text{H} & \text{H} \\
& | & \\
& \text{H} &
\end{array}
$$

Methyl alcohol does not dissolve in nonpolar solvents. The strong inter-molecular attractions of pure methyl alcohol are not overcome unless the solvent molecules can form attractions of equal, or almost equal, strength with the methyl alcohol molecules.

In general, then, polar materials dissolve only in polar solvents, and non-polar substances are soluble in nonpolar solvents. This is the first rule of solubility: "like dissolves like." Network crystals, such as the diamond, in which the atoms comprising the crystal are held together by covalent bonds, are insoluble in all liquids. This crystalline structure is far too stable to be broken down by a solution process, and any potential solute–solvent attractions cannot approach the strength of the covalent bonding of the crystal.

Polar liquids (water, in particular) can function as solvents for many ionic compounds. The ions of the solute are electrostatically attracted by the polar solvent molecules—negative ions by the positive poles of the solvent molecules, positive ions by the negative poles of the solvent molecules. These ion–dipole attractions can be relatively strong. Figure 9.1 diagrams the solution of an ionic crystal in water. The ions in the center of the crystal are attracted equally in all directions by the oppositely charged ions of the crystal. The electrostatic attractions on the ions of the surface of the crystal, however, are unbalanced, and these are the ions that are exposed to the solvent molecules. Water molecules are attracted to the surface ions of the crystal, the positive ends of the water molecules to the anions and the negative ends of the water molecules to the cations. The ion–dipole attractions thus formed allow the ions to escape from the crystal and drift off into the liquid phase. The dissolved ions are **hydrated** and move through the solution surrounded by a sheath of water molecules; all ions are hydrated in water solution.

Certain covalent molecules with relatively high dipole moments dissolve in water to produce solutions of ions (see Section 3.12). For example, hydro-

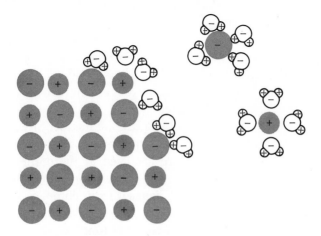

Figure 9.1 Solution of an ionic crystal in water.

gen chloride, which exists in the pure state as highly polar, covalent molecules, forms such aqueous solutions. When this substance is placed in water, the HCl molecules interact with the water molecules.

$$HCl(g) + H_2O \longrightarrow H_3O^+(aq) + Cl^-(aq)$$

Both the ions resulting from this reaction are, of course, hydrated.

A number of covalent compounds containing metals and nonmetals (e.g., aluminum chloride) also ionize in water solution. True cations with charges of $3+$ or higher (such as Al^{3+}) seldom exist in pure compounds; aluminum chloride is a covalent compound. In addition, other species with relatively high ratios of charge to size (e.g., the very small Be^{2+} ion) form pure compounds that are largely covalent. The same factor that is principally responsible for the covalent character of these compounds (a high ratio of ionic charge to radius) also leads to the formation of very stable hydrated ions (Section 9.3).

$$BeCl_2(s) + 4H_2O \longrightarrow Be(H_2O)_4^{2+}(aq) + 2Cl^-(aq)$$

9.3 Hydrates

The nature of the interactions between water molecules and ions in aqueous solution is a subject of extensive study. Negative ions in aqueous solution are hydrated by means of ion–dipole attractions or, where possible, by hydrogen bonding. Unless the positive ion itself contains hydrogen atoms (as, e.g., the ammonium ion, NH_4^+), hydrogen bonding between a positive ion and a water molecule is impossible.

Nevertheless, the attractions between water molecules and most metal cations are strong ones. At one time, coordinate covalent bonds were thought to bind these particles together into **complex ions**, such a bond being formed by the use of a vacant orbital of the metal cation and a pair of unshared electrons from the oxygen of a water molecule. This valence bond approach, especially when modified to take hybridized orbitals into account (Section 4.3), remains a useful one, but the ligand field theory and the molecular orbital theory (Section 19.4) offer interpretations that are more in agreement with the observed properties of these hydrated ions.

Most metal cations are hydrated by a definite number of water molecules; the most common number is six, although four is not rare. For sixfold coordination, the water molecules are arranged at the corners of a regular octahedron as illustrated in Figure 9.2 for the ion $[Cr(H_2O)_6]^{3+}$. Certain other molecules and anions (called **ligands**) form complex ions with metal cations (see Chapter 19). The number of ligands coordinated around the central ion is called the **coordination number** of that ion. In aqueous solution, hydrated complex cations are undoubtedly further hydrated by additional

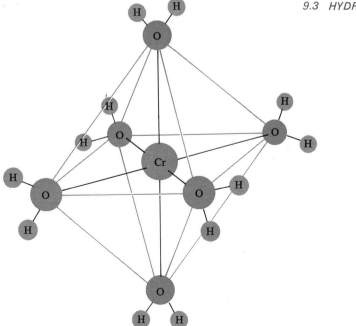

Figure 9.2 The hydrated Cr^{3+} ion.

water molecules that are hydrogen bonded to the coordinated water molecules; however, the water molecules of the outer layers are much more loosely held than those of the inner coordination sphere.

Frequently, hydrated ions persist in the crystalline materials obtained by the evaporation of aqueous solutions of salts. Thus the solid compound $FeCl_3 \cdot 6H_2O$ is actually $[Fe(H_2O)_6]Cl_3$, and $[Fe(H_2O)_6]^{3+}$ ions can be identified in the crystal. Other examples of solid hydrates in which the water of hydration is coordinated to the cation are $[Co(H_2O)_6]Cl_2$, $[Cr(H_2O)_6]Cl_3$, and $[Be(H_2O)_4]Cl_2$.

Solid hydrates in which water molecules are coordinated to anions by hydrogen bonding are known but are not common. For example, in the compound $ZnSO_4 \cdot 7H_2O$, six water molecules are coordinated around the zinc ion, and the seventh is hydrogen bonded to the sulfate anion. Other examples include the analogous compounds $NiSO_4 \cdot 7H_2O$ and $CoSO_4 \cdot 7H_2O$, as well as $CuSO_4 \cdot 5H_2O$ which may be represented $[Cu(H_2O)_4]SO_4 \cdot H_2O$.

There are two other ways in which water can occur in a crystalline hydrate in addition to association with cation or anion. The water molecules may assume positions in the crystal lattice without being associated with a specific ion. Such is the case for the compound $BaCl_2 \cdot 2H_2O$; removal of the water from this compound destroys the crystal lattice. Or, the water molecules may occur between the layers or in the interstices of a crystal lattice; the hydrates of the zeolites, a group of silicate minerals, incorporate water in such a manner. Removal of zeolitic water from a hydrate changes the crystal very little, if at all.

9.4   Heat of Solution

When a solute dissolves in a solvent, energy is absorbed or evolved, the actual quantity per mole of solute depending upon the concentration of the final solution. Thus, when a **heat of solution** is recorded, the number of moles of solvent used to dissolve 1 mole of solute in the determination of the heat effect must be indicated in some way. If no such distinction is made, it may be assumed that the heat of solution relates to a process in which 1 mole of solute is dissolved in an infinitely large quantity of solvent (heat of solution at infinite dilution); the heat of solution per mole of a given solute is virtually a constant when very dilute solutions are prepared.

The heat effect observed when a solution is prepared is the net result of the energy *required* to break apart certain chemical bonds or attractions (solute–solute and solvent–solvent) and the energy *released* by the formation of new ones (solute–solvent). Thus if an ionic solid (MX) dissolves in water, the heat of solution is a manifestation of the energy required to break apart the crystal lattice (the lattice energy; ΔH, positive):

$$MX(s) \longrightarrow M^+(g) + X^-(g)$$

and the energy liberated when the ions are hydrated (the heat of hydration; ΔH, negative):

$$M^+(g) + X^-(g) \longrightarrow M^+(aq) + X^-(aq)$$

The heat of hydration is itself the sum of two heat effects—the energy needed to break the hydrogen bonds between some of the solvent molecules and the energy released when these water molecules hydrate the ions of the solute. However, it is difficult to investigate these latter two effects separately.

The overall solution process is exothermic (ΔH, negative) if more energy is liberated by the hydration process than is required to break apart the crystal lattice (see data for AgF in Table 9.1). On the other hand, heat is absorbed

Table 9.1

Calculation of Heat of Solution[a]

Substance	Lattice Energy (kcal/mole)	Heat of Hydration (kcal/mole)	Heat of Solution (kcal/mole)
KCl	+167.6	−163.5	+4.1
AgF	+217.7	−222.6	−4.9

[a] Infinite dilution, 298°K.

(ΔH, positive) when the solute dissolves in water if the lattice energy cannot be supplied by the hydration energy (see data for KCl in Table 9.1). The data of Table 9.1 apply to the preparation of very dilute solutions.

The magnitude of the hydration energy of a salt depends upon the concentration of charge (ratio of charge to surface area) of its ions. In general, a high concentration of charge results when an ion has a small size, a high charge, or a combination of these two factors. Ions with high concentrations of charge attract water molecules strongly, and this leads to large heats of hydration. This is generally not reflected in the heat of solution because the same factor—high ionic charge concentration—also leads to very stable crystal structures and consequently large lattice energies.

Similar considerations apply to the solution of nonionic materials. The lattice energies of molecular crystals are not so large as those of ionic crystals since the forces holding molecular crystals together are not so strong; however, solvation energies for such covalent materials are also of a low order. For molecular substances that dissolve in nonpolar solvents without ionization and without appreciable solute–solvent interaction, the heat of solution is endothermic and has about the same magnitude as the heat of fusion of the solute.

Gases generally dissolve in liquids with the evolution of heat. Since no energy is required to separate the molecules of a gas, the predominant heat effect of such a solution process is the solvation of the gas molecules, and such is exothermic. The calculation of the heat of solution of hydrogen chloride gas in water, however, requires that the heat evolved by the formation of hydrated ions be reduced by the energy required for the ionization of the HCl molecules.

There is an entropy effect (Sections 7.5 and 13.5) when a solution is prepared. In some cases, the entropy increases (ΔS, positive); the change from pure substances to solution represents an increase in randomness, or disorder. In other instances (e.g., the dissolution of a gas in a liquid), the entropy, or disorder, of the system decreases when the solution is prepared (ΔS, negative); that is, the solution is more highly ordered (less disordered) than the pure components.

Entropy may be regarded as a probability function. A disordered condition is far more statistically probable than an ordered one. The probability that a bridge hand dealt from a well-shuffled deck of cards will contain a random mixture of suits is higher than the probability that it will contain thirteen cards of the same suit. In any natural process, there is a tendency for disorder, or randomness, to increase.

However, there is also a tendency for the energy of a system to decrease in the course of a natural process; that is, the system tends to go from a more energetic state to a less energetic state. Both of these factors (the tendency toward minimum energy and the tendency toward maximum entropy) must be considered in deciding whether a given process is spontaneous. It is convenient to use a function called the **Gibbs free energy**, *G*, for this purpose (Section 10.7).[1]

At constant temperature, the change in Gibbs free energy, ΔG, for a given process is

$$\Delta G = \Delta H - T\Delta S$$

A system is more ordered at low temperatures than at high temperatures; as the temperature increases, the randomness increases. The probability factor, $T\Delta S$, includes both temperature and change in entropy. Gibbs free energy and enthalpy are usually measured in cal or kcal; the factor $T\Delta S$ has comparable dimensions (°K times cal/°K or °K times kcal/°K). A favorable ΔH is negative (minimum energy), whereas a favorable $T\Delta S$ is positive (maximum entropy). In the equation for ΔG, the factor $T\Delta S$ appears with a negative sign, and ΔG values for spontaneous processes are negative.

We are now in a position to understand why endothermic solution processes occur. Why should KCl dissolve in water when more energy is required to break apart the crystal lattice than is supplied by the hydration of the ions? The increase in entropy for this process compensates for the unfavorable enthalpy change.

In the preparation of aqueous solutions of other ionic compounds (e.g., the preparation of dilute solutions of AgF), the entropy decreases, and dissolution occurs because a favorable enthalpy change overshadows an unfavorable entropy change. In this latter case, water molecules must hydrate the ions in a highly ordered manner to produce a solution which represents a decrease in randomness, or an increase in order (Figures 9.1 and 9.2). Entropy effects are difficult to predict qualitatively.

9.5 Effect of Temperature and Pressure on Solubility

The effect of a temperature change on the solubility of a substance depends upon whether heat is absorbed or evolved *when a saturated solution is prepared.* Suppose that a small quantity of solute dissolves in a nearly saturated solution with the absorption of heat. The crystallization of a small quantity of this solute from the saturated solution would evolve a commensurate quantity of heat. We can represent the equilibrium between excess solid solute and saturated solution as

$$\text{energy} + \text{solute} + H_2O \rightleftharpoons \text{saturated solution}$$

[1] This function was named in honor of J. Willard Gibbs, who developed the application of thermodynamic principles to chemistry.

The effect of adding heat to such a system can be predicted by means of a principle first proposed by Henri Le Chatelier in 1888. **Le Chatelier's principle** states that the application of a stress to a system in equilibrium results in the system reacting in such a way as to counteract the stress and establish a new equilibrium state. If the temperature of the system previously described is increased (energy added), the equilibrium point will shift to the right (the direction in which energy is absorbed), and hence more solute will dissolve. If the system is cooled, the point of equilibrium will shift to the left (the direction in which energy is evolved), and solute will precipitate out of solution. Hence, the solubility of materials that dissolve into nearly saturated solutions with the absorption of heat increases with increasing temperature; this is true of the solubility of most ionic solutes in water.

When a small amount of an ionic solute dissolves in a solution that is nearly saturated, the heat evolved by the hydration of ions is usually less than the heat evolved when the same amount of the solute dissolves in pure water. In a nearly saturated solution, such a large proportion of water molecules may be already involved in the hydration of ions that the proportion remaining is not sufficient to hydrate the added ions completely. The heat of solution is evidence of the deficit or surplus between what the heat of hydration supplies and the lattice energy requires, and the latter two are usually close in magnitude.

Therefore, even though a small amount of a solute may dissolve in pure water with the evolution of heat, the dissolution of a small amount of the same solute in a nearly saturated solution may proceed with the absorption of heat. The data of Table 9.1 pertain to the preparation of very dilute solutions. Many such preparations are exothermic; however, the large majority of ionic solutes dissolve into nearly saturated solutions with the absorption of heat.

When a substance dissolves with the evolution of heat.

$$\text{solute} + H_2O \rightleftharpoons \text{saturated solution} + \text{energy}$$

Le Chatelier's principle indicates that the solubility of the solute increases when the temperature is lowered, and the solubility decreases when the temperature is raised. There are a few ionic compounds (such as Li_2CO_3 and Na_2SO_4) that behave in this fashion. In addition, the solubility of all gases decreases as the temperature is raised; warming a soft drink causes bubbles of carbon dioxide gas to come out of solution.

The solubility differential with respect to change in temperature depends upon the magnitude of the heat of solution. The solubilities of substances with small heats of solution do not change much with changes in temperature.

Changes in pressure ordinarily have little effect upon the solubility of solid and liquid solutes. However, increasing or decreasing the pressure on a solution containing a dissolved gas has a definite effect. William Henry in 1803 discovered that the amount of a gas that dissolves in a given quantity of a liquid, at constant temperature, is directly proportional to the partial pressure of the gas above the solution. **Henry's law** is valid only for dilute solutions and relatively low pressures. Gases that are extremely soluble generally react chemically with the solvent (e.g., the solution of hydrogen chloride gas in water); such solutions do not follow Henry's law.

9.6   Concentration of Solutions

The concentration of solute in a solution may be expressed in several different ways.

1. The **weight percentage** of solute in a solution is 100 times the weight of solute divided by the *total* weight of the solution. Thus 100 g of a 10% aqueous solution of sulfuric acid contains 10 g of H_2SO_4 and 90 g of water. Notice that a solution of this concentration would contain 11 g of H_2SO_4 per 100 g of water. Volume percentages are not commonly employed; figures recorded as percentages should be understood to be based on weight unless specific notation to the contrary is made.

2. The **mole fraction** X, of a component of a solution is the ratio of the number of moles of that component to the total number of moles of all components present in the solution (Section 6.10, Example 6.14). A 100 g sample of a 10% H_2SO_4 solution contains $10/98 = 0.10$ mole of H_2SO_4 and $90/18 = 5.0$ moles of H_2O. The mole fraction of H_2SO_4 is, therefore,

$$X_{H_2SO_4} = \frac{0.10}{5.0 + 0.10} = 0.020$$

Since the mole fractions of all of the components of a solution taken together must equal 1.00, $X_{H_2O} = 0.98$.

3. The **molarity**, M, of a solution is the number of moles of solute per liter of solution. Thus a $6M$ solution of sulfuric acid is prepared by taking 6 moles of H_2SO_4 ($6 \times 98.08 = 588.48$ g) and adding the acid, with careful mixing, to sufficient water to make exactly 1 liter of solution.

Notice that the definition is based on the total *volume* of the solution. When a liquid solution is prepared, the volume of the solution rarely equals the sum of the volumes of the pure components. Usually, the final volume of the solution is larger or smaller than the total of the volumes of the constituents. Hence, it is not practical to attempt to predict the amount of solvent that should be employed to prepare a given solution; rather, molar solutions (as well as others that are based on total volume) are generally prepared by the use of the volumetric flasks (Figure 9.3). In the preparation of a solution, the correct amount of solute is placed in the flask, and water is then added, with careful and constant mixing, until the solution fills the flask to the calibration mark on the neck.

Figure 9.3 Volumetric flask.

It is a simple matter to calculate the quantity of solute present in a given sample of a solution when the concentration of the solution is expressed in terms of molarity. Concentrations defined on the basis of the total volume of solution have this decided advantage. Thus 1 liter of a $3M$ solution contains 3 moles of solute, 500 ml contains 1.5 moles, 250 ml contains 0.75 mole, and 100 ml contains 0.3 mole. A disadvantage, however, of basing concentrations on volume of solution is that such concentrations change slightly with temperature changes because of expansion or contraction of liquid solutions. For exact work, therefore, a solution should be prepared at the temperature at which it is to be used, and a volumetric flask calibrated for this temperature should be employed.

▶ **EXAMPLE 9.1**   What weight of concentrated nitric acid that is 70.0% HNO_3 should be used to prepare 250 ml of $2.00M$ HNO_3 ? If the density of the concentrated nitric acid is 1.42 g/ml, what volume of concentrated nitric acid should be used?

Solution   The molecular weight of HNO_3 is 63.0, and therefore, $2(63.0) = 126.0$ g of HNO_3 should be contained in 1000 ml of $2.00M$ solution. In 100 g of concentrated nitric acid (70.0%), there would be 70.0 g HNO_3. Therefore

$$? \text{ g concd. } HNO_3 = 250 \text{ ml soln.} \left(\frac{126.0 \text{ g } HNO_3}{1000 \text{ ml soln.}}\right)\left(\frac{100.0 \text{ g concd. } HNO_3}{70.0 \text{ g } HNO_3}\right)$$

$$= 45.0 \text{ g concd. } HNO_3$$

To convert this value into ml of concentrated acid,

$$? \text{ ml concd. } HNO_3 = 45.0 \text{ g concd. } HNO_3 \left(\frac{1.00 \text{ ml concd. } HNO_3}{1.42 \text{ g concd. } HNO_3}\right)$$

$$= 31.7 \text{ ml concd. } HNO_3$$

▶ **EXAMPLE 9.2** What is the molarity of a 20.0% H_2SO_4 solution if the density of the solution is 1.14 g/ml?

Solution

$$? \text{ moles } H_2SO_4 = 1000 \text{ ml soln.} \left(\frac{1.14 \text{ g soln.}}{1.00 \text{ ml soln.}}\right)\left(\frac{20.0 \text{ g } H_2SO_4}{100 \text{ g soln.}}\right)\left(\frac{1 \text{ mole } H_2SO_4}{98.08 \text{ g } H_2SO_4}\right)$$

$$= 2.32 \text{ moles } H_2SO_4$$

The solution is, therefore, 2.32M.

---

4. The **normality**, N, of a solution is the number of gram equivalent weights of solute per liter of solution. The equivalent weight of a substance depends upon the reaction that the substance undergoes. Hence, the normality of a solution depends upon the use that is to be made of the solution. If sulfuric acid is to be used in a neutralization reaction, the equivalent weight of H_2SO_4 is one-half the molecular weight, or we can say that 1 mole of H_2SO_4 is 2 equivalents (Section 8.7). Hence, a 1M solution of H_2SO_4 is 2N.

For solutions of $KMnO_4$ that are to be employed in oxidation-reduction reactions in which the equivalent weight of $KMnO_4$ is $\frac{1}{5}$ the molecular weight (Section 8.7), the normality of a given solution is five times the molarity since 1 mole of $KMnO_4$ is 5 equivalents. On the other hand, the normality of an NaOH solution, to be used in a neutralization reaction, is the same as its molarity since the equivalent weight of NaOH is the same as the molecular weight. The normality of a solution is always a simple whole number multiple (including 1) of the molarity of the solution.

Since the normality of a solution is based upon its total volume, the same volumetric technique is employed in the preparation of normal solutions as is used in the preparation of molar solutions. Similarly, the normality of a solution varies slightly with temperature.

▶ **EXAMPLE 9.3** What weight of $K_2Cr_2O_7$ should be used to prepare 500.0 ml of 0.1000N solution if the dichromate ion functions as an oxidizing agent?

$$6e^- + 14H^+ + Cr_2O_7^{2-} \longrightarrow 2Cr^{3+} + 7H_2O$$

What is the molarity of this solution?

Solution The molecular weight of $K_2Cr_2O_7$ is 294.19 and, according to the partial equation, the equivalent weight of $K_2Cr_2O_7$ is $\frac{1}{6}$ of the molecular weight, or 49.03. Thus

$$? \text{ g } K_2Cr_2O_7 = 500 \text{ ml soln.} \left(\frac{0.1(49.03) \text{ g } K_2Cr_2O_7}{1000 \text{ ml soln.}}\right)$$

$$= 2.452 \text{ g } K_2Cr_2O_7$$

Since 1 equivalent of $K_2Cr_2O_7$ is $\frac{1}{6}$ of a mole, this solution is $\frac{1}{6}(0.1)M$ or 0.01667M.

5. The **molality**, m, of a solution is the number of moles of solute per 1000 g of solvent. Thus a $1m$ aqueous solution of sulfuric acid can be prepared by adding 1 mole (98.08 g) of H_2SO_4 to 1000 g of water. The final volume of a molal solution is of no importance, and $1m$ aqueous solutions of different solutes, each containing 1000 g of water, will have different volumes. However, these solutions all will have the same mole fractions of solute and solvent (see Examples 9.4 and 9.5 following).

The molality of a given solution does not vary with temperature since such solutions are prepared on the basis of the masses of the components and mass does not change with temperature changes. The molality of a *very dilute* aqueous solution is approximately the same as the molarity of the solution since 1000 g of water occupies approximately 1000 ml.

▶ **EXAMPLE 9.4** What are the mole fractions of solute and solvent in a $1.0000m$ aqueous solution?

Solution The molecular weight of H_2O is 18.015. Hence,

$$? \text{ moles } H_2O = 1000 \text{ g } H_2O \left(\frac{1 \text{ mole } H_2O}{18.015 \text{ g } H_2O} \right) = 55.51 \text{ moles } H_2O$$

The total number of moles in a solution containing 1 mole of solute and 1000 g of H_2O is, therefore, $1 + 55.51 = 56.51$. Hence,

$$X_{H_2O} = \frac{55.51}{56.51} = 0.9823$$

$$X_{solute} = \frac{1.000}{56.51} = 0.0177$$

This last result could have been obtained by subtracting X_{H_2O} from 1.0000.

▶ **EXAMPLE 9.5** What are the mole fractions of solute and solvent in a $1.0000m$ solution employing CCl_4 as a solvent?

Solution The molecular weight of CCl_4 is 153.82.

$$? \text{ moles } CCl_4 = 1000 \text{ g } CCl_4 \left(\frac{1 \text{ mole } CCl_4}{153.82 \text{ g } CCl_4} \right) = 6.501 \text{ moles } CCl_4$$

The total number of moles in the solution is therefore $1 + 6.501 = 7.501$. Thus

$$X_{CCl_4} = \frac{6.501}{7.501} = 0.8667$$

$$X_{solute} = \frac{1.000}{7.501} = 0.1333$$

▶ **EXAMPLE 9.6** What is the molality of a $0.5000M$ aqueous solution of sucrose ($C_{12}H_{22}O_{11}$) if the density of the solution is 1.0638 g/ml?

Solution   The molecular weight of $C_{12}H_{22}O_{11}$ is 342.30. One liter of the solution weighs 1063.8 g and contains $342.30/2 = 171.15$ g $C_{12}H_{22}O_{11}$ and $(1063.8 - 171.2) = 892.6$ g H_2O.

$$? \text{ moles } C_{12}H_{22}O_{11} = 1000 \text{ g } H_2O \left(\frac{0.5 \text{ mole } C_{12}H_{22}O_{11}}{892.6 \text{ g } H_2O} \right)$$

$$= 0.5601 \text{ mole } C_{12}H_{22}O_{11}$$

The solution is, therefore, $0.5601m$.

9.7   Volumetric Analysis

The concentration of a given solution is constant from sample to sample no matter how much of the solution is taken, but the actual quantity of solute in a given sample is a different matter. Molar and normal concentrations state the amount of solute present in a liter of the solution. To determine the number of moles or the number of equivalents in a sample of a molar or normal solution, one must multiply the concentration of the solution by the volume, in liters, of the sample. Thus a $6M$ solution contains, by definition, 6 moles of solute in 1 liter of solution; 500 ml of this solution (0.5 liter) would contain 0.5(6) or 3 moles of solute; 100 ml of this solution (0.1 liter) would contain 0.1(6) or 0.6 mole of solute.

For a sample of a solution of volume V (*in liters*) and of molarity M or normality N:

$$V \times M = \text{number of moles of solute in sample}$$
$$V \times N = \text{number of equivalents of solute in sample}$$

Calculations for reactions that are run between substances in solution are simplified if the concentrations of the solutions are expressed in normalities. One equivalent weight of a substance will react with exactly 1 equivalent weight of another. Hence, n equivalents of 1 will react with exactly n equivalents of 2.

$$n_1 = n_2$$

But the number of equivalents of 1 in a sample of a solution of 1 is equal to the volume of the sample, in liters, times the normality of the solution.

$$n_1 = V_1 N_1 \quad \text{(volume in liters)}$$

Likewise,

$$n_2 = V_2 N_2 \quad \text{(volume in liters)}$$

We can therefore derive the relationship

$$V_1 N_1 = V_2 N_2$$

Since a volume term appears on both sides of the equality, any unit can be used to express V_1 and V_2 provided that both volumes are expressed in the same unit. This equation may be employed for calculations involving reactions between samples of two solutions.

Under some circumstances, another equation is useful. The number of equivalents in a sample is equal to the weight of the sample (g) divided by the equivalent weight (e) of the substance. Thus

$$n_2 = \frac{g_2}{e_2}$$

We can use this expression together with $n_1 = V_1 N_1$ to derive

$$V_1 N_1 = \frac{g_2}{e_2} \qquad \text{(volume in liters)}$$

If the volume is expressed in milliliters,

$$V_1 N_1 = \frac{1000\, g_2}{e_2} \qquad \text{(volume in milliliters)}$$

This expression is convenient for calculations for reactions between a weighed substance (2) and another (1) in solution. If sample 2 is impure, the actual weight of the reactive part of the sample is equal to the fractional purity (p_2) times the total weight of the sample (g_2); thus

$$V_1 N_1 = \frac{1000\, p_2 g_2}{e_2}$$

Solutions of known concentration are called **standard solutions**, and analytical procedures that make use of such solutions are called **volumetric analyses**. For example, a standard solution of an alkali may be used to determine the concentration of an acid solution in a process known as a **titration**. The standard solution of alkali is placed in a **buret** (Figure 9.4), which is a graduated tube fitted with a stopcock at the lower end to permit the solution to be withdrawn in controlled amounts. A carefully measured volume of the unknown acid solution is placed in a flask and a few drops of a colored substance known as an **indicator** are added. The standard alkali solution is gradually added to the flask from the buret until the indicator changes color; throughout the addition, the contents of the flask are kept well mixed by swirling. At the **end point**, shown by the color change of the indicator, we assume that all the acid has been neutralized, and equivalent amounts of acid and alkali have been used. The volume of the standard alkali used is read from the buret, and the concentration of the acid is calculated as illustrated in Example 9.7.

Figure 9.4 Buret.

▶ EXAMPLE 9.7 What is the normality of an acid solution if 50.00 ml of the solution requires 37.52 ml of 0.1429N alkali for neutralization?

Solution

$$V_1 N_1 = V_2 N_2$$
$$(50.00 \text{ ml})x = (37.52 \text{ ml})(0.1429N)$$
$$x = 0.1702N$$

▶ EXAMPLE 9.8 A 0.2676 g sample of a pure, solid acid dissolved in 100 ml of water requires 35.68 ml of 0.1190N alkali for neutralization. What is the equivalent weight of the acid? What is the molecular weight of the acid if it is diprotic?

Solution

$$V_1 N_1 = \frac{g_2}{e_2} \qquad \text{(volume in liters)}$$

$$(0.03568)(0.1190) = \frac{0.2676}{x}$$

$$x = 63.03$$

Since the acid is diprotic, the equivalent weight is $\frac{1}{2}$ the molecular weight, and the molecular weight must be 126.06.

▶ **EXAMPLE 9.9** A 0.4308 g sample of iron ore is dissolved in acid and the iron converted into the iron(II) state. This solution is titrated against permanganate; the titration employs 32.31 ml of $0.1248N$ $KMnO_4$ which oxidizes Fe^{2+} to Fe^{3+}. What is the percentage of iron in the ore?

Solution Since the oxidation number of iron increases by 1 unit, the equivalent weight of iron is the same as the atomic weight, 55.85.

$$V_1 N_1 = \frac{p_2 g_2}{e_2} \qquad \text{(volume in liters)}$$

$$(0.03231)(0.1248) = \frac{x(0.4308)}{55.85}$$

$$x = 0.5228$$

The ore is 52.28% iron.

9.8 Vapor Pressure of Solutions

The vapor pressure of any solution (P_{total}) is the sum of the partial pressure of the components (p_A, p_B, etc.). Thus for a binary solution,

$$P_{total} = p_A + p_B$$

For **ideal solutions**, the partial pressure of each component can be calculated from the mole fraction of the component present in the solution (X_A) and the vapor pressure of the pure component at the temperature in question ($p_A°$). Thus

$$p_A = X_A p_A° \qquad p_B = X_B p_B°$$
$$P_{total} = X_A p_A° + X_B p_B°$$

In other words, ideal solutions have properties that are the weighted averages of the properties of the components. This relationship was discovered by François Raoult in 1886 and is called **Raoult's law.**

Figure 9.5 illustrates partial pressure curves for components A and B of ideal binary solutions as well as the total pressure curve which is, of course, the sum of the two partial pressure curves. A and B represent liquids that are miscible in all proportions. In the figure, pressures are plotted versus mole fraction of A; since the mole fractions of A and B must add up to 1.0, the mole fraction of B is easily derived from the scale of the x axis.

Not all solutions are ideal. The vapor pressures of some solutions show negative deviations from Raoult's law (Figure 9.6); other nonideal solutions

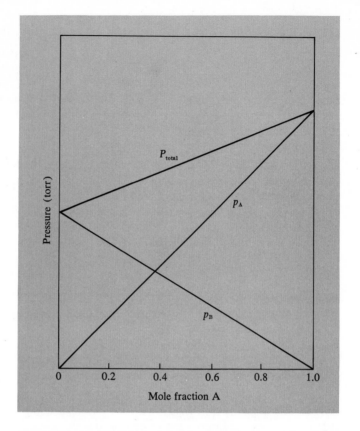

Figure 9.5 Typical total and partial vapor pressure curves for solutions that follow Raoult's law.

show positive deviations (Figure 9.7). The white lines of Figures 9.6 and 9.7 are the partial pressure and total pressure curves calculated by means of Raoult's law.

In ideal solutions, the intermolecular attractions between the components (A–B attractions) are of the same magnitude as the intermolecular attractions found in the pure components (A–A attractions and B–B attractions). Consequently, no heat effect is observed when an ideal solution is prepared. Negative deviations are observed when the intermolecular attractions of the solution (A–B) are stronger than those of either of the pure components (A–A and B–B); hence, the escaping tendencies of the components are reduced when they are mixed. Such solutions generally have exothermic heats of solution. Positive deviations result when the pure components have stronger intermolecular attractions (A–A and B–B) than the mixture (A–B); heat is absorbed when such solutions are prepared.

Even though a pair of components does not form ideal solutions over the entire range of concentrations, the behavior of the *solvent* of most *dilute* solu-

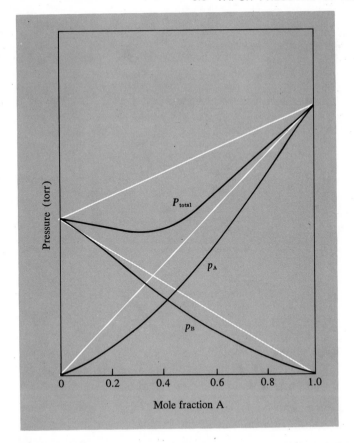

Figure 9.6 Typical total and partial vapor pressure curves for solutions that show negative deviations from Raoult's law. (White lines are based on Raoult's law.)

tions approaches ideality. In Figures 9.6 and 9.7, the extreme right portion of the p_A curve (where X_A approaches 1.0) and the extreme left portion of the p_B curve (where X_B approaches 1.0) are close to the curves calculated by means of Raoult's law.

Hence, dilute solutions of *nonvolatile* molecular solutes generally follow Raoult's law. When the solute has a very low vapor pressure, the vapor pressure of the solution is almost entirely due to the solvent. If component A is the solvent and B is the solute, then

$$P_{total} = X_A p_A{}^\circ$$

or

$$P_{total} = (1 - X_B)p_A{}^\circ$$

Therefore, the vapor pressure of a solution prepared from 1 mole of a nonvolatile nonionizing solute and 99 moles of solvent would be 99% of the vapor pressure of the pure solvent at the same temperature. The escape of solvent molecules to the vapor phase would be reduced because only 99%

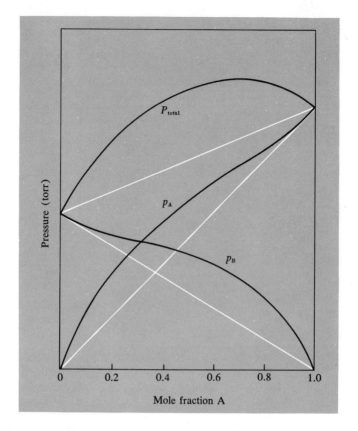

Figure 9.7 Typical total and partial vapor pressure curves for solutions that show positive deviations from Raoult's law. (White lines are based on Raoult's law.)

of the surface molecules in the solution are solvent molecules; 1% of the surface molecules are, by definition, nonvolatile.

Raoult's law is only strictly applicable to this type of solution when the solution is dilute and solvent–solute interactions are unimportant. Under this condition, the particular nonvolatile solute does not matter. It is the number of dissolved solute particles per given quantity of solvent that determines the vapor pressure lowering—not their size, shape, or weight. The properties of solutions containing nonvolatile solutes that are in ionic form are considered in Section 9.11.

▶ EXAMPLE 9.10 If heptane and octane form ideal solutions, what is the vapor pressure at 40°C of a solution containing 1.0 mole of heptane and 4.0 moles of octane? At 40°C, the vapor pressure of heptane is 92 torr, and the vapor pressure of octane is 31 torr.

Solution

$$X_{\text{heptane}} = \tfrac{1}{5} \quad \text{and} \quad X_{\text{octane}} = \tfrac{4}{5}$$

Hence

$$P_{\text{total}} = \tfrac{1}{5}(92 \text{ torr}) + \tfrac{4}{5}(31 \text{ torr}) = 43 \text{ torr}$$

▶ **EXAMPLE 9.11** Assuming ideality, calculate the vapor pressure of a 1.00m solution of a nonvolatile molecular solute in water at 50°C. The vapor pressure of water at 50°C is 92.5 torr.

Solution From Example 9.4, the mole fraction of water in a 1.00m solution is 0.982. Hence, the vapor pressure of a 1.00m solution at 50°C is

$$0.982(92.5 \text{ torr}) = 90.8 \text{ torr}$$

▶ **EXAMPLE 9.12** Assuming ideality, calculate the vapor pressure of a 1.00m solution of a nonvolatile molecular solute in carbon tetrachloride at 50°C. The vapor pressure of carbon tetrachloride at 50°C is 317 torr.

Solution From Example 9.5, the mole fraction of carbon tetrachloride in a 1.00m solution is 0.867. Hence, the vapor pressure of a 1.00m solution at 50°C is

$$0.867 (317 \text{ torr}) = 275 \text{ torr}$$

▶ **EXAMPLE 9.13** A solution is prepared from 2.00 g of a nonvolatile solute and 90.10 g of water. The vapor pressure of the solution, at 60°C, is 147.4 torr. According to Raoult's law, what is the approximate molecular weight of the solute? The vapor pressure of pure water at 60°C is 148.9 torr.

Solution

$$P_{\text{total}} = X_A p_A^{\circ}$$
$$147.4 \text{ torr} = X_A (148.9 \text{ torr})$$
$$X_A = 0.990$$

The amount of water employed in the preparation of the solution (90.10 g) is 5.000 moles. Hence, the mole fraction of water in the solution is given by

$$X_A = \frac{n_A}{n_A + n_B}$$

$$0.990 = \frac{5.000}{5.000 + n_B}$$

$$n_B = 0.0505 \text{ mole}$$

Thus the 2.00 g of solute used in the solution represents 0.0505 mole.

$$? \text{g} = 1.00 \text{ mole} \frac{2.00 \text{ g}}{0.0505 \text{ mole}} = 39.6 \text{ g}$$

9.9   Boiling Point and Freezing Point of Solutions

The effect of a dissolved nonvolatile solute on the vapor pressure of a liquid is difficult to measure, but the consequences of this vapor pressure depression —elevation of the boiling point and depression of the freezing point—are relatively easily determined with considerable accuracy.

The boiling point of a liquid is defined as the temperature at which the vapor pressure of the liquid is equal to the prevailing atmospheric pressure; boiling points measured under 760 torr pressure are termed normal boiling points (Section 7.4.) Since the addition of a nonvolatile solute decreases the vapor pressure of a liquid, a solution will not boil at the normal boiling point of the solvent. It is necessary to increase the temperature above this point in order to attain a vapor pressure over the solution of 760 torr. Hence, the boiling point of a solution containing a nonvolatile molecular solute is higher than that of the pure solvent, and the elevation is proportional to the concentration of solute in the solution.

This effect is illustrated by the vapor pressure curves plotted in Figure 9.8. The extent to which the vapor pressure curve of the solution lies below the vapor pressure curve of the solvent is proportional to the mole fraction of solute in the solution. The elevation of the boiling point, ΔT_b, follows from

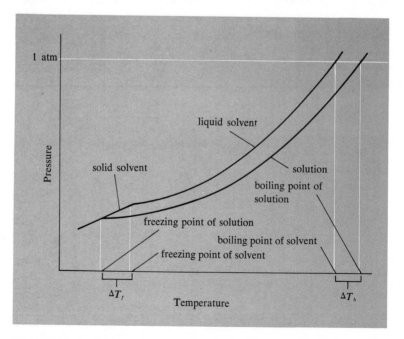

Figure 9.8 Vapor pressure curves of a pure solvent and a solution of a nonvolatile solute (not drawn to scale).

this displacement of the vapor pressure curve; for a given solvent, it is a constant for all solutions of the same concentration.

Concentrations are customarily expressed in molalities, rather than mole fractions, for problems involving boiling-point elevations. For example, the boiling point of a $1m$ aqueous solution is $0.512°C$ higher than the boiling point of water. Table 9.2 lists molal boiling-point elevation constants for

Table 9.2

Molal Boiling-point Elevation and Freezing-point Depression Constants

Solvent	Boiling Point (°C)	K_b (°/m)	Freezing Point (°C)	K_f (°/m)
acetic acid	118.1	3.07	16.6	3.90
benzene	80.1	2.53	5.5	5.12
camphor	—	—	179.	39.7
carbon tetrachloride	76.8	5.02	−22.8	29.8
chloroform	61.2	3.63	−63.5	4.68
ethyl alcohol	78.4	1.22	−114.6	1.99
naphthalene	—	—	80.2	6.80
water	100.0	0.512	0.0	1.86

several solvents. The boiling point of a $0.5m$ solution would be expected to be elevated by an amount equal to $\frac{1}{2}$ the molal constant. Thus the boiling-point elevation, ΔT_b, of a solution can be calculated by multiplying the molal boiling-point elevation constant of the solvent, K_b, by the molality of the solution, m.

$$\Delta T_b = mK_b$$

In reality, this relationship is only approximate; a more exact statement would require that the concentration be expressed in mole fraction of solute, not in molality. However, molalities of *dilute* solutions are proportional (at least with sufficient accuracy) to mole fractions of solute, and, since Raoult's law only describes the behavior of most real solutions satisfactorily if they are dilute, the use of molalities in these calculations is justified.

The mole fraction of solute in a solution, X_B, is

$$X_B = \frac{n_B}{n_A + n_B}$$

where n_B is the number of moles of solute, and n_A is the number of moles of solvent. If the solution is dilute, the number of moles of solute is negligible in comparison with the number of moles of solvent, and the denominator may be simplified by dropping the term n_B.

$$X_B \approx \frac{n_B}{n_A}$$

The molality of the solution, m, is the number of moles of solute per 1000 g of solvent. If the molecular weight of the solvent is M_A, $n_A = 1000/M_A$, and thus

$$X_B \approx \frac{m}{1000/M_A} \approx \frac{M_A}{1000} m$$

Hence, there is a direct relation between molality and mole fraction of solute for dilute solutions.

At the freezing point, the vapor pressure of solid and liquid are equal (Section 7.7). In Figure 9.8, the vapor pressure curves of the liquid solvent and the solid solvent intersect at the freezing point of the solvent. At this temperature, however, the vapor pressure of the solution is lower than the equilibrium vapor pressure of the pure solvent. The vapor pressure curve of the solution intersects the vapor pressure curve of the solid solvent at a lower temperature, and hence the freezing point of the solution is lower than that of the pure solvent. As in the case of boiling-point elevations, freezing-point depressions depend upon the concentration of the solution and the solvent employed. Molal freezing-point depression constants for some solvents are listed in Table 9.2, and the freezing-point depression, ΔT_f, of a solution can be calculated from the molality of the solution and the constant for the solvent K_f.

$$\Delta T_f = mK_f$$

This statement assumes that the solute does not form a solid solution with the solvent; if this is not the case, the relationship is not valid.

The following problems illustrate the use of these relations—for boiling-point elevation and freezing-point depression—in calculations of the boiling points and freezing points of solutions and, more importantly, the molecular weights of solutes.

▶ **EXAMPLE 9.14** What is the boiling point and freezing point of a solution prepared by dissolving 2.40 g of biphenyl ($C_{12}H_{10}$) in 75.0 g of benzene? The molecular weight of biphenyl is 154.

Solution   The molality of the solution is

$$? \text{ moles } C_{12}H_{10} = 1000 \text{ g benzene} \left(\frac{2.40 \text{ g } C_{12}H_{10}}{75.0 \text{ g benzene}} \right) \left(\frac{1 \text{ mole } C_{12}H_{10}}{154 \text{ g } C_{12}H_{10}} \right)$$

$$= 0.208 \text{ mole } C_{12}H_{10}$$

The boiling-point elevation is

$$? °C = 0.208m\ C_{12}H_{10}\left(\frac{2.53°C}{1m\ C_{12}H_{10}}\right) = 0.526°C$$

The boiling point of the solution is

$$80.1°C + 0.5°C = 80.6°C$$

The freezing-point depression is

$$? °C = 0.208m\ C_{12}H_{10}\left(\frac{5.12°C}{1m\ C_{12}H_{10}}\right) = 1.06°C$$

The freezing point of the solution is

$$5.5°C - 1.1°C = 4.4°C$$

▶ **EXAMPLE 9.15** A solution prepared from 0.300 g of an unknown nonvolatile solute in 30.0 g carbon tetrachloride has a boiling point 0.392°C higher than that of pure CCl_4. What is the molecular weight of the solute?

Solution K_b for CCl_4 is 5.02°C, and the molality of the solution is therefore

$$?m = 0.392°C\left(\frac{1m}{5.02°C}\right) = 0.0718m$$

Thus 1000 g of CCl_4 would contain 0.0781 moles of solute. The molecular weight of the solute, is, therefore,

$$? g = 1\ \text{mole solute}\left(\frac{1000\ \text{g } CCl_4}{0.0781\ \text{mole solute}}\right)\left(\frac{0.300\ \text{g solute}}{30.0\ \text{g } CCl_4}\right)$$

$$= 128\ \text{g}$$

9.10 Distillation

A solution of a nonvolatile solute can be separated into its components by **simple distillation**. Such a procedure consists of boiling away the volatile solvent from the solute. The solvent is obtained by condensing the vapor, and the solute is the residue remaining after the distillation.

A solution of two volatile components that follows Raoult's law (Figure 9.5) can be separated into its components by a process known as **fractional distillation**. According to Raoult's law, each component contributes to the vapor pressure of the solution in proportion to its mole fraction times its vapor pressure in the pure state. Let us assume that, at the temperature of the experiment, component A has a vapor pressure of 200 torr and component B has a vapor pressure of 400 torr. For a solution with a mole fraction of B equal to 0.60, the total vapor pressure is

$$P_{total} = X_A p_A^\circ + X_B p_B^\circ$$
$$= 0.40(200 \text{ torr}) + 0.60(400 \text{ torr})$$
$$= 80 \text{ torr} + 240 \text{ torr}$$
$$= 320 \text{ torr}$$

The composition of the *vapor* in equilibrium with this solution can be calculated by comparing the partial pressure of each component with the total vapor pressure of the solution (Section 6.10). Thus in the vapor,

$$X_{A, \text{ vapor}} = \frac{80 \text{ torr}}{320 \text{ torr}} = 0.25 \qquad X_{B, \text{ vapor}} = \frac{240 \text{ torr}}{320 \text{ torr}} = 0.75$$

Hence, a solution of concentration $X_B = 0.60$ would be in equilibrium with a vapor of concentration $X_{B, \text{ vapor}} = 0.75$. For ideal solutions, the vapor is always richer than the liquid in the more volatile component (which in this instance is B—it has the higher vapor pressure).

In a distillation of a solution of A and B, the vapor coming off, and being condensed, is richer in B than the liquid remaining behind. The actual compositions of vapor and liquid change as the distillation proceeds, but at any given time this generalization is true. By collecting the condensed vapor in several fractions and subjecting these fractions to repeated distillations, eventually the components of the original mixture can be obtained in substantially pure form.

For systems that deviate from Raoult's law, the situation is somewhat different. If the deviation is positive (Figure 9.7), there is a maximum in the total vapor pressure curve corresponding to a solution, of definite composition, that has a vapor pressure higher than either of the pure components. This means that such a solution, a **minimum boiling azeotrope**, will boil at a lower temperature than either of the two pure components. Ethyl alcohol and water form a minimum boiling azeotrope that contains 4.0 weight percent water and has a normal boiling point of 78.17°C (ethyl alcohol and water boil at 78.3°C and 100°C, respectively).

If a system shows a negative deviation from Raoult's law (Figure 9.6), there will be a minimum in the P_{total} curve. The solution that has a concentration corresponding to this minimum will have a vapor pressure, at any given temperature, lower than either pure component. Thus this solution boils at a temperature *higher* than either pure component and is called a **maximum boiling azeotrope**. Hydrochloric acid and water form such an azeotrope containing 20.22 weight percent HCl and boiling at 108.6°C (pure HCl has a boiling point of −80°C).

The vapor in equilibrium with a maximum or minimum boiling azeotrope is of the same concentration as the liquid; hence, azeotropes, like pure substances, distill without change. Fractional distillation of a solution containing components that form an azeotrope will eventually produce one pure component and the azeotrope but not both pure components.

9.11 Solutions of Electrolytes

Solutes may be classified according to the ability of their aqueous solutions to conduct electricity (Section 10.2). The electrical conductivity of a solution depends upon the presence of ions; pure water, itself, is very slightly ionized and is a poor conductor (Section 16.2). An **electrolyte** is a solute of a solution that is a better electrical conductor than the parent solvent alone; in solution, such a solute exists (in whole or in part) as ions. Covalent solutes that are exclusively molecular in solution, and hence do nothing to enhance the conductivity of the solvent, are called **nonelectrolytes**.

Electrolytes may be further divided into two groups: **strong electrolytes** and **weak electrolytes**. The conductivity of a $1m$ solution of a weak electrolyte is much inferior to the conductivity of a $1m$ solution of a strong electrolyte. Weak electrolytes are polar covalent materials that are incompletely dissociated into ions in solution; strong electrolytes are essentially completely ionic in solution.

In 1887, Svanté Arrhenius proposed his "chemical theory of electrolytes." In addition to data from electrical conductivity experiments, a principal source of evidence advanced by Arrhenius in support of his theory was derived from studies of the deviations from Raoult's law exhibited by solutions of electrolytes. The freezing points of *very dilute* solutions of electrolytes are lowered more than those of ideal solutions of nonelectrolytes with corresponding concentrations. The freezing-point depression for a dilute solution of a salt such as NaCl or $AgNO_3$ is approximately twice that of a solution of a nonelectrolyte with a similar molal concentration; the depression for a dilute solution of a salt such as K_2SO_4 or $BaCl_2$ is approximately three times as great as "expected" (see Table 9.3).

Table 9.3

Observed Freezing-point Depressions for Some Aqueous Solutions Compared to Calculated Depressions[a]

| Solute | Concentration of Solution | | |
	0.001 m	0.01 m	0.1 m
nonelectrolyte	0.00186°C	0.0186°C	0.186°C
sucrose	0.00186	0.0186	0.188
2 ions/formula	0.00372	0.0372	0.372
NaCl	0.00366	0.0360	0.348
3 ions/formula	0.00558	0.0558	0.558
K_2SO_4	0.00528	0.0501	0.432
4 ions/formula	0.00744	0.0744	0.744
$K_3[Fe(CN)_6]$	0.00710	0.0626	0.530

[a] Calculated on the assumptions that K_f for water is 1.86° C/molal over the entire range of concentrations, the salts are 100% ionic in solution, and the ions act independently of one another in their effect on the freezing point of the solution.

Arrhenius explained these results on the basis of the supposition that electrolytes are dissociated into ions in solution, NaCl and $AgNO_3$ forming two ions (Na^+, Cl^- and Ag^+, NO_3^-) per "molecule," whereas K_2SO_4 and $BaCl_2$ form three ions ($2K^+$, SO_4^{2+} and Ba^{2+}, $2Cl^-$) per "molecule." Today we know that these salts are ionic even when pure; "molecules" of these materials do not exist. Substances of this type are, therefore, completely ionic in solution and are strong electrolytes. Similar deviations are observed for boiling-point elevations.

Theoretically, the net effect on the freezing-point or boiling-point depends only on the number of nonvolatile particles in solution and not on their nature. The question, then, is not why the deviations for these salt solutions are larger than those expected for solutions of nondissociating solutes; it is, rather, why the deviations are not *exactly* twice the "expected" in the case of solutions of salts containing two ions per formula unit or three times the "expected" in the case of solutions of salts containing three ions per formula unit. This will be the topic of Section 9.12.

The hydroxides of the group I A metals are ionic crystalline materials, are water soluble, and are strong electrolytes; $Ba(OH)_2$, $Sr(OH)_2$, and $Ca(OH)_2$ are only moderately soluble in water,[2] but they too are strong electrolytes.

We have previously noted that certain covalent substances are ionized in water solution—a process more in harmony with Arrhenius' original views. Perchloric acid is completely ionic in water solution; it is virtually impossible to detect undissociated $HClO_4$ molecules.

$$H_2O + HClO_4 \longrightarrow H_3O^+ + ClO_4^-$$

Other acids, though covalent when pure, are strong electrolytes in aqueous solution; the common ones that may be considered ionic in solutions of $1M$ concentration or less are $HClO_4$, HCl, HBr, HI, HNO_3, and H_2SO_4.[3]

Some covalent materials may be ionized to a lesser extent in water and are classed as weak electrolytes—for example, acetic acid, $HC_2H_3O_2$:

$$H_2O + HC_2H_3O_2 \rightleftharpoons H_3O^+ + C_2H_3O_2^-$$

A $0.01m$ solution of acetic acid is approximately 4% ionic at room temperature; at any given time, 96% of the acetic acid present in the solution is in molecular form. This process is reversible and therefore a double arrow is shown in the preceding equation. In the solution, molecules are constantly dissociating into ions at the same rate that ions, upon interionic contact, are re-forming molecules. Thus this reversible system is in a state of chemical

---

[2] There is some evidence that in nearly saturated solutions of these compounds dissociation may be incomplete. Thus fairly large concentrations of the ion $CaOH^+$, as well as Ca^{2+} and OH^-, have been identified in such solutions, presumably from the dissociations: $Ca(OH)_2 \rightarrow CaOH^+ + OH^-$ and $CaOH^+ \rightleftharpoons Ca^{2+} + OH^-$.

[3] The first ionization only: $H_2O + H_2SO_4 \rightarrow H_3O^+ + HSO_4^-$.

equilibrium; such equilibria are the topic of Chapter 16. Most acids are weak electrolytes.

Certain covalent compounds, of which ammonia is the most common example, react with water to produce hydroxide ions.

$$NH_3 + H_2O \rightleftharpoons NH_4^+ + OH^-$$

Thus it is possible to have alkaline solutions of weak electrolytes.

Most salts are ionic compounds; such substances, if soluble, are strong electrolytes in aqueous solution. A number of covalent compounds containing metals and nonmetals (e.g., aluminum chloride, Section 9.2) are ionized virtually completely in water solution and are classed as strong electrolytes. A small number of covalent compounds of metals, however, dissolve in water but are not ionized completely; as such, they are weak electrolytes. Thus mercuric chloride solutions contain $HgCl_2$ molecules in addition to $HgCl^+$, Cl^-, and low concentrations of Hg^{2+}, as well as other more complicated species.

9.12   Interionic Attractions in Solution

The **van't Hoff factor**, i, may be defined as the ratio of the observed freezing-point depression for a solution (ΔT_f) to the depression calculated from the molality of the solution and the molal freezing-point constant for the solvent (mK_f).

$$i = \frac{\Delta T_f}{mK_f}$$

Since a similar relation is used for boiling-point elevations,

$$i = \frac{\Delta T_b}{mK_b}$$

we shall use unspecified ΔT and K in the discussion that follows.

If we rearrange the expression

$$\Delta T = imK$$

the significance of the i factor, which was named for Jacobus van't Hoff who first employed it, becomes clear. The expressions of Section 9.9, $\Delta T = mK$, were derived on the assumption that the solute *does not dissociate* ($i = 1$).

When dissociation of the solute occurs, it is necessary to correct the molality of the solution for freezing-point and boiling-point calculations. Thus if AB is a strong electrolyte and therefore dissociates completely in solution, in a $0.001m$ solution of AB there would be 0.001 mole of A^+ and 0.001 mole of B^- contained in 1000 g of water. On the assumption that each ion acts independently in its effect on the boiling point and freezing point, the effective concentration of this hypothetical solution would be 0.002m. Hence, in this simplified example, $i = 2$, $m = 0.001$, and

$$\Delta T = 2(0.001\ m)K$$

Inspection of the i values recorded in Table 9.4 (which were derived from

Table 9.4

van't Hoff Factor, i, for Various Strong Electrolytes in Solution[a]

	Concentration of Solution		
Electrolyte	0.001m	0.01m	0.1m
NaCl	1.97	1.94	1.87
$MgSO_4$	1.82	1.53	1.21
K_2SO_4	2.84	2.69	1.32
$K_3[Fe(CN)_6]$	3.82	3.36	2.85

[a] From freezing-point determinations.

freezing-point determinations) reveals that they do not exactly equal the number of ions per formula unit for each of the strong electrolytes listed. Thus for 0.001m solutions, the i value of NaCl is 1.97 (not 2), of K_2SO_4 it is 2.84 (not 3), and of $K_3[Fe(CN)_6]$ it is 3.82 (not 4). Furthermore, the i value changes with concentration of the solution approaching the value expected for complete dissociation as the solution becomes more and more dilute.

In 1923, Peter Debye and Erich Hückel proposed a quantitative theory to explain the behavior of dilute solutions of electrolytes.[4] According to the **Debye-Hückel theory**, there are interionic attractions in solutions of electrolytes so that the ions are not completely independent of one another as is the case for uncharged molecules in solution. (As has been noted in Section 9.8, solute–solute interactions cause deviations from Raoult's law.) Thus the electrical forces that operate between the oppositely charged ions reduce the effectiveness of these ions.

The i values in Table 9.4 show that the interionic attractions in solutions of $MgSO_4$ produce a stronger effect than those in solutions of NaCl of corresponding concentration even though both solutes contain 2 moles of ions per mole of compound; thus for 0.001m NaCl, $i = 1.97$, whereas for 0.001m

[4] It should be noted that the Debye-Hückel theory accounts only for the behavior of dilute solutions of electrolytes. Concentrated solutions are imperfectly understood at present. Among the factors that have been postulated to explain the anomolous behavior of concentrated solutions are the lack of sufficient water to hydrate the ions and the presence of ion pairs and ion triplets (ions closely associated with one another).

$MgSO_4$, $i = 1.82$. Both the ions of magnesium sulfate are doubly charged (Mg^{2+}, SO_4^{2-}), whereas the ions of sodium chloride are but singly charged (Na^+, Cl^-), and hence the interionic attractions are stronger in solutions of magnesium sulfate.

The effect of dilution upon i values can also be explained on the basis of these interionic attractions. As a solution is diluted, the ions spread farther and farther apart, their influence upon one another diminishes accordingly, and the i factor approaches its limiting value. Hence, in *very* dilute solutions, the Debye-Hückel effect is negligible, and the ions essentially behave independently.

Interionic attractions, therefore, make a solution behave as though its ion concentrations were less than they actually are. The **activity** of an ion, a, is defined as the "effective concentration" of that ion; it is related to the actual concentration of the ion, c, by an **activity coefficient**, γ.

$$a = \gamma c$$

The activity coefficient is always less than 1 and approaches unity as the concentration of the solution decreases. The calculation of activity coefficients from experimental data is complicated. It is important to recognize that the activity of a given ion depends upon the concentrations of all ions present in the solution whether they are all derived from the same compound or not, since all ions can enter into interionic attractions.

Some characteristics of solutes are summarized in Table 9.5.

Table 9.5

Characteristics of Solutes

Solute	Form of Solute in 1 m Solution	van't Hoff Factor for ΔT_f; Dilute Solutions of Molality, m $\Delta f_f = iK_f m$	Examples
nonelectrolytes	molecules	$i = 1$	$C_{12}H_{22}O_{11}$ (sucrose) CON_2H_4 (urea) $C_3H_5(OH)_3$ (glycerol)
strong electrolytes	ions	$i \approx n^a$	NaCl KOH
weak electrolytes	molecules and ions	$1 < i < n^a$	$HC_2H_3O_2$ NH_3 $HgCl_2$

^{a} n = number of moles of ions per mole of solute.

SOME SUGGESTED READINGS

Dreisbach, D., *Liquids and Solutions*, Boston, Houghton Mifflin, 1966 (paper).

Hildebrand, J. H., and Scott, R. L., *Regular Solutions*, Englewood Cliffs, N. J., Prentice-Hall, 1962.

Hildebrand, J. H., and Scott, R. L., *The Solubility of Nonelectrolytes*, New York, Dover, 1964 (paper).

Hunt, J. P., *Metal Ions in Aqueous Solution*, New York, Benjamin, 1963 (paper).

PROBLEMS

The more difficult problems are starred.

9.1 Define the following terms: maximum-boiling azeotrope, Debye-Hückle effect, volumetric analysis, heat of hydration, activity of ions, fractional distillation.

9.2 Describe three ways in which water occurs in crystalline hydrates.

9.3 Describe an experiment that can be run at a single temperature to determine whether the solubility of a given salt increases or decreases with an increase in temperature.

9.4 For the preparation of very dilute aqueous solutions at 298°K, the heats of solutions of KCl, AgF, and CaI_2 are $+4.1$ kcal/mole, -4.9 kcal/mole, and -28.7 kcal/mole, respectively. The entropy changes (ΔS) for the respective solution processes are $+18$ cal/°K mole, -4.7 cal/°K mole, and $+5.1$ cal/°K mole. Calculate the change in Gibbs free energy for the preparation of each solution and discuss the results.

*9.5 (a) The molecules in pure ethanol, CH_3CH_2OH, are extensively associated through hydrogen bonding; however, those in pure acetone,

$$CH_3-\overset{\overset{\displaystyle O}{\|}}{C}-CH_3,$$

and in pure chloroform, $CHCl_3$, are not. Explain why this is so. (b) On the basis of your answer to part (a), explain why the vapor pressures of chloroform and acetone solutions exhibit negative deviations from Raoult's law, whereas the vapor pressures of chloroform and ethanol solutions exhibit positive deviations.

9.6 For aqueous solutions of dinitrogen oxide gas, N_2O, at 20°C, the value of K in Henry's law equation, $p = KX$, is 1.55×10^6 torr. In the equation, p is the partial pressure of the gas over the saturated solution and X is the mole fraction of the dissolved gas in the solution. How many grams of N_2O dissolve in 100 g of water at 20°C if the pressure of N_2O over the solution is 760 torr?

*9.7 (a) Air is approximately 80.0% N_2 and 20.0% O_2 by volume. What are the partial pressures of N_2 and O_2 in air when the total pressure is 760 torr? (b) Henry's law may be stated as $p = KX$, where p is the partial pressure of the gas over a saturated solution, X is the mole fraction of the dissolved gas, and K is a constant. At 0°C, the values of K for N_2 and O_2 are 4.09×10^7 torr and 1.91×10^7 torr, respectively. What are the mole fractions of N_2 and O_2 in a saturated aqueous solution at 0°C under air at a pressure of 760 torr? (c) What is the freezing point of the solution?

9.8 The volume of an aqueous solution changes as the temperature changes. Thus, a concentration of a given solution determined at one temperature may not be correct for that same solution at another temperature. Which methods of expressing concentration yield results that are temperature-independent, and which yield results that are temperature-dependent?

*9.9 A given aqueous solution has a density of x g/ml and is y % solute by weight. Derive a mathematical equation relating the molarity of the solution, M, to the molality of the solution m.

9.10 (a) What is the molarity of a 0.050N solution of $Ba(OH)_2$ (calculated on the basis of complete neutralization of the alkali)? (b) What is the normality of 0.050M H_3PO_4 based on neutralization of the acid to the HPO_4^{2-} ion? (c) A potassium dichromate solution for use in a reaction in which $Cr_2O_7^{2-}$ is transformed into Cr^{3+} is labeled 0.100N. What is the molarity of the solution? (d) What is the normality of a 0.0500M $KBrO_3$ solution with regard to a reaction in which the $KBrO_3$ is transformed into KBr?

9.11 What volume of concentrated HNO_3 should be used to prepare 750 ml of 0.500M HNO_3? The concentrated acid is 70.0% HNO_3 and has a density of 1.42 g/ml.

9.12 What volume of concentrated H_3PO_4 should be used to prepare 100 ml of 2.00M H_3PO_4? The concentrated acid is 85.0% H_3PO_4 and has a density of 1.70 g/ml.

9.13 What weight of solid NaOH should be used to prepare 500 ml of 0.100M NaOH if the solid NaOH is 95.0% pure?

9.14 (a) What is the molarity of concentrated hydrobromic acid if the solution is 48.0% HBr and has a density of 1.50 g/ml? (b) What is the molality of this solution?

9.15 A 100 ml sample of concentrated acetic acid, $HC_2H_3O_2$, is diluted until the final volume is 500 ml. The density of the concentrated acid is 1.05 g/ml, and the acid is 98.0% pure $HC_2H_3O_2$. What is the molarity of the final solution?

*9.16 A quantity of Na added to water produces 609 ml of $H_2(g)$, collected at 20°C and 750 torr, and 400 ml of a solution of NaOH. What is the molarity of the NaOH solution?

9.17 How many ml of 0.300N H_2SO_4 would be required to neutralize 150 ml of 0.250N NaOH?

9.18 A 25.0 ml sample of a solution of an acid requires 36.2 ml of 0.132N NaOH for neutralization. What is the normality of the acid?

9.19 A 0.300 g sample of a pure solid acid requires 27.3 ml of 0.150N NaOH for neutralization. What is the equivalent weight of the acid?

9.20 A 25.0 ml sample of vinegar requires 35.0 ml of 0.500N NaOH for neutralization. The density of the vinegar is 1.00 g/ml. What is the concentration of acetic acid, $HC_2H_3O_2$, in the vinegar in terms of (a) normality, and (b) weight percent?

9.21 Potassium acid phthalate, $KHC_8H_4O_4$, functions as a monoprotic acid. If a 1.46 g sample of impure $KHC_8H_4O_4$ requires 34.3 ml of 0.145N NaOH for neutralization, what is the percentage of $KHC_8H_4O_4$ in the material?

9.22 Sodium carbonate reacts with acids:

$$Na_2CO_3 + 2HCl \longrightarrow 2NaCl + H_2O + CO_2(g)$$

(a) What is the equivalent weight of Na_2CO_3 for this reaction? (b) If a 0.338 g sample of impure Na_2CO_3 reacts with exactly 41.2 ml of 0.0960N HCl, what is the weight percentage of Na_2CO_3 in the material?

9.23 What weight sample of *pure* Na_2CO_3 (see Problem 9.22) should be taken so that a titration against 0.100N HCl will require 40.0 ml of HCl solution?

9.24 A 0.523 g sample of impure barium peroxide was dissolved in acid.

$$BaO_2 + 2H^+ \longrightarrow H_2O_2 + Ba^{2+}$$

The resulting solution was titrated against standard permanganate

$$6H^+ + 5H_2O_2 + 2MnO_4^- \longrightarrow 5O_2 + 2Mn^{2+} + 8H_2O$$

and required 34.5 ml of 0.120N $KMnO_4$. What percent of the material is BaO_2?

9.25 Potassium bromate, $KBrO_3$, reacts with hydrazine, N_2H_4, in acid solution.

$$2BrO_3^- + 3N_2H_4 \longrightarrow 2Br^- + 3N_2 + 6H_2O$$

If analyses are to be run on samples containing approximately 0.0300 g of hydrazine each, what concentration of $KBrO_3$ solution should be chosen so that each titration takes 35.0 ml?

*9.26 A sample of ammonia gas, NH_3, is absorbed in 100.00 ml of 0.150N HCl. The ammonia reacts with the hydrochloric acid to form ammonium chloride, NH_4Cl; however, the sample of NH_3 is insufficient to neutralize all the HCl. The solution is therefore titrated with 0.105N NaOH, and it is found that 63.2 ml of NaOH is required to neutralize the excess HCl. What was the weight of the original sample of NH_3 gas?

*9.27 A 50.0 ml sample of an OCl^- solution is added to 50.0 ml of a 0.0500M As_4O_6 solution. The OCl^- present reacts with part of the As_4O_6:

$$4OCl^- + As_4O_6 \longrightarrow 4Cl^- + 2As_2O_5$$

but some As_4O_6 remains unreacted. The excess As_4O_6 is reacted with I_2:

$$As_4O_6 + 4I_2 + 4H_2O \longrightarrow 2As_2O_5 + 8I^- + 8H^+$$

and 16.0 ml of 0.125M standard I_2 solution is required. (a) What are the normalities of the As_4O_6 and I_2 solutions? (b) What is the molarity and the normality of the OCl^- solution?

9.28 Benzene, C_6H_6, and n-octane, C_8H_{18}, form ideal solutions. At 60°C, the vapor pressure of pure benzene is 385 torr and the vapor pressure of n-octane is 78 torr. (a) What is the mole fraction of benzene in a solution that has a vapor pressure of 350 torr at 60°C? (b) What is the composition of the vapor (mole fraction of benzene) that is in equilibrium with the solution at 60°C?

9.29 (a) Use the data given in Problem 9.28 to calculate the vapor pressure at 60°C of a solution prepared from 9.75 g of benzene and 57.0 g of n-octane. (b) What is the composition of the vapor (mole fraction of benzene) in equilibrium with this solution at 60°C?

9.30 Liquids A and B form ideal solutions. The vapor pressure of pure B is 600 torr at the boiling point of a solution prepared from 1.00 mole of B and 4.00 moles of A. (a) What is the vapor pressure of pure A at this temperature? (b) What is the mole fraction of A in the vapor that is in equilibrium with the solution when the solution first begins to boil?

9.31 Liquids C and D form ideal solutions. The vapor pressure of pure D is 400 torr at the boiling point of a solution prepared from 1.00 mole of D and 4.00 moles of C. (a) What is the vapor pressure of pure C at this temperature? (b) What is the mole fraction of C in the vapor that is in equilibrium with the solution when the solution first begins to boil? (c) Compare your answers with the answers to question 9.30. What type of liquids are most readily separated by distillation?

9.32 A solution containing 7.36 g of ethanol, C_2H_5OH, and 4.78 g of chloroform, $CHCl_3$, has a vapor pressure of 190 torr at 35°C. At 35°C, the vapor pressure of pure ethanol is 104 torr and the vapor pressure of pure chloroform is 301 torr. (a) What would the vapor pressure of the solution be if ethanol and chloroform formed ideal solutions? (b) Does the vapor pressure of the solution show a positive or negative deviation from Raoult's law? (c) Is heat evolved or absorbed when this solution is prepared? (d) Do ethanol and chloroform form a maximum- or minimum-boiling azeotrope?

*9.33 A solution of 30.0 g of nonvolatile solute in exactly 1.00 mole of a volatile solvent has a vapor pressure of 300 torr at 20°C. A second mole of solvent is added to the mixture, and the resulting solution has a vapor pressure of 350 torr at 20°C. (a) What is the molecular weight of the solute? (b) What is the vapor pressure of the pure solvent at 20°C?

9.34 The boiling point of a solution prepared from 9.600 g of a nonvolatile, nondissociating solute in 400.0 g of chloroform, $CHCl_3$, is 0.605°C higher than the boiling point of pure chloroform. What is the molecular weight of the solute?

9.35 The boiling point of a water solution containing a nonvolatile solute is 100.2816°C. What is the freezing point of this solution?

9.36 A solution containing 5.23 g of a nonvolatile, nonelectrolyte in 168 g of water freezes at −0.510°C. What is the molecular weight of the solute?

9.37 (a) What is the boiling point of a solution prepared from 9.66 g of glycerol $C_3H_5(OH)_3$, and 300 g of CCl_4? (b) What is the freezing point of this solution?

9.38 What weight of sucrose, $C_{12}H_{22}O_{11}$, should be added to 250 g of water to produce a solution that freezes at $-2.50°C$?

9.39 A solution prepared by adding a given weight of a solute to 20.0 g of benzene freezes at a temperature $0.384°C$ below the freezing point of pure benzene. The freezing point of a solution prepared from the same weight of the solute and 20.00 g of water freezes at $-0.4185°C$. Assume that the solute is undissociated in benzene solution but is completely dissociated into ions in water solution. How many ions result from the dissociation of one molecule in water solution?

9.40 A solution containing 2.34 g $BaCl_2$ and 150 g of water freezes at $-0.356°C$. What is the van't Hoff factor, i, for the freezing point of this solution?

9.41 A solution is prepared from 38.0 g of H_2SO_4 and 100 g of water. If the van't Hoff factor, i, for this solution is 2.50, at what temperature will the solution freeze?

9.42 What is the freezing point of a $0.150m$ aqueous solution of a weak acid HX if the acid is 7.30% ionized? Ignore interionic attractions.

9.43 Ammonia ionizes in water:

$$NH_3 + H_2O \rightleftharpoons NH_4{}^+ + OH^-$$

A $0.0100m$ solution of NH_3 in water freezes at $-0.0193°C$. Ignore interionic attractions and calculate the percentage ionization of the ammonia.

10

ELECTRO-CHEMISTRY

The relations between chemical change and electrical energy are of theoretical and practical importance. Chemical reactions may be used to produce electrical energy (in **voltaic**, or **galvanic**, **cells**), or electrical energy may be used to bring about chemical transformations (in **electrolytic cells**). In addition, the study of electrochemical processes leads to an understanding, as well as the systemization, of oxidation-reduction phenomena that take place outside of cells. For example, data from electrochemical studies are useful in helping to determine the most favorable conditions for a given oxidation-reduction reaction, whether a proposed chemical transformation is possible, and the magnitude and nature of the energy effect that accompanies a given chemical change.

10.1 Metallic Conduction

An electric current is the flow of electric charge. In metals this charge is carried by electrons, and electrical conduction of this type is called

metallic (or **electronic**) **conduction**. The current moves as a result of the application of electric force supplied by a battery or some other source of electrical energy, and it is necessary to have a complete circuit in order to have current flow.

Metallic crystals have been described in terms of mobile electron clouds permeating relatively fixed lattices of positive metal ions (Section 4.6). When electrons are forced into one end of a metal wire, the impressed electrons displace other electrons of the cloud at the point of entry. The displaced electrons, in turn, assume new positions by pushing neighboring electrons ahead, and this effect is transmitted down the length of the wire until electrons are forced out of the wire at the opposite end. The current source may be regarded as an electron pump, for it serves to force electrons into one end of the circuit and drain them off from the other end. At any position in the wire, electrical neutrality is preserved, since the rate of electrons in equals the the rate of electrons out.

The analogy between the flow of electricity and the flow of a liquid is an old one; electricity was early described in terms of a current of "electric fluid." Conventions of long standing, which may be traced back to Benjamin Franklin (1747) and which were adopted before the electron was identified, ascribe a positive charge to this current. We shall interpret electrical circuits in terms of the movement of electrons. Remember, however, that conventional electric current is arbitrarily described as positive and as flowing in the opposite direction.

Quantity of electric charge is measured in **coulombs**; 1 coulomb is the charge carried by 6.2418×10^{18} electrons.[1] The rate of current flow is given by **amperes**; 1 amp is 1 coulomb/sec, and

$$I = Q/t \quad \text{or} \quad Q = It$$

where I is the current in amperes, Q is coulombs of charge transported, and t is time in seconds.

The current is forced through the circuit by an electrical potential difference which is measured in **volts**. It takes 1 joule of work[2] to move 1 coulomb from a lower to a higher potential when the potential difference is 1 v. One volt, therefore, equals 1 joule/coulomb, and 1 volt coulomb is a unit of energy and equals 1 joule.

The higher the potential difference between two points in a given wire, the more current the wire will carry between those two points. Georg Ohm

---

[1] One electrostatic unit of charge (esu) is the charge that will repel another like charge at a distance of 1 cm in a vacuum by a force of 1 dyne; 2.9979×10^9 esu = 1 coulomb.

[2] 1 joule = 10^7 erg = 2.3905×10^{-1} cal. One erg is the work done when a force of 1 dyne acts through a distance of 1 cm; 1 erg = 1 dyne cm = 1 g cm^2/sec^2.

(1826) expressed the quantitative relation between potential difference, $\mathscr{E}$, in volts and current, I, in amperes, as

$$I = \mathscr{E}/R \qquad \text{or} \qquad \mathscr{E} = IR$$

where the proportionality constant, R, of **Ohm's law** is called the resistance. Resistance is measured in **ohms**; 1 v is required to force a current of 1 amp through a resistance of 1 ohm.

Resistance to current flow in metals is probably caused by the vibration of the metal ions about their lattice positions; such vibrations interfere with the motion of the electrons and retard the flow of current. As the temperature is increased, the thermal motion of the metal ions is increased; hence, the resistance of metals increases, and metals become poorer conductors.

10.2 Electrolytic Conduction

Electrolytic conduction, in which the charge is carried by ions, will not occur unless the ions of the electrolyte are free to move. Hence, electrolytic conduction is exhibited principally by molten salts and by aqueous solutions of electrolytes. Furthermore, sustained current flow through an electrolytic conductor demands that chemical change accompany the movement of ions.

These principles of electrolytic conduction are best illustrated by reference to an electrolytic cell such as that diagramed in Figure 10.1 for the electrolysis

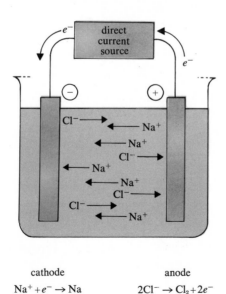

cathode $\qquad\qquad$ anode

$$Na^+ + e^- \rightarrow Na \qquad\qquad 2Cl^- \rightarrow Cl_2 + 2e^-$$

Figure 10.1 Electrolysis of molten sodium chloride.

of molten NaCl between inert electrodes.[3] The current source pumps electrons into the left-hand electrode which therefore may be considered to be negatively charged; electrons are drained from the right-hand, positive, electrode. In the electric field thus produced, sodium ions (cations) are attracted toward the negative pole (cathode), and chloride ions (anions) are attracted toward the positive pole (anode). Electric charge, in electrolytic conduction, is carried by cations moving toward the **cathode** and anions moving in the opposite direction, toward the **anode**.

For a complete circuit, electrode reactions must accompany the movement of ions. At the cathode, some chemical species (not necessarily the charge carrier) must accept electrons and be reduced; at the anode, electrons must be removed from some chemical species which is consequently oxidized. The conventions relating to the terms anode and cathode are summarized in Table 10.1.

Table 10.1

Electrode Conventions

	Cathode	Anode
ions attracted	cations	anions
direction of electron movement	into cell	out of cell
half reaction	reduction	oxidation
sign		
electrolysis cell	negative	positive
galvanic cell	positive	negative

In the diagramed cell, sodium ions are reduced at the cathode

$$Na^+ + e^- \longrightarrow Na$$

and chloride ions are oxidized at the anode

$$2Cl^- \longrightarrow Cl_2 + 2e^-$$

Proper addition of these two partial equations gives the reaction for the entire cell

$$2NaCl(l) \xrightarrow{\text{elec.}} 2Na(l) + Cl_2(g)$$

In the actual operation of the commercial cell used to produce metallic sodium, calcium chloride is added to lower the melting point of sodium chloride, and the cell is operated at a temperature of approximately 600°C. At this temperature, sodium metal is a liquid.

We can trace the flow of negative charge through the circuit of Figure 10.1 as follows. Electrons leave the current source and are pumped into the

---

[3] Inert electrodes are not involved in electrode reactions.

cathode where they are picked up by, and reduce, sodium ions that have been attracted to this negative electrode. Chloride ions move away from this pole, the cathode, toward the anode and thus carry negative charge in this direc- tion. At the anode, electrons are removed from the chloride ions oxidizing them to chlorine gas; these electrons are pumped out of the cell by the current source. In this manner the circuit is completed.

Electrolytic conduction, then, rests on the mobility of ions, and anything that inhibits the motion of ions causes resistance to current flow. Factors that influence the electrical conductivity of solutions of electrolytes include interionic attractions, solvation of ions, and viscosity of the solvent; these factors rest on solute–solute attractions, solute–solvent attractions, and solvent–solvent attractions, respectively. The average kinetic energy of the solute ions increases as the temperature is raised, and, therefore, the resistance of electrolytic conductors generally decreases as the temperature is raised (i.e., conduction increases). Furthermore, the effect of each of the three previously mentioned factors decreases as the temperature is increased.

At all times, electrical neutrality is preserved throughout all parts of the electrolytic liquid—there are as many cations per unit volume as there are anions.

10.3   Electrolysis

The electrolysis of molten sodium chloride serves as a commercial source of sodium metal and chlorine gas; analogous procedures are used to prepare other very active metals (such as potassium and calcium). When certain aqueous solutions are electrolyzed, however, water is involved in the electrode reactions rather than the ions derived from the solute. Hence, the current-carrying ions are not necessarily discharged at the electrodes.

In the electrolysis of aqueous sodium sulfate, sodium ions move toward the cathode and sulfate ions move toward the anode (Figure 10.2). Both these ions are difficult to discharge. When this electrolysis is conducted between inert electrodes, hydrogen gas is evolved at the cathode, and the solution surrounding the electrode becomes alkaline. Reduction occurs at the cathode, but rather than the reduction of the sodium ion

$$e^- + Na^+ \longrightarrow Na$$

the *net change* that occurs is the reduction of water

$$2e^- + 2H_2O \longrightarrow H_2(g) + 2OH^-$$

Water is an extremely weak electrolyte; pure water is approximately $2 \times 10^{-7}\%$ ionized at 25°C

$$2H_2O \rightleftharpoons H_3O^+ + OH^-$$

cathode

$$2e^- + 2H_2O \rightarrow$$
$$H_2(g) + 2OH^-$$

anode

$$2H_2O \rightarrow O_2(g) +$$
$$4H^+ + 4e^-$$

Figure 10.2 Electrolysis of aqueous sodium sulfate.

or, more briefly,

$$H_2O \rightleftharpoons H^+ + OH^-$$

The exact mechanism of the cathode reaction in the electrolysis of aqueous Na_2SO_4 is not known. It may be that the hydrogen ions from water are discharged and that the reaction proceeds as follows:

$$H_2O \rightleftharpoons H^+ + OH^-$$

$$2e^- + 2H^+ \longrightarrow H_2(g)$$

Multiplication of the first equation by 2 followed by addition of the equations gives the net change

$$2e^- + 2H_2O \longrightarrow H_2(g) + 2OH^-$$

In general, water is reduced at the cathode (producing hydrogen gas and hydroxide ions) whenever the cation of the solute is difficult to reduce.

Oxidation occurs at the anode, and in the electrolysis of aqueous Na_2SO_4, the anions (SO_4^{2-}) that migrate toward the anode are difficult to oxidize.

$$2SO_4^{2-} \longrightarrow S_2O_8^{2-} + 2e^-$$

Therefore the oxidation of water occurs preferentially. The mode of this reaction may be

$$H_2O \rightleftharpoons H^+ + OH^-$$

$$4OH^- \longrightarrow O_2(g) + 2H_2O + 4e^-$$

Multiplying the first equation by 4 and adding, we get the net change

$$2H_2O \longrightarrow O_2(g) + 4H^+ + 4e^-$$

At the anode, the evolution of oxygen gas is observed, and the solution surrounding the pole becomes acidic. In general, water is oxidized at the anode (producing oxygen gas and hydrogen ions) whenever the anion of the solute is difficult to oxidize.

The complete reaction for the electrolysis of aqueous Na_2SO_4 may be obtained by adding the cathode and anode reactions

$$2[2e^- + 2H_2O \longrightarrow H_2(g) + 2OH^-]$$
$$2H_2O \longrightarrow O_2(g) + 4H^+ + 4e^-$$
$$\overline{6H_2O \longrightarrow 2H_2(g) + O_2(g) + 4H^+ + 4OH^-}$$

If the solution is mixed, the hydrogen and hydroxide ions produced neutralize one another, and the net change

$$2H_2O \xrightarrow{\text{elec.}} 2H_2(g) + O_2(g)$$

is merely the electrolysis of water. In the course of the electrolysis, the hydrogen ions migrate away from the anode, where they are produced, toward the cathode. In like manner, the hydroxide ions move toward the anode. These ions neutralize one another in the solution between the two electrodes.

The electrolysis of an aqueous solution of NaCl between inert electrodes serves as an example of a process in which the anion of the electrolyte is discharged, but the cation is not.

anode: $\qquad 2Cl^- \longrightarrow Cl_2(g) + 2e^-$

cathode: $\quad 2e^- + 2H_2O \longrightarrow H_2(g) + 2OH^-$

$$\overline{2H_2O + 2Cl^- \longrightarrow H_2(g) + Cl_2(g) + 2OH^-}$$

Since the sodium ion remains in the solution unchanged, the reaction may be indicated

$$2H_2O + 2(Na^+, Cl^-) \xrightarrow{\text{elec.}} H_2(g) + Cl_2(g) + 2(Na^+, OH^-)$$

This process is a commercial source of hydrogen gas, chlorine gas, and, by evaporation of the solution left after electrolysis, sodium hydroxide.

In the electrolysis of a solution of $CuSO_4$ between inert electrodes (see right portion of Figure 10.4, given subsequently), the current is carried by the Cu^{2+} and SO_4^{2-} ions. The current-carrying cations are discharged, but the anions are not.

anode: $\qquad\quad 2H_2O \longrightarrow O_2(g) + 4H^+ + 4e^-$

cathode: $\quad 2e^- + Cu^{2+} \longrightarrow Cu(s)$

$$\overline{2Cu^{2+} + 2H_2O \longrightarrow O_2(g) + 2Cu(s) + 4H^+}$$

cathode   anode

$$2e^- + Cu^{2+} \rightarrow Cu(s) \qquad Cu(s) \rightarrow Cu^{2+} + 2e^-$$

Figure 10.3 Electrolysis of aqueous cupric sulfate between copper electrodes.

It is, of course, possible to have both ions of the solute discharged during the electrolysis of an aqueous solution. An example is the electrolysis of $CuCl_2$ between inert electrodes.

$$\begin{array}{lrcl} \text{anode:} & 2Cl^- & \longrightarrow & Cl_2(g) + 2e^- \\ \text{cathode:} & 2e^- + Cu^{2+} & \longrightarrow & Cu(s) \\ \hline & Cu^{2+} + 2Cl^- & \longrightarrow & Cu(s) + Cl_2(g) \end{array}$$

It is also possible to have the electrode itself enter into an electrode reaction. If aqueous $CuSO_4$ is electrolyzed between copper electrodes (Figure 10.3), Cu^{2+} ions are reduced at the cathode

$$2e^- + Cu^{2+} \longrightarrow Cu$$

but of the *three* possible anode oxidations

$$2SO_4^{2-} \longrightarrow 2S_2O_8^{2-} + 2e^-$$

$$2H_2O \longrightarrow O_2(g) + 4H^+ + 4e^-$$

$$Cu(s) \longrightarrow Cu^{2+} + 2e^-$$

the oxidation of the copper metal of the electrode is observed to occur. Hence, at the anode, copper from the electrode goes into solution as Cu^{2+} ions, and at the cathode, Cu^{2+} ions plate out as $Cu(s)$ on the electrode. This process is used to refine copper. Impure copper is used as the anode of an electrolytic cell, and a solution of $CuSO_4$ is electrolyzed; pure copper plates out on the cathode. Active electrodes are also used in electroplating processes; in silver plating, silver anodes are employed.

10.4 Faraday's Laws

The quantitative relationships between electricity and chemical change were first described by Michael Faraday. In 1832, he showed that the weight of a chemical substance liberated at an electrode is directly proportional to the amount of current passed through the cell. In 1833, he stated that the weights of different substances produced by a given amount of current are proportional to the equivalent weights of the substances.

Faraday's laws are readily interpreted by reference to the electrolysis of molten sodium chloride. The change at the cathode requires one electron for every sodium ion reduced.

$$Na^+ + e^- \longrightarrow Na$$

If Avogadro's number of electrons (1 mole) are consumed at this electrode, 22.9898 g of sodium metal (1 gram atom) is produced. The corresponding quantity of electricity is called the **faraday** (F) and has been found to equal 96,487 coulombs (for ordinary problem work, this value is customarily rounded off to 96,500 coulombs). If 2 F of electricity (2 moles of electrons) are used, 2 gram atoms of sodium are produced; 0.5 F would liberate 0.5 gram atom of sodium. Since the charge on the sodium ion is $1+$, the equivalent weight of sodium is the same as the atomic weight.

In the same time that electrons equivalent to 1 F are added to the cathode, that same number of electrons are removed from the anode.

$$2Cl^- \longrightarrow Cl_2 + 2e^-$$

The removal of 1 mole of electrons from this anode would result in the discharge of 35.453 g of chloride ion (1 gram atom), producing 0.5 mole of chlorine gas (1 gram equivalent). If 2 F of electricity flow through the cell, 2 gram atoms of chloride ions are discharged.

One faraday, then, will liberate 1 gram equivalent of an element or a compound. Rather than use equivalent weights, however, it is possible to interpret electrode reactions in terms of gram atoms, moles, and faradays. Thus the anode oxidation of the hydroxide ion,

$$4OH^- \longrightarrow O_2(g) + 2H_2O + 4e^-$$

may be read: four hydroxide ions produce one oxygen molecule, two water molecules, and four electrons, *or* 4 moles of hydroxide ion produce 1 mole of oxygen and 2 moles of water when 4 faradays of electricity is passed through the cell.

In Figure 10.4, two electrolytic cells are set up in series; electricity passes through one cell first and then through the other before returning to the current source. If silver nitrate is electrolyzed in one of the cells, the cathode reaction is

$$Ag^+ + e^- \longrightarrow Ag(s)$$

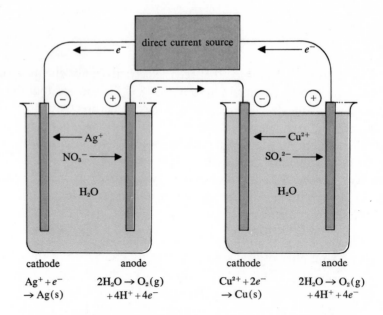

Figure 10.4 Silver coulometer in series with a cell for electrolysis.

and metallic silver is plated out on the electrode used for the electrolysis. By weighing the electrode before and after the electrolysis, one can determine the quantity of silver plated out and hence the number of coulombs that have passed through the cell. One faraday would plate out 107.868 g of silver; therefore, 1 coulomb is equivalent to

$$107.868/96{,}487 = 1.1180 \times 10^{-3} \text{ g of silver}$$

The same number of coulombs pass through both cells in a given time when these cells are arranged in series. Therefore the number of coulombs used in an electrolysis may be determined through the addition, in series, of this **silver coulometer** to the circuit of the experimental cell.

▶ EXAMPLE 10.1 The charge on a single electron is 1.6021×10^{-19} coulomb. Calculate Avogadro's number from the fact that 1 F = 96,487 coulombs.

Solution

$$? \text{ electrons} = 9.6487 \times 10^4 \text{ coulombs}\left(\frac{1 \text{ electron}}{1.6021 \times 10^{-19} \text{ coulomb}}\right)$$

$$= 6.0225 \times 10^{23} \text{ electrons}$$

▶ EXAMPLE 10.2 In the electrolysis of $CuSO_4$, what weight of copper is plated out on the cathode by a current of 0.750 amp flowing for 10.0 min?

Solution   The number of faradays employed may be calculated as follows:

$$? F = 10.0 \text{ min} \left(\frac{60 \text{ sec}}{1 \text{ min}}\right)\left(\frac{0.75 \text{ coulomb}}{1 \text{ sec}}\right)\left(\frac{1 F}{96,500 \text{ coulombs}}\right)$$

$$= 0.00466 \text{ F}$$

The cathode reaction is $Cu^{2+}(aq) + 2e^- \rightarrow Cu(s)$, and therefore 2 F plate out 63.5 g Cu(s)

$$? \text{ g Cu} = 0.00466 \text{ F}\left(\frac{63.5 \text{ g Cu(s)}}{2F}\right) = 0.148 \text{ g Cu(s)}$$

▶ **EXAMPLE 10.3**   (a) What volume of $O_2(g)$, at STP, is liberated at the anode in the electrolysis of $CuSO_4$ described in Example 10.2? (b) If 100 ml of $1.00M$ $CuSO_4$ is employed in the cell, what is the $H^+(aq)$ concentration at the end of the electrolysis? Assume that there is no volume change for the solution during the experiment and that the anode reaction is $2H_2O \rightarrow 4H^+(aq) + O_2(g) + 4e^-$

Solution   (a) Four faradays produce 22.4 liters of $O_2(g)$ at STP.

$$? \text{ liters } O_2(g) = 0.00466 \text{ F}\left(\frac{22.4 \text{ liters } O_2(g)}{4F}\right) = 0.0261 \text{ liter } O_2(g)$$

(b) Four faradays also produce 4 moles of $H^+(aq)$

$$? \text{ moles } H^+(aq) = 0.00466 \text{ F}\left(\frac{1 \text{ mole } H^+(aq)}{1F}\right) = 0.00466 \text{ mole } H^+(aq)$$

The small contribution of $H^+(aq)$ from the ionization of water may be ignored, and we may assume that there are 0.00466 mole $H^+(aq)$ in 100 ml of solution.

$$? \text{ moles } H^+(aq) = 1000 \text{ ml solution} \left(\frac{0.00466 \text{ mole } H^+(aq)}{100 \text{ ml solution}}\right)$$

$$= 0.0466 \text{ mole } H^+(aq)$$

The solution is therefore $0.0466M$ in hydrogen ion.

▶ **EXAMPLE 10.4**   (a) What weight of copper is plated out in the electrolysis of $CuSO_4$ in the same time that it takes to deposit 1.00 g of Ag in a silver coulometer that is arranged in series with the $CuSO_4$ cell? (b) If a current of 1.00 amp is used, how many minutes are required to plate out this quantity of copper?

Solution   (a) From the electrode reactions, we see that 2 F deposit 63.5 g Cu and 1 F deposits 107.9 g Ag.

$$? \text{ g Cu} = 1.00 \text{ g Ag}\left(\frac{1F}{107.9 \text{ g Ag}}\right)\left(\frac{63.5 \text{ g Cu}}{2F}\right) = 0.294 \text{ g Cu}$$

(b)

$$? \text{ min} = 1.00 \text{ g Ag}\left(\frac{96,500 \text{ coulombs}}{107.9 \text{ g Ag}}\right)\left(\frac{1 \text{ sec}}{1 \text{ coulomb}}\right)\left(\frac{1 \text{ min}}{60 \text{ sec}}\right) = 14.9 \text{ min}$$

10.5 Electrolytic Conductance

A material with a high electrical resistance is a poor electrical conductor; the ability of a substance to conduct electrical current is inversely related to that substance's electrical resistance. **Conductance** is defined as the reciprocal of resistance and has the units of reciprocal ohms (1/ohm). From Ohm's law,

$$R = \frac{\mathscr{E}}{I}$$

and

$$\text{conductance} = \frac{1}{R} = \frac{I}{\mathscr{E}}$$

Therefore, the conductance of a given solution is equal to the amount of current flowing (I) when the potential difference is 1 v ($\mathscr{E} = 1$ v). Conductance measurements are made using a rapidly alternating current (in which the direction of current flow reverses at regular time intervals) to minimize the effect of electrode reactions, which would change the composition of the solution.

The conductance of a given solution varies with the cell dimensions—directly with the area of the electrodes (A) and inversely with the distance between them (d). Thus

$$\text{conductance} = \frac{1}{R} = \frac{\kappa A}{d}$$

The proportionality constant, κ, is the **specific conductance**, or the conductance when A is 1 cm² and d is 1 cm; κ has the units 1/ohm cm.

It is not necessary to construct a cell of these exact dimensions in order to determine specific conductances. By measuring the resistance of a solution of known κ in an experimental cell, one can calculate the cell constant, k,

$$\kappa = \frac{k}{R}$$

and by means of this constant convert resistances measured in that cell into specific conductances. Since resistance (and hence conductance) varies with temperature, conductance measurements must be made at constant temperature.

The charges of solute ions are critical in determining how much current a solution may carry, and therefore comparisons of conductance data must be made between values for solutions of corresponding *normality*. The equivalent weight used in determining the normality is obtained by dividing the molecular weight of the solute by the total positive charge represented in the formula of the compound.

Equivalent conductance, Λ, is defined as the conductance, between electrodes 1 cm apart, of that volume of solution that contains 1 gram equivalent of solute; hence it represents the conductance of a collection of cations and anions equal to Avogadro's number of positive charges and Avogadro's number of negative charges. Since κ is the conductance of 1 cm^3 of solution, 1000κ is the conductance of 1 liter of solution. Hence

$$\Lambda = \frac{1000\,\kappa}{N}$$

where N, the normality of the solution, is the number of gram equivalents per liter; Λ therefore has the units cm^2/ohm equivalent.

▶ **EXAMPLE 10.5**   A conductance cell filled with $0.0200N$ KCl has a resistance of 163.3 ohms at 25°C. When filled with $0.0500N$ $AgNO_3$, it had a resistance of 78.5 ohms. The specific conductance of $0.0200N$ KCl is 2.768×10^{-3}/ohm cm. (a) What is the specific conductance of $0.500N$ $AgNO_3$? (b) What is the equivalent conductance of this solution?

Solution   (a) The cell constant may be determined by

$$\kappa = \frac{k}{R}$$

$$k = \kappa R = (2.768 \times 10^{-3}/\text{ohm cm})(163.3 \text{ ohm}) = 0.4520/\text{cm}$$

For $0.0500N$ $AgNO_3$,

$$\kappa = \frac{0.4520/\text{cm}}{78.5 \text{ ohm}} = 5.76 \times 10^{-3}/\text{ohm cm}$$

(b)

$$\Lambda = \frac{1000\,\kappa}{N} = \frac{(1000 \text{ cm}^3/\text{liter})(5.76 \times 10^{-3}/\text{ohm cm})}{5.00 \times 10^{-2} \text{ equivalent/liter}}$$

$$= 115 \text{ cm}^2/\text{ohm equivalent}$$

An examination of the data of Table 10.2 shows that the equivalent conductance of solutions of a given electrolyte, for example, NaCl, increases with decreasing concentration and approaches a limiting value, Λ_0, at infinite dilution. Owing to interionic attraction, any ion has a diffuse atmosphere of oppositely charged ions surrounding it; its motion in an electric field is therefore retarded. At infinite dilution, the ions are far enough apart to act independently of one another, and theoretically this ion-drag effect is eliminated.

Table 10.2

Equivalent Conductances, Λ, of Various Electrolytes at 25°C (in cm²/ohm equivalent)

Electrolyte	Concentration (equivalents/liter)			
	0.000	0.001	0.010	0.100
NaCl	126.5	123.7	118.5	106.7
KCl	149.9	147.0	141.3	129.0
BaCl$_2$	140.0	134.3	123.9	105.2
CuSO$_4$	133.0	115.2	83.3	50.5

As would be expected, the magnitude of the effect caused by interionic attractions depends upon the size of the charges of the solute ions. The equivalent conductance of $0.1N$ NaCl is about 84% of the Λ_0 value, the equivalent conductance of $0.1N$ BaCl$_2$ is about 75% of the Λ_0 value, and the equivalent conductance of $0.1N$ CuSO$_4$ is about 38% of the Λ_0 value.

Equivalent conductance measurements provide a method for the determination of the **degree of dissociation** (α) of a weak electrolyte in solution. In a solution of a weak electrolyte such as acetic acid

$$H_2O + HC_2H_3O_2 \;\rightleftharpoons\; H_3O^+ + C_2H_3O_2^-$$

the fraction of the compound in ionic form increases as the solution is diluted; weak electrolytes are theoretically 100% ionic at infinite dilution. At ordinary concentrations, the concentrations of ions in solutions of weak electrolytes are so small that interionic-attraction effects may be ignored. The undissociated compound, since it is uncharged, does not contribute to the conductance, and the equivalent conductance of a solution is attributed entirely to the fraction of the compound in ionic form. Since Λ_0 is the equivalent conductance that represents complete dissociation,

$$\Lambda = \alpha \Lambda_0$$

or

$$\alpha = \frac{\Lambda}{\Lambda_0}$$

The equivalent conductance at infinite dilution, Λ_0, of a strong electrolyte may be obtained by extrapolation of data obtained for solutions of various concentration (see Table 10.2). However, such a procedure cannot be used to secure Λ_0 values for weak electrolytes since equivalent conductance values for solutions of ordinary concentrations are low and rise very rapidly as the concentration approaches zero, at high dilutions. In order to get Λ_0 values for weak electrolytes, the assumption is made that Λ_0 values for compounds represent the sum of the equivalent conductances of the constituent ions; this procedure is illustrated in Example 10.6.

▶ **EXAMPLE 10.6** Given the following Λ_0 values (at 25°C): HCl, 426.2 cm²/ohm equivalent; $NaC_2H_3O_2$, 91.0 cm²/ohm equivalent; NaCl, 126.5 cm²/ohm equivalent. What is Λ_0 for acetic acid, $HC_2H_3O_2$, at 25°C?

Solution

$$\Lambda_0(HC_2H_3O_2) = \Lambda_0(HCl) + \Lambda_0(NaC_2H_3O_2) - \Lambda_0(NaCl)$$

$$= (426.2 + 91.0 - 126.5) \text{ cm}^2/\text{ohm equivalent}$$

$$= 390.7 \text{ cm}^2/\text{ohm equivalent}$$

▶ **EXAMPLE 10.7** At 25°C, the equivalent conductance of $0.100N$ $HC_2H_3O_2$ is 5.2 cm²/ohm equivalent; Λ_0 for acetic acid is 390.7 cm²/ohm equivalent. What is the degree of dissociation of $0.100N$ $HC_2H_3O_2$ at 25°C?

Solution

$$\alpha = \frac{\Lambda}{\Lambda_0}$$

$$\alpha = \frac{5.2 \text{ cm}^2/\text{ohm equivalent}}{390.7 \text{ cm}^2/\text{ohm equivalent}}$$

$$\alpha = 0.013$$

At 25°C, $0.100N$ acetic acid is 1.3% ionized.

10.6 Voltaic Cells

A cell that is used as a source of electrical energy is called a voltaic, or galvanic, cell after Alessandro Volta (1800) or Luigi Galvani (1780) who first experimented with the conversion of chemical energy into electrical energy.

The reaction between metallic zinc and copper(II) ions in solution is illustrative of a spontaneous change in which electrons are transferred.

$$Zn(s) + Cu^{2+}(aq) \longrightarrow Zn^{2+}(aq) + Cu(s)$$

The exact mechanism by which electron transfer occurs is not known; however, we may represent the above reaction as a combination of two half reactions.

$$Zn(s) \longrightarrow Zn^{2+}(aq) + 2e^-$$

$$2e^- + Cu^{2+}(aq) \longrightarrow Cu(s)$$

In a voltaic cell, these half reactions are made to occur at different electrodes so that the transfer of electrons takes place through the external electrical circuit rather than directly between zinc metal and copper(II) ions.

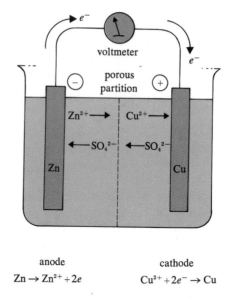

anode   cathode

$$Zn \rightarrow Zn^{2+} + 2e \qquad\qquad Cu^{2+} + 2e^- \rightarrow Cu$$

Figure 10.5   The Daniell Cell.

The cell diagramed in Figure 10.5 is designed to make use of this reaction to produce an electric current. The half cell on the left contains a zinc metal electrode and $ZnSO_4$ solution; the half cell on the right consists of a copper metal electrode in a solution of $CuSO_4$. The half cells are separated by a porous partition that prevents the mechanical mixing of the solutions but permits the passage of ions under the influence of the flow of electricity.

When the zinc and copper electrodes are joined by a wire, electrons flow from the zinc electrode to the copper electrode. At the zinc electrode, the zinc metal is *oxidized* to zinc ions; this electrode is the anode, and the electrons that are the product of the oxidation *leave* the cell from this pole (Table 10.1). The electrons travel the external circuit to the copper electrode where they are used in the reduction of copper(II) ions to metallic copper; the copper thus produced plates out on the electrode. The copper electrode is the cathode; here, the electrons *enter* the cell, and *reduction* occurs.

Since electrons are produced at the zinc electrode, this anode is designated as the negative pole. Electrons travel from the negative pole to the positive pole in the external circuit of any voltaic cell when the cell is operating. The cathode, where electrons are used in the electrode reaction, is therefore the positive pole. Within the cell, the movement of ions complete the electric circuit. At first glance, it is surprising that anions, being negatively charged, should travel toward an anode that is the negative electrode. Conversely, cations, which carry a positive charge, travel toward the cathode, which is the positive pole.

Careful consideration of the electrode reactions provides the answer to this apparent anomaly. At the anode, zinc ions are being produced and electrons left behind in the metal. At all times, the electrical neutrality of the solution is maintained; in the solution surrounding the electrode, there must be as much negative charge from anions as there is positive charge from cations. Hence, SO_4^{2-} ions move toward the anode to neutralize the effect of the Zn^{2+} ions being produced. At the same time, zinc ions move away from the anode toward the cathode. At the cathode, electrons are being used to reduce Cu^{2+} ions to copper metal. While the Cu^{2+} ions are being discharged, more Cu^{2+} ions move into the region surrounding the cathode to take the place of the ions being removed. If this did not occur, a surplus of SO_4^{2-} ions would build up around the cathode.

The porous partition is added to prevent mechanical mixing of the solutions of the half cells. If Cu^{2+} ions came into contact with the zinc metal electrode, electrons would be transferred directly rather than through the circuit. In the normal operation of the cell, this " short circuit " does not occur because the Cu^{2+} ions move in a direction away from the zinc electrode.

Actually, this cell would work if a solution of an electrolyte other than $ZnSO_4$ were used in the anode compartment, and if a metal other than copper were used for the cathode. However, the substitutes must be chosen so that the electrolyte in the anode compartment does not react with the zinc electrode and the cathode does not react with Cu^{2+} ions.

10.7 Electromotive Force

If $1M$ $ZnSO_4$ and $1M$ $CuSO_4$ solutions are employed in the Daniell cell, the cell may be represented by the notation

$$Zn(s) \,|\, Zn^{2+}(1M) \,|\, Cu^{2+}(1M) \,|\, Cu(s)$$

where the vertical lines represent phase boundaries. By convention, the substance forming the anode is listed first followed by the other materials comprising the cell listed in the order that one would encounter them leading away from the anode to the cathode, the composition of which is given last.

The voltage of a voltaic cell depends upon the concentrations of the materials used in the construction of the cell (Section 10.9). Standard voltages are determined at 25°C for cells with all reactants and products at unit *activity* (Section 9.12). For our discussion, we shall make the assumption that the activity of ions may be represented by their molar concentrations and the activity of gases by their pressures in atmospheres. Hence, according to this approximation, a standard cell would contain ions at $1M$ concentrations and gases at 1 atm pressures. In the cell notations that follow, concentrations will be indicated only if they deviate from standard.

Electric current flows through a circuit as a result of the **electromotive force** (emf), or voltage, of the cell. The greater the tendency of the cell reaction to occur, the higher the voltage. However, if emf is to be used as a reliable measure of this tendency, a voltage must be measured in a way that will ensure that the value secured is the maximum value obtainable for the particular cell under consideration. If an appreciable current flows during measurement, the voltage measured, $\mathscr{E}$, will be reduced by an amount, IR, equal to the product of the amount of current flowing, I, and the resistance of the cell, R. In addition, when the cell delivers current, the electrode reactions produce concentration changes which reduce the voltage.

The emf of a cell, therefore, must be measured with no appreciable current flowing through the cell, and such measurement is accomplished by the use of a potentiometer. The circuit of a potentiometer includes a current source of variable voltage and a means of measuring this voltage. The cell being studied is connected to the potentiometer circuit in such a way that the emf of the cell is opposed by the emf of the potentiometer current source.

If the emf of the cell is larger than that of the potentiometer, current will flow in the normal direction for a spontaneously discharging cell of that type. On the other hand, if the emf of the potentiometer current source is larger than that of the cell, current will flow in the opposite direction, causing the cell reaction to be reversed. When the two emf's are exactly balanced, no current will flow; this voltage is the **reversible emf** of the cell. The emf of a standard cell is given by the symbol $\mathscr{E}°$, and the $\mathscr{E}°$ for the Daniell cell is 1.10 v.

Faraday's laws apply to the cell reactions of voltaic, as well as electrolytic, cells. One precaution must be observed, however. Electricity is generated by simultaneous oxidation and reduction half reactions occurring at the anode and cathode, respectively; both must occur if the cell is to deliver current. Two faradays of electricity will be produced, therefore, by the oxidation of 1 gram atom of zinc at the anode *as well as* the reduction of 1 mole of Cu^{2+} ions at the cathode. The partial equations

$$\text{anode:} \qquad Zn \longrightarrow Zn^{2+} + 2e^-$$

$$\text{cathode:} \qquad 2e^- + Cu^{2+} \longrightarrow Cu$$

read in terms of gram atoms and moles, represent the flow of two times Avogadro's number of electrons or the production of 2 F of electricity.

The quantity of electrical energy, in joules, produced by a cell is the product of the quantity of electricity delivered, in coulombs, and the emf of the cell, in volts (see Section 10.1). The electrical energy *produced* by the reaction between 1 gram atom of zinc metal and 1 mole of copper(II) ions may be calculated as follows:

$$- 2(96,500 \text{ coulombs})(1.10 \text{ v}) = -212,000 \text{ joules}$$

or since 1 cal = 4.184 joule,

$$\frac{-212,000 \text{ joule}}{4.18 \text{ joule/cal}} = -50,700 \text{ cal}$$

The $\mathscr{E}°$ used in the preceding calculation is the reversible emf of the standard Daniell cell and hence the maximum voltage for this cell. Therefore, the value secured ($-50,700$ cal) is the maximum work that can be obtained from the operation of this type of cell. The maximum *net* work[4] that can be obtained from a chemical reaction conducted at a constant temperature and pressure is a measure of the *decrease* in the Gibbs free energy (Sections 9.4 and 13.6) of the system. Hence,

$$\Delta G = -nF\mathscr{E}$$

where n is the number of moles of electrons transferred in the reaction (or the number of faradays), F is the value of the faraday in appropriate units, and $\mathscr{E}$ is the emf in volts. If F is expressed as 96,487 coulombs, ΔG is obtained in joules; if the value 23,061 cal/v is used for F, ΔG is obtained in calories. A change in free energy derived from a standard emf, $\mathscr{E}°$, is given the symbol $\Delta G°$.

The free energy change of a reaction is a measure of the tendency of that reaction to occur. If work must be done on a system to bring about a change, the change is not spontaneous. At constant temperature and pressure, a spontaneous change is one from which net work can be obtained. Hence, for any spontaneous reaction, the free energy of the system decreases; ΔG is negative. Since $\Delta G = -nF\mathscr{E}$, only if $\mathscr{E}$ is positive will the cell reaction be spontaneous and serve as a source of electrical energy.

10.8 Electrode Potentials

In the same way that a cell reaction may be regarded as the sum of two half reactions, the emf of a cell may be thought of as the sum of two half-cell potentials. However, it is impossible to determine the absolute value of the potential of a single half cell. A relative scale has been established by assigning a value of zero to the voltage of a standard reference half cell and expressing all half-cell potentials relative to this reference electrode.

The reference half cell used is the **standard hydrogen electrode**, which consists of hydrogen gas, at 1 atm pressure, bubbling over a platinum electrode

---

[4] Some reactions proceed with an increase in volume, and the system must do work to expand against the atmosphere in order to maintain a constant pressure. The energy for this pressure-volume work is not available for any other purpose; it must be expended in this way if the reaction is to occur at constant pressure. Pressure-volume work is not included in the potentiometric measurement of the electrical work of any cell. Net work (or available work) is work other than pressure-volume work.

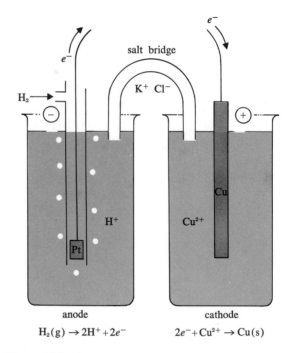

Figure 10.6 Standard hydrogen electrode and a Cu^{2+}/Cu electrode.

(coated with finely divided platinum to increase its surface) that is immersed in an acid solution containing $H^+(aq)$ at unit activity. In Figure 10.6, a standard hydrogen electrode is shown connected by means of a salt bridge to a standard Cu^{2+}/Cu electrode. A **salt bridge** is a tube filled with a concentrated solution of a salt (usually KCl), which permits current to flow between the half cells but prevents the mixing of the solutions of the half cells. The cell of Figure 10.6 may be diagramed as follows.

$$Pt \,|\, H_2 \,|\, H^+ \,\|\, Cu^{2+} \,|\, Cu$$

A double bar indicates a salt bridge. The hydrogen electrode is the anode, the copper electrode is the cathode, the emf of the cell is 0.34 v.

The cell emf is considered to be the sum of the half-cell potential for the oxidation half reaction (which we shall give the symbol $\mathscr{E}_{ox}$) and the half-cell potential for the reduction half reaction (which we shall indicate as $\mathscr{E}$ without subscript). For the cell of Figure 10.6,

anode:		$H_2 \longrightarrow 2H^+ + 2e^-$	$\mathscr{E}^\circ_{ox} = 0.00$ v
cathode:	$2e^- + Cu^{2+} \longrightarrow$	Cu	$\mathscr{E}^\circ = +0.34$ v

Since the hydrogen electrode is arbitrarily assigned a potential of zero, the entire cell emf is ascribed to the standard Cu^{2+}/Cu electrode. The value

$+0.34$ v is called the **standard electrode potential** of the Cu^{2+}/Cu electrode; notice that electrode potentials are given for reduction half reactions.

There are several interpretations of the meaning of the positive sign given to this electrode potential. (1) The copper electrode is the positive electrode (cathode). (2) Copper(II) ions are more active electron acceptors than $H^+(aq)$ ions (greater tendency for reduction). (3) The reduction of Cu^{2+} ions is the spontaneous direction of change for the Cu^{2+}/Cu electrode of this cell.

If a cell is constructed from a standard hydrogen electrode and a standard Zn^{2+}/Zn electrode, the zinc electrode is the anode, and the emf of the cell is 0.76 v. Thus

$$\text{anode:} \qquad Zn \longrightarrow Zn^{2+} + 2e^- \qquad \mathscr{E}^\circ_{ox} = +0.76 \text{ v}$$

$$\text{cathode:} \quad 2e^- + 2H^+ \longrightarrow H_2 \qquad \mathscr{E}^\circ = 0.00 \text{ v}$$

The value $+0.76$ v is sometimes called an **oxidation potential**, since it corresponds to an oxidation half reaction. An electrode potential, however, is a **reduction potential.** To obtain the electrode potential of the Zn^{2+}/Zn couple, we must change the sign of the oxidation potential so that the potential corresponds to the reverse half reaction, a reduction.

$$2e^- + Zn^{2+} \longrightarrow Zn \qquad \mathscr{E}^\circ = -0.76 \text{ v}$$

The negative sign of this electrode potential may be interpreted in several ways. (1) The zinc electrode is the negative electrode (anode). (2) Zinc ions are less active electron acceptors than $H^+(aq)$ ions (lesser tendency for reduction). (3) Oxidation of Zn (*not* reduction of Zn^{2+}) is the spontaneous direction of change for the Zn^{2+}/Zn electrode of this cell.

It is not necessary to use a cell containing a standard hydrogen electrode to obtain a standard electrode potential. For example, the standard potential of the Ni^{2+}/Ni electrode may be determined from the cell

$$Ni \,|\, Ni^{2+} \,\|\, Cu^{2+} \,|\, Cu$$

The emf of this cell is 0.59 v, and the nickel electrode functions as the anode.

$$Ni + Cu^{2+} \longrightarrow Ni^{2+} + Cu \qquad \mathscr{E}^\circ = +0.59 \text{ v}$$

The standard electrode potential of the Cu^{2+}/Cu electrode has been determined.

$$2e^- + Cu^{2+} \longrightarrow Cu \qquad \mathscr{E}^\circ = +0.34 \text{ v}$$

If we subtract the Cu^{2+}/Cu half reaction from the cell reaction and subtract the half-cell potential from the cell emf, we obtain

$$Ni \longrightarrow Ni^{2+} + 2e^- \qquad \mathscr{E}^\circ_{ox} = +0.25 \text{ v}$$

The electrode potential is therefore

$$2e^- + Ni^{2+} \longrightarrow Ni \qquad \mathscr{E}^\circ = -0.25 \text{ v}$$

Table 10.3

Standard Electrode Potentials at 25°C[a]   *(Reduction reactions)*

Half Reaction		$\mathscr{E}°$ (volts)
$Li^+ + e^-$ ⇌	Li	−3.045
$K^+ + e^-$ ⇌	K	−2.925
$Ba^{2+} + 2e^-$ ⇌	Ba	−2.906
$Ca^{2+} + 2e^-$ ⇌	Ca	−2.866
$Na^+ + e^-$ ⇌	Na	−2.714
$Mg^{2+} + 2e^-$ ⇌	Mg	−2.363
$Al^{3+} + 3e^-$ ⇌	Al	−1.662
$2H_2O + 2e^-$ ⇌	$H_2 + 2OH^-$	−0.82806
$Zn^{2+} + 2e^-$ ⇌	Zn	−0.7628
$Cr^{3+} + 3e^-$ ⇌	Cr	−0.744
$Fe^{2+} + 2e^-$ ⇌	Fe	−0.4402
$Cd^{2+} + 2e^-$ ⇌	Cd	−0.4029
$Ni^{2+} + 2e^-$ ⇌	Ni	−0.250
$Sn^{2+} + 2e^-$ ⇌	Sn	−0.136
$Pb^{2+} + 2e^-$ ⇌	Pb	−0.126
$2H^+ + 2e^-$ ⇌	H_2	0
$Cu^{2+} + 2e^-$ ⇌	Cu	+0.337
$Cu^+ + e^-$ ⇌	Cu	+0.521
$I_2 + 2e^-$ ⇌	$2I^-$	+0.5355
$Fe^{3+} + e^-$ ⇌	Fe^{2+}	+0.771
$Ag^+ + e^-$ ⇌	Ag	+0.7991
$Br_2 + 2e^-$ ⇌	$2Br^-$	+1.0652
$O_2 + 4H^+ + 4e^-$ ⇌	$2H_2O$	+1.229
$Cr_2O_7^{2-} + 14H^+ + 6e^-$ ⇌	$2Cr^{3+} + 7H_2O$	+1.33
$Cl_2 + 2e^-$ ⇌	$2Cl^-$	+1.3595
$MnO_4^- + 8H^+ + 5e^-$ ⇌	$Mn^{2+} + 4H_2O$	+1.51
$F_2 + 2e^-$ ⇌	$2F^-$	+2.87

Oxidation reactions have opposite sign.

[a] Data from A. J. de Bethune and N. A. Swendeman Loud, "Table of Electrode Potentials and Temperature Coefficients," pp. 414–424 in *Encyclopedia of Electrochemistry* (C. A. Hampel, editor), Van Nostrand Reinhold, New York, 1964, and from A. J. de Bethune and N. A. Swendeman Loud, *Standard Aqueous Electrode Potentials and Temperature Coefficients*, 19 pp., C. A. Hampel, publisher, Skokie, Illinois, 1964.

Standard electrode potentials are listed in Table 10.3, and a more complete list is found in the appendix.[5] The table is constructed with the most positive electrode potential (greatest tendency for reduction) at the bottom. Hence, if a pair of electrodes is combined to make a voltaic cell, the reduction half reaction (cathode) of the cell will be that listed for the electrode that stands lower in the table, and the oxidation half reaction (anode) will be the *reverse* of that shown for the electrode that stands higher in the table.

For example, consider a cell constructed from standard Ni^{2+}/Ni and Ag^+/Ag electrodes. The table entries for these electrodes are

$$Ni^{2+} + 2e^- \rightleftharpoons Ni \qquad \mathscr{E}° = -0.250 \text{ v}$$

$$Ag^+ + e^- \rightleftharpoons Ag \qquad \mathscr{E}° = +0.799 \text{ v}$$

[5] The definition of the standard electrode potential used agrees with that suggested by the International Union of Pure and Applied Chemistry (IUPAC) in 1953. Prior to this time, the common American practice was to tabulate oxidation potentials rather than electrode potentials.

Of the two ions, the Ag^+ ion shows the greater tendency for reduction. The Ag^+/Ag electrode is therefore the cathode, and the Ni^{2+}/Ni electrode is the anode. The half reaction that takes place at an anode is an oxidation, and the half-cell potential is an oxidation potential.

$$\text{anode:} \qquad Ni \longrightarrow Ni^{2+} + 2e^- \qquad \mathscr{E}^o_{ox} = +0.250 \text{ v}$$

$$\text{cathode:} \qquad 2e^- + 2Ag^+ \longrightarrow 2Ag \qquad \mathscr{E}^o = +0.799 \text{ v}$$

The cell reaction and cell emf may be obtained by addition.

$$Ni + 2Ag^+ \longrightarrow Ni^{2+} + 2Ag \qquad \mathscr{E}^o = +1.049 \text{ v}$$

Notice that the half reaction for the reduction of Ag^+ must be multiplied by 2 before the addition so that the electrons lost and gained in the half reactions will cancel. The $\mathscr{E}^o$ for the Ag^+/Ag electrode, however, is *not* multiplied by 2. The magnitude of an electrode potential depends upon the temperature and the concentrations of materials used in the construction of the half cell; these variables are fixed for *standard* electrode potentials. Indication of the stoichiometry of the cell reaction does not imply that a concentration change has been made.

Actually, the half reactions implied by the half-cell potentials are

$$\frac{\begin{array}{lcl} 2\cancel{H}^+ + Ni & \longrightarrow & \cancel{H_2} + Ni^{2+} \\ \cancel{H_2} + 2Ag^+ & \longrightarrow & 2\cancel{H}^+ + 2Ag \end{array}}{Ni + 2Ag^+ \quad \longrightarrow \quad Ni^{2+} + 2Ag}$$

Notice, however, that in the addition of these half reactions, the H_2 molecules and H^+ ions cancel.

An alternative way to use the table of electrode potentials to calculate a cell emf consists of subtracting the electrode potential of the anode (value nearer the top of the table column) from the electrode potential of the cathode (value nearer the bottom of the table column). This mathematical procedure amounts to the same thing as changing the sign of the electrode potential of the anode (to correspond to an oxidation) and adding the value to the electrode potential of the cathode.

By convention, the *anode* of a cell is indicated on the *left* in a cell notation. Thus the Cd^{2+}/Cd electrode is the anode of the cell

$$Cd \,|\, Cd^{2+} \,\|\, Ag^+ \,|\, Ag$$

and the cell reaction indicated is

$$Cd + 2Ag^+ \longrightarrow Cd^{2+} + 2Ag$$

The standard emf of the cell is

$$\mathscr{E}^o = \mathscr{E}^o_{right} - \mathscr{E}^o_{left}$$

Substitution of $\mathscr{E}^\circ$ values from the table gives

$$\mathscr{E}^\circ = (+0.799) - (-0.403)$$
$$= +1.202 \text{ v}$$

The positive sign of the cell emf indicates that the cell is properly diagramed and the reaction proceeds as indicated.

If we had mistakenly diagramed the cell as

$$Ag \,|\, Ag^+ \,\|\, Cd^{2+} \,|\, Cd$$

which corresponds to the reaction

$$2Ag + Cd^{2+} \longrightarrow 2Ag^+ + Cd$$

we would have obtained the result

$$\mathscr{E}^\circ = \mathscr{E}^\circ_{\text{right}} - \mathscr{E}^\circ_{\text{left}}$$
$$= (-0.403) - (+0.799)$$
$$= -1.202 \text{ v}$$

The negative sign of the cell emf means that the cell will not function in the manner indicated by the cell notation. Rather, the cell reaction would be the reverse of that shown, and the diagram should be reversed.

Electrode potentials are also useful for the evaluation of oxidation-reduction reactions that take place outside of electrochemical cells. Either of the two ways described for the analysis of a cell may be used to evaluate an oxidation-reduction reaction. The half reactions of Table 10.3 are listed as reductions, from left to right, with the oxidized form of the element, molecule, or ion accepting electrons to produce the reduced form.

$$(\text{oxidized form}) + ne^- \rightleftharpoons (\text{reduced form})$$

Because of the way in which the table is constructed (greatest tendency for reduction at the bottom), any *reduced form*, at unit activity, should be able to reduce the *oxidized form*, at unit activity, of a half reaction listed below it in the table. From the positions in the table of the following half reactions

$$2e^- + I_2 \rightleftharpoons 2I^- \qquad \mathscr{E}^\circ = +0.536 \text{ v}$$

$$2e^- + Cl_2 \rightleftharpoons 2Cl^- \qquad \mathscr{E}^\circ = +1.360 \text{ v}$$

one would correctly predict that the reduced form, I^-, should be able to reduce the oxidized form, Cl_2.

$$Cl_2(g) + 2I^-(aq) \longrightarrow 2Cl^-(aq) + I_2(s) \qquad \mathscr{E}^\circ = +0.824$$

The species with the greatest tendency toward oxidation (best reducing agent) is the reduced form of the half reaction at the top of the table (Li in Table 10.3); the oxidized form of the half reaction at the bottom of the table (F_2 in Table 10.3) has the greatest tendency to be itself reduced (best oxidizing agent).

There are several factors that must be kept in mind when using a table of electrode potentials to predict the course of a chemical reaction. Because $\mathscr{E}$ changes with changes in concentration, many presumably unfavored reactions can be made to occur by altering the concentrations of the reacting species. In addition, some theoretically favored reactions proceed at such a slow rate that they are of no practical consequence.

Correct use of the table also demands that all pertinent half reactions of a given element be considered before making a prediction. On the basis of the half reactions

$$3e^- + Fe^{3+} \rightleftharpoons Fe \qquad \mathscr{E}^\circ = -0.036 \text{ v}$$

$$2e^- + 2H^+ \rightleftharpoons H_2 \qquad \mathscr{E}^\circ = 0.000 \text{ v}$$

one would predict that the products of the reaction of iron with H^+ would be hydrogen gas and Fe^{3+} ions ($\mathscr{E}^\circ$ for the complete reaction, $+0.036$ v). However, the oxidation state iron(II) lies between metallic iron and the oxidation state iron(III). Once an iron atom has lost two electrons and becomes a Fe^{2+} ion, further oxidation is opposed, as may be seen from the reverse of the following

$$e^- + Fe^{3+} \rightleftharpoons Fe^{2+} \qquad \mathscr{E}^\circ = +0.771 \text{ v}$$

Thus the reaction yields Fe^{2+} ions only. This fact could have been predicted by an examination of the half reaction

$$2e^- + Fe^{2+} \rightleftharpoons Fe \qquad \mathscr{E}^\circ = -0.440 \text{ v}$$

The $\mathscr{E}_{ox}$ for the production of Fe^{2+} ions from the reaction of iron metal and H^+ ions ($+0.440$ v) is greater than that for the production of Fe^{3+} ions ($+0.036$ v), and hence the former is favored.

We may summarize the electrode potentials for iron and its ions as follows:

$$Fe^{3+} \xrightarrow{+0.771 \text{ v}} Fe^{2+} \xrightarrow{-0.440 \text{ v}} Fe$$
$$\underset{-0.036 \text{ v}}{\underline{\phantom{Fe^{3+} \xrightarrow{+0.771} Fe^{2+} \xrightarrow{-0.440}}}}$$

The preceding predictions are immediately evident from this diagram, if we remember that oxidation is the reverse of the relation corresponding to an electrode potential.

Occasionally, an oxidation state of an element is unstable toward disproportionation. The electrode potentials for copper and its ions may be summarized as follows:

$$Cu^{2+} \xrightarrow{+0.153 \text{ v}} Cu^+ \xrightarrow{+0.521 \text{ v}} Cu$$
$$\underset{+0.337 \text{ v}}{\underline{\phantom{Cu^{2+} \xrightarrow{+0.153} Cu^+ \xrightarrow{+0.521}}}}$$

From this we see that the Cu^+ ion is not a very stable one. In water, Cu^+ ions disproportionate to copper metal and Cu^{2+} ions.

$$2Cu^+(aq) \longrightarrow Cu(s) + Cu^{2+}(aq)$$

The $\mathscr{E}°$ for this reaction is $+0.521 - 0.153 = +0.368$ v. Species instable toward disproportionation may be readily recognized by the fact that the electrode potential for the reduction to the next lower oxidation state is more positive than the electrode potential for the couple with the next higher oxidation state. An inspection of the diagram for iron and its ions shows that the Fe^{2+} ion is stable toward such disproportionation.

10.9 Effect of Concentration on Cell Potentials

The potential of a cell in which the constituents are present at concentrations other than standard may be calculated by means of the **Nernst equation**, named for Walther Nernst, who developed it in 1889.

$$\mathscr{E} = \mathscr{E}° - \frac{RT}{nF} \ln Q$$

where $\mathscr{E}°$ is the standard cell emf, R is the gas constant (1.987 cal/°K), T is the absolute temperature, n is the number of moles of electrons transferred in the reaction (number of faradays), F is the faraday constant (23,060 cal/v), and $\ln Q$ is the natural logarithm of the reaction quotient.

The reaction quotient, Q, is a fraction derived from the activities of the dissolved substances and gases employed in the cell; the activity of each substance is raised to a power equal to the coefficient of that substance in the balanced chemical equation. The *numerator* of Q is the product of the activity terms for the materials on the *right* of the chemical equation; the *denominator* of Q is the product of the activity terms for the substances on the *left* of the chemical equation. Since the activity of a pure solid is assumed to be unity at all times, the activity term for a solid is always equal to 1, and such terms may be neglected in Q values.

For a hypothetical cell reaction,

$$wW + xX \longrightarrow yY + zZ$$

where the lower case letters represent the coefficients of the balanced chemical equation,

$$Q = \frac{(a_Y)^y (a_Z)^z}{(a_W)^w (a_X)^x}$$

For our work, we shall make the assumptions that the activity of a substance in solution is given by the molar concentration of the substance and the activity of a gas is equal to the partial pressure of the gas in atmospheres; such assumptions lead to $\mathscr{E}$ values that are approximately correct.

If we substitute the values of the constants into the Nernst equation and multiply by 2.303 to convert the natural logarithm into a logarithm to the base 10, for $T = 298.2°K$ (which is 25°C),

$$\mathscr{E} = \mathscr{E}° - \frac{0.05916}{n} \log Q$$

When the activities of all substances are unity (standard states), $Q = 1$, log $Q = 0$, and $\mathscr{E} = \mathscr{E}°$. The Nernst equation may be used to determine the voltage of a cell constructed from nonstandard electrodes or to calculate the electrode potential of a half cell in which all species are not present at unit activity.

▶ **EXAMPLE 10.7** What is the electrode potential of a Zn^{2+}/Zn electrode in which the concentration of Zn^{2+} ions is $0.1M$?

Solution The partial equation

$$2e^- + Zn^{2+} \longrightarrow Zn$$

shows 2 electrons gained. If the symbol $[Zn^{2+}]$ is used to designate the molar concentration of Zn^{2+} ions,

$$\mathscr{E} = \mathscr{E}° - \frac{0.0592}{2} \log \left(\frac{1}{[Zn^{2+}]}\right)$$

$\mathscr{E}°$ for the Zn^{2+}/Zn electrode is -0.76 v.

$$\mathscr{E} = -0.76 - \frac{0.0592}{2} \log \left(\frac{1}{0.1}\right)$$

$$\mathscr{E} = -0.76 - 0.0296(1) = -0.79 \text{ v}$$

▶ **EXAMPLE 10.8** (a) What is the potential for the cell

$$Ni \,|\, Ni^{2+}(0.01M) \,\|\, Cl^-(0.2M) \,|\, Cl_2(1 \text{ atm}) \,|\, Pt$$

(b) What is ΔG for the cell reaction?

Solution (a) Two faradays of electricity are involved in the cell reaction

$$Ni + Cl_2 \longrightarrow Ni^{2+} + 2Cl^-$$

and therefore $n = 2$. The standard cell emf is

$$\mathscr{E}° = \mathscr{E}°(Cl_2/Cl^-) - \mathscr{E}°(Ni^{2+}/Ni)$$

$$= (+1.36) - (-0.25) = +1.61 \text{ v}$$

Therefore,

$$\mathscr{E} = \mathscr{E}° - \frac{0.0592}{2} \log \left(\frac{[Cl^-]^2[Ni^{2+}]}{[Cl_2]}\right)$$

$$\mathscr{E} = +1.61 - \frac{0.0592}{2} \log \left(\frac{(0.2)^2(0.01)}{(1)}\right)$$

$$\mathscr{E} = +1.61 - 0.0296 \log (0.0004)$$

$$\mathscr{E} = +1.61 + 0.10 = +1.71 \text{ v}$$

(b)

$$\Delta G = -nF\mathscr{E}$$

$$\Delta G = -2(23,100 \text{ cal/v})(1.71 \text{ v}) = -79,000 \text{ cal}$$

▶ **EXAMPLE 10.9** What is the $\mathscr{E}$ of the cell

$$\text{Sn} \mid \text{Sn}^{2+}(1.0M) \parallel \text{Pb}^{2+}(0.0010 \ M) \mid \text{Pb}$$

Solution The following may be obtained from a table of standard electrode potentials

$$\text{Sn} \longrightarrow \text{Sn}^{2+} + 2e^- \qquad \mathscr{E}^0_{0x} = +0.136 \text{ v}$$

$$2e^- + \text{Pb}^{2+} \longrightarrow \text{Pb} \qquad \mathscr{E}^0 = -0.126 \text{ v}$$

Thus the reaction in a standard cell is

$$\text{Sn} + \text{Pb}^{2+} \longrightarrow \text{Sn}^{2+} + \text{Pb} \qquad \mathscr{E}^0 = +0.010 \text{ v}$$

For the cell as diagramed in the problem,

$$\mathscr{E} = \mathscr{E}^\circ - \frac{0.0592}{2} \log \left(\frac{[\text{Sn}^{2+}]}{[\text{Pb}^{2+}]} \right)$$

$$\mathscr{E} = +0.010 - \frac{0.0592}{2} \log \left(\frac{1.0}{0.0010} \right)$$

$$\mathscr{E} = +0.010 - 0.0296(3)$$

$$= +0.010 - 0.089 = -0.079 \text{ v}$$

This result means that the cell will not function in the manner implied by the diagram. Instead, it would operate in the reverse order and in a direction opposite to that of the standard cell. The cell is properly diagramed

$$\text{Pb} \mid \text{Pb}^{2+}(0.0010 \ M) \parallel \text{Sn}^{2+}(1.0 \ M) \mid \text{Sn}$$

and the reaction of the cell is

$$\text{Pb} + \text{Sn}^{2+} \longrightarrow \text{Pb}^{2+} + \text{Sn} \qquad \mathscr{E} = +0.079 \text{ v}$$

From this example, we see that concentration effects can sometimes reverse the direction that a reaction is expected to take.

Notice that the results of the preceding examples are qualitatively in agreement with predictions based on Le Chatelier's principle (Section 9.5). Increasing the concentrations of reactants and decreasing the concentrations of products would be expected to increase the driving force of the reaction and lead to a more positive $\mathscr{E}$. On the other hand, decreasing the concentrations of reactants and increasing the concentrations of products would be expected to retard a reaction and result in a more negative $\mathscr{E}$.

10.10 Concentration Cells

Since an electrode potential depends upon the concentration of the ions used in the electrode, a cell may be constructed from two electrodes composed of the same materials but differing in concentration of ions. For example,

$$Cu \mid Cu^{2+}(0.010M) \parallel Cu^{2+}(0.10M) \mid Cu$$

From the partial equation,

$$2e^- + Cu^{2+} \rightleftarrows Cu \qquad \mathscr{E}° = +0.34 \text{ v}$$

and Le Chatelier's principle, we can predict that *increasing* the concentration of Cu^{2+} ions would drive the reaction to the right and raise the reduction potential, whereas *decreasing* the concentration of Cu^{2+} ions would drive the reaction to the left and raise the oxidation potential (or, lower the reduction potential). Hence of the two electrodes in the cell diagramed, the left electrode would have the stronger tendency for oxidation and the right would have the stronger tendency for reduction. The "reaction" of the cell is

$$Cu + Cu^{2+}(0.10M) \longrightarrow Cu^{2+}(0.010M) + Cu$$

$\mathscr{E}°$ for this cell is zero since the same electrode is involved in each half cell. Then

$$\mathscr{E} = 0.00 - \frac{0.0592}{2} \log \left(\frac{0.010}{0.10} \right)$$

$$\mathscr{E} = -0.0296(-1) = +0.0296 \text{ v}$$

10.11 Electrode Potentials and Electrolysis

It should be kept in mind that electrode potentials are determined under reversible conditions. The measured voltage of a spontaneously discharging voltaic cell will not equal the calculated electromotive force for the cell since, in the production of an electric current, the cell is operating in an irreversible manner. The cell emf calculated by means of electrode potentials is the maximum voltage that the cell can develop and is determined by the application of a measured external voltage of a magnitude that will just stop the flow of electrons. If an external voltage infinitesimally greater than that which the cell develops were applied, the cell would run in the reverse direction; electrolysis would occur. Electrode potentials, therefore, give the minimum voltage necessary for electrolysis.

In practice, however, it is found that a higher voltage than calculated must be applied to effect electrolysis. Part of the increased voltage is required to overcome the electrical resistance of the cell, and the remainder is needed to overcome two additional effects. The first is called **concentration polarization** and is caused by the changes in the concentration of the electrolyte around the electrodes as the electrolysis proceeds, and ions are removed or produced. The concentration gradient set up within the cell is, in effect, a concentration cell and produces a back emf opposing the applied voltage. Concentration polarization can be reduced by stirring the electrolyte during the course of the electrolysis.

The other effect that makes the voltage required for an electrolysis higher than the reversible emf is called **overvoltage**. Overvoltage is thought to be caused by a slow rate of reaction at the electrodes so that an excess applied voltage is required to make the electrolysis proceed at an appreciable rate. Overvoltages for the deposition of metals are low, but those required for the liberation of hydrogen gas or oxygen gas are appreciable, vary with the material used for the electrode, and may amount to a volt or more.

Electrolysis is an important procedure for the quantitative analysis of ores, alloys, and other metal-containing compounds and mixtures. As the voltage is increased in the electrolysis of an aqueous solution, ions or molecules are discharged at the *cathode* in order of decreasing value of electrode potential— most positive value (nearest to the bottom of the table) first. In addition, the reduction of water is possible. The $\mathscr{E}°$ value for this reduction is -0.828 v, but in neutral aqueous solutions, the concentration of OH^- is $10^{-7}M$, not $1M$. The $\mathscr{E}$ value for neutral aqueous solutions, obtained by means of the Nernst equation, is

$$2e^- + 2H_2O \rightleftharpoons H_2 + 2OH^- \qquad \mathscr{E} = -0.414 \text{ v}$$

One would predict it to be impossible to reduce any aqueous species with an electrode potential more negative than -0.414 v, the reduction potential for water. However, because of the high hydrogen overvoltage, it is possible to plate out, on the cathode, metals that have electrode potentials more negative than the one for the reduction of water—down to, and including, zinc ($\mathscr{E}° = -0.763$ v).

At the *anode*, the species present are oxidized in inverse order of electrode potential—most negative value (uppermost on the table) first. The half reactions are the reverse of those listed in the table. In the electrolysis of aqueous solutions, the oxidation of water is possible. For neutral aqueous solutions (concentration of H^+, $10^{-7}M$), this oxidation is the reverse of

$$4e^- + 4H^+ + O_2 \rightleftharpoons 2H_2O \qquad \mathscr{E} = +0.815 \text{ v}$$

For the liberation of oxygen, however, high overvoltages are required. Thus the oxidation of chloride ion to chlorine gas takes place in the electrolysis of aqueous solutions of chlorides.

$$2e^- + Cl_2(g) \rightleftharpoons 2Cl^- \qquad \mathscr{E}° = +1.36 \text{ v}$$

The overvoltage of chlorine is less than the overvoltage of oxygen.

The products of electrolysis vary with the concentration of ions in the solution, since the half-cell emf's are dependent upon concentrations. For example, the electrolysis of *dilute* solutions of chlorides yields oxygen at the anode rather than chlorine. Furthermore, after the primary electrode reactions in which electrons are transferred, secondary reactions may occur. Thus, if chlorine is liberated in an alkaline solution, ClO^- or ClO_3^- ions are formed from the reaction of the chlorine with the hydroxide ions; if chlorine is liberated on a silver anode, AgCl is formed.

▶ **EXAMPLE 10.10**   A solution is $1M$ in each of the following: $AgNO_3$, $Cu(NO_3)_2$, $Fe(NO_3)_2$, and $NaNO_3$. In the electrolysis of this solution, between inert electrodes, the voltage is gradually increased. What would be the order in which materials would plate out on the cathode, and at what voltage would each be discharged? Assume that the overvoltage of oxygen is 0.600 v, the overvoltage of hydrogen is 0.300 v, and the solution is neutral. Ignore concentration polarization and cell resistance.

Solution   The only species at the anode (which is inert) are the nitrate ion and water. Since it is impossible to oxidize the nitrate ion, water will be oxidized:

$$2H_2O \longrightarrow O_2(g) + 4H^+ + 4e^- \qquad \mathscr{E}_{ox} = -0.815 \text{ v}$$

If the overvoltage of oxygen is taken into account, the half-cell potential for the oxidation is -1.415 v.

The following reductions should be considered as possible cathode half reactions:

$$e^- + Na^+ \longrightarrow Na \qquad \mathscr{E}^\circ = -2.714 \text{ v}$$

$$2e^- + Fe^{2+} \longrightarrow Fe \qquad \mathscr{E}^\circ = -0.440 \text{ v}$$

$$2e^- + Cu^{2+} \longrightarrow Cu \qquad \mathscr{E}^\circ = +0.337 \text{ v}$$

$$e^- + Ag^+ \longrightarrow Ag \qquad \mathscr{E}^\circ = +0.799 \text{ v}$$

In addition the reduction of water

$$2e^- + 2H_2O \longrightarrow H_2(g) + 2OH^- \qquad \mathscr{E} = -0.414 \text{ v}$$

must be considered. If the overvoltage of hydrogen is taken into account, the reduction potential for water is -0.714 v.

The silver will plate out first. The voltage at which this will occur will be equal to the oxidation potential of water (-1.415 v) plus the reduction potential of Ag($+0.799$ v), or -0.616 v. (The values are negative, since the voltage is applied.) After the silver has been removed, the copper will plate out at a voltage of -1.088 v, followed by the iron at a voltage of -1.855 v. The reduction of water (half-cell potential $= -0.714$ v) will occur before the reduction of sodium ions (half-cell potential $= -2.714$ v). Hence at a voltage of 2.129 v, hydrogen will be evolved at the cathode. Sodium ions can be reduced only in the absence of water, that is, by the electrolysis of molten sodium salts.

10.12   Some Commercial Voltaic Cells

Several voltaic cells are of commercial importance. The **dry cell** (Figure 10.7) consists of a zinc metal container (which serves as the anode) filled with a moist paste of ammonium chloride and zinc chloride and containing a graphite electrode (the cathode) surrounded by manganese dioxide. The electrode reactions are complex, but they may be approximately represented by

anode: $\qquad Zn \longrightarrow Zn^{2+} + 2e^-$

cathode: $\quad 2e^- + 2MnO_2 + 2NH_4^+ \longrightarrow Mn_2O_3 + H_2O + 2NH_3$

The dry cell generates a voltage of approximately 1.25 to 1.50 v.

A newer type of dry cell which has found use in small electrical devices (such as hearing aids) consists of a zinc container as the anode, a carbon rod as the cathode, and moist mercury(II) oxide mixed with potassium hydroxide as the electrolyte. A lining of porous paper keeps the electrolyte separated from the zinc anode. The cell has a potential of approximately 1.35 v.

anode: $\qquad Zn + 2OH^- \longrightarrow Zn(OH)_2 + 2e^-$

cathode: $\quad 2e^- + HgO + H_2O \longrightarrow Hg + 2OH^-$

The **lead storage cell** consists of a lead anode and a grid of lead packed with lead dioxide as the cathode. The electrolyte is sulfuric acid, and the half-cell reactions are

anode: $\qquad Pb(s) + SO_4^{2-} \longrightarrow PbSO_4(s) + 2e^-$

cathode: $\quad 2e^- + PbO_2(s) + SO_4^{2-} + 4H^+ \longrightarrow PbSO_4(s) + 2H_2O$

In practice, the current obtainable from a lead storage cell is increased by constructing the cell from a number of cathode plates joined together and arranged alternately with a number of anode plates, which are also joined

Figure 10.7   The dry cell.

together. The potential difference of one cell is approximately 2 v. A storage battery consists of three or six such cells joined in series to produce a 6- or a 12-volt battery.

The electrode reactions of the storage battery can be reversed by the application of an external current source and, in this manner, the battery can be recharged. Since sulfuric acid is consumed as the storage battery delivers current, the state of charge of the battery can be determined by measuring the density of the battery electrolyte.

The **nickel-cadmium storage cell** has a longer life than the lead storage cell but is more expensive to manufacture.

$$\text{anode:} \qquad Cd(s) + 2OH^- \longrightarrow Cd(OH)_2 + 2e^-$$

$$\text{cathode:} \quad 2e^- + NiO_2(s) + 2H_2O \longrightarrow Ni(OH)_2 + 2OH^-$$

The potential of each cell of a nickel-cadmium battery is approximately 1.4 v, and the battery is rechargeable.

10.13   Fuel Cells

Electrical cells that are designed to convert the energy from the combustion of fuels such as hydrogen, carbon monoxide, or methane directly into electrical energy are called fuel cells. Since, in theory, 100% of the free energy released by a combustion (ΔG) should be obtainable from an efficient fuel cell, extensive research into their development is currently being undertaken. Although approximately only 60 to 70% efficiency has been realized as yet, present fuel cells are about twice as efficient as processes in which the heat of combustion is used to generate electricity by mechanical means.

In a typical fuel cell, hydrogen and oxygen are bubbled through porous carbon electrodes into concentrated aqueous sodium hydroxide or potassium hydroxide. Catalysts are incorporated in the electrodes.

$$C \,|\, H_2(g) \,|\, OH^- \,|\, O_2(g) \,|\, C$$

The gaseous materials are consumed and are continuously supplied. The electrode reactions are

$$\text{anode:} \qquad 2H_2(g) + 4OH^- \longrightarrow 4H_2O + 4e^-$$

$$\text{cathode:} \quad 4e^- + O_2(g) + 2H_2O \longrightarrow 4OH^-$$

The complete cell reaction is

$$2H_2(g) + O_2(g) \longrightarrow 2H_2O(l)$$

The cell is maintained at an elevated temperature, and the water produced by the cell reaction evaporates as it is formed.

Research in the design of fuel cells is currently being directed toward lowering the cost of the processes. Another problem involves the development of electrode catalysts that will cause the half-cell reactions to occur more rapidly.

SOME SUGGESTED READINGS

Denaro, A. R., *Elementary Electrochemistry*, Washington, D. C., Butterworth, 1965 (paper).

Gurney, R. W., *Ionic Processes in Solution*, New York, Dover, 1962 (paper).

Latimer, W. M., *Oxidation Potentials*, 2nd ed., Englewood Cliffs, N. J., Prentice-Hall, 1952.

MacInnes, D. A., *The Principles of Electrochemistry*, New York, Dover, 1961 (paper).

Murray, R. E., and Reilley, C. N., *Electroanalytical Principles*, New York, Wiley, 1964 (paper).

PROBLEMS

The more difficult problems are starred.

A table of standard electrode potentials appears in the Appendix.

10.1 Given the following: 1 faraday equals 96,490 coulombs, 1 calorie is defined as 4.184 joules, 1 volt coulomb is 1 joule, and Avogadro's number is 6.023×10^{23}. Determine: (a) the charge on a single electron in coulombs, (b) the number of calories equal to 1 electron volt (1 ev), (c) the value of the electron volt in kilocalories per mole, (d) the equivalent of 1 faraday in calories per volt.

10.2 What is the effect of an increase in temperature on the conductivity of metals and on the conductivity of solutions of electrolytes. Discuss the causes of resistance to current flow in these two types of conductors.

10.3 Sketch a cell for the electrolysis of $CdCl_2$ between inert electrodes. On the sketch indicate: (a) the signs of the electrodes, (b) the cathode and anode, (c) the directions in which the ions move, (d) the direction in which the electrons move, (e) the electrode reactions.

10.4 Sketch a voltaic cell in which the reaction is

$$Cd + Cl_2 \longrightarrow Cd^{2+} + 2Cl^-$$

On the sketch indicate: (a) the signs of the electrodes, (b) the cathode and anode, (c) the directions in which the ions move, (d) the direction in which the electrons move, (e) the electrode reactions, (f) the cell voltage.

10.5   A Cu^{2+} solution is electrolyzed using a current of 3.00 amp. What weight of Cu is plated out in 30.0 minutes?

10.6   How many minutes will it take to plate out 10.0 g of Ni from a solution of $NiSO_4$ using a current of 2.50 amp?

10.7   (a) If 0.234 g of Ag is deposited on the cathode of a silver coulometer, how many coulombs passed through the circuit? (b) If the process described in part (a) took 15.0 minutes, at what rate did the current flow?

10.8   What is the equivalent weight of a metal if a current of 0.250 amp causes 0.262 g of the metal to plate out of a solution undergoing electrolysis in 30.0 minutes?

10.9   Aluminum is produced by the elecrolysis of molten Al_2O_3. The electrode reactions are

anode: $C + 2O^{2-} \longrightarrow CO_2 + 4e^-$

cathode: $3e^- + Al^{3+} \longrightarrow Al$

In the process, the carbon of which the anode is composed is gradually consumed by the anode reaction. What is the weight loss of the anode when 1.00 kg of aluminum is prepared?

10.10 In the electrolysis of a $CuSO_4$ solution, what volume of O_2 (measured at STP) is liberated at the anode in the time that it takes to plate out 5.08 g of Cu on the cathode?

10.11 What is the molarity of H^+ in the solution after the electrolysis described in Problem 10.10? The final volume of the solution is 300 ml.

10.12 How many hours will it take to plate out all of the copper in 150 ml of a $0.150M$ Cu^{2+} solution using a current of 0.150 amp?

10.13 If 250 ml of $0.200M$ $CuCl_2$ is electrolyzed using a current of 3.00 amp for 45.0 minutes, what is the final concentration of (a) Cl^-? (b) Cu^{2+}? Assume that the volume of the solution does not change during the course of the electrolysis.

10.14 The equivalent conductance of a $0.100N$ solution of $MgCl_2$ is 97.1 cm^2/ohm equivalent at 25°C. A cell with electrodes that are 1.50 cm^2 in surface area and 0.500 cm apart is filled with $0.100N$ $MgCl_2$. How much current will flow when the potential difference between the electrodes is 5.00 v?

10.15 A conductance cell is filled with $0.0500N$ KCl (specific conductance, κ, 6.67×10^{-3}/ohm cm) at 25°C, and the measured resistance is 243 ohms. When the cell is filled with $0.0100N$ NaOH, the measured resistance is 681 ohms at 25°C. What are the specific conductance and the equivalent conductance of $0.0100N$ NaOH?

10.16 Calcium fluoride is only slightly soluble in water, and a saturated solution of CaF_2 may be regarded as infinitely dilute. At 25°C, the specific conductance of a saturated solution of CaF_2 is 3.64×10^{-5}/ohm cm after correction for the conductance of pure water. At 25°C, the equivalent conductance of CaF_2 at infinite dilution, estimated from the Λ_0 values of other salts, is 85.4 cm^2/ohm equivalent. (a) What is the solubility of

CaF_2 in equivalents per liter? (b) What is the molar solubility of CaF_2? (c) How many grams of CaF_2 will dissolve in 100 ml of H_2O?

10.17 Given the following Λ_0 values at 25°C (in cm^2/ohm equivalent): HCl, 426.2; KCl, 149.9; $CaCl_2$, 135.8; NaCl, 126.5; Na_2SO_4, 129.9. Calculate the *equivalent* conductance at infinite dilution of: (a) H_2SO_4, (b) K_2SO_4, (c) $CaSO_4$.

10.18 (a) Given the following Λ_0 values at 25°C (in cm^2/ohm equivalent): $AgNO_3$, 133.4; KCl, 149.9; KNO_3, 144.9. What is the equivalent conductance at infinite dilution of AgCl? (b) Silver chloride is only slightly soluble in water, and a saturated solution of AgCl may be regarded as infinitely dilute. At 25°C, the specific conductance, κ, of a saturated solution is $1.80 \times 10^{-6}/ohm$ cm after correction for the conductance of pure water. What is the solubility of AgCl in moles per liter at 25°C?

10.19 Hydrofluoric acid is a weak electrolyte. At 25°C, the equivalent conductance of $0.00200M$ HF is 176.2 cm^2/ohm equivalent. The equivalent conductance at infinite dilution of HF is 405.2 cm^2/ohm equivalent. What is the degree of dissociation, α, of HF in a $0.00200M$ solution?

10.20 At 25°C, the specific conductance, κ, of a $0.0100N$ solution of propanoic acid, $HC_3H_5O_2$, is $1.41 \times 10^{-4}/ohm$ cm. The equivalent conductance at infinite dilution of propanoic acid, at 25°C, is 385.6 cm^2/ohm equivalent. Determine the degree of dissociation, α, of propanoic acid in a $0.0100N$ solution.

10.21 (a) What is $\mathscr{E}°$ for the cell

$$Sn \,|\, Sn^{2+} \,\|\, Ag^+ \,|\, Ag$$

(b) Write an equation for the cell reaction. (c) Which electrode is positive?

10.22 (a) Give the notation for a cell that utilizes the reaction

$$Cl_2(g) + 2I^-(aq) \longrightarrow 2Cl^-(aq) + I_2(s)$$

(b) What is $\mathscr{E}°$ for the cell? (c) Which electrode is the cathode?

10.23 For the cell

$$Zn \,|\, Zn^{2+} \,\|\, In^{3+} \,|\, In$$

$\mathscr{E}°$ is $+0.4198$ v. Use the emf of the cell and the $\mathscr{E}°$ for the Zn^{2+}/Zn couple to calculate $\mathscr{E}°$ for the In^{3+}/In half reaction.

10.24 From the table of standard electrode potentials (reactions in acid solution) that appears in the appendix, select a suitable substance for each of the following transformations (assume that all soluble substances are present in $1M$ concentrations): (a) an oxidizing agent capable of oxidizing Ni to Ni^{2+} but not Pb to Pb^{2+}, (b) an oxidizing agent capable of oxidizing H_2S to S but not H_2SO_3 to SO_4^{2-}, (c) a reducing agent capable of reducing Ce^{4+} to Ce^{3+} but not PbO_2 to Pb^{2+}, (d) a reducing agent capable of reducing Cr^{3+} to Cr^{2+} but not Cr^{3+} to Cr.

10.25 Use $\mathscr{E}^\circ$ values to predict whether or not the following skeleton equations represent reactions that will occur in acid solution with all soluble substances present in $1M$ concentrations. All reactants and products other than H^+ and H_2O are shown below. Complete and balance the equation for each reaction that is predicted to occur.

(a) $Au^+ \rightarrow Au + Au^{3+}$

(b) $Fe + Fe^{3+} \rightarrow Fe^{2+}$

(c) $Co^{2+} \rightarrow Co + Co^{3+}$

(d) $Cr_2O_7^{2-} + Cr \rightarrow Cr^{3+}$

10.26 Predict whether or not each of the following reactions will occur spontaneously in acid solution, and write a balanced chemical equation for each reaction that is predicted to occur. Assume that soluble reactants and products are present in $1M$ concentrations. (a) Oxidation of Co^{2+} to Co^{3+} by Br_2 (reduced to Br^-), (b) reduction of Br_2 to Br^- by H_2O_2 (oxidized to O_2), (c) oxidation of Mn^{2+} to MnO_4^- by Ce^{4+} (reduced to Ce^{3+}), (d) oxidation of Cl^- to Cl_2 by NO_3^- (reduced to NO), (e) reduction of Mn^{2+} to Mn by Zn (oxidized to Zn^{2+}).

10.27 The following reactions occur at 25°C with all soluble substances present in $1M$ concentrations:

$$Zn + 2Eu^{3+} \longrightarrow Zn^{2+} + 2Eu^{2+}$$

$$Zr + 2Zn^{2+} \longrightarrow Zr^{4+} + 2Zn$$

$$4Sc + 3Zr^{4+} \longrightarrow 4Sc^{3+} + 3Zr$$

From this information alone, predict whether the following reactions will occur under similar conditions.

(a) $Sc + 3Eu^{3+} \rightarrow Sc^{3+} + 3Eu^{2+}$

(b) $4Eu^{2+} + Zr^{4+} \rightarrow 4Eu^{3+} + Zr$

(c) $2Sc + 3Zn^{2+} \rightarrow 2Sc^{3+} + 3Zn$

*10.28 (a) For the reaction (at 25°C)

$$Pb(s) + Cl_2(g) \longrightarrow PbCl_2(s)$$

$\Delta G^\circ = -75.04$ kcal. Calculate $\mathscr{E}^\circ$ for a cell utilizing this reaction. (b) A half cell can be prepared in which a Pb electrode is in contact with $PbCl_2(s)$, which in turn is in contact with a solution containing Cl^- ions.

$$2e^- + PbCl_2(s) \rightleftharpoons Pb(s) + 2Cl^-(aq)$$

Determine $\mathscr{E}^\circ$ for this half reaction by designing a cell for the reaction given in part (a) and by using the cell emf calculated in part (a). (c) Diagram a cell, and calculate $\mathscr{E}^\circ$ for the cell, using the reaction:

$$Pb^{2+} + 2Cl^- \longrightarrow PbCl_2(s)$$

10.29 For the following standard cell

$$Ag \,|\, AgCl(s) \,|\, Cl^- \,\|\, Ag^+ \,|\, Ag$$

the anode reaction is $Ag + Cl^- \rightarrow AgCl + e^-$. (a) Write the equation for the cell reaction. (b) Calculate $\mathscr{E}^\circ$ for the cell. (c) Determine ΔG°.

10.30 (a) Diagram a cell for which the cell reaction is

$$H^+ + OH^- \longrightarrow H_2O$$

(b) Calculate $\mathscr{E}^\circ$ for the cell and ΔG° for the reaction.

10.31 (a) Diagram a cell for which the cell reaction (in acid solution) is

$$2H_2 + O_2 \longrightarrow 2H_2O$$

(b) Calculate $\mathscr{E}^\circ$ for the cell and ΔG° for the reaction.

10.32 Why does the measurement of the density of the electrolyte in a lead storage battery give an indication of the state of charge of the battery?

10.33 What is the concentration of Cd^{2+} in a cell

$$Cd \,|\, Cd^{2+}(?M) \,\|\, Ni^{2+}(2.00M) \,|\, Ni$$

if the emf of the cell is 0.200 v?

10.34 (a) Calculate the emf of the cell

$$Tl \,|\, Tl^+(0.0500M) \,\|\, H^+(2.00M) \,|\, H_2(0.100\ atm) \,|\, Pt$$

(b) Write an equation for the cell reaction. (c) Which electrode is negative?

10.35 (a) According to the $\mathscr{E}^\circ$ value, should the following reaction proceed spontaneously at 25°C with all soluble substances present at $1.00M$ concentration?

$$MnO_2(s) + 4H^+(aq) + 2Cl^-(aq) \longrightarrow Mn^{2+}(aq) + 2H_2O + Cl_2(g)$$

(b) Would the reaction be spontaneous if the concentrations of H^+ and Cl^- were each increased to $10.0M$?

10.36 For a half reaction of the form

$$M^{2+} + 2e^- \rightleftharpoons M$$

what would be the effect on the electrode potential if (a) the concentration of M^{2+} were doubled, (b) the concentration of M^{2+} were cut in half?

10.37 For the half reaction

$$Cr_2O_7^{2-} + 14H^+ + 6e^- \rightleftharpoons 2Cr^{3+} + 7H_2O$$

$\mathscr{E}^\circ$ is $+1.33$ v. What would the potential be if the concentration of $H^+(aq)$ were reduced to $0.100M$?

*10.38   Given the following standard cell:

$$Sn \mid Sn^{2+} \parallel Pb^{2+} \mid Pb$$

(a) Calculate the value of $\mathscr{E}°$ for the cell. (b) Initially both Sn^{2+} and Pb^{2+} are present in $1.00M$ concentrations. When the cell operates, the concentration of Sn^{2+} increases and the concentration of Pb^{2+} decreases. What are the concentrations of the ions when $\mathscr{E}$ is zero?

10.39   (a) Determine the emf, at 25°C, of the cell

$$Pt \mid H_2(g,\ 1.00\ atm) \mid H^+(0.0250M) \parallel H^+(5.00M) \mid H_2(g,\ 1.00\ atm) \mid Pt$$

(b) Write an equation for the "cell reaction." (c) Determine $\mathscr{E}$ for the cell if the pressure of $H_2(g)$ is changed to 2.00 atm in the anode half cell and to 0.100 atm in the cathode half cell.

10.40   (a) Determine the emf of a concentration cell prepared from two Al^{3+}/Al half cells, one in which the concentration of Al^{3+} is $2.00M$ and a second in which the concentration of Al^{3+} is $0.500M$. (b) Write an equation for the "cell reaction." (c) Which electrode is negative?

The very important nonmetals hydrogen and oxygen have been discussed in Chapter 8. In this chapter, we shall survey the chemistry of the group 0, group VII A, and group VI A nonmetals.

THE NONMETALS, PART I

THE NOBLE GASES

The outstanding characteristic of the noble gases is their low order of chemical reactivity. Until 1962, no true compounds of these elements were known, and hence they were called the "inert gases." Since 1962, approximately 25 compounds of the heavier elements of the group have been prepared.

11.1 Physical Properties of the Noble Gases

The properties of the noble gases reflect their very stable electronic configurations. Helium has a complete $n = 1$ shell $(1s^2)$; the outermost shell of each of the other noble gases consists of eight electrons arranged in the configuration $ns^2\ np^6$, where n, the principal quantum number, is the same as the number of the period in which the element is found.

The atoms of a group 0 element have no tendency to combine with each other to form polyatomic molecules; each element occurs in nature as a colorless monatomic gas. The low melting points and boiling points of these elements (Table 11.1) are evidence of the weak nature of the forces of attrac-

Table 11.1

Some Properties of the Noble Gases

Gas	Melting Point (°C)	Boiling Point (°C)	Ionization Potential (ev)	Abundance in Atmosphere (Volume %)[a]
He	—[b]	−268.9	24.6	5×10^{-4}
Ne	−248.6	−245.9	21.6	2×10^{-3}
Ar	−189.3	−185.8	15.8	0.94
Kr	−157	−152.9	14.0	1×10^{-4}
Xe	−112	−107.1	12.1	9×10^{-6}
Rn	−71	−61.8	10.8	trace

[a] Dry air at sea level.
[b] −272.2° C at 26 atm pressure.

tion between their atoms. These forces are van der Waals forces, caused by the motion of electrons (Section 3.10). Furthermore, each element has a melting point that lies close to its boiling point. Thus the elements exist as liquids over very narrow temperature ranges, and the forces of attraction of a crystal must be very similar to those of the corresponding liquid.

Within the group, the boiling point and melting point increase with increasing atomic number. This trend is expected, since the strength of van der Waals forces depends upon the number of electrons in the atoms. In addition, the size of the atom increases with increasing atomic number and the outer electrons become slightly less tightly held—a factor which also causes stronger van der Waals forces. This last effect is also shown by the ionization energies of the noble gases; the ionization potentials decrease in a regular fashion from helium to radon (Table 11.1).

All the noble gases occur in the atmosphere (Table 11.1), and Ne, Ar, Kr, and Xe are by-products of the fractionation of liquid air. Certain natural gas deposits (located principally in Kansas) contain a higher percentage of helium than is found in air; these constitute the major commercial source of helium. Isotopes of radon are produced in nature by the decay of certain radioactive elements. All the isotopes of radon are themselves radioactive;

$^{222}_{86}$Rn is produced by the radioactive decay of $^{226}_{88}$Ra and has a half-life of 3.82 days, the longest of any radon isotope.[1]

Cryogenics is the study of phenomena that occur at extremely low temperatures. Liquid helium may be cooled to a very low temperature by pumping away helium vapor from the evaporating liquid, and temperatures below 1°K have been reached in this manner. (Temperatures close to 0.001°K have been obtained by other techniques applied after initial cooling by helium evaporation.)

When liquid helium (helium I; normal boiling point 4.2°K) is cooled below 2.18°K, a new form of helium (helium II) is obtained. Whereas helium I has properties characteristic of ordinary liquids, helium II has such remarkable properties that it has been called a "fourth state of matter" or a "degenerate gas." Among the unusual properties of helium II are: an exceptionally low viscosity (about 1/1000 that of hydrogen gas), an extremely high thermal conductivity (about 600 times that of copper at room temperature), and a peculiar flow phenomenon in which the liquid climbs up the walls of the container and over the top, flows down the outside, and drips off the bottom. Helium II may be produced only from $^4_2$He. The other naturally occurring isotope of helium, $^3_2$He, which constitutes about $1.3 \times 10^{-4}\%$ of natural helium, exists in only one liquid state, helium I.

11.2   Chemistry of the Noble Gases

It has long been known that noble gases form **clathrates**, materials in which atoms or molecules of a guest substance (such as a noble gas) are trapped in cavities, or cages, of a crystal of a host substance (such as hydroquinone, $C_6H_4(OH)_2$). Clathrates are known for each of the noble gases except helium; the small size of helium atoms enables them to escape from the cages of any host crystal. The noble-gas hydrates are clathrates and are produced by crystallizing water under a high pressure of a noble gas. In none of these materials, however, does the noble gas atom form a chemical bond, and the clathrates cannot be regarded as authentic chemical compounds.

The first genuine chemical reaction of a noble gas to be observed, the reaction of xenon with platinum hexafluoride (PtF_6), was reported by Neil Bartlett in 1962. Platinum hexafluoride is a powerful oxidizing agent; it reacts with oxygen to give $[O_2^+][PtF_6^-]$. Since the first ionization potential of *molecular* oxygen (12.2 ev)

$$O_2 \longrightarrow O_2^+ + e^-$$

is close to the first ionization potential of xenon (12.1 ev), Bartlett reasoned that xenon should react with PtF_6. Experiment verified the prediction, and a

---

[1] The half-life is the period of time that it takes for half of the atoms of radioactive material to disappear (Section 21.3).

red crystalline solid, originally assigned the formula $Xe^+[PtF_6^-]$, is produced by the reaction. Subsequent study has shown that the composition of the product of this reaction is complex and conforms to the formula $Xe(PtF_6)_x$, where x lies between 1 and 2. Xenon also reacts with RuF_6, RhF_6, and PuF_6.

The best characterized noble-gas compounds are the xenon fluorides: XeF_2, XeF_4, and XeF_6. Each of these compounds may be prepared by direct reaction of Xe and F_2; the choice of reaction conditions, particularly the proportion of Xe to F_2 used, determines which fluoride is obtained. The xenon fluorides are colorless crystalline solids (Table 11.2).

Table 11.2

Properties of Some Compounds of Xenon

Oxidation State	Compound	Form	Melting Point (°C)	Heat of Formation (kcal/mole)
2+	XeF_2	colorless crystals	140	−37
4+	XeF_4	colorless crystals	114	−68
6+	XeF_6	colorless crystals	48	−96
	$XeOF_4$	colorless liquid	−28	
	XeO_3	colorless crystals		+96
8+	XeO_4	colorless gas		
	$Na_4XeO_6 \cdot 8H_2O$	colorless crystals		

Xenon hexafluoride reacts with alkali metal fluorides to produce fluoroxenates. For example,

$$CsF + XeF_6 \longrightarrow CsXeF_7$$

$$2CsXeF_7 \longrightarrow Cs_2XeF_8 + XeF_6$$

The compounds Cs_2XeF_8 and Rb_2XeF_8 are the most stable compounds of xenon known.

Oxygen-containing compounds of xenon are produced by reactions of the xenon fluorides with water. Partial hydrolysis of XeF_6 yields $XeOF_4$, a colorless liquid.

$$XeF_6(s) + H_2O \longrightarrow XeOF_4(l) + 2HF(g)$$

Complete hydrolysis of XeF_6, or hydrolysis of $XeOF_4$, produces a solution that yields solid XeO_3 upon evaporation.

$$XeF_6(s) + 3H_2O \longrightarrow XeO_3(aq) + 6HF(aq)$$

$$XeOF_4(l) + 2H_2O \longrightarrow XeO_3(aq) + 4HF(aq)$$

In addition, XeO_3 is also produced by the disproportionation of XeF_4 in water.

$$6XeF_4(s) + 12H_2O \longrightarrow 2XeO_3(aq) + 4Xe(g) + 3O_2(g) + 24HF(aq)$$

Xenon trioxide, or xenon(VI) oxide, functions as a strong oxidizing agent in aqueous solution, but the dry solid decomposes to the elements explosively. In alkaline solution, XeO_3 is converted into the xenate ion

$$XeO_3(aq) + OH^-(aq) \rightleftharpoons HXeO_4^-(aq)$$

which slowly disproportionates into a Xe(VIII) species, XeO_6^{4-}, and Xe gas

$$2HXeO_4^-(aq) + 2OH^-(aq) \longrightarrow XeO_6^{4-}(aq) + Xe(g) + O_2(g) + 2H_2O$$

The perxenate ion, XeO_6^{4-}, is a powerful oxidizing agent in aqueous solution. Solid perxenates, such as $Na_4XeO_6 \cdot 8H_2O$ and $[Ba_2XeO_6]_2 \cdot H_2O$, have been isolated. The explosively unstable xenon(VIII) oxide, XeO_4, has been prepared by the reaction of sodium perxenate with concentrated sulfuric acid.

$$Na_4XeO_6 + 2H_2SO_4 \longrightarrow XeO_4 + 2Na_2SO_4 + 2H_2O$$

The properties of some of the compounds of xenon are listed in Table 11.2.

The order of the group 0 elements according to decreasing reactivity (increasing ionization potential, Table 11.1) should be: $Rn > Xe > Kr > Ar > Ne > He$. Thus radon should be the most reactive noble gas. There is evidence that Rn reacts with fluorine; however, the radioactive disintegration of Rn isotopes makes the chemistry of Rn difficult to assess. Krypton is not so reactive as Xe, but a few compounds of Kr have been prepared. The most important of these compounds is KrF_2, which is made by subjecting a mixture of Kr and F_2 to an electric discharge. No compounds of He, Ne, or Ar have been prepared as yet.

The structures of most xenon compounds have been determined and may be interpreted by a valence bond approach. Each oxygen atom in XeO_4 may be considered to bond to the xenon atom by means of one of the four electron pairs in the valence level of the xenon atom. The observed tetrahedral structure of XeO_4 is consistent with the arrangement of these four electron pairs in a set of sp^3 hybrid orbitals. In like manner, the geometry of the XeO_3 molecule can be interpreted in terms of sp^3 hybridization with one of the hybrid orbitals occupied by an unshared electron pair (see the structure of NH_3 in Figure 4.8).

Each of the species XeF_4, $XeOF_4$, and XeO_6^{4-} may be considered to have six electron pairs surrounding the xenon atom and arranged in d^2sp^3 hybrid orbitals (Figure 11.1). In XeF_4, four electrons from the four F atoms together with four of the eight valence electrons of the Xe atom make up four bond pairs, and the remaining four electrons of Xe constitute two unshared electron pairs. The octahedral arrangement of these six electron pairs with

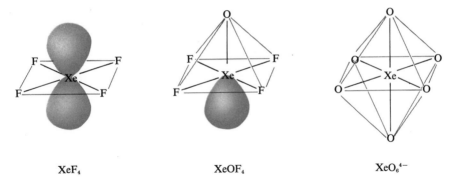

XeF₄   XeOF₄   XeO₆⁴⁻

Figure 11.1 Structures of XeF_4, $XeOF_4$, and XeO_6^{4-}.

unshared electron pairs at an angle of 180° from each other results in a square planar XeF_4 molecule.

An O atom needs two electrons to complete the $n = 2$ level; hence the O atom of $XeOF_4$ may be considered to supply no electrons to the bonding of the molecule but rather to bond through one of the unshared electron pairs of XeF_4. The resulting molecule is square pyramidal with the O atom at the apex.

For the bonding in the XeO_6^{4-} ion, we may imagine that the eight valence electrons of the Xe atom, together with the four electrons that account for the charge of the ion, constitute six bond pairs and that the six O atoms bond to the Xe atom by means of these six electron pairs. Use of d^2sp^3 hybrid orbitals for these bond pairs results in an octahedral structure.

The structures of XeF_2 and XeF_6 predicted by the valence bond approach are shown in Figure 11.2. In XeF_2, the ten electrons in the valence shell of Xe (eight from Xe and two from the two F atoms) are assumed to occupy dsp^3 hybrid orbitals. The five electron pairs are therefore directed toward the corners of a trigonal bipyramid with the bond pairs in polar positions. Thus

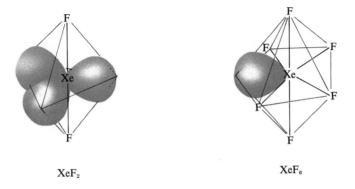

XeF₂   XeF₆

Figure 11.2 Structures of XeF_2 and XeF_6.

the XeF$_2$ molecular is linear. Analysis of the structure of XeF$_6$ leads to the prediction that the seven electron pairs in the valence shell of the Xe atom of the molecule are directed to the corners of a pentagonal bipyramid, in d^3sp^3 hybrid orbitals. The unshared electron pair is assumed to occupy one of the equatorial positions which gives the molecule the shape of a distorted octahedron.

The structures predicted by this valence bond treatment are qualitatively correct. Another approach to the bonding in xenon compounds, involving three-center molecular orbitals (Section 12.16), has been developed. Each of these theories has advantages and shortcomings, and both are currently used. However, in all of the xenon compounds, the Xe—F and Xe—O bonds are polar covalent in character, and no striking difference from other polar covalent bonds has been noted.

THE HALOGENS

The elements of group VII A, fluorine, chlorine, bromine, iodine, and astatine, are called the **halogens**. The name "halogen" is derived from Greek and means "salt former," and these elements, with the exception of astatine, occur extensively in nature in the form of halide salts. Astatine probably occurs in nature, in extremely small amounts, as a short-lived intermediate of natural radioactive decay processes. However, most of our meager information about the chemistry of astatine comes from the study of the small amounts of a radioactive isotope of this element prepared by nuclear transmutation reactions.

11.3 Group Properties

The electronic configurations of the halogens are listed in Table 11.3. Each halogen atom has one electron less than the noble gas following it in the periodic classification, and there is a marked tendency on the part of a halogen atom to attain a noble-gas configuration by the formation of a uninegative ion or a single covalent bond. Positive oxidation states exist for all the elements except fluorine.

Some properties of the halogens are summarized in Table 11.4; the symbol X stands for any halogen. Most of the properties listed increase or decrease in a regular fashion within the halogen series arranged by atomic number. The halogen of each period has a high ionization potential, second only to that of the noble gas of the period, and, within the group, ionization potential decreases with increasing atomic radius. It is easier to remove an electron

Table 11.3

Electronic Configurations of the Halogens

Element	Z	1s	2s	2p	3s	3p	3d	4s	4p	4d	4f	5s	5p	5d	6s	6p
F	9	2	2	5												
Cl	17	2	2	6	2	5										
Br	35	2	2	6	2	6	10	2	5							
I	53	2	2	6	2	6	10	2	6	10		2	5			
At	85	2	2	6	2	6	10	2	6	10	14	2	6	10	2	5

from an iodine atom than from the much smaller fluorine atom, and iodine apparently forms a unipositive ion in a few of its reactions. Fluorine, chlorine, and bromine do not form positive ions under any circumstance.

Within any A family of the periodic classification, metallic properties increase with increase in atomic number. The existence of compounds in which iodine exhibits cationic behavior illustrates the appearance of weak metallic character in group VII A. Presumably, astatine is more metallic than iodine.

Under ordinary conditions, the halogens exist as diatomic molecules with a single covalent bond joining the atoms of a molecule. The molecules are held together in the solid and liquid state by temporary dipoles caused by electron displacements within the molecules (van der Waals forces). Of all the halogen molecules, I_2 is the largest, has the most electrons, and is the most polarizable; it is not surprising that the intermolecular attractions of I_2 are the strongest and that iodine has the highest melting point and boiling point. At ordinary temperatures and pressures, I_2 is a solid, Br_2 is a liquid, and Cl_2 and F_2 are gases.

Table 11.4

Some Properties of the Halogens

	F_2	Cl_2	Br_2	I_2
color	pale yellow	yellow-green	red-brown	violet-black
melting point (°C)	−218	−101	−7	+113
boiling point (°C)	−188	−35	+59	+183
atomic radius (Å)	0.72	0.99	1.14	1.33
ionic radius, X^- (Å)	1.36	1.81	1.95	2.16
first ionization potential (ev)	17.4	13.0	11.8	10.4
electron affinity (ev)	−3.6	−3.8	−3.5	−3.2
electronegativity	4.0	3.0	2.8	2.5
bond energy (kcal/mole)	37	58	46	36
standard electrode potential (v) $2e^- + X_2 \rightleftharpoons 2X^-$	+2.87	+1.36	+1.07	+0.54

Each halogen is the most reactive nonmetal of its period, and fluorine is the most reactive of all the nonmetals. Fluorine has the highest electronegativity of any element and is one of the strongest oxidizing agents known. The electronegativity of the halogens decreases in the order $F > Cl > Br > I$, and the oxidizing power of the halogens decreases in the same order.

The values for electron affinity and bond energy are listed in Table 11.4 and do not change in a regular order from F_2 to I_2. One might expect that the values for fluorine would be the largest in view of the trends in electronegativities and electrode potentials. The reasons for the comparatively small electron affinity of fluorine and for the relatively low F—F bond energy are not completely understood; it is thought that the repulsion of the small, highly dense electron cloud of the fluorine atom is responsible for these effects.

Recall that electrode potentials refer to processes occurring in water solution in which all materials are present at unit activity. On this basis, the superior oxidizing ability of fluorine in comparison to the other halogens can be explained, in spite of fluorine's relatively small electron affinity, by consideration of the several steps involved in the conversion of the free halogens to halide ions in water solution (Table 11.5).

Table 11.5

Enthalpies of some Halogen Reactions (kcal)

Reaction			F_2	Cl_2	Br_2	I_2
X_2 (standard state)	$\longrightarrow$	$2X(g)$	+37	+58	+53	+51
$2X(g) + 2e^-(g)$	$\longrightarrow$	$2X^-(g)$	−167	−174	−163	−149
$2X^-(g)$	$\longrightarrow$	$2X^-(aq)$	−246	−178	−162	−144
X_2 (standard state) $+ 2e^-(g)$	$\longrightarrow$	$2X^-(aq)$	−376	−294	−272	−242

In the first step, heat is *absorbed* in the dissociation of the halogen molecules into gaseous halogen atoms. The enthalpy of dissociation of iodine includes the energy needed to convert $I_2(s)$ to $I_2(g)$ as well as the bond energy of I_2, and the enthalpy of dissociation of bromine includes the heat needed to convert $Br_2(l)$ to $Br_2(g)$. In the second step, heat is *evolved* (the electron affinity) by the formation of the gaseous halide ion. In the third step, heat is *evolved* by the hydration of the ions. The fluoride ion, which is the smallest of all the halide ions and has the highest charge density, has the highest enthalpy of hydration.

For each of the halogens, the algebraic sum of the enthalpies listed in Table 11.5 gives a measure of the vigor of the formation of the halide ion in water solution. It should be noted that the final equation of Table 11.5 involves gaseous electrons; however, the enthalpy values relating to this equation are adequate for the purpose of comparison. It is obvious that the high enthalpy of hydration of the fluoride ion (and to a lesser extent the low enthalpy of dissociation of the fluorine molecule) more than compensate for the difference in electron affinity. Therefore in water solution, fluorine is the most easily reduced halogen and consequently the strongest oxidizing agent.

In anhydrous reactions, fluorine is again the most reactive halogen; this is shown by the enthalpies of formation of the halides. The values listed in Table 11.6 are the heat effects when 1 mole of each of the compounds listed

Table 11.6

Enthalpies of Formation of Some Halides (kcal/mole)

	X = F	X = Cl	X = Br	X = I
NaX(s)	−136.0	−98.2	−86.3	−69.5
KX(s)	−134.5	−104.2	−94.2	−78.9
HX(g)	−64.2	−22.1	−8.7	+6.2

is prepared from the elements in their standard states (25°C). In each series, more heat is liberated in the preparation of the fluoride than in the production of any other halide, and the values decline in the expected order. The relatively low energy of the F—F bond (energy that is absorbed in the preparation) coupled with the relatively high energies of the short, strong bonds that fluorine forms with most other nonmetals (energy evolved) is believed to explain this effect for the covalent halides. Crystalline fluorides have high lattice energies because the F^- ion is relatively small and has a high charge density.

The relative oxidizing ability of the halogens may be observed in displacement reactions. Thus fluorine can displace chlorine, bromine, and iodine from their salts; chlorine can displace bromine and iodine from their salts; and bromine can displace iodine from iodides.

$$F_2(g) + 2NaCl(s) \longrightarrow 2NaF(s) + Cl_2(g)$$

$$Cl_2(g) + 2Br^-(aq) \longrightarrow 2Cl^-(aq) + Br_2(l)$$

$$Br_2(l) + 2I^-(aq) \longrightarrow 2Br^-(aq) + I_2(s)$$

Since fluorine actively oxidizes water (producing O_2), displacement reactions involving F_2 cannot be run in water solution.

11.4 Preparation of the Halogens

The principal natural sources of the halogens are listed in Table 11.7. Fluorine must be prepared by an electrochemical process because no suitable chemical agent is sufficiently powerful to oxidize fluoride ion to fluorine. Furthermore,

Table 11.7

Occurrence of the Halogens

Element	Percent of Earth's Crust	Occurrence
fluorine	0.1	CaF_2 (fluorspar), Na_3AlF_6 (cryolite)
chlorine	0.2	Cl^- (sea water and underground brines) $NaCl$ (rock salt)
bromine	0.001	Br^- (sea water, underground brines, solid salt beds)
iodine	0.001	I^- (oil-well brines, sea water) $NaIO_3$, $NaIO_4$ (impurities in Chilean saltpeter, $NaNO_3$)

since the oxidation of water is easier to accomplish than the oxidation of the fluoride ion, the electrolysis must be carried out under anhydrous conditions. In actual practice, anhydrous molten potassium hydrogen fluoride, KHF_2, is electrolyzed between carbon electrodes in a nickel or copper vessel.

$$2KHF_2(l) \xrightarrow[\text{heat}]{\text{elec.}} H_2(g) + F_2(g) + 2KF(l)$$

In the process, the nickel or copper container reacts with fluorine, and the fluoride coating thus formed protects the metal from further reaction. The KHF_2 for the electrolysis is prepared from KF and HF. Hydrogen fluoride is commercially derived from fluorospar, CaF_2 (Section 11.6), and KF is the product of the reaction of K_2CO_3 and HF.

The principal industrial source of chlorine is the electrolysis of aqueous sodium chloride, from which sodium hydroxide and hydrogen are also products.

$$2Na^+(aq) + 2Cl^-(aq) + 2H_2O \xrightarrow{\text{elec.}} H_2(g) + Cl_2(g) + 2Na^+(aq) + 2OH^-(aq)$$

Chlorine is also obtained, as a by-product, from the industrial processes in which the reactive metals Na, Ca, and Mg are prepared. In each of these processes, an anhydrous molten chloride is electrolyzed and Cl_2 gas is produced at the anode. For example,

$$2NaCl(l) \xrightarrow{\text{elec.}} 2Na(l) + Cl_2(g)$$

Bromine is commercially prepared by the oxidation of the bromide ion of salt brines or sea water with chlorine as the oxidizing agent.

$$Cl_2(g) + 2Br^-(aq) \longrightarrow 2Cl^-(aq) + Br_2(l)$$

The liberated Br_2 is removed from the solution by a stream of air and, in subsequent steps, collected from the air and purified.

In the United States, the principal commercial source of iodine is the iodide ion found in oil-well brines; free iodine is obtained by chlorine displacement.

$$Cl_2(g) + 2I^-(aq) \longrightarrow 2Cl^-(aq) + I_2(s)$$

In addition, iodine is commercially obtained from the iodate impurity found in Chilean nitrates; sodium bisulfite is used to reduce the iodate ion.

$$2IO_3^-(aq) + 5HSO_3^-(aq) \longrightarrow I_2(s) + 5SO_4^{2-}(aq) + 3H^+(aq) + H_2O$$

With the exception of fluorine (which must be prepared electrochemically), the free halogens are usually prepared in the laboratory by the action of oxidizing agents on aqueous solutions of the hydrogen halides or solutions containing the sodium halides and sulfuric acid.

From a table of standard electrode potentials, we can get an approximate idea of what oxidizing agents will satisfactorily oxidize a given halide ion. Thus any couple with a standard electrode potential more positive than $+1.36$ should oxidize chloride ion as well as bromide ion ($\mathscr{E}° = +1.07$ v) and iodide ion ($\mathscr{E}° = +0.54$ v). Recall, however, that standard electrode potentials are listed for half reactions at 25°C with all materials at unit activity. Thus, even though the standard electrode potential of $MnO_2 \rightarrow Mn^{2+}$ is only $+1.23$ v, MnO_2 is capable of oxidizing the chloride ion if concentrated HCl is used (rather than HCl at unit activity) and if the reaction is heated. In actual practice, $KMnO_4$, $K_2Cr_2O_7$, PbO_2, and MnO_2 are frequently used to prepare the free halogens from halide ions.

$$MnO_2(s) + 4H^+(aq) + 2Cl^-(aq) \longrightarrow Mn^{2+}(aq) + Cl_2(g) + 2H_2O$$

$$2MnO_4^-(aq) + 16H^+(aq) + 10Br^-(aq) \longrightarrow 2Mn^{2+}(aq) + 5Br_2(l) + 8H_2O$$

$$Cr_2O_7^{2-}(aq) + 14H^+(aq) + 6I^-(aq) \longrightarrow 2Cr^{3+}(aq) + 3I_2(s) + 7H_2O.$$

Some of the reactions of the halogens are summarized in Table 11.8.

Table 11.8

Some Reactions of the Halogens ($X_2 = F_2$, Cl_2, Br_2, or I_2)

General Reaction	Remarks
$nX_2 + 2M \longrightarrow 2MX_n$	F_2, Cl_2 with practically all metals; Br_2, I_2 with all except noble metals
$X_2 + H_2 \longrightarrow 2HX$	
$3X_2 + 2P \longrightarrow 2PX_3$	with excess P; similar reactions with As, Sb, and Bi
$5X_2 + 2P \longrightarrow 2PX_5$	with excess X_2, but not with I_2; SbF_5, $SbCl_5$, AsF_5, $AsCl_5$, and BiF_5 may be similarly prepared
$X_2 + 2S \longrightarrow S_2X_2$	with Cl_2, Br_2
$X_2 + H_2O \longrightarrow H^+ + X^- + HOX$	not with F_2
$2X_2 + 2H_2O \longrightarrow 4H^+ + 4X^- + O_2$	F_2 rapidly; Cl_2, Br_2 slowly in sunlight
$X_2 + H_2S \longrightarrow 2HX + S$	
$X_2 + CO \longrightarrow COX_2$	Cl_2, Br_2
$X_2 + SO_2 \longrightarrow SO_2X_2$	F_2, Cl_2
$X_2 + 2X'^- \longrightarrow X_2' + 2X^-$	$F_2 > Cl_2 > Br_2 > I_2$
$X_2 + X_2' \longrightarrow 2XX'$	formation of the interhalogen compounds (all except IF)

11.5   The Interhalogen Compounds

The halogens react with each other to produce a number of interhalogen compounds that conform to the general formula XX'_n, where X and X' are different halogen atoms and n is 1, 3, 5, or 7. All the compounds with the formula XX' (such as BrCl) are known except IF. Three XX'_3 compounds have been prepared (ClF_3, BrF_3, and ICl_3), and three XX'_5 compounds are known (ClF_5, BrF_5, and IF_5). The only XX'_7 compound that has been made is IF_7.

With the exception of ICl_3, all the molecules for which n of the formula XX'_n is greater than 1 are halogen fluorides in which fluorine atoms (the smallest and most electronegative of all the halogen atoms) surround a Cl, Br, or I atom. The stability of these compounds increases as the size of the central atom increases. Hence, neither BrF_7 nor ClF_7 has been prepared, although IF_7 is known; ClF_5 readily decomposes into ClF_3 and F_2, whereas BrF_5 and IF_5 are stable at temperatures above 400°C.

All the interhalogen compounds are very reactive oxidizing agents. The properties of ICl, a low-melting red solid, give evidence of the weakly metallic character of iodine. Molten ICl conducts electricity, and upon electrolysis, I_2 is discharged at the cathode. This electrochemical behavior has been interpreted as proof of the presence of I^+ ions in molten ICl.

The structures of the higher interhalogen compounds have received considerable attention because the bonding of the central atom in each of these

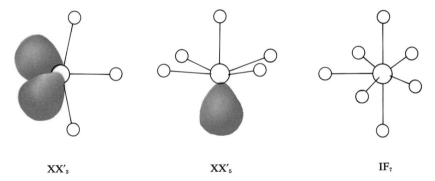

XX'_3 XX'_5 IF_7

Figure 11.3 Structures of XX'_3, XX'_5, and IF_7 molecules. The lone pairs in XX'_3 and XX'_5 molecules are responsible for some distortion from the regular T-shaped and square pyramidal structures.

molecules violates the octet principle (Figure 11.3). The X atom of the XX'_3 compounds utilizes dsp^3 hybrid orbitals for bonding, and the molecules are T-shaped. The XX'_5 molecules are square pyramidal and the central atoms use d^2sp^3 hybrid orbitals. The lone pairs of the central atoms of these two types of molecules introduce some distortion. The IF_7 molecule has a pentagonal bipyramidal structure and is bonded through d^3sp^3 hybrid orbitals of I.

All the interhalogen compounds are diamagnetic. Each halogen atom has one unpaired electron, and all the molecules have an even number of atoms. Uninegative interhalogen ions are known that are diamagnetic and contain an odd number of atoms. Ions such as ICl_2^-, IBr_2^-, and $BrCl_2^-$ are linear with the larger atom in the center. The central atom utilizes dsp^3 hybrid orbitals for bonding, and the unshared electron pairs assume positions similar to those of Xe in XeF_2 (Figure 11.2). Ions such as ICl_4^-, ClF_4^-, and IF_4^- are square planar with structures similar to the structure of XeF_4 (Figure 11.1), and they are bonded through d^2sp^3 hybrid orbitals of the central atom.

11.6 The Hydrogen Halides

Each of the hydrogen halides may be prepared by the direct reaction of hydrogen with the corresponding free halogen; the vigor of the reaction decreases markedly from fluorine to iodine.

Both HF and HCl are made industrially by the action of warm concentrated sulfuric acid on the corresponding naturally occurring halide, CaF_2 and NaCl.

$$CaF_2(s) + H_2SO_4(l) \longrightarrow CaSO_4(s) + 2HF(g)$$

$$NaCl(s) + H_2SO_4(l) \longrightarrow NaHSO_4(s) + HCl(g)$$

All the hydrogen halides are colorless gases at room temperature; sulfuric acid, on the other hand, is a high-boiling liquid. Thus the foregoing reactions are examples of a general method for the preparation of a volatile acid from its salts by means of a nonvolatile acid. At higher temperatures (ca. 500°C), further reaction occurs between $NaHSO_4$ and $NaCl$.

$$NaCl(s) + NaHSO_4(l) \longrightarrow HCl(g) + Na_2SO_4(s)$$

Hydrogen bromide and hydrogen iodide cannot be made by the action of concentrated sulfuric acid on bromides and iodides because hot, concentrated sulfuric acid oxidizes these anions to the free halogens. The bromide and iodide ions are easier to oxidize than the fluoride and chloride ions.

$$2NaBr(s) + 2H_2SO_4(l) \longrightarrow Br_2(g) + SO_2(g) + Na_2SO_4(s) + 2H_2O(g)$$

Since the iodide ion is a stronger reducing agent (more easily oxidized) than the bromide ion, S and H_2S, as well as SO_2, are obtained as reduction products from the reaction of NaI with hot concentrated sulfuric acid.

Pure HBr or HI can be obtained by the action of phosphoric acid on NaBr or NaI; phosphoric acid is an essentially nonvolatile acid and is a poor oxidizing agent.

$$NaBr(s) + H_3PO_4(l) \longrightarrow HBr(g) + NaH_2PO_4(s)$$

$$NaI(s) + H_3PO_4(l) \longrightarrow HI(g) + NaH_2PO_4(s)$$

The hydrogen halides may be prepared by the reaction of water on the appropriate phosphorus trihalide.

$$PX_3 + 3H_2O \longrightarrow 3HX(g) + H_3PO_3(aq)$$

Convenient laboratory preparations of HBr and HI have been developed in which red phosphorus, bromine or iodine, and a limited amount of water are employed and in which no attempt is made to isolate the phosphorus trihalide intermediate.

A convenient method for preparing aqueous hydrogen iodide involves the reduction of a water suspension of iodine by means of hydrogen sulfide gas.

$$H_2S(g) + I_2(s) \longrightarrow 2H^+(aq) + 2I^-(aq) + S(s)$$

Hydrogen fluoride molecules associate with each other through hydrogen bonding. The vapor consists of aggregates up to $(HF)_6$ at temperatures near the boiling point (19.4°C), but is less highly associated at higher temperatures. Gaseous HCl, HBr, and HI consist of single molecules. Liquid HF and solid HF are more highly hydrogen bonded than gaseous HF, and the boiling point and melting point of HF are abnormally high in comparison to those of the other hydrogen halides (Figure 8.2).

All the hydrogen halides are very soluble in water, and water solutions are called hydrohalic acids; for example, aqueous HI is called hydroiodic acid.

The H—F bond is stronger than any other H—X bond, and HF is a weak acid in water solution whereas HCl, HBr, and HI are completely dissociated.

$$HF(aq) \rightleftharpoons H^+(aq) + F^-(aq)$$

The F^- ions from this dissociation are largely associated with HF molecules.

$$F^-(aq) + HF(aq) \rightleftharpoons HF_2^-(aq)$$

Concentrated HF solutions are more strongly ionic than dilute solutions and contain high concentrations of ions of the type HF_2^-, $H_2F_3^-$, and higher.
   Hydrofluoric acid reacts with silica, SiO_2, and glass.

$$SiO_2(s) + 6HF(aq) \longrightarrow 2H^+(aq) + SiF_6^{2-}(aq) + 2H_2O$$

When warmed, the reaction is

$$SiO_2(g) + 4HF(aq) \longrightarrow SiF_4(g) + 2H_2O(g)$$

For this reason, hydrofluoric acid must be stored in wax or plastic containers instead of glass bottles.
   The fluorosilicate ion, SiF_6^{2-}, is an example of a large group of complex ions formed by the halide ions. Halo complexes are formed by most metals (with the notable exceptions of the group I A, group II A, and lanthanide metals) and with some nonmetals (e.g., BF_4^-). The formulas of these complex ions are most commonly of the types $(MX_4)^{n-4}$ and $(MX_6)^{n-6}$, where n is the oxidation number of the central atom of the complex.

11.7   The Metal Halides

The character of the bonding in metal halides varies widely as do the physical properties of these compounds. A metal that has a low ionization energy generally forms halides that are highly ionic and consequently have high melting and boiling points. On the other hand, metals that have comparatively high ionization energies react, particularly with halogens of low electron affinity, to form halides in which the bonding has a high degree of covalent character; such compounds have comparatively low melting points and boiling points. In general, the high-melting halides are, in the fused state, better conductors of electricity than are the low-melting compounds.
   In general, the halides of the I A metals, the II A metals (with the exception of Be), and most of the inner-transition metals are largely ionic; halides of the remaining metals are covalent to a varying degree. Within a series of halides of metals of the same period, covalent character increases from compound to compound as the oxidation number of the metal increases and the size of the cation undergoes a concomitant decrease. The equivalent conductances of the molten chlorides of some fourth-period metals are plotted in Figure 11.4. The "cations" of the compounds are isoelectronic. Potassium chloride is a

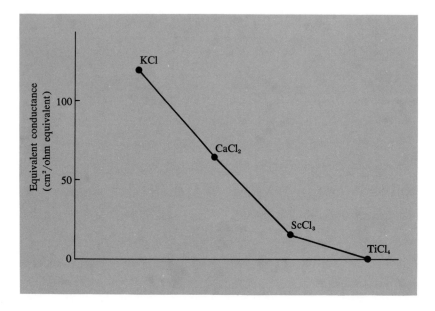

Figure 11.4 Equivalent conductances of some molten chlorides near the melting point.

completely ionic solid, and molten KCl has the highest conductance of the four compounds; $TiCl_4$ is a covalent liquid and is nonconducting.

If a metal exhibits more than one oxidation state, the halides of the highest oxidation state are the most covalent. Thus the second member of each of the following pairs is a highly covalent, volatile liquid (melting points are given in parentheses): $SnCl_2$ (246°C), $SnCl_4$ (−33°C); $PbCl_2$ (501°C), $PbCl_4$ (−15°C); $SbCl_3$ (73.4°C), $SbCl_5$ (2.8°C).

Since fluorine is the most electronegative halogen, fluorides are the most ionic of the halides, and ionic character decreases in the order: fluoride > chloride > bromide >iodide. The trend in the melting points of the sodium halides is typical:

NaF	NaCl	NaBr	NaI
993°C	801°C	755°C	651°C

The halides of aluminum are an excellent example of the relationship between ionic, or covalent, character and the size of the halide ion. Aluminum fluoride is an ionic substance. Aluminum chloride is semicovalent and crystallizes in a layer lattice in which electrically neutral layers are held together by van der Waals forces. Aluminum bromide and aluminum iodide are essentially covalent; the crystals consist of Al_2Br_6 and Al_2I_6 molecules.

The water solubility of fluorides is considerably different from that of the chlorides, bromides, and iodides. The fluorides of lithium, the group II A metals, and the lanthanides are only slightly soluble, whereas the other halides of these metals are relatively soluble.

Most chlorides, bromides, and iodides are soluble in water. The cations that form slightly soluble compounds with these halide ions include silver(I), mercury(I), lead(II), copper(I), and thallium(I).

The insolubility of the silver salts of Cl^-, Br^-, and I^- is the basis of a common test for these halide ions; AgCl is white, AgBr is cream, and AgI is yellow. The silver halide precipitates may be formed by the addition of a solution of silver nitrate to a solution containing the appropriate halide ion. Silver iodide is insoluble in excess ammonia; however, AgCl readily dissolves to form the $Ag(NH_3)_2^+$ complex ion and AgBr dissolves with difficulty. Silver fluoride is soluble; generally, MgF_2 or CaF_2 precipitates are used to confirm the presence of the fluoride ion in a solution.

If the iodide ion, in aqueous solution, is oxidized to iodine (the usual procedure employs chlorine), the I_2 can be extracted by carbon tetrachloride, which forms a two-liquid-layer system with water. The I_2 solution, in CCl_4, is violet colored. In the corresponding test for the bromide ion, the Br_2–CCl_4 solution is brown.

11.8 Oxyacids of the Halogens

The oxyacids of the halogens are listed in Table 11.9. Fluorine does not form compounds of this type. The acids of chlorine, and their salts, are the most important of these compounds.

Lewis formulas for the oxychlorine acids are shown in Figure 11.5; removal of H^+ from each of these structures gives the electronic formula of the corresponding anion. However, Lewis structures, in which each Cl and O atom has a valence-electron octet, do not show that the Cl—O bonds in these

Table 11.9

Oxyhalogen Acids

Oxidization State of the Halogen	Formula of Acid			Name of Acid	Name of Anion Derived from Acid
1+	HOCl	HOBr	HOI	hypohalous acid	hypohalite ion
3+	$HClO_2$	—	—	halous acid	halite ion
5+	$HClO_3^a$	$HBrO_3^a$	HIO_3^a	halic acid	halate ion
7+	$HClO_4$	$HBrO_4^a$	$\begin{cases} HIO_4 \\ H_4I_2O_9 \\ H_5IO_6 \end{cases}$	perhalic acid	perhalate ion

[a] Strong acids.

Figure 11.5 Lewis formulas for the oxychlorine acids.

compounds can have a considerable amount of double-bond character. For example, the experimentally observed Cl—O bond length in the ClO_4^- ion (1.46 Å) is appreciably shorter than the bond length predicted from atomic radii on the basis of single-bond formation (about 1.70 Å).

In these compounds, the Cl atom is assumed to use sp^3 hybrid orbitals for σ bonding with unshared electron pairs occupying some of the tetrahedral positions, and the observed structures are consistent with this view (Figure 11.6). The double-bond character of the bonds, which does not appreciably distort the geometry of the molecules, is assumed to arise from the overlap of unfilled $3d$ orbitals of Cl with filled $2p$ orbitals of O and is spoken of as **pπ-dπ bonding.**

Such $p\pi$-$d\pi$ bonding is particularly important in compounds in which a third-period nonmetal (Si, P, S, or Cl) is bonded to O, N, or F. Since the second-period nonmetals have no d orbitals in their valence levels, $p\pi$-$d\pi$ bonding does not occur in compounds of these elements (although double bonds may form by use of the s and p orbitals of these elements).

The oxybromine and oxyiodine anions have configurations similar to the analogous oxychlorine anions shown in Figure 11.6. The H_5IO_6 molecule is octahedral with five OH groups and one O atom in the six positions surrounding the central I atom. Presumably, this molecule is bonded by means of d^2sp^3 hybrid orbitals of I.

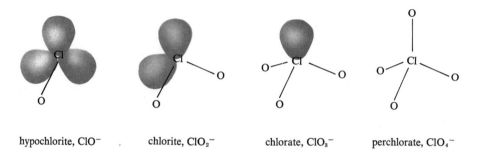

hypochlorite, ClO^- , chlorite, ClO_2^- , chlorate, ClO_3^- , perchlorate, ClO_4^-

Figure 11.6 Structures of the oxychlorine anions.

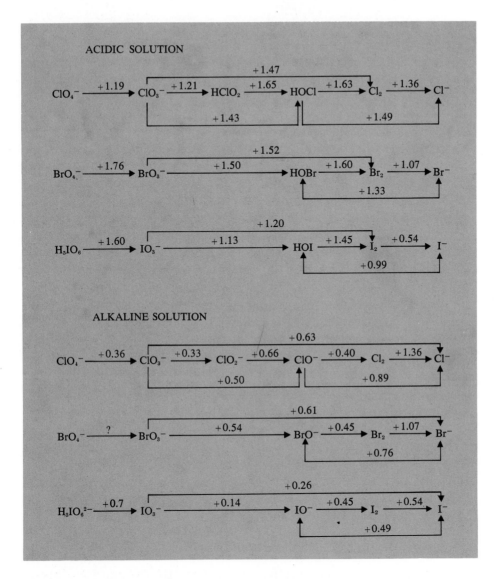

Figure 11.7 Standard electrode potential diagrams for chlorine, bromine, iodine, and their compounds.

The standard electrode potentials for Cl_2, Br_2, I_2, and the compounds of these elements in acidic and alkaline solution are summarized in Figure 11.7. The number shown over each arrow is the $\mathscr{E}°$, in volts, for the reduction of the species on the left to that on the right; an oxidation potential for a transformation from right to left may, of course, be obtained by changing the sign of $\mathscr{E}°$.

Perchloric acid ($HClO_4$), perbromic acid ($HBrO_4$), and the halic acids

($HClO_3$, $HBrO_3$, and HIO_3) are strong acids, but the remaining oxyacids are incompletely dissociated in water solution and exist in solution largely in molecular form. Hence, molecular formulas are shown in Figure 11.7 for the weak acids in acidic solution. In general, acid strength increases with increasing oxygen content.

Much of the chemistry of these compounds is effectively correlated by means of these electrode potential diagrams. Remember, however, that standard electrode potentials refer to reductions that take place at 25°C with all substances present at unit activity. Concentration changes and temperature changes alter $\mathscr{E}°$ values. Furthermore, a cell emf tells nothing about the speed of the transformation to which it applies; some reactions for which the cell emf's are positive occur so slowly that they are of no practical importance.

One of the outstanding characteristics of the oxyhalogen compounds is their ability to function as oxidizing agents; all the $\mathscr{E}°$ values are positive. The $\mathscr{E}°$ values also show that, in general, these compounds are stronger oxidizing agents in acidic solution than in alkaline solution.

Many of these oxyhalogen compounds are unstable toward disproportionation. Such materials are readily identified from the diagrams of Figure 11.7. A given substance is unstable toward disproportionation if the potential for a reduction to a lower oxidation state is more positive than the potential for a transformation from a higher oxidation state to the substance being studied. For example, in alkaline solution,

$$ClO^- \xrightarrow{+0.40} Cl_2 \xrightarrow{+1.36} Cl^-$$

Since $+1.36$ is more positive than $+0.40$, Cl_2 will disproportionate.

$$
\begin{array}{lll}
4OH^- + Cl_2 \longrightarrow 2ClO^- + 2H_2O + 2e^- & \mathscr{E}°_{ox} = -0.40 \text{ v} \\
2e^- + Cl_2 \longrightarrow 2Cl^- & \mathscr{E}° = +1.36 \text{ v} \\
\hline
2OH^- + Cl_2 \longrightarrow ClO^- + Cl^- + H_2O & \mathscr{E}° = +0.96 \text{ v}
\end{array}
$$

The $\mathscr{E}°$ values indicate that HOCl, HOBr, HOI, $HClO_2$, and ClO_3^- should disproportionate in acidic solution. In alkaline solution, all species should disproportionate except the halide ions, ClO_4^-, BrO_4^-, BrO_3^-, and $H_3IO_6^{2-}$.

In acidic solution, any reduction that has a potential more positive than $+1.23$ v theoretically can bring about the oxidation of water to O_2, since

$$2H_2O \longrightarrow O_2 + 4H^+ + 4e^- \qquad \mathscr{E}°_{ox} = -1.23 \text{ v}$$

In alkaline solution, any reduction that has a potential more positive than $+0.40$ v is theoretically capable of bringing about the oxidation:

$$4OH^- \longrightarrow O_2 + 2H_2O + 4e^- \qquad \mathscr{E}°_{ox} = -0.40 \text{ v}$$

Both these oxidations, however, occur slowly, so that it is possible to observe all the oxyhalogen compounds in solution.

The hypohalous acids (HOX) are the weakest of the halogen oxyacids. They exist in solution but cannot be prepared in pure form. Each of the three halogens is slightly soluble in water and reacts to produce a low concentration of the corresponding hypohalous acid.

$$X_2 + H_2O \longrightarrow H^+(aq) + X^-(aq) + HOX(aq)$$

All the standard potentials for these reactions are negative, and the reactions proceed to a very limited extent (see Example 10.9). Thus at 25°C, saturated solutions of the halogens contain the following HOX concentrations: HOCl, $3 \times 10^{-2} M$; HOBr, $1 \times 10^{-3} M$; HOI, $6 \times 10^{-6} M$.

The X_2-H_2O reactions may be driven to the right, and the yields of HOX increased, by the addition of Ag_2O or HgO to the reaction mixture (Section 14.11). These oxides precipitate the X^- ion and remove $H^+(aq)$.

$$2X_2 + Ag_2O(s) + H_2O \longrightarrow 2AgX(s) + 2HOX(aq)$$

$$2X_2 + 4HgO(s) + H_2O \longrightarrow HgX_2 \cdot 3HgO(s) + 2HOX(aq)$$

Each of the three halogens dissolves in alkaline solution to produce a hypohalite ion and a halide ion.

$$X_2 + 2OH^-(aq) \longrightarrow X^-(aq) + XO^-(aq) + H_2O$$

The emf for each of these reactions is positive, and each reaction is rapid. However, the hypohalite ions disproportionate in alkaline solution to the halate ions and halide ions. Fortunately, the disproportionation reactions of ClO^- and BrO^- are slow at temperatures around 0°C, so that these ions may be prepared by this method. The hypoiodite ion, however, disproportionates rapidly even at low temperatures.

Solutions of sodium hypochlorite, used commercially in cotton bleaching (e.g., Chlorox), are prepared by electrolyzing cold sodium chloride solutions as in the preparation of chlorine (Section 11.4). In this process, however, the products of the electrolysis are not kept separate; rather, the electrolyte is vigorously mixed so that the chlorine produced at the anode reacts with the hydroxide ion produced at the cathode.

anode: $$2Cl^- \longrightarrow Cl_2 + 2e^-$$

cathode: $$2e^- + 2H_2O \longrightarrow 2OH^- + H_2$$

$$Cl_2 + 2OH^- \longrightarrow OCl^- + Cl^- + H_2O$$

The overall equation for the entire process is

$$Cl^- + H_2O \xrightarrow[\text{cold}]{\text{elec.}} OCl^- + H_2$$

The hypohalous acids and hypohalites are good oxidizing agents, particularly in acidic solution. The compounds decompose not only by disproportionation but also by the liberation of O_2 from the solutions, since all the relevant $\mathscr{E}^\circ$ values for acidic half reactions are greater than $+1.23$ v and for alkaline half reactions are greater than $+0.40$ v. The reactions in which O_2 is liberated are slow, however, and are catalyzed by metal salts.

The only halous acid known is chlorous acid ($HClO_2$). This compound cannot be isolated in pure form, and even in aqueous solution it decomposes rapidly. Chlorous acid is a weak acid, but it is stronger than hypochlorous acid. The disproportionation of $HOCl$ in acidic solution does not yield $HClO_2$. The electrode potentials indicate, however, that it should be possible to make the chlorite ion by the disproportionation of ClO^- in alkaline solution; however, the disproportionation of ClO^- into ClO_3^- and Cl^- is more favorable, and ClO_2^- cannot be made from ClO^-.

Chlorites are comparatively stable in alkaline solution and may be prepared by passing chlorine dioxide gas (a very reactive odd-electron molecule) into a solution of an alkali.

$$2ClO_2(g) + 2OH^-(aq) \longrightarrow ClO_2^-(aq) + ClO_3^-(aq) + H_2O$$

A better preparation, in which no chlorate ion is produced, is the reaction of ClO_2 with an alkaline solution of sodium peroxide (which forms the hydroperoxide ion, HO_2^-, in water).

$$2ClO_2(g) + HO^-(aq) + OH^-(aq) \longrightarrow 2ClO_2^-(aq) + O_2(g) + H_2O$$

Solid chlorites are dangerous chemicals; they detonate when heated and are explosive in contact with combustible material.

We have mentioned the disproportionation reactions of the hypohalite ions.

$$3XO^- \longrightarrow XO_3^- + 2X^-$$

Thus if a free halogen is added to a hot, concentrated solution of alkali, the corresponding halide and halate ions are produced rather than the halide and hypohalite ions.

$$3X_2 + 6OH^-(aq) \longrightarrow 5X^-(aq) + XO_3^-(aq) + 3H_2O$$

The chlorates are commerically prepared by the electrolysis of hot, concentrated solutions of chlorides (instead of the cold solutions used for the electrochemical preparation of the hypochlorites). The electrolyte is stirred vigorously so that the chlorine produced at the anode reacts with the hydroxide ion that is a product of the reduction at the cathode.

anode: $$2Cl^- \longrightarrow Cl_2 + 2e^-$$

cathode: $$2e^- + 2H_2O \longrightarrow 2OH^- + H_2$$

$$3Cl_2 + 6OH^- \longrightarrow 5Cl^- + ClO_3{}^- + 3H_2O$$

If the three foregoing equations are added, after the first two equations have each been multiplied through by 3, the equation for the overall process is obtained.

$$Cl^- + 3H_2O \xrightarrow[\text{hot}]{\text{elec.}} ClO_3{}^- + 3H_2$$

The chlorate crystallizes from the concentrated solution employed as the electrolyte of the cell. Whereas chlorates are generally water soluble, they are much less soluble than the corresponding chlorides.

Solutions of a halic acid can be prepared by adding sulfuric acid to a solution of the barium salt of the acid.

$$Ba^{2+}(aq) + 2XO_3{}^-(aq) + 2H^+(aq) + SO_4^{2-}(aq) \longrightarrow BaSO_4(s)$$
$$+ 2H^+(aq) + 2XO_3{}^-(aq)$$

Pure $HBrO_3$ or $HClO_3$ cannot be isolated from aqueous solutions because of decomposition. Iodic acid, HIO_3, however, can be obtained as a white solid; this acid is generally prepared by oxidizing iodine with concentrated nitric acid. All the halic acids are strong. The halates, as well as the halic acids, are strong oxidizing agents. The reactions of chlorates with easily oxidized materials may be explosive.

Chlorine dioxide, which is used in the preparation of chlorites, may be prepared by the reduction of a chlorate, in aqueous solution, using sulfur dioxide gas as the reducing agent.

$$2ClO_3{}^-(aq) + SO_2(g) \longrightarrow ClO_2(g) + SO_4^{2-}(aq)$$

Chlorates decompose upon heating in a variety of ways. At high temperatures, and particularly in the presence of a catalyst, chlorates decompose into chlorides and oxygen (Section 8.1).

$$2KClO_3(s) \xrightarrow[\text{MnO}_2]{\text{heat}} 2KCl(s) + 3O_2(g)$$

At more moderate temperatures, in the absence of a catalyst, the decomposition yields perchlorates and chlorides.

$$4KClO_3(s) \xrightarrow{\text{heat}} 3KClO_4(s) + KCl(s)$$

Perchlorate salts are made by the controlled thermal decomposition of a chlorate or by the electrolysis of a cold solution of a chlorate. The free acid, a clear hygroscopic liquid, may be prepared by distilling a mixture of a perchlorate salt with concentrated sulfuric acid. A number of crystalline hydrates of perchloric acid are known. The compound $HClO_4 \cdot H_2O$ is of interest; the lattice positions of the crystal are occupied by H_3O^+ and ClO_4^- ions, and the solid is isomorphous (of the same crystalline structure) with NH_4ClO_4. Perchloric acid is a strong acid and a strong oxidizing agent. Concentrated $HClO_4$ may react violently when heated with organic substances; the reactions are frequently explosive.

Perbromates are prepared by the oxidation of bromates in alkaline solution using F_2 as the oxidizing agent. Several periodic acids have been prepared; the most common one is H_5IO_6. Periodates are made by the oxidation of iodates, usually by means of Cl_2 in alkaline solution. Salts of the anions IO_4^-, $I_2O_9^{4-}$, IO_6^{5-}, and IO_5^{3-} have been obtained.

SULFUR, SELENIUM, AND TELLURIUM

Group VI A includes oxygen, sulfur, selenium, tellurium, and polonium. The chemistry of oxygen, the most important and most abundant element of the group, has been discussed in Chapter 8. Polonium is produced by the radioactive disintegration of radium, and all the isotopes of polonium are radioactive. The most abundant isotope, ^{210}Po, has a half-life of only 138.7 days and not much is known definitely about the chemistry of this element.

11.9   Group Properties

The electronic configurations of the group VI A elements are listed in Table 11.10; each element is two electrons short of a noble-gas structure. Hence, these elements attain a noble-gas electronic configuration in the formation of ionic compounds by accepting two electrons per atom.

Table 11.10

Electronic Configurations of the Group VI A Elements

Element	Z	1s	2s	2p	3s	3p	3d	4s	4p	4d	4f	5s	5p	5d	6s	6p
O	8	2	2	4												
S	16	2	2	6	2	4										
Se	34	2	2	6	2	6	10	2	4							
Te	52	2	2	6	2	6	10	2	6	10		2	4			
Po	84	2	2	6	2	6	10	2	6	10	14	2	6	10	2	4

$$2Na^+ \quad :\overset{\cdot\cdot}{\underset{\cdot\cdot}{S}}:^{2-}$$

The elements also acquire noble-gas configurations through covalent-bond formation.

$$H:\overset{\cdot\cdot}{Se}:$$
$$\overset{\cdot\cdot}{H}$$

Certain properties of the group VI A elements are summarized in Table 11.11. Each member of the group is a less active nonmetal than the halogen of its period. The electronegatives of the elements decrease, in the expected manner, with increasing atomic number. Oxygen is the second most electronegative element (fluorine is first); sulfur is about as electronegative as iodine. Thus the oxides of most metals are ionic, whereas the sulfides, selenides, and tellurides of only the most active metals (such as the I A and II A metals) are truly ionic compounds.

Table 11.11

Some Properties of the Group VI A Elements

	Oxygen	*Sulfur*	*Selenium*	*Tellurium*
color	colorless	yellow	red to black	silver-white
molecular formula	O_2	S_8 rings	Se_8 rings $(Se)_n$ chains	$(Te)_n$ chains
melting point (°C)	−218.4	119	217	452
boiling point (°C)	−182.9	444.6	688	1390
atomic radius (Å)	0.74	1.04	1.17	1.37
ionic radius (2 − ion) (Å)	1.40	1.84	1.98	2.21
first ionization potential (ev)	13.6	10.4	9.8	9.0
electronegativity	3.5	2.5	2.4	2.1
bond energy (single bonds) (kcal/mole)	33	51	44	33
$\mathscr{E}°$ for reduction of element to H_2X in acidic solution (v)	+1.23	+0.14	−0.40	−0.72

The group VI A elements are predominantly nonmetallic in chemical behavior; however, metallic characteristics appear in the heavier members of the group. The trend in increasing metallic character parallels, as expected, increasing atomic number, increasing atomic radius, and decreasing ionization potential. Polonium is the most metallic member of the group; it appears to be capable of forming a Po^{2+} ion that exists in aqueous solution, and the 2 − state of polonium (e.g., in H_2Po) is unstable. Whereas tellurium is essentially nonmetallic in character, unstable salts of tellurium with anions of strong acids have been reported. The ordinary form of tellurium is metallic, and selenium exists in both metallic and nonmetallic crystalline modifications.

Sulfur, selenium, and tellurium exist in positive oxidation states in compounds in which they are combined with more electronegative elements (such as oxygen and the halogens); oxygen is considered to have a positive oxidation number only in the few compounds that it forms with fluorine. For sulfur, selenium, and tellurium, the oxidation states of 4+ and 6+ are particularly important.

The electrode potentials listed in Table 11.11 give an idea of the strength of of the group VI A elements as oxidizing agents. Oxygen is a strong oxidizing agent, but there is a striking decrease in this property from oxygen to tellurium; in fact, H_2Te and H_2Se are better *reducing* agents than hydrogen. Compare the $\mathscr{E}°$ values listed in Table 11.11 with those for the halogens in Table 11.4.

11.10   The Elements

All the members of this group exist in more than one allotropic modification. For a given element, the difference may be in molecular complexity (O_2 and O_3 for oxygen, Section 8.4), in crystalline form, or in both these factors.

The most important solid modifications of sulfur belong to the rhombic and monoclinic crystal systems (Section 7.9). The crystals of both allotropes are built up from S_8 molecules. These molecules are in the form of puckered, eight-membered rings of S atoms in which the S atoms are bonded to each other by single covalent bonds and the S—S—S bond angle is about 105° (Figure 11.8). In chemical equations, therefore, elementary sulfur should be indicated by the formula S_8. However, the usual practice is to designate sulfur

Figure 11.8   Structure of the S_8 molecule.

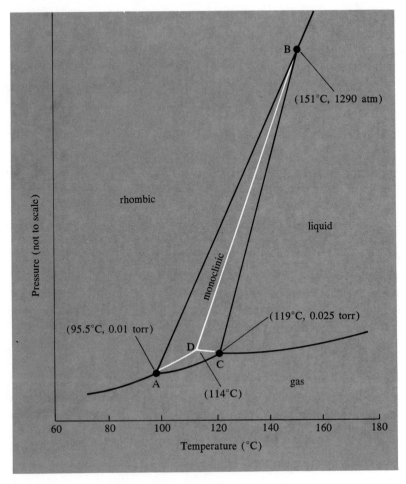

Figure 11.9   Phase diagram for sulfur.

by the symbol S; this practice leads to less complicated equations that are nevertheless stoichiometrically valid.

The phase diagram for sulfur is shown in Figure 11.9. The rhombic form of sulfur is the stable modification under ordinary conditions of temperature and pressure. Any point that falls within the triangle ABC of the diagram describes a set of temperature and pressure conditions under which monoclinic sulfur is the stable modification. If rhombic sulfur is heated under its own vapor pressure, it slowly undergoes a transition to monoclinic sulfur at 95.5°C, and the monoclinic sulfur, upon continued heating, melts at 119°C. The transition from one solid form to another is slow; rapid heating of the rhombic form causes it to melt, without going through the monoclinic form at 114°C (lines AD, DC, and DB of Figure 11.9). There are three triple, points (A, B, and C) and one metastable triple point (between rhombic, liquid, and gas at point D).

Liquid sulfur undergoes a series of changes as its temperature is increased. At the melting point, liquid sulfur is a light yellow, mobile liquid consisting principally of S_8 molecules. Upon continued heating, the sulfur changes into a red-brown highly viscous material. The viscosity reaches a maximum between 160°C and 200°C; upon further heating (up to the boiling point at 444.6°C), the viscosity of the liquid decreases. It is believed that the viscosity effect is caused by the dissociation of the S_8 rings and the formation of long chains of S atoms; at temperatures approaching the boiling point, it appears that these chains break into fragments. If sulfur is heated to approximately 200°C and then poured into cold water, a red-brown rubbery mass called plastic sulfur is obtained. It is assumed that plastic sulfur consists mainly of long chains of sulfur atoms, and the X-ray analysis of plastic sulfur has shown that it has the molecular structure characteristic of fibers. At room temperature, plastic sulfur, which is a supercooled liquid, slowly crystallizes and the S_8 rings re-form. Sulfur vapor has been shown to consist of S_8, S_6, S_4, and S_2 molecules; S_2 is paramagnetic, like O_2.

The stable modification of selenium at room temperature is a gray, metallic, hexagonal form, the crystals of which are constructed of zigzag chains of selenium atoms. It is this form that is used in photoelectric cells; the normally low electrical conductivity of hexagonal selenium is increased about 200 times by exposure of the element to light. There are two monoclinic forms of selenium, both red, and one of these has been shown to be made up of Se_8 rings that are similar to S_8 rings. In addition, amorphous forms of selenium have been described.

The common form of tellurium consists of silver-white, metallic hexagonal crystals built up from zigzag chains of tellurium atoms. A black, amorphous form of tellurium exists.

Table 11.12

Occurrence of Sulfur, Selenium, and Tellurium

Element	Percent of Earth's Crust	Occurrence
sulfur	0.05	native
		FeS_2 (pyrite), PbS (galena), HgS (cinnabar), ZnS (sphalerite), Cu_2S (chalcocite), $CuFeS_2$ (chalcopyrite)
		$CaSO_4 \cdot 2 H_2O$ (gypsum), $BaSO_4$ (barite), $MgSO_4 \cdot 7 H_2O$ (epsomite)
selenium	9×10^{-6}	small amounts of Se in some S deposits
		rare minerals: Cu_2Se, PbSe, Ag_2Se
		low concentrations in sufide ores of Cu, Fe, Pb, Ni
tellurium	2×10^{-7}	small amounts of Te in some S deposits
		rare minerals: $AuTe_2$, PbTe, Ag_2Te, Au_2Te, Cu_2Te
		low concentrations in sulfide ores of Cu, Fe

The two modifications of polonium that have been reported belong to the cubic and rhombohedral systems.

The principal forms in which sulfur, selenium, and tellurium occur in nature are listed in Table 11.12. Sulfur is obtained from large underground beds of the free element by the **Frasch process** (Figure 11.10). The sulfur is melted underground by water that is heated to approximately 170°C under pressure and forced down to the deposits. A froth of sulfur, air, and water is forced to the surface by hot, compressed air. The sulfur thus obtained is about 99.5% pure.

The principal commercial source of both selenium and tellurium is the anode sludge obtained from the electrolytic refining of copper (Section 18.5).

Some reactions of sulfur, selenium, and tellurium are summarized in Table 11.13.

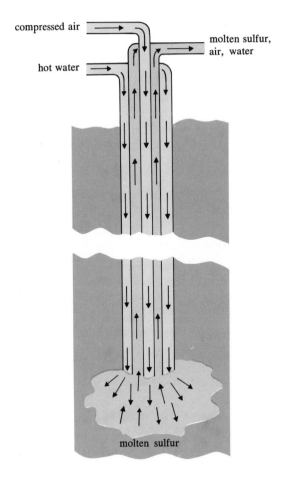

Figure 11.10 The Frasch process.

Table 11.13

Some Reactions of Sulfur, Selenium, and Tellurium

Reaction of Sulfur	Remarks
$nS + mM \longrightarrow M_mS_n$	Se, Te react similarly with many metals (not noble metals)
$nS + S^{2-} \longrightarrow S_{n+1}^{2-}$	for S and Te, $n = 1$ to 5; for Se, $n = 1$ to 4
$S + H_2 \longrightarrow H_2S$	S > Se > Te; elevated temperatures; compounds are better prepared by actions of dilute HCl on sulfides, selenides, or tellurides
$S + O_2 \longrightarrow SO_2$	S > Se > Te; dioxides of Se and Te are easier to prepare with a mixture of $O_2 + NO_2$
$S + 3F_2 \longrightarrow SF_6$	S, Se, Te with excess F_2
$S + 2F_2 \longrightarrow SF_4$	S, Se; TeF_4 is made indirectly ($TeF_6 + Te$)
$2S + X_2 \longrightarrow S_2X_2$	S, Se; $X_2 = Cl_2$ or Br_2
$S + 2X_2 \longrightarrow SX_4$	S, Se, Te with excess Cl_2; Se, Te with excess Br_2; Te with excess I_2
$S_2Cl_2 + Cl_2 \longrightarrow 2SCl_2$	SCl_2 only, SBr_2 unknown; $SeCl_2$, $SeBr_2$ (only in vapor state); $TeCl_2$, $TeBr_2$ are made by thermal decomposition of higher halides
$S + 4HNO_3 \longrightarrow SO_2 + 4NO_2 + 2H_2O$	hot, concentrated nitric acid; S yields mixtures of SO_2 and SO_4^{2-}; Se yields H_2SeO_3 ($SeO_2 \cdot H_2O$); Te yields $2TeO_2 \cdot HNO_3$

11.11 Hydrogen Compounds and Derivatives

The hydrogen compounds of sulfur, selenium, and tellurium can be prepared by the direct combination of the elements at elevated temperatures. However, direct combination is not a satisfactory laboratory source of the compounds; in addition to the inconvenience of this method of preparation, H_2S, H_2Se, and H_2Te are unstable at high temperatures, and the products are contaminated by starting materials.

The hydrogen compounds are readily obtained by the action of dilute acid on sulfides, selenides, and tellurides; for example,

$$FeS(s) + 2H^+(aq) \longrightarrow Fe^{2+}(aq) + H_2S(g)$$

The reaction of thioacetamide with water is a convenient laboratory source of H_2S.

thioacetamide   acetamide

Hydrogen sulfide, hydrogen selenide, and hydrogen telluride are colorless, unpleasant-smelling, highly poisonous gases; they are composed of angular molecules, similar to the water molecule (Figure 4.1). The physical properties of water are out of line in comparison to those of H_2S, H_2Se, and H_2Te because of the extensive hydrogen bonding that occurs between water molecules (Section 8.11).

Hydrogen sulfide reacts with oxygen to yield water and either SO_2 or free S depending upon the amount of oxygen employed. The combustion of H_2Se or H_2Te in oxygen produces water and either Se or Te.

The compounds H_2S, H_2Se, and H_2Te are all moderately soluble in water and are weak acids in aqueous solution. The trend in acid strength parallels that of the hydrogen halides—the elements of highest atomic number forming the strongest acid. Thus H_2Te is the strongest acid, and H_2S is the weakest acid of the group. The acids are diprotic and ionize in two steps.

$$H_2S(aq) \rightleftharpoons H^+(aq) + HS^-(aq)$$

$$HS^-(aq) \rightleftharpoons H^+(aq) + S^{2-}(aq)$$

The aqueous hydrogen sulfide system is discussed in Section 16.8.

The sulfides of the group I A and group II A metals are water soluble. The sulfides of the remaining metals are either very slightly soluble or decompose in the presence of water to form slightly soluble hydroxides.

$$Al_2S_3(s) + 6H_2O \longrightarrow 2Al(OH)_3(s) + 3H_2S(g)$$

Precipitation of the slightly soluble sulfides, under varying conditions, is extensively used in analytical procedures for the separation and identification of cations in solution (Section 17.3). An analytical test for the sulfide ion consists of generating H_2S gas by the addition of acid to the sulfide; the H_2S may be identified by its odor or by the formation of insoluble, black PbS on a filter paper wet with a solution of a soluble Pb^{2+} salt.

$$Pb^{2+}(aq) + H_2S(g) \longrightarrow PbS(s) + 2H^+(aq)$$

Sulfur dissolves in solutions of soluble sulfides and forms a mixture of polysulfide anions.

$$S^{2-}(aq) + nS(s) \longrightarrow S_{n+1}^{2-}(aq)$$

Polyselenide and polytelluride ions can be prepared by analogous reactions. For sulfur, ions varying in complexity from S_2^{2-} to S_6^{2-} have been prepared; Se_5^{2-} and Te_6^{2-} are the highest polyselenides and polytellurides known. The atoms of a polysulfide ion are joined into chains by single covalent bonds.

The structure of the disulfide ion, S_2^{2-}, is similar to that of the peroxide ion (Section 8.8). The mineral pyrite, FeS_2, is iron(II) disulfide.

At room temperature, polysulfides decompose in acid solution to yield mainly H_2S and free S; however, careful treatment of a polysulfide solution with concentrated HCl at $-15°C$ yields H_2S_2, H_2S_3, and small quantities of higher homologs. The hydrogen polysulfides are unstable, yellow oils.

11.12 The 4+ Oxidation State

The important compounds in which sulfur appears in a 4+ oxidation state are sulfur dioxide (SO_2), sulfurous acid (H_2SO_3), and the salts of sulfurous acid—the sulfites. Both selenium and tellurium form compounds analogous to those of sulfur.

Sulfur dioxide is commercially obtained by burning sulfur

$$S(s) + O_2(g) \longrightarrow SO_2(g)$$

or by roasting sulfide ores (such as ZnS, PbS, Cu_2S, and FeS_2) in air (Section 18.3)

$$2ZnS(s) + 3O_2(g) \longrightarrow 2ZnO(s) + 2SO_2(g)$$

Sulfur dioxide is a colorless gas. It has a sharp, irritating odor and is somewhat poisonous. The molecules of SO_2 are angular, and the structure of the compound may be represented as a resonance hybrid (Section 4.1).

The S—O bonds have additional double-bond character from $p\pi$-$d\pi$ bonding.

The polar nature of the SO_2 molecule is reflected in the ease with which sulfur dioxide may be liquefied. Sulfur dioxide liquefies at $-10°C$ (the normal boiling point) under a pressure of 1 atm, and, at 20°C, a pressure of about 3 atm will liquefy the gas. It is this property of SO_2 that makes the compound useful as a refrigerant.

Sulfur dioxide is moderately soluble in water—producing solutions of sulfurous acid, H_2SO_3. The acid is not very stable, and pure H_2SO_3 cannot be isolated. The extent of the reaction between dissolved SO_2 molecules and water is not known; probably both H_2SO_3 and SO_2 molecules exist in the solution in equilibrium.

$$SO_2(aq) + H_2O \rightleftharpoons H_2SO_3(aq)$$

Sulfurous acid is a weak, diprotic acid.

$$H_2SO_3(aq) \rightleftharpoons H^+(aq) + HSO_3^-(aq)$$

or

$$SO_2(aq) + H_2O \rightleftharpoons H^+(aq) + HSO_3^-(aq)$$

and

$$HSO_3^-(aq) \rightleftharpoons H^+(aq) + SO_3^{2-}(aq)$$

Therefore sulfurous acid forms two series of salts: normal salts (e.g., Na_2SO_3, sodium sulfite) and acid salts (e.g., $NaHSO_3$, sodium bisulfite or sodium hydrogen sulfite).

Sulfites are often prepared by bubbling SO_2 gas through a solution of a hydroxide.

$$2OH^- + SO_2(g) \longrightarrow SO_3^{2-}(aq) + H_2O$$

If the addition is continued, acid sulfites are produced.

$$H_2O + SO_3^{2-}(aq) + SO_2(g) \longrightarrow 2HSO_3^-(aq)$$

The salts of sulfurous acid can be isolated from solution.

Since sulfurous acid is unstable, the addition of an acid to a sulfite, or an acid sulfite, liberates SO_2 gas; this is a convenient way to prepare the gas in the laboratory.

$$SO_3^{2-}(aq) + 2H^+(aq) \longrightarrow SO_2(g) + H_2O$$

Sulfur dioxide, sulfurous acid, and sulfites can function as mild oxidizing agents; however, reactions in which these compounds react as reducing agents (and are oxidized to the sulfate ion, SO_4^{2-}) are more numerous and more important. Many substances (such as potassium permanganate, potassium dichromate, chlorine, and bromine) oxidize sulfite to sulfate. In fact, sulfites are usually contaminated by traces of sulfates because of oxidation by the oxygen of the air.

$$2SO_3^{2-} + O_2(g) \longrightarrow 2SO_4^{2-}$$

Sulfites may be identified by the production of SO_2 gas upon acidification and by oxidation to the sulfate ion,

$$6H^+(aq) + 5SO_3^{2-}(aq) + 2MnO_4^-(aq) \longrightarrow 5SO_4^{2-}(aq) + 2Mn^{2+}(aq) + 3H_2O$$

followed by the precipitation of the sulfate as the insoluble barium salt.

$$Ba^{2+}(aq) + SO_4^{2-}(aq) \longrightarrow BaSO_4(s)$$

The dioxides of selenium and tellurium may be prepared by direct combination of the elements with oxygen; however, SeO_2 and TeO_2 are usually made by heating the product obtained from the oxidation of selenium or tellurium by concentrated nitric acid (see Table 11.13). Both SeO_2 and TeO_2 are white solids.

Selenous acid, H_2SeO_3, is formed when the very soluble SeO_2 is dissolved in water; it is a weak, diprotic acid and may be obtained in pure form by the evaporation of a solution of SeO_2. Tellurium dioxide is only slightly soluble in water, and pure H_2TeO_3 has never been prepared. Consequently, only very dilute solutions of tellurous acid have been studied.

Tellerium dioxide, as well as selenium dioxide, will dissolve in aqueous solutions of hydroxides to produce tellurites and selenites. If an excess of the dioxide is employed, the corresponding acid salt is obtained.

The selenium and tellurium compounds of the 4+ oxidation state are better oxidizing agents, and poorer reducing agents, than the corresponding sulfur compounds: SeO_2 is a good oxidizing agent and is employed in certain organic syntheses.

11.13   The 6+ Oxidation State

Sulfur trioxide is produced when sulfur dioxide reacts with atmospheric oxygen. Since the reaction is very slow at ordinary temperatures, the commercial preparation is conducted at elevated temperatures (400° to 700°C) and in the presence of a catalyst (such as divanadium pentoxide or spongy platinum).

$$2SO_2(g) + O_2(g) \;\longrightarrow\; 2SO_3(g)$$

Sulfur trioxide is a volatile material (boiling point, 44.8°C); in the gas phase it consists of single molecules that are planar, triangular in form with O—S—O bond angles of 120°. The electronic structure of the molecule may be represented as a resonance hybrid:

Additional π bonding, over that represented by the resonance forms, arises from the overlap of filled $2p$ orbitals of O atoms with empty $3d$ orbitals of S. The compound exists in at least three solid modifications that are formed by the condensation of SO_3 units into larger molecules called polymers. The commercial product, which is a variable mixture of two forms of the compound, is a colorless solid that melts at approximately 40°C.

Sulfur trioxide is an extremely reactive substance and a strong oxidizing agent. It is the anhydride of sulfuric acid, H_2SO_4, and reacts vigorously with water to produce the acid and with metallic oxides to produce sulfates (Section 8.3).

Sulfuric acid is an important industrial chemical. Most sulfuric acid is made by the **contact process** in which SO_2 is catalytically oxidized to SO_3 in the manner previously described. The SO_3 vapor is bubbled through H_2SO_4 and pyrosulfuric acid ($H_2S_2O_7$) is formed.

$$SO_3(g) + H_2SO_4(l) \longrightarrow H_2S_2O_7(l)$$

Water is then added to the pyrosulfuric acid to give sulfuric acid of the desired concentration.

$$H_2S_2O_7(l) + H_2O \longrightarrow 2H_2SO_4(l)$$

This procedure, in which pyrosulfuric acid is formed, is easier to control than the direct reaction of SO_3 with water.

The **lead chamber process** is an older method for the manufacture of sulfuric acid. Sulfur dioxide, oxygen, water vapor, and oxides of nitrogen are mixed in a lead-lined chamber. The reactions are complex and are not completely understood, but it is recognized that nitrosylsulfuric acid, $HOSO_2(ONO)$, is formed as an intermediate and that this compound then reacts with water to form sulfuric acid. We may summarize the process by the simplified equations

$$2SO_2(g) + NO(g) + NO_2(g) + O_2(g) + H_2O(g) \longrightarrow 2HOSO_2(ONO)(s)$$

$$2HOSO_2(ONO)(s) + H_2O(g) \longrightarrow 2H_2SO_4(l) + NO(g) + NO_2(g)$$

The oxides of nitrogen are regenerated and are used over and over again. The sulfuric acid produced by the lead chamber process has a concentration of only 60 to 78% and is less pure than that made by the contact process.

Sulfuric acid is a colorless, oily liquid that freezes at 10.4°C and begins to boil at approximately 290°C with decomposition into water and sulfur trioxide. The electronic structure of sulfuric acid may be represented as

$$
\begin{array}{c}
:\!\ddot{O}\!: \\
| \\
H\!-\!\ddot{O}\!-\!S\!-\!\ddot{O}\!-\!H \\
| \\
:\!\ddot{O}\!:
\end{array}
$$

However, the S—O bonds have a considerable degree of double-bond character from $p\pi$-$d\pi$ bonding, and the electronic formula

$$
\begin{array}{c}
:\!O\!: \\
\| \\
H\!-\!\ddot{O}\!-\!S\!-\!\ddot{O}\!-\!H \\
\| \\
:\!O\!:
\end{array}
$$

is sometimes used. The H_2SO_4 molecule, as well as the SO_4^{2-} ion, is tetrahedral.

When concentrated sulfuric acid is added to water, a great deal of heat is evolved; this heat effect may be because of the formation of the hydronium ion, H_3O^+. Sulfuric acid has a strong affinity for water and forms a series of hydrates (such as $H_2SO_4 \cdot H_2O$, $H_2SO_4 \cdot 2H_2O$, and $H_2SO_4 \cdot 4H_2O$). Thus sulfuric acid is used as a drying agent, and gases that do not react with H_2SO_4 may be dried by being bubbled through the acid. The dehydrating power of sulfuric acid is also seen in the charring action of the acid on carbohydrates.

$$C_{12}H_{22}O_{11}(s) \xrightarrow{\;H_2SO_4\;} 12C(s) + 11H_2O(g)$$
$$\text{sucrose}$$

In aqueous solution, sulfuric acid ionizes in two steps.

$$H_2SO_4 \longrightarrow H^+(aq) + HSO_4^-(aq)$$

$$HSO_4^-(aq) \rightleftharpoons H^+(aq) + SO_4^{2-}(aq)$$

Sulfuric acid is a strong electrolyte as far as the first dissociation is concerned; however, the second dissociation is not complete. The acid forms two series of salts: normal salts (such as sodium sulfate, Na_2SO_4) and acid salts (such as sodium bisulfate, $NaHSO_4$). Most sulfates are soluble in water. However, barium sulfate ($BaSO_4$), strontium sulfate ($SrSO_4$), and lead sulfate ($PbSO_4$) are practically insoluble, and calcium sulfate ($CaSO_4$), mercury(I) sulfate (Hg_2SO_4), and silver sulfate (Ag_2SO_4) are but slightly soluble. The formation of white, insoluble barium sulfate, the least soluble of the substances listed, is commonly used as a laboratory test for the sulfate ion.

Since sulfuric acid has a relatively high boiling point (or decomposition temperature), it is used to secure more volatile acids from their salts. This use is illustrated by the preparations of HF and HCl (Section 11.6), as well as by the preparation of HNO_3 (Section 12.7).

Sulfuric acid at unit concentration and 25°C is not a particularly good oxidizing agent (note the relatively low standard electrode potential in Table 11.14); however, hot, concentrated sulfuric acid is a moderately effective oxidizing agent. The oxidizing ability of hot, concentrated H_2SO_4 on

Table 11.14

Standard Electrode Potentials of Sulfuric, Selenic, and Telluric Acids

$2e^- + 4H^+ + SO_4^{2-}$	$\rightleftharpoons$ $H_2SO_3 + H_2O$	$\mathscr{E}° = +0.17$ v
$2e^- + 4H^+ + SeO_4^{2-}$	$\rightleftharpoons$ $H_2SeO_3 + H_2O$	$\mathscr{E}° = +1.15$ v
$2e^- + 2H^+ + H_6TeO_6$	$\rightleftharpoons$ $TeO_2 + 4H_2O$	$\mathscr{E}° = +1.02$ v

bromides and iodides has already been noted (Section 11.6). This reagent will also oxidize many nonmetals.

$$C(s) + 2H_2SO_4(l) \longrightarrow CO_2(g) + 2SO_2(g) + 2H_2O(g)$$

Most metals are oxidized by hot, concentrated sulfuric acid, including those metals of relatively low reactivity that are not oxidized by hydronium ion. For example, copper will not displace hydrogen from aqueous acids; copper metal is, however, oxidized by hot, concentrated sulfuric acid, although hydrogen gas is not a product of the reaction.

$$Cu(s) + 2H_2SO_4(l) \longrightarrow CuSO_4(s) + SO_2(g) + 2H_2O(g)$$

Selenic acid, H_2SeO_4, is prepared by the oxidization of selenous acid, H_2SeO_3, and selenates may be prepared by the oxidation of the corresponding selenites. Selenium trioxide, the acid anhydride of selenic acid, is not very stable and decomposes to SeO_2 and O_2 on warming. Low yields of SeO_3 mixed with SeO_2 are produced when an electric discharge is passed through selenium vapor and oxygen; the trioxide may also be prepared by the reaction of potassium selenate, K_2SeO_4, and SO_3.

Selenic acid is very similar to sulfuric acid. In aqueous solution, the first dissociation of H_2SeO_4 is strong and the second dissociation weak. The acid forms normal and acid salts. Crystalline selenates are in most cases isomorphous with the corresponding sulfates. Like the sulfate ion, the selenate ion is tetrahedral.

Telluric acid is prepared by the action of vigorous oxidizing agents on elementary tellurium. Unlike H_2SO_4 and H_2SeO_4, the formula of telluric acid is H_6TeO_6, which may be regarded as a hydrated form of the nonexistent H_2TeO_4. No compound of formula H_2TeO_4 has ever been prepared, although salts of an acid corresponding to this formula exist. Tellurium, like iodine, is a large atom and can accommodate six oxygen atoms, and telluric acid, like IO_6^{5-}, is octahedral. Telluric acid is not very similar to sulfuric acid, and H_6TeO_6 functions in aqueous solution as a very weak diprotic acid. If H_6TeO_6 is heated to approximately 350°C, water is driven off and solid tellurium trioxide results. This compound is not very water soluble but reacts with alkalies to produce tellurates.

Both selenic and telluric acids are stronger oxidizing agents than sulfuric acid (Table 11.14), although the reactions of H_2SeO_4 and H_6TeO_6 often proceed slowly.

There are other acids of sulfur in which S is in a 6+ oxidation state. Pyrosulfuric acid (or disulfuric acid)

$$\begin{array}{ccc} & O & O \\ & \| & \| \\ H-O-&S-O-S&-O-H \\ & \| & \| \\ & O & O \end{array}$$

has been mentioned as the product of the reaction of SO_3 with H_2SO_4 in a 1:1 molar ratio. The pyrosulfate ion has been shown to have a structure in which two SO_4 tetrahedra are joined by an O atom common to both tetrahedra: $[O_3SOSO_3]^{2-}$. Pyrosulfuric acid is a stronger oxidizing agent and a stronger dehydrating agent than sulfuric acid.

A peroxy acid is an acid that contains a peroxide group $(-O-O-)$ somewhere in the molecule. Two peroxy acids of sulfur exist: peroxymonosulfuric acid (H_2SO_5) and peroxydisulfuric acid ($H_2S_2O_8$).

$$
\begin{array}{ccc}
& O & \\
& \| & \\
H-O-O-S-O-H & & \\
& | & \\
& O &
\end{array}
\qquad
\begin{array}{ccc}
O & & O \\
\| & & \| \\
H-O-S-O-O-S-O-H & \\
| & & | \\
O & & O
\end{array}
$$

The structure of the peroxydisulfate ion consists of two complete SO_4 tetrahedra joined by an O—O bond.

Peroxydisulfuric acid is prepared by the electrolysis of moderately concentrated solutions of sulfuric acid (50 to 70%) at temperatures below room temperature (5 to 10°C). Potassium and ammonium salts of this acid are prepared by the electrolysis of the corresponding acid sulfates. The anode reaction in these electrolyses may be represented by the partial equation

$$2HSO_4^- \longrightarrow S_2O_8^{2-} + 2H^+ + 2e^-$$

The reaction of peroxydisulfuric acid with water yields peroxymonosulfuric acid.

$$H_2S_2O_8 + H_2O \longrightarrow H_2SO_5 + H_2SO_4$$

Upon further hydrolysis, H_2SO_5 is decomposed into hydrogen peroxide and H_2SO_4.

$$H_2SO_5 + H_2O \longrightarrow H_2SO_4 + H_2O_2$$

The acids may also be prepared by the reaction of 1 mole of hydrogen peroxide with 1 or 2 moles of chlorosulfonic acid, $HOSO_2Cl$ (the product of the reaction of SO_3 and HCl).

Both peroxymonosulfuric acid and peroxydisulfuric acid are low melting solids. The first ionization of peroxydisulfuric acid is strong. The peroxydisulfate ion is one of the strongest oxidizing agents known.

$$2e^- + S_2O_8^{2-} \rightleftharpoons 2SO_4^{2-} \qquad E° = +2.01 \text{ v}$$

The oxidations, however, are slow and are usually catalyzed by Ag^+ ions. In both peroxy acids, sulfur is assumed to be in its highest oxidation state $(6+)$. However, the oxygen atoms of the peroxide grouping are each assigned an oxidation number of $1-$, and in the course of an oxidation, it is the peroxide oxygens that change oxidation state (from $1-$ to $2-$).

There is another significant group of sulfur-containing anions. The most important representative of the group is the thiosulfate ion, $S_2O_3^{2-}$.

$$\begin{bmatrix} & O & \\ & | & \\ O- & S & -O \\ & | & \\ & S & \end{bmatrix}^{2-}$$

This tetrahedral ion may be regarded as a sulfate ion in which one oxygen atom has been replaced by a sulfur atom. In fact, the prefix "thio-" is used when the species to be named may be considered to be derived from the compound described by the base name by replacing an oxygen atom by a sulfur atom. Thus CNO^- is the cyanate ion—CNS^- is the thiocyanate ion; $CO(NH_2)_2$ is urea—$CS(NH_2)_2$ is thiourea.

Thiosulfates may be prepared by the reaction of sulfur with sulfites in aqueous solution.

$$SO_3^{2-}(aq) + S(s) \longrightarrow S_2O_3^{2-}(aq)$$

The corresponding acid does not exist. Upon acidification, thiosulfates decompose to elementary sulfur and SO_2 gas.

$$S_2O_3^{2-}(aq) + 2H^+(aq) \longrightarrow S(s) + SO_2(g) + H_2O$$

The two sulfur atoms of the thiosulfate ion are not equivalent. This has been shown by the reactions of a compound derived from a sulfite and radioactive sulfur, $^{35}_{16}S$. When a compound thus prepared is decomposed by acidification, all of the activity ends in the elementary sulfur.

$$SO_3^{2-}(aq) + {}^{35}S(s) \longrightarrow {}^{35}SSO_3^{2-}(aq)$$

$${}^{35}SSO_3^{2-}(aq) + 2H^+(aq) \longrightarrow {}^{35}S(s) + SO_2(g) + H_2O$$

Hence, the central sulfur atom is generally assigned an oxidation number of $6+$ (as in the sulfate ion), and the coordinated sulfur is usually assigned an oxidation number of $2-$ (as the oxidation number of the oxygen it replaces); the average oxidation state of sulfur in the ion is $2+$.

The thiosulfate ion is readily oxidized to the tetrathionate ion, $S_4O_6^{2-}$. The tetrathionate ion may be regarded as an analog of the peroxydisulfate ion, $S_2O_8^{2-}$, in which the peroxide group $(-O-O-)$ is replaced by a disulfide group $(-S-S-)$. Other thionate ions exist—for example, the dithionate ion, $S_2O_6^{2-}$, and the trithionate ion, $S_3O_6^{2-}$; the latter is structurally similar to the pyrosulfate ion, $S_2O_7^{2-}$, with a sulfur atom replacing the central oxygen atom.

Figure 11.11   Electrode potential diagrams for sulfur and its compounds.

11.14   Sulfur Electrode Potential Diagrams

Electrode potential diagrams for sulfur and its compounds appear in Figure 11.11. On the basis of the $\mathscr{E}°$ values, several of the substances shown in the diagrams should be able to disproportionate. In alkaline solution (but not in acid), sulfur itself forms S^{2-} and $S_2O_3^{2-}$. The thiosulfate ion is stable in alkaline solution but disproportionates to S and SO_2 in acid. The electrode potentials also show that both SO_2, in acid, and SO_3^{2-}, in base, are unstable toward disproportionation. The latter two reactions, however, are slow under ordinary conditions. None of the materials shown in the diagrams are capable of liberating O_2 from solution.

At standard concentrations and in acidic solution, the oxysulfur compounds shown in the diagram are only moderately strong oxidizing agents. In alkaline solution, the oxysulfur compounds are poor oxidants. In fact, all the ions with the exception of SO_4^{2-} are easily oxidized in base and can function as reducing agents. The thiosulfate ion is easily oxidized to the tetrathionate ion $S_4O_6^{2-}$; $\mathscr{E}°_0$ for this transformation is only $+0.08$ v.

SOME SUGGESTED READINGS

Cotton, F. A., and Wilkinson, G., *Advanced Inorganic Chemistry*, 2nd ed., New York, Wiley, 1966.

Johnson, R. C., *Introductory Descriptive Chemistry*, New York, Benjamin, 1966 (paper).

Jolly, W. L., *The Chemistry of the Non-Metals*, Englewood Cliffs, N. J., Prentice-Hall, 1966 (paper).

Rich, R. L., *Periodic Correlations*, New York, Benjamin, 1965 (paper).

Sherwin, E., and Weston, G. J., *Chemistry of the Non-Metallic Elements*, Elmsford, N.Y., Pergamon, 1966 (paper).

Weeks, M. E., and Leicester, H. M., *Discovery of the Elements*, 7th ed., Easton, Penna., Chemical Education Publishing Co., 1968.

PROBLEMS

11.1 For each of the following, state the type of hybrid orbitals employed by Xe and draw diagrams to show the geometric configuration. (a) XeF_2, (b) XeF_4, (c) XeO_3, (d) $XeOF_4$, (e) XeO_4, (f) XeO_6^{4-}.

11.2 Write equations to show how to prepare (a) XeF_2, (b) XeF_6, (c) $CsXeF_7$, (d) $XeOF_4$, (e) XeO_3, (f) Na_4XeO_6, (g) XeO_4.

11.3 What are clathrates? Why have clathrates containing helium never been prepared?

11.4 What reasons can you give for the fact that the only binary noble-gas compounds known are the fluorides and oxides of Kr, Xe, and Rn?

11.5 Argon is used to fill electric light bulbs and to provide an atmosphere under which high-temperature welding may be carried out. Justify these uses.

11.6 Hydrogen and helium are used to fill balloons. (a) At STP, what is the weight of 22.4 liters of each of the following: H_2, He, and air? (Assume that air is 80.0% N_2 and 20.0% O_2 by volume.) (b) Compare the lifting power of a balloon filled with H_2 with that of a balloon filled with He. What must the volume of a He filled balloon be in order to compare in lifting power with a 100 liter balloon filled with H_2? Why should He be used in place of H_2?

11.7 (a) Use the ion-electron method to write an equation for the oxidation, in acid solution, of Mn^{2+} to MnO_4^- by XeO_3, which is reduced to Xe(g). (b) In a reaction between XeO_3 and Mn^{2+} that occurs in 200 ml of solution, the Xe(g) produced occupied a volume of 448 ml at STP. What is the normality and molarity of the MnO_4^- solution resulting from the reaction? What weight of XeO_3 was consumed by the reaction?

11.8 Write chemical equations to show how $Cl_2(g)$ may be prepared from $Cl^-(aq)$ by use of (a) $MnO_2(s)$, (b) $PbO_2(s)$, (c) $MnO_4^-(aq)$, (d) $Cr_2O_7^{2-}(aq)$. (e) Analogous equations may be written for reactions in which bromine and iodine are prepared from bromide ions and iodide ions. However, fluorine cannot be prepared from fluoride ions by use of these oxidizing agents. Why not?

11.9 Write chemical equations to show how to prepare the following: (a) F_2 from CaF_2, (b) Cl_2 from NaCl, (c) Br_2 from sea water, (d) I_2 from $NaIO_3$.

11.10 Write chemical equations for the reactions of Cl_2 with (a) H_2, (b) Zn, (c) P, (d) S, (e) H_2S, (f) CO, (g) SO_2, (h) $I^-(aq)$, (i) cold H_2O.

11.11 Explain why fluorine is a more reactive nonmetal than chlorine despite the fact that the electron affinity of chlorine is -3.8 ev, whereas that of fluorine is only -3.6 ev.

11.12 Since $HCl(g)$ can be prepared from $NaCl$ and H_2SO_4, why is it that the reaction of $NaBr$ and H_2SO_4 cannot be used to prepare $HBr(g)$?

11.13 From each of the following pairs of compounds, select the compound that would have the higher conductivity in the molten state. Explain the basis of your prediction in each case. (a) $FeCl_2$ or $FeCl_3$, (b) $RbCl$ or $SrCl_2$, (c) BeF_2 or $BeCl_2$.

11.14 Discuss the bonding and structure of the interhalogen compounds XX'_3, XX'_5, and XX'_7.

11.15 Write equations for the electrolysis of (a) dry, molten $NaCl$, (b) cold $NaCl$ solution, (c) cold $NaCl$ solution with the electrolyte stirred, (d) hot, concentrated $NaCl$ solution with the electrolyte stirred, (e) cold $NaClO_3$ solution.

11.16 Describe the changes in sulfur that occur as the temperature is increased.

11.17 Describe the Frasch process for mining elementary sulfur.

11.18 Write equations for the reactions of sulfur with (a) O_2, (b) $S^{2-}(aq)$, (c) $SO_3^{2-}(aq)$, (d) Fe, (e) F_2, (f) Cl_2, (g) HNO_3.

11.19 Compare the lead-chamber and contact processes for the manufacture of sulfuric acid. Which process yields the purer product?

11.20 Write equations for the reactions of H_2SO_4 with (a) $C_{12}H_{22}O_{11}$, (b) $NaNO_3$, (c) Cu, (d) Zn, (e) ZnS, (f) Fe_2O_3.

11.21 Write a sequence of equations representing reactions that could be used to synthesize each of the following and that start with elementary S. (a) H_2S (not by direct union of the elements), (b) H_2SO_3, (c) $Na_2S_2O_3$, (d) $NaHSO_4$, (e) $H_2S_2O_7$.

11.22 Write equations for the reaction of sulfur dioxide with (a) O_2 (Pt catalyst), (b) $Cl_2(g)$, (c) H_2O, (d) $ClO_3^-(aq)$, (e) $OH^-(aq)$, (f) $SO_3^{2-}(aq)$ and H_2O.

11.23 Draw Lewis structures for and describe the geometric structure of each of the following: (a) S_3^{2-}, (b) SO_3^{2-}, (c) SO_4^{2-}, (d) $S_2O_3^{2-}$, (e) $S_4O_6^{2-}$, (f) $H_2S_2O_7$, (g) $H_2S_2O_8$.

11.24 Write an equation for the reaction of each of the following with water: (a) $CH_3C(NH_2)S$, (b) Al_2S_3, (c) SeO_3, (d) TeO_3, (e) $H_2S_2O_7$, (f) $H_2S_2O_8$.

11.25 For each of the following acids, an oxide exists that reacts with water to produce the acid. What are these acid anhydrides? (a) H_2SO_3, (b) H_2SeO_4, (c) H_6TeO_6, (d) $HOCl$, (e) $HClO_4$, (f) HIO_3, (g) H_5IO_6.

11.26 Discuss $p\pi$-$d\pi$ bonding. What is the origin of the phenomenon and its effect on structures in which it occurs?

11.27 Explain why: (a) H_6SO_6 does not exist but H_6TeO_6 does, (b) HCl_2^- is not known but HF_2^- is, (c) OF_4 cannot be prepared but SF_4 can be.

11.28 What is the difference in meaning between the prefixes *per-* and *peroxy-* as applied in the naming of acids?

11.29 Describe a laboratory test for each of the following: (a) $F^-(aq)$, (b) $Cl^-(aq)$, (c) $Br^-(aq)$, (d) $I^-(aq)$, (e) $S^{2-}(aq)$, (f) $SO_3^{2-}(aq)$, (g) $SO_4^{2-}(aq)$, (h) $S_2O_3^{2-}(aq)$.

The group V A elements, as well as carbon and silicon of group IV A, and boron of group III A are discussed in this chapter.

THE GROUP V A ELEMENTS

THE NONMETALS, PART II

The elements of group V A—nitrogen, phosphorus, arsenic, antimony, and bismuth—collectively show a wider range of properties than is exhibited by either the elements of group VI A or the elements of group VII A.

12.1 Group Properties

Within any group of the periodic classification, metallic character increases (and nonmetallic character decreases) with increasing atomic number, atomic weight, and atomic size. This trend is particularly striking in group V A. Thus the electronegativities and first ionization potentials of the elements in the group decrease from

Table 12.1

Some Properties of the Group V A Elements

	Nitrogen	Phosphorus	Arsenic	Antimony	Bismuth
color	colorless	white, red, black	gray metallic, yellow	gray metallic, yellow	gray metallic
molecular formula	N_2	P_4 (white) P_n (black)	As_n (metallic) As_4 (yellow)	Sb_n (metallic) Sb_4 (yellow)	Bi_n
melting point (°C)	−210	44.1 (white)	814 (metallic) (36 atm)	630.5 (metallic)	271
boiling point (°C)	−195.8	280	633 (sublimes)	1325	1560
atomic radius (Å)	0.74	1.10	1.21	1.41	1.52
ionic radius (Å)	1.4(N^{3-})	1.85(P^{3-})		0.92(Sb^{3+})	1.08(Bi^{3+})
first ionization potential (ev)	14.5	11.0	10.0	8.6	8.0
electronegativity	3.0	2.1	2.0	1.9	1.9

values typical of a nonmetal (N) to those characteristic of a metal (Bi); these values are listed in Table 12.1. Nitrogen and phosphorus are generally regarded as nonmetals, arsenic and antimony as semimetals or metalloids, and bismuth as a metal. Bismuth, however, is not strongly metallic; its electrical and heat conductivities are low.

The electronic configurations of the elements are listed in Table 12.2. Each element has three electrons less than the noble gas of its period, and the formation of trinegative ions might be expected. Nitrogen forms the nitride ion, N^{3-}, in combination with certain reactive metals; phosphorus forms the phosphide ion, P^{3-}, less readily. The remaining elements of the group, however, have lower electronegativities and are more metallic than nitrogen

Table 12.2

Electronic Configurations of the Group V A Elements

Element	Z	1s	2s	2p	3s	3p	3d	4s	4p	4d	4f	5s	5p	5d	6s	6p
N	7	2	2	3												
P	15	2	2	6	2	3										
As	33	2	2	6	2	6	10	2	3							
Sb	51	2	2	6	2	6	10	2	6	10		2	3			
Bi	83	2	2	6	2	6	10	2	6	10	14	2	6	10	2	3

and phosphorus; hence, arsenic, antimony, and bismuth have no tendency to form comparable anions.

The loss of electrons and consequent formation of cations, which is characteristic of metals, is observed for the heavier members of the group. High ionization potentials prohibit the loss of all five valence electrons by any element; therefore, $5+$ ions do not exist, and the $5+$ oxidation state is only attained through covalent bonding. In addition, most of the compounds in which the group V A elements appear in the $3+$ oxidation state are covalent. However, antimony and bismuth can form inert-pair ions, Sb^{3+} and Bi^{3+}, through loss of the p electrons of their valence levels. The compounds $Sb_2(SO_4)_3$, BiF_3, and $Bi(ClO_4)_3 \cdot 5H_2O$ are ionic. The $3+$ ions of antimony and bismuth react with water to form antimonyl and bismuthyl ions (SbO^+ and BiO^+), as well as hydrated forms of these ions (e.g., $Bi(OH)_2{}^+$).

$$Bi^{3+}(aq) + H_2O \rightleftharpoons BiO^+(aq) + 2H^+(aq)$$

Nitrogen, phosphorus, and arsenic do not form simple cations.

The oxides of the group V A elements become less acidic, and more basic, as the metallic character of the element increases. Thus N_2O_3, P_4O_6, and As_4O_6 are acidic oxides; they dissolve in water to form acids, and they dissolve in solutions of alkalies to form salts of these acids. The compound Sb_4O_6 is amphoteric; it will dissolve in hydrochloric acid as well as in sodium hydroxide. The comparable oxide of bismuth is strictly basic; Bi_2O_3 is not soluble in alkalies, but the compound will dissolve in acids to produce bismuth salts.

All the oxides in which the elements exhibit a $5+$ oxidation state are acidic, but the acidity declines markedly from N_2O_5 to Bi_2O_5. In addition, the stability of the $5+$ oxidation state decreases with increasing atomic number; Bi_2O_5 is extremely unstable and has never been prepared in a pure state.

Many of the properties of nitrogen are anomalous in comparison to those of the other V A elements; this is characteristic of the first members of the groups of the periodic classification. Nitrogen is the smallest and the most electronegative atom of group V A; however, free nitrogen, N_2, has a low order of chemical reactivity (Section 12.2). In fact, phosphorus is more reactive toward oxygen than is nitrogen; phosphorus is the only member of group V A that does not occur in nature as an uncombined element.

Nitrogen has no d orbitals in its valence level ($n = 2$), and the maximum number of covalent bonds formed by nitrogen is four (e.g., in $NH_4{}^+$). In the valence levels of the other V A elements, there are empty d orbitals which may be utilized in covalent bond formation. Hence, P, As, Sb, and Bi form as many as six covalent bonds in such species as PCl_5, $PCl_6{}^-$, AsF_5, $SbCl_6{}^-$, and $BiCl_5^{2-}$.

For the group as a whole, the $3-$, $3+$, and $5+$ oxidation states are most common, the importance and stability of the 5+ and 3− states declining from the lighter to the heavier elements. Nitrogen, however, appears in every oxidation state from 3− to 5+. Nitrogen also has a tendency toward the formation of multiple bonds (e.g., in the cyanide ion, $C\equiv N^-$). The other V A elements do not form π bonds with p orbitals, but some multiple bond character can arise in the compounds of these elements (particularly those of P) from $p\pi$-$d\pi$ bonding.

12.2   The Elements

Nitrogen constitutes about 78% by volume of the earth's atmosphere and is produced commercially by the fractional distillation of liquid air. Very pure nitrogen is conveniently prepared by heating an aqueous solution saturated with ammonium chloride and sodium nitrite,

$$NH_4^+(aq) + NO_2^-(aq) \longrightarrow N_2(g) + 2H_2O$$

Free nitrogen is surprisingly unreactive partly because of the great strength of the bonding in the N_2 molecule.

$$:N\equiv N:$$

According to the molecular orbital theory, two π bonds and one σ bond join the atoms of a N_2 molecule, and the bond order is 3 (Section 4.4). The energy required to dissociate molecular N_5 into atoms is very high (225 kcal/mole).

Phosphorus is industrially prepared by heating a mixture of phosphate rock, sand, and coke in an electric furnace.

$$2Ca_3(PO_4)_2(s) + 6SiO_2(s) \longrightarrow 6CaSiO_3(l) + P_4O_{10}(g)$$

$$P_4O_{10}(g) + 10C(s) \longrightarrow P_4(g) + 10CO(g)$$

The calcium silicate is withdrawn, as a molten slag, from the bottom of the furnace, and the product gases are passed through water, which condenses the phosphorus vapor into a white solid.

Arsenic, antimony, and bismuth are obtained by carbon reduction of their oxides at elevated temperatures.

$$As_4O_6(s) + 6C(s) \longrightarrow As_4(g) + 6CO(g)$$

An important industrial source of the oxides is the flue dust obtained from the processes used in the production of certain metals, notably copper and lead. In addition, the oxides are obtained by roasting the sulfide ores of the elements in air; for example,

$$2Sb_2S_3(s) + 6O_2(g) \longrightarrow Sb_4O_6(g) + 6SO_2(g)$$

The ore arsenopyrite is decomposed by heating in the absence of air.

$$4FeAsS(s) \longrightarrow 4FeS(s) + As_4(g)$$

Stibnite may be reduced by iron at high temperatures.

$$Sb_2S_3(s) + 3Fe(s) \longrightarrow 3FeS(l) + 2Sb(l)$$

Although arsenic, antimony, and bismuth all occur as native ores, only the deposits of native bismuth are sufficiently large to be of commercial importance. The principal natural sources of the group V A elements are listed in Table 12.3.

Table 12.3

Occurrence of the Group V A Elements

Element	Percent of Earth's Crust	Occurrence
nitrogen	0.0046 (0.03 including atmosphere)	N_2 (atmosphere) $NaNO_3$ (Chilean saltpeter)
phosphorus	0.12	$Ca_3(PO_4)_2$ (phosphate rock), $Ca_5(PO_4)_3F$ and $Ca_5(PO_4)_3Cl$ (apatite)
arsenic	5×10^{-4}	$FeAsS$ (arsenopyrite), As_4S_4 (realgar), As_2S_3 (orpiment), As_4O_6 (arsenolite); native As; in ores of Cu, Pb, Co, Ni, Zn, Sn, Ag, and Au
antimony	5×10^{-5}	Sb_2S_3 (stibnite), Sb_4O_6 (senarmontite); native Sb; in ores of Cu, Pb, Ag, and Hg
bismuth	1×10^{-5}	Bi_2S_3 (bismuthinite), Bi_2O_3 (bismite); native Bi; in ores of Cu, Pb, Sn, Co, Ni, Ag, and Au

Phosphorus, arsenic, and antimony occur in allotropic modifications. There are three important forms of phosphorus: white, red, and black. White phosphorus, a waxy solid, is obtained by condensing phosphorus vapor. Crystals of white phosphorus are formed from P_4 molecules (Figure 12.1) in which each phosphorus atom has an unshared pair of electrons and completes its octet by forming single covalent bonds with the other three phosphorus atoms of the molecule.

White phosphorus is soluble in a number of nonpolar solvents (e.g., benzene, carbon disulfide, and ethyl ether). In such solutions, in liquid white

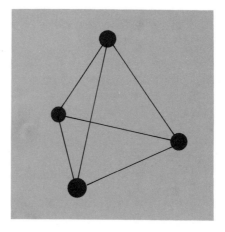

Figure 12.1 Structure of the P_4 molecule.

phosphorus, and in phosphorus vapor, the element exists as P_4 molecules. At temperatures above 800°C, a slight dissociation of the P_4 molecules of the vapor into P_2 molecules is observed; these latter molecules are assumed to have a structure similar to that of the N_2 molecule

$$:P \equiv P:$$

White phosphorus is the most reactive form of the element and is stored under water to protect it from atmospheric oxygen.

Red phosphorus may be prepared by heating white phosphorus to about 250°C in the absence of air. It is a polymeric material in which many phosphorus atoms are joined in a network, but the details of the structure of red phosphorus are not known. Red phosphorus is not soluble in common solvents and is considerably less reactive than the white variety. It does not react with oxygen at room temperature.

Black phosphorus, a less common allotrope, is made by subjecting the element to very high pressures or by a slow crystallization of liquid white phosphorus in the presence of mercury as a catalyst and a seed of black phosphorus. Crystalline black phosphorus consists of layers of phosphorus atoms covalently joined into a network (Figure 12.2). The distance between phosphorus atoms of adjacent layers is much greater than the distance between bonded phosphorus atoms of the same layer; it is assumed that the layers are held together by comparatively weak van der Waals forces. Hence, black phosphorus is a flaky material much like graphite (which also has a layer-type crystal, Section 12.10), and, like graphite, black phosphorus is an electrical conductor. Black phosphorus is the least soluble and least reactive form of the element.

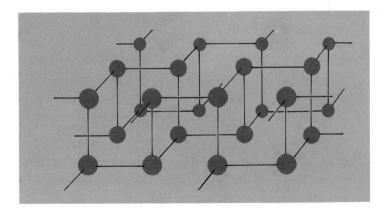

Figure 12.2 Structure of a layer of the black phosphorus crystal.

Arsenic and antimony exist in soft, yellow, nonmetallic modifications which are thought to be formed from tetrahedral As_4 and Sb_4 molecules analogous to the P_4 molecules of white phosphorus. These yellow forms may be obtained by the rapid condensation of vapors and are soluble in carbon disulfide. They are unstable and are readily converted into stable, gray, metallic modifications.

Bismuth commonly occurs as a light gray metal with a reddish cast; the element does not exist in a yellow modification. The metallic modifications of arsenic, antimony, and bismuth are comparatively soft and brittle and have a metallic luster. Their crystalline structures are similar to the structure of black phosphorus, and they are electrical conductors.

12.3 Nitrides and Phosphides

Elementary nitrogen reacts with a number of metals at high temperatures. It forms ionic compounds that contain the N^{3-} ion with lithium, the group II A metals, cadmium, and zinc. These **ionic nitrides** are high-melting, white, crystalline solids; they readily react with water to yield ammonia and hydroxides.

$$Li_3N(s) + 3H_2O \longrightarrow 3Li^+(aq) + 3OH^-(aq) + NH_3(g)$$

$$Ca_3N_2(s) + 6H_2O \longrightarrow 3Ca^{2+}(aq) + 6OH^-(aq) + 2NH_3(g)$$

Interstitial nitrides may be made, at elevated temperatures, from many transition metals, in powdered form, and nitrogen or ammonia. These substances, such as VN, Fe_4N, W_2N, and TiN, contain nitrogen atoms in the intersticies of the metal lattices; they frequently deviate slightly from exact stoichiometry. Interstitial nitrides have extremely high melting points, resemble metals in appearance, are good electrical conductors, are very hard, and are chemically inert.

Covalent nitrides include such compounds as S_4N_4, P_3N_5, Si_3N_4, Sn_3N_4, BN, and AlN. Some of these compounds are molecular in form; others are materials in which a large number of the constituent atoms are covalently joined into a crystal lattice. Aluminum nitride and boron nitride, which are representative of the latter type of compound, may be prepared by the reaction of the elements at high temperatures; AlN and BN react with water (BN only at red heat) to give ammonia and Al_2O_3 or B_2O_3. Since one B atom and one N atom may be considered to be equivalent to two C atoms, BN may be considered to be isoelectronic with carbon, and the compound is known in two crystalline modifications—one resembling graphite and another extremely hard form similar to the diamond.

Many metals unite with white phosphorus directly to form phosphides; these compounds have not been so well characterized as the nitrides. The group II A metals form phosphides of formula M_3P_2; lithium forms Li_3P, and sodium forms Na_3P. In addition, the I A metals form compounds with formulas corresponding to M_2P_5. All these compounds readily hydrolyze to form phosphine, PH_3. For example,

$$Ca_3P_2(s) + 6H_2O \longrightarrow 3Ca^{2+}(aq) + 6OH^-(aq) + 2PH_3(g)$$

The phosphides of the III A elements (such as BP, AlP, GaP, etc.) form covalent network crystals similar to silicon, and, like silicon, these substances are semiconductors. Many phosphides of the transition metals are known (e.g., FeP, Fe_2P, Co_2P_5, RuP, and OsP_2); these materials are gray-black, semimetallic substances that are electrical conductors and are insoluble in water.

The reactions of metals with arsenic, antimony, and, to a lesser extent, bismuth yield arsenides, stibnides, and bismuthides. The compounds of this series become progressively more difficult to prepare as the atomic number of the group V A element increases.

12.4   Hydrogen Compounds

The group V A elements all form hydrogen compounds, the most important of which is ammonia, NH_3. Large quantities of ammonia are commercially prepared by the direct union of the elements (**Haber process**).

$$N_2(g) + 3H_2(g) \rightleftharpoons 2NH_3(g)$$

Ammonia is the only hydrogen compound of the V A elements that can be prepared directly. The reaction is conducted under high pressures (from 100 to 1000 atm), at a temperature of approximately 1000°C, and in the presence of a catalyst. One catalyst, so employed, consists of finely divided iron and Fe_3O_4 containing small amounts of K_2O and Al_2O_3.

Smaller quantities of ammonia are produced as a by-product in the manufacture of coke by the destructive distillation of coal. Ammonia was formerly produced commercially by the reaction of calcium cyanamide, CaNCN, with steam under pressure.

$$CaNCN(s) + 3H_2O(g) \longrightarrow CaCO_3(s) + 2NH_3(g)$$

However, the Haber process has largely displaced this method as a commercial source of ammonia, and calcium cyanamide is produced chiefly as a fertilizer and as a raw material in the manufacture of certain nitrogen-containing organic compounds. Calcium cyanamide is produced in a two-step process. Calcium carbide, CaC_2, is made by the reaction of CaO and coke in an electric furnace

$$CaO(s) + 3C(s) \longrightarrow CaC_2(s) + CO(g)$$

and the calcium carbide is reacted with relatively pure nitrogen at approximately 1000°C to produce calcium cyanamide.

$$CaC_2(s) + N_2(g) \longrightarrow CaNCN(s) + C(s)$$

In the laboratory, ammonia is conveniently prepared by the hydrolysis of nitrides (Section 12.3) or by heating an ammonium salt with a strong alkali (such as NaOH or $Ca(OH)_2$) either dry or in solution.

$$NH_4^+(aq) + OH^-(aq) \longrightarrow NH_3(g) + H_2O$$

The ammonia molecule,

$$H-\overset{\cdot\cdot}{N}-H$$
$$\overset{|}{H}$$

is trigonal pyramidal with the nitrogen atom at the apex (Section 4.2), and the compound is associated through hydrogen bonding in the liquid and solid states (Section 8.11). Liquid ammonia chemistry is discussed in Section 15.2. Ammonia forms many complex ions (e.g., $Ag(NH_3)_2^+$, $Cu(NH_3)_4^{2+}$, and $Cr(NH_3)_6^{3+}$) through the unshared electron pair on nitrogen or through ion-dipole attractions (Sections 17.4 and 19.1).

Aqueous solutions of ammonia are alkaline (Sections 15.3 and 16.1).

$$NH_3(aq) + H_2O \rightleftharpoons NH_4^+(aq) + OH^-(aq)$$

In solution, or as a dry gas, ammonia reacts with acids to produce ammonium salts.

$$NH_3(g) + HCl(g) \longrightarrow NH_4Cl(s)$$

The ammonium ion is tetrahedral.

Nitrogen is formed when ammonia is burned in pure oxygen.

$$4NH_3(g) + 3O_2(g) \longrightarrow 2N_2(g) + 6H_2O(g)$$

However, when a mixture of ammonia and air is passed over platinum gauze at 1000°C, nitric oxide, NO, is produced.

$$4NH_3(g) + 5O_2(g) \longrightarrow 4NO(g) + 6H_2O(g)$$

This catalyzed oxidation of NH_3 is a part of the Ostwald process for the manufacture of nitric acid (see Section 12.7).

Hydrazine, N_2H_4, may be considered as derived from NH_3 by replacement of a H atom by an $-NH_2$ group.

$$H-\overset{..}{N}-\overset{..}{N}-H$$
$$\overset{|}{H}\quad\overset{|}{H}$$

The compound, which is a liquid, may be prepared by oxidizing NH_3 with NaOCl. Hydrazine is less basic than NH_3 but does form cations in which one proton or two protons are bonded to the free electron pairs of the molecule. For example,

$$\left[\begin{matrix} & H & \\ & | & \\ H-\overset{..}{N}-N-H \\ & | \quad | \\ & H \quad H \end{matrix} \right]^{+} Cl^{-} \qquad \left[\begin{matrix} H \quad H \\ | \quad | \\ H-N-N-H \\ | \quad | \\ H \quad H \end{matrix} \right]^{2+} 2Cl^{-}$$

Hydrazine is a strong reducing agent and has found some use in rocket fuels.

Hydroxylamine, NH_2OH, is another compound which, like hydrazine, may be considered as derived from the NH_3 molecule.

$$H-\overset{..}{N}-O-H$$
$$\overset{|}{H}$$

Like hydrazine, hydroxylamine is a weaker base than NH_3, but salts containing the $[NH_3OH]^+$ ion may be prepared.

Hydrazoic acid, HN_3, is another hydrogen compound of nitrogen. The structure of hydrazoic acid may be represented as a resonance hybrid.

$$H-\overset{..}{N}=\overset{\oplus}{N}=\overset{\ominus}{\overset{..}{N}}: \longleftrightarrow H-\overset{\ominus}{\underset{..}{N}}-\overset{\oplus}{N}\equiv N:$$

The two $N-N$ bond distances of the molecule are not the same; the distance from the central N to the N bearing the H atom (1.24 Å) is longer than the other (1.13 Å). Hydrazoic acid may be made by reacting hydrazine (which forms the $[N_2H_5]^+$ ion in acidic solution) with nitrous acid (HNO_2).

$$N_2H_5{}^+(aq) + HNO_2(aq) \longrightarrow HN_3(aq) + H^+(aq) + 2H_2O$$

The free acid, a low-boiling liquid, may be obtained by distillation of the water solution. Hydrazoic acid is a weak acid. The heavy metal salts of the acid, such as lead azide ($Pb(N_3)_2$), explode upon being struck and are used in detonation caps.

Phosphine, PH_3, a very poisonous, colorless gas is prepared by the hydrolysis of phosphides or by the reaction of white phosphorus with concentrated solutions of alkalies.

$$P_4(s) + 3OH^-(aq) + 3H_2O \longrightarrow PH_3(g) + 3H_2PO_2{}^-(aq)$$
$$\text{hypophosphite ion}$$

The PH_3 molecule is pyramidal, similar to the NH_3 molecule; however, unlike NH_3, the compound is not associated by hydrogen bonding in the liquid state.

Phosphine gas is only sparingly soluble in water; such solutions are not alkaline and decompose to yield phosphorus, hydrogen, and other products. Phosphonium compounds, analogous to ammonium compounds, can be prepared by reacting anhydrous phosphine gas with the anhydrous hydrogen halides.

$$PH_3(g) + HI(g) \longrightarrow PH_4I(s)$$

Phosphine is, however, much less basic than ammonia, and phosphonium compounds are unstable. They decompose at relatively low temperatures, or in aqueous solution, to yield phosphine and the acid halide.

Diphosphine, P_2H_4, is generally formed along with phosphine in the preparations of the latter compound. It is spontaneously flammable. Diphosphine has no basic properties in contrast to its nitrogen analog, hydrazine. Nitrogen and phosphorus are the only V A elements that form hydrides of general formula E_2H_4.

Arsine (AsH_3), stibine (SbH_3), and bismuthine (BiH_3) are extremely poisonous gases that may be produced by the hydrolysis of arsenides, stibnides, and bismuthides (e.g., Na_3As, Zn_3Sb_2, and Mg_3Bi_2). The yields of the hydrogen compounds become poorer with increasing molecular weight, and very poor yields of bismuthine are obtained by this method. The stability of the hydrogen compounds declines in the series form NH_3 to BiH_3, and bismuthine is very unstable, decomposing to the elements at room temperature. Consequently, bismuthine is poorly characterized. Arsine and stibine may be similarly decomposed by warming.

Compounds of these V A elements in higher oxidation states may be reduced by reactive metals in sulfuric acid solution to prepare the corresponding hydrogen compounds.

$$H_3AsO_3(aq) + 6H^+(aq) + 3Zn(s) \longrightarrow AsH_3(g) + 3Zn^{2+}(aq) + 3H_2O$$

In the Marsh test for arsenic or antimony, the material to be tested is subjected to a metal reduction such as is described by the preceding equation. If As or Sb is present in the sample, either AsH_3 gas or SbH_3 gas is produced The gas issuing from the reaction flask is passed through a heated tube in which it thermally decomposes and deposits, in the case of a positive test, either an As or an Sb mirror on the tube.

Arsine, stibine, and bismuthine have no basic properties and do not form salts with acids.

12.5 Halogen Compounds

The most important halides of the V A elements are the trihalides (e.g., NF_3) and the pentahalides (e.g., PF_5). All four binary trihalides of each of the V A elements have been made, but the tribromide and triiodide of nitrogen can be isolated only in the form of ammoniates ($NBr_3 \cdot 6NH_3$ and $NI_3 \cdot xNH_3$). The nitrogen trihalides are prepared by the halogenation of ammonia gas (NF_3, NBr_3), of an ammonium salt in acidic solution (NCl_3, NBr_3), or of concentrated aqueous ammonia (NI_3). Each of the trihalides of P, As, Sb, and Bi is prepared by direct halogenation of the V A element using a stoichiometric excess of the V A element to prevent pentahalide formation.

Bismuth trifluoride is an ionic compound, but the other trihalides are covalent. In the gaseous state, the covalent trihalides exist as trigonal pyramidal molecules, which is the expected configuration for sp^3 hybridization with an unshared electron pair occupying one of the hybrid orbitals (Figure 12.3). This molecular form persists in the liquid state and in all of the solids except AsI_3, SbI_3, and BiI_3, which crystallize in covalent layer lattices.

Nitrogen trifluoride is a very stable colorless gas in contrast to the other trihalides of nitrogen, which are explosively unstable. The NF_3 molecule has the typical trigonal pyramidal structure but a low dipole moment (Section 4.2).

The trihalides undergo hydrolysis:

$$NCl_3(l) + 3H_2O \longrightarrow NH_3(g) + 3HOCl(aq)$$

$$PCl_3(l) + 3H_2O \longrightarrow H_3PO_3(aq) + 3H^+(aq) + 3Cl^-(aq)$$

$$AsCl_3(l) + 3H_2O \longrightarrow H_3AsO_3(aq) + 3H^+(aq) + 3Cl^-(aq)$$

$$SbCl_3(s) + H_2O \longrightarrow SbOCl(s) + 2H^+(aq) + 2Cl^-(aq)$$

$$BiCl_3(s) + H_2O \longrightarrow BiOCl(s) + 2H^+(aq) + 2Cl^-(aq)$$

Figure 12.3
Molecular structure of the covalent tri-halides of the VA elements.

Nitrogen is more electronegative than Cl, and in the hydrolysis of NCl_3, N and Cl appear in 3— and 1+ oxidation states, respectively. In each of the other hydrolysis reactions, the V A element appears in a 3+ oxidation state and Cl in a 1— state. The metallic character of the V A elements increases with increasing atomic number, and Sb and Bi occur as oxo cations (SbO^+ and BiO^+) in the hydrolysis products of $SbCl_3$ and $BiCl_3$.

The pentahalide series is not so complete as the trihalide series. Since N has no *d* orbitals in its valence level, N can form no more than four covalent bonds, and hence pentahalides of N do not exist. All the pentahalides of phosphorus are known with the exception of the pentaiodide; presumably, there is not sufficient room around a phosphorus atom to accommodate five large iodine atoms. In addition, AsF_5, SbF_5, BiF_5, and $SbCl_5$ have been prepared.

The pentahalides may be prepared by direct reaction of the elements using an excess of the halogen and by the reaction of the halogen with the trihalide.

$$PCl_3(l) + Cl_2(g) \longrightarrow PCl_5(s)$$

The preceding reaction is reversible. In the gas phase, the pentahalides dissociate in varying degrees:

$$PCl_5(g) \rightleftharpoons PCl_3(g) + Cl_2(g)$$

The pentahalides are trigonal bipyramidal molecules (dsp^3 hybridization) in the gaseous and liquid state (Figure 12.4). The crystal lattice of $SbCl_5$ consists of such molecules; however, solid PCl_5 and PBr_5 form ionic lattices composed of PCl_4^+ and PCl_6^- and PBr_4^+ and Br^-, respectively. Apparently, it is impossible to pack six bromine atoms around a phosphorous atom since PBr_6^- does not form. The cations are tetrahedral (sp^3) and the PCl_6^- ion is octahedral (d^2sp^3); see Figure 12.5.

Figure 12.4 Structure of the gaseous PCl_5 molecule.

The phosphorus pentahalides undergo hydrolysis in two steps; for example,

$$PCl_5(s) + H_2O \longrightarrow POCl_3(l) + 2H^+(aq) + 2Cl^-(aq)$$

$$POCl_3(l) + 3H_2O \longrightarrow H_3PO_4(aq) + 3H^+(aq) + 3Cl^-(aq)$$

A number of mixed trihalides (e.g., NF_2Cl, $PFBr_2$, and $SbBrI_2$) and mixed pentahalides (e.g., PCl_2F_3, $PClF_4$, and $SbCl_3F_2$) have been prepared. In addition, halides are known that conform to the general formula E_2X_4: N_2F_4, P_2Cl_4, P_2I_4, and As_2I_4. These compounds have molecular structures similar to the structure of hydrazine, N_2H_4.

Isomers are substances that have the same molecular formula but differ in the way the constituent atoms are arranged into molecules. Dinitrogen difluoride exists in two isomeric forms.

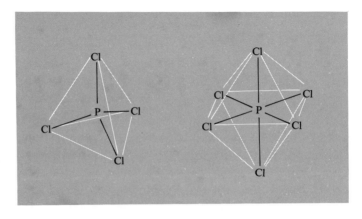

Figure 12.5 Structures of PCl_4^+ and PCl_6^-.

$$\begin{array}{cc} \underset{\textit{trans}}{\overset{\displaystyle F}{\underset{\displaystyle}{\Large N=N}}\overset{\displaystyle}{\underset{\displaystyle F}{}}} & \underset{\textit{cis}}{\overset{\displaystyle N=N}{\underset{\displaystyle F}{\overset{\displaystyle}{}}\underset{\displaystyle F}{}}} \end{array}$$

The double bond, a σ bond and a π bond, between the two nitrogen atoms prevents free rotation about the nitrogen-nitrogen axis. In the *cis* isomer, both fluorine atoms are on the same side of the doubly bonded nitrogen atoms, whereas in the *trans* isomer, the fluorine atoms are on opposite sides; both molecules are planar.

Two series of nitrogen oxyhalides are known: the nitrosyl halides, XNO (X = F, Cl, and Br), and the nitryl halides, XNO_2 (X = F and Cl). These compounds are relatively unstable and are very reactive.

The most important oxyhalides of phosphorus are the phosphoryl halides, POX_3 (X = F, Cl, or Br). These compounds may be prepared by the hydrolysis of the appropriate pentahalide in a limited amount of water or by the reaction of the trihalide with oxygen.

$$2PCl_3(l) + O_2(g) \longrightarrow 2POCl_3(l)$$

Molecules of the phosphoryl halides have a PX_3 grouping arranged as a trigonal pyramide (Figure 12.2) with an oxygen atom bonded to the phosphorus atom, thus forming a distorted tetrahedron.

12.6 Sulfides

The sulfides of the V A elements are listed in Table 12.4; other sulfides have been reported, but their existence is questioned. Tetranitrogen tetrasulfide, N_4S_4, is obtained by the reaction of anhydrous ammonia with either disulfur dichloride, S_2Cl_2, or sulfur dichloride, SCl_2; it is a yellow-orange crystalline solid.

With the exception of N_4S_4, all the sulfides listed in Table 12.4 may be prepared by the direct reaction of the elements. Each of the four phosphorus sulfides is a yellow crystalline material; P_4S_3 is used in the manufacture of strike-anywhere matches.

The sulfides of bismuth and antimony, as well as As_2S_3 and As_2S_5, may be precipitated from acidic solutions of appropriate compounds of these V A elements by hydrogen sulfide; As_2S_3 and As_2S_5 are yellow; Sb_2S_3 is orange-red to black; Sb_2S_5 is orange; and Bi_2S_3 is dark brown. The arsenic and antimony sulfides are dissolved by excess sulfide ion to form thio anions; the 3+ compounds form the thioarsenite, AsS_3^{3-}, and thioantimonite, SbS_3^{3-}, ions, and the 5+ compounds form the thioarsenate, AsS_4^{3-}, and the thioantimonate, SbS_4^{3-}, ions. Bismuth sulfide, Bi_2S_3, is not dissolved by sulfide ion. The formation of thio anions is used in qualitative analysis to effect separations of sulfide precipitates (Section 17.4).

Table 12.4

Sulfides of the V A Elements

Nitrogen	Phosphorus	Arsenic	Antimony	Bismuth
N_4S_4	P_4S_3	As_4S_3	Sb_2S_3	Bi_2S_3
	P_4S_5	As_4S_4	Sb_2S_5	
	P_4S_7	As_2S_3		
	P_4S_{10}	As_2S_5		

12.7 Oxides and Oxyacids of Nitrogen

Oxides are known for every oxidation state of nitrogen from $1+$ to $5+$. Nitrous oxide (or dinitrogen oxide), N_2O, is prepared by gently heating molten ammonium nitrate.

$$NH_4NO_3(l) \longrightarrow N_2O(g) + 2H_2O(g)$$

It is a colorless gas and is relatively unreactive. However, at temperatures around 500°C, nitrous oxide decomposes to nitrogen and oxygen, and hence, N_2O supports combustion. Molecules of N_2O are linear, and the electronic structure of the compound may be represented as a resonance hybrid.

$$\overset{\ominus}{:}\overset{..}{N}=N=\overset{..}{\overset{\oplus}{O}}: \longleftrightarrow :N\equiv\overset{\oplus}{N}-\overset{..}{\underset{..}{O}}\overset{\ominus}{:}$$

Dinitrogen oxide is commonly called "laughing gas" because of the effect it produces when breathed in small amounts. The gas is used as a general anesthetic, and because of its solubility in cream, it is the gas used to charge whipped cream aerosol cans.

Nitric oxide (or nitrogen oxide), NO, may be prepared by the direct reaction of the elements at high temperatures.

$$N_2(g) + O_2(g) \longrightarrow 2NO(g)$$

The reaction is endothermic ($\Delta H = +21.6$ kcal/mole), but even at 3000°C, the yield of NO is only approximately 4%. In a successful preparation, the hot gases from the reaction must be rapidly cooled to prevent the decomposition of NO back into nitrogen and oxygen. By this reaction, atmospheric nitrogen is fixed during lightning storms, and the reaction serves as the basis of the **arc process** of nitrogen fixation in which an electric arc is used to provide the high temperatures necessary for the direct combination of nitrogen and oxygen. As a commercial source of NO, the arc process has been supplanted by the catalytic oxidation of ammonia from the Haber process (Section 12.4).

Nitric oxide is conveniently prepared in the laboratory by the reaction of copper and dilute nitric acid.

$$3Cu(s) + 8H^+(aq) + 2NO_3^-(aq) \longrightarrow 3Cu^{2+}(aq) + 2NO(g) + 4H_2O$$

The NO molecule contains an odd number of electrons, which means that one electron must be unpaired; for this reason, NO is paramagnetic. The electronic structure of the molecule may be represented by the resonance forms

$$:\!\overset{\displaystyle\cdot}{N}\!=\!\overset{\displaystyle\cdot\cdot}{O}\!: \longleftrightarrow :\!\overset{\displaystyle\cdot\cdot}{\overset{\ominus}{N}}\!=\!\overset{\oplus}{\overset{\displaystyle\cdot}{O}}\!:$$

However, the structure is best described by molecular orbital theory which assigns a bond order of $2\frac{1}{2}$ to the molecule and indicates that the odd electron is in a π^* orbital (Section 4.4). The loss of an electron from NO produces the nitrosonium ion, NO^+. Since the electron is lost from an antibonding orbital, the NO^+ ion has a bond order of 3, and the bond distance in NO^+ (1.06 Å) is shorter than the bond distance in the NO molecule (1.14 Å). Ionic compounds of NO^+ are known (e.g., $NO^+\ HSO_4^-$, $NO^+\ ClO_4^-$, and $NO^+\ BF_4^-$).

Whereas odd-electron molecules are generally very reactive and highly colored, nitric oxide is only moderately reactive and is a colorless gas (condensing to a blue liquid and blue solid at low temperatures). In addition, NO shows little tendency to associate into N_2O_2 molecules by electron pairing. Nitrogen oxide reacts instantly with oxygen at room temperature to form nitrogen dioxide.

$$2NO(g) + O_2(g) \longrightarrow 2NO_2(g)$$

Dinitrogen trioxide, N_2O_3, forms as a blue liquid when an equimolar mixture of nitric oxide and nitrogen dioxide is cooled to $-20°C$.

$$NO(g) + NO_2(g) \longrightarrow N_2O_3(l)$$

The compound is unstable under ordinary conditions and decomposes into NO and NO_2. Both NO and NO_2 are odd-electron molecules; N_2O_3 is formed by electron pairing, and the N_2O_3 molecule is thought to contain a $N{-}N$ bond. It is the anhydride of nitrous acid, HNO_2, and dissolves in aqueous alkali to produce the nitrite ion, NO_2^-.

Nitrogen dioxide, NO_2, and dinitrogen tetroxide, N_2O_4, exist in equilibrium with each other.

$$2NO_2 \rightleftharpoons N_2O_4$$

Nitrogen dioxide consists of odd-electron molecules, is paramagnetic, and is brown in color; the dimer, in which the electrons are paired, is diamagnetic and colorless. In the solid state, the oxide is colorless and consists of pure N_2O_4. The liquid is yellow in color and consists of a dilute solution of NO_2 in N_2O_4. As the temperature is raised, the gas contains more and more NO_2 and becomes deeper and deeper brown in color. At 135°C, approximately 99% of the mixture is NO_2.

Nitrogen dioxide molecules are angular.

The structure of N_2O_4 is thought to be planar with two NO_2 units joined by a N—N bond.

Nitrogen dioxide is produced by the reaction of nitric oxide with oxygen. In the laboratory, the compound is conveniently prepared by heating lead nitrate.

$$2Pb(NO_3)_2(s) \longrightarrow 2PbO(s) + 4NO_2(g) + O_2(g)$$

Dinitrogen pentoxide, N_2O_5, is the acid anhydride of nitric acid from which it may be prepared by dehydration using phosphorus (V) oxide.

$$4HNO_3(g) + P_4O_{10}(s) \longrightarrow 4HPO_3(s) + N_2O_5(g)$$

The compound is a colorless, crystalline material that sublimes at 32.5°C. The vapor consists of N_2O_5 molecules which are thought to be planar with the two nitrogen atoms joined through an oxygen atom (O_2NONO_2).

The electronic structure of the molecule may be represented as a resonance hybrid between

and other equivalent structures with different arrangements of the double bonds. The compound is unstable in the vapor state and decomposes according to the equation

$$2N_2O_5(g) \longrightarrow 4NO_2(g) + O_2(g)$$

Crystals of N_2O_5 are composed of nitronium, NO_2^+, and nitrate, NO_3^-, ions; the compound is dissociated into these two ions in solutions in anhydrous sulfuric acid, nitric acid, and phosphoric acid. The nitrate ion is triangular planar. The nitronium ion is linear; it is isoelectronic with CO_2 and may be considered as a nitrogen dioxide molecule minus the odd electron. The ion is probably a reaction intermediate in certain reactions of nitric acid in the presence of sulfuric acid (nitrations) and ionic nitronium compounds have been prepared (e.g., $NO_2^+ClO_4^-$, $NO_2^+BF_4^-$, $NO_2^+PF_6^-$).

There is chemical and spectroscopic evidence for the existence of NO_3 and N_2O_6. However, these substances have not been isolated in the pure condition.

The most important oxyacid of nitrogen is nitric acid, HNO_3, in which nitrogen exhibits an oxidation number of $5+$. Commercially, nitric acid is produced by the **Ostwald process**. Nitric oxide, from the catalytic oxidation of ammonia, is reacted with oxygen to form nitrogen dioxide. This gas, together with excess oxygen, is passed into a tower where it reacts with warm water.

$$3NO_2(g) + H_2O \longrightarrow 2H^+(aq) + 2NO_3^-(aq) + NO(g)$$

The excess oxygen converts the NO from the preceding reaction into NO_2 which reacts with water as before. In this manner, the nitric oxide is eventually completely converted into nitric acid. The product of the Ostwald process is about 70% HNO_3 and is known as concentrated nitric acid; more concentrated solutions may be prepared from it by distillation.

Pure nitric acid is a colorless liquid that boils at 83°C. It may be prepared in the laboratory by heating sodium nitrate with concentrated sulfuric acid.

$$NaNO_3(s) + H_2SO_4(l) \longrightarrow NaHSO_4(s) + HNO_3(g)$$

This preparation (from Chilean saltpeter) is a minor commercial source of the acid.

The HNO_3 molecule is planar and may be represented as a resonance hybrid.

Nitric acid is a strong acid, almost completely dissociated in aqueous solution. Most of the salts of nitric acid, the nitrates, are very soluble in water. The nitrate ion is triangular planar.

Nitric acid is a powerful oxidizing agent; it oxidizes most nonmetals (generally to oxides or oxyacids of their highest oxidation state) and all metals with the exception of a few of the noble metals. Many unreactive metals, such as silver and copper, that do not react to yield hydrogen with nonoxidizing acids, such as HCl, dissolve in nitric acid.

In nitric acid oxidations, hydrogen is almost never obtained; instead, a variety of nitrogen-containing compounds, of lower oxidation state, is produced (Table 12.5). The product to which HNO_3 is reduced depends upon the

Table 12.5

Standard Electrode Potentials for Reductions of the Nitrate Ion

$e^- + 2H^+ + NO_3^- \rightleftharpoons NO_2 + H_2O$		$\mathscr{E}° = +0.80$ v
$8e^- + 10H^+ + NO_3^- \rightleftharpoons NH_4^+ + 3H_2O$		$\mathscr{E}° = +0.88$ v
$2e^- + 3H^+ + NO_3^- \rightleftharpoons HNO_2 + H_2O$		$\mathscr{E}° = +0.94$ v
$3e^- + 4H^+ + NO_3^- \rightleftharpoons NO + 2H_2O$		$\mathscr{E}° = +0.96$ v
$8e^- + 10H^+ + 2NO_3^- \rightleftharpoons N_2O + 5H_2O$		$\mathscr{E}° = +1.12$ v
$10e^- + 6H^+ + 2NO_3^- \rightleftharpoons N_2 + 6H_2O$		$\mathscr{E}° = +1.25$ v

concentration of the acid, the temperature, and the nature of the material being oxidized. Generally, a mixture of products is obtained, but the principal product, in many cases, is NO when dilute HNO_3 is employed and the nitrogen(IV) oxides when concentrated HNO_3 is used.

Dilute:

$$3Cu(s) + 8H^+(aq) + 2NO_3^-(aq) \longrightarrow 3Cu^{2+}(aq) + 2NO(g) + 4H_2O$$

concentrated:

$$Cu(s) + 4H^+(aq) + 2NO_3^-(aq) \longrightarrow Cu^{2+}(aq) + 2NO_2(g) + 2H_2O$$

In some instances, however, strong reducing agents are known to produce almost pure compounds of nitrogen in lower oxidation states; for example, the reaction of zinc and dilute nitric acid yields NH_3 as the reduction product of HNO_3.

The half reactions for the reduction of the nitrate ion in acid solution (Table 12.5) show the $\mathscr{E}°$ values to be strongly dependent upon the $H^+(aq)$ concentration. This concentration dependence is experimentally observed; below a concentration of $2M$, nitric acid has little more oxidizing power than solutions of HCl of corresponding concentration.

Pure nitrous acid, HNO_2, has never been isolated, but a solution of this acid may be prepared by adding an equimolar mixture of NO and NO_2 to water.

$$NO(g) + NO_2(g) + H_2O \rightleftharpoons 2HNO_2(aq)$$

The reaction is exothermic and reversible; when warmed, nitrous acid decomposes, and the NO_2, thus produced, reacts with water to give nitric acid. The overall reaction may be indicated

$$3HNO_2(aq) \longrightarrow H^+(aq) + NO_3^-(aq) + H_2O + 2NO(g)$$

Consequently, solutions of the acid are usually prepared by adding a strong acid to a cold aqueous solution of a nitrite.

$$H^+(aq) + NO_2^-(aq) \longrightarrow HNO_2(aq)$$

The acid is weak and may function as an oxidizing agent or a reducing agent. The electronic structure may be represented as

Nitrites are prepared by the addition of NO and NO_2 to solutions of alkalies. The nitrites of the I A metals are formed when the nitrates are heated, or they may be prepared by heating the nitrate with a reducing agent, such as lead, iron, or coke.

$$NaNO_3(l) + C(s) \longrightarrow NaNO_2(l) + CO(g)$$

The nitrite ion is angular.

Hyponitrous acid, $H_2N_2O_2$, is a relatively unimportant oxyacid of nitrogen. It is a very weak acid and readily decomposes to yield nitrous oxide.

$$H_2N_2O_2(aq) \longrightarrow H_2O + N_2O(g)$$

Although nitrous oxide is formally the acid anhydride of hyponitrous acid, neither the acid nor its salts may be prepared from N_2O.

Electrode potential diagrams for N_2 and some of its compounds appear in Figure 12.6. Except for NH_4^+ and NH_3 (which cannot function as oxidizing agents), the compounds of nitrogen shown in the diagrams are much stronger oxidizing agents in acidic solution than in alkaline solution. In fact, the NO_3^- ion is a very weak oxidant in alkaline solution. Conversely, a given compound of nitrogen is easier to oxidize in alkaline solution than in acidic solution with the exception of NO_3^- which cannot be oxidized. The potentials also indicate that HNO_2 is unstable toward disproportionation to NO and NO_3^- in acid, whereas in alkaline solution, the NO_2^- ion is stable toward such disproportionation.

ACIDIC SOLUTION

$$NO_3^- \xrightarrow{+0.94} HNO_2 \xrightarrow{+1.00} NO \xrightarrow{+1.59} N_2O \xrightarrow{+1.77} N_2 \xrightarrow{+0.27} NH_4^+$$

(with +0.96 over NO₃⁻ to NO, and +1.12 under HNO₂ to NO)

ALKALINE SOLUTION

$$NO_3^- \xrightarrow{+0.01} NO_2^- \xrightarrow{-0.46} NO \xrightarrow{+0.76} N_2O \xrightarrow{+0.94} N_2 \xrightarrow{-0.73} NH_3$$

(with −0.15 over NO₃⁻ to NO, and +0.10 under NO₂⁻ to NO)

Figure 12.6 Electrode potential diagrams for nitrogen and some of its compounds.

12.8 Oxides, and Oxyacids of Phosphorus, Arsenic, Antimony, and Bismuth

When white phosphorus is burned in a limited supply of air, the chief product is phosphorus(III) oxide (or phosphor*ous* oxide), P_4O_6. It is a colorless material that melts at 23.8°C. The combustion of phosphorus in excess oxygen yields phosphorus(V) oxide (or phosphor*ic* oxide), P_4O_{10}, a white powder that sublimes at approximately 360°C. The structures of these molecules are based on P_4 tetrahedra (Figure 12.7). Before the true molecular structures of these compounds were known, empirical formulas were used; consequently, the compounds are often designated as P_2O_3, phosphorus trioxide, and P_2O_5, phosphorus pentoxide. Phosphorus(V) oxide exists in three crystalline modifications, two of which are polymeric. When P_4O_6 is heated above 210°C, red

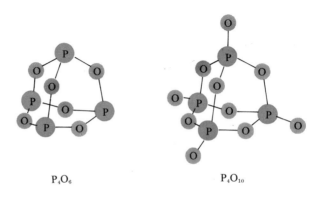

P_4O_6 P_4O_{10}

Figure 12.7 Structures of P_4O_6 and P_4O_{10}.

phosphorus and a third oxide, $(PO_2)_n$, are formed; $(PO_2)_n$ is a polymeric material and is relatively unimportant.

Phosphorus(V) oxide has a great affinity for water and is a very effective drying agent. Many different phosphoric acids may be prepared by the addition of water to P_4O_{10}. The most important acid of phosphorus in the 5+ state, orthophosphoric acid (or merely phosphoric acid) results from the complete hydration of the oxide.

$$P_4O_{10} + 6H_2O \longrightarrow 4H_3PO_4$$

Phosphoric acid is obtained commercially by this means or by treating phosphate rock with sulfuric acid.

$$Ca_3(PO_4)_2(s) + 3H_2SO_4(l) \longrightarrow 2H_3PO_4(l) + 3CaSO_4(s)$$

The compound is a colorless solid but is generally sold as an 85% solution. The electronic structure of H_3PO_4 may be represented as

since the P—O bond has double-bond character from $p\pi$-$d\pi$ bonding. The H_3PO_4 molecule and the ions derived from it are tetrahedral (Figure 12.8).

Phosphoric acid is a weak, triprotic acid without effective oxidizing power.

$$H_3PO_4(aq) \rightleftharpoons H^+(aq) + H_2PO_4^-(aq)$$

$$H_2PO_4^-(aq) \rightleftharpoons H^+(aq) + HPO_4^{2-}(aq)$$

$$HPO_4^{2-}(aq) \rightleftharpoons H^+(aq) + PO_4^{3-}(aq)$$

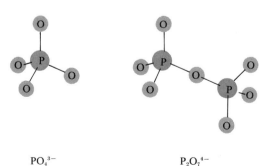

$PO_4{}^{3-}$ $P_2O_7{}^{4-}$

Figure 12.8 Structures of PO_4^{3-} and $P_2O_7^{4-}$ ions.

Hence, three series of salts may be derived from H_3PO_4: the dihydrogen phosphates (e.g., NaH_2PO_4), the monohydrogen phosphates (e.g., Na_2HPO_4), and the normal phosphates (e.g., Na_3PO_4). The product of a given neutralization depends upon the stoichiometric ratio of H_3PO_4 to alkali.

Phosphates are important ingredients of commercial fertilizers. Phosphate rock is too insoluble in water to be used for this purpose; however, the more soluble calcium dihydrogen phosphate may be obtained by treatment of phosphate rock with an acid.

$$Ca_3(PO_4)_2(s) + 2H_2SO_4(l) \longrightarrow Ca(H_2PO_4)_2(s) + 2CaSO_4(s)$$

The mixture of $Ca(H_2PO_4)_2$ and $CaSO_4$ is called **superphosphate fertilizer**. A higher yield of the dihydrogen phosphate is obtained if phosphoric acid is employed in the reaction instead of sulfuric acid.

$$Ca_3(PO_4)_2(s) + 4H_3PO_4(l) \longrightarrow 3Ca(H_2PO_4)_2(s)$$

Since nitrates are also important constituents of fertilizers, the mixture obtained by treatment of phosphate rock with nitric acid is a highly effective fertilizer.

$$Ca_3(PO_4)_2(s) + 4HNO_3(l) \longrightarrow Ca(H_2PO_4)_2(s) + 2Ca(NO_3)_2(s)$$

Condensed phosphoric acids have more than one P atom per molecule. The members of one group of condensed phosphoric acids, the **polyphosphoric acids,** conform to the general formula $H_{n+2}P_nO_{3n+1}$. Examples are:

$H_4P_2O_7$, diphosphoric acid $H_5P_3O_{10}$, triphosphoric acid

The polyphosphoric acids and polyphosphates have chain structures based on PO_4 tetrahedra which are joined through O atoms common to adjacent tetrahedra (Figure 12.8).

The **metaphosphoric acids** constitute another group of condensed phosphoric acids. These compounds have the general formula $H_nP_nO_{3n}$. Some of the metaphosphoric acids are cyclic. For example,

$H_3P_3O_9$, trimetaphosphoric acid $H_4P_4O_{12}$, tetrametaphosphoric acid

In addition, there are high-molecular-weight, long-chain metaphosphoric acids which are always obtained as complex mixtures that are assigned the formula $(HPO_3)_n$. The molecules of these mixtures are based on long chains

$$
\begin{array}{c}
\text{O} \\
| \\
\text{of } -\text{P}-\text{O}- \\
| \\
\text{OH}
\end{array}
\text{ units joined in such a way that each P atom is tetrahedrally}
$$

bonded to four O atoms, but the complete structures are very complicated and involve phosphorus-oxygen units that link two chains together.

The condensed phosphoric acids may be obtained by the controlled addition of water to P_4O_{10}. For example,

$$P_4O_{10}(s) + 4H_2O \longrightarrow \underset{\text{diphosphoric acid}}{2H_4P_2O_7(s)}$$

$$P_4O_{10}(s) + 2H_2O \xrightarrow{0°C} \underset{\text{tetrametaphosphoric acid}}{H_4P_4O_{12}(s)}$$

The dehydration of H_3PO_4 by heating also yields condensed acids. For example,

$$2H_3PO_4(l) \xrightarrow{215°C} \underset{\text{diphosphoric acid}}{H_4P_2O_7(l)} + H_2O(g)$$

$$nH_3PO_4(l) \xrightarrow{325°C} \underset{\text{metaphosphoric acid mixture}}{(HPO_3)_n(l)} + nH_2O(g)$$

On standing in water, all the condensed phosphoric acids revert to H_3PO_4.

The condensed phosphates may be prepared by neutralization of the acids or by thermal dehydration of mixtures of appropriate orthophosphates. For example,

$$2Na_2HPO_4(l) + NaH_2PO_4(l) \longrightarrow \underset{\text{sodium triphosphate}}{Na_5P_3O_{10}(l)} + 2H_2O(g)$$

Phosphor*ous* acid, H_3PO_3, may be prepared by adding P_4O_6 to cold water,

$$P_4O_6(s) + 6H_2O \longrightarrow 4H_3PO_3(aq)$$

or by the hydrolysis of PCl_3 (Section 12.5). Condensed phosphorous acids also exist. Even though the H_3PO_3 molecule contains three hydrogen atoms, phosphorous acid is a weak, *diprotic* acid and is probably better formulated as $H_2(HPO_3)$.

$$H_2(HPO_3)(aq) \rightleftharpoons H^+(aq) + H(HPO_3)^-(aq)$$

$$H(HPO_3)^-(aq) \rightleftharpoons H^+(aq) + HPO_3^{2-}(aq)$$

The sodium salts NaH_2PO_3 and Na_2HPO_3 are known, but it is impossible to prepare Na_3PO_3.

Solutions of salts of hypophosphorous acid, H_3PO_2, are prepared by boiling white phosphorus with solutions of alkalies (Section 12.4). The acid, which is a colorless crystalline material, may be obtained by treating a solution of barium hypophosphite with sulfuric acid, removing the precipitated barium sulfate by filtration, and evaporating the solution. Hypophosphorous acid is a weak monoprotic acid; hence the formula of the compound is sometimes written $H(H_2PO_2)$.

$$H(H_2PO_2)(aq) \rightleftharpoons H^+(aq) + H_2PO_2^-(aq)$$

The numbers of protons released by orthophosphoric, phosphorous, and hypophosphorous acids may be explained by the electronic structures of these compounds.

```
          O                        H
          |                        |
  H—O—P—O—H              H—O—P—O
          |                        |
          H                        H
  phosphorous acid        hypophosphorous acid
```

Only the hydrogen atoms bonded to oxygen atoms are acidic; those bonded to phosphorus atoms do not dissociate as $H^+(aq)$ in water. In each of these molecules, the P—O bonds have $p\pi$-$d\pi$ double-bond character.

Electrode potential diagrams for phosphorus and some of its compounds appear in Figure 12.9. The most striking feature of the diagrams is that all the potentials are negative in contrast to the potentials of the nitrogen diagram. Thus none of the substances is a good oxidizing agent, particularly in

Figure 12.9 Electrode potential diagrams for phosphorus and some of its compounds.

alkaline solution. Rather, H_3PO_3, H_3PO_2, and the salts of these acids have strong reducing properties, the acids being readily oxidized to H_3PO_4 and the anions being readily oxidized to PO_4^{3-}. With the exception of HPO_3^{2-} in alkaline solution, all the species of intermediate oxidation state disproportionate, PH_3 being one of the products of each disproportionation.

When arsenic, antimony, or bismuth is burned in air, a $3+$ oxide is formed: As_4O_6, Sb_4O_6, or Bi_2O_3. The arsenic(III) and antimony(III) oxides have molecular structures similar to P_4O_6 (Figure 12.7). Bismuth(III) oxide exists in an ionic lattice, and the empirical formula, Bi_2O_3, is used for this compound. All these oxides are solids; As_4O_6 and Sb_4O_6 are white, and Bi_3O_2 is yellow.

Arsenic(III) oxide is slightly soluble in water, but Sb_4O_6 and Bi_2O_3 are practically insoluble. Solutions of As_4O_6 are acidic; however, the form of the weak acid, "arsenious acid," thus produced is unknown, and the formula H_3AsO_3 (an ortho- formula) is usually used. The free "acid" is probably a hydrated oxide. Most of the known arsenites are metaarsenites (e.g., $NaAsO_2$), but orthoarsenites (e.g., $Cu(HAsO_3)$ and Na_3AsO_3) as well as other types are known.

The increasing metallic character in the series As, Sb, Bi is apparent in the decreasing acidic character of the corresponding $3+$ oxides. The compound As_4O_6 is predominantly an acidic oxide, and it readily dissolves in alkaline solutions to produce arsenites. However, As_4O_6 is also weakly basic; it dissolves in hot, concentrated HCl to give solutions of $AsCl_3$. The oxide Sb_4O_6 is amphoteric, dissolving readily in both alkalies (to give antimonites, such as $NaSbO_2$) and acids (to give salts of the SbO^+ ion). Bismuth(III) oxide is completely basic; it will not dissolve in alkalies but is soluble in acids. Evaporation of these acidic solutions yields Bi^{3+} salts (e.g., $Bi(NO_3)_3$). However, if these solutions are diluted, or if Bi^{3+} salts are dissolved in water, bismuthyl salts precipitate (such as $BiONO_3$, $BiOCl$, and $(BiO)_2SO_4$). Most bismuthyl compounds are insoluble. The addition of OH^- to a solution of a bismuth salt precipitates $Bi(OH)_3$; this compound is a true hydroxide, and no similar compound of arsenic or antimony is known. Under different conditions, bismuthyl hydroxide, BiO(OH), can be prepared.

The structures of the $5+$ oxides of arsenic and antimony are not known and empirical formulas (As_2O_5 and Sb_2O_5) are employed. These compounds are acidic oxides and possess no amphoteric characteristics. Neither As_2O_5 nor Sb_2O_5 may be made by direct reaction of the elements. Arsenic(V) oxide, a white solid, is prepared by heating the hydrate of orthoarsenic acid $(2H_3AsO_4 \cdot H_2O)$ that is obtained from the reaction of concentrated HNO_3 with either As or As_4O_6. Orthoarsenic acid is produced when As_2O_5 is dissolved in water. Metaarsenic acid $HAsO_3$, and pyroarsenic acid, $H_4As_2O_7$, may be prepared by heating orthoarsenic acid; they revert to the ortho- form in water. The arsenates, which may be prepared by neutralizing arsenic acid or by dissolving As_2O_5 in alkali, resemble phosphates in crystal form and solubility.

The reaction of Sb or Sb_4O_6 with concentrated HNO_3 gives hydrated Sb_2O_5 which may be heated to obtain anhydrous Sb_2O_5, a yellow powder. Free antimonic acid is unknown, but antimonates may be produced by dissolving Sb_2O_5 in alkalies. Sodium antimonate, $NaSb(OH)_6$, is one of the least soluble salts of Na^+, and its formation is often used as a test for this ion. The antimonate ion $(Sb(OH)_6^-)$ is octahedral in contrast to the tetrahedral AsO_4^{3-} and PO_4^{3-} ions; antimony is a sufficiently large atom to accommodate six oxygen atoms.

Bismuth(V) oxide has never been prepared in the pure state; it is unstable and readily loses oxygen. The red-brown product obtained by the action of strong oxidizing agents (such as Cl_2, OCl^-, and $S_2O_8^{2-}$) on a suspension of Bi_2O_3 in an alkaline solution is thought to be impure Bi_2O_5 Bismuth(V) oxide dissolves in sodium hydroxide to produce a yellow-brown substance known as sodium bismuthate and assigned the formula $NaBiO_3$. This material, which may also be prepared by fusing Na_2O_2 and Bi_2O_3, is probably a mixture of oxides containing some Bi_2O_5. Bismuthic acid is not known.

In contrast to the phosphate ion, the arsenate ion and the antimonate ion are relatively good oxidizing agents in acidic solution. Sodium bismuthate, in acidic solution, is an extremely powerful oxidizing agent.

CARBON AND SILICON

Carbon, silicon, germanium, tin, and lead comprise group IV A. The compounds of carbon are more numerous than the compounds of any other element with the exception of hydrogen. In fact, approximately ten compounds that contain carbon are known for every one compound that does not. The chemistry of the compounds of carbon (most of which also contain hydrogen) is the subject of **organic chemistry** (Chapter 20.).

12.9 Group Properties

The transition from nonmetallic character to metallic character with increasing atomic number that is exhibited by the elements of group V A is also evident in the chemistry of the IV A elements. Carbon is strictly a nonmetal (although graphite is an electrical conductor). Silicon is essentially a nonmetal in its chemical behavior; however, its electrical and physical properties are those of a semimetal. Germanium is a semimetal; its properties are more metallic than nonmetallic. Tin and lead are truly metallic, although some

Table 12.6

Some Properties of the Group IV A Elements

	Carbon	Silicon	Germanium	Tin	Lead
melting point (°C)	3570	1420	959	232	327
boiling point (°C)	4200	2355	2700	2360	1755
atomic radius (Å)	0.77	1.17	1.22	1.41	1.54
ionization potential (ev)					
first	11.3	8.1	8.1	7.3	7.4
second	24.4	16.3	15.9	14.5	15.0
third	47.9	33.5	34.1	30.5	32.0
fourth	64.5	45.1	45.5	39.4	42.1
electronegativity	2.5	1.8	1.8	1.8	1.8

vestiges of nonmetallic character remain (e.g., the oxides and hydroxides of tin and lead are amphoteric).

Carbon exists in network crystals with the atoms of the crystal held together by covalent bonds (Section 12.10). A large amount of energy is required to rupture some or all of these bonds in fusion or vaporization; hence, carbon has the highest melting point and boiling point of the family (Table 12.6). The heaviest member of the family, lead, exists in a typical metallic lattice. The crystalline forms of the intervening members show a transition between the two extremes displayed by carbon and lead, and this accounts for the trend in melting points and boiling points of the elements (Table 12.6).

The crystalline forms of silicon and germanium are similar to the diamond; however, the bonds are not so strong as those in the diamond, and silicon and germanium are semiconductors (the diamond is not). Silicon and germanium may be used to prepare impurity semiconductors (Section 7.14) that are employed in transistors. Although one modification of tin has a diamond-type structure, the principal form of tin is metallic.

The electronic configurations of the elements are listed in Table 12.7. With the possible exception of carbon, the assumption of a noble-gas configuration

Table 12.7

Electronic Configurations of the Group IV A Elements

Element	Z	1s	2s	2p	3s	3p	3d	4s	4p	4d	4f	5s	5p	5d	6s	6p
C	6	2	2	2												
Si	14	2	2	6	2	2										
Ge	32	2	2	6	2	6	10	2	2							
Sn	50	2	2	6	2	6	10	2	6	10		2	2			
Pb	82	2	2	6	2	6	10	2	6	10	14	2	6	10	2	2

through the formation of a 4— ion by electron gain is not observed; the electronegativities of the group IV A elements are generally low (Table 12.6). Carbon forms saltlike carbides with certain strongly metallic elements (Section 12.11); however, the bonding in these compounds probably has a significant degree of covalent character.

The ionization potentials of the elements (Table 12.6) show that the energy required for the removal of all four valence electrons from any given element is extremely high. Consequently, simple 4+ ions of group IV A elements are unknown. Germanium, tin, and lead appear to be able to form inert-pair ions by the loss of two electrons. However, only some of the compounds of Pb^{2+} (such as PbF_2 and $PbCl_2$) are ionic. The compounds of Ge^{2+} and Sn^{2+} are predominantly covalent, and those of Ge^{2+} are relatively unstable toward disproportionation to the 4+ and 0 states.

In the majority of their compounds, the IV A elements are covalently bonded. Through the formation of four covalent bonds per atom, an element can attain the electronic configuration of the noble gas of its period. These bonds may be regarded as having been formed by the use of sp^3 hybrid orbitals, and compounds of the type AB_4 are tetrahedral. All the carbon family elements can form such compounds, but only a few compounds of this type are known for lead (PbF_4, $PbCl_4$, and PbH_4) and they, with the exception of PbF_4, are thermally unstable.

In the case of carbon, the formation of four covalent bonds saturates the valence level. However, the other members of the group have empty d orbitals available in their valence levels and can form species in which the atom of the IV A element exhibits a covalence greater than four. The ions SiF_6^{2-}, $GeCl_6^{2-}$, $SnBr_6^{2-}$, $Sn(OH)_6^{2-}$, $Pb(OH)_6^{2-}$, and $PbCl_6^{4-}$ utilize d^2sp^3 hybrid bonding orbitals; they are octahedral.

The most important way in which carbon differs from the remaining elements of group IV A (as well as from all other elements) is the pronounced ability of carbon to form compounds in which many carbon atoms are bonded to each other in chains or rings. This property, called **catenation**, is exhibited by other elements near carbon in the periodic classification (such as boron, nitrogen, phosphorus, sulfur, oxygen, silicon, germanium, and tin) but to a much lesser extent than carbon, and it is this property of carbon that makes for the large number of organic compounds.

In group IV A, the tendency for self-linkage diminishes markedly with increasing atomic number. The hydrides, which have the general formula E_nH_{2n+2} (where E is a group IV A elements), illustrate this trend. There appears to be no limit to the number of carbon atoms that can bond together to form chains, and a very large number of hydrocarbons are known. For the other IV A elements, the most complex hydrides that have been prepared are Si_6H_{14}, Ge_9H_{20}, Sn_2H_6, and PbH_4. The carbon–carbon single bond energy (82 kcal/mole) is much greater than that of the silicon–silicon bond

(43 kcal/mole), the germanium–germanium bond (40 kcal/mole), or the tin–tin bond (37 kcal/mole).

In addition, carbon chains are much more stable than the chains of any other element. The reason for this difference in stability may be derived, in part, from a comparison of some bond energies:

C—C	82 kcal/mole	Si—Si	43 kcal/mole
C—O	84 kcal/mole	Si—O	89 kcal/mole
C—H	99 kcal/mole	Si—H	81 kcal/mole
C—Cl	78 kcal/mole	Si—Cl	86 kcal/mole
C—F	105 kcal/mole	Si—F	128 kcal/mole

The C—C bond energy is approximately of the same order of magnitude as the energies of the bond between carbon and other elements. The Si—Si bond, however, is weaker than the bonds that silicon forms with other elements.

Another characteristic of carbon is its pronounced ability to form multiple bonds with itself and with other nonmetals. Such groupings as

$$\text{>C=C<}, \quad -C\equiv C-, \quad -C\equiv N, \quad \text{>C=O, and} \quad \text{>C=S}$$

are frequently encountered. No other IV A element uses p orbitals to form π bonds. Double-bond character arises in some of the bonds of Si (such as Si—O and Si—N) from the overlap of a filled p orbital of the substituent atom with an empty d orbital of Si. This $p\pi$-$d\pi$ bonding, however, does not occur to any extent in the bonds of the other IV A elements.

Only the truly nonmetallic members of the family, carbon, and silicon will be treated in the sections that follow.

12.10 The Elements

Carbon constitutes approximately 0.03 % of the earth's crust; in addition, the atmosphere contains 0.03 % CO_2, by volume, and carbon is an important constituent of all plant and animal matter. The allotropes of carbon, diamond and graphite, as well as impure forms of the element such as coal (which also contains combined carbon) are naturally occurring. In combined form, the element occurs in compounds with hydrogen, called **hydrocarbons**, found in natural gas and petroleum, in the atmosphere as CO_2, and in carbonate minerals such as limestone ($CaCO_3$), dolomite ($CaCO_3 \cdot MgCO_3$), siderite ($FeCO_3$), witherite ($BaCO_3$), and malachite ($CuCO_3 \cdot Cu(OH)_2$).

In diamond, each carbon atom is bonded, through sp^3 hybrid orbitals, to four other carbon atoms arranged tetrahedrally (Figure 12.10). Strong bonds

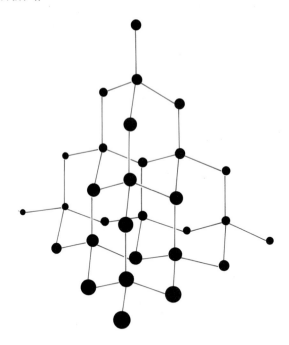

Figure 12.10 Arrangement of atoms in a diamond crystal.

hold this network crystal together; furthermore, all the valence electrons of each carbon atom are paired in bonding orbitals, and the valence level of each carbon atom can hold no more than eight electrons. Thus the diamond is extremely hard, high melting, stable, and a nonconductor of electricity.

Whereas the diamond is a colorless, transparent material with a high refractivity, graphite is a soft, black solid with a slight metallic luster. The graphite crystal is composed of layers formed from hexagonal rings of carbon atoms (Figure 12.11). The layers are held together by relatively weak van der Waals forces, and the distance from carbon atom to carbon atom in adjacent planes is 3.35 Å as compared to a distance of 1.415 Å between bonded carbon atoms of a plane. Since it is easy for the layers to slide over one another, graphite is soft and has a slippery feel; it is less dense than diamond.

The nature of the bonding in the layers of the graphite crystal accounts for some of the properties of this substance. Each carbon atom is bonded to three other carbon atoms, and all the bonds are perfectly equivalent. The C—C bond distance in graphite (1.415 Å) compared to that in the diamond (1.54 Å) suggests that a degree of multiple bonding exists in the former, and graphite may be represented as a resonance hybrid (Figure 12.12) in which each bond is a $1\frac{1}{3}$ bond.

Each C atom in graphite forms σ bonds with three other C atoms through the use of sp^2 hybrid orbitals. Therefore, the structure is planar with the

Figure 12.11 Arrangement of atoms in a graphite crystal.

three σ bonds of each atom directed to the corners of equilateral triangles. Such bonding accounts for three of the four valence electrons of each C atom; the fourth, a p electron, is not involved in σ bond formation (Figure 12.13a).

If only two adjacent atoms in a molecule had this electron arrangement, the additional p electrons would pair to form a localized π bond, and thus the atoms would be joined by a double bond. However, in graphite, *each* C atom has an additional p electron, and the resonance forms depict the possibility of forming conventional double bonds in three ways. Since each p orbital overlaps with more than one other p orbital, an extended π bonding system forms encompassing the entire structure (Figure 12.13b). The electrons in this π bonding system are not localized between two atoms but are free to move throughout the entire layer. Hence, graphite has a metallic luster and is an electrical conductor. The conductivity is fairly large in a direction parallel to the layers but is small in a direction perpendicular to the planes of the crystal.

Silicon, which constitutes approximately 28% of the earth's crust, is the second most abundant element (oxygen is first). The element does not occur

Figure 12.12 Resonance forms for a fragment of a graphite layer.

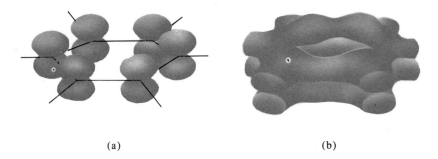

(a)   (b)

Figure 12.13 Schematic representation of the formation of the multicenter π bonding system of a graphite. (σ bonds are shown as lines.)

free in nature; rather, it is found as silicon dioxide (sometimes called silica) and in an enormous variety of silicate minerals.

Silicon is prepared by the reduction of silicon dioxide by coke, at high temperatures, in an electric furnace.

$$SiO_2(l) + 2C(s) \longrightarrow Si(l) + 2CO(g)$$

If a larger quantity of carbon is employed, silicon carbide, (or "Carborundum"), SiC, is produced rather than silicon. The only known modification of silicon has a structure similar to diamond. Crystalline silicon is a gray, lustrous solid that is a semiconductor. The bonds in silicon are not so strong as those in diamond, and the bonding electrons are not so firmly localized. Evidently, in silicon, electrons may be thermally excited to a conductance band that is energetically close to the valence band (Section 4.6).

Very pure silicon, for use in transistors, is prepared by a series of steps. First, impure silicon is reacted with chlorine to produce $SiCl_4$. The tetrachloride, a volatile liquid, is purified by fractional distillation and then reduced, by hydrogen, to elementary silicon. This product is further purified by zone refining. In this process, a short section of one end of a silicon rod is melted, and this melted zone is caused to move slowly along the rod to the other end by the movement of the heater. Pure silicon crystallizes from the melt, and the impurities are swept along, in the melted zone, to one end of the rod which is subsequently sawed off and discarded.

12.11   Carbides and Silicides

A large number of carbides and silicides are known—the carbides having been much more extensively studied than the silicides. Carbides may be made by heating the metal or its oxide with carbon, carbon monoxide, or a hydrocarbon. As is the case with the hydrides and nitrides, carbides may be classified as **saltlike**, **interstitial**, or **covalent**.

The saltlike carbides may be divided into two types. The I A and II A metals, as well as Cu^+, Ag^+, Au^+, Zn^{2+}, and Cd^{2+}, form carbides that are believed to contain the acetylide ion, C_2^{2-}, which has the structure

$$[:C \equiv C:]^{2-}$$

Upon hydrolysis, acetylides yield acetylene, C_2H_2,

$$H-C \equiv C-H$$

$$CaC_2(s) + 2H_2O \longrightarrow Ca(OH)_2(aq) + C_2H_2(g)$$

Beryllium carbide, Be_2C, and aluminum carbide, Al_4C_3, contain the methanide ion, C^{4-}, and yield methane, CH_4, upon hydrolysis.

$$Al_4C_3(s) + 12H_2O \longrightarrow 4Al(OH)_3(s) + 3CH_4(g)$$

Interstitial carbides are formed by transition elements and consist of metallic lattices with carbon atoms in the interstices. These materials, such as TiC, TaC, W_2C, VC, and Mo_2C, are in general very hard, high melting, and chemically inert. They resemble metals in appearance and electrical conductivity.

For the formation of interstitial carbides, the interstices of the metallic crystal must be sufficiently large to accommodate carbon atoms, and this requires that the metals have a radius greater than 1.3 Å. Some transition metals, with radii less than 1.3 Å, form carbides intermediate in character between the saltlike carbides and the interstitial carbides. The metal lattices of these substances, such as Fe_3C, Cr_3C_2, Co_3C, and Ni_3C, are distorted, and these materials are readily hydrolyzed.

Silicon carbide, produced by the reaction of SiO_2 and C, is a covalent carbide. It is hard, stable, and chemically inert. The silicon carbide crystal consists of a three-dimensional network formed from tetrahedra of alternating carbon and silicon atoms. Boron carbide, B_4C, which is even harder than silicon carbide, is made by the reduction of B_2O_3 by carbon in an electric furnace.

Silicon dissolves in almost all molten metals, and in many of these instances, definite compounds, called silicides, are produced. The compounds Mg_2Si, $CaSi_2$, Li_3Si, FeSi, Fe_2Si, Ni_2Si, NiSi, VSi_2, and $CoSi_3$ are among those known. Although probably none of the silicides are truly ionic, certain of them hydrolyze to produce hydrogen-silicon compounds, called **silicon hydrides** or **silanes**.

The silanes are compounds of general formula Si_nH_{2n+2}, and compounds where n equals 1 to 6 are well characterized. The hydrolysis of Mg_2Si, by dilute acids, gives a mixture of silanes; for example,

$$Mg_2Si(s) + 4H^+(aq) \longrightarrow 2Mg^{2+}(aq) + SiH_4(g)$$

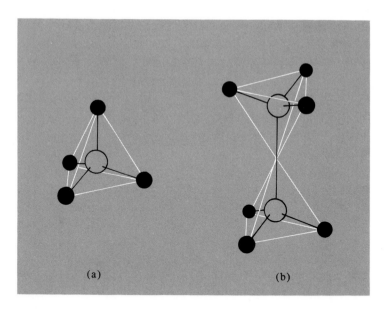

(a)   (b)

Figure 12.14   Arrangement of atoms in (a) CH_4 and SiH_4 and (b) C_2H_6 and Si_2H_6. Open circles, C or Si; black circles, H.

The silanes structurally resemble the hydrocarbons of formula C_nH_{2n+2} called the **alkanes** (Figure 12.14). However, there is presumably no limit to the number of carbon atoms that can join together to form alkanes, whereas the number of silanes appears to be limited owing to the comparative weakness of the Si—Si bond. In addition, the alkanes are much less reactive than the silanes, which are spontaneously flammable in air.

$$2Si_2H_6(g) + 7O_2(g) \longrightarrow 4SiO_2(s) + 6H_2O(g)$$

The C—C bonds of the alkanes are all σ bonds, but there are hydrocarbons, such as acetylene, which contain multiple bonds between carbon atoms. Silicon hydrides that contain multiple bonds are unknown. The hydrocarbons are discussed in Chapter 20.

12.12   Oxides and Oxyacids

Three oxides of carbon are well characterized: C_3O_2 (carbon suboxide), CO (carbon monoxide), and CO_2 (carbon dioxide). Carbon monoxide is formed by the combustion of carbon in a limited supply of oxygen at high temperatures (ca. 1000°C).

$$2C(s) + O_2(g) \longrightarrow 2CO(g)$$

It is also produced by the reaction of CO_2 and C at high temperatures and is a constituent of water gas (Section 8.9).

Carbon monoxide is isoelectronic with nitrogen (Section 4.4),

$$:C \equiv O:$$

with two π bonds and a σ bond joining the atoms. Certain transition metals and transition metal salts react with CO to produce metal carbonyls in which the CO molecule uses the unshared electron pair of the C atom for bond formation. Nickel carbonyl, $Ni(CO)_4$, is formed by the reaction of finely divided Ni and CO. The $Ni(CO)_4$ molecule is diamagnetic with a tetrahedral arrangement of four CO groups around a central Ni atom and may be assumed to be bonded through sp^3 hybrid orbitals of Ni. The electronic configuration of the outer sublevels of Ni is

	3d	4s	4p
Ni	⇅ ⇅ ⇅ ↑ ↑	⇅	— — —

In the carbonyl, the electronic structure of the Ni atom is

	3d	sp^3
Ni (hybridized)	⇅ ⇅ ⇅ ⇅ ⇅	— — — —

with the four electron pairs from the CO molecules occupying the sp^3 orbitals. In like manner, the Fe atom in $Fe(CO)_5$ exhibits dsp^3 hybridization (the molecule is trigonal bipyramidal and diamagnetic), and the Cr atom in $Cr(CO)_6$ displays d^2sp^3 hybridization (the molecule is octahedral and diamagnetic).

Since each CO molecule contributes a pair of electrons to the bonding, a metal with an odd number of electrons might be expected to form a carbonyl that would have an unpaired electron. In these cases, metal–metal bonds are usually formed, and a binuclear carbonyl results. For example, the electron configuration of the outer sublevels of Mn is

	3d	4s	4p
Mn	↑ ↑ ↑ ↑ ↑	⇅	— — —

In a hypothetical $Mn(CO)_5$ formed by using d^2sp^3 hybrid orbitals of Mn, five of the hybrid orbitals would be occupied by the five electron pairs from the CO molecules, and the sixth would contain an unpaired electron from the Mn atom.

	3d	d^2sp^3
Mn (hybridized)	⇅ ⇅ ⇅	↑ — — — — —

The odd electron is paired by the formation of a Mn−Mn bond between two $Mn(CO)_5$ units, and the formula of the compound is $Mn_2(CO)_{10}$. A large number of carbonyl compounds are known.

Carbon monoxide burns in air.

$$2CO(g) + O_2(g) \longrightarrow 2CO_2(g)$$

The reaction is highly exothermic ($\Delta H = -67.6$ kcal/mole) which accounts for the use of carbon monoxide as a fuel. The compound reacts with the halogens, in sunlight, to produce the carbonyl halides (COX_2) and with sulfur vapor, at high temperatures, to form carbonyl sulfide (COS).

Carbon monoxide is used as a reducing agent in metallurgical processes; at high temperatures, it reacts with many metal oxides to yield the free metal and CO_2.

$$FeO(s) + CO(g) \longrightarrow Fe(1) + CO_2(g)$$

The catalyzed reactions of carbon monoxide and hydrogen are commercially important for the production of hydrocarbons and methanol. Carbon monoxide is a poisonous gas because it combines, in the lungs, with the hemoglobin of the blood, thus preventing the hemoglobin from combining with oxygen.

Carbon dioxide is formed by the complete combustion of carbon or compounds of carbon (principally the hydrocarbons). It is also produced by the reaction of carbonates or hydrogen carbonates with acids.

$$CaCO_3(s) + 2H^+(aq) \longrightarrow Ca^{2+}(aq) + CO_2(g) + H_2O$$

and by heating carbonates,

$$CaCO_3(s) \longrightarrow CaO(s) + CO_2(g)$$

The molecule is linear and nonpolar. The electronic structure:

$$:\ddot{O}=C=\ddot{O}:$$

is only an approximation because the bonds of CO_2 are shorter and stronger than carbon-to-oxygen double bonds of other molecules. A treatment of the bonding has been proposed that incorporates delocalized π molecular orbitals, extending over all three atoms, together with the σ bonds that join the O atoms to the C atom.

Plants convert carbon dioxide and water vapor, from air, into carbohydrates (compounds of general formula $(C_x(H_2O)_y)$). The energy for this process, called **photosynthesis**, is supplied by sunlight, and the process is catalyzed by the green-coloring matter of plants, **chlorophyll**.

Carbon dioxide is moderately soluble in water; it is the acid anhydride of carbonic acid, H_2CO_3. The acid, however, has never been obtained in the pure state, and solutions of CO_2 in water consist mainly of dissolved CO_2 molecules, less than 1% of the dissolved material being in the form of H_2CO_3

molecules. Carbonic acid is a weak, diprotic acid, and equations for the ionizations are best written

$$CO_2(aq) + H_2O \rightleftharpoons H^+(aq) + HCO_3^-(aq)$$

$$HCO_3^-(aq) \rightleftharpoons H^+(aq) + CO_3^{2-}(aq)$$

Two series of salts are formed: the normal carbonates (such as Na_2CO_3 and $CaCO_3$) and the hydrogen carbonates (such as $NaHCO_3$ and $Ca(HCO_3)_2$). The structure of the carbonate ion has been discussed in Section 4.5 (Figure 4.24).

Sodium carbonate is an important industrial chemical, and more than 90% of the compound is produced commercially by the **Solvay process**. Ammonia and carbon dioxide, under pressure, are passed into a saturated solution of sodium chloride. The ammonia and carbon dioxide react:

$$NH_3(g) + CO_2(g) + H_2O \rightleftharpoons NH_4^+(aq) + HCO_3^-(aq)$$

Sodium bicarbonate precipitates from the solution because of the high concentration of sodium ion, and ammonium chloride is left behind.

$$Na^+(aq) + HCO_3^-(aq) \longrightarrow NaHCO_3(s)$$

The sodium bicarbonate is removed by filtration and washed; heating decomposes it into the normal carbonate.

$$2NaHCO_3(s) \longrightarrow Na_2CO_3(s) + CO_2(g) + H_2O(g)$$

The ammonia is recovered, for reuse, from the mother liquor by heating this solution with quicklime, CaO.

$$2NH_4^+(aq) + CaO(s) \longrightarrow 2NH_3(g) + Ca^{2+}(aq) + H_2O$$

The calcium oxide is obtained from limestone, $CaCO_3$, by heating; the CO_2 produced as a by-product of the preparation of CaO, as well as that produced by heating $NaHCO_3$, is used in the initial step of the process.

Although it is postulated that silicon monoxide exists in the vapor state, the only well-characterized oxide of silicon is SiO_2. In contrast to the oxides of carbon, which are volatile molecular species, held together by weak van der Waals forces in the solid state, SiO_2 forms very stable, nonvolatile, three-dimensional network crystals (melting point, $\sim 1700°C$). One of the three crystal modifications of SiO_2 has a lattice that may be considered to be derived from the diamond lattice with silicon atoms replacing carbon atoms and an oxygen atom midway between each pair of silicon atoms.

Of all the bonds that silicon forms, the $Si-O$ bond has a larger bond energy than any other with the exception of the $Si-F$ bond. It is not surprising that the chemistry of silicon is dominated by compounds containing the $Si-O$ linkage, and that SiO_2 is a chemically stable substance. Silicon dioxide is the product of the reaction of the elements; it is produced by reaction of the spontaneously flammable silicon hydrides with air, and hydrous SiO_2 is the product of the hydrolysis of many silicon compounds. Silicon dioxide occurs in several forms in nature; among them are sand, flint, agate, jasper, onyx, and quartz.

Silicon dioxide is an acidic oxide; however, no acids of silicon have ever been isolated. The oxide does not react directly with water, and acidification of a water solution of a soluble silicate yields only hydrous SiO_2. Silicates may be made by heating metal oxides, or metal carbonates, with SiO_2. Certain silicates of the I A metals (with a molar ratio of silicon dioxide to metal oxide of not more than 2 to 1) are water soluble.

A large number of silicates, of various types, occur in nature. The basic structure of all silicates is a tetrahedral SiO_4 unit (Figure 12.15). The simple ion SiO_4^{4-} occurs in certain minerals, for example, zircon ($ZrSiO_4$). More complicated ions are known in which two or more SiO_4 tetrahedra are joined through common oxygen atoms. In the simple ion SiO_4^{4-}, each oxygen completes its octet by accepting an electron; when tetrahedra are joined, the bridge oxygens complete their octets exclusively through covalent bond formation with two silicon atoms. Thus the ion containing two tetrahedral units has the formula $Si_2O_7^{6-}$; the mineral thortveitite ($Sc_2Si_2O_7$) contains this ion. Cyclic silicate ions are known in which two oxygen atoms of each SiO_4 unit act as bridge atoms; bentonite ($BaTiSi_3O_9$) and beryl ($Be_3Al_2Si_6O_{18}$) contain such ions.

The sharing of two oxygen atoms per SiO_4 tetrahedron can lead to polymeric anion chains of the type $(SiO_3^{2-})_n$ found in the pyroxenes (e.g., spodumene, $LiAl(SiO_3)_2$) and the double-chain type $(Si_4O_{11}^{6-})_n$ found in the amphiboles (e.g., the asbestos minerals). These **anion** chains extend throughout the crystal and, consequently, minerals **of these** types have a fibrous nature.

If three oxygen atoms of each SiO_4 tetrahedron are used as bridge atoms, a sheetlike anion results. The anion $(Si_2O_5^{2-})_n$ occurs in talc ($Mg_3(Si_2O_5)(OH)_2$), the layer structure giving the slippery feel of this material. Occasionally, aluminum atoms take the places of some of the silicon atoms in certain anions. The hypothetical AlO_4 tetrahedron would have a 5— charge, however, because aluminum has one less proton in the nucleus than silicon; consequently, such substitutions increase the negative charge on the anion. Muscovite ($KAl_3Si_3O_{10}(OH)_2$) contains a sheetlike aluminosilicate anion with one-fourth of the silicon atoms of the $(Si_2O_5^{2-})_n$ structure replaced by aluminum atoms.

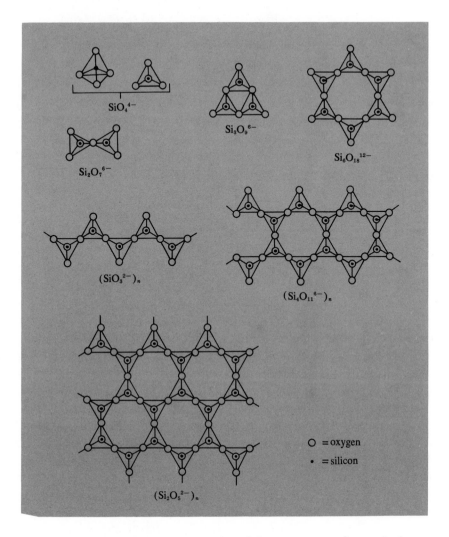

Figure 12.15 Schematic representation of the arrangement of atoms in the silicate ions.

If all four oxygen atoms of each SiO_4 tetrahedron are used as bridge atoms, SiO_2 results. However, if some of the silicon atoms of this three-dimensional network are replaced by aluminum atoms, an anion results. Framework aluminosilicates, such as the feldspars and the zeolites, are of this type.

Glass is a mixture of silicates made by fusing SiO_2 with metal oxides and carbonates. Common soda-lime glass is made from Na_2CO_3, $CaCO_3$, and SiO_2. Special glasses may be made by the addition of other acidic and basic oxides (such as Al_2O_3, B_2O_3, PbO, and K_2O). Cement is a complex aluminosilicate mixture made from limestone ($CaCO_3$) and clay ($H_4Al_2Si_2O_9$).

12.13 Sulfur Compounds and Halogen Compounds

Carbon disulfide, CS_2, is a volatile liquid prepared by heating carbon and sulfur together in an electric furnace. The electronic structure of the molecule is analogous to CO_2. Silicon disulfide, SiS_2, prepared by the reaction of the elements at high temperatures, is a colorless, crystalline material that hydrolyzes to SiO_2 and H_2S. Solid SiS_2 has a chainlike structure

Carbon tetrachloride is made by heating chlorine with carbon disulfide

$$CS_2(g) + 3Cl_2(g) \longrightarrow CCl_4(g) + S_2Cl_2(g)$$

Carbon tetrachloride, which is a liquid under ordinary conditions, is a good solvent for many nonpolar materials. Carbon tetrafluoride, CF_4, which may be obtained by the fluorination of almost any carbon-containing compound, is a very stable gas. The mixed halide CCl_2F_2, "Freon," is a very stable, odorless, nontoxic gas used as a refrigerant. Carbon tetrabromide, CBr_4, and carbon tetraiodide, CI_4, are solids; they are thermally unstable, presumably because of the difficulty of carbon in accommodating four large atoms around itself.

The silicon tetrahalides, SiX_4, are formed by the reactions of the elements; SiF_4 is a gas; $SiCl_4$ and $SiBr_4$ are liquids; and SiI_4 is a solid. Unlike the tetrahalides of carbon, the silicon tetrahalides readily hydrolyze

$$SiX_4 + (n + 2)H_2O \longrightarrow SiO_2 \cdot nH_2O(s) + 4H^+(aq) + 4X^-(aq)$$

The difference in chemical reactivity of the tetrahalides of carbon and silicon is attributed to the availability of unoccupied d orbitals in silicon which make it possible for a water molecule to attach itself and thus facilitate hydrolysis.

With SiF_4, a secondary reaction follows the one previously given. The hydrofluoric acid formed in the initial reaction reacts with SiF_4 to form fluosilicic acid, a strong acid.

$$SiF_4(g) + 2HF(aq) \longrightarrow 2H^+(aq) + SiF_6^{2-}(aq)$$

The SiF_6^{2-} ion is octahedral and uses d^2sp^3 hybrid bonding orbitals of silicon.

Catenated halides of carbon and silicon are known (e.g., C_2Cl_6 and Si_2Cl_6).

12.14   Carbon-Nitrogen Compounds

There are many compounds in which carbon is bonded to nitrogen. Sodium cyanide is commercially prepared by the reaction of sodium amide with carbon at red heat. Sodium amide is a product of the iron-catalyzed reaction of Na metal and liquid ammonia.

$$2Na(s) + 2NH_3(l) \longrightarrow 2Na^+ + 2NH_2^- + H_2(g)$$

$$NaNH_2(l) + C(s) \longrightarrow NaCN(l) + H_2(g)$$

The cyanide ion is isoelectronic with N_2 and CO (Section 4.4)

$$[:C \equiv N:]^-$$

and it has a strong tendency to form covalent complexes with metal cations (such as $Ag(CN)_2^-$, $Cd(CN)_4^{2-}$, $Ni(CN)_4^{2-}$, $Hg(CN)_4^{2-}$, $Fe(CN)_6^{4-}$, $Fe(CN)_6^{3-}$, and $Cr(CN)_6^{3-}$).

Treatment of a cyanide with dilute sulfuric acid produces hydrogen cyanide, HCN. The compound is a low-boiling liquid (boiling point, 26.5°C) and is readily soluble in water to produce solutions of hydrocyanic acid, a weak acid. Hydrogen cyanide and the cyanides are extremely poisonous.

The thermal decomposition of certain heavy metal cyanides (such as AgCN, $Hg(CN)_2$, and AuCN) yields the metal and cyanogen, C_2N_2, or $(CN)_2$. The molecule is linear,

$$:N \equiv C - C \equiv N:$$

This very poisonous, colorless gas is sometimes called a pseudohalogen because it resembles the halogens in its chemical reactions. For example,

$$Cl_2(g) + 2OH^-(aq) \longrightarrow Cl^-(aq) + OCl^-(aq) + H_2O$$

$$(CN)_2(g) + 2OH^-(aq) \longrightarrow CN^-(aq) + OCN^-(aq) + H_2O$$

Cyanides resemble chlorides in their water solubility.

The ion OCN^-, produced by the disproportionation reaction of cyanogen in alkaline solution, is the cyanate ion; the corresponding acid, cyanic acid (HOCN), is not stable. An analogous ion, the thiocyanate ion, SCN^-, is prepared by fusing I A cyanides with sulfur.

BORON

Of the group III A elements—boron, aluminum, gallium, indium, and thallium—boron alone is a nonmetal.

12.15   Group Properties

The electronic configurations of the elements are listed in Table 12.8, and properties of the elements appear in Table 12.9. Boron is a much smaller atom

Table 12.8

Electronic Configurations of the Group III A Elements

Element	Z	1s	2s	2p	3s	3p	3d	4s	4p	4d	4f	5s	5p	5d	6s	6p
B	5	2	2	1												
Al	13	2	2	6	2	1										
Ga	31	2	2	6	2	6	10	2	1							
In	49	2	2	6	2	6	10	2	6	10		2	1			
Tl	81	2	2	6	2	6	10	2	6	10	14	2	6	10	2	1

Table 12.9

Some Properties of the Group III A Elements

	Boron	Aluminum	Gallium	Indium	Thallium
melting point (°C)	2300	659	30	155	304
boiling point (°C)	2550	2500	2070	2100	1457
atomic radius (Å)	0.80	1.25	1.25	1.50	1.55
ionic radius, M^{+3} (Å)	0.20	0.52	0.62	0.81	0.95
ionization potential (ev)					
first	8.3	6.0	6.0	5.8	6.1
second	25.1	18.8	20.4	18.8	20.3
third	37.9	28.4	30.6	27.9	29.7
heat of hydration, M^{3+} (kcal/mole)	—	−1121	−1124	−994	−984
electrode potential, $\mathscr{E}°$, (M^{3+}/M)(v)	—	−1.67	−0.52	−0.34	+0.72

than the others of the group, which accounts for the sharp distinction in properties between the nonmetallic boron and the other, metallic, group members. The atomic sizes of Ga, In, and Tl are influenced by the electronic inner-building of elements immediately preceding them in the periodic classification (particularly in the case of Tl which follows the lanthanides); hence, atomic radius does not rapidly and regularly increase with increasing atomic number for these elements. The comparatively small sizes of the elements account for the relatively high ionization potentials which do not decline in the expected manner as the group is descended.

None of the elements has the slightest tendency to form simple anions. Rather, as would seem reasonable from the electronic configurations of the elements, the most important oxidation state is 3+. This relatively high charge coupled with comparatively small ionic radii leads to species with significant polarizing abilities.

Hence, the compounds of the elements in the 3+ state are predominantly covalent, which also follows from the comparatively high values of the first three ionization potentials of the elements. With the exception of boron, which is exclusively nonmetallic in its chemistry, the III A elements exist as 3+ ions in water solution; these ions are strongly hydrated, however, and the heats of hydration are high.

The electrode potentials are indicative of a higher order of metallic reactivity than the ionization potentials of the gaseous ions might lead one to expect. This is because of the high heats of hydration that result from the high charge concentration of the small ions. The high charge density also accounts for the marked tendency of the elements to form complex ions.

The oxides and hydroxides (or hydrous oxides) exhibit the usual trend in decreasing acidic character with increasing atomic number. Thus B_2O_3 and $B(OH)_3$ (or H_3BO_3) are acidic; the compounds of aluminum and gallium are amphoteric; and In_2O_3 and Tl_2O_3 have no acidic character at all.

The $ns^2 np^1$ configuration of the valence level would lead one to anticipate the existence of 1+, inert-pair ions for the larger members of the group. This is indeed the case for thallium. The 1+ state of this element is considerably more stable than the 3+ state; TlOH is a strong electrolyte. Compounds of indium and gallium in which these elements are in a 1+ state are known, but this state is less important, and less stable, than the 3+ state.

Boron has a slight tendency for catenation (in e.g., B_2Cl_4 the atoms of which are arranged Cl_2BBCl_2), but no other member of the family displays this characteristic.

In some instances, similarities exist between elements that are not members of the same group of the periodic table but adjoin each other diagonally. Such a diagonal relationship exists between boron and silicon.

B	C
Al	Si

Indeed, in some ways, boron resembles silicon more than it resembles aluminum. Boron and silicon form volatile, covalent hydrides that are spontaneously flammable in air; the halides of both elements are easily, and extensively, hydrolyzed. Both B_2O_3 and SiO_2 are acidic and are the precursors of complex, and in some instances structurally similar, anions; with metallic oxides, the oxides of boron and silicon form glasses. Neither boron nor silicon will liberate hydrogen from acids, but these elements react with alkalies to produce hydrogen gas and borates or silicates.

12.16   The Element

Boron ($3 \times 10^{-4}\%$ of the earth's crust) does not occur free in nature; the principal ores of boron are borates such as kernite ($Na_2B_4O_7 \cdot 4H_2O$), borax ($Na_2B_4O_7 \cdot 10H_2O$), colemanite ($Ca_2B_6O_{11} \cdot 5H_2O$), and ulexite ($NaCaB_5O_9 \cdot 8H_2O$). A somewhat impure, dark-brown, amorphous form of the element is prepared by heating boric oxide, B_2O_3, with powdered magnesium. Pure, crystalline boron may be obtained by reducing BBr_3 by hydrogen on a hot tungsten filament (approximately 1500°C).

$$2BBr_3(g) + 3H_2(g) \longrightarrow 2B(s) + 6HBr(g)$$

The crystals, which condense on the filament, are black with a metallic luster.

The structures of three types of boron crystals have been determined, and at least one other allotrope is known to exist. Groups of 12 B atoms arranged in regular icosohedra (solid figures, each with 20 equilateral-triangular faces) occur in each of these crystalline modifications (Figure 12.16). In the α-rhombohedral form, each B atom participates not only in the bonding of its icosohedron but also in bonding that icosohedron to others. Ordinary electron-pair bonds cannot account for the large number of B to B interactions of the structure since a boron atom has only three electrons and four oribtals in its valence level.

In metallic crystals, there are too few valence electrons to form covalent bonds between neighboring metal atoms of the crystal lattice; the electrons belong to the crystal as a whole and serve to bind many nuclei together. However, boron is a nonmetal, and the properties of crystalline boron (low electrical conductivity, extreme hardness, brittleness, and high melting point) are more typical of a covalent, network type of crystal than a metallic crystal.

The bonding in elementary boron has been interpreted as involving **three-center bonds** as well as the more common two-center bonds. In a three-center bond, three atoms are held together by an electron pair in a single molecular

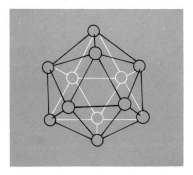

Figure 12.16   Arrangement of atoms in a B_{12} icosohedron.

Figure 12.17 Formation of a three-center B—B—B bond.

orbital. The molecular orbital is assumed to arise from the overlap of three atomic orbitals, one from each of the three bonded atoms. Several types of three-center bonds have been postulated, including the BBB bond found in crystalline boron (Figure 12.17) and a BHB bond found in the boron hydrides (Section 12.17).

The bonding of α-rhombohedral boron may be described by assuming that a number of three-center BBB bonds, together with two-center BB bonds, are used to hold each icosohedron together as well as to bond it to neighboring icosohedra. Such a description is not without its defects, however, since more than 70 equivalent resonance forms can be drawn for the structure that includes the proper number of bonds of each type.

12.17 Compounds of Boron

At very high temperatures (about 2000°C) boron reacts with many metals to form borides. These substances are very hard, are chemically stable, and have metallic conductivity. In the crystals of some metallic borides, the boron atoms are interstitial; in others, chains, octahedra, or layers of boron atoms are present. Magnesium boride, MgB_2, unlike the other borides, is readily hydrolyzed to produce a mixture of boron hydrides.

Boron reacts with ammonia or nitrogen at elevated temperatures to produce boron nitride, BN. This material is isoelectronic with carbon and has a crystal structure similar to graphite but with alternating boron and nitrogen atoms. At very high temperatures and pressures, this modification of BN is converted to another form that has a diamond-type lattice and is harder than diamond.

At high temperatures, boron reacts with the halogens to yield the trihalides: BF_3 and BCl_3 are gases, BBr_3 is a liquid, and BI_3 is a solid. The molecules of the trihalides are triangular planar. Presumably sp^2 hybrid orbitals of boron are used for bonding.

$$\ddot{X}$$
$$|$$
$$B$$
$$\diagup \diagdown$$
$$\ddot{X} \qquad \ddot{X}$$

Since the boron atom does not have an octet of electrons in each of these molecules, the trihalides react as electron acceptors (Lewis acids, Section 15.7).

$$\left[:\ddot{F}:\right]^- \;+\; \overset{:\ddot{F}:}{\underset{:\ddot{F}:}{B-\ddot{F}:}} \;\longrightarrow\; \left[:\ddot{F}-\overset{:\ddot{F}:}{\underset{:\ddot{F}:}{B}}-\ddot{F}:\right]^-$$

$$NH_3 + BF_3 \longrightarrow H_3N{:}BF_3$$

$$H_2O + BF_3 \longrightarrow H_2O{:}BF_3$$

The fluoborate ion, $BF_4{}^-$, is tetrahedral, and is bonded by sp^3 hybrid bonds.

Many borates occur in nature; some may be prepared by fusion of metallic oxides with B_2O_3 or boric acid, and hydrated borates may be obtained by crystallization of the solution resulting from the neutralization of boric acid with aqueous alkali. The borate anions may be considered to be built up from triangular BO_3 units, with or without BO_4 tetrahedra, by the sharing of oxygen atoms between units in much the same way as the silicates are constructed. Examples are illustrated in Figure 12.18.

Two BO_3 triangles with an oxygen atom in common form the $B_2O_5^{4-}$ ion (found in $Co_2B_2O_5$). By sharing two oxygen atoms per BO_3 unit, a cyclic structure (in $K_3B_3O_6$) or a polymeric chain structure (in CaB_2O_4) results.

The anions exclusively formed from BO_3 triangles are not stable in water and are readily hydrated into forms containing one or more BO_4 tetrahedra. For example, the hydrated anion $B_4O_5(OH)_4^{2-}$ is composed of two tetrahedra and two triangles (Figure 12.18); it exists in borax, $Na_2B_4O_5(OH)_4 \cdot 8H_2O$ (commonly written as $Na_2B_4O_7 \cdot 10H_2O$) and results from the neutralization of boric acid by NaOH in aqueous solution.

The acidification of an aqueous solution of any borate precipitates orthoboric acid (or merely boric acid), $B(OH)_3$, as soft, white crystals. This acid, which may also be prepared by the complete hydration of B_2O_3, has a layer-type crystal lattice in which there is extensive hydrogen bonding between $B(OH)_3$ molecules (Figure 12.19). The crystal structure of the material accounts for its cleavage into sheets and its slippery feel. Boric acid and the borates are toxic.

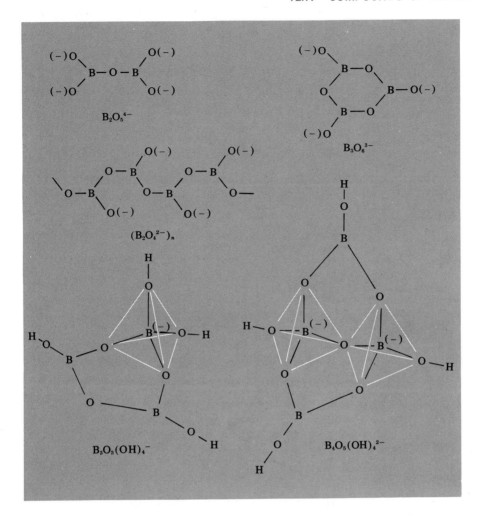

Figure 12.18 Arrangement of atoms in borate ions.

Boric acid is a very weak, *monobasic* acid in solution. Its ionization in fairly dilute solution may be represented as

$$B(OH)_3(aq) + H_2O \rightleftharpoons H^+(aq) + B(OH)_4^-(aq)$$

or

$$(H_2O)B(OH)_3(aq) \rightleftharpoons H^+(aq) + B(OH)_4^-(aq)$$

The $B(OH)_4^-$ ion is tetrahedral. In more concentrated solutions, polymeric anions, such as $B_3O_3(OH)_4^-$, exist (Figure 12.18).

When boric acid is heated to about 175°C, metaboric acid, HBO_2, results. The meta- acid reverts to the more highly hydrated ortho- form in water. Although salts of many hypothetical boric acids are known, these are the only two acids that exist in the pure condition.

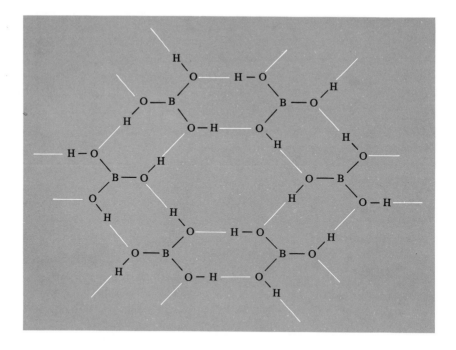

Figure 12.19 Arrangement of atoms in a layer of H_3BO_3 crystal. (White lines represent hydrogen bonds.)

Metaboric acid may be dehydrated, by heating, into boric oxide, B_2O_3. The oxide may also be prepared by heating boron in air. Crystals of B_2O_3 consist of interconnected spiral chains of BO_4 tetrahedra. The material, however, is usually obtained as a glass.

Boron forms two series of hydrides: B_nH_{n+4}, where $n = 2, 5, 6, 8, 10$, or 18, and B_nH_{n+6}, where $n = 4, 5, 6, 9$, or 10. A few compounds that do not conform to either of these formulas have been reported. The simplest hydride of boron is diborane, B_2H_6. The molecule BH_3 cannot be isolated but is thought to be a transitory intermediate in some of the reactions of the boron hydrides.

Diborane, which is a gas under ordinary conditions, may be prepared by the reaction of BF_3 and lithium hydride, in ether.

$$6LiH + 8BF_3 \longrightarrow 6LiBF_4 + B_2H_6$$

A mixture of higher boranes is obtained by heating diborane.

The compounds of formula B_nH_{n+4} are thermally more stable (with regard to decomposition to the elements) than the second group, B_nH_{n+6}. The compounds B_2H_6, B_5H_9, and B_5H_{11} are spontaneously flammable in air, and all the boranes hydrolyze, at various rates, to yield boric acid and hydrogen.

Figure 12.20   (a) Structure of diborane. (b) Formation of bonding orbitals. (Shapes of orbitals simplified.)

The molecular structure of diborane is shown in Figure 12.20. In the molecule, each B atom has two H atoms (called terminal hydrogen atoms) bonded to it by regular two-center, electron-pair bonds, and the resulting BH_2 fragments are joined together by two hydrogen bridges (three-center BHB bonds). The two B atoms and the four terminal H atoms are coplanar, and the bridge H atoms lie above and below this plane.

Each B atom may be considered to use sp^3 hybrid orbitals for the formation of the molecule. Two of the sp^3 orbitals of each B atom are used to form ordinary two-center bonds with terminal H atoms, and the other two hybrid orbitals are used to form three-center BHB bonds. Each three-center bond consists of a pair of electrons in a bonding molecular orbital formed by the overlap of the $1s$ orbital of the H atom with orbitals of the two B atoms (Figure 12.20). Of the twelve valence electrons in the molecule (six from the two B atoms and six from the six H atoms), four pairs are utilized in the two-center bonds to the four terminal H atoms, and two pairs are used in the two BHB three-center bonds. The molecule is diamagnetic. The bond distance between a B atom and a terminal H is shorter than the distance between a B atom and a bridge H, indicating a stronger bond in the former case.

The structures of the higher boranes involve BBB as well as BHB three-center bonds. Several of the higher boranes have skeletons of boron atoms that are fragments of the B_{12} icosohedron found in crystalline boron.

Boron forms a series of borohydride ions. The most important one is $BH_4{}^-$, a tetrahedral ion that may be prepared by the reaction of lithium hydride and B_2H_6 in ether.

$$2LiH + B_2H_6 \longrightarrow 2LiBH_4$$

Lithium borohydride, and the alkali borohydrides in general, are ionic materials that are important reducing agents. Other borohydride ions are known, such as $B_3H_8{}^-$, $B_{10}H_{13}{}^-$, and $B_{12}H_{12}^{2-}$. The boron skeleton of the $B_{12}H_{12}^{2-}$ ion is a B_{12} icosohedron.

SOME SUGGESTED READINGS

Cotton, F. A., and Wilkinson, G., *Advanced Inorganic Chemistry*, 2nd ed., New York, Wiley, 1966.

Johnson, R. C., *Introductory Descriptive Chemistry*, New York, Benjamin, 1966 (paper).

Jolly, W. L., *The Chemistry of the Non-Metals*, Englewood Cliffs, N. J., Prentice-Hall, 1966 (paper).

Rich, R. L., *Periodic Correlations*, New York, Benjamin, 1965 (paper).

Sherwin, E., and Weston, G. J., *Chemistry of the Non-Metallic Elements*, Elmsford, N.Y., Pergamon, 1966 (paper).

Weeks, M. E., and Leicester, H. M., *Discovery of the Elements*, 7th ed., Easton, Penna., Chemical Education Publishing Co., 1968.

PROBLEMS

12.1 Discuss how the properties of the elements of group V A and their compounds change with increasing atomic number.

12.2 Write all the equations that you can for the reactions of elementary nitrogen. Explain the low order of chemical reactivity of N_2.

12.3 Discuss the comparative reactivities, solubilities, and electrical conductivities of the three allotropic forms of phosphorus in terms of molecular structure.

12.4 Write chemical equations for all of the reactions that occur between (a) P_4O_6, (b) Sb_4O_6, and (c) Bi_2O_3 and H_2O, aqueous NaOH, and aqueous HCl.

12.5 What are the characteristics of the three types of nitrides?

12.6 Boron nitride, BN, exists in two crystalline modifications—one resembling diamond and the other graphite. Describe, using drawings, the structures of these four substances.

12.7 Discuss the preparation, structure, and properties of ammonia. Why is the boiling point of NH_3 high in comparison to the boiling points of PH_3, AsH_3, and SbH_3?

12.8 Write equations for the following reactions of ammonia:

(a) $NH_3(aq) + Ag^+(aq) \longrightarrow$

(b) $NH_3(aq) + H^+(aq) \longrightarrow$

(c) $NH_3(aq) + H_2O + CO_2(aq) \longrightarrow$

(d) $NH_3(g) + O_2(g) \xrightarrow{\text{heat}}$

(e) $NH_3(g) + O_2(g) \xrightarrow[\text{heat}]{\text{Pt}}$

(f) $NH_3(g) + HCl(g) \longrightarrow$

(g) $NH_3(g) + V(s) \xrightarrow{\text{heat}}$

(h) $NH_3(l) + Na(s) \longrightarrow$

12.9 Write a series of equations for the preparation of nitric acid starting with N_2 as the source of nitrogen.

12.10 Write an equation for the reaction of HNO_3 with (a) Cu, (b) Zn, (c) P_4O_{10}, (d) NH_3, (e) $Ca(OH)_2$.

12.11   (a) List the oxides of nitrogen. (b) Write a chemical equation for the preparation of each of them. (c) Diagram the electronic structure of each oxide.

12.12   (a) Diagram the isomers of N_2F_2. (b) Diagram the theoretically possible isomers of PCl_2F_3. Note that the equatorial and polar positions of a trigonal bipyramid are not equivalent.

12.13   State the products of the thermal decomposition of (a) NH_4NO_3, (b) NH_4NO_2, (c) $Pb(NO_3)_2$, (d) $NaNO_3$, (e) NaN_3.

12.14   Write equations for the following oxidation-reduction reactions: (a) The reaction of NH_3 with OCl^- that produces N_2H_4 and Cl^-. (b) The reaction of NO_2 with H_2 in HCl solution that produces $[NH_3OH]Cl$. (c) The electrolysis of NH_4F in anhydrous HF that produces NF_3 and H_2.

12.15   Draw electronic structures for orthophosphoric, phosphorous, and hypophosphorous acids. Tell how these structures explain the number of $H^+(aq)$ dissociated per mole when each of these compounds is dissolved in water.   ·

12.16   Write equations for the preparations of all of the acids that may be obtained by the hydrolysis of P_4O_{10}.

12.17   Write an equation for the reaction of each of the following with water: (a) Li_3N, (b) AlN, (c) Ca_3P_2, (d) $CaNCN$, (e) NCl_3, (f) PCl_3, (g) PCl_5, (h) $H_4P_2O_7$, (i) NO_2, (j) CaC_2, (k) Be_2C, (l) $SiCl_4$, (m) BF_3.

12.18   What is the acid anhydride of each of the following? (a) $H_2N_2O_2$, (b) HNO_2, (c) HNO_3, (d) $H_4P_2O_7$, (e) $H_3P_3O_9$, (f) H_3PO_3, (g) H_3AsO_4, (h) H_2CO_3, (i) $B(OH)_3$.

12.19   Discuss the ways in which the chemistry of carbon differs from the chemistry of the other elements of group IV A.

12.20   What explanation may be offered for the fact that carbon has a greater tendency toward catenation than any other element?

12.21   For each of the following carbonyls, all of which are diamagnetic, describe the geometric configuration of the molecule and the type of hybrid orbitals employed by the metal atom. (a) $C_2(CO)_8$, (b) $Mo(CO)_6$, (c) $Re_2(CO)_{10}$, (d) $Ru(CO)_5$.

12.22   Write a series of equations that lead to the preparation of Na_2CO_3 and that employ only N_2, H_2O, NaCl, $CaCO_3$, and substances derived from this list.

12.23   Explain the cause of the difference in reactivity toward water of CF_4 and SiF_4.

12.24   Write an equation for the reaction that occurs when each of the following is heated with carbon. (a) P_4O_{10}, (b) As_4O_6, (c) CaO, (d) $NaNO_3$, (e) $NaNH_2$, (f) SiO_2.

12.25   Write an equation for the reaction that occurs when each of the following is heated. (a) $NaHCO_3$, (b) $CaCO_3$, (c) AgCN, (d) H_3PO_4, (e) $Ca_3(PO_4)_2$ and SiO_2, (f) $CaCO_3$ and SiO_2.

12.26   Describe the ways in which the chemistry of boron resembles the chemistry of silicon.

12.27 Write an equation to show how orthoboric acid ionizes in water solution.

12.28 Complete and balance the following:

(a) $B_2O_3 + Mg \xrightarrow{\text{heat}}$ (f) $B_2O_3 + H_2O \longrightarrow$

(b) $BBr_3 + H_2 \xrightarrow{\text{heat}}$ (g) $B(OH)_3 + Na^+ + OH^- \longrightarrow$

(c) $B + N_2 \xrightarrow{\text{heat}}$ (h) $B(OH)_3 \xrightarrow[\text{heating}]{\text{mild}}$

(d) $B + Mg \xrightarrow{\text{heat}}$ (i) $B(OH)_3 \xrightarrow[\text{heating}]{\text{strong}}$

(e) $BF_3 + F^- \longrightarrow$ (j) $LiH + B_2H_6 \longrightarrow$

12.29 In a molecule of B_4H_{10}, the four boron atoms form a puckered square and are joined by B—H—B three-center bonds. Two of the boron atoms, diagonally across the square from one another, are joined by an electron-pair bond. Diagram the structure of the molecule.

12.30 What is a three-center bond?

ELEMENTS OF CHEMICAL THERMODYNAMICS

We have repeatedly referred to the energy effects accompanying chemical and physical changes. **Thermodynamics** is the study of these energy effects; in particular, it summarizes the relations between heat, work, and other forms of energy that are involved in all types of change. The laws of thermodynamics can be used to predict whether a particular chemical or physical transformation is theoretically possible under a given set of conditions. Furthermore, if a study shows that a desired change will not occur under the conditions assumed, thermodynamic principles can be used to determine how the conditions can be altered to make the change theoretically possible.

13.1   First Law of Thermodynamics

Thermodynamics had its origin in the investigation of the relation between mechanical work and heat. Many scientists of the late eighteenth and early nineteenth centuries studied the conversion of mechanical work into heat. However, the careful and convincing studies of James Joule, in the years 1840 to 1849, firmly established the principle that work could be converted into heat and provided a quantitative value for the mechanical equivalent of heat.

Joule studied the conversion of work into heat in many ways. He used the work done by a falling weight to turn a paddle wheel immersed in a container of water and determined the heat produced by measuring the increase in temperature of the water. In a series of such experiments, he used different weights and different quantities of water, as well as mercury in place of the water. Joule also studied the heating effects of electric currents and the conversion of work into heat by the compression of gases. In all his experiments, Joule found that a given amount of work produces a definite quantity of heat. In modern terms, the relation is

$$4.1840 \text{ joules} = 1 \text{ cal}$$

One joule, the unit of work, is 10^7 ergs, and 1 erg is the work done when a force of 1 dyne (or 1 g cm/sec^2) acts through a distance of 1 cm. The **calorie,** which was originally defined as the amount of heat required to raise the temperature of 1 g of water from 14.5° to 15.5°C, is now defined by its joule equivalent.

The recognition that heat and work are quantitatively related led to the concept that they are manifestations of a larger classification, energy, which is conserved. The **first law of thermodynamics**, which is the law of conservation of energy, states that energy can be converted from one form into another but cannot be created or destroyed.

In applying thermodynamic concepts, we frequently confine our attention to the changes that occur within definite boundaries. That portion of the universe included within these boundaries is called a **system**; the remainder of the universe is called the **surroundings**. If there is no exchange of mass between a system and its surroundings, the system is spoken of as a **closed system**. If, in addition, energy is not exchanged between the system and its surroundings, the system is referred to as an **isolated system**. Work done on a system need not always result in an increase in the temperature of the system or the conversion of work into heat. For example, the charging of a storage battery by an automobile engine results in an increase of the "chemical energy" of the battery; doing work on (or adding heat to) a sample of ice at 0°C could result in melting a part of the ice with no increase in the temperature of the system. A system is assumed to have an **internal energy**, E, which includes all possible forms of energy attributable to the system.

According to the first law of thermodynamics, the internal energy of an isolated system is constant. The actual value of E for any system is not known, nor can it be determined. However, thermodynamics is concerned only with *changes* in internal energy, and such changes are measurable.

The internal energy of a system depends upon the state of the system and not upon how the system arrived at that state. Internal energy is therefore called a **state function**. Consider a sample of an ideal gas that occupies a volume of 1 liter at 100°K and 1 atm pressure (state A). At 200° K and 0.5 atm (state B), the sample occupies a volume of 4 liters. According to the first law, the internal energy of the system in state A, E_A, is a constant, as is the internal energy of the system in state B, E_B. It follows that the difference in the internal energies of the two states, ΔE, is also a constant and is independent of the path taken between state A and state B. It makes no difference whether the gas is first heated and then the pressure changed, whether the heating is done after the pressure change, or indeed whether the total change is brought about in several steps,

$$\Delta E = E_B - E_A$$

If ΔE were not independent of the manner in which the corresponding change was brought about, it would be possible to create or destroy energy, in violation of the first law, by taking a system from A to B by one route and then returning it to state A by a different route. Instead, in a cyclic process (in which a system is returned to its original state), the increase in E in one direction exactly equals the decrease in E in the opposite direction so that for the cycle there is no net gain or loss in energy.

The change in internal energy of a system may be determined by measurement of the heat absorbed by the system from its surroundings, q, and the work done by the system on its surroundings, w. In these terms,

$$\Delta E = q - w$$

It is important to keep in mind the conventions regarding the signs of these quantities:

q, positive $=$ heat *absorbed* by the system

q, negative $=$ heat *evolved* by the system

w, positive $=$ work done *by* the system

w, negative $=$ work done *on* the system

The values of q and w involved in changing a system from state A to state B depend upon the way in which the change is carried out. However, the value of $(q - w)$ is a constant, equal to ΔE, for the change no matter how it is brought about. If a system undergoes a change in which the internal energy of the system remains constant, the work done by the system equals the heat absorbed by the system. If a system undergoes a change that reduces its internal energy, the energy released will be the sum of the heat evolved and the work done.

13.2 Enthalpy

Two types of changes that give rise to work terms are of especial interest to chemists. For electrochemical systems, the work term results, in whole or in part, from the production or use of electrical energy. For ordinary chemical reactions, the work term generally arises as a consequence of pressure-volume changes—for example, the work done against the atmosphere if the system expands in the course of the reaction. The term PV has the dimensions of work. Pressure (force per unit area) may be expressed in dynes per square centimeter; multiplying pressure by volume (in cubic centimeters) gives a product in dyne centimeters (or ergs) which is a dimension of work (force times distance). In like manner, liter atmospheres are units of work. If the pressure is held constant, the work done in expansion from V_A to V_B is

$$w = P(V_B - V_A) = P\Delta V$$

No pressure-volume work can be done by a **process** carried out at constant volume. Since $w = 0$,

$$\Delta E = q_V$$

Processes carried out at constant pressure are far more common in chemistry than those conducted at constant volume. If we restrict our attention to pressure-volume work, again, in the case of constant pressure processes, the work done is $P\Delta V$. Thus

$$\Delta E = q_p - P\Delta V$$

or

$$q_P = \Delta E + P\Delta V$$

This relationship may be written

$$q_P = (E_B - E_A) + P(V_B - V_A)$$

or, by rearranging,

$$q_P = (E_B + PV_B) - (E_A + PV_A)$$

The thermodynamic function **enthalpy**, H, is defined by the equation

$$H = E + PV$$

Therefore,

$$q_P = H_B - H_A = \Delta H$$

Thus the heat absorbed by a process conducted at constant pressure is equal to the change in enthalpy, and ΔH is related to the change in the internal energy of the system by the expression

$$\Delta H = \Delta E + P\Delta V$$

Enthalpy, like internal energy, is a function of the state of the system and is independent of the manner in which that state was achieved. This fact is the basis of the law of Hess (see the discussion of heats of reaction in Section 5.8 and the Born-Haber cycle in Section 5.10). Standard enthalpies of formation for a number of compounds are listed in Table 13.1.

Table 13.1

Enthalpy of Formation at 25°C and 1 Atm

Compound	ΔH_f° (kcal/mole)	Compound	ΔH_f° (kcal/mole)
$H_2O(g)$	−57.80	$CO(g)$	−26.42
$H_2O(l)$	−68.32	$CO_2(g)$	−94.05
$HF(g)$	−64.2	$NO(g)$	+21.60
$HCl(g)$	−22.06	$NO_2(g)$	+8.09
$HBr(g)$	−8.66	$NaCl(s)$	−98.23
$HI(g)$	+6.20	$MgO(s)$	−143.84
$H_2S(g)$	−4.82	$CaO(s)$	−151.9
$NH_3(g)$	−11.04	$Ca(OH)_2(s)$	−235.80
$CH_4(g)$	−17.89	$CaCO_3(s)$	−288.45
$C_2H_6(g)$	−20.24	$BaO(s)$	−133.4
$C_2H_4(g)$	+12.50	$BaCO_3(s)$	−291.3
$C_2H_2(g)$	+54.19	$Al_2O_3(s)$	−399.09
$CH_3OH(l)$	−57.02	$Fe_2O_3(s)$	−196.5
$C_6H_6(l)$	+11.72	$AgCl(s)$	−30.36
$SO_2(g)$	−70.96	$ZnO(s)$	−83.17

When a bomb calorimeter is used to make a calorimetric determination (Section 5.8), the heat effect is measured at constant volume; ordinarily, reactions are run at constant pressure. The relationship between change in enthalpy and change in internal energy is used to convert heats of reaction at constant volume ($q_V = \Delta E$) to heats of reaction at constant pressure ($q_P = \Delta H$). The appropriate conversion is made by considering the change in volume of the system—the total volume of the reactants subtracted from the total volume of the products. The changes in the volumes of liquids and solids are so small that they are neglected; if only liquids and solids are involved in the reaction, the equation $q_V = q_P$ is sufficiently accurate for most purposes.

For reactions involving gases, however, volume changes may be signifi-cant. Let us say that: V_A is the total volume of gaseous reactants; V_B is the total volume of gaseous products; n_A is the number of moles of gaseous reactants; n_B is the number of moles of gaseous products; and the pressure and temperature are constant. (Calorimetric values are usually recorded at 25°C.) From the ideal gas law,

$$PV_A = n_A RT \quad \text{and} \quad PV_B = n_B RT$$

Thus

$$P\Delta V = PV_B - PV_A$$
$$= n_B RT - n_A RT$$
$$= (\Delta n)RT$$

Therefore,

$$\Delta H = \Delta E + (\Delta n)RT$$

where Δn is the number of moles of gaseous products minus the number of moles of gaseous reactants.

In order to solve problems using this equation, we must express the value of R in appropriate units. As noted previously in this section, liter atmospheres are the dimensions of energy; therefore the value of R in liter atm/°K mole may be converted to cal/°K mole or to joules/°K mole (see Table 13.2).

Table 13.2

Value of the Gas Constant, R, in Various Units

R	Units
0.082056	liter atm/°K mole
8.3143	joules/°K mole
1.9872	cal/°K mole

▶ **EXAMPLE 13.1** The heat of combustion at constant volume of $CH_4(g)$ is measured in a bomb calorimeter at 25°C as $-211,613$ cal/mole. What is the ΔH?

Solution For the reaction

$$CH_4(g) + 2O_2(g) \longrightarrow CO_2(g) + 2H_2O(l) \qquad \Delta E = -211,613 \text{ cal}$$
$$\Delta n = 1 - (2 + 1) = -2$$

Therefore,

$$\Delta H = \Delta E + (\Delta n)RT$$
$$\Delta H = -211,613 \text{ cal} + (-2 \text{ mole})(1.987 \text{ cal/°K mole})(298.2°K)$$
$$= -211,613 \text{ cal} - 1185 \text{ cal}$$
$$= -212,798 \text{ cal} = -212.798 \text{ kcal}$$

It is convenient to note that a difference of 1 mole between the gaseous products and the gaseous reactants makes a change of 592.5 cal at 25°C.

▶ **EXAMPLE 13.2**   Calculate ΔH and ΔE at 25°C for the reaction

$$OF_2(g) + H_2O(g) \longrightarrow O_2(g) + 2HF(g)$$

The enthalpies of formation are: $OF_2(g)$, $+5.5$ kcal/mole; $H_2O(g)$, -57.8 kcal/mole; and $HF(g)$, -64.2 kcal/mole.

Solution   The enthalpies of formation are used to calculate the ΔH for the reaction (Section 5.9).

$$\begin{aligned}
\Delta H &= 2\Delta H_f(HF) - [\Delta H_f(OF_2) + \Delta H_f(H_2O)] \\
&= 2(-64.2) - [(+5.5) + (-57.8)] \\
&= -128.4 + 52.3 = -76.1 \text{ kcal}
\end{aligned}$$

This value of ΔH is used to calculate ΔE. For the reaction, $\Delta n = +1$ mole.

$$\begin{aligned}
\Delta E &= \Delta H - (\Delta n)RT \\
&= -76.1 \text{ kcal} - (1 \text{ mole})(1.99 \text{ cal/°K mole})(298°K) \\
&= -76.1 \text{ kcal} - 593 \text{ cal} = -76.7 \text{ kcal}
\end{aligned}$$

Therefore, the internal energy of the system decreases by 76.7 kcal ($\Delta E = -76.7$ kcal). At a constant pressure of 1 atm, only 76.1 kcal of this quantity are given off as heat ($\Delta H = -76.1$ kcal). The remainder is used for the work of expansion against the atmosphere.

13.3   Bond Energies

The value of ΔH for the dissociation of a gaseous diatomic molecule into gaseous atoms is a measure of the strength of the covalent bond of the molecule and is called the **bond dissociation energy**. For example, 118.3 kcal are absorbed when 1 mole of $O_2(g)$ is dissociated into oxygen atoms.

$$O_2(g) \longrightarrow 2O(g) \qquad \Delta H = +118.3 \text{ kcal}$$

This value is also called the **heat of atomization** of $O_2(g)$.

A bond dissociation energy of a polyatomic molecule refers to a process in which a specific bond of the molecule is broken. The dissociation of the molecule may be imagined to occur in steps, and the ΔH values for the steps are not the same. For example,

$$\begin{aligned}
HOH(g) &\longrightarrow H(g) + OH(g) \qquad \Delta H = +119.7 \text{ kcal} \\
OH(g) &\longrightarrow H(g) + O(g) \qquad \Delta H = +101.5 \text{ kcal}
\end{aligned}$$

The sum of these bond dissociation energies is the heat of atomization of gaseous H_2O.

$$H_2O(g) \longrightarrow 2H(g) + O(g) \qquad \Delta H = +221.2 \text{ kcal}$$

In many instances, the individual ΔH values pertaining to the successive dissociations of a polyatomic molecule are now known. However, the heat of atomization can be calculated by use of the heat of formation of the gaseous compound and the heats of atomization of the elements that make up the compound (Example 13.3). An **average bond energy** can be derived from the heat of atomization for a molecule in which all of the bonds are alike. For the O—H bond of the water molecule, the average bond energy is 221.2/2 or 110.6 kcal/mole.

▶ **EXAMPLE 13.3** The bond dissociation energies of $H_2(g)$ and $O_2(g)$ are $+104.2$ kcal/mole and $+118.3$ kcal/mole, respectively, and the heat of formation of $H_2O(g)$ is -57.8 kcal/mole. What is the heat of atomization of $H_2O(g)$?

Solution   The following equations and corresponding ΔH values are derived from the thermochemical data given.

$$H_2O(g) \longrightarrow H_2(g) + \tfrac{1}{2}O_2(g) \qquad \Delta H = +\ 57.8 \text{ kcal}$$
$$H_2(g) \longrightarrow 2H(g) \qquad \Delta H = +104.2 \text{ kcal}$$
$$\tfrac{1}{2}O_2(g) \longrightarrow O(g) \qquad \Delta H = +\ 59.2 \text{ kcal}$$

The sum of these enthalpy changes is the heat of atomization.

$$H_2O(g) \longrightarrow 2H(g) + O(g) \qquad \Delta H = +221.2 \text{ kcal}$$

The average bond energy of a given type of bond is not the same in all of the molecules containing that bond. However, the variation from compound to compound is small in most cases, and an average value is usually a satisfactory approximation. Hence, average bond energies can be obtained from heats of atomization by use of established bond energies. For example, the hydrogen peroxide molecule (H—O—O—H) contains two H—O bonds and one O—O bond. The heat of atomization of hydrogen peroxide, which is the energy required to break all three bonds, is 254.3 kcal/mole, and subtraction of 221.2 kcal for the two H—O bonds from 254.3 kcal, gives 33.1 kcal/mole as the bond energy of the O—O bond.

Average bond energies are given in Table 13.3. The values listed for diatomic molecules are, of course, also bond dissociation energies. Average bond energies may be used to obtain approximate heats of reaction.

▶ **EXAMPLE 13.4** Use average bond energies to calculate the ΔH of the reaction

$$OF_2(g) + H_2O(g) \longrightarrow O_2(g) + 2HF(g)$$

Solution   We can imagine the reaction to take place by a series of steps. Energy is absorbed (ΔH, positive) when a bond is broken, and energy is evolved (ΔH, negative) when a bond is formed.

$$F-O-F(g) \longrightarrow 2F(g) + O(g) \qquad \Delta H = 2(+44) \ \ = \ +88 \text{ kcal}$$
$$H-O-H(g) \longrightarrow 2H(g) + O(g) \qquad \Delta H = 2(+111) = +222 \text{ kcal}$$
$$2O(g) \longrightarrow O_2(g) \qquad \Delta H = -118 \ \ \ = -118 \text{ kcal}$$
$$2H(g) + 2F(g) \longrightarrow 2H-F(g) \qquad \Delta H = 2(-135) = -270 \text{ kcal}$$

The sum of these steps is

$$OF_2(g) + H_2O(g) \longrightarrow O_2(g) + 2HF(g) \qquad \Delta H = -78 \text{ kcal}$$

The result of Example 13.2 is a more reliable value for the ΔH of this reaction. Since most average bond energies are approximations, a ΔH obtained by use of these values must be regarded as an estimate.

Table 13.3

Average Bond Energies (kcal/mole)

H—H	104	N—Cl	48
H—F	135	C—C	83
H—Cl	103	C=C	148
H—Br	87	C≡C	194
H—I	71	C—H	99
F—F	37	C—O	84
Cl—Cl	58	C=O	169
O—O	33	C—Cl	78
$O_2{}^a$	118	C—N	70
O—H	111	C≡N	210
O—F	44	S—S	63
O—Cl	49	S—H	81
N—N	38	S—Cl	66
N≡N	225	P—H	76
N—H	93	P—Cl	76

^{a} Double bond of molecular oxygen.

13.4 Second Law of Thermodynamics

A chemical reaction, or a physical change, is said to be **spontaneous** if it has the potential to proceed of its own accord under the conditions specified. The first law of thermodynamics puts only one restriction on chemical or physical changes—energy must be conserved. However, the first law provides no basis for determining whether or not a proposed change will occur spontaneously. The second law of thermodynamics establishes criteria for making such predictions.

An important thermodynamic function, **entropy, S,** is central to the second law. Entropy may be interpreted as a measure of the randomness, or disorder, of a system. Since a disordered state is more statistically probable than an ordered one, entropy may be regarded as a probability function (Section 9.4). One statement of the **second law of thermodynamics** is: every spontaneous change is accompanied by an increase in entropy.

As an example of a spontaneous change, consider the expansion of a gas into a vacuum. A flask of gas under pressure is connected, by means of a stopcock, to an evacuated flask (Figure 13.1). When the stopcock is opened, the gas spontaneously expands into the second flask until the pressure is the same in both flasks.

The random distribution of a gas in the apparatus shown in Figure 13.1 would result in as many gas molecules occupying the left-hand flask as the right-hand flask. Thus the change represents an increase in randomness—an increase in entropy. If both flasks are of equal volume, the chance of finding a certain molecule in the left-hand flask is $\frac{1}{2}$; the chance of finding the molecule in the whole apparatus is 1. If 1 mole of gas is used, the probability that it will occupy only the left-hand flask is 1 out of $10^{1.8 \times 10^{23}}$. This is 1 chance out of a number so large that there is no name for it—1 followed by 180 sextillion zeros. Thus with the stopcock open, the probability that the gas will occupy the entire apparatus is much higher than the probability that it will occupy only half of the apparatus, and the expansion of the gas represents an increase in entropy.

The interpretation of entropy as a measure of randomness was introduced by Ludwig Boltzmann in 1896. However, no such model is necessary for the application of thermodynamic concepts, and, as a matter of fact, the second

compressed gas   evacuated

(a)

expanded gas

(b)

Figure 13.1 Spontaneous expansion of a gas.

law was developed without the use of a molecular interpretation. The formulation of the second law was a result of the study of the operation of heat engines and of physical changes, but we shall discuss the law by centering on a chemical system.

Any spontaneous reaction has the capacity to do work. If work must be done on a system to effect a chemical change, that change is not spontaneous. However, the amount of work obtained from a chemical change depends upon the way in which the change is carried out. If the value derived for a given change is to have any meaning, it must be a measure of the *maximum* work that can be derived from the change, and the maximum quantity of work can be obtained only if the change is carried out in a **reversible** manner. When a change is carried out in a reversible manner, it occurs in such a way that the process could at any moment be reversed by an infinitesimal change in one of the conditions. A reversible process proceeds infinitely slowly by a series of equilibrium states.

For example, consider the reversible expansion of a gas occurring in a cylinder with the expansion opposed by a pressure exerted by a piston. In order for the expansion to occur, the applied pressure must be lower than the pressure of the gas, but this difference is infinitesimally small in the reversible process. A maximum amount of work would have to be done by the gas to effect the expansion, since the expansion is constantly opposed by the maximum pressure that will permit the gas to expand. If stored, the energy from the work of expansion would be sufficient to effect the compression of the gas.

It is impossible to conduct an experimental change in a completely reversible manner, although in certain instances (notably, the operation of voltaic cells) reversibility may be approximated. When a spontaneous change occurs, it does so in an irreversible manner. It is the lack of balance that provides the driving force for a spontaneous change. In the expansion of a gas into a vacuum, an example of an irreversible change, no work is done against a confining pressure, and no energy may be stored to bring about recompression.

The reversible emf of a cell, $\mathscr{E}$, pertains to the reversible operation of the cell and is the maximum voltage that the cell can develop (Section 10.7). Therefore, the reversible emf of a cell can be used to calculate the maximum quantity of electrical work that can be obtained from the cell. This quantity is a measure of the decrease in Gibbs free energy of the cell reaction, $-\Delta G$. The ΔG value for a chemical reaction is itself an important criterion of spontaneity. The use of ΔG values has been discussed in Section 10.7 and will be developed more fully in Sections 13.5 and 14.10. It is important to note that the free energy change is defined on the basis of a reversible process and that ΔG pertains to maximum work other than pressure-volume work. For voltaic cells, ΔG is a measure of maximum electrical work.

For the cell

$$Ag(s) \,|\, AgCl(s) \,|\, Cl^-(aq) \,|\, Cl_2(1 \text{ atm}) \,|\, Pt(s)$$

the half-cell reactions are

$$2Ag(s) + 2Cl^-(aq) \rightleftharpoons 2AgCl(s) + 2e^- \qquad \mathscr{E}_{ox} = -0.222 \text{ v}$$

$$2e^- + Cl_2(g) \rightleftharpoons 2Cl^-(aq) \qquad \mathscr{E} = +1.359 \text{ v}$$

and the cell reaction is

$$2Ag(s) + Cl_2(g) \longrightarrow 2AgCl(s) \qquad \mathscr{E} = +1.137 \text{ v}$$

The free energy change is

$$\Delta G = -nF\mathscr{E}$$
$$= -2(23.06 \text{ kcal/v})(1.137 \text{ v}) = -52.44 \text{ kcal}$$

The enthalpy change for the reaction, conducted outside the cell at 25°C and 1 atm, is twice the heat of formation of AgCl (-30.36 kcal/mole).

$$\Delta H = -60.72 \text{ kcal}$$

The ΔE for the reaction at 25°C is -60.13 kcal, since $\Delta n = -1$ and $\Delta E = \Delta H - \Delta nRT$. However, we will restrict our attention to the heat effect at constant pressure, ΔH. At 25°C and 1 atm, the reaction liberates 60.72 kcal of heat, but a maximum of 52.44 kcal of electrical work can be obtained from it.

If the reaction proceeds in an irreversible manner, less than the maximum amount of work is obtained. The difference between $-\Delta H$ and the actual quantity of work obtained is given off as heat—the less work obtained, the more heat evolved. In the most irreversible process possible, heat equivalent of $-\Delta H$ is evolved and no work other than pressure-volume work is done.

In the reversible operation of the cell, the maximum amount of electrical work is obtained and the minimum amount of heat is evolved.

$$\Delta H = \Delta G + q_{rev}$$
$$-60.72 \text{ kcal} = -52.44 \text{ kcal} + q_{rev}$$
$$q_{rev} = -8.28 \text{ kcal}$$

The value q_{rev} is interpreted in terms of the change in entropy accompanying the reaction. An isothermal process is one that occurs at a constant temperature. For a reversible isothermal process, the change in entropy, ΔS, is defined as the quantity of heat absorbed divided by the absolute temperature at which it is absorbed.

$$\Delta S = \frac{q_{rev}}{T}$$

Therefore,

$$q_{rev} = T\Delta S$$

and for the cell reaction at 298°K,

$$T\Delta S = -8.28 \text{ kcal}$$

$$\Delta S = \frac{-8,280 \text{ cal}}{298°K} = -27.8 \text{ kcal/°K}$$

The reaction is accompanied by a decrease in entropy of 27.8 cal/°K.

Like ΔG, the ΔS for a reaction is defined on the basis of a reversible process. Nevertheless, entropy and free energy, as well as enthalpy, are state functions, and the values of ΔS, ΔG, and ΔH depend only upon the final and initial states of the system and not upon the path taken between these two states. When a spontaneous reaction occurs, the free energy of the system declines. Even if the reaction is carried out in a completely irreversible manner and no electrical work obtained from it, the possibility of getting the work defined by ΔG is lost. In like manner, no matter how the reaction is carried out, the ΔS calculated on the basis of the reversible process is the entropy change for the reaction.

Since ΔS for the reaction of Ag and Cl_2 is negative, the system becomes more ordered as the reaction proceeds. It appears that the system expends 8.28 kcal to achieve a less probable state. However, if entropy is to be used to determine whether a change can occur, the entropy change of the surroundings, as well as the entropy change of the system, must be considered.

$$\Delta S_{total} = \Delta S_{system} + \Delta S_{surroundings}$$

The heat evolved by the system is isothermally absorbed by the surroundings. Such a transfer of heat may be regarded as a reversible process, since the direction of heat flow can be reversed by an infinitesimal change in the temperature of either the system or the surroundings. Therefore, the entropy change of the surroundings is equal to the quantity of heat absorbed by the surroundings divided by 298°K, the temperature at which the process is conducted.

For the reversible process, $q_{rev} = -8.28$ kcal. Therefore, 8.28 kcal of heat is theoretically *evolved* by the system and *absorbed* by the surroundings in the reversible process. It follows that the *total* change in entropy is zero.

$$\Delta S_{total} = \Delta S_{system} + \Delta S_{surroundings}$$

$$= -27.8 \text{ cal/°K} + \frac{8,280 \text{ cal}}{298°K}$$

$$= -27.8 \text{ cal/°K} + 27.8 \text{ cal/°K} = 0$$

When the reaction occurs by the completely irreversible path, 60.72 kcal of heat (which is $-\Delta H$) is *evolved* by the system and *absorbed* by the surroundings. The value of ΔS_{system}, however, is defined on the basis of the reversible process.

$$\Delta S_{\text{total}} = \Delta S_{\text{system}} + \Delta S_{\text{surroundings}}$$

$$= -27.8 \text{ cal/°K} + \frac{60,720 \text{ cal}}{298°K}$$

$$= -27.8 \text{ cal/°K} + 203.8 \text{ cal/°K} = +176 \text{ cal/°K}$$

Therefore, whenever the reaction occurs at 1 atm and 25°C by any irreversible process, ΔS_{total} will have a value between 0 and $+176$ cal/°K and will have a positive sign. The more irreversible the process, the larger the value of ΔS_{total} will be within these limits. All naturally occurring processes are irreversible, and every spontaneous change is accompanied by an increase in entropy.

Thus the ΔS_{total} of a postulated change may be used as a criterion for whether the change will occur spontaneously. The entropy of the universe is steadily increasing as spontaneous changes occur. Rudolf Clausius summarized the first and second laws of thermodynamics as: "The energy of the universe is constant; the entropy of the universe tends toward a maximum."

It must be emphasized that, whereas thermodynamic concepts can be used to determine what changes are possible, thermodynamics has nothing to say about the rapidity of change. Some thermodynamically favored changes occur very slowly. Although reactions between carbon and oxygen, as well as between hydrogen and oxygen, at 25°C and 1 atm pressure are definitely predicted by theory, mixtures of carbon and oxygen and mixtures of hydrogen and oxygen can be kept for prolonged periods without significant reaction; such reactions are generally initiated by suitable means. Thermodynamics can authoritatively indicate postulated changes that will *not* occur and need not be attempted, and it can tell us how to alter the conditions of a presumably unfavored reaction in such a manner that the reaction will then be thermodynamically possible.

13.5   Gibbs Free Energy

The change in entropy of the surroundings often plays a dominant role in determining whether the total entropy change of an experimental process is positive and the process, therefore, spontaneous. Gibbs free energy is a criterion for spontaneity that centers on the system only and that takes into account the entropy change of the surroundings. The chemist is primarily concerned with chemical reactions conducted at constant temperature and pressure, and ΔG is defined in such a way that it applies to chemical systems under these conditions.

In the last section, we noted that

$$\Delta S_{\text{total}} = \Delta S_{\text{system}} + \Delta S_{\text{surroundings}}$$

The ΔS_{system}, which we will hereafter indicate merely as ΔS, is defined by the reversible process. For the completely irreversible process conducted at *constant temperature and pressure*, $\Delta S_{\text{surroundings}} = -\Delta H/T$ (see Section 13.4). Therefore,

$$\Delta S_{\text{total}} = \Delta S - \frac{\Delta H}{T}$$

or

$$\Delta S_{\text{total}} = \frac{T\Delta S - \Delta H}{T}$$

The Gibbs free energy function is defined by the equation

$$G = H - TS$$

For a change at constant temperature,

$$\Delta G = \Delta H - T\Delta S$$

or

$$-\Delta G = T\Delta S - \Delta H$$

Therefore, if we substitute in the preceding expression for ΔS_{total},

$$\Delta S_{\text{total}} = \frac{-\Delta G}{T}$$

or

$$T\Delta S_{\text{total}} = -\Delta G$$

In any spontaneous process, ΔS_{total} is greater than zero and therefore,

$$T\Delta S_{\text{total}} > 0$$

It follows that

$$-\Delta G > 0$$

or

$$\Delta G < 0$$

The free energy change is negative for any spontaneous chemical reaction conducted at constant temperature and pressure.

Some insight into the meaning of free energy may be gained in the following way. According to the first law, for any isolated system,

$$\Delta E = q - w$$

The maximum quantity of work of any kind that can be derived from a change is obtained by means of the reversible process. If we view the system and surroundings as an isolated system,

$$\Delta E = q_{\text{rev}} - w_{\text{max}}$$

At constant temperature,

$$\Delta S = \frac{q_{rev}}{T}$$

or

$$T\Delta S = q_{rev}$$

Therefore,

$$\Delta E = T\Delta S - w_{max}$$

Addition of $P\Delta V$ to both sides of the equation gives

$$\Delta E + P\Delta V = T\Delta S - (w_{max} - P\Delta V)$$

At constant pressure,

$$\Delta H = \Delta E + P\Delta V$$

Therefore,

$$\Delta H = T\Delta S - (w_{max} - P\Delta V)$$

and

$$\Delta H - T\Delta S = -(w_{max} - P\Delta V)$$

But

$$\Delta G = \Delta H - T\Delta S$$

Therefore,

$$\Delta G = -(w_{max} - P\Delta V)$$

or

$$-\Delta G = w_{max} - P\Delta V$$

At constant temperature and pressure, the decrease in free energy (note minus sign) for any change is a measure of the maximum work that the system can do minus pressure-volume work. The change in free energy is sometimes said to measure *net* work or *available* work. Some chemical reactions are accompanied by an increase in volume. If such a reaction is run at constant pressure, the system must do work to push back the atmosphere. The free energy change, ΔG, for the reaction does not include such pressure-volume work, which must be done if the reaction is to take place and is therefore available for no other purpose. On the other hand, some reactions are accompanied by a decrease in volume. At constant pressure such a system receives energy as the reaction proceeds by having work done on it by the atmosphere. The change in free energy is therefore larger than would be the case if the contraction did not occur. The change in free energy is the maximum amount of work that can be derived from a reaction other than pressure-volume work.

Gibbs free energy is an important thermodynamic function for the chemist. Why some chemical reactions are possible and others are not is of fundamental importance. The earliest answer to the question was that reactions proceed because the reactants have a chemical affinity for each other; this "explanation" is still valid but, unfortunately, not very illuminating. In an effort to relate chemical affinity to some measurable quantity, Julius Thomsen and Marcellin Berthelot (1878) proposed that chemical reactions proceed spontaneously only if they evolve heat; presumably the heat evolved measures the chemical affinity of the reactants in going from a more energetic to a lesser energetic (more stable) state. Most chemical reactions are exothermic; however, the hypothesis of Thomsen and Berthelot is not tenable because spontaneous endothermic reactions are known and many spontaneous physical processes absorb heat (e.g., the melting of ice at room temperature).

The flaw of the hypothesis of Thomsen and Berthelot is that it ignores the role of entropy. The materials of a chemical reaction do indeed seek a minimum in energy, but they also seek a maximum in randomness (entropy). At times, these two factors work together; at other times, they oppose one another. The change in free energy takes into account both factors

$$\Delta G = \Delta H - T\Delta S$$

A system is more ordered at low temperatures than high temperatures; as the temperature increases, the randomness increases. The probability factor, $T\Delta S$, includes both temperature and change in entropy.

The most favorable circumstance for a negative value of ΔG, which indicates a spontaneous reaction, is a negative value of ΔH together with a positive value of ΔS. However, a large negative value of ΔH can outweigh an unfavorable entropy change resulting in a negative value of ΔG, and a large positive value of $T\Delta S$ can overshadow an unfavorable enthalpy change giving rise to a negative value of ΔG. For most chemical reactions at 25°C and 1 atm, the absolute value of ΔH is much larger than the value of $T\Delta S$, and hence, under these conditions, exothermic reactions are usually spontaneous no matter how the entropy changes.

However, with increasing temperature, the value of $T\Delta S$ increases and the influence of the entropy effect on ΔG increases. Both ΔH and ΔS usually do not change greatly with increasing temperature. However, the term $T\Delta S$ includes the temperature itself so that at high temperatures $T\Delta S$ can be sufficiently large to be the dominant influence on ΔG. Thus a reaction for which ΔH is positive and ΔS is positive (such as a decomposition reaction) may have a positive value of ΔG at ordinary temperatures because the absolute value of ΔH is larger than $T\Delta S$, but, at higher temperatures, $T\Delta S$ may be larger than the absolute value of ΔH and the value of ΔG may be negative.

▶ **EXAMPLE 13.5**   For the standard cell

$$Ag(s) \,|\, AgCl(s) \,|\, Cl^-(aq) \,|\, Hg_2Cl_2(s) \,|\, Hg(l) \,|\, Pt$$

$\mathscr{E}$ is 0.0454 v and the cell reaction is

$$2Ag(s) + Hg_2Cl_2(s) \longrightarrow 2Hg(l) + 2AgCl(s)$$

The heat of formation of $AgCl(s)$ is -30.36 kcal/mole and of Hg_2Cl_2 is -63.32 kcal/mole. Calculate (a) ΔH, (b) ΔG, and (c) ΔS for the cell reaction at 25°C.

Solution   (a) The enthalpy change for the reaction may be obtained from the ΔH_f values.

$$\begin{aligned} \Delta H &= 2\Delta H_f(AgCl) - \Delta H_f(Hg_2Cl_2) \\ &= 2(-30.36) - (-63.32) \\ &= +2.60 \text{ kcal} \end{aligned}$$

The reaction is endothermic.
(b) The free energy change may be calculated from the emf of the cell.

$$\begin{aligned} \Delta G &= -nF\mathscr{E} \\ &= -2(23.1 \text{ kcal/v})(0.0454 \text{ v}) \\ &= -2.10 \text{ kcal} \end{aligned}$$

The cell reaction is spontaneous.
(c) The value of ΔS may be obtained from the relation

$$\begin{aligned} \Delta G &= \Delta H - T\Delta S \\ -2.10 \text{ kcal} &= +2.60 \text{ kcal} - T\Delta S \\ T\Delta S &= +4.70 \text{ kcal} \\ \Delta S &= \frac{+4,700 \text{ cal}}{298°\text{K}} = +15.8 \text{ cal}/°\text{K} \end{aligned}$$

The ΔG value for the reaction is negative because this favorable entropy change outweighs an unfavorable change in enthalpy.

13.6   Standard Free Energies

A standard free energy change, given the symbol $\Delta G°$, applies to a reaction run at 25°C and 1 atm pressure with reactants and products in their standard states. The standard state of a substance is that state in which the substance occurs under these conditions. For materials in solution, the standard state is unit activity. Similar conventions are used for standard changes in enthalpy (Sections 5.8 and 13.2) and standard electrode potentials (Section 10.8).

The **standard free energy of formation**, ΔG_f°, is defined as the change in standard free energies when 1 mole of a substance is prepared from its constituent elements. In this system, an element in its standard state at 25°C and 1 atm is assigned a standard free energy of zero. Chemical equations for which standard free energy changes are known may be added or subtracted in the same way as thermochemical equations are (law of Hess, Section 5.9).

In this manner, ΔG_f° values may be used to calculate standard free energy changes for many reactions. The value of ΔG_f° for a reaction is equal to the sum of the standard free energies of formation of the products minus the sum of the standard free energies of the reactants. Remember that the value of ΔG_f° of a compound is recorded for 1 mole; if 2 moles of a compound appear in the equation, the value of ΔG_f° for that compound must be multiplied by 2.

Some ΔG_f° values are given in Table 13.4. A negative value means that the

Table 13.4

Gibbs Free Energy of Formation at 25°C and 1 Atm

Compound	ΔG_f° (kcal/mole)	Compound	ΔG_f° (kcal/mole)
$H_2O(g)$	−54.64	$CO(g)$	−32.81
$H_2O(l)$	−56.69	$CO_2(g)$	−94.26
$HF(g)$	−64.7	$NO(g)$	+20.72
$HCl(g)$	−22.77	$NO_2(g)$	+12.39
$HBr(g)$	−12.72	$NaCl(s)$	−91.79
$HI(g)$	+0.31	$MgO(s)$	−136.13
$H_2S(g)$	−7.89	$CaO(s)$	−144.4
$NH_3(g)$	−3.98	$Ca(OH)_2(s)$	−214.33
$CH_4(g)$	−12.14	$CaCO_3(s)$	−269.78
$C_2H_6(g)$	−7.86	$BaO(s)$	−126.3
$C_2H_4(g)$	+16.28	$BaCO_3(s)$	−272.2
$C_2H_2(g)$	+50.00	$Al_2O_3(s)$	−376.77
$CH_3OH(l)$	−39.73	$Fe_2O_3(s)$	−177.1
$C_6H_6(l)$	+30.99	$AgCl(s)$	−26.22
$SO_2(g)$	−71.79	$ZnO(s)$	−76.05

reaction in which the compound is prepared from its constituent elements under standard conditions is spontaneous.

▶ EXAMPLE 13.6 (a) What is ΔG° for the reaction

$$Cl_2(1 \cdot atm) + 2I^-(aq) \longrightarrow 2Cl^-(aq) + I_2(s)$$

For I^-, $\Delta G_f^\circ = -12.35$ kcal/mole; for Cl^-, $\Delta G_f^\circ = -31.35$ kcal/mole. (b) On the basis of ΔG° calculated, determine the $\mathscr{E}^\circ$ for the cell

$$Pt \,|\, I_2(s) \,|\, I^-(aq) \,\|\, Cl^-(aq) \,|\, Cl_2(1\ atm) \,|\, Pt$$

Solution (a)

$$\Delta G^\circ = 2[\Delta G_f^\circ(Cl^-)] - 2[\Delta G_f^\circ(I^-)]$$
$$= 2(-31.35\ kcal) - 2(-12.35\ kcal)$$
$$= -38.00\ kcal$$

(b)

$$\Delta G^\circ = -nF\mathscr{E}^\circ$$

$$\mathscr{E}^\circ = \frac{-37.0\ kcal}{-(2)(23.1\ kcal/v)}$$

$$\mathscr{E}^\circ = +0.822\ v$$

The value of $\mathscr{E}^\circ$ derived from standard electrode potentials is $+0.82$ v.

13.7 Absolute Entropies

The entropy of a substance increases as the temperature is increased; this fact is readily understood on the basis of the concept that entropy is a measure of disorder. The addition of heat to a substance results in an increase in molecular randomness. Conversely, cooling a substance makes a substance more ordered and decreases its entropy. At absolute zero, the entropy of a perfect crystalline substance may be taken as zero. This statement is sometimes called the **third law of thermodynamics** and was first formulated by Walther Nernst in 1906. The entropy of an imperfect crystal, a glass, or a solid solution is not zero at $0°K$.

On the basis of the third law, absolute entropies can be calculated from heat capacity data by extrapolating to absolute zero. Standard third-law entropies are recorded for substances in their standard states at 25°C and may be used to calculate ΔS° values for reactions. The ΔS° for a reaction is equal to the sum of the entropies of the products minus the sum of the entropies of the reactants.

▶ **EXAMPLE 13.7** For the reaction

$$2Hg(l) + O_2(g) \longrightarrow 2HgO(s)$$

the third law entropies are

$$S^\circ(Hg) = 18.5\ cal/°K\ mole$$
$$S^\circ(O_2) = 49.0\ cal/°K\ mole$$
$$S^\circ(HgO) = 17.2\ cal/°K\ mole$$

The heat of formation, ΔH_f°, of HgO is -21.68 kcal/mole. What is the standard free energy of formation of HgO(s)? Is the reaction, at 25°C, for the production of HgO in its standard state from Hg and O_2 in their standard states spontaneous?

Solution

$$\Delta S^\circ = 2S^\circ(\text{HgO}) - [2S^\circ(\text{Hg}) + S^\circ(O_2)]$$
$$= 2(17.2) - [2(18.5) + 49.0]$$
$$= -51.6 \text{ cal}/°\text{K}$$

For the reaction as written

$$\Delta H^\circ = 2\Delta H_f^\circ = -43,400 \text{ cal}$$
$$\Delta G^\circ = \Delta H^\circ - T\Delta S^\circ$$
$$= -43,400 - (298)(51.6)$$
$$= -28,000 \text{ cal}$$

the equation shows the formation of 2 moles of HgO; for 1 mole, $\Delta G_f^\circ = -14.0$ kcal/mole.

The reaction is spontaneous; the change in enthalpy compensates for the unfavorable change in entropy so that the free energy change is negative.

SOME SUGGESTED READINGS

Bent, H. A., *The Second Law*, New York, Oxford University Press, 1965 (paper).

Campbell, A. J., *Why Do Chemical Reactions Occur?*, Englewood Cliffs, N. J., Prentice-Hall, 1965 (paper).

Luder, W. F., *A Different Approach to Thermodynamics*, New York, Van Nostrand Reinhold, 1967 (paper).

Mahan, B. H., *Elementary Chemical Thermodynamics*, New York, Benjamin 1963 (paper).

Nash, L., *Elements of Chemical Thermodynamics*, 2nd ed., Reading, Mass., Addison-Wesley, 1970 (paper).

Thompson, J. J., *An Introduction to Chemical Energetics*, Boston, Houghton Mifflin, 1968 (paper).

PROBLEMS

13.1 (a) The combustion of 1.000 g of benzene, $C_6H_6(l)$, in a bomb calorimeter (at constant volume) evolves 9.987 kcal of heat at 25°C. The products of the combustion are $CO_2(g)$ and $H_2O(l)$. What is ΔE°, in kcal/mole, for the combustion of benzene? The molecular weight of benzene is 78.11. (b) Write the equation for the reaction. What is the value of ΔH°? (c) Use the enthalpies of formation for $CO_2(g)$ and $H_2O(l)$ given in Table 13.1 and your answer to part (b) to calculate ΔH°_f for benzene.

13.2 (a) The combustion of 1.000 g of thiourea, $CS(NH_2)_2(s)$, in a bomb calorimeter evolves 3.673 kcal of heat at 25°C. The products of the combustion are $CO_2(g)$, $SO_2(g)$, $N_2(g)$, and $H_2O(l)$. What is $\Delta E°$, in kcal/mole, for the combustion of thiourea? The molecular weight of thiourea is 76.12. (b) Write the equation for the reaction. What is the value of $\Delta H°$? (c) Use the values given in Table 13.1 and your answer to part (b) to calculate $\Delta H°_f$ for thiourea.

13.3 Calculate $\Delta E°$ for the combustion of ethene, $C_2H_4(g)$ to $CO_2(g)$ and $H_2O(l)$ at 25°C. The enthalpy of combustion, $\Delta H°$, of ethene is -337.2 kcal/mole.

13.4 (a) Use the values given in Table 13.1 to calculate $\Delta H°$ for the reaction

$$2NO(g) + O_2(g) \longrightarrow 2NO_2(g)$$

(b) What is $\Delta E°$ for the reaction?

13.5 Calculate $\Delta H°$ and $\Delta E°$ for the reaction

$$NH_4NO_3(s) \longrightarrow N_2O(g) + 2H_2O(l)$$

The enthalpies of formation are: $NH_4NO_3(s)$, -87.27 kcal/mole; $N_2O(g)$, $+19.49$ kcal/mole; $H_2O(l)$, -68.32 kcal/mole.

13.6 The bond dissociation energies of $H_2(g)$ and $N_2(g)$ are $+104.2$ kcal/mole and $+225.1$ kcal/mole and the heat of formation of $NH_3(g)$ is -11.0 kcal/mole. (a) What is the heat of atomization of $NH_3(g)$ in kcal/mole? (b) What is the average bond energy of the N—H bond?

13.7 Use the value of the heat of formation of acetylene, $C_2H_2(g)$, found in Table 13.1 and the values for the H—H, C—H, and C≡C bond energies found in Table 13.3 to calculate the heat of sublimation of graphite.

13.8 The heat of atomization of phosphine, PH_3, is $+228$ kcal/mole and the heat of atomization of diphosphine, P_2H_4, is $+355$ kcal/mole. What is the bond energy of the P—P bond?

13.9 (a) Use bond energies (Table 13.3) to calculate ΔH for the reaction

$$4NH_3(g) + 3O_2(g) \longrightarrow 2N_2(g) + 6H_2O(g)$$

(b) Use enthalpies of formation (Table 13.1) to calculate a ΔH value for the reaction. How well do the values agree?

13.10 Use bond energies to calculate the enthalpy of formation of HF(g) and of HCl(g). Compare your results with the values in Table 13.1.

13.11 (a) Use bond energies to calculate ΔH for the reaction

$$CH_4(g) + 4Cl_2(g) \longrightarrow CCl_4(l) + 4HCl(g)$$

(b) Use the values in Table 13.1 and the answer to part (a) to calculate an approximate enthalpy of formation for $CCl_4(l)$. (c) The correct value for the $\Delta H°_f$ of CCl_4 is -33.3 kcal. What are the percentage errors in your answers to parts (a) and (ʋ)?

13.12 (a) Use the average bond energies (Table 13.3) to calculate ΔH for the reaction

$$\begin{matrix} H & H \\ | & | \\ C{=}C(g) \\ | & | \\ H & H \end{matrix} + H_2(g) \longrightarrow \begin{matrix} H & H \\ | & | \\ H{-}C{-}C{-}H(g) \\ | & | \\ H & H \end{matrix}$$

(b) Calculate ΔH for the reaction by using enthalpies of formation (Table 13.1). How do the two values compare?

13.13 (a) Use free energies of formation (Table 13.4) to calculate ΔG for the reaction given in Problem 13.12. (b) Use your answer to part (a) and the ΔH calculated for Problem 13.12 (b) to calculate ΔS for the reaction.

13.14 Consider the standard cell:

$$Ag(s) | AgI(s) | I^-(aq) | I_2(s) | Pt(s)$$

(a) Write the equation for the cell reaction. (b) Calculate $\mathscr{E}°$ for the half reaction

$$e^- + AgI(s) \longrightarrow Ag(s) + I^-(aq)$$

given that the free energy of formation of AgI(s) is -15.85 kcal/mole and $\mathscr{E}°$ for the I^-/I_2 electrode is $+0.5355$ v.

13.15 Consider the standard cell:

$$Tl(s) | TlCl(s) | Cl^-(aq) | Cl_2(g) | Pt(s)$$

(a) Write the equation for the cell reaction. (b) Calculate $\mathscr{E}°$ for the half reaction

$$e^- + TlCl(s) \longrightarrow Tl(s) + Cl^-(aq)$$

given that the free energy of formation of TlCl(s) is -44.19 kcal/mole and $\mathscr{E}°$ for the Cl^-/Cl_2 electrode is $+1.3593$ v.

13.16 For the half reaction

$$XeO_3(aq) + 6H^+(aq) + 6e^- \longrightarrow Xe(g) + 3H_2O$$

$\mathscr{E}°$ is $+1.80$ v. (a) Calculate $\Delta G°$ for the reaction:

$$XeO_3(aq) + 3H_2(g) \longrightarrow Xe(g) + 3H_2O$$

(b) Use the answer to part (a) to calculate the free energy of formation, $\Delta G°_f$, of $XeO_3(aq)$.

13.17 (a) Use electrode potentials to determine the value of $\Delta G°$ for the reaction

$$Zn(s) + 2H^+(aq) \longrightarrow Zn^{2+}(aq) + H_2(g)$$

(b) If we adopt the convention that the free energy of formation of H^+(aq) is zero, what is $\Delta G°_f$ of Zn^{2+}(aq)? (c) Standard thermodynamic values pertain to aqueous ions at unit activity. What is the ΔG_f for Zn^{2+}(aq) at an activity of 0.100?

13.18 (a) Determine the emf of the standard cell:

$$Cd(s)\,|\,Cd^{2+}(aq)\,\|\,Cu^{2+}(aq)\,|\,Cu(s)$$

(b) For the cell reaction

$$Cd(s) + Cu^{2+}(aq) \longrightarrow Cd^{2+}(aq) + Cu(s)$$

$\Delta H°$ is -32.7 kcal. What is $\Delta E°$? Calculate: (c) $\Delta G°$ and (d) $\Delta S°$ for the reaction.

13.19 (a) Determine the emf of the standard cell:

$$Zn(s)\,|\,Zn^{2+}(aq)\,\|\,Ag^+(aq)\,|\,Ag(s)$$

(b) For the cell reaction

$$Zn(s) + 2Ag^+(aq) \longrightarrow Zn^{2+}(aq) + 2Ag$$

$\Delta H°$ is -87.05 kcal. What is $\Delta E°$? Calculate (c) $\Delta G°$, and (d) $\Delta S°$ for the reaction.

13.20 For the cell

$$Pb(s)\,|\,PbBr_2(s)\,|\,Br^-(aq)\,|\,Br_2(l)\,|\,Pt(s)$$

$\mathscr{E}°$ is $+1.349$ v. The absolute entropy of Pb(s) is $+15.5$ cal/°K mole, of $Br_2(l)$ is $+36.4$ cal/°K mole, and of $PbBr_2(s)$ is $+38.6$ cal/°K mole. Write the equation for the cell reaction and calculate $\Delta H°$ for the reaction.

13.21 For the reaction

$$In(s) + 3H^+(aq) \longrightarrow In^{3+}(aq) + \tfrac{3}{2}H_2(g)$$

$\Delta H°$ is -32.0 kcal. The absolute entropies of the reactants and products are: In^{3+}(aq), -62.0 cal/°K mole; H_2(g), $+31.2$ cal/°K mole; H^+(aq), 0.0 cal/°K mole; In(s), $+12.5$ cal/°K mole. Calculate (a) $\Delta S°$ and (b) $\Delta G°$ for the reaction. (c) Determine $\mathscr{E}°$ for the half reaction,

$$3e^- + In^{3+}(aq) \longrightarrow In(s)$$

13.22 The heat of vaporization of ethyl alcohol, C_2H_5OH, is 204.3 cal/g at 78.3°C, which is the normal boiling point of ethyl alcohol. For the vaporization of one mole of liquid C_2H_5OH, calculate (a) ΔH, (b) ΔE, (c) ΔS, (d) ΔG.

13.23 For the reaction

$$CO(g) + 2H_2(g) \longrightarrow CH_3OH(l)$$

Calculate: (a) $\Delta H°$ (b) $\Delta G°$, (c) $\Delta S°$. (d) Is the reaction spontaneous at 25°C?

13.24 The $\Delta G°_f$ of ethanol, C_2H_5OH, is -41.77 kcal/mole. Is it possible to make ethanol by a reaction of $C(s)$ with $H_2(g)$ and $O_2(g)$ at $25°C$? Examine the $\Delta G°_f$ values in Table 13.4 before you make your decision.

13.25 Use the data given in Table 13.4 to calculate $\Delta G°$ values for the following postulated reactions:

$$SO_2(g) + H_2(g) \longrightarrow H_2S(g) + O_2(g)$$
$$SO_2(g) + 3H_2(g) \longrightarrow H_2S(g) + 2H_2O(l)$$

What would you predict the products of the reaction of $SO_2(g)$ and $H_2(g)$ at $25°C$ to be?

13.26 A chemist claims that the following reaction occurs at $25°C$:

$$SF_6(g) + 8HI(g) \longrightarrow H_2S(g) + 6HF(g) + 4I_2(s)$$

Is it thermodynamically possible? Use the data in Table 13.4 plus the fact that $\Delta G°_f$ for $SF_6(g)$ is -237 kcal/mole to calculate $\Delta G°$ for the reaction.

13.27 The $\Delta G°_f$ of $CCl_4(l)$ is -16.4 kcal/mole. Is it thermodynamically possible to make $CCl_4(l)$ from $C(s)$ and $Cl_2(g)$ at $25°C$? Are there any conditions attached to your answer?

13.28 Consider the transformation:

$$CaCO_3(s) \longrightarrow CaO(s) + CO_2(g)$$

(a) Use the $\Delta H°_f$ values of Table 13.1 to calculate $\Delta H°$. (b) Use the $\Delta G°_f$ values of Table 13.4 to calculate $\Delta G°$. (c) Calculate $\Delta S°$ from your answers to parts (a) and (b). (d) Is the reaction spontaneous at $25°C$? Interpret your answer.

13.29 Calculate $\Delta G°$ for the reaction

$$PCl_3(g) + Cl_2(g) \longrightarrow PCl_5(g)$$

The absolute entropies of reactants and products (in cal/$°K$ mole) are: $PCl_3(g)$, $+74.49$; $Cl_2(g)$, $+53.286$; $PCl_5(g)$, $+84.3$. The enthalpy of formation of $PCl_3(g)$ is -73.22 kcal/mole, and $\Delta H°_f$ of $PCl_5(g)$ is -95.35 kcal/mole.

13.30 (a) From the following data, calculate the entropy change at $25°C$, $\Delta S°$, for the preparation of each of the hydrogen halides from the elements:

	HF	HCl	HBr	HI
$\Delta H°_f$ (kcal/mole)	-64.2	-22.063	-8.66	$+6.20$
$\Delta G°_f$ (kcal/mole)	-64.7	-22.769	-12.72	$+0.31$

(b) Discuss the practicality of preparing each hydrogen halide in essentially pure form by reaction of the elements. Use both $\Delta G°$ and $\Delta S°$ as the basis of your discussion. For each reaction, how can the change in entropy of the immediate surroundings be calculated?

13.31 What is the absolute entropy at 25°C, $S°$, of carbon disulfide, $CS_2(l)$? For $CS_2(l)$, $\Delta H°_f$ is $+21.0$ kcal/mole and $\Delta G°_f$ is $+15.2$ kcal/mole. The absolute entropy of C (graphite) is $+1.36$ cal/°K mole and of S (rhombic) is $+7.62$ cal/°K mole.

13.32 Calculate the value of $\Delta H°$ for the combustion of ethyl alcohol, $C_2H_5OH(l)$, to $CO_2(g)$ and $H_2O(l)$. The absolute entropies, in cal/°K mole, of reactants and products are: $C_2H_5OH(l)$, $+38.4$; $O_2(g)$, $+49.0$; $CO_2(g)$, $+51.1$; $H_2O(l)$, $+16.7$. The free energies of formation of $CO_2(g)$ and $H_2O(l)$ are listed in Table 13.4, and $\Delta G°_f$ of $C_2H_5OH(l)$ is -41.77 kcal/mole.

14

CHEMICAL KINETICS AND CHEMICAL EQUILIBRIUM

Chemical kinetics is the study of the rates of chemical reactions, the means by which reaction rates may be controlled, and the ways in which reactions proceed on the atomic-molecular level.

Reactions are frequently classed as **homogeneous** or **heterogeneous**. A homogeneous reaction occurs in a single phase; for example,

$$H^+(aq) + OH^-(aq) \longrightarrow H_2O(l)$$
$$2NO(g) + O_2(g) \longrightarrow 2NO_2(g)$$

Heterogeneous reactions take place on a phase boundary; for example,

$$Zn(s) + 2H^+(aq) \longrightarrow Zn^{2+}(aq) + H_2(g)$$
$$2Mg(s) + O_2(g) \longrightarrow 2MgO(s)$$

Many chemical reactions are reversible. For example, the reaction

$$N_2(g) + 3H_2(g) \rightleftharpoons 2NH_3(g)$$

may be made to give a good yield of ammonia through a judicious choice of conditions; under other reaction conditions, virtually complete dissociation of ammonia is observed.

14.1 Molecular Collisions and Reaction Rates

Consider a hypothetical homogeneous gas phase reaction between two diatomic molecules A_2 and B_2.

$$A_2(g) + B_2(g) \rightleftharpoons 2AB(g)$$

Not every reaction proceeds in a manner described by the net chemical equation; many reactions occur through a series of steps (called the **reaction mechanism**), and the net equation represents the sum of the equations for the steps. In the case of the reaction between A_2 and B_2, however, let us assume that the reaction proceeds, as depicted by the equation, through the collisions of A_2 and B_2 molecules (Figure 14.1).

Not every collision between molecules results in a reaction. Comparison of the calculated total number of collisions per unit time with the observed rate of a reaction shows that generally only a small fraction of the total number of collisions is effective.

There are two reasons why a given collision may not be effective. First, the molecules may be improperly aligned (Figure 14.2). Second, the impact of the collision may be so gentle that the molecules rebound unchanged. The negatively charged electron clouds surrounding molecules produce a force of repulsion that acts between molecules; this repulsion causes molecules with low energies to rebound when they collide. In a collision between

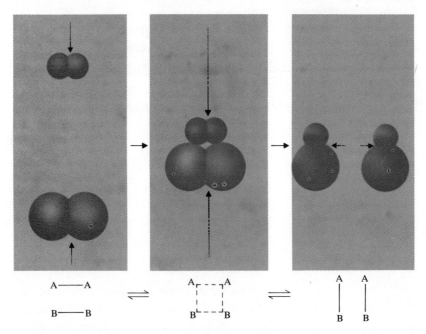

Figure 14.1 Collision between an A_2 molecule and a B_2 molecule resulting in a reaction.

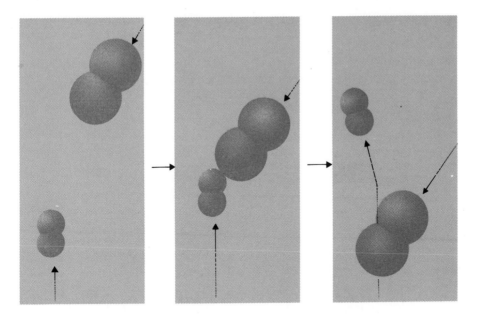

Figure 14.2 Collision between an A_2 molecule and a B_2 molecule producing no reaction.

high-energy molecules, however, the molecules possess sufficient energy to overcome the forces of repulsion, and the rearrangement typical of the chemical reaction may then follow. For an effective collision, the sum of the energies of the colliding molecules must equal or exceed some minimum value.

Therefore, when the rate of a given reaction is increased through an alteration in an experimental condition, this increase is brought about by either an increase in the total number of collisions per unit time, an increase in the fraction of the total number of collisions that are effective, or a combination of both factors.

14.2 Temperature and Reaction Rate

The rate of any chemical reaction is increased when the temperature is raised; this effect is observed for endothermic as well as exothermic reactions. The more rapid molecular motion resulting from an increase in temperature brings about a larger number of molecular collisions per unit time. However, raising the temperature from 25°C to 35°C causes the average speed of the molecules to increase by about 2%, whereas the same temperature rise brings about an increase in the reaction rate of approximately 200 to 300%. Obviously, increasing the temperature must increase the fraction of molecular collisions that are effective, and this factor must far outweigh the concomitant increase in the total number of collisions per unit time.

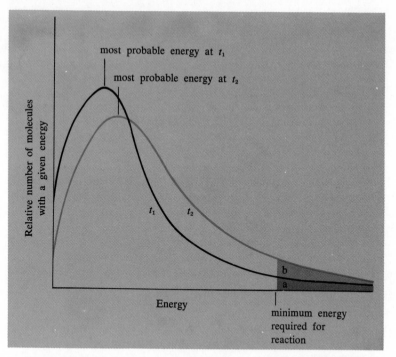

Figure 14.3 Molecular energy distributions at temperatures t_1 and t_2.

By an examination of Figure 14.3, we can understand why proportionately more molecular collisions result in reactions at a higher temperature than at a lower temperature. Two molecular energy distribution curves are shown—one for a temperature, t_1, and another for a higher temperature, t_2. The minimum energy required for reaction is indicated on the diagram; the number of molecules at t_1 with energies equal to or greater than this minimum energy is proportional to the area, a, under the curve for t_1. The curve for temperature t_2 is shifted only slightly in the direction of higher energy; however, at t_2 the number of molecules possessing sufficient energy to react successfully upon collision is greatly increased and is proportional to the area $a + b$. Thus a temperature rise produces an increase in reaction rate principally because the proportion of effective collisions is increased. The increase in the total number of collisions per unit time is only a minor factor. The influence of temperature on reaction rates is analyzed mathematically in Section 14.6.

In a successful collision between reacting molecules, the molecules form a transitory intermediate called an **activated complex**. Let us again consider the reaction between A_2 and B_2. In a gentle collision, the A_2 and B_2 molecules are repelled by the molecular electron clouds and never get close enough for A—B bonds to form. However, a collision between high-energy molecules results in the formation of a short-lived molecule, A_2B_2, which is the activated complex for the reaction; the atoms of the complex assume the square configuration diagramed in Figure 14.1. The A_2B_2 complex may split to form two

AB molecules or may decompose to re-form A_2 and B_2 molecules. In fact, this same activated complex is produced by the collision of two high-energy AB molecules and is the intermediate in the reverse reaction—the formation of A_2 and B_2 from AB.

$$A_2 + B_2 \rightleftharpoons \begin{matrix} A\text{---}A \\ \vdots \quad \vdots \\ B\text{---}B \end{matrix} \rightleftharpoons 2AB$$

The bonding arrangement of the activated complex is not so stable as that of either the reactants or the products; the activated complex represents a state of relatively high potential energy. A potential energy diagram for the hypothetical reaction

$$A_2 + B_2 \rightleftharpoons A_2B_2 \rightleftharpoons 2AB$$

is shown in Figure 14.4; potential energy is plotted against a reaction coordinate that may be interpreted as showing the progress of the reaction. The difference between the potential energy of the reactants, $A_2 + B_2$, and the potential energy of the activated complex is called the **energy of activation** and is given the symbol E_a; typical values of E_a range from 15 to 60 kcal/mole.

The energy of activation constitutes a potential energy barrier between the reactants and products. Even though the energy of the reactants, $A_2 + B_2$,

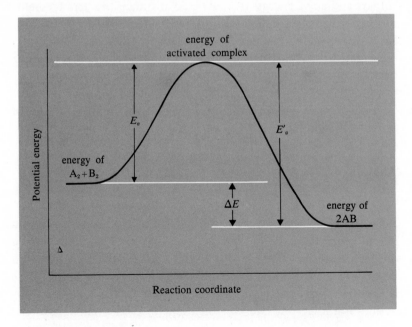

Figure 14.4 Potential energy diagram for the hypothetical reaction $A_2 + B_2 \rightleftharpoons A_2B_2 \rightleftharpoons 2AB$.

is higher than that of the products and the overall reaction is exothermic, the system must climb a potential energy hill before it can coast down to a state of lower potential energy. In a successful collision, part of the kinetic energy of the fast-moving A_2 and B_2 molecules is used to provide the energy of activation and thus produce the high-energy molecular arrangement of the activated complex. If the activated complex re-forms A_2 and B_2 molecules, the energy of activation is released in the form of the kinetic energy of the molecules. If the activated complex splits into the product, two molecules of AB, the energy indicated as E_a' on the diagram is released as kinetic energy. The overall difference between the energy released and the energy absorbed is the ΔE (or ΔH, depending on conditions) for the reaction.

$$\Delta E = E_a - E_a'$$

As shown in Figure 14.4, $E_a' > E_a$; therefore ΔE is negative, and the forward reaction is exothermic.

The reaction diagramed in Figure 14.4 is reversible; E_a' is the energy of activation of the reverse reaction. If the diagram is read from right to left, then E_a' is absorbed and E_a evolved.

$$\Delta E = E_a' - E_a$$

The reverse reaction is endothermic; ΔE is positive, since $E_a' > E_a$.

If molecules of A_2 and B_2 with relatively low kinetic energies approach each other, sufficient energy is lacking to produce the arrangement of the activated complex by forcing the molecules together in opposition to the repulsive forces. In this instance, the molecules possess only sufficient energy between them to get part way up the hill; then, repelling each other, they coast back down the hill and fly apart unchanged. Since only high-energy molecules can get over the hill, it is easy to understand the role of temperature in influencing reaction rate through changes in the fraction of high-energy molecules.

14.3 Catalysts

A **catalyst** is a substance that increases the rate of a chemical reaction without being used up in the reaction; the catalyst may be recovered unchanged at the conclusion of the process. For example, the decomposition of $KClO_3$ can be greatly accelerated by the addition of a small quantity of MnO_2. In the equation for the change, the catalyst is indicated over the arrow since its use does not affect the overall stoichiometry of the reaction.

$$2KClO_3 \xrightarrow{\text{MnO}_2} 2KCl + 3O_2$$

Catalysts cannot cause thermodynamically impossible reactions to occur. Furthermore, it is not the mere *presence* of a catalyst (presumably acting as a cheering section) that causes the effect on the reaction rate. In a catalyzed reaction, the catalyst is actually consumed in one step and regenerated in a subsequent step; thus it is used over and over again without undergoing any permanent change.

A catalyst, then, functions by opening an alternative path by which a reaction can proceed, and the mechanism of the catalyzed reaction is different from that of the uncatalyzed reaction. The catalyzed path has a lower energy of activation than the uncatalyzed path (Figure 14.5) which accounts for the more rapid reaction rate. When a catalyst is used, proportionately more molecules possess the energy required for a successful collision (Figure 14.6); thus, of the total number of collisions per unit time, the fraction that results in reaction is increased.

Two additional observations may be derived from an examination of Figure 14.5. First, ΔE for the catalyzed reaction is the same as ΔE for the uncatalyzed reaction. Second, the energy of activation for the reverse reaction, E_a', is lowered by the use of the catalyst to the same extent that the energy of activation of the forward reaction, E_a, is lowered. This means that a catalyst has the same effect on the reverse reaction that it has on the forward reaction. If a catalyst doubles the speed of a forward reaction, the same catalyst will double the speed of the reverse reaction.

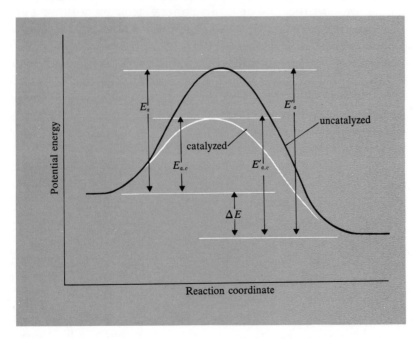

Figure 14.5   Potential energy diagrams for catalyzed and uncatalyzed reactions.

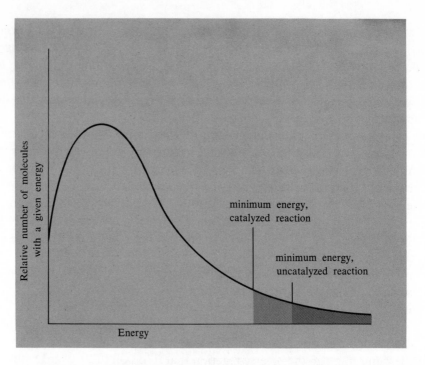

Figure 14.6 Molecular energy distribution showing the effect of a catalyst on the number of molecules possessing sufficient energy to react.

Many industrial processes depend upon catalytic procedures, but even more important to man are the natural catalysts known as **enzymes**. These extremely complicated substances catalyze life processes such as digestion and cell synthesis. The large number of complex chemical reactions that occur in the body, and are necessary for life, can occur at the relatively low temperature of the body because of the action of enzymes. Thousands of enzymes are known to exist, each serving a specific function. Reasearch into the structure and action of enzymes offers great promise for the advancement of knowledge of the causes of disease and the mechanism of growth.

In **homogeneous** catalysis, the substance serving as a catalyst is present in the same phase as the reactants; in **heterogeneous**, or **surface**, catalysis, the reactants and catalyst comprise two separate phases, and the reaction occurs on a catalytic surface. An example of homogeneous catalysis in the gas phase is the effect of chlorine on the decomposition of dinitrogen oxide.

Gaseous N_2O is a relatively inert substance at room temperature; however, at temperatures in the neighborhood of 1000°K it decomposes according to the equation

$$2N_2O(g) \longrightarrow 2N_2(g) + O_2(g)$$

Kinetic studies show that the reaction proceeds by means of collisions between two molecules of N_2O. The reaction is catalyzed by traces of chlorine gas.

A proposed mechanism for the catalyzed path follows. At the temperature of the experiment, and particularly in the presence of light, some chlorine molecules are dissociated into chlorine atoms.

$$Cl_2(g) \longrightarrow 2Cl(g)$$

These chlorine atoms readily react with N_2O

$$N_2O(g) + Cl(g) \longrightarrow N_2(g) + ClO(g)$$

and the decomposition of ClO is rapid

$$2ClO(g) \longrightarrow Cl_2(g) + O_2(g)$$

In this last step, the catalyst is returned to its original form; the final products of the catalyzed reaction are the same as those of the uncatalyzed reaction.

Another example of homogeneous catalysis is the decomposition of ozone in the presence of N_2O_5. Dinitrogen pentoxide decomposes readily into oxygen and lower oxides of nitrogen. For example,

$$2N_2O_5(g) \longrightarrow 2N_2O_4(g) + O_2(g)$$

Ozone reacts rapidly with N_2O_4 producing oxygen and regenerating the catalyst, N_2O_5.

$$O_3(g) + N_2O_4(g) \longrightarrow O_2(g) + N_2O_5(g)$$

The proper addition of these two equations gives the net change

$$2O_3(g) \xrightarrow{\text{N}_2\text{O}_5} 3O_2(g)$$

It must be emphasized that these mechanisms are merely plausible hypotheses. Undoubtedly, the actual mechanism of the N_2O_5-catalyzed decomposition of ozone is much more complicated and may involve steps such as

$$N_2O_4(g) \longrightarrow 2NO_2(g)$$

$$NO_2(g) + O_3(g) \longrightarrow NO_3(g) + O_2(g)$$

$$NO_2(g) + NO_3(g) \longrightarrow N_2O_5(g)$$

Homogeneous catalysis also occurs in aqueous solution; many reactions are catalyzed by acids and bases. The decomposition of hydrogen peroxide

$$2H_2O_2(aq) \longrightarrow 2H_2O(l) + O_2(g)$$

is catalyzed by the presence of iodide ion. A postulated mechanism for the catalyzed reaction is

$$H_2O_2(aq) + I^-(aq) \longrightarrow H_2O(l) + IO^-(aq)$$

$$H_2O_2(aq) + IO^-(aq) \longrightarrow H_2O(l) + O_2(g) + I^-(aq)$$

Heterogeneous catalysis generally proceeds, through **chemical adsorption** (or **chemisorption**) of the reactants on the surface of the catalyst. Adsorption is a process in which molecules adhere to the surface of a solid; charcoal is used in gas masks as an adsorbent for noxious gases. In ordinary **physical adsorption** the molecules are held to the surface of the adsorbent by van der Waals forces; thus the adsorbed gas molecules are affected to about the same extent that they would be if the gas were liquefied.

In chemisorption, the adsorbed molecules are held to the catalytic surface by bonds comparable to those of chemical compounds. In the process of forming bonds with the adsorbent, chemisorbed molecules undergo internal electron rearrangements. The bonding within certain molecules is stretched and weakened, and the bonds of some molecules are even broken. For example, hydrogen is adsorbed in atomic form on the surface of platinum. Thus the chemisorbed layer of molecules functions as an activated complex in a surface-catalyzed reaction.

At the present time, chemisorption and surface catalysis are far from completely understood; we can only make reasonable postulates for the mechanisms of specific reactions. A suggested mechanism for the decomposition of N_2O on gold is diagramed in Figure 14.7. Molecules of N_2O are chemisorbed on the surface of the gold, and the following reactions take place on this surface.

$$N_2O \longrightarrow N_2(g) + O$$
$$O + O \longrightarrow O_2(g)$$

The release of the gaseous products from the surface is called **desorption**.

Some empirical observations have great utility in the selection of suitable catalysts for particular reactions; for example, most reactions of gaseous hydrogen are catalyzed by platinum. However, the fundamental theory of

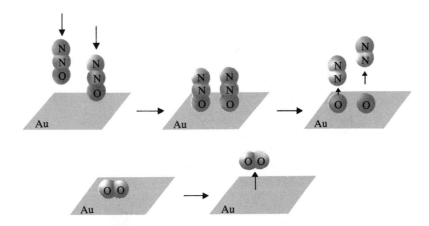

Figure 14.7 Proposed mode of decomposition of N_2O on Au.

catalytic processes has not been developed to the point where it can be used to select or design a catalyst for a specific use. It appears that the electronic structure of the solid, as well as the geometric arrangement and spacing of the atoms on the surface of the solid, is a critical consideration.

It has been proposed that lattice defects or irregularities in the surface of the catalyst are active sites for catalysis; this hypothesis has been used to explain the action of **promoters**, which are materials that enhance the activity of catalysts. For example, in the synthesis of ammonia,

$$2N_2(g) + 3H_2(g) \xrightarrow{\text{Fe}} 2NH_3(g)$$

an iron catalyst is made more effective by incorporating traces of potassium or vanadium.

Catalytic **poisons** are substances that inhibit the activity of catalysts. For example, small amounts of arsenic destroy the power of platinum to catalyze the preparation of sulfur trioxide from sulfur dioxide.

$$2SO_2(g) + O_2(g) \xrightarrow{\text{Pt}} 2SO_3(g)$$

Presumably, platinum arsenide forms on the surface of the platinum and destroys its catalytic activity.

Catalysts are generally highly specific in their activity. In some cases, a given substance will catalyze the synthesis of one set of products from certain reagents, whereas another substance will catalyze the synthesis of completely different products from the same reactants. In these instances, of course, both reactions are thermodynamically sound. Carbon monoxide and hydrogen can be made to yield a wide variety of products depending upon the catalyst employed and the conditions of the reaction.

If a cobalt or nickel catalyst is used, CO and H_2 produce mixtures of hydrocarbons. For example,

$$CO(g) + 3H_2(g) \xrightarrow{\text{Ni}} CH_4(g) + H_2O(g)$$

On the other hand, methanol is the product of the reaction of CO and H_2 when a mixture of zinc and chromic oxides is employed as a catalyst.

$$CO(g) + 2H_2(g) \xrightarrow{ZnO/Cr_2O_3} CH_3OH(g)$$

14.4 Heterogeneous Reactions

Heterogeneous reactions occur on a surface or phase boundary; hence, the rate of such a reaction can be greatly increased if the surface is increased. In a reaction between a solid and a gas, or a solid and a liquid, the total number of collisions per unit time can be increased by pulverizing the solid. A finely divided combustible material may burn with such rapidity as to produce an explosion. The rate of a heterogeneous process may be increased by agitation of the reacting mixture, since agitation keeps the reactive surface continuously exposed. Thus sugar dissolves more quickly in coffee if the mixture is stirred.

For this same reason, surface catalysts are usually prepared in a way that will produce a large surface area for a given amount of solid. Solids used as catalysts are generally porous and extremely finely divided.

14.5 Concentrations and Reaction Rates

Reaction rate is generally dependent upon the concentrations of the reacting substances. When the concentration of a reactant is increased, more molecules are crowded into a given volume, and the total number of molecular collisions per unit time is increased; this results in an increase in the rate of the reaction. If all other conditions are held constant, there is no change in the proportion of collisions that are effective.

Many different techniques are employed to study reaction rates—the appropriate one depending upon the reaction under consideration. In addition to chemical analysis, physical methods are sometimes used to follow the progress of chemical reactions. These physical methods are applicable only when some measurable change takes place in the course of the reaction; for example, physical methods have been devised to study reactions in which there is a change in one of the following: total pressure, color (appearance or disappearance of a colored substance), acidity or alkalinity, conductivity, volume, or viscosity.

Since the concentrations of the reactants decrease as the reaction proceeds, the rate of a chemical reaction decreases with time as well. In Figure 14.8 concentrations are plotted against time for the hypothetical reaction

$$A_2 + B_2 \longrightarrow 2AB$$

The rate of the reaction, in terms of the change in concentration of A_2, B_2, or AB per unit time is given by the slope of the appropriate curve. The rate of this reaction may be expressed in terms of the rate of disappearance of A_2 and B_2 or the rate of appearance of AB; because of the stoichiometry of the reaction, these rates are not equal. The rate of appearance of AB is twice that of the rate of disappearance of A_2 and B_2.

Concentrations are generally expressed in moles per liter (molarity for substances in solution); in mathematical expressions, the concentration of a substance is usually represented by its formula enclosed in brackets. Since the pressure of a gas is a measure of its concentration, expressions are

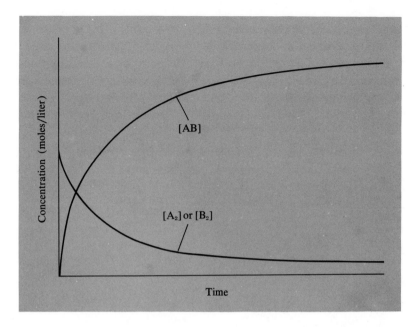

Figure 14.8   Curves showing changes in concentrations of materials with time for the reaction $A_2 + B_2 \rightarrow 2AB$.

frequently derived on the basis of the partial pressures of reacting gases (in torr or atm); the partial pressure of nitrogen is given the symbol p_{N_2}.

For a chemical reaction, a mathematical expression (a **rate equation**) relating the concentrations of reactants to the reaction rate may usually be determined experimentally. The chemical equation for a reaction stoichiometrically describes only the initial reactants and final products; frequently, the chemical change itself occurs by way of a mechanism consisting of several steps. Each of these steps proceeds at its own rate—some rapid, some slow—and each is dependent upon the concentrations of the initial reactants and/or the reaction intermediates. Therefore, the rate expression for the chemical reaction may not generally be derived from an inspection of the balanced chemical equation for the overall chemical change but must be determined experimentally.

For reactions that are known to be simple one-step processes (which must be determined experimentally), a rate expression can be derived from the chemical equation; such reactions are not numerous. For example, we have assumed the reaction

$$A_2(g) + B_2(g) \longrightarrow 2AB(g)$$

proceeds in one step through collisions between A_2 molecules and B_2 molecules. If the concentration of A_2 is doubled in a given system, the number of A_2 molecules is doubled. In this instance, the number of A_2—B_2 collisions per second is doubled, and the reaction rate is doubled. If the concentration of B_2 is doubled and the concentration of A_2 is constant, the same effect on the rate is observed. Doubling both the A_2 and B_2 concentrations increases the reaction rate by a factor of four. The rate of the reaction, then, is proportional to the product of the concentrations of A_2 and B_2, or

$$\text{rate} = k[A_2][B_2]$$

The proportionality constant, k, is called the **rate constant**; its numerical value is dependent upon temperature, catalysis, and the terms in which the reaction rate is expressed.

The rate equation may also be expressed in terms of pressures,

$$\text{rate} = k p_{A_2} p_{B_2}$$

The value of k in this equation is not the same as that of the previous rate equation.

The reaction

$$2N_2O(g) \longrightarrow 2N_2(g) + O_2(g)$$

proceeds by means of collisions between two N_2O molecules. For a given system of definite volume, the number of collisions per second for a *single* N_2O molecule is proportional to the total number of molecules present less one $(n - 1)$. Inasmuch as this is true of all n of the molecules present, the total number of collisions per second is proportional to $\frac{1}{2}n(n - 1)$. The factor $\frac{1}{2}$ must be included so that a given collision is not counted twice—once for each molecule in the collision. The number of molecules in a sample is so large that $(n - 1)$ is approximately equal to n; thus the total number of collisions per second is proportional to $\frac{1}{2}n^2$ to a good approximation. The constant $\frac{1}{2}$ may be incorporated into the rate constant and the number of molecules of N_2O in the system is proportional to the concentration of N_2O. Thus

$$\text{rate} = k[N_2O]^2$$

In general, for any single step reaction (or for one step of a multistep mechanism) such as

$$wW + xX + \cdots \longrightarrow \text{products}$$

the rate equation is

$$\text{rate} = k[W]^w [X]^x \cdots$$

This is a statement of the **law of mass action** which was first expressed in general form by Cato Guldberg and Peter Waage in 1864. If the reactants are gases, similar expressions using partial pressures may be derived.

The **order** of a rate equation is given by the sum of the exponents of the concentrations appearing in the equation. Thus for the reaction between NO and O_2 listed in Table 14.1, the rate expression is said to be second order in

Table 14.1

Rate Equations for Some Gas Phase Reactions

First Order	
$2N_2O_5 \longrightarrow 4NO_2 + O_2$	rate $= k[N_2O_5]$
$2N_2O \xrightarrow{Au} 2N_2 + O_2$	rate $= k[N_2O]$
$SO_2Cl_2 \longrightarrow SO_2 + Cl_2$	rate $= k[SO_2Cl_2]$
$2NO_2Cl \longrightarrow 2NO_2 + Cl_2$	rate $= k[NO_2Cl]$
$N_2O_4 \longrightarrow 2NO_2$	rate $= k[N_2O_4]$
Second Order	
$2N_2O \longrightarrow 2N_2 + O_2$	rate $= k[N_2O]^2$
$2NOCl \longrightarrow 2NO + Cl_2$	rate $= k[NOCl]^2$
$2NO_2 \longrightarrow 2NO + O_2$	rate $= k[NO_2]^2$
Third Order	
$2NO + O_2 \longrightarrow 2NO_2$	rate $= k[NO]^2[O_2]$
$2NO + Cl_2 \longrightarrow 2NOCl$	rate $= k[NO]^2[Cl_2]$
$2NO + Br_2 \longrightarrow 2NOBr$	rate $= k[NO]^2[Br_2]$

NO, first order in O_2, and third order overall. Since experimentally determined rate expressions may represent a mathematical summary of several rate equations (one for each step of a multistep mechanism), equations of fractional order are sometimes obtained.

▶ **EXAMPLE 14.1** The data of the following table were obtained at 25°C for the

$$S_2O_8^{2-}(aq) + 2I^-(aq) \longrightarrow 2SO_4^{2-}(aq) + I_2(aq)$$

What is the rate equation for the reaction and the value of k?

Experiment	Initial Conc. $S_2O_8^{2-}$ (M)	Initial Conc. I^- (M)	Initial Rate— Increase in Conc. of I_2 (M/min)
A	1.0×10^{-4}	1.0×10^{-2}	0.65×10^{-6}
B	2.0×10^{-4}	1.0×10^{-2}	1.30×10^{-6}
C	2.0×10^{-4}	0.5×10^{-2}	0.65×10^{-6}

Solution Comparison of the data from experiment A with that from experiment B shows that the rate is doubled when the concentration of $S_2O_8^{2-}$ is doubled.

According to the data from experiments B and C, doubling the concentration of I^- has the same effect on the reaction rate. The reaction, therefore, is first order in $S_2O_8^{2-}$, first order in I^-, and second order overall.

$$\text{rate} = k[S_2O_8^{2-}][I^-]$$

Note that the chemical equation for the reaction might lead one to expect a rate expression of third order.

The data from any of the experiments may be used to derive the value for the rate constant; $k = 0.65/M$ min.

▶ **EXAMPLE 14.2** The mechanism of the thermal decomposition of gaseous acetaldehyde, CH_3CHO, is complicated, and the order of the reaction changes with changes in the conditions under which the reaction is run. The following data pertain to the decomposition at $800°K$. Find the order of the reaction under the conditions specified.

Experiment	Initial Pressure of Acetaldehyde (torr)	Initial Rate of Increase in Total Pressure (torr/sec)
A	300	0.61
B	200	0.27

Solution The rate of the thermal decomposition of acetaldehyde vapor

$$CH_3CHO(g) \longrightarrow CH_4(g) + CO(g)$$

may be obtained by measuring the rate of increase in the total pressure of the system. At any time, the total pressure, P, is equal to the sum of the partial pressures of all gases present.

$$P = p_{CH_3CHO} + p_{CH_4} + p_{CO}$$

If we let a equal the original pressure of acetaldehyde and x equal the decrease in the partial pressure of this gas, the partial pressure of acetaldehyde is $(a - x)$. At the same time, the partial pressures of CH_4 and CO are each equal to x, since the decomposition of 1 mole of CH_3CHO yields 1 mole of CH_4 and 1 mole of CO. Therefore,

$$p = (a - x) + x + x = a + x$$

Hence, the rate of *increase* in the total pressure is also the rate of *decrease* in the partial pressure of CH_3CHO vapor and represents the rate of decomposition of CH_3CHO.

For a rate expression of the form, rate $= k[CH_3CHO]^n$, n represents the order of the reaction. If we take the logarithm of this equation, we derive

$$\log \text{rate} = \log k + n \log [CH_3CHO]$$

Both k and n are constants, and for two different sets of data

$$\log \text{rate}_1 = \log k + n \log [CH_3CHO]_1$$

$$\log \text{rate}_2 = \log k + n \log [CH_3CHO]_2$$

Subtraction of the second equation from the first gives

$$\log \text{rate}_1 - \log \text{rate}_2 = n(\log [CH_3CHO]_1 - \log [CH_3CHO]_2)$$

or

$$\log (\text{rate}_1/\text{rate}_2) = n \log ([CH_3CHO]_1/[CH_3CHO]_2)$$

Therefore,

$$n = \frac{\log (\text{rate}_1/\text{rate}_2)}{\log ([CH_3CHO]_1/[CH_3CHO]_2)}$$

Since, the pressure of a gas is proportional to its concentration, we may substitute our values.

$$n = \frac{\log (0.61/0.27)}{\log (300/200)} = \frac{\log 2.26}{\log 1.50}$$

$$= \frac{0.354}{0.176} = 2.0$$

The reaction is second order under the conditions of the study and

$$\text{rate} = k[CH_3CHO]^2$$

14.6 Rate Equations and Temperature

The rate constant, k, varies with temperature in a manner described by the following equation

$$k = Ae^{-E_a/RT}$$

where A is a constant that is characteristic of the reaction being studied, e is the base of natural logarithms (2.718), E_a is the energy of activation for the reaction (in calories), R is the molar gas constant (1.987 cal/mole °K), and T is the absolute temperature. This equation was first proposed by Svanté Arrhenius in 1889 and is known as the **Arrhenius equation.**

The factor $e^{-E_a/RT}$ represents the fraction of molecules that have energies equal to or greater than the energy of activation, E_a, and may be derived from the Maxwell-Boltzmann distribution law (Sections 6.11 and 14.2).

The constant A incorporates terms for other factors that influence reaction rate, such as the frequency of molecular collisions and the geometric requirements for the alignment of colliding molecules that react. The equation is only approximate, but in most cases, the approximation is a good one.

If we take the natural logarithm of the Arrhenius equation, we get

$$\ln k = \ln A - \frac{E_a}{RT}$$

which may be transformed into

$$2.303 \log k = 2.303 \log A - \frac{E_a}{RT}$$

or

$$\log k = \log A - \frac{E_a}{2.303 RT}$$

▶ **EXAMPLE 14.3** For the reaction

$$2N_2O_5(g) \longrightarrow 4NO_2(g) + O_2(g)$$

A is 4.3×10^{13}/sec and E_a is 24,700 cal. What is k at $300°K$?

Solution

$$\log k = \log A - \frac{E_a}{2.303 RT}$$

$$= \log (4.3 \times 10^{13}) - \frac{24,700}{(2.30)(1.99)(300)}$$

$$= 13.63 - \frac{24,700}{1370}$$

$$= -4.40 = 0.60 - 5.00$$

$$k = 4.0 \times 10^{-5}/sec$$

Since the relation between k and T is exponential, a small change in T causes a relatively large change in k. For example, as the data of Table 14.2 show, a $10°$ rise in temperature (from $300°K$ to $310°K$) causes an approximately fourfold increase in the rate of decomposition of N_2O_5. The larger the activation energy, the greater the effect of a given temperature rise on k. For example, E_a for the decomposition of C_2H_5Cl is more than double E_a for the decomposition of N_2O_5, and increasing the temperature from $300°K$ to $310°K$ causes the theoretical rate of decomposition of C_2H_5Cl to increase by a factor of about 300 (Table 14.2).

Table 14.2

Effect of Temperature on Some First-Order Rate Constants

Reaction	A (1/sec)	E_a (cal)	k (1/sec)	T (°K)
$2N_2O_5(g) \rightarrow 4NO_2(g) + O_2(g)$	4.3×10^{13}	24,700	4.0×10^{-5}	300
			1.7×10^{-4}	310
$C_2H_5Cl(g) \rightarrow C_2H_4(g) + HCl(g)$	1.6×10^{14}	59,000	5.9×10^{-30}	300
			1.9×10^{-28}	310
			4.2×10^{-5}	700
			7.2×10^{-5}	710

The values of k for the decomposition of C_2H_5Cl at 300°K and 310°K in Table 14.2 are of theoretical significance only; they are so small that the reaction would not occur at an appreciable rate at these temperatures. Nevertheless, the data of Table 14.2 illustrate not only the effect of the magnitude of E_a on the variation of k and T but also the fact that the effect of a 10° temperature rise is greater at low temperatures than at high temperatures. Whereas an increase from 300°K to 310°K causes an approximate 300-fold increase in k for the C_2H_5Cl decomposition, an increase from 700°K to 710°K approximately doubles k.

Since the equation

$$\log k = -\frac{E_a}{2.303R} \left(\frac{1}{T}\right) + \log A$$

is in the form of the equation for a straight line ($y = mx + b$), a plot of $\log k$ against $1/T$ is a straight line with a slope of $-E_a/2.303 R$ and a y-intercept of $\log A$ (Figure 14.9). Thus, if values of k for a reaction are determined at several temperatures and the data plotted in this manner, E_a for the reaction may be calculated from the slope of the curve and A may be obtained by taking the antilogarithm of the intercept. For the curve shown in Figure 14.9, E_a is 24,000 cal and A is 9.0×10^{12} liter/mole sec. The values of E_a and A are usually obtained from experimental data either graphically or by the method illustrated in the following example.

▶ **EXAMPLE 14.4** For the reaction

$$2NOCl(g) \longrightarrow 2NO(g) + Cl_2(g)$$

the rate constant is 2.8×10^{-5} liter/mole sec at 300°K and 7.0×10^{-1} liter/mole sec at 400°K. What is the energy of activation for the reaction?

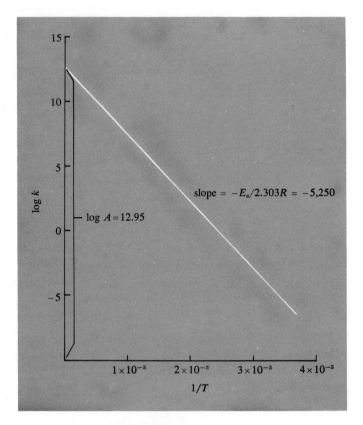

Figure 14.9 Plot of log K versus $1/T$ for the reaction $2NOCl(g) \rightarrow 2NO(g) + Cl_2(g)$.

Solution For two temperatures T_1 and T_2, where the corresponding rate constants are k_1 and k_2, we may write

$$\log k_2 = \log A - \frac{E_a}{2.303 R T_2}$$

and

$$\log k_1 = \log A - \frac{E_a}{2.303 R T_1}$$

Subtraction of the second equation from the first gives

$$\log k_2 - \log k_1 = \frac{E_a}{2.303 R T_1} - \frac{E_a}{2.303 R T_2}$$

or

$$\log \left(\frac{k_2}{k_1} \right) = \frac{E_a}{2.303 R} \left(\frac{T_2 - T_1}{T_1 T_2} \right)$$

If this equation is solved for E_a, we get

$$E_a = 2.303R \left(\frac{T_1 T_2}{T_2 - T_1}\right) \log\left(\frac{k_2}{k_1}\right)$$

In this case,

$$E_a = 2.30(1.99) \left(\frac{(300)(400)}{(400 - 300)}\right) \log \left(\frac{7.0 \times 10^{-1}}{2.8 \times 10^{-5}}\right)$$

$$= 5490 \log(2.5 \times 10^4) = 5490(4.38)$$

$$= 24{,}000 \text{ cal} = 24 \text{ kcal}$$

14.7 Reaction Mechanisms and Rate Equations

Mechanisms of chemical reactions are generally proposed on the basis of experimentally derived rate equations and other experimental evidence (e.g., the detection of short-lived reaction intermediates). It is practically impossible to be completely certain of the mechanism of any reaction; mechanisms are only plausible hypotheses consistent with all known facts.

Table 14.1 lists the uncatalyzed decomposition of N_2O as a second-order reaction, whereas the gold-catalyzed decomposition of the same compound is listed as a first-order reaction. The uncatalyzed reaction is thought to be a simple one-step process involving bimolecular collisions (Section 14.5).

$$2N_2O \longrightarrow 2N_2 + O_2$$

Such a mechanism would call for a second-order rate expression.

$$\text{rate} = k[N_2O]^2$$

On the other hand, the gold-catalyzed decomposition (Section 14.3, Figure 14.7) is thought to occur by a three-step mechanism in which N_2O molecules are chemisorbed on the surface of the gold in the first step.

(i) $\qquad N_2O(g) \longrightarrow N_2O(\text{on Au})$

(ii) $\qquad N_2O(\text{on Au}) \longrightarrow N_2(g) + O(\text{on Au}) \quad$ (slow)

(iii) $\quad O(\text{on Au}) + O(\text{on Au}) \longrightarrow O_2(g) \qquad\qquad$ (rapid)

The rate expression for either step (i) or step (ii) is first order. The rate of the chemisorption is determined by the pressure of gaseous N_2O and the rate of step (ii) is determined by the number of chemisorbed N_2O molecules, which in turn is determined by the pressure of gaseous N_2O. There is evidence however, that step (ii) is the slower process and as such is the **rate-determining step.** Step (iii) occurs much more rapidly than step (ii). As fast as (ii) produces O atoms, step (iii) uses them up. The second step, therefore, is the bottleneck and determines the overall rate of the entire decomposition.

At relatively high pressures of N_2O gas, the gold-catalyzed decomposition is observed to be **zero-order** that is, the rate is presumably unaffected by the concentration of gaseous N_2O. When the surface of the gold holds all the N_2O molecules that it can, the rate of decomposition is constant. Under these conditions, small changes in the pressure of gaseous N_2O do not cause the chemisorbed N_2O molecules to decompose any more slowly or rapidly, and there is always a supply of gaseous N_2O molecules sufficient to keep the surface saturated.

The decomposition of NO_2 is second order.

$$2NO_2(g) \longrightarrow 2NO(g) + O_2(g)$$

$$\text{rate} = k[NO_2]^2$$

Even though the chemical equation for the uncatalyzed decomposition of N_2O_5 is very similar,

$$2N_2O_5(g) \longrightarrow 4NO_2(g) + O_2(g)$$

this reaction has been found to be first order.

$$\text{rate} = k[N_2O_5]$$

We could account for the observed rate expression for the decomposition of N_2O_5 by visualizing a simple one-step unimolecular decomposition or a rate-determining unimolecular decomposition followed by one or more rapid steps.

However, there is evidence that the following is the mechanism for the decomposition of N_2O_5, with the third step being the slowest one.

(i) $\qquad\qquad N_2O_5 \xrightarrow{k_1} NO_2 + NO_3$

(ii) $\qquad\quad NO_2 + NO_3 \xrightarrow{k_2} N_2O_5$

(iii) $\qquad\quad NO_2 + NO_3 \xrightarrow{k_3} NO + O_2 + NO_2$

(iv) $\qquad\quad NO + NO_3 \xrightarrow{k_4} 2NO_2$

In the first step, the N_2O_5 molecule splits into two fragments, NO_2 and NO_3. The second step is the reverse of the first; NO_2 and NO_3 recombine to give the starting molecule. In the third step, NO_2 and NO_3 react in a different way from step (ii), and in the collision of NO_2 and NO_3, each molecule gives up an O atom to form O_2, so that NO and NO_2 are left. Step (iv) is a bimolecular collision of NO and NO_3.

The substances NO and NO_3 are **reaction intermediates**; they do not appear as final products. The molecule NO is a well-known oxide of nitrogen, but NO_3 is an unstable substance that does not exist for any length of time under ordinary conditions. The detection of NO_3 in systems in which N_2O_5 is decomposing is one of the lines of evidence used to support the mechanism.

We can reconcile the mechanism with the experimentally determined, first-order rate expression by the use of a **steady-state approximation.** It is assumed that, after the reaction has proceeded for a while, each of the reaction intermediates, NO and NO_3, attains a steady state in which its concentration is approximately constant and, therefore, the *net* rate of change in its concentration is zero. The concentrations of the intermediates are low at all times, and the *net* rate of change in the concentration of an intermediate is negligible in comparison to the rate at which the intermediate is produced or consumed; therefore, the approximation is a good one.

Applying the law of mass action to the appropriate steps, we derive an expression for the rate of increase in the concentration of NO which, according to the steady-state approximation, is equal to zero. Nitrogen oxide is *produced* in the third step at a rate equal to $+k_3[NO_2][NO_3]$; it is *used* in the fourth step at a rate equal to $-k_4[NO][NO_3]$. Therefore the rate of *production* of NO is

$$+k_3[NO_2][NO_3] - k_4[NO][NO_3] = 0$$

From this, we derive

$$[NO] = \frac{k_3}{k_4}[NO_2] \tag{1}$$

In like manner, we can derive an expression for the net rate of *production* of NO_3, which is produced in step (i) and used in steps (ii), (iii), and (iv).

$$+k_1[N_2O_5] - k_2[NO_2][NO_3] - k_3[NO_2][NO_3] - k_4[NO][NO_3] = 0$$

Solving for $[NO_3]$, we get

$$[NO_3] = \frac{k_1[N_2O_5]}{(k_2 + k_3)[NO_2] + k_4[NO]}$$

If we substitute equation (1) into this expression, we derive

$$[NO_3] = \frac{k_1[N_2O_5]}{(k_2 + 2k_3)[NO_2]} \tag{2}$$

We are now ready to find a single rate equation for the overall reaction in terms of the concentration of the starting material, N_2O_5. From the equations for the first two steps of the mechanism,

$$\text{rate of } \textit{decrease} \text{ in } [N_2O_5] = +k_1[N_2O_5] - k_2[NO_2][NO_3]$$

Substitution of (2) yields

$$\text{rate of } \textit{decrease} \text{ in } [N_2O_5] = k_1[N_2O_5] - k_2[NO_2]\left(\frac{k_1[N_2O_5]}{(k_2 + 2k_3)[NO_2]}\right)$$

$$= \frac{2k_1k_3}{k_2 + 2k_3}[N_2O_5]$$

If we combine all the rate constants into a single constant, we get

$$\text{rate of } \textit{decrease} \text{ in } [N_2O_5] = k[N_2O_5]$$

which is the experimentally determined rate equation.

The mathematical treatment of mechanisms of other chemical reactions may be much more involved; it is not surprising that complicated rate equations, which may be of fractional order, are often derived from the data obtained from experimental studies of chemical reactions.

The study of reactions that are initiated by means of light is called **photochemistry.** The most famous example of a photochemical reaction is photosynthesis, which occurs in plants and converts carbon dioxide and water into plant carbohydrates. The green coloring matter in plants, chlorophyll, acts as a catalyst for photosynthesis.

Light also initiates the reaction between hydrogen and chlorine. The primary, light-induced, step of the reaction is the dissociation of chlorine molecules into chlorine atoms.

$$Cl_2 \longrightarrow 2Cl$$

These chlorine atoms initiate a **chain reaction** in which the cycle

$$Cl + H_2 \longrightarrow HCl + H$$
$$H + Cl_2 \longrightarrow HCl + Cl$$

is repeated again and again. A chain may be terminated by such reactions as

$$2H \longrightarrow H_2$$
$$2Cl \longrightarrow Cl_2$$

or

$$H + Cl \longrightarrow HCl$$

Chain reactions usually proceed very rapidly. Many explosive reactions occur by a chain mechanism; atomic fission and atomic fusion are of this type. In the reaction of hydrogen and chlorine, the chain is sustained by the chlorine atoms and the hydrogen atoms; these extremely reactive intermediates are called chain propagators.

A branched-chain reaction, such as that between hydrogen and oxygen, is a reaction in which one or more of the steps produce more than one chain propagator. Following are some of the steps that have been postulated for the reaction between H_2 and O_2.

(i) $$H_2 + O_2 \longrightarrow 2OH$$

(ii) $$OH + H_2 \longrightarrow H_2O + H$$

(iii) $$H + O_2 \longrightarrow OH + O$$

(iv) $$O + H_2 \longrightarrow OH + H$$

Reaction (i) is a chain-initiating step, and reaction (ii) merely sustains the chain. The chain propagators are OH, H, and O, and steps (iii) and (iv) are chain-branching steps. Each of these steps produces two chain propagators, and thus two reactions follow from either reaction (iii) or reaction (iv); this increases the overall rate of the reaction. Chains terminate upon collisions of the chain propagators—usually at the walls of the container. Generally, a third body is necessary in these collisions to absorb the energy evolved by the highly exothermic recombination.

14.8 Reversible Reactions and Chemical Equilibrium

In Sections 14.1 and 14.2 we discussed the reversible reaction

$$A_2(g) + B_2(g) \rightleftharpoons 2AB(g)$$

This equation may be read either forward or backward. If A_2 and B_2 are mixed, they react to produce AB. The rate of this forward reaction declines as the reaction proceeds, since A_2 and B_2 are used up and their concentrations decrease. If no AB is present at the start, the backward reaction is initially impossible. However, the forward reaction produces AB, so that the backward reaction begins soon after the A_2 and B_2 are mixed. This reaction starts slowly (the concentration of AB is low) but picks up speed as the concentration of AB is built up by more rapid forward reaction.

With time, the forward reaction rate decreases and the backward reaction rate increases until eventually a condition is reached in which the two rates are equal. At this point, chemical equilibrium is established, and the concentrations of all chemical species are constant. The rate at which AB is produced by the forward reactions equals the rate at which AB is consumed by the backward reaction. In like manner, A_2 and B_2 are produced at rates exactly equal to the rates at which they are used.

It is important to note that equilibrium is a dynamic condition; equilibrium concentrations are constant because the rates of the opposing reactions are equal and not because all activity has ceased. Typical data for this reaction are plotted in Figure 14.10; equilibrium is attained at t_e.

The rate of the forward reaction is given by

$$\text{rate}_f = k[A_2][B_2]$$

and the rate of the backward reaction is

$$\text{rate}_b = k'[AB]^2$$

At equilibrium these rates are equal, and therefore,

$$k[A_2][B_2] = k'[AB]^2$$

or

$$\frac{k}{k'} = \frac{[AB]^2}{[A_2][B_2]}$$

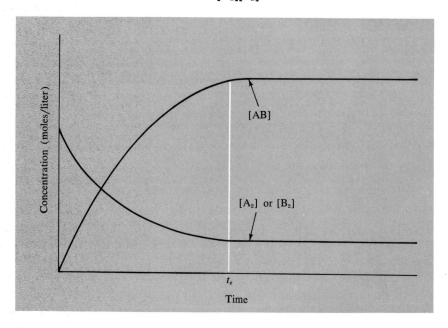

Figure 14.10 Curves showing changes in concentrations of materials with time **for** the reaction $A_2 + B_2 \rightleftharpoons 2AB$; equilibrium is attained at time t_e.

The rate constant of the forward reaction, k, divided by the rate constant of the backward reaction, k', is equal to a third constant—the **equilibrium constant** K.

$$K = \frac{[AB]^2}{[A_2][B_2]}$$

The numerical value of K varies with temperature. There are an infinite number of possible equilibrium systems for this reaction. However, the concentrations of A_2, B_2, and AB for any system in equilibrium will, when expressed in the preceding manner, equal K for the particular temperature under consideration.

In general, for any reversible reaction

$$wW + xX + \cdots \rightleftharpoons yY + zZ + \cdots$$

at equilibrium,

$$K = \frac{[Y]^y [Z]^z \cdots}{[W]^w [X]^x \cdots}$$

By convention, the concentration terms for the materials on the right of the chemical equation are written in the numerator of the expression for the equilibrium constant. If the equation is written in reverse form, the equilibrium constant becomes the reciprocal of that for the original equation. The preceding equation constitutes a statement of the **law of chemical equilibrium** which Guldberg and Waage derived from their law of mass action (Section 14.5).

In the rate equation for the reaction of A_2 and B_2 and the rate equation for the decomposition of AB, the exponents of the concentrations correspond to the coefficients of the balanced chemical equation. In this instance, both the forward and backward reactions occur through single-step bimolecular collisions, and the rate expressions may be derived from the chemical equation. It is not immediately apparent that the law of chemical equilibrium holds for a reaction that occurs by means of a mechanism of more than one step. However, an equilibrium constant may be derived for any reversible chemical change on the basis of the overall equation for the change.

For example, the forward reaction

$$2NO_2Cl \rightleftharpoons 2NO_2 + Cl_2$$

is first order; $rate_f = k[NO_2Cl]$. The reaction is assumed to follow the mechanism

$$NO_2Cl \xrightarrow{k_1} NO_2 + Cl$$

$$NO_2Cl + Cl \xrightarrow{k_2} NO_2 + Cl_2$$

Both steps of the mechanism must be reversible, and when equilibrium is established for the overall change, each step of the mechanism must exist in equilibrium. Thus

$$K_a = \frac{k_1}{k_1'} = \frac{[NO_2][Cl]}{[NO_2Cl]}$$

and

$$K_b = \frac{k_2}{k_2'} = \frac{[NO_2][Cl_2]}{[NO_2Cl][Cl]}$$

By combining these expressions, we get

$$K_a K_b = \frac{k_1 k_2}{k_1' k_2'} = \frac{[NO_2][Cl]}{[NO_2Cl]} \frac{[NO_2][Cl_2]}{[NO_2Cl][Cl]} = \frac{[NO_2]^2 [Cl_2]}{[NO_2Cl]^2}$$

which is the same as the expression for the equilibrium constant that would have been derived directly from the equation for the overall change. In this case, the equilibrium constant for the overall change is the product of the equilibrium constants of each of the steps.

14.9   Equilibrium Constants

For the reaction

$$H_2(g) + I_2(g) \rightleftharpoons 2HI(g)$$

the equilibrium constant at 425°C is

$$K = \frac{[HI]^2}{[H_2][I_2]} = 54.8$$

The numerical value of K must be determined experimentally. At 425°C, the concentrations of the materials present in any equilibrium mixture when expressed in the manner prescribed by the equilibrium constant will equal 54.8; if this is not the case, the mixture is not in equilibrium.

The equilibrium condition may be approached from either direction. That is, an equilibrium mixture can be obtained by mixing hydrogen and iodine, by allowing pure hydrogen iodide to dissociate, or by mixing all three materials.

The magnitude of the value of the equilibrium constant gives an indication of the position of equilibrium. Recall that the concentration terms of materials on the right of the equation are written in the numerator of the expression for the equilibrium constant. For the reaction

$$CO(g) + Cl_2(g) \rightleftharpoons COCl_2(g)$$

at 100°C,

$$K = \frac{[COCl_2]}{[CO][Cl_2]} = 4.57 \times 10^9$$

From this relatively large value of K, we conclude that equilibrium concentrations of CO and Cl_2 are small and that the synthesis of $COCl_2$ is virtually complete. In other words, the reaction to the right is fairly complete at equilibrium.

For the reaction

$$N_2(g) + O_2(g) \rightleftharpoons 2NO(g)$$

at 2000°C,

$$K = \frac{[NO]^2}{[N_2][O_2]} = 4.08 \times 10^{-4}$$

We conclude from this small value of K that NO is largely dissociated into N_2 and O_2 at equilibrium; the reaction to the left is fairly complete.

Equilibria between substances in two or more phases are called **heterogeneous equilibria**. The concentrations of pure solids or pure liquids are proportional to their densities and are constant at constant temperature. Hence, for any heterogeneous equilibrium, the values of the concentrations of solids or liquids involved are included in the value of K, and concentration terms for these substances do not appear in the expression for the equilibrium constant.

For example, for the reaction

$$CaCO_3(s) \rightleftharpoons CaO(s) + CO_2(g)$$

the values for the concentrations of CaO and $CaCO_3$ are included in the value of K, and the expression for the equilibrium constant is

$$K = [CO_2]$$

Hence, at any temperature, the equilibrium concentration of CO_2 over a mixture of the solids is a definite value. The equilibrium constant for the reaction

$$3Fe(s) + 4H_2O(g) \rightleftharpoons Fe_3O_4(s) + 4H_2(g)$$

is expressed in the following terms

$$K = \frac{[H_2]^4}{[H_2O]^4}$$

Since the partial pressure of a gas is a measure of its concentration, equilibrium constants for reactions involving gases may be given in terms of the partial pressures of the reacting gases; such an equilibrium constant is given the designation K_p. For the calcium carbonate equilibrium, the constant in terms of partial pressures is

$$K_p = p_{CO_2}$$

For the equilibrium

$$N_2(g) + 3H_2(g) \; \rightleftharpoons \; 2NH_3(g)$$

the K_p is

$$K_p = \frac{(p_{NH_3})^2}{(p_{N_2})(p_{H_2})^3}$$

There is a simple relation between the K_p for a reaction and the equilibrium constant derived from concentrations. Consider the reaction

$$wW + xX \; \rightleftharpoons \; yY + zZ$$

If all these materials are gases,

$$K_p = \frac{(p_Y)^y (p_Z)^z}{(p_W)^w (p_X)^x}$$

If we assume that these gases follow the ideal gas law, the partial pressure of any gas is

$$p = \frac{n}{V} RT$$

The concentration of a gas in moles per liter is equal to n/V. Hence, for W,

$$p_W = [W]RT$$

If we substitute terms such as this for the partial pressures in the expression for K_p, we get

$$K_p = \frac{[Y]^y (RT)^y [Z]^z (RT)^z}{[W]^w (RT)^w [X]^x (RT)^x} = K(RT)^{+y+z-w-x}$$

We shall designate the quantity $(+y + z - w - x)$, which is equal to the number of moles of products minus the number of moles of reactants, as Δn. Therefore,

$$K_p = K(RT)^{\Delta n}$$

Generally, partial pressures are expressed in atmospheres; concentrations are expressed in moles per liter; R is 0.08206 liter atm/°K mole; and T is the absolute temperature.

It is obvious that $K = K_p$ when $\Delta n = 0$, as in the reaction

$$H_2(g) + I_2(g) \rightleftharpoons 2HI(g)$$

To be strictly accurate, equations for equilibrium constants should be given in terms of activities rather than concentrations or partial pressures. The activity of a substance may be regarded as its effective concentration and may be obtained by multiplying the actual concentration by an activity co-efficient (Section 9.12). By this means, deviations, due principally to the existence of intermolecular forces of attraction, may be minimized. However, at low concentrations and pressures up to a few atmospheres, ideality may be assumed, and concentrations may be used with reasonable accuracy.

▶ **EXAMPLE 14.5** For the reaction

$$N_2O_4(g) \rightleftharpoons 2NO_2(g)$$

the concentrations of an equilibrium mixture at 25°C are $[N_2O_4] = 4.50 \times 10^{-2}$ mole/liter and $[NO_2] = 1.61 \times 10^{-2}$ mole/liter. What is K?

Solution

$$K = \frac{[NO_2]^2}{[N_2O_4]}$$

$$= \frac{(1.61 \times 10^{-2} \text{ mole/liter})^2}{(4.50 \times 10^{-2} \text{ mole/liter})}$$

$$= 5.76 \times 10^{-3} \text{ mole/liter}$$

▶ **EXAMPLE 14.6** What is K for the reaction

$$N_2(g) + 3H_2(g) \rightleftharpoons 2NH_3(g)$$

at 500°C if $K_p = 1.50 \times 10^{-5}/\text{atm}^2$ at this temperature?

Solution For the reaction, $\Delta n = -2$

$$K = K_p(RT)^{-\Delta n}$$

$$= (1.50 \times 10^{-5}/\text{atm}^2)[(0.08206 \text{ liter atm}/°K \text{ mole})(773°K)]^2$$

$$= 6.04 \times 10^{-2} \text{ liter}^2/\text{mole}^2$$

▶ **EXAMPLE 14.7** K for the reaction

$$H_2(g) + CO_2(g) \rightleftharpoons H_2O(g) + CO(g)$$

at 750°C is 0.771. If 1 mole of H_2 and 1 mole of CO_2 are mixed in a 1 liter con-tainer at 750°C, what are the concentrations of all substances at equilibrium?

Solution If x moles of H_2 react with x moles of CO_2, then x moles of H_2O and x moles of CO will be produced. Since the container has a volume of 1 liter, at equilibrium the concentrations are (in moles/liter):

$$H_2(g) + CO_2(g) \rightleftharpoons H_2O(g) + CO(g)$$
$$\underset{(1-x)}{} \quad \underset{(1-x)}{} \qquad \underset{x}{} \quad \underset{x}{}$$

$$K = \frac{[H_2O][CO]}{[H_2][CO_2]} = 0.771$$

$$= \frac{x^2}{(1-x)(1-x)} = 0.771$$

If we extract the square root of both sides of this equation, we get

$$\frac{x}{(1-x)} = 0.878$$

$$x = 0.468$$

Therefore, at equilibrium,

$$[H_2] = [CO_2] = (1-x) = 0.532 \text{ mole/liter}$$

$$[H_2O] = [CO] = x = 0.468 \text{ mole/liter}$$

14.10 Free Energy and Chemical Equilibrium

The law of chemical equilibrium can be derived from thermodynamics as well as from kinetics. At constant temperature and pressure, any spontaneous chemical change results in a decrease in the Gibbs free energy of a system (Section 13.6). If the ΔG for a proposed reaction is positive, net work must be done on the system to bring about the change; the reaction is not spontaneous. If ΔG is negative, the reaction is spontaneous and, in theory, can be used to accomplish net work. At equilibrium, $\Delta G = 0$, since there is no *net* change in the system that requires work or that can be harnessed to do work. The macroscopic properties of a system in equilibrium do not change with time (the concentrations of all substances present are constant) even though the reversible reaction is proceeding in both directions.

If we assign the Gibbs free energy of a *mole* of substance W in its standard state (unit activity) the symbol of G_W°, the Gibbs free energy of a mole of this substance at another activity is given by the equation

$$G_W = G_W^\circ + RT \ln a_W$$

where R is the gas constant, T is the absolute temperature, and $\ln a_W$ is the natural logarithm of the activity of W. For w moles of material

$$wG_W = wG_W^\circ + wRT \ln a_W$$

or

$$wG_W = wG_W^\circ + RT \ln (a_W)^w \qquad (3)$$

The absolute values of free energies are not known; however, changes in free energies can be determined. For the hypothetical reaction

$$wW + xX \longrightarrow yY + zZ$$

the change in free energy is given by the equation

$$\Delta G = yG_Y + zG_Z - (wG_W + xG_X) \qquad (4)$$

In like manner,

$$\Delta G^\circ = yG_Y^\circ + zG_Z^\circ - (wG_W^\circ + xG_X^\circ) \qquad (5)$$

By substituting expressions similar to (3) into equation (4), we get

$$\Delta G = yG_Y^\circ + RT \ln (a_Y)^y + zG_Z^\circ + RT \ln (a_Z)^z - wG_W^\circ - RT \ln (a_W)^w - xG_X^\circ - RT \ln (a_X)^x$$

Combining terms, we get

$$\Delta G = yG_Y^\circ + zG_Z^\circ - wG_W^\circ - xG_X^\circ + RT \ln \left(\frac{(a_Y)^y (a_Z)^z}{(a_W)^w (a_X)^x} \right)$$

From equation (5),

$$\Delta G = \Delta G^\circ + RT \ln \left(\frac{(a_Y)^y (a_Z)^z}{(a_W)^w (a_X)^x} \right)$$

In this equation, ΔG° is the change in free energy for the preparation of the products in their standard states from the reactants in their standard states; the logarithmic term corrects the standard free-energy change to the free-energy change for a more general condition in which the activities of the substances are not unity. We shall use the approximations that the activity of gases are given by their partial pressures and the activities of substances in solution equal their concentrations.

At equilibrium, $\Delta G = 0$, and if we assume that the preceding reaction takes place in the gas phase,

$$0 = \Delta G^\circ + RT \ln \left(\frac{(p_Y)^y (p_Z)^z}{(p_W)^w (p_X)^x} \right)$$

But this fraction is simply an equilibrium constant in terms of partial pressures. Therefore,

$$\Delta G^\circ = -RT \ln K_p$$

If $\Delta G°$ is expressed in terms of kilocalories and the natural logarithm is converted to a base 10 logarithm, at 25°C,

$$\Delta G° = -1.364 \log K_p$$

The partial pressures used in K_p are expressed in atmospheres. A similar expression can be derived for equilibrium constants that apply to equilibria occurring in solutions and that are based on concentrations of dissolved substances (in moles per liter).

This relationship between $\Delta G°$ and K is an important one since it may be used to calculate equilibrium constants from thermochemical data. Furthermore, since

$$\Delta G° = -nF\mathscr{E}°$$

(Section 10.7), electrochemical data can be used to calculate equilibrium constants for reactions that can be studied in voltaic cells.

The change in free energy of a system in which the reaction

$$N_2O_4(g) \; \rightleftharpoons \; 2NO_2(g)$$

occurs is plotted in Figure 14.11. The curve is plotted for the reaction at 25°C and a total pressure of 1 atm, and for a system containing the equivalent of 1 mole of N_2O_4. Point A, therefore, represents the free energy of 1 mole of N_2O_4; point B represents the free energy of 2 moles of NO_2; and the intervening points on the curve represent mixtures of N_2O_4 and NO_2 such that a material balance exists. The absolute values of free energies are not known, and no scale is indicated on the vertical axis of the diagram; however, differences in free energies may be calculated so that the shape of the curve is accurately represented.

The free energy of the system exhibits a minimum at the equilibrium point, E, where 18.5% of the N_2O_4 is dissociated; $K_p = 0.141$. Since standard free energies are defined in terms of a total pressure of 1 atm, the difference between the free energy at point B and the free energy at point A ($+1.15$ kcal) is the $\Delta G°$ of the reaction. On this basis alone, one might predict that the formation of NO_2 from N_2O_4 is impossible. However, the difference between the free energy of pure N_2O_4 (point A) and the free energy of the equilibrium mixture (point E), which is -0.22 kcal, shows that N_2O_4 will dissociate into NO_2 until equilibrium is reached.

The graph shows that equilibrium may be approached from either direction, and experiment bears this out. Thus $\Delta G = -1.37$ kcal for the preparation of the equilibrium mixture (point E) from pure NO_2 (point B). The negative values of ΔG for both changes (from A to E and from B to E) indicate that both changes are spontaneous.

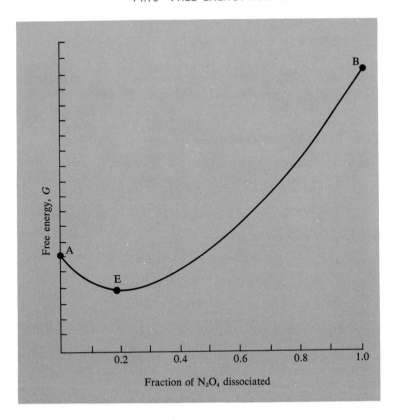

Figure 14.11 Free energy of a system that contains the equivalent of 1 mole of N_2O_4 as the reaction $N_2O_4(g) \rightleftharpoons 2NO_2(g)$ occurs ($25°C$ and 1 atm pressure).

▶ **EXAMPLE 14.8** Calculate K_p for the following reaction at $25°C$.

$$2SO_2(g) + O_2(g) \rightleftharpoons 2SO_3(g)$$

$\Delta G_f^\circ(SO_2) = -71.79$ kcal/mole; $\Delta G_f^\circ(SO_3) = -88.52$ kcal/mole.

Solution The standard free energy change for the reaction is

$$\Delta G^\circ = 2 \text{ moles } (-88.52 \text{ kcal/mole}) - 2 \text{ moles } (-71.79 \text{ kcal/mole})$$
$$\Delta G^\circ = -33.46 \text{ kcal}$$

K_p may be calculated from this value.

$$\Delta G^\circ = -1.364 \log K_p$$

$$\log K_p = \frac{-33.46 \text{ kcal}}{-1.364 \text{ kcal}} = 22.09$$

$$K_p = 1.2 \times 10^{22}$$

The reaction to the right is virtually complete.

▶ **EXAMPLE 14.9** Using electrochemical data, calculate K for the reaction

$$Fe^{2+}(aq) + Ag^+(aq) \rightleftharpoons Fe^{3+}(aq) + Ag(s)$$

Solution The half reactions are

$$Fe^{2+} \longrightarrow Fe^{3+} + e^- \qquad \mathscr{E}^\circ_{ox} = -0.771 \text{ v}$$

$$e^- + Ag^+ \longrightarrow Ag(s) \qquad \mathscr{E}^\circ = +0.799 \text{ v}$$

Therefore, $\mathscr{E}^\circ = +0.028$ v and 1 F of electricity is involved. The standard change in free energy is

$$\Delta G^\circ = -nF\mathscr{E}^\circ$$

$$= -1(23.1 \text{ kcal/v})(0.028 \text{ v})$$

$$= -0.65 \text{ kcal}$$

The equilibrium constant may be calculated from:

$$\Delta G^\circ = -1.36 \log K$$

$$\log K = \frac{-0.65 \text{ kcal}}{-1.36 \text{ kcal}} = 0.48$$

$$K = 3.0$$

14.11   Le Chatelier's Principle

The effect of an alteration in a reaction condition on a system in equilibrium was summarized in 1884 by Henri Le Chatelier. **Le Chatelier's principle** may be stated as: an alteration in any condition that determines the state of a system in equilibrium will cause the position of equilibrium to shift in a manner that tends to counteract the alteration. This important and powerful generalization is very simple to apply.

Alterations in three conditions cause changes in the position of equilibrium: concentration, pressure, and temperature. Of these three, only a change in temperature will affect the value of the equilibrium constant. The presence or absence of a catalyst has no effect on the position of equilibrium, since a catalyst will affect the rate of the forward and backward reaction to an equal extent (Section 14.3). However, the introduction of a catalyst into a system not in equilibrium will cause the system to attain equilibrium more rapidly than it otherwise would.

If we have a system in equilibrium,

$$H_2(g) + I_2(g) \rightleftharpoons 2HI(g)$$

and we increase the concentration of H_2, the equilibrium will be upset and the system will react to establish a new equilibrium condition. When equilibrium is again attained, the concentration of HI will be increased over its initial value; the concentration of I_2 will be decreased in comparison to its initial value; and the concentration of H_2 will be lower than its value after the addition. In summary, the reaction will proceed to the right, thereby partially counteracting the alteration and decreasing the concentration of H_2.

If additional HI is added to a system in equilibrium, the reaction will proceed to the left, thus increasing the concentrations of H_2 and I_2 and using up HI. Removal of one of the substances from an equilibrium system also causes the position of equilibrium to shift. For example, removal of HI would cause the reaction to proceed to the right, thus producing more HI and decreasing the concentrations of H_2 and I_2.

▶ **EXAMPLE 14.10** K for the HI equilibrium

$$H_2(g) + I_2(g) \rightleftharpoons 2HI(g)$$

is 54.8 at 425°C, and for a particular equilibrium system the concentrations are: $[H_2] = [I_2] = 0.010$ mole/liter and $[HI] = 0.074$ mole/liter. If the concentration of HI is momentarily increased to 0.100 mole/liter, what will be the concentrations of all substances when a new equilibrium is established?

Solution   If we consider 1 liter of the reaction mixture and let $2x$ be the number of additional moles of HI dissociated at equilibrium, then x additional moles of H_2 and x additional moles of I_2 will be formed at equilibrium. The new equilibrium concentrations will be (in moles/liter):

$$\underset{(0.010 + x)}{H_2(g)} + \underset{(0.010 + x)}{I_2(g)} \rightleftharpoons \underset{(0.100 - 2x)}{2HI(g)}$$

$$K = \frac{[HI]^2}{[H_2][I_2]} = 54.8$$

$$= \frac{(0.100 - 2x)^2}{(0.010 + x)^2} = 54.8$$

$$= \frac{(0.100 - 2x)}{(0.010 + x)} = 7.4$$

$$x = 0.0028$$

The new equilibrium concentrations are

$$[H_2] = [I_2] = 0.010 + x = 0.013 \text{ mole/liter}$$

$$[HI] = 0.100 - 2x = 0.094 \text{ mole/liter}$$

Le Chatelier's principle predicts that the position of equilibrium will shift to the left for a change of this type; this prediction is borne out by the calculation.

Le Chatelier's principle may also be used to make qualitative predictions of the effect of pressure changes on systems in equilibrium. Consider the effect of a pressure increase on an equilibrium mixture of SO_2, O_2, and SO_3.

$$2SO_2(g) + O_2(g) \;\rightleftharpoons\; 2SO_3(g)$$

In the forward reaction, two gas molecules ($2SO_3$) are produced by the disappearance of three gas molecules ($2SO_2 + O_2$); two gas molecules do not exert as high a pressure as three gas molecules. Hence, when the pressure on an epuilibrium mixture is increased (or the volume of the system decreased), the position of equilibrium shifts to the right and thus counteracts the change. Alternativeiy, decreasing the pressure (or increasing the volume) would cause the position of this equilibrium to shift to the left.

For certain reactions, in which $\Delta n = 0$, pressure changes have no effect on the epuilibria. For example, equilibria involving the systems

$$H_2(g) + I_2(g) \;\rightleftharpoons\; 2HI(g)$$

$$N_2(g) + O_2(g) \;\rightleftharpoons\; 2NO(g)$$

$$H_2(g) + CO_2(g) \;\rightleftharpoons\; H_2O(g) + CO(g)$$

are not influenced by changing the pressure, since there is no difference in the totol volume in either the forward or backward direction for any one of these reactions.

For a system that involves only liquids and solids, the effect of pressure on the position of equilibrium is slight and may usually be ignored for ordinary changes in pressure. However, large pressure changes can significantly alter such equilibria, and, at times, even slight changes in such equilibria are of interest. For example, the equilibrium

$$H_2O(s) \;\rightleftharpoons\; H_2O(l)$$

is forced to the right by an increase in pressure because a given quantity of water occupies a smaller volume in the liquid state than in the solid state (its density is higher).

Pressure changes affect equilibria involving gases to a much greater degree and are much more important. For example, a high pressure would favor the production of a high yield of ammonia from the equilibrium

$$N_2(g) + 3H_2(g) \rightleftharpoons 2NH_3(g)$$

Hence, Le Chatelier's principle is of practical importance as an aid in determining favorable reaction conditions for the production of a desired substance.

For heterogeneous equilibria, the effect of pressure is predicted by counting the number of *gas* molecules on each side of the equation. For example, the equilibrium

$$3Fe(s) + 4H_2O(g) \rightleftharpoons Fe_3O_4(s) + 4H_2(g)$$

is virtually unaffected by pressure because there are four gas molecules on each side of the equation.

▶ **EXAMPLE 14.11** For the equilibrium

$$PCl_5(g) \rightleftharpoons PCl_3(g) + Cl_2(g)$$

$K = 4.16 \times 10^{-2}$ mole/liter at 250°C. In a given system at 250°C, the equilibrium concentrations are $[PCl_5] = 1$ mole/liter and $[PCl_3] = [Cl_2] = 0.204$ mole/liter. If the pressure is reduced by half (volume doubled), what are the new equilibrium concentrations?

Solution One would predict, by Le Chatelier's principle, that a decrease in pressure would favor the forward reaction, since there are two gas molecules on the right and only one gas molecule on the left. Immediately after the initial change, the concentrations are each cut in half. For example, the concentration of PCl_5, instead of being 1 mole/liter, is now 1 mole/2 liters, or 0.5 mole/liter.

If when equilibrium is reestablished, x additional moles/liter of PCl_5 have dissociated, then x moles/liter of PCl_3 and x moles/liter of Cl_2 have been formed. The new equilibrium concentrations are (in moles/liter):

$$PCl_5(g) \rightleftharpoons PCl_3(g) + Cl_2(g)$$
$$(0.500 - x) \qquad (0.102 + x) \qquad (0.102 + x)$$

$$K = \frac{[PCl_3][Cl_2]}{[PCl_5]} = 4.16 \times 10^{-2} \text{ mole/liter}$$

$$\frac{(0.102 + x)^2}{(0.500 - x)} = 4.16 \times 10^{-2} \text{ mole/liter}$$

Expanding,

$$x^2 + 0.246x - 0.0104 = 0$$

By use of the quadratic formula,[1]

$$x = 0.0365$$

[1] For an equation in the form $ax^2 + bx + c = 0$, $x = \frac{-b \pm \sqrt{b^2 - 4ac}}{2a}$.

Therefore the new equilibrium concentrations are

$$[PCl_5] = 0.464 \text{ mole/liter}$$
$$[PCl_3] = [Cl_2] = 0.138 \text{ mole/liter}$$

In order to predict the effect of a temperature change on a system in equilibrium, the thermochemical nature of the chemical reaction must be known. At 25°C, the thermochemical equation for the synthesis of ammonia is

$$N_2(g) + 3H_2(g) \rightleftharpoons 2NH_3(g) + 22.1 \text{ kcal}$$

The forward reaction is exothermic, and the backward reaction is endothermic. If the temperature of an equilibrium mixture is raised, the equilibrium will shift to the left—the direction that absorbs heat. Lowering the temperature favors the reaction to the right in which heat is produced. We conclude that the highest yields of ammonia are obtained at the lowest temperatures.

Thermochemical equations for reversible reactions may be written with the heat term on either the left or the right side of the equation. In each case, increasing the temperature favors the endothermic change, and decreasing the temperature favors the exothermic change. The reaction (ΔH measured at 25°C)

$$9.83 \text{ kcal} + CO_2(g) + H_2(g) \rightleftharpoons CO(g) + H_2O(g)$$

is forced to the right by an increase in temperature.

The numerical value of the equilibrium constant changes with a change in temperature. For the preceding reaction, the position of equilibrium is displaced to the right by an increase in temperature. Thus the concentrations of the materials on the right are increased; concentration terms for these materials appear in the numerator of the expression for K. Hence, as the temperature is increased, the value of K for this reaction increases; at 700°C, $K = 0.63$, and at 1000°C, $K = 1.66$.

An equation relating the equilibrium constant and temperature may be derived from the Arrhenius equation (Section 14.6). The Arrhenius equation for the rate constant for the forward reaction is

$$k = Ae^{-E_a/RT}$$

and the corresponding equation for the reverse equation is

$$k' = A'e^{-E_a'/RT}$$

Since the equilibrium constant, K is equal to k/k'

$$K = \frac{Ae^{-E_a/RT}}{A'e^{-E_a'/RT}}$$

or

$$K = Ce^{(-E_a + E_a')/RT}$$

Since ΔE for the forward reaction, or ΔH if the pressure is held constant, is equal to $E_a - E_a'$ (Section 14.2), we may write

$$-\Delta H = -E_a + E_a'$$

Therefore,

$$K = Ce^{-\Delta H/RT}$$

or

$$\ln K = \ln C - \frac{\Delta H}{RT}$$

$$\log K = \log C - \frac{\Delta H}{2.303RT}$$

For two temperatures T_1 and T_2 for which the equilibrium constants are K_1 and K_2,

$$\log K_2 = \log C - \frac{\Delta H}{2.303RT_2}$$

$$\log K_1 = \log C - \frac{\Delta H}{2.303RT_1}$$

Subtraction of the second equation from the first gives

$$\log K_2 - \log K_1 = -\frac{\Delta H}{2.303RT_2} + \frac{\Delta H}{2.303RT_1}$$

or

$$\log\left(\frac{K_2}{K_1}\right) = \frac{\Delta H}{2.303R}\left(\frac{1}{T_1} - \frac{1}{T_2}\right)$$

which is

$$\log\left(\frac{K_2}{K_1}\right) = \frac{\Delta H}{2.303R}\left(\frac{T_2 - T_1}{T_1T_2}\right)$$

Since ΔH varies with temperature, the equation is only approximate. However, over a narrow temperature range, the value of ΔH may be assumed to be constant and an average value for the temperature range used.

▶ EXAMPLE 14.12 For the reaction

$$CO_2(g) + H_2(g) \rightleftharpoons CO(g) + H_2O(g)$$

K is 0.63 at 700°C and 1.66 at 1000°C. (a) What is the average ΔH for the temperature range considered? (b) What is the value of K at 800°C?

Solution   (a) Let $T_1 = 973°K$. $K_1 = 0.63$, $T_2 = 1273°K$, and $K_2 = 1.66$.

$$\log\left(\frac{1.66}{0.63}\right) = \frac{\Delta H}{2.30(1.99)}\left(\frac{1273 - 973}{(973)(1273)}\right)$$

$$0.421 = \frac{\Delta H}{4.58}\left(\frac{3 \times 10^2}{1.24 \times 10^6}\right)$$

$$\Delta H = 8.0 \times 10^3 \text{ cal}$$

(b) Let the unknown equilibrium constant be K_2, then $T_2 = 1073°K$, $K_1 = 0.63$, and $T_1 = 973°K$.

$$\log\left(\frac{K_2}{0.63}\right) = \frac{8.0 \times 10^3}{2.30(1.99)}\left(\frac{1073 - 973}{(973)(1073)}\right)$$

$$\log K_2 - (-0.201) = 0.167$$

$$\log K_2 = -0.033 = 0.967 - 1$$

$$K_2 = 0.93$$

SOME SUGGESTED READINGS

Back, M. A., and Laidler, K. J., *Chemical Kinetics*, Elmsford, N. Y., Pergamon, 1967 (paper).

Basolo, F., and Pearson, R. G., *Mechanisms of Inorganic Reactions*, 2nd ed., New York, Wiley, 1967.

Campbell, A. J., *Why Do Chemical Reactions Occur?*, Englewood Cliffs, N. J., Prentice-Hall, 1965 (paper).

Denbigh, K., *Principles of Chemical Equilibrium*, 2nd ed., New York, Cambridge University Press, 1966 (paper).

Edwards, J. O., *Inorganic Reaction Mechanisms: An Introduction*, New York, Benjamin, 1964 (paper).

Eyring, H., and Eyring, E. M., *Modern Chemical Kinetics*, New York, Van Nostrand Reinhold, 1963 (paper).

Harris, G. M., *Chemical Kinetics*, Boston, Heath, 1966 (paper).

King, E. L., *How Chemical Reactions Occur*, New York, Benjamin, 1963 (paper).

Morris, K., *Principles of Chemical Equilibrium*, 2nd ed., New York, Van Nostrand Reinhold, 1967 (paper).

Sykes, A. G., *Kinetics of Inorganic Reactions*, Elmsford, N. Y., Pergamon, 1966 (paper).

PROBLEMS

The more difficult problems are starred.

14.1   List four factors that influence the rate of a chemical reaction and explain on the atomic-molecular level how each exerts its influence.

14.2 Define the following: (a) activated complex, (b) energy of activation, (c) reaction order, (d) catalyst, (e) chemisorption, (f) rate-determining step, (g) reaction intermediate, (h) zero-order reaction, (i) steady state.

14.3 Draw a potential energy diagram for the hypothetical reaction $A(g) + B(g) \rightleftharpoons 2C(g)$ for which E_a is 37 kcal and E'_a is 25 kcal. Indicate the magnitude of ΔH on the diagram. Is the reaction exothermic or endothermic? Draw a curve for a catalyzed reaction on the diagram.

14.4 The systhesis of perbromates has only recently been accomplished. The best preparation involves the oxidation of bromates, in alkaline solution, by fluorine. For the half reaction

$$2e^- + 2H^+ + BrO_4^- \longrightarrow BrO_3^- + H_2O$$

$\mathcal{E}°$ is $+1.763$ v. Although this potential is fairly high, it alone cannot account for the difficulty encountered in the synthesis of perbromates. What explanation can you give for this difficulty, and how well would you expect perbromates to function as oxidizing agents?

14.5 A common, and serious, mistake is to assume that the rate equation for reaction can be derived from the balanced chemical equation for the reaction by using the coefficients of the chemical equation as exponents in the rate expression. Why cannot rate equations be derived in this way? How do you reconcile your answer with the law of mass action?

14.6 The rate equation for the reaction

$$2NO(g) + 2H_2(g) \longrightarrow N_2(g) + 2H_2O(g)$$

is second order in $NO(g)$ and first order in $H_2(g)$. (a) Write an equation for the rate of appearance of $N_2(g)$. (b) If concentrations are expressed in moles/liter, what units would the rate constant, k, have? (c) If concentrations are expressed in atmospheres, what units would k have? (d) Give an equation for the rate of disappearance of $NO(g)$. Would k in this equation have the same numerical value as k in the equation of part (a)?

14.7 For a reaction of A and B to form C, the following data were obtained from three experiments:

Experiment	[A]	[B]	Rate (Formation of C)
1	0.60M	0.15M	$6.3 \times 10^{-3}M$/min
2	0.20M	0.60M	$2.8 \times 10^{-3}M$/min
3	0.20M	0.15M	$7.0 \times 10^{-4}M$/min

(a) What is the rate equation for the reaction? (b) What is the numerical value of the rate constant, k?

14.8 Assume that the rate-determining step of a reaction is

$$2A(g) + B(g) \longrightarrow C(g)$$

and that 2 moles of $A(g)$ and 1 mole of $B(g)$ are mixed in a 1 liter container.

Compare the following to the initial reaction rate of this mixture: (a) rate when half of both A(g) and B(g) have been consumed, (b) rate when two-thirds of both A(g) and B(g) have been consumed, (c) initial reaction rate of a mixture of 2 moles of A(g) and 2 moles of B(g) in a 1 liter container, (d) initial reaction rate of a mixture of 4 moles of A(g) and 2 moles of B(g) in a 1 liter container.

14.9 Calculate the value of the specific rate constant, (a) in 1/torr sec and (b) in liter/mole sec, for the decomposition of acetaldehyde vapor at 800°K using the data given in Example 14.2.

14.10 The following data pertain to the decomposition of sulfuryl chloride gas at 320°C:

$$SO_2Cl_2(g) \longrightarrow SO_2(g) + Cl_2(g)$$

Experiment	Initial Pressure of $SO_2Cl_2(g)$	Initial Rate of Increase in Total Pressure
1	550 torr	0.0121 torr/sec
2	650 torr	0.0143 torr/sec

(a) What is the order of the rate equation for the reaction? (b) What is the value of the specific rate constant, k?

14.11 Use data from Table 14.2 to calculate the specific rate constant for the decomposition of chloroethane, $C_2H_5Cl(g)$, at 500°K.

14.12 For the reaction

$$C_2H_5Br(g) \longrightarrow C_2H_4(g) + HBr(g)$$

the rate constant is 2.0×10^{-5}/sec at 650°K and 7.0×10^{-5}/sec at 670°K. What is the energy of activation for the reaction?

14.13 What is the activation energy of a reaction that doubles in rate when the temperature is increased from 300°K to 310°K?

14.14 The specific rate constant for the decomposition of $N_2O_5(g)$ at 300°K is 4.0×10^{-5}/sec. At what temperature is k equal to 8.0×10^{-5}/sec? Use data from Table 14.2.

14.15 At 300°K, a certain reaction is 50.0% complete in 20.0 minutes. At 350°K, the same reaction is 50.0% complete in 5.00 minutes. Calculate the activation energy for the reaction.

14.16 The reaction

$$CH_4(g) + Cl_2(g) \longrightarrow CH_3Cl(g) + HCl(g)$$

proceeds by a chain mechanism. The chain propagators are Cl atoms and CH_3 radicals, and it is believed that free H atoms are not involved. Write a series of equations showing the mechanism and identify the chain-initiating, chain-sustaining, and chain-terminating steps.

14.17 (a) A proposed mechanism for the reaction

$$2NO_2Cl(g) \longrightarrow 2NO_2(g) + Cl_2(g)$$

consists of the following two steps:

(1) $$NO_2Cl(g) \xrightarrow{k_1} NO_2(g) + Cl(g)$$

(2) $$NO_2Cl(g) + Cl(g) \xrightarrow{k_2} NO_2(g) + Cl_2(g)$$

Assume that the concentration of Cl(g) reaches a steady state, and show that the rate equation for the overall reaction is first order. (b) What is the value of k for the rate equation in terms of k_1 and k_2?

*14.18 The rate expression for the reaction

$$2O_3 \longrightarrow 3O_2$$

has been determined experimentally as

$$\text{rate of decrease of } [O_3] = k\,\frac{[O_3]^2}{[O_2]}$$

The following mechanism has been postulated for the decomposition of ozone:

(1) $$O_3 \underset{k_2}{\overset{k_1}{\rightleftharpoons}} O_2 + O$$

(2) $$O + O_3 \xrightarrow{k_3} 2O_2$$

The first step is a rapidly established equilibrium (for which an equilibrium constant may be derived), and the slower second step is rate determining. Show how the suggested mechanism leads to the observed rate expression.

14.19 The reaction $A(g) + B(g) \rightleftharpoons C(g)$ is exothermic as written. (a) What effect would an increase in temperature have on the numerical value of K? (b) How would the numerical values of K and K_p vary with an increase in total pressure?

14.20 A mixture consisting of 1.000 mole of $H_2(g)$ and 1.000 mole of $CO_2(g)$ is placed in a 1.000 liter container at 800°C. At equilibrium, 0.491 mole of CO(g) and 0.491 mole of $H_2O(g)$ are present.

$$H_2(g) + CO_2(g) \rightleftharpoons H_2O(g) + CO(g)$$

(a) What are the equilibrium concentrations of $H_2(g)$ and $CO_2(g)$?
(b) What is the value of K? (c) What is K_p?

14.21 For the equilibrium

$$C(s) + CO_2(g) \rightleftharpoons 2CO(g)$$

K_p is 167.5 atm at 1000°C. What is the partial pressure of CO(g) in equilibrium with $CO_2(g)$ at a partial pressure of 10.0 torr?

14.22 K_p for the equilibrium

$$FeO(s) + CO(g) \rightleftharpoons Fe(s) + CO_2(g)$$

at 1000°C is 0.403. If CO(g), at a pressure of 1.000 atm, and excess FeO(s) are confined in a container at 1000°C, what are the partial pressures of CO(g) and $CO_2(g)$ when equilibrium is attained?

14.23 A mixture, containing 0.075 mole/liter of HCl(g) and 0.033 mole/liter of $O_2(g)$, is allowed to come to equilibrium at 480°C.

$$4HCl(g) + O_2(g) \rightleftharpoons 2Cl_2(g) + 2H_2O(g)$$

At equilibrium, the concentration of $Cl_2(g)$ is 0.030 mole/liter. (a) What are the equilibrium concentrations of HCl(g), $O_2(g)$, and $H_2O(g)$? (b) What is the value of K at 480°C? (c) What is K_p at this temperature?

14.24 At 1100°K and a total pressure of 1.00 atm, $SO_3(g)$ is 75.0% dissociated:

$$2SO_3(g) \rightleftharpoons 2SO_2(g) + O_2(g)$$

Assume that 1.00 mole of $SO_3(g)$ was present before dissociation. (a) How many moles of $SO_3(g)$, $SO_2(g)$, and $O_2(g)$ are present at equilibrium? (b) What is the total number of moles of gas present at equilibrium? (c) What are the equilibrium partial pressures of the three gases? (d) What is the numerical value of K_p at 1100°K?

*14.25 At a given temperature and a total pressure of 1.00 atm, the partial pressures of an equilibrium mixture

$$N_2O_4(g) \rightleftharpoons 2NO_2(g)$$

are $p_{N_2O_4} = 0.50$ atm and $p_{NO_2} = 0.50$ atm. (a) What is K_p at this temperature? (b) If the total pressure is increased to 2.00 atm, temperature constant, what are the partial pressures of the components of an equilibrium mixture?

*14.26 At 425°C, K is 54.8 for the equilibrium

$$H_2(g) + I_2(g) \rightleftharpoons 2HI(g)$$

If 1.000 mole of $H_2(g)$, 1.000 mole of $I_2(g)$, and 1.000 mole of HI(g) are placed in a liter container at 425°C, what are the concentrations of all gases present at equilibrium?

14.27 At 100°C, the equilibrium constant, K, for the reaction

$$CO(g) + Cl_2(g) \rightleftharpoons COCl_2(g)$$

is 4.57×10^9 liters/mole. If 1.00 mole of $COCl_2$ is confined in a 1.00 liter container, what is the concentration of CO after equilibrium has been established? Note that the subtraction of a very small number from a large number may be neglected.

14.28 At 250°C, K is 24.0 liters/mole for the equilibrium

$$PCl_3(g) + Cl_2(g) \rightleftharpoons PCl_5(g)$$

What is (a) K and (b) K_p for the equilibrium

$$PCl_5(g) \rightleftharpoons PCl_3(g) + Cl_2(g)$$

at this temperature?

*****14.29** If C(s) and $O_2(g)$ are placed in a container at 1000°C, several equilibria involving C(s), $O_2(g)$, CO(g), and $CO_2(g)$ are established. Given (at 1000°C)

$$C(s) + CO_2(g) \rightleftharpoons 2CO(g) \qquad K_p = 1.68 \times 10^2 \text{ atm}$$
$$2CO(g) + O_2(g) \rightleftharpoons 2CO_2(g) \qquad K_p = 7.41 \times 10^{13}/\text{atm}$$

(a) Determine the value of K_p for the equilibrium

$$C(s) + O_2(g) \rightleftharpoons CO_2(g)$$

(b) Determine the value of K_p for the equilibrium

$$2C(s) + O_2(g) \rightleftharpoons 2CO(g)$$

14.30 Use the data of Table 13.4 to calculate K_p for the equilibrium (at 25°C)

$$2NO(g) + O_2(g) \rightleftharpoons 2NO_2(g)$$

14.31 (a) Use data from Table 13.4 to determine the K_p values for the following:

$$4NH_3(g) + 3O_2(g) \rightleftharpoons 2N_2(g) + 6H_2O(g)$$
$$4NH_3(g) + 5O_2(g) \rightleftharpoons 4NO(g) + 6H_2O(g)$$

(b) When a pair of substances can react in two different ways, what determines which reaction will occur?

14.32 (a) Calculate K_p for the equilibrium system (at 25°C)

$$CdCl_2 \cdot H_2O(s) \rightleftharpoons CdCl_2(s) + H_2O(g)$$

Relevant values of $\Delta G°_f$ are: $CdCl_2 \cdot H_2O(s)$, -140.13 kcal/mole; $CdCl_2(s)$, -81.88 kcal/mole; $H_2O(g)$, -54.64 kcal/mole. (b) What is the equilibrium vapor pressure of water, in torr, at 25°C?

*****14.33** For $N_2O_4(g)$, $\Delta G°_f$ is $+23.49$ kcal/mole and $\Delta H°_f$ is $+2.31$ kcal/mole. For $NO_2(g)$, $\Delta G°_f$ is $+12.39$ kcal/mole and $\Delta H°_f$ is $+8.09$ kcal/mole. (a) According to this data, what is K_p for the following equilibrium at 25°C:

$$N_2O_4(g) \rightleftharpoons 2NO_2(g)$$

(b) Assume that ΔH is constant over the temperature range from 25°C to 100°C, and calculate K_p for the equilibrium at 100°C.

*14.34 For the equilibrium

$$2SO_2(g) + O_2(g) \rightleftharpoons 2SO_3(g)$$

K_p is 42.8/atm at 900°K and 3.44/atm at 1000°K. (a) What is the average value of ΔH for the temperature range considered? (b) What is the value of K_p at 950°K?

14.35 From the electrode potentials

$$2H_2O + 2e^- \rightleftharpoons H_2 + 2OH^- \qquad \mathscr{E}° = -0.828 \text{ v}$$

$$2H^+ + 2e^- \rightleftharpoons H_2 \qquad \mathscr{E}° = 0$$

calculate the equilibrium constant for

$$H_2O \rightleftharpoons H^+(aq) + OH^-(aq)$$

14.36 Use electrode potentials (given in the appendix) to calculate the equilibrium constant for the reaction (at 25°C)

$$Cl_2(g) + 2Br^-(aq) \rightleftharpoons 2Cl^-(aq) + Br_2(l)$$

14.37 Use electrode potentials (given in the appendix) to calculate the equilibrium constant for the reaction (at 25°C)

$$2Fe^{3+}(aq) + Fe(s) \rightleftharpoons 3Fe^{2+}(aq)$$

*14.38 Calculate $\mathscr{E}°$ for the half reaction

$$2e^- + Hg_2Cl_2 \longrightarrow 2Hg + 2Cl^-$$

given the following data:

$$Hg_2SO_4(s) + 2Cl^-(aq) \rightleftharpoons Hg_2Cl_2(s) + SO_4^{2-}(aq) \qquad K = 5.6 \times 10^{11}$$

$$2e^- + Hg_2SO_4 \longrightarrow 2Hg + SO_4^{2-} \qquad \mathscr{E}° = +0.615 \text{ v}$$

14.39 State the direction that each of the following equilibrium systems would be shifted upon the application of the stress listed beside the equation:

(a) $CO(g) + H_2O(g) \rightleftharpoons CO_2(g) + H_2(g)$
(exothermic) — increase temperature

(b) $N_2(g) + O_2(g) \rightleftharpoons 2NO(g)$ (endothermic) — decrease temperature

(c) $2NOBr(g) \rightleftharpoons 2NO(g) + Br_2(g)$ — decrease total pressure

(d) $3Fe(s) + 4H_2O(g) \rightleftharpoons Fe_3O_4(s) + 4H_2(g)$ — increase total pressure

(e) $C(s) + CO_2(g) \rightleftharpoons 2CO(g)$ — decrease total pressure

(f) $C(s) + CO_2(g) \rightleftharpoons 2CO(g)$ — add C(s)

(g) $N_2O_4(g) \rightleftharpoons 2NO_2(g)$ — increase concentration of NO_2

(h) $N_2(g) + 3H_2(g) \rightleftharpoons 2NH_3(g)$ — add a catalyst

(i) $BaCl_2 \cdot H_2O(s) \rightleftharpoons BaCl_2(s) + H_2O(g)$ — remove $H_2O(g)$

Throughout the history of chemistry, various acid-base concepts have been proposed and used. In this chapter, four concepts in current use are reviewed. Each of the definitions can be applied with advantage in appropriate circumstances; in a given situation, the chemist uses the concept that best suits his purpose.

ACIDS AND BASES

15.1 The Arrhenius Concept

The earliest criteria for the characterization of acids and bases were the experimentally observed properties of aqueous solutions of these substances (taste, effect on indicators, neutralization of one by the other, etc.). Concurrent with the development of generalizations concerning the structure of matter, scientists searched for a correlation between acidic and basic properties and the structure of the compounds exhibiting these properties.

Acids, bases, and salts were classified as electrolytes by Faraday in 1834. Justus von Liebig proposed (1838) that acids are compounds containing hydrogen that can be replaced by metals. The role of water as an ionizing solvent was emphasized by Svanté Arrhenius in his theory of electrolytic dissociation (1884), which led to the definition of acids and bases in terms of the ions of water; Arrhenius' views were vigorously championed and developed by Wilhelm Ostwald.

At the time of Arrhenius, the distinction between ionic and covalent compounds was not clear, and the nature of $H^+(aq)$ was not understood. Consequently, the **water system** (or **Arrhenius concept**) has been modified throughout its history. In present-day terms an **acid** is a substance that ionizes in water solution to produce $H^+(aq)$, or the hydronium ion; a **base** is a substance that dissolves in water to produce hydroxide ion, $OH^-(aq)$. The strength of an acid is defined in terms of the concentration of $H^+(aq)$ that is present in a water solution of given concentration of acid, and the strength of a base depends upon the relative concentration of $OH^-(aq)$ in an aqueous solution of base.

Neutralization, then, may be represented by the equation

$$H^+(aq) + OH^-(aq) \longrightarrow H_2O + 13.7 \text{ kcal}$$

As indicated in the preceding equation, the enthalpy for the neutralization of a dilute solution of any strong acid by a dilute solution of any strong base is a constant value. If a weak acid or a weak base is involved in the neutralization, or if a slightly soluble salt is formed from the cation derived from the base and the anion derived from the acid, the enthalpy of the reaction is different; in such cases, the total enthalpy includes heat effects due to the ionization of the weak acid or base or due to the precipitation of a salt, as well as the enthalpy of neutralization.

The properties that all Arrhenius acids have in common are those of $H^+(aq)$; chemical properties include such reactions as those of acids with reactive metals and with the bicarbonate ion.

$$2H^+(aq) + Zn(s) \longrightarrow H_2(g) + Zn^{2+}(aq)$$

$$H^+(aq) + HCO_3^-(aq) \longrightarrow H_2O + CO_2(g)$$

The properties that are characteristic of Arrhenius bases are due to the $OH^-(aq)$ ion; among the reactions of strong bases are

$$2OH^-(aq) + H_2O + Si(s) \longrightarrow SiO_3^{2-}(aq) + 2H_2(g)$$

$$OH^-(aq) + NH_4^+(aq) \longrightarrow H_2O + NH_3(g)$$

The oxides of many nonmetals react with water to form acids and are called **acidic oxides**, or **acid anhydrides**.

$$N_2O_5(s) + H_2O \longrightarrow 2H^+(aq) + 2NO_3^-(aq)$$

Many oxides of metals dissolve in water to form hydroxides; such compounds are called **basic oxides**.

$$Na_2O(s) + H_2O \longrightarrow 2Na^+(aq) + 2OH^-(aq)$$

Acidic oxides and basic oxides react to produce salts in the absence of water. It must be noted, however, that not all acids and bases may be derived from oxides (e.g., HCl and NH_3).

The Arrhenius concept is severely limited by its emphasis on water and reactions in aqueous solution. Later definitions are more general, serve to correlate more reactions, and are applicable to reactions in nonaqueous media.

15.2 The Solvent System Concept

The principles of the Arrhenius-water concept can be used to devise acid-base schemes for many solvents. In a **solvent system**, an **acid** is a substance that gives the cation characteristic of the solvent, and a **base** is a substance that yields the anion characteristic of the solvent. Thus the reaction of an acid and a base, a **neutralization**, yields the solvent as one of its products. Many solvent systems of acids and bases have been developed (Table 15.1); the water concept is but a single example of a solvent system.

Table 15.1

Some Solvent Systems

Solvent	Acid Ion	Base Ion	Typical Acid	Typical Base
H_2O	H_3O^+ $(H^+ \cdot H_2O)$	OH^-	HCl	$NaOH$
NH_3	NH_4^+ $(H^+ \cdot NH_3)$	NH_2^-	NH_4Cl	$NaNH_2$
NH_2OH	NH_3OH^+ $(H^+ \cdot NH_2OH)$	$NHOH^-$	$NH_2OH \cdot HCl$ (NH_3OH^+, Cl^-)	$K(NHOH)$
$HC_2H_3O_2$	$H_2C_2H_3O_2^+$ $(H^+ \cdot HC_2H_3O_2)$	$C_2H_3O_2^-$	HCl	$NaC_2H_3O_2$
SO_2	SO^{2+}	SO_3^{2-}	$SOCl_2$	Cs_2SO_3
N_2O_4	NO^+	NO_3^-	$NOCl$	$AgNO_3$
$COCl_2$	$COCl^+$	Cl^-	$(COCl)AlCl_4$	$CaCl_2$

The ammonia system has been investigated more extensively than any other with the exception of the water system. The properties of liquid ammonia (boiling point, $-33.4°C$) are strikingly similar to those of water. Liquid ammonia is associated through hydrogen bonding (Section 8.11), and the

NH_3 molecule is polar (Section 4.3). Hence, liquid ammonia is an excellent solvent for ionic and polar compounds, and it functions as an ionizing solvent for electrolytes. Many compounds form ammoniates, which are analogous to hydrates (e.g., $BaBr_2 \cdot 8NH_3$ and $CaCl_2 \cdot 6NH_3$), and ions are solvated in liquid ammonia solutions (e.g., $Ag(NH_3)_2{}^+$ and $Cr(NH_3)_6^{3+}$). Whereas solutions of electrolytes in ammonia are good conductors of electricity, pure liquid ammonia, like water, has a relatively low conductance.

The autoionization of ammonia

$$2NH_3 \rightleftharpoons NH_4{}^+ + NH_2{}^-$$

which occurs only to a low degree, is responsible for the electrical conductivity of pure solvent, just as the autoionization of water

$$2H_2O \rightleftharpoons H_3O^+ + OH^-$$

is responsible for the electrical properties of this compound.

Any compound that produces ammonium ion, $NH_4{}^+$, in liquid ammonia solution is an acid, and any compound that yields amide ion, $NH_2{}^-$, is a base. Thus the neutralization reaction is the reverse of the autoionization reaction.

$$NH_4{}^+ + NH_2{}^- \longrightarrow 2NH_3$$

Indicators may be used to follow an acid-base reaction in liquid ammonia. For example, phenolphthalein is red in a liquid ammonia solution of potassium amide, KNH_2, and the indicator becomes colorless after a stoichiometrically equivalent amount of ammonium chloride has been added.

In addition to the neutralization reaction, the ammonium ion in liquid ammonia undergoes other reactions analogous to the reactions of the hydronium ion in water. For example, metals such as sodium react with the ammonium ion to liberate hydrogen.

$$2Na(s) + 2NH_4{}^+ \longrightarrow 2Na^+ + H_2(g) + 2NH_3(l)$$

The reactions of the amide ion are analogous to those of the hydroxide ion.

$$Zn(OH)_2(s) + 2OH^- \longrightarrow Zn(OH)_4^{2-}$$

$$Zn(NH_2)_2(s) + 2NH_2{}^- \longrightarrow Zn(NH_2)_4^{2-}$$

$$Hg^{2+} + 2OH^- \longrightarrow HgO(s) + H_2O$$

$$3Hg^{2+} + 6NH_2{}^- \longrightarrow Hg_3N_2(s) + 4NH_3$$

The analogy can be extended to derive a nitrogen system of compounds comparable to the oxygen system (Table 15.2). The comparison is somewhat complicated by the fact that nitrogen is customarily trivalent, whereas

Table 15.2

Comparable Compounds of the Nitrogen System and
the Oxygen System

Nitrogen System		Oxygen System	
KNH_2	potassium amide	KOH	potassium hydroxide
$Ca(NH_2)_2$	calcium amide	$Ca(OH)_2$	calcium hydroxide
PbNH	lead(II) imide	PbO	lead(II) oxide
Ca_3N_2	calcium nitride	CaO	calcium oxide
H_2NCl	chloramine	HOCl	hypochlorous acid
HNNN	hydrazoic acid	$HONO_2$	nitric acid
$(HNPN)_n$	phospham	$(HOPO_2)_n$	metaphosphoric acid
P_3N_5	phosphorus(V) nitride	P_4O_{10}	phosphorus(V) oxide
CaNCN	calcium cyanamide	$CaCO_3$	calcium carbonate
H_2NNH_2	hydrazine	HOOH	hydrogen peroxide
CH_3NH_2	methyl amine	CH_3OH	methyl alcohol

oxygen is divalent; thus the analog of the hydroxide ion, OH^-, or $-OH$ group is the amide ion, NH_2^-, or $-NH_2$ group, whereas the oxide ion, O^{2-}, or $=O$ group must be compared to both the imide ion, NH^{2-}, or $=NH$ group and the nitride ion, N^{3-}, or $\equiv N$ group. Nevertheless, the analogy is a good one; ammonium ion will neutralize the imide and nitride ions as well as the amide ion.

$$2NH_4^+ + NH^{2-} \longrightarrow 3NH_3$$

$$3NH_4^+ + N^{3-} \longrightarrow 4NH_3$$

Therefore metal nitrides and imides are basic compounds in the nitrogen system in the same way that metal oxides are classified as basic oxides in the oxygen system. In addition, the nitrides of the nonmetals have acidic properties similar to the acidic characteristics of the nonmetal oxides of the oxygen system.

Many properties and reactions of compounds belonging to the nitrogen-ammonia system have been predicted and correlated by comparison to the better known chemistry of the compounds of the oxygen-water system. In fact, the study of various solvent systems has been responsible for greatly increasing our knowledge of the reactions that occur in solvents other than water. The solvent system approach, however, is compartmentalized and does not offer extensive correlation or generalization.

A unique aspect of liquid-ammonia chemistry deserves special mention, although it is not related to acid-base phenomena. Liquid ammonia dissolves the group I A metals, thereby producing unusual solutions. In the presence of catalysts (such as iron) a reaction occurs

$$2Na(s) + 2NH_3 \longrightarrow 2Na^+ + 2NH_2^- + H_2(g)$$

(Compare the reaction of sodium with water.) In the absence of catalysts however, the solutions are stable for some time.

Dilute solutions of the metals are blue, and concentrated solutions have a bronze color. Evaporation of a solution yields the original metal. The conductance of a solution is higher than that of any known electrolytic solution and, for a concentrated solution, approaches metallic conductance. Conductance studies also show that the negative species is the same no matter what metal is dissolved. Dilute solutions are strongly paramagnetic. All solutions of the same concentration have identical absorption spectra, indicating that the same species causes the blue color in each case; since the I A metal cations are colorless, the blue color is due to the negative species.

On the basis of the preceding studies, and many more, it has been postulated that metal atoms in the solutions exist in equilibrium with metal cations and electrons, both of which are solvated. The essentially free electrons are responsible for the strong reducing properties of the solutions that are experimentally observed.

15.3 The Brønsted-Lowry Concept

In 1923, Johannes Brønsted and Thomas Lowry independently proposed a broader concept of acids and bases. According to the Brønsted-Lowry definitions, an **acid** is a substance that can donate protons, and a **base** is a substance that can accept protons. In these terms, the reaction of an acid with a base constitutes a transfer of a proton from the acid to the base, and this is the only characteristic reaction of these substances treated by the Brønsted-Lowry concept. We shall see, however, that many reactions are included in this classification.

The dissolution of ammonia in water may be represented by the equation

$$H_2O + NH_3 \rightleftharpoons NH_4^+ + OH^-$$

In the reaction as written, H_2O is serving as an acid and is releasing a proton to the base, NH_3. Whereas the solution resulting from the addition of NH_3 to H_2O is alkaline, conductivity and i factor measurements show that the ionization is incomplete. Furthermore, if a solution of an ammonium salt is made strongly alkaline, ammonia gas is released. The reaction, therefore, is reversible, and the system exists in equilibrium.

According to the Brønsted-Lowry concept, acids and bases may be molecules or ions. In the reverse reaction, NH_4^+ is serving as an acid and OH^- is a base since the equation, from right to left, shows NH_4^- releasing a proton to OH^-. It follows, then, that in this Brønsted acid-base reaction, two acids (H_2O and NH^+) and two bases (OH^- and NH_3) are involved; the reaction is actually a competition between the two bases for a proton.

The base NH_3 gains a proton and thereby forms the acid NH_4^+, and the acid NH_4^+ upon the loss of a proton forms the base NH_3. Such an acid-base pair, related through the loss or gain of a proton, is called a **conjugate pair**; NH_4^+ is the conjugate acid of the base NH_3, and NH_3 is the conjugate base of the acid NH_4^+. In like manner, the acid H_2O and the base OH^- constitute a second conjugate pair in the preceding reaction. We may indicate conjugate relationships by the use of subscripts in the following manner:

$$\underset{\text{Acid}_1}{H_2O} + \underset{\text{Base}_2}{NH_3} \;\rightleftharpoons\; \underset{\text{Acid}_2}{NH_4^+} + \underset{\text{Base}_1}{OH^-}$$

There are many molecules and ions that can function as acids in certain reactions and as bases in other reactions; such species are called **amphiprotic**. For example, in the reaction with ammonia, water acts as an acid (conjugate base, OH^-); in the reaction with acetic acid, water is a base (conjugate acid, H_3O^+).

$$\underset{\text{Acid}_1}{HC_2H_3O_2} + \underset{\text{Base}_2}{H_2O} \;\rightleftharpoons\; \underset{\text{Acid}_2}{H_3O^+} + \underset{\text{Base}_1}{C_2H_3O_2^-}$$

In like manner, NH_3 is seen as a base (conjugate acid, NH_4^+) in its reaction with water. In the reaction of the hydride ion, H^-, with liquid ammonia, NH_3 acts as an acid (conjugate base, NH_2^-).

$$\underset{\text{Acid}_1}{NH_3} + \underset{\text{Base}_2}{H^-} \;\longrightarrow\; \underset{\text{Acid}_2}{H_2} + \underset{\text{Base}_1}{NH_2^-}$$

Several amphiprotic substances are listed in Table 15.3.

Table 15.3

Some Amphiprotic Substances

Amphiprotic Substance	Typical Reaction				
	$Acid_1$	$Base_2$		$Acid_2$	$Base_1$
H_2O	H_2O	$+ H^-$	$\rightleftharpoons$	H_2	$+ OH^-$
	HCN	$+ H_2O$	$\rightleftharpoons$	H_3O^+	$+ CN^-$
NH_3	H_2O	$+ NH_2^-$	$\rightleftharpoons$	NH_3	$+ OH^-$
	HCl	$+ NH_3$	$\rightleftharpoons$	NH_4^+	$+ Cl^-$
H_2SO_4	H_2SO_4	$+ H_2O$	$\rightleftharpoons$	H_3O^+	$+ HSO_4^-$
	$HClO_4$	$+ H_2SO_4$	$\rightleftharpoons$	$H_3SO_4^+$	$+ ClO_4^-$
HSO_4^-	H_2SO_4	$+ H_2O$	$\rightleftharpoons$	H_3O^+	$+ HSO_4^-$
	HSO_4^-	$+ H_2O$	$\rightleftharpoons$	H_3O^+	$+ SO_4^{2-}$
$Al(OH)(H_2O)_5^{2+}$	$Al(H_2O)_6^{3+}$	$+ OH^-$	$\rightleftharpoons$	H_2O	$+ Al(OH)(H_2O)_5^{2+}$
	$Al(OH)(H_2O)_5^{2+} + OH^-$		$\rightleftharpoons$	H_2O	$+ Al(OH)_2(H_2O)_4^+$

The neutralization reactions of the Arrhenius system and certain solvent systems may, therefore, be interpreted in terms of the Brønsted definitions.

Such neutralizations are merely acid-base reactions between the conjugate acid and the conjugate base of an amphiprotic solvent. Thus

$$\underset{\text{Acid}_1}{H_3O^+} + \underset{\text{Base}_2}{OH^-} \rightleftharpoons \underset{\text{Acid}_2}{H_2O} + \underset{\text{Base}_1}{H_2O}$$

$$NH_4^+ + NH_2^- \rightleftharpoons NH_3 + NH_3$$

15.4 Strengths of Brønsted Acids and Bases

In Brønsted terms, the strength of an acid is determined by its tendency to donate protons, and the strength of a base is dependent upon its tendency to receive protons. The reaction

$$\underset{\text{Acid}_1}{HCl} + \underset{\text{Base}_2}{H_2O} \rightleftharpoons \underset{\text{Acid}_2}{H_3O^+} + \underset{\text{Base}_1}{Cl^-}$$

proceeds virtually to completion (from left to right). We must conclude, therefore, that HCl is a stronger acid than H_3O^+, since it has the stronger tendency to lose protons and the equilibrium is displaced far to the right. In addition, it is apparent that H_2O is a stronger base than Cl^-, since, in the competition for protons, water molecules succeed in holding practically all of them. The strong acid, HCl, has a weak conjugate base, Cl^-.

A strong acid, with a great tendency to lose protons, is necessarily conjugate to a weak base, with a small tendency to gain, and hold, protons. Hence, the stronger the acid, the weaker is its conjugate base. In like manner, a strong base attracts protons strongly and is necessarily conjugate to a weak acid, one that does not readily lose protons. The stronger the base, the weaker is its conjugate acid.

Acetic acid, in $1.0M$ solution, is 0.42% ionized at 25°C (Section 16.1). The equilibrium

$$\underset{\text{Acid}_1}{HC_2H_3O_2} + \underset{\text{Base}_2}{H_2O} \rightleftharpoons \underset{\text{Acid}_2}{H_3O^+} + \underset{\text{Base}_1}{C_2H_3O_2^-}$$

is displaced to the left. This equation may be said to represent a competition between bases, acetate ions and water molecules, for protons. The position of the equilibrium shows that the $C_2H_3O^-$ ion is a stronger base than H_2O; at equilibrium, more protons form $HC_2H_3O_2$ molecules than form H_3O^+ ions. We may also conclude that H_3O^+ is a stronger acid than $HC_2H_3O_2$; at equilibrium, more H_3O^+ ions than $HC_2H_3O_2$ molecules have lost protons. In the preceding example, we note again that the stronger acid, H_3O^+, is conjugate to the weaker base, H_2O, and the stronger base, $C_2H_3O_2^-$, is conjugate to the weaker acid, $HC_2H_3O_2$.

One further conclusion should be stated. In a given reaction, the position of equilibrium favors the formation of the weaker acid and the weaker base. Thus, in the reaction of HCl and H_2O, the equilibrium concentrations of H_3O^+ and Cl^- (the *weaker* acid and base, respectively) are *high*, whereas in the solution of acetic acid, the equilibrium concentrations of H_3O^+ and $C_2H_3O_2^-$ (the *stronger* acid and base, respectively) are *low*.

Notice that the Brønsted concept is an extension of the Arrhenius concept. According to the Arrhenius scheme, strong acids, such as HCl, are strong electrolytes, virtually 100% ionized in water solution to produce solutions with relatively high concentrations of H_3O^+. According to the Arrhenius concept, weak acids, such as acetic acid, are weak electrolytes, incompletely ionized in water solution to produce solutions with relatively low concentrations of H_3O^+. Although the Brønsted system classifies many more substances as acids, compounds that qualify as acids according to the Arrhenius definition are also acids in the Brønsted concept; that is, they are proton donors.

In the Brønsted system, acids are classified according to their ability to donate protons to the specific base under consideration. If water is used as a reference base, the acid strengths of the Arrhenius-water concept may be explained in terms of the Brønsted concept. Thus strong Arrhenius acids are those compounds that are stronger acids than H_3O^+, and weak Arrhenius acids are those compounds that are weaker acids than H_3O^+.

It is apparent that acid strengths are influenced by the solvent water. Acids that are stronger than H_3O^+ are essentially completely ionized in water solution.

$$HClO_4 + H_2O \; \rightleftharpoons \; H_3O^+ + ClO_4^-$$

$$HCl + H_2O \; \rightleftharpoons \; H_3O^+ + Cl^-$$

$$HNO_3 + H_2O \; \rightleftharpoons \; H_3O^+ + NO_3^-$$

Aqueous solutions of $HClO_4$, HCl, and HNO_3 of the same concentration appear to be of the same acid strength. The acid properties of the solutions are due to the H_3O^+ ion which the compounds produce to an equivalent extent in their reactions with water. Water is said to have a **leveling effect** on acids stronger than H_3O^+. The strongest acid that can exist in water solution is the conjugate acid of water, H_3O^+. Acids that are weaker than H_3O^+ are not leveled by water. Thus $HC_2H_3O_2$, H_3PO_4, HNO_2, H_2S, and other weak acids show a wide variation in their degree of ionization—the extent to which they form H_3O^+ in their reactions with water (Section 16.1).

The leveling effect is also observed for solvents other than water. The strongest acid in liquid ammonia solutions is the conjugate acid of ammonia, NH_4^+. Acetic acid, in liquid ammonia solution, is essentially completely ionized, since $HC_2H_3O_2$ is a stronger acid than NH_4^+.

$$HC_2H_3O_2 + NH_3 \; \rightleftharpoons \; NH_4^+ + C_2H_3O_2^-$$

Nitric acid, in methanol (CH_3OH) solution, is incompletely dissociated, since HNO_3 is a weaker acid than the conjugate acid of methanol, $CH_3OH_2{}^+$.

$$HNO_3 + CH_3OH \rightleftharpoons CH_3OH_2{}^+ + NO_3{}^-$$

Solvents that can function as acids exert a leveling effect on bases. The strongest base capable of existing in water solution is the conjugate base of water, OH^-. Many substances, such as $NH_2{}^-$ and H^-, are stronger bases than OH^-. However, in water solution, these strongly basic substances accept protons from water to form OH^- ions; these reactions are essentially complete. The apparent basicity of strongly basic materials in water solution is reduced to the level of the OH^- ion.

$$H_2O + NH_2{}^- \rightleftharpoons NH_3 + OH^-$$
$$H_2O + H^- \rightleftharpoons H_2 + OH^-$$

Materials, such as ammonia, that are less basic than OH^- are not leveled by water and show varying degrees of ionization in aqueous solution (Section 16.1).

Other solvents, in addition to water, level bases. Since H^- and $NH_2{}^-$ appear equally strong in water solution, we must examine their reactions in other solvents to compare their relative basicities. It would be surprising if both ions had exactly the same basic character. In liquid ammonia, the hydride ion reacts rapidly and essentially completely to form hydrogen and the amide ion.

$$NH_3 + H^- \rightleftharpoons H_2 + NH_2{}^-$$

We conclude that the hydride ion is a stronger base than the amide ion; liquid ammonia reduces H^- to the level of the conjugate base of ammonia, $NH_2{}^-$—the strongest base possible in liquid ammonia solution.

The Brønsted definition enlarges the Arrhenius concept even more for bases than it does for acids. In essence, the Arrhenius concept treats only one Brønsted base—the hydroxide ion. According to the Arrhenius concept, strong bases are completely ionic in water solution and form solutions with high concentrations of OH^- ion. In fact, a compound such as NaOH is ionic when pure; molecules of NaOH do not exist. Solutions of weak bases, according to the Arrhenius concept, are prepared from compounds that produce low concentrations of OH^- ion in water (such as NH_3).

The Brønsted system classifies many more substances as bases, and, in this system, it is the OH^- ion of NaOH that is the base, not the compound itself. From the Arrhenius view, solutions resulting from the addition of such compounds as NaH or Na_2O to water owe their basic character to the fact that they are merely solutions of NaOH after the reaction of H^- or O^{2-} with water.

$$H_2O + H^- \longrightarrow H_2 + OH^-$$

$$H_2O + O^{2-} \longrightarrow OH^- + OH^-$$

15.5 Hydrolysis

The reaction of an ion with water in which either H_3O^+ or OH^- is produced is called a **hydrolysis**. Such reactions are Brønsted acid-base reactions. Anions that function as bases in water solution (B^- in the equation that follows) are hydrolyzed.

$$\underset{\text{Acid}_1}{H_2O} + \underset{\text{Base}_2}{B^-} \rightleftharpoons \underset{\text{Acid}_2}{HB} + \underset{\text{Base}_1}{OH^-}$$

In the reaction, water acts as an acid, and a proton is transferred to the anion. The extent of hydrolysis of a given anion depends upon the base strength of the anion, and an indication of the degree of hydrolysis is given by the concentration of OH^- relative to the concentration of anion present in the solution. Anions that are extensively hydrolyzed are strong bases with weak conjugate acids.

Hydrolysis is complete in the reaction

$$H_2O + H^- \longrightarrow H_2 + OH^-$$

The anion undergoing hydrolysis, H^-, is a stronger base than OH^-, and the conjugate acid of the anion, H_2, is a much weaker acid than H_2O; complete hydrolysis is characteristic of such anions. This equation, in fact, illustrates the leveling effect of water on bases stronger than OH^-.

At the other extreme, some anions, such as Cl^-, do not hydrolyze at all.

$$H_2O + Cl^- \longleftarrow HCl + OH^-$$

The Cl^- ion is a very weak base, and its conjugate acid, HCl, is not only stronger than H_2O but is also stronger than H_3O^+. In fact, HCl is leveled in water solution to H_3O^+, and therefore HCl molecules do not exist in measurable quantities in aqueous solutions of moderate concentrations. The chloride ion is simply too weak a base to accept a proton from water to a significant extent. Anions that have conjugate acids stronger than H_3O^+ do not hydrolyze.

The behavior of many anions in water solution is intermediate between the two extremes represented by H^- and Cl^-. For example,

$$H_2O + C_2H_3O_2^- \rightleftharpoons HC_2H_3O_2 + OH^-$$

The $C_2H_3O_2^-$ ion is a weaker base than OH^- but not so weak as Cl^-. Even though $HC_2H_3O_2$, the conjugate acid of $C_2H_3O_2^-$, is a stronger acid than water, it is a weaker acid than HCl or H_3O^+. Acetic acid is not leveled by water; molecules of the weak acid $HC_2H_3O_2$ can exist in aqueous solution. The hydrolysis represented by the equation occurs only to a slight extent; the equilibrium, as written, is displaced to the left because the substances written on the left are the weaker acid and the weaker base of the reaction. Nevertheless, in a solution of sodium acetate, there is a measurable concentration of OH^- from the hydrolysis of the acetate ion—enough to cause red litmus to turn blue. Anions, such as $C_2H_3O_2^-$, CN^-, NO_2^-, and S^{2-}, that have conjugate acids stronger than water but weaker than H_3O^+ are measurably, but not completely, hydrolyzed in water solution.

There are some hydrogen-containing cations, of which the ammonium ion is the principal example, that hydrolyze to produce H_3O^+.

$$NH_4^+ + H_2O \; \rightleftharpoons \; H_3O^+ + NH_3$$

Ammonia is a stronger base than water, and therefore the position of equilibrium is to the left. However, water is a sufficiently strong base to gain some of the protons in the competition; although the hydrolysis is far from complete, a solution of NH_4Cl gives an acid reaction toward litmus because of the hydrolysis of the NH_4^+ ion.

There are a few relatively unimportant cations that hydrolyze completely. For example, the phosphonium ion, PH_4^+, is a stronger acid than the hydronium ion; in water solution, the phosphonium ion is leveled.

$$PH_4^+ + H_2O \; \longrightarrow \; H_3O^+ + PH_3$$

Metal cations are hydrated in water solution, and some of these hydrated cations hydrolyze. For example, solutions of aluminum chloride, zinc chloride, and iron(III) chloride show acidic characteristics because of the hydrolysis of the cations. The hydrolysis of the aluminum ion (which we shall indicate as $Al(H_2O)_6^{3+}$) may be represented as follows:

$$Al(H_2O)_6^{3+} + H_2O \; \rightleftharpoons \; H_3O^+ + Al(H_2O)_5(OH)^{2+}$$

In the hydrolysis, $Al(H_2O)_6^{3+}$ functions as an acid and donates a proton to H_2O which acts as a base. A water molecule coordinated to the Al^{3+} ion has an enhanced acidic character because the $O-H$ bonds of

$$Al\text{---}O\underset{\diagdown H}{\overset{\diagup H}{}}$$

are weakened by the displacement of electrons toward the positively charged central ion. Thus the coordinated water molecules release protons and act as Brønsted acids.

In general, small ions with high positive charges form hydrated species that act as Brønsted acids in hydrolysis reactions. The cations of the group I A and group II A metals have comparatively low charges for their relatively large sizes; the hydrated species of these ions have no significant acid character and consequently do not hydrolyze appreciably. The hydrolysis of ions is discussed in more detail in Section 17.6.

The amphoteric nature of some hydroxides (e.g., $Al(OH)_3$ and $Zn(OH)_2$) may be explained by means of the Brønsted theory. These substances, normally insoluble in water, dissolve in both acidic solution and alkaline solution. In acid, a typical reaction is

$$H_3O^+ + Al(OH)_3(H_2O)_3(s) \rightleftharpoons Al(OH)_2(H_2O)_4^+ + H_2O$$

A proton is transferred from H_3O^+ to the hydrated hydroxide, which acts as a base. A coordinated OH of the aluminum complex accepts the proton and is transformed into a coordinated H_2O. The other coordinated OH groups can also accept protons, and the reaction continues until $Al(H_2O)_6^{3+}$ is formed.

In alkaline solution, the reaction is

$$Al(OH)_3(H_2O)_3(s) + OH^- \rightleftharpoons H_2O + Al(OH)_4(H_2O)_2^-$$

The hydrated aluminum hydroxide acts as an acid, and a coordinated H_2O of the aluminum compound loses a proton to the OH^- ion. The loss of a proton transforms this H_2O into an OH group, and the aluminate ion, $Al(OH)_4(H_2O)_2^-$ results. Whereas all hydroxides react with H_3O^+, only those hydroxides that are classed as amphoteric react with OH^-. Amphoterism is discussed further in Section 17.5.

15.6 Acid and Base Strengths and Structure

The correlation between molecular structure and acid or base strength is complex and involves many factors. Polar molecules with a hydrogen atom situated at the positive end of the dipole are acids; in such molecules, electrons are withdrawn from the hydrogen atom, thereby facilitating its release as a proton. For the hydrogen compounds of the elements of a given period, increasing acid strength parallels increasing electronegativity of the atom combined with hydrogen. For the elements of the second period, the order of increasing acid strength of the hydrogen compounds of the last three elements is

$$NH_3 < H_2O < HF$$

However, increasing acid strength does not always parallel increasing electronegativity of the atom bonded to hydrogen; evidently other factors are also involved. There is an increase in acid strength of the hydro acids of the elements in any group of the periodic classification with increasing atomic size of the electronegative element. For example, the hydrogen compounds of the group VI A and group VII A elements arranged according to increasing acid strength are

$$H_2O < H_2S < H_2Se < H_2Te$$

$$HF < HCl < HBr < HI$$

In each series, the last compound is the strongest acid and is formed by the element of lowest electronegativity.

When the hydrogen compounds of a period are compared, the small differences in the atomic radius of the electronegative elements are unimportant. However, in the hydrogen halide series, the bond distance increases from 1.0 Å for HF to 1.7 Å for HI, and with it the bond energy decreases from 135 kcal/mole for HF to 71 kcal/mole for HI (Section 11.6). The bond energy pertains to a process in which the molecule is broken into atoms, not ions. However, the energy required for the removal of a proton from each hydrogen halide may be calculated by adding the bond energy

$$HX(g) \longrightarrow H(g) + X(g)$$

the ionization energy of hydrogen

$$H(g) \longrightarrow H^+(g) + e^-$$

and the electron affinity of the halogen

$$e^- + X(g) \longrightarrow X^-(g)$$

The values for the hydrogen halides fall in the same order as do the bond energies themselves. If the reaction of HX with water is of interest, the heats of hydration of the ions may be added without altering the observed order. The actual process

$$HX + H_2O \rightleftharpoons H_3O^+ + X^-$$

does not, of course, occur by the mechanism used for the analysis of the energy effect.

A base must have an unshared electron pair in order to attract and hold a proton; a polar molecule that has an electron pair situated at the negative end of the dipole is a base. Trends in the base strength of anions are readily derived from conjugate relationships. Thus, since H_2S is a stronger acid than H_2O, S^{2-} is a weaker base than O^{2-}; for monatomic anions of similar charge, base strength decreases with increasing size.

The base strength of the uninegative ions of elements of the second period

$$NH_2^- > OH^- > F^-$$

parallels a decrease in the electronegativity for the element of the second period; a similar trend is observed for the hydrogen-containing molecules of these elements

$$NH_3 > H_2O > HF$$

In these series, size differences are small and unimportant; the trend is set by the decreasing electronegativity of the central element. Both small size and low electronegativity are found in the hydride ion, H^-, which is a powerful base.

A third factor that influences the base strength of anions is the charge on the ion. Thus the base strength of the monatomic anions of the elements of the second period

$$N^{3-} > O^{2-} > F^-$$

decreases with increasing electronegativity and with decreasing negative charge on the ion.

The oxy acids have been studied more extensively than any other type of acids. For acids with the structure

$$H-O-Z$$

the acid strength increases with increasing electronegativity of Z. The higher the electronegativity of Z, the more the electrons of the molecule are displaced toward Z, and the more readily the proton is removed. For example,

$$HOCl > HOBr > HOI$$

is the order of decreasing acidity of the hypohalous acids.

In compounds in which additional oxygen atoms are bonded to Z, the electron-withdrawing power of the group bonded to hydrogen is increased; thus the proton is more readily removed. This effect is illustrated by the series

$$H-\overset{\cdot\cdot}{\underset{\cdot\cdot}{O}}-\overset{\cdot\cdot}{\underset{\cdot\cdot}{Cl}}\colon \quad < \quad H-\overset{\cdot\cdot}{\underset{\cdot\cdot}{O}}-\overset{\oplus}{\underset{\cdot\cdot}{Cl}}-\overset{\cdot\cdot}{\underset{\cdot\cdot}{O}}\colon^{\ominus} \quad < \quad H-\overset{\cdot\cdot}{\underset{\cdot\cdot}{O}}-\overset{\overset{\displaystyle :\overset{\cdot\cdot}{O}:^{\ominus}}{|}}{\underset{(2+)}{Cl}}\overset{\cdot\cdot}{=}\overset{\cdot\cdot}{\underset{\cdot\cdot}{O}}:^{\ominus} \quad < \quad H-\overset{\cdot\cdot}{\underset{\cdot\cdot}{O}}-\overset{\overset{\displaystyle :\overset{\cdot\cdot}{O}:^{\ominus}}{|}}{\underset{\underset{\displaystyle :\overset{\cdot\cdot}{O}:^{\ominus}}{|}}{\underset{(3+)}{Cl}}}\overset{\cdot\cdot}{=}\overset{\cdot\cdot}{\underset{\cdot\cdot}{O}}:^{\ominus}$$

in which acidity increases with increasing oxidation state of chlorine (from $1+$ in HOCl to $7+$ in $HClO_4$). However, the formal charge of the central atom of an oxy acid (determined from a structure written in conformity with the octet principle) is a better indicator of acid strength than oxidation number. For the oxy acids of chlorine, increasing formal charge on the chlorine atom (indicated in the preceding structures) parallels an increase in the oxidation number of the chlorine atom, and either serves to indicate increasing acid strength. However, for the oxy acids of phosphorus, oxidation number fails to give a true indication of acid strength. The acids

are approximately of equal strength, and in each case, the formal charge on the phosphorus atom is $1+$. Note however, that the oxidation number of P in H_3PO_2 is $1+$, in H_3PO_3 it is $3+$, and in H_3PO_4 it is $5+$.

The number of O atoms bonded to the central atom but *not* bonded to H atoms influences the formal charge of the central atom, and therefore a qualitative indication of the strength of acids of general formula $(HO)_m ZO_n$ is provided by the value of n in the formula. In general, acids are very strong when $n = 3$ ($HOClO_3$, $HOIO_3$), strong when $n = 2$ ($HOClO_2$, $(HO)_2SO_2$, $HONO_2$), weak when $n = 1$ ($HOClO$, $(HO)_3PO$, $HONO$), and very weak when $n = 0$ ($HOCl$, $(HO)_3B$). There are, of course, variations within any of the groups, and the electronegativity of the central atom provides the key to these variations. Thus, for the halic acids, the oxidation state of each halogen atom is $5+$, and $n = 2$; the acidity of the compounds in the series increases with increasing electronegativity of the halogen atom.

$$HOClO_2 > HOBrO_2 > HOIO_2$$

Increasing acid strength parallels decreasing base strength of the conjugate base. Thus for the series

$$HOCl < HOClO < HOClO_2 < HOClO_3$$

the order of base strengths of the anions is

$$OCl^- > ClO_2^- > ClO_3^- > ClO_4^-$$

The addition of oxygen atoms provides a larger volume to accommodate the charge of the ion. A large uninegative ion attracts and holds a proton less strongly than a small uninegative ion.

15.7 The Lewis Concept

In reality, the Brønsted concept enlarges the definition of a base much more than it does that of an acid. In the Brønsted system, a base is a molecule or ion that has an unshared electron pair with which it can attract and hold a proton, and an acid is a substance that can supply a proton to a base. If a molecule or ion can share an electron pair with a proton, it can do the same thing with other substances as well.

Gilbert N. Lewis proposed a broader concept of acids and bases that liberated acid-base phenomena from the proton; although Lewis first proposed his system in 1923, he did little to develop it until 1938. Lewis defined a **base** as a substance that has an unshared electron pair with which it can form a covalent bond with an atom, molecule, or ion. An **acid** is a substance that can form a covalent bond by accepting an electron pair from a base. The emphasis has been shifted, by the Lewis concept, from the proton to the electron pair and covalent-bond formation.

An example of a Lewis acid-base reaction that is not treated as such by any other acid-base concept is

Many Lewis acids and bases of this type can be titrated against one another by the use of suitable indicators in the same way that traditional acids and bases can be titrated.

Substances that are bases in the Brønsted system are also bases according to the Lewis concept. However, the Lewis definition of an acid considerably expands the number of substances that are classified as acids. A Lewis acid must have an empty orbital capable of receiving the electron pair of the base; the proton is but a single example of a Lewis acid.

Lewis acids include molecules or atoms that have incomplete octets.

Aluminum chloride, although it reacts as $AlCl_3$, is actually a dimer—Al_2Cl_6. The formation of the dimer from the monomer may be regarded as a Lewis acid-base reaction in itself, since a chlorine atom in each $AlCl_3$ unit supplies an electron pair to the aluminum atom of the other $AlCl_3$ unit to complete the octet of the aluminum atom; these bonds are indicated by $\cdots$ in the diagram

$$\begin{array}{ccc} Cl & Cl & Cl \\ \diagdown & \diagdown\cdots & \diagup \\ & Al\cdots\quad\cdots Al \\ \diagup & \cdots\diagdown & \diagdown \\ Cl & Cl & Cl \end{array}$$

Many simple cations can function as Lewis acids; for example,

$$Cu^{2+} + 4:NH_3 \longrightarrow Cu(:NH_3)_4^{2+}$$

$$Fe^{3+} + 6:C\equiv N:^- \longrightarrow Fe(:C\equiv N:)_6^{3-}$$

Some metals atoms can function as acids in the formation of compounds such as the carbonyls, which are produced by the reaction of the metal with carbon monoxide.

$$Ni + 4:C\equiv O: \longrightarrow Ni(:C\equiv O:)_4$$

Compounds that have central atoms capable of expanding their valence shells are Lewis acids in reactions in which this expansion occurs. Examples are

$$SnCl_4 + 2Cl^- \longrightarrow SnCl_6^{2-}$$

$$SiF_4 + 2F^- \longrightarrow SiF_6^{2-}$$

$$PF_5 + F^- \longrightarrow PF_6^-$$

In each of the first two reactions, the valence shell of the central atom (Sn and Si) is expanded from eight to twelve electrons, and in the third reaction, the valence shell of P goes from ten to twelve electrons.

In addition, some compounds have an acidic site because of one or more multiple bonds in the molecule. Examples are

$$\begin{array}{ccc} :\overset{\displaystyle :O:}{\underset{\displaystyle :O:}{S}} + :\overset{..}{O}{-}H^- & \longrightarrow & \left[:\overset{\displaystyle :O:}{\underset{\displaystyle :O:}{S}}{-}\overset{..}{O}{-}H \right] \end{array}$$

$$\begin{array}{ccc} \overset{\displaystyle :O:}{\underset{\displaystyle :O:}{C}} + :\overset{..}{\underset{..}{O}}:^{2-} & \longrightarrow & \left[\overset{\displaystyle :O:}{\underset{\displaystyle :O:}{C}}{-}\overset{..}{\underset{..}{O}}: \right]^{2-} \end{array}$$

The reactions of silica, SiO_2, with metal oxides are analogous to the reaction of carbon dioxide with the oxide ion, although both silica and the silicate products (compounds of SiO_3^{2-}) are polymeric. This reaction is important in high-temperature metallurgical processes where a basic oxide is added to an ore to remove silica in the form of silicates (slag). Many of the processes used in the manufacture of glass, cement, and ceramics involve the reaction of the base O^{2-} (from metal oxides, carbonates, etc.) with acid oxides (such as SiO_2, Al_2O_3, and B_2O_3).

Arrhenius and Brønsted acid-base reactions may be interpreted in Lewis terms by focusing attention on the proton, as a Lewis acid

$$H^+(aq) + OH^-(aq) \longrightarrow H_2O$$

in which case the Brønsted acid is termed a **secondary** Lewis acid since it serves to provide the **primary** Lewis acid, the proton. Probably a better interpretation is that which classifies Brønsted acid-base reactions as Lewis base displacements. The Brønsted acid is interpreted as a complex in which the Lewis acid (proton) is already combined with a base; the reaction is viewed as a displacement of this base by another, stronger, base.

$$H_3O^+ + OH^- \longrightarrow H_2O + H_2O$$

In this reaction, the base OH^- displaces the weaker base H_2O from its combination with the acid, the proton.

All Brønsted acid-base reactions are Lewis base displacements. In the reaction

$$HCl + H_2O \longrightarrow H_3O^+ + Cl^-$$

the base H_2O displaces the weaker base, Cl^-. A base supplies an electron pair to a nucleus and is, therefore, called **nucleophilic** (Greek, nucleus loving). Base displacements are nucleophilic displacements.

Nucleophilic displacements may be identified among reactions that are not Brønsted acid-base reactions. The formation of $Cu(NH_3)_4^{2+}$ has been previously used as an illustration of a Lewis acid-base reaction. Since the reaction occurs in water, the formation of this complex is more accurately interpreted as the displacement of the base H_2O from the complex $Cu(H_2O)_4^{2+}$ by the stronger base NH_3.

$$Cu(H_2O)_4^{2+} + 4NH_3 \longrightarrow Cu(NH_3)_4^{2+} + 4H_2O$$

Lewis acids accept an electron pair in a reaction with a base; they are **electrophilic** (Greek, electron loving). Acid displacements, or electrophilic displacements, are not so common as base displacements, but this type of reaction is known. For example, if $COCl_2$ is viewed as a combination of $COCl^+$ (an acid) with Cl^- (a base), the reaction

$$COCl_2 + AlCl_3 \longrightarrow COCl^+ + AlCl_4^-$$

is an electrophilic displacement in which the acid $AlCl_3$ displaces the weaker acid $COCl^+$ from its complex with the base Cl^- (Table 15.1). The reaction

$$SeOCl_2 + BCl_3 \longrightarrow SeOCl^+ + BCl_4^-$$

may be similarly interpreted.

The Lewis theory is frequently used to interpret reaction mechanisms. Examples of such interpretations are found in Sections 20.5 and 20.6.

SOME SUGGESTED READINGS

Drago, R. S., and Matiwiyoff, N. A., *Acids and Bases*, Boston, Heath, 1968 (paper).

Holliday, A. K., and Massey, A. G., *Inorganic Chemistry in Non-Aqueous Solvents*, Elmsford, N.Y., Pergamon, 1965 (paper).

Kolthoff, I. M., and Bruckenstein, S., *Acid-Bases in Analytical Chemistry*, New York, Wiley, 1964 (paper).

Luder, W. F., and Zuffanti, S., *The Electronic Theory of Acids and Bases*, New York, Dover, 1961 (paper).

Sisler, H. H., *Chemistry in Non-Aqueous Solvents*, New York, Van Nostrand Reinhold, 1961 (paper).

VanderWerf, C. A., *Acids, Bases and the Chemistry of the Covalent Bond*, New York, Van Nostrand Reinhold, 1961 (paper).

Waddington, T. C., *Non-Aqueous Solvents*, New York, Appleton-Century-Crofts, 1970 (paper).

PROBLEMS

15.1 Give one-sentence descriptions of an *acid*, a *base*, and a *neutralization reaction* based on (a) the Arrhenius concept, (b) the solvent system concept, (c) the Brønsted-Lowry concept, and (d) the Lewis concept.

15.2 Write equations analogous to the following but employing compounds of the oxygen system in place of the nitrogen-system compounds:
  (a) $KNH_2 + NH_4NO_3 \rightarrow KNO_3 + 2NH_3$
  (b) $Ca_3N_2 + 4NH_3 \rightarrow 3Ca(NH_2)_2$
  (c) $xP_3N_5 + xNH_3 \rightarrow 3(HNPN)_x$
  (d) $Cl_2 + 2NH_3 \rightarrow NH_4Cl + H_2NCl$
  (e) $Pb(NH_2)_2 \rightarrow PbNH + NH_3$
  (f) $2Na + 2NH_3 \rightarrow 2NaNH_2 + H_2$
  (g) $Zn(NH_2)_2 + 2NaNH_2 \rightarrow Na_2[Zn(NH_2)_4]$

15.3 What is the conjugate base of (a) H_3PO_4, (b) $H_2PO_4^-$, (c) NH_3, (d) HS^-, (e) H_3O^+, (f) $HOCl$, (g) $Al(H_2O)_6^{3+}$?

15.4 What is the conjugate acid of (a) F^-, (b) OH^-, (c) PO_4^{3-}, (d) NH_3, (e) NH_2^-, (f) HS^-, (g) $Zn(OH)(H_2O)_5^+$?

15.5 Identify the Brønsted acids and bases in the following:
(a) $NH_3 + HCl \rightleftharpoons NH_4^+ + Cl^-$
(b) $NH_4^+ + OH^- \rightleftharpoons NH_3 + H_2O$
(c) $HS^- + OH^- \rightleftharpoons S^{2-} + H_2O$
(d) $H_3O^+ + HS^- \rightleftharpoons H_2S + H_2O$
(e) $HSO_4^- + CN^- \rightleftharpoons HCN + SO_4^{2-}$

15.6 Write chemical equations to illustrate the behavior of the following as Brønsted acids: (a) $H_2AsO_4^-$, (b) HF, (c) $Zn(H_2O)_6^{2+}$, (d) H_2O.

15.7 Write chemical equations to illustrate the behavior of the following as Brønsted bases: (a) $H_2AsO_4^-$, (b) CO_3^{2-}, (c) H^-, (d) O^{2-}.

15.8 (a) What is an amphiprotic substance? (b) Give four examples of such substances. Select both molecules and ions as your examples. (c) Write chemical equations to illustrate the characteristic behavior of the substances that you listed in part (b).

15.9 What is the leveling effect of a solvent? Use chemical equations in your answer, and describe the leveling of both acids and bases.

15.10 What is the difference in meaning between the terms amphiprotic and amphoteric?

15.11 Each of the following reactions is displaced to the right. (a) Arrange all the Brønsted acids that appear in these equations according to decreasing acid strength. (b) Make a similar list for the Brønsted bases.
(a) $H_3O^+ + H_2PO_4^- \rightleftharpoons H_3PO_4 + H_2O$
(b) $HCN + OH^- \rightleftharpoons H_2O + CN^-$
(c) $H_3PO_4 + CN^- \rightleftharpoons HCN + H_2PO_4^-$
(d) $H_2O + NH_2^- \rightleftharpoons NH_3 + OH^-$

15.12 On the basis of your lists from Problem 15.11, would you expect an appreciable reaction (over 50%) between the species listed in each of the following?
(a) $H_3O^+ + CN^- \rightarrow$ (c) $HCN + H_2PO_4^- \rightarrow$
(b) $NH_3 + CN^- \rightarrow$ (d) $H_3PO_4 + NH_2^- \rightarrow$

15.13 Each of the following reactions is displaced to the right. (a) Arrange all the Brønsted acids that appear in these equations according to decreasing acid strength. (b) Make a similar list for the Brønsted bases.
(a) $HCO_3^- + OH^- \rightleftharpoons H_2O + CO_3^{2-}$
(b) $HC_2H_3O_2 + HS^- \rightleftharpoons H_2S + C_2H_3O_2^-$
(c) $H_2S + CO_3^{2-} \rightleftharpoons HCO_3^- + HS^-$
(d) $HSO_4^- + C_2H_3O_2^- \rightleftharpoons HC_2H_3O_2 + SO_4^{2-}$

15.14 On the basis of your lists from Problem 15.13, would you expect an appreciable reaction (over 50%) between the species listed in each of the following?
(a) $HCO_3^- + C_2H_3O_2^- \rightarrow$ (c) $HC_2H_3O_2 + CO_3^{2-} \rightarrow$
(b) $HSO_4^- + HS^- \rightarrow$ (d) $H_2S + C_2H_3O_2^- \rightarrow$

15.15 Briefly discuss, using chemical equations, how the compound H_2O is classified according to the (a) Arrhenius concept, (b) the Brønsted-Lowry concept, and (c) the Lewis concept.

15.16 Do acid-base reactions ever involve oxidation and reduction? Consider all of the acid-base theories presented in this chapter.

15.17 Write equations for the hydrolysis of the following ions: (a) $C_2H_3O_2^-$, (b) CN^-, (c) NO_2^-, (d) NH_4^+, (e) PH_4^+, (f) $Cu(H_2O)_4^{2+}$.

15.18 Ammonium chloride (NH_4Cl) reacts with sodium amide ($NaNH_2$) in liquid ammonia to produce sodium chloride and ammonia. Interpret this reaction in terms of the solvent system, Brønsted, and Lewis theories of acids and bases. State clearly what acid(s) and base(s) are involved in each case.

15.19 Which compound of each of the following pairs is the stronger acid?
(a) H_3PO_4 or H_3AsO_4 (d) H_3BO_3 or H_2CO_3
(b) H_3AsO_3 or H_3AsO_4 (e) H_2Se or HBr
(c) H_2SO_4 or H_2SO_3

15.20 Which compound of each of the following pairs is the stronger base?
(a) P^{3-} or S^{2-} (d) NO_2^- or NO_3^-
(b) PH_3 or NH_3 (e) Br^- or F^-
(c) SiO_3^{2-} or SO_3^{2-}

15.21 Perchloric acid, $HClO_4$, is a stronger acid than chloric acid, $HClO_3$. On the other hand, periodic acid, H_5IO_6, is a weaker acid than iodic acid, HIO_3. (a) Draw Lewis structures for the four compounds, and assign formal charges to the atoms of the molecules. (b) Explain the differences in acid strength on the basis of your structures of part (a).

15.22 (a) Draw Lewis structures (include formal charges) for selenic acid, H_2SeO_4, and telluric acid, H_6TeO_6. (b) Which is the stronger acid?

15.23 Interpret the following reactions in terms of the Lewis theory:
(a) $BeF_2 + 2F^- \rightarrow BeF_4^{2-}$ (d) $H^- + H_2C{=}O \rightarrow H_3CO^-$
(b) $H_2O + BF_3 \rightarrow H_2OBF_3$ (e) $AuCN + CN^- \rightarrow Au(CN)_2^-$
(c) $S + S^{2-} \rightarrow S_2^{2-}$

15.24 Interpret the following as Lewis displacement reactions. For each, state the type of displacement, what is displaced, and the agent for the displacement.
(a) $NH_3 + H^- \rightarrow H_2 + NH_2^-$
(b) $HONO_2 + H_2SO_4 \rightarrow NO_2^+ + H_2O + HSO_4^-$
(c) $[Co(NH_3)_5(H_2O)]^{3+} + Cl^- \rightarrow [Co(NH_3)_5Cl]^{2+} + H_2O$
(d) $Ge + GeS_2 \rightarrow 2GeS$
(e) $O^{2-} + H_2O \rightarrow 2OH^-$
(f) $Br_2 + FeBr_3 \rightarrow Br^+ + FeBr_4^-$
(g) $CH_3Cl + AlCl_3 \rightarrow CH_3^+ + AlCl_4^{4-}$
(h) $CH_3I + OH^- \rightarrow CH_3OH + I^-$

15.25 Sulfur dioxide is a significant contributor to atmospheric pollution. The sulfurous acid produced by the reaction of SO_2 and atmospheric moisture adversely effects the eyes, skin, and respiratory systems of humans and causes the corrosion of metals and the deterioration of other materials. The reaction of SO_2 and water can be roughly indicated:

$$H_2O + SO_2 \longrightarrow H_2OSO_2 \longrightarrow (HO)_2SO$$

(a) Draw Lewis structures (complete with formal charges) for the compounds given. (b) Interpret the two steps of the sequence in terms of the Lewis acid-base theory. (c) Why does the proton migration of the second step occur?

The principles of chemical equilibrium may be applied to equilibria involving ions in aqueous solution. An understanding of such equilibria is especially important to the study of analytical chemistry.

IONIC EQUILIBRIA, PART I

16.1 Weak Electrolytes

Strong electrolytes are completely ionic in water solution. For example, a $0.01M$ solution of $CaCl_2$ is $0.01M$ in calcium ions and $0.02M$ in chloride ions. Interionic attractions (the Debye-Hückel effect, Section 9.12) account for the observed deviations in the properties of solutions of strong electrolytes from the properties calculated on the basis of complete dissociation; such deviations are not large.

Weak electrolytes, however, are incompletely ionized in water solution; dissolved molecules exist in equilibrium with ions in such solutions. For example, the following equation represents the dissociation of acetic acid in water

$$HC_2H_3O_2 + H_2O \rightleftharpoons H_3O^+ + C_2H_3O_2^-$$

and the equilibrium constant for this reaction as written is

$$K' = \frac{[H_3O^+][C_2H_3O_2^-]}{[HC_2H_3O_2][H_2O]}$$

In dilute solutions, the molar concentration of water is virtually a constant (approximately 1000/18, or 55.5M); the number of moles of water consumed in the formation of hydronium ion (approximately 10^{-3} mole per liter in a 0.1M acetic acid solution) is negligible in comparison with the large number of moles of water present. Thus

$$K = K'[H_2O] = \frac{[H_3O^+][C_2H_3O_2^-]}{[HC_2H_3O_2]}$$

We shall follow the practice of representing the concentration of hydronium ion by the symbol [H$^+$], and thus the expression for the equilibrium constant reduces to a form consistent with the simplified equation

$$HC_2H_3O_2 \rightleftharpoons H^+ + C_2H_3O_2^-$$

$$K = \frac{[H^+][C_2H_3O_2^-]}{[HC_2H_3O_2]}$$

For complete accuracy, equilibrium constants should be expressed in terms of activities instead of concentrations. However, the concentrations of ions present in dilute solutions of weak electrolytes are so small that interionic attractions are negligible. Under these conditions, molar concentrations may be used, rather than activities, to give reasonably accurate results. By convention, the ions are written on the right of an equation for the reversible dissociation of a weak electrolyte; hence, the concentration terms for ions appear in the numerator of the expression for the equilibrium constant.

The degree of dissociation, α, of a weak electrolyte in aqueous solution may be determined by conductance measurements (Section 10.5) or, not as accurately, by measurements of colligative properties (Section 9.11). Potentiometric methods for such determinations are also used (Sections 16.4 and 17.8). From the degree of dissociation, the value of the equilibrium constant (or ionization constant) may be calculated.

▶ **EXAMPLE 16.1**   At 25°C, a 0.100M solution of acetic acid is 1.34% ionized. What is the ionization constant for acetic acid?

Solution Since $\alpha = 0.0134$, in 1 liter of solution $(0.0134)(0.100) = 0.00134$ mole of acetic acid would be in ionic form, and $0.100 - 0.00134 = 0.09866$ mole of acetic acid would remain in molecular form. According to the chemical equation for the ionization, 1 mole of H^+ and 1 mole of $C_2H_3O_2^-$ are produced for every mole of acetic acid that ionizes. Therefore the equilibrium concentrations are

$$\underset{0.09866M}{HC_2H_3O_2} \rightleftharpoons \underset{0.00134M}{H^+} + \underset{0.00134M}{C_2H_3O_2^-}$$

These concentrations may be used to find the numerical value of the equilibrium constant.

$$K = \frac{[H^+][C_2H_3O_2^-]}{[HC_2H_3O_2]}$$

$$= \frac{(0.00134)(0.00134)}{(0.09866)}$$

$$= 1.81 \times 10^{-5}$$

In future problem work, we shall express equilibrium constants to two significant figures; higher accuracy is generally not warranted when molar concentrations are used instead of activities.

▶ **EXAMPLE 16.2** What are the concentrations of all species present in $1.0M$ acetic acid at $25°C$? What is the degree of ionization?

Solution If we let x equal the number of moles of acetic acid in ionic form in 1 liter of solution, the equilibrium concentrations are

$$\underset{(1.0-x)M}{HC_2H_3O_2} \rightleftharpoons \underset{(x)M}{H^+} + \underset{(x)M}{C_2H_3O_2^-}$$

Hence, we find

$$1.8 \times 10^{-5} = \frac{[H^+][C_2H_3O_2^-]}{[HC_2H_3O_2]}$$

$$= \frac{x^2}{(1.0-x)}$$

which can be expanded to

$$x^2 + 1.8 \times 10^{-5}x - 1.8 \times 10^{-5} = 0$$

This equation may be solved by means of the quadratic formula (Section 14.11); we find

$$x = [H^+] = [C_2H_3O_2^-] = 4.2 \times 10^{-3}M$$

$$(1.0 - x) = [HC_2H_3O_2] = 9.958 \times 10^{-1}M$$

(Note that this last concentration is $1.0M$ to two significant figures.) The degree of ionization can be calculated by dividing the number of ionized moles of acetic acid in 1 liter of solution by the total number of moles of acetic acid present in 1 liter.

$$\alpha = \frac{4.2 \times 10^{-3}}{1.0} = 4.2 \times 10^{-3}$$

The use of the quadratic formula in problem solving may be avoided by making an approximation that is frequently employed in calculations involving aqueous equilibria. The subtraction of a very small number from a larger number does not significantly alter the value of the larger number and may be neglected. Thus, in the preceding example, such a small amount of acetic acid is ionized (x) that the quantity $(1.0 - x)$ used to represent the concentration of undissociated acetic acid molecules is, for all practical purposes, equal to 1.0 (as previously noted). By using 1.0 instead of $(1.0 - x)$ for the concentration of $HC_2H_3O_2$, we find

$$1.8 \times 10^{-5} = \frac{[H^+][C_2H_3O_2^-]}{[HC_2H_3O_2]}$$

$$= \frac{x^2}{1.0}$$

$$x = 4.2 \times 10^{-3}M$$

which is the same as the result obtained through the use of the quadratic formula.

The subtraction of a small number from another small number may not be neglected; therefore the quadratic formula must be employed to solve some problems. As a rule of thumb, if the number to be subtracted is more than 5% of the number from which it is to be subtracted, the simplified procedure should not be used; the final result of such a calculation would not have two significant figures. Thus the result of a calculation obtained by the use of the simplified procedure may be used to check whether the use of the procedure was justified.

In Table 16.1, the molar concentrations of ions are listed for solutions of acetic acid of various concentrations. The percent ionized increases with dilution; at infinite dilution, all electrolytes are completely dissociated. This is consistent with Le Chatelier's principle. Addition of water to an equilibrium system of a weak electrolyte,

$$HC_2H_3O_2 + H_2O \;\rightleftharpoons\; H_3O^+ + C_2H_3O_2^-$$

shifts the equilibrium to the right so that proportionately more of the electrolyte is found in ionic form.

Table 16.1

Ion Concentrations and Percent Ionization of Solutions
of Acetic Acid at 25°C

Concentration of Solution (M)	[H$^+$] or [C$_2$H$_3$O$_2$$^-$] (M)	Percent Ionization
1.00	0.00420	0.420
0.100	0.00134	1.34
0.0100	0.000420	4.20
0.00100	0.000125	12.5

The values of ionization constants change with temperature; most values are reported at 25°C. At 25°C, K for acetic acid is 1.8×10^{-5}; at 100°C, the numerical value of the constant for this equilibrium is 1.1×10^{-5}.

An equilibrium system of a weak electrolyte may not only be prepared from the pure compound but also from compounds that supply the component ions of the electrolyte; this is illustrated in the following example.

▶ **EXAMPLE 16.3** What are the concentrations of all species present in a solution made by diluting 0.10 mole of HCl and 0.50 mole of NaC$_2$H$_3$O$_2$ to 1.0 liter?

Solution Hydrochloric acid and sodium acetate are strong electrolytes. We may assume, therefore, that before equilibrium is attained, the concentration of H$^+$ is 0.10M, and the concentration of C$_2$H$_3$O$_2$$^-$ is 0.50M. If we let x equal the number of moles per liter of acetic acid at equilibrium, the equilibrium concentrations are

$$\underset{(x)M}{HC_2H_3O_2} \rightleftharpoons \underset{(0.10-x)M}{H^+} + \underset{(0.50-x)M}{C_2H_3O_2^-}$$

If we solve the problem using these quantities, the quadratic formula must be employed, since x is not negligible in comparison to 0.10 or 0.50.

A simpler way to solve the problem is to assume that the reaction goes as far to the left as is possible and that then a portion of the acetic acid thus formed dissociates into ions. In this instance, let y equal the number of moles of acetic acid that is dissociated at equilibrium.

$$HC_2H_3O_2 \rightleftharpoons H^+ + C_2H_3O_2^-$$

	HC$_2$H$_3$O$_2$	H$^+$	C$_2$H$_3$O$_2$$^-$
after mixing:	—	0.10M	0.50M
reaction to left:	0.10M	—	0.40M
equilibrium:	(0.10 − y)M	(y)M	(0.40 + y)M

Now, y is indeed negligible in comparison to both 0.10 and 0.40, and we may simplify the problem by neglecting y in the terms for the concentrations of acetic acid and acetate ion. Thus

$$1.8 \times 10^{-5} = \frac{[H^+][C_2H_3O_2^-]}{[HC_2H_3O_2]}$$

$$= \frac{y(0.40)}{(0.10)}$$

$$y = 4.5 \times 10^{-6} M$$

We can see, from the value obtained for y, that the approximations applied to $[C_2H_3O_2^-]$ and $[HC_2H_3O_2]$ are warranted. To two significant figures, the equilibrium concentrations are

$$[H^+] = 4.5 \times 10^{-6} M$$

$$[C_2H_3O_2^-] = 0.40 M$$

$$[HC_2H_3O_2] = 0.10 M$$

The hydroxides of most metals are either strong electrolytes or slightly soluble compounds. There are some water-soluble compounds, however, that produce alkaline solutions in which equilibria exist between molecules and ions. The most important such compound is ammonia, and the chemical equation for the reversible reaction is

$$H_2O + NH_3 \rightleftharpoons NH_4^+ + OH^-$$

The expression for the equilibrium constant for this reaction

$$K' = \frac{[NH_4^+][OH^-]}{[NH_3][H_2O]}$$

simplifies to the following if the concentration of water is assumed to be a constant,

$$K = K'[H_2O] = \frac{[NH_4^+][OH^-]}{[NH_3]}$$

Formerly it was assumed that ammonia gas dissolves in water to produce ammonium hydroxide molecules, NH_4OH, and that these molecules dissociate into NH_4^+ and OH^- ions. Currently, however, the existence of such ammonium hydroxide molecules is questioned. Considerable experimental evidence suggests that in aqueous solutions of ammonia, each NH_3 molecule is hydrogen bonded to several H_2O molecules; if NH_4OH molecules exist at all in such solutions, they constitute a minor component. The ammonia equilibrium, therefore, is probably best represented in the manner employed in the preceding equation.

Table 16.2

Ionization Constants at 25°C

	Weak Acids		
acetic	$HC_2H_3O_2$	$\rightleftharpoons$ $H^+ + C_2H_3O_2^-$	1.8×10^{-5}
benzoic	$HC_7H_5O_2$	$\rightleftharpoons$ $H^+ + C_7H_5O_2^-$	6.0×10^{-5}
chlorous	$HClO_2$	$\rightleftharpoons$ $H^+ + ClO_2^-$	1.1×10^{-2}
cyanic	$HOCN$	$\rightleftharpoons$ $H^+ + OCN^-$	1.2×10^{-4}
formic	$HCHO_2$	$\rightleftharpoons$ $H^+ + CHO_2^-$	1.8×10^{-4}
hydrazoic	HN_3	$\rightleftharpoons$ $H^+ + N_3^-$	1.9×10^{-5}
hydrocyanic	HCN	$\rightleftharpoons$ $H^+ + CN^-$	4.0×10^{-10}
hydrofluoric	HF	$\rightleftharpoons$ $H^+ + F^-$	6.7×10^{-4}
hypobromous	$HOBr$	$\rightleftharpoons$ $H^+ + BrO^-$	2.1×10^{-9}
hypochlorous	$HOCl$	$\rightleftharpoons$ $H^+ + ClO^-$	3.2×10^{-8}
nitrous	HNO_2	$\rightleftharpoons$ $H^+ + NO_2^-$	4.5×10^{-4}

	Weak Bases		
ammonia	$NH_3 + H_2O$	$\rightleftharpoons$ $NH_4^+ + OH^-$	1.8×10^{-5}
aniline	$C_6H_5NH_2 + H_2O$	$\rightleftharpoons$ $C_6H_5NH_3^+ + OH^-$	4.6×10^{-10}
dimethylamine	$(CH_3)_2NH + H_2O$	$\rightleftharpoons$ $(CH_3)_3NH_2^+ + OH^-$	7.4×10^{-4}
hydrazine	$N_2H_4 + H_2O$	$\rightleftharpoons$ $N_2H_5^+ + OH^-$	9.8×10^{-7}
methylamine	$CH_3NH_2 + H_2O$	$\rightleftharpoons$ $CH_3NH_3^+ + OH^-$	5.0×10^{-4}
pyridine	$C_5H_5N + H_2O$	$\rightleftharpoons$ $C_5H_5NH^+ + OH^-$	1.5×10^{-9}
trimethylamine	$(CH_3)_3N + H_2O$	$\rightleftharpoons$ $(CH_3)_3NH^+ + OH^-$	7.4×10^{-5}

Table 16.2 lists the ionization constants of some weak acids and some weak bases. Since the terms for the ion concentrations appear in the numerator of the ionization-constant expression, the magnitude of the value of K gives a qualitative idea of the strength of the electrolyte. Thus HOCN ($K = 1.2 \times 10^{-4}$) is a stronger acid than HCN ($K = 4.0 \times 10^{-10}$). The relative acidity of solutions of the two acids, however, must be found by comparing the concentrations of hydrogen ion in the solutions and not by comparing the equilibrium constants.

▶ **EXAMPLE 16.4** Compare the acidity of $0.10M$ HOCN with the acidity of $0.10M$ HCN.

Solution Let x equal the concentration of hydrogen ion in $0.10M$ HOCN and y equal the concentration of hydrogen ion in $0.10M$ HCN.

$$HOCN \rightleftharpoons H^+ + OCN^-$$
$$\underset{0.10M}{} \quad \underset{(x)M}{} \quad \underset{(x)M}{}$$

$$HCN \rightleftharpoons H^+ + CN^-$$
$$\underset{0.10M}{} \quad \underset{(y)M}{} \quad \underset{(y)M}{}$$

$$1.2 \times 10^{-4} = \frac{[H^+][OCN^-]}{[HOCN]}$$

$$4.0 \times 10^{-10} = \frac{[H^+][CN^-]}{[HCN]}$$

$$= \frac{x^2}{0.10}$$

$$= \frac{y^2}{0.10}$$

$$x = \sqrt{1.2 \times 10^{-4}(0.10)}$$

$$y = \sqrt{4.0 \times 10^{-10}(0.10)}$$

$$\frac{\text{acidity } 0.10M \text{ HOCN}}{\text{acidity } 0.10M \text{ HCN}} = \frac{x}{y} = \frac{\sqrt{1.2 \times 10^{-4}(0.10)}}{\sqrt{4.0 \times 10^{-10}(0.10)}}$$

$$= \sqrt{0.30 \times 10^6}$$

$$= 5.5 \times 10^2$$

The solution of HOCN is 550 times more acidic than the solution of HCN.

16.2 The Ionization of Water

Pure water is itself a very weak electrolyte and ionizes according to the equation

$$H_2O + H_2O \rightleftharpoons H_3O^+ + OH^-$$

In simplified form, this is

$$H_2O \rightleftharpoons H^+ + OH^-$$

The expression for the ionization constant derived from this equation is

$$K = \frac{[H^+][OH^-]}{[H_2O]}$$

In dilute solutions, the concentration of water is virtually a constant, and we may combine $[H_2O]$ with the constant K. Thus

$$K[H_2O] = [H^+][OH^-]$$

This constant, $K[H_2O]$, is called the ion product of water, or the water constant, and is given the symbol K_w. At 25°C,

$$K_w = 1.0 \times 10^{-14} = [H^+][OH^-]$$

In pure water,

$$[H^+] = [OH^-] = x$$

$$[H^+][OH^-] = 1.0 \times 10^{-14}$$

$$x^2 = 1.0 \times 10^{-14}$$

$$x = 1.0 \times 10^{-7} M$$

Thus the concentrations of both of the ions of water are equal to $1.0 \times 10^{-7} M$ in pure water or in any neutral solution at 25°C. Hence, in 1 liter, only 10^{-7} mole of water is in ionic form out of a total of approximately 55.5 moles.

In any aqueous solution, both hydronium and hydroxide ions exist. In an acid solution, the concentration of hydronium ions is larger than $1.0 \times 10^{-7} M$ and larger than the hydroxide ion concentration. In an alkaline solution, the hydroxide ion concentration is larger than $1.0 \times 10^{-7} M$ and larger than the hydronium ion concentration.

▶ **EXAMPLE 16.5** What are $[H^+]$ and $[OH^-]$ in a $0.020M$ solution of HCl?

Solution   The quantity of hydronium ion obtained from the ionization of water is negligible compared to that derived from the hydrochloric acid. Furthermore, since HCl is a strong electrolyte, $[H^+] = 0.020M$.

$$[H^+][OH^-] = 1.0 \times 10^{-14}$$

$$(2.0 \times 10^{-2})[OH^-] = 1.0 \times 10^{-14}$$

$$[OH^-] = \frac{1.0 \times 10^{-14}}{2.0 \times 10^{-2}}$$

$$[OH^-] = 5.0 \times 10^{-13} M$$

Thus there are hydroxide ions present in this acidic solution. Notice, however, that $[OH^-]$ is extremely small; in this solution, there would be one hydroxide ion for every 40 billion hydronium ions.

▶ **EXAMPLE 16.6** What are $[H^+]$ and $[OH^-]$ in a $0.0050M$ solution of NaOH?

Solution   Sodium hydroxide is a strong electrolyte, and therefore $[OH^-] = 5.0 \times 10^{-3} M$.

$$[H^+][OH^-] = 1.0 \times 10^{-14}$$

$$[H^+](5.0 \times 10^{-3}) = 1.0 \times 10^{-14}$$

$$[H^+] = \frac{1.0 \times 10^{-14}}{5.0 \times 10^{-3}}$$

$$[H^+] = 2.0 \times 10^{-12} M$$

16.3 pH (potency of Hydrogen)

A convenient method for expressing the hydronium ion concentration of a solution is in terms of the pH scale. The **pH** of a solution may be defined as the logarithm of the reciprocal of the hydronium ion concentration. Since the logarithm of 1 is 0, pH may also be defined as the negative logarithm of the hydronium ion concentration. Thus

$$pH = \log \left(\frac{1}{[H^+]} \right) = -\log [H^+]$$

or

$$[H^+] = 10^{-pH} = \text{antilog} \, (-pH)$$

For a neutral solution, therefore,

$$[H^+] = 1.0 \times 10^{-7}$$

$$pH = -\log (10^{-7}) = -(-7)$$

$$pH = 7$$

For a 0.001M solution of HCl,

$$[H^+] = 1 \times 10^{-3}$$

$$pH = -\log (10^{-3}) = 3$$

We can define **pOH** in the same terms—as the negative logarithm of the hydroxide ion concentration. Such values generally are not quoted; the pH value of a solution is used to define the acidity or alkalinity of the solution. However, it is frequently convenient to use pOH's in calculations involving alkaline solutions or solutions for which the hydroxide ion concentration is known. The water constant is

$$[H^+][OH^-] = 10^{-14}$$

By taking the logarithm of each term and multiplying through by -1, we find

$$-\log[H^+] - \log[OH^-] = -\log(10^{-14})$$

or

$$pH + pOH = 14$$

Thus for a 0.01 M solution of NaOH, the pOH is 2. Since the sum of the pH and the pOH equals 14, the pH of this solution is 12.

▶ **EXAMPLE 16.7**   What is the pH of a solution $0.050M$ in H^+?

Solution

$$[H^+] = 5.0 \times 10^{-2}$$

$$\log[H^+] = \log 5.0 + \log 10^{-2}$$

$$= 0.7 - 2.0 = -1.3$$

$$pH = 1.3$$

▶ **EXAMPLE 16.8**   What is the pH of a solution for which $[OH^-] = 0.15M$?

Solution

$$[OH^-] = 1.5 \times 10^{-1}$$

$$\log[OH^-] = \log 1.5 + \log 10^{-1}$$

$$= 0.2 - 1.0 = -0.8$$

$$pOH = 0.8$$

$$pH = 13.2$$

An alternative solution is

$$[H^+][OH^-] = 1.0 \times 10^{-14}$$

$$[H^+] = \frac{1.0 \times 10^{-14}}{1.5 \times 10^{-1}} = 6.7 \times 10^{-14}$$

$$\log[H^+] = \log 6.7 + \log 10^{-14}$$

$$= 0.8 - 14.0 = -13.2$$

$$pH = 13.2$$

▶ **EXAMPLE 16.9**   What is the $[H^+]$ of a solution with a pH of 10.6?

Solution

$$\log[H^+] = -10.6 = 0.4 - 11.0$$

$$[H^+] = \text{antilog } 0.4 \times \text{antilog}(-11)$$

$$[H^+] = 2.5 \times 10^{-11}$$

It should be kept in mind that pH relates to a power of 10. Hence, a solution of pH $= 1$ has a hydronium ion concentration 100 times that of a solution of pH $= 3$ (not three times). Furthermore, since the pH is related to a *negative* exponent, the lower the pH value, the larger the concentration of hydronium ion. At pH $= 7$, a solution is neutral. Solutions with pH's below 7 are acidic; those with pH's above 7 are alkaline. These relationships are summarized in Table 16.3.

Table 16.3

The pH Scale

pH	$[H^+]$	$[OH^-]$	
14	10^{-14}	10^0	
13	10^{-13}	10^{-1}	
12	10^{-12}	10^{-2}	
11	10^{-11}	10^{-3}	increasing
10	10^{-10}	10^{-4}	alkalinity
9	10^{-9}	10^{-5}	
8	10^{-8}	10^{-6}	
7	10^{-7}	10^{-7}	neutrality
6	10^{-6}	10^{-8}	
5	10^{-5}	10^{-9}	
4	10^{-4}	10^{-10}	
3	10^{-3}	10^{-11}	increasing
2	10^{-2}	10^{-12}	acidity
1	10^{-1}	10^{-13}	
0	10^0	10^{-14}	

16.4 Determination of pH

Potentiometric methods are commonly employed for pH determination. Since the emf of a cell is dependent upon activities and not concentrations, we redefine pH as the negative logarithm of the activity of the hydronium ion concentration. However, this redefinition introduces a problem since it is experimentally impossible to determine activities of single ions, and, as we shall see, it is necessary to introduce an assumption into the treatment.

The following cell might be used for the determination of pH's

$$Pt|H_2(1 \text{ atm})|H^+(a = ?)\|Cl^-(1N)|Hg_2Cl_2(s)|Hg$$

This cell is diagramed in Figure 16.1. The left-hand electrode is a hydrogen electrode (Section 10.8) in which the electrolyte is the solution being studied. This electrode is connected by means of a salt bridge to a normal calomel electrode. The calomel electrode utilizes, as the electrolyte, a normal solution of potassium chloride which is saturated with mercurous chloride (Hg_2Cl_2); the electrode proper consists of mercury metal, at the bottom of the tube, overlayed with a paste of mercurous chloride (calomel) and mercury.

Figure 16.1 Hydrogen electrode and normal calomel electrode.

The half reactions for the cell are:

$$H_2(g) \longrightarrow 2H^+(aq) + 2e^-$$

$$2e^- + Hg_2Cl_2(s) \longrightarrow 2Hg(l) + 2Cl^-(aq)$$

and the corresponding net chemical change is

$$H_2(g) + Hg_2Cl_2(s) \longrightarrow 2H^+(aq) + 2Cl^-(aq) + 2Hg(l)$$

The cell is not thermodynamically reversible (Section 10.7). When the cell is discharging, $H^+(aq)$ ions leave the test solution and enter the salt bridge, and Cl^- ions leave the salt bridge and enter the test solution. When the operation of the cell is reversed, K^+ ions enter the test solution from the salt bridge, and ions from the test solution (not necessarily Cl^- ions) enter the salt bridge. Hence, there is an indeterminable liquid-junction potential at the salt bridge. The dependence of the emf of the cell upon the activities of the species present may be expressed by adapting the Nernst equation (Section 10.9),

$$\mathscr{E} = \mathscr{E}^\circ - \frac{0.05916}{2} \log \left(\frac{(a_{H^+})^2 (a_{Cl^-})^{-2}}{(a_{H_2})} \right) + \mathscr{E}_{\text{liquid junction}}$$

Upon expansion, this becomes

$$\mathscr{E} = \mathscr{E}^\circ + \frac{0.05916}{2} \log(a_{H_2}) - 0.05916 \log(a_{Cl^-}) + \mathscr{E}_{\text{liquid junction}} - 0.05916 \log(a_{H^+})$$

We shall assume that the pressure of H_2 gas is maintained at 1 atm, that the salt bridge is effective in maintaining a constant Cl^- ion concentration in the calomel electrode, and that the liquid-junction potential is a constant value that is negligibly small. Hence, the first four terms of the expression for the emf of the cell may be combined into an experimentally determined constant, $\mathscr{E}'$.

$$\mathscr{E} = \mathscr{E}' - 0.05916 \log(a_{H^+})$$

For the normal calomel electrode in air at 25°C, $\mathscr{E}'$ is 0.2825 v.[1] Therefore,

$$\mathscr{E} = 0.2825 + 0.05916(\text{pH})$$

$$\text{pH} = \frac{\mathscr{E} - 0.2825}{0.05916}$$

This expression may be regarded as an operational definition of pH. For problem work, we shall use pH's based on concentrations and activities interchangeably, since the activities of $H^+(aq)$ approximate the concentrations of $H^+(aq)$ in dilute solutions.

In place of the hydrogen electrode, a glass electrode is usually employed for the determination of pH's. The hydrogen electrode is easily poisoned and requires the use of gaseous hydrogen. A glass electrode consists of a reference electrode containing a solution of known pH sealed in a membrane of special glass. In the determination of the pH of a solution, the glass electrode and another reference electrode are immersed in the solution being studied.

The emf of the complete cell depends upon the difference in potential across the glass membrane that separates solutions of different pH's and is found to respond to changes in pH in the same way that an assembly using a hydrogen electrode does. The value of $\mathscr{E}'$ for a cell using a glass electrode depends upon the electrode used in the construction of the glass electrode as well as the other reference electrode employed in the complete cell. Instruments known as pH meters employ glass electrodes and are usually calibrated in pH units rather than volts; such instruments are standardized with solutions of known pH.

---

[1] In the absence of air, the normal potassium chloride-calomel electrode has an $\mathscr{E}'$ of 0.2812 v. Frequently, a saturated solution of KCl is employed; the generally accepted value of $\mathscr{E}'$ for such an electrode is 0.2415 v.

▶ **EXAMPLE 16.10**   For a cell containing a solution of unknown pH and utilizing a hydrogen electrode and a normal calomel electrode, the potential is 0.608 v at 25°C. Calculate the pH of the solution and the approximate concentration of H^+ (aq).

Solution

$$pH = \frac{\mathscr{E} - 0.283}{0.0592}$$

$$= \frac{0.608 - 0.283}{0.0592}$$

$$pH = 5.5$$

$$\log[H^+] = -5.5 = 0.5 - 6.0$$

$$[H^+] = 3.1 \times 10^{-6}M$$

An approximate value of the ionization constant of a weak acid or a weak base may be determined by measuring the pH of a solution of known concentration of the weak electrolyte. A more exact method for the determination of ionization constants based on pH determinations is described in Section 17.7.

▶ **EXAMPLE 16.11**   The pH of a $0.10M$ solution of a weak base, B, is 10.6. What is the ionization constant of B?

Solution

$$\log[H^+] = -10.6 = 0.4 - 11.0$$

$$[H^+] = 2.5 \times 10^{-11}$$

$$[OH^-] = \frac{1.0 \times 10^{-14}}{2.5 \times 10^{-11}} = 4.0 \times 10^{-4}M$$

Since the solution was prepared from the base alone,

$$[BH^+] = [OH^-] = 4.0 \times 10^{-4}M$$

The concentration of B in the solution is, for all practical purposes, equal to $0.10M$; the small quantity of B dissociated need not be considered. Thus the equilibrium concentrations are

$$\underset{0.10M}{B} + H_2O \rightleftharpoons \underset{4.0 \times 10^{-4}M}{BH^+} + \underset{4.0 \times 10^{-4}M}{OH^-}$$

The value of the ionization constant is

$$K = \frac{[BH^+][OH^-]}{[B]}$$

$$= \frac{(4.0 \times 10^{-4})^2}{1.0 \times 10^{-1}} = \frac{16 \times 10^{-8}}{1.0 \times 10^{-1}}$$

$$K = 1.6 \times 10^{-6}$$

16.5 Indicators

Indicators are colored, organic compounds of complex structure that change color in solution as the pH of the solution changes. For example, methyl orange is red in solutions of pH below 3.1 and yellow in solutions of pH above 4.5; the color of this indicator is a varying mixture of yellow and red in the pH range between 3.1 and 4.5. Many indicators have been described and used; a few are listed in Table 16.4.

Table 16.4

Some Indicators

Indicator	Acid Color	pH Range of Color Change	Alkaline Color
thymol blue	red	1.2–2.8	yellow
methyl orange	red	3.1–4.5	yellow
bromcresol green	yellow	3.8–5.5	blue
methyl red	red	4.2–6.3	yellow
litmus	red	5.0–8.0	blue
bromthymol blue	yellow	6.0–7.6	blue
thymol blue	yellow	8.0–9.6	blue
phenolphthalein	colorless	8.3–10.0	red
alizarin yellow	yellow	10.0–12.1	lavender

By the use of indicators, one may determine the pH of a solution. If thymol blue is yellow in a test solution and methyl orange is red in another sample of the same solution, the pH of the solution is between 2.8 and 3.1. Reference to Table 16.4 shows that thymol blue is yellow only in solutions of pH greater than 2.8, and methyl orange is red only in solutions of pH less than 3.1. If enough indicators are employed, it is possible to determine pH values that are accurate to the first decimal place; potentiometric measurements of pH's are, however, more accurate.

Indicators are weak acids or weak bases. Since they are intensely colored, only a few drops of a dilute solution of an indicator need be employed in any determination; hence, the acidity of the solution in question is not significantly altered by the addition of the indicator.

If we let the symbol HIn stand for the litmus molecule (which is red) and the symbol In^- stand for the anion (which is blue) derived from the weak acid, the equation for the litmus equilibrium may be written

$$\underset{\text{red}}{HIn} \rightleftharpoons \underset{\text{blue}}{H^+ + In^-}$$

According to the principle of Le Chatelier, increasing the concentration of H^+ shifts the equilibrium to the left, and the red (or acid) color of HIn is observed. On the other hand, addition of OH^- decreases the concentration of H^+; the equilibrium shifts to the right, and the blue (or alkaline) color of In^- is observed.

The ionization constant for litmus is approximately equal to 10^{-7}.

$$10^{-7} = \frac{[H^+][In^-]}{[HIn]}$$

We may rearrange this expression in the following manner

$$\frac{10^{-7}}{[H^+]} = \frac{[In^-]}{[HIn]}$$

At a pH of 5 or below, the red color of litmus is observed. If we substitute $[H^+] = 10^{-5}$, which corresponds to pH = 5, into the preceding expression, we get

$$\frac{10^{-7}}{10^{-5}} = \frac{1}{100} = \frac{[In^-] \longleftarrow \text{blue}}{[HIn] \longleftarrow \text{red}}$$

Thus, the mixture appears red to the eye when the concentration of the red HIn is 100 times (or more) that of the blue In^-.

The blue color of litmus is observed in solutions of pH = 8 or higher. If $[H^+] = 10^{-8}$, then

$$\frac{10^{-7}}{10^{-8}} = \frac{10}{1} = \frac{[In^-] \longleftarrow \text{blue}}{[HIn] \longleftarrow \text{red}}$$

When the concentration of the blue In^- ion is 10 times that of the red HIn, or approximately 91% of the indicator is in ionic form, the blue color of the In^- ions completely masks the red color of the HIn molecules, and the mixture appears blue.

Thus the blue color predominates when the concentration of the blue species is 10 times that of the red, whereas the red color predominates only when the concentration of the red form is 100 times that of the blue. This is not surprising, since the blue color of litmus is a much stronger color than the red. Only when $[H^+] = K = 10^{-7}$ will the factor $K/[H^+] = 1$ and $[In^-] = [HIn]$. Hence, at pH $= 7$, litmus exhibits its "neutral" color (purple).

Therefore the pH range over which a given indicator changes color depends upon the ionization constant of the indicator. For indicators that are weak acids, the smaller the value of K, the higher is the pH range of the color change.

▶ **EXAMPLE 16.12** An indicator is a weak acid and the pH range of its color change is 3.1 to 4.5. If the neutral point of the indicator is in the center of this pH range, what is the ionization constant of the indicator.

Solution The center of the range may *not* be calculated by averaging the pH values, since pH's are exponential in form. We may find the center of the range by averaging the corresponding concentrations of H^+, however.

$$pH = 3.1$$

$$\log[H^+] = -3.1 = 0.9 - 4.0$$

$$[H^+] = 7.9 \times 10^{-4}$$

$$pH = 4.5$$

$$\log[H^+] = -4.5 = 0.5 - 5.0$$

$$[H^+] = 3.2 \times 10^{-5}$$

To average these two hydronium ion concentrations, we must express both to the same power of 10. Thus

$$\frac{79.0 \times 10^{-5} + 3.2 \times 10^{-5}}{2} = 4.1 \times 10^{-4}$$

When $[H^+] = 4.1 \times 10^{-4}M$, $K = [H^+]$. Therefore

$$K = 4.1 \times 10^{-4}$$

16.6 The Common-Ion Effect

In a $0.1M$ solution of acetic acid, methyl orange assumes its acid color, red. If sodium acetate is added to this solution, the color changes to yellow, showing that the addition causes the acidity of the solution to decrease. This experimental observation is readily explained on the basis of Le Chatelier's principle. The equilibrium

$$HC_2H_3O_2 \rightleftharpoons H^+ + C_2H_3O_2^-$$

is shifted to the left by the addition of the acetate ion from the sodium acetate, and the concentration of hydronium ion correspondingly decreases. Since acetic acid and sodium acetate have the acetate ion in common, this phenomenon is called the **common-ion effect.**

The concentration of hydronium ion in a solution of acetic acid to which acetate ion has been added can be calculated by means of the ionization constant of acetic acid.

▶ **EXAMPLE 16.13**   What is the concentration of hydronium ion in a $0.10M$ solution of acetic acid that has been made $0.15M$ in sodium acetate?

Solution   Sodium acetate is a strong electrolyte; the concentration of acetate ion derived from this source is, therefore, $0.15M$. In a $0.10M$ solution of pure acetic acid $[H^+] = [C_2H_3O_2^-] = 0.00134M$ (Table 16.1). In a $0.10M$ solution of acetic acid to which sodium acetate has been added, the concentration of acetate ion derived from the ionization of acetic acid is much less than $0.00134M$ because of the common-ion effect. Therefore the concentration of acetate ion may be regarded as $0.15M$ and the contribution from acetic acid ignored. Likewise, the concentration of acetic acid may be taken as equal to the total concentration of acetic acid present, $0.10M$, since such a small amount of the acetic acid is ionized. Thus

$$\underset{0.10M}{HC_2H_3O_2} \rightleftharpoons \underset{(x)M}{H^+} + \underset{0.15M}{C_2H_3O_2^-}$$

$$1.8 \times 10^{-5} = \frac{[H^+][C_2H_3O_2^-]}{[HC_2H_3O_2]}$$

$$= \frac{[H^+](0.15)}{(0.10)}$$

$$[H^+] = 1.2 \times 10^{-5}M$$

Therefore, when a $0.10M$ solution of acetic acid is made $0.15M$ in sodium acetate, the concentration of hydronium ion is reduced from $1.3 \times 10^{-3}M$ to $1.2 \times 10^{-5}M$.

▶ **EXAMPLE 16.14**   What is the concentration of hydroxide ions in a solution made by dissolving 0.020 mole of ammonium chloride in 100 ml of $0.15M$ ammonia? Assume that the addition of the solid does not cause the volume of the solution to change.

Solution   Ammonium chloride is a strong electrolyte. The concentration of NH_4^+ from the NH_4Cl added is

$$? \text{ moles } NH_4^+ = 1000 \text{ ml soln.} \left(\frac{0.020 \text{ mole } NH_4^+}{100 \text{ ml soln.}} \right) = 0.20 \text{ mole } NH_4^+$$

Therefore,

$$\underset{0.15M}{NH_3 + H_2O} \rightleftharpoons \underset{0.20M}{NH_4^+} + \underset{(x)M}{OH^-}$$

$$1.8 \times 10^{-5} = \frac{[NH_4^+][OH^-]}{[NH_3]}$$

$$= \frac{(0.20)[OH^-]}{(0.15)}$$

$$[OH^-] = 1.4 \times 10^{-5}M$$

16.7   Buffers

It is sometimes necessary that a solution of definite pH be prepared and stored. The preservation of such a solution is even more difficult than its preparation. If the solution comes in contact with the air, it will absorb carbon dioxide (an acid anhydride) and become more acidic. If the solution is stored in a glass bottle, alkaline impurities leached from the glass may alter the pH. **Buffer solutions** are capable of maintaining their pH at some fairly constant value even when small amounts of acid or base are added.

A buffer may be prepared from a weak acid or a weak base and a salt of the weak electrolyte. For example, a buffer can be prepared from acetic acid and sodium acetate. If both these materials are present in the same concentration, for example, $1.00M$, then

$$1.8 \times 10^{-5} = \frac{[H^+][C_2H_3O_2^-]}{[HC_2H_3O_2]}$$

$$[H^+] = 1.8 \times 10^{-5} \left(\frac{[HC_2H_3O_2]}{[C_2H_3O_2^-]} \right) = 1.8 \times 10^{-5}M$$

$$pH = -\log(1.8 \times 10^{-5}) = 4.7$$

the pK of a weak electrolyte may be defined in a manner analogous to pH or pOH,

$$pK = -\log K$$

A solution of a weak acid in which the concentration of the anion is the same as the concentration of the undissociated acid has a pH equal to the pK of the acid.

In a sample of the buffer previously described, the quantities of acetic acid molecules and acetate ion are much larger than the quantity of hydronium ion present—approximately 50,000 times larger.

$$\text{HC}_2\text{H}_3\text{O}_2 \; \rightleftharpoons \; \underset{1.8 \times 10^{-5}M}{\text{H}^+} + \underset{1.0M}{\text{C}_2\text{H}_3\text{O}_2^-}$$

$$\underset{1.0M}{}$$

If a small quantity of hydronium ion is added, the large reservoir of acetate ion will quickly convert it to acetic acid. If a small amount of hydroxide ion is added to the buffer, it will neutralize hydronium ion, but the large quantity of acetic acid present will, by dissociation, replace any hydronium ion removed and maintain the pH at a fairly constant value.

The action of buffers may be interpreted in terms of the Brønsted concept. Thus an acetic acid-acetate buffer

$$\overset{\text{Acid}_1}{\text{HC}_2\text{H}_3\text{O}_2} + \overset{\text{Base}_2}{\text{H}_2\text{O}} \; \rightleftharpoons \; \overset{\text{Acid}_2}{\text{H}_3\text{O}^+} + \overset{\text{Base}_1}{\text{C}_2\text{H}_3\text{O}_2^-}$$

effectively neutralizes small additions of hydronium ion because of the presence of a relatively large concentration of the base $\text{C}_2\text{H}_3\text{O}_2^-$. Similarly, small additions of hydroxide ion are effectively neutralized by the acid $\text{HC}_2\text{H}_3\text{O}_2$ which is present in relatively large concentration. In either instance, the change in the pH of the solution brought about by the addition is slight.

Buffers are not called upon to withstand the addition of large amounts of acids or alkalies. The addition of 0.01 mole per liter of H^+ or OH^- is about the maximum shock that any buffer can be expected to withstand. How successfully a buffer withstands such an addition is illustrated in the following example.

▶ **EXAMPLE 16.15** The ionization constant of acetic acid to three significant figures is 1.81×10^{-5}. A buffer containing $1.00M$ concentrations of acetic acid and sodium acetate has a pH of 4.74. (a) What is the pH of the solution after 0.0100 mole of HCl has been added to 1 liter of the buffer? (b) What is the pH of the solution after the addition of 0.0100 mole/liter of NaOH?

Solution (a) The 0.0100 mole/liter of H^+ converts an equivalent amount of acetate ion into acetic acid. Thus the concentrations are

$$\text{HC}_2\text{H}_3\text{O}_2 \; \rightleftharpoons \; \text{H}^+ + \text{C}_2\text{H}_3\text{O}_2^-$$

	$\text{HC}_2\text{H}_3\text{O}_2$	H^+	$\text{C}_2\text{H}_3\text{O}_2^-$
buffer:	$1.00M$	1.81×10^{-5}	$1.00M$
after H^+ addition:	$1.01M$	?	$0.99M$

$$\frac{[\text{H}^+][\text{C}_2\text{H}_3\text{O}_2^-]}{[\text{HC}_2\text{H}_3\text{O}_2]} = 1.81 \times 10^{-5}$$

$$\frac{[\text{H}^+](0.99)}{(1.01)} = 1.81 \times 10^{-5}$$

$$[\text{H}^+] = 1.81 \times 10^{-5} \frac{(1.01)}{(0.99)}$$

$$= 1.85 \times 10^{-5}M$$

$$\text{pH} = 4.73$$

Thus the addition causes the pH to change 0.01 pH units. A similar addition to pure water would change the pH from 7.0 to 2.0—a change of 5.0 pH units.

(b) The addition of 0.0100 mole of OH^- would change the concentration of acetate ion to $1.01M$ and the concentration of acetic acid to $0.99M$. Thus

$$\frac{[H^+][C_2H_3O_2^-]}{[HC_2H_3O_2]} = 1.81 \times 10^{-5}$$

$$\frac{[H^+](1.01)}{(0.99)} = 1.81 \times 10^{-5}$$

$$[H^+] = 1.81 \times 10^{-5}\frac{(0.99)}{(1.01)}$$

$$= 1.77 \times 10^{-5}M$$

$$pH = 4.75$$

A similar addition to water would have caused the pH to rise from 7.0 to 12.0.

Alkaline buffers may also be prepared. If the base and its derived ion are present in equal concentrations,

$$pOH = pK$$

$$pH = 14.0 - pK$$

A solution with $[NH_3] = 0.10M$ and $[NH_4^+] = 0.10M$ is an example of this type of buffer.

$$\underset{0.10M}{NH_3 + H_2O} \rightleftharpoons \underset{0.10M}{NH_4^+} + \underset{?}{OH^-}$$

$$\frac{[NH_4^+][OH^-]}{[NH_3]} = 1.8 \times 10^{-5}$$

$$[OH^-] = 1.8 \times 10^{-5}M$$

$$pOH = 4.7$$

$$pH = 9.3$$

Buffers may also be prepared in which the ratio of the concentration of weak electrolyte to the concentration of common ion is not $1 : 1$; this technique may be used to obtain a buffer that has a pH (or pOH) different from the pK of the weak acid (or base). Let us assume that a buffer is to be prepared from a hypothetical weak acid, HA,

$$HA \rightleftharpoons H^+ + A^-$$

for which

$$\frac{[H^+][A^-]}{[HA]} = K$$

The concentration of hydronium ion is

$$[H^+] = \frac{K[HA]}{[A^-]}$$

Taking the negative logarithm of each term, we get

$$-\log[H] = -\log K - \log\left(\frac{[HA]}{[A^-]}\right)$$

or

$$pH = pK - \log\left(\frac{[HA]}{[A^-]}\right)$$

In general, for an effective buffer, the ratio of the concentration of the molecular species to the concentration of the ionic species should be between 1/10 and 10/1. This concentration range is equivalent to the following pH range.

$$pH = pK - \log\left(\frac{1}{10}\right) = pK - \log 10^{-1}$$

$$= pK + 1$$

$$pH = pK - \log\left(\frac{10}{1}\right)$$

$$= pK - 1$$

Therefore an efficient buffer may be prepared from acetic acid ($pK = 4.7$) having any desired pH between 3.7 and 5.7.

The use of buffers is an important part of many industrial processes; examples are electroplating and the manufacture of leather, photographic materials, and dyes. In bacteriological research, culture media are generally buffered to maintain the pH required for the growth of the bacteria being studied. Buffers are used extensively in analytical chemistry and are used to calibrate pH meters. Human blood is buffered to a pH of 7.4 by means of bicarbonate, phosphate, and complex protein systems.

▶ **EXAMPLE 16.16** What concentrations should be used to prepare a cyanic acid–cyanate buffer of pH = 3.50?

Solution

$$pH = 3.50$$

$$\log[H^+] = -3.50 = 0.50 - 4.00$$

$$[H^+] = 3.1 \times 10^{-4} M$$

$$HOCN \rightleftharpoons H^+ + OCN^-$$

$$1.2 \times 10^{-4} = \frac{[H^+][OCN^-]}{[HOCN]}$$

$$= \frac{3.1 \times 10^{-4}[OCN^-]}{[HOCN]}$$

$$\frac{[HOCN]}{[OCN^-]} = \frac{3.1 \times 10^{-4}}{1.2 \times 10^{-4}}$$

$$\frac{[HOCN]}{[OCN^-]} = 2.6$$

Any solution in which $[HOCN]/[OCN^-]$ is 2.6 will have a pH of 3.5. For example, if $[HOCN] = 0.26M$, $[OCN^-]$ must be $0.10M$; or if $[HOCN] = 0.52M$, $[OCN^-] = 0.20M$.

An alternative solution of the problem utilizes the relationship

$$pH = pK - \log\frac{[HOCN]}{[OCN^-]}$$

$$3.50 = 3.92 - \log\frac{[HOCN]}{[OCN^-]}$$

$$\log\frac{[HOCN]}{[OCN^-]} = 0.42$$

$$\frac{[HOCN]}{[OCN^-]} = 2.6$$

▶ **EXAMPLE 16.17**   What is the pH of a solution made by mixing 100 ml of $0.15M$ HCl and 200 ml of $0.20M$ aniline $(C_6H_5NH_2)$? Assume that the volume of the final solution is 300 ml.

Solution   The number of moles of HCl used and the number of moles of aniline used are

$$? \text{ moles HCl} = 100 \text{ ml soln.} \left(\frac{0.15 \text{ mole HCl}}{1000 \text{ ml soln.}}\right) = 0.015 \text{ mole HCl}$$

$$? \text{ moles aniline} = 200 \text{ ml soln.} \left(\frac{0.20 \text{ mole aniline}}{1000 \text{ ml soln.}}\right) = 0.040 \text{ mole aniline}$$

One mole of aniline reacts with 1 mole of H^+. Thus

	$C_6H_5NH_2$	+	H^+	$\longrightarrow$	$C_6H_5NH_3^+$
before reaction:	0.040 mole		0.015 mole		—
after reaction: ′	0.025 mole		—		0.015 mole

The molar concentrations in the final solution are

$$? \text{ moles } C_6H_5NH_3{}^+ = 1000 \text{ ml soln.} \left(\frac{0.015 \text{ mole } C_6H_5NH_3{}^+}{300 \text{ ml soln.}} \right)$$

$$= 0.050 \text{ mole } C_6H_5NH_3{}^+$$

$$? \text{ moles } C_6H_5NH_2 = 1000 \text{ ml soln.} \left(\frac{0.025 \text{ mole } C_6H_5NH_2}{300 \text{ ml soln.}} \right)$$

$$= 0.083 \text{ mole } C_6H_5NH_2$$

Therefore the concentrations in the solution are

$$C_6H_5NH_2 + H_2O \rightleftharpoons C_6H_5NH_3{}^+ + OH^-$$
$$\underset{0.083M}{} \qquad\qquad \underset{0.050M}{} \quad \underset{?}{}$$

$$\frac{[C_6H_5NH_3{}^+][OH^-]}{[C_6H_5NH_2]} = 4.6 \times 10^{-10}$$

$$\frac{(0.050)[OH^-]}{(0.083)} = 4.6 \times 10^{-10}$$

$$[OH^-] = 7.6 \times 10^{-10} M$$

$$[H^+] = 1.3 \times 10^{-5} M$$

$$pH = 4.9$$

16.8 Polyprotic Acids

Polyprotic acids are those that contain more than one acid hydrogen per molecule; examples include sulfuric acid (H_2SO_4), oxalic acid ($H_2C_2O_4$), phosphoric acid (H_3PO_4), and arsenic acid (H_3AsO_4). Polyprotic acids ionize in a stepwise manner, and there is an ionization constant for each step. Subscripts are added to the symbol K in order to specify the step to which the constant applies.

Phosphoric acid is triprotic and ionizes in three steps.

$$H_3PO_4 \rightleftharpoons H^+ + H_2PO_4{}^- \qquad \frac{[H^+][H_2PO_4{}^-]}{[H_3PO_4]} = K_1 = 7.5 \times 10^{-3}$$

$$H_2PO_4{}^- \rightleftharpoons H^+ + HPO_4^{2-} \qquad \frac{[H^+][HPO_4^{2-}]}{[H_2PO_4{}^-]} = K_2 = 6.2 \times 10^{-8}$$

$$HPO_4^{2-} \rightleftharpoons H^+ + PO_4^{3-} \qquad \frac{[H^+][PO_4^{3-}]}{[HPO_4^{2-}]} = K_3 = 1 \times 10^{-12}$$

Thus in a solution of phosphoric acid, three equilibria occur together with the water equilibrium; H_3PO_4, $H_2PO_4^-$, HPO_4^{2-}, PO_4^{3-}, H^+, OH^-, and H_2O are present.

The ionization of phosphoric acid is typical of all polyprotic acids in that the primary ionization is stronger than the secondary, and the secondary ionization is stronger than the tertiary. This trend in the value of the ionization constant is consistent with the nature of the particle that ionizes in each step. One would predict that a proton would be released more readily by an uncharged molecule than by a uninegative ion and more readily by a uninegative ion than by a binegative ion.

No polyprotic acid is known for which all ionizations are strong. The primary ionization of sulfuric acid is essentially complete,

$$H_2SO_4 \longrightarrow H^+ + HSO_4^-$$

but the secondary ionization is weak,

$$HSO_4^- \rightleftharpoons H^+ + SO_4^{2-} \qquad \frac{[H^+][SO_4^{2-}]}{[HSO_4^-]} = K_2 = 1.3 \times 10^{-2}$$

Solutions of carbon dioxide are acidic. Carbon dioxide reacts with water to form carbonic acid, H_2CO_3; however, the reaction is not complete, and most of the carbon dioxide exists in solution as CO_2 molecules. Therefore, we shall indicate the primary ionization as follows:

$$CO_2 + H_2O \rightleftharpoons H^+ + HCO_3^- \qquad \frac{[H^+][HCO_3^-]}{[CO_2]} = K_1 = 4.2 \times 10^{-7}$$

where the symbol $[CO_2]$ is used to represent the total concentration of $CO_2(aq)$ and H_2CO_3. The second ionization step is

$$HCO_3^- \rightleftharpoons H^+ + CO_3^{2-} \qquad \frac{[H^+][CO_3^{2-}]}{[HCO_3^-]} = K_2 = 4.8 \times 10^{-11}$$

An analogous situation exists for solutions of sulfur dioxide in water. The acidity of aqueous SO_2 has been attributed to the ionization of sulfurous acid, H_2SO_3. However, H_2SO_3 has never been isolated in pure form; in solution, it apparently exists in equilibrium with $SO_2(aq)$

$$SO_2(aq) + H_2O \rightleftharpoons H_2SO_3(aq)$$

and we shall represent the primary ionization of sulfurous acid as

$$SO_2 + H_2O \rightleftharpoons H^+ + HSO_3^-$$

The ionization constants of some polyprotic acids are listed in Table 16.5.

Table 16.5

Ionization Constants of Some Polyprotic Acids at 25°C

arsenic	H_3AsO_4	$\rightleftharpoons$	$H^+ + H_2AsO_4^-$	$K_1 = 2.5 \times 10^{-4}$
	$H_2AsO_4^-$	$\rightleftharpoons$	$H^+ + HAsO_4^{2-}$	$K_2 = 5.6 \times 10^{-8}$
	$HAsO_4^{2-}$	$\rightleftharpoons$	$H^+ + AsO_4^{3-}$	$K_3 = 3 \times 10^{-13}$
carbonic	$CO_2 + H_2O$	$\rightleftharpoons$	$H^+ + HCO_3^-$	$K_1 = 4.2 \times 10^{-7}$
	HCO_3^-	$\rightleftharpoons$	$H^+ + CO_3^{2-}$	$K_2 = 4.8 \times 10^{-11}$
hydrosulfuric	H_2S	$\rightleftharpoons$	$H^+ + HS^-$	$K_1 = 1.1 \times 10^{-7}$
	HS^-	$\rightleftharpoons$	$H^+ + S^{2-}$	$K_2 = 1.0 \times 10^{-14}$
oxalic	$H_2C_2O_4$	$\rightleftharpoons$	$H^+ + HC_2O_4^-$	$K_1 = 5.9 \times 10^{-2}$
	$HC_2O_4^-$	$\rightleftharpoons$	$H^+ + C_2O_4^{2-}$	$K_2 = 6.4 \times 10^{-5}$
phosphoric	H_3PO_4	$\rightleftharpoons$	$H^+ + H_2PO_4^-$	$K_1 = 7.5 \times 10^{-3}$
	$H_2PO_4^-$	$\rightleftharpoons$	$H^+ + HPO_4^{2-}$	$K_2 = 6.2 \times 10^{-8}$
	HPO_4^{2-}	$\rightleftharpoons$	$H^+ + PO_4^{3-}$	$K_3 = 1 \times 10^{-12}$
phosphorous (diprotic)	H_3PO_3	$\rightleftharpoons$	$H^+ + H_2PO_3^-$	$K_1 = 1.6 \times 10^{-2}$
	$H_2PO_3^-$	$\rightleftharpoons$	$H^+ + HPO_3^{2-}$	$K_2 = 7 \times 10^{-7}$
sulfuric	H_2SO_4	$\longrightarrow$	$H^+ + HSO_4^-$	strong
	HSO_4^-	$\rightleftharpoons$	$H^+ + SO_4^{2-}$	$K_2 = 1.3 \times 10^{-2}$
sulfurous	$SO_2 + H_2O$	$\rightleftharpoons$	$H^+ + HSO_3^-$	$K_1 = 1.3 \times 10^{-2}$
	HSO_3^-	$\rightleftharpoons$	$H^+ + SO_3^{2-}$	$K_2 = 5.6 \times 10^{-8}$

Polyprotic acids form more than one salt. Depending upon the stoichiometric ratio of reactants, the reaction of NaOH and H_2SO_4 yields either the normal salt, Na_2SO_4 (sodium sulfate) or the acid salt $NaHSO_4$ (sodium bisulfate or sodium hydrogen sulfate). Three salts may be derived from phosphoric acid: NaH_2PO_4 (sodium dihydrogen phosphate), Na_2HPO_4 (sodium hydrogen phosphate), and Na_3PO_4 (sodium phosphate).

▶ **EXAMPLE 16.18** Calculate $[H^+]$, $[H_2PO_4^-]$, $[HPO_4^{2-}]$, $[PO_4^{3-}]$, and $[H_3PO_4]$ in a $0.10M$ solution of phosphoric acid.

Solution The principal source of H^+ is the primary ionization; the H^+ produced by the other ionizations, as well as that from the ionization of water, is negligible in comparison. Furthermore, the concentration of $H_2PO_4^-$ derived from the primary ionization is not significantly diminished by the secondary ionization. Thus we write

$$H_3PO_4 \rightleftharpoons H^+ + H_2PO_4^-$$
$$(0.10 - x)M \quad\quad (x)M \quad (x)M$$

The problem must be solved by means of the quadratic formula.

$$\frac{[H^+][H_2PO_4{}^-]}{[H_3PO_4]} = 7.5 \times 10^{-3}$$

$$\frac{x^2}{(0.10 - x)} = 7.5 \times 10^{-3}$$

$$x = [H^+] = [H_2PO_4{}^-] = 2.4 \times 10^{-2}M$$

$$(0.10 - x) = [H_3PO_4] = 7.6 \times 10^{-2}M$$

The $[H^+]$ and $[H_2PO_4{}^-]$ apply to the secondary ionization. Therefore,

$$H_2PO_4{}^- \;\; \rightleftharpoons \;\; H^+ \;\; + \;\; HPO_4^{2-}$$
$$2.4 \times 10^{-2}M \qquad\quad 2.4 \times 10^{-2}M \qquad ?$$

$$\frac{[H^+][HPO_4^{2-}]}{[H_2PO_4{}^-]} = 6.2 \times 10^{-8}$$

$$\frac{(2.4 \times 10^{-2})[HPO_4^{2-}]}{(2.4 \times 10^{-2}]} = 6.2 \times 10^{-8}$$

$$[HPO_4^{2-}] = 6.2 \times 10^{-8}M$$

In any solution of H_3PO_4 that does not contain ions derived from another electrolyte, the concentration of the secondary ion is equal to K_2.

For the tertiary ionization,

$$HPO_4^{2-} \;\; \rightleftharpoons \;\; H^+ \;\; + \;\; PO_4^{3-}$$
$$6.2 \times 10^{-8}M \qquad\quad 2.4 \times 10^{-2}M \qquad ?$$

$$\frac{[H^+][PO_4^{3-})}{[HPO_4^{2-}]} = 1 \times 10^{-12}$$

$$\frac{(2.4 \times 10^{-2})[PO_4^{3-}]}{(6.2 \times 10^{-8})} = 1 \times 10^{-12}$$

$$[PO_4^{3-}] = 3 \times 10^{-18}M$$

▶ **EXAMPLE 16.19** What are $[H^+]$, $[HS^-]$, $[S^{2-}]$, and $[H_2S]$ in a $0.10M$ solution of H_2S?

Solution K_1 for H_2S is 1.1×10^{-7}; therefore, the small amount of H_2S that ionizes is negligible in comparison to the original concentration of H_2S. In addition, the concentrations of H^+ and HS^- are not significantly altered by the secondary ionization ($K_2 = 1.0 \times 10^{-14}$). Thus

$$H_2S \;\; \rightleftharpoons \;\; H^+ \;\; + \;\; HS^-$$
$$0.10M \qquad\quad (x)M \qquad (x)M$$

$$\frac{[H^+][HS^-]}{[H_2S]} = 1.1 \times 10^{-7}$$

$$\frac{x^2}{0.10} = 1.1 \times 10^{-7}$$

$$x = [H^+] = [HS^-] = 1.0 \times 10^{-4}M$$

These concentrations also apply to the secondary ionization.

$$HS^- \rightleftharpoons H^+ + S^{2-}$$
$$\quad 1.0 \times 10^{-4}M \qquad 1.0 \times 10^{-4}M \qquad ?$$

$$\frac{[H^+][S^{2-}]}{[HS^-]} = 1.0 \times 10^{-14}$$

$$\frac{(1.0 \times 10^{-4})[S^{2-}]}{(1.0 \times 10^{-4})} = 1.0 \times 10^{-14}$$

$$[S^{2-}] = 1.0 \times 10^{-14}M$$

The concentration of the secondary ion is equal to K_2 in any solution of H_2S that does not contain ions derived from another electrolyte.

The product of the expressions for the two ionizations of H_2S is

$$\left(\frac{[H^+][HS^-]}{[H_2S]}\right)\left(\frac{[H^+][S^{2-}]}{[HS^-]}\right) = K_1 K_2$$

$$\frac{[H^+]^2[S^{2-}]}{[H_2S]} = (1.1 \times 10^{-7})(1.0 \times 10^{-14}) = 1.1 \times 10^{-21}$$

This very convenient relationship can be misleading. Superficially, it looks as though it applies to a process in which one sulfide ion is produced for every two hydronium ions. However, the ionization of H_2S does not proceed in this manner; in any solution of H_2S, the concentration of hydronium ion is much larger than the concentration of sulfide ion (Example 16.19). The majority of the H_2S molecules that ionize do so only to the HS^- stage, and S^{2-} ions result only from the small ionization of the secondary ion.

At 25°C, a saturated solution of H_2S is 0.10M. For a *saturated solution*, therefore,

$$\frac{[H^+]^2[S^{2-}]}{(0.10)} = 1.1 \times 10^{-21}$$

$$[H^+]^2[S^{2-}] = 1.1 \times 10^{-22}$$

This relation can be used to calculate the sulfide ion concentration of a solution of known pH that has been saturated with H_2S. We shall see later that acidic solutions of H_2S are frequently employed laboratory reagents.

A similar relationship may be derived for carbonic acid.

$$\left(\frac{[H^+][HCO_3{}^-]}{[CO_2]}\right)\left(\frac{[H^+][CO_3^{2-}]}{[HCO_3{}^-]}\right) = K_1 K_2$$

$$\frac{[H^+]^2\,[CO_3^{2-}]}{[CO_2]} = (4.2 \times 10^{-7})(4.8 \times 10^{-11}) = 2.0 \times 10^{-17}$$

Carbon dioxide is less soluble than H_2S; a saturated solution is $0.034M$ in CO_2.

$$\frac{[H^+]^2\,[CO_3^{2-}]}{(3.4 \times 10^{-2})} = 2.0 \times 10^{-17}$$

$$[H^+]^2\,[CO_3^{2-}] = 6.8 \times 10^{-19}$$

▶ **EXAMPLE 16.20** What is the sulfide ion concentration of a dilute HCl solution that has been saturated with H_2S if the pH of the solution is 3.0?

Solution Since the pH $= 3.0$,

$$[H^+] = 1.0 \times 10^{-3}M$$

Therefore

$$[H^+]^2\,[S^{2-}] = 1.1 \times 10^{-22}$$

$$(1.0 \times 10^{-3})^2\,[S^{2-}] = 1.1 \times 10^{-22}$$

$$[S^{2-}] = 1.1 \times 10^{-16}M$$

In a saturated solution of pure H_2S (Example 16.19), $[S^{2-}] = 1.0 \times 10^{-14}M$. In the H_2S solution described in the problem, the common ion, H^+, has repressed the ionization of H_2S. In addition, since the solution contains H^+ ions from a source other than H_2S, $[H^+]$ does not equal $[HS^-]$, and consequently, $[S^{2-}]$ does not equal K_2.

SOME SUGGESTED READINGS

Blackburn, T. R., *Equilibrium—A Chemistry of Solutions*, New York, Holt, Rinehart, and Winston, 1969 (paper).

Butler, J. N., *Solubility and pH Calculations*, Reading, Mass., Addison-Wesley, 1964 (paper).

Guyon, J. C., and Jones, B. E., *Introduction to Solution Equilibrium*, Boston, Allyn and Bacon, 1969 (paper).

Lee, T. S., and Sillen, L. G., *Chemical Equilibrium in Analytical Chemistry*, New York, Wiley, 1964 (paper).

Margolis, E. J., *Princples in the Calculation of Ionic Equilibrium*, New York, Macmillan, 1966 (paper).

Morris, K., *Principles of Chemical Equilibrium*, New York, Van Nostrand Reinhold, 1965 (paper).

Robbins, O., Jr., *Ionic Reactions and Equilibria*, New York, Macmillan, 1967 (paper).

PROBLEMS

The more difficult problems are starred.

16.1 (a) What are the concentrations of H^+, $C_7H_5O_2^-$ and $HC_7H_5O_2$ in a $0.20M$ solution of benzoic acid? (b) What is the degree of ionization of $HC_7H_5O_2$ in this solution?

16.2 The ionization constant for lactic acid, a weak monobasic acid, is 1.4×10^{-4}. What is the concentration of H^+ in a $0.25M$ solution of lactic acid?

16.3 In an aqueous solution of NH_3, the concentration of OH^- is $1.8 \times 10^{-3}M$. What is the concentration of NH_3?

16.4 Propanoic acid, $HC_3H_5O_2$, is 0.72% ionized in $0.25M$ solution. What is the ionization constant for this acid?

16.5 A solution is prepared by dissolving 0.30 mole of chloroacetic acid, a weak monobasic acid, in sufficient water to make exactly one liter. The concentration of H^+ in the resulting solution is $0.020M$. What is the ionization constant for chloroacetic acid?

16.6 What is the concentration of OH^- in a $0.15M$ solution of hydrazine (N_2H_4)?

*16.7 What are the concentrations of H^+, F^-, and HF in a $0.15M$ solution of HF?

16.8 A weak acid, HX, is 0.80% ionized in $0.015M$ solution. What percent of HX is ionized in a $0.10M$ solution?

16.9 A weak acid, HX, is 0.10% ionized in $0.10M$ solution. At what concentration is the acid 1.0% ionized?

16.10 What are the concentrations of H^+, F^-, and HF in a solution prepared by adding 10 ml of $0.50M$ NaF to 10 ml of $0.30M$ HCl? Assume that the total volume of the solution is 20 ml.

16.11 What is the concentration of H^+ in a solution prepared from 0.22 mole of sodium formate $(NaCHO_2)$ and 0.15 mole of HCl in a total volume of 1.0 liter?

16.12 What are the concentrations of H^+ and OH^- in: (a) a $0.015M$ solution of HCl, (b) a $0.015M$ solution of $Ca(OH)_2$?

16.13 What pH corresponds to each of the following? (a) $[H^+] = 0.65M$, (b) $[OH^-] = 6.0 \times 10^{-4}M$, (c) $[OH^-] = 3.0 \times 10^{-10}M$, (d) $[H^+] = 4.0 \times 10^{-4}M$.

16.14 What concentration of H^+ corresponds to each of the following?
(a) pH = 4.40, (b) pOH = 4.40, (c) pOH = 12.22, (d) pH = 5.55.

16.15 What is the pH of a $0.25M$ NH_3 solution?

16.16 A $0.37M$ solution of a weak acid, HX, has a pH of 3.70. What is the ionization constant of the acid?

16.17 How many moles of chlorous acid, $HClO_2$, must be used to prepare 1.00 liter of solution that has a pH of 2.60?

*16.18 $\mathscr{E}°$ is $+0.536$ v for the following cell:

$$Pt\,|\,H_2(g)\,|\,H^+(aq),\,I^-(aq)\,|\,I_2(s)\,|\,Pt$$

(a) Write the equation for the cell reaction. (b) The emf of the cell is $+0.737$ v when the pressure of $H_2(g)$ is maintained at 1 atm and a HI solution of unknown concentration is employed. What is the pH of the HI solution?

16.19 A cell consisting of a hydrogen electrode and a normal calomel electrode contains a solution of unknown pH. The emf of the cell is $+0.478$ v at 25°C. Calculate the pH of the solution and the concentration of H^+.

16.20 The cell described in Problem 16.19 is filled with a solution that has a pH of 5.50. What is the emf of the cell at 25°C?

16.21 Given the following standard electrode potentials:

$$2H_2O + 2e^- \rightleftharpoons H_2 + 2OH^- \qquad \mathscr{E}° = -0.828 \text{ v}$$

$$O_2 + 4H^+ + 4e^- \rightleftharpoons 2H_2O \qquad \mathscr{E}° = +1.229 \text{ v}$$

Calculate the potentials corresponding to half reactions that occur in a solution with a pH of 7.00. Assume that the gas pressures are maintained at exactly 1 atm.

16.22 An indicator, HIn, has an ionization constant of 9.0×10^{-9}. The acid color of the indicator is yellow, and the alkaline color is red. The yellow color is visible when the ratio of yellow form to red form is 30 to 1, and the red color is predominant when the ratio of red form to yellow form is 2 to 1. What is the pH range of color change for the indicator?

16.23 An indicator is a weak acid and the pH range of its color change is 4.3–5.7. Assuming that the neutral point of the indicator is the center of this range, calculate the ionization constant of the indicator.

16.24 A solution prepared from 0.060 mole of a weak acid, HX, diluted to 250 ml has a pH of 2.89. What is the pH of the solution after 0.030 mole of solid NaX is dissolved in it? Assume that no significant volume change occurs when the NaX is dissolved in the solution.

16.25 A solution prepared from 0.028 mole of a weak acid, HX, and 0.0070 mole of NaX diluted to 200 ml has a pH of 3.66. What is the ionization constant of HX?

16.26 A solution is prepared by adding 0.010 mole of sodium formate, $Na(CHO_2)$, to 100 ml of $0.025M$ formic acid, $HCHO_2$. Assume that no volume change occurs. Calculate (a) the pH of the solution and (b) the percent ionization of $HCHO_2$.

16.27 A $0.10M$ solution of hydrazine, N_2H_4, containing an unknown concentration of hydrazine hydrochloride, $N_2H_5^+ Cl^-$, has a pH of 7.15. What is the concentration of hydrazine hydrochloride in the solution?

16.28 A $0.20M$ solution of nitrous acid, HNO_2, containing an unknown quantity of sodium nitrite, $NaNO_2$, has a pH of 3.80. What is the concentration of sodium nitrite in the solution?

16.29 What concentrations should be used to prepare an acetic acid–acetate buffer with a pH equal to 5.00?

16.30 What concentrations should be used to prepare an ammonia–ammonium ion buffer with a pH equal to 9.50?

16.31 How many moles of sodium benzoate, $NaC_7H_5O_2$, should be added to 250 ml of $0.30M$ benzoic acid, $HC_7H_5O_2$, to prepare a buffer with a pH of 5.00? Assume that no volume change occurs when the sodium benzoate is added to the solution.

16.32 What is the pH of a buffer prepared from 0.25 mole of trimethylamine, $(CH_3)_3N$, and 0.40 mole of trimethylammonium chloride, $(CH_3)_3NH^+ Cl^-$, in 500 ml of solution?

*16.33 What volume of a $0.80M$ solution of NaOH should be added to 100 ml of $0.80M$ solution of benzoic acid, $HC_7H_5O_2$, in order to prepare a buffer with a pH of 4.00?

16.34 Calculate the concentrations of H^+, $H_2AsO_4^-$, $HAsO_4^{2-}$, AsO_4^{3-}, and H_3AsO_4 in a $0.50M$ solution of arsenic acid.

16.35 (a) What are the concentrations of H^+, HCO_3^-, CO_3^{2-}, and CO_2 in a saturated solution of carbonic acid ($0.034M$ in CO_2)? (b) What is the pH of the solution?

*16.36 What are the concentrations of H^+, $HC_2O_4^-$, $C_2O_4^{2-}$, and $H_2C_2O_4$ in a $0.10M$ solution of oxalic acid?

*16.37 What are the concentrations of H^+, HSO_4^-, SO_4^{2-}, and H_2SO_4 in a $0.20M$ solution of sulfuric acid?

16.38 A solution with a pH of 3.55 is saturated with H_2S. What is the sulfide ion concentration?

16.39 (a) What is the sulfide ion concentration of a solution prepared by saturating a $0.20M$ HCl solution with H_2S? (b) What is the concentration of HS^-?

16.40 What should be the concentration of H^+ in a solution in order to have a sulfide ion concentration of $2.0 \times 10^{-19}M$ when the solution is saturated with H_2S?

IONIC EQUILIBRIA, PART II

Homogeneous equilibria between dissolved molecules of weak electrolytes and ions derived from them were discussed in Chapter 16. In this chapter, other homogeneous systems will be studied, including equilibria between oxidizing and reducing agents in solution, as well as heterogeneous systems in which solids are in equilibrium with the constituent ions in solution.

17.1 The Solubility Product

Most substances are soluble in water to at least some slight extent. If an "insoluble" or "slightly soluble" material is placed in water, an equilibrium is established when the rate of dissolution of ions from the solid equals the rate of precipitation of ions from the *saturated solution*. Thus an equilibrium exists between solid silver chloride and a saturated solution of silver chloride.

$$AgCl(s) \rightleftharpoons Ag^+(aq) + Cl^-(aq)$$

The equilibrium constant is

$$K' = \frac{[Ag^+][Cl^-]}{[AgCl]}$$

Since the concentration of a pure solid is a constant, $[AgCl]$ may be combined with K' to give

$$K_{SP} = K'[AgCl] = [Ag^+][Cl^-]$$

The constant K_{SP} is called a **solubility product;** the ionic concentrations of the expression are those for a saturated solution at the reference temperature.

Since the solubility of a salt usually varies widely with temperature, the numerical value of K_{SP} for a salt changes with temperature; values are usually recorded at 25°C. The ionic concentrations of a saturated solution of a slightly soluble material are low; therefore, concentrations may be satisfactorily employed in equilibrium expressions. For the more soluble salts, interionic attractions cause the activity coefficients to deviate significantly from unity, and activities, rather than concentrations, must be employed for the mathematical analysis of these systems. Fortunately, it is the slightly soluble substances that are of primary interest in analytical chemistry. A table of solubility products, at 25°C, is given in the appendix.

The numerical value of K_{SP} for a salt may be found from the molar solubility of the salt.

▶ EXAMPLE 17.1   At 25°C, 0.00188 g of AgCl dissolves in 1 liter of water. What is the K_{SP} of AgCl?

Solution   The molar solubility of AgCl (molecular weight, 143) is

$$? \text{ moles AgCl} = 0.00188 \text{ g AgCl}\left(\frac{1 \text{ mole AgCl}}{143 \text{ g AgCl}}\right) = 1.31 \times 10^{-5} \text{ mole AgCl}$$

For each mole of AgCl dissolving, 1 mole of Ag^+ and 1 mole of Cl^- are formed.

$$AgCl(s) \rightleftharpoons \underset{1.31 \times 10^{-5}M}{Ag^+} + \underset{1.31 \times 10^{-5}M}{Cl^-}$$

$$K_{SP} = [Ag^+][Cl^-]$$
$$= (1.31 \times 10^{-5})^2$$
$$= 1.7 \times 10^{-10}$$

The K_{SP} of a substance may also be found by conductance measurements (if the equivalent conductances of the ions are known) or by potentiometric measurements.

▶ **EXAMPLE 17.2**   Calculate the K_{SP} of AgCl from the electrode potentials

$$e^- + AgCl(s) \rightleftharpoons Ag(s) + Cl^-(aq) \qquad \mathscr{E}° = +0.222v$$

$$e^- + Ag^+(aq) \rightleftharpoons Ag(s) \qquad\qquad \mathscr{E}° = +0.799\ v$$

(See Example 14.9, Section 14.10.)

Solution   The theoretical cell

$$Ag\,|\,Ag^+,\ Cl^-\,|\,AgCl\,|\,Ag$$

would have the following electrode reactions

$$Ag \longrightarrow Ag^+ + e^- \qquad \mathscr{E}°_{ox} = -0.799\ v$$

$$e^- + AgCl \longrightarrow Ag + Cl^- \qquad \mathscr{E}° = +0.222\ v$$

The cell reaction is

$$AgCl \longrightarrow Ag^+ + Cl^- \qquad \mathscr{E}° = -0.577\ v$$

Notice that the reaction for the standard cell is not spontaneous as written. For this reaction, $n = 1$.

$$\Delta G° = -nF\mathscr{E}°$$

$$= -1(23.1\ \text{kcal/v})(-0.577\ v)$$

$$= +13.3\ \text{kcal}$$

$$\Delta G° = -RT \ln K$$

$$+13.3\ \text{kcal} = -1.36\ \text{kcal}\ (\log K)$$

$$\log K = -9.78$$

$$K = 1.7 \times 10^{-10}$$

For salts that have more than two ions per formula unit, the ion concentrations must be raised to the powers indicated by the coefficients of the balanced chemical equation.

$$Mg(OH)_2(s) \rightleftharpoons Mg^{2+} + 2OH^- \qquad K_{SP} = [Mg^{2+}][OH^-]^2$$

$$Bi_2S_3(s) \rightleftharpoons 2Bi^{3+} + 3S^{2-} \qquad K_{SP} = [Bi^{3+}]^2\,[S^{2-}]^3$$

$$Hg_2Cl_2(s) \rightleftharpoons Hg_2^{2+} + 2Cl^- \qquad K_{SP} = [Hg_2^{2+}][Cl^-]^2$$

For a salt of this type, the calculation of the K_{SP} from the molar solubility requires that the chemical equation representing the dissociation process be carefully interpreted.

▶ **EXAMPLE 17.3** At 25°C, 7.8×10^{-5} mole of silver chromate dissolves in 1 liter of water. What is the K_{SP} of Ag_2CrO_4?

Solution For each mole of Ag_2CrO_4 that dissolves, 2 moles of Ag^+ and 1 mole of CrO_4^{2-} are formed. Therefore

$$Ag_2CrO_4(s) \;\rightleftharpoons\; \underset{2(7.8 \times 10^{-5})M}{2Ag^+} + \underset{7.8 \times 10^{-5}M}{CrO_4^{2-}}$$

$$K_{SP} = [Ag^+]^2[CrO_4^{2-}]$$

$$= (1.56 \times 10^{-4})^2(7.8 \times 10^{-5})$$

$$= 1.9 \times 10^{-12}$$

▶ **EXAMPLE 17.4** The K_{SP} of CaF_2 is 3.9×10^{-11} at 25°C. What is the concentration of Ca^{2+} and of F^- in the saturated solution? How many grams of calcium fluoride will dissolve in 100 ml of water at 25°C?

Solution Let x equal the molar solubility of CaF_2.

$$CaF_2(s) \;\rightleftharpoons\; \underset{x}{Ca^{2+}} + \underset{2x}{2F^-}$$

$$K_{SP} = [Ca^{2+}][F^-]^2 = 3.9 \times 10^{-11}$$

$$x(2x)^2 = 3.9 \times 10^{-11}$$

$$4x^3 = 3.9 \times 10^{-11}$$

$$x = 2.1 \times 10^{-4}M$$

Therefore,

$$[Ca^{2+}] = x = 2.1 \times 10^{-4}M$$

$$[F^-] = 2x = 4.2 \times 10^{-4}M$$

$$? \text{ g } CaF_2 = 100 \text{ ml } H_2O \left(\frac{2.1 \times 10^{-4} \text{ mole } CaF_2}{1000 \text{ ml } H_2O}\right)\left(\frac{78 \text{ g } CaF_2}{1 \text{ mole } CaF_2}\right)$$

$$= 1.6 \times 10^{-3} \text{ g } CaF_2$$

There is evidence that some salts ionize in a stepwise manner. For example, lead chloride

$$PbCl_2(s) \;\rightleftharpoons\; Pb^{2+}(aq) + 2Cl^-(aq) \qquad K_{SP} = [Pb^{2+}][Cl^-]^2$$

is thought to ionize according to the equations

$$PbCl_2(s) \rightleftharpoons PbCl_2(aq) \qquad\qquad K_1 = [PbCl_2(aq)]$$

$$PbCl_2(aq) \rightleftharpoons PbCl^+(aq) + Cl^-(aq) \qquad K_2 = \frac{[PbCl^+][Cl^-]}{[PbCl_2(aq)]}$$

$$PbCl^+(aq) \rightleftharpoons Pb^{2+}(aq) + Cl^-(aq) \qquad K_3 = \frac{[Pb^{2+}][Cl^-]}{[PbCl^+]}$$

The product of the stepwise constants is

$$K_1 K_2 K_3 = [PbCl_2(aq)] \left(\frac{[PbCl^+][Cl^-]}{[PbCl_2(aq)]} \right) \left(\frac{[Pb^{2+}][Cl^-]}{[PbCl^+]} \right) = [Pb^{2+}][Cl^-]^2 = K_{SP}$$

In these expressions, $PbCl_2(aq)$ is a neutral molecule in solution.

Thus the solubility product principle applies to all solutions of slightly soluble materials whether they dissociate in a stepwise manner or not. However, the K_{SP}'s of salts that dissociate in steps must be carefully interpreted. For example, in a saturated solution of $PbCl_2$, the concentration of Cl^- is not twice the concentration of Pb^{2+} as the expression for the K_{SP} might lead one to expect; such an erroneous deduction ignores the existence of $PbCl_2(aq)$ molecules and $PbCl^+$ ions. The value of the K_{SP} applies only if the *actual* concentrations of Pb^{2+} and Cl^- are employed, and the stepwise mechanism must be considered in order to deduce the correct concentration terms.

Other factors introduce errors into solubility calculations for certain salts. The solubility of lead chloride is enhanced in moderately concentrated solutions of chloride ion because of the formation of the *complex ion*, $PbCl_3{}^-$.

$$PbCl_2(s) + Cl^-(aq) \rightleftharpoons PbCl_3{}^-(aq)$$

Also, the hydrolysis of the Pb^{2+} ion

$$Pb^{2+}(aq) + H_2O \rightleftharpoons Pb(OH)^+(aq) + H^+(aq)$$

reduces the concentration of Pb^{2+} so that the solubility of $PbCl_2$ is actually higher than the value obtained from a calculation that ignores hydrolysis. Complex-ion and hydrolysis equilibria are discussed in Sections 17.4 and 17.6.

The solubility of any solid is increased by the presence of the ions of another salt in the solution; thus $PbCl_2$ is more soluble in moderately concentrated solutions of $NaNO_3$ than it is in pure water. This **salt effect** also increases the degree of ionization of soluble weak electrolytes. The effect is due to interionic attractions, and these do not depend upon the nature of the dissolved ions but on their concentrations and charges. Therefore, foreign ions reduce the activities of the ions of the substance under study. Since the equilibrium constant is properly a function of activities (rather than concentrations), more of the substance ionizes to realize the activity required to satisfy the mathematical relationship.

17.2 Precipitation and the Solubility Product

The numerical value of the solubility product of a salt is a quantitative statement of the limit of solubility of the salt. For a specific solution of a salt, the product of the concentrations of the ions, each raised to the proper power, is called the **ion product.** Thus, for a saturated solution in equilibrium with excess solid, the ion product equals the K_{SP}. If the ion product of a solution is less than the K_{SP}, the solution is unsaturated; additional solid can dissolve in this solution. On the other hand, if the ion product is greater than the K_{SP}, the solution is momentarily supersaturated; precipitation will occur until the ion product equals the K_{SP}.

▶ **EXAMPLE 17.5**   Will a precipitate form if 10 ml of $0.010M$ $AgNO_3$ and 10 ml of $0.00010M$ NaCl are mixed? Assume that the final volume of the solution is 20 ml. For AgCl, $K_{SP} = 1.7 \times 10^{-10}$.

Solution   Diluting a solution to twice its original volume reduces the concentrations of ions in the solution to half their original value. Therefore, if there were no reaction, the ion concentrations would be

$$[Ag^+] = 5.0 \times 10^{-3}M$$
$$[Cl^-] = 5.0 \times 10^{-5}M$$

The ion product is

$$[Ag^+][Cl^-] = ?$$
$$(5.0 \times 10^{-3})(5.0 \times 10^{-5}) = 2.5 \times 10^{-7}$$

Therefore the ion product is larger than the K_{SP} (1.7×10^{-10}), and precipitation of AgCl will occur.

▶ **EXAMPLE 17.6**   Will a precipitate of $Mg(OH)_2$ form in a $0.0010M$ solution of $Mg(NO_3)_2$ if the pH of the solution is adjusted to 9.0? The K_{SP} of $Mg(OH)_2$ is 8.9×10^{-12}.

Solution   If the pH = 9.0,

$$[OH^-] = 1.0 \times 10^{-5}M$$

Since $[Mg^{2+}] = 1.0 \times 10^{-3}$, the ion product is

$$[Mg^{2+}][OH^-]^2 = ?$$

$$(1 \times 10^{-3})(1 \times 10^{-5}) = 1 \times 10^{-13}$$

Since the ion product is less than 8.9×10^{-12}, no precipitate will form.

The common-ion effect pertains to solubility equilibria. As an example, consider the system

$$BaSO_4(s) \rightleftharpoons Ba^{2+}(aq) + SO_4^{2-}(aq)$$

The addition of sulfate ion, from sodium sulfate, to a saturated solution of barium sulfate will cause the equilibrium to shift to the left; the concentration of Ba^{2+} will decrease, and $BaSO_4$ will precipitate. Since the product $[Ba^{2+}][SO_4^{2-}]$ is a constant, increasing $[SO_4^{2-}]$ will cause $[Ba^{2+}]$ to decrease.

The amount of barium ion in a solution may be determined by precipitating the Ba^{2+} as $BaSO_4$. The precipitate is then removed by filtration and is dried and weighed. The concentration of Ba^{2+} left in solution after the precipitation may be reduced to a very low value if excess sulfate ion is employed in the precipitation. As a general rule, however, too large an excess of the common ion should be avoided. At high ionic concentrations, the salt effect increases the solubility of a salt, and, for certain precipitates, the formation of a complex ion may lead to enhanced solubility.

▶ **EXAMPLE 17.7**   At 25°C, a saturated solution of $BaSO_4$ is $3.9 \times 10^{-5}M$; the K_{SP} of $BaSO_4$ is 1.5×10^{-9}. What is the solubility of $BaSO_4$ in $0.050M$ Na_2SO_4?

Solution   The sulfate ion derived from $BaSO_4$ may be ignored. Thus

$$BaSO_4(s) \rightleftharpoons \underset{?}{Ba^{2+}} + \underset{5.0 \times 10^{-2}}{SO_4^{2-}}$$

$$[Ba^{2+}][SO_4^{2-}] = 1.5 \times 10^{-9}$$

$$[Ba^{2+}](5.0 \times 10^{-2}) = 1.5 \times 10^{-9}$$

$$[Ba^{2+}] = 3.0 \times 10^{-8}M$$

The solubility of $BaSO_4$ has been reduced from $3.9 \times 10^{-5}M$ to $3.0 \times 10^{-8}M$ by the common ion effect.

Frequently, a solution contains more than one ion capable of forming a precipitate with another ion which is to be added to the solution. For example, a solution might contain both Cl^- and CrO_4^{2-} ions, both of which form insoluble salts with Ag^+. When Ag^+ is added to the solution, the less soluble silver salt will precipitate first. If the addition is continued, eventually a point will be reached where the more soluble salt will begin to precipitate along with the less soluble.

▶ **EXAMPLE 17.8** A solution is $0.10M$ in Cl^- and $0.10M$ in CrO_4^{2-}. If solid $AgNO_3$ is gradually added to this solution, which will precipate first, $AgCl$ or Ag_2CrO_4? Assume that the addition causes no change in volume. For $AgCl$, $K_{SP} = 1.7 \times 10^{-10}$; for Ag_2CrO_4, $K_{SP} = 1.9 \times 10^{-12}$.

Solution When a precipitate *begins* to form, the pertinent ion product *just* exceeds the K_{SP} of the solid. Therefore, we calculate the concentrations of Ag^+ needed to precipitate $AgCl$ and Ag_2CrO_4.

$$AgCl(s) \rightleftharpoons \underset{?}{Ag^+} + \underset{0.10M}{Cl^-} \qquad Ag_2CrO_4(s) \rightleftharpoons \underset{?}{2Ag^+} + \underset{0.10M}{CrO_4^{2-}}$$

$$[Ag^+][Cl^-] = 1.7 \times 10^{-10} \qquad\qquad [Ag^+]^2 [CrO_4^{2-}] = 1.9 \times 10^{-12}$$

$$[Ag^+](0.10) = 1.7 \times 10^{-10} \qquad\qquad [Ag^+]^2 (0.10) = 1.9 \times 10^{-12}$$

$$[Ag^+] = 1.7 \times 10^{-9}M \qquad\qquad [Ag^+]^2 = 1.9 \times 10^{-11}$$

$$[Ag^+] = 4.4 \times 10^{-6}M$$

Therefore, $AgCl$ will precipitate first.

▶ **EXAMPLE 17.9** (a) In the experiment described in Example 17.8, what will be the concentration of the Cl^- ion when Ag_2CrO_4 begins to precipitate? (b) At this point, what percent of the chloride ion originally present remains in solution?

Solution (a) From the preceding example, we see that $[Ag^+] = 4.4 \times 10^{-6}$ M when Ag_2CrO_4 starts to precipitate. At this point, the concentration of chloride ion will be

$$[Ag^+][Cl^-] = 1.7 \times 10^{-10}$$

$$(4.4 \times 10^{-6})[Cl^-] = 1.7 \times 10^{-10}$$

$$[Cl^-] = \frac{1.7 \times 10^{-10}}{4.4 \times 10^{-6}} = 3.9 \times 10^{-5}M$$

Thus until the $[Cl^-]$ is described to $3.9 \times 10^{-5}M$, no Ag_2CrO_4 will form.

(b) Since the original concentration of chloride was $0.10M$, the percent of Cl^- remaining in solution when Ag_2CrO_4 starts to precipitate is

$$\frac{3.9 \times 10^{-5}}{1.0 \times 10^{-1}} 100 = 0.039\%$$

Chromate ion is used as a **precipitation indicator**. The concentration of chloride ion in a solution can be determined by titrating a sample of the solution against a standard $AgNO_3$ solution using a few drops of K_2CrO_4 as an indicator. In the course of the titration, white AgCl precipitates. The appearance of red Ag_2CrO_4 indicates that the precipitation of chloride ion is essentially complete. In a quantitative procedure of this type, the concentration of CrO_4^{2-} used is much less than that employed in the preceding problem. Hence, a higher concentration of Ag^+ is required to start the precipitation of Ag_2CrO_4, and a lower concentration of Cl^- will be present in the solution when the Ag_2CrO_4 begins to precipitate.

▶ **EXAMPLE 17.10** What concentration of NH_4^+, derived from NH_4Cl, is necessary to prevent the formation of a $Mg(OH)_2$ precipitate in a solution that is $0.050M$ in Mg^{2+} and $0.050M$ in NH_3? The K_{SP} of $Mg(OH)_2$ is 8.9×10^{-12}.

Solution We first calculate the maximum concentration of hydroxide ion that can be present in the solution without causing $Mg(OH)_2$ to precipitate.

$$[Mg^{2+}][OH^-]^2 = 8.9 \times 10^{-12}$$

$$(5.0 \times 10^{-2})[OH^-]^2 = 8.9 \times 10^{-12}$$

$$[OH^-]^2 = 1.8 \times 10^{-10}$$

$$[OH^-] = 1.3 \times 10^{-5}M$$

From the expression for the ionization constant for NH_3, we can derive the concentration of NH_4^+ that will maintain the concentration of OH^- at this level.

$$\frac{[NH_4^+][OH^-]}{[NH_3]} = 1.8 \times 10^{-5}$$

$$\frac{[NH_4^+](1.3 \times 10^{-5})}{(5.0 \times 10^{-2})} = 1.8 \times 10^{-5}$$

$$[NH_4^+] = 6.9 \times 10^{-2} M$$

Thus the minimum concentration of NH_4^+ that must be present is $0.069M$.

17.3 Precipitation of Sulfides

The sulfide ion concentration in an acid solution that has been saturated with H_2S is extremely low. In 10 ml of a saturated H_2S solution that has been made $0.3M$ in H^+, there are approximately seven S^{2-} ions. Nevertheless, when

Pb^{2+} ions are added to such a solution, PbS precipitates immediately. It seems unlikely that the precipitate forms as a result of the reaction of Pb^{2+} ions with S^{2-} ions.

There is evidence that in this and in similar sulfide precipitations, a hydrosulfide forms initially and then decomposes to give the normal sulfide.

$$Pb(HS)_2(s) \rightleftharpoons PbS(s) + H_2S(aq)$$

The hydroxides of many metals are known to produce oxides in a parallel manner, and, in fact, what is known as lead hydroxide, $Pb(OH)_2$, is in reality hydrous lead oxide, $PbO \cdot xH_2O$. The hydrosulfide of lead could form as a result of the reaction of Pb^{2+} ions with either H_2S molecules or HS^- ions; the concentrations of H_2S and HS^- are much higher than the concentration of S^{2-}.

However, an equilibrium constant does not depend upon the reaction mechanism by which the equilibrium is attained (Section 14.9). Provided the system is in equilibrium, the relationship expressed by the solubility product principle is valid no matter what series of reactions produces the precipitate. Thus we may use K_{SP}'s to calculate favorable reaction conditions for the formation of a desired precipitate or reaction conditions that will prevent the formation of a precipitate.

▶ **EXAMPLE 17.11** A solution that is $0.30M$ in H^+, $0.050M$ in Pb^{2+}, and $0.050M$ in Fe^{2+} is saturated with H_2S; should PbS and/or FeS precipitate? The K_{SP} of PbS is 7×10^{-29} and the K_{SP} of FeS is 4×10^{-19}.

Solution For any saturated solution of H_2S,

$$[H^+]^2 [S^{2-}] = 1.1 \times 10^{-22}$$

Since this solution is $0.30M$ in H^+,

$$(3.0 \times 10^{-1})^2 [S^{2-}] = 1.1 \times 10^{-22}$$

$$[S^{2-}] = 1.2 \times 10^{-21}M$$

Both Pb^{2+} and Fe^{2+} are $2+$ ions, and the form of the ion product is

$$[M^{2+}][S^{2-}]$$

where M^{2+} stands for either metal ion. Since both are present in concentrations of $0.050M$,

$$[M^{2+}][S^{2-}]$$

$$(5.0 \times 10^{-2})(1.2 \times 10^{-21}) = 6.0 \times 10^{-23}$$

This ion product is greater than the K_{SP} of PbS; therefore PbS will precipitate. However, the ion product is less than the K_{SP} of FeS; the solubility of FeS has not been exceeded; no FeS will form.

▶ **EXAMPLE 17.12** What must be the hydronium ion concentration of a solution that is $0.050M$ in Ni^{2+} to prevent the precipitation of NiS when the solution is saturated with H_2S? The K_{SP} of NiS is 3×10^{-21}.

Solution

$$[Ni^{2+}][S^{2-}] = 3 \times 10^{-21}$$

$$(0.050)[S^{2-}] = 3 \times 10^{-21}$$

$$[S^{2-}] = 6 \times 10^{-20}M$$

Therefore the $[S^{2-}]$ must be less than $6 \times 10^{-20}M$ if NiS is not to precipitate. For a solution saturated with H_2S,

$$[H^+]^2 [S^{2-}] = 1.1 \times 10^{-22}$$

$$[H^+]^2 (6 \times 10^{-20}) = 1.1 \times 10^{-22}$$

$$[H^+] = 0.04M$$

The $[H^+]$ must be greater than $0.04M$ to prevent the precipitation of NiS.

The preceding examples illustrate an important analytical technique. In the usual qualitative analysis scheme, certain cations are separated into groups on the basis of whether their sulfides form in acidic solution. Thus, in a solution that has a H^+ concentration of $0.3M$, the sulfides of Hg^{2+}, Pb^{2+}, Cu^{2+}, Bi^{3+}, Cd^{2+}, and Sn^{2+} are insoluble, whereas the sulfides of Fe^{2+}, Co^{2+}, Ni^{2+}, Mn^{2+}, and Zn^{2+} are soluble.

In considering systems that involve sulfide precipitation, one must note that the H^+ concentration of a solution increases when a sulfide precipitates from the solution.

▶ **EXAMPLE 17.13** A solution that is $0.050M$ in Cd^{2+} and $0.10M$ in H^+ is saturated with H_2S. What concentration of Cd^{2+} remains in solution after CdS has precipitated? The K_{SP} of CdS is 1.0×10^{-28}.

Solution For each Cd^{2+} ion precipitated, two H^+ ions are added to the solution.

$$Cd^{2+}(aq) + H_2S(aq) \rightleftharpoons CdS(s) + 2H^+(aq)$$

We shall assume that virtually all the Cd^{2+} precipitates as CdS. Hence, the precipitation introduces 0.10 mole of H^+ per liter of solution, and the final $[H^+]$ is 0.20M. Therefore,

$$[H^+]^2[S^{2-}] = 1.1 \times 10^{-22}$$

$$(0.20)^2[S^{2-}] = 1.1 \times 10^{-22}$$

$$[S^{2-}] = 2.8 \times 10^{-21}$$

The concentration of Cd^{2+} after the CdS has precipitated may be derived from the K_{SP} of CdS.

$$[Cd^{2+}][S^{2-}] = 1.0 \times 10^{-28}$$

$$[Cd^{2+}](2.8 \times 10^{-21}) = 1.0 \times 10^{-28}$$

$$[Cd^{2+}] = 3.6 \times 10^{-8}M$$

From our answer, we can see that our assumption was justified. The value of $[H^+]$ that we used was well within our limits of accuracy.

It must be emphasized that calculations such as the preceding, although illustrative of principles, are only approximate. Exact mathematical treatment of sulfide systems is complicated and must take into account complex-ion formation (Section Section 17.4) and hydrolysis (Section 17.6). In addition, the solubility-product constants for the sulfides are generally less reliable than those for other slightly soluble solids. The attainment of equilibrium in sulfide systems is slow, and measurement of equilibrium constants for these systems is difficult. The precipitated sulfides of some cations (notably Ni^{2+}, Co^{2+}, and Zn^{2+}) become less soluble upon standing. The decrease in solubility may be caused by the transition from hydrosulfide to sulfide, but more probably it is the result of the rearrangement of the ions into a more stable crystalline form. Thus, for all practical purposes, the K_{SP}'s for some sulfides change with time. The values of the solubility products of the sulfides listed in the appendix are for the freshly precipitated, or more soluble, modifications.

17.4 Equilibria Involving Complex Ions

Complex ions are discussed in Chapter 19. However, these ions take part in some aqueous equilibria that properly constitute a part of the topic of this chapter. A **complex ion** is an aggregate consisting of a central metal cation (usually a transition-metal ion) surrounded by a number of ligands. The **ligands** of a complex may be anions, molecules, or a combination of the two, and the charge of a complex ion is obtained by adding the charges of its constituent particles. Examples of complex ions are: $Co(NH_3)_6^{3+}$, $Cu(H_2O)_4^{2+}$, $CdCl_4^{2-}$, $Fe(CN)_6^{4-}$, $Ag(S_2O_3)_2^{3-}$, and $Co(NH_3)_5Cl^{2+}$.

A ligand must have an unshared pair of electrons with which it can bond to the central ion. Thus the ammonia molecule, NH_3, functions as a ligand in the formation of complex ions—the ammonium ion, NH_4^+, does not.

$$H-\ddot{N}-H \qquad \left[H-N-H \right]^+$$

In addition to ammonia, the requirement is met by many molecules and anions.

$$H-\ddot{O}: \qquad [:C\equiv N:]^- \qquad :\ddot{Cl}:^- \qquad \left[:\ddot{S}-S-\ddot{O}: \right]^{2-} \qquad [:\ddot{O}-H]^-$$

The stabilities of complex ions vary widely. The group I A and group II A cations only form aggregates that are loosely held together by weak ion–dipole or ion–ion electrostatic attractions; these are probably better described as ion pairs rather than complex ions. At the other extreme are the very stable complex ions, such as $Co(NH_3)_6^{3+}$ and $Fe(CN)_6^{4-}$, in which the strength of the attractions between the central ions and the ligands is of the same order as the covalent bond. We shall restrict our attention to those complex ions that are formed in definite stoichiometric ratios and that exist in solution as reversibly dissociated entities.

All ions are hydrated in water solution, and most hydrated metal ions should be regarded as complex ions since each metal ion has a definite number of water molecules tightly bonded to it. This number is difficult to determine and is not known with certainty for some species. Nevertheless, in water solution, complexes probably form by the replacement of water ligands by other ligands. For example,

$$Cu(H_2O)_6^{2+} + NH_3 \;\rightleftharpoons\; Cu(H_2O)_5(NH_3)^{2+} + H_2O$$

For simplicity, however, the coordinated water molecules are usually not shown.

$$Cu^{2+} + NH_3 \;\rightleftharpoons\; Cu(NH_3)^{2+}$$

The dissociation, as well as the formation, of a complex ion occurs in steps.

Thus, the $Ag(NH_3)_2{}^+$ ion dissociates as follows:

$$Ag(NH_3)_2{}^+ \rightleftharpoons Ag(NH_3){}^+ + NH_3 \qquad K_1 = \frac{[Ag(NH_3){}^+][NH_3]}{[Ag(NH_3)_2{}^+]}$$

$$= 1.4 \times 10^{-4}$$

$$Ag(NH_3){}^+ \rightleftharpoons Ag^+ + NH_3 \qquad K_2 = \frac{[Ag^+][NH_3]}{[Ag(NH_3){}^+]}$$

$$= 4.3 \times 10^{-4}$$

The product of the two constants is called the **instability constant** of the $Ag(NH_3)_2{}^+$ ion. This instability constant corresponds to the overall dissociation of the ion.

$$Ag(NH_3)_2{}^+ \rightleftharpoons Ag^+ + 2NH_3$$

$$\left(\frac{[Ag(NH_3){}^+][NH_3]}{[Ag(NH_3)_2{}^+]}\right)\left(\frac{[Ag^+][NH_3]}{[Ag(NH_3){}^+]}\right) = \frac{[Ag^+][NH_3]^2}{[Ag(NH_3)_2{}^+]}$$

$$K_{inst} = K_1 K_2 = (1.4 \times 10^{-4})(4.3 \times 10^{-4}) = 6.0 \times 10^{-8}$$

For many complexes, the values of the equilibrium constants for the individual steps of the dissociation are not known, although the value for the overall dissociation may have been determined. However, an overall instability constant for a complex ion must be cautiously interpreted since the chemical equation to which it applies does not take into consideration any intermediate species.

▶ **EXAMPLE 17.14** A $1.0 \times 10^{-3}M$ solution of $AgNO_3$ is made $0.10M$ in NH_3. What are the concentrations of Ag^+, $Ag(NH_3){}^+$, and $Ag(NH_3)_2{}^+$ in the resulting solution?

Solution We shall assume that the Ag^+ is practically completely converted into the higher complex, $Ag(NH_3)_2{}^+$, by this excess of NH_3. Therefore,

$$[Ag(NH_3)_2{}^+] = 1.0 \times 10^{-3}M$$

The formation of this concentration of $Ag(NH_3)_2{}^+$ would reduce the concentration of NH_3 by $2.0 \times 10^{-3}M$, but this, as well as the amount of NH_3 that reacts with H_2O to form $NH_4{}^+$, is negligible in comparison with the original concentration of NH_3. From the instability constant, we see

$$\frac{[Ag^+][NH_3]^2}{[Ag(NH_3)_2{}^+]} = 6.0 \times 10^{-8}$$

$$\frac{[Ag^+](1.0 \times 10^{-1})^2}{(1.0 \times 10^{-3})} = 6.0 \times 10^{-8}$$

$$[Ag^+] = 6.0 \times 10^{-9}M$$

The concentration of $Ag(NH_3)^+$ may be obtained from either of the stepwise dissociation constants. Thus

$$\frac{[Ag(NH_3)^+][NH_3]}{[Ag(NH_3)_2{}^+]} = 1.4 \times 10^{-4}$$

$$\frac{[Ag(NH_3)^+](1.0 \times 10^{-1})}{(1.0 \times 10^{-3})} = 1.4 \times 10^{-4}$$

$$[Ag(NH_3)^+] = 1.4 \times 10^{-6} M$$

By comparing the concentrations of all of the cations in the solution, we can see that the assumption that $Ag(NH_3)_2{}^+$ is the principal silver-containing ion is a valid one.

▶ **EXAMPLE 17.15** What is the solubility of AgCl in $0.10M$ NH_3?

Solution If we let x equal the solubility of AgCl in moles per liter, then $[Cl^-] = x$. From the K_{SP} for AgCl, we derive

$$[Ag^+][Cl^-] = 1.7 \times 10^{-10}$$

$$[Ag^+] = \frac{1.7 \times 10^{-10}}{x}$$

If we assume that the majority of the dissolved Ag^+ goes into solution as $Ag(NH_3)_2{}^+$, then

$$[Ag(NH_3)_2{}^+] = x$$

Since two molecules of NH_3 are required for every $Ag(NH_3)_2{}^+$ ion formed,

$$[NH_3] = 0.10 - 2x$$

Therefore,

$$\frac{[Ag^+][NH_3]^2}{[Ag(NH_3)_2{}^+]} = 6.0 \times 10^{-8}$$

$$\frac{\left(\dfrac{1.7 \times 10^{-10}}{x}\right)(0.10 - 2x)^2}{x} = 6.0 \times 10^{-8}$$

from which we derive

$$\frac{(0.10 - 2x)^2}{x^2} = \frac{6.0 \times 10^{-8}}{1.7 \times 10^{-10}} = 3.5 \times 10^2$$

By extracting the square root of both sides of this equation, we get the relation

$$\frac{(0.10 - 2x)}{x} = 19$$

$$x = [Ag(NH_3)_2{}^+] = 4.8 \times 10^{-3}M.$$

which is the solubility of AgCl in $0.10M$ NH_3. The concentration of NH_3 is

$$[NH_3] = 0.10 - 2x = 9.0 \times 10^{-2}M$$

The concentration of Ag^+ is

$$[Ag^+] = \frac{1.7 \times 10^{-10}}{x}$$

$$= 3.5 \times 10^{-8}M$$

The concentration of $Ag(NH_3)^+$ can be derived from

$$\frac{[Ag(NH_3)^+][NH_3]}{[Ag(NH_3)_2{}^+]} = 1.4 \times 10^{-4}$$

$$\frac{[Ag(NH_3)^+](9.0 \times 10^{-2})}{4.8 \times 10^{-3}} = 1.4 \times 10^{-4}$$

$$[Ag(NH_3)^+] = 7.5 \times 10^{-6}M$$

Comparison of the concentrations of all of the species in the solution will show that our assumptions were justified.

As an alternative solution to this problem, we write the equation for the complete transformation and let x equal the molar solubility of AgCl.

$$\underset{0.10 - 2x}{AgCl(s)} \; + \; 2NH_3 \; \rightleftharpoons \; \underset{x}{Ag(NH_3)_2{}^+} + \underset{x}{Cl^-}$$

An equilibrium constant corresponding to this equation may be derived by dividing the K_{SP} of AgCl by the K_{inst} of $Ag(NH_3)_2{}^+$.

$$K_{SP}\left(\frac{1}{K_{inst}}\right) = [Ag^+][Cl^-]\left(\frac{[Ag(NH_3)_2{}^+]}{[Ag^+][NH_3]^2}\right)$$

$$(1.7 \times 10^{-10})\left(\frac{1}{6.0 \times 10^{-8}}\right) = 2.8 \times 10^{-3}$$

Therefore,

$$\frac{[Ag(NH_3)_2{}^+][Cl^-]}{[NH_3]^2} = 2.8 \times 10^{-3}$$

$$\frac{x^2}{(0.10 - 2x)^2} = 2.8 \times 10^{-3}$$

$$\frac{x}{(0.10 - 2x)} = 5.3 \times 10^{-2}$$

$$x = 4.8 \times 10^{-3} M$$

If a large excess of ligand is employed and if each of the stepwise dissociation constants is small, then the assumption may be made that the principal complex in solution is the one with the highest number of ligands. Such an assumption greatly simplifies problem solving (Examples 17.14 and 17.15). Unfortunately, there are many situations in which such an assumption may not be made because either or both of the criteria are not satisfied. For example, in solving problems concerning the complexes formed by Ag^+ and the thiosulfate ion, the assumption cannot be made that the concentrations of all Ag^+ containing species are negligible except for $Ag(S_2O_3)_3^{5-}$, the highest complex. The equations and corresponding constants for the stepwise dissociation of the $Ag(S_2O_3)_3^{5-}$ ion are

$$Ag(S_2O_3)_3^{5-} \; \rightleftharpoons \; Ag(S_2O_3)_2^{3-} + S_2O_3^{2-} \quad K_1 = 2.0 \times 10^{-1}$$

$$Ag(S_2O_3)_2^{3-} \; \rightleftharpoons \; Ag(S_2O_3)^- + S_2O_3^{2-} \quad K_2 = 3.3 \times 10^{-5}$$

$$Ag(S_2O_3)^- \; \rightleftharpoons \; Ag^+ + S_2O_3^{2-} \quad K_3 = 1.5 \times 10^{-9}$$

The constant for the first step of the dissociation is comparatively large. Therefore, even at high concentrations of $S_2O_3^{2-}$, significant concentrations of both $Ag(S_2O_3)_3^{5-}$ and $Ag(S_2O_3)_2^{3-}$ exist. Notice that this conclusion can not be reached by an examination of the instability constant (9.9×10^{-15}) alone.

Slightly soluble substances can often be dissolved through the formation of complex ions. The dissolution of AgCl in NH_3 (Example 17.15) illustrates this technique, which is an important one in analytical chemistry. The equilibrium between solid AgCl and its ions

$$AgCl(s) \; \rightleftharpoons \; Ag^+(aq) + Cl^-(aq)$$

is forced to the right by the removal of Ag^+ ions through the formation of the silver-ammonia complex ion, and therefore AgCl dissolves.

A few metals form thio complex ions (e.g., HgS_2^{2-}, AsS_3^{3-}, SbS_2^{3-}, SnS_3^{2-}); the true structure of these anions may involve the HS^- ion. The formation of a thio complex ion may be used to separate sulfide precipitates. For example, a mixture of CuS (which does not form a thio complex) and As_2S_3 may be separated by dissolving the As_2S_3 in an alkaline solution containing S^{2-} ion. The solution must have a high pH to maintain a relatively high concentration of S^{2-}.

$$CuS(s) + S^{2-}(aq) \longrightarrow \text{no reaction}$$

$$As_2S_3(s) + 3S^{2-}(aq) \rightleftharpoons 2AsS_3^{3-}(aq)$$

The reaction of As_2S_3 may involve HS^- ions or H_2S molecules, and the actual structure of the complex ion may be $As(SH)_4^-$.

If a solution containing Al^{3+} and Zn^{2+} is treated with a buffer of NH_3 at a controlled alkaline pH, $Al(OH)_3$ will precipitate, but Zn^{2+} will stay in solution as $Zn(NH_3)_4^{2+}$. The precipitation of $Zn(OH)_2$ is prevented by the formation of the complex ion; Al^{3+} does not form an ammonia complex.

$$Al^{3+}(aq) + 3OH^-(aq) \rightleftharpoons Al(OH)_3(s)$$

$$Zn^{2+}(aq) + 4NH_3(aq) \rightleftharpoons Zn(NH_3)_4^{2+}(aq)$$

Complex ions are frequently highly colored; $Fe(SCN)^{2+}$ is deep red. Thus the production of a deep red color when SCN^- is added to a solution serves as a test for the Fe^{3+} ion.

17.5 Amphoterism

The hydroxides of certain metals can function as both bases and acids. Thus these water-insoluble compounds dissolve in solutions of high pH or of low pH. Examples of these compounds, which are called **amphoteric hydroxides**, are $Al(OH)_3$, $Zn(OH)_2$, $Sn(OH)_2$, $Cr(OH)_3$, $Be(OH)_2$, $Sb(OH)_3$ (or Sb_2O_3), and $As(OH)_3$ (or As_2O_3); many other compounds including $Cu(OH)_2$ and $AgOH$ (or Ag_2O) exhibit this property to a lesser degree.

The explanation of amphoteric behavior hinges on the ability of the metal cation of the amphoteric hydroxide to form complex ions with H_2O and with OH^-. For a example, a series of complexes, each with six ligands, is formed by the hydrated Al^{3+} ion in a solution as the pH is increased.

$$Al(H_2O)_6^{3+} + OH^- \rightleftharpoons Al(OH)(H_2O)_5^{2+} + H_2O$$

$$Al(OH)(H_2O)_5^{2+} + OH^- \rightleftharpoons Al(OH)_2(H_2O)_4^+ + H_2O$$

$$Al(OH)_2(H_2O)_4^+ + OH^- \rightleftharpoons Al(OH)_3(H_2O)_3(s) + H_2O$$

$$Al(OH)_3(H_2O)_3(s) + OH^- \rightleftharpoons Al(OH)_4(H_2O)^- + H_2O$$

The formation and dissociation of these complexes follow the principles discussed in Section 17.4. These equations are usually written without showing the coordinated water. Notice that aluminum hydroxide precipitates at a certain pH and that at a higher pH, it dissolves to form the aluminate ion $(Al(OH)_4(H_2O)_2^-$, or simply $Al(OH)_4^-)$. These reactions may be interpreted as proton exchanges. In each of them, a proton from a coordinated water of an aluminum complex (a Brønsted acid) is transferred to a OH^- ion (a Brønsted base). If the equations are read from right to left, they describe the stepwise dissociation of the aluminum complexes and appear similar to equations for the ionizations of weak bases (such as NH_3) in water.

Amphoteric hydroxides are amphiprotic. When the pH of a solution containing the aluminate ion is decreased slightly, the complex functions as a Brønsted base, and a coordinated OH group accepts a proton from H_3O^+, a Brønsted acid.

$$Al(OH)_4(H_2O)_2^- + H_3O^+ \rightleftharpoons Al(OH)_3(H_2O)_3(s) + H_2O$$

Continued gradual addition of H_3O^+ results in the successive formation of the lower hydroxy complexes. Read from right to left, the preceding equation is analogous to equations for the dissociations of weak acids.

▶ **EXAMPLE 17.16** (a) At what minimum pH will 1.0×10^{-3} mole of $Al(OH)_3$ go into solution (1 liter) as $Al(OH)_4^-$? (b) At what maximum pH will 1.0×10^{-3} mole of $Al(OH)_3$ go into solution (1 liter) as Al^{3+}? K_{SP} of $Al(OH)_3$ is 5.0×10^{-33}, and K_{inst} of $Al(OH)_4^-$ is 1.3×10^{-34}.

Solution (a) At the point at which $Al(OH)_3$ just dissolves,

$$K_{SP} = [Al^{3+}][OH^-]^3 = 5.0 \times 10^{-33} \qquad (1)$$

If the $Al(OH)_3$ is substantially completely converted into $Al(OH)_4^-$, then,

$$[Al(OH)_4^-] = 1.0 \times 10^{-3} M$$

and

$$\frac{[Al^{3+}][OH^-]^4}{[Al(OH)_4^-]} = 1.3 \times 10^{-34}$$

$$\frac{[Al^{3+}][OH^-]^4}{(1.0 \times 10^{-3})} = 1.3 \times 10^{-34}$$

$$[Al^{3+}][OH^-]^4 = 1.3 \times 10^{-37} \qquad (2)$$

If we divide equation (2) by equation (1), we get

$$\frac{[Al^{3+}][OH^-]^4}{[Al^{3+}][OH^-]^3} = \frac{1.3 \times 10^{-37}}{5.0 \times 10^{-33}}$$

$$[OH^-] = 2.6 \times 10^{-5} M$$

$$pH = 9.4$$

(b) The way the problem is stated, the $Al(OH)_3$ is to be completely converted into Al^{3+}. This may *not* be the pH at which the solid disappears into solution since the intermediate ions ($Al(OH)_2{}^+$ and $Al(OH)^{2+}$) are ignored. If, however,

$$[Al^{3+}] = 1.0 \times 10^{-3} M$$

then

$$[Al^{3+}][OH^-]^3 = 5.0 \times 10^{-33}$$

$$(1.0 \times 10^{-3})[OH^-]^3 = 5.0 \times 10^{-33}$$

$$[OH^-]^3 = 5.0 \times 10^{-30}$$

$$[OH^-] = 1.7 \times 10^{-10} M$$

$$pH = 4.2$$

The results of calculations such as those of Example 17.16 are not completely reliable. The constants are of doubtful validity, and the stepwise constants for many hydroxide systems are not known. Indeed, there is evidence that not all the ions and equilibria in solutions of this type have been identified, and probably the situation is much more complicated than we have depicted it. In theory, the ions $Al(OH)_5^{2-}$ and $Al(OH)_6^{3-}$ should be possible, but their existence in solution has never been firmly established. We have considered only mononuclear complexes (complexes with only one central metal atom). However, polynuclear complexes have been identified in some hydroxide systems. For example, $Sn_2(OH)_2^{2+}$ and $Sn_3(OH)_4^{2+}$, as well as $SnOH^+$, are postulated as occurring in acidic solutions of Sn^{2+} ion.

Advantage is taken of the amphoteric nature of some hydroxides in analytical chemistry and in some commercial processes. For example, Mg^{2+} and Zn^{2+} may be separated from a solution containing the two ions by making the solution alkaline.

$$Mg^{2+} + 2OH^- \rightleftharpoons Mg(OH)_2(s)$$

$$Zn^{2+} + 4OH^- \rightleftharpoons Zn(OH)_4^{2-}$$

The insoluble magnesium hydroxide may be removed by filtration from the solution containing the zincate ion.

In the production of aluminum metal from bauxite (impure hydrated Al_2O_3), the ore is purified prior to its reduction to aluminum metal. This purification is accomplished by dissolving the aluminum oxide in a solution of sodium hydroxide and removing the insoluble impurities by filtration.

$$Al_2O_3(s) + 2OH^- + 3H_2O \longrightarrow 2Al(OH)_4^-$$

17.6 Hydrolysis

Certain ions react with water to produce acidic or alkaline solutions. For example, the acetate ion can accept a proton from a water molecule to form an acetic acid molecule (a weak electrolyte) and a hydroxide ion.

$$C_2H_3O_2^- + H_2O \rightleftharpoons HC_2H_3O_2 + OH^-$$

This reaction of the acetate ion is similar to that of any other weak base, such as NH_3, with water. The fact that the acetate ion has a charge, whereas the ammonia molecule does not, is unimportant. Nevertheless, the reaction of an ion with water is customarily called a hydrolysis reaction and interpreted by reference to the weak electrolyte from which the ion is derived.

Ions derived from acids or alkalies that are strong electrolytes (such as Cl^- and Na^+) do not hydrolyze, and the weaker the electrolyte from which an ion is derived, the more extensive is its hydrolysis. A $0.1M$ solution of sodium acetate has a pH of 8.9 (Example 17.17), and the pH of a $0.1M$ solution of sodium cyanide is 11.2. In each case, it is the hydrolysis of the anion that causes the solution to be alkaline; the sodium ion does not undergo hydrolysis.

$$C_2H_3O_2^- + H_2O \rightleftharpoons HC_2H_3O_2 + OH^-$$

$$CN^- + H_2O \rightleftharpoons HCN + OH^-$$

Since HCN (ionization constant, 4.0×10^{-10}) is a weaker electrolyte than $HC_2H_3O_2$ (ionization constant, 1.8×10^{-5}), HCN does a better job of tying up protons than $HC_2H_3O_2$ does. Therefore, the hydrolysis of CN^- is more complete than that of $C_2H_3O_2^-$, and the concentration of OH^- is higher in the NaCN solution than in the $NaC_2H_3O_2$ solution. Note, however, that in both of these systems, the position of equilibrium is such that the reverse reaction, which may be regarded as a neutralization, proceeds to a greater extent than the forward reaction since H_2O is a weaker electrolyte than either HCN or $HC_2H_3O_2$.

The equilibrium constant for a hydrolysis equilibrium such as

$$C_2H_3O_2^- + H_2O \rightleftharpoons HC_2H_3O_2 + OH^-$$

may be obtained by dividing the water constant by the ionization constant for the weak acid.

$$[H^+][OH^-]\left(\frac{[HC_2H_3O_2]}{[H^+][C_2H_3O_2^-]}\right) = \frac{[HC_2H_3O_2][OH^-]}{[C_2H_3O_2^-]}$$

$$K_w\left(\frac{1}{K_{HC_2H_3O_2}}\right) = K_H$$

$$(1.0 \times 10^{-14})\left(\frac{1}{1.8 \times 10^{-5}}\right) = 5.6 \times 10^{-10}$$

▶ **EXAMPLE 17.17** What is the pH of a $0.10M$ solution of $NaC_2H_3O_2$?

Solution If we let x equal the equilibrium concentration of $HC_2H_3O_2$, we derive the following concentration terms.

$$\underset{0.10M}{C_2H_3O_2^-} + H_2O \rightleftharpoons \underset{(x)M}{HC_2H_3O_2} + \underset{(x)M}{OH^-}$$

In arriving at these concentration expressions, we assume that the decrease in the concentration of $C_2H_3O_2^-$ because of hydrolysis is negligible in comparison with the original concentration of $C_2H_3O_2^-$; also, we assume that the contribution to the concentration of OH^- from the ionization of water is negligible in comparison to that derived from the hydrolysis.

$$\frac{[HC_2H_3O_2][OH^-]}{[C_2H_3O_2^-]} = 5.6 \times 10^{-10}$$

$$\frac{x^2}{0.10} = 5.6 \times 10^{-10}$$

$$x^2 = 5.6 \times 10^{-11}$$

$$x = [HC_2H_3O_2] = [OH^-] = 7.5 \times 10^{-6}M$$

We can see that our assumptions were justified; 7.5×10^{-6} is indeed negligible in comparison to 0.10, and for all practical purposes $[C_2H_3O_2^-] = 0.10M$. Also the concentration of OH^- in pure water is only approximately 1.3% of the concentration of OH^- determined here; in a solution of sodium acetate, the OH^- produced by the hydrolysis would repress the ionization of water so that any additional OH^- from this source would be even more insignificant.

Since,

$$[OH^-] = 7.5 \times 10^{-6}M$$

$$[H^+] = 1.3 \times 10^{-9}M$$

$$pH = 8.9$$

The hydrolysis of cations produces acidic solutions.

$$NH_4^+ + H_2O \rightleftharpoons NH_3 + H_3O^+$$

This reaction of NH_4^+ is similar to the ionization of any other weak acid, such as $HC_2H_3O_2$, and rests on the ability of H_2O to accept a proton from a donor. The reverse reaction, a neutralization, proceeds to a greater extent than the forward reaction. Ammonia is a stronger base than water, and in the competition for protons, NH_3 is more effective than H_2O. Therefore, the concentration of NH_4^+ is higher than the concentration of H_3O^+.

The equilibrium constant for this hydrolysis equilibrium is obtained by dividing the water constant by the ionization constant for ammonia.

$$K_H = \frac{[NH_3][H_3O^+]}{[NH_4^+]}$$

$$K_H = \frac{K_w}{K_{NH_3}} = \frac{1.0 \times 10^{-14}}{1.8 \times 10^{-5}} = 5.6 \times 10^{-10}$$

▶ **EXAMPLE 17.18** What is the pH of a $0.30M$ solution of NH_4Cl?

Solution

$$\underset{0.30M}{H_2O + NH_4^+} \rightleftharpoons \underset{(x)M}{NH_3} + \underset{(x)M}{H_3O^+}$$

$$\frac{[NH_3][H_3O^+]}{[NH_4^+]} = 5.6 \times 10^{-10}$$

$$\frac{x^2}{0.30} = 5.6 \times 10^{-10}$$

$$x^2 = 1.7 \times 10^{-10}$$

$$x = [NH_3] = [H_3O^+] = 1.3 \times 10^{-5}M$$

$$pH = 4.9$$

In the hydrolysis of a metal cation, a coordinated water molecule of the hydrated cation donates a proton to a water molecule.

$$Al(H_2O)_6^{3+} + H_2O \rightleftharpoons Al(OH)(H_2O)_5^{2+} + H_3O^+$$

Usually these reactions are written without showing the coordinated water.

$$Al^{3+} + H_2O \rightleftharpoons Al(OH)^{2+} + H^+$$

Mathematical analysis of the hydrolysis of metal cations is complicated by several factors. Usually more than one hydrolytic product results from the hydrolysis of a metal cation, and often the values of the successive equilibrium constants do not decrease from step to step in the manner characteristic of the polyprotic acids. In some systems, hydrolysis proceeds to the point where the hydroxide of the metal cation precipitates. Furthermore, the constants have not been accurately determined for many systems, and in some systems, polynuclear complexes are thought to exist.

▶ **EXAMPLE 17.19**   What is the pH of a $0.10M$ solution of $Fe(NO_3)_2$?

Solution   The stepwise constants for the ionization of $Fe(OH)_2$ are

$$Fe(OH)_2(s) \rightleftharpoons Fe(OH)_2(aq) \qquad K_1 = 7.2 \times 10^{-6}$$

$$Fe(OH)_2(aq) \rightleftharpoons Fe(OH)^+ + OH^- \qquad K_2 = 1.0 \times 10^{-4}$$

$$Fe(OH)^+ \rightleftharpoons Fe^{2+} + OH^- \qquad K_3 = 2.5 \times 10^{-6}$$

The species $Fe(OH)_2(aq)$ is a neutral molecule in solution. From K_2 and K_3, we derive the constants for the steps of the hydrolysis.

$$Fe^{2+} + H_2O \rightleftharpoons Fe(OH)^+ + H^+ \qquad K_{H_1} = \frac{K_w}{K_3} = 4.0 \times 10^{-9}$$

$$Fe(OH)^+ + H_2O \rightleftharpoons Fe(OH)_2(aq) + H^+ \qquad K_{H_2} = \frac{K_w}{K_2} = 1.0 \times 10^{-10}$$

From the values of the constants, we see that the first step of the hydrolysis proceeds to a limited extent only and that the concentration of $Fe(OH)^+$, from this step, is low. The hydrolysis of this low concentration of $Fe(OH)^+$, described in the second hydrolysis step (which also occurs to a very limited extent), is therefore negligible, and we shall ignore the second step in our calculations.

$$\underset{(0.10-x)M}{Fe^{2+}} + H_2O \rightleftharpoons \underset{(x)M}{Fe(OH)^+} + \underset{(x)M}{H^+}$$

The x is negligible in comparison to 0.10 in the term for the concentration of Fe^{2+}.

$$\frac{[Fe(OH)^+][H^+]}{[Fe^{2+}]} = 4.0 \times 10^{-9}$$

$$\frac{x^2}{0.10} = 4.0 \times 10^{-9}$$

$$x = [H^+] = 2.0 \times 10^{-5}M$$

$$pH = 4.7$$

The concentrations of the species of interest present in this solution are

$$[H^+] = 2.0 \times 10^{-5} M$$

$$[Fe^{2+}] = 1.0 \times 10^{-1} M$$

$$[Fe(OH)^+] = 2.0 \times 10^{-5} M$$

$$[Fe(OH)_2(aq)] = 1.0 \times 10^{-10} M$$

The concentration of $Fe(OH)_2(aq)$ is readily calculated by means of K_{H_2}. From these concentration figures, we see that we were justified in neglecting the second step of the hydrolysis.

Notice that the equilibrium

$$Fe(OH)_2(s) \rightleftharpoons Fe(OH)_2(aq) \qquad K_1 = 7.2 \times 10^{-6}$$

defines the concentration of $Fe(OH)_2(aq)$ that exists in equilibrium with solid $Fe(OH)_2$, in a saturated solution. Since the concentration of $Fe(OH)_2(aq)$ in this $0.10M$ solution of $Fe(NO_3)_2$ is less than $7.2 \times 10^{-6} M$, the solution is not saturated with respect to $Fe(OH)_2$ and $Fe(OH)_2$ does not precipitate. The same conclusion could be reached by use of the K_{SP} of $Fe(OH)_2$.

The hydrolyses of anions derived from weak polyprotic acids are similar to the hydrolyses of multivalent cations. The ionization constants for H_2S are

$$H_2S \rightleftharpoons H^+ + HS^- \qquad K_1 = 1.1 \times 10^{-7}$$

$$HS^- \rightleftharpoons H^+ + S^{2-} \qquad K_2 = 1.0 \times 10^{-14}$$

Therefore the hydrolysis constants for the sulfide ion are

$$S^{2-} + H_2O \rightleftharpoons HS^- + OH^- \qquad K_{H_1} = \frac{K_w}{K_2} = 1.0$$

$$HS^- + H_2O \rightleftharpoons H_2S + OH^- \qquad K_{H_2} = \frac{K_w}{K_1} = 9.1 \times 10^{-8}$$

Notice that the *first* hydrolysis constant is obtained by dividing the water constant by the *second* ionization constant of H_2S.

In solutions of a soluble sulfide, the first step of the hydrolysis of the sulfide ion is so nearly complete that it far overshadows the second, and the acidity of the solution may be calculated by neglecting the hydrolysis of the HS^- ion.

▶ **EXAMPLE 17.20** What is the pH of a $0.10M$ solution of Na_2S?

Solution

$$S^{2-} + H_2O \rightleftharpoons HS^- + OH^-$$
$$\underset{(0.10-x)M}{} \qquad\qquad \underset{(x)M}{} \quad \underset{(x)M}{}$$

$$\frac{[HS^-][OH^-]}{[S^{2-}]} = 1.0$$

$$\frac{x^2}{(0.10-x)} = 1.0$$

$$x = 9.16 \times 10^{-2}$$

$$(0.10 - x) = [S^{2-}] = 8.4 \times 10^{-3}M$$

$$[HS^-] = [OH^-] = 9.2 \times 10^{-2}M$$

$$[H^+] = 1.1 \times 10^{-13}M$$

$$pH = 13.0$$

The pH of a solution of an acid salt (such as NaHS, NaH_2PO_4, Na_2HPO_4, and $NaHCO_3$) is affected not only by the hydrolysis of the anion but also by the dissociation of the anion. In a solution of NaHA, a salt of a hypothetical weak acid H_2A, the following equilibria are of importance.

$$HA^- \rightleftharpoons H^+ + A^{2-} \tag{3}$$

$$HA^- + H_2O \rightleftharpoons H_2A + OH^- \tag{4}$$

Since the concentrations of H_2A and A^{2-} are low, the ionization of H_2A and the hydrolysis of A^{2-} may be neglected.

The $[H^+]$ produced by the dissociation of HA^- (equation 3) is equal to $[A^{2-}]$. However, the OH^- produced by the hydrolysis of HA^- (equation 4) reduces the concentration of H^+ by an amount equal to $[H_2A]$. If we neglect the $[H^+]$ from the ionization of H_2O, then

$$[H^+] = [A^{2-}] - [H_2A] \tag{5}$$

Expressions for $[A^{2-}]$ and $[H_2A]$ may be derived from the appropriate ionization constants.

$$K_1 = \frac{[H^+][HA^-]}{[H_2A]}$$

therefore,

$$[H_2A] = \frac{[H^+][HA^-]}{K_1} \tag{6}$$

$$K_2 = \frac{[H^+][A^{2-}]}{[HA^-]}$$

and

$$[A^{2-}] = \frac{K_2[HA^-]}{[H^+]} \tag{7}$$

Substitution of equations (6) and (7) in (5) gives

$$[H^+] = \frac{K_2[HA^-]}{[H^+]} - \frac{[H^+][HA^-]}{K_1}$$

By clearing fractions, we derive

$$[H^+]^2 K_1 = K_1 K_2 [HA^-] - [H^+]^2 [HA^-]$$

Rearranging terms gives

$$[H^+]^2 K_1 + [H^+]^2 [HA^-] = K_1 K_2 [HA^-]$$
$$[H^+]^2 (K_1 + [HA^-]) = K_1 K_2 [HA^-]$$

If the concentration of HA^- is moderately large, K_1 will be negligible in comparison to $[HA^-]$ and $(K_1 + [HA^-]) \cong [HA^-]$. Therefore,

$$[H^+]^2 [HA^-] = K_1 K_2 [HA^-]$$
$$[H^+]^2 = K_1 K_2$$
$$[H^+] = \sqrt{K_1 K_2}$$

Thus for any solution of NaHS of moderate concentration, $[H^+]$ is equal to the square root of the product of the ionization constants of H_2S. For a solution of NaH_2PO_4, $[H^+] = \sqrt{K_1 K_2}$, and a for a solution of Na_2HPO_4, $[H^+] = \sqrt{K_2 K_3}$, where K_1, K_2, and K_3 are the successive ionization constants of H_3PO_4.

The hydrolysis of ions influences the solubility of slightly soluble substances. For example, in a solution of lead sulfide,

$$PbS(s) \rightleftharpoons Pb^{2+} + S^{2-}$$

the concentrations of Pb^{2+} and S^{2-} are reduced by hydrolysis (in which

$Pb(OH)^+$, HS^-, and H_2S are formed), and, therefore, more PbS dissolves than would be the case if hydrolysis did not occur.

▶ **EXAMPLE 17.21**   What is the molar solubility of PbS?

Solution   If the hydrolysis of ions is ignored,

$$K_{SP} = [Pb^{2+}][S^{2-}] = 7.0 \times 10^{-29}$$

$$x^2 = 7.0 \times 10^{-29}$$

$$x = 8.4 \times 10^{-15} M$$

As a first approximation, therefore, $[Pb^{2+}] = [S^{2-}] = 8.4 \times 10^{-15} M$, and any H^+ or OH^- obtained from the hydrolysis of such low concentrations of ions may be ignored in comparison to that derived from the ionization of water. Therefore,

$$[H^+] = [OH^-] = 1.0 \times 10^{-7} M$$

The hydrolysis equilibria in this solution are:

$$Pb^{2+} + H_2O \rightleftharpoons Pb(OH)^+ + H^+ \qquad K_H = \frac{1.0 \times 10^{-14}}{1.5 \times 10^{-8}} = 6.7 \times 10^{-7}$$

$$S^{2-} + H_2O \rightleftharpoons HS^- + OH^- \qquad K_{H_1} = \frac{1.0 \times 10^{-14}}{1.0 \times 10^{-14}} = 1.0$$

$$HS^- + H_2O \rightleftharpoons H_2S + OH^- \qquad K_{H_2} = \frac{1.0 \times 10^{-14}}{1.1 \times 10^{-7}} = 9.1 \times 10^{-8}$$

The sum of the concentrations of all sulfur-containing species must equal the sum of the concentrations of all lead-containing species since both types were derived from PbS. Therefore,

$$[Pb^{2+}] + [Pb(OH)^+] = [S^{2-}] + [HS^-] + [H_2S] \qquad (8)$$

By use of the hydrolysis constants, we can derive expressions in terms of $[Pb^{2+}]$ or $[S^{2-}]$ for the concentrations of all species. Thus

$$\frac{[Pb(OH)^+][H^+]}{[Pb^{2+}]} = 6.7 \times 10^{-7}$$

$$\frac{[Pb(OH)^+](1.0 \times 10^{-7})}{[Pb^{2+}]} = 6.7 \times 10^{-7}$$

Therefore,

$$[Pb(OH)^+] = 6.7[Pb^{2+}] \tag{9}$$

$$\frac{[HS^-][OH^-]}{[S^{2-}]} = 1.0$$

$$\frac{[HS^-](1.0 \times 10^{-7})}{[S^{2-}]} = 1.0$$

and

$$[HS^-] = 1.0 \times 10^7[S^{2-}] \tag{10}$$

$$\frac{[H_2S][OH^-]}{[HS^-]} = 9.1 \times 10^{-8}$$

$$\frac{[H_2S](1.0 \times 10^{-7})}{1.0 \times 10^7[S^{2-}]} = 9.1 \times 10^{-8}$$

Thus,

$$[H_2S] = 9.1 \times 10^6[S^{2-}] \tag{11}$$

Substitution of equations (9), (10), and (11) into (8) gives

$$[Pb^{2+}] + 6.7[Pb^{2+}] = [S^{2-}] + 1.0 \times 10^7[S^{2-}] + 9.1 \times 10^6[S^{2-}]$$

$$7.7[Pb^{2+}] = 1.9 \times 10^7[S^{2-}] \tag{12}$$

From the K_{SP} of PbS,

$$[S^{2-}] = \frac{7.0 \times 10^{-29}}{[Pb^{2+}]} \tag{13}$$

Substitution of (13) into (12) gives

$$7.7[Pb^{2+}] = 1.9 \times 10^7 \frac{7.0 \times 10^{-29}}{[Pb^{2+}]}$$

$$[Pb^{2+}]^2 = 1.7 \times 10^{-22}$$

$$[Pb^{2+}] = 1.3 \times 10^{-11}M$$

From (9),

$$[Pb(OH)^+] = 6.7(1.3 \times 10^{-11}) = 8.7 \times 10^{-11}M$$

The molar solubility of PbS is

$$[Pb^{2+}] + [Pb(OH)^+] = 1.0 \times 10^{-10}M$$

This value is 12,000 times that obtained by ignoring hydrolysis.

17.7 Titration of Acids and Alkalies

We are now in a position to study acid-alkali titrations in some detail. Let us consider the titration of a 50.0 ml sample of $0.100N$ HCl with a solution of $0.100N$ NaOH. Since HCl and NaOH are both strong electrolytes, the only equilibrium to be considered is the water equilibrium. Furthermore, for either solution, the molarity is equal to the normality. We shall assume, in the calculations that follow, that when a sample of NaOH solution is added to 50.0 ml of the HCl solution, the resulting volume is equal to the sum of the volumes of the two solutions.

The concentration of H^+ in the original 50.0 ml sample of acid in the titration flask is $0.100M$, and therefore the pH is 1.00.

After 10.0 ml of $0.100N$ NaOH has been added from the buret, the total volume of the solution is 60.0 ml, and the equivalent of 40.0 ml of $0.100N$ HCl remains unneutralized.

$$VN = VN$$

$$40.0(0.100) = 60.0x$$

$$x = [H^+] = 0.0667N$$

$$pH = 1.18$$

When 50.0 ml of $0.100N$ NaOH has been added, the "end point" of the titration is reached; all the acid is neutralized, and the $pH = 7.00$.

As NaOH solution is added beyond the equivalent point, the solution in the titration flask becomes increasingly alkaline. For example, when 60.0 ml of $0.100N$ NaOH has been added (total volume, 110 ml), the solution contains the equivalent of 10.0 ml of $0.100N$ NaOH.

$$VN = VN$$

$$10.0(0.100) = 110.0x$$

$$x = [OH^-] = 0.00909N$$

$$pOH = 2.04$$

$$pH = 11.96$$

The values in Table 17.1 were obtained from calculations such as these, and the data of Table 17.1 are plotted in Figure 17.1. Notice that the curve rises sharply in the section around the equivalence point. Whereas the first 49.9 ml of NaOH solution added causes the pH to change by three units, the next 0.2 ml added causes a change of *six* units in the pH. If an indicator is to be used in this titration to locate the equivalence point, any indicator may be employed that changes color in the pH range of the straight portion

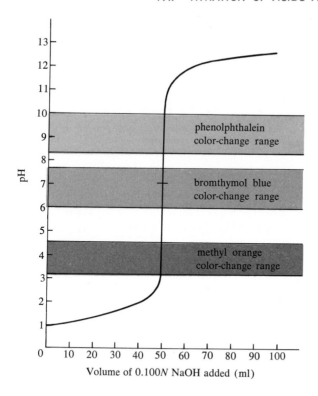

Figure 17.1 Titration of 50.0 ml of 0.100N HCl with 0.100N NaOH.

Table 17.1

Titration of 50.0 ml of 0.100N HCl with 0.100N NaOH

Volume of 0.100N NaOH Added (ml)	pH
0.0	1.00
10.0	1.18
20.0	1.37
30.0	1.60
40.0	1.96
49.0	3.00
49.9	4.00
50.0	7.00
50.1	10.00
51.0	11.00
60.0	11.96
70.0	12.22
80.0	12.36
90.0	12.46
100.0	12.52

of the curve. Around this point, the addition of one drop of NaOH solution causes a sharp increase in the pH. Any one of the three indicators indicated in Figure 17.1 would be satisfactory.

Let us now consider the titration of 50.0 ml of $0.100N$ acetic acid—a weak acid—with $0.100N$ sodium hydroxide. The concentration of H^+ in the original 50.0 ml sample of acid may be calculated by using the equilibrium constant (Example 16.2). From Table 16.1, we see that $[H^+] = 1.34 \times 10^{-3}M$, and the pH of the solution is, therefore, 2.87.

The solution resulting from the addition of 10.0 ml of $0.100N$ NaOH to the 50.0 ml sample of $0.100N$ $HC_2H_3O_2$ is, in effect, a buffer since it contains a mixture of $C_2H_3O_2^-$ ions, produced by the neutralization, together with unneutralized $HC_2H_3O_2$. The pH of a buffer is conveniently calculated by use of the relation

$$pH = pK - \log \left(\frac{[HA]}{[A^-]} \right)$$

which was derived in Section 16.7. For acetic acid, the pK is 4.75 (the negative logarithm of 1.80×10^{-5}). The ratio $[HC_2H_3O_2]/[C_2H_3O_2^-]$ is easily calculated. After 10.0 ml of NaOH is added, 40/50 of the acid of the original 50.0 ml sample remains unneutralized and 10/50 has, in effect, been converted into the salt sodium acetate. The ratio is, therefore, 4 to 1. Thus

$$pH = pK - \log \left(\frac{[HC_2H_3O_2]}{[C_2H_3O_2^-]} \right)$$

$$= 4.75 - \log(4/1)$$

$$= 4.15$$

At the equivalence point, all of the acid has been neutralized, and the solution (100 ml) is effectively $0.0500M$ in sodium acetate. The calculation of the pH of this solution must take into account the hydrolysis of the $C_2H_3O_2^-$ ion (Example 17.17).

$$C_2H_3O_2^- + H_2O \rightleftharpoons HC_2H_3O_2 + OH^-$$

$$\underset{0.0500M}{} \qquad \underset{(x)M}{} \quad \underset{(x)M}{}$$

$$\frac{[HC_2H_3O_2][OH^-]}{[C_2H_3O_2^-]} = 5.56 \times 10^{-10}$$

$$\frac{x^2}{5.00 \times 10^{-2}} = 5.56 \times 10^{-10}$$

$$x = [OH^-] = 5.27 \times 10^{-6}$$

$$pOH = 5.28$$

$$pH = 8.72$$

Notice that the equivalence point in this titration does not occur at the "neutral" pH, 7.

After the equivalence point, the addition of NaOH causes the solution to become increasingly alkaline. The added OH^- represses the hydrolysis of the acetate ion, and the contribution of the hydrolysis to the concentration of OH^- is negligible in comparison to the added OH^-. Thus the calculations from this point on are identical to those for the HCl–NaOH titration.

Data for a $HC_2H_3O_2$–NaOH titration are summarized in Table 17.2 and plotted in Figure 17.2. The equivalence point of this titration occurs at a

Table 17.2

Titration of 50.0 ml of 0.100N $HC_2H_3O_2$ with 0.100N NaOH

Volume of 0.100N NaOH Added (ml)	pH
0.0	2.87
10.0	4.15
20.0	4.57
30.0	4.93
40.0	5.35
49.0	6.44
49.9	7.45
50.0	8.72
50.1	10.00
51.0	11.00
60.0	11.96
70.0	12.22
80.0	12.36
90.0	12.46
100.0	12.52

higher pH than that of the preceding titration, and all pH values on the acid side of the equivalence point are higher. Therefore, the rapidly ascending portion of the curve around the equivalence point is reduced in length. From the curve of Figure 17.2, we can see that methyl orange is not a suitable indicator for this titration. Neither is bromthymol blue suitable, since its color change would start after 47.34 ml of NaOH has been added and continue until 49.97 ml has been added; this would hardly constitute a sharp end point for a titration. Phenolphthalein, however, would be a satisfactory indicator to employ.

Other titration curves may be drawn following the general line of approach outlined here. Figure 17.3 represents the titration curve for the titration of 50.0 ml of 0.100N NH_3 with 0.100N HCl. In this instance, methyl orange could be used as the indicator. Figure 17.4 is the titration curve for the

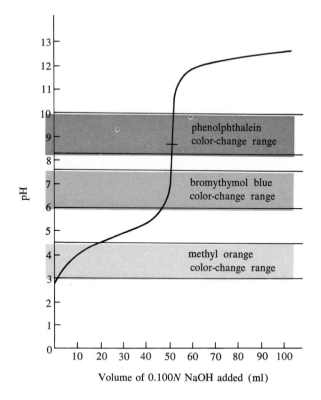

Figure 17.2 Titration of 50.0 ml of 0.100N HC$_2$H$_3$O$_2$ with 0.100N NaOH.

titration of 50.0 ml of 0.100N HC$_3$H$_3$O$_2$ with 0.100N NH$_3$; both solutes are weak electrolytes. No indicator can be found that would function satisfactorily for this titration, and such titrations—between weak electrolytes—are not usually run.

Titrations may be conducted potentiometrically. For example, a titration may be performed with the electrodes of a pH meter immersed in the solution being analyzed. The pH of the solution is determined after successive additions of reagent. The equivalence point of the titration is indicated by an abrupt change in the pH, but additions and readings are continued beyond this point. The equivalence point may be determined by graphing the data and estimating the volume corresponding to the midpoint of the steeply rising portion of the titration curve. A plot of cell potential has the same shape as a titration curve based on pH, and titrations may be conducted using such measurements instead of pH determinations. The same considerations apply for the determination of the equivalence point for curves based on either type of measurement.

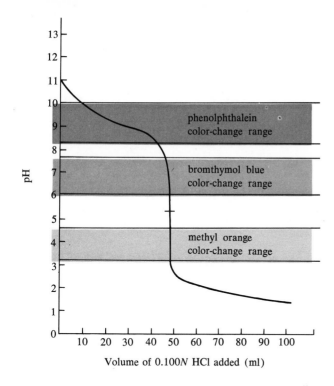

Figure 17.3 Titration of 50.0 ml of 0.100N NH₃ with 0.100N HCl.

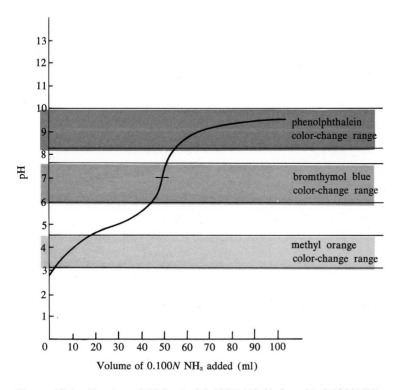

Figure 17.4 Titration of 50.0 ml of 0.100N HC₂H₃O₂ with 0.100N NH₃.

The potentiometric titration of a weak electrolyte serves as an important method of determining the dissociation constant of the electrolyte. Since

$$pH = pK - \log([HA]/[A^-])$$

the pK of the electrolyte is equal to the pH of the solution at half neutralization (where $[HA] = [A^-]$), but the pK, and hence the K itself, may be determined from any point on the titration curve.

▶ **EXAMPLE 17.22** The equivalence point in titration of 40.00 ml of a solution of a weak monoprotic acid occurs when 35.00 ml of a 0.100N NaOH solution has been added. The pH of the solution is 5.75 after 20.00 ml of the NaOH solution has been added. What is the dissociation constant of the acid?

Solution Since 35.00 ml of NaOH is required for complete neutralization, the acid has been 20/35 neutralized after 20.00 ml of NaOH has been added. In other words, 15/35 of the acid is in the form HA, and 20/35 is in the form A^-. The ratio $[HA]/[A^-]$ is, therefore, 15 to 20 or 0.75.

$$pH = pK - \log\left(\frac{[HA]}{[A^-]}\right)$$

$$5.75 = pK - \log(0.75)$$

$$pK = 5.63$$

$$K = 2.4 \times 10^{-6}$$

17.8 Oxidation-Reduction Equilibria

The ionic equilibria we have thus far considered in this chapter have not involved oxidation and reduction. Electrochemical measurements are the principal source of data for the study of oxidation-reduction equilibria. As we have seen, electrochemical measurements are used in the study of certain equilibria that do not involve oxidation-reduction—such as the determination of pH (Section 16.4), K_{SP}'s (Section 17.1), and titration curves (Section 17.7).

The equilibrium constant for an oxidation-reduction equilibrium is readily calculated from the standard cell potential of the reaction which in turn may be calculated from the standard electrode potentials for the half reactions. The change in standard Gibbs free energy for the reaction under consideration is given by the equation

$$\Delta G° = -nF\mathscr{E}° \tag{14}$$

and $\Delta G°$ is related to the equilibrium constant by the expression

$$\Delta G° = -RT \ln K \qquad (15)$$

An expression that relates the equilibrium constant directly to the cell potential is obtained by combining equations (14) and (15).

$$\mathscr{E}° = \left(\frac{RT}{nF}\right) \ln K$$

At 25°C,

$$\mathscr{E}° = \frac{0.05916}{n} \log K$$

This expression may also be derived from the Nernst equation (Section 10.9). A convenient, and equivalent expression is

$$\log K = 16.90 \, n\mathscr{E}°$$

As a rule, an ionic reaction that does not involve oxidation-reduction reaches equilibrium very rapidly—usually in the time that it takes to prepare the solution. Although many oxidation-reduction reactions occur rapidly in solution, a large number do not; in this latter instance, equilibrium is attained very slowly. Therefore even a large value for an equilibrium constant does not necessarily mean that the reaction to which it pertains will occur at an appreciable rate.

Oxidation-reduction reactions can be followed potentiometrically in much the same way as acid-alkali reactions, and redox titrations are extensively used in analysis. For example, the amount of iron in a sample of an ore can be determined by dissolving the ore, converting all of the iron in the resulting solution into the ferrous state, and titrating this solution against a standard solution of an oxidizing agent (such as ceric sulfate, potassium permanganate, or potassium dichromate). Let us consider the titration of 50.0 ml of $0.10M$ Fe^{2+} solution with a $0.10M$ solution of Ce^{4+}.

▶ **EXAMPLE 17.23** A 50.0 ml sample of $0.10M$ ferrous sulfate is titrated with $0.10M$ ceric sulfate. (a) What is the equilibrium constant for the reaction? (b) What are the concentrations of ions in equilibrium at the equivalence point?

Solution The electrode potentials for the half reactions are

$$e^- + Fe^{3+} \rightleftharpoons Fe^{2+} \qquad \mathscr{E}° = +0.77 \text{ v}$$

$$e^- + Ce^{4+} \rightleftharpoons Ce^{3+} \qquad \mathscr{E}° = +1.61 \text{ v}$$

and the potential for the reaction is

$$Fe^{2+} + Ce^{4+} \;\rightleftharpoons\; Fe^{3+} + Ce^{3+} \qquad \mathscr{E}^{\circ} = +0.84 \text{ v}$$

$$\log K = 16.9\, n\mathscr{E}^{\circ}$$

$$= 16.9\,(1)\,(0.84)$$

$$K = 1.6 \times 10^{14}$$

(b) To reach the equivalence point, as much Ce^{4+} will have to be added as there is Fe^{2+} in the original solution. At the equivalence point, therefore,

$$[Fe^{3+}] = [Ce^{3+}]$$

and

$$[Fe^{2+}] = [Ce^{4+}]$$

From the equilibrium constant,

$$\frac{[Fe^{3+}][Ce^{3+}]}{[Fe^{2+}][Ce^{4+}]} = 1.6 \times 10^{14}$$

$$\frac{[Fe^{3+}]^2}{[Fe^{2+}]^2} = 1.6 \times 10^{14}$$

$$\frac{[Fe^{3+}]}{[Fe^{2+}]} = 1.3 \times 10^{7}$$

We can see that the reaction proceeds essentially to completion, and, on this basis, we can calculate the concentrations of ions. Since the volume of the solution equals 100 ml at the equivalence point, $[Fe^{3+}] = [Ce^{3+}] = 0.050M$. If we let $x = [Fe^{2+}] = [Ce^{4+}]$,

$$\frac{(0.050)}{x} = 1.3 \times 10^{7}$$

$$x = [Fe^{2+}] = [Ce^{4+}] = 3.8 \times 10^{-9}M$$

and

$$[Fe^{3+}] = [Ce^{3+}] = 5.0 \times 10^{-2}M$$

At every point in the titration of Fe^{2+} with Ce^{4+}, the $\mathscr{E}$ of a theoretical cell

$$Pt\,|\,Ce^{4+},\,Ce^{3+}\,|\,Fe^{3+},\,Fe^{2+}\,|\,Pt$$

would be zero since equilibrium is established at each point. However, if the titration is run in a cell containing a standard hydrogen electrode (the reference electrode) and a platinum electrode (the indicator electrode), a difference in potential may be read as the titration proceeds.

The $\mathscr{E}$ of the cell

$$Pt|\,H_2|\,H^+|\,Fe^{3+},\,Fe^{2+}|\,Pt$$

where the left-hand electrode is a standard hydrogen electrode, varies with the concentrations of the iron ions

$$\mathscr{E} = \mathscr{E}° - \left(\frac{0.059}{1}\right)\log\frac{[Fe^{2+}]}{[Fe^{3+}]}$$

Initially, before any Ce^{4+} is added to the 50.0 ml sample of $0.10M$ Fe^{2+}, $\mathscr{E}$ is theoretically equal to $-\infty$, although traces of Fe^{3+}, due to air oxidation, will give a small positive reading.

After 10.0 ml of $0.10M$ Ce^{4+} is added, 40/50 of the iron is in the original form, Fe^{2+}, and 10/50 of the iron is in the oxidized form, Fe^{3+}. The ratio of $[Fe^{2+}]$ to $[Fe^{3+}]$ is, therefore, 4 to 1, and

$$\mathscr{E} = +0.77 - (0.059)\log 4$$

$$= +0.77 - (0.059)(0.60)$$

$$= +0.73 \text{ v}$$

At the half-titration point, when 25.0 ml of Ce^{4+} has been added, $[Fe^{2+}] = [Fe^{3+}]$, and $[Fe^{2+}]/[Fe^{3+}] = 1$. Since the logarithm of 1 is 0,

$$\mathscr{E} = +0.77 \text{ v}$$

At the equivalence point, $[Fe^{3+}]/[Fe^{2+}] = 1.3 \times 10^7$ (Example 17.23). Therefore,

$$\frac{[Fe^{2+}]}{[Fe^{3+}]} = \frac{1}{1.3 \times 10^7} = 7.7 \times 10^{-8}$$

and

$$\mathscr{E} = +0.77 - 0.059 \log(7.7 \times 10^{-8})$$

$$= +0.77 - 0.059(-7.11)$$

$$= +1.19 \text{ v}$$

After the equivalence point, the concentration of Fe^{2+} becomes vanishingly small. We may calculate points for the titration curve by remembering that at each point of the curve the $\mathscr{E}$ for the reduction of Ce^{4+} equals the $\mathscr{E}$ for the reduction of Fe^{3+}, since $\mathscr{E}$ for the couple is zero whenever equilibrium is established. Prior to the equivalence point, the Ce^{4+} is consumed in the oxidation of Fe^{2+} as fast as it is added; after the equivalence point, Ce^{4+} is present in excess. The cell, in effect, is

$$Pt \mid H_2 \mid H^+ \mid Ce^{4+}, Ce^{3+} \mid Pt$$

After 60.0 ml of $0.100M$ Ce^{4+} has been added, 10.0 ml is present in excess. The concentration of Ce^{4+} is proportional to the 10.0 ml added above the amount needed for equivalence, and the concentration of Ce^{3+} is proportional to 50.0 ml (the volume needed to react with the 50.0 ml of Fe^{2+}). Therefore the ratio of $[Ce^{3+}]$ to $[Ce^{4+}]$ is equal to 50/10 or 5.

$$\mathscr{E} = +1.61 - 0.059 \log\left(\frac{[Ce^{3+}]}{[Ce^{4+}]}\right)$$

$$= +1.61 - 0.059 \log(5)$$

$$= +1.56 \text{ v}$$

Notice that $\mathscr{E}°$ for the $Ce^{4+}-Ce^{3+}$ couple (1.61 v) is reached when 100.0 ml of Ce^{4+} solution has been added.

The titration curve of Figure 17.5 was plotted from data obtained from calculations such as the foregoing. The equivalence point of an actual titration may be obtained by taking readings of the potential after successive additions of the oxidizing agent, plotting the data, and finding the inflection point of the titration curve in the same manner as that employed for acid-alkali titrations.

In addition to potentiometric determinations, oxidation-reduction indicators may be used to locate the end point of an oxidation-reduction titration. For the titration of Fe^{2+} by Ce^{4+}, ferroin is a suitable indicator. Ferroin undergoes a conversion from a pale blue form to a red form at approximately 1.11 v, a value suitably close to the equivalence point voltage of 1.19 v.

The data plotted in Figure 17.5 were calculated for a cell utilizing a standard hydrogen electrode ($\mathscr{E}° = 0.00$ v) as a reference electrode. In actual practice calomel electrodes (Section 16.4) or silver–silver chloride electrodes are generally employed in place of hydrogen electrodes since the latter are inconvenient to use. If a normal calomel electrode is employed as the reference electrode ($\mathscr{E} = +0.283$ v), every potential measured will be displaced by 0.283 v. For example, the equivalence point of the titration would occur at 0.91 v instead of 1.19 v. The actual $\mathscr{E}$ measurements are of no concern, since the equivalence point is derived from the titration curve and the curve is merely displaced to lower $\mathscr{E}$ values by the use of a calomel electrode in place of a hydrogen electrode.

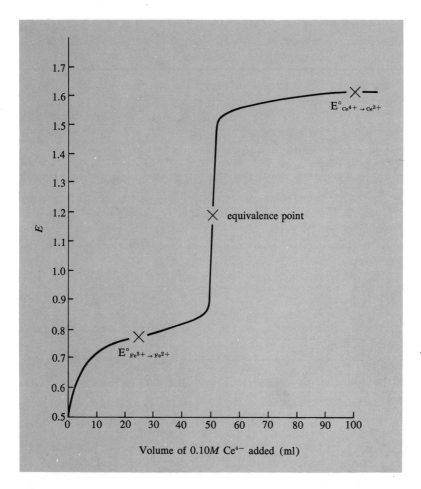

Figure 17.5 Titration of 50.0 ml 0.10*M* Fe²⁺ with 0.10*M* Ce⁴⁺. Potential of a platinum electrode is referred to a standard hydrogen electrode.

As a matter of fact, for a given oxidation-reduction reaction, a titration curve based on actual $\mathscr{E}$ measurements would be slightly different from a titration curve derived from $\mathscr{E}°$ values. $\mathscr{E}°$ values are based on activities rather than concentrations; the difference between the activity and the concentration of a multivalent ion can be appreciable. If so-called "formal potentials" are used instead of standard potentials, a titration curve is obtained that is more in harmony with that plotted from the data obtained from an actual titration. Formal potentials are based on concentrations rather than activities. In any event, the equivalence point is located from the titration curve rather than from a calculated equivalence-point potential, and the principles of an oxidation-reduction titration are adequately illustrated by the use of $\mathscr{E}°$'s.

SOME SUGGESTED READINGS

Blackburn, T. R., *Equilibrium—A Chemistry of Solutions*, New York, Holt, Rinehart, and Winston, 1969 (paper).

Butler, J. N., *Solubility and pH Calculations*, Reading, Mass. Addison-Wesley, 1964 (paper).

Guyon, J. C., and Jones, B. E., *Introduction to Solution Equilibrium*,, Boston, Allyn and Bacon, 1969 (paper).

Lee, T. S., and Sillen, L. G., *Chemical Equilibrium in Analytical Chemistry*, New York, Wiley, 1964 (paper).

Margolis, E. J., *Principles in the Calculation of Ionic Equilibrium*, New York, Macmillan, 1966 (paper).

Morris, K., *Principles of Chemical Equilibrium*, New York, Van Nostrand Reinhold, 1965 (paper).

Robbins, O., Jr., *Ionic Reactions and Equilibria*, New York, Macmillan, 1967 (paper).

PROBLEMS

The more difficult problems are starred.

17.1 At 25°C, 3.4×10^{-6} mole of $Ni(OH)_2$ dissolves in 1.0 liter of water. Calculate the K_{SP} of $Ni(OH)_2$.

17.2 The K_{SP} of $CaCO_3$ is 4.7×10^{-9}. What is the molar solubility of $CaCO_3$?

17.3 How many moles of SrF_2 will dissolve in 150 ml of $0.30M$ NaF solution? Neglect the hydrolysis of the F^- ion.

17.4 How many moles of $Mg(OH)_2$ will dissolve in 250 ml of a solution with a pH of 12.70?

17.5 In a saturated solution of calcium phosphate, the concentration of PO_4^{3-} ion is $3.3 \times 10^{-7}M$. Calculate the K_{SP} of $Ca_3(PO_4)_2$.

*17.6 The K_{SP} of Ag_3PO_4 is 1.8×10^{-18}. What is the molar solubility of Ag_3PO_4?

17.7 Which oxalate has the lower molar solubility, $Ag_2C_2O_4$ (K_{SP}, 1.1×10^{-11}) or CaC_2O_4 (K_{SP}, 1.3×10^{-9})?

17.8 Calculate the K_{SP} of thallium(I) chloride from the following standard electrode potentials:

$$TlCl(s) + e^- \rightleftharpoons Tl(s) + Cl^-(aq) \qquad \mathscr{E}° = -0.557 \text{ v}$$

$$Tl^+(aq) + e^- \rightleftharpoons Tl(s) \qquad \mathscr{E}° = -0.336 \text{ v}$$

17.9 The K_{SP} of Ag_2CrO_4 is 1.9×10^{-12} and the Ag^+/Ag electrode potential is

$$e^- + Ag^+(aq) \rightleftharpoons Ag(s) \qquad \mathscr{E}° = +0.799 \text{ v}$$

Calculate $\mathscr{E}°$ for the half reaction

$$Ag_2CrO_4(s) + 2e^- \rightleftharpoons 2Ag(s) + CrO_4^{2-}(aq)$$

17.10 Calculate the K_{SP} of bismuthyl chloride, BiOCl, from the following standard electrode potentials:

$$BiOCl(s) + 2H^+(aq) + 3e^- \rightleftharpoons Bi(s) + H_2O + Cl^-(aq) \quad \mathscr{E}° = +0.160 \text{ v}$$
$$BiO^+(aq) + 2H^+(aq) + 3e^- \rightleftharpoons Bi(s) + H_2O \quad \mathscr{E}° = +0.320 \text{ v}$$

17.11 Given the following standard electrode potentials:

$$Ag_2MoO_4(s) + 2e^- \rightleftharpoons 2Ag(s) + MoO_4^{2-}(aq) \quad \mathscr{E}° = +0.486 \text{ v}$$
$$Ag^+(aq) + e^- \rightleftharpoons Ag(s) \quad \mathscr{E}° = +0.799 \text{ v}$$

What is the molar solubility of silver molybdate?

17.12 Calculate the final concentrations of Ca^{2+}, NO_3^-, Na^+, and F^- in a solution prepared by adding 100 ml of $0.20M$ $Ca(NO_3)_2$ to 150 ml of $0.25M$ NaF. Neglect the hydrolysis of the F^- ion.

17.13 The formula of the mercurous ion is Hg_2^{2+}, and the K_{SP} of mercurous carbonate, Hg_2CO_3, is 9.0×10^{-17}. (a) Determine the molar solubility of Hg_2CO_3. (b) What would the K_{SP} of this compound be if the mercurous ion were Hg^+?

17.14 What concentration of F^- is necessary to start the precipitation of SrF_2 from a saturated solution of $SrSO_4$?

17.15 What minimum concentration of NH_4^+ is necessary to prevent the formation of a $Fe(OH)_2$ precipitate from a solution that is $0.020M$ in Fe^{2+} and $0.020M$ in NH_3?

17.16 A solution is $0.030M$ in Mn^{2+} and $0.025M$ in NH_4^+. What should the concentration of NH_3 be in order to cause $Mn(OH)_2$ to start to precipitate?

*17.17 Will $Mg(OH)_2$ precipitate from a solution prepared by adding 5.0 ml of a $0.090M$ NH_3 solution to 10 ml of a solution in which the concentration of H^+ is $0.030M$ and the concentration of Mg^{2+} is $0.030M$? Remember that NH_3 and H^+ react to form NH_4^+.

17.18 The concentration of Ba^{2+} in a solution is $0.30M$. What should the concentration of Pb^{2+} be so that, when solid Na_2SO_4 is gradually added, $PbSO_4$ precipitates before $BaSO_4$?

17.19 (a) A solution is $0.15M$ in Pb^{2+} and $0.20M$ in Ag^+. If solid Na_2SO_4 is very slowly added to this solution, which will precipitate first, $PbSO_4$ or Ag_2SO_4? Neglect volume changes. (b) The addition of Na_2SO_4 is continued until the second cation just starts to precipitate as the sulfate. What is the concentration of the first cation at this point?

17.20 (a) A solution is $0.10M$ in CrO_4^{2-} and $0.15M$ in SO_4^{2-}. Solid $Ba(NO_3)_2$ is gradually added to the solution. Neglect volume changes, and calculate the concentrations of Ba^{2+} required to start the precipitation of $BaCrO_4$

and $BaSO_4$. Which compound precipitates first? (b) What is the concentration of CrO_4^{2-} when $BaSO_4$ starts to precipitate? (c) What is the concentration of CrO_4^{2-} when half of the SO_4^{2-} has been precipitated as $BaSO_4$?

17.21 Calculate the number of S^{2-} ions in 10 ml of a solution that is $0.30M$ in H^+ and that has been saturated with H_2S.

17.22 A solution that is $0.30M$ in H^+ and $0.15M$ in Ni^{2+} is saturated with H_2S. Should NiS precipitate?

17.23 A solution that is $0.20M$ in H^+ and $0.050M$ in Cd^{2+} is saturated with H_2S. Should CdS precipitate?

17.24 What should the H^+ concentration be in a solution that is $0.25M$ in Co^{2+} to prevent the precipitation of CoS when the solution is saturated with H_2S?

17.25 A solution that is $0.10M$ in H^+ and $0.10M$ in Cu^2 is saturated with H_2S. What is the concentration of Cu^{2+} after CuS has precipitated? Note that it is necessary to take into account the increase in acidity caused by the precipitation. Neglect the hydrolysis of ions.

17.26 (a) What concentration of H^+ should be present in a solution that is $0.20M$ in Pb^{2+} and $0.20M$ in Zn^{2+} so that upon saturation with H_2S, the maximum amount of PbS precipitates but no ZnS precipitates at any stage? (b) What concentration of Pb^{2+} remains in the solution after the PbS has precipitated? Ignore the hydrolysis of ions, but do not neglect the increase in acidity caused by the precipitation.

17.27 (a) Will a precipitate of MnS form when a solution that is $0.10M$ in acetic acid, $HC_2H_3O_2$, and $0.10M$ in Mn^{2+} is saturated with H_2S? (b) If the solution described in part (a) also is $0.10M$ in sodium acetate, $NaC_2H_3O_2$, will MnS precipitate?

17.28 A solution is $0.30M$ in H^+, $0.030M$ in $Cr_2O_7^{2-}$, and $0.030M$ in Fe^{3+}. Saturation of the solution with H_2S reduces $Cr_2O_7^{2-}$ to Cr^{3+} and Fe^{3+} to Fe^{2+}. In these reactions, which may be considered to be complete, H_2S is oxidized to S. (a) Write equations for the two oxidation-reduction reactions. (b) What is the final concentration of H^+? (c) Will FeS precipitate? (d) What is the total weight of solid that precipitates out of 100 ml of solution?

17.29 Compare the molar solubilities of (a) AgCl, (b) AgBr, and (c) AgI in $0.50M$ NH_3 solution.

17.30 Why is it incorrect to assume that the concentration of NH_3 is exactly four times the concentration of Cu^{2+} in a solution of $Cu(NH_3)_4^{2+}$?

17.31 A $0.010M$ solution of $AgNO_3$ is made $0.50M$ in NH_3 thus forming the $Ag(NH_3)_2^+$ complex ion. (a) Will AgCl precipitate if sufficient NaCl is added to make the solution $0.010M$ in Cl^-? (b) Will AgI precipitate if the solution is made $0.010M$ in I^-?

*17.32 Use the constants for the stepwise dissociation of the $Ag(S_2O_3)_3^{5-}$ ion given in Section 17.4 to determine the concentrations of Ag^+, $Ag(S_2O_3)^-$, $Ag(S_2O_3)_2^{3-}$, $Ag(S_2O_3)_3^{5-}$, and $S_2O_3^{2-}$ in a solution prepared by dissolving 1.0 mole of $Ag(S_2O_3)_3^{5-}$ in 1.0 liter of water.

17.33 (a) At what minimum concentration of OH^- will 1.0×10^{-3} mole of $Zn(OH)_2$ into solution (1.0 liter) as $Zn(OH)_4^{2-}$? (b) At what maximum concentration of OH^- will 1.0×10^{-3} mole of $Zn(OH)_2$ go into solution (1.0 liter) as Zn^{2+}?

17.34 What is the pH of a $0.10M$ solution of sodium benzoate $(NaC_7H_5O_2)$?

17.35 What is the pH of a $0.20M$ solution of hydrazine hydrochloride (N_2H_5Cl)?

17.36 What concentration of sodium acetate, $NaC_2H_3O_2$, will produce a solution with a pH of 9.00?

17.37 The pH of a $0.20M$ solution of NaX is 9.30. What is the ionization constant of the weak acid HX?

17.38 What is the pH of a $0.10M$ solution of $Cu(NO_3)_2$? Consider only the first step of the hydrolysis.

17.39 How many moles of $ZnCl_2$ are present in 1.0 liter of a solution that has a pH of 5.92? Consider only the first step of the hydrolysis.

17.40 A $0.25M$ solution of NaX has a pH of 9.60. Determine the ionization constant of the weak acid HX.

17.41 Determine the pH of (a) a $0.10M$ solution of Na_2CO_3, and (b) a $0.10M$ solution of $NaHCO_3$.

17.42 Determine the concentration of H^+ of a $0.10M$ solution of (a) Na_3PO_4, (b) Na_2HPO_4, (c) NaH_2PO_4.

*17.43 Determine the molar solubility of CuS (a) neglecting the hydrolysis of ions and (b) taking hydrolysis into account.

*17.44 Determine the molar solubility of ZnS (a) neglecting the hydrolysis of ions and (b) taking hydrolysis into account.

17.45 Determine pH values for the titration curve pertaining to the titration of 30.00 ml of $0.100N$ benzoic acid, $HC_7H_5O_2$, with $0.100N$ NaOH (a) after 10.00 ml of NaOH solution has been added, (b) after 30.00 ml of NaOH solution has been added, (c) after 40.00 ml of NaOH solution has been added.

17.46 Determine pH values for the titration curve pertaining to the titration of 25.00 ml of $0.100N$ NH_3 solution with a $0.100N$ solution of HCl (a) after 10.00 ml of the HCl solution has been added, (b) after 25.00 ml of HCl solution has been added, and (c) after 35.00 ml of HCl solution has been added.

17.47 The equivalence point in a titration of 25.00 ml of a weak acid HX occurs when 32.30 ml of $0.250N$ NaOH solution has been added. The pH of the solution is 4.66 after 5.00 ml of the NaOH solution has been added. What is the equilibrium constant for the ionization of HX?

17.48 The equivalence point in the titration of 50.00 ml of a solution of formic acid, $HCHO_2$, occurs when 38.75 ml of a $0.360N$ solution of NaOH has been added. How many ml of the NaOH solution should be added to 50.00 ml of the formic acid solution to produce a solution with a pH of 4.00?

*17.49 In the titration of a solution of a weak acid, HX, with NaOH solution, the pH is 5.80 after 10.00 ml of the NaOH solution has been added and 6.40 after 20.00 ml of the NaOH solution has been added. What is the equilibrium constant for the ionization of HX?

17.50   (a) Calculate the equilibrium constant for the reaction

$$Zn(s) + Cu^{2+} \rightleftharpoons Zn^{2+} + Cu(s)$$

(b) If metallic zinc is added to a $0.10M$ Cu^{2+} solution, what are the concentrations of Zn^{2+} and Cu^{2+} ions at equilibrium? (c) In theory, what volume of solution, at equilibrium, would contain one Cu^{2+} ion?

17.51   (a) Calculate the equilibrium constant for the reaction

$$Sn(s) + Pb^{2+} \rightleftharpoons Sn^{2+} + Pb(s)$$

(b) If solid Sn is added to a $0.10M$ Pb^{2+} solution, what are the concentrations of Sn^{2+} and Pb^{2+} at equilibrium?

17.52   (a) Calculate the equilibrium constant for the reaction

$$Cr^{2+} + Fe^{3+} \rightleftharpoons Cr^{3+} + Fe^{2+}$$

(b) Determine the concentrations of ions present at equilibrium in a solution prepared by the addition of 50.0 ml of a $0.050M$ Cr^{2+} solution to 50.0 ml of a $0.050M$ Fe^{3+} solution.

*17.53   A 50.00 ml sample of a $0.10M$ Sn^{2+} solution is titrated with a $0.20M$ Ce^{4+} solution. (a) Determine the equilibrium constant for the reaction

$$Sn^{2+} + 2Ce^{4+} \rightleftharpoons Sn^{4+} + 2Ce^{3+}$$

(b) What are the concentrations of ions in equilibrium at the equivalence point?

METALS

More than three-quarters of all the known elements are metals. Although metals vary widely with respect to a given property, several chemical and physical properties are typical of metals and generally serve as the basis of the definition of this class of elements. Metals have superior electrical and thermal conductivities, characteristic luster, and the ability to be deformed, without cleaving, under stress. Among the chemical characteristics of most metals is their tendency to donate electrons thus producing positive ions and their formation of basic oxides. Much of the chemistry of the metals has been included in the discussion of the nonmetals in Chapters 11 and 12.

18.1 Physical Properties of Metals

The densities of metals show a wide variation. Of all the *solid* elements, lithium has the lowest density and osmium has the highest. The large majority of metals, however, have relatively high densities in comparison to the densities of the solid nonmetals. The metals of groups I A and II A are referred to as the light metals because they are exceptions to the preceding generalization. The close-packed arrangement of the atoms of most metallic crystals (Section 7.11) helps to explain the relatively high densities of metals.

The trend in the magnitude of the density across a period (Figure 18.1) reflects the variation in atomic radius of the elements of the period. Thus the atomic radii of the elements of the fourth, fifth, and sixth periods reach a minimum approximately at group VIII, and the densities are at a maximum at this point. The I A metals have the largest atomic radii and the smallest atomic masses of their periods; these factors coupled with their crystal structure give them comparatively low densities.

The densities of the elements of a group increase with increasing atomic number; this trend corresponds to an increase in atomic mass which is not offset by a proportionate increase in atomic radius. Data for the lanthanides of period 6 are not plotted in Figure 18.1, but the lanthanide contraction causes the pronounced difference between the curves for period 5 and period 6.

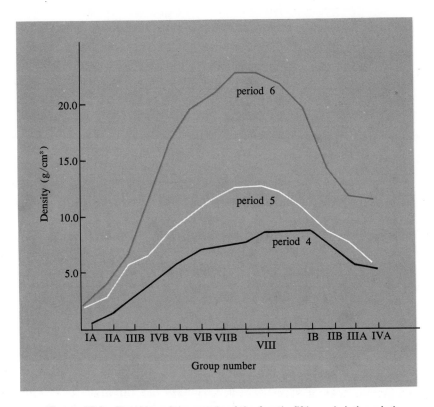

Figure 18.1 Densities of the metals of the fourth, fifth, and sixth periods.

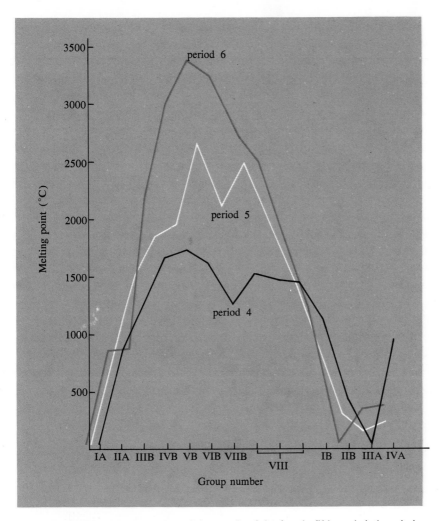

Figure 18.2   Melting points of the metals of the fourth, fifth, and sixth periods.

The melting points and boiling points of the nonmetals show extreme variations—from the very low values of the gaseous elements to the extremely high values of the elements that crystallize in covalent network lattices, such as the diamond. There is considerable variation in the melting and boiling points of the metals, although low values, such as those of the gaseous nonmetals, are not observed. In general, most metals have comparatively high melting and boiling points.

The striking feature of the curves of Figure 18.2 is the maximum that occurs at approximately the center of each curve. Curves for the boiling point, heat of fusion, heat of vaporization, and hardness of metals have approximately the same appearance. For a given period, therefore, the strength of the metallic bonding (Section 4.6) must reach a maximum around the center of the transition series.

The strength of the metallic bonding is, of course, related to the number of delocalized electrons per atom used in the bonding. If we count only the ns, np, and unpaired $(n-1)$ d electrons of a metal as bonding electrons, we get an order that approximates that of the properties under discussion. This analysis is a decided oversimplification; other factors, such as atomic radius, nuclear charge, number of bonding orbitals, overlap of orbital energies, and crystal form, are involved.

The deformability, luster, thermal conductivity, and electrical conductivity of metals are the properties most characteristic of metallic bonding and the metallic state (Section 4.6). Electrical conductivity is measured in units of 1/ohm cm; a conductivity of 1.0/ohm cm means that a current of 1.0 amp flows when a potential of 1.0 v is applied to opposite faces of a 1.0 cm^3 cube of the material being studied (Section 10.1). The conductivities of metals, or conductors, lie in the general range of 10^4 to 10^6/ohm cm at room temperature and decrease with increasing temperature. These conductivities are approximately 1 million to 1 billion times the conductivities of the semimetals, or semiconductors (Section 7.14), which range from 10^{-5} to 10/ohm cm at room temperature and increase with rising temperature. The nonmetals, or insulators, have negligible conductivities—from 10^{-22} to 10^{-10}/ohm cm at room temperature, increasing with increasing temperature.

The conductivities of some metals are listed in Table 18.1. The metals of

Table 18.1

Electrical Conductivities of the Metals at 0°C in Units of 10^4/Ohm cm

Li 11.8	Be 18													
Na 23	Mg 25											Al 40		
K 15.9	Ca 23	Sc	Ti 1.2	V 0.6	Cr 6.5	Mn 20	Fe 11.2	Co 16	Ni 16	Cu 65	Zn 18	Ga 2.2		
Rb 8.6	Sr 3.3	Y	Zr 2.4	Nb 4.4	Mo 23	Tc	Ru 8.5	Rh 22	Pd 10	Ag 66	Cd 15	In 12	Sn 10	Sb 2.8
Cs 5.6	Ba 1.7	La 1.7	Hf 3.4	Ta 7.2	W 20	Re 5.3	Os 11	Ir 20	Pt 10	Au 49	Hg 4.4	Tl 7.1	Pb 5.2	Bi 1

group I B (copper, silver, and gold) are outstanding electrical conductors. Except for similarities in the relative standing in a period of elements of the same group, periodic trends in the conductivities are difficult to discern. Nor is it easy to explain the lack of a close correlation between the general trend in melting points and the pattern of the conductivities.

The thermal conductivity, luster, and deformability of metals have been discussed in Section 4.6. In general, thermal conductivities parallel electrical conductivities. The nondirectional character of metallic bonding accounts for the ease with which planes of atoms slide across one another under stress so that the crystal may be deformed without shattering. When the planes of an ionic crystal are displaced (Figure 3.14), the new alignment brings ions of the same charge into proximity and results in the cleavage of the crystal. Covalent network crystals are deformed only by breaking the covalent bonds of the crystal, a process which also results in the fragmentation of the crystal.

18.2 Natural Occurrence of Metals

An **ore** is a naturally occurring material from which one or more metals can be profitably extracted. The principal types of ores and examples of each are listed in Table 18.2. A few of the less reactive metals occur in nature in elementary form; for many of these metals, native ores constitute the most important source. The greatest tonnage of metals is derived from oxides— either oxide ores or metal oxides that are produced by the calcining of carbonate or sulfide ores.

Table 18.2

Occurrence of Metals

Type of Ore	*Examples*
native metals	Cu, Ag, Au, As, Sb, Bi, Pd, Pt
oxides	Al_2O_3, Fe_2O_3, Fe_3O_4, SnO_2, MnO_2, TiO_2, $FeO \cdot Cr_2O_3$, $FeO \cdot WO_3$, Cu_2O, ZnO
carbonates	$CaCO_3$, $CaCO_3 \cdot MgCO_3$, $MgCO_3$, $FeCO_3$, $PbCO_3$, $BaCO_3$, $SrCO_3$, $ZnCO_3$, $MnCO_3$, $CuCO_3 \cdot Cu(OH)_2$, $2CuCO_3 \cdot Cu(OH)_2$
sulfides	Ag_2S, Cu_2S, CuS, PbS, ZnS, HgS, $FeS \cdot CuS$, FeS_2, Sb_2S_3, Bi_2S, MoS_2, NiS, CdS
halides	$NaCl$, KCl, $AgCl$, $KCl \cdot MgCl_2 \cdot 6H_2O$, $NaCl$ and $MgCl_2$ in sea water
sulfates	$BaSO_4$, $SrSO_4$, $PbSO_4$, $CaSO_4 \cdot 2H_2O$, $CuSO_4 \cdot 2Cu(OH)_2$
silicates	$Be_3AlSi_6O_{18}$, $ZrSiO_4$, $Sc_2Si_2O_7$, $(NiSiO_3, MgSiO_3)^a$
phosphates	$(CePO_4, LaPO_4, NdPO_4, PrPO_4, Th_3(PO_4)_4)^a$, $LiF \cdot AlPO_4$

a Occur in a single mineral but not in fixed proportions.

Silicate minerals are abundant in nature. However, the extraction of metals from silicates is difficult, and the cost of such processes may be prohibitive. Consequently, only the less common metals are commercially derived from silicate ores. Phosphate minerals are, in general, rare and frequently occur in low concentrations.

A number of metals occur as impurities in the ores of other metals so that both metals are derived from the same commercial operation. For example, cadmium metal is obtained as a by-product in the production of zinc.

Ores, as mined, generally contain variable amounts of unwanted materials (such as silica, clay, and granite), which are called **gangue**. The concentration of the desired metal must be sufficiently high to make its extraction chemically feasible and economically competitive. Ores of low concentration are worked only if they can be processed comparatively easily and inexpensively or if the metal product is scarce and valuable. The required concentration varies greatly from metal to metal. For aluminum or iron, it should be 30% or more; for copper, it may be 1% or less.

18.3 Metallurgy: Preliminary Treatment of Ores

Metallurgy is the science of extracting metals from their ores and preparing them for use. Metallurgical processes may be conveniently divided into three principal operations: (1) **preliminary treatment**, in which the desired component of the ore is concentrated, specific impurities removed, and/or the mineral is put into a suitable form for subsequent treatment, (2) **reduction**, in which the metal compound is reduced to the free metal, and (3) **refining**, in which the metal is purified and, in some cases, substances added to give desired properties to the final product. The problems encountered in each step vary from metal to metal so that many different metallurgical procedures exist.

The processing of many ores requires, as a first step, that much of the gangue be removed. Such **concentration** procedures, which are usually carried out on ores that have been crushed and ground, may be based on physical or chemical properties. **Physical separations** are based on differences between the physical properties of the mineral and the gangue. Thus through washing with water, the particles of rocky impurities may often be separated from the heavier mineral particles. This may be accomplished by shaking the crushed ore in a stream of water on an inclined table; the heavier mineral particles settle to the bottom and are collected. Adaptations of this process exist.

Flotation is a method of concentration applied to many ores, especially those of copper, lead, and zinc. The finely crushed ore is mixed with a suitable oil and water in large tanks. The mineral particles are wetted by the oil, whereas the gangue particles are wetted by the water. Agitation of the mixture with air produces a froth, containing the oil and mineral particles, which floats on the top of the water and is then skimmed off.

Magnetic separation is employed to separate Fe_3O_4 (the mineral magnetite) from gangue. The ore is crushed, and electromagnets are used to attract the particles of Fe_3O_4, which is ferromagnetic.

The removal of free metals from native ores may be considered to be a type of concentration. Certain ores, such as native bismuth and native copper, are heated to a temperature just above the melting point of the metal and the liquid metal poured away from the gangue. The process is called **liquation.**

Mercury will dissolve silver and gold to form what are called **amalgams**. Hence, the native ores of silver and gold are treated with mercury, the resulting liquid amalgam collected, and the free silver or gold recovered from the amalgam by distilling away the mercury.

The chemical properties of minerals are the basis of **chemical separations**. An important example is the **Bayer method** of obtaining pure aluminum oxide from the ore bauxite. Since aluminum hydroxide is amphoteric, the alumina is dissolved away from the ore impurities (principally ferric oxide and silicates) by treatment of the crushed ore with hot sodium hydroxide solution.

$$Al_2O_3(s) + 2OH^-(aq) + 3H_2O \longrightarrow 2Al(OH)_4^-(aq)$$

The solution of sodium aluminate is filtered and cooled; its pH is adjusted downward by dilution and/or neutralization with carbon dioxide so that aluminum hydroxide precipitates (Section 17.5). Pure aluminum oxide, ready for reduction, is obtained by heating the aluminum hydroxide.

$$2Al(OH)_3(s) \longrightarrow Al_2O_3(s) + 3H_2O(g)$$

The first step in the extraction of magnesium from sea water is a chemical concentration. The Mg^{2+} in sea water (approximately 0.13%) is precipitated as magnesium hydroxide by treatment of the sea water with a slurry of calcium hydroxide. The calcium hydroxide is produced by roasting oyster shells.

$$CaCO_3(s) \longrightarrow CaO(s) + CO_2(g)$$

$$CaO(s) + H_2O \longrightarrow Ca(OH)_2(s)$$

$$Mg^{2+}(aq) + Ca(OH)_2(s) \longrightarrow Mg(OH)_2(s) + Ca^{2+}(aq)$$

The magnesium hydroxide is converted to magnesium chloride by reaction with hydrochloric acid, and the magnesium chloride solution is evaporated to produce the dry $MgCl_2$ necessary for electrolytic reduction.

The metal component of some ores may be obtained by **leaching**. Thus, low-grade carbonate and oxide ores of copper may be leached with dilute sulfuric acid

$$CuO(s) + 2H^+(aq) \longrightarrow Cu^{2+}(aq) + H_2O$$

$$CuCO_3(s) + 2H^+(aq) \longrightarrow Cu^{2+}(aq) + CO_2(g) + H_2O$$

and the resulting copper sulfate solutions directly subjected to electrolysis.

Silver and gold ores are leached with solutions of sodium cyanide in the presence of air, since these metals form very stable complex ions with the cyanide ion. For native silver, argentite (Ag_2S), and cerargyrite ($AgCl$), the reactions are

$$4Ag(s) + 8CN^-(aq) + O_2(g) + 2H_2O \longrightarrow 4Ag(CN)_2^-(aq) + 4OH^-(aq)$$

$$Ag_2S(s) + 4CN^-(aq) \longrightarrow 2Ag(CN)_2^-(aq) + S^{2-}(aq)$$

$$AgCl(s) + 2CN^-(aq) \longrightarrow Ag(CN)_2^-(aq) + Cl^-(aq)$$

After concentration, many ores are **roasted** in air. The sulfide ores of the less reactive metals are directly reduced to the free metal by heating (see Section 18.4). However, the majority of the sulfide ores, as well as the carbonate ores, are converted into oxides by roasting.

$$2ZnS(s) + 3O_2(g) \longrightarrow 2ZnO(s) + 2SO_2(g)$$

$$PbCO_3(s) \longrightarrow PbO(s) + CO_2(g)$$

Oxides are more readily reduced than sulfides or carbonates.

18.4 Metallurgy: Reduction

By far the largest quantity of metals, as well as the largest number of metals, are produced by **smelting** operations—high-temperature reduction processes in which the metal is usually secured in a molten state. In most of these processes, a **flux** (such as limestone, $CaCO_3$) is added to the ore and the reducing agent to remove the gangue that remains after ore concentration. The flux forms a **slag** with the silica and silicate impurities; for limestone and silica the simplified equations are

$$CaCO_3(s) \longrightarrow CaO(s) + CO_2(g)$$

$$CaO(s) + SiO_2(s) \longrightarrow CaSiO_3(l)$$

The slag is liquid at the smelting temperatures, generally floats on top of the molten metal, and hence is readily separated from the metal.

The reducing agent employed for a given smelting operation is, of course, the least expensive material that is capable of yielding a product of the required purity. For the ores of the metals of low reactivity—for example, the sulfide ores of mercury, copper, and lead—no chemical agent is required. Mercury is produced by roasting cinnabar, HgS, in air.

$$HgS(s) + O_2(g) \longrightarrow Hg(g) + SO_2(g)$$

The mercury vapor is condensed in a receiver and requires no further purification.

Copper sulfide ores, after concentration by flotation, are smelted not to the metal but to a material called **matte**, which is essentially cuprous sulfide, Cu_2S. In this operation, a flux is employed to remove ore impurities in the form of a slag composed principally of calcium and ferrous silicates. A prior roasting may be used to reduce the sulfur content of the ore. The matte is reduced by blowing air through the molten material.

$$Cu_2S(l) + O_2(g) \longrightarrow 2Cu(l) + SO_2(g)$$

Any cuprous oxide that forms is reduced by stirring the molten metal by poles of green wood. The copper produced by this method (blister copper) is about 99% pure and is refined by electrolysis.

Lead sulfide ores (galena) are subjected to a roasting operation in which a portion of the PbS is converted into lead oxide and lead sulfate.

$$2PbS(s) + 3O_2(g) \longrightarrow 2PbO(s) + 2SO_2(g)$$

$$PbS(s) + 2O_2(g) \longrightarrow PbSO_4(s)$$

The resulting PbS, PbO, and $PbSO_4$ mixture, together with fluxes, is smelted in the absence of air. The reactions, in which sulfur is oxidized and lead reduced, are

$$PbS(s) + 2PbO(s) \longrightarrow 3Pb(l) + SO_2(g)$$

$$PbS(s) + PbSO_4(s) \longrightarrow 2Pb(l) + 2SO_2(g)$$

Some lead is also produced by smelting PbO with coke. The lead oxide is obtained by roasting the sulfide ore in an excess of air so that virtually complete conversion to the oxide results.

Iron, zinc, tin, cadmium, antimony, nickel, cobalt, molybdenum, lead, and other metals are produced by **carbon reduction** of oxides, obtained as ores or as the products of roasting operations.

The reactions that occur in a high-temperature carbon reduction are complex. In most cases, the reduction is effected principally by carbon monoxide, not carbon. Since both the mineral and coke are solids that are not readily fusible, contact between them is poor and direct reaction slow.

$$MO(s) + C(s) \longrightarrow M(l) + CO(g)$$

(M stands for a metal.) However, a gas and a solid make better contact and react more readily.

$$2C(s) + O_2(g) \longrightarrow 2CO(g)$$
$$MO(s) + CO(g) \longrightarrow M(l) + CO_2(g)$$

The carbon dioxide produced is converted into carbon monoxide by reaction with coke.

$$C(s) + CO_2(g) \longrightarrow 2CO(g)$$

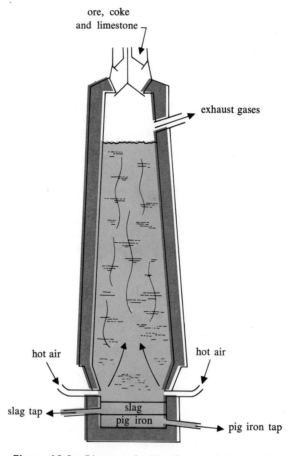

Figure 18.3 Diagram of a blast furnace (schematic).

The most important commercial metal, iron, is produced by carbon reduction is a **blast furnace** designed to operate continuously (Figure 18.3). The ore, coke, and a limestone flux are charged into the top of the furnace and heated air, which is sometimes enriched with oxygen, is blown in at the bottom. The incoming air reacts with carbon to form carbon monoxide and liberate considerable amounts of heat; at this point, the temperature of the furnace is the highest (ca. 1500°C).

The iron ore (usually Fe_2O_3) is reduced in stages depending upon the temperature. Near the top of the furnace, where the temperature is lowest, Fe_3O_4 is the reduction product.

$$3Fe_2O_3(s) + CO(g) \longrightarrow 2Fe_3O_4(s) + CO_2(g)$$

The descending Fe_3O_4 is reduced to FeO in a lower, hotter, zone.

$$Fe_3O_4(s) + CO(g) \longrightarrow 3FeO(s) + CO_2(g)$$

In the hottest zone, reduction to metallic iron occurs.

$$FeO(s) + CO(g) \longrightarrow Fe(l) + CO_2(g)$$

The molten iron collects in the bottom of the furnace. Molten slag, principally calcium silicate which is produced by the ultimate action of the flux on the gangue, also collects on the bottom. The slag floats on top of the molten iron, thus protecting the metal from oxidation by the incoming air. The slag and iron are periodically drawn off. The hot exhaust gases are used to heat incoming air and some slag is used in making cement.

The impure iron produced by the blast furnace (**pig iron**) contains up to 4% carbon, up to 2% silicon, some phosphorus, and a trace of sulfur. In the manufacture of steel (Section 18.5), these impurities are removed or their concentrations adjusted; in addition, certain metallic ingredients are added. The presence of some carbon in steel is desirable, and the amount of carbon in the final product is readily controlled in the refining process.

The carbon reduction of some oxides yields products (such as chromium, manganese, and tungsten) that contain an appreciable quantity of carbon. If these metals are to be used in the manufacture of steel, the carbon content does not matter. However, since carbon impurities are difficult to remove from many metals, carbon reduction is not a satisfactory method for preparing these metals in a pure form. In such instances, as well as those in which carbon is incapable of effecting a reduction, reactive metals (such as Na, Mg, and Al) may be used as reducing agents. Processes that use metals as reducing agents are more expensive than those that employ carbon because the cost of the production of the metal used as a reducing agent must be taken into account.

The reduction of an oxide by aluminum is called the **Goldschmidt**, or **thermite, process**.

$$Cr_2O_3(s) + 2Al(s) \longrightarrow 2Cr(l) + Al_2O_3(l)$$

$$3MnO_2(s) + 4Al(s) \longrightarrow 3Mn(l) + 2Al_2O_3(l)$$

$$3BaO(s) + 2Al(s) \longrightarrow 3Ba(l) + Al_2O_3(l)$$

The reactions are highly exothermic, and molten metals are produced. The reaction of Fe_2O_3 and aluminum is used at times for the production of molten iron in welding operations and as the basis of incendiary (thermite) bombs. Other oxides commercially reduced by metals include: UO_3 (by Al or Ca), V_2O_5 (by Al), Ta_2O_5 (by Na), MoO_3 (by Al), ThO_2 (by Ca), and WO_3 (by Al).

The **Kroll process** involves the reduction of metal halides (such as $TiCl_4$, $ZrCl_4$, UF_4, and $LaCl_3$) by magnesium, sodium, or calcium. In the production of titanium, titanium tetrachloride is prepared by the reaction of titanium dioxide, carbon, and chlorine. The chloride is a liquid and is readily purified by distillation. Purified $TiCl_4$ is passed into molten magnesium or sodium at approximately 700°C under an atmosphere of argon or helium (which prevents oxidation of the product).

$$TiCl_4(g) + 2Mg(l) \longrightarrow Ti(s) + 2MgCl_2(l)$$

A **metal displacement** reaction employing zinc is used to obtain silver and gold from solutions resulting from cyanide leaching operations.

$$2Ag(CN)_2^-(aq) + Zn(s) \longrightarrow 2Ag(s) + Zn(CN)_4^{2-}(aq)$$

Hydrogen can be used, at high temperatures, in place of carbon for metallurgical reductions, but it is more expensive than coke. **Hydrogen reduction** is used for the preparation of some metals when carbon reduction yields an unsatisfactory product. Examples are

$$GeO_2(s) + 2H_2(g) \longrightarrow Ge(s) + 2H_2O(g)$$

$$WO_3(s) + 3H_2(g) \longrightarrow W(s) + 3H_2O(g)$$

$$MoO_3(s) + 3H_2(g) \longrightarrow Mo(s) + 3H_2O(g)$$

The metals are produced as powders by this method. Germanium is melted and cast into ingots, but tungsten (wolfram) and molybdenum have high melting points. They are heated and pounded into compact form. Hydrogen cannot be used to reduce the oxides of some metals because of the formation of undesirable hydrides.

Figure 18.4 Schematic diagram of the Downs cell for the production of sodium and chlorine.

The most reactive metals are prepared by **electrolytic reduction** of molten compounds. Sodium and magnesium (as well as the other I A and II A metals) are prepared by electrolysis of the fused chlorides. Sodium chloride is electrolyzed in a **Downs cell** (Figure 18.4), which is designed to keep the products separate from one another so that they do not react.

$$\text{anode:} \qquad 2Cl^- \longrightarrow Cl_2(g) + 2e^-$$

$$\text{cathode:} \qquad e^- + Na^+ \longrightarrow Na(l)$$

Purified Al_2O_3 is electrolyzed in the **Hall process** for the production of aluminum (Figure 18.5). Alumina dissolved in cryolite, Na_3AlF_6, produces a solution that will conduct electric current. The carbon lining of the cell serves as the cathode, and carbon anodes are used. The primary reaction at the anode may be considered to be the discharge of oxygen from oxide ions. However, the oxygen reacts with the carbon anodes so that the cell reactions are

$$\text{anode:} \qquad C(s) + 2O^{2-} \longrightarrow CO_2(g) + 4e^-$$

$$\text{cathode:} \qquad 3e^- + Al^{3+} \longrightarrow Al(l)$$

The molten aluminum collects at the bottom of the cell and is periodically withdrawn.

Figure 18.5 Schematic diagram of an electrolytic cell for the production of aluminum.

Some metals are prepared by the electrolysis of aqueous solutions of their salts. Very pure zinc is produced by the electrolysis of zinc sulfate solutions. The zinc sulfate is obtained by treating zinc oxide (from zinc sulfide ores, by roasting) with sulfuric acid, and the sulfuric acid for the process is made from the sulfur dioxide derived from the roasting of the sulfide ore.

anode: $2H_2O \longrightarrow O_2(g) + 4H^+(aq) + 4e^-$

cathode: $2e^- + Zn^{2+}(aq) \longrightarrow Zn(s)$

Aqueous solutions of salts of copper, cadmium, chromium, cobalt, gallium, indium, manganese, and thorium are electrolyzed to produce the corresponding metals. Electrolytically prepared metals generally require no further refining.

18.5 Metallurgy: Refining

Most of the metals obtained from reduction operations require refining to rid them of objectionable impurities. Refining processes vary widely from metal to metal, and, for a given metal, the method employed may vary with the proposed use of the final product. Along with the removal of material that impart undesirable properties to the metal, the refining step may include the addition of substances to give the product desired characteristics. Some refining processes are designed to recover valuable metal impurities, such as gold, silver, and platinum.

Crude tin, lead, and bismuth are purified by **liquation**. Ingots of the impure metals are placed at the top of a sloping hearth maintained at a temperature slightly above the melting point of the metal. The metal melts and flows down the inclined hearth into a well leaving behind the solid impurities.

Some low-boiling metals (such as zinc and mercury) are purified by **distillation**.

The **Parkes process** for refining lead, which also is a concentration method for silver, relies upon the selective dissolution of silver in molten zinc. A small amount of zinc (1 to 2%) is added to molten lead that contains silver as an impurity. Silver is much more soluble in zinc than in lead; lead and zinc are insoluble in each other. Hence, most of the silver concentrates in the zinc, which comes to the top of the molten lead. The zinc layer solidifies first upon cooling; it is removed and the silver obtained by distilling away the zinc, which is collected and used over again.

In the **Mond process**, impure nickel is treated with carbon monoxide at 60°C to 80°C. The nickel reacts to form gaseous nickel carbonyl leaving solid impurities, including cobalt, behind.

$$Ni(s) + 4CO(g) \longrightarrow Ni(CO)_4(g)$$

Pure nickel is recovered from the carbonyl by heating the gas to temperatures of from 180°C to 200°C.

$$Ni(CO)_4(g) \longrightarrow Ni(s) + 4CO(g)$$

The carbon monoxide is recirculated.

The **Van Arkel process** is also based upon the thermal decomposition of a metal compound. The method, which is used for the purification of titanium, hafnium, and zirconium, involves the decomposition of a metal iodide on a hot metal filament. For example, impure zirconium is heated with a limited amount of iodine in an evacuated glass apparatus.

$$Zr(s) + 2I_2(g) \longrightarrow ZrI_4(g)$$

The gaseous zirconium tetraiodide is decomposed upon contact with a hot filament and pure zirconium metal is deposited upon the filament.

$$ZrI_4(g) \longrightarrow Zr(s) + 2I_2(g)$$

The regenerated iodine reacts with more zirconium. The process is very expensive and is employed for the preparation of limited amounts of very pure metals for special uses.

Another process capable of producing metals of very high purity is **zone refining**. A circular heater is fitted around a rod of an impure metal, such as

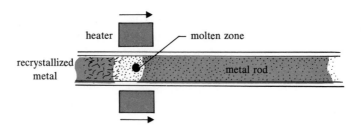

Figure 18.6 Schematic diagram of zone refining.

germanium (Figure 18.6). The heater, which is slowly moved down the rod, melts a band of the metal. As the heater moves along, pure metal recrystallizes out of the melt, and impurities are swept along in the molten zone to one end of the rod which is subsequently discarded. More than one pass of the heater may be made on the same rod.

Electrolytic refining is an important, and widely used, method of purification. Many metals, including copper, tin, lead, gold, zinc, chromium, and nickel, are refined electrolytically. Plates of the impure metal are used as anodes, the electrolyte is a solution of a salt of the metal, and the pure metal plates out on the cathode. For copper, copper sulfate is employed as the electrolyte, and the electrode reactions are

$$\text{anode:} \qquad \text{Cu}(s) \longrightarrow \text{Cu}^{2+}(aq) + 2e^-$$

$$\text{cathode:} \qquad 2e^- + \text{Cu}^{2+}(aq) \longrightarrow \text{Cu}(s)$$

The more reactive metals in the crude copper anode, such as iron, are oxidized and pass into solution where they remain; they are not reduced at the cathode. The less reactive metals, such as silver, gold, and platinum, are not oxidized. As the copper anode dissolves away, they fall to the bottom of the cell from where they are recovered as a valuable "anode sludge."

Pig iron is refined into steel by the **Bessemer process** or by the **open hearth process.** In both processes, the impurities (carbon from the coke used in the reduction, and such substances as silicon, phosphorus, and sulfur from the ore) are oxidized and volatilize out of the iron or go into the slag.

In the Bessemer process, molten pig iron from the blast furnace is poured into egg-shaped converters and a blast of air blown through the melt to oxidize the impurities. The heat required to keep the charge molten is supplied by these oxidations. The process is rapid (10 to 15 min); however, it is difficult to control, and the quality of the product is variable.

By far the largest percentage of steel is manufactured by the open hearth process. A charge of pig iron, scrap iron, and iron oxide is heated in a shallow hearth lined with calcium oxide or magnesium oxide. A blast of burning fuel and hot air is directed on the molten iron, and the oxidation of the impurities is accomplished by reaction with excess air or with iron oxide. The carbon monoxide escapes and burns, and the oxides of silicon, phosphorus, and sulfur combine with the oxides of the hearth lining to form a slag.

Since it takes about 8 to 10 hours to produce a batch of steel by the open hearth process, the quality of the final product is readily controlled and is uniform. Alloying metals, such as manganese, chromium, nickel, tungsten, molybdenum, and vanadium, may be added before the charge is poured.

18.6   The Group I A Metals

The I A metals, also called the **alkali metals**, constitute the most reactive group of metals. None of the elements is found free in nature, and all are prepared by the electrolysis of dry, molten salts. The element francium, $Z = 87$, is formed in certain natural radioactive processes; all of its isotopes are radioactive with short half-lives, and the element is extremely rare.

The group I A elements are silvery metals; cesium has a slight golden-yellow cast. The elements are comparatively soft (they can be cut by a knife) and have low melting points and boiling points (Table 18.3). Melting point,

Table 18.3

Some Properties of the I A Metals

	Lithium	Sodium	Potassium	Rubidium	Cesium
outer electronic configuration	$2s^1$	$3s^1$	$4s^1$	$5s^1$	$6s^1$
melting point (°C)	179	97.5	63.7	39.0	28.5
boiling point (°C)	1336	880	760	700	670
density (g/cm³)	0.53	0.97	0.86	1.53	1.90
atomic radius (Å)	1.23	1.57	2.03	2.16	2.35
ionic radius, M^+ (Å)	0.60	0.95	1.33	1.48	1.69
ionization potential (ev)					
first	5.4	5.1	4.3	4.2	3.9
second	75.6	47.3	31.8	27.4	23.4
electrode potential, $\mathscr{E}°$,					
(M^+/M) (v)	−3.05	−2.71	−2.93	−2.93	−2.92

boiling point, and hardness decrease with increasing atomic number. The metals are good conductors of heat and electricity. They have very low densities. Compare the densities given in Table 18.3 with the densities of the metals of the first transition series which range from 2.5 g/cm³ for $_{21}$Sc to 8.9 g/cm³ for $_{30}$Cu.

The alkali metals emit electrons when irradiated (the photoelectric effect).

Cesium, which ejects electrons most readily, is used in the manufacture of photocells (employed in light meters and electric eyes) which convert light signals into electric signals.

The electronic configuration of each of the alkali metals is that of the preceding noble gas (a noble gas core) plus a single s valence electron in the outer shell. These valence electrons are easily lost to give $1+$ ions that are isoelectronic with noble gases. Thus an element of group I A has the lowest first ionization potential of any element of its period. The ease with which these elements lose electrons makes them extremely strong reducing agents.

The second ionization potentials of the I A metals are so much higher than the first ionization potentials that the $1+$ oxidation state is the only one observed for these metals. With few exceptions, alkali metal compounds are ionic.

In general, the reactivity of the elements increases with increasing atomic number paralleling the decrease in first ionization potential. Thus in most cases, cesium is the most reactive element of the group and lithium is the least reactive. This order of reactivity is expected since a large atom holds its valence electron less tightly than a small atom; in a large atom, the electron is farther from the nucleus and is screened from the positive nuclear charge by a large number of underlying electron shells.

Each I A element has the largest atomic radius and largest ionic radius or any element of its period. This comparatively large size combined with the low charge of the I A ions leads to species that have little polarizing ability (and hence form strongly ionic compounds) and that do not readily form complex ions.

Since the alkali metal ions have comparatively low charge/size ratios, the hydration energies of the ions are low. The lithium ion, which is the smallest ion and has the least effectively screened nuclear charge of the group, has the largest hydration energy. The hydration energies decrease with increasing ion size (Table 18.4).

Although all the I A ions are loosely hydrated in water solution, only salts of lithium and sodium (the two smallest ions) form hydrates in which the water may be considered to be coordinated around the cation, and in these substances the metal ion–water attractions are electrostatic. Hydrates of salts of the other I A metals are known, but the water is not present in these crystals as coordination water.

The trend in the magnitudes of the hydration energies of the ions helps to explain why the order of the electrode potentials is different from that of the ionization potentials (Table 18.3). Of all the alkali metals, lithium is the most difficult to oxidize to the $1+$ state, and lithium has the highest ionization potential of any member of the group. On the other hand, lithium is the I A metal most readily converted to *hydrated* $1+$ ions, and lithium has the lowest standard electrode potential.

Table 18.4

Enthalpy Changes of Some I A Metal Transformations
(Kcal)

	Li	Na	K	Rb	Cs
$M(s) \longrightarrow M(g)$	+37	+26	+22	+20	+19
$M(g) \longrightarrow M^+(g) + e^-$	+124	+118	+100	+96	+89
$M^+(g) \longrightarrow M^+(aq)$	−121	−95	−76	−69	−62
$M(s) \longrightarrow M^+(aq) + e^-$	+40	+49	+46	+47	+46

The relationship between ionization potential and electrode potential may be clarified by means of a Born-Haber treatment of the half reaction

$$M(s) \longrightarrow M^+(aq) + e^-$$

For the purpose of analysis, the enthalpy change for this half reaction may be considered to be derived from the enthalpy of sublimation (energy absorbed),

$$M(s) \longrightarrow M(g)$$

the ionization energy (energy absorbed),

$$M(g) \longrightarrow M^+(g) + e^-$$

and the enthalpy of hydration (energy evolved),

$$M^+(g) \longrightarrow M^+(aq)$$

The sums of these energy effects actually apply to transformations in which the electrons are left in the gaseous state; however, the values derived, which are listed in Table 18.4, permit some valid comparisons to be made. Each of the factors listed in Table 18.4 varies in a regular, and predictable, manner. The sums of the energy effects, however, indicate that the oxidation of lithium to produce hydrated lithium ions requires less energy than the oxidation of any other I A metal and that the corresponding oxidation of sodium requires more energy than the oxidation of any other I A metal. This conclusion is supported by the electrode potentials of the alkali metals. In an oxidation-reduction reaction involving the alkali metals, the energy required to effect one of these oxidations is usually more than adequately supplied by the reduction.

Rigorously, electrode potentials can only be derived from changes in Gibbs free energy, which include not only changes in enthalpy but also changes in entropy. These entropy effects are not large; but since we have ignored them, and also used ΔH values correct only to 1 kcal, not much importance should be attached to the order of the values for K, Rb, and Cs recorded in Table 18.4, other than to note that they lie between the values for Li and Na.

All the hydroxides of the alkali metals are strong electrolytes. Alkali metal compounds are generally quite soluble in water. However, the hydroxide, carbonate, phosphate, and fluoride of lithium are much less soluble than the corresponding salts of the other I A metals. Sodium ion may be precipitated from solution as sodium zinc uranyl acetate, $NaZn(UO_2)_3(C_2H_3O_2)_9 \cdot 6H_2O$. The perchlorate ion, ClO_4^-, the hexachloroplatinate ion, $[PtCl_6]^{2-}$, and the cobaltinitrite ion, $[Co(NO_2)_6]^{3-}$, may be used to precipitate K^+, Rb^+, and Cs^+.

The unipositive ammonium ion has a radius that lies between those of K^+ and Rb^+, and ammonium salts have solubilities that resemble those of the alkali metal salts. The ionic radius of the thallous ion, Tl^+, is similar to that of the rubidium ion. Not only do thallous compounds resemble rubidium compounds in solubility, but TlOH is also a strong electrolyte.

Some of the reactions of the I A metals are summarized in Table 18.5. Whereas the properties of lithium are similar in most respects to those of the other members of group I A, there are some dissimilarities which may be traced to the comparatively small size of Li and Li^+. The first members of the groups of the periodic table often deviate slightly in character from the remaining members of their groups. In addition, similarities may be observed between these first members and elements that adjoin them diagonally on the periodic table (diagonal relationships).

$$\begin{array}{cccc} \text{Li} & \text{Be} & \text{B} & \text{C} \\ \text{Na} & \text{Mg} & \text{Al} & \text{Si} \end{array}$$

Thus lithium resembles magnesium in some of its properties. The magnesium ion has a slightly larger ionic radius (0.65 Å) than the lithium ion (0.60 Å), but the charge on the magnesium ion is $2+$.

Lithium resembles magnesium and differs from its congeners in the following ways. The carbonate, phosphate, and fluoride of lithium are but slightly soluble in water. Lithium forms a normal oxide, rather than a peroxide or a superoxide, upon burning in oxygen. Lithium ions are more strongly hydrated than those of any other I A element. Lithium reacts directly with nitrogen to give a nitride. Lithium hydroxide may be decomposed to Li_2O and water

Table 18.5

Reaction of the I A Metals[a]

Reaction	Remarks
$2M + X_2 \longrightarrow 2MX$	X_2 = all halogens
$4Li + O_2 \longrightarrow 2Li_2O$	excess oxygen
$2Na + O_2 \longrightarrow Na_2O_2$	
$M + O_2 \longrightarrow MO_2$	M = K, Rb, Cs
$2M + S \longrightarrow M_2S$	also with Se and Te
$6Li + N_2 \longrightarrow 2Li_3N$	Li only
$12M + P_4 \longrightarrow 4M_3P$	also with As, Sb
$2M + 2C \longrightarrow M_2C_2$	M = Li and Na; other I A metals give nonstoichiometric interstitial compounds
$2M + H_2 \longrightarrow 2MH$	
$2M + 2H_2O \longrightarrow 2MOH + H_2$	room temperature
$2M + 2H^+ \longrightarrow 2M^+ + H_2$	violent reaction
$2M + 2NH_3 \longrightarrow 2MNH_2 + H_2$	liquid NH_3 in presence of catalysts such as Fe; gaseous NH_3, heated

[a] M = any I A metal, except where noted.

upon heating, and lithium carbonate decomposes to Li_2O and CO_2 upon ignition. Lithium nitrate decomposes upon heating.

$$4LiNO_3(s) \longrightarrow 2Li_2O(s) + 4NO_2(g) + O_2(g)$$

The nitrates of the other alkali metals form nitrites upon heating,

$$2MNO_3(s) \longrightarrow 2MNO_2(s) + O_2(g)$$

and the hydroxides and carbonates of Na, K, Rb, and Cs are thermally stable.

18.7   The Group II A Metals

The group II A metals, or **alkaline earth metals**, are highly electropositive and constitute the second most reactive group of metals. They are not found free in nature and are commonly produced by the electrolysis of molten chlorides. Radium is a comparatively scarce element and all its isotopes are radioactive.

Because of its larger nuclear charge, each II A metal has a smaller atomic radius than that of the I A metal of its period. Since atoms of the II A metals are smaller and have two valence electrons instead of one, the II A metals have higher melting and boiling points and greater densities than the I A metals (Table 18.6). In addition, the alkaline earth metals are harder than the

Table 18.6

Some Properties of the II A Metals

	Beryllium	Magnesium	Calcium	Strontium	Barium
outer electronic configuration	$2s^2$	$3s^2$	$4s^2$	$5s^2$	$6s^2$
melting point (°C)	1280	651	851	800	850
boiling point (°C)	1500	1107	1440	1366	1537
density (g/cm³)	1.86	1.75	1.55	2.6	3.59
atomic radius (Å)	0.89	1.36	1.74	1.91	1.98
ionic radius, M^{2+} (Å)	0.31	0.65	0.99	1.13	1.35
ionization potential (ev)					
first	9.3	7.6	6.1	5.7	5.2
second	18.2	15.0	11.9	11.0	10.0
third	153.9	80.1	51.2	–	–
electrode potential, $\mathscr{E}°$,					
(M^{2+}/M) (v)	−1.85	−2.36	−2.87	−2.89	−2.91

alkali metals. Beryllium is hard enough to scratch glass and has a tendency toward brittleness; the degree of hardness declines with increasing atomic number. The alkaline earth metals are white metals with a silvery luster. They are good conductors of electricity.

Each of the II A metals has an electronic configuration consisting of a noble gas core plus two s electrons in the outer, valence, level. The loss of the two valence electrons produces an ion that is isoelectronic not only with a noble gas but also with the I A metal ion of the same period. However, the alkaline earth metal ions have a larger nuclear charge than the alkali metal ions and are therefore considerably smaller. The beryllium ion is an exceptionally small cation.

In comparison to the I A metal ions, the II A metal ions, therefore, have considerably greater ratios of ionic charge to ionic radius. There are several important consequences of this fact. They hydration energy of a given alkaline earth ion is about five times that of the alkali metal ion of the same period. Furthermore, whereas the compounds of calcium, strontium, and barium are essentially ionic, the compounds of the smaller members of the group, magnesium and beryllium, have appreciable covalent character because the cations of these metals have a stronger polarizing effect on anions. This tendency for covalent bond formation is particularly pronounced for beryllium; all compounds of this metal, even those with the most electronegative elements such as oxygen and fluorine, have significant covalent character.

Beryllium has the greatest tendency of the group toward the formation of complex ions; examples are $[Be(H_2O)_4]^{2+}$, $[Be(NH_3)_4]^{2+}$, BeF_4^{2-}, and $[Be(OH)_4]^{2-}$. Beryllium hydroxide is the only amphoteric hydroxide formed by a group II A metal.

The covalent nature of beryllium halides is indicated by the poor electrolytic conduction of the anhydrous molten compounds; NaCl is generally added to anhydrous molten $BeCl_2$ in the electrolytic preparation of beryllium.

Gaseous $BeCl_2$ molecules are linear and presumably of the *sp* hybrid type. In most solid compounds, beryllium is tetrahedrally disposed, in many through sp^3 hybrid bonding. Such a configuration is observed in the complex ions of beryllium. Beryllium chloride is polymeric; each beryllium atom is joined to four chlorine atoms.

The BeO crystal may be considered to be composed of BeO_4 tetrahedra.

The ionization potentials of the II A metals are higher than those of the I A metals because of differences in atomic size and nuclear charge. Nevertheless, the II A metals are very reactive, although not so reactive as the I A metals. The ionization potentials recorded in Table 18.6 show that it is distinctly more difficult to remove three electrons than it is to remove two; hence, the production of 3+ ions is not likely. However, these values also show that the second electron is significantly more difficult to remove than the first; the production of 1+ ions might appear reasonable.

A 1+ ion would have a much smaller hydration energy then a 2+ ion. In addition, because of the less intense electric field surrounding a 1+ ion (the 1+ ion would be larger as well as having a lower positive charge), the lattice energies of crystalline compounds of such ions would be smaller. Therefore the additional energy required to remove the second electron is more than supplied by the larger hydration energy of the 2+ ion or, in the case of solids, by the larger lattice energy of the M^{2+} salt. Stable 1+ ions of the II A metals do not exist in the solid state or in solution.

It is because of these comparatively large hydration energies that the electrode potentials of the II A metals (despite larger enthalpies of sublimation and larger ionization energies) are rather similar in magnitude to those of the I A metals. The hydration energy is largest for Be^{2+} and smallest for Ba^{2+}, but nevertheless the electrode potentials fall in the same order as the ionization potentials: Ba is the strongest reducing agent of the group and Be is the weakest.

This order of reactivity is illustrated by the reactions of the alkaline earth metals with water. Beryllium fails to react at red heat. Magnesium will react with boiling water or steam. Calcium, strontium, and barium react vigorously with cold water. Some chemical reactions of the group II A metals are summarized in Table 18.7.

Table 18.7

Reactions of the II A Metals[a]

Reactions		Remarks
$M + X_2$	$\longrightarrow$ MX_2	X_2 = all halogens
$2M + O_2$	$\longrightarrow$ $2MO$	Ba also gives BaO_2
$M + S$	$\longrightarrow$ MS	also with Se and Te
$3M + N_2$	$\longrightarrow$ M_3N_2	at high temperatures
$6M + P_4$	$\longrightarrow$ $2M_3P_2$	at high temperatures
$M + 2C$	$\longrightarrow$ MC_2	all except Be which forms Be_2C; high temperatures
$M + H_2$	$\longrightarrow$ MH_2	M = Ca, Sr, Ba; high temperatures; Mg with H_2 under pressure
$M + 2H_2O$	$\longrightarrow$ $M(OH)_2 + H_2$	M = Ca, Sr, Ba; room temperature
$Mg + H_2O$	$\longrightarrow$ $MgO + H_2$	steam; Be does not react at red heat
$M + 2H^+$	$\longrightarrow$ $M^{2+} + H_2$	
$Be + 2OH^- + 2H_2O$	$\longrightarrow$ $Be(OH)_4^{2-} + H_2$	Be only
$M + 2NH_3$	$\longrightarrow$ $M(NH_2)_2 + H_2$	M = Ca, Sr, Ba; liquid ammonia in presence of catalysts
$3M + 2NH_3$	$\longrightarrow$ $M_3N_2 + 3H_2$	gaseous NH_3; high temperatures

[a] M = any II A metal, except where noted.

Almost all the salts of the I A metals are very soluble in water. In contrast, a number of II A metal compounds are not appreciably water soluble; the solubility products of some of these insoluble compounds are listed in Table 18.8.

Table 18.8

Solubility Product Constants of Some II A Metal Salts

	OH^-	SO_4^{2-}	CO_3^{2-}	$C_2O_4^{2-}$	F^-	CrO_4^{2-}
Be^{2+}	1.6×10^{-26}	—	—	—	—	—
Mg^{2+}	8.9×10^{-12}	—	10^{-5}	8.6×10^{-5}	8×10^{-8}	—
Ca^{2+}	1.3×10^{-6}	2.4×10^{-5}	4.7×10^{-9}	1.3×10^{-9}	1.7×10^{-10}	7.1×10^{-4}
Sr^{2+}	3.2×10^{-4}	7.6×10^{-7}	7×10^{-10}	5.6×10^{-8}	7.9×10^{-10}	3.6×10^{-5}
Ba^{2+}	5.0×10^{-3}	1.5×10^{-9}	1.6×10^{-9}	1.5×10^{-8}	2.4×10^{-5}	8.5×10^{-11}

The solubility of a salt depends upon the lattice energy of the salt (energy absorbed in the solution process)

$$MA(s) \longrightarrow M^{2+}(g) + A^{2-}(g)$$

and the hydration energies of the ions (energy evolved)

$$M^{2+}(g) \longrightarrow M^{2+}(aq)$$
$$A^{2-}(g) \longrightarrow A^{2-}(aq)$$

When the solubilities of salts containing the same anion are compared, the hydration energy of the anion may be neglected and solubility differences attributed to the combination of the other two factors.

The solubility of the alkaline earth sulfates decreases with increasing cation size; $BeSO_4$ is very soluble, and $BaSO_4$ is very insoluble. The lattice energies of the sulfates do not change greatly in the sequence from $BeSO_4$ to $BaSO_4$, presumably because the anion is so much larger than any II A cation. The trend in the solubility of the sulfates, therefore, parallels the trend in hydration energies of the ions. The hydration of the small Be^{2+} ion is by far the most exothermic of any ion of the group, and $BeSO_4$ is by far the most soluble sulfate formed by any ion of the group.

The trend in the solubility of hydroxides is the reverse of that of the sulfates; $Be(OH)_2$ is the least soluble alkaline earth hydroxide, and the solubility increases down the group. For hydroxides, the lattice energy is dependent upon cation size. The strength of the crystal forces decreases with increasing cation size; $Be(OH)_2$ has the largest lattice energy of any alkaline earth hydroxide. Apparently, the trend in lattice energy (energy required) overshadows the trend in hydration energy (energy released).

Solubility data cannot always be so simply interpreted. In the preceding solubility considerations, we have ignored entropy effects. In addition, even though the lattice energies and hydration energies of a group of salts may vary regularly, the sum of the two energy effects, and hence the solubilities of the salts, may vary in an irregular manner in the same way that the standard electrode potentials of the I A metals vary.

The lattice energies of the oxides of the II A metals decrease regularly from BeO to BaO, and the effect of this trend is seen in the series of reactions of the alkaline earth oxides with water. Beryllium oxide is insoluble in, and unreactive toward, water. Magnesium oxide reacts very slowly with water; MgO that has been ignited at high temperatures, however, is practically inert. The oxides of calcium, strontium, and barium readily react with water to form hydroxides

$$MO + H_2O \longrightarrow M(OH)_2$$

The carbonates of the alkaline earth metals decompose upon heating

$$MCO_3(s) \longrightarrow MO(s) + CO_2(g)$$

The thermal stability of the carbonates varies directly with the size of the cation. Beryllium carbonate is very unstable and can be prepared only in an atmosphere of carbon dioxide presumably because of the enhanced stability of BeO over $BeCO_3$.

The tendency of the II A metal ions toward hydration causes a number of the compounds of these ions to hydrate with ease; $Mg(ClO_4)_2$, $CaCl_2$, $CaSO_4$, and $Ba(ClO_4)_2$ are used as desiccants.

The beryllium ion hydrolyzes in solution

$$[Be(H_2O)_4]^{2+} + H_2O \rightleftharpoons [Be(H_2O)_3(OH)]^+ + H_3O^+$$

but the other cations do not hydrolyze. The hydroxides of beryllium and magnesium may be regarded as insoluble (Table 18.8). Even though the hydroxides of calcium, strontium, and barium are limitedly soluble in water, these compounds are completely dissociated in aqueous solution.

The sulfides of the group are water soluble, and solutions of these compounds are alkaline due to the hydrolysis of the sulfide ion. In quantitative determinations, barium ion is usually precipitated as barium sulfate, strontium ion as strontium sulfate or strontium oxalate, and calcium ion as calcium oxalate. Magnesium ion is precipitated as $Mg(NH_4)PO_4 \cdot 6H_2O$ by the HPO_4^{2-} ion in the presence of ammonia. Beryllium may be determined as the hydroxide.

Barium ion may be separated from Sr^{2+}, Ca^{2+}, and Mg^{2+} in solution, by taking advantage of the fact that the chromate of barium is the least soluble chromate of any ion of the group. The chromate ion, CrO_4^{2-}, exists in equilibrium with the dichromate ion, $Cr_2O_7^{2-}$, in acid solution.

$$2CrO_4^{2-}(aq) + 2H^+(aq) \rightleftharpoons Cr_2O_7^{2-}(aq) + H_2O$$

The pH of the solution is carefully adjusted by means of an acetic acid buffer so that the concentration of CrO_4^{2-} is maintained at a low value. This concentration is sufficient to precipitate only $BaCrO_4$.

After the $BaCrO_4$ has been removed, $SrCrO_4$ may be made to precipitate by the addition of ammonia and ethyl alcohol. Increasing the pH of the solution increases the concentration of chromate ions by shifting the chromate-dichromate equilibrium. When the concentration of CrO_4^{2-} is sufficiently high, $SrCrO_4$ precipitates. Calcium chromate does not precipitate under these conditions.

The calcium ion may be separated from the magnesium ion by the careful addition of ammonium oxalate, $(NH_4)_2C_2O_4$. Magnesium oxalate is much more soluble than calcium oxalate. The magnesium ion may be precipitated as magnesium ammonium phosphate.

Because of the extremely small size of Be and Be^{2+}, beryllium is even more exceptional with regard to the other members of group II A than lithium is with regard to the other members of group I A. The diagonal relationship between beryllium and aluminum is particularly striking. Although Al^{3+} is larger than Be^{2+}, the two ions have similar electric fields because of the higher charge of Al^{3+}.

Both elements have a strong tendency toward the formation of covalent compounds. The halides are largely covalent in nature, soluble in organic solvents, and strong Lewis acids. Both aluminum hydroxide and beryllium hydroxide are amphoteric, and both metals dissolve in solutions of hydroxides to give hydrogen. The standard electrode potential of beryllium is similar in magnitude to that of aluminum but much smaller than those of the other II A metals.

The carbides of beryllium and aluminum yield methane, CH_4, on hydrolysis

$$Be_2C(s) + 4H_2O \longrightarrow 2Be(OH)_2(s) + CH_4(g)$$

$$Al_4C_3(s) + 12H_2O \longrightarrow 4Al(OH)_3(s) + 3CH_4(g)$$

The hydrolysis of the other II A metal carbides yields acetylene, C_2H_2.

Aluminum and beryllium (as well as magnesium in this case) have thin protective oxide coatings, which make them resistant to attack by dilute nitric acid. Beryllium oxide and aluminum oxide are hard, extremely high melting, insoluble solids. Beryllium and aluminum form the stable fluoro complex anions BeF_4^{2-} and AlF_6^{3-}. The other II A metals do not form complexes with the fluoride ion that are stable in solution. Normal beryllium carbonate is unstable, and aluminum carbonate cannot be made at all.

18.8   The Transition Metals

The transition metals are found in groups III B to II B in the periodic table. Some chemists do not include group II B (the zinc group) in this classification, and some exclude group I B (the copper group), as well. However, there are advantages in classifying the copper- and zinc-group elements as transition elements, and we shall follow this practice.

In general, the transition metals have high melting and boiling points, high heats of fusion, and high heats of vaporization. The group II B elements (zinc, cadmium, and mercury) are exceptions to this generalization. Mercury is a liquid under ordinary conditions, and all of the II B elements are comparatively low melting and relatively easy to volatilize (distillation constitutes a method of refining the metals). Most of the transition metals are good conductors of heat and electricity; the I B elements are outstanding in these respects (Table 18.1).

The significant feature of the electronic configurations of the transition elements (Table 18.9) is the gradual build up of the *d* subshell of the next to

Table 18.9

Postulated Electronic Configurations of the Valence
Subshells of the Transition Metals

Sc	$3d^1\ 4s^2$	Y	$4d^1\ 5s^2$	La	$5d^1\ 6s^2$
Ti	$3d^2\ 4s^2$	Zr	$4d^2\ 5s^2$	Hf	$5d^2\ 6s^2$
V	$3d^3\ 4s^2$	Nb	$4d^4\ 5s^1$	Ta	$5d^3\ 6s^2$
Cr	$3d^5\ 4s^1$	Mo	$4d^5\ 5s^1$	W	$5d^4\ 6s^2$
Mn	$3d^5\ 4s^2$	Tc	$4d^6\ 5s^1$	Re	$5d^5\ 6s^2$
Fe	$3d^6\ 4s^2$	Ru	$4d^7\ 5s^1$	Os	$5d^6\ 6s^2$
Co	$3d^7\ 4s^2$	Rh	$4d^8\ 5s^1$	Ir	$5d^7\ 6s^2$
Ni	$3d^8\ 4s^2$	Pd	$4d^{10}$	Pt	$5d^9\ 6s^1$
Cu	$3d^{10}4s^1$	Ag	$4d^{10}5s^1$	Au	$5d^{10}6s^1$
Zn	$3d^{10}4s^2$	Cd	$4d^{10}5s^2$	Hg	$5d^{10}6s^2$

the outer shell. Included in the sixth and seventh periods are the lanthanides and actinides, respectively. These are the inner-transition elements in which inner f orbitals are being filled (Section 18.9).

The transition elements exhibit a wide variation in chemical properties. Many compounds of the transition elements are colored and paramagnetic because of unpaired electrons. Since the inner d orbitals are energetically close to the s orbital of the outer level, both ns and $(n-1)d$ electrons are involved in compound formation. With the exceptions of zinc, cadmium, and the elements of group III B, all the transition elements exhibit more than one oxidation state in compound formation. The largest number of oxidation states, as well as the maximum oxidation number, is observed for the fifth transition element of period 4 (Mn) and the sixth elements of periods 5 and 6 (Ru and Os, respectively). For these elements and the ones preceding them in each transition series, the maximum oxidation number corresponds to the total number of ns and $(n-1)d$ electrons (Table 18.10). The higher oxidation numbers of a given element are most frequently seen in compounds containing the more electronegative elements: fluorine, oxygen, and chlorine.

After the maximum oxidation state of a period is reached in each transition series, there is a decrease in the highest oxidation number observed for each subsequent element, and these oxidation states are, in general, difficult to obtain and unstable. Less common and unstable oxidation states are enclosed in parentheses in Table 18.10.

In general, the lowest oxidation number observed is $2+$; notable exceptions are Cu^+, Ag^+, Au^+, and Hg_2^{2+}. The mercury(I), or mercurous, ion is unique; evidence for its dimeric structure includes the following. Mercurous salts are diamagnetic in agreement with the formula Hg_2^{2+}; the ion Hg^+ would have one unpaired electron. X-ray studies of mercurous salts indicate discrete Hg_2^{2+} ions. The interpretations of certain equilibria involving the mercurous

Table 18.10

Oxidation States of the Transition Elements
(Less Common, or Unstable, States in Parentheses)

Sc	Ti	V	Cr	Mn	Fe	Co	Ni	Cu	Zn
								1+	
	(2+)	(2+)	2+	2+	2+	2+	2+	2+	2+
3+	3+	3+	3+	(3+)	3+	3+	(3+)	(3+)	
	4+	4+	(4+)	4+	(4+)	(4+)	(4+)		
		5+	(5+)		(5+)				
			6+	(6+)	(6+)				
				7+					

Y	Zr	Nb	Mo	Tc	Ru	Rh	Pd	Ag	Cd
						(1+)		1+	
	(2+)	(2+)	(2+)	(2+)	2+	(2+)	2+	(2+)	2+
3+	(3+)	(3+)	3+	(3+)	3+	3+	(3+)	(3+)	
	4+	(4+)	4+	4+	4+	4+	4+		
		5+	5+	5+	(5+)	(5+)			
			6+	6+	(6+)	(6+)			
				7+	7+				
			(8+)		(7+)				
					(8+)				

La	Hf	Ta	W	Re	Os	Ir	Pt	Au	Hg
						(1+)		1+	1+
		(2+)	(2+)		(2+)	(2+)	2+		2+
(3+)	(3+)	(3+)	(3+)	3+	(3+)	3+	(3+)	3+	
	4+	(4+)	4+	4+	4+	4+	4+		
		5+	5+	(5+)	(5+)	(5+)	(5+)		
			6+	(6+)	6+	(6+)	(6+)		
				7+					
					8+				

ion are in agreement with experimentally derived values for the equilibrium constants only if the formula Hg_2^{2+} is used.

Within each group, the higher oxidation states become more stable, and more important, with increasing atomic number; a corresponding decline in the stability and importance of the lower oxidation states is also observed. The gain in stability of the higher states with increasing atomic number may be attributed to the increasing atomic size which makes the d electrons more available for compound formation.

Thus the 2+ ions of many of the fourth period transition elements are stable and characteristic of the elements, whereas the 2+ states of the heavier elements are not particularly common or stable. The most important oxidation states of iron are $2+$ and $3+$; for osmium, the heaviest member of the same group, the most important states are $4+$, $6+$, and $8+$.

The maximum oxidation number of manganese (which is the first member of its group) is attained in the permanganate ion, MnO_4^-. This ion is a strong oxidizing agent in acidic solution.

$$5e^- + 8H^+ + MnO_4^- \longrightarrow Mn^{2+} + 4H_2O \qquad \mathscr{E}^\circ = +1.51 \text{ v}$$

In contrast, the analogous perrhenate ion, ReO_4^-, formed by the heaviest member of the group, is stable under comparable conditions.

The transition elements of group VI B form series of oxy anions in which the central metal ion is in an oxidation state of $6+$; the simplest members of these series are the chromate ion, CrO_4^{2-}, the molybdate ion, MoO_4^{2-}, and the tungstate ion, WO_4^{2-}. Only a few polynuclear complexes of chromium have been reported; the most important of these is the dichromate ion, $Cr_2O_7^{2-}$, which results when chromate solutions are acidified.

$$2H^+ + CrO_4^{2-} \longrightarrow Cr_2O_7^{2-} + H_2O$$

The dichromate ion is easily reduced in acid and consequently is a strong oxidizing agent.

$$6e^- + 14H^+ + CrO_7^{2-} \longrightarrow 2Cr^{3+} + 7H_2O \qquad \mathscr{E}^\circ = +1.33 \text{ v}$$

In contrast, molybdenum and tungsten form very extensive series of poly-nuclear molybdates and tungstates, and these compounds, as well as the corresponding acids, are very stable and without significant oxidizing power. The formation of such polynuclear oxy anions is not a common phenomenon in transition metal chemistry.

With increasing oxidation number, the oxides of a given element become less basic and more acidic. Thus CrO is an exclusively basic oxide and dissolves in acids to form Cr^{2+} salts; Cr_2O_3 is amphoteric and forms Cr^{3+} salts with acids and the chromite ion, $Cr(OH)_4^-$, in alkaline solution; CrO_3 is entirely acidic in character and gives rise to chromates, CrO_4^{2-}, and dichromates, $Cr_2O_7^{2-}$.

The atomic and ionic radii of the transition elements are, in general, smaller than those of the representative elements of the same period (Figure 3.1) since, for the transition elements, electrons are being added to an inner d sublevel where the effect of the nuclear charge is greater than it is in the outer shell. This relatively small size causes the transition element ions to have comparatively high charge densities; this, plus the availability of d orbitals for bonding, accounts for the pronounced tendency of most transition elements to form numerous stable complex ions (Chapter 19).

There are horizontal (or period) similarities as well as vertical (or group) similarities between the transition metals. The elements Cr through Cu, of the first transition series, have very similar atomic radii and ionic radii for ions of the same charge (Table 18.11), and horizontal similarities follow (such as

Table 18.11

Atomic and Ionic Radii of the Transition Elements of the Fourth Period

	Sc	Ti	V	Cr	Mn	Fe	Co	Ni	Cu	Zn
atomic radii	1.44	1.32	1.22	1.17	1.17	1.17	1.16	1.15	1.17	1.25
ionic radii										
M^{2+}	—	0.90	0.88	0.84	0.80	0.76	0.74	0.72	0.72	0.74
M^{3+}	0.81	0.76	0.74	0.69	0.66	0.64	0.63	—	—	—

the formation of compounds of formula MO, MS, MCl_2, etc.). Among the heavier elements, horizontal similarities are also evident (e.g., the formation of MO_2 compounds), and such similarities are particularly striking among the transition triads of group VIII (Fe, Co, and Ni; Ru, Rh, and Pd; and Os, Ir, and Pt). The elements of the two heavier triads are similar both physically and chemically.

The lanthanides occur at the beginning of the transition series of the sixth period. For the lanthanides, electrons are being added to the $4f$ sublevel without significant change in the $5s$, $5p$, $5d$, and $6s$ sublevels. The nuclear charge increases as this $4f$ sublevel deep within the atom is being filled, and there is a consequent decrease in the atomic and ionic radii of the lanthanides which is known as the **lanthanide contraction.**

The lanthanide contraction has an important effect on the properties of the transition elements following the lanthanides in the sixth period. Because of the lanthanide contraction, the atomic radii of these elements are not much different from those of the corresponding elements of the fifth period (Figure 18.7). Consequently, the second and third members of each group resemble each other much more than they resemble the first member of the group; there is no regular increase in size with increasing atomic number such as is observed for the A family elements.

Even though 32 elements intervene, hafnium $(Z = 72)$ is notably similar to zirconium $(Z = 40)$. Both elements have approximately the same atomic and ionic radii, and the chemical properties of the two elements are very similar; the separation of the two elements, which occur together in nature, is extremely difficult.

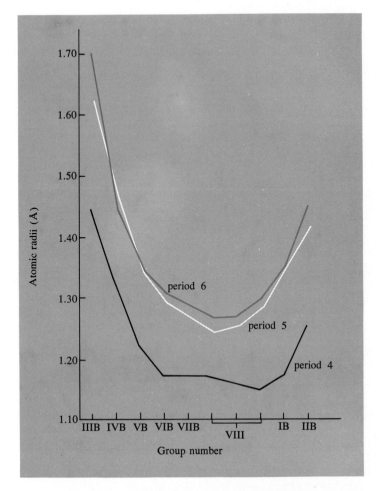

Figure 18.7 Atomic radii of the transition elements.

Some of the standard electrode potentials of the transition elements are listed in Table 18.12. For the most part, the potentials listed for the heavier elements, since they are for lower oxidation states, are not particularly important; however, they do serve to illustrate several trends.

Many of the metals react with dilute acids, as well as water or steam, to liberate hydrogen. Some of the metals, however, are poor reducing agents— notably, mercury, the group I B elements (copper, silver and gold), and the transition triads of the fifth and sixth periods (ruthenium, rhodium, palladium, osmium, iridium, and platinum). Frequently, these six elements of the transition triads, silver, and gold are referred to as noble metals.

Thus the elements of low reactivity appear to be concentrated toward the end of the transition series, particularly those of the fifth and sixth periods, and, in general, there is a decrease in electropositive character (or strength

Table 18.12

Standard Electrode Potentials of the Transition Elements (Volts)

	Sc	Ti	V	Cr	Mn	Fe	Co	Ni	Cu	Zn
M^+/M	—	—	—	—	—	—	—	—	+0.52	—
M^{2+}/M	—	−1.63	−1.19	−0.91	−1.18	−0.44	−0.28	−0.25	+0.34	−0.76
M^{3+}/M	−2.08	−1.21	−0.88	−0.74	−0.28	−0.04	+0.42	—	—	—

	Y	Zr	Nb	Mo	Tc	Ru	Rh	Pd	Ag	Cd
M^+/M	—	—	—	—	—	—	+0.6	—	+0.80	—
M^{2+}/M	—	—	—	—	+0.4	+0.45	+0.6	+0.99	—	−0.40
M^{3+}/M	−2.37	—	−1.1	−0.2	—	—	+0.8	—	—	—

	La	Hf	Ta	W	Re	Os	Ir	Pt	Au	Hg
M^+/M	—	—	—	—	—	—	—	—	+1.69	+0.79
M^{2+}/M	—	—	—	—	—	+0.85	—	+1.2	—	+0.85
M^{3+}/M	−2.52	—	—	−0.11	+0.3	—	+1.15	—	+1.50	—

of the metals as reducing agents) across a period and down a group. The decreasing size of the atoms across a period causes the electrons to be held increasingly tightly. The vertical trend is more surprising in view of the trends established by the A families. However, for transition elements, the increasing nuclear charge with increasing atomic number down a group is not accompanied by a large increase in atomic size, and the electrons are held more tightly. This is particularly true of the transition elements of the sixth period that follow the lanthanides. Here, the unusually small sizes of the atoms cause the electrons to be very tightly held; with the exceptions of La and Hf, the least electropositive member of each group is the sixth period element.

Although a given electrode potential may indicate a thermodynamic tendency for a reaction to occur, at times the rates at which some transition elements react are extremely slow. Thus chromium is a moderately strong reducing agent and reacts with nonoxidizing acids, such as HCl, to liberate hydrogen. Chromium does not, however, react with nitric acid, a strong oxidizing agent. It is said that the metal is made passive by the nitric acid. The phenomenon of passivity, which is displayed by many transition elements, is not well understood. In some instances, it may be that the metal is protected by a thin, transparent, impervious, oxide coating.

The products of some of the reactions of the transition metals of the fourth period, which are the most common of the transition elements, are given in Table 18.13.

Table 18.13

Products of Some Reactions of the Transition Elements
of the Fourth Period

	Sc	Ti	V	Cr	Mn
O_2	Sc_2O_3	TiO_2	V_2O_5, VO_2	Cr_2O_3	Mn_3O_4
X_2	ScX_3	TiX_4	VF_5, VCl_4, VBr_3, VI_3	CrX_3 (except CrI_2)	MnX_2
S	Sc_2S_3	TiS_2	V_2S_5, VS_2	CrS	MnS
N_2	ScN	TiN	VN	CrN	Mn_3N_2
HCl	$Sc^{3+} + H_2$	$Ti^{3+} + H_2$	—	$Cr^{2+} + H_2$	$Mn^{2+} + H_2$
H_2O	$Sc(OH)_3 + H_2$	$TiO_2 + H_2$[a]	—	$Cr_2O_3 + H_2$[a]	$Mn(OH)_2 + H_2$
NaOH	—	—	—	$Cr(OH)_6^{3-} + H_2$	—

	Fe	Co	Ni	Cu	Zn
O_2	Fe_3O_4, Fe_2O_3	Co_3O_4	NiO	Cu_2O, CuO	ZnO
X_2	FeX_3 (except FeI_2)	CoX_2	NiX_2	CuX_2 (except CuI)	ZnX_2
S	FeS	CoS	NiS	Cu_2S	ZnS
N_2	—	—	—	—	—
HCl	$Fe^{2+} + H_2$	$Co^{2+} + H_2$	$Ni^{2+} + H_2$	—	$Zn^{2+} + H_2$
H_2O	$Fe_3O_4 + H_2$[a]	$CoO + H_2$[a]	$NiO + H_2$[a]	—	$ZnO + H_2$[a]
NaOH	—	—	—	—	$[Zn(OH)_4]^{2-} + H_2$

[a] Steam

18.9 The Lanthanides

Postulated electronic configurations for the lanthanides are given in Table
18.14; there is some uncertainty to the assignment listed. The differentiating
electrons of the lanthanides, or inner-transition elements, are lodged in the
third from the outer shell in $4f$ orbitals. This factor accounts for some of the
unusual aspects of the chemistry of these elements. The atomic and ionic
radii of the elements show a regular decrease with increasing atomic number
(the lanthanide contraction).

The outstanding feature of the chemistry of the lanthanides is their similarity. The differentiating $4f$ electrons lie deep within the lanthanide atoms; thus
these f electrons are shielded from the surroundings of the atom and do not
cause strong variations in properties. In contrast, the properties of the transition elements vary widely. The d electrons project from transition element
atoms and ions and interact with the surroundings (Chapter 19). Hence, the
number and arrangement of the d electrons of the transition elements is
significant, whereas the number and arrangement of the f electrons of the
inner-transition elements cause only minor variations in properties.

All the lanthanides form ions in the characteristic group III B oxidation state, 3+ (Table 18.14). For some of the elements, other oxidation states are known, but these are less stable. The 3+ ions are formed through the loss of the two $6s$ electrons and one $4f$ electron (or one $5d$ electron, if such is available).

There is some evidence that f^0, f^7 (half-filled), and f^{14} (filled) ions have stable configurations. Thus La^{3+}, (f^0), Gd^{3+} (f^7), and Lu^{3+} (f^{14}) are the only ions that these elements form, and the most stable 2+ and 4+ ions are Eu^{2+} (f^7), Yt^{2+} (f^{14}), Ce^{4+} (f^0), and Tb^{4+} (f^7). The ceric ion, Ce^{4+}, is a good oxidizing agent.

Table 18.14

Some Properties of the Lanthanides

	Z	Postulated Electronic Configurations of Valence Subshells	Oxidation States	Atomic Radius, Å	Ionic Radius, M^{3+}, Å	$\mathscr{E}^\circ$ $3e^- +$ $M^{3+} \to M$ (volts)
La	57	$5d^1\ 6s^2$	3+	1.69	1.06	−2.52
Ce	58	$4f^2\ 6s^2$	3+, 4+	1.65	1.03	−2.48
Pr	59	$4f^3\ 6s^2$	3+, 4+	1.65	1.01	−2.46
Nd	60	$4f^4\ 6s^2$	2+, 3+, 4+	1.64	1.00	−2.43
Pm	61	$4f^5\ 6s^2$	3+	—	0.98	−2.42
Sm	62	$4f^6\ 6s^2$	2+, 3+	1.66	0.96	−2.41
Eu	63	$4f^7\ 6s^2$	2+, 3+	1.85	0.95	−2.41
Gd	64	$4f^7\ 5d^1 6s^2$	3+	1.61	0.94	−2.40
Tb	65	$4f^9\ 6s^2$	3+, 4+	1.59	0.92	−2.39
Dy	66	$4f^{10} 6s^2$	3+, 4+	1.59	0.91	−2.35
Ho	67	$4f^{11} 6s^2$	3+	1.58	0.89	−2.32
Er	68	$4f^{12} 6s^2$	3+	1.57	0.88	−2.30
Tm	69	$4f^{13} 6s^2$	2+, 3+	1.56	0.87	−2.28
Yb	70	$4f^{14} 6s^2$	2+, 3+	1.70	0.86	−2.27
Lu	71	$4f^{14} 5d^1 6s^2$	3+	1.56	0.85	−2.26

The elements occur together in nature because of their great chemical similarity. Promethium, which is radioactive and probably occurs only in trace amounts, is an exception. The elements are extremely difficult to separate; repeated fractional crystallization and ion-exchange techniques have been employed to effect separations.

All of the lanthanides are silvery white, very reactive metals. The electrode potentials for the reduction of the 3+ ions are strikingly similar (Table 18.14). Some reactions of the lanthanides are given in Table 18.15; a number of the metals are also known to react with carbon to produce saltlike carbides and with hydrogen to give saltlike hydrides. The M_2O_3 oxides react with water to form insoluble hydroxides, $M(OH)_3$, that are not amphoteric. Insoluble

Table 18.15

Reactions of the Lanthanides[a]

Reaction	Remarks
$2M + 3X_2 \longrightarrow 2MX_3$	$X_2 =$ all halogens; Ce gives CeF_4 with F_2
$4M + 3O_2 \longrightarrow 2M_2O_3$	Ce gives CeO_2
$2M + 3S \longrightarrow M_2S_3$	not Eu; reactions with Se similar
$2M + N_2 \longrightarrow 2MN$	high temperatures; reactions with P_4, As, Sb, and Bi similar
$2M + 6H^+ \longrightarrow 2M^{3+} + 3H_2$	
$2M + 6H_2O \longrightarrow 2M(OH)_3 + 3H_2$	slow with cold water

[a] M = any lanthanide, except where noted.

carbonates, $M_2(CO_3)_3$, may be produced by the reactions of carbon dioxide with the oxides or hydroxides. The halides (with the exception of fluorides), nitrates, chlorates, acetates, and sulfates of the $3+$ ions are water soluble; the phosphates, fluorides, oxalates, hydroxides, and carbonates are insoluble. The precipitation of the elements as oxalates serves as the basis of an analytical determination. Generally, the compounds are paramagnetic and highly colored.

18.10 The Metals of Group III A

The characteristics of the group III A elements have been discussed in Section 12.15, and some of the properties of the metals are listed in Table 12.9.

Aluminum, the most abundant metal of the earth's crust (approximately 8%), is obtained by the electrolysis of molten Al_2O_3 (the Hall process, Section 18.4). Gallium, indium, and thallium are widely distributed in nature but occur only in trace amounts; they may be prepared by the electrolysis of aqueous solutions of salts of the metals. They are soft, white metals with relatively low melting points (Figure 18.2). Gallium has an unusually low melting point (30°C). Since its boiling point is not abnormally low (2070°C), gallium has an exceptional liquid range and has found use as a thermometer fluid.

The metals are fairly reactive (Table 18.16). Aluminum, gallium, and indium (but not thallium) have protective oxide coatings and are passive toward nitric acid. However, all the metals react with nonoxidizing acids to liberate hydrogen. As expected from their $ns^2 np^1$ electronic configurations, the most important oxidation state is $3+$. Most of the compounds of the metals in the $3+$ oxidation state are covalent. In water, however, the M^{3+} ions are stabilized through hydration (Section 12.15), and the heats of hydration are high.

Table 18.16

Reactions of Aluminum, Gallium, Indium, and Thallium [a]

Reaction	Remarks
$2M + 3X_2 \longrightarrow 2MX_3$	X_2 = all halogens; Tl also gives TlX; no iodide of Tl^{3+}
$4M + 3O_2 \longrightarrow 2M_2O_3$	high temperatures; Tl also gives Tl_2O
$2M + 3S \longrightarrow M_2S_3$	high temperatures; Tl also gives Tl_2S; also with Se and Te
$2Al + N_2 \longrightarrow 2AlN$	Al only; GaN and InN may be prepared indirectly
$2M + 6H^+ \longrightarrow 2M^{3+} + 3H_2$	M = Al, Ga, and In; Tl gives Tl^+
$2M + 2OH^- + 6H_2O \longrightarrow 2M(OH)_4^- + 3H_2$	M = Al and Ga

[a] M = Al, Ga, In, and Tl, except where noted.

The sulfates, nitrates, and halides are water soluble, but the M^{3+} ions hydrolyze readily.

$$[M(H_2O)_6]^{3+} + H_2O \longrightarrow [M(H_2O)_5(OH)]^{2+} + H_3O^+$$

For this reason, salts of weak acids (such as acetates, carbonates, sulfides, and cyanides) do not exist in water solution. Such salts are completely hydrolyzed.

$$[M(H_2O)_6]^{3+} + 3C_2H_3O_2^- \longrightarrow M(OH)_3(s) + 3H_2O + 3HC_2H_3O_2$$

In addition, complexes with ammonia do not exist in water.

$$[M(H_2O)_6]^{3+} + NH_3 \longrightarrow [M(H_2O)_5(OH)]^{2+} + NH_4^+$$

The hydroxides, $M(OH)_3$, are insoluble in water. Aluminum hydroxide and gallium hydroxide are amphoteric.

$$Al(OH)_3 + OH^- \longrightarrow [Al(OH)_4]^-$$
$$Ga(OH)_3 + OH^- \longrightarrow [Ga(OH)_4]^-$$

Aluminum sulfate forms an important series of double salts called alums, $MAl(SO_4)_2 \cdot 12H_2O$ (or $M_2SO_4 \cdot Al_2(SO_4)_3 \cdot 24H_2O$), where M may be almost any univalent cation (Na^+, K^+, Rb^+, Cs^+, NH_4^+, Ag^+, and Tl^+) except Li^+ (which is too small). In addition to Al^{3+}, other M^{3+} species form series of such double sulfates: Fe^{3+}, Cr^{3+}, Mn^{3+}, Ti^{3+}, Co^{3+}, Ga^{3+}, In^{3+}, Rh^{3+}, and Ir^{3+}.

Hydrides, analogous to those of boron, are not formed by aluminum, gallium, indium, and thallium. However, $[MH_4]^-$ ions, analogous to the borohydride ion, are formed.

Among the heavier members of the group, compounds with the metal in a 1+ oxidation state are known. The np^1 electron is more readily removed than the ns^2 electrons, which comprise an inert pair. This effect is also seen for the M^{2+} ions of group IV A, and the low reactivity of mercury has been ascribed to the $6s^2$ inert pair of its valence level.

Unlike the transition elements, however, the 1+ state of the III A elements (their lowest state) is most stable among the heavier members of the group. No 1+ compounds of aluminum are known. Gallium and indium form a few compounds (such as Ga_2S, Ga_2O at high temperatures, InCl, InBr, and In_2O). The Ga^+ and In^+ ions are not stable in water solution.

For thallium, however, the 1+ state is important and stable. In fact, Tl^+ is more stable in water than Tl^{3+} (which is a strong oxidizing agent).

$$2e^- + Tl^{3+} \rightleftharpoons Tl^+ \qquad \mathscr{E}° = +1.25 \text{ v}$$

The oxide Tl_2O dissolves in water to form the soluble hydroxide TlOH. Whereas the Tl^{3+} ion is extensively hydrolyzed in aqueous solution, the Tl^+ ion is not. A wide variety of Tl^+ compounds are known. The sulfate, nitrate, acetate, and fluoride are water soluble; the chloride, bromide, iodide, sulfide, and chromate are insoluble.

18.11   The Metals of Group IV A

Of the elements of group IV A, germanium, tin, and lead are classified as metals. The characteristics of the group as a whole are discussed in Section 12.9, and some of the properties of the metals are listed in Table 12.6. The metals are not abundant in nature; germanium is a rare element.

Germanium is a semiconductor and is used in the manufacture of transistors. It is a hard, brittle, white metal and has the highest melting point of the metals of the group. Tin and lead have relatively low melting points and low tensile strengths. Lead is especially soft and malleable.

The metals are fairly reactive (Table 18.17). Lead frequently appears less reactive than the electrode potential

$$2e^- + Pb^{2+} \rightleftharpoons Pb \qquad \mathscr{E}° = -0.13 \text{ v}$$

would indicate because of the formation of surface coatings. Thus the reaction of lead with sulfuric acid or hydrochloric acid is impeded by the formation of insoluble lead sulfate or lead chloride on the surface of the metal.

Since the elements have $ns^2 np^2$ valence shell configurations, two oxidation states are observed: 4+ and 2+ (inert pair species). The 4+ state declines in importance, and the 2+ state becomes increasingly important down the

Table 18.17

Reactions of Germanium, Tin, and Lead [a]

Reaction	Remarks
$M + 2X_2 \longrightarrow 2MX_4$	X_2 = any halogen; M = Ge and Sn; Pb yields PbX_2
$M + O_2 \longrightarrow MO_2$	M = Ge and Sn; high temperatures; Pb yields PbO or Pb_3O_4
$M + 2S \longrightarrow MS_2$	M = Ge and Sn; high temperatures; Pb yields PbS
$M + 2H^+ \longrightarrow M^{2+} + H_2$	M = Sn and Pb
$3M + 4H^+ + 4NO_3^- \longrightarrow 3MO_2 + 4NO + 2H_2O$	M = Ge and Sn
$3Pb + 8H^+ + 2NO_3^- \longrightarrow 3Pb^{2+} + 2NO + 4H_2O$	
$M + OH^- + 2H_2O \longrightarrow M(OH)_3^- + H_2$	M = Sn and Pb; slow
$Ge + 2OH^- + 4H_2O \longrightarrow Ge(OH)_6^{2-} + 2H_2$	

[a] M = Ge, Sn, and Pb, except where noted.

series: Ge, Sn, Pb. Thus only a few 2+ germanium compounds are of importance (GeO, GeS, $GeCl_2$, $GeBr_2$, and GeI_2), whereas only a few 4+ lead compounds are important (PbO_2, $Pb(C_2H_3O_2)_4$, PbF_4, and $PbCl_4$). The Sn^{2+} (stannous, or tin(II) ion) and Pb^{2+} (plumbous, or lead(II) ion) are the only cationic species of the group that exist in water; 4+ ions probably do not exist. Most of the pure 2+ and 4+ compounds are covalent, although PbF_2 is known to be ionic.

All the metals form dioxides; GeO_2 and SnO_2 are the products of the reactions of the metals with oxygen. Lead dioxide may be prepared by the oxidation of PbO or Pb^{2+} salts in alkaline solution.

$$Pb(OH)_3^-(aq) + OCl^-(aq) \longrightarrow PbO_2(s) + Cl^-(aq) + OH^-(aq) + H_2O$$

Lead dioxide is a strong oxidizing agent.

$$2e^- + 4H^+ + PbO_2 \longrightarrow Pb^{2+} + 2H_2O \qquad \mathscr{E}° = +1.46\,v$$

In acid solution, PbO_2 oxidizes Mn^{2+} to MnO_4^- and Cl^- to Cl_2. In contrast to GeO_2 and SnO_2, PbO_2 is thermally unstable. Upon gentle heating, PbO_2 decomposes to Pb_3O_4 (red lead); stronger heating gives PbO (litharge). The compound Pb_3O_4 contains lead in two oxidation states and may be represented as $Pb_2^{II}Pb^{IV}O_4$ like the compounds Fe_3O_4 and Co_3O_4, both of which conform to the formula $M^{II}(M^{III}O_2)_2$.

Germanates, stannates, and plumbates may be derived from the dioxides by reactions with aqueous alkali or, in the case of PbO_2, fusion with alkali metal oxides or alkaline earth oxides. The stannates and plumbates form trihydrates in which the anion is an octahedral hydroxy complex: $[M(OH)_6]^{2-}$; a few germanates of similar structure are known (e.g., $Fe[Ge(OH)_6]$). Crystalline metagermanates (e.g., Na_2GeO_3) and orthogermanates (e.g., Mg_2GeO_4) are known; these compounds have structures analogous to the meta- and orthosilicates. There are no hydroxides of formula $M(OH)_4$, but hydrous MO_2 oxides may be prepared.

Treatment of the Sn^{2+} and Pb^{2+} ions, in water solution, with OH^- ion gives hydrous-oxide precipitates that are commonly assigned the formulas $Sn(OH)_2$ and $Pb(OH)_2$. By heating these products, SnO and PbO can be prepared; PbO is also the product of the reaction of lead and oxygen as well as the decompositions of Pb_3O_4 and PbO_2. The compound GeO may be prepared by the hydrolysis of $GeCl_2$.

All the monoxides, as well as the hydrous oxides (or hydroxides), are amphoteric and dissolve in either acid or alkaline solution. In excess alkali, germanites, stannites, and plumbites are produced. For example,

$$PbO(s) + OH^-(aq) + H_2O \longrightarrow Pb(OH)_3{}^-(aq)$$

The stannite ion is a strong reducing agent.

$$2e^- + Sn(OH)_6^{2-} \longrightarrow Sn(OH)_3{}^- + 3OH^- \qquad \mathscr{E}° = -0.93 \text{ v}$$

All the metals form monosulfides, MS, but only germanium and tin form disulfides, MS_2. The disulfides of germanium and tin may be prepared by the reactions of the metals and sulfur and may be precipitated from solutions of Ge^{IV} or Sn^{IV} compounds by H_2S. The disulfides, like the dioxides, are amphoteric. In solutions of alkali metal sulfides or ammonium sulfide, GeS_2 and SnS_2 dissolve to form thioanions; compounds of the SnS_3^{2-} and SnS_4^{4-} ions have been isolated from such solutions, but thiogermanates have not been obtained in pure form.

$$SnS_2(s) + S^{2-}(aq) \longrightarrow SnS_3^{2-}(aq)$$

Insoluble PbS and SnS may be precipitated from solutions by means of H_2S. Lead(II) sulfide is also the product of the direct union of the elements, and SnS may be prepared by the thermal decomposition of SnS_2. Germanium-(II) sulfide may be derived from the disulfide of germanium by the reaction

$$GeS_2 + Ge \longrightarrow 2GeS$$

None of the monosulfides are soluble in sulfide solutions.

Complete series of the tetrahalides of germanium, tin, and lead are known except for $PbBr_4$ and PbI_4. Lead in a 4+ state has strong oxidizing power and cannot exist in a compound with bromine and iodine in 1− states (which have reducing abilities). Lead(IV) chloride readily decomposes at 100°C.

$$PbCl_4(l) \longrightarrow PbCl_2(s) + Cl_2(g)$$

The tetrahalides, in general, are volatile covalent substances. They hydrolyze readily, producing hydrous dioxides.

The tetrahalides of germanium and tin form complex anions, such as GeF_6^{2-} and $SnCl_6^{2-}$; a few compounds containing such anions of lead(IV) have been prepared. Whereas the halo complexes GeF_6^{2-}, SnF_6^{2-}, and $SnCl_6^{2-}$ are stable in water, the others are readily hydrolyzed to give the corresponding dioxides.

All the dihalides of germanium, tin, and lead are known. Germanium(II) halides, as well as tin(II) halides, may be prepared by the reaction of the appropriate tetrahalide and metal.

$$GeCl_4 + Ge \longrightarrow 2GeCl_2$$

The reactions of tin and the hydrohalic acids yield tin(II) halides. Lead(II) halides may be produced by the direct reaction of the elements, and since all PbX_2 compounds are insoluble in water, they may be precipitated from solutions containing Pb^{2+} by the addition of halide ions.

The dihalides are much less volatile than the tetrahalides indicating an increased degree of ionic character; PbF_2, $PbCl_2$, and $PbBr_2$ are ionic in the solid state. The dihalides of germanium are not particularly stable. Complex anions, such as $GeCl_3^-$, $SnCl_4^{2-}$, $PbCl_3^-$, $PbCl_4^{2-}$, and $PbCl_6^{4-}$ are known. Both Sn^{2+} and Pb^{2+} form such ions in aqueous solution in the presence of halide ions; in general, the ions MX^+ and MX_3^- are most important. Insoluble lead(II) halides dissolve in solutions containing excess halide ions because of the formation of such complexes.

All three metals form covalent, volatile hydrides: GeH_4, germane; SnH_4, stannane; and PbH_4, plumbane. The hydride of lead is thermally unstable and decomposes to the elements at $0°C$; SnH_4 decomposes at approximately $150°C$. Continuing the trend established by carbon and silicon, germanium forms catenated hydrides of formula Ge_nH_{2n+2}, where n is any number from 2 to 8. Tin or lead form only the simple hydrides.

The Sn^{2+} and Pb^{2+} ions are extensively hydrolyzed in water.

$$[Sn(H_2O)_6]^{2+} + H_2O \rightleftharpoons [Sn(H_2O)_5(OH)]^+ + H_3O^+ \qquad K_H \cong 10^{-2}$$

$$[Pb(H_2O)_6]^{2+} + H_2O \rightleftharpoons [Pb(H_2O)_5(OH)]^+ + H_3O^+ \qquad K_H \cong 10^{-8}$$

The hydrolysis is particularly pronounced in the case of tin(II) compounds; excess acid is generally added to aqueous solutions of such compounds to inhibit hydrolysis and prevent the precipitation of basic salts, such as $Sn(OH)Cl$.

Lead(II) nitrate and lead(II) acetate are soluble in water; the acetate is only slightly dissociated. The sulfate, chromate, carbonate, sulfide, and all of the halides, of Pb^{2+} are only slightly soluble in water.

SOME SUGGESTED READINGS

Cotton, F. A., and Wilkinson, G., *Advanced Inorganic Chemistry*, 2nd ed., New York, Wiley, 1966.

Larsen, E. M., *Transitional Elements*, New York, Benjamin, 1965 (paper).

Lingane, J. J., *Analytical Chemistry of Selected Metallic Elements*, New York, Van Nostrand Reinhold, 1965 (paper).

Moeller, T., *The Chemistry of the Lanthanides*, New York, Van Nostrand Reinhold, 1963 (paper).

Rich, R. L., *Periodic Correlations*, New York, Benjamin, 1965 (paper).

Weeks, M. E., and Leicester, H. M., *Discovery of the Elements*, 7th ed., Easton, Penna., Chemical Education Publishing Co., 1968.

PROBLEMS

The more difficult problems are starred.

18.1 What properties distinguish metals from nonmetals?

18.2 What evidence supports the belief that the strength of the metallic bonding of the metals of the fourth and subsequent periods reaches a maximum around the center of the transition series? How can the trend be explained?

18.3 What diameter of iron wire must be used so that a given length will have an electrical conductivity equal to that of the same length of copper wire that is 1.0 cm in diameter? Electrical conductivities are listed in Table 18.1.

18.4 What are the principal types of ores? Give an example of each type.

18.5 Explain why it is not surprising that the following ores are found in nature: (a) native ores of platinum, gold, and silver, (b) sulfate ores of barium, strontium, and lead, (c) Na^+ and Mg^{2+} in sea water, (d) sulfide ores of lead, bismuth, and nickel.

18.6 What types of ores are roasted? Write a chemical equation for the roasting of an ore of each type. Why is this procedure used?

18.7 Give equations for reactions that occur in the blast furnace for the production of pig iron.

18.8 Describe the following metallurgical processes. Use equations when possible. (a) Froth flotation, (b) Parkes process, (c) Mond process, (d) Van Arkel process, (e) Kroll process, (f) liquation, (g) zone refining, (h) thermite process.

18.9 Identify the following: (a) ore, (b) gangue, (c) alum, (d) amalgam, (e) flux, (f) slag, (g) smelting.

18.10 Describe, with equations, the steps in the production of aluminum metal from bauxite.

18.11 Use equations to show how magnesium is obtained from sea water.

18.12 Compare the metallurgical processes used to obtain copper from (a) low-grade $CuCO_3$ ores, (b) CuS ores.

18.13 Explain, using chemical equations, how silver is obtained from low-grade ores of native silver.

18.14 Use equations to compare the processes used to obtain lead from (a) $PbCO_3$ by roasting and carbon reduction, (b) PbS by incomplete roasting and smelting in the absence of air.

18.15 Write an equation for each reaction that occurs between Na and the following: (a) H_2, (b) N_2, (c) O_2, (d) Cl_2, (e) S, (f) P_4, (g) C, (h) H_2O, (i) NH_3.

18.16 According to first ionization potentials, the most reactive I A metal is cesium. According to electrode potentials, the most reactive I A metal is lithium. Reconcile these observations.

18.17 Discuss the ways in which the chemistry of lithium and its compounds differs from the chemistry of sodium and its compounds.

18.18 Write an equation for each reaction that occurs between Ca and the following: (a) H_2, (b) N_2, (c) O_2, (d) Cl_2, (e) S, (f) P_4, (g) C, (h) H_2O, (i) NH_3.

18.19 The second ionization potentials of the II A metals are much larger than the first ionization potentials. Why don't these elements form $1+$ ions instead of $2+$ ions in their reactions?

18.20 An aqueous solution contains Ba^{2+}, Sr^{2+}, Ca^{2+}, and Mg^{2+}. How can these ions be separated from each other?

18.21 Explain why the compounds of beryllium are far more covalent than those of any other II A metal.

18.22 Write equations to compare the reactions of Fe, Cr, and Zn with the following: (a) Cl_2, (b) O_2, (c) S, (d) N_2, (e) H_2O, (f) $H^+(aq)$, (g) $OH^-(aq)$.

18.23 In what ways do the properties of the transition metals differ from those of the A family metals?

18.24 Group IV B consists of Ti, Zr, and Hf. Why do Zr and Hf resemble each other chemically much more than either of them resemble Ti?

18.25 Write equations for the reactions of CrO, Cr_2O_3, and CrO_3 with $H^+(aq)$ and $OH^-(aq)$.

18.26 What reasons can you give to explain the low order of reactivity of the noble metals?

*18.27 The standard electrode potential, $\mathscr{E}°$, for the Hg_2^{2+}/Hg half reaction is $+0.788$ v. For the cell

$$Pt \,|\, Hg \,|\, Hg_2^{2+}(10^{-3}M) \,\|\, Hg_2^{2+}(10^{-2}M) \,|\, Hg \,|\, Pt$$

$\mathscr{E}$ equals $+0.0296$ v. (a) What would be the emf of this concentration cell if the mercurous ion had the formula Hg^+? Notice that the ion concentrations given apply to the formula Hg_2^{2+}. (b) What would be the standard electrode potential of the mercurous ion/mercury couple if the formula of the mercurous ion were Hg^+? Notice that a liter of a $1M$ Hg^+ solution would contain one-half the weight of "mercurous" ion that a liter of $1M$ Hg_2^{2+} solution would contain. (c) Explain why measurement of the emf of the concentration cell proves that the formula of the mercurous ion is Hg_2^{2+} whereas measurement of the $\mathscr{E}°$ for the mercurous ion/mercury couple does *not* establish the formula of the ion.

*18.28   The crystalline structures of three oxides of iron are related. (a) In the first, oxide ions form a face-centered cubic lattice and iron ions fill all of the octahedral holes. What type of iron ion, Fe^{2+} or Fe^{3+}, satisfies this requirement? What is the formula of this oxide? (b) The crystalline structure of the second type of oxide can be derived from the first structure by removing three-quarters of the iron ions and replacing them with the electrically equivalent number of ions of the other type. This second group of ions, however, is distributed equally between octahedral holes and tetrahedral holes. What is the formula of this oxide? What fraction of the total number of octahedral holes is filled? What fraction of the total number of tetrahedral holes is filled? (c) The crystalline structure of the third oxide can be derived by removing all the iron ions from the first crystal and replacing them with the electrically equivalent number of ions of the other type distributed randomly between octahedral and tetrahedral holes. What is the formula of this oxide? What fraction of the total number of octahedral and tetrahedral holes, taken together, is filled?

18.29   Write an equation for each reaction that occurs between La and (a) Cl_2, (b) O_2, (c) S, (d) N_2, (e) H_2O, (f) $H^+(aq)$.

18.30   The chemical properties of the transition metals vary widely from element to element. In contrast, the inner-transition metals markedly resemble each other chemically. Explain why this difference exists.

18.31   Write an equation for each reaction that occurs between Al and the following: (a) Cl_2, (b) O_2, (c) S, (d) N_2, (e) H_2O, (f) $H^+(aq)$.

18.32   Why do Al and Pb appear at times to be less reactive than electrode potentials would indicate?

18.33   A "diagonal relationship" exists between Al and Be. Explain the atomic-ionic properties that cause such a relationship and cite evidence for its existence.

18.34   Why is it impossible to precipitate Al_2S_3 from aqueous solutions containing $Al^{3+}(aq)$ ions?

18.35   Write an equation for each reaction that occurs between Sn and the following: (a) Cl_2, (b) O_2, (c) S, (d) $H^+(aq)$, (e) $OH^-(aq)$, (f) HNO_3.

18.36   Complete the following equations:
(a) $PbO_2(s) + H_2O + OH^-(aq) \rightarrow$
(b) $PbO_2(s) \xrightarrow[\text{heating}]{\text{mild}}$
(c) $PbO_2(s) \xrightarrow[\text{heating}]{\text{strong}}$
(d) $PbO(s) + H_2O + OH^-(aq) \rightarrow$
(e) $SnS(s) + S^{2-}(aq) \rightarrow$
(f) $SnS_2(s) + S^{2-}(aq) \rightarrow$
(g) $PbCl_2(s) + Cl^-(aq) \rightarrow$
(h) $SnF_4 + F^-(aq) \rightarrow$

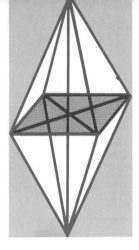

19
COMPLEX COMPOUNDS

The chemistry of complex compounds is the subject of much of the current research in inorganic chemistry. Innumerable practical applications have derived from these studies; advances have occurred in such fields as metallurgy, analytical chemistry, biochemistry, water softening, textile dyeing, ion exchange, electrochemistry, and bacteriology. In addition, the study of complex compounds has enlarged our understanding of chemical bonding, certain physical properties (such as spectral and magnetic properties), minerals (many minerals are complex compounds), and metabolic processes (both heme of blood and chlorophyll of plants are complex compounds).

19.1 Structure

A complex ion, or complex compound, consists of a central metal cation to which several anions and/or molecules (called **ligands**) are bonded. With few exceptions, free ligands have at least one electron pair that is not engaged in bonding.

665

$$:\ddot{\underset{..}{Cl}}:^- \qquad :C\equiv N:^- \qquad \underset{\overset{|}{H}}{H-\ddot{O}:} \qquad \underset{\overset{|}{H}}{H-\overset{..}{N}-H}$$

It is these electron pairs that may be considered to be donated to the electron-deficient metal ions in the formation of complexes, and ligands are substances capable of acting as Lewis bases. The bonding of complexes, however, shows a wide variation in character—from strongly covalent to predominantly ionic (Section 19.5).

The ligands are said to be coordinated around the central cation in a **first coordination sphere**; in the formulas of complex compounds (such as $K_3[Fe(CN)_6]$ and $[Cu(NH_3)_4]Cl_2$), the first coordination sphere is indicated by square brackets. The ligands are disposed about the central ion in a regular geometric manner (Figure 19.1), and the number of atoms *directly* bonded to the central metal ion, or the number of coordination positions, is called the **coordination number** of the central ion.

The charge of a complex is the sum of the charges of the constituent parts, and complexes may be cations, anions, or neutral molecules. Thus in each of the following complexes of platinum(IV): $[Pt(NH_3)_5Cl]^{3+}$, $[Pt(NH_3)_2Cl_4]^0$, and $[PtCl_6]^{2-}$, the platinum contributes $4+$, each chlorine contributes $1-$,

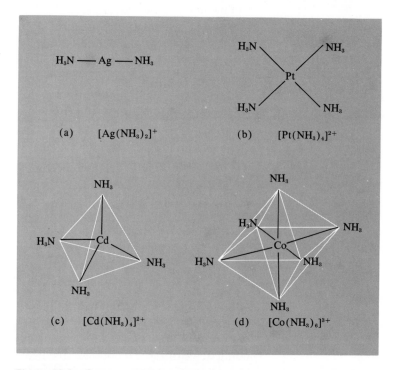

Figure 19.1 Common configurations of complex ions: (a) linear, (b) square planar, (c) tetrahedral, and (d) octahedral.

and the coordinated ammonia molecules do not contribute to the charge of the whole.

An interesting series of platinum(IV) complexes appears in Table 19.1.

Table 19.1

Some Platinum(IV) Complex Compounds

	Molar Conductance 0.001 N Solution[a] (25°C)	Number of Ions per Formula Unit	Number of Cl^- Ions per Formula unit
$[Pt(NH_3)_6]Cl_4$	523	5	4
$[Pt(NH_3)_5Cl]Cl_3$	404	4	3
$[Pt(NH_3)_4Cl_2]Cl_2$	228	3	2
$[Pt(NH_3)_3Cl_3]Cl$	97	2	1
$[Pt(NH_3)_2Cl_4]$	0	0	0
$K[Pt(NH_3)Cl_5]$	108	2	0
$K_2[PtCl_6]$	256	3	0

[a] Cm^2/ohm mole.

The list is headed by the chloride of the $[Pt(NH_3)_6]^{4+}$ ion, and in each subsequent entry an ammonia molecule of the coordination sphere is replaced by a chloride ion. The coordinated ammonia molecules and chloride ions are tightly held and do not dissociate in water solution; however, those chloride ions of the compound that are not coordinated to the platinum are ionizable. Hence, aqueous solutions of the last three compounds of the table do not precipitate silver chloride upon the addition of silver nitrate, whereas solutions of the first four precipitate AgCl in amounts proportional to 4/4, 3/4, 2/4, and 1/4, respectively, of their total chlorine content. In addition, in each case, the total number of ions per formula unit derived from conductance data agrees with the formula listed in the table.

In general, the most stable complexes are formed by metal ions that have a high positive charge and a small ionic radius. The transition elements and the metals immediately following (notably the III A and IV A metals) have a marked tendency to form complexes. Few complexes are known for the lanthanides and the I A and II A metals (with the exception of beryllium). The bonding of transition-metal complexes involves the d orbitals of the central metal atom.

Complexes are known containing metal ions with coordination numbers of from two to nine. However, the majority of complexes are two-, four-, and sixfold coordinate (Figure 19.1), and the coordination number six is by far the most common.

Six-coordinate complexes are octahedral. The regular octahedral arrangement of atoms is frequently represented

This is a convenient way to create a three-dimensional illusion in the depiction of this configuration. However, no difference between the bonds of the vertical axis and the other bonds should be inferred from this drawing; all the bonds are equivalent. Tetragonal geometry is a distorted form of the octahedral in which the bond distances along one of the axes are longer or shorter than the remaining bonds.

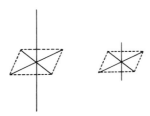

Four-coordinate complexes are known in tetrahedral and square-planar configurations. The square-planar configuration is the usual one for Pt^{II}, Pd^{II}, and Au^{III}, and is assumed by many complexes of Ni^{II} and Cu^{II}. Examples include $[Pt(NH_3)_4]^{2+}$, $[PdCl_4]^{2-}$, $[AuCl_4]^-$, $[Ni(CN)_4]^{2-}$, and $[Cu(NH_3)_4]^{2+}$. There is evidence that square complexes may be, in reality, tetragonal forms with two groups, along a vertical axis, located at greater distances from the central ion than the ligands of the plane. Thus $[Cu(NH_3)_4]^{2+}$, in water solution, may have two water molecules coordinated in the manner shown in Figure 19.2. Hence, square-planar and octahedral geometries may be considered to merge.

The tetrahedral configuration, for four-coordinate complexes, is encountered more frequently than the square-planar and is particularly common for complexes of the nontransition elements. Certain complexes of Cu^I, Ag^I, Au^I, Be^{II}, Zn^{II}, Cd^{II}, Hg^{II}, Al^{III}, Ga^{III}, In^{III}, Fe^{III}, Co^{II}, and Ni^0 are of this type; examples include $[Cu(CN)_4]^{3-}$, $[BeF_4]^{2-}$, $[AlF_4]^-$, $[FeCl_4]^-$, $[Cd(CN)_4]^{2-}$, $[ZnCl_4]^{2-}$, and $[Ni(CO)_4]^0$. The oxyanions of certain transition metals (such as VO_4^{3-}, CrO_4^{2-}, FeO_4^{2-}, and MnO_4^-) are tetrahedral, resem-

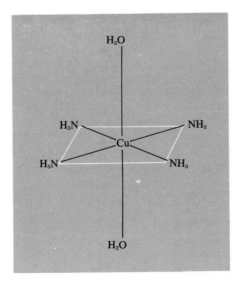

Figure 19.2 Configuration of
$[Cu(NH_3)_4(H_2O)_2]^{2+}$

bling the tetrahedral oxyanions of nonmetals (such as SiO_4^{4-}, PO_4^{3-}, AsO_4^{3-}, SO_4^{2-}, and ClO_4^-). Whereas a number of tetrahedral complexes of transition elements are known, the majority of complexes of these elements are octahedral.

Linear, two-coordinate, complexes are not so common as the other forms previously mentioned. However, well-characterized complexes of this type are known for Cu^I, Ag^I, and Hg^{II}; examples are $[CuCl_2]^-$, $[Ag(NH_3)_2]^+$, $[Au(CN)_2]^-$, $[Hg(NH_3)_2]^{2+}$, and $[Hg(CN)_2]^0$.

In general, there is no one characteristic coordination number and geometry for each metal ion. Whereas all the known complexes of Co^{III} are octahedral, most cations form more than one type of complex. Thus tetrahedral and octahedral complexes of Al^{III} are known; Cu^I forms linear and tetrahedral complexes; and square-planar, tetrahedral, and octahedral complexes of Ni^{II} exist.

Complexes of the transition elements are frequently highly colored. Examples of complexes that exhibit a wide range of colors are $[Co(NH_3)_6]^{3+}$ (yellow), $[Co(NH_3)_5(H_2O)]^{3+}$ (pink), $[Co(NH_3)_5Cl]^{2+}$ (violet), $[Co(H_2O)_6]^{3+}$ (purple), and $[Co(NH_3)_4Cl_2]^+$ (a violet form and a green form—see Section 19.4).

The ligands we have discussed thus far have been capable of forming only one bond with the central ion; they are referred to as **unidentate** (Latin, one toothed) ligands. Certain ligands are capable of occupying more than one coordination position of a metal ion. Ligands that coordinate through two bonds from different parts of the molecule or anion are called **bidentate**. Examples are

carbonate ion   oxalate ion   ethylenediamine

The carbonate and oxalate ions each coordinate through two oxygen atoms; the ethylenediamine molecule (abbreviated *en*) coordinates through both nitrogen atoms. These positions are marked with arrows. Bidentate ligands form rings with the central metal ions

and the resulting metal complexes are called **chelates** (Greek, claw). The formation of five- or six-membered rings is generally favored.

Multidentate ligands have been prepared that can coordinate at 2, 3, 4, 5, or 6 positions. In general, chelates are more stable than complexes containing only unidentate ligands. Thus the sexadentate complexing agent ethylenediaminetetraacetate ion (EDTA)

is capable of forming a very stable complex with the calcium ion—an ion with one of the least tendencies toward the formation of complexes (Figure 19.3).

Heme, of hemoglobin, is a chelate of Fe^{2+}, and chlorophyll is a chelate of Mg^{2+}. In both these substances, the metal atom is coordinated to a quadridentate ligand, which may be considered to be derived from a porphin structure (Figure 19.4) by the substitution of various groups for the H atoms of the porphin. The substituted porphins are called **porphyrins**.

Coordination around the iron atom of heme is octahedral. Four of the coordination positions are utilized in the formation of the heme (which is essentially planar), the fifth is used to bond the heme to a protein molecule (globin), and the sixth is used to coordinate either H_2O (hemoglobin) or O_2 (oxyhemoglobin). Coordination about this sixth position is reversible

$$\text{hemoglobin} + O_2 \rightleftharpoons \text{oxyhemoglobin} + H_2O$$

Figure 19.3   Ethylenediaminetetraacetate complex of Ca^{2+} ($[Ca(EDTA)]^{2-}$).

and dependent upon the pressure of O_2. Hence, hemoglobin picks up O_2 in the lungs and releases it in the body tissues, where it is used for the oxidation of food. Hemoglobin reacts with carbon monoxide to form a complex that is more stable than oxyhemoglobin, and therefore CO is toxic.

Chlorophyll, the green pigment of plants, serves as a catalyst for the process of photosynthesis in which CO_2 and H_2O are converted into a carbohydrate

Figure 19.4   Metal porphin.

(glucose) and O_2. The energy for photosynthesis comes from sunlight and the chlorophyll molecule initiates the process by absorbing a quantum of light.

19.2 Labile and Inert Complexes

Certain complexes (which are called **labile**) rapidly undergo reactions in which ligands are replaced; other complexes (**nonlabile**, or **inert, complexes**) do not undergo these substitution reactions or do so only slowly. The distinction applies to the rate of attainment of equilibrium and has no bearing on the position of equilibrium. With the exception of the complexes of Cr^{III} and Co^{III}, most of the octahedral complexes of the fourth period transition elements are very labile; exchange reactions come to equilibrium almost as fast as the reagents are mixed. The reason that the complexes of Co^{III} have been studied more than any other group of complexes is that these substances undergo ligand exchange reactions at a slower, more convenient, rate.

The inertness of a complex should not be confused with its thermodynamic stability. Although $[Co(NH_3)_6]^{3+}$ is stable in aqueous solution

$$(Co(NH_3)_6]^{3+} + 6H_2O \rightleftharpoons [Co(H_2O)_6]^{3+} + 6NH_3 \qquad K \cong 10^{-34}$$

the complex is unstable in aqueous acid

$$[Co(NH_3)_6]^{3+} + 6H_3O^+ \rightleftharpoons [Co(H_2O)_6]^{3+} + 6NH_4^+ \qquad K \cong 10^{22}$$

Nevertheless, the $[Co(NH_3)_6]^{3+}$ ion can exist in dilute acid for weeks; the latter reaction must have a high activation energy. Thus the complex is thermodynamically unstable and, at the same time, inert.

Examples of the reverse situation are also known. The stable complex $[FeCl_6]^{3-}$ is very labile and undergoes rapid exchange with radioactive chloride in aqueous solution.

In many cases, complex formation results in the stabilization of metal ions toward oxidation or reduction. Electrode potentials for Zn^{2+} and some complexes of this ion are

$$2e^- + Zn^{2+}(aq) \rightleftharpoons Zn(s) \qquad \mathscr{E}^\circ = -0.763 \text{ v}$$
$$2e^- + [Zn(NH_3)_4]^{2+} \rightleftharpoons Zn(s) + 4NH_3 \qquad \mathscr{E}^\circ = -1.04 \text{ v}$$
$$2e^- + [Zn(CN)_4]^{2-} \rightleftharpoons Zn(s) + 4CN^- \qquad \mathscr{E}^\circ = -1.26 \text{ v}$$

The increasing stability toward reduction observed in this series parallels increasing stability of the complexes toward dissociation in aqueous solution. The instability constant of $[Zn(NH_3)_4]^{2+}$ is approximately 10^{-10} and that of the $[Zn(CN)_4]^{2-}$ ion is about 10^{-18}.

It is tempting to ascribe the lower electrode potentials of the complexes to the decreased concentrations of Zn^{2+}(aq) in the solutions of these complexes, and such an interpretation is in agreement with the concentration effects predicted by the Nernst equation (Section 10.9). However, this explanation implies a mechanism for the reductions that has not been confirmed. The "free" zinc ion, Zn^{2+}(aq), is in reality an aquo complex, and it is difficult to see why the reduction of every other complex of Zn^{2+} should be required to proceed through, and be dependent upon, the aquo complex. Mechanism studies of the oxidation-reduction reactions of complexes indicate that the actual situation is not this simple. There is, however, a relationship between the stability of a complex toward dissociation and its tendency to undergo oxidation or reduction.

In many instances, complex formation results in the stabilization of a metal in a rare, or otherwise unknown, oxidation state. A classic example is afforded by the complexes of Co^{III}. Simple compounds containing cobalt in an oxidation state of $3+$ are rare. The electrode potential

$$e^- + [Co(H_2O)_6]^{3+} \rightleftharpoons [Co(H_2O)_6]^{2+} \qquad \mathscr{E}^\circ = +1.81 \text{ v}$$

indicates that the hydrated Co^{3+} ion is a strong oxidizing agent, capable of oxidizing water to oxygen and hence incapable of prolonged existence in water.

In the presence of many complexing agents, such as NH_3, the $3+$ oxidation state of cobalt is much more stable toward reduction.

$$e^- + [Co(NH_3)_6]^{3+} \rightleftharpoons [Co(NH_3)_6]^{2+} \qquad \mathscr{E}^\circ = +0.11 \text{ v}$$

The $[Co(NH_3)_6]^{3+}$ ion can exist in aqueous solution. It does not oxidize water to oxygen, and, in fact, the reverse reaction—the oxidation of Co^{II} complexes by a stream of air—is used to prepare Co^{III} complexes. The ammonia complex of Co^{III}, with an instability constant of about 10^{-34}, is much more stable toward dissociation than the ammonia complex of Co^{II}, which has an instability constant of approximately 10^{-5}.

The electrode potentials for copper and its ions may be diagramed

$$Cu^{2+} \xrightarrow{\text{+0.153 v}} Cu^+ \xrightarrow{\text{+0.521 v}} Cu$$

from which we can see that the Cu^+ ion is unstable in water solution and disproportionates (Section 10.11).

$$2Cu^+(aq) \rightleftharpoons Cu^{2+}(aq) + Cu(s) \qquad \mathscr{E}^\circ = +0.368 \text{ v}$$

The equilibrium constant for this disproportionation may be derived from the cell potential.

$$K = \frac{[Cu^{2+}]}{[Cu^+]^2} \cong 10^6$$

With certain complexing agents, the stability of the $1+$ state is enhanced more than that of the $2+$ state. For example, with ammonia $K \cong 10^{-2}$, and the $[Cu(NH_3)_2]^+$ ion is stable toward disproportionation. Other complexing agents, such as ethylenediamine, have a greater affinity for Cu^{II} than Cu^I. For ethylenediamine, $K \cong 10^5$, and an ethylenediamine complex of Cu^I does not exist in water solution.

A similar situation is observed for the ions of gold; Au^+ is theoretically unstable toward disproportionation into Au^{3+} and Au metal. In addition, this case is complicated by the fact that both ions are strong oxidizing agents and are capable of oxidizing water. However, stable complexes of both Au^I and Au^{III} are known.

The stability of complex ions toward dissociation in aqueous solution is discussed in Section 17.4.

19.3 Nomenclature

Since there are thousands of complexes known and the number is constantly expanding, a system of nomenclature has been adopted for these compounds. The following paragraphs summarize the important rules of the I.U.P.A.C. system; they are adequate for naming the simple, and frequently encountered, complexes.

1. If the complex compound is a salt, the cation is named first whether or not it is the complex ion.

2. The constituents of the complex are named in the following order: anions, neutral molecules, central metal ion.

3. Anionic ligands are given -o endings; examples are: OH^-, hydroxo; S^{2-}, thio; Cl^-, chloro; F^-, fluoro; CO_3^{2-}, carbonato; CN^-, cyano; CNO^-, cyanato; $C_2O_4^{2-}$, oxalato; NO_3^-, nitrato; NO_2^-, nitro; SO_4^{2-}, sulfato; and $S_2O_3^{2-}$, thiosulfato.

4. The names of neutral ligands are not changed. Exceptions to this rule are: H_2O, aquo; NH_3, ammine; CO, carbonyl; and NO, nitrosyl.

5. The number of ligands of a particular type is indicated by a prefix: di-, tri-, tetra-, penta-, and hexa- (for two to six). For complicated ligands (such as ethylenediamine), the prefixes bis-, tris, and tetrakis- (two to four) are employed.

6. The oxidation number of the central ion is indicated by a Roman numeral, set off by parentheses, and placed after the name of the complex.

7. If the complex is an anion, the ending -ate is employed. If the complex is a cation or a neutral molecule, the name is not changed. Examples follow:

$[Ag(NH_3)_2]Cl$	Diamminesilver(I) chloride
$[Co(NH_3)_3Cl_3]$	Trichlorotriamminecobalt(III)

$K_4[Fe(CN)_6]$	Potassium hexacyanoferrate(II)
$[Ni(CO)_4]$	Tetracarbonylnickel(0)
$[Cu(en)_2]SO_4$	Bis(ethylenediamine)copper(II) sulfate
$[Pt(NH_3)_4][PtCl_6]$	Tetraammineplatinum(II) hexachloroplatinate(IV)
$[Co(NH_3)_4(H_2O)Cl]Cl_2$	Chloroaquotetraamminecobalt(III) chloride

Common names are frequently employed when they are clearly more convenient than the systematic name (e.g., ferrocyanide rather than hexacyanoferrate(II) for $[Fe(CN)_6]^{4-}$) or when the structure of the complex is not certain (e.g., the aluminate ion).

19.4 Isomerism

Two compounds with the same molecular formula but different arrangements of atoms are called **isomers**; such compounds, of course, differ in their chemical and physical properties. **Structural isomerism** is displayed by compounds that have different ligands within their coordination spheres; several types of structural isomers may be identified.

The following pair of compounds of Co^{III} serve as an example of **ionization isomers**.

(a) $[Co(NH_3)_5(SO_4)]Br$ (b) $[Co(NH_3)_5Br]SO_4$
red   violet

Conductance data show that both compounds dissociate into two ions in aqueous solution. In the first compound, the SO_4^{2-} ion is a part of the coordination sphere, and the Br^- ion is ionizable. Hence, an aqueous solution of compound (a) gives an immediate precipitate of AgBr upon the addition of $AgNO_3$, but since the SO_4^{2-} ion is not free, no precipitate forms upon the addition of $BaCl_2$. For compound (b), the reverse is true. An aqueous solution of this compound gives a precipitate of $BaSO_4$ but not AgBr, since the SO_4^{2-} is ionizable and the Br^- is coordinated. Note that SO_4^{2-} functions as a unidentate ligand and that the charge on the complex ion of compound (a) is $1+$ and of compound (b) is $2+$.

There are numerous additional examples of ionization isomers; for example,

$[Pt(NH_3)_4Cl_2]Br_2$ $[Pt(NH_3)_4Br_2]Cl_2$

Hydrate isomerism is analogous to ionization isomerism and is probably best illustrated by the following series of compounds of formula $CrCl_3 \cdot 6H_2O$.

(a) $[Cr(H_2O)_6]Cl_3$
violet

(b) $[Cr(H_2O)_5Cl]Cl_2 \cdot H_2O$
green

(c) $[Cr(H_2O)_4Cl_2]Cl \cdot 2H_2O$
green

In a mole of each of these compounds there are six moles of water. However, in compound (a) six water molecules are coordinated; in compound (b), five; and in compound (c), four. The uncoordinated water, which probably occurs in the crystals as lattice water, is readily lost when compounds (b) and (c) are exposed to desiccants; however, the coordinated water is not so easily removed. Further evidence for the structures of the compounds is afforded by conductance data (the compounds are composed of four, three, and two ions, respectively) and the quantity of AgCl precipitated (the compounds have three, two, and one ionizable chloride ions, respectively).

Another example of hydrate isomerism is given by the following pair of compounds.

$$[Co(NH_3)_4(H_2O)Cl]Cl_2 \qquad [Co(NH_3)_4Cl_2]Cl \cdot H_2O$$

Coordination isomers are compounds that have at least two centers of coordination and which may be considered to have been formed through the exchange of ligands between these coordination centers. In simple examples, involving only two complex ions per compound, the coordinated metal ions may be the same

$$[Cr(NH_3)_6][Cr(SCN)_6] \qquad [Cr(NH_3)_4(SCN)_2][Cr(NH_3)_2(SCN)_4]$$

or different

$$[Cu(NH_3)_4][PtCl_4] \qquad [Pt(NH_3)_4][CuCl_4]$$

and the oxidation state of the metals may vary

$$[Pt(NH_3)_4][PtCl_6] \qquad [Pt(NH_3)_4Cl_2][PtCl_4]$$

tetraammineplatinum(II)-   dichlorotetraammineplatinum(IV)-
hexachloroplatinate(IV)   tetrachloroplatinate(II)

Linkage isomerism is a rare, but interesting type; it arises when ligands are capable of coordinating in two ways. For example, the nitrite ion, NO_2^-, can coordinate through an oxygen atom ($-ONO$, nitrito compounds) or through the nitrogen atom ($-NO_2$, nitro compounds).

$$[Co(NH_3)_5(NO_2)]Cl_2 \qquad [Co(NH_3)_5(ONO)]Cl_2$$

(yellow)   (red)
nitropentaamminecobalt(III)-   nitritopentaamminecobalt(III)-
chloride   chloride

Theoretically, many ligands might be capable of forming linkage isomers: CN^- might coordinate either through the C atom or the N atom; SCN^-, through N or S; CO, through C or O. However, few authentic cases of linkage isomerism are known.

Figure 19.5   (a) *Cis* and (b) *trans* isomers of dichlorodiammine-
platinum(II).

Stereoisomerism is a second general classification of isomers. Compounds
are stereoisomers when they both contain the same ligands in their coordination spheres but differ in the way that these ligands are arranged in space. One
type of stereoisomerism is **geometric**, or **cis-trans, isomerism**.

An example of geometric isomerism is afforded by the *cis* and *trans*
isomers of the square planar dichlorodiammineplatinum(II); see Figure 19.5.
In the *cis* isomer, the chlorine atoms are situated on adjacent corners of the
square (along an edge), whereas in the *trans* isomer, they occupy opposite
corners (along the diagonal).

Since all the ligands of a tetrahedral complex have the same relationship
to one another, *cis-trans* isomerism does not exist for this geometry. Many
geometric isomers are known for octahedral complexes, however. There are
two isomers of the dichlorotetraamminecobalt(III) ion: a violet *cis* form and
a green *trans* form (Figure 19.6).

A second type of stereoisomerism is **optical isomerism**. Some molecules and
ions can exist in two forms that are not superimposable and that bear the
same relationship that a right hand (or glove) bears to a left hand (or glove).
That the hands, or gloves, are not superimposable is readily demonstrated by
attempting to put a left-handed glove on a right hand. Such molecules and

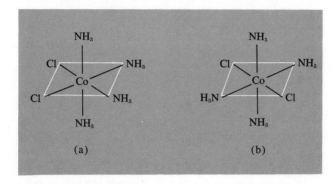

Figure 19.6   (a) *Cis* and (b) *trans* isomers of the dichlorotetra-
amminecobalt(III) ion.

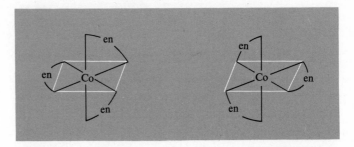

Figure 19.7 Dextro and levo forms of the tris(ethylenediamine) cobalt(III) ion.

ions are spoken of as being **dissymmetric** and the forms are called **enantiomorphs** (Greek, opposite forms) or **mirror images** (since the one may be considered to be a mirror reflection of the other).

Enantiomorphs have identical physical properties except for their effects on plane-polarized light. Light that has been passed through a polarizer consists of waves that vibrate in a single plane. One enantiomorph (the **dextro** form), pure or in solution, will rotate the plane of the plane-polarized light to the right; the other (the **levo** form) will rotate the plane an equal extent to the left.

It is for this reason that enantiomorphs are called optical isomers or **optical antipodes** An equimolar mixture of enantiomorphs, called a **racemic modification**, has no effect on plane-polarized light since it contains an equal number of *dextro*rotary and *levo*rotary forms.

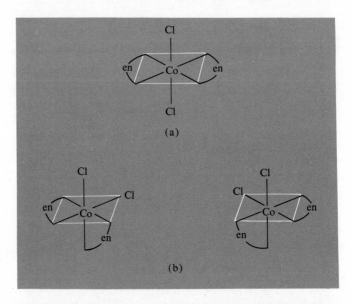

Figure 19.8 Isomers of the dichlorobis(ethylenediamine)cobalt-(III) ion: (a) *trans* isomer, (b) optical isomers of the *cis* form.

The tris(ethylenediamine)cobalt(III) ion exists in enantiomorphic forms. Examination of the diagrams of Figure 19.7 confirms that the enantiomorphs are not superimposable and that the ions are dissymmetric. Note that bidentate chelating agents can span only *cis* positions.

Both types of stereoisomerism—geometric and optical—are illustrated by the isomers of the dichlorobis(ethylenediamine)cobalt(III) ion (Figure 19.8). The *trans* configuration of this ion is optically inactive and a mirror image would be identical to the original. The *cis* arrangement, however, is dissymmetric and exists in *dextro* and *levo* forms. The *trans* modification is said to be a *diastereoisomer* of either the *dextro* or *levo cis* modification.

19.5 The Bonding in Complexes

There are several approaches to the theoretical treatment of the bonding in complexes. The **valence bond theory** describes the bonding in terms of hybridized orbitals of the central metal ion. The metal ion is assumed to have a number of unoccupied orbitals available for complex formation equal to its coordination number. Each ligand donates a pair of electrons toward the formation of a coordinate covalent bond, and a bond arises from the overlap of a vacant hybrid orbital of the metal atom and a filled orbital of a ligand. The bonds usually have an appreciable degree of polarity. The types of hybridization commonly encountered (Section 4.2) are

sp	linear
sp^3	tetrahedral
dsp^2	square planar
d^2sp^3	octahedral

For octahedral coordination, d_{z^2} and $d_{x^2-y^2}$ orbitals, as well as p_x, p_y, and p_z orbitals, are directed toward ligands; it is these orbitals that are combined with an s orbital into a $d^2 sp^3$ set (Figure 4.7). Square-planar (dsp^2) hybridization utilizes the $d_{x^2-y^2}$, p_x, p_y, and s orbitals (Figure 4.4).

The valence bond diagrams of some simple complexes together with the electronic configurations of the central metal ions are shown in Figure 19.9. Hund's rule applies to the electrons occupying the nonbonding d orbitals, and, accordingly, some of these electrons are unpaired. In each of the complexes shown, the number of unpaired electrons determined by magnetic susceptibility measurement agrees with the structure diagramed. Thus $[Co(en)_3]^{3+}$ and $[Ni(CN)_4]^{2-}$ are diamagnetic, and the others are paramagnetic. In addition, the experimentally determined geometry of each complex agrees with that predicted on the basis of the type of hybridization displayed.

There are some defects in this attractively simple picture. From the dia-

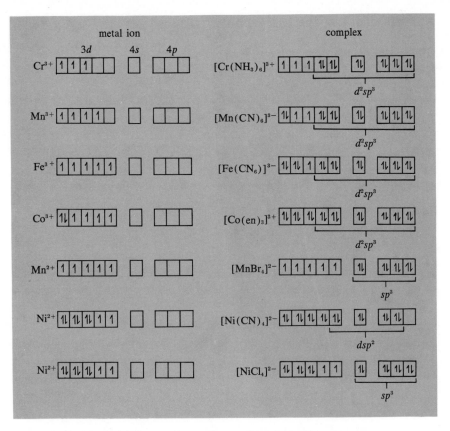

Figure 19.9 Valence-bond diagrams for some simple complexes.

grams of Figure 19.9, one might suppose that all of the octahedral complexes of Fe^{III} would have one unpaired electron (as in $[Fe(CN)_6]^{3-}$) and that all of the octahedral complexes of Co^{III} would be diamagnetic (like $[Co(en)_3]^{3+}$). Such is not the case. The magnetic moments of $[FeF_6]^{3-}$ and $[CoF_6]^{3-}$ indicate the existence of five and four unpaired electrons, respectively, in these complexes; these are the same numbers of unpaired electrons as are found in the free Fe^{3+} and Co^{3+} ions. At one time, the bonding in this type of complex was thought to be ionic with the d orbitals of the central ion undisturbed by complex formation. According to a later explanation, the $4d$, rather than the $3d$, orbitals are assumed to be used for the octahedral hybridization. Hence, **inner** (d^2sp^3) and **outer** (sp^3d^2) **complexes** are postulated (Figure 19.10). Since it is impossible to clear two inner d orbitals of the Ni^{2+} ion for inner d^2sp^3 hybridization, all octahedral Ni^{II} complexes must be assumed to be of the outer type.

A further complication arises in the case of $[Co(NO_2)_6]^{4-}$—an octahedral complex with one unpaired electron. In order to fit this complex into the d^2sp^3 category, it is necessary to postulate the promotion of an electron into the $4d$ sublevel.

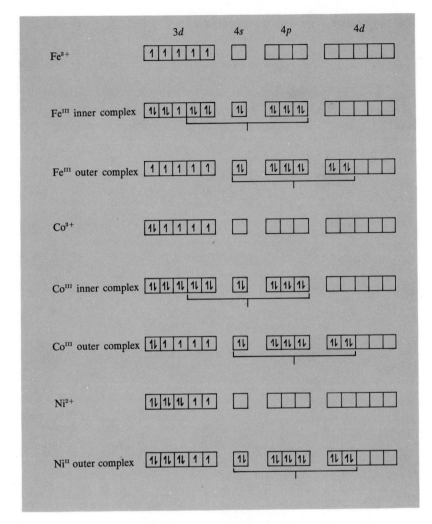

Figure 19.10 Inner and outer complexes of Fe^{III}, Co^{III}, and Ni^{II}.

	3d					4s	4p			4d			
Co^{2+}	⇅	⇅	↑	↑	↑	—	—	—	—	—	—	—	—

	3d			d^2sp^3						4d			
$[Co(NO_2)_6]^{4-}$	⇅	⇅	⇅	⇅	⇅	⇅	⇅	⇅	⇅	↑	—	—	—

It is also necessary to assume such an unlikely promotion for all of the square complexes of Cu^{II}.

	3d					4s	4p		
Cu^{2+}	⇅	⇅	⇅	⇅	↑	—	—	—	—

	3d				dsp^2				4p	
$[CuCl_4]^{2-}$	⇅	⇅	⇅	⇅	⇅	⇅	⇅	⇅	↑	—

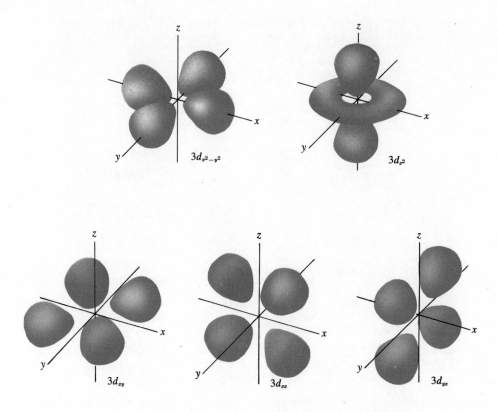

Figure 19.11   Boundary surface diagrams for the d orbitals.

The fundamental defect of the valence bond theory is that it fails to take into account the existence of antibonding molecular orbitals which are produced, along with bonding molecular orbitals, by the overlap of atomic orbitals. Many of the experimental observations that are difficult to explain on the basis of the valence bond approach are readily understood in terms of electrons occupying antibonding orbitals.

The **crystal field theory** and its more acceptable outgrowth, the **ligand field theory** center on the d orbitals of the metal ion. In a free transition-metal ion, all five of the d orbitals have equal energies, or are **degenerate**. All of the d orbitals are not equivalent, however, when the metal ion engages in complex formation; the degeneracy is split.

Consider the relation of the d orbitals (Figure 19.11) to the arrangement of the ligands of an octahedral complex (Figure 19.12). The d_{z^2} and $d_{x^2-y^2}$ orbitals have lobes that point toward ligands, whereas the lobes of the d_{xy}, d_{xz}, and d_{yz} orbitals lie between ligands. Thus in the complex, two sets of d orbitals exist; the d_{xy}, d_{xz}, and d_{yz} orbitals (or t_{2g} orbitals) are equivalent to each other, and the d_{z^2} and $d_{x^2-y^2}$ orbitals (or e_g orbitals) are equivalent to

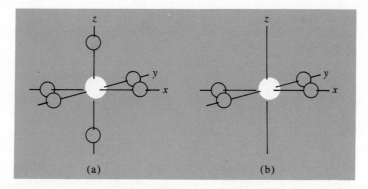

Figure 19.12 Arrangement of ligands of (a) octahedral and (b) square planar complexes in relation to sets of Cartesian coordinates.

each other and different from the first three. The symbols t_{2g} and e_g are applied to threefold degenerate and twofold degenerate sets of orbitals, respectively.

It is not immediately obvious that the d_{z^2} orbital is perfectly equivalent to the $d_{x^2-y^2}$ orbital. The d_{z^2} orbital may be regarded as a combination, in equal parts, of two hypothetical orbitals, $d_{z^2-y^2}$ and $d_{z^2-x^2}$, which have shapes exactly like that of the $d_{x^2-y^2}$ orbital (see Figure 19.13). Since the number of d orbitals is limited to five, the $d_{z^2-y^2}$ and $d_{z^2-x^2}$ orbitals have no independent existence.

In the crystal field theory, the assumption is made that an electrostatic field surrounding the central metal ion is produced by the negative ends of the dipolar molecules, or by the anions, that function as ligands. A metal-ion electron in a d orbital that has lobes directed toward ligands has a higher energy (owing to electrostatic repulsion) than an electron in an orbital with lobes that point between ligands. In octahedral complexes, the orbitals of the e_g group, therefore, have higher energies than those of the t_{2g} group. The

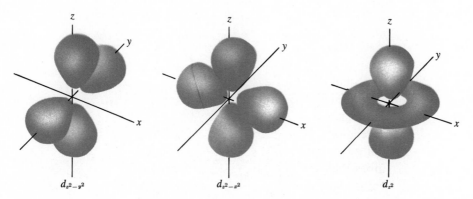

Figure 19.13 Diagram showing that the d_{z^2} orbital may be considered to be a combination of the $d_{z^2-y^2}$ and $d_{z^2-x^2}$ orbitals.

difference between the energies of the t_{2g} and e_g orbitals in an octahedral complex is given the symbol Δ_o.

In a square-planar complex (see Figure 19.12), the d orbitals exhibit four different relationships. The lobes of the $d_{x^2-y^2}$ orbital point toward ligands, and this orbital has the highest energy. The lobes of the d_{xy} orbital lie between orbitals but are coplanar with them, and hence this orbital is next highest in energy. The lobes of the d_{z^2} orbital point of the plane of the complex, but the belt around the center of the orbital (which contains about a third of the electron density) lies in the plane; therefore, the d_{z^2} orbital is next highest in energy. The d_{xz} and d_{yz} orbitals, which are degenerate, are least affected by the electrostatic field of the ligands, since their lobes point out of the plane of the complex, and these orbitals are lowest in energy.

The order of splitting of the d orbitals in a tetrahedral complex may be derived from an examination of Figure 19.14, which shows the relation of tetrahedrally arranged ligands to a system of Cartesian coordinates and a hypothetical cube. The lobes of the d_{xy}, d_{xz}, and d_{yz} orbitals point toward cube edges, and the lobes of the d_{z^2} and $d_{x^2-y^2}$ orbitals point toward the centers of cube faces. Notice that the distance from the center of a cube face to a ligand is farther than the distance from the center of a cube edge to a ligand. Therefore, the order of orbital energies is the reverse of that for octahedral coordination, and the threefold degenerate set, t_{2g}, is of higher energy than the twofold degenerate set, e_g, The difference in energy is given the symbol Δ_t.

The splitting of d-orbital energies in tetrahedral, octahedral, and square-planar complexes is summarized in Figure 19.15. The crystal field theory fails to take into account the mixing of metal and ligand orbitals and the covalent character of the bonding in complexes, and hence it is ultimately unsatisfactory. The ligand field theory offers a more realistic explanation which

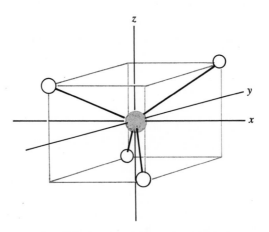

Figure 19.14 The relation of tetrahedrally arranged ligands to a set of Cartesian coordinates.

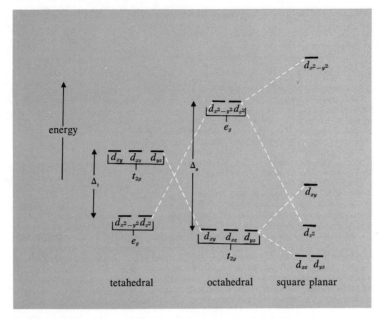

Figure 19.15 The splitting of *d*-orbital energies by ligand fields of three different geometries.

derives from molecular orbital theory. In both theories, the orders of splitting are those shown in Figure 19.15.

In an octahedral complex, the $3d_{z^2}$ and $3d_{x^2-y^2}$ orbitals along with the $4s$ and three $4p$ orbitals are assumed to overlap the six ligand σ orbitals with the attendant formation of six bonding molecular orbitals and six antibonding molecular orbitals (Section 4.4). The d_{xy}, d_{xz}, and d_{yz} orbitals (the t_{2g} set), which do not overlap the σ orbitals of the ligands, are essentially nonbonding. (The t_{2g} set can be used in π bonding, however.)

A bonding molecular orbital concentrates electron density between the atoms and is of relatively low energy in comparison to an antibonding molecular orbital, which has a low electron density between the atoms and acts as a disruptive force. A molecular orbital energy level diagram for an octahedral complex with no π bonding is given in Figure 19.16.

Whenever two atomic orbitals of different energies combine, the character of the resulting bonding molecular orbital is predominantly that of the atomic orbital of lower energy, and the antibonding molecular orbital has mainly the character of the higher energy atomic orbital. In an octahedral complex, the bonding orbitals have predominantly the character of ligand orbitals. The antibonding orbitals resemble metal orbitals more than ligand orbitals and the t_{2g} set, which are nonbonding, may be considered as purely metal orbitals.

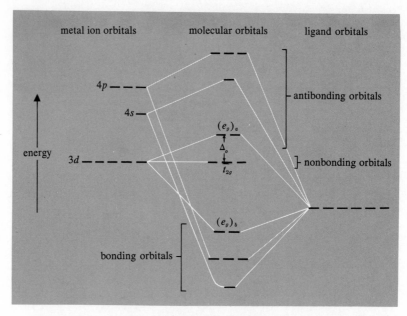

Figure 19.16 Diagram indicating the formation of molecular orbitals for an octahedral complex with no π bonding.

In an octahedral complex, the six electron pairs from the ligands completely occupy the bonding molecular orbitals. The d electrons of the central metal ion are accommodated in the t_{2g} nonbonding orbitals and the $(e_g)_a$ antibonding orbitals; the difference between the energies of these sets is Δ_o. The four remaining antibonding orbitals are never occupied in the ground states of any known complex.

Hence, the conclusion reached by this treatment is much the same as that postulated by the crystal field theory: in an octahedral complex, the degeneracy of the metal d orbitals may be considered to be split into a threefold degenerate set, t_{2g}, and a higher energy, metal-like, twofold degenerate set which may be labeled $(e_g)_a$ or simply e_g.

The molecular orbital treatment may be applied to tetrahedral and square-planar complexes, but the applications are more complicated. The conclusions reached are in essential agreement with the splittings diagramed in Figure 19.15.

For the octahedral complexes of a given metal ion, the magnitude of Δ_o is different for each set of ligands, and the electronic configurations of many complexes depend upon the size of Δ_o.

For complexes of transition-element ions with one, two, or three d electrons (which are referred to as d^1, d^2, or d^3 ions), the orbital occupancy is certain and is independent of the magnitude of Δ_o. The electrons enter the lower energy t_{2g} orbitals singly with their spins parallel. For d^4, d^5, d^6, and d^7 ions, a choice of two configurations is possible (see Figure 19.17).

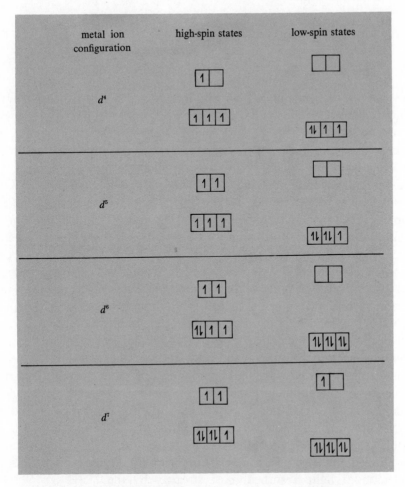

Figure 19.17 Arrangements of electrons in high-spin and low-spin octahedral complexes of d^4, d^5, d^6, and d^7 ions.

In the case of an octahedral complex of a d^4 ion, the fourth electron can singly occupy a higher energy e_g orbital, or it can enter a t_{2g} orbital, thus pairing with an electron already present. The former configuration has four unpaired electrons and is called the **high-spin state**, the latter configuration, with two unpaired electrons, is called the **low-spin state**. Which configuration is assumed depends upon which is energetically more favorable.

If Δ_o is small, the electron may be promoted to the e_g level where it occupies an orbital singly. However, if Δ_o is large, the electron may be forced to pair with an electron in a t_{2g} orbital even though this pairing occurs against interelectronic repulsion and requires the expenditure of a pairing energy, P. Thus the high-spin configuration results when

$$\Delta_o < P$$

and the low-spin configuration is assumed when

$$\Delta_o > P$$

The value of P depends upon the metal ion; Δ_o is different for each complex.

This conclusion is also valid for complexes of d^5, d^6, and d^7 ions. For a complex of a d^8 ion, there is only one possible configuration: six electrons paired in the t_{2g} orbitals and two unpaired electrons in the e_g orbitals. Likewise, complexes of d^9 and d^{10} ions exist in only one configuration.

The complexes that were fitted into the valence-bond scheme only with difficulty are readily classified by the ligand field theory. Hence, the inner complex $[Fe(CN)_6]^{3-}$ with one unpaired electron is in reality a low-spin state of this d^5 ion, and the outer complex $[FeF_6]^{3-}$ with five unpaired electrons has the high-spin configuration of a d^5 ion. The octahedral complexes of Ni^{II}, all of which must be assumed to be of the outer valence-bond type, have the only configuration possible for a complex of a d^8 ion: six electrons in the t_{2g} orbitals and two unpaired electrons in the e_g orbitals. The complex $[Co(NO_2)_6]^{4-}$, for which it was necessary to postulate the promotion of an electron to a $4d$ atomic orbital in the valence-bond treatment, is a low-spin d^7 complex according to the ligand field theory.

Values of Δ_o can be obtained from studies of the absorption spectra of complexes. In the complex $[Ti(H_2O)_6]^{3+}$, there is only one electron to be accommodated in either the t_{2g} or e_g orbitals. In the ground state, this electron occupies a t_{2g} orbital. However, excitation of the electron to an e_g orbital is possible when the energy required for this transition, Δ_o, is supplied, and the absorption of light by the complex can bring about such excitations. The wavelength of light absorbed most strongly by the $[Ti(H_2O)_6]^{3+}$ ion is approximately 4900 Å, which corresponds to a Δ_o of about 58 kcal/mole. The single absorption band of this complex spreads out over a considerable portion of the visible spectrum; however, most of the red and violet light is not absorbed, and this causes the red-violet color of the complex.

The interpretation of the absorption spectra of complexes with more than one d electron is considerably more complicated, since more than two arrangements of d electrons are possible. In general, for a given metal ion, the replacement of one set of ligands by another causes a change in the energy difference between the t_{2g} and e_g orbitals, Δ_o, which gives rise to different light-absorption properties. Hence, in many instances, a striking color change is observed when the ligands of a complex are replaced by other ligands.

Ligands may be arranged in a **spectrochemical series** according to the magnitude of Δ_o they bring about. From the experimental study of the spectra of many complexes, it has been found that the order is the same for the complexes of all of the transition elements in their common oxidation states with only occasional inversions of order between ligands that stand near to one another on the list. The order of some common ligands is

$$I^- < Br^- < Cl^- < F^- < OH^- < C_2O_4^{2-} < H_2O < NH_3 < en < NO_2^- < CN^-$$

The values of Δ_o induced by the halide ions are generally low, and complexes of these ligands usually have high-spin configurations. The cyanide ion, which stands at the opposite end of the series from the halide ions, induces the largest d-orbital splittings of any ligand listed; cyano complexes generally have low-spin configurations.

A given ligand, however, does not always produce complexes of the same spin type. Thus the hexaammine complex of Fe^{2+} has a high-spin configuration, whereas the hexaammine complex of Co^{3+} (which is isoelectronic with Fe^{2+}) has a low-spin configuration.

For each metal ion, there is a point in the series that corresponds to the change from ligands that produce high-spin complexes to ligands that form low-spin complexes. For example, Co^{II} forms high-spin complexes with NH_3 and ethylenediamine, but the NO_2^- and CN^- complexes of Co^{II} have low-spin configurations. The actual position in the series, when this change from high- to low-spin complex formation occurs, depends upon the electron-pairing energy, P, for the metal ion, as well as the values of Δ_o for the complexes under consideration.

SOME SUGGESTED READINGS

Basolo, F., and Johnson, R. C., *Coordination Chemistry*, New York, Benjamin, 1964 (paper).

Day, M. C., Jr., and Selbin, J., *Theoretical Inorganic Chemistry*, 2nd ed., New York, Van Nostrand Reinhold, 1969.

Kettle, S. F. A., *Coordination Compounds*, New York, Appleton-Century-Crofts, 1970 (paper).

Murmann, R. K., *Inorganic Complex Compounds*, New York, Van Nostrand Reinhold, 1964 (paper).

Quagliano, J. V., and Vallarino, L. M., *Coordination Chemistry*, Boston, Heath, 1969 (paper).

Werner, A., *Classics in Coordination Chemistry*, New York, Dover, 1968 (paper).

PROBLEMS

The more difficult problems are starred.

19.1 Define the following: (a) coordination number, (b) ligand, (c) chelate, (d) enantiomorph, (e) racemic modification, (f) inert complex.

19.2 Write formulas for:

    (a) hexacarbonylvanadium(0)

    (b) zinc hexachloroplatinate(IV)

    (c) chloronitrotetraaminecobalt(III) sulfate

    (d) sodium dithiosulfatoargentate(I)

    (e) tetraamineplatinum(II) trichloroammineplatinate(II)

    (f) tetachlorodiammineplatinum(IV)

    (g) potassium hexabromoaurate(III)

    (h) hexaamminenickel(II) hexanitrocobaltate(III)

19.3 Name the following compounds:

    (a) $K_4[Ni(CN)_4]$ (d) $[Cu(NH_3)_4][PtCl_4]$

    (b) $K_2[Ni(CN)_4]$ (e) $[Ir(NH_3)_5(ONO)]Cl_2$

    (c) $(NH_4)_2[Fe(H_2O)Cl_5]$ (f) $[Co(NH_3)_6]_2[Ni(CN)_4]_3$

19.4 Write formulas for (a) iron(II) hexacyanoferrate(II), (b) iron (II) hexacyanoferrate(III), (c) iron(III) hexacyanoferrate(II), (d) iron(III) hexacyanoferrate(III).

19.5 Two compounds have the same empirical formula: $Co(NH_3)_3(H_2O)_2$-$ClBr_2$. One mole of compound A readily loses one mole of water in a desiccator, whereas compound B does not lose any water under the same conditions. An aqueous solution of A has a conductivity equivalent to that of a compound with two ions per formula unit; the conductivity of an aqueous solution of B corresponds to that of a compound with three ions per formula unit. When $AgNO_3$ is added to a solution of compound A, one mole of AgBr is precipitated per mole of A; a solution of compound B yields two moles of AgBr per mole of B. (a) Write the formulas of A and B. (b) What type of isomers are A and B?

19.6 Write a formula for an example of each of the following: (a) a linkage isomer of $[Cr(NH_3)_5(ONO)]Br_2$, (b) an ionization isomer of $[Co(en)_2$-$Cl(NO_2)]NO_2$, (c) a coordination isomer of $[Co(en)_3][Cr(C_2O_4)_3]$, (d) a hydrate isomer of $[Co(NH_3)_5(H_2O)](NO_3)_3$.

19.7 Identify all of the possible isomers (stereoisomers as well as coordination isomers) of the compound $[Pt(NH_3)_4][PtCl_6]$.

19.8 Diagram the structures of all of the possible stereoisomers of each of the following octahedral complexes. Classify the structures as geometric or optical isomers. (a) $[Cr(NH_3)_2Cl_4]^-$, (b) $[Cr(NH_3)_3Br_3]$, (c) $[Cr(NH_3)_4$-$(en)]^{3+}$, (d) $[Cr(en)_2(NO_2)Cl]^+$, (e) $[Cr(en)_2(C_2O_4)]^+$.

19.9 Diagram all of the stereoisomers of each of the following molecules. In the formulas, py stands for pyridene, C_5H_5N, a unidentate ligand. (a) $[Pt(NH_3)(py)ClBr]$ (square planar), (b) $[Pt(NH_3)(py)Cl_2]$ (square planar), (c) $[Pt(py)_2Cl_2]$ (square planar), (d) $[Co(py)_2Cl_2]$ (tetrahedral).

19.10 How can dipole-moment measurement distinguish between the *cis*- and *trans*-isomers of the square planar $[Pt(NH_3)_2Cl_2]$?

*19.11 Diagram the four stereoisomers of $[Pt(en)(NO_2)_2Cl_2]$.

19.12 Draw valance bond diagrams for the bonding in the following, each of which is diamagnetic. What geometric configuration does each have? (a) $AuCl_2^-$, (b) $AuCl_4^-$, (c) $Cd(CN)_4^{2-}$, (d) $BeCl_4^{2-}$, (e) $PdCl_6^{2-}$.

19.13 The complex $[Ni(CN)_4]^{2-}$ is square planar, and the complex $[NiCl_4]^{2-}$ is tetrahedral. Draw valence bond diagrams for these complexes and predict the number of unpaired electrons in each.

19.14 The octahedral complexes $[Fe(CN)_6]^{3-}$ and $[FeF_6]^{3-}$ have one and five unpaired electrons, respectively. Offer an explanation for these observations based on (a) the valence bond theory, (b) the ligand field theory.

19.15 (a) Contrast the valence bond and ligand field explanations for the electronic structures of the two types of octahedral Co^{2+} complexes (one with three unpaired electrons and another with only one unpaired electron). (b) Why is the valence bond description of the complex with one unpaired electron unsatisfactory?

19.16 For Mn^{3+}, the electron-pairing energy, P, is about 80 kcal/mole. Approximate values of Δ_o for the complexes $[Mn(H_2O)_6]^{3+}$ and $[Mn(CN)_6]^{3-}$ are 60 kcal/mole and 110 kcal/mole, respectively. (a) Do these complexes have high-spin or low-spin configurations? (b) Draw a d-orbital splitting diagram for each.

19.17 (a) Draw d-orbital splitting diagrams for $[Fe(NH_3)_6]^{2+}$ and $[Co(NH_3)_6]^{3+}$. Δ_o values for these two complex ions are approximately 35 kcal/mole and 66 kcal/mole, respectively. The pairing energy of Fe^{2+} is about 50 kcal/mole, and that of Co^{3+} is about 60 kcal/mole. (b) How many unpaired electrons are present in each of the complex ions?

19.18 Draw d-orbital splitting diagrams for the high-spin and low-spin octahedral complexes of (a) Cr^{2+}, (b) Co^{2+}, (c) Fe^{3+}, (d) Co^{3+}, (e) Mn^{2+}.

19.19 Draw d-orbital splitting diagrams for (a) the octahedral complexes of Cr^{3+}, (b) the octahedral complexes of Ni^{2+}, (c) the square planar complexes of Ni^{2+} (all of which are diamagnetic), (d) the square planar complexes of Co^{2+} (all of which have one unpaired electron), (e) the tetrahedral complexes of Co^{2+}, (f) the octahedral complexes of Ru^{2+} (all of which are diamagnetic), (g) the octahedral complexes of Ir^{4+} (all of which have one unpaired electron).

19.20 The $[Ti(H_2O)_6]^{3+}$ complex is red-violet. What change in color would be expected if the ligands of this complex were replaced by ligands that induce a larger Δ_o? Note that the color of the complex corresponds to light transmitted, not absorbed.

*19.21 A complex of Fe^{3+} has a magnetic moment of 5.9 Bohr magnetons (see Section 2.16). (a) How many unpaired electrons are present in the complex? (b) Is this a high- or low-spin complex?

*19.22 Given the following data, calculate the instability constant, K_{inst}, of the $Al(OH)_4^-$ ion.

$$3e^- + Al(OH)_4^- \rightleftharpoons Al + 4OH^- \qquad \mathscr{E}^\circ = -2.330 \text{ v}$$

$$3e^- + Al^{3+} \rightleftharpoons Al \qquad \mathscr{E}^\circ = -1.662 \text{ v}$$

20

ORGANIC CHEMISTRY

The name organic chemistry derives from the early concept that substances of plant or animal origin (organic substances) were different from those of mineral origin (inorganic substances). In the middle of the nineteenth century, however, the idea that organic substances could only be synthesized by living organisms was gradually discounted. Not only have a large number of natural products been synthesized in the laboratory, but also countless related materials have been made that do not occur in nature. All these compounds contain carbon, and over a million carbon compounds are known.

Because it represents a convenient division of chemistry, the term organic chemistry is retained, but it is now commonly defined as the chemistry of carbon and its compounds. Some carbon compounds, such as carbonates, carbides, and cyanides, are traditionally classed as inorganic compounds, and organic chemistry is probably better defined as the chemistry of the hydrocarbons (compounds containing only carbon and hydrogen) and their derivatives.

Carbon forms an unusually large number of

compounds because of its exceptional ability to catenate (Section 12.9). In addition, the carbon atom can form four, very stable, single-covalent bonds, and it also has the ability to form multiple bonds with other carbon atoms or with atoms of other elements.

20.1   The Alkanes

In the first four sections of this chapter, various types of hydrocarbons are characterized. The reactions of the hydrocarbons is the topic of Section 20.5. The simplest hydrocarbon is methane, CH_4. This molecule contains four, equivalent, carbon–hydrogen bonds arranged tetrahedrally (Figure 20.1), and the bonding may be considered to arise through the use of sp^3 hybrid orbitals of the carbon atom. Each of the bonds of methane is of the same length (1.095 Å), and each of the H—C—H bond angles is 109° 28′ (the so-called tetrahedral angle). The commonly employed structural formula of methane,

$$
\begin{array}{c}
\text{H} \\
| \\
\text{H}-\text{C}-\text{H} \\
| \\
\text{H}
\end{array}
$$

does not accurately represent the tetrahedral arrangement of the molecule.

The **alkanes** are hydrocarbons in which all of the carbon–carbon bonds are single bonds; they may be considered to be derived from methane by the successive addition of $-CH_2-$ units. Such a series of compounds is said to

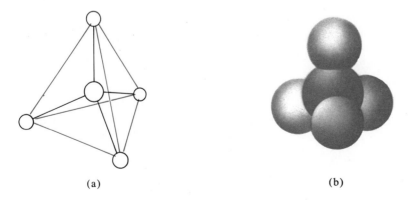

(a)   (b)

Figure 20.1   Representations of the structure of methane, CH_4. The bonds in diagram (a) are of exaggerated length in comparison to the atomic sizes.

be **homologous**. Thus the formula of the second member of the family, ethane

$$
\begin{array}{c}
H\ \ H \\
|\ \ \ | \\
H-C-C-H \\
|\ \ \ | \\
H\ \ H
\end{array}
$$

may be formally derived by the introduction of a $-CH_2-$ unit between the carbon and a hydrogen of methane. This molecule is also represented by the formula CH_3-CH_3.

The alkanes conform to the general formula C_nH_{2n+2}, where n is the number of carbon atoms in the compound. A few subsequent members of the family, and their names, are

$$
\begin{array}{c}
H\ \ H\ \ H \\
|\ \ \ |\ \ \ | \\
H-C-C-C-H \\
|\ \ \ |\ \ \ | \\
H\ \ H\ \ H \\
CH_3CH_2CH_3 \\
\text{propane}
\end{array}
\qquad
\begin{array}{c}
H\ \ H\ \ H\ \ H \\
|\ \ \ |\ \ \ |\ \ \ | \\
H-C-C-C-C-H \\
|\ \ \ |\ \ \ |\ \ \ | \\
H\ \ H\ \ H\ \ H \\
CH_3CH_2CH_2CH_3 \\
\text{butane}
\end{array}
$$

$$
\begin{array}{c}
H\ \ H\ \ H\ \ H\ \ H \\
|\ \ \ |\ \ \ |\ \ \ |\ \ \ | \\
H-C-C-C-C-C-H \\
|\ \ \ |\ \ \ |\ \ \ |\ \ \ | \\
H\ \ H\ \ H\ \ H\ \ H \\
CH_3CH_2CH_2CH_2CH_3 \\
\text{pentane}
\end{array}
$$

These compounds are spoken of as **straight-chain** compounds even though the carbon chains are far from linear (Figure 20.2); all the bond angles are

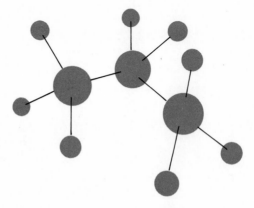

Figure 20.2 Representation of the structure of propane, $CH_3CH_2CH_3$.

approximately tetrahedral, and axial rotation of any carbon atom around a single bond of the chain is possible.

There is only one compound for each of the formulas CH_4, C_2H_6, and C_3H_8. However, there are two compounds with the formula C_4H_{10}: the compound with a straight chain and one with a **branched chain**.

$$CH_3CHCH_3$$
$$|$$
$$CH_3$$

methylpropane

The two compounds of formula C_4H_{10} are **structural isomers** (compounds with the same molecular formula but different structural formulas); they have different properties.

There are three structural isomers of C_5H_{12}: pentane (the straight-chain compound),

$$CH_3CH_2CHCH_3 \quad \text{and} \quad CH_3-\overset{\displaystyle CH_3}{\underset{\displaystyle CH_3}{\overset{|}{\underset{|}{C}}}}-CH_3$$
$$|$$
$$CH_3$$

methylbutane   dimethylpropane

In the alkane series, the number of possible structural isomers increases rapidly: there are five structural isomers for C_6H_{14}, nine for C_7H_{16}, 75 for $C_{10}H_{22}$, and it has been calculated that more than 4 billion isomers are possible for $C_{30}H_{62}$.

A branched-chain compound may be named in terms of the longest straight chain in the molecule. The side chains are named as alkyl radicals, and their positions on the straight chain are usually indicated by a numbering system. Alkyl radicals are fragments of alkane molecules from which a hydrogen atom has been removed; their names are derived from the name of the parent alkane with the ending changed to —*yl*. A list of common alkyl radicals appears in Table 20.1.

For example, the longest straight chain in the molecule

$$CH_3$$
$$|$$
$$CH_3C\!\!-\!\!-\!\!-CHCH_2CH_3$$
$$|\quad\;\; |$$
$$CH_3\; CH_2$$
$$|$$
$$CH_3$$

consists of five carbon atoms, and the compound is named as a derivative of

Table 20.1

Simple Alkyl Radicals

Formula	Name
CH_3-	methyl
CH_3CH_2-	ethyl
$CH_3CH_2CH_2-$	*normal*-propyl or *n*-propyl
CH_3CH- $\quad\mid$ $\quad CH_3$	isopropyl
$CH_3CH_2CH_2CH_2-$	*normal*-butyl or *n*-butyl
CH_3CHCH_2- $\quad\mid$ $\quad CH_3$	isobutyl
CH_3CH_2CH- $\qquad\mid$ $\qquad CH_3$	*secondary*-butyl or *sec*-butyl
$\quad CH_3$ $\quad\mid$ CH_3C- $\quad\mid$ $\quad CH_3$	*tertiary*-butyl or *tert*-butyl

pentane. The pentane chain is numbered starting at the end that will give the side chains the lowest numbers.

$$
\begin{array}{c}
CH_3 \\
| \\
CH_3C\text{---}CHCH_2CH_3 \\
|\quad\ | \\
CH_3\ CH_2 \\
\quad\ | \\
\quad\ CH_3 \\
\end{array}
$$
$$\;1\quad 2\quad\ 3\ \ 4\quad 5$$

In the name, a number is used to indicate the position of each substituent radical. Thus the name of the compound is

2,2-dimethyl-3-ethylpentane

No numbers appear in the names of our earlier examples of structural isomers. The name methylpropane requires no number to indicate the position of the methyl radical with regard to the propane chain since there is only one possible position for the methyl group (number 2). If the methyl group were placed on either terminal carbon atom (number 1 or number 3), the compound would be the straight-chain isomer, butane. In like manner, the names methylbutane and dimethylpropane do not require the use of numbers; there is only one possible structure corresponding to each name.

Names for some of the higher straight-chain homologs may be obtained from Table 20.2 which lists the melting points and boiling points of some of

Table 20.2

Physical Properties of Some Straight-Chain Alkanes

Compound	Formula	Melting Point (°C)	Boiling Point (°C)
methane	CH_4	-183	-162
ethane	C_2H_6	-172	-88
propane	C_3H_8	-187	-42
butane	C_4H_{10}	-135	1
pentane	C_5H_{12}	-131	36
hexane	C_6H_{14}	-94	69
heptane	C_7H_{16}	-91	99
octane	C_8H_{18}	-57	126
nonane	C_9H_{20}	-54	151
decane	$C_{10}H_{22}$	-30	174
hexadecane	$C_{16}H_{34}$	20	288
heptadecane	$C_{17}H_{36}$	23	303

the straight-chain alkanes. With increasing molecular weight, the melting points and boiling points increase. The first four compounds are gases under ordinary conditions; higher homologs are liquids (C_5H_{12} to $C_{15}H_{32}$) and solids (from $C_{16}H_{34}$ on).

Aliphatic hydrocarbons are open-chain structures; in addition, **cyclic hydrocarbons** are known. The **cycloalkanes** are ring structures that contain only single carbon–carbon bonds; they have the general formula C_nH_{2n}. Examples are

cyclopropane   cycloxehane

The cyclohexane ring is not planar but is puckered in such a way that the C–C–C bond angles are 109°28′, the tetrahedral angle. Three- and four-membered rings are strained because the C–C–C bond angles deviate significantly from the tetrahedral angle. The strain is greatest in cyclopropane, where the C atoms form an equilateral triangle and the bond angles are 60°. Thus the cyclopropane ring is readily broken by H_2 (Ni catalyst) to give propane. Cyclobutane reacts with H_2 in an analagous manner (to give butane), but a higher temperature is required.

Petroleum is the principle source of alkanes and cycloalkanes. In the refining of petroleum, the crude oil is first separated into fractions by distillation (Table 20.3). Some higher-boiling fractions are subjected to **cracking processes**

Table 20.3

Petroleum Fractions

Fraction	Boiling Range (°C)	Carbon Content of Compounds	Use
gas	below 20	C_1-C_4	fuel
petroleum ether	20–90	C_5-C_7	solvent
gasoline	35–220	C_5-C_{12}	motor fuel
kerosene	200–315	$C_{12}-C_{16}$	jet fuel
fuel oil	250–375	$C_{15}-C_{18}$	diesel fuel
lubricating oils, greases	350 up	$C_{16}-C_{20}$	lubrication
paraffin wax	50–60 (m.p.)	$C_{20}-C_{30}$	candles
asphalt	viscous liquid		paving
residue	solid		fuel

in which large molecules are broken down into smaller molecules, thus increasing the yield of the most valuable fraction, gasoline. In addition, small molecules are converted into larger ones in what are called **alkylation processes**. Gases that are by-products of these processes, together with the petroleum fractions and substances obtained from the fractions, comprise important starting materials for the manufacture of many chemical products. More than 2000 such products (such as rubber, detergents, plastics, and textiles) are derived from the substances obtained from petroleum and natural gas.

20.2 The Alkenes

The **alkenes**, or **olefins**, are aliphatic hydrocarbons that have a carbon–carbon double bond somewhere in their molecular structure. The first member of the series is ethene (or ethylene),

$$\overset{H}{\underset{H}{\diagdown}}C=C\overset{H}{\underset{H}{\diagup}}$$

Each carbon atom of ethene uses sp^2 hybrid orbitals to form three sigma bonds: one with the other C atom and two with H atoms. Thus all six atoms lie in the same plane, and all bond angles are approximately 120°. In addition, each carbon atom has an electron in a p orbital that is not engaged in the formation of sp^2 σ bonds. These two p orbitals are coplanar and perpendicular to the plane of the molecule; they overlap to form a π bonding orbital with regions of charge density above and below the plane of the molecule (Section 4.5, Figure 4.21).

The p orbitals can overlap and form a π bonding orbital only when they lie in the same plane. Consequently, free rotation around the carbon–carbon double bond is not possible without breaking the π bond. The carbon–carbon bond distance in ethene (1.33 Å) is shorter than that in ethane (1.54 Å) because of the double bond. The π bond is not so strong as the σ bond; the carbon–carbon bond energy in ethane is approximately 81 kcal/mole, and the bond energy of the carbon–carbon double bond in ethene is about 145 kcal/mole.

Alkanes are called **saturated** compounds because all the valence electrons of the carbon atoms are engaged in single bond formation, and no more hydrogen atoms, or atoms of other elements, can be accommodated by the carbon atoms of the chain. **Unsaturated** compounds, such as the alkenes, can undergo **addition reactions** (Section 20.5) because of the availability of the π electrons of the double bond. In one such reaction, hydrogen adds to ethene to form ethane.

$$CH_2=CH_2 + H_2 \longrightarrow CH_3-CH_3$$

Alkenes conform to the general formula C_nH_{2n}. The name of an alkene is derived from the name of the corresponding alkane by changing the ending from -*ane* to -*ene*; a number is used, where necessary, to indicate the position of the double bond. The second member of the series is propene.

$$CH_2=CH-CH_3$$

New types of isomerism arise in the alkene series. The type of structural isomerism displayed by the alkanes (e.g., butane and methylpropane) is known as **chain isomerism**. In addition to chain isomerism, **position isomerism** occurs in the olefin series. There is only one straight-chain butane. There are, however, two straight-chain butenes, and they differ in the *position* of the double bond.

$$\underset{\text{1-butene}}{CH_2=CH-CH_2-CH_3} \qquad \underset{\text{2-butene}}{CH_3-CH=CH-CH_3}$$

In the first compound, the double bond is located between carbon atoms number 1 and number 2, and the lower number (1) is used to indicate its position. In like manner, the lower number is used to indicate the position of the double bond (which occurs between carbon atoms number 2 and number 3) in the name of the second compound. In each case the chain is numbered from the end that gives the lowest possible number for the name.

The name of a branched-chain alkene is derived from that of the longest straight chain that contains the double bond.

The alkenes also exhibit **geometric (or cis-trans) isomerism** which is a type of **stereoisomerism.** Stereoisomers have the same structural formula but differ in the arrangement of the atoms in space. An example is provided by the isomers of 2-butene. Because of the restricted rotation around the double bond, one isomer exists with both methyl groups on the same side of the double bond (the *cis* isomer), and another isomer exists with the methyl groups on opposite sides of the double bond (the *trans* isomer). All the carbon atoms of the molecule lie in the same plane.

cis-2-butene
boiling point, 1°C

trans-2-butene
boiling point, 2.5°C

The properties of the 2-butenes do not differ greatly. Other *cis-trans* isomers exhibit wide variation in their physical properties.

cis-1,2-dichloroethane
boiling point, 60.1°C

trans-1,2-dichloroethane
boiling point, 48.4°C

The physical properties of the alkenes are very similar to the alkanes. The C_2H_4, C_3H_6, and C_4H_8 compounds are gases under ordinary conditions; the C_5H_{10} to $C_{18}H_{36}$ compounds are liquids; and the higher alkenes are solids. All the compounds are only slightly soluble in water.

Molecules can contain more than one double bond. For example,

$$CH_2=CH-CH=CH_2$$
1,3-butadiene

which is used to produce a type of synthetic rubber (Section 20.12). Cycloalkenes are known, for example,

cycloxhexene

20.3 The Alkynes

Molecules that contain carbon–carbon triple bonds are known as alkynes. These unsaturated hydrocarbons have the general formula C_nH_{2n-2} and constitute the **alkyne**, or **acetylene, series.** The first member of the series is ethyne, or acetylene.

$$H-C\equiv C-H$$

In acetylene, each carbon atom uses sp hybrid orbitals to form a σ bond with a hydrogen atom and a σ bond with the other carbon atom. Consequently, the four atoms of the molecule lie in a straight line. In addition to the carbon–carbon σ bond, two π bonds are formed between the carbon atoms by the overlap of p orbitals (Section 4.5, Figure 4.23). The resultant carbon–carbon bond distance (1.21 Å) is shorter than the carbon–carbon double-bond distance (1.33 Å). The π bonds are weaker than the C–C σ bond; the bond energy of the triple bond is approximately 198 kcal/mole (compared to the single bond energy of 81 kcal/mole). Alkynes readily undergo addition reactions across the triple bond because of the availability of the four electrons of the π bonds.

Alkynes are named in a manner analogous to that employed in naming alkenes; the ending -*yne* is used in place of -*ene*. Their physical properties are similar to those of the other aliphatic hydrocarbons. Both chain and position isomerism occur in the alkyne series, but *cis-trans* isomerism is not possible because of the linear geometry of the grouping $X-C\equiv C-X$, where X is a carbon atom or an atom of another element.

Notice that a branched-chain isomer of C_4H_6 is impossible; only two isomers of C_4H_6 exist

$$HC\equiv CCH_2CH_3 \qquad CH_3C\equiv CCH_3$$
1-butyne   2-butyne

Both branched-chain and straight-chain isomers of C_5H_8 are known.

$$HC\equiv CCH_2CH_2CH_3 \qquad CH_3C\equiv CCH_2CH_3 \qquad HC\equiv CCHCH_3$$
$$| $$
$$CH_3$$
1-pentyne   2-pentyne   methyl-1-butyne

20.4 Aromatic Hydrocarbons

Aromatic hydrocarbons are compounds that have molecular structures based on that of benzene, C_6H_6. The six carbon atoms of benzene are arranged in a ring from which the hydrogen atoms are radially bonded (Figure 20.3).

Figure 20.3 Geometry of the benzene molecule.

The entire structure is planar, and all of the bond angles are 120°. The carbon–carbon bond distance is 1.39 Å, which is between the single-bond distance of 1.54 Å and the double-bond distance of 1.33 Å.

The electronic structure of benzene may be represented as a resonance hybrid

This representation correctly shows that all of the carbon–carbon bonds are equivalent and that each one is intermediate between a single bond and a double bond.

Each carbon atom of the ring uses sp^2 hybrid orbitals to form σ bonds with two adjacent carbon atoms and with a hydrogen atom. Therefore, the resulting framework of the molecule is planar with bond angles of 120° (Figure 20.3). A $2p$ electron of each carbon atom is not employed in the formation of the sp^2-hybrid, σ bonds. The axes of these p orbitals are perpendicular to the plane of the molecule, and each p orbital can overlap two adjacent p orbitals. The result is the formation of a system of π orbitals with

Figure 20.4 The π bonding system of benzene; σ bonds are indicated as black lines.

regions of charge density above and below the plane of the ring (Figure 20.4).

The electron pairs of the σ bonds of the benzene molecule (as well as the electron pair of an ordinary π bond) are localized with respect to the two nuclei that they serve to bond. However, the six electrons that occupy the π bonding system (one contributed by each carbon atom) are delocalized. On the average, the π electrons tend to be distributed evenly about the benzene ring, which explains the bond length and equivalence of all the C to C bonds. Since delocalization minimizes electron–electron repulsion, the structure, which is reminiscent of that of graphite (Section 12.10), is very stable and is responsible for the properties that are typical of aromatic compounds. The benzene ring does not readily undergo addition reactions in the way that alkenes and alkynes do.

Notice that the resonance and molecular-orbital pictures of benzene are qualitatively equivalent. If the overlap of the p orbitals is imagined to occur only between orbitals of adjacent carbon atoms in such a way that traditional electron-pair bonds between only two atoms result, then the two resonance forms are derived (Figure 20.4). According to the resonance theory, neither of these forms is correct; the true structure is a hybrid of both of them.

The benzene ring is usually represented as

The carbon and hydrogen atoms of the ring are not shown. In benzene derivatives, such as

toluene
methylbenzene

and

ethylbenzene

it is understood that the substituents replace hydrogen atoms of the ring. The radical formed from benzene by the removal of a hydrogen atom,

is called a **phenyl radical**.

There are three position isomers of any disubstituted benzene derivative. For example,

o-xylene   m-xylene   p-xylene

The prefixes *ortho-* (*o-*), *meta-* (*m-*), and *para-* (*p-*) are used to designate the positions of the two substituent groups. Numbers are used when more than two substituents are present on the ring.

1,3,5-trinitrobenzene

Compounds are known in which several rings are fused together. For example, naphthalene, $C_{10}H_8$, is a planar molecule that is a resonance hybrid,

There are no hydrogen atoms bonded to the carbon atoms through which the rings are fused.

Coal is a major source of aromatic compounds. In the preparation of coke for industrial use (principally the reduction of iron ore), bituminous coal is heated out of contact with air in retorts. Coal tar, a by-product of this process, is a black, viscous material from which various aromatic compounds may be separated. Aromatic compounds are also obtained from processes that utilize the alkanes and cycloalkanes derived from petroleum.

20.5 Reactions of the Hydrocarbons

Combustion of any hydrocarbon in excess oxygen yields carbon dioxide and water.

$$CH_4(g) + 2O_2(g) \longrightarrow CO_2(g) + 2H_2O(g)$$

The reactions are highly exothermic, which accounts for the use of hydrocarbons as fuels. Carbon compounds exist in oxidation states intermediate between the hydrocarbons and carbon dioxide. These compounds are discussed in sections that follow; they are not generally prepared by direct reaction with elementary oxygen.

The replacement of a hydrogen atom of a hydrocarbon molecule by another atom or group of atoms is called a **substitution reaction**. The alkanes react with chlorine, or bromine, in the presence of sunlight, or ultraviolet light, by means of a free-radical chain mechanism (Section 14.7). The chain is initiated by the light-induced dissociation of a chlorine molecule into atoms.

$$Cl_2 \longrightarrow 2Cl\cdot$$

Propagation of the chain occurs by the reactions

$$Cl\cdot + CH_4 \longrightarrow CH_3\cdot + HCl$$
$$CH_3\cdot + Cl_2 \longrightarrow CH_3Cl + Cl\cdot$$

The chain is terminated by the reactions

$$CH_3\cdot + Cl\cdot \longrightarrow CH_3Cl$$
$$Cl\cdot + Cl\cdot \longrightarrow Cl_2$$
$$CH_3\cdot + CH_3\cdot \longrightarrow CH_3CH_3$$

The reactions that terminate the chain occur at the walls of the container, which carry away the energy liberated by the formation of the new bond. In a collision between radicals in the gas phase, the united fragments fly apart almost immediately because of the lack of a third body to carry away the energy released by bond formation. Hence, the chain terminators do not occur with great frequency, and all the reactants are rapidly consumed in the reactions.

The overall reaction for the preceding mechanism is

$$CH_4 + Cl_2 \longrightarrow CH_3Cl + HCl$$

In addition to chloromethane, CH_3Cl, the reaction produces dichloromethane, CH_2Cl_2, trichloromethane (chloroform), $CHCl_3$, and tetrachloromethane (carbon tetrachloride), CCl_4. In terms of the chain mechanism, these compounds arise through collisions of chlorine atoms with already chlorinated methane molecules. For example,

$$Cl\cdot + CH_3Cl \longrightarrow CH_2Cl\cdot + HCl$$
$$CH_2Cl\cdot + Cl_2 \longrightarrow CH_2Cl_2 + Cl\cdot$$

Complex mixtures of mono- and polysubstituted isomers are obtained as products of the chlorination of higher alkanes.

Addition reactions are characteristic of unsaturated hydrocarbons; examples follow.

$$CH_2=CH_2 + Br_2 \longrightarrow CH_2Br-CH_2Br$$
1,2-dibromoethane

$$HC\equiv CH + HCl \longrightarrow CH_2=CHCl$$
1-chloroethene

$$CH_2=CHCl + HCl \longrightarrow CH_3-CHCl_2$$
1.1-dichloroethane

$$\underset{\overset{|}{CH_3}}{CH_3CH_2C}=CH_2 + HOH \xrightarrow{H_2SO_4} \underset{\overset{|}{OH}}{\overset{\overset{CH_3}{|}}{CH_3CH_2CCH_3}}$$
2-methyl-2-butanol

$$CH_3CH=CH_2 + HBr \longrightarrow \underset{\overset{|}{Br}}{CH_3CHCH_3}$$
2-bromopropane

When unsymmetrical molecules (such as HBr) add to the double bond of an olefin, two isomeric compounds are sometimes produced. Thus, in the last reaction of the previous series, two compounds are obtained.

$$\underset{\overset{|}{Br}}{CH_3CHCH_3} \qquad CH_3CH_2CH_2Br$$
2-bromopropane   1-bromopropane

Over 90% of the product, however, is the 2-bromo-isomer. The principal product of such an addition is that in which the hydrogen atom of the addend is bonded to the carbon that originally had the larger number of hydrogen atoms (**Markovnikov's rule**).

The initial step of the mechanism of the addition of HBr is thought to be an electrophilic attack by a proton (a Lewis acid) on the π electrons of the double bond (a Lewis base). The product of this step is a positive ion called a **carbonium ion**, and, for propene, two such ions are possible.

$$
CH_3-\underset{H}{\overset{H}{C}}=\underset{H}{\overset{H}{C}}-H \;+\; H^+
\begin{cases}
CH_3-\underset{+}{\overset{H}{C}}-\underset{H}{\overset{H}{C}}-H \\[2em]
CH_3-\underset{H}{\overset{H}{C}}-\underset{+}{\overset{H}{C}}-H
\end{cases}
$$

The π electrons are used to bond the incoming proton to one of the carbon atoms of the double bond which leaves the other carbon atom with a positive charge. The stability of carbonium ions is known to decrease in the order

$$
\underset{+}{R-\overset{R}{C}-R} \;>\; \underset{+}{R-\overset{H}{C}-R} \;>\; \underset{+}{R-\overset{H}{C}-H}
$$

where R is an alkyl radical. Consequently, in the reaction of propene with HBr, the carbonium ion produced in larger quantity is the first one shown.

Carbonium ions are highly reactive Lewis acids; they exist only transiently and rapidly combine with bromide ion (a Lewis base).

$$
\underset{+}{CH_3CHCH_3} + Br^- \longrightarrow \underset{\underset{Br}{|}}{CH_3CHCH_3}
$$

$$
CH_3CH_2CH_2{}^+ + Br^- \longrightarrow CH_3CH_2CH_2Br
$$

Thus the relative stabilities of the carbonium ions are responsible for the fact that 2-bromopropane is the principal product of the reaction.

In contrast to unsaturated aliphatic hydrocarbons, the principal reactions of benzene are substitutions, not additions.

nitrobenzene

bromobenzene

toluene

The last reaction is the Friedel-Crafts synthesis for the preparation of aromatic hydrocarbons.

The catalysts, which are indicated over the arrows in the preceding equations, produce powerful Lewis acids (NO_2^+, Br^+, and CH_3^+) as follows:

$$HNO_3 + 2H_2SO_4 \longrightarrow NO_2^+ + H_3O^+ + 2HSO_4^-$$

$$Br_2 + FeBr_3 \longrightarrow Br^+ + FeBr_4^-$$

$$CH_3Cl + AlCl_3 \longrightarrow CH_3^+ + AlCl_4^-$$

These cationic Lewis acids, which are short-lived reaction intermediates, are electrophilic, and we shall indicate them as E^+ in the mechanism that follows.

The benzene ring is attacked by the electrophilic group, E^+, which bonds to a carbon atom by means of a pair of π electrons and creates an activated complex with a positive charge.

Notice that the carbon atom to which E is bonded holds two groups in the complex; the remaining five carbon atoms hold only their customary hydrogen atoms. The complex is a resonance hybrid, and the charge is delocalized, thus providing a degree of stability. The π bonding system of benzene is more stable, however, and is restored by the loss of a proton.

The proton is lost to the anion produced in the reaction that generated the cationic electrophile.

$$H^+ + HSO_4^- \longrightarrow H_2SO_4$$
$$H^+ + FeBr_4^- \longrightarrow HBr + FeBr_3$$
$$H^+ + AlCl_4^- \longrightarrow HCl + AlCl_3$$

20.6 Alcohols and Ethers

The alcohols may be considered as derivatives of hydrocarbons in which a hydroxyl group, OH, replaces a hydrogen. The hydroxyl group is one of a number of **functional groups**, which are groups of atoms that give organic compounds bearing them characteristic chemical and physical properties.

The compounds are named as derivatives of a hydrocarbon consisting of the longest straight chain that contains the OH group. The ending of the parent hydrocarbon is changed from -*ane* to -*anol*, and numbers are used to indicate the positions of substituents, the lowest possible number being assigned to the OH group. Alcohols may be classified as *primary, secondary,* or *tertiary*, according to the number of alkyl radicals on the carbon atom holding the OH. Thus

Alcohols associate through hydrogen bonding,

For this reason, the melting points and boiling points of the alcohols are higher than those of alkanes of corresponding molecular weight (Table 20.4). The lower alcohols are miscible with water in all proportions because of intermolecular hydrogen bonding.

Table 20.4

Physical Properties of Some Alcohols

Name	Formula	Melting Point (°C)	Boiling Point (°C)	Solubility in Water (g/100 g H_2O, 20°C)
methanol	CH_3OH	-98	65	miscible
ethanol	CH_3CH_2OH	-115	78	miscible
1-propanol	$CH_3(CH_2)_2OH$	-127	97	miscible
1-butanol	$CH_3(CH_2)_3OH$	-90	117	7.9
1-pentanol	$CH_3(CH_2)_4OH$	-79	138	2.4
1-hexanol	$CH_3(CH_2)_5OH$	-52	157	0.6

However, as the size of the alkyl radical increases, the alcohols become more like alkanes in their physical properties, and the higher alcohols are only slightly soluble in water.

Alcohols, like water, are amphiprotic substances. They can act as Brønsted bases (proton acceptors) with very strong acids.

$$H_2SO_4 + ROH \rightleftharpoons ROH_2^+ + HSO_4^-$$

With very strong bases, they are Brønsted acids (proton donors).

$$ROH + H^- \longrightarrow OR^- + H_2$$

Alcohols, however, are more weakly acidic and basic than water; consequently, the conjugate acids (ROH_2^+) and conjugate bases (OR^-) are stronger than H_3O^+ and OH^-. The anion OR^-, known as an alkoxide ion, results from the reaction of an alcohol with a reactive metal (compare the reaction of water with sodium).

$$2CH_3CH_2OH + 2Na \longrightarrow 2CH_3CH_2ONa + H_2$$

The first member of the series, methanol or methyl alcohol, is known as wood alcohol because it can be obtained by the destructive distillation of wood. The principal commercial source of this alcohol is the catalytic hydrogenation of carbon monoxide.

$$CO + 2H_2 \longrightarrow CH_3OH$$

The alcohol of alcoholic beverages is ethanol, or ethyl alcohol. It is prepared by the fermentation of starches or sugars. Ethanol is also commercially prepared from ethene. The indirect addition of water to olefins by means of sulfuric acid is a general method of preparing alcohols. The synthesis of ethanol proceeds by the following steps.

$$CH_2{=}CH_2 + H_2SO_4 \longrightarrow CH_3CH_2OSO_2OH$$
$$CH_3CH_2OSO_2OH + H_2O \longrightarrow CH_3CH_2OH + H_2SO_4$$

Alcohols can be prepared from alkyl halides by displacement, or nucleophilic substitution, reactions.

$$RX + OH^- \longrightarrow ROH + X^-$$

This is an important classification of organic reactions and includes reactions of the alklyl halides, as well the alcohols themselves, with a wide variety of nucleophilic substances. The reactions are usually reversible and are run under conditions that favor the formation of the desired compound; an excess of the nucleophilic reagent may be employed or the product removed from the reaction mixture as it forms (e.g., by distillation).

Primary and secondary halides or alcohols generally react by what is called an S_N2 mechanism, which can be illustrated by the reaction of hydroxide ion with methyl bromide. The hydroxide ion, a Lewis base, attacks the carbon atom and displaces the bromide ion (also a Lewis base) which takes along the electron pair with which it had been bonded.

$$OH^- + H-\underset{\underset{H}{|}}{\overset{\overset{H}{|}}{C}}-Br \longrightarrow \left[HO\text{---}\underset{\underset{H}{|}}{C}\text{---}Br \right]^- \longrightarrow HO-\underset{\underset{H}{\diagup}}{\overset{\overset{H}{\diagdown}}{C}}-H + Br^-$$

activated complex

The attack of the OH^- ion takes place on the opposite side of the carbon atom from that holding the bromine atom. As the OH^- ion approaches, it begins to form a covalent bond, and the bromide ion begins to break away; the activated complex of the reaction is the form in which both nucleophilic groups are partially bonded to the carbon atom. The reaction causes inversion of the geometric arrangement of the groups attached to the carbon atom, a process that is customarily compared to the inversion of an umbrella in a high wind. The mechanism is given the designation S_N2 because it is the substitution of one nucleophilic group for another, and the rate-determining step (the formation of the activated complex) is bimolecular. The nucleophilic substitution reaction of HBr with CH_3OH proceeds through the formation of $CH_3OH_2^+$ and the displacement of H_2O from this ion by Br^-.

In the case of tertiary alkyl halides, the three alkyl groups bonded to the carbon atom bearing the halogen inhibit the rearward approach of the OH^- ion, and it is thought that tertiary alkyl halides undergo displacement reactions by a different mechanism. The rate-determining step is the formation of a carbonium ion,

$$CH_3-\underset{\underset{CH_3}{|}}{\overset{\overset{CH_3}{|}}{C}}-Br \longrightarrow CH_3\underset{\underset{CH_3}{|}}{\overset{\overset{CH_3}{|}}{C}}{}^+ + Br^-$$

The central carbon atom of the carbonium ion has only six electrons in its valence level and displays sp^2 hybridization; the carbonium ion is, therefore, planar. It is a powerful Lewis acid and rapidly adds hydroxide ion (a Lewis base).

$$\begin{array}{ccc} & CH_3 & & CH_3 \\ & | & & | \\ CH_3-C^+ + OH^- & \longrightarrow & CH_3-C-OH \\ & | & & | \\ & CH_3 & & CH_3 \end{array}$$

This mechanism is given the designation S_N1 because it is a nucleophilic substitution in which the rate-determining step is unimolecular. The S_N1 mechanism is favored when the reaction is run in polar solvents (such as water) which aids the first-step ionization of the halide.

Tertiary alcohols also undergo S_N1 reactions. The steps of a typical substitution involving HBr are

$$\begin{array}{ll} (CH_3)_3COH + H^+ \rightleftharpoons (CH_3)_3COH_2^+ & \text{(rapid, equilibrium)} \\ (CH_3)_3COH_2^+ \longrightarrow (CH_3)_3C^+ + H_2O & \text{(rate determining)} \\ (CH_3)_3C^+ + Br^- \longrightarrow (CH_3)_3CBr \end{array}$$

In all these nucleophilic substitution reactions, appreciable quantities of olefins are formed along with the substitution products; this is particularly true of the reactions of the tertiary compounds, and olefin formation is thought to proceed by the elimination of a proton by a carbonium ion.

$$\begin{array}{ccc} H \ \ CH_3 & & H \ \ CH_3 \\ | \ \ \ | & & | \ \ \ | \\ H-C-C^+ & \longrightarrow & H^+ + C=C \\ | \ \ \ | & & | \ \ \ | \\ H \ \ CH_3 & & H \ \ CH_3 \end{array}$$

Tertiary carbonium ions are formed more readily than any other type (Section 20.5); elimination reactions of primary and secondary alcohols are thought to occur by a mechanism that does not involve the formation of carbonium ions.

The elimination of one water molecule from one molecule of an alcohol produces an olefin.

$$CH_3CH_2OH \xrightarrow[\text{above 150° C}]{H_2SO_4} CH_2{=}CH_2 + H_2O$$

Under milder conditions, only one molecule of water is removed from two molecules of alcohol, and an ether is produced.

$$CH_3CH_2OH + HOCH_2CH_3 \xrightarrow[\text{130-140° C}]{H_2SO_4} \underset{\text{diethyl ether}}{CH_3CH_2OCH_2CH_3} + H_2O$$

Ethers may be regarded as derivatives of water, HOH, in which both hydrogen atoms are replaced by alkyl groups, ROR. The alkyl groups may be alike or different. Ethers are also produced by nucleophilic substitution reactions involving alkoxide ions and alkyl halides.

$$CH_3CH_2O^- + CH_3CH_2CH_2Br \longrightarrow CH_3CH_2OCH_2CH_2CH_3 + Br^-$$
ethyl propyl ether

Unlike alcohols, ethers do not associate by hydrogen bonding. Therefore the boiling points of ethers are much lower than those of alcohols of corresponding molecular weight, and the ethers are much less soluble in water.

CH_3CH_2OH CH_3OCH_3

ethanol   dimethyl ether

boiling point, 78°C   boiling point, −24°C

Notice that ethanol and dimethyl ether are isomeric; the type of isomerism displayed by this pair of compounds is known as **functional group isomerism.** The ethers are less reactive than the alcohols.

Polyhydroxy alcohols contain more than one OH group. Examples include 1,2-ethanediol (ethylene glycol),

CH_2-CH_2

$\quad|\qquad\quad|$

$OH\quad\ OH$

and 1,2,3-propanetriol (glycerol), which is derived from fats,

$CH_2-CH-CH_2$

$\quad|\qquad\ |\qquad\ |$

$OH\quad OH\quad OH$

Unlike aliphatic alcohols, which do not dissociate in water solution, the aromatic alcohols are weak acids in water.

phenol   phenoxide ion

The acidity of phenol (carbolic acid) is attributed to the stability of the phenoxide ion in which the charge is delocalized by the π bonding system of the aromatic ring.

Aromatic halides do not readily undergo displacement reactions. Sodium phenoxide is commercially obtained from chlorobenzene by reaction with NaOH at elevated temperatures and under high pressure.

$$\text{Cl} \quad + \quad 2\text{NaOH} \quad \longrightarrow \quad \text{ONa} \quad + \quad \text{NaCl} \quad + \quad \text{H}_2\text{O}$$

Phenol is derived by acidification of the phenoxide.

20.7 Carbonyl Compounds

A carbon atom can form a double bond with an oxygen atom to produce what is called a **carbonyl group**

$$\overset{\text{O}}{\underset{}{\overset{\|}{-\text{C}-}}}$$

The double bond, like the carbon–carbon double bond, consists of a σ bond and a π bond between the bonded atoms. The carbon atom of the carbonyl group and the atoms bonded to it are coplanar and form bond angles of 120°, a geometry that is typical of sp^2 hybridized species. The carbonyl double bond differs from the olefinic double bond in that it is markedly polar since oxygen is more electronegative than carbon.

If the carbonyl group is bonded to one alkyl group and a hydrogen, or to two hydrogens, the compound is an **aldehyde**.

$$\overset{\text{O}}{\underset{\substack{\text{formaldehyde}\\\text{methanal}}}{\overset{\|}{\text{H}-\text{C}-\text{H}}}} \qquad \overset{\text{O}}{\underset{\substack{\text{acetaldehyde}\\\text{ethanal}}}{\overset{\|}{\text{CH}_3-\text{C}-\text{H}}}} \qquad \underset{\text{3-methylbutanal}}{\overset{\text{CH}_3}{\overset{|}{\text{CH}_3-\text{C}-\text{CH}_2-\overset{\overset{\text{O}}{\|}}{\text{C}}-\text{H}}}}$$

Systematic nomenclature of aldehydes employs the ending *-al*; substituent groups are given numbers based on the assignment of the number 1 (understood) to the carbonyl carbon.

In a **ketone**, the carbonyl groups is bonded to two alkyl groups which may be alike or different.

$$\underset{\substack{\text{acetone}\\\text{propanone}}}{\overset{\text{O}}{\overset{\|}{\text{CH}_3-\text{C}-\text{CH}_3}}} \qquad \underset{\substack{\text{methyl ethyl ketone}\\\text{butanone}}}{\overset{\text{O}}{\overset{\|}{\text{CH}_3-\text{C}-\text{CH}_2\text{CH}_3}}} \qquad \underset{\text{5-methyl-3-hexanone}}{\overset{\text{O}\qquad\text{CH}_3}{\overset{\|\qquad|}{\text{CH}_3\text{CH}_2-\text{C}-\text{CH}_2\text{CHCH}_3}}}$$

The ending *-one* is used to designate a ketone. Numbers are employed to indicate the positions of substituents on the longest continuous chain containing the carbonyl group, which is assigned the lowest possible number.

Aldehydes may be prepared by the mild oxidation of primary alcohols. An oxidizing agent such as potassium dichromate in dilute sulfuric acid may be used.

$$3RCH_2OH + Cr_2O_7^{2-} + 8H^+ \longrightarrow 3R\overset{\overset{\displaystyle O}{\|}}{C}-H + 2Cr^{3+} + 7H_2O$$

Equations for a reaction such as this are usually written with the oxidizing agent indicated over the arrow and only the organic reactant and product shown. Thus

$$CH_3CH_2OH \xrightarrow{\ Cr_2O_7^{2-}/H^+\ } CH_3\overset{\overset{\displaystyle O}{\|}}{C}-H$$

When an aldehyde is prepared by the oxidation of a primary alcohol, provision must be made to prevent the aldehyde from being destroyed by further oxidation, since aldehydes are easily oxidized to carboxylic acids (Section 20.8). Many aldehydes may be distilled out of the reaction mixture as they are formed.

Some aldehydes are made commercially by reacting alcohol vapors with air over a copper catalyst at elevated temperatures.

$$2CH_3OH + O_2 \xrightarrow{\ Cu\ } 2H-\overset{\overset{\displaystyle O}{\|}}{C}-H + 2H_2O$$

The oxidation of alcohols may also be conducted by passing the hot alcohol vapor over a heated copper catalyst in the absence of oxygen. This process results in the removal of a molecule of hydrogen from an alcohol molecule and is called a **dehydrogenation**; it avoids the danger of secondary oxidation of the aldehyde product.

$$CH_3CH_2CH_2OH \xrightarrow{\ Cu\ } CH_3CH_2\overset{\overset{\displaystyle O}{\|}}{C}-H + H_2$$

The oxidation of secondary alcohols produces ketones.

$$CH_3CH_2\overset{\overset{\displaystyle OH}{|}}{C}HCH_3 \xrightarrow{\ Cr_2O_7^{2-}/H^+\ } CH_3CH_2\overset{\overset{\displaystyle O}{\|}}{C}CH_3$$

Acetone (propanone) may be prepared by the oxidation of 2-propanol with oxygen or by the dehydrogenation of the alcohol.

$$CH_3\overset{\overset{\displaystyle OH}{|}}{C}HCH_3 \xrightarrow{\ Cu\ } CH_3\overset{\overset{\displaystyle O}{\|}}{C}CH_3 + H_2$$

The oxidation of tertiary alcohols results in the destruction of the carbon skeleton of the molecule.

The double bond of the carbonyl group readily undergoes many addition reactions. Reduction of aldehydes or ketones with hydrogen in the presence of a nickel or platinum catalyst yields primary or secondary alcohols.

$$
\begin{array}{c}
\text{O} \\
\parallel \\
\text{R}-\text{C}-\text{H} + \text{H}_2
\end{array}
\longrightarrow
\begin{array}{c}
\text{OH} \\
\mid \\
\text{R}-\text{CH}_2
\end{array}
$$

$$
\begin{array}{c}
\text{O} \\
\parallel \\
\text{R}-\text{C}-\text{R} + \text{H}_2
\end{array}
\longrightarrow
\begin{array}{c}
\text{OH} \\
\mid \\
\text{R}-\text{CH}-\text{R}
\end{array}
$$

When an unsymmetrical reagent (such as HCN) adds to the double bond, the positive part of the addend (the hydrogen) adds to the oxygen, and the negative part of the addend (the cyanide group) bonds to the carbon. This mode of addition reflects the polarity of a carbonyl double bond; the oxygen is negative with respect to the carbon.

$$
\begin{array}{c}
\text{O} \\
\parallel \\
\text{R}-\text{C}-\text{R} + \text{H}-\text{C}\equiv\text{N}
\end{array}
\longrightarrow
\begin{array}{c}
\text{OH} \\
\mid \\
\text{R}-\text{C}-\text{R} \\
\mid \\
\text{C}\equiv\text{N}
\end{array}
$$

a cyanohydrin

The proposed mechanism for additions of this type consists of the electrophilic attack of the anionic Lewis base

$$
\begin{array}{c}
\text{O} \\
\parallel \\
\text{R}-\text{C}-\text{R} + \text{CN}^-
\end{array}
\longrightarrow
\begin{array}{c}
\text{O}^- \\
\mid \\
\text{R}-\text{C}-\text{R} \\
\mid \\
\text{CN}
\end{array}
$$

followed by combination with a proton

$$
\begin{array}{c}
\text{O}^- \\
\mid \\
\text{R}-\text{C}-\text{R} + \text{H}^+ \\
\mid \\
\text{CN}
\end{array}
\longrightarrow
\begin{array}{c}
\text{OH} \\
\mid \\
\text{R}-\text{C}-\text{R} \\
\mid \\
\text{CN}
\end{array}
$$

An important addition reaction involves organomagnesium compounds known as **Grignard reagents**. Alkyl halides react with magnesium metal in dry diethyl ether

$$\text{R}-\text{X} + \text{Mg} \longrightarrow \text{R}-\text{Mg}-\text{X}$$

These reagents are usually given the formula RMgX; however, the materials possess a high degree of ionic character and may be mixtures of magnesium dialkyls (MgR_2) and magnesium halides (MgX_2). Water must be excluded from a Grignard reaction because these reagents are easily hydrolyzed.

$$\text{R}-\text{Mg}-\text{X} + \text{HOH} \longrightarrow \text{R}-\text{H} + \text{Mg(OH)X}$$

The formula Mg(OH)X stands for an equimolar mixture of magnesium hydroxide and magnesium halide.

A Grignard reagent adds to an aldehyde as follows

$$
\underset{\substack{\text{O}\\\|\\}}{R'-C-H} + R-Mg-X \longrightarrow \underset{\substack{\text{OMgX}\\|\\R}}{R'-C-H}
$$

where the alkyl groups R and R′ may be alike or different. The addition compound is readily decomposed by water or by dilute acid.

$$
\underset{\substack{\text{OMgX}\\|\\R}}{R'-C-H} + HX \longrightarrow \underset{\substack{\text{OH}\\|\\R}}{R'-C-H} + MgX_2
$$

Thus the ultimate product of the reaction of a Grignard reagent and an aldehyde is a secondary alcohol.

Hydrolysis of an addition compound formed by a Grignard reagent and a ketone yields a tertiary alcohol.

$$
\underset{\substack{\text{O}\\\|}}{R'-C-R''} + RMgX \longrightarrow \underset{\substack{\text{OMgX}\\|\\R}}{R'-C-R''}
$$

$$
\underset{\substack{\text{OMgX}\\|\\R}}{R'-C-R''} + HX \longrightarrow \underset{\substack{\text{OH}\\|\\R}}{R'-C-R''} + MgX_2
$$

The alkyl groups may be alike or different.

In these reactions of Grignard reagents, new carbon–carbon bonds are formed, and the reactions are frequently useful as steps in organic syntheses. The alcohols produced may be oxidized to carbonyl compounds, subjected to displacement reactions, or dehydrated to olefins. Thus a series of reactions may be employed to synthesize a desired compound from compounds of lower molecular weight.

20.8 Carboxylic Acids and Esters

Oxidation of the aldehyde group yields a **carboxyl group**

$$
\underset{\substack{\text{O}\\\|}}{-C-H} \longrightarrow \underset{\substack{\text{O}\\\|}}{-C-OH}
$$

Compounds containing the −COOH group are weak acids (**carboxylic**

Table 20.5

Properties of Some Carboxylic Acids

Acid	Formula	Melting Point (°C)	Boiling Point (°C)	Ionization Constant at 25°C
methanoic (formic)	HCOOH	8	101	1.8×10^{-4}
ethanoic (acetic)	CH_3COOH	17	118	1.8×10^{-5}
propanoic (propionic)	CH_3CH_2COOH	-22	141	1.4×10^{-5}
butanoic (butyric)	$CH_3(CH_2)_2COOH$	-8	164	1.5×10^{-5}
pentanoic (valeric)	$CH_3(CH_2)_3COOH$	-35	187	1.6×10^{-5}
benzoic	C_6H_5COOH	122	249	6.0×10^{-5}

acids); ionization constants for some of these acids are listed in Table 20.5.

$$
\underset{\substack{\| \\ R-C-OH}}{O} + H_2O \rightleftharpoons \underset{\substack{\| \\ R-C-O^-}}{O} + H_3O^+
$$

The charge of the carboxylate anion is delocalized.

$$
\underset{\substack{\| \\ R-C-O^-}}{O} \longleftrightarrow \underset{\substack{| \\ R-C=O}}{O^-}
$$

The acids are associated through hydrogen bonding. Lower members of the series form dimers in the vapor state.

$$
R-C\underset{O-H\cdots O}{\overset{O\cdots H-O}{\diagup\diagdown}}C-R
$$

According to systematic nomenclature, the name of a carboxylic acid is derived from the parent hydrocarbon by elision of the final -*e*, addition of the ending -*oic*, and addition of the separate word *acid*. The numbers used to designate the positions of substituents on the carbon chain are derived by numbering the chain starting with the carbon of the carboxyl group.

$$
\underset{\text{propanoic acid}}{\underset{\substack{\| \\ CH_3CH_2C-OH}}{O}} \qquad \underset{\text{3-methylbutanoic acid}}{\underset{\substack{| \qquad \| \\ CH_3CHCH_2C-OH}}{\overset{CH_3 \quad O}{}}}
$$

Carboxylic acids may be prepared by the oxidation of primary alcohols or aldehydes. Potassium dichromate or potassium permanganate are frequently employed as the oxidizing agent.

$$CH_3CH_2CH_2CH_2OH \xrightarrow{Cr_2O_7^{2-}/H^+} CH_3CH_2CH_2\overset{\overset{\displaystyle O}{\|}}{C}-OH$$

Acetic acid is commercially prepared by the air oxidation of acetaldehyde.

$$2CH_3\overset{\overset{\displaystyle O}{\|}}{C}-H + O_2 \xrightarrow{Mn(C_2H_3O_2)_2} 2CH_3\overset{\overset{\displaystyle O}{\|}}{C}-OH$$

Vigorous oxidation of an alkyl-substituted aromatic compound converts the side chain to a carbonyl group and thus yields benzoic acid.

toluene   benzoic acid

These oxidations do not touch the aromatic ring, an illustration of the stability of this structure.

The oxidation of an unsaturated hydrocarbon yields a variety of products, including carboxylic acids, depending upon conditions. Dilute aqueous permanganate at room temperature oxidizes olefins to glycols.

$$R-CH=CH-R \xrightarrow{MnO_4^-} R-\underset{\underset{\displaystyle OH}{|}}{C}H-\underset{\underset{\displaystyle OH}{|}}{C}H-R$$

Under more vigorous conditions (more concentrated solutions and heating), the carbon chain is cleaved at the double bond and carboxylic acids produced.

$$R-CH=CH-R \xrightarrow{MnO_4^-} R-\overset{\overset{\displaystyle O}{\|}}{C}-OH + HO-\overset{\overset{\displaystyle O}{\|}}{C}-R$$

Alkynes also may be cleaved to yield acids.

$$R-C\equiv C-R \xrightarrow{MnO_4^-} R-\overset{\overset{\displaystyle O}{\|}}{C}-OH + HO-\overset{\overset{\displaystyle O}{\|}}{C}-R$$

Oxidation of some olefins yields ketones.

$$R-\underset{\underset{\displaystyle R}{|}}{C}=\underset{\underset{\displaystyle R}{|}}{C}-R \xrightarrow{MnO_4^-} R-\underset{\underset{\displaystyle R}{|}}{C}=O + O=\underset{\underset{\displaystyle R}{|}}{C}-R$$

Carboxylic acids may be produced by the alkaline hydrolysis of alkyl cyanides; the cyanides are the product of nucleophilic substitution reactions of the CN^- ion with alkyl halides.

$$CH_3CH_2Br + CN^- \longrightarrow CH_3CH_2CN + Br^-$$

$$CH_3CH_2CN + OH^- + H_2O \longrightarrow CH_3CH_2\overset{\displaystyle O}{\overset{\|}{C}}-O^- + NH_3$$

Some compounds contain more than one carboxyl group. Examples include

$$\begin{array}{cc}
\begin{array}{c} COOH \\ | \\ COOH \end{array} & \text{and} \quad
\begin{array}{c} CH_2COOH \\ | \\ HO-C-COOH \\ | \\ CH_2COOH \end{array}
\end{array}$$

oxalic acid   citric acid

Carboxylic acids react with alcohols to produce compounds known as esters.

$$CH_3\overset{\displaystyle O}{\overset{\|}{C}}-OH + CH_3CH_2OH \longrightarrow \left[CH_3\overset{\displaystyle OH}{\underset{\displaystyle OCH_2CH_3}{\overset{|}{\underset{|}{C}}}}-OH \right] \longrightarrow CH_3\overset{\displaystyle O}{\overset{\|}{C}}-OCH_2CH_3 + H_2O$$

ethyl acetate

Esterification reactions are reversible and proceed to equilibrium; they may be forced in either direction by the appropriate choice of conditions. The name of an ester reflects the alcohol and acid from which it is derived, the ending *-ate* being employed with the base of the name of the acid to give the second portion of the name of the ester.

The lower molecular weight esters have pleasant, fruity odors. Esters of high-molecular-weight carboxylic acids and glycerol are animal and vegetable **fats:** glyceryl esters that are liquids at room temperature are commonly called **oils.**

$$\begin{array}{c}
R-\overset{\displaystyle O}{\overset{\|}{C}}-O-CH_2 \\ | \\
R'-\overset{\displaystyle O}{\overset{\|}{C}}-O-CH \\ | \\
R''-\overset{\displaystyle O}{\overset{\|}{C}}-O-CH_2
\end{array}$$

The alkyl groups indicated in the preceding general formula are part of the carboxylic acids from which the compound may be considered to have been derived; they may be alike or different. The carboxylic acids are long-chain structures and may be saturated

$$CH_3(CH_2)_{14}COOH$$

palmitic acid

or unsaturated

$$CH_3(CH_2)_7CH=CH(CH_2)_7COOH$$

oleic acid

Liquid fats, or oils, contain a high percentage of glyceryl esters of unsaturated acids. Hydrogenation of vegetable oils produces solid fats. In commercial practice, the process is run only until a solid of the desired consistency is obtained; not all of the olefinic linkages are saturated.

The alkaline hydrolysis of an ester produces an alcohol and a salt of a carboxylic acid.

$$\underset{\text{RCOR}'}{\overset{O}{\|}} + OH^- \longrightarrow \underset{R-C-O^-}{\overset{O}{\|}} + R'OH$$

The salts of long-chain carboxylic acids are soaps. These compounds, together with glycerol, are produced by the alkaline hydrolysis of fats, and the process is commonly called **saponification** (soap making).

20.9 Amines and Amides

The **amines** may be considered as derivatives of ammonia with one, two, or three hydrogen atoms replaced by alkyl groups.

$$\underset{\substack{\text{methylamine}\\\text{a primary amine}}}{\overset{\overset{\displaystyle H}{|}}{CH_3-N-H}} \qquad \underset{\substack{\text{dimethylamine}\\\text{a secondary amine}}}{\overset{\overset{\displaystyle CH_3}{|}}{CH_3-N-H}} \qquad \underset{\substack{\text{trimethylamine}\\\text{a tertiary amine}}}{\overset{\overset{\displaystyle CH_3}{|}}{CH_3-N-CH_3}}$$

The amines resemble ammonia in that they are weak bases.

$$CH_3NH_2 + H_2O \rightleftharpoons CH_3NH_3^+ + OH^-$$
$$(CH_3)_2NH + H_2O \rightleftharpoons (CH_3)_2NH_2^+ + OH^-$$
$$(CH_3)_3N + H_2O \rightleftharpoons (CH_3)_3NH^+ + OH^-$$

Ionization constants for some amines are listed in Table 20.6. The amines form ionic salts with acids

$$CH_3NH_2 + HCl \longrightarrow CH_3NH_3^+ + Cl^-$$

which may be decomposed by hydroxides

$$CH_3NH_3^+ + OH^- \longrightarrow CH_3NH_2 + H_2O$$

Table 20.6

Properties of Some Amines

Amine	Formula	Melting Point (°C)	Boiling Point (°C)	Ionization Constant at 25°C
methylamine	CH_3NH_2	−93	−7	5×10^{-4}
dimethylamine	$(CH_3)_2NH$	−96	7	7.4×10^{-4}
trimethylamine	$(CH_3)_3N$	−124	4	7.4×10^{-5}
ethylamine	$CH_3CH_2NH_2$	−81	17	5.6×10^{-4}
propylamine	$CH_3CH_2CH_2NH_2$	−83	49	4.7×10^{-4}
aniline	$C_6H_5NH_2$	−6	184	4.6×10^{-10}

The last reaction is the reverse of the ionization of methylamine in water; it is forced to yield the free amine by employment of an excess of OH^- or by warming.

Amines may be prepared by reacting alkyl halides with ammonia. These reactions are nucleophilic substitutions.

$$NH_3 + CH_3CH_2Br \longrightarrow CH_3CH_2NH_3^+ + Br^-$$

Treatment of the amine salt with hydroxide ion yields the free amine. Mixtures of primary, secondary, and tertiary amines are produced by this type of reaction.

Primary amines may be produced by the catalytic hydrogenation of alkyl cyanides.

$$CH_3CH_2C \equiv N + 2H_2 \longrightarrow CH_3CH_2CH_2-NH_2$$

Aniline is produced by the reduction of nitrobenzene. Iron and steam, with a trace of hydrochloric acid, serve as the reducing agent.

nitrobenzene   aniline

Some compounds that contain more than one amino group are important. Ethylenediamine (1,2-diaminoethane, $H_2N-CH_2-CH_2-NH_2$) is a useful chelating agent (Section 19.1), and hexamethylenediamine (1,6-diaminohexane $H_2N(CH_2)_6NH_2$) is used in the manufacture of nylon.

Amides may be produced from ammonia and carboxylic acids. The preparation proceeds through the formation of ammonium salts which eliminate water upon heating.

$$CH_3\overset{\overset{\displaystyle O}{\|}}{C}-OH + NH_3 \longrightarrow CH_3\overset{\overset{\displaystyle O}{\|}}{C}-O^-NH_4{}^+$$

$$\underset{\text{ammonium acetate}}{CH_3\overset{\overset{\displaystyle O}{\|}}{C}-O^-NH_4{}^+} \longrightarrow \underset{\text{acetamide}}{CH_3\overset{\overset{\displaystyle O}{\|}}{C}-NH_2 + H_2O}$$

Amides may also be prepared by the nucleophilic substitution reaction of ammonia on an ester.

$$NH_3 + CH_3\overset{\overset{\displaystyle O}{\|}}{C}-OCH_2CH_3 \longrightarrow CH_3\overset{\overset{\displaystyle O}{\|}}{C}-NH_2 + CH_3CH_2OH$$

Primary and secondary amines react with acids in a similar manner to produce substituted amides, compounds in which one or two alkyl radicals replace hydrogen atoms of the $-NH_2$ group.

20.10 Amino Acids and Proteins

Carboxylic acid molecules that contain an amino group, $-NH_2$, on the carbon atom adjacent to the carboxyl carbon (the so-called α-carbon atom) are called **amino acids.** The simplest such compound is aminoacetic acid, or glycine.

$$\underset{NH_2}{\overset{\displaystyle CH_2}{|}}-\overset{\overset{\displaystyle O}{\|}}{C}-OH$$

Amino acids are both acidic and basic

$$H_2N-CH_2\overset{\overset{\displaystyle O}{\|}}{C}-OH + OH^- \rightleftharpoons H_2N-CH_2\overset{\overset{\displaystyle O}{\|}}{C}-O^- + H_2O$$

$$H_2N-CH_2\overset{\overset{\displaystyle O}{\|}}{C}-OH + H_3O^+ \rightleftharpoons {}^+H_3N-CH_2\overset{\overset{\displaystyle O}{\|}}{C}-OH + H_2O$$

Thus internal neutralization, producing a **zwitter ion,** can occur.

$$^+H_3N-CH_2-\overset{\overset{\displaystyle O}{\|}}{C}-O^-$$

For a given compound, the acid strength and base strength, which depend upon molecular structure, are generally not exactly equal. The **isoelectric point** is the pH at which the internal neutralization of a given amino acid is at a maximum.

The acid hydrolysis of proteins yields amino acids. Many different amino acids have been synthesized, but only about two dozen have been obtained from proteins. The general formula of these compounds is

$$H_2N-\underset{\underset{R}{|}}{CH}-\overset{\overset{O}{\|}}{C}-OH$$

The radicals, R in the preceding formula, vary considerably in structure. Some of the radicals contain additional amino groups or carboxyl groups; a number include rings (some of them aromatic rings); some incorporate sulfur atoms or hydroxyl groups in their structures; and one contains iodine.

In protein molecules, many amino acid units are linked together in long chains so that the molecular weights of proteins range from approximately 10^4 to about 10^7. When two amino acids combine, the amino group of one molecule joins, with the elimination of water, to the carboxyl group of the second molecule, and a **peptide linkage** $-\overset{\overset{O}{\|}}{C}-\overset{\overset{H}{|}}{N}-$, is formed.

$$H_2N-\underset{\underset{R}{|}}{CH}-\overset{\overset{O}{\|}}{C}-OH + H_2N-\underset{\underset{R}{|}}{CH}-\overset{\overset{O}{\|}}{C}-OH \longrightarrow H_2N-\underset{\underset{R}{|}}{CH}-\overset{\overset{O}{\|}}{C}-\overset{\overset{H}{|}}{N}-\underset{\underset{R}{|}}{CH}-\overset{\overset{O}{\|}}{C}-OH + H_2O$$

This product has a free amino group and a free carboxyl group and can condense with other amino acid molecules to form long chains, or polypeptides. The hydrolysis of polypeptide chains is the reverse of the condensation process and produces amino acids.

The amino acids provide examples of a type of stereoisomerism called **optical isomerism** (Section 19.4). The simplest optical isomers are compounds that contain asymmetric carbon atoms—carbon atoms to which four different types of groups are bonded (Figure 20.5). Such molecules are dissymmetric—that is, the mirror image (enantiomorph) of the molecule is not superimposable on the original. Thus the structures shown in Figure 20.5 are mirror reflections of one another, and a study of the figure reveals that the two configurations cannot be superimposed. If groups 1 and 3 of the structures are superimposed, group 4 of one structure coincides with group 2 of the other. No matter how the two structures are oriented, it is impossible to make all four groups of one structure coincide with the same four groups of the other structure; two different isomers exist.

The physical properties of optical isomers are identical except for their effects on plane-polarized light. The isomers are said to be optically active because they rotate the plane of plane-polarized light in either a clockwise

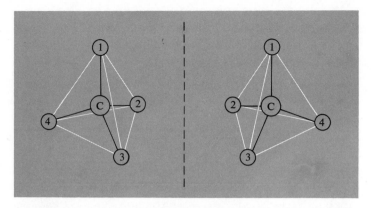

Figure 20.5   Optical isomers of a compound containing an asymmetric carbon atom. (Dashes represent reflection plane.)

or a counterclockwise direction. The isomer that rotates the plane to the right (clockwise) is said to be **dextrorotatory** $(+)$; the other isomer rotates the plane an equal amount to the left and is said to be **levorotatory** $(-)$.

With the exception of glycine (aminoacetic acid), the α-carbon atoms of all α-amino acids are asymmetric.

$$\underset{\underset{R}{|}}{H_2N-\overset{\overset{H}{|}}{C}-\overset{\overset{O}{\|}}{C}-OH}$$

The two-dimensional representation of optical isomers is difficult; structures of the optical isomers of amino acids are usually diagramed

$$\begin{array}{cc}
\overset{O}{\underset{\|}{}} & \overset{O}{\underset{\|}{}} \\
\text{C-OH} & \text{C-OH} \\
| & | \\
\text{H}_2\text{N-C-H} & \text{H-C-NH}_2 \\
| & | \\
\text{R} & \text{R} \\
\text{L-amino acid} & \text{D-amino acid}
\end{array}$$

The diagrams represent structures in which the asymmetric carbon atoms are in the plane of the paper, the $-$COOH and $-$R groups are behind the plane of the paper, and the $-$H and $-$NH$_2$ groups are in front of the plane of the paper. With such an arrangement of groups, the L-form is that in which the amino group is to the left of the chain, and the D-form is that in which the amino group is to the right. The structures can be related to the diagrams of Figure 20.5; the L-form is the one on the left in the figure if group $1 = -$COOH, $2 = -$R, $3 = -$H, and $4 = -$NH$_2$.

All the amino acids derived from proteins are L-amino acids. Only the L-forms can be utilized in the metabolic processes of the body. The sign of rotation should not be confused with the symbols D- or L- which are used to designate the configuration of the asymmetric carbon atom. Thus the L-isomer of alanine (2-aminopropanoic acid) is dextrorotatory.

$$
\begin{array}{c}
\text{O} \\
\parallel \\
\text{C}-\text{OH} \\
| \\
\text{H}_2\text{N}-\text{C}-\text{H} \\
| \\
\text{CH}_3
\end{array}
$$

L-(+)-alanine

20.11 Carbohydrates

Sugars, starches, and cellulose belong to a group of organic compounds called **carbohydrates**; the name derives from the fact that most (but not all) such compounds have the general formula $C_x(H_2O)_y$. Carbohydrates are hydroxy aldehydes, hydroxy ketones, or substances that yield hydroxy carbonyl compounds upon hydrolysis.

The optical isomers of glucose, an important simple sugar, have the formulas

$$
\begin{array}{c}
\text{H} \\
| \\
\text{C}=\text{O} \\
| \\
\text{H}-\text{C}-\text{OH} \\
| \\
\text{HO}-\text{C}-\text{H} \\
| \\
\text{H}-\text{C}-\text{OH} \\
| \\
\text{H}-\text{C}-\text{OH} \\
| \\
\text{CH}_2\text{OH}
\end{array}
\qquad
\begin{array}{c}
\text{H} \\
| \\
\text{C}=\text{O} \\
| \\
\text{HO}-\text{C}-\text{H} \\
| \\
\text{H}-\text{C}-\text{OH} \\
| \\
\text{HO}-\text{C}-\text{H} \\
| \\
\text{HO}-\text{C}-\text{H} \\
| \\
\text{CH}_2\text{OH}
\end{array}
$$

D-(+)-glucose   L-(−)-glucose

There are four asymmetric carbon atoms in the molecule (the terminal carbon atoms do not hold four different groups and are not asymmetric). Sixteen optical isomers (eight D,L pairs) of this formula exist; only the preceding pair are called glucose.

D-glucose forms a cyclic molecule by an addition reaction involving the carbonyl group and a hydroxy group.

Ring formation generates a new asymmetric center, and two ring isomers of D-glucose exist which differ in the orientation of the new OH group.

$$\alpha\text{-D-glucose} \qquad \beta\text{-D-glucose}$$

In these diagrams, the carbon atoms of the ring are not shown. The rings are actually puckered, not planar. Notice that in the α form, the OH group of the extreme right-hand carbon atom is on the same side of the ring as the OH group of the adjacent carbon atom; these OH groups may be said to be *cis* to each other. In aqueous solution, α and β forms of D-glucose exist in equilibrium, together with a low concentration of the open-chain form.

Fructose is a hydroxy ketone.

$$
\begin{array}{ccc}
& CH_2OH & & CH_2OH \\
& | & & | \\
& C=O & & C=O \\
& | & & | \\
HO-&C-H & & H-C-OH \\
& | & & | \\
H-&C-OH & & HO-C-H \\
& | & & | \\
H-&C-OH & & HO-C-H \\
& | & & | \\
& CH_2OH & & CH_2OH \\
& \text{D-(−)-fructose} & & \text{L-(+)-fructose}
\end{array}
$$

There are three asymmetric carbon atoms in this molecule and eight stereoisomers (or four D,L pairs) of this formula are known. Cyclic forms of D-fructose are known with five- or six-membered rings.

Glucose and fructose are known as monosaccharides. Sucrose, cane sugar, is a disaccharide. Acid hydrolysis of sucrose yields the two simple sugars D-glucose and D-fructose. In the sucrose molecule, an α D-glucose unit and the β five-membered ring form of a D-fructose unit are joined through two OH groups by the elimination of a molecule of water.

$$\text{D-glucose unit} \qquad \text{D-fructose unit}$$

Cellulose and starch are polysaccharides that yield only D-glucose upon hydrolysis. It is estimated that the number of D-glucose units in the molecular structures of these substances may be as high as several thousand. The D-glucose units of cellulose are linked in long chains in β combination.

The D-glucose units of starch are linked in a different manner; there are occasional cross links between long chains of D-glucose units arranged in α combination.

Starch is an important food material, and cellulose cannot be digested by man—an important distinction brought about by difference in the way that the D-glucose units are linked together.

20.12 Polymers

Starch, cellulose, and proteins are examples of natural **polymers**—molecules of high molecular weight that are formed from simpler molecules, called **monomers**. Important polymers, or **macromolecules**, that do not occur in nature have been synthesized; most of these are linear, or chain-type, structures although some are cross-linked.

Many polymers are formed from compounds that contain carbon–carbon double bonds by a process that is called **addition polymerization**. For example, ethene (ethylene) polymerizes upon heating (100°C–400°C) under high pressure (1000 atm); the product is called polyethylene.

The preceding equation shows the combination of only two molecules of ethene; the actual polymerization process continues, by successive additions of $CH_2=CH_2$ molecules, until chains of hundreds or thousands of $-CH_2-CH_2-$ units are produced. The product, polyethylene, is a tough, waxy solid.

Important polymers have been made from ethene derivatives. Orlon and acrilan are polymers of acrylonitrile, $CH_2=CH-C\equiv N$; the polymers have the structure

$$-CH_2-\underset{\underset{CN}{|}}{CH}\left(CH_2-\underset{\underset{CN}{|}}{CH}\right)_n CH_2-\underset{\underset{CN}{|}}{CH}-$$

Teflon is a polymer of tetrafluoroethene, $CF_2=CF_2$. Vinyl chloride, $CH_2=CHCl$, and vinyl acetate, $CH_2=CH-O-\overset{\overset{O}{\|}}{C}-CH_3$, are important monomers in the preparation of vinyl plastics. Lucite, or Plexiglas, is a polymer of methyl methacrylate, $CH_2=C(CH_3)COOCH_3$.

Natural rubber is a polymer of the diolefin 2-methyl-1,3-butadiene, or isoprene.

$$CH_2=\underset{\underset{CH_3}{|}}{C}-CH=CH_2$$

Such a system of alternating double and single bonds is called a **conjugated system.** Rubber consists of thousands of these units joined in a chain.

$$-CH_2-\underset{\underset{CH_3}{|}}{C}=CH-CH_2\left(CH_2-\underset{\underset{CH_3}{|}}{C}=CH-CH_2\right)_n CH_2-\underset{\underset{CH_3}{|}}{C}=CH-CH_2-$$

Notice that the polymer contains double bonds. Crude rubber is vulcanized by heating with sulfur. It is thought that the sulfur atoms add to some of the double bonds, thereby linking adjacent chains into a complex network. This process adds strength to the final product.

A number of types of synthetic rubber have been made utilizing such monomers as 1,3-butadiene ($CH_2=CH-CH=CH_2$), 2-chloro-1,3-butadiene (chloroprene, $CH_2=C(Cl)-CH=CH_2$), and 2,3-dimethyl-1,3-butadiene ($CH_2=C(CH_3)-C(CH_3)=CH_2$) alone or in combination. The product formed by the polymerization of two different monomers is called a **copolymer;** the molecular structures and properties of such materials depend upon the proportions of the two monomers employed. Buna S rubber is a copolymer of 1,3-butadiene and styrene ($C_6H_5CH=CH_2$). A section of the chain of this material has the structure

$$-CH_2-CH=CH-CH_2-CH-CH_2-$$

An addition polymerization is thought to proceed by either a free-radical or a carbonium-ion chain mechanism. The free-radical type may be initiated by small amounts of hydrogen peroxide or organic peroxides, which are readily split into free radicals (indicated by $Z\cdot$ in the equations that follow).

$$Z_2 \longrightarrow 2Z\cdot$$

A free radical from an initiator combines with one of the π electrons of a molecule of the monomer to form a new free radical.

$$Z\cdot + CH_2=CH_2 \longrightarrow Z-CH_2-CH_2\cdot$$

Chain propagation occurs by the combination of this free radical with another molecule of the monomer

$$Z-CH_2-CH_2\cdot + CH_2=CH_2 \longrightarrow Z-CH_2-CH_2-CH_2-CH_2\cdot$$

and the molecule grows by repeated additions. Chain termination is caused by the combination of two free radicals or by other means, such as the elimination of a hydrogen atom.

A carbonium-ion chain polymerization is initiated by a Lewis acid, such as $AlCl_3$ or BF_3. In the equations that follow, the proton is used to indicate the Lewis-acid, or electrophilic, initiator, although stronger Lewis acids are more frequently employed. Combination of the initiator with a molecule of the monomer produces a carbonium ion.

$$H^+ + CH_2=CH_2 \longrightarrow CH_3-CH_2^+$$

Chain propagation occurs through the combination of the carbonium ion with both π electrons of a molecule of the monomer.

$$CH_3-CH_2^+ + CH_2=CH_2 \longrightarrow CH_3-CH_2-CH_2-CH_2^+$$

Chain termination may occur by the elimination of a proton from a long-chain carbonium ion.

$$CH_3-CH_2(CH_2-CH_2)_nCH_2-CH_2^+ \longrightarrow CH_3-CH_2(CH_2-CH_2)_nCH=CH_2 + H^+$$

Condensation polymerization occurs between molecules of monomers by the elimination of a small molecule, usually water. Proteins and polysaccharides are condensation polymers. Nylon, like the proteins, is a polyamide. It is formed by the condensation of a diamine (such as hexamethylenediamine, $H_2N(CH_2)_6NH_2$) and a dicarboxylic acid (such as adipic acid, $HOOC(CH_2)_4COOH$). The polymerization is accompanied by the loss of water, and the chain has the structure

$$-\underset{\underset{H}{|}}{N}-\underset{\overset{\|}{O}}{C}-(CH_2)_4-\underset{\overset{\|}{O}}{C}-\underset{\underset{H}{|}}{N}-(CH_2)_6-\underset{\underset{H}{|}}{N}-\underset{\overset{\|}{O}}{C}-$$

Dacron is a polyester formed by the elimination of water between ethylene glycol ($HOCH_2CH_2OH$) and a dicarboxylic acid (such as terephthalic acid, $p\text{-}HOOCC_6H_4COOH$).

Bakelite is a cross-linked polymer formed from phenol and formaldehyde by the elimination of water. Notice that the formaldehyde units condense in the *ortho* and *para* positions of phenol.

SOME SUGGESTED READINGS

Benfey, O. T., *From Vital Force to Structural Formulas*, Boston, Houghton Mifflin, 1964 (paper).

Benfey, O. T., *Introduction to Organic Reaction Mechanisms*, New York, McGraw-Hill, 1970 (paper).

Bonner, W. A., and Castro, A. J., *Essentials of Modern Organic Chemistry*, New York, Van Nostrand Reinhold, 1965.

Herz, W., *The Shape of Carbon Compounds: An Introduction to Organic Chemistry*, New York, Benjamin, 1963 (paper).

Morrison, R. T., and Boyd, R. N., *Organic Chemistry*, 2nd ed., Boston, Allyn and Bacon, 1966.

O'Driscoll, K., *The Nature and Chemistry of High Polymers*, New York, Van Nostrand Reinhold, 1964 (paper).

Smith, L. O., Jr., and Cristol, S. J., *Organic Chemistry*, New York, Van Nostrand Reinhold, 1966.

VanderWerf, C. A., *Acids, Bases and the Chemistry of the Covalent Bond*, New York, Van Nostrand Reinhold, 1961 (paper).

Whitfield, R. C., *A Guide to Understanding Basic Organic Reactions*, Boston, Houghton Mifflin, 1966 (paper).

PROBLEMS

The more difficult problems are starred.

20.1 Write structural formulas for the following compounds: (a) 3,5-dimethyl-3-ethyl-4-isopropylheptane, (b) 3-methyl-1,4-pentadiene, (c) 2,2-dibromo-propane, (d) 1,2-diphenylethane, (e) *m*-nitrophenol, (f) 2,2,5,5-tetra-methyl-3-hexyne, (g) 1,2,4-trichlorobenzene.

20.2 Write structural formulas for the following compounds: (a) cyclohexanone, (b) 3-methyl-2-butanone, (c) methyl ethyl ether, (d) methyl ethyl ketone, (e) methyl ethyl amine, (f) aniline, (g) 2,3,4-trimethylpentanoic acid, (h) *n*-propyl acetate.

20.3 Name each of the following compounds:

(a) $CH_3-CH-CH_2-CH-CH_3$
             | |
             CH_3 OH

(d) $CH_3-CH-O-CH_2-CH_3$
            |
            CH_3

(b) OH
          |
   $CH_3-C-CH_2-CH_2-CH_3$
          |
          CH_3

(e) O
            ||
   $CH_3-CH-C-O-CH_3$
         |
         CH_3

(c) O
          ||
   $CH_3-CH-C-CH_2-CH_3$
        |
       CH_3

(f) O
                   ||
   $CH_3-CH-CH_2-CH_2-C-OH$
        |
       CH_3

20.4 What is incorrect about each of the following names? (a) 2-Ethylhexane, (b) 3-methyl-3-pentene, (c) 4-hexyne, (d) 2-methyl-2-hexyne, (e) 3,3-dimethyl-2-hexene, (f) 3-methyl-3-pentanone.

20.5 The general formula for the alkanes is C_nH_{2n+2}. What are the general formulas for the (a) alkenes, (b) alkynes, (c) alkadienes, (d) cycloalkanes, (e) alcohols?

20.6 When the terms primary, secondary, and tertiary are applied to amines, their meanings are not the same as when they are applied to alcohols. Explain the distinction.

20.7 Write structural formulas for all of the isomers that have the formula C_5H_{10}.

20.8 Write structural formulas for all of the isomers that have the formula $C_4H_8Cl_2$.

***20.9** Write structural formulas for all of the isomers that have the formula $C_4H_8O_2$.

20.10 Give examples of each of the following types of isomers: (a) chain, (b) position, (c) functional group, (d) geometric, (e) optical.

20.11 Write structural formulas for all of the isomers of each of the following: (a) dinitrobenzene, (b) trinitrobenzene, (c) chlorodinitrobenzene.

20.12 Write structural formulas for the ten dichloro substitution isomers of naphthalene.

20.13 *Cis-* and *trans*-isomers are known for certain alkenes. Why do not the alkynes display this type of isomerism?

20.14 For which of the following compounds are *cis-* and *trans*-isomers possible? (a) 2,3-Dimethyl-2-butene, (b) 3-methyl-2-pentene, (c) 2-methyl-2-pentene, (d) CH(COOH)=CH(COOH).

20.15 For which of the following are optical isomers possible? (a) 2-Hydroxy-propanoic acid, (b) hydroxyacetic acid, (c) 2-bromo-2-chloropropane, (d) 1-bromo-1-chloroethane, (e) the cyanohydrin prepared from butanone.

20.16 Define the following: (a) olefin, (b) homologous series, (c) cracking, (d) conjugated system, (e) saponification, (f) carbohydrate, (g) cyanohydrin, (h) zwitter ion.

20.17 Why do alcohols have higher boiling points than hydrocarbons of corresponding molecular weight?

20.18 What is the difference between: (a) an amine and an amide, (b) an ester and an ether, (c) a fat and an oil, (d) an aliphatic hydrocarbon and an aromatic hydrocarbon, (e) α-D-glucose and β-D-glucose.

20.19 What is the product of the reaction of bromoethane with (a) OH^-(aq), (b) Mg, (c) NaCN, (d) $NaOCH_2CH_3$, (e) NH_3, (f) CH_3NH_2.

20.20 What are the products when the following compounds are oxidized under vigorous conditions? (a) 2-Pentyne, (b) 2-pentene, (c) 2,3-dimethyl-2-butene, (d) 1-butanol, (e) 2-butanol, (f) butanal, (g) toluene. What are the products when the following compounds are oxidized using mild conditions? (h) 2-pentene, (i) 1-butanol.

20.21 What are the products when the following compounds are reacted with hydrogen in the presence of a suitable catalyst? (a) Butanal, (b) butanone, (c) 2-butene, (d) 2-butyne, (e) propyl cyanide, (f) nitrobenzene.

20.22 State the formulas of all products formed by the reaction of HBr with each of the following. If more than one compound is formed, tell which is produced in the greatest quantity.

(a) CH_3CH_2OH
(b) CH_3CH_2MgBr
(c) $(CH_3CH_2)_2C=CH_2$
(d) $CH_3C\equiv CH$
(e) $CH_3CH_2COO^-Na^+$
(f) $(CH_3CH_2)_2NH$

20.23 State the compound formed when each of the following is treated with aqueous NaOH.

(a) $(CH_3)_2CHCOOH$

(d) $CH_3CH_2CH_2COOCH_2CH_3$

(b) $(CH_3)_2CHBr$

(e) $CH_3CH_2NH_3{}^+Cl^-$

(c) $CH_3CH_2CH_2CN$

20.24 Write equations to show the reactions of NH_3 with each of the following: (a) 2-bromopropane, (b) propanoic acid, (c) methyl propanoate.

20.25 What is the final product (obtained by hydrolysis of the initial product) of the reaction of ethyl magnesium bromide with (a) methanal, (b) butanal, (c) butanone.

20.26 What Grignard reagent and what carbonyl compound should be used to prepare the following alcohols? (a) 3-Methyl-2-butanol, (b) 2-methyl-2-butanol, (c) 2-methyl-1-butanol.

20.27 Write equations to show how the following can be made by means of addition reactions: (a) 1,2-dibromoethane from ethene, (b) 1,1-dibromoethane from acetylene, (c) cyclohexanol from cyclohexene.

20.28 Write equations to show how ethanol may be converted into the following substances. More than one step may be required for a given preparation. (a) Ethene, (b) ethanal, (c) diethyl ether, (d) ethane, (e) acetic acid, (f) bromoethane, (g) ethyl cyanide, (h) 2-hydroxypropanoic acid.

*20.29 Using 1-propanol and 2-propanol as the only organic starting materials, write a series of equations to show how to prepare: (a) 3-hexanol, (b) 2,3-dimethyl-2-butanol, (c) 2-methyl-2-pentanol, (d) 2-methyl-3-pentanol. Use a Grignard reaction as one of the steps in each preparation.

*20.30 Write structural formulas for the compounds indicated by Roman numerals in the following sequence: (a) $CH_3CH_2OH \xrightarrow[200°C]{H_2SO_4}$ I, (b) I $\xrightarrow{Br_2}$ II, (c) II $\xrightarrow{NaCN}$ III, (d) III $\xrightarrow{NaOH}$ IV, (e) III $\xrightarrow{H_2/Ni}$ V, (f) IV + V → VI.

*20.31 Write structural formulas for the compounds indicated by Roman numerals in the following sequence: (a) 2-methylpropanal $\xrightarrow{H_2/Pt}$ I, (b) I $\xrightarrow[200°C]{H_2SO_4}$ II, (c) II $\xrightarrow{HBr}$ III, (d) III $\xrightarrow{OH^-(aq)}$ IV.

20.32 Write an equation to show how a soap may be made from a fat.

20.33 Why are vegetable oils hydrogenated? What occurs chemically in the process?

20.34 Valine is 2-amino-3-methylbutanoic acid. Write the structural formula of a polypeptide containing three valine units.

20.35 What is the difference in meaning between the designations D and (+) as applied to amino acids?

20.36 Describe, with examples: (a) addition polymers, (b) copolymers, (c) condensation polymers.

20.37 (a) What is Markovnikov's rule? (b) How does the mechanism of the addition of HBr to an alkene explain why such an addition follows Markovnikov's rule?

20.38 Compare and contrast the mechanism of a substitution reaction of an alkane with the mechanism of a substitution reaction of an aromatic hydrocarbon.

20.39 Interpret the following in terms of the Lewis theory: (a) an S_N1 reaction of a alkyl halide, (b) an S_N2 reaction of an alcohol, (c) the addition of HBr to an olefin, (d) the addition of HCN to a ketone.

20.40 Describe the function of $AlCl_3$ in (a) a Friedel-Crafts reaction, (b) a polymerization.

20.41 Arrange the following compounds in decreasing order of strength as Brønsted acids: CH_3CH_2OH, $CH_3CH_2OH_2{}^+$, H_2O, H_3O^+, CH_3COOH, $CH_3CH_2NH_2$.

20.42 Arrange the following compounds in decreasing order of strength as Brønsted bases: CH_3CH_2OH, $CH_3CH_2O^-$, OH^-, CH_3COO^-, $CH_3CH_2NH_2$.

20.43 Draw the resonance structures of (a) benzene, (b) naphthalene, (c) the acetate ion.

20.44 (a) Why is phenol a stronger acid then methanol? (b) Why is aniline a weaker base than methylamine?

20.45 Cite a compound in which carbon may be assumed to employ the following: (a) *sp* hybrid orbitals, (b) sp^2 hybrid orbitals, (c) sp^3 hybrid orbitals.

*20.46 (a) What quantity of ethyl acetate is, in theory, obtainable from a preparation employing 30.0 g of ethanol and 30.0 g of acetic acid? (b) If 30.0 g of ethyl acetate is isolated, what percent of the theoretical yield was obtained?

*20.47 (a) A 3.00 g sample of tartaric acid is burned in oxygen; 1.79 liters of CO_2 (measured at STP) and 1.08 g of H_2O are collected from the combustion. Tartaric acid contains only carbon, hydrogen, and oxygen. What is the empirical formula of this compound? (b) A mixture of 0.050 g of tartaric acid and 0.50 g of camphor melts at 153°C. The melting point of pure camphor is 179°C, and the molal freezing point depression constant is 39.7°/m. What is the molecular formula of tartaric acid? (c) A 0.300 g sample of pure tartaric acid requires 25.0 ml of 0.160N NaOH for complete neutralization. What is the equivalent weight of the acid? (d) Draw a structural formula for tartaric acid consistent with the data given in this problem.

21

NUCLEAR CHEMISTRY

Ordinary chemical reactions involve only the extranuclear electrons; in such reactions, the nucleus is important only insofar as it influences the electrons. However, matter does undergo important transformations that involve the nucleus directly. The study of nuclear reactions and radioactivity has enlarged our understanding of the nature of matter and the courses of chemical and biological processes, and many technological applications have been developed as a result of these investigations.

21.1 The Nucleus

The nuclei of atoms are thought to contain protons and neutrons, particles that are collectively called **nucleons.** The number of protons in a specific atomic nucleus corresponds to the atomic number (or nuclear charge), Z, and the total number of nucleons is given by the mass number, A. Thus the number of neutrons equals $(A-Z)$. This information is indicated on the chemical symbol of a given nuclide by appending the atomic number as a subscript and the mass number as a superscript. The symbols for the two naturally occurring isotopes of lithium are

$$_3^6\text{Li} \quad \text{and} \quad _3^7\text{Li}$$

Much is known about the structure of the nucleus, but much more remains to be learned. Determination of the radii of a large number of atomic nuclei show that the radius of a given nucleus, r, is directly related to the cube root of its mass number.

$$r = (1.3 \times 10^{-13} \text{ cm})A^{1/3}$$

The volume of a sphere is $\frac{4}{3}\pi r^3$, and, if we assume a spherical nucleus, it follows that nuclear volume varies directly with mass number. In other words, the mass of a nucleus determines its volume, and nuclear density is, therefore, approximately constant for all atomic nuclei. This density is about 2.44×10^{14} g/cm^3, an amazingly high value; 1 cm^3 of this nuclear matter would weigh more than 250 million tons.

The density of a liquid is constant and independent of the size of any drop considered. Since all nuclei have approximately the same density, a fluid-droplet model of the nucleus has been proposed. The nature of the cohesive forces holding the nucleons into a nuclear fluid is far from completely understood.

It is clear that powerful cohesive forces between nucleons exist and that they effectively overcome the electrostatic forces of repulsion between the protons of the nucleus. The attractive forces between nucleons are charge independent, that is, proton–proton, proton–neutron, and neutron–neutron attractions are identical. The range of the force is believed to be on the order of 2×10^{-13} cm, the diameter of a nucleon.

In 1935, Hidekei Yukawa postulated that neutrons and protons are bound together by the very rapid exchange of a nuclear particle, later identified as a π meson, or pion. Three types of pions are known to exist: positive, π^+, negative, π^-, and neutral, π^0. According to the exchange theory, a neutron, n_A^0, is converted into a proton, p_A^+, by the emission of a negative pion. The emitted π^- is accepted by a proton, p_B^+, which is converted into a neutron, n_B^0.

$$n_A^0 \longrightarrow p_A^+ + \pi^-$$

$$\pi^- + p_B^+ \longrightarrow n_B^0$$

If we consider the deuterium nucleus, which consists of one proton and one neutron, this exchange then reverses, the neutron n_B^0 becoming a proton, p_B^+, and the proton p_A^+ becoming a neutron, n_A^0. The exchange is extremely rapid; approximately 10^{24} transfers occur in one second.

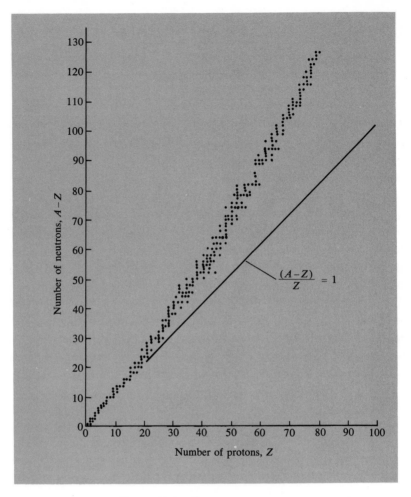

Figure 21.1 Neutron/proton ratio.

The same type of interaction can be postulated for the positive pion,

$$p_A^+ \longrightarrow n_A^0 + \pi^+$$

$$\pi^+ + n_B^0 \longrightarrow p_B^+$$

or the neutral pion,

$$p_A^+ \longrightarrow p_A^+ + \pi^0$$

$$\pi^0 + n_B^0 \longrightarrow n_B^0$$

The exchange of a neutral pion can also be used to account for the existence of neutron–neutron and proton–proton forces.

In Figure 21.1, the number of neutrons is plotted against the number of protons for the naturally occurring, nonradioactive nuclei. The points, representing stable combinations of protons and neutrons, lie in what may be called a **zone of stability.** Nuclei that have compositions represented by points that lie outside of this zone spontaneously undergo radioactive transformations that tend to bring their compositions into, or closer to, this zone (Section 21.2).

The stable nuclei of the lighter elements contain approximately equal numbers of neutrons and protons, a neutron/proton ratio of 1. The heavier nuclei contain more neutrons than protons. With increasing atomic number, more and more protons are packed into a tiny nucleus, and the electrostatic forces of repulsion increase sharply. A larger and larger excess of neutrons is required to diminish the effect of these repulsion forces, and the neutron/proton ratio increases with increasing atomic number until the ratio is approximately 1.5 at the end of the curve of Figure 21.1. There appears to be an upper limit to the number of protons that can be packed into a nucleus, no matter how many neutrons are present. The largest stable nucleus is $^{209}_{83}Bi$; nuclei that are larger than this exist, but all of them are radioactive.

Most naturally occurring stable nuclides have an even number of protons and an even number of neutrons; only five ($^{2}_{1}H$, $^{6}_{3}Li$, $^{10}_{5}B$, $^{14}_{7}N$, and $^{180}_{73}Ta$) have an odd number of protons and an odd number of neutrons (Table 21.1).

Table 21.1

Distribution of Naturally Occurring Stable Nuclides

Protons	Neutrons	Number of Nuclides	
even	even	157	⎫ 209
even	odd	52	⎭
odd	even	50	⎫ 55
odd	odd	5	⎭

For each odd atomic number, there are never more than two stable nuclides, whereas for an even atomic number, as many as ten stable nuclides may occur. The two elements of atomic number less than 83 that have never been proven to be naturally existing ($_{43}Tc$ and $_{61}Pm$) have odd atomic numbers. Empirical observations such as these suggest that there is a periodicity in nuclear structure similar to the periodicity of atomic structure, and a nuclear shell model, as yet incompletely developed, has been suggested.

Periodic variations are observed in many nuclear properties. Certain nuclides have relatively high binding energies (indicative of comparatively great stability; Sections 2.9 and 21.7) compared to nuclides of close atomic number or mass number. Exceptional nuclear stability is also shown by certain nuclides that have a poor ability to capture neutrons (Section 21.5).

Comparison of data from these and other studies of nuclear properties indicates that unusual nuclear stability is associated with nuclides having either a number of protons, or a number of neutrons, equal to a magic number: 2, 8, 20, 28, 50, 82, and 126. It is thought that the magic numbers indicate closed nuclear shells in the same way that the atomic numbers of the noble gases: 2, 10, 18, 36, 54, and 86, indicate stable electronic configurations. In general, elements that have an atomic number equal to a magic number have a larger number of stable isotopes than neighboring elements. The nuclides with a magic number of protons as well as a magic number of neutrons, $_2^4$He, $_8^{16}$O, $_{20}^{40}$Ca, and $_{82}^{208}$Pb, have notably high stabilities in terms of such factors as neutron capture (Section 21.5), binding energy (Section 21.6), and relative abundance.

21.2 Radioactivity

Unstable nuclei spontaneously undergo certain changes that result in the attainment of more stable nuclear compositions. Some unstable nuclides are naturally occurring; others are man-made. Certain synthetic radioactive nuclides undergo some types of radioactive decay that have not been observed for any naturally occurring unstable nuclide.

Alpha emission consists of the ejection of α particles, which have an atomic number of 2 and a mass number of 4 and may be considered to be $_2^4$He nuclei. Both synthetic and natural nuclides undergo α decay, which is common only for nuclides of mass number greater than 209 and atomic number greater than 82. Nuclides such as these have too many protons for stability; points indicating the composition of these nuclides fall outside the plot of Figure 21.1, to the upper right, beyond the zone of stability. The emission of α particles reduces the number of protons by two and the number of neutrons by two and adjusts the composition of the nucleus downward, closer to the stability zone.

An example of α decay is

$$_{84}^{210}\text{Po} \longrightarrow {}_{82}^{206}\text{Pb} + {}_2^4\text{He}$$

Notice that the equation indicates the conservation of mass number (superscripts) and atomic number (subscripts). Equations such as these are written to indicate nuclear changes only; the extranuclear electrons are customarily ignored. An α particle is emitted as a $_2^4$He nucleus, without electrons, and with a 2+ charge. Subsequent to its emission, however, the particle attracts electrons from other atoms (which become cations), and the α particle becomes a neutral atom of $_2^4$He. The $_{82}^{206}$Pb is left, therefore, with a surplus of two electrons and a 2− charge; these excess electrons are rapidly lost to surrounding cations.

The energy released in this process is readily calculated in the same way that binding energy is calculated (Section 2.9); it is the energy equivalent of the difference in mass between the reactant (parent nucleus) and products (daughter nucleus and α particle). The masses of neutral *atoms*, rather than the masses of *nuclei*, are generally recorded, but this causes no trouble in the calculation. If the mass of the $^{210}_{84}$Po *atom* is used, the mass of 84 electrons is included; for the products, the mass of the $^{206}_{82}$Pb *atom* includes the mass of 82 electrons, and the mass of the $^4_2$He *atom* includes the mass of two electrons. Thus the masses of the extranuclear electrons cancel when atomic masses are employed for the calculation.

$$(\text{mass } ^{210}_{84}\text{Po}) - (\text{mass } ^{206}_{82}\text{Pb} + \text{mass } ^4_2\text{He})$$

$$209.9829 \text{ u} - (205.9745 \text{ u} + 4.0026 \text{ u}) = 0.0058 \text{ u}$$

The energy equivalent of this mass difference may be calculated by means of Einstein's equation, $E = mc^2$. The energy unit customarily employed is the Mev (million electron volts). An electron volt (ev) is the energy acquired by an electron when it is accelerated through a potential difference of 1 v; it is the unit we employed in discussing ionization potentials (Section 3.2). The energy equivalent of 1 u is 931.478 Mev, and therefore the energy released by the α decay of $^{210}_{84}$Po is

$$0.0058 \text{ u} \times 931 \text{ Mev/u} = 5.4 \text{ Mev}$$

If the daughter nucleus in an α-decay process is left in the ground state, the kinetic energy of the emitted α particle accounts for most of the energy released, and the kinetic energy of the recoiling daughter nucleus accounts for the remainder. If all the daughter nuclei are left in the ground state, all the α particles emitted have the same energy. In some α-decay processes, however, several energy groups of α particles are emitted. In these cases, the α particles of highest energy correspond to daughter nuclei in the ground state, and the α particles of lower energy originate from nuclei left in excited states. A nucleus in an excited state subsequently emits energy, in the form of γ radiation, to reach the ground state, and the sum of the kinetic energy of the α particle, the recoil energy of the daughter nucleus, and the energy of the γ radiation equals the decay energy.

Gamma radiation is electromagnetic radiation of very short wavelength; its emission is caused by energy changes within the nucleus, and its emission alone does not cause changes in the mass number or the atomic number of the nucleus. At times, nuclides are produced in excited states by nuclear reactions (Section 21.5), and such nuclides revert to their ground states by the emission of the excess energy in the form of γ radiation.

$$[^{125}_{52}\text{Te}]^* \longrightarrow ^{125}_{52}\text{Te} + \gamma$$

excited state   ground state

The γ rays emitted by a specific nucleus have a definite energy value, or set of energy values, because they correspond to transitions between discrete energy levels of the nucleus. Thus an emission spectrum of γ radiation is analogous to the line spectrum that results from transitions of electrons between energy levels in an excited atom.

Gamma radiation frequently accompanies all other types of radioactive decay. The following α-decay process is an example.

$$^{240}_{94}\text{Pu} \longrightarrow [^{236}_{92}\text{U}]^* + ^4_2\text{He}$$

$$[^{236}_{92}\text{U}]^* \longrightarrow ^{236}_{92}\text{U} + \gamma$$

In cases such as this, deductions can be made concerning the energy levels of the daughter nucleus. The emission of a 5.16 Mev α particle results directly in the production of $^{236}_{92}\text{U}$ in the ground state; no γ radiation accompanies such α particles. However, for the process outlined in the set of equations, a 5.12 Mev α particle is emitted along with a 0.04 Mev γ ray. It is assumed that the energy of the γ ray corresponds to the energy difference between the ground state and the first excited state of $^{236}_{92}\text{U}$. Alpha particles of other energies are also emitted, and the complete analysis of these energies results in a more detailed picture of the energy levels of the $^{236}_{92}\text{U}$ nucleus.

Beta emission is observed for nuclides that have too high a neutron/proton ratio for stability; points representing such nuclides lie to the left of the zone of stability of Figure 21.1. The β particle is an electron, indicated $_{-1}^{0}e$, which may be considered to result from the transformation of a nuclear neutron into a nuclear proton; electrons, as such, do not exist in the nucleus. The net effect of β emission is that the number of neutrons is decreased by 1 and the number of protons is increased by 1. Thus the neutron/proton ratio is decreased; the mass number does not change.

Beta decay is a very common mode of radioactive disintegration and is observed for both natural and synthetic nuclides. Examples include

$$^{186}_{73}\text{Ta} \longrightarrow ^{186}_{74}\text{W} + _{-1}^{0}e$$

$$^{82}_{35}\text{Br} \longrightarrow ^{82}_{36}\text{Kr} + _{-1}^{0}e$$

$$^{27}_{12}\text{Mg} \longrightarrow ^{27}_{13}\text{Al} + _{-1}^{0}e$$

$$^{14}_{6}\text{C} \longrightarrow ^{14}_{7}\text{N} + _{-1}^{0}e$$

Notice that the sums of the subscripts and superscripts on the right side of the equation equal the subscript and superscript of the parent nucleus on the left.

The last equation represents the mode of decay of the radioactive carbon isotope that is present in small amount in the atmosphere. The energy released by this process may be calculated by using atomic masses instead of nuclear masses. If we add six orbital electrons to both sides of the equation, we have the equivalent of the *atomic* mass of $^{14}_{6}C$ (which includes the mass of six electrons) on the left and, taking into account the electron ejected as a β particle, the equivalent of the *atomic* mass of $^{14}_{7}N$ (which includes the mass of seven electrons) on the right. Therefore,

$$(\text{mass } ^{14}_{6}C) - (\text{mass } ^{14}_{7}N)$$

$$14.00324 \text{ u} - 14.00307 \text{ u} = 0.00017 \text{ u} = 0.16 \text{ Mev}$$

In β decay, the recoil energy of the daughter nucleus is negligible, since the ejected electron has a small mass. One would expect that the decay energy would be taken up by the kinetic energy of the β particle and that all the β particles emitted would have energies corresponding to this value. Instead, however, a continuous spectrum of β-particle energies is observed with the highest energy almost equal to the decay energy. It is postulated that when a β particle of less than maximum energy is ejected, a **neutrino**, v, that carries off the excess energy is emitted at the same time.

$$^{14}_{6}C \longrightarrow ^{14}_{7}N + _{-1}^{0}e + v$$

The neutrino is assumed to be a chargeless particle of a vanishingly small mass.

Unstable nuclides that have neutron/proton ratios below those required for stability (points below the zone of stability of Figure 21.1) do not occur in nature. Many such artificial nuclides are known, however, and two types of radioactive processes are observed that increase the neutron/proton ratio of this type of nuclide; positron emission and electron capture.

Positron emission, or β^+ emission, consists of the ejection of a positive electron, called a positron and indicated $^{0}_{1}e$, from the nucleus. A positron has the same mass as an electron but an opposite charge; it arises from the conversion of a nuclear proton into a neutron. Positron emission results in a decrease of *one* in the number of protons and an increase of *one* in the number of neutrons; no change in mass number occurs. Hence, positron emission raises the numerical value of the neutron/proton ratio.

Examples of this mode of radioactive decay include

$$^{122}_{53}I \longrightarrow ^{122}_{52}Te + ^{0}_{1}e$$

$$^{38}_{19}K \longrightarrow ^{38}_{18}Ar + ^{0}_{1}e$$

$$^{23}_{12}Mg \longrightarrow ^{23}_{11}Na + ^{0}_{1}e$$

$$^{15}_{8}O \longrightarrow ^{15}_{7}N + ^{0}_{1}e$$

We can use atomic masses to calculate the energy released by the process described by the last equation. If we add eight orbital electrons to both sides of the equation, the equivalent of the atomic mass of $^{15}_{8}O$ (eight electrons) would be indicated on the left. The equivalent of the atomic mass of $^{15}_{7}N$

(seven electrons) plus the mass of one orbital electron (making up the eight added) plus the mass of the ejected positron would be indicated on the right. Thus the mass difference is

$$(\text{mass } {}^{15}_{8}O) - (\text{mass } {}^{15}_{7}N + \text{mass } {}_{-1}^{0}e + \text{mass } {}^{0}_{1}e)$$

Since the mass of a positron is identical to that of an electron,

$$(\text{mass } {}^{15}_{8}O) - [\text{mass } {}^{15}_{7}N + 2(\text{mass } {}_{-1}^{0}e)]$$

$$15.00308 \text{ u} - [15.00011 \text{ u} + 2(0.00055 \text{ u})]$$

$$15.00308 \text{ u} - 15.00121 \text{ u} = 0.00187 \text{ u} = 1.74 \text{ Mev}$$

For spontaneous positron emission, the atomic mass of the parent must exceed the atomic mass of the daughter by at least 0.00110 u, the mass of two electrons.

In positron emission, a spectrum of β^{+} energies is observed similar to that observed for β emission, and the simultaneous ejection of neutrinos is postulated.

$$ {}^{15}_{8}O \longrightarrow {}^{15}_{7}N + {}^{0}_{1}e + \nu $$

The positron was the first antiparticle to be observed. It is similar to the electron in all respects, except charge. When a positron and an electron collide, they annihilate each other, and γ radiation equivalent to the masses of the two particles is produced. It is believed that antiparticles exist for all particles except the neutral pion, π^{0}, and the photon. The negative proton (antiproton) has been detected; the annihilation of proton with antiproton usually produces several high-energy pions. Since the antineutron, like the neutron, has no charge, its detection rests on annihilation phenomena.

Electron capture (ec), sometimes called K capture, is another process through which the neutron/proton ratio of an unstable, proton-rich, nuclide may be increased. Unlike positron emission, electron capture can occur when the mass difference between parent and daughter does not exceed 0.00110 u. In this process, the nucleus captures an orbital electron from the K or L shell, and the captured electron converts a nuclear proton into a neutron. The transformation results in a daughter nuclide with *one* less proton and *one* more neutron than the parent; consequently, the atomic number of the daughter is *one* less than that of the parent, and the mass number does not change. Examples are

$$ {}_{-1}^{0}e + {}^{197}_{80}Hg \xrightarrow{\text{ec}} {}^{197}_{79}Au $$

$$ {}_{-1}^{0}e + {}^{106}_{47}Ag \xrightarrow{\text{ec}} {}^{106}_{46}Pd $$

$$ {}_{-1}^{0}e + {}^{37}_{18}Ar \xrightarrow{\text{ec}} {}^{37}_{17}Cl $$

$$_{-1}^{0}e + {}_{4}^{7}\text{Be} \xrightarrow{\text{ec}} {}_{3}^{7}\text{Li}$$

$$_{-1}^{0}e + {}_{26}^{55}\text{Fe} \xrightarrow{\text{ec}} {}_{25}^{55}\text{Mn}$$

The energy released can be calculated directly from the atomic masses of the parent and daughter. Thus, for the last example,

$$(\text{mass } {}_{26}^{55}\text{Fe}) - (\text{mass } {}_{25}^{55}\text{Mn})$$

$$54.93830 \text{ u} - 54.93805 \text{ u} = 0.00025 \text{ u} = 0.23 \text{ Mev}$$

The recoil energy of the daughter nucleus is negligible, and if the daughter nucleus is left in the ground state, all the available energy is carried away by a neutrino that is ejected in the process. In addition, electron capture is accompanied by the production of X rays. The capture of an orbital electron leaves a vacancy in the K or L shell, and when an outer electron falls into this vacancy, X-ray emission follows (Section 2.12).

21.3 Rate of Radioactive Decay

Many techniques are employed to study the emissions of radioactive substances. Radiations from these materials affect photographic film in the same way that ordinary light does. In fact, radioactivity was discovered in 1896 by Henri Becquerel when he noticed that a photographic plate that had been placed in a drawer with uranium minerals had become fogged. Photographic techniques for the qualitative and quantitative detection of radiation are employed, but they are not very accurate nor are they suitable for rapid analysis.

The energy of emissions from radioactive sources are absorbed by some materials (e.g., zinc sulfide) and transformed into radiant energy of visible wavelength. The zinc sulfide is said to **fluoresce**, and a little flash of light may be observed from the impact of each particle from the radiactive source. This property has been put to use in an instrument known as a **scintillation counter**. The window of a sensitive photoelectric tube is coated with ZnS, and the flash of light emitted by the ZnS when it is struck by a particle causes a pulse of electric current to pass through the photoelectric tube. These signals are amplified and made to operate various kinds of counting devices.

The **Wilson cloud chamber** enables the path of ionizing radiation to be seen. The chamber contains air saturated with water vapor. By the movement of a piston, the air in the chamber is suddenly expanded and cooled; this causes droplets of water to condense on the ions that are formed by the particles as they move through the vapor, and makes the paths of the particles visible. Photographs of these cloud tracks may be made and studied. Such photographs

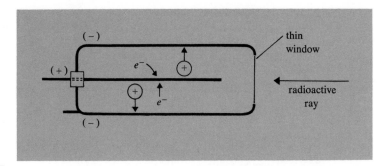

Figure 21.2   Essential features of a Geiger-Müller counter tube.

provide information on the length of the paths, collisions undergone by the particles, the speed of the particles, and the effects of external forces on the behavior of the particles.

The essential features of a **Geiger-Müller counter** are diagramed in Figure 21.2. The radiation enters the tube through a thin window. As a particle or a γ ray traverses the tube, which contains argon gas, it knocks electrons off the argon atoms in its path and forms Ar^+ ions. A potential of about 1000 to 1200 v is applied between the electrodes of the tube, and the electrons and Ar^+ ions cause a pulse of electric current to flow through the circuit. This pulse is amplified to cause a clicker to sound or an automatic counting device to operate.

The rates of decay of all radioactive substances have been found to be of first order (Section 14.5) and independent of temperature. This lack of temperature dependence implies that the activation energy of any radioactive-decay process is zero. The rate of decay, therefore, depends upon the amount of radioactive material present—a relationship similar to the rate at which money accumulates at compound interest, with the distinction that radio-active decay represents a loss, not an accumulation. We may express this relationship as

$$-\frac{\Delta N}{\Delta t} = kN$$

where N is the number of atoms of radioactive material; t is time; and k is the rate constant; the rate expression is negative because it represents the disappearance of the radioactive substance.

Rearrangement of the rate expression gives

$$-\frac{\Delta N}{N} = k\Delta t$$

which states that the fraction lost $(-\Delta N/N)$ in a given time interval (Δt) is directly proportional to the length of the time interval. Therefore the time required for half of the sample to decay (the **half-life,** $t_{1/2}$) is a constant.

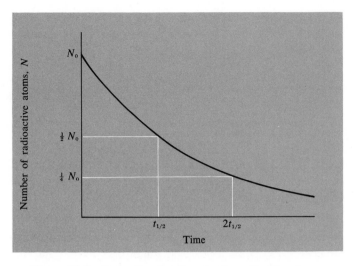

Figure 21.3 Curve showing the rate of a radioactive decay.

The curve of Figure 21.3, showing number of radioactive atoms versus time, is typical of first-order processes. After a single half-life period has elapsed, one-half of the original number of atoms remain ($\frac{1}{2}N_0$). This number is reduced by half (to $\frac{1}{4}N_0$) by the time that another half-life has passed. Each radioactive isotope has a characteristic half-life, and these vary widely; for example, $^{5}_{3}$Li has a half-life estimated to be 10^{-21} sec, and $^{238}_{92}$U has a half-life of 4.51×10^9 years.

The rate equation may be written in its differential form,

$$-\frac{dN}{dt} = kN$$

and by means of the calculus, this equation may be integrated,

$$-2.303 \log\left(\frac{N}{N_0}\right) = kt$$

where N_0 is the amount present at time zero, and N is the amount present at time t. The last equation may be rearranged to give

$$\log\left(\frac{N_0}{N}\right) = \frac{kt}{2.303}$$

An expression for the half-life may be derived by allowing

$$N = \tfrac{1}{2}N_0$$

$$\frac{N_0}{N} = 2$$

Therefore,

$$\log 2 = \frac{k(t_{1/2})}{2.303}$$

$$t_{1/2} = \frac{2.303 \log 2}{k} = \frac{0.693}{k}$$

According to the rate law, a radioactive substance never completely disappears. However, the rate law describes the behavior of a sample containing a large number of atoms. When the number of atoms in the sample declines to a very small value, the rate law is no longer followed exactly. How can a fraction of an atom disintegrate?

▶ **EXAMPLE 21.1**   The isotope $^{60}_{27}Co$ has a half-life of 5.27 years. What amount of a 0.0100 g sample of $^{60}_{27}Co$ remains after 1.00 year?

Solution   The rate constant for this disintegration is

$$k = \frac{0.693}{t_{1/2}}$$

$$= \frac{0.693}{5.27 \text{ years}} = 0.132/\text{year}$$

The fraction remaining undecomposed at the end of 1.00 year may be found in the following way.

$$\log \left(\frac{N_0}{N} \right) = \frac{kt}{2.30}$$

$$= \frac{(0.132/\text{year})(1.00 \text{ year})}{2.30} = 0.0573$$

$$\log \left(\frac{N}{N_0} \right) = -0.0573$$

$$\frac{N}{N_0} = 0.876$$

Therefore the amount remaining after 1.00 year is

$$0.876 \times 0.0100 \text{ g} = 0.0088 \text{ g}$$

The radioactive isotope $^{14}_{6}C$ is produced in the atmosphere by the action of cosmic-ray neutrons on $^{14}_{7}N$.

$$^{14}_{7}N + ^{1}_{0}n \longrightarrow ^{14}_{6}C + ^{1}_{1}H$$

The $^{14}_{6}C$ is oxidized to CO_2, and this radioactive CO_2 mixes with non-radioactive CO_2. The radiocarbon disappears through radioactive decay, but it is also constantly being made. The steady state is reached when the proportion is one atom of $^{14}_{6}C$ to 10^{12} ordinary carbon atoms, which represents 15.3 ± 0.1 disintegrations per minute per gram of carbon.

The CO_2 of the atmosphere is absorbed by plants through the process of photosynthesis, and the ratio of $^{14}_{6}C$ to ordinary carbon in plant materials that are alive and growing is the same ratio as that in the atmosphere. When the plant dies, however, the amount of $^{14}_{6}C$ diminishes through radioactive decay and is not replenished by the assimilation of atmospheric CO_2 by the plant.

The half-life of $^{14}_{6}C$, a β emitter, is 5770 years. The age of a wooden object can be determined by comparing the radiocarbon activity of the object with that of growing trees. This method of **radiocarbon dating** has been applied to many archeological finds and objects of historical interest. By this means, the Dead Sea scrolls were determined to be 1917 ± 200 years old.

▶ **EXAMPLE 21.2** A sample of carbon from a wooden artifact is found to give 700 $^{14}_{6}C$ counts per minute per gram of carbon. What is the approximate age of the artifact?

Solution The half-life of $^{14}_{6}C$ is 5770 years. Therefore,

$$k = \frac{0.693}{t_{1/2}}$$

$$= \frac{0.693}{5770 \text{ years}} = 1.20 \times 10^{-4}/\text{year}$$

The $^{14}_{6}C$ from wood recently cut down decays at the rate of 15.3 disintegrations per minute per gram of carbon. Therefore,

$$\log\left(\frac{N_0}{N}\right) = \frac{kt}{2.30}$$

$$\log\left(\frac{15.3 \text{ disintegrations/min}}{7.00 \text{ disintegrations/min}}\right) = \frac{(1.20 \times 10^{-4}/\text{year})t}{2.30}$$

$$t = \frac{2.30 \log 2.19}{1.20 \times 10^{-4}/\text{year}} = 6520 \text{ years}$$

The amount of radiation emanating from a source per unit time is termed the **activity** of the source.

$$\text{activity} = -\frac{dN}{dt} = kN$$

Activities are generally expressed in curies; 1 curie (c) is defined as 3.70×10^{10} disintegrations per second, and 1 microcurie (μc) is 3.70×10^4 disintegrations per second.

▶ **EXAMPLE 21.3**　The half-life of $^{100}_{43}$Tc, a β emitter, is 16 sec. How many atoms of $^{100}_{43}$Tc are present in a sample with an activity of 0.200 μc? What is the weight of the sample?

Solution　For this radioactive decay, the rate constant, k, is

$$k = \frac{0.693}{t_{1/2}}$$

$$= \frac{0.693}{16 \text{ sec}} = 0.0433/\text{sec}$$

The activity of the sample in terms of disintegrations per second is

$$0.200(3.70 \times 10^4 \text{ disintegrations/sec}) = 7.40 \times 10^3 \text{ disintegrations/sec}$$

This represents the decay of 7.40×10^3 atoms/sec and

$$\text{activity} = kN$$

$$(7.40 \times 10^3 \text{ atoms/sec}) = (4.33 \times 10^{-2}/\text{sec})N$$

$$N = 1.71 \times 10^5 \text{ atoms}$$

The weight of the sample can be derived from the fact that the atomic weight of ^{100}Tc to three significant figures is 100; thus,

$$? \text{ g Tc} = 1.71 \times 10^5 \text{ atoms Tc} \left(\frac{100 \text{ g Tc}}{6.02 \times 10^{23} \text{ atoms Tc}} \right)$$

$$= 2.84 \times 10^{-19} \text{ g Tc}$$

21.4　Radioactive Disintegration Series

The examples of α, β^-, and β^+ emission and of electron capture given in Section 21.2 are one-step processes that lead to stable nuclides. Frequently, however, the daughter nucleus produced by a radioactive process is itself radioactive. The repetition of this situation creates a chain, or series, of disintegration processes involving many radioactive nuclides and leading ultimately to the production of a stable nuclide.

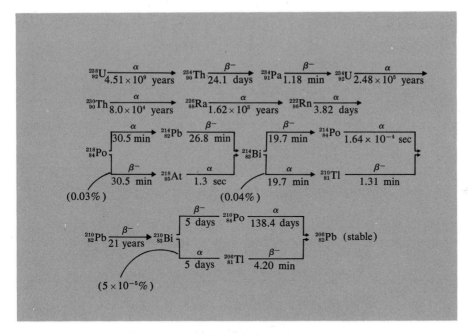

Figure 21.4 Disintegration series of $^{238}_{92}$U. Half-lives of isotopes are indicated.

Three such **disintegration series**, involving only α and β emission, occur in nature: the $^{232}_{90}$Th, $^{238}_{92}$U, and $^{235}_{92}$U series. The $^{238}_{92}$U series, which leads finally to the stable nuclide $^{206}_{82}$Pb, is diagrammed in Figure 21.4. In several places in the series, branching occurs, and the series proceeds by two different routes. The branches, however, always rejoin at a later point, and commonly one branch is preferred over the other (note the percentage figures in Figure 21.4). By any given route, the $^{238}_{92}$U series consists of 14 steps—8 involving α decay, and 6 involving β decay.

The radioactive nuclides that occur in nature are those that have very long half-lives or those that are constantly being produced by the disintegration of other nuclides. This last type of naturally occurring radioactive nuclide eventually exists in a steady state at which time the amount of the nuclide remains essentially constant because the material is being produced at the same rate that it is decomposing.

The natural disintegration series serve as the basis of a method of geological dating. A sample of rock may be analyzed for its $^{206}_{82}$Pb and $^{238}_{92}$U content, and the length of time to produce this ratio of lead to uranium may be calculated from the decay constants of the series. Results from studies such as these place the age of some rocks at from 3 to 3.5 billion years; the age of the earth is estimated to be 4.5 billion years.

Decay series, some more elaborate than others, are known for artificial nuclides. Positron emission and K capture are observed in some of these series as well as α and β emission. Following are three examples of simple, two-step, disintegration series of artificial nuclides.

$$^{20}_{8}O \xrightarrow[14 \text{ sec}]{\beta^-} {}^{20}_{9}F \xrightarrow[11 \text{ sec}]{\beta^-} {}^{20}_{10}Ne$$

$$^{30}_{16}S \xrightarrow[1.4 \text{ sec}]{\beta^+} {}^{30}_{15}P \xrightarrow[2.6 \text{ min}]{\beta^+} {}^{30}_{14}Si$$

$$^{76}_{36}Kr \xrightarrow[10 \text{ hours}]{ec} {}^{76}_{35}Br \xrightarrow[16.5 \text{ hours}]{\beta^+ \text{ or ec}} {}^{76}_{34}Se$$

21.5   Nuclear Reactions

In 1915, Ernest Rutherford reported that the following transformation occurs when α particles, from $^{214}_{84}Po$, are passed through nitrogen.

$$^{14}_{7}N + {}^{4}_{2}He \longrightarrow {}^{17}_{8}O + {}^{1}_{1}H$$

This was the first artificial transmutation of one element into another to be reported; in the years following, thousands of such nuclear transformations have been studied. It is assumed that the projectile (in this case, an α particle) forms a compound nucleus with the target ($^{14}_{7}N$) and that the compound nucleus very rapidly ejects a subsidiary particle ($^{1}_{1}H$) to form the product nucleus ($^{17}_{8}O$). Other projectiles, such as neutrons, deuterons ($^{2}_{1}H$), protons, and ions of low atomic number, are used in addition to α particles.

Particle-particle reactions are usually classified according to the type of projectile employed and the subsidiary particle ejected. Thus the preceding reaction is called an (α, p) reaction, and the complete transformation is indicated by the notation $^{14}_{7}N$ (α, p) $^{17}_{8}O$. Examples of several of the more common types of nuclear transformations are listed in Table 21.2.

Table 21.2

Examples of Nuclear Reactions

Type	Reaction		Radioactivity of Product Nuclide
(α, n)	$^{75}_{33}As + {}^{4}_{2}He$	$\longrightarrow {}^{78}_{35}Br + {}^{1}_{0}n$	β^+
(α, p)	$^{106}_{46}Pd + {}^{4}_{2}He$	$\longrightarrow {}^{109}_{47}Ag + {}^{1}_{1}H$	stable
(p, n)	$^{7}_{3}Li + {}^{1}_{1}H$	$\longrightarrow {}^{7}_{4}Be + {}^{1}_{0}n$	ec
(p, γ)	$^{14}_{7}N + {}^{1}_{1}H$	$\longrightarrow {}^{15}_{8}O + \gamma$	β^+
(p, α)	$^{9}_{4}Be + {}^{1}_{1}H$	$\longrightarrow {}^{6}_{3}Li + {}^{4}_{2}He$	stable
(d, p)	$^{31}_{15}P + {}^{2}_{1}H$	$\longrightarrow {}^{32}_{15}P + {}^{1}_{1}H$	β^-
(d, n)	$^{209}_{83}Bi + {}^{2}_{1}H$	$\longrightarrow {}^{210}_{84}Po + {}^{1}_{0}n$	α
(n, γ)	$^{59}_{27}Co + {}^{1}_{0}n$	$\longrightarrow {}^{60}_{27}Co + \gamma$	β^-
(n, p)	$^{45}_{21}Sc + {}^{1}_{0}n$	$\longrightarrow {}^{45}_{20}Ca + {}^{1}_{1}H$	β^-
(n, α)	$^{27}_{13}Al + {}^{1}_{0}n$	$\longrightarrow {}^{24}_{11}Na + {}^{4}_{2}He$	β^-

The first artificial, radioactive nuclide produced was made by the (α, n) reaction

$$^{27}_{13}Al + ^{4}_{2}He \longrightarrow ^{30}_{15}P + ^{1}_{0}n$$

The product, $^{30}_{15}P$, decays by positron emission,

$$^{30}_{15}P \longrightarrow ^{30}_{14}Si + ^{0}_{1}e$$

Except for the nature of the product, there is no difference between nuclear reactions that produce stable nuclides and those that yield radioactive nuclides.

Projectile particles that bear a positive charge are repelled by target nuclei; this is particularly true of the heavier nuclei, which have high charges. Consequently, only a small number of nuclear transformations can be brought about by the positive particles emitted by radioactive sources. Various particle accelerators are used to give protons, deuterons, α particles, and other cationic projectiles sufficiently high kinetic energies to overcome the electrostatic repulsions of the target nuclei. The **cyclotron**, Figure 21.5, is one such instrument.

The ion source is located between two hollow D-shaped plates (D_1 and D_2), called dees, that are separated by a gap. The dees are enclosed in an evacuated chamber located between the poles of a powerful electromagnet (not shown in the figure). A high-frequency generator keeps the dees oppositely charged. Under the influence of the magnetic and electrical fields, the ions move from the source in a circular path. Each time they reach the gap between the dees, the polarity of the dees is reversed. Thus the positively charged particles are pushed out of a positive dee and attracted into a negative dee. Each time they traverse the gap, therefore, they are accelerated. Because of this, the particles

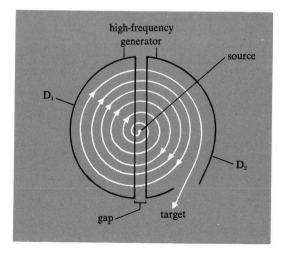

Figure 21.5 Path of a particle in a cyclotron.

Figure 21.6 Schematic representation of a linear accelerator.

travel an ever-increasing spiral path; eventually they penetrate a window in the instrument and, moving at extremely high speed, impinge on a target.

The **linear accelerator** (Figure 21.6) operates in much the same way except that no magnetic field is employed. The particles are accelerated through a series of tubes enclosed in an evacuated chamber. A positive ion from the source is attracted into tube 1, which is negatively charged. At this time, the odd-numbered tubes have negative charges and the even-numbered tubes have positive charges. As the particle emerges from tube 1, the charges of the tubes are reversed so that the even-numbered tubes are now negatively charged. The particle is repelled out of tube 1 (now positive) and attracted into tube 2 (now negative); as a result, it is accelerated.

Each time the particle leaves one tube to enter another, the charges of the tubes are reversed. Since the polarity of the tubes is reversed at a constant time interval, and since the speed of the particle increases constantly, each tube must be longer than the preceding one. The accelerated particles leave the last tube at high speed and strike the target.

Neutrons are particularly important projectiles because they bear no charge and therefore are not repelled by the positive charge of the target nuclei. A mixture of beryllium and an α emitter (such as $^{222}_{86}\text{Rn}$) is a convenient neutron source.

$$^9_4\text{Be} + {}^4_2\text{He} \longrightarrow {}^{12}_6\text{C} + {}^1_0\text{n}$$

This reaction was used by James Chadwick in his experiments that characterized the neutron (1932). The bombardment of beryllium by accelerated deuterons, from a cyclotron, is a more intense source of neutrons.

$$^9_4\text{Be} + {}^2_1\text{H} \longrightarrow {}^{10}_5\text{B} + {}^1_0\text{n}$$

A very important source of neutrons is the nuclear reactor (Section 21.6).

Neutrons from nuclear reactions are known as **fast neutrons**; they cause reactions in which a subsidiary particle is ejected [such as (n, α) and (n, p) reactions]. **Slow neutrons**, or **thermal neutrons**, are produced when the neutrons derived from a nuclear reaction are passed through a moderator (such as carbon, paraffin, hydrogen, deuterium, or oxygen). Through collisions with the nuclei of the moderator, the kinetic energies of the neutrons are decreased to values approximating those of ordinary gas molecules. Bombardments using slow neutrons bring about (n, γ) reactions which are also called **neutron-capture reactions** since no subsidiary particle is ejected.

$$^{34}_{16}S + ^{1}_{0}n \longrightarrow ^{35}_{16}S + \gamma$$

Isotopes of practically every element have been prepared by this type of reaction.

Nuclear reactions have been used to prepare isotopes belonging to elements that do not exist in nature or that exist in extremely minute concentrations. Thus isotopes of technetium and astatine have been prepared by the reactions

$$^{96}_{42}Mo + ^{2}_{1}H \longrightarrow ^{97}_{43}Tc + ^{1}_{0}n$$

$$^{209}_{83}Bi + ^{4}_{2}He \longrightarrow ^{211}_{85}At + 2^{1}_{0}n$$

The elements following uranium in the periodic classification are called the **transuranium elements**; none of these elements are naturally occurring, but many have been made by nuclear reactions. Some of these reactions use targets of artificial nuclides, and in these cases, the final products are therefore the result of syntheses consisting of several steps. Examples of these preparations are

$$^{238}_{92}U + ^{1}_{0}n \longrightarrow ^{239}_{92}U + \gamma$$

$$^{239}_{92}U \longrightarrow ^{239}_{93}Np + _{-1}^{0}e$$

$$^{239}_{93}Np \longrightarrow ^{239}_{94}Pu + _{-1}^{0}e$$

$$^{239}_{94}Pu + ^{2}_{1}H \longrightarrow ^{240}_{95}Am + ^{1}_{0}n$$

$$^{239}_{94}Pu + ^{4}_{2}He \longrightarrow ^{242}_{96}Cm + ^{1}_{0}n$$

In addition to the common projectiles, ions of elements of low atomic number are used in some bombardment reactions.

$$^{238}_{92}U + ^{12}_{6}C \longrightarrow ^{244}_{98}Cf + 6^{1}_{0}n$$

$$^{238}_{92}U + ^{14}_{7}N \longrightarrow ^{246}_{99}Es + 6^{1}_{0}n$$

$$^{238}_{92}U + ^{16}_{8}O \longrightarrow ^{250}_{100}Fm + 4^{1}_{0}n$$

$$^{252}_{98}Cf + ^{10}_{5}B \longrightarrow ^{257}_{103}Lr + 5^{1}_{0}n$$

21.6 Nuclear Fission and Fusion

Nuclear fission reactions are more famous, and infamous, than particle–particle or particle–capture transformations. In a **fission** process, a heavy nucleus is split into nuclei of lighter elements and several neutrons. The fission of a given nuclide results in more than one set of products. Two possible reactions for the slow neutron induced fission of $^{235}_{92}U$ are

$$^{235}_{92}U + ^{1}_{0}n \longrightarrow ^{93}_{36}Kr + ^{140}_{56}Ba + 3\,^{1}_{0}n$$

$$^{235}_{92}U + ^{1}_{0}n \longrightarrow ^{90}_{38}Sr + ^{144}_{54}Xe + 2\,^{1}_{0}n$$

Heavy nuclei have much larger neutron/proton ratios than nuclei of moderate mass (Figure 21.1). The neutrons released in the fission process lower the neutron/proton ratios of the product nuclei; nevertheless, these nuclei are generally radioactive, and further adjustment of the neutron/proton ratios occurs, usually through β emission. Certain fissions can be induced by protons, deuterons, or α particles, but the most important are those that are brought about by neutrons.

The **binding energy** of a nucleus may be considered to be the energy *required* to pull the nucleons of the nucleus apart or the energy *released* by the hypothetical formation of the nucleus by the condensation of the individual nucleons. The binding energy of a nucleus may be calculated from the difference between the sum of the masses of the constituent nucleons and the mass of the corresponding nucleus (Section 2.9). For $^{35}_{17}Cl$, this mass difference is 0.320 u, and therefore

$$0.320 \text{ u} \times 931 \text{ Mev/u} = 298 \text{ Mev}$$

The magnitude of the binding energy of a given nucleus indicates the stability of that nucleus toward radioactive decay. For the purpose of comparison, the values are usually given in terms of binding energy per nucleon, and the largest values are characteristic of the most stable nuclei. The binding energy per nucleon in the case of $^{35}_{17}Cl$ is

$$\frac{298 \text{ Mev}}{35 \text{ nucleons}} = 8.5 \text{ Mev/nucleon}$$

In Figure 21.7, mass number is plotted against binding energy per nucleon for the nuclides. Inspection of the curve shows that nuclides of intermediate mass have larger values of binding energy per nucleon than the heavier nuclides. Thus the fission of $^{235}_{92}U$ produces lighter nuclei with higher binding energy/nucleon values, and energy is liberated. The sum of the masses of the products of a fission reaction is less than the sum of the masses of the reactants. A typical fission of a single $^{235}_{92}U$ nucleus releases approximately 200 Mev.

The fission of each $^{235}_{92}U$ nucleus is induced by a single neutron and produces several neutrons; in the overall process, an average of approximately 2.5 neutrons are produced per fission. If each neutron causes the fission of another $^{235}_{92}U$ nucleus, an explosively rapid chain reaction ensues. Using a reproduction factor of 2 for simplicity, the first fission would cause 2 first-

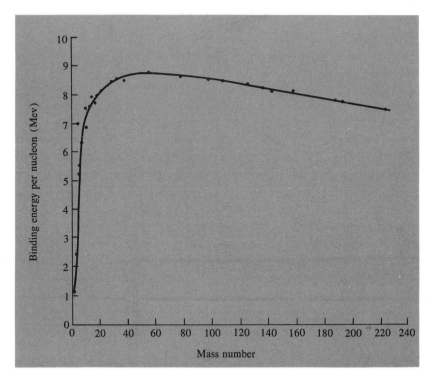

Figure 21.7 Binding energy per nucleon versus mass number.

generation fissions. Each of these would cause 2 fissions—a total of 4 second-generation fissions; these would be followed by 8, 16, 32, etc., fissions in succeeding generations. In the nth generation, 2^n fissions would occur. Since each fission is extremely rapid, an explosion results, and if 200 Mev are released by each fission, a tremendous amount of energy is liberated.

In a small amount of $^{235}_{92}U$ undergoing fission, many of the neutrons produced are lost from the surface of the mass before they can bring about nuclear reactions. If the size of the fissionable material exceeds a certain **critical mass,** however, the neutrons are captured before they can leave the mass and an explosive chain reaction results. An atomic bomb is detonated by bringing together two pieces of fissionable material, each of subcritical size, together into one piece of supercritical size. The reaction is started by a stray neutron.

A number of nuclei, such as $^{238}_{92}U$, $^{231}_{91}Pa$, $^{237}_{93}Np$, and $^{232}_{90}Th$, undergo fission with fast, but not with slow, neutrons. Slow neutrons, however, can induce fission in $^{233}_{92}U$, $^{235}_{92}U$ and $^{239}_{94}Pu$. The latter two isotopes are those commonly employed as nuclear fuels. The isotope $^{235}_{92}U$, which comprises only about 0.7% of natural uranium, was employed in the construction of the first atomic bomb. The separation of $^{235}_{92}U$ from the principal uranium isotope, $^{238}_{92}U$, was carried out in many ways, the most successful being the separation of gaseous $^{235}UF_6$ from $^{238}UF_6$ by thermal diffusion through porous barriers (Section 6.12). The isotope $^{239}_{94}Pu$ does not occur in nature but may be prepared from $^{238}_{92}U$ by the series of nuclear reactions given in Section 21.5.

The controlled fission of nuclear fuels in a **nuclear reactor** serves as a source of energy or as a source of neutrons and γ radiation for scientific research and the production of artificial isotopes. In a nuclear reactor, cylinders containing at least a critical mass of nuclear fuel ($^{235}_{92}U$, $^{233}_{92}U$, $^{239}_{94}Pu$, natural U, or natural U enriched with $^{235}_{92}U$) are surrounded by a moderator (graphite, water, or heavy water). The moderator serves to slow down the neutrons produced by the fission, thus increasing the possibility of their capture.

The neutron reproduction factor must be maintained at a value close to 1. If it falls below this value, the reaction will eventually stop, and if it increases much above this value, the reaction may become explosively violent. Control rods of cadmium, boron steel, or other materials, which may be inserted into the reactor to any desired depth, serve to capture excess neutrons and control the rate of the reaction.

$$^{113}_{48}Cd + ^{1}_{0}n \longrightarrow ^{114}_{48}Cd + \gamma$$

$$^{10}_{5}B + ^{1}_{0}n \longrightarrow ^{11}_{5}B + \gamma$$

The $^{114}_{48}Cd$ and $^{11}_{5}B$ isotopes are not radioactive. Provision is made for the insertion of research samples into the reactor.

Early reactors that used natural uranium as a fuel and graphite blocks as a moderator were large—cubes on the order of 20 to 25 feet on an edge. The use of enriched fuels and moderators other than graphite has reduced the size required considerably. Breeder reactors produce a fissionable isotope (e.g., $^{239}_{94}Pu$ from $^{238}_{92}U$) within the reactor and thus provide for the maintenance of a supply of nuclear fuel. Nuclear reactors that are designed as sources of energy employ a circulating coolant to remove the heat from the reactor to the outside where it is used in power production. All nuclear reactors must be heavily shielded.

Nuclear **fusion** is a process in which very light nuclei are fused into a heavier nucleus. The curve of Figure 21.7 shows that such processes should liberate more energy than fission processes. The hydrogen bomb is based on nuclear fusion. Extremely high activation energies are required for fusion reactions, and, in actual practice, a fission bomb is used to supply the high temperatures required. The energy of the sun is believed to be derived from the conversion of hydrogen nuclei into helium nuclei by nuclear fusion. Such reactions as the following are postulated.

$$^{1}_{1}H + ^{1}_{1}H \longrightarrow ^{2}_{1}H + ^{0}_{1}e$$

$$^{2}_{1}H + ^{1}_{1}H \longrightarrow ^{3}_{2}He + \gamma$$

$$^{3}_{2}He + ^{3}_{2}He \longrightarrow ^{4}_{2}He + 2^{1}_{1}H$$

The liquid drop model of the nucleus interprets fusion and fission in terms of the forces of repulsion and attraction between the nucleons in the nucleus. The size of the nucleus is critical in determining the total effect of these two opposing forces. The nucleons on the surface of the nucleus are subjected to fewer forces of attraction than the nucleons that are surrounded on all sides by other nucleons in the center of the nucleus (Figure 7.1). Therefore, the total effect of the attractive forces is increased when the surface area is decreased. One large drop has a smaller surface area than several small drops comprising the same amount of nuclear fluid.

On the other hand, the electrostatic forces of repulsion between protons tend to disrupt a large drop into smaller ones. Whether the process of fusion or fission occurs depends upon the balance between these two effects, which do not vary with the size of the drop in a parallel manner. Since the surface area of a sphere is $4\pi r^2$, the increase or decrease in the energy of attraction brought about by a change in surface area is proportional to the square of the radius, r^2 or $A^{2/3}$. The coulombic forces of repulsion, however, are proportional to the square of the nuclear charge divided by the radius, Z^2/r or $Z^2/A^{1/3}$. For light nuclei, the increase in the effect of the attractive forces brought about by the reduction in nuclear surface area more than offsets the increase in the effect of the forces of repulsion, and fusion occurs. For heavy nuclei, the reverse applies; fission occurs since it leads to a reduction in the effect of the forces of repulsion that is of more significance than the accompanying reduction in the effect of the forces of attraction.

21.7 Uses of Isotopes

A large number of uses have been developed for the isotopes that are the products of the processes run in nuclear reactors. Thickness gauges have been developed in which a radioactive source is placed on one side of the material to be tested (cigarettes, metal plates, etc.) and a counting device on the other. The amount of radiation reaching the counter is a measure of the thickness of the material.

The effectiveness of lubricating oils is measured in an engine constructed from metal into which radioactive isotopes have been incorporated. After the engine has been run for a fixed time period, the oil is withdrawn and tested for the presence of radioactive particles accumulated through engine wear.

When a single pipeline is used to transfer more than one petroleum derivative, a small amount of a radioactive isotope is placed in the last portion of one substance to signal its end and the start of another. The radiation may be used to activate an automatic valve system so that the liquids are diverted into different tanks.

The use of radiocarbon in determining the age of materials of plant origin has been mentioned. Photosynthesis has been studied by tracing the absorption of CO_2 containing $^{14}_6C$ by plants. In this way much has been learned about the conversion of CO_2 into sugars, starches, and cellulose.

Radioactive isotopes have found many uses in medical research, therapy, and diagnosis. The radiations from $^{60}_{27}Co$, a β and γ emitter, are used in cancer therapy. The isotope $^{131}_{53}I$ is used in the diagnosis and treatment of thyroid disorders, since this gland concentrates ingested iodine.

Radioactive tracers have found wide use in chemical studies. The following structure of the thiosulfate ion

$$\left[\begin{array}{c} S \\ | \\ O-S-O \\ | \\ O \end{array} \right]^{2-}$$

is indicated by studies using $^{35}_{16}S$. The thiosulfate ion is prepared by heating a sulfite with the radioactive sulfur.

$$^{35}S(s) + SO_3^{2-}(aq) \longrightarrow [^{35}SSO_3]^{2-}(aq)$$

Upon the acidification of this thiosulfate solution, the radioactive sulfur is quantitatively precipitated; none is found in the resulting SO_2 gas.

$$[^{35}SSO_3]^{2-}(aq) + 2H^+(aq) \longrightarrow {}^{35}S(s) + SO_2(g) + H_2O$$

In addition, upon the decomposition of silver thiosulfate derived from this ion, all the radioactive sulfur ends in the silver sulfide.

$$Ag_2[^{35}SSO_3](s) + H_2O \xrightarrow{\text{heat}} Ag_2{}^{35}S(s) + SO_4^{2-}(aq) + 2H^+(aq)$$

These results indicate that the two sulfur atoms of the thiosulfate ion are not equivalent and that the proposed structure is likely.

Radioactive isotopes have been used to study reaction rates and mechanisms as well as the action of catalysts. By using radioactive tracers, it becomes possible to follow the progress of tagged molecules and atoms through a chemical reaction.

For example, the mechanism of the reaction between the sulfite ion and the chlorate ion

$$SO_3^{2-} + ClO_3^- \longrightarrow SO_4^{2-} + ClO_2^-$$

has been shown to proceed by the exchange of an oxygen atom. The SO_3^{2-} ion used contained ordinary oxygen atoms, but the ClO_3^- ion was prepared with $^{18}_8O$, which is not radioactive but which may be detected by using a mass spectrograph. The SO_4^{2-} ion produced by the reaction contained $^{18}_8O$ in an amount that would indicate that one $^{18}_8O$ atom had been added to each SO_3^{2-} ion.

The mechanism proposed, therefore, is a Lewis nucleophilic displacement of ClO_2^- by SO_3^{2-} on one of the oxygen atoms of the ClO_3^- ion. The $^{18}_8O$ atoms are marked with asterisks.

$$
\begin{bmatrix} & O & \\ & \| & \\ O-&S& \\ & | & \\ & O & \end{bmatrix}^{2-}
+
\begin{bmatrix} & O^* & \\ & | & \\ O^*-&Cl&-O^* \end{bmatrix}^{-}
\longrightarrow
\begin{bmatrix} & O & & O^* & \\ & \| & & | & \\ O-&S&\cdots O^* \cdots &Cl&-O^* \\ & | & & & \\ & O & & & \end{bmatrix}^{3-}
\longrightarrow
$$

$$
\begin{bmatrix} & O & \\ & \| & \\ O-&S&-O^* \\ & | & \\ & O & \end{bmatrix}^{2-}
+
\begin{bmatrix} & O^* & \\ & | & \\ & Cl&-O^* \end{bmatrix}^{-}
$$

Activation analysis is the determination of the quantity of an element in a sample by bombarding the sample with suitable nuclear projectiles and measuring the intensity of the radioactivity induced in the element being investigated. The induced activity is not influenced by the chemical bonding of the element. Neutrons are the most frequently employed projectiles. Techniques have been developed for the determination of more than 50 elements and the method is particularly valuable for the determination of elements present in extremely low concentrations.

Determinations of very small vapor pressures and very low solubilities may be made conveniently by using tagged materials. For example, the solubility of water in benzene may be determined by using water that has been enriched with the radioactive ^3_1H and measuring the activity of the water-saturated benzene.

SOME SUGGESTED READINGS

Bethe, H. A., and Morrison, P., *Elementary Nuclear Theory*, New York, Wiley, 1966 (paper).

Choppin, G. R., *Nuclei and Radioactivity*, New York, Benjamin, 1964 (paper).

Cook, C. S., *Structure of Atomic Nuclei*, New York, Van Nostrand Reinhold, 1964 (paper).

Cunninghamme, J. G., *Introduction to the Atomic Nucleus*, New York, Elsevier, 1964 (paper).

Harvey, B. G., *Nuclear Chemistry*, Englewood Cliffs, N. J., Prentice-Hall, 1965 (paper).

Katz, J., and Rabinowich, E., *The Chemistry of Uranium*, New York, Dover, 1961 (paper).

Lane, A. M., *Nuclear Theory*, New York, Benjamin, 1963 (paper).

Overman, R. T., *Basic Concepts of Nuclear Chemistry*, New York, Van Nostrand Reinhold, 1963 (paper).

Seaborg, G. T., *Man-Made Transuranium Elements*, Englewood Cliffs, N. J., Prentice-Hall, 1963 (paper).

PROBLEMS

21.1 Briefly describe the exchange theory of nuclear bonding.

21.2 Define the following terms: nuclide, nucleon, radioactive activity, critical mass, thermal neutrons, fission, fusion.

21.3 Write equations for the following examples of radioactive decay: (a) alpha emission by $^{221}_{87}Fr$, (b) beta emission by $^{66}_{29}Cu$, (c) positron emission by $^{18}_{9}F$, (d) electron capture by $^{133}_{56}Ba$.

21.4 Write equations for the following examples of radioactive decay:
(a) alpha emission by $^{227}_{91}Pa$, (b) beta emission by $^{114}_{47}Ag$, (c) positron emission by $^{39}_{20}Ca$, (d) electron capture by $^{55}_{26}Fe$.

21.5 The nuclide $^{213}_{85}At$ decays to $^{209}_{83}Bi$ by alpha emisssion. The mass of $^{213}_{85}At$ is 212.9931 u, and the mass of $^{209}_{83}Bi$ is 208.9804 u. Calculate the energy released in this process.

21.6 When $^{222}_{88}Ra$ decays, 6.56 Mev and 6.23 Mev α particles are emitted. What is the energy and the source of the γ radiation accompanying this α emission?

21.7 The disintegration energy is 11.5 Mev for the β decay of $^{11}_{4}Be$ to $^{11}_{5}B$ (mass, 11.00931 u). What is the mass of $^{11}_{4}Be$?

21.8 The nuclide $^{18}_{10}Ne$ (mass, 18.00572 u) decays to $^{18}_{9}F$ (mass, 18.00095 u) by positron emission. What is the energy released by this radioactive decay process?

21.9 The energy released by the decay of $^{27}_{14}Si$ by position emission is 3.80 Mev. The daughter nuclide $^{27}_{13}Al$ has a mass of 26.98154 u. What is the mass of $^{27}_{14}Si$?

21.10 The daughter of the radioactive decay of $^{41}_{20}Ca$ is $^{41}_{19}K$. Is it energetically possible for $^{41}_{20}Ca$ (mass, 40.96227 u) to decay to $^{41}_{19}K$ (mass, 40.96183 u) by positron emission, or must the process occur by electron capture?

21.11 Why is electron capture accompanied by the production of X rays?

21.12 The nuclide $^{198}_{79}Au$ has a half-life of 64.8 hours. How much of a 0.0100 g sample remains at the end of 1.00 day?

21.13 The nuclide $^{22}_{11}Na$ decays by positron emission. The rate is such that 76.6% of the original quantity remains after 1.00 year. (a) What is the rate constant? (b) What is the half-life of $^{22}_{11}Na$?

21.14 The half-life of $^{35}_{16}S$ is 86.7 days. How long will it take for 90.0% of a sample to disappear?

21.15 The half-life of $^{35}_{16}S$ is 86.7 days. What is the activity, in curies, of a 0.000100 g sample of $^{35}_{16}S$? The atomic weight of $^{35}_{16}S$, to three significant figures, is 35.0.

21.16 A sample of a radioactive nuclide gives 3000 counts/minute and 20 minutes later gives 2500 counts/minute. What is the half-life of the nuclide?

21.17 The half-life of $^{45}_{20}Ca$ is 163 days. (a) How many atoms of $^{45}_{20}Ca$ are in a sample that has an activity of 0.500 curie? (b) What is the weight of the sample?

21.18 The half-life of $^{23}_{12}Mg$ is 12 sec. If a sample of $^{23}_{12}Mg$ has an activity of 5.00 microcuries, what is the activity of the sample after 1.00 minute?

21.19 The carbon from the heartwood of a giant sequoia tree gives 10.8 $^{14}_{6}C$ counts per minute per gram of carbon, whereas the wood from the outer portion of the tree gives 15.3 $^{14}_{6}C$ counts per minute per gram of carbon. How old is the tree?

21.20 Starting with $^{154}_{68}Er$, the successive steps in an artificial decay chain are: α, β^{+}, ec, α, α. What are the daughter members of the chain?

21.21 It is believed that a $^{237}_{93}Np$ disintegration series existed in nature at one time. However, the members of the series (with the exception of the stable nuclide that ends the series) have virtually disappeared, through radioactive decay, in the time since the earth was created. The particles successively emitted in the $^{237}_{93}Np$ series are: α, β, α, α, β, α, α, α, β, α, β. Determine, in order, the daughter members of the chain.

21.22 The half-life of $^{237}_{93}Np$ is 2.1×10^{6} years, and the age of earth is approximately 3.5×10^{9} years. What fraction of the quantity of $^{237}_{93}Np$ that was formed when the earth was created is now present?

21.23 Write equations for the following induced nuclear reactions:

(a) $^{10}_{5}B(\alpha, n)$ (e) $^{96}_{42}Mo(p, n)$

(b) $^{6}_{3}Li(n, \alpha)$ (f) $^{75}_{33}As\,(d, p)$

(c) $^{7}_{3}Li\,(d, n)$ (g) $^{45}_{21}Sc\,(\alpha, p)$

(d) $^{12}_{6}C(p, \gamma)$ (h) $^{51}_{23}V\,(d, 2n)$

21.24 Following are listed some transuranium nuclides and the types of induced nuclear reactions that have been used to prepare them. In each case, what isotope was used as the starting material?

(a) $(d, 6n)^{231}_{93}Np$ (e) $(^{16}_{8}O, 5n)\,^{249}_{100}Fm$

(b) $(d, 3n)\,^{243}_{97}Bk$ (f) $(\alpha, 2n)\,^{255}_{101}Md$

(c) $(\alpha, ^{3}_{1}H)\,^{250}_{99}Es$ (g) $(^{22}_{10}Ne, 4n)\,^{256}_{102}No$

(d) $(^{12}C, 4n)\,^{245}_{99}Es$ (n) $(^{10}_{5}B, 3n)\,^{257}_{103}Lr$

21.25 An isotope of element 105 was recently prepared by bombarding a $^{249}_{98}Cf$ target with $^{15}_{7}N$ nuclei. Four neutrons were emitted when a $^{249}_{98}Cf$ nucleus absorbed a $^{15}_{7}N$ nucleus. Write an equation for the transformation.

21.26 Calculate the binding energy per nucleon of $^{235}_{92}U$ (mass, 325.0439 u). The masses of the proton, neutron, and electron are 1.007277 u, 1.008665 u, and 0.0005486 u, respectively.

21.27 (a) Calculate the energy released by the fission:

$$^{235}_{92}U + {}^{1}_{0}n \longrightarrow {}^{94}_{38}Sr + {}^{139}_{54}Xe + 3\,{}^{1}_{0}n$$

The atomic masses are: $^{235}_{92}U$, 235.0439 u; $^{94}_{38}Sr$, 93.9154 u; $^{139}_{54}Xe$, 138.9179 u. The mass of the neutron is 1.0087 u. (b) What percent of the total mass of the starting materials is converted into energy?

21.28   (a) Calculate the energy released by the fusion:

$$^1_1H + {}^2_1H \longrightarrow {}^3_2He$$

The atomic masses are: ^1_1H, 1.0078 u; ^2_1H, 2.0141 u; ^3_2He, 3.0160 u. (b) What percent of the total mass of the starting materials is converted into energy?

21.29   Each of the following nuclides represents one of the products of a neutron-induced fission of $^{235}_{92}U$. In each case, another nuclide and three neutrons are also produced. Identify the other nuclides. (a) $^{148}_{58}Ce$, (b) $^{95}_{37}Rb$, (c) $^{134}_{52}Te$.

21.30   What are the functions of the moderator and the control rods in a nuclear reactor? Of what are they composed?

Appendix A
Values of Some Constants and Conversion Factors

Avogadro's number (N)	6.02252×10^{23}/mole
Bohr radius (a_0)	5.29167×10^{-9} cm
Defined calorie (cal)	4.1840 joules
Electronic charge, unit charge (e)	1.60210×10^{-19} coulomb
	4.80298×10^{-10} $g^{1/2}cm^{3/2}$/sec (or esu)
Electron rest mass (m)	9.1091×10^{-28} g
	5.48597×10^{-4} u
Proton rest mass	1.67252×10^{-24} g
	1.00727663 u
Neutron rest mass	1.67482×10^{-24} g
	1.0086654 u
Electron volt (ev)	1.60210×10^{-12} erg/electron
	2.3061×10^4 cal/mole
Electrostatic unit (esu)	3.33564×10^{-10} coulomb
Faraday (F)	9.64870×10^4 coulombs/mole
Gas constant (R)	8.2056×10^{-2} liter atm/°K mole
	8.3143 joule/°K mole
	1.9872 cal/°K mole
Kelvin temperature scale	Triple point of water (0.01°C) is 273.16°K
	Freezing point of water (0°C) is 273.15°K
Molar volume, ideal gas at STP	22.4136 liters
Planck's constant (h)	6.6256×10^{-27} erg sec
Speed of light in vacuum (c)	2.997925×10^{10} cm/sec
Unified atomic mass unit (u)	1.66037×10^{-24} g
	931.478 Mev

Appendix B
Standard Electrode Potentials at 25°C[a]

Acid Solution

Half Reaction	$\mathscr{E}°$ (volts)
$Li^+ + e^- \rightleftharpoons Li$	-3.045
$K^+ + e^- \rightleftharpoons K$	-2.925
$Rb^+ + e^- \rightleftharpoons Rb$	-2.925
$Cs^+ + e^- \rightleftharpoons Cs$	-2.923
$Ra^{2+} + 2e^- \rightleftharpoons Ra$	-2.916
$Ba^{2+} + 2e^- \rightleftharpoons Ba$	-2.906
$Sr^{2+} + 2e^- \rightleftharpoons Sr$	-2.888
$Ca^{2+} + 2e^- \rightleftharpoons Ca$	-2.866
$Na^+ + e^- \rightleftharpoons Na$	-2.714
$Ce^{3+} + 3e^- \rightleftharpoons Ce$	-2.483
$Mg^{2+} + 2e^- \rightleftharpoons Mg$	-2.363
$Be^{2+} + 2e^- \rightleftharpoons Be$	-1.847
$Al^{3+} + 3e^- \rightleftharpoons Al$	-1.662
$Mn^{2+} + 2e^- \rightleftharpoons Mn$	-1.180
$Zn^{2+} + 2e^- \rightleftharpoons Zn$	-0.7628
$Cr^{3+} + 3e^- \rightleftharpoons Cr$	-0.744
$Ga^{3+} + 3e^- \rightleftharpoons Ga$	-0.529
$Fe^{2+} + 2e^- \rightleftharpoons Fe$	-0.4402
$Cr^{3+} + e^- \rightleftharpoons Cr^{2+}$	-0.408
$Cd^{2+} + 2e^- \rightleftharpoons Cd$	-0.4029
$PbSO_4 + 2e^- \rightleftharpoons Pb + SO_4^{2-}$	-0.3588
$Tl^+ + e^- \rightleftharpoons Tl$	-0.3363
$Co^{2+} + 2e^- \rightleftharpoons Co$	-0.277
$H_3PO_4 + 2H^+ + 2e^- \rightleftharpoons H_3PO_3 + H_2O$	-0.276
$Ni^{2+} + 2e^- \rightleftharpoons Ni$	-0.250
$Sn^{2+} + 2e^- \rightleftharpoons Sn$	-0.136
$Pb^{2+} + 2e^- \rightleftharpoons Pb$	-0.126
$2H^+ + 2e^- \rightleftharpoons H_2$	0.0000
$S + 2H^+ + 2e^- \rightleftharpoons H_2S$	$+0.142$
$Sn^{4+} + 2e^- \rightleftharpoons Sn^{2+}$	$+0.15$
$SO_4^{2-} + 4H^+ + 2e^- \rightleftharpoons H_2SO_3 + H_2O$	$+0.172$

[a] Data from A. J. de Bethune and N. A. Swendeman Loud, "Table of Electrode Potentials and Temperature Coefficients," pp. 414–424 in *Encyclopedia of Electrochemistry* (C. A. Hampel, editor), Van Nostrand Reinhold, New York, 1964, and from A. J. de Bethune and N. A. Swendeman Loud, *Standard Aqueous Electrode Potentials and Temperature Coefficients*, 19 pp., C. A. Hampel, publisher, Skokie, Illinois, 1964.

Half Reaction	$\mathscr{E}°$ *(volts)*
$AgCl + e^- \rightleftharpoons Ag + Cl^-$	$+0.2222$
$Cu^{2+} + 2e^- \rightleftharpoons Cu$	$+0.337$
$H_2SO_3 + 2H^+ + 4e^- \rightleftharpoons S + 3H_2O$	$+0.450$
$Cu^+ + e^- \rightleftharpoons Cu$	$+0.521$
$I_2 + 2e^- \rightleftharpoons 2I^-$	$+0.5355$
$MnO_4^- + e^- \rightleftharpoons MnO_4^{2-}$	$+0.564$
$O_2 + 2H^+ + 2e^- \rightleftharpoons H_2O_2$	$+0.6824$
$Fe^{3+} + e^- \rightleftharpoons Fe^{2+}$	$+0.771$
$Hg_2^{2+} + 2e^- \rightleftharpoons 2Hg$	$+0.788$
$Ag^+ + e^- \rightleftharpoons Ag$	$+0.7991$
$2NO_3^- + 4H^+ + 2e^- \rightleftharpoons N_2O_4 + 2H_2O$	$+0.803$
$Hg^{2+} + 2e^- \rightleftharpoons Hg$	$+0.854$
$2Hg^{2+} + 2e^- \rightleftharpoons Hg_2^{2+}$	$+0.920$
$NO_3^- + 4H^+ + 3e^- \rightleftharpoons NO + 2H_2O$	$+0.96$
$Br_2 + 2e^- \rightleftharpoons 2Br^-$	$+1.0652$
$O_2 + 4H^+ + 4e^- \rightleftharpoons 2H_2O$	$+1.229$
$MnO_2 + 4H^+ + 2e^- \rightleftharpoons Mn^{2+} + 2H_2O$	$+1.23$
$Tl^{3+} + 2e^- \rightleftharpoons Tl^+$	$+1.25$
$Cr_2O_7^{2-} + 14H^+ + 6e^- \rightleftharpoons 2Cr^{3+} + 7H_2O$	$+1.33$
$Cl_2 + 2e^- \rightleftharpoons 2Cl^-$	$+1.3595$
$Au^{3+} + 2e^- \rightleftharpoons Au^+$	$+1.402$
$PbO_2 + 4H^+ + 2e^- \rightleftharpoons Pb^{2+} + 2H_2O$	$+1.455$
$Au^{3+} + 3e^- \rightleftharpoons Au$	$+1.498$
$Mn^{3+} + e^- \rightleftharpoons Mn^{2+}$	$+1.51$
$MnO_4^- + 8H^+ + 5e^- \rightleftharpoons Mn^{2+} + 4H_2O$	$+1.51$
$Ce^{4+} + e^- \rightleftharpoons Ce^{3+}$	$+1.61$
$2HOCl + 2H^+ + 2e^- \rightleftharpoons Cl_2 + 2H_2O$	$+1.63$
$PbO_2 + SO_4^{2-} + 4H^+ + 2e^- \rightleftharpoons PbSO_4 + 2H_2O$	$+1.682$
$Au^+ + e^- \rightleftharpoons Au$	$+1.691$
$MnO_4^- + 4H^+ + 3e^- \rightleftharpoons MnO_2 + 2H_2O$	$+1.695$
$H_2O_2 + 2H^+ + 2e^- \rightleftharpoons 2H_2O$	$+1.776$
$Co^{3+} + e^- \rightleftharpoons Co^{2+}$	$+1.808$
$S_2O_8^{2-} + 2e^- \rightleftharpoons 2SO_4^{2-}$	$+2.01$
$O_3 + 2H^+ + 2e^- \rightleftharpoons O_2 + H_2O$	$+2.07$
$F_2 + 2e^- \rightleftharpoons 2F^-$	$+2.87$

Alkaline Solution

$Al(OH)_4^- + 3e^- \rightleftharpoons Al + 4OH^-$	-2.33
$Zn(OH)_4^{2-} + 2e^- \rightleftharpoons Zn + 4OH^-$	-1.215
$Fe(OH)_2 + 2e^- \rightleftharpoons Fe + 2OH^-$	-0.877
$2H_2O + 2e^- \rightleftharpoons H_2 + 2OH^-$	-0.82806
$Cd(OH)_2 + 2e^- \rightleftharpoons Cd + 2OH^-$	-0.809
$S + 2e^- \rightleftharpoons S^{2-}$	-0.447

Half Reduction	$\mathscr{E}°$ *(volts)*
$CrO_4^{2-} + 4H_2O + 3e^- \rightleftharpoons Cr(OH)_3 + 5OH^-$	-0.13
$NO_3^- + H_2O + 2e^- \rightleftharpoons NO_2^- + 2OH^-$	$+0.01$
$O_2 + 2H_2O + 4e^- \rightleftharpoons 4OH^-$	$+0.401$
$NiO_2 + 2H_2O + 2e^- \rightleftharpoons Ni(OH)_2 + 2OH^-$	$+0.490$
$HO_2^- + H_2O + 2e^- \rightleftharpoons 3OH^-$	$+0.878$

Appendix C
Equilibrium Constants at 25°C

I Ionization Constants

Monoprotic Acids

acetic	$HC_2H_3O_2 \rightleftharpoons H^+ + C_2H_3O_2{}^-$	1.8×10^{-5}
benzoic	$HC_7H_5O_2 \rightleftharpoons H^+ + C_7H_5O_2{}^-$	6.0×10^{-5}
chlorous	$HClO_2 \rightleftharpoons H^+ + ClO_2{}^-$	1.1×10^{-2}
formic	$HCHO_2 \rightleftharpoons H^+ + CHO_2{}^-$	1.8×10^{-4}
hydrazoic	$HN_3 \rightleftharpoons H^+ + N_3{}^-$	1.9×10^{-5}
hydrocyanic	$HCN \rightleftharpoons H^+ + CN^-$	4.0×10^{-10}
hydrofluoric	$HF \rightleftharpoons H^+ + F^-$	6.7×10^{-4}
hypobromous	$HOBr \rightleftharpoons H^+ + OBr^-$	2.1×10^{-9}
hypochlorous	$HOCl \rightleftharpoons H^+ + OCl^-$	3.2×10^{-8}
nitrous	$HNO_2 \rightleftharpoons H^+ + NO_2{}^-$	4.5×10^{-4}

Polyprotic Acids

arsenic	$H_3AsO_4 \rightleftharpoons H^+ + H_2AsO_4{}^-$	$K_1 = 2.5 \times 10^{-4}$
	$H_2AsO_4{}^- \rightleftharpoons H^+ + HAsO_4^{2-}$	$K_2 = 5.6 \times 10^{-8}$
	$HAsO_4^{2-} \rightleftharpoons H^+ + AsO_4^{3-}$	$K_3 = 3 \times 10^{-13}$
carbonic	$CO_2 + H_2O \rightleftharpoons H^+ + HCO_3{}^-$	$K_1 = 4.2 \times 10^{-7}$
	$HCO_3{}^- \rightleftharpoons H^+ + CO_3^{2-}$	$K_2 = 4.8 \times 10^{-11}$
hydrosulfuric	$H_2S \rightleftharpoons H^+ + HS^-$	$K_1 = 1.1 \times 10^{-7}$
	$HS^- \rightleftharpoons H^+ + S^{2-}$	$K_2 = 1.0 \times 10^{-14}$
oxalic	$H_2C_2O_4 \rightleftharpoons H^+ + HC_2O_4{}^-$	$K_1 = 5.9 \times 10^{-2}$
	$HC_2O_4{}^- \rightleftharpoons H^+ + C_2O_4^{2-}$	$K_2 = 6.4 \times 10^{-5}$
phosphoric	$H_3PO_4 \rightleftharpoons H^+ + H_2PO_4{}^-$	$K_1 = 7.5 \times 10^{-3}$
	$H_2PO_4{}^- \rightleftharpoons H^+ + HPO_4^{2-}$	$K_2 = 6.2 \times 10^{-8}$
	$HPO_4^{2-} \rightleftharpoons H^+ + PO_4^{3-}$	$K_3 = 1 \times 10^{-12}$
phosphorous	$H_3PO_3 \rightleftharpoons H^+ + H_2PO_3{}^-$	$K_1 = 1.6 \times 10^{-2}$
(diprotic)	$H_2PO_3{}^- \rightleftharpoons H^+ + H_2PO_3^{2-}$	$K_2 = 7 \times 10^{-7}$
sulfuric	$H_2SO_4 \rightarrow H^+ + HSO_4{}^-$	strong
	$HSO_4{}^- \rightleftharpoons H^+ + SO_4^{2-}$	$K_2 = 1.3 \times 10^{-2}$
sulfurous	$SO_2 + H_2O \rightleftharpoons H^+ + HSO_3{}^-$	$K_1 = 1.3 \times 10^{-2}$
	$HSO_3{}^- \rightleftharpoons H^+ + SO_3^{2-}$	$K_2 = 5.6 \times 10^{-8}$

Bases

ammonia	$NH_3 + H_2O \rightleftharpoons NH_4{}^+ + OH^-$	1.8×10^{-5}
aniline	$C_6H_5NH_2 + H_2O \rightleftharpoons C_6H_5NH_3{}^+ + OH^-$	4.6×10^{-10}
dimethylamine	$(CH_3)_2NH + H_2O \rightleftharpoons (CH_3)_2NH_2{}^+ + OH^-$	7.4×10^{-4}

hydrazine	$N_2H_4 + H_2O \rightleftharpoons N_2H_5^+ + OH^-$	9.8×10^{-7}
methylamine	$CH_3NH_2 + H_2O \rightleftharpoons CH_3NH_3^+ + OH^-$	5.0×10^{-4}
pyridine	$C_5H_5N + H_2O \rightleftharpoons C_5H_5NH^+ + OH^-$	1.5×10^{-9}
trimethylamine	$(CH_3)_3N + H_2O \rightleftharpoons (CH_3)_3NH^+ + OH^-$	7.4×10^{-5}

II Solubility Products

Bromides

$PbBr_2$	4.6×10^{-6}
Hg_2Br_2	1.3×10^{-22}
$AgBr$	5.0×10^{-13}

Carbonates

$BaCO_3$	1.6×10^{-9}
$CdCO_3$	5.2×10^{-12}
$CaCO_3$	4.7×10^{-9}
$CuCO_3$	2.5×10^{-10}
$FeCO_3$	2.1×10^{-11}
$PbCO_3$	1.5×10^{-15}
$MgCO_3$	1×10^{-15}
$MnCO_3$	8.8×10^{-11}
Hg_2CO_3	9.0×10^{-17}
$NiCO_3$	1.4×10^{-7}
Ag_2CO_3	8.2×10^{-12}
$SrCO_3$	7×10^{-10}
$ZnCO_3$	2×10^{-10}

Chlorides

$PbCl_2$	1.6×10^{-5}
Hg_2Cl_2	1.1×10^{-18}
$AgCl$	1.7×10^{-10}

Chromates

$BaCrO_4$	8.5×10^{-11}
$PbCrO_4$	2×10^{-16}
Hg_2CrO_4	2×10^{-9}
Ag_2CrO_4	1.9×10^{-12}
$SrCrO_4$	3.6×10^{-5}

Fluorides

BaF_2	2.4×10^{-5}
CaF_2	3.9×10^{-11}
PbF_2	4×10^{-8}
MgF_2	8×10^{-8}
SrF_2	7.9×10^{-10}

Hydroxides

$Al(OH)_3$	5×10^{-33}
$Ba(OH)_2$	5.0×10^{-3}
$Cd(OH)_2$	2.0×10^{-14}
$Ca(OH)_2$	1.3×10^{-6}
$Cr(OH)_3$	6.7×10^{-31}
$Co(OH)_2$	2.5×10^{-16}
$Co(OH)_3$	2.5×10^{-43}
$Cu(OH)_2$	1.6×10^{-19}
$Fe(OH)_2$	1.8×10^{-15}
$Fe(OH)_3$	6×10^{-38}
$Pb(OH)_2$	4.2×10^{-15}
$Mg(OH)_2$	8.9×10^{-12}
$Mn(OH)_2$	2×10^{-13}
$Hg(OH)_2$ (HgO)	3×10^{-26}
$Ni(OH)_2$	1.6×10^{-16}
$AgOH$ (Ag_2O)	2.0×10^{-8}
$Sr(OH)_2$	3.2×10^{-4}
$Sn(OH)_2$	3×10^{-27}
$Zn(OH)_2$	4.5×10^{-17}

Iodides

PbI_2	8.3×10^{-9}
Hg_2I_2	4.5×10^{-29}
AgI	8.5×10^{-17}

Oxalates

BaC_2O_4	1.5×10^{-8}
CaC_2O_4	1.3×10^{-9}
PbC_2O_4	8.3×10^{-12}
MgC_2O_4	8.6×10^{-5}
$Ag_2C_2O_4$	1.1×10^{-11}
SrC_2O_4	5.6×10^{-8}

Phosphates

$Ba_3(PO_4)_2$	6×10^{-39}
$Ca_3(PO_4)_2$	1.3×10^{-32}
$Pb_3(PO_4)_2$	1×10^{-54}
Ag_3PO_4	1.8×10^{-18}
$Sr_3(PO_4)_2$	1×10^{-31}

Sulfates

$BaSO_4$	1.5×10^{-9}
$CaSO_4$	2.4×10^{-5}
$PbSO_4$	1.3×10^{-8}
Ag_2SO_4	1.2×10^{-5}
$SrSO_4$	7.6×10^{-7}

Sulfides

Bi_2S_3	1.6×10^{-72}
CdS	1.0×10^{-28}
CoS	5×10^{-22}
CuS	8×10^{-37}
FeS	4×10^{-19}
PbS	7×10^{-29}
MnS	7×10^{-16}
HgS	1.6×10^{-54}
NiS	3×10^{-21}
Ag_2S	5.5×10^{-51}
SnS	1×10^{-26}
ZnS	2.5×10^{-22}

Miscellaneous

$NaHCO_3$	1.2×10^{-3}
$KClO_4$	8.9×10^{-3}
$K_2[PtCl_6]$	1.4×10^{-6}
$AgC_2H_3O_2$	2.3×10^{-3}
$AgCN$	1.6×10^{-14}
$AgCNS$	1.0×10^{-12}

III   Instability Constants

AlF_6^{3-}	1.4×10^{-20}
$Al(OH)_4^-$	1.3×10^{-34}
$Al(OH)^{2+}$	7.1×10^{-10}
$Cd(NH_3)_4^{2+}$	7.5×10^{-8}
$Cd(CN)_4^{2-}$	1.4×10^{-19}
$Cr(OH)^{2+}$	5×10^{-11}
$Co(NH_3)_6^{2+}$	1.3×10^{-5}
$Co(NH_3)_6^{3+}$	2.2×10^{-34}
$Cu(NH_3)_2^+$	1.4×10^{-11}
$Cu(NH_3)_4^{2+}$	4.7×10^{-15}
$Cu(CN)_2^-$	1×10^{-16}
$Cu(OH)^+$	1×10^{-8}
$Fe(CN)_6^{4-}$	1×10^{-35}
$Fe(CN)_6^{3-}$	1×10^{-42}
$Pb(OH)^+$	1.5×10^{-8}

$HgBr_4^{2-}$	2.3×10^{-22}
$HgCl_4^{2-}$	1.1×10^{-16}
$Hg(CN)_4^{2-}$	4×10^{-42}
HgI_4^{2-}	5.3×10^{-31}
$Ni(NH_3)_4^{2+}$	1×10^{-8}
$Ni(NH_3)_6^{2+}$	1.8×10^{-9}
$Ag(NH_3)_2^+$	6.0×10^{-8}
$Ag(CN)_2^-$	1.8×10^{-19}
$Ag(S_2O_3)_2^{3-}$	5×10^{-14}
$Ag(S_2O_3)_3^{5-}$	9.9×10^{-15}
$Zn(NH_3)_4^{2+}$	3.4×10^{-10}
$Zn(CN)_4^{2-}$	1.2×10^{-18}
$Zn(OH)_4^{2-}$	3.6×10^{-16}
$Zn(OH)^+$	4.1×10^{-5}

Appendix D
Logarithms

	0	1	2	3	4	5	6	7	8	9
10	0000	0043	0086	0128	0170	0212	0253	0294	0334	0374
11	0414	0453	0492	0531	0569	0607	0645	0682	0719	0755
12	0792	0828	0864	0899	0934	0969	1004	1038	1072	1106
13	1139	1173	1206	1239	1271	1303	1335	1367	1399	1430
14	1461	1492	1523	1553	1584	1614	1644	1673	1703	1732
15	1761	1790	1818	1847	1875	1903	1931	1959	1987	2014
16	2041	2068	2095	2122	2148	2175	2201	2227	2253	2279
17	2304	2330	2355	2380	2405	2430	2455	2480	2504	2529
18	2553	2577	2601	2625	2648	2672	2695	2718	2742	2765
19	2788	2810	2833	2856	2878	2900	2923	2945	2967	2989
20	3010	3032	3054	3075	3096	3118	3139	3160	3181	3201
21	3222	3243	3263	3284	3304	3324	3345	3365	3385	3404
22	3424	3444	3464	3483	3502	3522	3541	3560	3579	3598
23	3617	3636	3655	3674	3692	3711	3729	3747	3766	3784
24	3802	3820	3838	3856	3874	3892	3909	3927	3945	3962
25	3979	3997	4014	4031	4048	4065	4082	4099	4116	4133
26	4150	4166	4183	4200	4216	4232	4249	4265	4281	4298
27	4314	4330	4346	4362	4378	4393	4409	4425	4440	4456
28	4472	4487	4502	4518	4533	4548	4564	4579	4594	4609
29	4624	4639	4654	4669	4683	4698	4713	4728	4742	4757
30	4771	4786	4800	4814	4829	4843	4857	4871	4886	4900
31	4914	4928	4942	4955	4969	4983	4997	5011	5024	5038
32	5051	5065	5079	5092	5105	5119	5132	5145	5159	5172
33	5185	5198	5211	5224	5237	5250	5263	5276	5289	5302
34	5315	5328	5340	5353	5366	5378	5391	5403	5416	5428
35	5441	5453	5465	5478	5490	5502	5514	5527	5539	5551
36	5563	5575	5587	5599	5611	5623	5635	5647	5658	5670
37	5682	5694	5705	5717	5729	5740	5752	5763	5775	5786
38	5798	5809	5821	5832	5843	5855	5866	5877	5888	5899
39	5911	5922	5933	5944	5955	5966	5977	5988	5999	6010
40	6021	6031	6042	6053	6064	6075	6085	6096	6107	6117
41	6128	6138	6149	6160	6170	6180	6191	6201	6212	6222
42	6232	6243	6253	6263	6274	6284	6294	6304	6314	6325
43	6335	6345	6355	6365	6375	6385	6395	6405	6415	6425
44	6435	6444	6454	6464	6474	6484	6493	6503	6513	6522
45	6532	6542	6551	6561	6571	6580	6590	6599	6609	6618
46	6628	6637	6646	6656	6665	6675	6684	6693	6702	6712
47	6721	6730	6739	6749	6758	6767	6776	6785	6794	6803
48	6812	6821	6830	6839	6848	6857	6866	6875	6884	6893
49	6902	6911	6920	6928	6937	6946	6955	6964	6972	6981
50	6990	6998	7007	7016	7024	7033	7042	7050	7059	7067
51	7076	7084	7093	7101	7110	7118	7126	7135	7143	7152
52	7160	7168	7177	7185	7193	7202	7210	7218	7226	7235
53	7243	7251	7259	7267	7275	7284	7292	7300	7308	7316
54	7324	7332	7340	7348	7356	7364	7372	7380	7388	7396

	0	1	2	3	4	5	6	7	8	9
55	7404	7412	7419	7427	7435	7443	7451	7459	7466	7474
56	7482	7490	7497	7505	7513	7520	7528	7536	7543	7551
57	7559	7566	7574	7582	7589	7597	7604	7612	7619	7627
58	7634	7642	7649	7657	7664	7672	7679	7686	7694	7701
59	7709	7716	7723	7731	7738	7745	7752	7760	7767	7774
60	7782	7789	7796	7803	7810	7818	7825	7832	7839	7846
61	7853	7860	7868	7875	7882	7889	7896	7903	7910	7917
62	7924	7931	7938	7945	7952	7959	7966	7973	7980	7987
63	7993	8000	8007	8014	8021	8028	8035	8041	8048	8055
64	8062	8069	8075	8082	8089	8096	8102	8109	8116	8122
65	8129	8136	8142	8149	8156	8162	8169	8176	8182	8189
66	8195	8202	8209	8215	8222	8228	8235	8241	8248	8254
67	8261	8267	8274	8280	8287	8293	8299	8306	8312	8319
68	8325	8331	8338	8344	8351	8357	8363	8370	8376	8382
69	8388	8395	8401	8407	8414	8420	8426	8432	8439	8445
70	8451	8457	8463	8470	8476	8482	8488	8494	8500	8506
71	8513	8519	8525	8531	8537	8543	8549	8555	8561	8567
72	8573	8579	8585	8591	8597	8603	8609	8615	8621	8627
73	8633	8639	8645	8651	8657	8663	8669	8675	8681	8686
74	8692	8698	8704	8710	8716	8722	8727	8733	8739	8745
75	8751	8756	8762	8768	8774	8779	8785	8791	8797	8802
76	8808	8814	8820	8825	8831	8837	8842	8848	8854	8859
77	8865	8871	8876	8882	8887	8893	8899	8904	8910	8915
78	8921	8927	8932	8938	8943	8949	8954	8960	8965	8971
79	8976	8982	8987	8993	8998	9004	9009	9015	9020	9025
80	9031	9036	9042	9047	9053	9058	9063	9069	9074	9079
81	9085	9090	9096	9101	9106	9112	9117	9122	9128	9133
82	9138	9143	9149	9154	9159	9165	9170	9175	9180	9186
83	9191	9196	9201	9206	9212	9217	9222	9227	9232	9238
84	9243	9248	9253	9258	9263	9269	9274	9279	9284	9289
85	9294	9299	9304	9309	9315	9320	9325	9330	9335	9340
86	9345	9350	9355	9360	9365	9370	9375	9380	9385	9390
87	9395	9400	9405	9410	9415	9420	9425	9430	9435	9440
88	9445	9450	9455	9460	9465	9469	9474	9479	9484	9489
89	9494	9499	9504	9509	9513	9518	9523	9528	9533	9538
90	9542	9547	9552	9557	9562	9566	9571	9576	9581	9586
91	9590	9595	9600	9605	9609	9614	9619	9624	9628	9633
92	9638	9643	9647	9652	9657	9661	9666	9671	9675	9680
93	9685	9689	9694	9699	9703	9708	9713	9717	9722	9727
94	9731	9736	9741	9745	9750	9754	9759	9763	9768	9773
95	9777	9782	9786	9791	9795	9800	9805	9809	9814	9818
96	9823	9827	9832	9836	9841	9845	9850	9854	9859	9863
97	9868	9872	9877	9881	9886	9890	9894	9899	9903	9908
98	9912	9917	9921	9926	9930	9934	9939	9943	9948	9952
99	9956	9961	9965	9969	9974	9978	9983	9987	9991	9996

Appendix E

Answers to Selected Numerical Problems

Chapter 2

2.4 69.17% ^{63}Cu, 30.83% ^{65}Cu. **2.7** 7.016 u. **2.10** 4.29 × 10^{14}/sec,
2.84 × 10^{-12} erg; 7.50 × 10^{14}/sec, 4.97 × 10^{-12} erg.
2.14 (a) 0.529 Å, 2.12 Å, 4.76 Å. (b) −2.17 × 10^{-11} erg,
−5.42 × 10^{-12} erg, −2.42 × 10^{-12} erg. (c) 2.91 × 10^{15}/sec, 1030 Å;
4.52 × 10^{14}/sec, 6640 Å; 2.46 × 10^{15}/sec, 1220 Å.
2.18 (a) 6.6 × 10^{-19} cm/sec. (b) 7.3 × 10^8 cm/sec.

Chapter 3

3.15 4.9%. **3.27** 13.6 ev.

Chapter 5

5.1 1.99 × 10^{-23} g, 5.02 × 10^{22} atoms. **5.7** 60.6% W. **5.10** 726 lb Zr.
5.13 (a) As$_2$O$_3$. (b) As$_4$O$_6$. **5.21** (b) 79.8 g P$_4$O$_{10}$, 20.2 g H$_2$O.
5.26 23.9 g. **5.29** 76.9% BaO. **5.32** −1.35 × 10^3 kcal/mole.
5.34 −424.7 kcal, 2.58 × 10^3 kcal. **5.38** −53.3 kcal/mole.
5.41 −164.6 kcal/mole.

Chapter 6

6.1 5.05 × 10^{13} atoms. **6.3** (a) 12.7 atm. (b) 313°C. **6.7** 154 ml.
6.11 136 ml. **6.16** 28.0. **6.21** (b) 14 liters. **6.26** (a) C$_2$H$_5$. (b) C$_4$H$_{10}$.
6.28 24.6 liters. **6.32** 69%. **6.36** (a) 1.69. (b) 0.31 mole N$_2$O$_4$,
1.38 moles NO$_2$. (c) 69%. (d) 0.817. (e) 0.183 atm, 0.817 atm.
6.39 48.1.

Chapter 7

7.3 8.7 kcal/mole, 68 cal/g. **7.17** 2.04 Å. **7.20** 3.62 Å.
7.26 (a) 5.71 Å. (b) 1.43 Å. **7.27** (a) 66.4 Å^3. (b) 49.0 Å^3. (c) 26%.
7.30 (a) 2r. (b) 8r^3. (c) 4.19r^3. (d) 4.76%. **7.33** 0.73.
7.36 (a) 4Zn^{2+}, 4S^{2-}. (b) 5.41 Å.
7.38 (a) −206 kcal/mole. (b) 11% too large.

Chapter 8

8.11 (a) 3+. (b) 4+. (c) 7+. (d) 6+. (e) 6+. (f) 2−. (g) 5+.
(h) 4+. **8.23** (a) 1/2. (b) 1/3. (c) 1/6. (d) 1/4. (e) 1. **8.25** 23.0.

Chapter 9

9.6 0.120 g. **9.9** $mx\left(1 - \dfrac{y}{100}\right) = M$. **9.11** 23.8 ml.
9.14 (a) $8.90M$. **(b)** $11.4m$. **9.17** 125 ml. **9.21** 69.6%. **9.24** 67.0%.
9.26 0.142 g. **9.28 (a)** 0.886. **(b)** 0.974. **9.34** 144. **9.39** Three.
9.40 2.56.

Chapter 10

10.5 1.78 g. **10.10** 0.896 liter. **10.11** $0.533M$. **10.14** 0.146 amp.
10.18 (a) 138.4 cm²/ohm equivalent. **(b)** $1.30 \times 10^{-5}M$.
10.21 (a) $+0.935$ v. **(b)** $Sn + 2Ag^+ \rightarrow Sn^{2+} + 2Ag$. **(c)** Ag electrode.
10.29 (a) $Ag^+ + Cl^- \rightarrow AgCl$. **(b)** $+0.5769$ v. **(c)** -13.3 kcal.
10.33 $0.050M$. **10.37** $+1.19$ v.
10.38 (a) $+0.010$ v. **(b)** Sn^{2+}, $1.38M$; Pb^{2+}, $0.62M$.

Chapter 11

11.6 (a) 2.0 g 4.0 g, 28.8 g. **(b)** 108 liters.

Chapter 13

13.1 (a) -780.08 kcal/mole.
(b) $C_6H_6(l) + \tfrac{15}{2}O_2(g) \rightarrow 6CO_2(g) + 3H_2O(l)$, -780.97 kcal.
(c) $+11.71$ kcal/mole. **13.4 (a)** -27.02 kcal. **(b)** -26.43 kcal.
13.6 (a) 279.9 kcal/mole. **(b)** 93.3 kcal/mole. **13.9 (a)** -312 kcal.
(b) -302.64 kcal. **13.14 (a)** $2Ag + I_2 \rightarrow 2AgI$. **(b)** -0.1518 v.
13.18 (a) $+0.740$ v. **(b)** -32.7 kcal. **(c)** -34.1 kcal.
(d) 4.7 cal/°K. **13.21 (a)** -27.7 cal/°K. **(b)** -23.7 kcal. **(c)** -0.343 v.
13.23 (a) -30.60 kcal. **(b)** -6.92 kcal. **(c)** -79.5 cal/°K. **(d)** Yes.
13.29 -9.1 kcal.

Chapter 14

14.8 (a) $1/8 \times$. **(b)** $1/27 \times$. **(c)** $2 \times$. **(d)** $8 \times$.
14.9 (a) 6.8×10^{-6}/torr sec. **(b)** 3.4×10^{-1} liter/mole sec.
14.12 54.2 kcal. **14.14** 305°K.
14.20 (a) 0.509 mole/liter. **(b)** 0.930. **(c)** 0.930.
14.25 (a) 0.50 atm. **(b)** NO_2, 0.78 atm; N_2O_4, 1.22 atm.
14.27 1.48×10^{-5} mole/liter. **14.30** 6.4×10^{19}/atm. **14.36** 9.0×10^9

Chapter 16

16.1 (a) $[H^+] = [C_7H_5O_2{}^-] = 3.5 \times 10^{-3}M$, $[HC_7H_5O_2] = 0.20M$.
(b) 1.8×10^{-2}. **16.4** 1.3×10^{-5}. **16.10** $[H^+] = 1.0 \times 10^{-3}M$,
$[F^-] = 0.10M$, $[HF] = 0.15M$.

16.13 (a) 0.19. (b) 10.78. (c) 4.48. (d) 3.40.
16.15 11.32. **16.19** 3.29, $5.1 \times 10^{-4}M$. **16.22** 6.57–8.35. **16.24** 4.85.
16.31 0.45 mole.
16.34 $1.1 \times 10^{-3}M$, $1.1 \times 10^{-3}M$, $5.6 \times 10^{-8}M$, $1.5 \times 10^{-17}M$, $0.50M$.
16.38 $1.4 \times 10^{-15}M$.

Chapter 17

17.1 1.6×10^{-16}. **17.6** $1.6 \times 10^{-5}M$. **17.8** 1.7×10^{-4}.
17.12 $5.0 \times 10^{-3}M$, $0.16M$, $0.15M$, $8.8 \times 10^{-5}M$. **17.15** $1.2M$.
17.19 (a) $PbSO_4$, (b) $4.3 \times 10^{-5}M$. **17.24** $0.23M$. **17.25** $6.7 \times 10^{-16}M$
17.33 (a) $9.0 \times 10^{-2}M$. (b) $2.1 \times 10^{-7}M$. **17.37** 5.0×10^{-6}.
17.39 $6.0 \times 10^{-3}M$. **17.42** (a) $3.7 \times 10^{-13}M$ (b) $2.5 \times 10^{-10}M$.
(c) $2.2 \times 10^{-5}M$.
17.45 (a) 3.92. (b) 8.46. (c) 12.16.
17.50 (a) 1.5×10^{37}. (b) $0.10M$, $6.7 \times 10^{-39}M$. (c) 2.5×10^{14} liters.

Chapter 18

18.27 (a) $+0.0592$ v. (b) $+0.770$ v.
18.28 (a) Fe^{2+}, FeO. (b) Fe_3O_4, 1/2 octahedral, 1/8 tetrahedral.
(c) Fe_2O_3, 2/9.

Chapter 19

19.21 (a) 5. (b) High-spin. **19.22** 1.3×10^{-34}.

Chapter 20

20.46. (a) 44.0 g. (b) 68.2%. **20.47** (a) $C_2H_3O_3$. (b) $C_4H_6O_6$.
(c) 75. (d) COOHCHOHCHOHCOOH.

Chapter 21

21.5 9.40 Mev. **21.9** 26.98672 u. **21.12** 7.7×10^{-3} g.
21.17 (a) 2.61×10^{14} atoms. (b) 1.74×10^{-8} g. **21.19** 2890 years.
21.26 7.59 Mev/nucleon.

Index

PERIODIC CLASSIFICATION OF

IA	IIA	IIIB	IVB	VB	VIB	VIIB	VIIIB	
1 **H** 1.0080								
3 **Li** 6.941	4 **Be** 9.01218							
11 **Na** 22.9898	12 **Mg** 24.305							
19 **K** 39.102	20 **Ca** 40.08	21 **Sc** 44.9559	22 **Ti** 47.90	23 **V** 50.9414	24 **Cr** 51.996	25 **Mn** 54.9380	26 **Fe** 55.847	27 **Co** 58.9332
37 **Rb** 85.4678	38 **Sr** 87.62	39 **Y** 88.9059	40 **Zr** 91.22	41 **Nb** 92.9064	42 **Mo** 95.94	43 **Tc** 98.9062a	44 **Ru** 101.07	45 **Rh** 102.9055
55 **Cs** 132.9055	56 **Ba** 137.34	57* **La** 138.9055	72 **Hf** 178.49	73 **Ta** 180.9479	74 **W** 183.85	75 **Re** 186.2	76 **Os** 190.2	77 **Ir** 192.22
87 **Fr** (223)b	88 **Ra** 226.0254a	89 ** **Ac** (227)b	104 (260)b	105 (260)b				

*	58 **Ce** 140.12	59 **Pr** 140.9077	60 **Nd** 144.24	61 **Pm** (147)b	62 **Sm** 150.4
**	90 **Th** 232.0381a	91 **Pa** 231.0359a	92 **U** 238.029	93 **Np** 237.0482a	94 **Pu** (242)b

aMass of most commonly available, long-lived isotope.
bMass number of most stable or best known isotope.